W9-AAT-960

PRENTICE HALL ②

Realidades

Teacher's Edition
Level 2

Peggy Palo Boyles
Oklahoma City, OK

Myriam Met
Rockville, MD

Richard S. Sayers
Longmont, CO

Carol Eubanks Wargin

PEARSON

Prentice
Hall

Boston, Massachusetts
Upper Saddle River, New Jersey

**This work is protected by United States copyright laws
and is provided *solely for the use of teachers and
administrators* in teaching courses and assessing
student learning in their classes and schools.
Dissemination or sale of any part of this work (including
on the World Wide Web) will destroy the integrity of the
work and is *not* permitted.**

Inset image, front cover: Indian woman at market carrying carrots, Guatemala

Front cover (background) and back cover: Market day in Sololá, near Lake Atitlán, Guatemala

 Special thanks to the American Council on the Teaching of Foreign Languages for the use of the logo that accompanies
the references to the Standards for Foreign Learning.

**Copyright © 2008 by Pearson Education, Inc., publishing as Pearson Prentice Hall, Boston,
Massachusetts 02116.** All rights reserved. Printed in the United States of America.
This publication is protected by copyright, and permission should be obtained from the
publisher prior to any prohibited reproduction, storage in a retrieval system, or transmission
in any form or by any means, electronic, mechanical, photocopying, recording, or likewise.
For information regarding permission(s), write to: Rights and Permissions Department, 1 Lake
Street, Upper Saddle River, NJ 07458.

Pearson Prentice Hall™ is a trademark of Pearson Education, Inc.
Pearson® is a registered trademark of Pearson plc.
Prentice Hall® is a registered trademark of Pearson Education, Inc.

ISBN 0-13-134098-0

5 6 7 8 9 10   10 09

Realidades 2 Professional Development

Table of Contents

In-Service
prentice ● hall
On Demand

PHSchool.com

REALIDADES, Research, and the Standards

Topics covered:

▶ **REALIDADES and Research-based Instruction**

▶ **Achieving the Standards with REALIDADES**

REALIDADES is based on the belief that the purpose of learning Spanish is to communicate with the people who speak it and to understand their cultures. **REALIDADES** presents a fresh, exciting approach to Spanish by making language learning real for today's students.

....

REALIDADES and Research-based Instruction

REALIDADES reflects the most current research on how students learn languages and what teachers and materials need to do to help them become proficient language users. Let's take a look at some of the basic premises about language and language learning.

Communication

Communication is an authentic exchange of information for a real purpose between two or more people. By this we mean that people tell each other (through speech or writing) something the other person doesn't already know.

Communicating meaning has several aspects. Students needs to listen to and read Spanish in order to interpret intended meanings. Students need to express meaning by conveying their own messages for a purpose and to a real audience. They also need to negotiate meaning through the natural give-and-take involved in understanding and making oneself understood. Research tells us that classroom activities must provide students practice in interpreting, expressing, and negotiating meaning through extensive and frequent peer interactions.

Throughout *REALIDADES*, students are engaged in understanding messages, in sending their own messages, and thus in communicating real ideas and real meanings for real purposes.

Comprehensible input

Research states that students learn best when they have ample opportunities to internalize meanings before they have to produce them. In other words, comprehension precedes production. The term "comprehensible input" suggests that learners acquire language by understanding what they hear and read. Students need many opportunities to match what they hear with visual cues (pictures, video, or teacher pantomime) or experiences (physical actions). Reading input should be supported by a close connection between text and visuals. All these strategies for comprehensible input help students associate meaning with forms.

In keeping with this research, *REALIDADES* begins each chapter with a section call *A primera vista.* These four pages of language input give students opportunities to comprehend new language before producing it. The visualized presentation of vocabulary in context, the reading input in the *Videohistoria,* and the listening input in the *A primera vista* video segment provide a wide range of comprehensible input of new language that addresses all students and all learning styles.

Practice activities

Research tells us that students need extensive practice in using their new language to create and convey their own messages. The *Manos a la obra* section provides a wide range of practice activities. New vocabulary and grammar are first practiced in skill-getting activities that provide concrete practice. This basic practice helps to develop accuracy in using the language and prepares students to transition into more communicative tasks. In these transitional activities, students work with a partner or in small groups with information- or opinion-gap activities that are characteristic of real-life communication. Students then continue on to more open-ended, personalized speaking or writing tasks.

> **❝Communication is an authentic exchange of information for for a real purpose between two or more people.❞**

Meaningful context in language learning

All effective learning is rooted in a meaningful context. We know from research that information is most likely to be retained when it is connected to other information in a meaningful way. Thus, language learning is most successful and retention more likely when we present new language organized into topics or by situations.

REALIDADES is organized into themes. All material in a chapter—vocabulary, grammar, culture—is rooted in a context and used meaningfully. Students engage in communicative tasks that are relevant to their lives. Students work with readings, realia, photography, and art that are authentic to the Spanish-speaking world. The video programs and Internet links show native speakers engaged in real-life situations and experiences.

Understanding grammar

Students learn grammar most effectively when it is presented and practiced in a meaningful context and when it connects to real communication needs. Students also benefit when shown how the patterns of grammar work.

In *REALIDADES,* new structures are foreshadowed through lexical presentation (grammar is presented as vocabulary) in the *A primera vista* language input section. In addition, early vocabulary activities in the *Manos a la obra* section have students work with the grammar lexically. This allows students to see the grammar and work with it in a meaningful context before being formally presented with the rules or paradigms.

Grammar is formally presented with clear explanations and examples. Comparisons between English and Spanish grammar are made whenever possible. Students then practice the grammar concepts in a variety of tasks that range from concrete activities that focus primarily on the structures to more open-ended tasks that focus on communication.

To further facilitate the learning of grammar, *REALIDADES* offers *GramActiva,* a multi-modality approach to grammar that includes grammar videos and hands-on grammar activities. By teaching and practicing grammar through different learning styles, more students will be able to learn grammar.

Building cultural perspectives

The *Standards for Foreign Language Learning* have expanded how culture is taught in today's classroom. We want students to understand the *why* (perspectives) of culture that determines the *what* (products and practices).

The approach to culture in *REALIDADES* not only teaches students the *what* but asks students to explore the *why.* Cultural products, practices, and comparisons are presented throughout *REALIDADES* in features such as *Fondo cultural, La cultura en vivo,* and *Perspectivas del mundo hispano,* and in *REALIDADES 3, Puente a la cultura.* Students read information about cultures that offer different perspectives and they are asked questions that encourage them to think and make observations about cultures.

Strategies for success

Research shows that effective learners know how to help themselves become successful learners. One way they do this is by using specific problem-solving strategies.

REALIDADES teaches students strategies to be effective communicators whether listening, speaking, reading, or writing. Each reading selection is supported by a reading strategy. Each performance-based task includes a useful strategy that connects to a step-by-step approach that helps students plan, rehearse, and present or publish. Each also includes a rubric so students know how they might be evaluated.

We know more than ever about how foreign languages are learned. *REALIDADES* is based on solid research in second-language acquisition, on accepted theories about the teaching of culture, and on sound pedagogical practices that are common to all disciplines. We are sure that you and your students will find this an exciting, motivating, and enormously successful approach to learning Spanish.

Achieving the Standards with *REALIDADES*

The *Standards for Foreign Language Learning* provide an important and useful framework to guide the teaching and learning of foreign languages. This framework should result in a new generation of language learners prepared to meet the demand for competence in other languages that our nation will face as we move into an increasingly interdependent world.

REALIDADES is written based upon the Standards. This means that instruction used in REALIDADES will help students develop the competencies delineated in the *Standards for Foreign Language Learning.* Teachers will find a correlation to the Standards at the beginning of each chapter and with the notes that accompany each activity (if appropriate) in the Teacher's Edition.

Goal 1: Communication

1.1 (Interpersonal): Each chapter provides a wide range of paired and group activities. Students speak with a partner, work in small groups, and interview classmates.

1.2 (Interpretive): *REALIDADES* builds the interpretive listening skill through the Audio Program. This CD program supports activities in the Student Edition (input checks, dictations, listening comprehension, and test preparation) and the *Writing, Audio, & Video Workbook.* The Video Program also develops listening through the different language, grammar, and storyline mystery video segments.

REALIDADES provides extensive support for the interpretive reading skill. Students read throughout the chapter: comprehensible input, practice activities, realia, culture notes, and reading selections. Reading is seamlessly integrated with practice and anchored in real-life contexts. Whenever possible, readings are supported by focused strategies.

1.3 (Presentational): Each chapters ends with a performance-based task: in the "A" chapters, a speaking task, in the "B" chapters a presentation writing task. Both presentations are supported by strategies and the speaking or writing process, step-by-step support to help students successfully complete the task.

Goal 2: Culture

2.1 (Practices and Perspectives): 2.2 (Products and Perspectives) Each chapter in *REALIDADES* explores a cultural theme through a wide range of practices, products, and perspectives. Students see authentic culture through realia, art, photographs, popular sayings, tongue twisters, rhymes and songs, hands-on projects, readings, and authentic literature. In addition, the unique *Fondo cultural* readings generally include a Standards-based critical thinking question.

Goal 3: Connections

3.1 (Cross-curricular Connections): *REALIDADES* integrates cross-curricular activities within the *Manos a la obra* section. Students make connections to a variety of disciplines through activities that integrate the language of the chapter.

3.2 (Connections to Target Culture): *REALIDADES* exposes students to perspectives only available within the target culture through art, realia, pronunciation activities, and readings.

Goal 4: Comparisons

4.1 (Language Comparisons): *REALIDADES* enables students to see comparisons between languages in both the grammar explanations in the text, on the *GramActiva* video, and in a unique section called *Exploración de lenguaje*. Students learn to look for language connections, to understand how language works, and to integrate these new skills as they continue in their study of Spanish.

4.2 (Cultural Comparisons): *REALIDADES* is rich in cultural comparisons. A unique feature called *Fondo cultural* generally informs students about a cultural product or practice and is followed by a question that challenges students to think critically and make comparisons between cultures.

Goal 5: Communities

5.1 (Outside the Classroom): *REALIDADES* provides informative features called *El español en la comunidad* and *El español en el mundo del trabajo*. These sections help students see how to use Spanish beyond the classroom, in their communities, and in the world of work.

5.2 (Lifelong Learners): For a textbook to help students achieve this goal, it must motivate students to want to communicate and want to learn more about the culture. The core of *REALIDADES*—real language, real culture, real tasks—motivates students. The video programs and other technology support engage learners in ways that may encourage them to continue their exploration of the Spanish language and cultures.

Standards for Foreign Language Learning

Goal 1: Communicate In Languages Other Than English

- Standard 1.1: Students engage in conversation, provide and obtain information, express feelings and emotions, and exchange opinions.
- Standard 1.2: Students understand and interpret written and spoken language on a variety of topics.
- Standard 1.3: Students present information, concepts and ideas to an audience of listeners or readers on a variety of topics.

Goal 2: Gain Knowledge And Understanding Of Other Cultures

- Standard 2.1: Students demonstrate an understanding of the relationship between the practices and perspectives of the culture studied.
- Standard 2.2: Students demonstrate an understanding of the relationship between the products and perspectives of the culture studied.

Goal 3: Connect With Other Disciplines And Acquire Information

- Standard 3.1: Students reinforce and further their knowledge of other disciplines through the foreign language.
- Standard 3.2: Students acquire information and recognize the distinctive viewpoints that are only available through the foreign language and its cultures.

Goal 4: Gain Insight Into The Nature Of Language And Culture

- Standard 4.1: Students demonstrate understanding of the nature of language through comparisons of the language studied and their own.
- Standard 4.2: Students demonstrate understanding of the concept of culture through comparisons of the cultures studied and their own.

Goal 5: Participate In Multilingual Communities At Home And Around The World

- Standard 5.1: Students use the language both within and beyond the school setting.
- Standard 5.2: Students show evidence of becoming life-long learners by using the language for personal enjoyment and enrichment.

Program Organization

REALIDADES is a communication-based five-level series with a full range of printing and technology components that allow teachers to meet the needs of the different students in today's Spanish classroom.

....

Middle School

REALIDADES A and *B* are separate middle school books that meet the needs of the younger learners. Each Student Edition provides the same content of *REALIDADES 1* but has been adapted with new art, photographs, and activities that are age-appropriate for the younger learner. Students completing *REALIDADES B* will make a smooth transition into *REALIDADES 2.*

High School

Each high school Student Edition provides the complete curriculum for one year of instruction. The spiraling of themes and extensive recycling of content allows for smooth articulation between the three levels. Students completing *REALIDADES 3* will have a solid foundation for advanced Spanish study.

REALIDADES A
• Introductory section *Para empezar*
• Themes 1–4

REALIDADES B
• Review section *Para empezar*
• Themes 5–9

REALIDADES 1
• Introductory section *Para empezar*
• Themes 1–9

REALIDADES 2
• Review section *Para empezar*
• Themes 1–9

REALIDADES 3
• Review section *Para empezar*
• Chapters 1–10

Chapter Organization

▶ Temas

REALIDADES 2 begins with an introductory section followed by nine thematic chapters. Each chapter is divided into two sections.

Tema	Capítulo	
Para empezar	1. ¿Cómo eres tú? 2. ¿Qué haces?	
	A	**B**
1: Tu día escolar	1A ¿Qué haces en la escuela?	1B: ¿Qué haces después de las clases?
2: Un evento especial	2A: ¿Cómo te preparas?	2B: ¿Qué ropa compraste?
3: Tú y tu comunidad	3A: ¿Qué hiciste ayer?	3B: ¿Cómo se va . . . ?
4: Recuerdos del pasado	4A: Cuando éramos niños	4B: Celebrando los días festivos
5: En las noticias	5A: Un acto heroico	5B: Un accidente
6: La televisión y el cine	6A: ¿Viste el partido en la televisión?	6B: ¿Qué película has visto?
7: Buen provecho	7A: ¿Cómo se hace la paella?	7B: ¿Te gusta comer al aire libre?
8: Cómo ser un buen turista	8A: Un viaje en avión	8B: Quiero que disfrutes de tu viaje
9: ¿Cómo será el futuro?	9A: ¿Qué profesión tendrás?	9B: ¿Qué haremos para mejorar el mundo?

▶ Chapters

Each chapter in *REALIDADES* is built around a clear sequence of instruction.

Chapter Section	Pedagogical support
A primera vista	Provides comprehensible language input for the chapter's new vocabulary and grammar within an authentic context. Input includes words, dialogues, narration, visuals, audio, and video. Students' language production focuses on comprehension and limited production.
Manos a la obra	Provides productive language practice with a variety of concrete, transitional, and open-ended activities. The activities develop all four language skills and focus on relevant language tasks. Many activities build off of authentic documents, *realia,* and photographs.
¡Adelante!	Provides culminating theme-based activities that have students apply what they have learned. The section features a culturally-based reading, performance-based speaking or writing tasks, cultural activities, and the storyline mystery video *En busca de la verdad.*
Repaso del capítulo	Provides complete support for the end-of-chapter assessment. One page summarizes what students need to know (vocabulary and grammar). The second page outlines the proficiency and culture sections of the test by describing the task, providing a practice task, and referring students to chapter activities for review.

Program Organization

Articulation

REALIDADES offers a completely articulated Scope and Sequence across all levels. The recursive themes allow for the recycling, review, and reteaching of vocabulary and grammar.

REALIDADES 1

Tema	Capítulo	
Para empezar	• En la escuela: greetings; introductions; leave-takings; numbers; time; body parts • En la clase: classroom, date, asking for help • El tiempo: weather, seasons	
	(A)	**(B)**
1: Mis amigos y yo	**1A ¿Qué te gusta hacer?** **Vocabulary:** activities and expressions for saying what you like and don't like to do **Grammar:** infinitives; making negative statements	**1B Y tú, ¿cómo eres?** **Vocabulary:** adjectives and vocabulary to ask about and describe someone's personality **Grammar:** adjectives; definite and indefinite articles; word order
2: La escuela	**2A Tu día en la escuela** **Vocabulary:** classroom items and furniture; parts of the classroom; prepositions of location **Grammar:** subject pronouns; the present tense of *-ar* verbs	**2B Tu sala de clases** **Vocabulary:** classroom items and furniture; parts of the classroom; prepositions of location **Grammar:** the verb *estar*; plurals of nouns and articles
3: La comida	**3A ¿Desayuno o almuerzo?** **Vocabulary:** foods; beverages; adverbs of frequency; expressions to show surprise **Grammar:** present tense of *-er* and *-ir* verbs; *me gusta(n), me encanta(n)*	**3B Para mantener la salud** **Vocabulary:** food; beverages; expressions to discuss health; expressions to discuss preferences, agreement, disagreement, and quantity; adjectives to describe food **Grammar:** the plural of adjectives; the verb *ser*
4: Los pasatiempos	**4A ¿Adónde vas?** **Vocabulary:** leisure activities; places; expressions to tell where and with whom you go; expressions to talk about when things are done **Grammar:** the verb *ir*; interrogative words	**4B ¿Quieres ir conmigo?** **Vocabulary:** leisure activities; feelings; expressions for extending, accepting, and declining invitations; expressions to tell when something happens **Grammar:** *ir + a +* infinitive; the verb *jugar*
5: Fiesta en familia	**5A Una fiesta de cumpleaños** **Vocabulary:** family and parties **Grammar:** the verb *tener;* possessive adjectives	**5B ¡Vamos a un restaurante!** **Vocabulary:** describing people and ordering a meal **Grammar:** the verb *venir;* the verbs *ser* and *estar*
6: La casa	**6A En mi dormitorio** **Vocabulary:** bedroom items; electronic equipment; colors; adjectives to describe things **Grammar:** comparisons and superlatives; stem-changing verbs: *poder* and *dormir*	**6B ¿Cómo es tu casa?** **Vocabulary:** rooms in a house and household chores **Grammar:** affirmative *tú* commands; the present progressive tense
7: De compras	**7A ¿Cuánto cuesta?** **Vocabulary:** clothing; shopping; numbers 200–1,000 **Grammar:** stem-changing verbs: *pensar, querer,* and *preferir;* demonstrative adjectives	**7B ¡Qué regalo!** **Vocabulary:** places to shop; gifts; accessories; buying and selling **Grammar:** preterite of *-ar, -car,* and *-gar* verbs; direct object pronouns *lo, la, los, las*
8: Experiencias	**8A De vacaciones** **Vocabulary:** vacation places; activities; modes of transportation **Grammar:** preterite of *-er* and *-ir* verbs; preterite of *ir;* the personal *a*	**8B Ayudando en la comunidad** **Vocabulary:** recycling and volunteer work; places in a community **Grammar:** the verb *decir;* indirect object pronouns; preterite of *hacer* and *dar*
9: Medios de comunicación	**9A El cine y la televisión** **Vocabulary:** television shows; movie genres; giving opinions **Grammar:** *acabar de +* infinitive; *gustar* and similar verbs	**9B La tecnología** **Vocabulary:** computers; communication; computer-related activities **Grammar:** the verbs *pedir* and *servir; saber* and *conocer*

REALIDADES A and B provide the same Scope and Sequence as *REALIDADES 1*.

REALIDADES A covers the same content as the *Para empezar* section and *Temas* 1–4.

Tema	Capítulo
Para empezar	• En la escuela: greetings; introductions; leave-takings; numbers; time; body parts • En la clase: classroom, date, asking for help • El tiempo: weather, seasons

Tema	Capítulo (A)	Capítulo (B)
1: Mis amigos y yo	**1A ¿Qué te gusta hacer?** **Vocabulary:** activities and expressions for saying what you like and don't like to do **Grammar:** infinitives; making negative statements	**1B Y tú, ¿cómo eres?** **Vocabulary:** adjectives and vocabulary to ask about and describe someone's personality **Grammar:** adjectives; definite and indefinite articles; word order
2: La escuela	**2A Tu día en la escuela** **Vocabulary:** classroom items and furniture; parts of the classroom; prepositions of location **Grammar:** subject pronouns; the present tense of -ar verbs	**2B Tu sala de clases** **Vocabulary:** classroom items and furniture; parts of the classroom; prepositions of location **Grammar:** the verb estar; plurals of nouns and articles
3: La comida	**3A ¿Desayuno o almuerzo?** **Vocabulary:** foods; beverages; adverbs of frequency; expressions to show surprise **Grammar:** present tense of -er and -ir verbs; me gusta(n), me encanta(n)	**3B Para mantener la salud** **Vocabulary:** food; beverages; expressions to discuss health; expressions to discuss preferences, agreement, disagreement, and quantity; adjectives to describe food **Grammar:** the plural of adjectives; the verb ser
4: Los pasatiempos	**4A ¿Adónde vas?** **Vocabulary:** leisure activities; places; expressions to tell where and with whom you go; expressions to talk about when things are done **Grammar:** the verb ir; interrogative words	**4B ¿Quieres ir conmigo?** **Vocabulary:** leisure activities; feelings; expressions for extending, accepting, and declining invitations; expressions to tell when something happens **Grammar:** ir + a + infinitive; the verb jugar

REALIDADES B provides a review section called *Para empezar* and continues with *Temas* 5–9.

Tema	Capítulo (A)	Capítulo (B)
5: Fiesta en familia	**5A Una fiesta de cumpleaños** **Vocabulary:** family and parties **Grammar:** the verb tener; possessive adjectives	**5B ¡Vamos a un restaurante!** **Vocabulary:** describing people and ordering a meal **Grammar:** the verb venir; the verbs ser and estar
6: La casa	**6A En mi dormitorio** **Vocabulary:** bedroom items; electronic equipment; colors; adjectives to describe things **Grammar:** comparisons and superlatives; stem-changing verbs: poder and dormir	**6B ¿Cómo es tu casa?** **Vocabulary:** rooms in a house and household chores **Grammar:** affirmative tú commands; the present progressive tense
7: De compras	**7A ¿Cuánto cuesta?** **Vocabulary:** clothing; shopping; numbers 200–1,000 **Grammar:** stem-changing verbs: pensar, querer, and preferir; demonstrative adjectives	**7B ¡Qué regalo!** **Vocabulary:** places to shop; gifts; accessories; buying and selling **Grammar:** preterite of -ar, -car, and -gar verbs; direct object pronouns lo, la, los, las
8: Experiencias	**8A De vacaciones** **Vocabulary:** vacation places; activities; modes of transportation **Grammar:** preterite of -er and -ir verbs; preterite of ir; the personal a	**8B Ayudando en la comunidad** **Vocabulary:** recycling and volunteer work; places in a community **Grammar:** the verb decir; indirect object pronouns; preterite of hacer and dar
9: Medios de comunicación	**9A El cine y la televisión** **Vocabulary:** television shows; movie genres; giving opinions **Grammar:** acabar de + infinitive; gustar and similar verbs	**9B La tecnología** **Vocabulary:** computers; communication; computer-related activities **Grammar:** the verbs pedir and servir; saber and conocer

Program Organization

REALIDADES 2 uses a recursive Scope and Sequence that revisits the themes from *REALIDADES A, B,* or *1*. This natural recycling allows for important review and reteaching. In addition, students expand their vocabulary, grammar, and cultural understanding as they revisit each theme in greater depth.

REALIDADES 2

Tema	Capítulo	
Para empezar	A. **¿Cómo eres tú?** *Repaso:* describing people; asking for information; nationalities; adjective agreement; the verb *ser* B. **¿Qué haces?** *Repaso:* leisure activities; seasons of the year; regular *-ar, -er,* and *-ir* verbs	
1: Tu día escolar	**1A ¿Qué haces en la escuela?** **Vocabulary:** classroom items, activities, and rules **Grammar:** *(Repaso)* stem-changing verbs; affirmative and negative words	**1B ¿Qué haces después de las clases?** **Vocabulary:** extracurricular activities **Grammar:** making comparisons; *(Repaso)* the verbs *saber* and *conocer; hace* + time expressions
2: Un evento especial	**2A ¿Cómo te preparas?** **Vocabulary:** daily routines, getting ready for an event **Grammar:** reflexive verbs; *(Repaso)* the verbs *ser* and *estar;* possessive adjectives *mío, tuyo, suyo*	**2B ¿Qué ropa compraste?** **Vocabulary:** shopping vocabulary, prices, money **Grammar:** *(Repaso)* the preterite of regular verbs; demonstrative adjectives
3: Tú y tu comunidad	**3A ¿Qué hiciste ayer?** **Vocabulary:** running errands; locations in a downtown; items purchased **Grammar:** *(Repaso)* direct object pronouns; the irregular preterite of the verbs *ir, ser, hacer, tener, estar, poder*	**3B ¿Cómo se va . . . ?** **Vocabulary:** places in a city or town; driving terms; modes of transportation **Grammar:** *(Repaso)* direct object pronouns: *me, te, nos;* irregular affirmative *tú* commands; *(Repaso)* present progressive: irregular forms
4: Recuerdos del pasado	**4A Cuando éramos niños** **Vocabulary:** toys; play terms; describing children **Grammar:** the imperfect tense: regular verbs and irregular verbs; *(Repaso)* indirect object pronouns	**4B Celebrando los días festivos** **Vocabulary:** expressions describing etiquette; holiday and family celebrations **Grammar:** the imperfect tense: describing a situation; reciprocal actions
5: En las noticias	**5A Un acto heroico** **Vocabulary:** natural disasters; emergencies; rescues; heroes **Grammar:** the imperfect tense: other uses; the preterite of the verbs *oír, leer, creer,* and *destruir*	**5B Un accidente** **Vocabulary:** parts of the body; accidents; events in the emergency room **Grammar:** the irregular preterites: *venir, poner; decir, traer;* the imperfect progressive and preterite
6: La televisión y el cine	**6A ¿Viste el partido en la televisión?** **Vocabulary:** watching television programs; sporting events **Grammar:** the preterite of *-ir* stem-changing verbs; other reflexive verbs	**6B ¿Qué película has visto?** **Vocabulary:** movies; making a movie **Grammar:** verbs that use indirect objects; the present perfect
7: Buen provecho	**7A ¿Cómo se hace la paella?** **Vocabulary:** cooking expressions; food; appliances; following a recipe; giving directions in a kitchen **Grammar:** negative *tú* commands; the impersonal *se*	**7B ¿Te gusta comer al aire libre?** **Vocabulary:** camping and cookouts; food **Grammar:** *usted* and *ustedes* commands; uses of *por*
8: Cómo ser un buen turista	**8A Un viaje en avión** **Vocabulary:** visiting an airport; planning a trip; traveling safely **Grammar:** the present subjunctive; irregular verbs in the subjunctive	**8B Quiero que disfrutes de tu viaje** **Vocabulary:** staying in a hotel; appropriate tourist behaviors; traveling in a foreign city **Grammar:** the present subjunctive with impersonal expressions; the present subjunctive of stem-changing verbs
9: ¿Cómo será el futuro?	**9A ¿Qué profesión tendrás?** **Vocabulary:** professions; making plans for the future; earning a living **Grammar:** the future tense; the future tense of irregular verbs	**9B ¿Qué haremos para mejorar el mundo?** **Vocabulary:** environment; environmental issues and solutions **Grammar:** the future tense: other irregular verbs; the present subjunctive with expressions of doubt

REALIDADES 3 offers ten thought-provoking thematic chapters that integrate rich vocabulary groups and a thorough presentation of grammar. Chapter activities combine communication, culture, and cross-curricular content with authentic literature and poetry.

REALIDADES 3

Capítulo	Each thematic chapter is divided into two sections. Each of these sections (1 and 2) present and practice vocabulary and grammar.	
Para empezar	1. Tu vida diaria *Repaso:* daily routines; school life; eisure activities; present tense verbs; reflexive verbs 2. Días especiales *Repaso:* weekend activities; celebrations; special events; verbs like *gustar;* possessive adjectives	
	①	**②**
1: Días inolvidables	**Vocabulary:** hiking objects, activities, and perils; weather **Grammar:** *(Repaso)* preterite verbs with the spelling change *i→y; (Repaso)* preterite of irregular verbs; *(Repaso)* preterite of verbs with the spelling change *e→i* and *o→u*	**Vocabulary:** getting ready for an athletic or academic competition; emotional responses to competition; awards and ceremonies **Grammar:** *(Repaso)* the imperfect; uses of the imperfect
2: ¿Cómo te expresas?	**Vocabulary:** describing art and sculpture; tools for painting; describing what influences art **Grammar:** *(Repaso)* the preterite vs. the imperfect; *estar +* participle	**Vocabulary:** musical instruments; describing dance; describing drama **Grammar:** *(Repaso) ser* and *estar;* verbs with special meanings in the preterite vs. the imperfect
3: ¿Qué haces para estar en forma?	**Vocabulary:** nutrition; illnesses and pains; medicine; habits for good health **Grammar:** *(Repaso)* affirmative *tú* commands; *(Repaso)* affirmative and negatives commands with *Ud.* and *Uds.*	**Vocabulary:** exercises; getting and staying in shape; health advice **Grammar:** *(Repaso)* the subjunctive: regular verbs; *(Repaso)* the subjunctive: irregular verbs; *(Repaso)* the subjunctive with stem-changing *-ar* and *-er* verbs
4: ¿Cómo te llevas con los demás?	**Vocabulary:** personality traits; interpersonal behavior; friendship **Grammar:** *(Repaso)* the subjunctive with verbs of emotion; *(Repaso)* the uses of *por* and *para*	**Vocabulary:** expressing and resolving interpersonal problems; interpersonal relationships **Grammar:** commands with *nosotros;* possessive pronouns
5: Trabajo y comunidad	**Vocabulary:** after-school work; describing a job **Grammar:** *(Repaso)* the present perfect; *(Repaso)* the past perfect	**Vocabulary:** volunteer activities; the benefits and importance of volunteer work **Grammar:** the present perfect subjunctive; demonstrative adjectives and pronouns
6: ¿Qué nos traerá el futuro?	**Vocabulary:** jobs and professions; qualities of a good employee **Grammar:** *(Repaso)* the future; *(Repaso)* the future of probability	**Vocabulary:** technology; inventions; jobs in the future **Grammar:** the future perfect; *(Repaso)* the use of direct and indirect object pronouns
7: ¿Mito o realidad?	**Vocabulary:** archaeological terms and activities; describing archaeological sites **Grammar:** the present and past subjunctive in expressions of doubt	**Vocabulary:** myths and legends; ancient beliefs; pre-Columbian scientific discoveries **Grammar:** the subjunctive in adverbial clauses
8: Encuentro entre culturas	**Vocabulary:** architecture and history of Spain **Grammar:** the conditional	**Vocabulary:** Spain in the Americas; the encounter between Cortés and the Aztecs; family heritage **Grammar:** the past subjunctive; the past subjunctive with *si* clauses
9: Cuidemos nuestro planeta	**Vocabulary:** caring for the environment **Grammar:** present subjunctive with conjunctions (*mientras, tan pronto como,* etc.); relative pronouns *que, quien, lo que*	**Vocabulary:** environmental issues; endangered animals **Grammar:** present subjunctive with other conjunctions (*a menos que, sin que, para que,* etc.)
10: ¿Cuáles son tus derechos y deberes?	**Vocabulary:** rights and responsibilties **Grammar:** the passive voice: *ser +* past participle; the present vs. the past subjunctive	**Vocabulary:** government; the role of government; individual rights **Grammar:** the past perfect subjunctive; the conditional perfect

Program Organization

Student Print Resources

Practice Workbook
- focused practice for new vocabulary and grammar
- end-of-chapter Crossword Puzzle and Organizer
- go online Web Codes for linking to Companion Web Site

Writing, Audio & Video Activities
- additional writing practice
- student response pages for the Audio Program and *A primera vista* video segments
- lyrics to songs

REALIDADES para hispanohablantes
- all-Spanish companion worktext to Student Edition
- grammar explanations in Spanish
- more practice for language mechanics, usage, vocabulary, grammar, reading, and writing

Guided Practice Activities for Vocabulary and Grammar
- ideal for students that need extra help
- reinforcement and reteaching for vocabulary and grammar

Lecturas para hispanohablantes
- literature anthology for additional reading

Reading and Writing for Success
- thematic readings that prepare students for standarized assessments
- one workbook for all levels

Grammar Study Guide
- laminated cards summarize grammar for Spanish 1–2

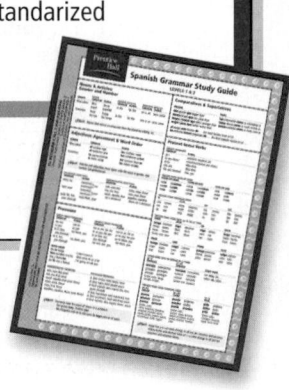

Student Technology

REALIDADES Companion Web Site
- instant access using Web Codes
- tutorial practice for vocabulary and grammar
- Internet links and activities
- four puzzles per chapter
- end-of-chapter self-test

MindPoint™ Quiz Show CD-ROM
- interactive game show format for review
- competition against computer, a partner, or entire class
- detailed report provides instant overview of student performance against the National Standards and chapter objectives

Interactive Textbook
- interactive Student Edition online or on CD-ROM
- access to audio and video
- interactive activities

Downloadable audio files
- audio for vocabulary, Student Edition activities, and pronunciation for students to download
- Web Codes listed in Student Edition

Teacher Print Resources

Teacher's Resource Books

Organized by chapters:

- Input Script
- Video and Audio Scripts
- *Practice Workbook* Answer Key
- *Writing, Audio & Video Activities* Answer Sheet
- Communication Activities on Blackline Masters
- Vocabulary Clip Art
- Situation Cards on Blackline Masters
- School to Home Letters
- *GramActiva* and *Juego* Blackline Masters

TPR Stories

- Complete support for integrating TPR storytelling with *REALIDADES*
- Written by Karen Rowan

Pre-AP* Resource Book

- Strategies for developing Pre-AP* skills
- Correlations per chapter
- Support for all levels

Guided Practice Activities Teacher's Guide with Audio CDs

- Answer Key to workbook
- Audio end-of-chapter vocabulary lists on two CDs

REALIDADES para hispanohablantes Answer Key

- Answer Key for heritage learner workbook

Reading and Writing for Success Answer Key

- Answer key to workbook

Teacher Assessment

Three programs for assessing all students

Assessment Program

- for use with students using Student Edition

Assessment Program *REALIDADES para hispanohablantes*

- for use with heritage learners

Alternate Assessment Program

- for use with students needing alternate assessment or retesting

ExamView® Computer Test Bank

Available per chapter

- Two different sets of question banks
- Additional question bank for heritage learners
- Additional question bank for Pre-AP* learners
- Create tests and alternate versions
- Questions correlated to the Florida Benchmarks

Teacher Technology

PHSchool.com

TeacherEXPRESS™ CD-ROM

- Lesson Planner
- Teacher's Edition
- Teaching Resources
- Vocabulary Clip Art
- Computer Test Bank
- Web Resources

PresentationEXPRESS™ CD-ROM

PowerPoint-based teaching tool

- Vocabulary images and clip art
- Grammar transparencies and teaching tools
- *ExamView®* QuickTake quizzes
- Answers on transparencies

Video Program (VHS or DVD)

- *A primera vista* segments expand each chapter's *Videohistoria*
- *GramActiva* segments teach the new grammar using humor and graphics
- *En busca de la verdad* mystery video

PHSchool.com

Companion Web Site

- teaching ideas
- links to other resources

Audio Program (22 CDs)

- *A primera vista*
  - *Vocabulario y gramática en contexto*
  - *Videohistoria*
- Student Edition *Escuchar* Activities
- *Pronunciación*
- *Writing, Audio & Video Workbook* Listening Activities
- Listening section of *Examen del capítulo*
- Songs

Guided Practice Audio CDs

- CDs (two) contain end-of-chapter audio of vocabulary lists

SuccessNet™ Online Access Pack

- Registration code to activate online Interactive Textbook

MindPoint™ Quiz Show CD-ROM

Teacher Transparencies

Vocabulary and Grammar Transparencies

- Maps
- Graphic Organizers
- *A primera vista*
  - *Vocabulario y gramática en contexto*
  - *Videohistoria*
- *Gramática*
  - verb paradigms and grammar charts
- Realia
- Rapid Review

Answers on Transparencies

- Student Edition answers
- *Practice Workbook* answers

Fine Art Transparencies

- 72 fine art transparencies to be used across all levels
- accompanying notes and activities

Getting Started

Students get started in *REALIDADES 2* with these colorful reference and introductory sections:

▷ **Mapas**

▷ **Study Tips**

▷ **Para empezar**

▷ **A ver si recuerdas**

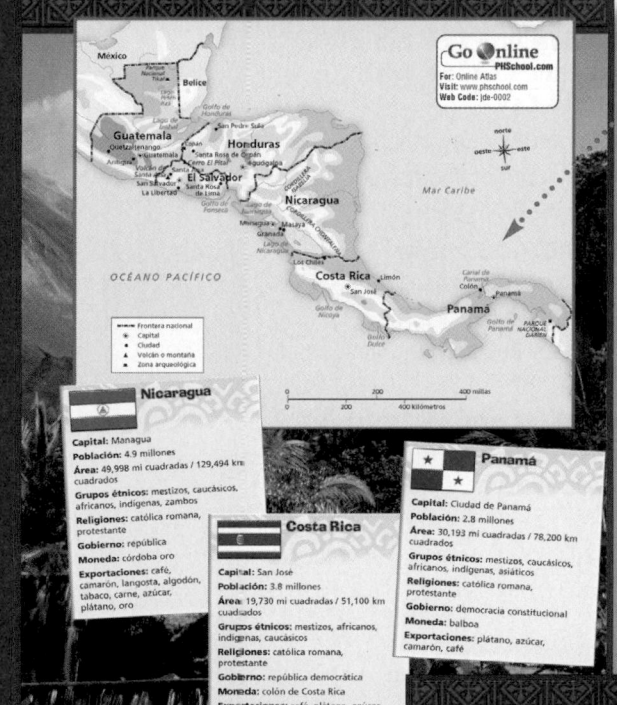

Mapas

Colorful atlas pages support geography skills. Students can go online to learn more about each country.

Study Tips

Students are reminded of study tips as they begin *REALIDADES 2*.

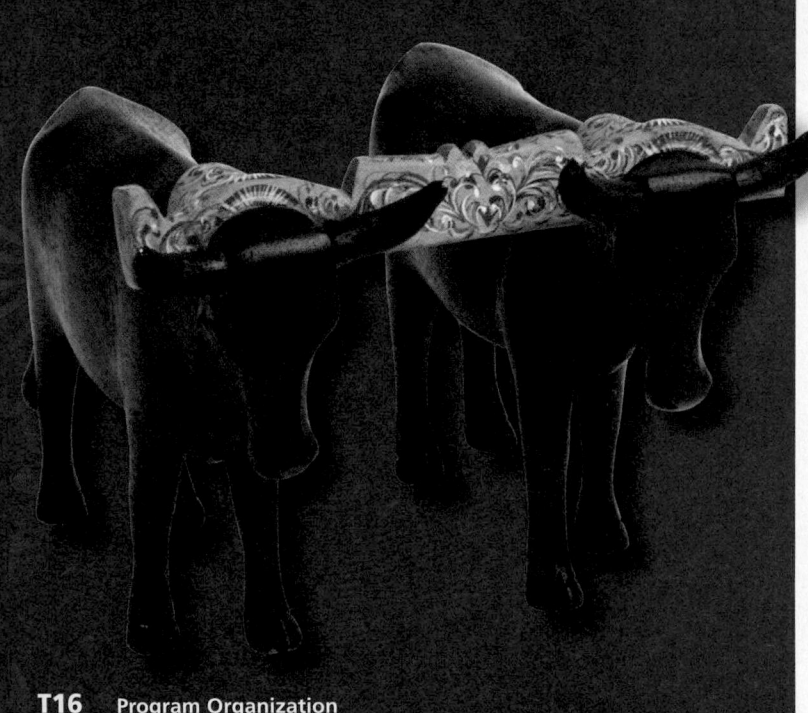

Para empezar

This bridge section provides a basic review of key content from *REALIDADES 1*.

Basic Review

The quick review covers concepts from the first year.

A ver si recuerdas...

This section helps students review the key vocabulary and grammar learned in first-year Spanish as it relates to the themes for the upcoming chapter.

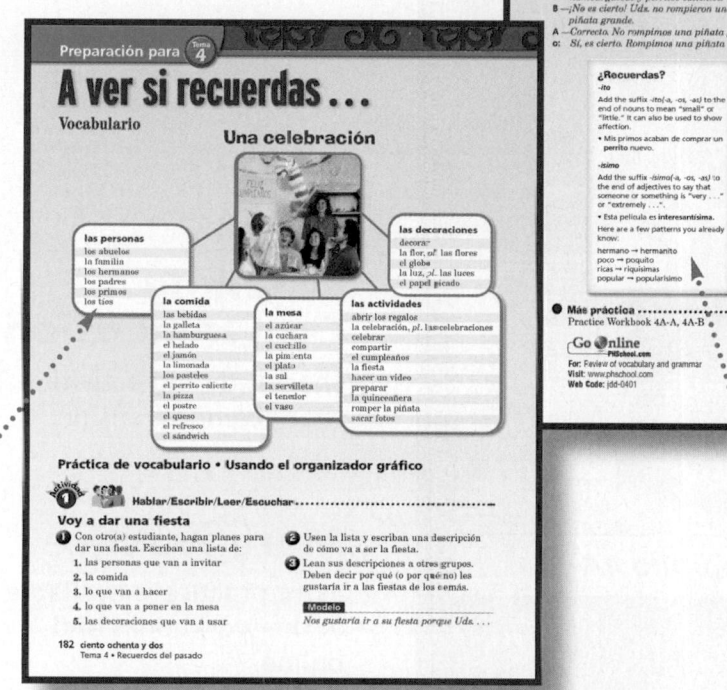

Vocabulary Review

Thematic vocabulary is reviewed using a graphic organizer.

Grammar Review

Students review and practice key grammar concepts.

Chapter Organization

Chapter Sequence

▷ **A primera vista**

▷ **Manos a la obra**

▷ **¡Adelante!**

▷ **Repaso del capítulo**

▷ **Chapter Opener** *Capítulo 4A*

A primera vista

This four-page section gives students a "first look" at the new vocabulary and grammar through comprehensible input that integrates visuals and text with audio and video.

Visualized Vocabulary

New words are presented visually and in context.

Language Input

Input continues with visuals accompanied by narrative. All new vocabulary words and grammar are highlighted in blue.

Listening Comprehension

Short listening activities check comprehension.

More Practice

Extra practice is available in the workbooks and online.

Reading and Language Input

The input of new vocabulary and grammar continues through a short, engaging reading written as a *videohistoria*. This story is based upon the accompanying *A primera vista* video segment.

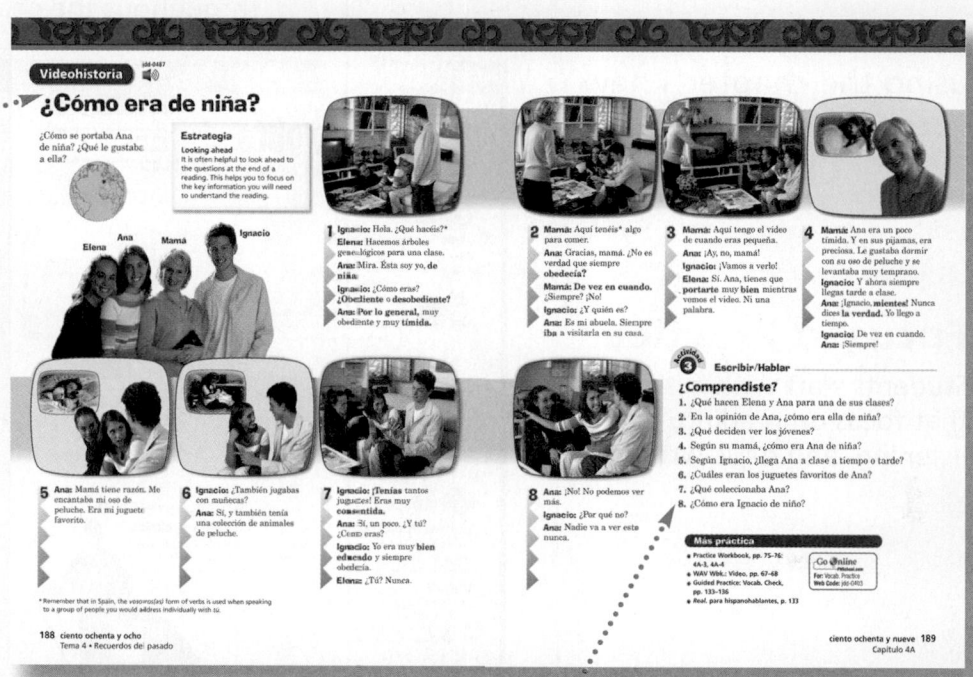

Reading Comprehension

Questions check students' comprehension of the story while practicing the new vocabulary and grammar.

Videos and Language Input

The language, characters, and culture of the *Videohistoria* come to life in the *A primera vista* video segment. Each video segment is approximately 5 minutes in length. The videos were filmed in San Antonio, Mexico City, Costa Rica, and Spain (Madrid and Toledo). To help students with language input, each video is shown twice. The first time, key vocabulary is labeled on the screen. The second time, the words are not shown. Additional video activities can be found in the Writing, Audio & Video Workbook.

From the *A primera vista* video segment

Manos a la obra

Students "get to work" using the chapter's new vocabulary and grammar.

Integrated Culture

Cultural notes are embedded throughout the chapter.

Focused Practice

Students start with activities that focus on reading, listening, and basic writing.

Paired Practice

Students transition to paired practice activities that focus on the new vocabulary.

Grammar Integrated with Communication

The complete grammar presentation features clear explanations and examples.

Review and Recycling

¿Recuerdas? notes help students remember what they've already learned about the grammar point.

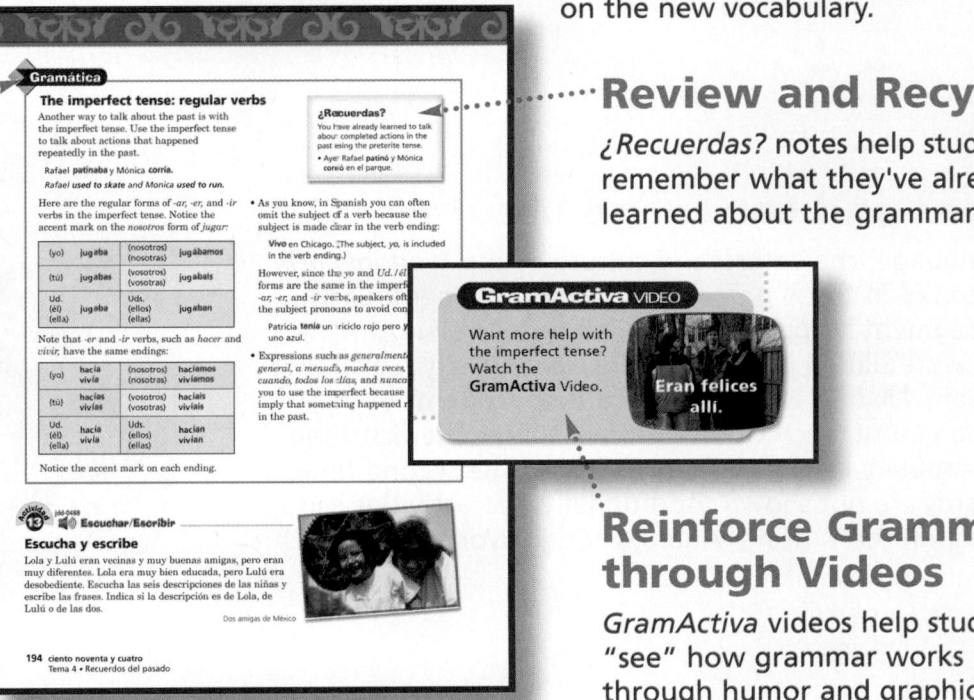

Reinforce Grammar through Videos

GramActiva videos help students "see" how grammar works through humor and graphics.

Language and Culture

Culture is woven together with language practice.

Connections to Other Disciplines

Cross-curricular connections are integrated into the language practice.

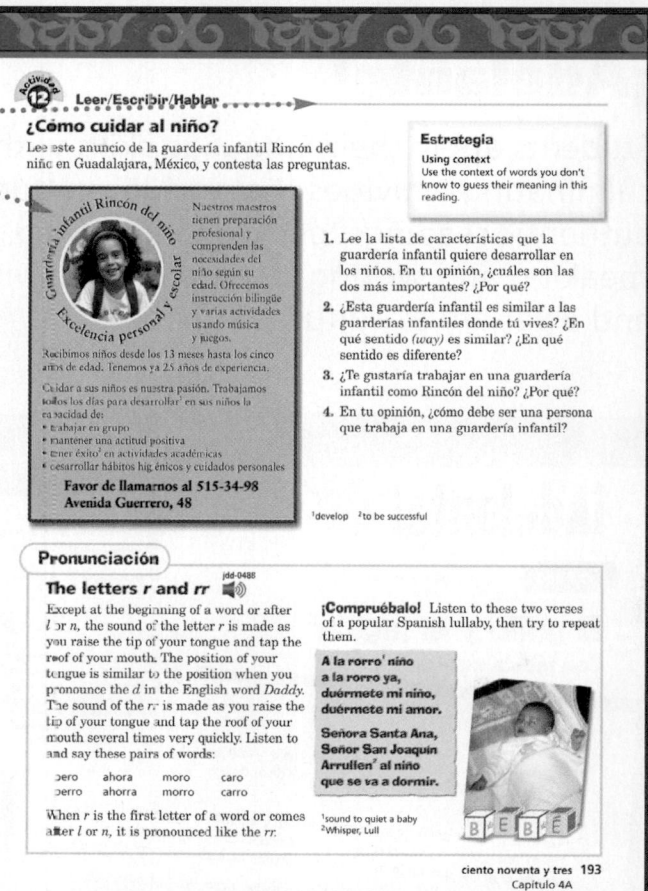

Actividad 12 Leer/Escribir/Hablar

¿Cómo cuidar al niño?

Lee este anuncio de la guardería infantil Rincón del niño en Guadalajara, México, y contesta las preguntas.

Estrategia
Using context
Use the context of words you don't know to guess their meaning in this reading.

Guardería infantil Rincón del niño

Nuestros maestros tienen preparación profesional y comprenden las necesidades del niño según su edad. Ofrecemos instrucción bilingüe y varias actividades usando música y juegos.

Excelencia personal y escolar

Recibimos niños desde los 13 meses hasta los cinco años de edad. Tenemos ya 25 años de experiencia.

Cuidar a sus niños es nuestra pasión. Trabajamos todos los días para desarrollar¹ en sus niños la capacidad de:
• trabajar en grupo
• mantener una actitud positiva
• tener éxito² en actividades académicas
• desarrollar hábitos higiénicos y cuidados personales

Favor de llamarnos al 515-34-98
Avenida Guerrero, 48

¹develop ²to be successful

1. Lee la lista de características que la guardería infantil quiere desarrollar en los niños. En tu opinión, ¿cuáles son las dos más importantes? ¿Por qué?

2. ¿Esta guardería infantil es similar a las guarderías infantiles donde tú vives? ¿En qué sentido (way) es similar? ¿En qué sentido es diferente?

3. ¿Te gustaría trabajar en una guardería infantil como Rincón del niño? ¿Por qué?

4. En tu opinión, ¿cómo debe ser una persona que trabaja en una guardería infantil?

Pronunciación

The letters r and rr jdd-0488

Except at the beginning of a word or after *l* or *n*, the sound of the letter *r* is made as you raise the tip of your tongue and tap the roof of your mouth. The position of your tongue is similar to the position when you pronounce the *d* in the English word *Daddy*. The sound of the *rr* is made as you raise the tip of your tongue and tap the roof of your mouth several times very quickly. Listen to and say these pairs of words:

| pero | ahora | moro | caro |
| perro | ahorra | morro | carro |

When *r* is the first letter of a word or comes after *l* or *n*, it is pronounced like the *rr*.

¡Compruébalo! Listen to these two verses of a popular Spanish lullaby, then try to repeat them.

A la rorro¹ niño
a la rorro ya,
duérmete mi niño,
duérmete mi amor.

Señora Santa Ana,
Señor San Joaquín
Arrullen² al niño
que se va a dormir.

¹sound to quiet a baby
²Whisper, Lull

ciento noventa y tres **193**
Capítulo 4A

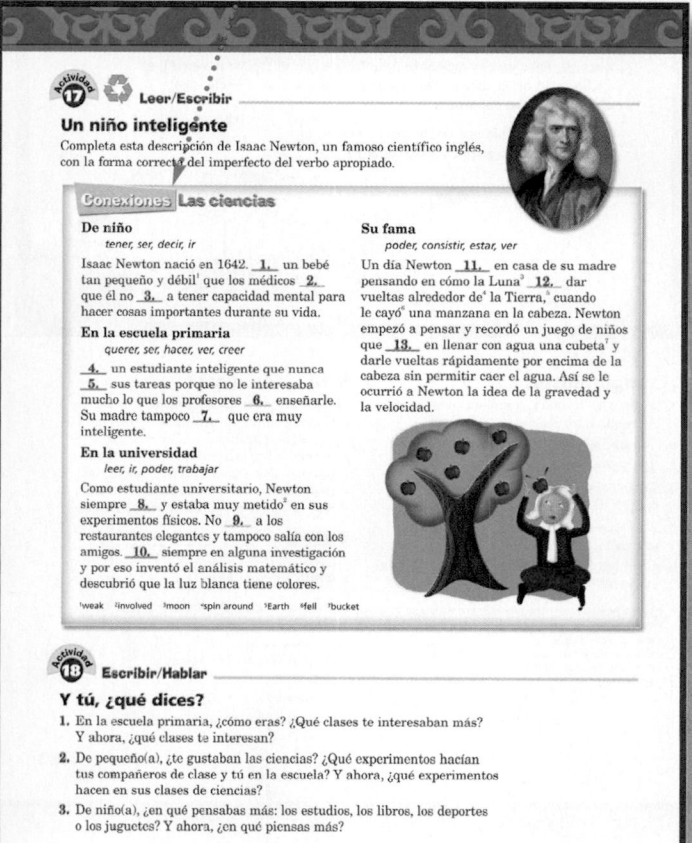

Actividad 17 Leer/Escribir

Un niño inteligente

Completa esta descripción de Isaac Newton, un famoso científico inglés, con la forma correcta del imperfecto del verbo apropiado.

Conexiones | Las ciencias

De niño
tener, ser, decir, ir

Isaac Newton nació en 1642. **1.** un bebé tan pequeño y débil¹ que los médicos **2.** que él no **3.** a tener capacidad mental para hacer cosas importantes durante su vida.

En la escuela primaria
querer, ser, hacer, ver, creer

4. un estudiante inteligente que nunca **5.** sus tareas porque no le interesaba mucho lo que los profesores **6.** enseñarle. Su madre tampoco **7.** que era muy inteligente.

En la universidad
leer, ir, poder, trabajar

Como estudiante universitario, Newton siempre **8.** y estaba muy metido² en sus experimentos físicos. No **9.** a los restaurantes elegantes y tampoco salía con los amigos. **10.** siempre en alguna investigación y por eso inventó el análisis matemático y descubrió que la luz blanca tiene colores.

Su fama
poder, consistir, estar, ver

Un día Newton **11.** en casa de su madre pensando en cómo la Luna³ **12.** dar vueltas alrededor de⁴ la Tierra,⁵ cuando le cayó⁶ una manzana en la cabeza. Newton empezó a pensar y recordó un juego de niños que **13.** en llenar con agua una cubeta⁷ y darle vueltas rápidamente por encima de la cabeza sin permitir caer el agua. Así se le ocurrió a Newton la idea de la gravedad y la velocidad.

¹weak ²involved ³moon ⁴spin around ⁵Earth ⁶fell ⁷bucket

Actividad 18 Escribir/Hablar

Y tú, ¿qué dices?

1. En la escuela primaria, ¿cómo eras? ¿Qué clases te interesaban más? Y ahora, ¿qué clases te interesan?

2. De pequeño(a), ¿te gustaban las ciencias? ¿Qué experimentos hacían tus compañeros de clase y tú en la escuela? Y ahora, ¿qué experimentos hacen en sus clases de ciencias?

3. De niño(a), ¿en qué pensabas más: los estudios, los libros, los deportes o los juguetes? Y ahora, ¿en qué piensas más?

ciento noventa y siete **197**
Capítulo 4A

Personal Responses

The sequence of exercises culminates with personalized speaking and writing tools.

Hands-on Learning

Fun, interactive games help students learn new concepts.

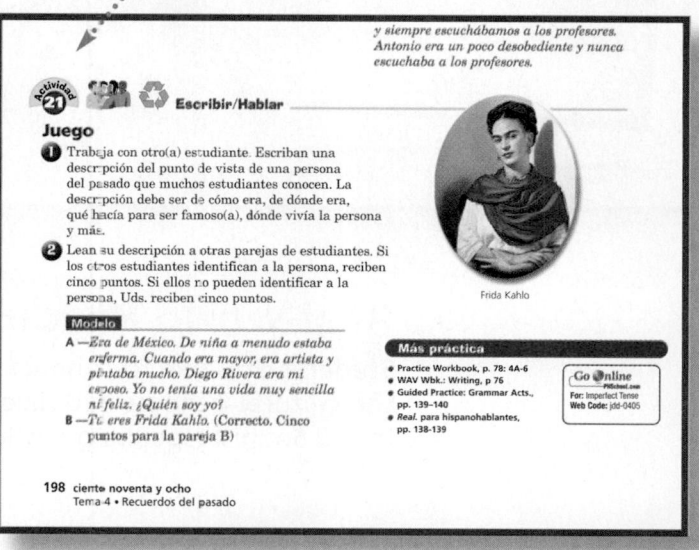

y siempre escuchábamos a los profesores. Antonio era un poco desobediente y nunca escuchaba a los profesores.

Actividad 21 Escribir/Hablar

Juego

1 Trabaja con otro(a) estudiante. Escriban una descripción del punto de vista de una persona del pasado que muchos estudiantes conocen. La descripción debe ser de cómo era, de dónde era, qué hacía para ser famoso(a), dónde vivía la persona y más.

2 Lean su descripción a otras parejas de estudiantes. Si los otros estudiantes identifican a la persona, reciben cinco puntos. Si ellos no pueden identificar a la persona, Uds. reciben cinco puntos.

Frida Kahlo

Modelo

A —Era de México. De niña a menudo estaba enferma. Cuando era mayor, era artista y pintaba mucho. Diego Rivera era mi esposo. Yo no tenía una vida muy sencilla ni feliz. ¿Quién soy yo?

B —Tú eres Frida Kahlo. (Correcto. Cinco puntos para la pareja B)

Más práctica

• Practice Workbook, p. 78: 4A-6
• WAV Wbk.: Writing, p 76
• Guided Practice: Grammar Acts., pp. 139-140
• Real. para hispanohablantes, pp. 138-139

Go Online
PHSchool.com
For: Imperfect Tense
Web Code: jdd-0405

198 ciento noventa y ocho
Tema 4 • Recuerdos del pasado

¡Adelante!

Students apply their language skills with culminating activities that include culturally authentic readings, performance-based speaking and writing tasks, a mystery video, and a variety of cultural activities.

Reading Strategies

Reading strategies help students become better readers.

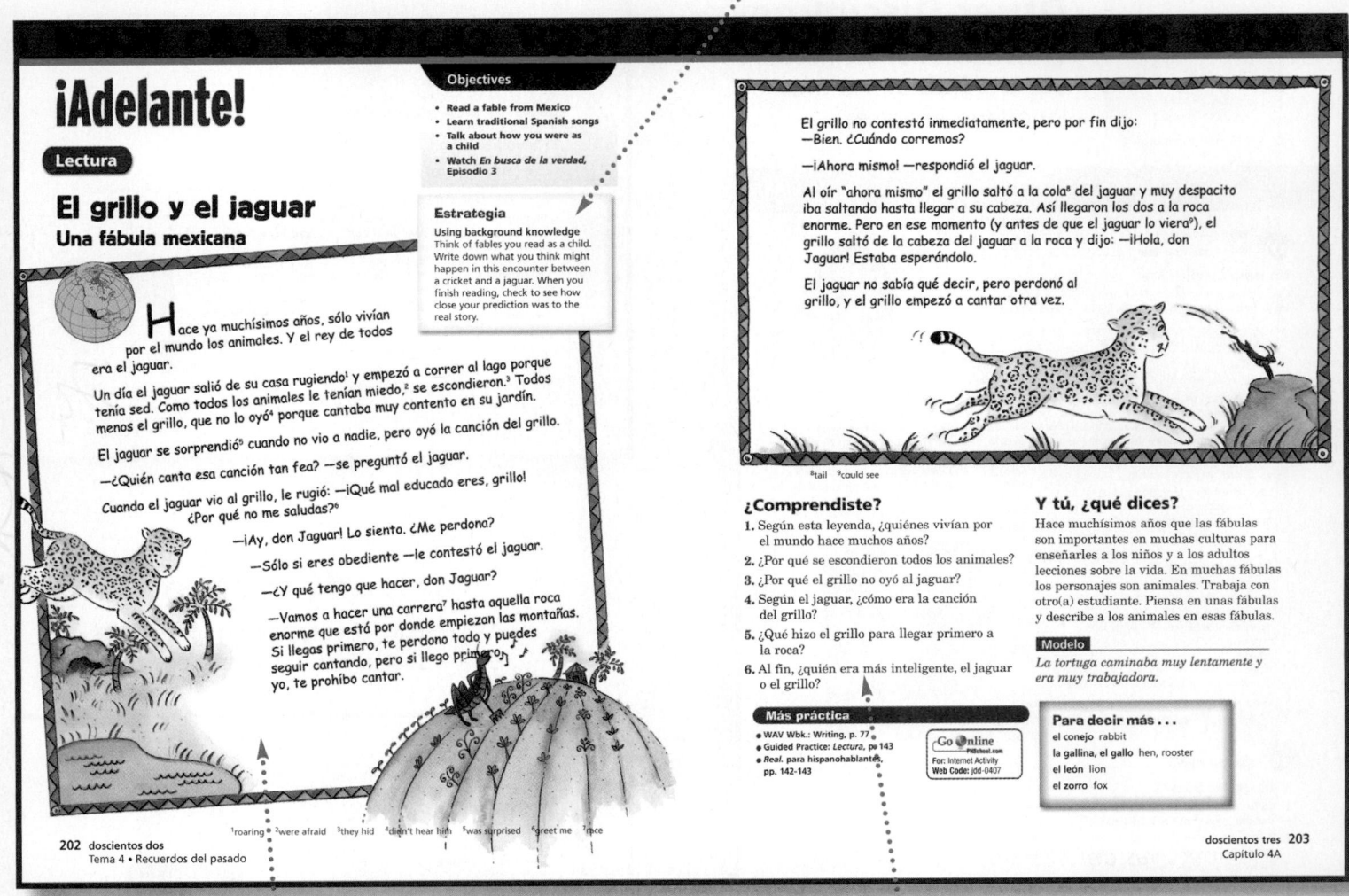

¡Adelante!

Lectura

El grillo y el jaguar
Una fábula mexicana

Objectives
- Read a fable from Mexico
- Learn traditional Spanish songs
- Talk about how you were as a child
- Watch *En busca de la verdad,* Episodio 3

Estrategia
Using background knowledge
Think of fables you read as a child. Write down what you think might happen in this encounter between a cricket and a jaguar. When you finish reading, check to see how close your prediction was to the real story.

Hace ya muchísimos años, sólo vivían por el mundo los animales. Y el rey de todos era el jaguar.

Un día el jaguar salió de su casa rugiendo[1] y empezó a correr al lago porque tenía sed. Como todos los animales le tenían miedo,[2] se escondieron.[3] Todos menos el grillo, que no lo oyó[4] porque cantaba muy contento en su jardín.

El jaguar se sorprendió[5] cuando no vio a nadie, pero oyó la canción del grillo.

—¿Quién canta esa canción tan fea? —se preguntó el jaguar.

Cuando el jaguar vio al grillo, le rugió: —¡Qué mal educado eres, grillo! ¿Por qué no me saludas?[6]

—¡Ay, don Jaguar! Lo siento. ¿Me perdona?

—Sólo si eres obediente —le contestó el jaguar.

—¿Y qué tengo que hacer, don Jaguar?

—Vamos a hacer una carrera[7] hasta aquella roca enorme que está por donde empiezan las montañas. Si llegas primero, te perdono todo y puedes seguir cantando, pero si llego primero yo, te prohíbo cantar.

[1]roaring [2]were afraid [3]they hid [4]didn't hear him [5]was surprised [6]greet me [7]race

202 doscientos dos
Tema 4 • Recuerdos del pasado

El grillo no contestó inmediatamente, pero por fin dijo:
—Bien. ¿Cuándo corremos?

—¡Ahora mismo! —respondió el jaguar.

Al oír "ahora mismo" el grillo saltó a la cola[8] del jaguar y muy despacito iba saltando hasta llegar a su cabeza. Así llegaron los dos a la roca enorme. Pero en ese momento (y antes de que el jaguar lo viera[9]), el grillo saltó de la cabeza del jaguar a la roca y dijo: —¡Hola, don Jaguar! Estaba esperándolo.

El jaguar no sabía qué decir, pero perdonó al grillo, y el grillo empezó a cantar otra vez.

[8]tail [9]could see

¿Comprendiste?

1. Según esta leyenda, ¿quiénes vivían por el mundo hace muchos años?
2. ¿Por qué se escondieron todos los animales?
3. ¿Por qué el grillo no oyó al jaguar?
4. Según el jaguar, ¿cómo era la canción del grillo?
5. ¿Qué hizo el grillo para llegar primero a la roca?
6. Al fin, ¿quién era más inteligente, el jaguar o el grillo?

Más práctica
- WAV Wbk.: Writing, p. 77
- Guided Practice: *Lectura,* pp 143
- *Real.* para hispanohablantes, pp. 142-143

Go Online
PHSchool.com
For: Internet Activity
Web Code: jdd-0407

Y tú, ¿qué dices?

Hace muchísimos años que las fábulas son importantes en muchas culturas para enseñarles a los niños y a los adultos lecciones sobre la vida. En muchas fábulas los personajes son animales. Trabaja con otro(a) estudiante. Piensa en unas fábulas y describe a los animales en esas fábulas.

Modelo
La tortuga caminaba muy lentamente y era muy trabajadora.

Para decir más . . .
el conejo rabbit
la gallina, el gallo hen, rooster
el león lion
el zorro fox

doscientos tres **203**
Capítulo 4A

Real-world Readings

Students are able to connect to the cultural richness and diversity in the Spanish-speaking world.

Comprehension Checks

Follow-up questions check students' comprehension.

La cultura en vivo
jdd-0488

Canciones infantiles

A todos los niños les encanta cantar. Aquí están dos canciones populares que cantan los niños en algunos países hispanohablantes mientras *(while)* juegan con sus amigos.

El columpio

Yo tengo un columpio[1]
de suave vaivén[2]
y en él muy contento
me vengo a mecer[3].

En la fuerte rama[4]
de un fuerte laurel[5],
mi buen papacito
lo vino a poner.

Qué suave columpio
qué rico vaivén
¿muchachos, no quieren
venirse a mecer?

Los elefantes

Un elefante se balanceaba
sobre la tela de una araña[6]
como veía que resistía
fue a buscar a otro elefante.

Dos elefantes se balanceaban
sobre la tela de una araña
como veían que resistía
fueron a buscar a otro elefante.

Tres elefantes se balanceaban . . .
Cuatro elefantes se balanceaban . . .
Cinco elefantes se balanceaban . . .
Seis elefantes se balanceaban . . .
Siete elefantes se balanceaban . . .
Ocho elefantes se balanceaban . . .
Nueve elefantes se balanceaban . . .

Diez elefantes se balanceaban
sobre la tela de una araña,
como veían que se rompía,
fueron a dejar a un elefante.

Nueve elefantes se balanceaban . . .

[6]spider web

[1]swing [2]swaying motion [3]to swing
[4]branch [5]laurel tree

¡Compruébalo! En grupos de cuatro, practiquen en voz alta *(aloud)* una de las canciones. Presten atención a la pronuncia y al ritmo de los versos. Presenten su canc la clase.

204 doscientos cuatro
Tema 4 • Recuerdos del pasado

Hands-on Culture

La cultura en vivo offers a fun, hands-on experience with a wide range of cultural products and practices.

Perspectivas del mundo hispano

El Roscón de Reyes

Es el Día de los Reyes Magos, el seis de enero, y mientras los niños juegan con sus regalos, los mayores preparan la merienda[1] de Reyes para sus amigos y familia. Esta merienda incluye un postre especial que se llama el roscón (o en México, la rosca) de Reyes. Cuando es la hora de comer el roscón, todo el mundo se acerca a la mesa y una persona empieza a cortarlo. Cada persona corta una rebanada[2] del roscón. Todos comen su porción cuando una persona grita, "¡Lo tengo!".

¿Qué es lo que tiene? Pues, dentro del roscón hay un muñequito de plástico. Según la tradición la persona que encuentra el muñequito debe pagar por la cena u otro roscón. Según otra tradición, la persona que encuentra el muñequito es el rey o la reina[3] de la fiesta.

El roscón es dulce, parecido a un pan dulce o a una torta, que se hace y se come sólo una vez al año. Está hecho con harina,[4] huevos, azúcar, mantequilla y frutas confitadas.[5] Como toda comida tradicional, la receta puede variar según la familia o la región. En ciertos países, el roscón se acompaña[6] con una taza de chocolate caliente.

¡Compruébalo! ¿Hay una tradición o celebración de tu familia en la que comen algo especial? ¿Qué es? ¿Cómo se prepara? ¿Hay algo especial que hacen mientras la preparan?

¿Qué te parece? ¿Crees que es importante mantener la tradición de preparar una comida especial? ¿Por qué?

[1]snack [2]slice [3]king or queen [4]flour
[5]candied [6]is accompanied

Un roscón de Reyes

Un vendedor de roscas de Reyes en México

230 doscientos treinta
Tema 4 • Recuerdos del pasado

Cultural Perspectives

Perspectivas del mundo hispano provides a thought-provoking overview of a product or practice (and its related perspectives) from the Spanish-speaking world.

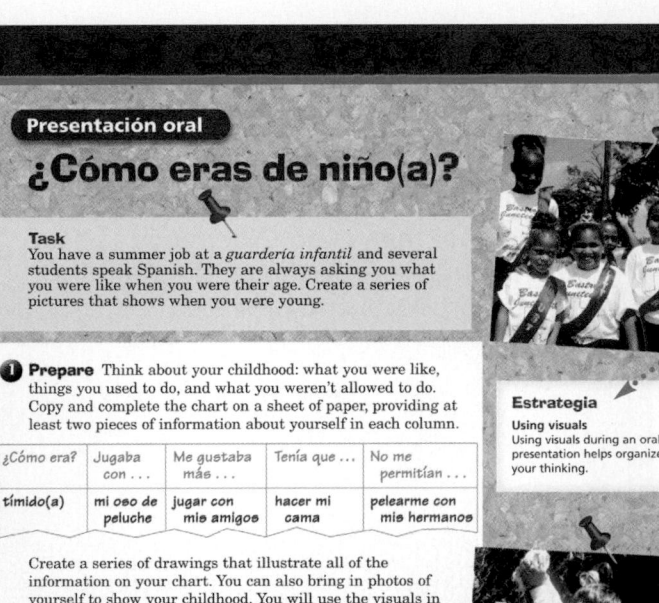

Presentación oral

¿Cómo eras de niño(a)?

Task
You have a summer job at a *guardería infantil* and several students speak Spanish. They are always asking you what you were like when you were their age. Create a series of pictures that shows when you were young.

1 Prepare Think about your childhood: what you were like, things you used to do, and what you weren't allowed to do. Copy and complete the chart on a sheet of paper, providing at least two pieces of information about yourself in each column.

¿Cómo era?	Jugaba con . . .	Me gustaba más . . .	Tenía que . . .	No me permitían . . .
tímido(a)	mi oso de peluche	jugar con mis amigos	hacer mi cama	pelearme con mis hermanos

Create a series of drawings that illustrate all of the information on your chart. You can also bring in photos of yourself to show your childhood. You will use the visuals in your presentation. Be sure they are easy to understand and represent you when you were young!

2 Practice Go through your presentation several times. You can use your chart to practice, but not when you present. Use your drawings and photos when you practice to help you recall what you want to say. Try to:
• provide as much information as possible on each point
• use complete sentences
• speak clearly so that you can be understood

3 Present Talk about what you were like as a child. Be sure to use your drawings during your presentation.

4 Evaluation Your teacher may give you a rubric for how the presentation will be graded. You will probably be graded on:
• amount of information you communicate
• how easy it is to understand you
• quality of visuals

Estrategia
Using visuals
Using visuals during an oral presentation helps organize your thinking.

doscientos ci...
Capítulo

Performance-based Speaking Tasks

Real-life speaking tasks are supported by strategies and a step-by-step process that helps all students to be successful. The *Assessment Program* contains the rubric for this task.

Presentación escrita

Mi celebración favorita

Task
You have an e-mail pal who wants to know about your favorite holiday or celebration. Write an e-mail message describing an event from your childhood.

1 Prewrite Think of an event you used to celebrate and want to write about. Copy the chart below on a sheet of paper. Using the questions on the top of each column as a guide, write words or expressions related to your topic.

¿Qué hacían?	¿Dónde se reunían?	¿Cómo era?	¿Quiénes estaban?	¿Por qué te gustaba?

2 Draft Use the ideas from the chart to write the first draft of your e-mail message.

Modelo

Mi celebración favorita era El Día de la Madre. Celebrábamos este día con toda la familia y, claro, con mi mamá. Íbamos a su restaurante favorito, Las Palomas. Siempre le regalábamos algo, como un collar o perfume. Ella siempre lloraba porque estaba muy contenta.

3 Revise Read your e-mail and check for correct spelling and vocabulary use. Be sure that you used the imperfect tense to describe events that used to take place. Share the e-mail with a partner, who should check the following:
• Is the e-mail easy to read and understand?
• Does it provide an interesting description of the event?
• Is there anything you should add?
• Are there any errors?

4 Publish Rewrite the e-mail, making necessary changes or corrections. Make a copy for your teacher or add it to your portfolio.

5 Evaluation Your teacher may give you a rubric for how the e-mail will be graded. You will probably be graded on:
• amount of information you provide
• accuracy in describing events in the past
• variety of vocabulary

Estrategia
Using a chart
Thinking through categories and writing down key words and expressions will give you more ideas for writing.

doscientos treinta y uno **231**
Capítulo 4B

Performance-based Writing Tasks

Students become better writers with real-life tasks that are supported with the writing process and focused strategies. As with the speaking tasks, a rubric has been specially written for each *Presentación escrita*.

Motivate and Build Confidence with a Mystery Video

Starting in *Tema 3*, students join Roberto Toledo as he searches for the truth behind the mysterious disappearance of his grandfather.

Después de ver el video

¿Comprendiste?

A. Escoge la palabra correcta de las tres que están entre paréntesis.

1. "Me parece estupendo. Saben que ustedes siempre son (esperados/bienvenidos/queridos) en esta casa".

2. "Su mamá está aquí arreglando un programa de (juegos/televisión/intercambio) con nuestra escuela".

3. "Mañana viene el carpintero a reparar algunas (cosas/plantas/mesas) en mi casa".

4. "Hoy hablé con la maestra Toledo. Ella dice que todo está (caminando/progresando/funcionando) muy bien para el intercambio".

5. "Bueno, tengo que volver a la (escuela/clínica/casa). ¡Mis pacientes me esperan!".

6. "Dani, tengo un (mensaje/regalo/pastel) para la abuela".

7. "Ella sabe más que yo. Ahora, tengo que (vestirme/irme/dormirme)".

B. ¿Por qué crees que Roberto empieza a pensar en su abuelo con la llegada de Linda? Escribe lo que piensas.

C. Mira las fotos de Roberto y su abuela mientras hablan por teléfono. Escribe un resumen de la conversación.

Go Online
PHSchool.com
For: More on *En busca de la verdad*
Web code: jdd-0209

doscientos siete **207**
Capítulo 4A

Videomisterio

En busca de la verdad

Episodio 3

Antes de ver el video

"Vamos a ver . . . ¿Qué hay de nuevo en el correo electrónico?".

"Tu abuelo se llamaba Federico Toledo. Es todo lo que puedo decirte".

Nota cultural El mercado es el lugar donde la gente va a comprar comida fresca. En Guanajuato está el famoso mercado Hidalgo, donde venden frutas, verduras, carnes y muchas cosas más.

Resumen del episodio

En este episodio van a conocer a Nela, la abuela de Roberto. Él hace planes para visitarla al día siguiente. La familia Toledo almuerza en casa. Después de comer, Roberto le pregunta a su papá sobre su abuelo.

Palabras para comprender
catrina artistic rendering of a skull
una cosa más one more thing
carpintero carpenter
conocerse mejor to know each other better
a propósito by the way

206 doscientos seis
Tema 4 • Recuerdos del pasado

Comprehension Checks

A variety of questions check students' comprehension of the video.

Repaso del capítulo

These two pages provide complete review and preparation for the chapter test.

Online Self-test.

Students can get extra test practice online.

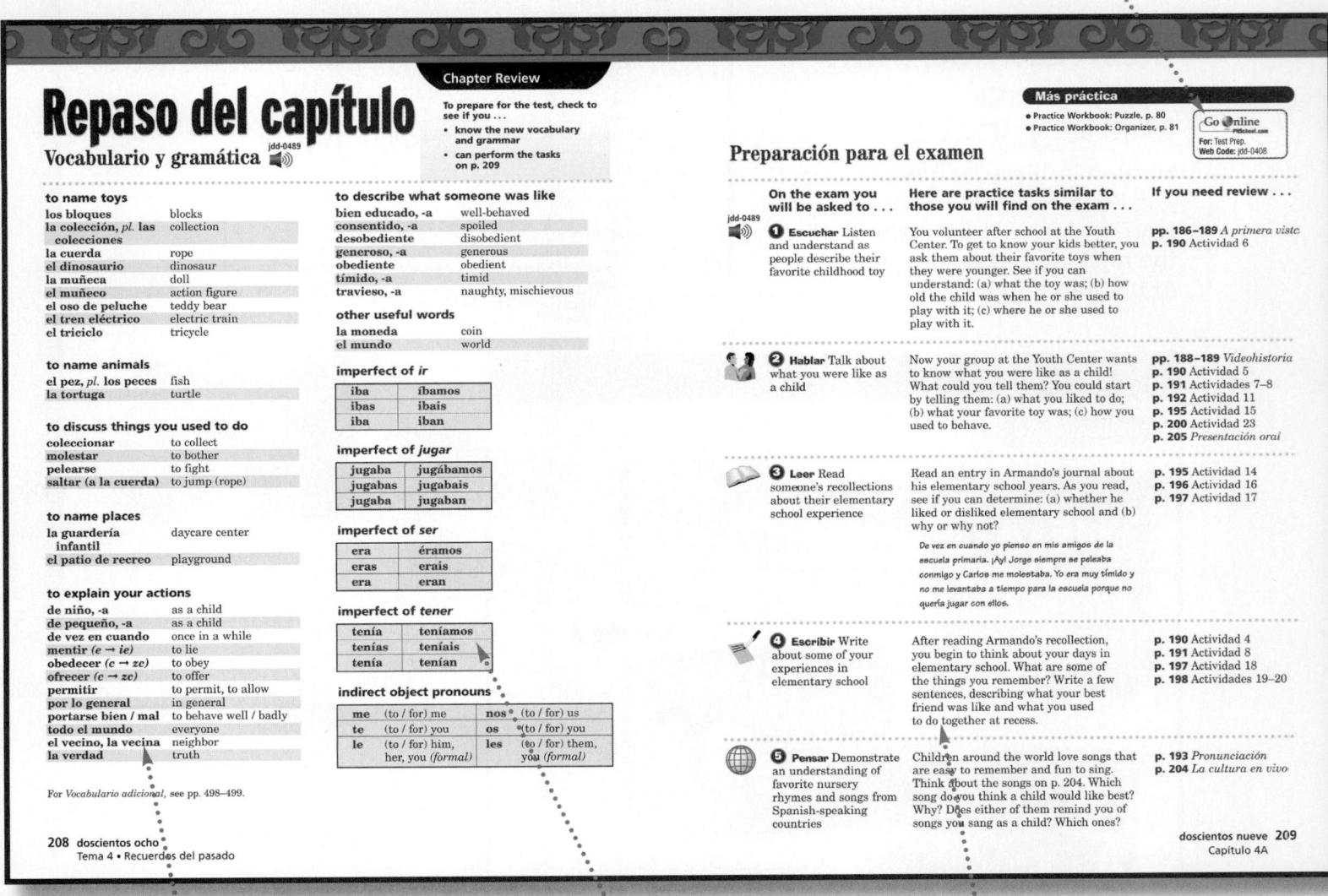

Vocabulary List

Chapter vocabulary is listed as language functions and with English translations.

Grammar Summary

Chapter grammar is conveniently summarized.

Complete Test Preparation

This page prepares students for the proficiency and culture sections of the chapter test. Students are told how they will be tested, what the task might be like, and how to review.

End-of-Book Student Resources

Additional thematic vocabulary

Useful lists provide additional thematic vocabulary.

Grammar summary and charts

This quick reference guide helps students build a strong grammar foundation.

End glossaries

Helpful Spanish-English and English-Spanish glossaries are located at the end of the book.

Using the Teacher's Edition

- ▷ **Teaching the Theme**
- ▷ **Planning for Instruction**
- ▷ **Alignment with the Standards for Foreign Language Learning**
- ▷ **Complete Teaching Support**

Teaching the Theme

The Teacher's Edition provides complete planning support for teaching the themes.

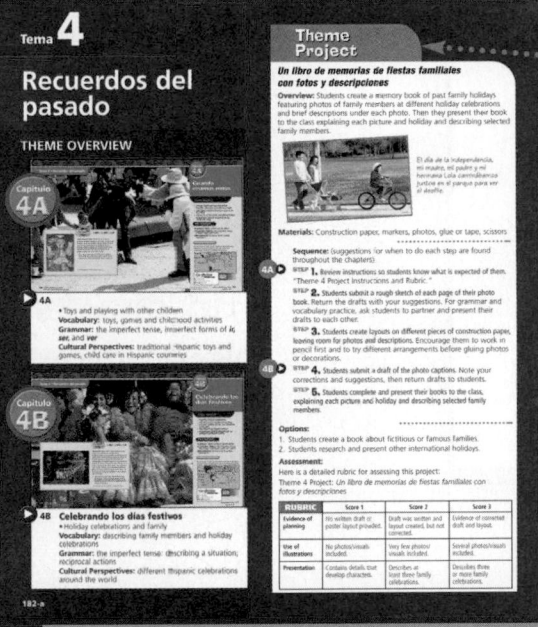

Theme Project

Each theme begins with an optional project. The project is divided into manageable steps and includes a rubric.

Theme Support

Additional support per theme includes bulletin board ideas, games, hands-on culture activities, and teaching resources.

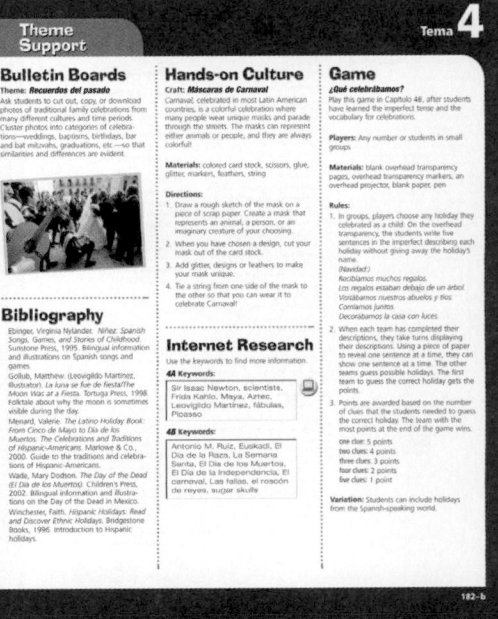

Planning for Instruction

The Teacher's Edition provides four pages of planning support interleaved at the beginning of each chapter.

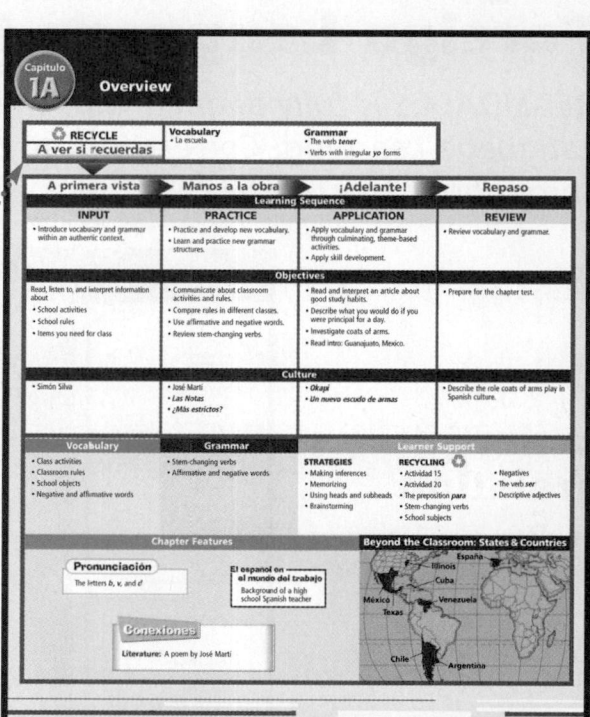

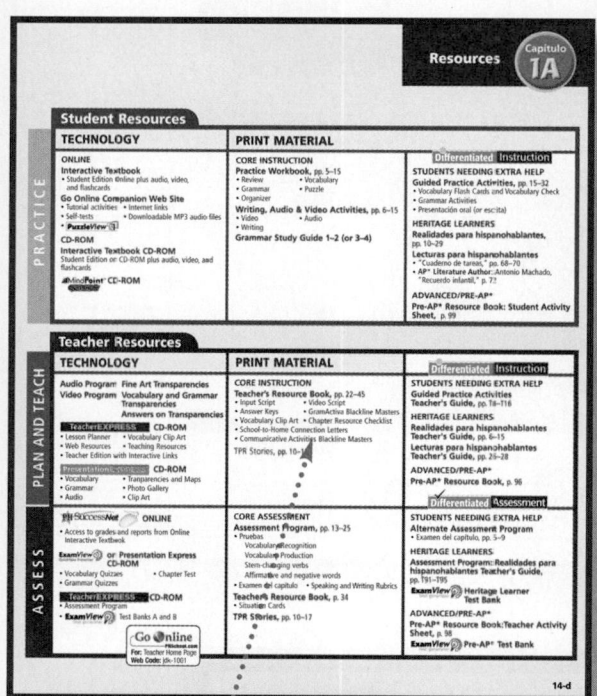

Scope and Sequence

This section gives a quick overview of the chapter sections, objectives, and content.

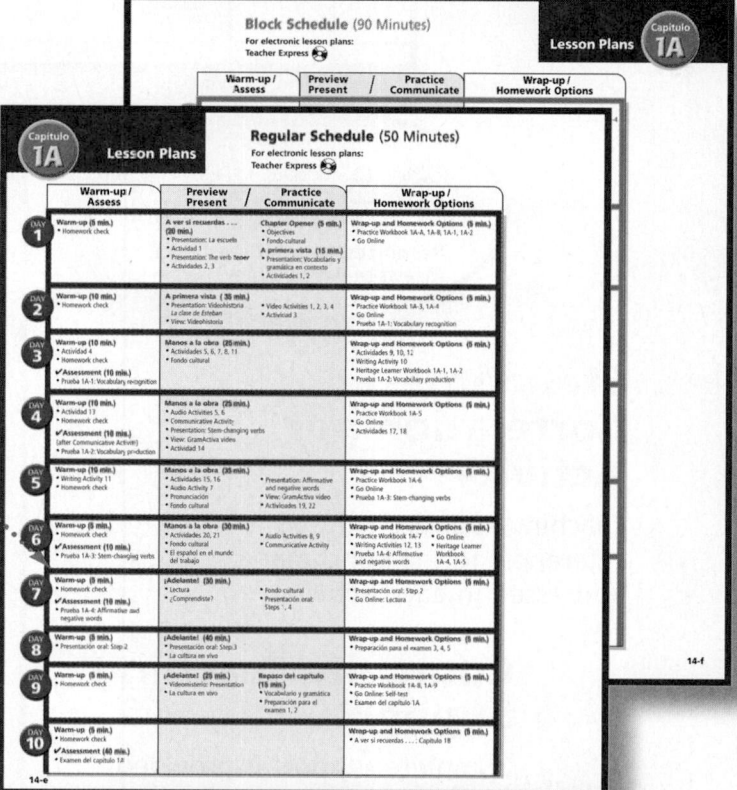

Program Resources

This section shows all the program resources available for this chapter. All resources are conveniently referenced at point of use in the chapter.

Lesson Plans

Lesson Plans are provided for instruction on the regular or block schedule.

Alignment with the Standards for Foreign Language Learning

REALIDADES is fully aligned with the Standards for Foreign Language Learning. Correlations to the Standards are provided throughout the Teacher's Edition.

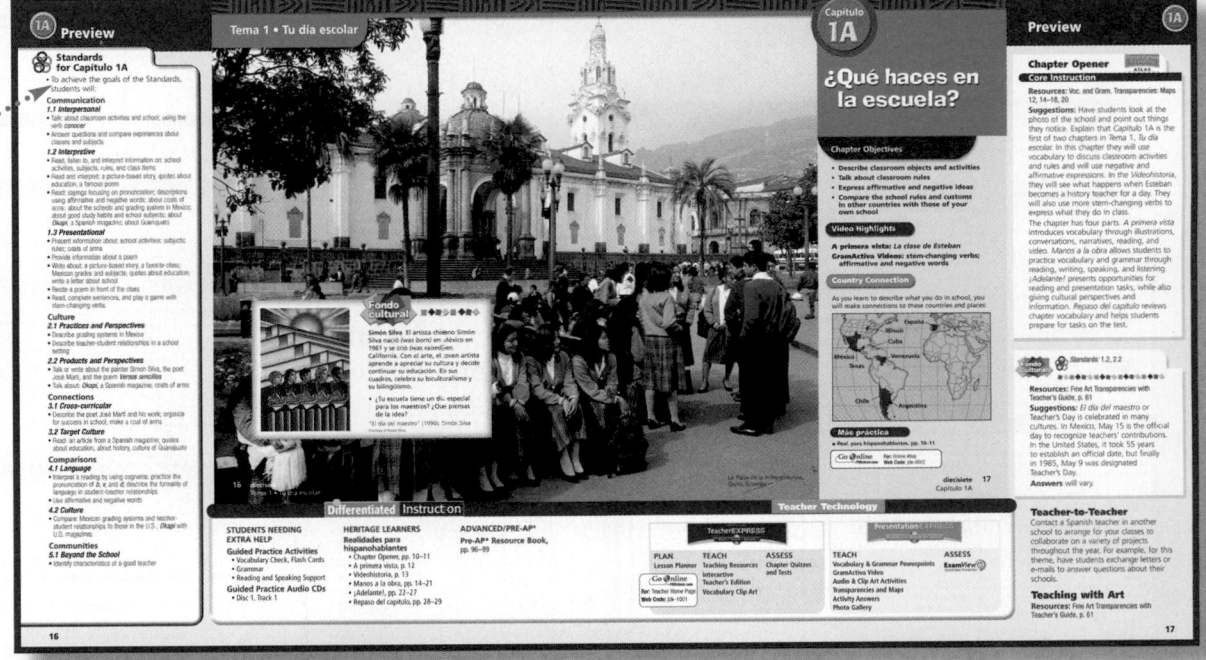

Standards Correlation

A complete correlation of chapter activities to the standards is provided at the beginning of each chapter.

Standards Correlation per Activity

Teaching support includes references to the benchmarks addressed in each activity.

Complete Teaching Support

Complete support is provided for each activity.

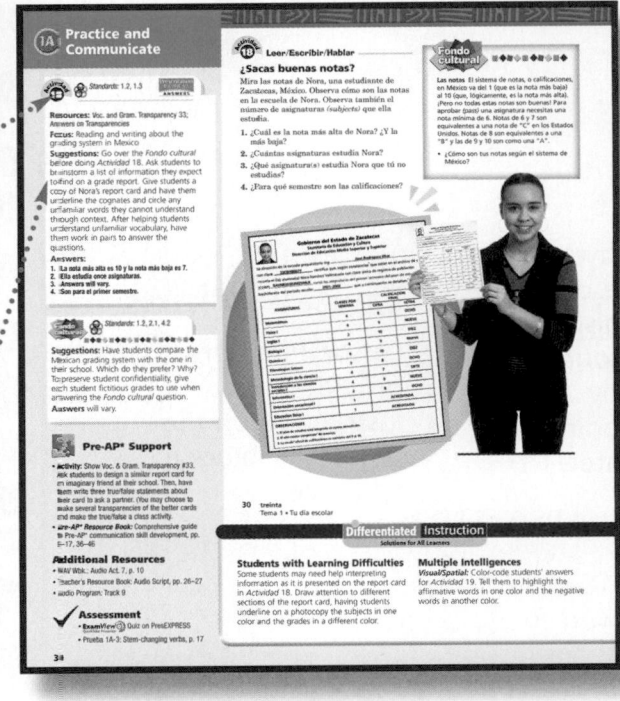

Complete Teaching Support

REALIDADES provides teachers with complete instructional support in both print and technology formats.

Chapter Objectives

- Discuss childhood toys and games
- Describe what you were like as a child
- Talk about activities that you used to do as a child
- Discuss to or for whom something is done
- Understand cultural perspectives on childhood songs

Program Organization

Each chapter provides a well-organized structure, clear student outcomes based upon the standards, and a variety of activities that develop all language skills.

✓ Assessment
- Prueba 5A-3: The verb *tener*

Assessment

Teachers are provided with multiple print and technology tools that measure student progress in listening, speaking, reading, and writing.

Go Online
PHSchool.com
For: Test preparation
Visit: www.phschool.com
Web Code: jdd-0408

Presentación oral

¿Cómo eras de niño(a)?

Task
You have a summer job at a *guardería infantil* and several students speak Spanish. They are always asking you what you were like when you were their age. Create a series of pictures that shows when you were young.

Differentiated Instruction
Solutions for All Learners

Heritage Language Learners
Students who have not been exposed to written Spanish may tend to omit diacritical marks. Encourage them to keep a list of words with accent marks and add to it throughout the year.

Advanced Learners/Pre-AP*
Students can work in pairs to write a short paragraph about what they like and don't like to do. Each pair takes turns reading their paragraph to another pair who write down what they hear.

Differentiated Instruction

REALIDADES provides teaching suggestions to help all students learn Spanish. Each level also provides differentiated assessment.

Differentiated Assessment
Solutions for All Learners

STUDENTS NEEDING EXTRA HELP
- Alternate Assessment Program: Examen del Capítulo 1A
- Audio Program CD 20: Chap. 1A, Track 3

HERITAGE LEARNERS
- Assessment Program: Realidades para-hispanohablantes: Examen del Capítulo 1A
- **ExamView** Heritage Learner Test Bank

ADVANCED/PRE-AP*
- **ExamView** Pre-AP* Test Bank
- Pre-AP* Resource Book, pp. 58–61

Instructional Planning and Support

REALIDADES provides complete planning and teaching support. The Teacher's Edition, the TeacherEXPRESS™ CD-ROM, the PresentationEXPRESS™ CD-ROM, and other program components provide time-saving teaching tools that will enable all students to become proficient in Spanish.

Assessment

An assessment program in a second language classroom should be based on the premise that the main purpose of learning a language is to communicate in a meaningful and culturally appropriate way. As you begin to teach a unit of instruction, you might want to start by asking a few key questions: What do I expect my students to learn? What do I want them to be able to do? How can I assess what I am looking for in student performance?

....

Assessing Student Progress

There are several assessment strategies that will enable students to develop proficiency in a language other than English. This particular list comes from *The Foreign Language Framework for California Public Schools.* These strategies include:

- Have a clear purpose readily communicated to teachers, students, and parents;
- Provide information to guide the teacher in planning instruction;
- Measure how well students perform in reading, writing, listening, and speaking;
- Have clear and concise criteria;
- Include instruments that provide representative samples of what students know and are able to do;
- Integrate the speaking, listening, reading, and writing skills;
- Include a wide range of assessment strategies that allow for a variety of responses;
- Provide students and parents with ongoing information on their progress;
- Allow students to monitor and adjust their individual learning strategies; and
- Employ various forms of assessment.

Topics covered:

- ▷ **Assessing Student Progress**
- ▷ **Purposes of Assessment**
- ▷ **Forms of Assessment**
- ▷ **Portfolios and Assessment**
- ▷ **Self-Assessment**
- ▷ **Making Assessment Real**

❝What do I expect my students to learn? What do I want them to be able to do? How can I assess what I am looking for in student performance?❞

Purposes of Assessment

The following chart outlines the various purposes for assessment:

Purposes of Assessment

Entry-level assessment	• Analyzes students' ability to communicate as a basis for placing students at an appropriate level in an established foreign language program.
Progress/monitoring assessment	• Gathers evidence about students' progress towards achieving objectives as measured in relation to the stage of the curriculum. • Will occur on an ongoing basis. • May occur at any point in an instructional sequence other than at the end of the course of study.
Summative assessment	• Judges students' achievement at the end of a unit, chapter, or course of study.

Forms of Assessment

Achievement assessment determines what students know by evaluating them on specific, previously learned material, such as the names of items of clothing or the conjugation of *-ar* verbs. They test for discrete bits of information. Achievement tests are used to measure the incremental steps involved in learning a second language—for example, to cover what was taught in a specific chapter. Achievement may be quizzed or tested with some frequency as proof of regular progress for both student and teacher.

Proficiency or **performance-based assessment** measures what students can do with this knowledge and how well they can perform in the language. These tests do not involve testing specific items; rather they are performance-based, checking how well students integrate what they have learned. Their characteristic open-endedness permits students to use what they know to receive or communicate a message, since the emphasis is on communication needs. Proficiency tests address the questions: How well and at what level can the student use the language to receive and express meaningful communication?

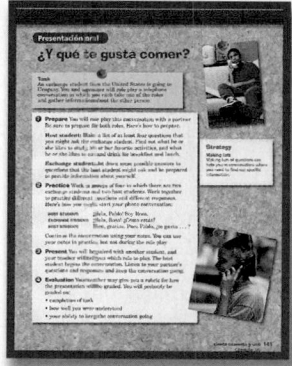

Performance-based speaking task

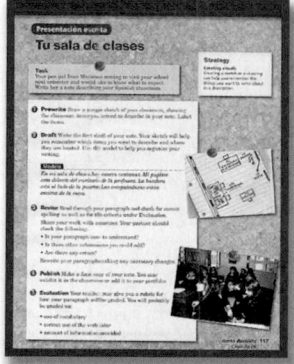

Performance-based writing task

Assessment

Portfolios and Assessment

Portfolios are another form of assessment that can measure student progress and growth. Portfolios contain samples of a student's work collected over time. This enables both the teacher and the student to observe the progress being made. Portfolios provide students the opportunity to examine and reflect upon what they have produced so that they become more involved in improving their work. The portfolio can be useful to determine grade/level placement.

Chapter Assessment in *REALIDADES*

REALIDADES offers a wide variety of options for chapter assessment. There are three different Assessment Programs in *REALIDADES* to evaluate the different students in your classroom:

- monolingual students needing no accommodation
- students using *REALIDADES para hispanohablantes*
- students who need alternate assessment

There is also a Placement Test for heritage learners.

Contents of the Portfolio

- ☐ written work, such as short paragraphs, compositions, short stories, poems, or journals
- ☐ audio and/or video cassettes of student performance
- ☐ quizzes and tests
- ☐ evidence of reading comprehension
- ☐ evidence of listening comprehension
- ☐ individual student projects
- ☐ art work
- ☐ cultural projects
- ☐ technology projects and Web research
- ☐ picture dictionaries
- ☐ story boards
- ☐ evidence that language skills were practiced outside the classroom
- ☐ evidence of contact with Hispanic cultures in the community
- ☐ evidence of student reflection on his or her own writing or speaking

✓ Teacher Assessment

Assessment Program
- Placement Test
- chapter quizzes and tests
- cumulative tests
- rubrics and portfolio support

Placement Test for Heritage Learners
- leveled Placement Tests with audio CD
- vocabulary, grammar, and proficiency assessment

Alternate Assessment Program
- assessment options for students needing extra help and alternate assessment

Assessment Program: *REALIDADES para hispanohablantes*
- chapter quizzes and tests with directions
- cumulative tests with directions in Spanish
- rubrics in Spanish and portfolio support

Assessment Resources in *REALIDADES*

REALIDADES offers a wide range of assessment resources. These include activities in the Student Editions, various print ancillaries, the different Placement and Assessment Programs, and technology. Teachers are encouraged to pick and choose from the many resources.

▶ Assessment Resources	Informal	Formal	Chapter	Summative
Student Edition				
• *Actividades* (various)	✔	✔		✔
• *Lectura*		✔	✔	✔
• *Presentación oral*		✔	✔	✔
• *Presentación escrita*		✔	✔	✔
• *Preparación para el examen*		✔	✔	✔
Assessment Programs				
• Placement Tests		✔	✔	✔
• Chapter Quizzes		✔	✔	✔
• Chapter Tests		✔	✔	✔
• Cumulative Tests		✔	✔	✔
• Rubrics		✔		✔
• Portfolio Assessment				✔
• Chapter Checklist and Self-Assessment Worksheet	✔		✔	
Reading and Writing for Success				
• Additional Readings with Standardized Test Practice		✔		✔
• Short Response Writing				✔
Teacher Resource Book				
• Communicative Activities	✔	✔	✔	
• Situation Cards	✔		✔	✔
Technology				
• QuickTake Quizzes	✔	✔		
• Interactive Textbook	✔	✔	✔	
• MindPoint™ Quiz Show CD-ROM	✔	✔		
• Exam*View*® Test Bank with CD-ROM	✔	✔	✔	
• Companion Web Site	✔			

Differentiated Instruction

All students are capable of and can benefit from learning a second language. However, today's students bring into the classroom a wide range of needs, interests, motivations, home languages, and literacy levels. This diversity presents heightened challenges to both curriculum and instruction. It should be clearly acknowledged that individual needs of some students require additional specialized support. However, the goal of a comprehensive Spanish program remains the provision of teaching all students to develop proficiency. All students should have access to a communicative and culturally rich program in addition to whatever specialized intervention may be required. *REALIDADES* has been developed especially to meet the diverse needs of students in Spanish classrooms.

....

Success in Teaching All Students

All students are able to access learning when teachers provide curriculum and instruction in ways that allow all learners in the classroom to participate and achieve the instructional and behavioral goals of general education, as well as those of the core curriculum. Success is achieved in classrooms that consistently and systematically integrate instructional strategies that are responsive to the needs of all learners with a special focus on students that need extra help—students with learning difficulties, heritage learners, and students who are eligible for and receiving special education services.

Effective Instructional Strategies

Here are general strategies that deliver effective instruction for all learners in the Spanish classroom.

- **Clarify the objectives for a chapter.** Students need to understand the outcomes for which they will be assessed.

- **Provide "thinking time" before students have to talk.** You may want to ask a question and then count to 10 before expecting a response. If a student is struggling, state that you want him/her to think about it, and indicate that you'll be back for the response in a minute. Move on to another student, and then return to the student for his/her response.

- **Write all assignments on the board.** Assignments given both verbally and visually are clearer to all students.

- **Use visuals throughout the lesson.** Present vocabulary visually. Use charts to present grammar. Use video that provides visual support (such as vocabulary words highlighted on the screen) and grammar videos that visualize grammar patterns. Use graphic organizers whenever possible. Connect communicative tasks to photos, art, and realia.

- **Assist in time management.** When requiring students to complete projects or long-term assignments, provide a calendar that breaks down requirements by due dates. Many students experience significant difficulties in self-managing the time needed to complete complex projects.

- **Build in opportunities for reteaching and practicing vocabulary words and grammar.** Students need many opportunities to learn new concepts and need to practice in a variety of formats.

- **Build vocabulary skills by teaching the patterns of language.** Teach the meaning of prefixes, suffixes, and the role of cognates. Point out connections between English, Spanish, and Latin.

- **Work with students based on their strengths rather than their weaknesses.** Allow students to experience success by using their strengths while working on areas of weakness.

- **Consider alternative means for demonstrating understanding.** Think beyond the common modes of reading and writing. Students could present information orally,

> **"All students are capable of and can benefit from learning a second language."**

create a poster or visual representation of work, tape-record their ideas, or act out their understanding.

- **Have students begin all work in class.** Prior to class dismissal, check to ensure that each student has a good start and understands what is expected.

- **Consider setting up a homework hotline using voicemail or e-mail.** Homework assignments could be posted and easily accessed by parents and students outside of school hours.

Teaching Today's Students

The strategies presented on these pages provide an overview of instructional strategies that are effective with all learners. Today's students need instruction that enables them to see how learning is relevant, that helps them organize their time and learning, that provides focus on what is important (either within instructional materials or with classroom activities), that provides multiple opportunities to learn utilizing different modalities, and that assures students know what is expected of them whether in the classroom or for homework.

Differentiated Instruction

Teaching Spanish to Students with Learning Disabilities

There are many reasons why students may experience difficulties in learning a second language. In general, these difficulties may be characterized by the inability to spell or read well, problems with auditory discrimination and in understanding auditory input, and difficulty with abstract thinking. Research by Ganchow and Sparks (1991) indicates that difficulties with one's first language are a major factor in foreign language learning difficulties.

It is not always evident which students will experience difficulties with learning a second language. Many times these students are bright and outgoing. They may have experienced reading or spelling problems in elementary school, but they have learned to compensate over time. Ask students what problems they may have experienced with their first language, especially in the areas of reading and dictation.

Accommodating Instruction

Students with learning disabilities can develop a level of proficiency in a second language with some modifications to instruction and testing. These learners benefit from a highly structured approach that teaches new content in context and in incremental amounts. Teach, practice, and assess using multisensory strategies. Many students benefit when instruction combines seeing, hearing, saying, and writing. For example, a teacher would first show a visual of a word and say it aloud. This is followed by using the new word in context. The teacher then writes the word on the board. Students would say the word aloud with the teacher. They then write it down and say it aloud again. In subsequent days, many students benefit from frequent reviews of learned auditory materials.

Accommodations for Students with Special Needs

Here are suggestions for instruction for students with special needs. For additional support, see the *REALIDADES* Alternate Assessment Program.

Hearing impairments

- Help students comprehend oral information or instructions. Provide written directions/materials and/or visual cues to support what is presented orally. Face the students when speaking, repeat as needed, and speak clearly. Seat these students in the front of the classroom. Provide outlines of lectures or oral presentations. Have another student take notes and makes copies of notes available to all students. Use the audio and video scripts of the *REALIDADES* Audio or Video Program. Utilize the close-captioned version of the Video Program.

- Allow students to refer to their textbooks or to other written materials during oral presentations.

- Limit background noises that may distract students. Avoid seating these students where they may hear extraneous noise.

- Change listening activities and assessments to reading/writing activities. In activities that require aural/oral skills, let students demonstrate skills through alternative responses such as writing.

- Provide access to the audio and video materials. When using *REALIDADES*, students can download all Student Edition audio material from the Companion Web Site. The Interactive Textbook (online or CD-ROM) provides pronunciation support for all vocabulary, access to all Student Edition listening activities, and access to the vocabulary and grammar videos.

Visual perception problems

- Help students access information provided visually. Allow for preferred seating in the front of the class, including providing space for a guide dog, if necessary. Avoid seating students where they will be distracted by extraneous auditory or visual stimuli. Give students additional time to review visual input prior to an oral or written task. Highlight important information by providing key words, visuals, and simple outlines.

- Provide support for accessing printed information. Make sure the print is easy to read. The readings should be designed to maximize readability: easy-to-read font, layout, and design. Teach reading strategies that highlight the visual aspects of a selection: text organization, use of visuals, titles and headers, and the use of color. Provide copies of reading selections with additional support: underline key words/sentences/concepts or magnify the text in duplication.
- Teach, practice, and assess using multi-sensory strategies.

ADHD/ADD

- Provide additional support that enables students to focus. Present information in small "chunks." This includes new content, short instructions or directions, and shorter assignments, or break assignments into steps. Limit extraneous auditory and visual stimulation. Provide visual and written support for aural instructions or input. Repeat and explain (again) as needed. Provide outlines of oral presentations. Support readings with strategies similar to those for students with visual perception problems. Use graphic organizers.
- Verify that students "got it." Check that students are looking at you (eye contact) when providing oral instructions. Ask students to repeat what you just told them. Move closer to students to increase attention. Provide preferential seating that allows you to monitor students' focus and attention. Allow extra wait time when students are responding.
- Provide a variety of different learning activities that reach different learning styles. This will also allow for frequent changes of activities within a class. Provide for hands-on activities, vocabulary clip art, and grammar manipulatives.
- Use technology to provide interactive learning. These students benefit from using interactive textbooks, CD-ROMs, and Web sites.
- Be predictable. Establish a daily routine for managing the classroom and be consistent. Avoid surprises with these students.
- Help students organize themselves and their learning. Ask students to maintain notebooks that are organized by dividers. Provide study guides, summary sheets, and organizers for daily or weekly assignments.

Differentiated Instruction

Accommodation in *REALIDADES*

REALIDADES 2 provides a wide range of support for accommodating instruction.

Student Edition
- clean design and layout of pages
- visualized presentation of vocabulary
- step-by-step scaffolding of activities
- Companion Web Site: interactive practice activities, downloadable audio files

Teacher's Edition
- Differentiated Instruction article
- Differentiated Instruction suggestions

Guided Practice Activities for Vocabulary and Grammar
- audio support and CD for pronunciation
- vocabulary clip art to create flashcards
- focused vocabulary practice
- simplified grammar instruction
- separate Teacher's Guide

Alternate Assessment Program
- additional suggestions for accommodating assessment
- alternate assessments for students with special needs

Differentiated Instruction

Teaching Heritage Learners

A diverse background

Those who have a home language other than English bring a wider range of language abilities to the classroom. These abilities range from students who are minimally functional in the language to those who are completely fluent and literate. It is important for teachers to assess the language skills of the different heritage learners in the classroom.
This diversity includes:

- Students who are able to understand the spoken language, but are unable to respond in the language beyond single-word answers.

- Students who are able to understand the language and communicate at a minimal level. These students may be able to read some items, but because of their limited vocabulary, they may not comprehend much information. They may write what they are able to sound out, but errors are evident.

- Students who can speak the language fluently but who have little to no experience with the language in its written form.

- Students who have come to the United States from non-English-speaking countries. They can understand and speak the language fluently; however, their reading and writing skills may be limited due to lack of a formal education in their country of origin.

- Fluent bilingual students who can understand, speak, read, and write another language very well and have possibly received formal instruction in that language in the United States or in another country.

Program goals

Heritage learners bring rich home language experiences to the classroom that can serve as a foundation for learning. Because of their language background, these students have the potential to be bilingual, biliterate, and bicultural. Heritage learners need to be exposed to a program that can improve and maintain the home language. Students need to study the grammar and focus on vocabulary development. Emphasis should be placed on building reading and writing skills. It is important that students develop a sensitivity to, when in a social situation, standard and non-standard language should be employed and comfortably adjust their language accordingly. In addition, students should be exposed to the diverse cultures within the Spanish-speaking community while developing a sense of pride in their own heritage. Heritage learners need to reach a high level of proficiency and accuracy that will ensure success at the advanced level of language study and testing. These students should also be ready to transition into a focused study of Spanish in specific professional areas.

Focus on individual needs

Due to their diverse backgrounds, heritage learners differ greatly in language skills and may need individualized instruction. In many of today's classrooms, teachers encounter classes that contain a mixture of beginning-level students and heritage learners. These groups need different materials, different instructional approaches, and different objectives. Here are several strategies that may be helpful for heritage learners:

- Build upon their background knowledge. Develop instructional units around themes and topics that relate to their life experiences. Encourage students to use these experiences as the foundation for building language skills through vocabulary development, reading, and writing.

- Help students connect aural with written language. If students don't understand a word in a reading, have them read it aloud or ask a friend or teacher to read it aloud. Often they can recognize the word once hearing it. Allow for opportunities for students to follow along as a story is read aloud.

- Use the strategies that are effective in a language arts classroom, such as building schema, teaching language-learning strategies, using graphic organizers, and incorporating pre- and post-reading tasks. Use the writing process to develop good writers.

- Encourage students to begin communicating, especially in writing. Have them write down their thoughts in the way they sound to them. Then have students work with the teacher or another student for corrections. Students can also look through textbooks and dictionaries to assist with error correction.

- Maintain high standards. Require students to focus on accuracy and proficient communication. Many heritage learners experience frustration with reading and writing in the home language when they have good aural/oral skills. Building language skills takes time.

Teaching Heritage Learners with *REALIDADES 2*

REALIDADES 2 offers ideal support for teaching heritage learners at the novice level of proficiency. The Student Edition, the *REALIDADES para hispanohablantes* all-Spanish worktext, the *Lecturas para hispanohablantes* literature anthology, and the varied assessment options offer a rich and varied curriculum. With *REALIDADES*, teachers have three options (1) the Student Edition with English support for the students who need it; (2) the companion all-Spanish worktext; and (3) a combination of both.

Teaching All Students: Summary

The diverse needs of today's Spanish students pose a challenge to teachers, curriculum developers, and school administrators as they design programs to ensure that all students develop language proficiency. With *REALIDADES*, teachers have at their disposal a variety of materials and strategies to enable them to provide access to Spanish for all learners. Clearly, some students will require additional tutoring and specialized services to reach their full learning potential. However, the activities and materials that accompany *REALIDADES*, coupled with instructional strategies described within this article, constitute a viable framework for reaching and teaching all learners.

Differentiated Instruction

Teaching Heritage Learners with *REALIDADES para hispanohablantes*

REALIDADES 2 provides extensive support for teaching heritage learners.

Student Edition
- focused vocabulary and grammar
- integrated language and culture
- extensive reading and writing
- test preparation

REALIDADES para hispanohablantes

- all-Spanish companion worktext
- all-Spanish grammar explanations
- companion pages for each section of Student Edition
- increased emphasis on reading and writing
- accompanying Teacher's Guide

Lecturas para hispanohablantes
- literature anthology for additional readings

Assessment Program: *REALIDADES para hispanohablantes*

- direction lines in Spanish
- complete assessment support
- rubrics in Spanish

Instructional Planning and Support

Topics covered:

- ▷ **Creating a Communicative Learning Community**

- ▷ **The Role of Grammar in a Communicative Classroom**

- ▷ **Pair and Group Activities in a Communicative Classroom**

- ▷ **Integrating Technology in the Classroom**

- ▷ **Teaching Culture and Language**

prentice • hall
In-Service On Demand
PHSchool.com

Today's Spanish classroom is a vibrant and interactive learning community, integrating language with culture. Teachers are planning for instruction that is communicative, motivating, and real for *all* students. They are incorporating a wide range of strategies, activities, and technology to achieve clearly defined teaching objectives. This section provides an overview of instructional strategies that will help teachers achieve these goals.

....

Creating a Communicative Learning Community

A communicative classroom is built upon activities that enable students to use language in meaningful and purposeful ways. One of the challenges is to get students ready, willing, and able to communicate. Here are several strategies that can be built into communicative tasks to help all students be successful.

Teach and use learning strategies

Research states that successful language students use a wide range of learning strategies. In contrast, unsuccessful students employ fewer strategies and tend to give up quickly. Strategies are inherently student-centered and when employed by learners, allow them to become more independent and more successful. Learning strategies enable students to:

- Learn and recall information more efficiently

- Interpret and comprehend language when reading or writing

- Speak more effectively

- Write more effectively

- Take more risks and be more positive

- Work more cooperatively with others

Use activities based upon multiple intelligences

The Multiple Intelligences Theory tells us that students learn in different ways. If new material is presented in a variety of formats, more students will likely learn and be able to demonstrate proficiency with the new material. Howard Gardner in 1983 proposed the theory of Multiple Intelligences in his book, *Frames of Mind.* This theory states that a person has many different ways of acquiring and demonstrating intelligence. Some people remember just about anything if learned to the tune of a jingle or chant, while someone else may be able to grasp an idea, concept, or grammatical point if presented as a graph, chart, or picture.

Gardner presents the notion that there is no "general intelligence," but rather that the mind is organized around distinct functional capacities, which he defines as "intelligences". Though each of the intelligences is developed independently of the others over the course of a lifetime, they usually work together and do not often appear in isolation. Gardner has identified and labeled eight main styles of acquiring and demonstrating knowledge; those eight intelligences are:

- Verbal/Linguistic
- Visual/Spatial
- Bodily/Kinesthetic
- Logical/Mathematical
- Interpersonal/Social
- Intrapersonal/Introspective
- Musical/Rhythmic
- Naturalist

In the Teacher's Edition, you will find frequent specific suggestions for accommodating and teaching to the Multiple Intelligences. This is not meant to be construed as a paradigm for labeling every student in your class. On the contrary, they are presented as tools to help more students access content while recognizing that they are intelligent in many ways and that their overall "intelligence" is based upon the sum of all their intelligences.

Activities that incorporate critical thinking tend to be more interesting for students as they are guided to think differently in ways such as:

⊔ **use or apply**

⊔ **illustrate / sketch / diagram**

⊔ **compare and contrast**

⊔ **analyze**

⊔ **categorize**

⊔ **create**

⊔ **organize / prepare**

⊔ **evaluate**

⊔ **revise**

⊔ **value**

Provide activities that require critical thinking

All students learn more effectively when activities help them make connections and see and use information in new and different ways. Critical thinking skills can be used as tools for learning and are easily integrated in a variety of tasks beginning in the first year of language study in both communication and culture activities.

Scaffolded tasks

Step-by-step support builds success.

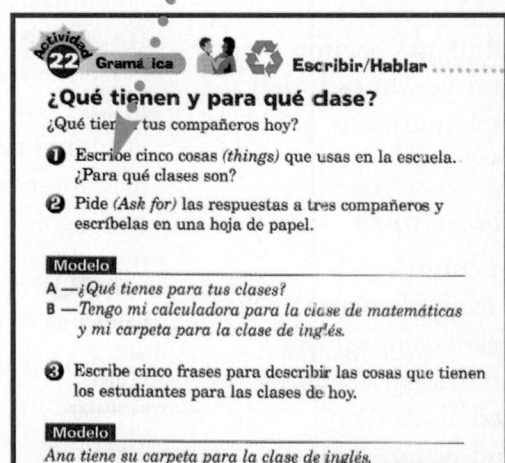

Scaffold communicative tasks

Communicating in a second language is a complicated task. There are mental steps that take place as a student attempts to communicate a message. Activities that help students get through these mental steps allow students to be successful. This "scaffolded" support is provided throughout *REALIDADES.*

For example, in preparing for a speaking task, students think through what they might want to say using a chart. In writing, they might fill out a word web before attempting the first draft. By providing a scaffold that asks students to think, plan, process, and then communicate, more students will become effective communicators.

The Role of Grammar in a Communicative Classroom

In a proficiency-based curriculum, vocabulary and grammar are viewed as tools that students need in order to communicate, rather than as ends in themselves.

Input grammar in context

For students to internalize grammar, it needs to be presented in a meaningful context. For example, students can grasp the concept of the preterite more easily if it is presented within a topic, like shopping. As the teacher presents clothing and store vocabulary, she can tell the class what items of clothing she or another person bought, when it was purchased, and how much was paid. As the teacher points to a picture of a sweater on an overhead transparency or clip art or an actual sweater, she begins with comprehensible input that uses the *yo* form of the preterite: *Ayer, yo fui de compras y compré un suéter nuevo. Y pagué veinte dólares. No es mucho, ¿verdad?* Repetition of the input can continue with other articles of clothing, allowing students to easily deduce and internalize the meaning of *compré* and *pagué*. The teacher then begins to ask students questions using *compraste* and *pagaste* and makes summary comments about what is said in the class, drawing other students into the discussion as she introduces other preterite forms. As students begin to internalize these forms and the chapter vocabulary, they begin to make simple statements or ask questions to a partner about shopping for clothing.

Input grammar in small, manageable chunks

Present new grammar in manageable chunks that can be immediately practiced. In the example above, students can use a few preterite forms of *comprar* and *pagar* as they talk about shopping. Additional *-ar* verbs and other preterite forms can be added as students become comfortable using *comprar* and *pagar*.

Input grammar in readings

Grammar input can also take place through reading. As students read sentences, short paragraphs, and dialogues with supporting contextual and visual cues, they can understand new grammatical forms. Through carefully planned out questions asked by their teacher, students can be led to explain grammatical concepts.

Teach what is needed for the immediate communication objectives

Teach students the grammar needed to accomplish the communicative objective. This allows students to learn the concept in context and practice. For example, if you teach *pensar* or *querer* in connection with a theme, don't give students an additional list of all *-ie* stem-changing verbs. Rather, teach additional *-ie* verbs in later chapters as they connect to the themes.

Practice grammar in a variety of activities

Just as there are several ways to provide input, there are many useful methods for practicing grammar. This practice can involve hands-on activities and games that let students manipulate grammatical structures. Grammar practice is effectively integrated into communicative activities such as surveys, Venn diagrams, and paired and group activities. In addition, practice can involve comput- erized activities on a Web site where students practice grammar again and again at their own pace.

Grammar and communication

Grammar can be successfully integrated in a communicative classroom with activities that deal with grammatical accuracy at different levels. When presented in meaningful contexts, in manageable chunks, and with presentation and practice that incorporate a variety of activities, students will develop increasing accuracy with grammar.

Pair and Group Activities in a Communicative Classroom

Benefits of group work

Effective group work develops a friendly and cooperative atmosphere by giving students a chance to get to know each other better. This sense of camaraderie leads to a more relaxed classroom in which students are more willing to talk and to participate. Group work also allows more opportunity for "student talk," thereby increasing the quantity of student practice in the target language.

Grouping options and techniques

The communicative activities in a Spanish classroom allow for a variety of grouping options.

The most common option is random grouping that includes pairing up two students or creating small groups of three to five students. Some possible ways to randomly group students include:

- Count off by going left to right or up and down in rows.
- Write on pieces of paper vocabulary words (English/Spanish), countries/capitals, opposites, colors, or categories that can be matched up, in a bag. Have students draw a piece of paper and find their partner(s).
- Order students along a continuum by birthday, height, phone numbers, etc.
- Place numbers or a deck of cards in a hat, bag, or box and have students draw.
- Turn to the student to the left or right, front or back.

Another grouping option is to place students by their ability level. Homogeneous grouping allows students of similar ability to work together. In this case, teachers assign tasks based upon the ability level of the group. Advanced students are given a more challenging task. Other students are given tasks that they can success-fully complete. Heterogeneous grouping places students of varying abilities together. This allows for stronger students to help weaker students.

Grouping students by interest level is another option to consider. Students could group themselves for an activity or longer project based upon mutual interest.

Planning and facilitating an effective group activity

- Make sure that the task involves a true exchange of information.
- Think through the language functions and content information to make certain students can complete the task.
- Prepare all materials in advance and anticipate questions.
- Explain the task before the students break up into groups. Be sure to model the task if necessary.
- Determine in advance how students will be evaluated and share those criteria with the class.
- Allow adequate time for the task. Make sure at least three quarters of the students at different ability levels can complete it. Tell students how much time they have and stick to the plan.
- Encourage students to stay on-task by walking around the class and monitoring the groups.
- Build into your grading system a way to include group participation and staying on task.
- Develop some sort of follow-up upon completion of the task.

Error correction

As students work in groups, they will be making mistakes. Here are strategies that can help students to focus on accuracy while doing group work.

- Listen for common errors while monitoring the class. If the error is one of vocabulary usage or grammar, discuss the error with the class and do some focused practice once the task is completed. If the error is one of meaning (very common in beginning writing), have the class work together to determine how best to express the message.
- If you want to correct an individual student error, correct the student only after he or she has spoken. Restate the student's response using the correction in your restatement.

Integrating Technology in the Classroom

Technology offers teachers and students a wide range of useful, creative, and motivating tools that build language proficiency. The varied learning experiences available through audio, video, CD-ROMs, and the Internet address different learning styles through multi-sensory and interactive tasks.

REALIDADES 2 Video Program

Student Technology in REALIDADES

REALIDADES offers technology-based learning tools.

- **Interactive Textbook** The Student Edition comes alive with interactive learning. The Interactive Textbook provides the same instruction as in the Student Edition but with additional features that include built-in audio, pronunciation practice, video, interactive activities, links to workbook pages, links to the Companion Web Site plus other learning resources. Available online or on CD-ROM.

- **Companion Web Site** The online interactive activities, easily accessed by Web Codes, provide additional practice for vocabulary and grammar, end-of-chapter self-tests, and Internet links.

- **MindPoint™ Quiz Show CD-ROM** The interactive games offer a fun end-of-chapter review while providing students and teachers with detailed reports on how well individual students and/or the class have performed on questions based upon the National Standards and chapter objectives.

- **Downloadable audio files** Students can download all the Student Edition listening activities to a computer or audio player. The audio activities are easily accessed through Web Codes provided in the front matter of the Student Edition.

Teacher Technology in REALIDADES

- **PresentationEXPRESS™ CD-ROM** Present vocabulary and grammar using this time-saving teacher presentation tool that integrates audio, images, vocabulary clip art, grammar slides, video, answers, and interactive QuickTake Quizzes.

- **TeacherEXPRESS™ CD-ROM** Teach, plan, and assess with this interactive Teacher's Edition. The CD-ROM provides instant access to Lesson Planning, Teacher Edition pages, Teaching Resources, Exam*View*™ Computer Test Bank on CD-ROM, Vocabulary Clip Art, and Web Resources.

- **Video Program** The innovative videos on DVD or VHS accompany each chapter.

> **❝ Technology provides new ways to reach and teach today's learners. ❞**

- **Audio Program** Audio supports the *A primera vista* language input, pronunciation, Student Edition listening activities, audio activities that accompany the *Writing, Audio & Video Activities,* songs, and the listening tasks from the chapter tests.

- **Exam*View*™ Test Bank on CD-ROM** The Test Bank allows provides two chapter tests plus a test bank per chapter to use with Heritage Learners and Pre-AP* students. It allows you to edit questions and tests or create new tests.

- **Transparencies** Three different sets of transparencies include Vocabulary and Grammar Transparencies, Answers on Transparencies, and Fine Art Transparencies.

▶ Technology in *REALIDADES 2*

REALIDADES 2 provides a complete, state-of-the-art technology package for each chapter at all levels of the program. Technology is integrated into the instruction design of each chapter as follows:

Chapter Section	▶ Chapter Opener	A primera vista	Manos a la obra	¡Adelante!	Repaso del capítulo
Student Learning Tools	**Web Site** • Atlas **Interactive Textbook**	**Web Site** • Vocabulary practice • Audio files **Interactive Textbook**	**Web Site** • Grammar practice • Audio files **Interactive Textbook**	**Web Site** • Internet link and activity • *En busca de la verdad* link **Interactive Textbook**	**Web Site** • *Vocabulario y gramática* • Self-test • Audio files **Interactive Textbook** **MindPoint™ Quiz Show CD-ROM**
Teacher Planning	**TeacherEXPRESS™ CD-ROM** **Web Site**	**TeacherEXPRESS™ CD-ROM** **Web Site**	**TeacherEXPRESS™ CD-ROM** **Web Site**	**TeacherEXPRESS™ CD-ROM** **Web Site**	**TeacherEXPRESS™ CD-ROM** **Web Site**
Instruction	**Presentation EXPRESS™ CD-ROM** **Fine Art Transparencies** **Vocabulary and Grammar Transparencies** • Maps Videohistoria  **A primera vista**	**Presentation EXPRESS™ CD-ROM** **Vocabulary and Grammar Transparencies** • *Vocabulario y gramática en contexto* • *Videohistoria* **Answers on Transparencies** **Audio Program** • *Vocabulario y gramática en contexto* • *Actividades 1* and *2* • Audio Activities (*Writing, Audio & Video Workbook*) **Video Program** • *A primera vista* segments	**Presentation EXPRESS™ CD-ROM** **Vocabulary and Grammar Transparencies** • *Gramática* (verbs and charts) • Rapid Review • Graphic Organizers **Answers on Transparencies** **Fine Art Transparencies** **Audio Program** • *Actividades* • *Pronunciación* • Audio Activities (*Writing, Audio & Video Workbook*) **Video Program** • *GramActiva* segments	**Presentation EXPRESS™ CD-ROM** **Vocabulary and Grammar Transparencies** • Graphic Organizers **Answers on Transparencies** **Video Program** • *En busca de la verdad* (starting *Tema 3*) GramActiva mi perro **GramActiva**	**Presentation EXPRESS™ CD-ROM** **Audio Program** • *Repaso del capítulo (Vocabulario y gramática)* • *Escuchar (Preparación para el examen)* • *Canciones* Videomisterio **En busca de la verdad**
Assessment		**QuickTake Quiz**	**QuickTake Quiz**		**QuickTake Quiz** **ExamView® Test Bank with CD-ROM** **Audio Program** • Listening Assessment

Instructional Planning and Support

Teaching Culture and Language

Culture is communication that extends beyond words. Language is part of a culture, but it is only part of how a people communicate. Culture is two people greeting each other on the street with a kiss. Culture is an energetic *salsa*. Culture is spending Sundays with *los abuelos, tíos, sobrinos, y nietos.* Culture is a warm tortilla prepared by experienced hands. Culture is a vibrant mural painted in downtown Chicago, or Mexico City, or Los Angeles. Culture is a poem by Neruda. Culture is your favorite Mexican *telenovela*. Culture is another form of communication and one of the goals of today's Spanish classroom is to guide students to accepting, understanding, and appreciating the rich cultures of the Spanish-speaking world.

The *Standards for Foreign Language Learning* represents culture learning as the development of an understanding of the practices and products of a culture in terms of the perspectives (its attitudes, values, beliefs) of the culture that creates and maintains them. Too often in teaching foreign languages, it is easier to focus on the informational aspects of culture and to ignore the perspectives that underlie them. In other words, we now want students to understand the *why* of culture that determines the *what*.

Cultural understandings are developed through activities that lead students to thoughtful observation, to knowledge and understanding of Hispanic cultures, as well as to reflect on their own culture. This can be accomplished through questions that relate to art or photographs. Informative cultural readings can provide information, insights, and thought-provoking questions that allow students to reflect upon cultural perspectives.

Another cultural goal in the *Standards for Foreign Language Learning* is to provide opportunities for students to compare and contrast culture with the goal of developing cross-cultural understanding. Cultural comparison may represent a challenge for students as they are asked to think not only about another culture, but about their own. As students think about similarities and differences, they often arrive at insight about their own experiences and communities.

As culture and language are inseparable, it is important to weave culture into the learning experience. Technology can play an important part of bringing culture into the classroom through video and internet activities. Readings should be rich in culture information that leads students to reflect upon cultural perspectives and comparisons. Authentic materials such as menus, advertisements, songs, and nursery rhymes can be woven into practice.

The goal of a proficiency-based classroom is to develop in students the ability to use language for real world purposes in culturally appropriate ways. The teaching of language and culture go hand-in-hand. As culture is woven with language in the classroom, students gain a deeper understanding of culture. And with new perspectives, many students are willing to seek out opportunities to communicate in Spanish in their school, in their community, and in the global community that awaits them in the 21st century.

Professional Resources

- ▶ Professional Organizations
- ▶ Regional Conferences
- ▶ Listservs
- ▶ Web Sites

National Organizations

These national organizations provide an annual conference and a wide range of teaching support.

The American Council on the Teaching of Foreign Languages (ACTFL)
http://www.actfl.org

American Association of Teachers of Spanish and Portuguese (AATSP)
http://www.aatsp.org

State Organizations

Each state offers the support of a language association. These organizations provide workshops, conferences, job placement, networking opportunities, and updates on state and second language issues. Teachers are encouraged to contact their state organizations and get involved.

Regional Conferences

Central States Conference on the Teaching of Foreign Languages
http://www.centralstates.cc

Northeast Conference on the Teaching of Foreign Languages
http://www.dickinson.edu/nectfl

Southern Conference on Language Teaching
http://www.valdosta.edu/scolt

Southwest Conference on the Teaching of Foreign Languages
http://www.swcolt.org

Listservs

The following electronic resources are helpful to language teachers and curriculum developers. To subscribe to a listserv, send a message with no subject line as follows:

subscribe [name of listserv] your first name your last name

for example: subscribe *FLTEACH* Abraham Lincoln

FLTEACH: a forum for discussion among foreign language educators

listserv@listserv.acsu.buffalo.edu

SLART-L: focuses on second language acquisition research and teaching

listserv@cunyvm.cuny.edu

IECC: an e-mail listserv that helps teachers find partners for intercultural e-mail classroom connections

iecc-request@stolaf.edu

LLTI: a forum to discuss language learning and technology

listserv@dartcms1.dartmouth.edu

Web Sites

The number of Web sites of interest to foreign language educators is too large to list. Below are some places to begin.

http://www.clta.net/lessons
- excellent source of Web-based activities for the foreign language classroom

http://www.cortland.edu/flteach
- accesses the wide range of archives and resources offered by the Foreign Language Teaching Forum

http://www.cal.org
- wide range of resources for language-related issues

http://www.eric.ed.gov
- bibliographic database for journal articles and other published and unpublished education materials

http://www.nclrc.org
- one of nine federally-funded language resource centers

http://www.carla.umn.edu
- resources related to second language teaching

NOTE: Web site addresses are subject to change.

Bibliography

Assessment

Boyles, Peggy. *"Assessing the Speaking Skill in the Classroom: New Solutions to an Ongoing Problem."* Northeast Conference Reports: Testing, Teaching, and Assessment, ed. Charles R. Hancock. Lincolnwood, IL: National Textbook Company, 1994.

Burke, K., R. Fogarty, and S. Belgard. *The Mindful School: The Portfolio Connection.* Palatine, IL: IRI/Skylight Publishing Inc., 1994.

Cohen, Andrew D. *Assessing Language Ability in the Classroom,* 2nd ed. Boston: Heinle and Heinle, 1994.

Liskin-Gasparro, Judith. *"Assessment: From Content Standards to Student Performance."* National Standards. A Catalyst for Reform, ed. Robert Lafayette. Lincolnwood, IL: National Textbook Company, 1996.

National K–12 Foreign Language Resource Center. "National Assessment Summit Papers", New Visions in Action, Iowa State University, 2005.

Pettigrew, Frances and Ghislaine Tulou. *"Performance Assessment for Language Students."* Language Learners of Tomorrow: Process and Promise, ed. Margaret Ann Kassen. Lincolnwood, IL: National Textbook Company, 1999.

Block Scheduling

Blaz, Deborah. *Teaching Foreign Languages on the Block.* Larchmont, NY: Eye on Education, 1998.

Canady, R. L., and M. D. Rettig. *Block Scheduling: A Catalyst for Change in High Schools.* Larchmont, NY: Eye on Education, 1995.

———. *Teaching on the Block: Strategies for Engaging Active Learners.* Larchmont, NY: Eye on Education, 1996.

Culture

Byram, Michael. *Teaching and Assessing Intercultural Competence.* Clevedon, U.K.: Multilingual Matters, 1997.

Fantini, Alvino. *"Comparisons: Towards the Development of Intercultural Competence."* Foreign Language Standards: Linking Theory, Research, and Practice, ed. June Phillips. Lincolnwood, IL: National Textbook Co., 1999.

Galloway, Vicki. *"Bridges and Boundaries: Growing the Cross-Cultural Mind."* Language Learners of Tomorrow: Process and Promise. Lincolnwood, IL: National Textbook Co., 1999.

Heusvinkveld, Paula R., ed. *Pathways to Culture.* Yarmouth, ME: Intercultural Press, Inc. 1997.

Curriculum and Instruction

A Texas Framework for Languages Other Than English. Austin, TX: Texas Education Agency, 1997.

ACTFL Performance Guidelines for K–12 Learners. Yonkers, NY: ACTFL, 1999.

"Challenge for a New Era." Nebraska K–12 Foreign Language Frameworks. Lincoln: Nebraska Department of Education, 1996.

Chamot, Anna U. *"Reading and Writing Processes: Learning Strategies in Immersion Classrooms."* Language Learners of Tomorrow: Process and Promise, ed. Margaret Ann Kassen. Lincolnwood, IL: National Textbook Company, 1999.

Davis, Robert. *"Group Work is NOT Busy Work: Maximizing Success of Group Work in the L2 Classroom."* Foreign Language Annals, Vol. 30 (1997): 265–279.

Ferguson, Susan, *"Breathing Life Into Foreign Language Reading".* Educational Leadership, Vol. 63 No. 2 (2005): 63–65.

Foreign Language Framework for California Public Schools Kindergarten Through Grade Twelve. Sacramento: California State Department of Education, 2002.

Guntermann, G., ed. *Teaching Spanish with the Five C's: A Blueprint for Success.* New York: Harcourt College Publishers, 2000.

Hall, Joan Kelly. *"The Communication Standards."* Foreign Language Standards: Linking Theory, Research, and Practice, ed. June Phillips. Lincolnwood, IL: National Textbook Co., 1999.

Heining-Boyton, Audrey L., and David B. Heining-Boyton. *"Incorporating Higher-Order Thinking Skills in the Foreign Language Curriculum."* Foreign Languages: Internationalizing the Future, ed. Robert M. Terry. Valdosta, GA: Southern Conference on Language Teaching, 1993.

Jackson, Claire, et al. *Articulation & Achievement: Connecting Standards, Performance, and Assessment in Foreign Language.* New York: College Board of Publications, 1996.

Klee, Carol A. *"Communication as an Organizing Principle in the National Standards: Sociolinguistic Aspects of Spanish Language Teaching."* Hispania. Vol. 81 (2) (1998), pp. 339–351.

Knerr, Jennifer and Charles James. *"Partner Work and Small-Group Work for Cooperative and Communicative Learning."* Focus on the Foreign Language Learner: Priority and Strategies, ed. Lorraine Strasheim. Lincolnwood, IL: National Textbook Co., 1991.

Krashen, Stephen. *Principles and Practice in Second Language Acquisition.* Oxford: Pergamon Press, 1982.

Met, Myriam, with J. Phillips. *Curriculum Handbook.* Association for Supervision and Curriculum Development, 1999.

———. *"Making Connections."* Foreign Language Standards: Linking Theory, Research, and Practice, ed. June Phillips. Lincolnwood, IL: National Textbook Co., 1999.

Moeller, Aleidine. *"Optimizing Student Success: Focused Curriculum, Meaningful Assessment, and Effective Instruction,"* The 2005 Report of the Central States Conference on the Teaching of Foreign Languages. The Year of Languages: Challenges, Changes, and Choices, ed. Peggy Boyles and Paul Sandrock. Eau Claire, WI: Crown Prints. 2005.

National K–12 Foreign Language Resource Center. *"A Guide to Aligning Curriculum with the Standards."* Ames: Iowa State University, 1996.

———. *Bringing the Standards into the Classroom: A Teacher's Guide.* Ames: Iowa State University, 1997.

Standards for Foreign Language Learning in the 21st Century: *Including Chinese, Classical Languages, French, German, Italian, Japanese, Portuguese, Russian, and Spanish.* Lawrence, KS: Allen Press, 1999.

Zaslow, Brandon. *"Teaching Language for Proficiency: From Theory to Practice (An Instructional Framework)."* Unpublished document. School of Education, University of California, Los Angeles, 2001.

Heritage Learners

Blanco, George. *"El hispanohablante y la gramática."* Bilingual Research Journal 18 (1995): 23–46.

Colombi, Cecilia M. and Francisco X. Alarcón, eds. *La enseñanza del español a hispanohablantes: Praxis y teoría.* Boston: Houghton Mifflin Co., 1997.

Miller, Barbara L., and John B. Webb, eds. *Teaching Heritage Language Learners: Voices from the Classroom, ACTFL Series.* Princeton: Princeton University, 2000.

Rodríguez-Pino, Cecilia, and Daniel Villa. *"A Student-Centered Spanish for Native Speakers Program: Theory, Curriculum Design, and Outcome Assessment."* Faces in a Crowd: The Individual Learner in Multisection Courses, ed. Carol Klee. Boston: Heinle and Heinle, 1994.

Methodology

Hadley, Alice Omaggio. *Teaching Language in Context, 3rd ed.* Boston: Heinle and Heinle, 2001.

Hall, Joan Kelly. *Methods for Teaching Foreign Languages: Creating a Community of Learners in the Classroom.* Upper Saddle River, NJ: Merrill Prentice Hall, 2001.

Hamilton, Heidi E., Crane, Cori, Bartoshesky, Abigal. *"Doing Foreign Language: Bringing Concordia Language Villages into Language Classrooms."* Pearson Education, Inc. 2005.

Lee, James, and Bill Van Patten. *Making Communicative Language Teaching Happen.* New York: McGraw Hill, 1995.

Oxford, Rebecca L. *Language Learning Strategies: What Every Teacher Should Know.* New York: Newbury House, 1990.

Shrum, Judith, and Eileen Glisan. *Teacher's Handbook: Contextualized Language Instruction.* Boston: Heinle and Heinle, 1994.

Multiple Intelligences

Armstrong, Thomas. *Awakening Your Child's Natural Genius.* Los Angeles, CA: Jeremy P. Tarcher, Inc., 1991.

Armstrong, Thomas. *Multiple Intelligences in the Classroom.* Alexandria, VA: Association for Supervision and Curriculum Development, 1994.

Gardner, Howard. *Frames of Mind: The Theory of Multiple Intelligences.* New York, NY: Basic Books, 1983.

Lazear, David. *Seven Pathways of Learning: Teaching Students and Parents about Multiple Intelligences.* Tucson, AZ: Zephyr Press, 1994.

Middle School

Raven, Patrick T. and Jo Anne S. Wilson. *"Middle-School Foreign Language: What Is It? What Should It Be?,"* Visions and Reality in Foreign Language Teaching: Where We Are, Where We Are Going, ed. William N. Hatfield. Lincolnwood, IL: National Textbook Co., 1993.

Verkler, Karen W. *"Middle School Philosophy and Second Language Acquisition Theory: Working Together for Enhanced Proficiency."* Foreign Language Annals, Vol. 27 (1994): 19–42.

Inclusion

Ganschow, Leonore, and Richard Sparks. *"A Screening Instrument for the Identification of Foreign Language Learning Problems."* Foreign Language Annals, Vol. 24 (1991): 383–398.

———, and James Javorsky, John Patton, Jane Pohlman, Richard Sparks. *"Test Comparisons among Students Identified as High-Risk, Low-Risk, and Learning Disabled in High School Foreign Language Courses."* The Modern Language Journal, Vol. 76 (1992): 142–159.

Sax Mabbott, Ann. *"An Exploration of Reading Comprehension, Oral Reading Errors, and Written Errors by Subjects Labeled Learning Disabled."* Foreign Language Annals, Vol. 27 (1994): 294–324.

Sheppard, Marie. *"Proficiency as an Inclusive Orientation: Meeting the Challenge of Diversity."* Reflecting on Proficiency from the Classroom Perspective, ed. June Phillips. Lincolnwood, IL: National Textbook Co., 1993.

Treviño, María. *"Inclusion in the languages other than English classroom."* LOTE CED Communiqué, Issue 9. Austin, TX: 2003.

Technology

Blyth, C. S. *Untangling the Web.* New York: St. Martin's Press, 1998.

Bush, M.D., R. M. Terry., eds. *Technology-Enhanced Language Learning.* Lincolnwood, IL: National Textbook Co., 1997.

Muyskens, Judith Ann., ed. *New Ways of Learning and Teaching: Focus on Technology and Foreign Language Education.* Boston: Heinle and Heinle, 1997.

Index of Cultural References

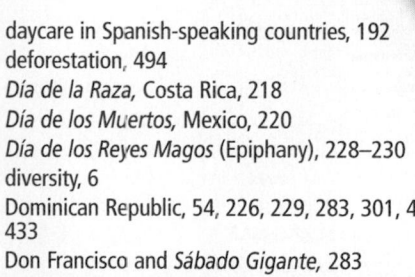

pre-Columbian civilizations, 200, 420, 424
prescriptions and pharmacies, 137
proverbs, 29, 89, 482, 491
Puerto Rico, 54, 164, 301, 335, 390–391, 407, 438

Q

quesadillas, 367
quiz shows, 308

R

rain forests, 494
recipes
    arepas (Venezuelan cornmeal pancakes), 358
    arroz a banda (striped saffron rice), 349
    quesadillas, 367
    tacos, 366
    tostones, 355
relief efforts: Hurricane Mitch, 254
REMAJ (Mexican youth hostel network), 436
RENFE (Spanish train system), 444
Reventador, Ecuador (volcano), 247
Richter scale, 256
riddles, 308, 416
Río, Dolores del, 326
Rivera, Diego, 72, 156, 264
Rodríguez, Narciso, 117
Ronaldo (Luiz Nazario da Lima), 280
Ruiz, Antonio M., 210

S

Sábado Gigante, 283
salsa (dance), 61
salsa (music), 59
San Juan, Puerto Rico: Old San Juan, 164
Sapia, Mariano, 307
school life
    early language learning, 201
    education systems, 458
    formality and familiarity, 32
    grading systems, 30
    school calendar, xxvi
    school names, 178
    study habits, 412
    university studies, 466
Serie de Béisbol del Caribe, 301
shoes, sizing in Spain and Mexico, 109
shopping
    bargaining in open-air markets, 431
    bilingual product labels, 137
    clothing and shoe sizes, 109
    pharmacies, 137
    proverbs, 89
    Spanish-speaking customers, 115
Silva, Simón, 16, 346

Siqueiros, David Alfaro, 450
sister cities: Ciudades Hermanas Internacional, 146–147
sleep needs, teenagers, 83
soccer, 54, 280
social activities, recreation, and customs, 51, 91, 212, 227, 320, 368, 384, 385, 387. *See also* celebrations, festivals, and parades; family life.
social security and socialized medicine in Latin America, 284
sombreros in Mexico, Peru, and Ecuador, 72
songs, 25, 193, 204, 271, 391. *See also* poems.
Sosa, Mercedes, 283
South America. *See individual countries.*
Spain
    ambulance service, 271
    anti-noise pollution campaign, 489
    Basque Country, 216, 280
    clothing and shoe sizes, 109
    Dalí, Salvador, 292, 448b
    driving ages, 172
    euskera, 216
    Ferrer y Miró, Juan, 171
    film industry, 332
    Goya, Francisco de, 201
    independence from France, 223
    jai alai, 280
    Las Fallas de Valencia, 227
    Madrid, 165
    paradores, 440
    Picasso, Pablo, 184
    postage stamps, 145
    RENFE (train system), 444
    royal family, 36, 100, 251
    social security, 284
    summer vacations, 384
    television shows, 308
    traditional clothing, 145
    Velázquez, Diego, 100
Spanish in the workplace. *See* work life and Spanish.
Spanish language, words borrowed from Arabic, 113
Spanish-language videos, 334
sports
    baseball, 54, 301
    Club Deportivo Acuasol, 61
    extracurricular activities, 42, 48, 51
    jai alai, 280
    Olympic Games, 303
    Pan-American games, 310–311
    Ronaldo (soccer), 280
    soccer, 54
    sports injuries, 279
    surfing, 461
    water sports, Punta del Este, Uruguay, 432
survival shows, 308
swing dancing, 62–63

T

tacos, 366
tamales, 380, 392
Tamborrada, festival of San Sebastián, Basque Country, Spain, 216
tango dancing, 62–63
Teatro Colón, Buenos Aires, 90–91
teenagers
    annual youth art contest, 147
    dressing up, 79
    driver's licenses, 172
    exchange programs, 412
    extracurricular activities, 51
    favorite sports, 54
    sleep needs, 83
    study habits, 412
    theater auditions, *Teatro Colón,* Buenos Aires, 91
    youth hostels (REMAJ), 436
television, 293, 304, 307, 308, 312
Texas
    cascarones (confetti-filled eggshells), 227
    Dallas, Texas, 156
    Hinojosa, Celina, 463
theater companies in the Spanish-speaking world, 91
tongue twister, 308, 459
Torres-García, Joaquín, 490
tortillas, 366
tostones (plantain dish), 355
tourism in the United States, 173
toys, 200
transportation and travel. *See also individual countries;* vacation destinations.
    buses in the Spanish-speaking world, 409
    consulates, 417
    ecotourism in Ecuador, 485
    indigenous American *códices,* 420
    Mexican youth hostel network, 436
    Mexico City subway, 169
    money on trips, 414
    paradores in Spain, 440
    train travel in Spain, 444
tropical storms, 254

U

United States. *See also* Americans of Spanish-speaking origin.
    decorations and ornaments from Spanish-speaking countries, 227
    film festival, 332
    growing Spanish-speaking consumer population, 115
    hospital interpreters, 276

PRENTICE HALL 2
Realidades

Peggy Palo Boyles
Oklahoma City, OK

Myriam Met
Rockville, MD

Richard S. Sayers
Longmont, CO

Carol Eubanks Wargin

PEARSON
Prentice Hall

Boston, Massachusetts
Upper Saddle River, New Jersey

Inset image, front cover: Indian woman at market carrying carrots, Guatemala
Front cover (background) and back cover: Market day in Sololá, near Lake Atitlán, Guatemala

Copyright © 2008 by Pearson Education, Inc., publishing as Pearson Prentice Hall, Boston, Massachusetts, 02116. All rights reserved. Printed in the United States of America. This publication is protected by copyright, and permission should be obtained from the publisher prior to any prohibited reproduction, storage in a retrieval system, or transmission in any form or by any means, electronic, mechanical, photocopying, recording, or likewise. For information regarding permission(s), write to: Rights and Permissions Department, One Lake Street, Upper Saddle River, New Jersey 07458.

Pearson Prentice Hall™ is a trademark of Pearson Education, Inc.
Pearson® is a registered trademark of Pearson plc.
Prentice Hall® is a registered trademark of Pearson Education, Inc.

ISBN 0-13-134092-1

4 5 6 7 8 9 10   11 10 09 08 07

Realidades Authors

Peggy Palo Boyles

During her foreign language career of over thirty years, Peggy Palo Boyles has taught elementary, secondary, and university students in both private and public schools. She is currently an independent consultant who provides assistance to schools, districts, universities, and other organizations of foreign language education in the areas of curriculum, assessment, professional development and program evaluation. She s also a part-time instructor at Oklahoma State University She was a member of the ACTFL Performance Guidelines for the K–12 Learners task force and served as a Senior Editor for the project. She currently serves on the Advisory Committee for the ACTFL Assessment for Performance and Proficiency of Languages (AAPPL). Ms. Boyles is the Past-President of the National Association of District Supervisors of Foreign Language (NADSFL) and is the Advocacy Chair for the National Network of Early Language Learners (NNELL).

Myriam Met

For most of her professional life, Myriam (Mimi) Met has worked in the public schools, first as a high school teacher in New York, then as K–12 supervisor of language programs in the Cincinnati Public Schools, and finally as a Coordinator of Foreign Language in Montgomery County (MD) Public Schools. She is currently a Senior Research Associate at the National Foreign Language Center, University of Maryland, where she works on K–12 language policy and infrastructure development. Mimi Met has served on the Advisory Board for the National Standards for Foreign Language Learning, on the Executive Council of ACTFL, and as President of the National Association of District Supervisors of Foreign Languages (NADSFL). She has been honored by ACTFL with the Steiner Award for Leadership in K–12 Foreign Language Education and the Papalia Award for Excellence in Teacher Education.

Richard S. Sayers

Rich Sayers has been an educator in world languages for 28 years. He taught Spanish at Niwot High School in Longmont, CO for 18 years, where he taught levels 1 through AP Spanish. While at Niwot High School, Rich served as department chair, district foreign language coordinator, and board member of the Colorado Congress of Foreign Language Teachers. Rich has also served on the Board of the Southwest Conference on Language Teaching. In 1991, Rich was selected as one of the Disney Company's Foreign Language Teacher Honorees for the American Teacher Awards. Rich serves as National Consultant Training Manager for Prentice Hall. He has been a national consultant for modern and classical languages for Scott Foresman/Addison Wesley and Prentice Hall since 1996. He is also one of the co-authors of the PASO A PASO and REALIDADES Spanish series. Rich lives in Longmont, CO with his wife, Debbie. Their two sons, Todd and Scott, attend college in southern California.

Carol Eubanks Wargin

Carol Eubanks Wargin taught Spanish for 20 years at Glen Crest Middle School, Glen Ellyn, IL, and also served as Foreign Languages department chair. In 1997, Ms. Wargin's presentation "From Text to Test: How to Land Where You Planned" was honored as the best presentation at the Illinois Conference on the Teaching of Foreign Languages (ICTFL) and at the Central States Conference on the Teaching of Foreign Languages (CSC). She was twice named Outstanding Young Educator by the Jaycees.

Contributing Writers

Sheree Altmann
Lassiter High School
Marietta, GA

Madela Ezcurra
New York, NY

Thomasina Pagán Hannum
Albuquerque, NM

Norah L. Jones
Gladys, VA

Mary A. Mosley, Ph.D.
Fulton, MO

Craig Reubelt
The University of Chicago Laboratory Schools
Chicago, IL

National Consultants

María R. Hubbard
Braintree, MA

Jan Polumbus
Tulsa, OK

Patrick T. Raven
Milwaukee, WI

Joseph Wieczorek
Baltimore, MD

Tabla de materias

Go Online
PHSchool.com

For: Online Table of Contents
Web Code: jdk-0001

Tema 2 Un evento especial

Capítulo 3A
¿Qué hiciste ayer?

Objectives

- Talk about things you did and where you did them
- Explain why you couldn't do certain things
- Describe things you bought and where you bought them
- Understand cultural perspectives on shopping

Video Highlights

- **A primera vista:** *¿Qué hiciste esta mañana?*
- **GramActiva Videos:** direct object pronouns: *lo, la, los, las*; irregular preterite verbs: *ir, ser, hacer, tener, estar, poder*
- **Videomisterio:** *En busca de la verdad*, Episodio 1

Capítulo 3B
¿Cómo se va . . . ?

Objectives

- Give directions for getting to places
- Give a friend directions for a task
- Discuss driving and good driving habits
- Understand cultural perspectives on neighborhoods

Video Highlights

- **A primera vista:** *¿Cómo llegamos a la plaza?*
- **GramActiva Videos:** irregular affirmative *tú* commands; present progressive: irregular forms
- **Videomisterio:** *En busca de la verdad*, Episodio 2

Tema 4 — Recuerdos del pasado

Capítulo 5A
Un acto heroico

Objectives

- Discuss emergencies, crises, rescues, and heroic acts
- Describe past situations and settings
- Describe weather conditions
- Understand cultural perspectives on natural disasters and legends

Video Highlights

- **A primera vista:** *En el noticiero*
- **GramActiva Videos:** the imperfect tense: other uses; the preterite of the verbs *oír, leer, and creer*
- **Videomisterio:** *En busca de la verdad,* Episodio 5

Capítulo 5B
Un accidente

Objectives

- Describe an accident scene
- Talk about injuries and treatments
- Talk about what you were doing when an accident occurred
- Understand cultural perspectives on health

Video Highlights

- **A primera vista:** *¡El pobrecito soy yo!*
- **GramActiva Videos:** irregular preterites: *venir, poner, decir,* and *traer;* imperfect progressive and preterite
- **Videomisterio:** *En busca de la verdad,* Episodio 6

Tema 9 ¿Cómo será el futuro?

Capítulo 9A
¿Qué profesión tendrás?

Objectives

- Discuss professions and making plans for the future
- Talk about future events
- Understand cultural perspectives on folk art

Video Highlights

- **A primera vista:** *Y tú, ¿qué vas a ser?*
- **GramActiva Videos:** the future tense; the future tense: irregular verbs

Capítulo 9B
¿Qué haremos para mejorar el mundo?

Objectives

- Make predictions about the future
- Express doubts about ecological issues
- Discuss environmental problems and possible solutions
- Understand cultural perspectives on ecological problems and solutions

Video Highlights

- **A primera vista:** *¡Caramba, qué calor!*
- **GramActiva Videos:** the future tense: other irregular verbs; the present subjunctive with expressions of doubt

México

La Pirámide del Sol, Teotihuacán, México

Geography

Mexico is the fifth largest country in the Western Hemisphere. Its geography ranges from the rugged mountains of the Sierra Madre Occidental and Sierra Madre Oriental to tropical rain forests, volcanic peaks, and world-renowned beaches.

The central area of the country, a high plateau between the ranges of the Sierra Madre, is dry, with limited rainfall. Most of the population lives in this area. Its hub is México, D.F. (Distrito Federal), the nation's capital. The city is located in a basin known historically as the Valley of Mexico. Earthquakes are not uncommon. In 1985 one of the worst earthquakes in Mexican history shook Mexico City and its environs, causing many deaths and extensive damage.

The central plateau is also home to Mexico's highest peaks and volcanoes, including Popocatépetl and Iztaccíhuatl. Pico de Orizaba is the highest mountain in Mexico at 5,610 meters (18,406 feet).

To the north of the central plateau is the Sierra Tarahumara, or Copper Canyon, the largest canyon system in North America. The climate varies dramatically here. At the rim of the canyons the weather is temperate, with cold winters and mild summers, punctuated by heavy rainfall. Deep below the canyon rims, the climate is tropical, wet, and hot for most of the year.

North of the Sierra Tarahumara is the border with the United States, most of which is formed by the Rio Grande, known in Mexico as the Río Bravo.

To the southwest of Mexico City is Acapulco. Mexican vacationers and tourists from around the world visit the heavily populated city and its tropical ocean beaches. Southeast of the capital, on the Yucatan peninsula, is Cancún. Tourists flock to this area's white sandy beaches and the turquoise waters of the Caribbean.

One of the highlights of southern Mexico is Oaxaca, where the climate is spring-like throughout the year. Here archeological sites dot the landscape, revealing the ancient remains of pre-Columbian settlements.

Día de la Independencia, México

México

Capital: México, D.F.

Población: 106.2 millones

Área: 761,606 mi cuadradas / 1,972,550 km cuadrados

Lenguas: español (oficial), náhuatl, lenguas maya, y otras lenguas indígenas

Religiones: católica romana, protestante

Gobierno: república federal

Moneda: peso mexicano

Exportaciones: productos manufacturados, petróleo y sus derivados, plata, café, algodón

Differentiated Instruction
Solutions for All Learners

Advanced Learners

Teotihuacán, which means "the place where men become gods," was a thriving city in 400 A.D., with over 200,000 inhabitants. The large pyramids that remain hint at the mysteries of a vanished civilization. *La pirámide del Sol,* the third-largest pyramid in the world, was probably a religious monument. Though experts are still not sure why the city began to decline after 650 A.D., a large fire that destroyed part of the city seems to have been a significant factor. Ask students to speculate both on what might have happened to the city and on the function of the pyramids.

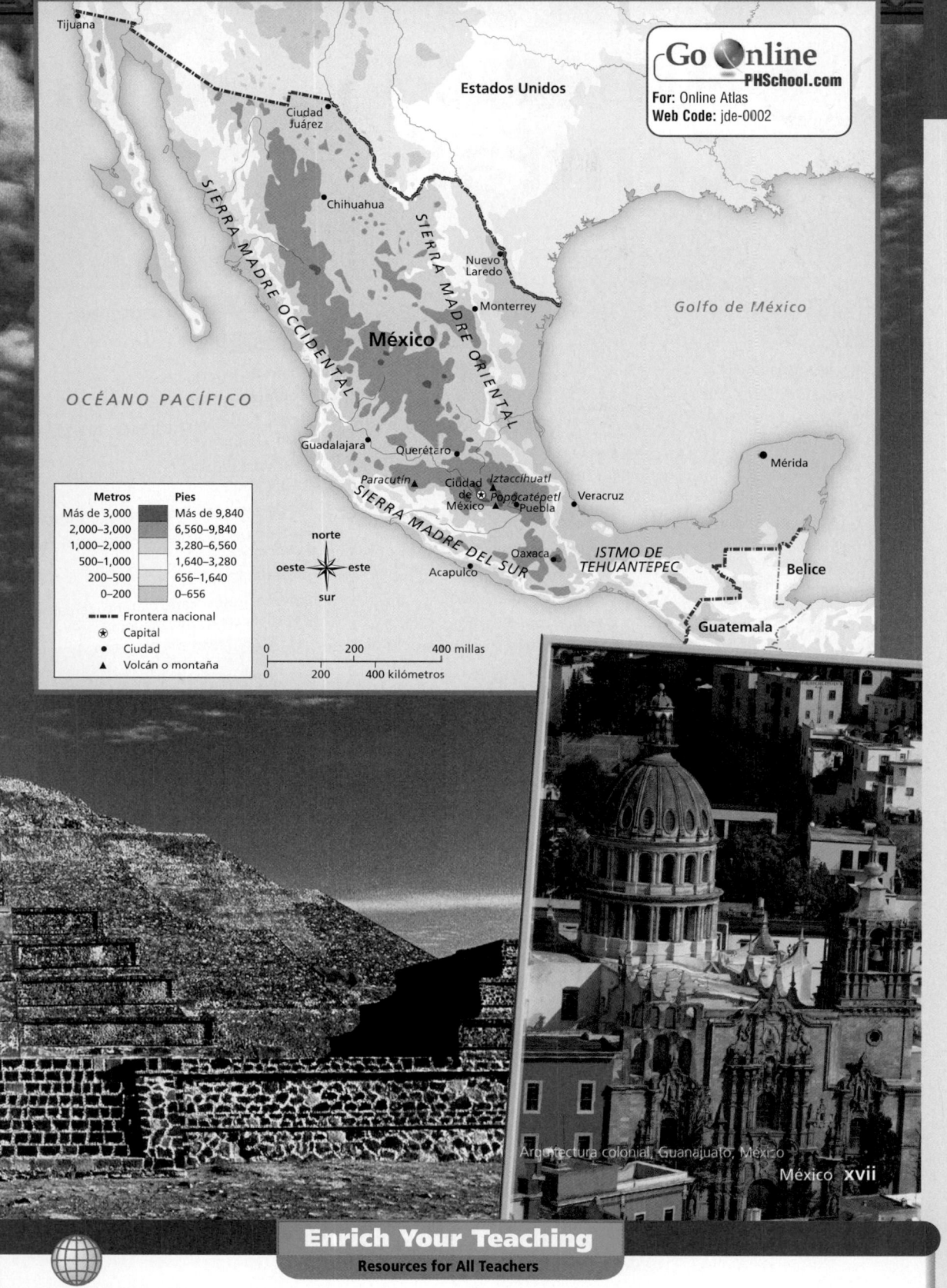

Metros	**Pies**
Más de 3,000	Más de 9,840
2,000–3,000	6,560–9,840
1,000–2,000	3,280–6,560
500–1,000	1,640–3,280
200–500	656–1,640
0–200	0–656

—···— Frontera nacional
⊛ Capital
● Ciudad
▲ Volcán o montaña

norte
oeste — este
sur

0   200   400 millas
0   200   400 kilómetros

Estados Unidos

Tijuana
Ciudad Juárez
Chihuahua
SIERRA MADRE OCCIDENTAL
Nuevo Laredo
Monterrey
México
SIERRA MADRE ORIENTAL
OCÉANO PACÍFICO
Golfo de México
Guadalajara
Querétaro
Paracutín ▲
Ciudad de México ⊛
Iztaccíhuatl ▲
Popocatépetl ▲
Puebla
Veracruz
Mérida
SIERRA MADRE DEL SUR
Oaxaca
Acapulco
ISTMO DE TEHUANTEPEC
Belice
Guatemala

Go Online
PHSchool.com
For: Online Atlas
Web Code: jde-0002

Arquitectura colonial, Guanajuato, México

México **xvii**

History

1519 Hernán Cortés conquers the Aztec emperor Moctezuma II and establishes the first Spanish settlement in Mexico.

1810 Mexico declares its independence from Spain.

1845 Mexican-American War begins as U.S. troops capture Mexico City in an effort to annex Texas.

1862–1864 French troops, led by Napoleon III, march into Mexico City. Maximilian of Austria is declared Emperor of Mexico.

1867 Mexican forces regain control of the country. Maximilian is assassinated.

1876 Porfirio Díaz becomes president of the Republic and eventual dictator (1876–80, 1884–1911).

1910–1911 The Mexican Revolution begins. Francisco I. Madero becomes president.

1913 Madero is assassinated and civil war breaks out.

1940 The Party of Institutionalized Revolution (PRI) is formed and is in power for the next 60 years.

1968 Over 300 protesters against the government are killed during the Mexico City Olympic Games.

1992 The North American Free Trade Agreement (NAFTA) between Canada, the United States, and Mexico is signed.

1994 The Zapatista National Liberation Army (a group of Native American rebels) declares war on the government.

1995–2000 The PRI grip begins to loosen in Mexico with a variety of parties winning provincial elections.

2000–2006 Vicente Fox Quesada, from the *Partido Acción Nacional* (PAN) party, is President of Mexico.

Social Background

Mexico has a diverse population made up of many cultures and customs. The majority of the people are **mestizo,** or a mix of indigenous and European (mostly Spanish) ancestry. Most of the population speaks Spanish as its first language. Indigenous people make up the second largest ethnic group of the population.

Enrich Your Teaching
Resources for All Teachers

Culture Note

Located to the north of Mexico City is Guanajuato, whose name means "Place of Frogs" because the indigenous people thought it only fit for frogs! When large silver deposits were found nearby during colonial times, however, it quickly became an important economic center. Guanajuato represents one of Mexico's best-preserved colonial regions, and UNESCO declared it a World Heritage site in 1988 for its charming architecture and underground streets.

Geography

A series of islands were once scattered between what is now the Caribbean Sea and the Pacific Ocean. Three million years ago (relatively recently in geological terms) they merged to form Central America, a land bridge that links North and South America.

The region is geographically unstable. It is home to at least 14 active volcanoes and experiences frequent earthquakes. Managua, capital of Nicaragua, has been nearly destroyed by earthquakes twice in the last 100 years.

The land is marked by volcanic mountains and **calderas,** lakes that have formed in the volcanic craters. Central America's western coastal plain is fairly narrow, sloping dramatically up to the central mountain region. A less dramatic plateau slopes eastward to the Caribbean.

The climate is diverse, mostly due to a variety of altitudes rather than to topography. There are three major areas. The hottest (**tierra caliente**) is the lowest area, ranging from sea level to an altitude of roughly 915 meters (3,000 feet). The **tierra templada** ranges from 1,830 meters to 3,050 meters (6,000–10,000 feet) and averages temperatures of 65–75° F. The coldest area (**tierra fría**) is the highest and encompasses the mountain peaks.

Water is key to Central American geography. Bordered on east and west by enormous bodies of water, the region also has several rivers and two very large lakes—Lake Nicaragua and Lake Managua. The Panama Canal is a commercial waterway that links the Caribbean and the Pacific. It was constructed at the narrowest point of Central America so that ships carrying goods between distant ports would not have to sail all the way around the southern tip of South America.

The countries of Central America offer a variety of products and resources that are traded worldwide. Honduras and Nicaragua are rich in minerals, including gold and silver. Honduras also has significant deposits of lead, zinc, copper, and iron ore, while Nicaragua offers offshore oil. Bananas and coffee are key to the economies of Costa Rica and Panama, which are the chief exporters of these products to the United States.

América Central

Guatemala

Capital: Guatemala
Población: 14.7 millones
Área: 42,043 mi cuadradas / 108,890 km cuadrados
Lenguas: español (oficial), Quiché, cakchiquel, kekchi, mam, garifuna, xinca, y otras lenguas indígenas
Religiones: católica romana, protestante, creencias tradicionales mayas
Gobierno: república democrática constitucional
Moneda: quetzal, dólar
Exportaciones: combustibles, maquinaria y equipos de transporte, materiales para construcción, granos

Honduras

Capital: Tegucigalpa
Población: 7 millones
Área: 43,278 mi cuadradas / 112,090 km cuadrados
Lenguas: español (oficial), lenguas indígenas
Religiones: católica romana, protestante
Gobierno: república constitucional democrática
Moneda: lempira
Exportaciones: café, plátano, camarón, langosta, carne, cinc, madera

El Salvador

Capital: San Salvador
Población: 6.7 millones
Área: 8,124 mi cuadradas / 21,040 km cuadrados
Lenguas: español (oficial), nahua
Religiones: católica romana, protestante
Gobierno: república
Moneda: colón salvadoreño, dólar
Exportaciones: elaboración de productos con materiales fabricados en el extranjero, equipos, café, azúcar, camarón, textiles, productos químicos, electricidad

Piscinas termales, cerca del Volcán Arenal, Costa Rica

xviii América Central

Differentiated Instruction
Solutions for All Learners

Teaching with Photos

Ecotourism is popular in some Central American countries, such as Costa Rica. Using the picture as a starting point, discuss with your students why it would be important to preserve our natural resources. Can they think of national parks in the United States similar to those in Costa Rica?

Multiple Intelligences

Naturalist: Ask students to compare this picture with a city landscape. What feelings do they associate with the two places? You might want to start by putting a list of emotions on the board, such as **contento(a), tranquilo(a), nervioso(a),** and **cansado(a).**

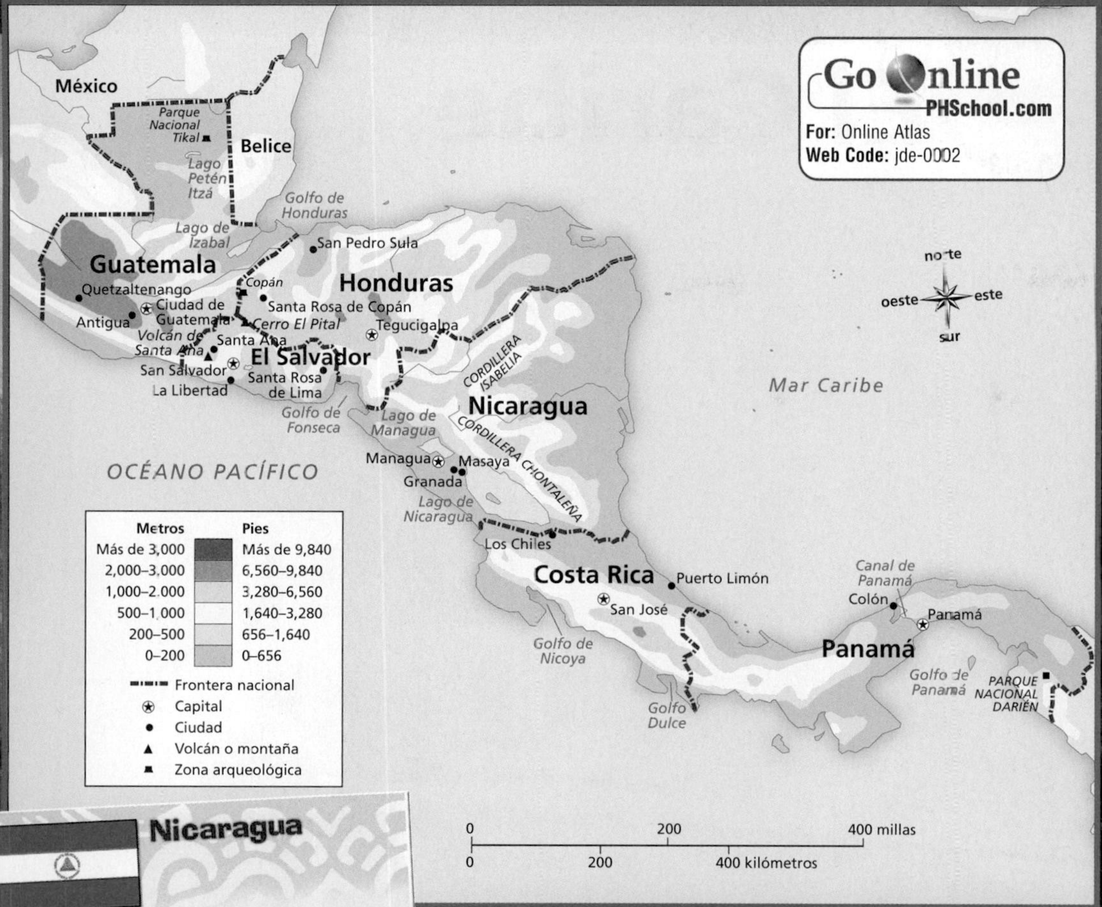

Go Online
PHSchool.com

For: Online Atlas
Web Code: jde-0002

Map of Central America

México
Belice
Parque Nacional Tikal ▲
Lago Petén Itzá
Golfo de Honduras
Lago de Izabal
San Pedro Sula
Guatemala
Quetzaltenango
Copán
Honduras
Ciudad de Guatemala
Santa Rosa de Copán
Antigua
Cerro El Pital ▲
Tegucigalpa
Volcán de Santa Ana ▲
Santa Ana
El Salvador
San Salvador
Santa Rosa de Lima
La Libertad
Golfo de Fonseca
Lago de Managua
Nicaragua
CORDILLERA ISABELIA
CORDILLERA CHONTALEÑA
Mar Caribe
norte
oeste — este
sur

OCÉANO PACÍFICO
Managua
Masaya
Granada
Lago de Nicaragua
Los Chiles
Costa Rica
Puerto Limón
San José
Golfo de Nicoya
Golfo Dulce
Canal de Panamá
Colón
Panamá
Panamá
Golfo de Panamá
PARQUE NACIONAL DARIÉN

Metros / Pies
Metros	Pies
Más de 3,000	Más de 9,840
2,000–3,000	6,560–9,840
1,000–2,000	3,280–6,560
500–1,000	1,640–3,280
200–500	656–1,640
0–200	0–656

- – Frontera nacional
- ⊛ Capital
- • Ciudad
- ▲ Volcán o montaña
- ▪ Zona arqueológica

0   200   400 millas
0   200   400 kilómetros

Nicaragua
Capital: Managua
Población: 5.5 millones
Área: 49,998 mi cuadradas / 129,494 km cuadrados
Lenguas: español (oficial), inglés, miskito, otras lenguas indígenas
Religiones: católica romana, protestante
Gobierno: república
Moneda: córdoba oro
Exportaciones: café, camarón, langosta, algodón, tabaco, carne, azúcar, plátano, oro

Costa Rica
Capital: San José
Población: 4 millones
Área: 19,730 mi cuadradas / 51,100 km cuadrados
Lenguas: español (oficial), inglés
Religiones: católica romana, protestante
Gobierno: república democrática
Moneda: colón de Costa Rica
Exportaciones: café, plátano, azúcar, textiles, componentes electrónicos

Panamá
Capital: Ciudad de Panamá
Población: 3 millones
Área: 30,193 mi cuadradas / 78,200 km cuadrados
Lenguas: español (oficial), inglés
Religiones: católica romana, protestante
Gobierno: democracia constitucional
Moneda: balboa, dólar
Exportaciones: plátano, azúcar, camarón, café

América Central **xix**

Enrich Your Teaching
Resources for All Teachers

Culture Note
Costa Rica has one of the oldest democracies in the Americas. It is known as the Switzerland of the Americas because it promotes peace and maintains neutrality during international conflicts. In 1987, Dr. Óscar Arias, the president of Costa Rica, won the Nobel Peace Prize.

Internet Search
Keyword:

ecotourism, travel + (Spanish-speaking country)

History

1502 On his fourth voyage, Columbus establishes Spain's claim to Central America.

1510–1519 Explorers create and settle colonies. The region is divided into two jurisdictions.

1821–1822 Guatemala, El Salvador, Honduras, Nicaragua, and Costa Rica declare their independence from Spain and create The United Provinces of Central America.

1823 U.S. President James Monroe and Secretary of State John Quincy Adams develop the Monroe Doctrine, warning Europe against intervening in the government or trade of countries in the Western Hemisphere.

1840 Guatemala, Honduras, El Salvador, Nicaragua, and Costa Rica become independent republics.

1855 The Panama Railroad is completed, improving commerce to the Pacific coast ports.

1903 Panama becomes independent from Colombia.

1960 Guatemala, Honduras, El Salvador, and Nicaragua create the Central American Common Market (CACM).

1979 The Sandinistas in Nicaragua overthrow the government of Anastasio Somoza.

1987 Costa Rican president Oscar Arias Sánchez wins the Nobel Peace Prize for creating a peace plan for Central America.

1992 Guatemalan indigenous activist Rigoberta Menchú Tum wins the Nobel Peace Prize for her work in Social Justice and ethno-cultural reconciliation.

2005 The Central America Free Trade Agreement (CAFTA) is signed.

2005–present The nations of Central America continue to strive for political stability and economic modernization.

Social Background
The majority of people in Central America are ***mestizo,*** a mix of Native American and European—mostly Spanish. Though the first language of most of the population is Spanish, in Guatemala 23 dialects of Mayan are also spoken.

Geography

The Spanish-speaking islands of the Caribbean share common and dramatic geographical features, including a similar topography of mountain ranges and extensive shorelines.

Cuba consists of one main island and several small ones, including la *Isla de la Juventud* (The Isle of Youth) and four small archipelagos.

Cuba is the largest island in the Caribbean. It is unusual in that three quarters of the country are fertile farmland, where crops such as sugar, tobacco, citrus fruits, and coffee grow in abundance. Cuba's shoreline is home to spectacular beaches, coral reefs, and deep harbors.

The Dominican Republic shares the island of Hispaniola with Creole-speaking Haiti. It, too, has fertile farmland, but the majority of the island consists of mountain ranges. Its most valuable crops are sugar, cocoa, and tobacco.

Puerto Rico's landscape is marked by steep mountains. The Cordillera Central extends from east to west and divides the country into northern and southern regions. The island's mountain peak of *El Yunque* (The Anvil) attracts tourists throughout the year. The warm, sunny beaches of the coastline are also a major tourist destination. Puerto Rico's economy relies on industry and tourism rather than agriculture. An estimated five million tourists visit the island each year.

The three countries share a similar climate. Generally, the temperatures are moderate to tropical all year round. The mountainous areas receive the most rainfall, while the beaches remain fairly warm and sunny throughout the year.

El Capitolio, La Habana, Cuba

Rio Yaque Norte, República Dominicana

XX El Caribe

Differentiated Instruction
Solutions for All Learners

Multiple Intelligences

Mathematical/Logical: Have students calculate population densities for Cuba, the Dominican Republic, and Puerto Rico. Tell them to use the population data and area in square miles for each island. Encourage them to compile their data in a graph or table and present their findings to the class.

Cuba

Capital: La Habana

Población: 11.3 millones

Área: 42,803 mi cuadradas / 110,860 km cuadrados

Lenguas: español (oficial)

Religiones: católica romana, protestante, y otras religiones

Gobierno: estado comunista

Moneda: peso cubano

Exportaciones: azúcar, níquel, tabaco, mariscos, productos médicos, cítricos, café

República Dominicana

Capital: Santo Domingo

Población: 9 millones

Área: 18,815 mi cuadradas / 48,730 km cuadrados

Lenguas: español (oficial)

Religiones: católica romana, protestante

Gobierno: democracia representativa

Moneda: peso dominicano

Exportaciones: ferroníquel, azúcar, oro, plata, cacao, tabaco, carne

Puerto Rico

Capital: San Juan

Población: 3.9 millones

Área: 3,515 mi cuadradas / 9,104 km cuadrados

Lenguas: español e inglés (lenguas oficiales)

Religiones: católica romana, protestante

Gobierno: estado libre asociado de los Estados Unidos

Moneda: dólar estadounidense

Exportaciones: productos manufacturados, petróleo y productos derivados, plata, café, algodón

El Caribe **xxi**

Go Online
PHSchool.com
For: Online Atlas
Web Code: jde-C002

History

1492 Christopher Columbus explores Hispaniola and Cuba on his first voyage to the Americas.

1493 Puerto Rico is claimed by Spain during Columbus's second voyage.

1496 Santo Domingo, the oldest Spanish settlement in the Western Hemisphere and the capital of the Dominican Republic, is founded.

1898 Puerto Rico is ceded to the U.S. after the Spanish-American War.

1899 Cuba becomes an independent republic under U.S. protection.

1917 Residents of Puerto Rico are granted U.S. citizenship.

1934 Cuba terminates its alliance with the U.S.

1952 Puerto Rico enacts its first constitution for internal self-government.

1956–1959 Fidel Castro launches the Cuban Revolution. Many Cubans flee to Florida.

1961 The U.S. suspends diplomatic relations with Cuba due to Castro's ties with Communist U.S.S.R.

1996 The Dominican Republic holds its first free elections.

1997 Puerto Rican voters decide to maintain their Commonwealth status.

2002 Castro claims he has 99% of the Cuban electorate's backing to retain its socialist system.

2005 The Dominican Republic decides to participate in the Dominican Republic-Central America Free Trade Agreement (DR-CAFTA).

Social Background

Cuba and the Dominican Republic have similar populations, which are largely *mestizo,* and African. Puerto Rico is different in that most of its inhabitants are Caucasian decendants of Spanish settlers.

Enrich Your Teaching
Resources for All Teachers

Culture Note

Each island of the Caribbean has its own unique cuisine. When traveling to Cuba, a visitor might enjoy rice and beans, fried plantains, and pork stew. In the Dominican Republic, you might indulge in fresh seafood, including crayfish, crab, or frog's legs. In Puerto Rico, traditional dishes are spiced with three staples of the country's diet: *achiote,* a mixture of seeds and oils; *sofrito,* herbs and spices ground together; and *adobo,* salt and garlic flavored with lime juice.

Geography

The countries of northern South America share dramatic landscapes of high mountains, lush tropical rainforests, and striking coastlines. Yet each country has a unique geography that distinguishes it from its neighbors.

Venezuela is the continent's northernmost nation. Most of its population lives in the northern highlands or the coastal regions, where the capital, Caracas, is located. The rest of the country is divided between the *Llanos,* tropical grasslands, and the Guiana Highlands, a mountainous area comprising over half of the country. The highlands have recently become more populated due to large deposits of iron, manganese, and bauxite that have been discovered there.

Colombia's landscape is divided between east and west by the spectacular Andes Mountains, which extend southward, dividing Ecuador, Peru, and Bolivia as well. Most of the population of Colombia lives in the basins around the *Cordillera Oriental.* One of the highest ranges of the Andes, the *Cordillera's* peaks reach to 5,500 meters (18,000 feet). To the east lies a jungle lowland, thinly populated and one of the last minimally explored areas on earth.

Ecuador, named for its location on the Equator, has four distinct geographic regions, including the coastal plain and the *Sierra,* where the Andes mountains and one of the world's highest volcanoes, Cotopaxi, are found. The *Oriente* jungle covers almost half the country, while the Galapagos Islands are a series of 15 offshore islands dotted with volcanic peaks.

Peru lies just south of Ecuador and Colombia. Peru's Andean peaks are some of the highest in the world. *Huascarán,* at 6,768 meters (22,205 feet), is the highest mountain in the country. Earthquakes occur in this part of Peru, and these mountains are virtually impassable. Peru's long coast is dry and wide and is the economic and population center of the country.

Bolivia is nicknamed "Rooftop of the World," because most of the country sits at a high elevation atop the Andes. Most of the people live in the mountains and in cities like La Paz, Santa Cruz, and Cochabamba.

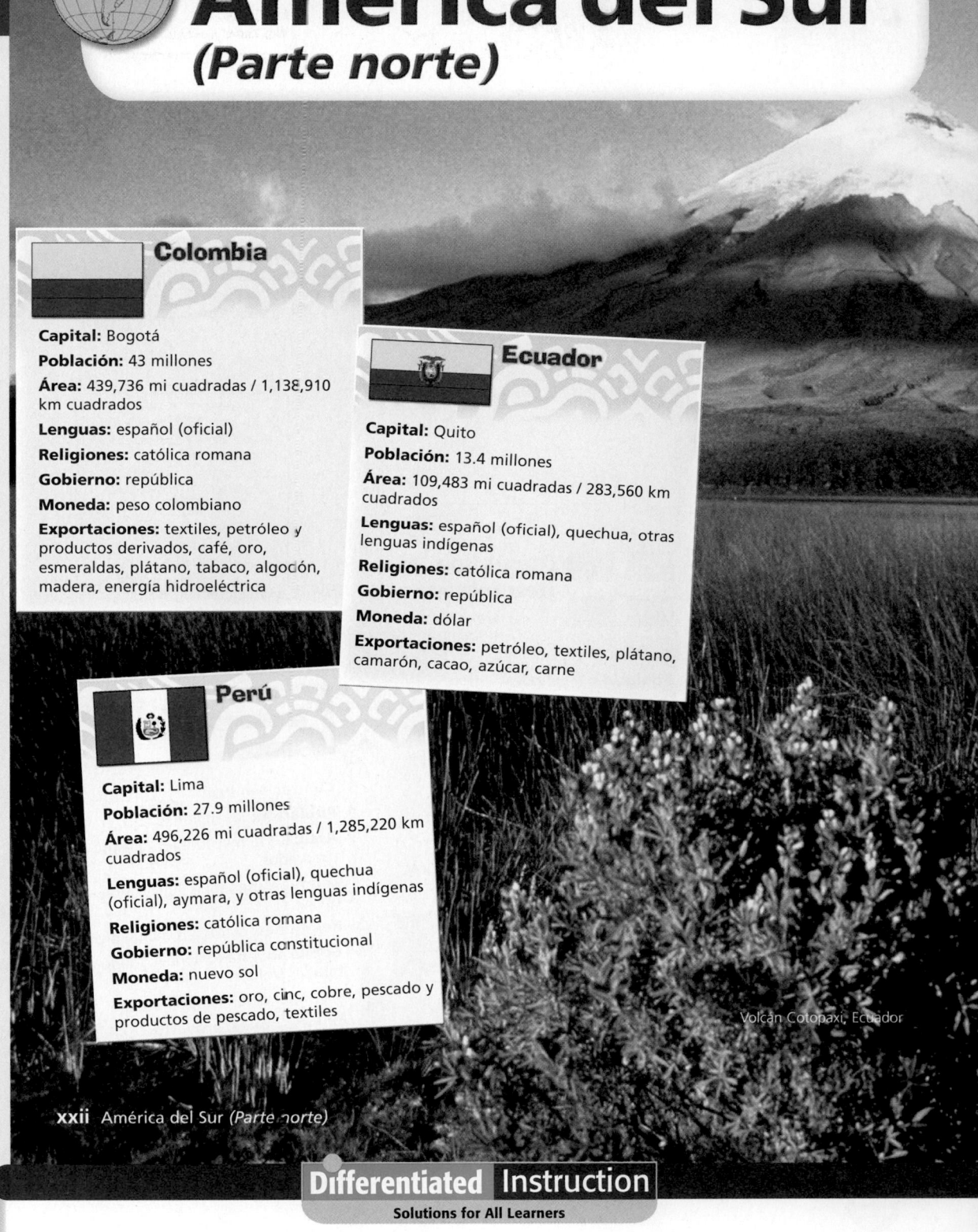

América del Sur
(Parte norte)

Colombia

Capital: Bogotá

Población: 43 millones

Área: 439,736 mi cuadradas / 1,138,910 km cuadrados

Lenguas: español (oficial)

Religiones: católica romana

Gobierno: república

Moneda: peso colombiano

Exportaciones: textiles, petróleo y productos derivados, café, oro, esmeraldas, plátano, tabaco, algodón, madera, energía hidroeléctrica

Ecuador

Capital: Quito

Población: 13.4 millones

Área: 109,483 mi cuadradas / 283,560 km cuadrados

Lenguas: español (oficial), quechua, otras lenguas indígenas

Religiones: católica romana

Gobierno: república

Moneda: dólar

Exportaciones: petróleo, textiles, plátano, camarón, cacao, azúcar, carne

Perú

Capital: Lima

Población: 27.9 millones

Área: 496,226 mi cuadradas / 1,285,220 km cuadrados

Lenguas: español (oficial), quechua (oficial), aymara, y otras lenguas indígenas

Religiones: católica romana

Gobierno: república constitucional

Moneda: nuevo sol

Exportaciones: oro, cinc, cobre, pescado y productos de pescado, textiles

Volcán Cotopaxi, Ecuador

Differentiated Instruction
Solutions for All Learners

Teaching with Photos

Natural disasters are quite common in this part of the world. The photo on this page shows a volcano in Ecuador. Ask students if there are natural disasters in the United States. What are some examples? What can we do to protect ourselves from natural disasters?

Map Labels

Mar Caribe
Maracaibo
Cartagena
Caracas
Medellín
Venezuela
Río Orinoco
Cali
Bogotá
Colombia
Ecuador
Ecuador
Quito
ISLAS GALÁPAGOS (Ecuador)
Chimborazo
Guayaquil
Golfo de Guayaquil
Perú
Brasil
Huascarán
CORDILLERA DE LOS ANDES
Callao
Machu Picchu
Cuzco
Lima
Bolivia
La Paz
Cochabamba
Titicaca
Sucre
Nevado Sajama
Potosí
OCÉANO PACÍFICO
Trópico de Capricornio
Chile
Paraguay
Trópico de Capricornio
Argentina
OCÉANO ATLÁNTICO
Uruguay

Go Online
PHSchool.com
For: Online Atlas
Web Code: jde-0002

Map Legend

Metros	Pies
Más de 3,000	Más de 9,840
2,000–3,000	6,560–9,840
1,000–2,000	3,280–6,560
500–1,000	1,640–3,280
200–500	656–1,640
0–200	0–656

- - - - - Frontera nacional
✪ Capital
● Ciudad
▲ Volcán o montaña
■ Zona arqueológica

norte
oeste · este
sur

0   400   800 millas
0   400   800 kilómetros

América del Sur (Parte norte) **xxiii**

Venezuela

Capital: Caracas

Población: 25.4 millones

Área: 352,144 mi cuadradas / 912,050 km cuadrados

Lenguas: español (oficial), varias lenguas indígenas

Religiones: católica romana, protestante

Gobierno: república federal

Moneda: bolívar

Exportaciones: petróleo y productos derivados, azúcar, plátano, acero, aluminio, energía hidroeléctrica

Bolivia

Capital: La Paz, Sucre

Población: 8.9 millones

Área: 424,164 mi cuadradas / 1,098,580 km cuadrados

Lenguas: español, quechua, aymara (todas lenguas oficiales)

Religiones: católica romana, protestante

Gobierno: república

Moneda: boliviano

Exportaciones: soya, gas natural, cinc, madera, oro

History

1498 Christopher Columbus sights Venezuela on his third voyage.

1502 On his fourth voyage, Columbus explores the Colombian coast.

1532 Francisco Pizarro lands in Peru.

1533 Sebastián de Benalcázar enters Ecuador under the auspices of Pizarro.

1538 Hernando Pizarro, son of Francisco, conquers Bolivian territory.

1811 Venezuela declares its independence from Spain.

1819 Simón Bolívar leads the revolution that unites present-day Colombia and Venezuela as la República de Gran Colombia.

1821 Peru declares its independence from Spain.

1822 Ecuador is liberated from Spain and joins Gran Colombia.

1825 Bolivia declares its independence from Spain.

1830 Ecuador becomes an independent country.

1879 War begins over land disputes between Chile, Peru, and landlocked Bolivia over access to the Pacific.

1970s Ecuador becomes South America's second largest producer of oil.

1980 Peru begins an economic decline that leads to depression.

1994 Under President Alberto Fujimori, Peru's economy begins to recover.

2000 Fujimori loses popularity and is forced to flee the country.

2002 Venezuela's controversial president, Hugo Chávez, is ousted from power. Three days later he is reinstated.

2005 Evo Morales is elected President of Bolivia. He is the first indigenous leader to become president of a South American nation.

Social Background

Bolivia and Peru have very large indigenous populations. The two largest groups are the Quechua, descended from the ancient Incas, and the Aymará. The entire Aymará population of the world—roughly 1.2 million people—live in the area around Lake Titicaca on the border between Peru and Bolivia.

Culture Note

The Quechua languages derived from the languages of the ancient Inca people. These languages were spoken in the Inca Empire and are still used in some parts of South America. They are the source for several words that have become a part of our vocabulary in English. Have you ever tried beef jerky? The word *jerky* comes from Quechua as do *llama, condor,* and *gaucho.*

Internet Search
Keyword:

volcanoes, earthquakes + (Spanish-speaking country)

Geography

The southern part of South America has dramatic contrasts between the west coast of Chile and the eastern plains of Uruguay. This part of the world, south of the massive country of Brazil, has fascinating culture, geography, and history.

Chile's footprint is easy to remember. The country is long and extremely narrow, with a rugged desert coastline punctuated by dozens of undersea volcanic peaks that form islands along its southernmost coast. Like its neighbors to the north—Peru, Ecuador, and Colombia—Chile's principal geographic landmark is the Andes Mountains, which extend the entire length of the country. Chile's population is centered in the Central Valley. This area is only 40 to 80 kilometers wide.

Argentina is almost as long as Chile, but it is much wider. It is geographically and topographically quite diverse. Along its western border, it shares the Andes with Chile. Eastward from the Andes is a flat, rolling plain divided into two territories: *Gran Chaco,* which it shares with neighboring Paraguay, and the *Pampas,* which are treeless plains that are the center of the country's prosperous agriculture. The southernmost plains are part of Patagonia, a dry, desolate, sparsely inhabited region.

Uruguay is one of the smallest countries of South America. Its landscape offers a sharp contrast to the Andean countries. Due to its relatively uniform elevation, Uruguay has a moderate temperature. Along its Atlantic coast, there are beaches, deep lagoons, and wide sand dunes, which extend almost as much as eight kilometers inland. The economy is based largely on agriculture.

Paraguay, to the northeast of Argentina, is characterized mainly by the Paraná plateau, which is 300–600 meters (1,000–2,000 feet) high. The area slopes gently to the Paraná River and boasts spectacular waterfalls. Paraguay's weather averages 60–80° F year round.

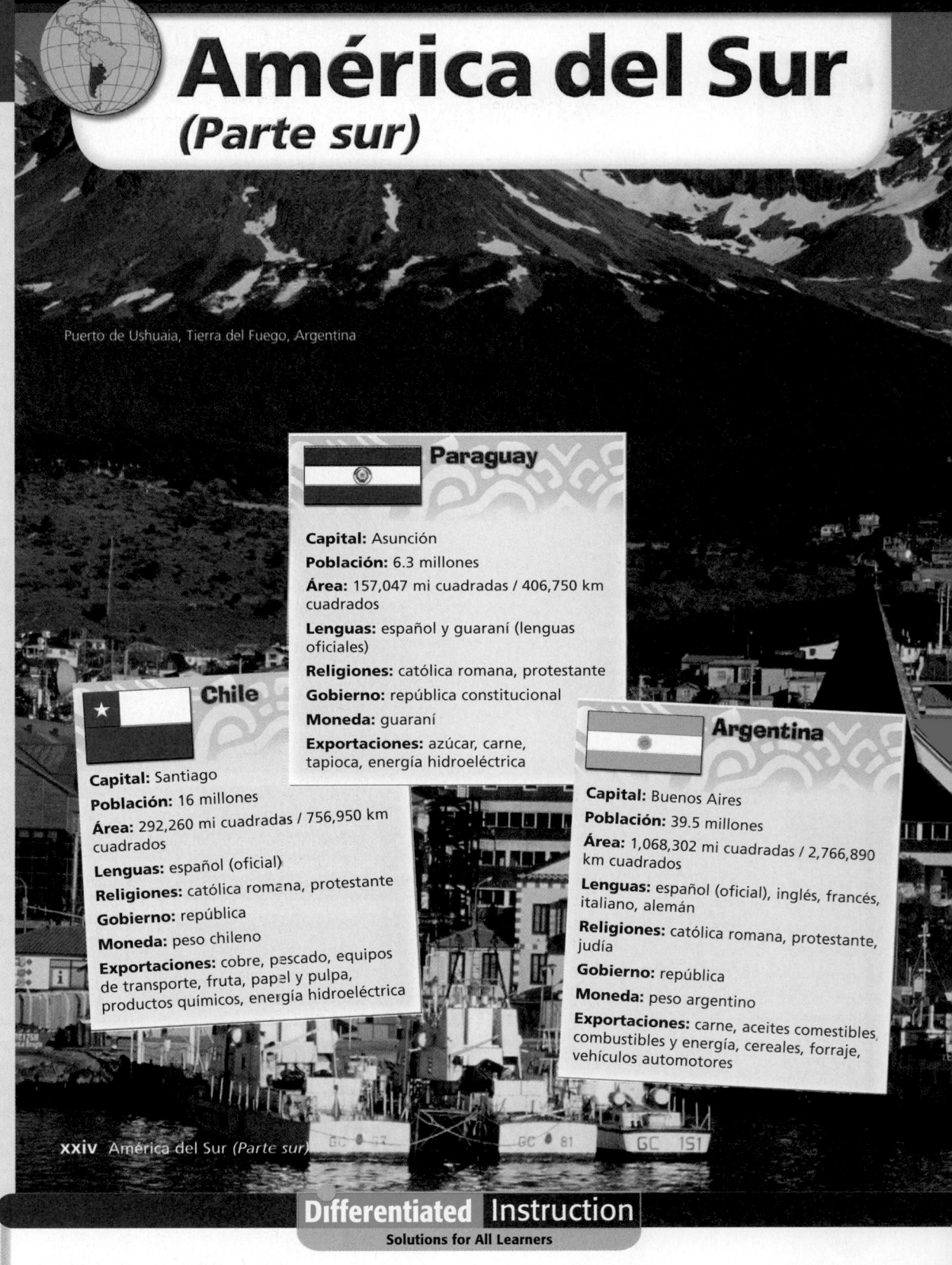

América del Sur
(Parte sur)

Puerto de Ushuaia, Tierra del Fuego, Argentina

Paraguay

Capital: Asunción

Población: 6.3 millones

Área: 157,047 mi cuadradas / 406,750 km cuadrados

Lenguas: español y guaraní (lenguas oficiales)

Religiones: católica romana, protestante

Gobierno: república constitucional

Moneda: guaraní

Exportaciones: azúcar, carne, tapioca, energía hidroeléctrica

Chile

Capital: Santiago

Población: 16 millones

Área: 292,260 mi cuadradas / 756,950 km cuadrados

Lenguas: español (oficial)

Religiones: católica romana, protestante

Gobierno: república

Moneda: peso chileno

Exportaciones: cobre, pescado, equipos de transporte, fruta, papel y pulpa, productos químicos, energía hidroeléctrica

Argentina

Capital: Buenos Aires

Población: 39.5 millones

Área: 1,068,302 mi cuadradas / 2,766,890 km cuadrados

Lenguas: español (oficial), inglés, francés, italiano, alemán

Religiones: católica romana, protestante, judía

Gobierno: república

Moneda: peso argentino

Exportaciones: carne, aceites comestibles, combustibles y energía, cereales, forraje, vehículos automotores

Differentiated Instruction
Solutions for All Learners

Multiple Intelligences

Visual/Spatial: Tell students that from north to south, Chile is as long as the distance between the east and west coast of the United States. In other words, northern Chile is as far away from southern Chile as New York is from California. The country averages only 100 miles in width.

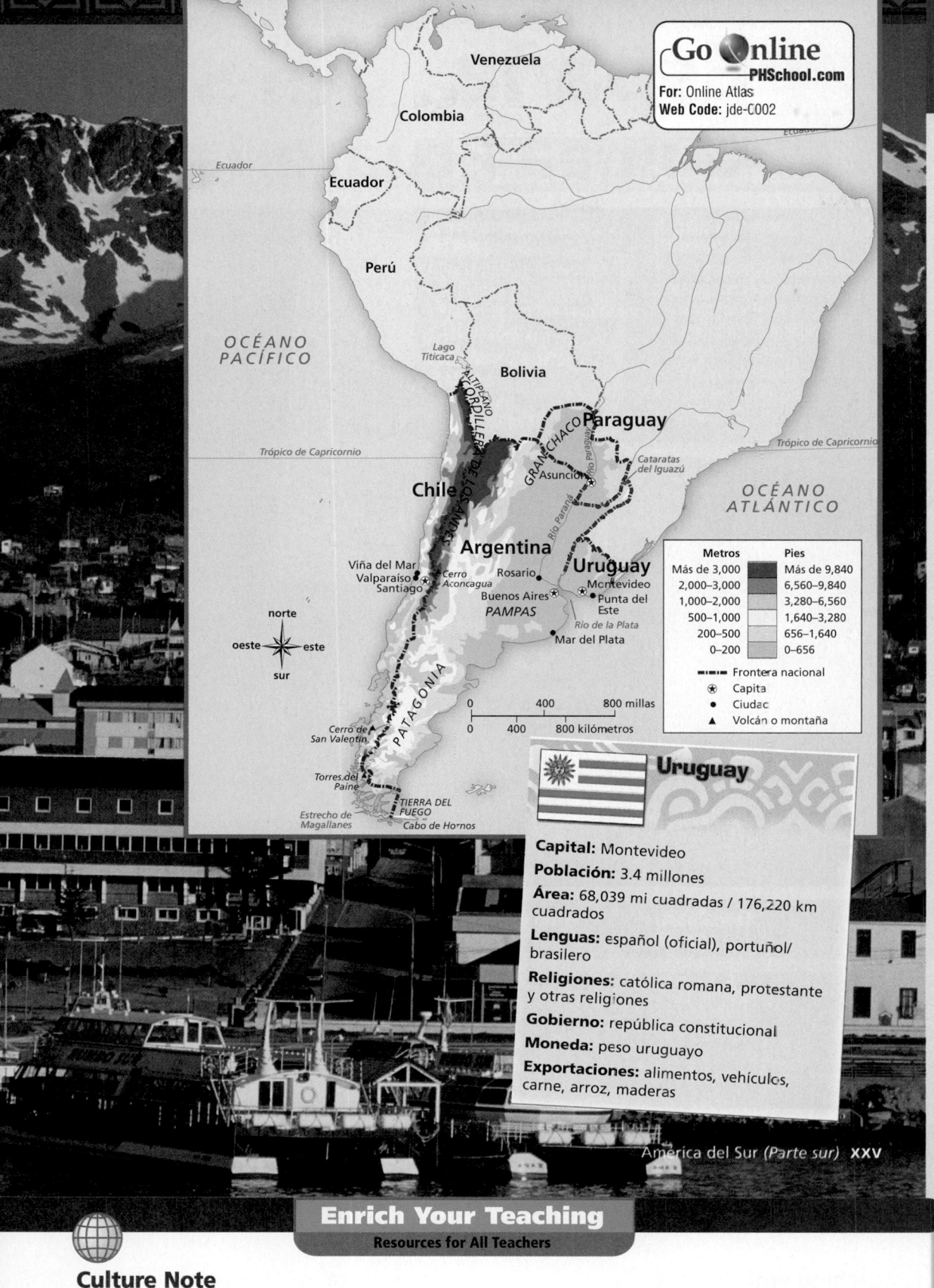

Venezuela

Colombia

Ecuador

Ecuador

Perú

OCÉANO
PACÍFICO

Lago
Titicaca

Bolivia

ALTIPLANO
CORDILLERA

Trópico de Capricornio

GRAN CHACO **Paraguay**

Asunción ✷

Cataratas
del Iguazú

Trópico de Capricornio

Río Paraná

OCÉANO
ATLÁNTICO

Chile

CORDILLERA DE LOS ANDES

Río Paraná

Argentina

Viña del Mar
Valparaíso ✷
Santiago

Cerro
Aconcagua ▲

Rosario

Uruguay

Montevideo ✷
Punta del
Este

norte

Buenos Aires ✷
PAMPAS

Río de la Plata

oeste ✦ este

sur

Mar del Plata

PATAGONIA

Metros	Pies
Más de 3,000	Más de 9,840
2,000–3,000	6,560–9,840
1,000–2,000	3,280–6,560
500–1,000	1,640–3,280
200–500	656–1,640
0–200	0–656

▪▫▪ Frontera nacional
✷ Capital
● Ciudad
▲ Volcán o montaña

Cerro de
San Valentín

0   400   800 millas
0   400   800 kilómetros

Torres del
Paine

TIERRA DEL
FUEGO

Estrecho de
Magallanes

Cabo de Hornos

Uruguay

Capital: Montevideo

Población: 3.4 millones

Área: 68,039 mi cuadradas / 176,220 km cuadrados

Lenguas: español (oficial), portuñol/brasilero

Religiones: católica romana, protestante y otras religiones

Gobierno: república constitucional

Moneda: peso uruguayo

Exportaciones: alimentos, vehículos, carne, arroz, maderas

América del Sur *(Parte sur)* **XXV**

History

1520 Portuguese explorer Ferdinand Magellan lands in Chile.

1536 Buenos Aires is founded.

1540 Chile becomes colonial vice-regency of Spain.

1624 First permanent Spanish settlement in Uruguay is founded.

1810 Chile breaks ties with Spain.

1811 Paraguay declares independence.

1814 The Spanish governor is driven from Uruguay.

1815 Representatives from various provinces in Argentina declare independence from Spain.

1816 Bernardo O'Higgins is named supreme dictator of Chile.

1828 Uruguay officially becomes an independent nation.

1839 Chile invades Peru for territorial reasons.

1864–1870
      After years of growth under President Carlos Antonio López, Paraguay is devastated in a war with the Triple Alliance (Argentina, Brazil, and Uruguay) over borders.

1906 An earthquake devastates the city of Santiago, Chile.

1946 Juan Perón becomes head of state in Argentina.

1955 Perón's government is ousted.

1970 Salvador Allende Gossens is elected president of Chile.

1973 Perón is reinstated as Argentina's president.
      Allende of Chile dies during Augusto Pinochet's military coup.

1974 Isabel Perón, third wife of Juan Perón, is elected first woman head of state in the Western Hemisphere.

1990 Pinochet is ousted as president of Chile.

2000 Ricardo Lagos is elected president of Chile.

2003 Néstor Kirchner is elected president of Argentina. Nicanor Duarte is elected president of Paraguay.

2005 Tabaré Vásquez is elected president of Uruguay.

2006 Michelle Bachelet, a former victim of Pinochet's repressive government, becomes President of Chile.

Enrich Your Teaching
Resources for All Teachers

Culture Note

Ushuaia, located in Argentina's Tierra del Fuego, is the southernmost inhabited city in the world. Close to Antarctica, the surrounding areas boast a variety of unusual fauna, including penguins, sea lions, and exotic birds. The city is surrounded by stunning vistas of snow-capped mountains and glaciers.

España
Guinea Ecuatorial

Geography

Spain, in the southwest of Europe, occupies most of the Iberian peninsula, which it shares with Portugal. It is surrounded on three sides by the Mediterranean and the Atlantic. The Pyrenees Mountains extend across the northeastern border with France.

The most pronounced topographical feature in Spain is the *Meseta Central,* or Central Plateau, which slopes downward from north to south and east to west. The eastern coastal plain is narrow, broken by rocky mountains that slope directly to the sea. Barcelona is the best harbor on Spain's Mediterranean coast.

Spain is separated from Africa by only 13 kilometers at the Strait of Gibraltar. On the southern coast, the people enjoy a subtropical climate; the coldest it gets is around 57° F. It does not rain often, except in the northern mountains. In fact, along the central plateau, the summers are so dry that droughts are not uncommon.

Spain has many environmental concerns, and has embraced international agreements on air quality, marine dumping, and endangered species protection.

Equatorial Guinea is located in Western Africa between Gabon and Cameroon. It includes a mainland territory, known as Mbini, and several islands, the largest of which is Bioko Island. The entire country is smaller than the state of Maryland.

The mainland is covered with gently rolling forests and woodland. In contrast, Bioko Island was formed by volcanic eruptions and is quite mountainous, with a steep and rocky coast. Inland, the island is made up of fertile volcanic soils.

Equatorial Guinea has a climate similar to that of the Canary Islands (see inset), its Spanish island neighbor off the coast of Morocco. The weather on Bioko is hot and humid, with a rainy season from December through February.

The primary occupation of the country's nearly half million residents is agriculture. In 1995, however, offshore oil deposits were discovered, which could transform the country's economy.

Un molino en Castilla-La Mancha, España

España

Capital: Madrid
Población: 40.3 millones
Área: 194,897 mi cuadradas / 504,782 km cuadrados
Lenguas: castellano (oficial), catalán, gallego, vasco
Religiones: católica romana
Gobierno: monarquía parlamentaria
Moneda: euro
Exportaciones: alimentos, maquinaria, vehículos automotores

La Sagrada Familia, Barcelona, España

Differentiated Instruction
Solutions for All Learners

Teaching with Photos

La Sagrada Familia is an architectural treasure strongly associated with the city of Barcelona. Ask students to identify any monuments that might represent your city. Have students research Gaudí and his unique architectural style.

Culture Note

The windmills in the photo are typical of *La Mancha,* a region of Spain located on a plateau just south of Madrid. These windmills are a symbol of Cervantes's masterpiece, *Don Quijote.* The main character, *Don Quijote de la Mancha,* mistakes the windmills for giants and attacks them in a comical scene in the novel.

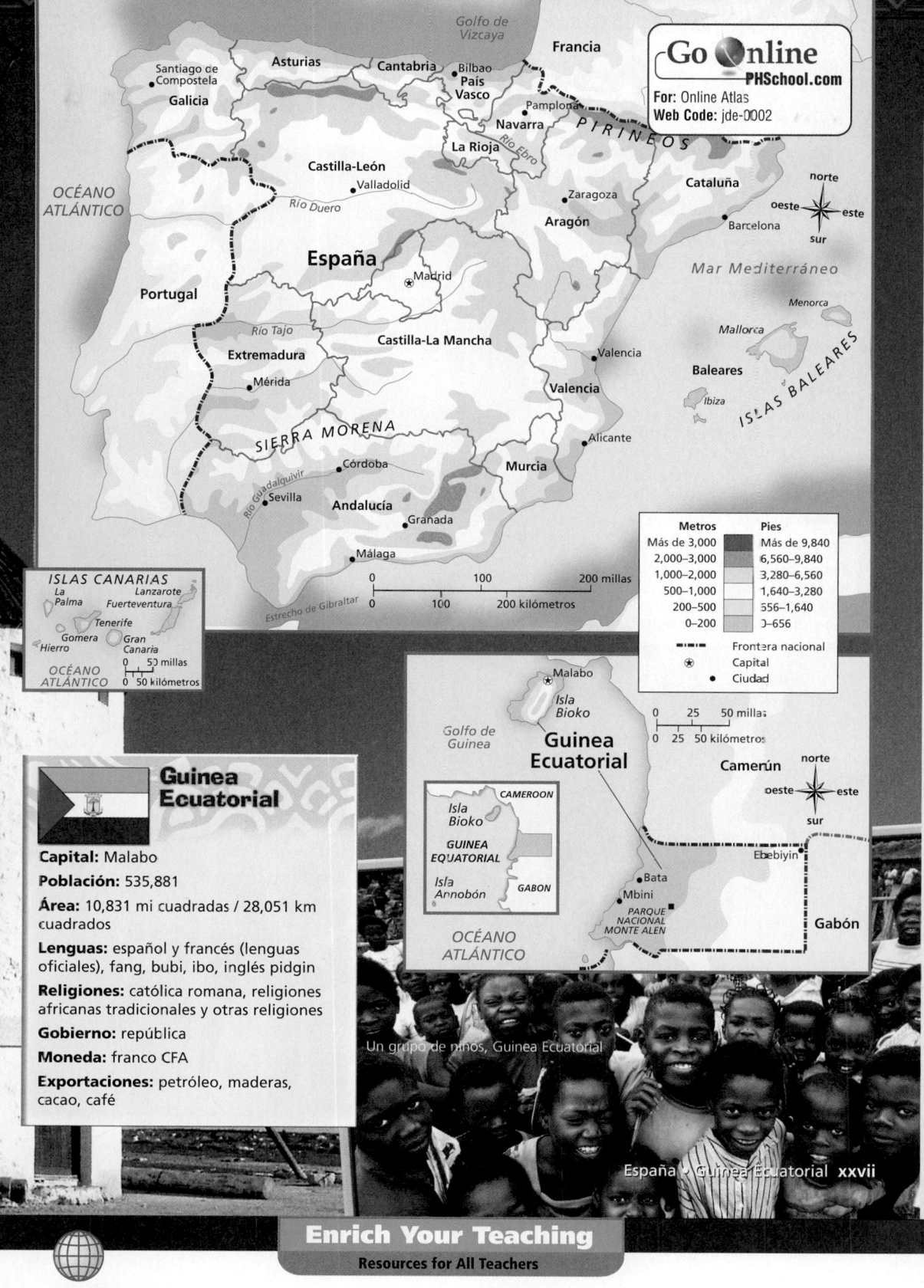

Golfo de Vizcaya
Francia
Santiago de Compostela
Galicia
Asturias
Cantabria
Bilbao
País Vasco
Pamplona
Navarra
La Rioja
Río Ebro
PIRINEOS
Castilla-León
Valladolid
Río Duero
OCÉANO ATLÁNTICO
Zaragoza
Aragón
Cataluña
Barcelona
norte
oeste
este
sur
Mar Mediterráneo
España
Madrid
Portugal
Río Tajo
Castilla-La Mancha
Menorca
Mallorca
Extremadura
Mérida
Valencia
Valencia
Baleares
Ibiza
ISLAS BALEARES
SIERRA MORENA
Alicante
Córdoba
Murcia
Río Guadalquivir
Sevilla
Andalucía
Granada
Málaga
Estrecho de Gibraltar
0 100 200 millas
0 100 200 kilómetros
Metros
Pies
Más de 3,000
Más de 9,840
2,000–3,000
6,560–9,840
1,000–2,000
3,280–6,560
500–1,000
1,640–3,280
200–500
656–1,640
0–200
0–656
Frontera nacional
Capital
Ciudad

ISLAS CANARIAS
La Palma
Lanzarote
Fuerteventura
Tenerife
Gomera
Gran Canaria
Hierro
OCÉANO ATLÁNTICO
0 50 millas
0 50 kilómetros

Go Online
PHSchool.com
For: Online Atlas
Web Code: jde-0002

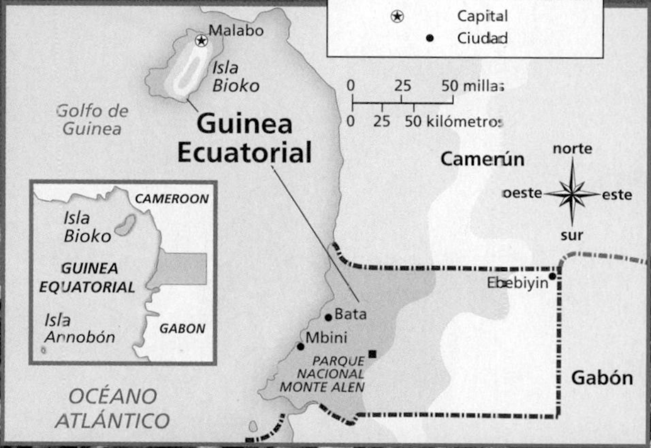

Malabo
Isla Bioko
Golfo de Guinea
Guinea Ecuatorial
0 25 50 millas
0 25 50 kilómetros
Camerún
norte
oeste
este
sur
CAMEROON
Isla Bioko
GUINEA EQUATORIAL
Isla Annobón
GABON
Ebebiyín
Bata
Mbini
PARQUE NACIONAL MONTE ALEN
Gabón
OCÉANO ATLÁNTICO

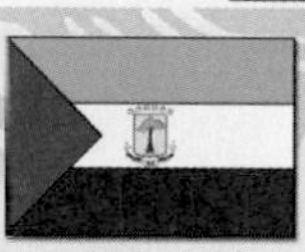

Guinea Ecuatorial

Capital: Malabo
Población: 535,881
Área: 10,831 mi cuadradas / 28,051 km cuadrados
Lenguas: español y francés (lenguas oficiales), fang, bubi, ibo, inglés pidgin
Religiones: católica romana, religiones africanas tradicionales y otras religiones
Gobierno: república
Moneda: franco CFA
Exportaciones: petróleo, maderas, cacao, café

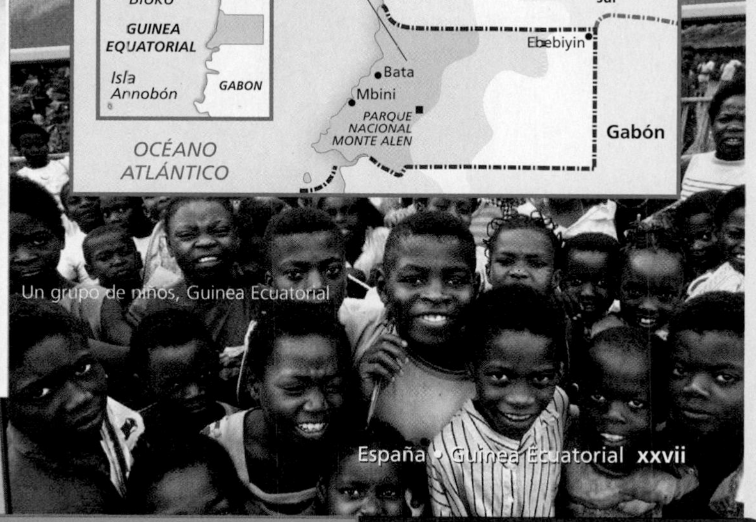

Un grupo de niños, Guinea Ecuatorial

History

España

1469 The marriage of Ferdinand and Isabella unites the kingdoms of Aragon and Castille.

1492 Spain is created after Granada falls to Ferdinand and Isabella.

1492 Queen Isabella finances Columbus's first voyage to the Americas.

1493–1580 Spain explores and colonizes throughout the Americas.

1588 The British defeat the Armada, beginning the decline of Spain's hold on large parts of the world.

1826 By 1826, all of the Spanish colonies in the Americas have won their independence.

1898 The Spanish-American War marks the end of the Spanish Empire.

1936–1939 Civil War breaks out. Franco becomes dictator of Spain.

1947 Franco declares Spain a monarchy, but continues to rule.

1955 The United Nations admits Spain as a member.

1975 Franco dies; Juan Carlos I de Borbón becomes king.

1978 A constitution is drafted.

2004 José Luis Rodríguez Zapatero becomes Prime Minister. Madrid suffers a terrorist attack on March 11.

Guinea Ecuatorial

1473 Explorer Fernando Poo claims Equatorial Guinea for Portugal.

1778 Portugal relinquishes the area to Spain.

1904 Bioki Island (known as Fernando Poo) and the mainland (known as Río Muni) become known as Spanish Guinea.

1959 Spanish Guinea becomes an official province of Spain.

1963 Spanish Guinea is granted autonomy.

1968 Spanish Guinea becomes an independent country and is renamed Equatorial Guinea.

2004 Prime Minister Miguel Abia Biteo Borico becomes head of government.

Enrich Your Teaching

Resources for All Teachers

Culture Note

La Sagrada Familia in Barcelona is characteristic of the unusual style of Antonio Gaudí, one of Spain's most important and influential architects. Its construction began at the end of the nineteenth century and it is still unfinished.

Culture Note

The Bubi were the original inhabitants of Equatorial Guinea. The Fang were indigenous to the mainland and, with the Bubi, have migrated to Bioki. The Fernandinos are a mix of Spanish and African people. In Equatorial Guinea, most of the people have Spanish first names and African middle and last names, giving them a total of four names.

Geography

The geography of the United States is as diverse as its people.

The United States is made up of fifty states and a number of territories, including Puerto Rico, the U.S. Virgin Islands, American Samoa, and Guam. The states vary in size from the largest (Alaska) at 1,593,438 square km (615,230 square miles) to Rhode Island, which is just 3,188 square km (1,231 square miles).

The United States is mountainous, with the Appalachians in the east and the Rocky Mountains, which run north to south, in the west-central part of the country. In the center of the country lie flat, fertile plains.

Like its geography, the climate varies greatly from region to region. In general, the northern half of the country experiences cold winters and mild summers. The southern coastal areas are semi-tropical, with mild winters and hot, humid summers, while inland areas in the southwest have a desert climate. The southeastern and east central parts of the country also see more violent weather patterns, such as tornados and hurricanes.

The country is rich in natural resources and has a diverse economy that includes industry, agriculture, technology, and financial services. The eastern part of the country includes uninterrupted urban centers extending from Massachusetts to the Carolinas and is home to one third of the nation's largest corporations. Many of the area's cities are also major tourist attractions.

The central U.S. is home to both industry and agriculture. Rich soils, abundant rainfall, and a long growing season offer ideal conditions for its soybean, wheat, corn, and alfalfa crops. Livestock and dairy farms dot the landscape. Manufacturing includes the auto industry, with Ohio and Michigan as its chief centers.

Agriculture, industry, and tourism also dominate the western part of the United States. Wine, cotton, citrus fruits, and vegetables are the region's principal crops. Aircraft manufacturing, computer technology, aerospace technology, and entertainment are all key factors in the region's economy.

Estados Unidos

Estados Unidos

Capital: Washington, D.C.

Población: 296 millones

Área: 3,717,813 mi cuadradas / 9,629,091 km cuadrados

Lenguas: inglés, español, otras lenguas indoeuropeas, lenguas asiáticas y del Pacífico, otras lenguas

Religiones: protestante, católica romana, judía, musulmana y otras religiones

Gobierno: república federal

Moneda: dólar estadounidense

Exportaciones: vehículos automotores, equipos aeroespaciales, telecomunicaciones, equipos electrónicos, bienes de consumo, productos químicos, alimentos, trigo, maíz

Ruinas de Cliff Palace, Mesa Verde, CO

Un chilenoamericano con la bandera de los Estados Unidos

xxviii Estados Unidos

Differentiated Instruction
Solutions for All Learners

Advanced Learners
Ask students to talk about their heritage. Where did their family come from? Ask if their parents or grandparents speak another language. Have them interview family members about their family history and share it with the class.

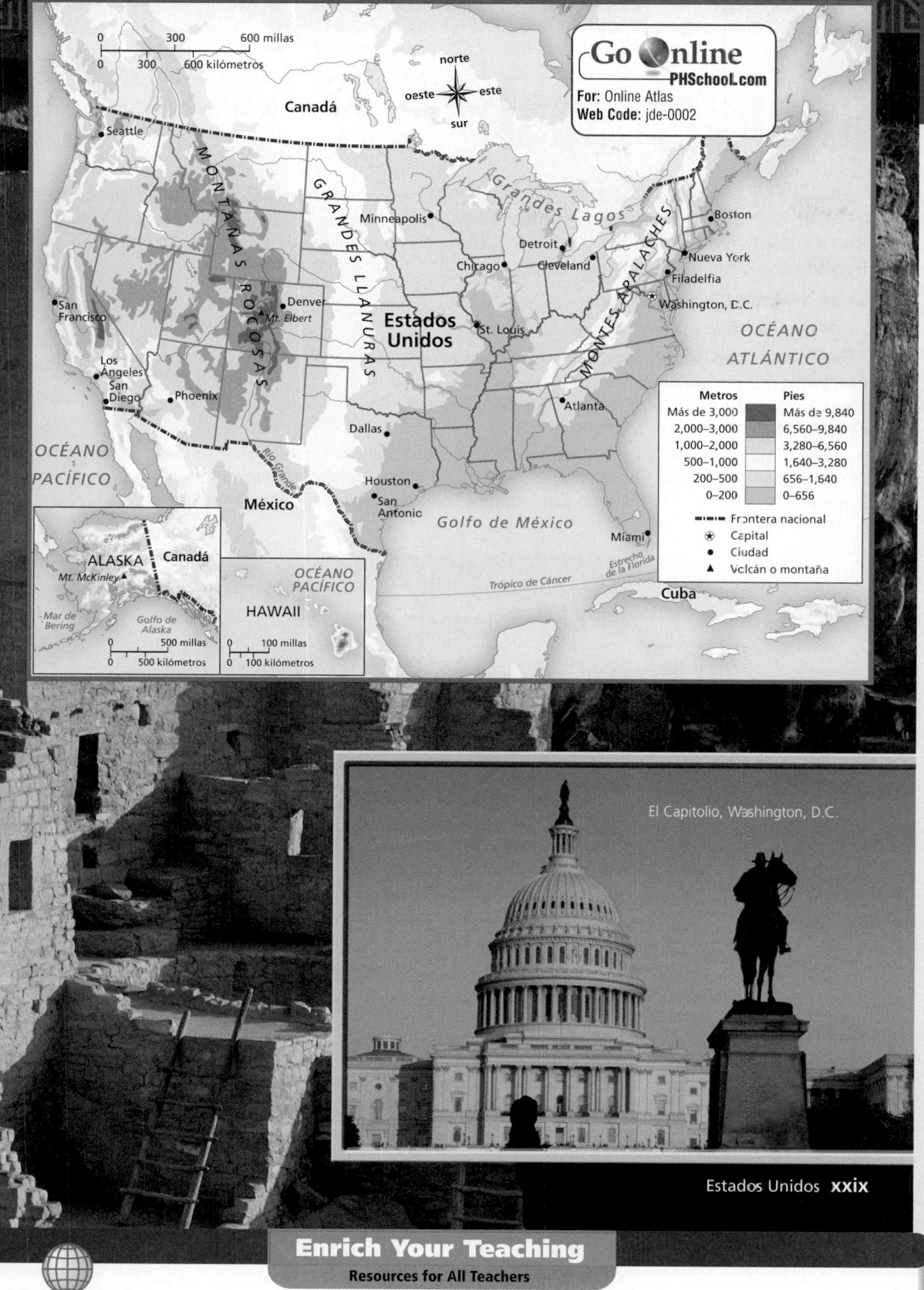

Metros / Pies

Metros	Pies
Más de 3,000	Más de 9,840
2,000–3,000	6,560–9,840
1,000–2,000	3,280–6,560
500–1,000	1,640–3,280
200–500	656–1,640
0–200	0–656

- - - Frontera nacional
✪ Capital
● Ciudad
▲ Volcán o montaña

El Capitolio, Washington, D.C.

Estados Unidos **xxix**

Enrich Your Teaching
Resources for All Teachers

Culture Note

In the 1100s indigenous North Americans built high cliff dwellings in the canyon walls of the U.S. southwest. Cliff Palace is the largest of these dwellings. It has more than 200 rooms and was home to about 400 people. The U.S. Congress meets in the Capitol, located on Capitol Hill, which is also home to the Library of Congress and the Supreme Court. These institutions symbolize the values of the nation's democracy. The Statue of Freedom rests on top of the Capitol's dome, beneath which is the Great Rotunda. The equestrian statue in the foreground is of Ulysses S. Grant, 18th President and commander of the Union forces during the Civil War.

History

1492   Christopher Columbus is the first European to encounter America.

1497–1620   Explorers from Spain, France, Portugal, and England explore and establish colonies.

1763   Britain defeats France in the French and Indian War and gains control of eastern North America.

1775–1781   The Revolutionary War ends with U.S. independence.

1787   U.S. Constitution is ratified.

1803   Louisiana Purchase doubles the size of the U.S.

1821   U.S. purchases Florida from Spain.

1823   The Monroe Doctrine warns European nations not to interfere in the Western Hemisphere.

1848   U.S. wins the Mexican War and obtains huge areas of land from Texas to California.

1861–1865   U.S. Civil War.

1898   U.S. defeats Spain in the Spanish-American War.

1917   The U.S. joins European allies in fighting World War I.

1941   Japanese attack the U.S. at Pearl Harbor, Hawaii, and U.S. enters World War II.

1945   President Truman orders the use of the atomic bomb against Japan.

1962   U.S.S.R. removes missiles from Cuba, averting war with the U.S.

1969   U.S. astronauts walk on the moon.

2001   Terrorists attack New York (World Trade Center) and Washington (Pentagon).

2003   Beginning of II Iraq War.

Social Background

Spanish speakers are rapidly becoming the largest minority group in the United States. Forty-one million, or 14% of the U.S. population, is considered to be Hispanic. Mexicans make up the majority.

Spanish speakers are active in the workforce, and many of their customs and celebrations are becoming part of mainstream U.S. culture.

Most U.S. citizens of Hispanic origin live in five states—California, Texas, New York, Florida, and Illinois.

Suggestions: Discuss with students their experience in Spanish class last year. How did they feel at the end of the year? Have they had a chance to use Spanish since then? Have them explain where or when. Explain to students that they will be reviewing what they learned last year and adding onto that foundation in this second year. Some students will be more confident than others as they start the second year. Reassure all students that they probably remember a lot more than they think.

Tips for reviewing:

Para empezar: Use the *Para empezar* section as necessary based on the language skills of your class. Some students may need more review than others. The time you need to cover this section with your class will vary.

The activities in this section review the basic material covered in the first year: talking about yourself, friends, and activities. In answering the activity questions, students will also have a chance to get to know their peers for the new school year. Have students tell their names and their favorite activities. Model for students by first talking about yourself.

A ver si recuerdas: This section provides a comprehensive review of thematic vocabulary presented in *Realidades* 1. Vocabulary is presented in a graphic organizer and is linked thematically to the chapter that follows it. Also available on transparencies, the organizers provide a quick review of vocabulary and grammar that will be built upon in the related chapter.

You may want to encourage students to keep a vocabulary notebook or to dedicate a section of their class notebook solely to vocabulary. Give them tips for organizing their notebook, such as listing a noun with the definite article or highlighting the verb ending to differentiate between the *-ar, -er* or *-ir* groups.

Grammar Summary and Glossaries: Point out to students the Grammar Summary and Glossaries at the end of the book. Show them how the section is organized and give them ideas on how to use this section of the book. Show them how, if they are having problems with a vocabulary word or verb conjugation, they can always turn to this section for help.

¡Bienvenidos!

Welcome back to **Realidades 2!** You've already begun to understand, speak, read, and write in Spanish. You've also explored many different Spanish-speaking countries and their cultures. Because learning language is a process in which you build upon what you already know, in **Realidades 2** you'll be using and building on what you learned in your first year of study.

Tips for Reviewing

Here are some ways you can review.

• **Para empezar Realidades 2** begins with a review chapter that focuses on the basics from first year: talking about yourself, friends, and activities. It is likely that you'll remember this vocabulary and grammar. If not, use the textbook activities and the **Go Online** links at **PHSchool.com** for extra practice.

• **A ver si recuerdas** Prior to each theme and some chapters, you'll find this section, the title of which means "Let's see if you remember." It contains a quick summary of vocabulary and grammar from first-year Spanish that connects to the upcoming theme or chapter.

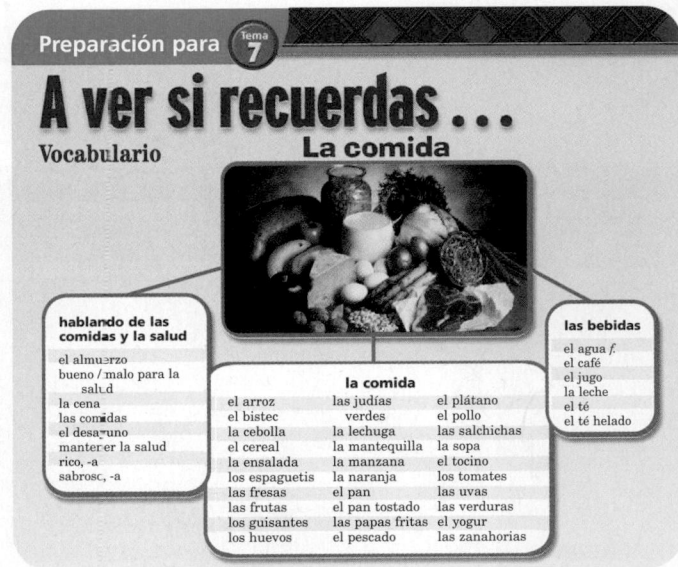

• **Grammar Summary and Glossaries** At the end of the book, you'll find grammar and vocabulary references from both first- and second-year Spanish.

• **Go Online** Be sure to use the online activities as a review. These will provide further practice in grammar, reading, and writing. You will also find some fun activities to help you practice even more!

xxx ¡Bienvenidos!

Advanced Learners

Ask students to mention some of the Spanish-speaking countries they encountered in their first year of study. Ask them if they remember any cultural information associated with each country. You can use a map of the region and ask students to identify each country and their corresponding capitals. This is a good opportunity to remind your students that culture is central to language learning. By speaking a second language, they will be able to speak with people from other cultures and understand how other countries are different from their own.

Study Tips

Go Online
PHSchool.com

For: More Tips for Studying Spanish
Web Code: jde-0003

Here are some tips to help you learn Spanish.

You don't need to understand everything. When reading a text or listening to someone speak Spanish, don't worry about knowing the meaning of every word. Focus on what you *do* know, and look for context clues to help you with the rest. You'll be surprised at how much you understand!

Look for opportunities to practice your Spanish. If you wait to speak until you think your Spanish is perfect, you will have missed many opportunities to use it. Take risks! You will learn from your mistakes. Concentrate on *what* you are saying, and *how* you say it will soon come naturally.

Look for Estrategia and ¿Recuerdas? boxes. Throughout **Realidades,** you will see boxes that provide a useful strategy or remind you of something you have already learned.

Go beyond the book. Look for ways to practice your Spanish outside of class. You know more language now that you are in Spanish 2, so practice with a friend, watch Spanish television programs, speak with Spanish speakers, or use the Internet. You can also visit the Web site for **Realidades** at **PHSchool.com.** Throughout the book you'll find **Go Online** icons with **Web Codes** that give you direct access to additional practice and information.

Estrategia

Taking notes
When you are retelling information for a report, it is helpful to jot down key details to include in the report. When you write the report, you build the narrative around retelling the facts.

¿Recuerdas?

You know how to use the imperfect tense to say what someone used to do.

- Siempre **nos reuníamos** para los días festivos.
- Mis primos y yo **jugábamos** mucho.

Enrich Your Teaching
Resources for All Teachers

Teacher to Teacher

Talk to your students about your personal experiences as a learner of a second language. Include an anecdote in which you (or a friend) communicated successfully without full comprehension. Remind your students that the ultimate goal of learning a language is to communicate with other people. If you have achieved communication, you have successfully used language!

Study Tips
Core Instruction

Suggestions:

You don't need to understand everything: Point out to students that the best way to learn a language is to be exposed to it as much as possible: by reading a passage, listening to a conversation, or watching a video. Play a news clip or short ad in Spanish. Point out to students that it may not be possible to understand every word, but if they listen for cognates and watch for visual cues, they will understand more than they can speak.

Look for opportunities to practice your Spanish: Practice does make perfect! Discuss with students the importance of practicing their Spanish. Encourage them to participate actively in class. Explain that learning a language is dependent on their communicating both with you and their peers. Highlight the "fun" in language learning: talking with their classmates as they practice Spanish.

Remind students not to be afraid of making mistakes, since these are a natural part of language learning. It is only by learning from their mistakes that they will become better language students.

Look for ... boxes: Have students flip through the book to find examples of *¿Recuerdas?* and *Estrategia* boxes and to become better acquainted with the organization of the material. Read a sample box and discuss how these notes will help them incorporate what they already know with the new material they will be learning.

Go beyond the book: Tell students where they might find other resources to use their Spanish. Contact your local cable company to look for the specific channels that offer Spanish programming. See if there are any local radio stations that play Spanish music. Search the Internet for Spanish-language newspapers, radio stations, or Web sites that are appropriate for students.

Para empezar

OVERVIEW

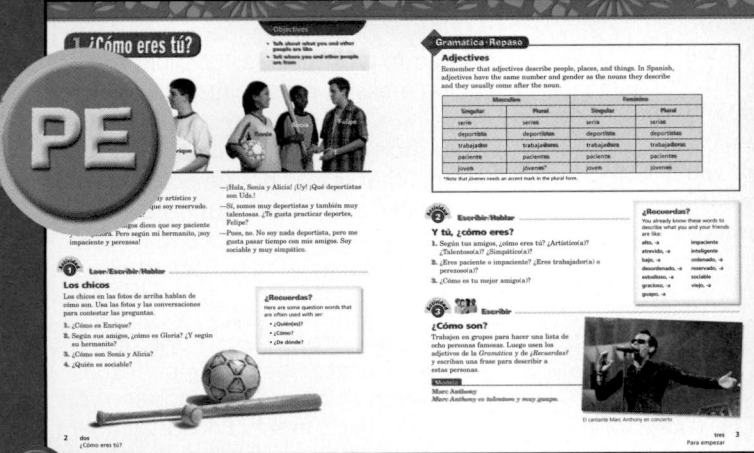

▶ 1 ¿Cómo eres tú?
- Describing people

Vocabulary: descriptive adjectives; adjectives of nationality

Grammar: adjective agreement; the present tense of the verb *ser;* adjective agreement

Cultural Perspectives: the first day of school; Hispanic population in the U.S.

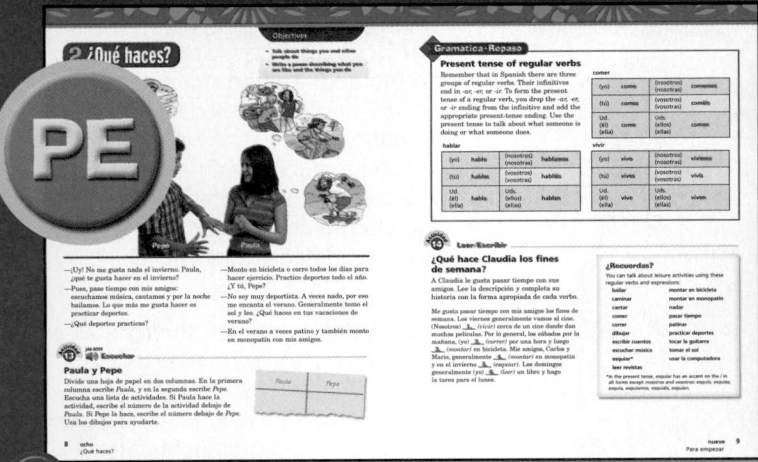

▶ 2 ¿Qué haces?
- Leisure activities

Vocabulary: common verbs; question words; seasons; adverbs of time

Grammar: present tense of regular verbs

Theme Project

¿Quién soy yo?

Overview: Students create a four-page "Who am I?" book by folding pieces of paper. They write two sentences per page to describe themselves and their activities without revealing their identity. On the last page, they use the verb **ser** to identify themselves. They can then share their "books" and try to guess the authors.

Materials: construction paper, markers, photos, glue or tape, scissors

Sequence: (suggestions for when to do each step are found throughout the chapter)

① ▶ STEP 1. Review instructions so students know what is expected of them. Hand out the *"Para empezar* Project Instructions and Rubric" from the *Teacher's Resource Book.*

STEP 2. Students submit a rough sketch of each page of their "book." Return the drafts with your suggestions. Ask students to partner and present their drafts to each other.

STEP 3. Students create layouts on different pieces of construction paper, leaving room for photos and descriptions. Encourage them to work in pencil first and to try different arrangements before gluing photos or decorations.

② ▶ STEP 4. Students submit a draft of each page of the book. Note your corrections and suggestions, then return drafts to students.

STEP 5. Students share their "books" with other members of the class. Students must try to guess the author of each book before they reach the last page.

Options:
1. Students create books about fictitious or famous people.
2. Students create books about cartoon characters or characters from television shows.

Assessment:
Here is a detailed rubric for assessing this project:

Para empezar Project: *¿Quién soy yo?*

RUBRIC	Score 1	Score 3	Score 5
Your evidence of planning	You provide no written draft or sketch.	Your draft was written and layout created, but not corrected.	You show evidence of corrected draft and layout.
Your use of illustrations	You include no photos or visuals.	You include very few photos or visuals.	You include several photos or visuals.
Your presentation	You include little of the required information.	You provide one sentence per page.	You provide two or more sentences per page.

Theme Support

Bulletin Boards

Theme: *¿Cómo eres tú? ¿Qué haces?*

Cover the bulletin board with questions such as: *¿Cómo eres tú? ¿Qué haces? ¿Cómo es tu amigo(a)? ¿Qué deportes juegas? ¿Cuál es tu nacionalidad? ¿De dónde es tu familia?* (Create questions in a large font, on the computer.) Using the same font, post lists of adjectives of description and personality, adjectives of nationality, and regular verbs. Have students bring in pictures (from magazines or other sources) of people participating in activities and neatly mount them on construction paper to post on the bulletin board.

Bibliography

Amparano, Julie, and Penny Dann. *America's Latinos: Their Rich History, Culture, and Traditions.* Child's World, 2003. Information on Latino culture in the United States.

Marvis, Barbara J. *Contemporary American Success Stories: Famous People of Hispanic Heritage.* Mitchell Lane Publishers, 1995. Information on several well-known Hispanics in the U.S.

Montes, Marisa. *A Crazy, Mixed-Up Spanglish Day.* Scholastic Paperbacks, 2003.

Rodriguez, Bruce Markusen. *¡Béisbol! Latino Baseball Pioneers and Legends.* Lee & Low Books, 2001.

Soto, Gary. *Baseball in April and Other Stories.* Harcourt, 2000.

Hands-on Culture

Craft: *Ojo de Dios*

Ojo de Dios is a yarn craft made in different forms by indigenous peoples of Mexico and South America.

Materials:
   2 craft sticks
   yarn in varying colors and lengths

Directions:

1. With one color of yarn, tie the two craft sticks together in an X pattern. Leave about one foot of yarn hanging from the center of the X.

2. Take the remaining yarn and wind it around one arm of the X, closest to the middle. Wind either clockwise or counter-clockwise as desired. Be sure to wind the yarn behind the stick and to loop it completely around the stick. Continue on to the next arm of the X.

3. Change the color of your yarn by tying a new color to the previous one. Continue the wrapping with the new color.

4. Continue changing colors and wrapping until you fill the entire X.

5. Hang your decoration!

Game

¡Batalla en el mar!

Play this game in *Para empezar* 2, after students have reviewed the present tense forms of regular verbs.

Players: Any number of students in pairs

Materials: blank paper, pen

Rules:

1. In pairs, students create grids that are seven squares wide and ten squares long. Along the top of the grid, students write the subject pronouns *yo, tú, él, ella, nosotros, ellos,* and *ellas.* Down the left side of the grid, the students agree on and write ten regular verbs from the chapter. Both students need a copy of the grid.

2. After the students have completed two identical copies of the grid, they sit back-to-back. Each student shades seven boxes in his or her grid. The shaded boxes represent boats.

3. The students try to find one another's boats by taking turns creating short phrases using the subject pronouns and the verbs on the grid. Students must conjugate correctly. If there is a boat at the point where the subject pronoun meets the verb on the grid, the owner of the boat will say *"¡Encontraste mi barco!".* The first student to find all of the partner's boats is the winner.

Variation: In order to get the point for finding each boat, the student must create a complete sentence by adding an ending to the short phrase.

Chapter Overview

¿Cómo eres tú?	¿Qué haces?	Presentación escrita

Learning Sequence

PRACTICE	PRACTICE	APPLICATION
• Practice vocabulary and grammar structures.	• Practice vocabulary and grammar structures.	• Apply vocabulary and grammar through culminating, theme-based writing activity.

Objectives

• Talk about what you and other people are like. • Tell where you and other people are from.	• Talk about things you and other people do. • Write a poem describing what you are like and the things you do.	• Write a poem.

Culture

• Nationalities	• Enrique Iglesias	

Vocabulary	Grammar	Strategies
• Personalities • Nationalities	• Adjectives • The verb *ser* • Question words • Present tense of regular verbs • Question words • Frequency vocabulary	• Organizing your thoughts

Chapter Features

Beyond the Classroom: States & Countries

Exploración del lenguaje

Nationalities—adjectives of nationality

Conexiones

Social Studies: The percentage of Spanish speakers in the population of the United States

Texas
España
Florida
República Dominicana

Student Resources

TECHNOLOGY

PRACTICE

ONLINE
Interactive Textbook
• Student Edition Online plus audio, video, and flashcards

Go Online Companion Web Site
• Tutorial activities • Internet links
• Self-tests • Downloadable MP3 audio files
• *PuzzleView*

CD-ROM
Interactive Textbook CD-ROM
Student Edition on CD-ROM plus audio, video, and flashcards

MindPoint™ CD-ROM
QUIZSHOW

PRINT MATERIAL

CORE INSTRUCTION
Practice Workbook, pp. 1–4
• Review • Vocabulary
• Grammar • Puzzle
• Organizer

Writing, Audio & Video Activities, pp. 1–5
• Video • Audio
• Writing

Grammar Study Guide 1–2 (or 3–4)

Differentiated Instruction

STUDENTS NEEDING EXTRA HELP
Guided Practice Activities, pp. 1–14
• Vocabulary Flash Cards and Vocabulary Check
• Grammar Activities
• Presentación escrita

HERITAGE LEARNERS
Realidades para hispanohablantes, pp. x–9

Teacher Resources

TECHNOLOGY

PLAN AND TEACH

Audio Program Fine Art Transparencies
Video Program Vocabulary and Grammar
  Transparencies
  Answers on Transparencies

TeacherEXPRESS CD-ROM
• Lesson Planner • Vocabulary Clip Art
• Web Resources • Teaching Resources
• Teacher Edition with Interactive Links

PresentationEXPRESS CD-ROM
• Vocabulary • Tranparencies and Maps
• Grammar • Photo Gallery
• Audio • Clip Art

PRINT MATERIAL

CORE INSTRUCTION
Teacher's Resource Book, pp. 1–18
• Input Script • Video Script
• Answer Keys • GramActiva Blackline Masters
• Vocabulary Clip Art • Chapter Resource Checklist
• School-to-Home Connection Letters
• Communicative Activities Blackline Masters

Differentiated Instruction

STUDENTS NEEDING EXTRA HELP
Guided Practice Activities
Teacher's Guide, pp. T1–T7

HERITAGE LEARNERS
Realidades para hispanohablantes
Teacher's Guide, pp. 1–5

ASSESS

PH SuccessNet ONLINE
• Access to grades and reports from Online Interactive Textbook

ExamView on Presentation Express
QuickTake Presenter
CD-ROM
• Vocabulary Quizzes • Chapter Test
• Grammar Quizzes

TeacherEXPRESS CD-ROM
• Assessment Program
• **ExamView** Test Banks A and B
  test generator

Go Online
PHSchool.com
For: Teacher Home Page
Web Code: jdk-1001

CORE ASSESSMENT
Assessment Program, pp. 7–10
• Pruebas
  Prueba P-1
  Prueba P-2
• Examen del capítulo • Speaking and Writing Rubrics
Teacher's Resource Book, p. 12
• Situation Cards

Differentiated Assessment

STUDENTS NEEDING EXTRA HELP
Alternate Assessment Program
• Examen del capítulo, pp. 1–4

HERITAGE LEARNERS
Assessment Program: Realidades para hispanohablantes Teacher's Guide,
pp. T89–T81
ExamView Heritage Learner
test generator Test Bank
ExamView Pre-AP* Test Bank
test generator

	Warm-up / Assess	Preview Present / Practice Communicate	Wrap-up / Homework Options
DAY 1	**Warm-up (5 min.)** • Chapter Opener • Fondo cultural	**¿Cómo eres tú? (40 min.)** • Presentation • Actividad 1 • Presentation: Adjectives • Actividades 2, 3, 4, 5, 6	**Wrap-up and Homework Options (5 min.)** • Practice Workbook P-1 • Go Online
DAY 2	**Warm-up (10 min.)** • Homework check	**¿Cómo eres tú? (35 min.)** • Presentation: The verb *ser* • Actividades 7, 8, 9 • Exploración del lenguaje • Actividades 11, 12	**Wrap-up and Homework Options (5 min.)** • Practice Workbook P-2, P-3 • Go Online
DAY 3	**Warm-up (10 min.)** • Actividad 10 • Homework check	**¿Qué haces? (35 min.)** • Presentation • Actividad 13 • Presentation: Present tense of regular verbs • Actividades 14, 15 • Presentación escrita: Steps 1, 5	**Wrap-up and Homework Options (5 min.)** • Presentación escrita: Step 2 • Go Online
DAY 4	**Warm-up (5 min.)** • Homework check	**¿Qué haces? (40 min.)** • Actividades 16, 17, 18 • Presentación escrita: Step 3	**Wrap-up and Homework Options (5 min.)** • Presentación escrita: Step 4 • Practice Workbook P-4 • Go Online
DAY 5	**Warm-up (5 min.)** • Homework check	**¿Qué haces? (40 min.)** • Actividades 19, 20, 21 • Share Presentación escrita with class	**Wrap-up and Homework Options (5 min.)** • Go Online • A ver sí recuerdas . . . :Tema 1A

Block Schedule (90 Minutes)

For electronic lesson plans:
Teacher Express

Warm-up / Assess	Preview Present / Practice Communicate		Wrap-up / Homework Options
DAY 1 **Warm-up (10 min.)** • Chapter Opener • Fondo cultural	**¿Cómo eres tú? (65 min.)** • Presentation • Actividad 1 • Presentation: Adjectives • Actividades 2, 3, 4, 5, 6 • Presentation: The verb *ser* • Actividades 7, 8, 9 • Exploración del lenguaje		**Wrap-up and Homework Options (5 min.)** • Presentation escrita: Step 2 • Practice Workbook P-1, P-2 • Go Online
DAY 2 **Warm-up (10 min.)** • Homework check **¿Cómo eres tú? (15 min.)** • Actividades 10, 11, 12	**¿Qué haces? (40 min.)** • Presentation • Actividad 13 • Presentation: Present tense of regular verbs • View: GramActiva video • Actividades 14, 15, 16, 17, 18		**Wrap-up and Homework Options (5 min.)** • Presentation escrita: Step 4 • Go Online • Practice Workbook P-3, P-4
DAY 3 **Warm-up (10 min.)** • Homework check	**¿Qué haces? (75 min.)** • Actividades 19, 20, 21 • Share Presentación escrita poem with class		**Wrap-up and Homework Options (5 min.)** • Go Online • A ver sí recuerdas . . . : Tema 1A

Standards for Para empezar

- To achieve the goals of the Standards, students will:

Communication
1.1 Interpersonal
- Talk about place of origin and nationality of people
- Talk about activities people do and how frequently they do them

1.2 Interpretive
- Read and interpret information about the first day of class in Spanish-speaking countries
- Listen to, read, and interpret information that describes people
- Read information about population in the United States
- Listen to, read, and interpret information about activities people do
- Read and interpret an article about singer Enrique Iglesias

1.3 Presentational
- Present information about describing people
- Summarize information about the immigrant population in the United States
- Present detailed information about activities people do and how frequently they are done
- Write a diamond-shaped poem describing themselves

Culture
2.1 Practices and Perspectives
- Describe the first day of class in Spanish-speaking countries

2.2 Products and Perspectives
- Read and write about Enrique Iglesias and his songs

Connections
3.1 Cross-curricular
- Read and write about the immigrant population in the United States
- Make a written presentation

Comparisons
4.1 Language
- Review adjectives
- Use adjectives of nationality in relation to country of origin

Fondo cultural

El primer día de clases En los países hispanohablantes, los estudiantes regresan a las clases en diferentes meses. Por ejemplo, en Uruguay y Chile los estudiantes regresan en marzo porque las vacaciones de verano son de noviembre a febrero. En Colombia, hay tres calendarios para las escuelas. Unas escuelas van de enero a noviembre, el horario tradicional, y otras van de agosto a junio. El tercer calendario va de septiembre a junio, que es igual a los calendarios de los Estados Unidos y de México.

- ¿En qué mes regresas a la escuela después de las vacaciones de verano?

El primer día de clases en el Perú

Differentiated Instruction
Solutions for All Learners

STUDENTS NEEDING EXTRA HELP

Guided Practice Activities
- Vocabulary Check, Flash Cards
- Grammar
- Reading and Writing Support

HERITAGE LEARNERS

Realidades para hispanohablantes
- Chapter Opener, pp. x–1
- ¿Cómo eres tú?, pp. 2–5
- ¿Qué haces?, pp. 6–8
- Presentación escrita, p. 9

Para empezar

Objectives

1 ¿Cómo eres tú?

- Talk about what you and other people are like
- Tell where you and other people are from

2 ¿Qué haces?

- Talk about things you and other people do
- Talk about how often you do certain things

Más práctica

- *Real.* para hispanohablantes, p. x

uno **1**
Para empezar

Chapter Opener

Core Instruction

The *Para empezar* section is designed to give a quick reentry into the new school year by allowing students to talk about themselves and the things they enjoy doing. It reviews fundamental structures such as **ser,** adjectives, and regular present-tense verbs, and also covers adjectives of nationality. Review of additional topics and structures will be woven throughout the book in the *A ver si recuerdas . . .* sections and in the regular chapters. Throughout the review, you should feel free to incorporate any favorite activities or materials from *Realidades 1* that deal with the same topics or structures.

Suggestions: Introduce yourself and give a few adjectives that describe you. Tell where you are from and some activities that you like to do. Then have students turn to a partner to find out the same information: the name of the student, what the student is like, where the student is from, some favorite activities he or she likes to do, and how often he or she does those activities. You can then summarize the objectives of the unit by saying that students will review how to say some of these things in Spanish. Point out that students may have forgotten things over the summer, but that with practice, the language they learned last year will come back to them quickly.

 **Fondo cultural**  *Standards:* 1.2, 2.1

Suggestions: Ask students why they think the school calendar is different depending on the country. You might suggest that they look at a globe when they consider their answers. Remind students that in the Southern Hemisphere the seasons are the opposite of those in the Northern Hemisphere. When it is summer in Chile (December and January), it is winter in the United States. In some cases, school schedules may be different to accommodate overcrowding in schools or to be sure that not everyone in the country is taking vacations at the same time, or to match the agricultural cycles in a given region.

Teacher Technology

TeacherEXPRESS
Plan · Teach · Assess

PLAN
Lesson Planner

TEACH
Teaching Resources
Interactive
Teacher's Edition
Vocabulary Clip Art

ASSESS
Chapter Quizzes
and Tests

Go Online
PHSchool.com
For: Teacher Home Page
Web Code: jdk-1001

PresentationEXPRESS
Dynamic Presentations for Teachers

TEACH
Vocabulary & Grammar Powerpoints
GramActiva Video
Audio & Clip Art Activities
Transparencies and Maps
Activity Answers
Photo Gallery

ASSESS
ExamView
QuickTake Presenter

1

¿Comó eres tú?

Core Instruction

Resources: Teacher's Resource Book: Input Script, p. 6, Audio Script, p. 7; Audio Program: Track 1

Focus: Reviewing personal characteristics and descriptions

Suggestions: Use the *Audio CD* or have students perform the dialogues. Use gesture and over-acting to convey meaning. Use transparencies from *Realidades* 1 or the lists in the *Gramática • Repaso* and *¿Recuerdas?* on p. 3 to review the adjectives that students have learned. Vary the dialogues with other adjectives.

Standards: 1.2

Resources: Answers on Transparencies

Focus: Reading comprehension

Suggestions: Select four pairs of students to go to the board. Read the questions aloud, pausing after each to give the students time to answer by drawing pictures of the various characters. Call on students to answer the question orally and present their corresponding drawings. Have the class determine if the pictures on the board are accurate according to the dialogues.

Answers:

1. Enrique es muy artístico y estudioso. También es reservado.
2. Según sus amigos, Gloria es paciente y trabajadora. Según su hermanito, es impaciente y perezosa.
3. Sonia y Alicia son deportistas y también muy talentosas.
4. Felipe es muy sociable.

Common Errors: Students may say that Gloria is *pacienta,* rather than *paciente.* Remind students that not all feminine adjectives end in *-a.*

Block Schedule

Cut out photos of people from magazines. Number them and post them around the room. Type up a handout that has a description to match each photo. Have students walk around the room and match the descriptions to the photos. Ask them to write an additional sentence for each photo's description.

---

1 ¿Cómo eres tú?

jdd-0099

Objectives

- Talk about what you and other people are like
- Tell where you and other people are from

—Oye, Enrique, ¿eres artístico?

—Sí, según mis amigos soy muy artístico y estudioso. También dicen que soy reservado. Y Gloria, ¿cómo eres tú?

—Bueno . . . mis amigos dicen que soy paciente y trabajadora. Pero según mi hermanito, ¡soy impaciente y perezosa!

—¡Hola, Sonia y Alicia! ¡Uy! ¡Qué deportistas son Uds.!

—Sí, somos muy deportistas y también muy talentosas. ¿Te gusta practicar deportes, Felipe?

—Pues, no. No soy nada deportista, pero me gusta pasar tiempo con mis amigos. Soy sociable y muy simpático.

 Leer/Escribir/Hablar

Los chicos

Los chicos en las fotos de arriba hablan de cómo son. Usa las fotos y las conversaciones para contestar las preguntas.

1. ¿Cómo es Enrique?
2. Según sus amigos, ¿cómo es Gloria? ¿Y según su hermanito?
3. ¿Cómo son Sonia y Alicia?
4. ¿Quién es sociable?

¿Recuerdas?

Here are some question words that are often used with *ser:*

- ¿Quién(es)?
- ¿Cómo?
- ¿De dónde?

2 dos
¿Cómo eres tú?

Differentiated Instruction
Solutions for All Learners

Advanced Learners

Have students go on a photo safari at your school, taking pictures of people demonstrating each trait reviewed here. They can print the pictures out and mount them on poster board, labeling each with a sentence identifying the trait, or use presentation software to create a slide show with graphics and narration.

Students with Learning Difficulties

To help students grasp the gender and number distinctions underlying adjective agreement, make an overhead of the *Gramática* chart and add photos or drawings of males and females. For example, place one serious boy's face beside *serio* and two serious boys' faces beside *serios.* Give this to students as a handout.

Gramática·Repaso

Adjectives

Remember that adjectives describe people, places, and things. In Spanish, adjectives have the same number and gender as the nouns they describe and they usually come after the noun.

Masculine		Feminine	
Singular	**Plural**	**Singular**	**Plural**
serio	serios	seria	serias
deportista	deportistas	deportista	deportistas
trabajador	trabajadores	trabajadora	trabajadoras
paciente	pacientes	paciente	pacientes
joven	jóvenes*	joven	jóvenes

*Note that *jóvenes* needs an accent mark in the plural form.

Escribir/Hablar

Y tú, ¿cómo eres?

1. Según tus amigos, ¿cómo eres tú? ¿Artístico(a)? ¿Talentoso(a)? ¿Simpático(a)?
2. ¿Eres paciente o impaciente? ¿Eres trabajador(a) o perezoso(a)?
3. ¿Cómo es tu mejor amigo(a)?

Escribir

¿Cómo son?

Trabajen en grupos para hacer una lista de ocho personas famosas. Luego usen los adjetivos de la *Gramática* y de *¿Recuerdas?* y escriban una frase para describir a estas personas.

Modelo

Marc Anthony
Marc Anthony es talentoso y muy guapo.

¿Recuerdas?

You already know these words to describe what you and your friends are like:

alto, -a	impaciente
atrevido, -a	inteligente
bajo, -a	ordenado, -a
desordenado, -a	reservado, -a
estudioso, -a	sociable
gracioso, -a	viejo, -a
guapo, -a	

El cantante Marc Anthony en concierto

tres 3
Para empezar

Enrich Your Teaching
Resources for All Teachers

Teacher-to-Teacher

Have teams of students stand at a distance from you. Call out an adjective. Each team will send a student or students whom the adjective could describe. For example, for **inteligente,** they could send a boy or a girl, but for **serio,** they would have to send a boy. The first team to reach you with the correct answer wins a point.

Culture Note

Actors and singers from Spanish-speaking countries are crossing over to the American market and gaining popularity with English-speaking audiences. Their success is due in part to an increase in the Spanish-speaking population of the United States, which is expected to reach 70 million by 2020.

Practice and Communicate

PE

Gramática·Repaso

Presentation EXPRESS
GRAMMAR

Core Instruction

 Standards: 4.1

Resources: Voc. and Gram. Transparency 21
Suggestions: Have two male students and two female students stand in front of the class. Make statements using different adjective forms (*Es muy serio. Son trabajadores.*). Have the rest of the class tell which students you could be talking about. Remind them that if the group is mixed you use the masculine plural form of the adjective.

  Standards: 1.3

Focus: Describing oneself and others
Suggestions: Direct attention to the *¿Recuerdas?* for more adjectives and review the meanings. Check comprehension by calling out adjectives and having students act them out.
Answers will vary.
Common Errors: Remind students to check the endings of the adjectives to be sure they agree with their subjects.
Extension: Have students write a fourth question to ask a classmate, such as: *¿Cómo es tu hermano?*

  Standards: 1.3

Pre-AP*

Focus: Using adjectives to describe people
Suggestions: Write on the board roles for carrying out group assignments, for example, expediter / leader, recorder, timekeeper, and spokesperson. Have students decide which roles the people in their group will perform as they work together on the activity. Make it clear to students if they should write the descriptive sentences as a group, or if you would like each student to write eight sentences about the famous people their group listed.
Answers will vary.

3

Actividad 4

Standards: 1.2

Presentation EXPRESS AUDIO

Resources: Teacher's Resource Book: Audio Script, p. 7; Audio Program: Track 2; Answers on Transparencies

Focus: Listening comprehension

Suggestions: Can students guess the meaning of ***edades?*** Ask students questions about the reading to give them practice locating the information before you play the *Audio CD.*

Script and Answers:

1. Alicia y Carmen tienen 18 años. *(C)*
2. Alicia es de Puerto Rico, y Carmen es de Cuba. *(F)*
3. Alicia es poeta. *(C)*
4. Carmen es muy sociable. *(C)*
5. A Carmen no le gusta escuchar los poemas de Alicia. *(F)*
6. Los amigos de las jóvenes son negativos y serios. *(F)*

Actividad 5

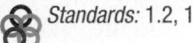

Standards: 1.3

Focus: Writing descriptions of oneself and others

Suggestions: For the *Cómo son* section, have students create two cluster diagrams to organize their ideas, one about themselves and one about their friend.

Answers will vary.

Actividad 6

Standards: 1.2, 1.3

Focus: Using a visual prompt for writing

Suggestions: Check comprehension by asking why Carlos's friend has a surprised expression in the last frame of the comic strip *(he didn't know that Carlos and the girls were cousins).* Then brainstorm as a class what the girls might be saying. Remind students that the girls are Carlos's cousins, so their conversation will be different from the one in the comic strip.

Answers will vary.

Additional Resources

- WAV Wbk.: Audio Act. 1, p. 1
- Teacher's Resource Book: Audio Script, p. 7, Communicative Activity BLM, p. 9
- Audio Program: Track 3

Actividad 4 jdd-0099 **Leer/Escuchar**

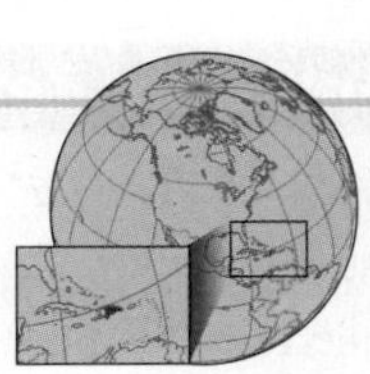

Dos jóvenes

Lee esta descripción de dos chicas latinoamericanas. Luego escribe los números del 1 al 6 en una hoja de papel. Escucha las frases y escribe *C* si la información es cierta y *F* si es falsa.

Nombres: Alicia Menéndez García y Carmen Díaz Ortiz

Edades: Tienen 18 años.

Residencia: Viven en Santiago de los Caballeros, República Dominicana, con sus familias.

Cómo son: Alicia es una poeta joven. Lee sus poemas en público. Ella es muy inteligente y artística. Carmen no es artística pero le gusta escuchar los poemas de Alicia. Carmen es muy sociable y deportista. Las dos jóvenes son amigas inseparables.

Amigos: "Nuestros amigos son graciosos y simpáticos," dicen Alicia y Carmen. "No tenemos tiempo para las personas negativas."

Actividad 5 **Escribir**

¿Y cómo son tú y tus amigos?

Ahora escribe una descripción de tu mejor amigo(a) y de ti. Usa la información de la descripción en la Actividad 4: nombres, edades, residencia y cómo son.

Actividad 6 **Leer/Escribir/Hablar**

Amigos y primos

Lee la conversación entre los dos chicos del dibujo. Imagina lo que dicen las chicas sobre los chicos. Escribe la conversación de las chicas usando la conversación de los chicos como modelo. Presenta la conversación a la clase.

Esas chicas son muy bonitas. ¿Sabes cómo se llaman, Carlos?
Sí, hombre. Se llaman Dolores y Marisa. Son de Buenos Aires.
¿Cómo son?
Las dos son simpáticas. Dolores es seria y reservada. Le gusta leer. Marisa es graciosa y muy sociable. Le gusta pasar tiempo con sus amigos.
¿Uds. son muy buenos amigos?
Pues, sí, pero también somos primos.

Más práctica

- Practice Workbook, p. 1: P-1
- WAV Wbk.: Writing, p. 3
- Guided Practice, pp. 1–6
- *Real.* para hispanohablantes, pp. 2–3

Go Online PHSchool.com
For: Adjectives
Web Code: jdd-0001

Differentiated Instruction

Solutions for All Learners

Multiple Intelligences

Visual/Spatial: Have students treat *Actividad* 5 as if it were a magazine article. They should include a photo, write a title for the interview, and type the interview to look like it came from a magazine. They should bo dface the headings ***nombres, edades,*** etc., and of course, include a byline.

Students with Special Needs

Using the script for *Actividad* 4, create a chart for hearing impaired students. In the first column, list the dictated sentences describing Alicia and Carmen. In the second column, have students write ***C*** for ***cierta*** if the information is true. If it is false, have them rewrite the sentence with correct information.

Gramática · Repaso

The verb *ser*

You have learned to use the verb *ser* with adjectives to tell what someone is like.

Esas chicas **son bonitas.**

You have also learned to use *ser* with *de* to tell where someone is from.

Son de Buenos Aires.

Remember that *ser* is irregular. Here are its present-tense forms:

(yo)	soy	(nosotros) (nosotras)	somos
(tú)	eres	(vosotros) (vosotras)	sois
Ud. (él) (ella)	es	Uds. (ellos) (ellas)	son

 Actividad 7 — Leer/Escribir

Así son los compañeros de Alejandro

Escribe la forma correcta del verbo *ser* para completar lo que Alejandro escribe sobre los estudiantes en su clase de español.

Así son los estudiantes en mi clase de español. Ana María __1.__ estudiosa y le gusta mucho leer. Manuel y Marianela practican muchos deportes y __2.__ deportistas. A José Luis le gusta nadar en la piscina grande en el gimnasio; él __3.__ atrevido. A mi compañero Juanito y a mí nos gusta ir a la escuela porque nosotros __4.__ trabajadores. Pero a Mercedes y a Eduardo no les gusta ir a la escuela porque __5.__ perezosos. Carolina dibuja bien y __6.__ muy artística. Manolito y Victoria tocan la guitarra y __7.__ muy talentosos. A mi compañero Ignacio y a mí nos gusta mucho hablar por teléfono y pasar tiempo con amigos porque __8.__ sociables. Pero a mí no me gusta ir al gimnasio porque no __9.__ deportista. Y tú, ¿cómo __10.__?

Más práctica

- Practice Workbook, p. 2: P-2
- WAV Wbk., Writing, p. 4
- Guided Practice: Grammar Act. p. 7
- *Real.* para hispanohablantes, p. 4

 Go Online PHSchool.com
For: Ser
Web Code: jdd-0002

 Actividad 8 — Escribir

¿Y cómo son tus compañeros?

¿Cómo son los estudiantes en tu clase de español? Usa la descripción de Alejandro como modelo y escribe cinco o seis frases para describir a tus compañeros.

Actividad 9 — Escribir/Hablar

Juego

Tu profesor(a) te va a dar una tarjeta con el nombre de otro(a) estudiante de la clase. Escribe una descripción de esta persona en la tarjeta. Luego vas a leer la descripción y tus compañeros tienen que adivinar (*guess*) quién es.

Modelo
Es seria y trabajadora, pero muy simpática. Le gusta la música. Ella e Isabel son buenas amigas. ¿Quién es?

cinco 5
Para empezar

 PE

Practice and Communicate

Gramática · Repaso — GRAMMAR

Core Instruction

Resources: Voc. and Gram. Transparency 22
Suggestions: Bring a light bulb to class. Hold the light bulb over your head and say *¡Soy muy inteligente! ¡Tengo muchas buenas ideas!* Have a student stand under the lightbulb with you and say *¡Somos inteligentes!* Hold the light bulb over other students' heads to present the other forms of *ser.* You might also want to show the *GramActiva* Video on *ser* from *Realidades* 1, *Capítulo* 3B as a review. *Estar* will be reviewed in *Capítulo* 2A.

Standards: 1.2 — ANSWERS

Resources: Answers on Transparencies
Focus: Using the present-tense forms of *ser* to complete a paragraph
Suggestions: Point out to students that in this activity the adjectives will help them decide which form of *ser* to use.

Answers:
1. es 3. es 5. son 7. son 9. soy
2. son 4. somos 6. es 8. somos 10. eres

Standards: 1.3

Focus: Using *ser* to describe people
Suggestions: Write *Así son los estudiantes en mi clase de español* on the board. Brainstorm the subjects and descriptions students could use.
Answers will vary.

Standards: 1.3 — Pre-AP*

Focus: Describing people
Suggestions: Prepare the cards in advance. Read each student's description before it is read aloud to make sure there are no inappropriate descriptions.
Answers will vary.

Enrich Your Teaching
Resources for All Teachers

Teacher-to-Teacher
Have students bring in props or costumes identified with the various adjectives. Have an "adjective parade" in which students walk in front of the class while the others call out statements: *Es deportista. Es inteligente.* Students can then group themselves with others who have chosen the same adjective and repeat the parade.

Culture Note
Santiago de los Caballeros, mentioned in *Actividad* 4, is the second largest city in the Dominican Republic. Founded in the 1490s by members of Columbus' second expedition to the Americas, it is often referred to simply as "Santiago." The city is known for its beauty and for its vital manufacturing industry.

5

Exploración del lenguaje

Core Instruction

Resources: Voc. and Gram. Transparency 23

Focus: Reviewing adjectives of nationality

Suggestions: Have students choose 16 of the countries listed in *Exploración del lenguaje* and write them on a sheet of paper in a four-by-four grid. Play "Bingo" by calling out the names of countries randomly. Students will place a check by the countries they hear. Students who check off four in a row and call out "Bingo!" will win that round only if they correctly say the male and female nationalities of all the countries in that row.

Bellringer Review

Put *América del Sur, América Central, América del Norte, El Caribe* y *Europa* on the board. Ask students to list as many Spanish-speaking countries as they can under each location.

Standards: 1.2, 1.3, 3.1

Focus: Summarizing information from a chart; connection to social studies

Suggestions: Tell students that when they write a summary of a paragraph they are expected to describe its main ideas. The same is true when summarizing information in a chart or graph. Help students identify the main ideas of the chart before they begin to write. Model commentary for them that they can then use in creating their summaries.

Answers will vary.

Extension: Have pairs of students work together to create a list of cognates in the introductory paragraph and the chart.

Block Schedule

Distribute a photocopied map of Central and South America that does not have the countries or cities labeled on it. You could also use an overhead of the same map. As a class, fill in the country names of all the Spanish-speaking countries, as well as their capitals and important cities. Ask students to pick a country and tell the class that they are from a city in that country. Tell them to mention their new nationality.

Exploración del lenguaje

Nationalities

You have already learned many adjectives of nationality. The Spanish words for these nationalities are based on the country name. Review the chart to see how each nationality relates to the country of origin. Remember that since the nationalities are adjectives, they agree in gender and number with the nouns they describe. They are usually used with the verb *ser*.

País	Nacionalidad	País	Nacionalidad	País	Nacionalidad
Argentina	argentino, -a	El Salvador	salvadoreño, -a	Paraguay	paraguayo, -a
Bolivia	boliviano, -a	España	español, española	Perú	peruano, -a
Chile	chileno, -a	Guatemala	guatemalteco, -a	Puerto Rico	puertorriqueño, -a
Colombia	colombiano, -a	Honduras	hondureño, -a	República Dominicana	dominicano, -a
Costa Rica	costarricense	México	mexicano, -a		
Cuba	cubano, -a	Nicaragua	nicaragüense	Uruguay	uruguayo, -a
Ecuador	ecuatoriano, -a	Panamá	panameño, -a	Venezuela	venezolano, -a

10 Leer/Escribir

Una población diversa

Los Estados Unidos es un país de inmigrantes, donde hay gente de todas partes del mundo. Un grupo importante de los inmigrantes está formado por hispanohablantes. La población hispana representa más de 35 millones de personas, o el 13 por ciento *(percent)* de la población total. Es muy diversa porque hay hispanohablantes de muchos países hispanos. Lee la gráfica sobre esta población y escribe un resumen.

Modelo
El grupo más grande de hispanohablantes en los Estados Unidos es el grupo de México. Los mexicanos son el 58.5 por ciento...

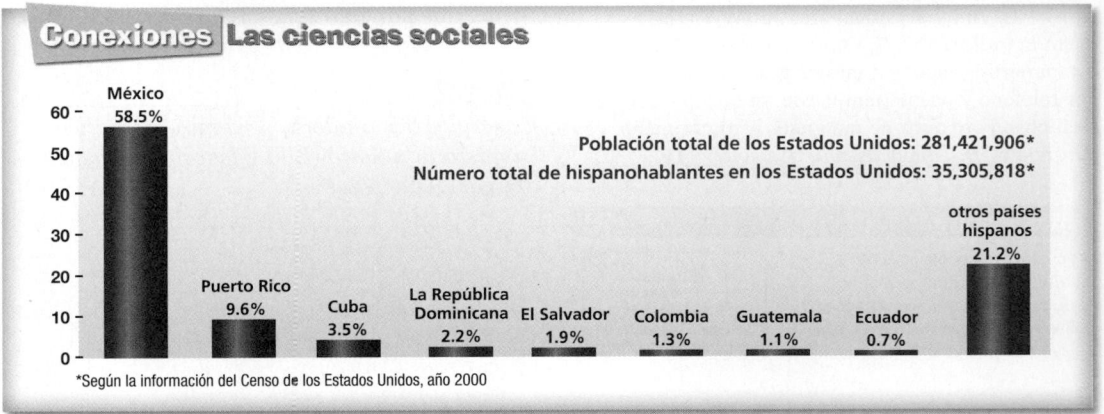

Conexiones Las ciencias sociales

México 58.5%

Población total de los Estados Unidos: 281,421,906*
Número total de hispanohablantes en los Estados Unidos: 35,305,818*

otros países hispanos 21.2%

Puerto Rico 9.6%
Cuba 3.5%
La República Dominicana 2.2%
El Salvador 1.9%
Colombia 1.3%
Guatemala 1.1%
Ecuador 0.7%

*Según la información del Censo de los Estados Unidos, año 2000

6 seis
¿Cómo eres tú?

Differentiated Instruction
Solutions for All Learners

Multiple Intelligences

Verbal/Linguistic: Photocopy the nationalities chart and distribute to students. Have students analyze the chart to form general rules about how nationality adjectives are formed. Have them color-code the different forms and then come up with general rules and exceptions.

Students with Learning Difficulties

For *Actividad* 10, make a transparency of the *Conexiones*. Explain that a bar graph presents information in a visual format, making comparisons more apparent. Ask questions to highlight facts, for example: Among the countries listed, which is least represented in the United States?

Actividad 11 — Hablar

¿De dónde son?

Estos estudiantes le escriben a tu clase por correo electrónico. Trabaja con otro(a) estudiante y pregúntale de dónde es cada estudiante y de qué nacionalidad. Después de hablar de estos chicos, pregunta a tu compañero(a) de dónde es.

Modelo
A —¿De dónde es *Teresa?*
B —Es de *Asunción. Es paraguaya.*

Para decir más . . .
estadounidense U.S. citizen
norteamericano, -a North American (including Canada, Mexico, and the United States)
canadiense Canadian

Estados Unidos — Juanita, La Habana
México — José, Tegucigalpa — Cuba
Ricardo, Santo Domingo
República Dominicana — Puerto Rico
Guatemala — Honduras
El Salvador — Nicaragua
Costa Rica
Panamá — Venezuela — Linda, Caracas
Colombia
Ecuador — Sergio, Madrid
Mercedes, La Ciudad de Panamá
Perú — España
Bolivia
Paraguay — Teresa, Asunción
Chile
Esteban, Lima — Uruguay
Argentina — Benjamín, Montevideo
María José, Madrid

Actividad 12 — Hablar

¿Y de dónde eres tú?

Imagina que eres de uno de los países hispanohablantes que está en el mapa de la Actividad 11. Con otro(a) estudiante, pregunta y contesta según el modelo.

Modelo
A —¿De dónde eres tú?
B —Soy de San Juan.
A —Ah, eres puertorriqueño(a).

Más práctica
- Practice Workbook, p. 3: P-3
- *Real.* para hispanohablantes, pp. 1, 5

Go Online
PHSchool.com
For: Nationalities
Web Code: jdd-0003

siete **7**
Para empezar

Actividad 11  *Standards:* 1.1

Resources: Voc. and Gram. Transparencies: Maps 12–18, 20; Answers on Transparencies

Focus: Asking and telling where someone is from

Suggestions: Call out the names of the cities the students in the activity are from and have students guess the countries without looking at their books. Point out that Mexicans are also North Americans, so the adjective *estadounidense* is used to specify an "American" from the United States.

Answers:
Juanita es de La Habana. Es cubana. José es de Tegucigalpa. Es hondureño. Ricardo es de Santo Domingo. Es dominicano. Linda es de Caracas. Es venezolana. Teresa es de Asunción. Es paraguaya. Benjamín es de Montevideo. Es uruguayo. Esteban es de Lima. Es peruano. Mercedes es de la Ciudad de Panamá. Es panameña. Sergio es de Madrid. Es español. María José es de Madrid. Es española.

Actividad 12   *Standards:* 1.1

Focus: Asking and telling where someone is from

Suggestions: Have students imagine that they are having the conversation in the activity with a stranger on an airplane. Place three chairs in a row at the front of the room and have volunteers perform their conversations for the class. You will be the flight attendant.

Answers will vary.

Common Errors: Students may say ¿Dónde eres tú? Remind them that they must use **de dónde** to ask where someone is from.

Additional Resources
- WAV Wbk.: Audio Act. 2, p. 1
- Teacher's Resource Book: Audio Script, p. 7
- Audio Program: Track 4

✓ Assessment
- **ExamView** Quiz on PresEXPRESS
  QuickTake Presenter
- Prueba P-1, pp. 7–8

Enrich Your Teaching
Resources for All Teachers

Teacher-to-Teacher
Have a group of students draw the flag of each Spanish-speaking country on white index cards (see *El mundo hispano* on pp. xvi–xxvi). On the back, they will write each country's name and nationality upside down. Tape the flags on the bulletin board. Students can guess the countries and nationalities, then flip up the flag to see if they are correct.

🌐 Culture Note
There are roughly 420 million Spanish speakers worldwide: United States—41 million; Spain—40 million; Central America—38 million; Mexico—103 million; South America—178 million; Caribbean nations—20 million.

¿Qué haces?

Core Instruction

Resources: Teacher's Resource Book: Audio Script, p. 7; Audio Program: Track 5

Suggestions: Use the transparency to aid understanding as students listen to the dialogue. Then draw a large Venn diagram on the board. Label the left side **invierno,** the right side **verano,** and the section where the circles overlap, **las dos.** Mime activities that can be done in winter, in summer, or in both seasons and have students guess the activity and the season. Have volunteers write the activities on the diagram. Have pairs of students reread the dialogue, replacing the activities shown with other activities from the Venn diagram.

Bellringer Review

Place a four column chart on the board. Write the four seasons at the top of each column. Students suggest activities for each season.

Actividad 13  *Standards:* 1.2   **Presentation EXPRESS AUDIO**

Resources: Teacher's Resource Book: Audio Script, p. 8; Audio Program: Track 6; Answers on Transparencies

Focus: Reading and listening comprehension

Suggestions: Ask students how they would describe Sonia **(deportista, sociable, talentosa)** and Pepe **(no deportista, un poco perezoso, reservado).** Tell students that keeping Sonia and Pepe's personality traits in mind will help them identify the activities that each likes.

 Script and Answers:

1. bailar *(Paula)*
2. leer *(Pepe)*
3. escuchar música *(Paula)*
4. montar en bicicleta *(Paula)*
5. tocar la guitarra *(Paula)*
6. nadar *(Pepe)*
7. correr *(Paula)*
8. escribir canciones *(Pepe)*

Extension: Play the *Audio CD* again and have students act out the activities.

Block Schedule

Assign each student a regular verb. Have one student start a story by forming a sentence using their verb. Have that student pick the next student who will continue the story by creating a sentence with his or her verb. Continue until the story ends or every student has had a turn.

Objectives
• Talk about things you and other people do
• Write a poem describing what you are like and the things you do

2 ¿Qué haces?

jcd-0099

—¡Uy! No me gusta nada el invierno. Paula, ¿qué te gusta hacer en el invierno?

—Pues, paso tiempo con mis amigos: escuchamos música, tocamos la guitarra y por la noche bailamos. Lo que más me gusta hacer es practicar deportes.

—¿Qué deportes practicas?

—Monto en bicicleta o corro todos los días para hacer ejercicio. Practico deportes todo el año. ¿Y tú, Pepe?

—No soy muy deportista. A veces nado, por eso me encanta el verano. Generalmente tomo el sol y leo. También escribo canciones. ¿Qué haces en tus vacaciones de verano?

—En el verano a veces patino y también monto en monopatín con mis amigos.

Actividad 13   jdd-0099  **Escuchar**

Paula y Pepe

Divide una hoja de papel en dos columnas. En la primera columna escribe *Paula,* y en la segunda escribe *Pepe.* Escucha una lista de actividades. Si Paula hace la actividad, escribe el número de la actividad debajo de *Paula.* Si Pepe la hace, escribe el número debajo de *Pepe.* Usa los dibujos para ayudarte.

Paula	Pepe

8 ocho
¿Qué haces?

 Differentiated Instruction
Solutions for All Learners

Advanced Learners/Pre-AP*

Have students prepare a four-seasons guide to recreational activities in your area for Spanish-speaking tourists. They can group activities according to type, and then tell where each can be performed.

Students with Learning Difficulties

Give students three sets of index cards: one set with subjects and subject pronouns, one with the regular stems, and a third with the regular verb endings. Have them draw random cards from the first two sets, and then choose the correct ending from the third set.

Present tense of regular verbs

Remember that in Spanish there are three groups of regular verbs. Their infinitives end in *-ar, -er,* or *-ir*. To form the present tense of a regular verb, you drop the *-ar, -er,* or *-ir* ending from the infinitive and add the appropriate present-tense ending. Use the present tense to talk about what someone is doing or what someone does.

hablar

(yo)	hablo	(nosotros) (nosotras)	hablamos
(tú)	hablas	(vosotros) (vosotras)	habláis
Ud. (él) (ella)	habla	Uds. (ellos) (ellas)	hablan

comer

(yo)	como	(nosotros) (nosotras)	comemos
(tú)	comes	(vosotros) (vosotras)	coméis
Ud. (él) (ella)	come	Uds. (ellos) (ellas)	comen

vivir

(yo)	vivo	(nosotros) (nosotras)	vivimos
(tú)	vives	(vosotros) (vosotras)	vivís
Ud. (él) (ella)	vive	Uds. (ellos) (ellas)	viven

Actividad 14 Leer/Escribir

¿Qué hace Claudia los fines de semana?

A Claudia le gusta pasar tiempo con sus amigos. Lee la descripción y completa su historia con la forma apropiada de cada verbo.

Me gusta pasar tiempo con mis amigos los fines de semana. Los viernes generalmente vamos al cine. (Nosotros) __1.__ *(vivir)* cerca de un cine donde dan muchas películas. Por lo general, los sábados por la mañana, (yo) __2.__ *(correr)* por una hora y luego __3.__ *(montar)* en bicicleta. Mis amigos, Carlos y Mario, generalmente __4.__ *(montar)* en monopatín y en el invierno __5.__ *(esquiar)*. Los domingos generalmente (yo) __6.__ *(leer)* un libro y hago la tarea para el lunes.

¿Recuerdas?

You can talk about leisure activities using these regular verbs and expressions:

bailar	montar en bicicleta
caminar	montar en monopatín
cantar	nadar
comer	pasar tiempo
correr	patinar
dibujar	practicar deportes
escribir cuentos	tocar la guitarra
escuchar música	tomar el sol
esquiar*	usar la computadora
leer revistas	

*In the present tense, *esquiar* has an accent on the *i* in all forms except *nosotros* and *vosotros*: *esquío, esquías, esquía, esquiamos, esquiáis, esquían.*

nueve 9
Para empezar

Teacher-to-Teacher

Divide the class into groups. Have each group pick an *-ar, -er,* or *-ir* verb and create a *Sesame Street*–style video to teach the verb and its endings to elementary school students. They could also create a slide show using presentation software.

Teacher-to-Teacher

Have students take pictures of one another performing the various activities listed here, either singly or in groups. Have them label the pictures using complete sentences and create an album for the class.

Practice and Communicate

Core Instruction

Resources: Voc. and Gram. Transparency 24

Suggestions: Make two sets of 13 ping-pong balls with the regular *-ar, -er,* and *-ir* verb endings (*-o, -as, -a, -amos, -áis, -an, -es, -e, -emos, -éis, -en, -imos, -ís*) written on them. Place each set in a box. After reviewing the *Gramática,* divide the class into two teams. Give a student from each team one box. Call out a verb. The first student to pull out six correct verb endings for that verb and place them in order on the chalk rail wins a point for the team. For more variety, use other infinitives.

 Pre-AP* Support

- **Activity:** Play "*Secretos*". Write sentences about Pepe and Paula on slips of paper. Divide the class into teams. Each team sits in a row. Distribute a slip with the same sentence to the last person in each row. On cue, students whisper the sentence to the person seated directly in front. Continue until the last person has heard the "secret." This person must correctly write the sentence on the board for the team to score a point.

- ***Pre-AP* Resource Book:*** Comprehensive guide to Pre-AP* comunication skill development, pp. 9–17, 36–46

 Standards: 1.2   Presentation EXPRESS ANSWERS

Resources: Answers on Transparencies

Focus: Using the present tense of regular verbs to complete a paragraph

Suggestions: Point out that in items 1, 2, and 6, students are given the subject pronouns, but they will need to determine which verb forms to use in the other items by looking at the sentences.

Answers:

1. vivimos   3. monto   5. esquían
2. corro   4. montan   6. leo

Common Errors: Students may forget the accent mark on *esquían.* Direct their attention to the note at the bottom of *¿Recuerdas?* before they begin writing their responses.

Extension: Have students imagine they just moved to Beverly Hills, California. Have them write a letter to their friends back home, bragging about the activities they do with their new movie star friends.

Additional Resources

- Teacher's Resource Book: GramActiva BLM, p. 13

9

Standards: 1.2

Presentation EXPRESS ANSWERS

Resources: Answers on Transparencies

Focus: Reviewing interrogative words

Suggestions: Review the *¿Recuerdas?* by giving students situations in English, such as: "You can't find your favorite T-shirt." Students will tell you which question word they would use to ask about their T-shirt's whereabouts *(¿dónde?).* Remind them of the importance of writing the accent marks on question words. Review the expressions of time and frequency by asking choice-forcing questions: *¿Montas en bicicleta todos los días o solamente los fines de semana?*

Answers:

1. quién	3. Dónde	5. Cuál	7. Cuántas
2. Cuándo	4. Qué	6. Cuándo	

Extension: As homework, have students write an e-mail to a student in one of your other Spanish classes or to a Spanish student at another school. In their e-mail, they should ask five questions.

 Standards: 1.1, 1.3

Focus: Asking and answering questions about activities and writing summaries

Suggestions: Have students create a two-column chart with the headings *Actividad* and *Frecuencia* to record their partner's answers to their questions.

Answers will vary.

 Standards: 1.1

Pre-AP*

Focus: Writing, reading, and responding to questions about activities

Suggestions: Write the names of activities on the board with the letters scrambled. Have the class unscramble them and leave them on the board for reference as students do the activity. Remind students to write complete questions.

Answers will vary.

 **Escribir**

Unas preguntas

Vas a contestar unas preguntas, pero primero tienes que completarlas. En una hoja de papel, escribe los números del 1 al 7. Luego escribe la palabra apropiada para completar cada pregunta.

1. ¿Con ___ pasas tiempo los fines de semana?
2. ¿ ___ vas al cine, los viernes, los sábados o los domingos?
3. ¿ ___ vives? ¿Está cerca de la escuela?
4. ¿ ___ deportes practicas?
5. ¿ ___ es tu restaurante favorito?
6. ¿ ___ usas la computadora, después de las clases o por la noche?
7. ¿ ___ veces vas a la biblioteca durante la semana?

¿Recuerdas?

Here are the question words you already know:

¿Adónde?	¿Cuánto, -a?	¿Por qué?
¿Cómo?	¿Cuántos, -as?	¿Qué?
¿Cuál(es)?	¿De dónde?	¿Quién(es)?
¿Cuándo?	¿Dónde?	

And here are words you can use to talk about how often you do an activity:

a menudo	el (los) fin(es) de semana	siempre
a veces		todos los días
después de	nunca	

 Hablar/Escribir

¿A menudo o nunca?

Usa las preguntas de la Actividad 15 para hacer una conversación con otro(a) estudiante. Pregúntale con qué frecuencia hace estas actividades. Escribe las respuestas de tu compañero(a) y úsalas para escribir un párrafo.

Modelo

A veces paso los fines de semana con mis amigos. Siempre vamos al cine los sábados . . .

 Escribir/Hablar

Dos preguntas, por favor

1 Van a trabajar en grupos de tres. Cada estudiante debe escribir en una hoja de papel una actividad que hace.

Modelo

Monto en bicicleta.

2 Pasen la hoja de papel a la persona a su izquierda. Esta persona va a escribir una pregunta usando la información de la primera frase y una palabra interrogativa.

Modelo

¿Cuándo montas en bicicleta?

3 Pasen la hoja de papel a la persona a su izquierda que va a escribir otra pregunta usando la información de la primera frase y otra palabra interrogativa.

Modelo

¿Dónde montas en bicicleta?

4 Pasen la hoja a la persona que escribió la primera frase. Esta persona tiene que leer las preguntas y contestarlas.

Modelo

Monto en bicicleta a menudo. Monto en bicicleta en el parque.

10 diez
¿Qué haces?

Differentiated Instruction
Solutions for All Learners

Heritage Language Learners

Have students research a popular entertainer and write a report on his or her life and career. They should follow the model shown in *Actividad* 19. Have them begin by writing six to eight questions to which they would like to find the answers. They should turn in both their questions and their report.

Students with Learning Difficulties

Some students will have difficulty understanding which interrogative words elicit which kinds of information. You may want to give them a simple chart that makes the relationships clear. It could be organized according to the categories *Who? What / Which? When? Where? Why?* and *How?*

Actividad 18 — Hablar

Tu tiempo libre

Trabaja con otro(a) estudiante y pregúntale adónde va en su tiempo libre. Tu compañero(a) te va a contestar y va a decir con qué frecuencia va.

Estudiante A

1. en el invierno
2. los fines de semana
3. después de las clases
4. en la primavera
5. en el otoño
6. de vacaciones

Modelo

A —¿Adónde vas en el verano?
B —En el verano voy a la piscina todos los días.

Estudiante B

¿Dónde?	¿Cuándo?
la piscina	todos los días
el centro comercial	siempre
la playa	a veces
el parque	nunca
el gimnasio	a menudo
¡Respuesta personal!	¡Respuesta personal!

Actividad 19 — Leer/Escribir

¡Enrique!

Lee este artículo de una revista sobre el cantante Enrique Iglesias. Luego contesta las preguntas.

Enrique Iglesias

El cantante Enrique Iglesias es de España pero ahora vive en Miami. Su padre es el famosísimo cantante Julio Iglesias, pero los jóvenes de todo el mundo conocen a Enrique por sus canciones populares como "Bailamos," "Be With You," y "Hero." Por primera vez en la historia de la música latina, recibe en 1996 el premio Grammy como Mejor Artista Latino con su primer disco. Enrique dice que la inspiración de su música viene de la música rock norteamericana y por las influencias latinas, caribeñas y europeas. Dice que "Soy y voy a ser siempre latino, pero mi música no lo es." Cuando no está escribiendo música o cantando en conciertos, le gusta practicar deportes acuáticos, pasar tiempo con su perro, Grammy, y ver la tele, especialmente los programas musicales. Sus amigos dicen que es gracioso, independiente, romántico y optimista.

1. ¿Cómo se llama el padre de Enrique?
2. ¿De dónde es Enrique?
3. ¿Dónde vive ahora?
4. ¿Cuándo recibe el premio Grammy?
5. ¿Qué tipo de música le inspira a Enrique?
6. ¿Quién es Grammy?
7. ¿Quién es tu cantante favorito(a)? ¿Por qué te gusta?

once **11**
Para empezar

Enrich Your Teaching
Resources for All Teachers

Teacher-to-Teacher
Have students turn *Actividad* 18 into a skit about a journalist interviewing someone who just won $100 million about his or her daily activities. Allow them to add additional places to the list.

Culture Note
The Grammy Award for "Best Latin Recording" was first awarded (to Eddie Palmieri) in 1975, 18 years after the first Grammy Awards ceremony was held in 1958. The separate Latin Grammy Awards ceremony was first held in 2000.

Actividad 18 Standards: 1.1

Focus: Asking and telling where one goes and how often

Suggestions: Before they begin their conversations, ask students what the weather is like in each season and what activities they are likely to do in each one.

Answers will vary.

Common Errors: Student B may respond with answers in the order they are listed in the box. Remind students to give appropriate responses based on the season, day of the week, or time.

Extension: Encourage Student B to give longer responses by using *y, pero,* or *o* to connect phrases.

Bellringer Review

Write these words on the board: *todos los días, a menudo, nunca.* Ask students to tell activities that they do using these expressions. (Ex. *Todos los días monto en bicicleta.*)

Actividad 19 Standards: 1.2, 2.2 Presentation EXPRESS ANSWERS

Resources: Answers on Transparencies
Focus: Reading comprehension

Suggestions: Read items 1–6 and have students write their guesses on a sheet of paper. Have volunteers read the article aloud and see who guessed the most answers correctly.

Answers:
1. El padre de Enrique se llama Julio Iglesias.
2. Enrique es de España.
3. Ahora vive en Miami.
4. Recibe el premio Grammy en 1996.
5. La música rock norteamericana, la música latina, caribeña y europea le inspiran a Enrique.
6. Grammy es su perro.
7. Answers will vary.

Common Errors: Students may confuse *el premio Grammy* with *el perro Grammy.* Advise them to read items 4 and 6 carefully.

Focus: Describing images

Suggestions: Have students write the questions in Step 1 on a sheet of paper and then give them a time limit in which to write words for each question.

Answers will vary.

Extension: Have students compete to see who can describe one of the images for the longest time without pausing for more than three seconds or saying "Umm . . ." or "Uh . . .".

Actividad 21 *Standards:* 1.1, 1.3

Focus: Writing about and discussing activities

Suggestions: For item 1, suggest that students review the *¿Recuerdas?* on p. 9 for activity ideas. Point out that item 2 has a follow-up question. Tell students that they may make up an answer for item 3 if they like.

Answers will vary.

Block Schedule

Divide the class into small groups and give each group the name of a popular Spanish-speaking singer. Have the groups research their singer on the Internet and give a brief report to the class about what he or she is like.

Additional Resources

• WAV Wbk.: Audio Act. 3, p. 2
• Teacher's Resource Book: Audio Script, p. 8, Communicative Activity BLM, pp. 10–11
• Audio Program: Track 7

 ### Assessment

• **ExamView** Quiz on PresEXPRESS
• Prueba P-2, pp. 9–10

  Actividad 20 Pensar/Escribir/Hablar

Juego

1 Escribe palabras que puedes usar para hablar de los tres dibujos. No tienes que escribir frases completas. Piensa en estas preguntas:

¿Qué hacen los jóvenes?

¿Dónde están?

¿Cuándo es?

¿Cómo se llaman ellos?

¿Cómo son ellos?

2 Formen grupos de tres. Decidan quién va a empezar *(start)*. La primera persona habla del primer dibujo por 20 segundos. Su profesor(a) va a decirles cuándo se termina el tiempo. La segunda persona habla del mismo dibujo por 15 segundos sin repetir nada. Su profesor(a) va a decirles cuándo se termina el tiempo. Luego la tercera persona habla del mismo dibujo por diez segundos.

3 Ahora repitan el Paso 2, pero describan el segundo dibujo. Luego repitan lo mismo, pero con el tercer dibujo.

 Actividad 21 Escribir/Hablar

Y tú, ¿qué dices?

1. ¿Qué haces los fines de semana?

2. ¿Cuándo vas al gimnasio: nunca, a veces o todos los días? ¿Por qué?

3. ¿Qué hace tu familia en el verano?

Más práctica

• Practice Workbook, p. 4: P-4
• WAV Wbk.: Writing, p. 5
• Guided Practice: Grammar Acts., pp. 8–14
• *Real.* para hispanohablantes, pp. 6–8

 **Go Online** PHSchool.com
For: Regular Verbs
Web Code: jdd-0004

12 doce
¿Qué haces?

Differentiated Instruction
Solutions for All Learners

Heritage Language Learners

To extend *Actividad* 20, ask students to write a letter to a long-lost relative that describes what they typically do on the weekends. Encourage them to give as many details as possible, and to use adjectives. Remind students to check their work for spelling, punctuation, and grammar errors.

Students with Special Needs

For *Actividad* 20, pair advanced learners with visually impaired students. For each illustration, have the advanced learner briefly describe the illustration. The visually impaired student then can use interrogatives to elicit additional details.

Poemas en diamante

Task
Write a poem in the shape of a diamond. The poem is going to describe you.

1 **Prewrite** Follow these instructions to write your poem:

1. Escribe tu nombre.
2. Escribe dos adjetivos que no te describen.
3. Escribe tres adjetivos que te describen.
4. Escribe cuatro actividades que haces todos los días.
5. Escribe tres actividades que tú y tus amigos hacen en el verano.
6. Escribe dos actividades que nunca haces.
7. Escribe "¡Así soy yo!"

2 **Draft** Use the information above and write your poem in the shape of a diamond.

3 **Revise** Show your poem to a partner. Your partner will check the following:

• Does the poem include all the information from the *Prewrite* section?

• Did you use the correct forms of the adjectives and verbs?

• Is there anything you should add or change?

Decide whether you want to use your partner's suggestions. Rewrite your draft.

4 **Publish** Put your poem on an $8\frac{1}{2}$" × 11" sheet of paper or poster board. Decorate the sheet or poster with photos, drawings, and other items that are descriptive of you.

5 **Evaluation** Your teacher may give you a rubric for grading the poem. You will probably be graded on:

• correct completion of the task

• use of adjectives and verbs

• attractiveness of the project

Estrategia

Organizing your thoughts
Follow the guidelines of a graphic organizer in a diamond shape as you write your poem. This will help you organize your ideas and improve your writing.

Me llamo Linda.
No soy ni seria ni vieja.
Soy alta, sociable, estudiosa.
Todos los días yo escucho música, leo, corro, uso la computadora.
En el verano mis amigos y yo nadamos, cantamos, bailamos.
Nunca patino ni monto en bicicleta.
¡Así soy yo!

trece **13**
Para empezar

Presentación escrita
Creative

 Standards: 1.3, 3.1

Focus: Writing a poem that follows a model

Suggestions: Read through the task and the outline for the assignment. Suggest that students spend ample time planning. Before students decide on the information to include for lines 1–7, ask them to consider the answers to questions such as the following: What is your favorite thing to do when you are not in school? What do you like to do in school? What kind of person do you think you are? How do other people describe you? What makes you angry? What makes you happy? Remind students that they might have to revise the sentences to make sure the poem has a diamond shape. You may want to display students' poems in the classroom and have volunteers read their poems to the class.

Portfolio
Have students include their poem in their portfolio.

Pre-AP* Support
• **Pre-AP* Resource Book:** Comprehensive guide to Pre-AP* writing skill development, pp. 25–35

Teacher-to-Teacher
Give students copies of the rubric before they begin the activity. Go over the descriptions of the different levels of performance. After assessing students, help individuals understand how their performance could be improved.

Additional Resources
Student Resources: Realidades para hispanohablantes, p. 9; Guided Practice: Presentación escrita, pp. 13–14

Enrich Your Teaching
Resources for All Teachers

RUBRIC	Score 1	Score 3	Score 5
Completeness of your task	You provide some of the information required.	You provide most of the information required.	You provide all of the information required.
Your use of adjectives and verbs	You use adjectives and verbs with many grammatical errors.	You use adjectives and verbs with occasional grammatical errors.	You use adjectives and verbs with very few grammatical errors.
Neatness and attractiveness of your presentation	You provide no visuals and your poster contains visible error corrections and smudges.	You provide few visuals and your poster contains visible error corrections and smudges.	You provide several visuals, have no error corrections and smudges, and your poster is attractive.

Tu día escolar
THEME OVERVIEW

▶ **1A ¿Qué haces en la escuela?**
- School activities and rules

Vocabulary: school activities; school rules; classroom objects

Grammar: the verb *tener;* stem-changing verbs; affirmative and negative words

Cultural Perspectives: grading systems; student-teacher interaction

▶ **1B ¿Qué haces después de las clases?**
- Extracurricular activities

Vocabulary: extracurricular activities and pastimes

Grammar: making comparisons; *saber* and *conocer; hace* + time expressions; the verb *ir*

Cultural Perspectives: extracurricular activities

Theme Project

Mi escuela: Una guía

Overview: Students create a trifold brochure in which they describe their school for incoming students. In the brochure, students must: compare their school, teams, and subject areas with those of other schools; describe the possible extracurricular activities their school offers; list the school rules. Students should decorate their brochures with pictures or drawings and present them to the class.

Materials: Construction paper, markers, photos, glue or tape, scissors

Sequence: (suggestions for when to do each step are found throughout the chapters)

1A ▶ **STEP 1.** Review instructions so students know what is expected of them. Hand out the "Theme 1 Project Instructions and Rubric" from the *Teacher's Resource Book.*

STEP 2. Students submit a rough sketch of each page of their brochures. Return the drafts with your suggestions. For grammar and vocabulary practice, ask students to partner and present their drafts to each other.

STEP 3. Students create layouts on different pieces of construction paper, leaving room for photos and descriptions. Encourage them to work in pencil first and to try different arrangements before gluing photos or decorations.

1B ▶ **STEP 4.** Students submit a draft of the brochures. Note your corrections and suggestions, then return drafts to students.

STEP 5. Students present their brochures to the class, explaining each page and describing selected pictures.

Options:

1. Students research and make a brochure about a school in a Spanish-speaking country.
2. Students write about a fictitious school.

Assessment:
Here is a detailed rubric for assessing this project:
Theme 1 Project: *Mi escuela: Una guía*

RUBRIC	Score 1	Score 3	Score 5
Your evidence of planning	You provide no written draft or sketch.	Your draft was written and layout created, but not corrected.	You show evidence of corrected draft and layout.
Your use of illustrations	You include no photos or visuals.	You include very few photos or visuals.	You include several photos or visuals.
Your presentation	You include little of the required information.	You include at least three rules, extracurricular activities, and comparisons.	You include three or more rules, extracurricular activities, and comparisons.

Bulletin Boards

Theme: *En la escuela*

Ask students to cut out, copy, or download photos of school activities, extracurricular activities, school uniforms, and classroom activities from different Spanish-speaking cultures. Cluster photos into several categories—sports, arts and music, school subjects, school uniforms, etc.—so that similarities and differences are evident.

Bibliography

Colon-Vila, Lilian. *Salsa.* Arte Público Pr., 1998.

DK Hornby, Hugh. *Soccer.* DK Eyewitness Books. New York: Dorling Kindersley, 2000. The inside story of soccer, from its origins to the latest World Cup finals.

Klickman, F. Henri. *How to Play Latin American Rhythm Instruments.* Warner Brothers, 1995. Explains the rhythmic contributions of Latin American instruments.

Hands-on Culture

Game: *El balero*

El balero is a traditional Mexican children's game commonly played in schoolyards and at home. The *balero* is a wooden cup attached by a string to a smaller wooden ball. The object is to swing the wooden cup and try to get the ball to land inside.

Materials:

>   paper cups
>   yarn
>   1 buttons
>   craft sticks or pencils
>   tape

Directions:

1. With the craft stick or pencil, make a hole in the center of the bottom of the cup. Tape the stick in place so that the cup has a handle.

2. Tie a foot-long piece of yarn to the bottom of the handle. Secure with tape.

3. Tie a button onto the other end of the yarn.

4. Holding the cup by the handle, try to get the button to land inside of the cup.

Internet Search

Use the keywords to find more information.

1A Keywords:

> Simón Silva, José Martí

1B Keywords:

> Antonio Berni, Rubén Blades, fútbol, Fernando Botero, ballet, merengue, tango, flamenco

Game

¿Aprendes de memoria?

Play this game after any chapter to review vocabulary.

Players: Any number of students in small groups

Materials: Index cards or small squares of construction paper, markers

Rules:

1. Give each group of students 36 blank index cards or squares of paper.

2. In groups, players choose 18 vocabulary words from the chapter. On one card, students write the Spanish word; on another, they write the English word.

3. When each team has completed their cards, they shuffle them and lay them face-down in a 6 x 6 grid. Each student takes turns flipping two cards at a time and trying to make a match.

4. If a student finds a match, that student must create a complete Spanish sentence using that word. A correct sentence earns a point. The student with the most points at the end of the game wins.

5. Students can continue playing and practicing new vocabulary by switching their deck of cards with another group.

Variation: Instead of writing the English word, students can draw a picture of the Spanish word or activity.

RECYCLE
A ver si recuerdas

Vocabulary
- La escuela

Grammar
- The verb *tener*
- Verbs with irregular *yo* forms

A primera vista	Manos a la obra	¡Adelante!	Repaso

Learning Sequence

INPUT	PRACTICE	APPLICATION	REVIEW
• Introduce vocabulary and grammar within an authentic context.	• Practice and develop new vocabulary. • Learn and practice new grammar structures.	• Apply vocabulary and grammar through culminating, theme-based activities. • Apply skill development.	• Review vocabulary and grammar.

Objectives

• Read, listen to, and interpret information about • School activities • School rules • Items you need for class	• Communicate about classroom activities and rules. • Compare rules in different classes. • Use affirmative and negative words. • Review stem-changing verbs.	• Read and interpret an article about good study habits. • Describe what you would do if you were principal for a day. • Investigate coats of arms. • Read intro: Guanajuato, Mexico.	• Prepare for the chapter test.

Culture

• Simón Silva	• *José Martí* • *Las Notas* • *¿Más estrictos?*	• *Okapi* • *Un nuevo escudo de armas*	• Describe the role coats of arms play in Spanish culture.

Vocabulary
- Class activities
- Classroom rules
- School objects
- Negative and affirmative words

Grammar
- Stem-changing verbs
- Affirmative and negative words

Learner Support

STRATEGIES
- Making inferences
- Memorizing
- Using heads and subheads
- Brainstorming

RECYCLING
- Actividad 15
- Actividad 20
- The preposition *para*
- Stem-changing verbs
- School subjects

- Negatives
- The verb *ser*
- Descriptive adjectives

Chapter Features

Pronunciación

The letters *b*, *v*, and *d*

El español en el mundo del trabajo

Background of a high school Spanish teacher

Conexiones

Literature: A poem by José Martí

Beyond the Classroom: States & Countries

España
Illinois
Cuba
México
Venezuela
Texas
Chile
Argentina

Student Resources

TECHNOLOGY

ONLINE

Interactive Textbook
• Student Edition Online plus audio, video, and flashcards

Go Online Companion Web Site
• Tutorial activities   • Internet links
• Self-tests   • Downloadable MP3 audio files
• **PuzzleView**

CD-ROM

Interactive Textbook CD-ROM
Student Edition on CD-ROM plus audio, video, and flashcards

MindPoint CD-ROM
QUIZSHOW

PRINT MATERIAL

CORE INSTRUCTION

Practice Workbook, pp. 5–15
• Review   • Vocabulary
• Grammar   • Puzzle
• Organizer

Writing, Audio & Video Activities, pp. 6–15
• Video   • Audio
• Writing

Grammar Study Guide 1–2 (or 3–4)

Differentiated Instruction

STUDENTS NEEDING EXTRA HELP

Guided Practice Activities, pp. 15–32
• Vocabulary Flash Cards and Vocabulary Check
• Grammar Activities
• Presentación oral

HERITAGE LEARNERS

Realidades para hispanohablantes, pp. 10–29

Lecturas para hispanohablantes
• "Cuaderno de tareas," pp. 68–70
• AP* Literature Author: Antonio Machado, "Recuerdo infantil," p. 72

ADVANCED/PRE-AP*

Pre-AP* Resource Book: Student Activity Sheet, p. 99

Teacher Resources

TECHNOLOGY

Audio Program   Fine Art Transparencies
Video Program   Vocabulary and Grammar
                Transparencies
                Answers on Transparencies

TeacherEXPRESS CD-ROM
• Lesson Planner   • Vocabulary Clip Art
• Web Resources   • Teaching Resources
• Teacher Edition with Interactive Links

PresentationEXPRESS CD-ROM
• Vocabulary   • Transparencies and Maps
• Grammar   • Photo Gallery
• Audio   • Clip Art

PH SuccessNet ONLINE
• Access to grades and reports from Online Interactive Textbook

ExamView on Presentation Express
QuickTake Presenter CD-ROM
• Vocabulary Quizzes   • Chapter Test
• Grammar Quizzes

TeacherEXPRESS CD-ROM
• Assessment Program
• **ExamView** Test Banks A and B
  test generator

Go Online
PHSchool.com
For: Teacher Home Page
Web Code: jdk-1001

PRINT MATERIAL

CORE INSTRUCTION

Teacher's Resource Book, pp. 22–45
• Input Script   • Video Script
• Answer Keys   • GramActiva Blackline Masters
• Vocabulary Clip Art   • Chapter Resource Checklist
• School-to-Home Connection Letters
• Communicative Activities Blackline Masters

TPR Stories, pp. 10–17

CORE ASSESSMENT

Assessment Program, pp. 13–25
• Pruebas
    Vocabulary Recognition
    Vocabulary Production
    Stem-changing verbs
    Affirmative and negative words
• Examen del capítulo   • Speaking and Writing Rubrics

Teacher's Resource Book, p. 34
• Situation Cards

TPR Stories, pp. 10–17

Differentiated Instruction

STUDENTS NEEDING EXTRA HELP

Guided Practice Activities Teacher's Guide, pp. T8–T16

HERITAGE LEARNERS

Realidades para hispanohablantes Teacher's Guide, pp. 6–15

Lecturas para hispanohablantes Teacher's Guide, pp. 26–28

ADVANCED/PRE-AP*

Pre-AP* Resource Book, p. 96

Differentiated Assessment

STUDENTS NEEDING EXTRA HELP

Alternate Assessment Program
• Examen del capítulo, pp. 5–9

HERITAGE LEARNERS

Assessment Program: Realidades para hispanohablantes Teacher's Guide, pp. T91–T95

ExamView Heritage Learner
test generator Test Bank

ADVANCED/PRE-AP*

Pre-AP* Resource Book:Teacher Activity Sheet, p. 98

ExamView Pre-AP* Test Bank
test generator

Capítulo 1A — Lesson Plans

Regular Schedule (50 Minutes)

For electronic lesson plans:
Teacher Express

	Warm-up / Assess	Preview Present	/ Practice Communicate	Wrap-up / Homework Options
DAY 1	**Warm-up (5 min.)** • Homework check	**A ver si recuerdas . . . (20 min.)** • Presentation: La escuela • Actividad 1 • Presentation: The verb *tener* • Actividades 2, 3	**Chapter Opener (5 min.)** • Objectives • Fondo cultural **A primera vista (15 min.)** • Presentation: Vocabulario y gramática en contexto • Actividades 1, 2	**Wrap-up and Homework Options (5 min.)** • Practice Workbook 1A-A, 1A-B, 1A-1, 1A-2 • Go Online
DAY 2	**Warm-up (10 min.)** • Homework check	**A primera vista (35 min.)** • Presentation: Videohistoria *La clase de Esteban* • View: Videohistoria	• Video Activities 1, 2, 3, 4 • Actividad 3	**Wrap-up and Homework Options (5 min.)** • Practice Workbook 1A-3, 1A-4 • Go Online • Prueba 1A-1: Vocabulary recognition
DAY 3	**Warm-up (10 min.)** • Actividad 4 • Homework check ✔**Assessment (10 min.)** • Prueba 1A-1: Vocabulary recognition	**Manos a la obra (25 min.)** • Actividades 5, 6, 7, 8, 11 • Fondo cultural		**Wrap-up and Homework Options (5 min.)** • Actividades 9, 10, 12 • Writing Activity 10 • Heritage Learner Workbook 1A-1, 1A-2 • Prueba 1A-2: Vocabulary production
DAY 4	**Warm-up (10 min.)** • Actividad 13 • Homework check ✔**Assessment (10 min.)** (after Communicative Activity) • Prueba 1A-2: Vocabulary production	**Manos a la obra (25 min.)** • Audio Activities 5, 6 • Communicative Activity • Presentation: Stem-changing verbs	• View: GramActiva video • Actividad 14	**Wrap-up and Homework Options (5 min.)** • Practice Workbook 1A-5 • Go Online • Actividades 17, 18
DAY 5	**Warm-up (10 min.)** • Writing Activity 11 • Homework check	**Manos a la obra (35 min.)** • Actividades 15, 16 • Audio Activity 7 • Pronunciación • Fondo cultural	• Presentation: Affirmative and negative words • View: GramActiva video • Actividades 19, 22	**Wrap-up and Homework Options (5 min.)** • Practice Workbook 1A-6 • Go Online • Prueba 1A-3: Stem-changing verbs
DAY 6	**Warm-up (5 min.)** • Homework check ✔**Assessment (10 min.)** • Prueba 1A-3: Stem-changing verbs	**Manos a la obra (30 min.)** • Actividades 20, 21 • Fondo cultural • El español en el mundo del trabajo	• Audio Activities 8, 9 • Communicative Activity	**Wrap-up and Homework Options (5 min.)** • Practice Workbook 1A-7 • Writing Activity 12, 13 • Prueba 1A-4: Affirmative and negative words • Go Online • Heritage Learner Workbook 1A-4, 1A-5
DAY 7	**Warm-up (5 min.)** • Homework check ✔**Assessment (10 min.)** • Prueba 1A-4: Affirmative and negative words	**¡Adelante! (30 min.)** • Lectura • ¿Comprendiste? • Fondo cultural • Presentación oral: Steps 1, 4		**Wrap-up and Homework Options (5 min.)** • Presentación oral: Step 2 • Go Online: Lectura
DAY 8	**Warm-up (5 min.)** • Presentación oral: Step 2	**¡Adelante! (40 min.)** • Presentación oral: Step 3 • La cultura en vivo		**Wrap-up and Homework Options (5 min.)** • Preparación para el examen 3, 4, 5
DAY 9	**Warm-up (5 min.)** • Homework check	**¡Adelante! (25 min.)** • Videomisterio: Presentation • La cultura en vivo	**Repaso del capítulo (15 min.)** • Vocabulario y gramática • Preparación para el examen 1, 2	**Wrap-up and Homework Options (5 min.)** • Practice Workbook 1A-8, 1A-9 • Go Online: Self-test • Examen del capítulo 1A
DAY 10	**Warm-up (5 min.)** • Homework check ✔**Assessment (40 min.)** • Examen del capítulo 1A			**Wrap-up and Homework Options (5 min.)** • A ver si recuerdas . . . : Capítulo 1B

	Warm-up / Assess	Preview Present / Practice Communicate		Wrap-up / Homework Options
DAY 1	**Warm-up (5 min.)** • Homework check	**A ver si recuerdas . . . (20 min.)** • Presentation: La escuela • Actividad 1 • Presentation: The verb *tener* • Actividades 2, 3 **Chapter Opener (5 min.)** • Objectives • Fondo cultural	**A primera vista (55 min.)** • Presentation: Vocabulario y gramática en contexto • Actividades 1, 2 • Presentation: Videohistoria: *La clase de Esteban* • View: Videohistoria • Video Activities 1, 2, 3, 4 • Actividad 3	**Wrap-up and Homework Options (5 min.)** • Practice Workbook 1A-A, 1A-B, 1A-1, 1A-2, 1A-3, 1A-4 • Go Online • Prueba 1A-1: Vocabulary recognition
DAY 2	**Warm-up (10 min.)** • Actividad 4 • Homework check ✔**Assessment (10 min.)** • Prueba 1A-1: Vocabulary recognition	**Manos a la obra (65 min.)** • Actividades 5, 6, 7, 8, 9, 10, 11, 12 • Fondo cultural • Audio Activities 5, 6 • Communicative Activity		**Wrap-up and Homework Options (5 min.)** • Writing Activity 10 • Go Online • Heritage Learner Workbook 1A-1, 1A-2 • Prueba 1A-2: Vocabulary production
DAY 3	**Warm-up (10 min.)** • Actividad 13 • Homework check ✔**Assessment (10 min.)** • Prueba 1A-2: Vocabulary production	**Manos a la obra (65 min.)** • Presentation: Stem-changing verbs • View: GramActiva video • Actividades 14, 15, 16, 17 • Pronunciación • Actividad 18 • Fondo cultural • Audio Activity 7 • Writing Activity 11 • Presentation: Affirmative and negative words • View: GramActiva video • Actividad 19		**Wrap-up and Homework Options (5 min.)** • Practice Workbook 1A-5, 1A-6 • Go Online • Prueba 1A-3: Stem-changing verbs
DAY 4	**Warm-up (5 min.)** • Homework check ✔**Assessment (10 min.)** • Pruebas 1A-3: Stem-changing verbs	**Manos a la obra (45 min.)** • Actividades 20, 21, 22, 23 • Fondo cultural • El español en el mundo del trabajo • Audio Activities 8, 9 • Writing Activity 12 • Communicative Activity	**¡Adelante! (25 min.)** • Presentación oral: Steps 1, 4 • La cultura en vivo	**Wrap-up and Homework Options (5 min.)** • Practice Workbook 1A-7 • Presentación oral: Step 2 • Writing Activity 13 • Go Online • Heritage Learner Workbook 1A-4, 1A-5 • Prueba 1A-4: Affirmative and negative words
DAY 5	**Warm-up (5 min.)** • Homework check ✔**Assessment (10 min.)** • Prueba 1A-4: Affirmative and negative words	**¡Adelante! (45 min.)** • Presentación oral: Step 3 • Lectura • ¿Comprendiste? • Fondo cultural	**Repaso del capítulo (25 min.)** • Vocabulario y gramática • Preparación para el examen 1, 2, 3, 4, 5	**Wrap-up and Homework Options (5 min.)** • Practice Workbook 1A-8, 1A-9 • Go Online: Self-test • Examen del capítulo 1A
DAY 6	**Warm-up (10 min.)** • Homework check • Answer questions **Repaso del capítulo (15 min.)** • Situation Cards ✔**Assessment (40 min.)** • Examen del capítulo 1A	**¡Adelante! (20 min.)** • Videomisterio: Presentation		**Wrap-up and Homework Options (5 min.)** • Go Online: Lectura

Vocabulario

Core Instruction

 Standards: 1.1, 1.3

Resources: Voc. and Gram. Transparency 25

Focus: Reviewing vocabulary related to classes, supplies, and objects found in school

Suggestions: The *A ver si recuerdas* sections are designed to provide quick review of material from *Realidades* 1 over which students should have a reasonable level of control. These reviews are spread across the first several chapters of the book. In addition, more intensive review of additional structures is built into the chapters themselves. Use the transparencies to review the vocabulary sets and grammar topics. Feel free to re-enter favorite activities that students used in *Realidades* 1 should they need more practice.

Have students look around the room and name as many objects as they can in Spanish. Then ask: *¿Qué clases tienen en la primera hora?* Ask a volunteer to write the responses on the board. Ask students to vote on which classes they consider most difficult (**difícil**), interesting (**interesante**), practical (**práctica**), etc.

 Actividad 1 *Standards:* 1.1, 1.3

Focus: Writing and speaking about topics related to school

Suggestions: To encourage variety, assign students different classes. Tell students to avoid personal criticisms of teachers.

Answers will vary.

Extension: Have students write a list of questions and interview a partner about a particular class.

A ver si recuerdas...

Vocabulario

La escuela

las clases
el arte
las ciencias naturales
las ciencias sociales
la educación física
el español
el inglés
las matemáticas
la tecnología

mi horario
primera hora
segunda hora
tercera hora
cuarta hora
quinta hora
sexta hora
séptima hora
octava hora
novena hora
décima hora

descripciones de las clases
aburrido, -a
difícil
divertido, -a
fácil
interesante
práctico, -a

en mi mochila
un bolígrafo
una calculadora
una carpeta
una carpeta de argollas
un cuaderno
un diccionario
una hoja de papel
un lápiz
un libro
la tarea

en la sala de clases
un asiento
una bandera
un cartel
un escritorio
una mesa
la papelera
la puerta
un pupitre
un reloj
un sacapuntas
una silla
la ventana

Práctica de vocabulario • Usando el organizador gráfico

 Actividad 1 **Hablar/Escribir** ——————

Tu escuela

Un estudiante de América Central estudia en tu escuela este año.
Usa la información del organizador gráfico y dile *(tell him)*:

- una clase que tienes   *Tengo . . .*
- el nombre del profesor / de la profesora
  El (La) profesor(a) se llama . . .
- cómo es la clase   *La clase es . . .*

- las cosas que traes a la clase todos los días
  Todos los días traigo . . .
- a qué hora tienes la clase   *Tengo la clase a las . . .*
- si te gusta o no te gusta la clase y por qué
  Me gusta / No me gusta la clase porque . . .

14 catorce
Tema 1 • Tu día escolar

Differentiated Instruction
Solutions for All Learners

Advanced Learners
Have students write a short description of their ideal class. Tell them to include the subject, what the teacher is like, at what time of day it takes place, and what is used on a daily basis.

Students with Learning Difficulties
For *Actividad 3*, break the directions down into three steps. For each sentence, have students first select the appropriate verb, then circle the subject, and finally determine the correct form of the verb.

Gramática·Repaso

The verb *tener*

Use the verb *tener* to show relationship, possession, or age, or in other expressions such as *tener hambre/sueño/sed*.

(yo)	**tengo**	(nosotros) (nosotras)	**tenemos**
(tú)	**tienes**	(vosotros) (vosotras)	**tenéis**
Ud. (él) (ella)	**tiene**	Uds. (ellos) (ellas)	**tienen**

Use *tener que* + infinitive to say that something has to be done.

Tenemos que escribir mucho en la clase de inglés.

Verbs with irregular *yo* forms

Some verbs are irregular in the *yo* form only.

hacer (to do, to make)	poner (to put)	traer (to bring)
hago	**pongo**	**traigo**

Hago la tarea de español todos los días.
Pongo los libros en el escritorio.
Traigo una carpeta a la clase.

Práctica de gramática

 Actividad 2 Escribir

¿Qué tienen que hacer?

¿Qué tienen que hacer estas personas en sus clases? Escribe frases con una actividad diferente para cada persona.

Modelo

mi amiga *(nombre)*
Mi amiga Gloria tiene que usar la computadora.

1. yo
2. mi amigo *(nombre)*
3. nosotros
4. mis amigos
5. la profesora
6. tú

Más práctica

- Practice Workbook, pp. 5–6: 1A-A, 1A-B
- Guided Practice Acts., pp. 15–16: 1A-1, 1A-2
- *Real.* para hispanohablantes, p. 10

 **Go Online** PHSchool.com
For: Vocab. and Grammar
Web Code: jdd-0101

 Actividad 3 Leer/Escribir

¿Cómo son las clases?

Completa la siguiente conversación con la forma correcta del verbo apropiado. Luego escribe un párrafo para describir tus clases.

A —¿Qué __1.__ *(traer/hacer)* Uds. en la clase de ciencias?

B —Nosotros __2.__ *(tener/hacer)* muchas cosas diferentes. Estudiamos plantas y animales. A veces el profesor __3.__ *(poner/hacer)* un experimento y nosotros __4.__ *(tener/traer)* que escribir nuestras observaciones.

A —¿El profesor __5.__ *(traer/hacer)* animales o insectos a la clase para estudiar?

B —Sí, él __6.__ *(poner/hacer)* un animal sobre la mesa y nosotros lo describimos. A veces los estudiantes __7.__ *(poner/traer)* una planta o una piedra interesante a la clase también.

A —¿ __8.__ *(Traer/Tener)* Uds. mucha tarea en la clase?

B —Sí. Leemos mucho y __9.__ *(Traer/Hacer)* una prueba cada semana. Yo siempre __10.__ *(poner/hacer)* mi libro de ciencias en mi mochila porque hay tarea todos los días.

quince 15
Preparación: Vocabulario y gramática

Enrich Your Teaching

Resources for All Teachers

Culture Note

To avoid overcrowded classes, high schools in larger cities in Mexico often have split schedules. One group starts in the morning and finishes in the early afternoon. The second group arrives around 1:30 P.M. and finishes their school day around 8:30 P.M.

Teacher-to-Teacher

To provide students with visual cues for school-related vocabulary, create picture cards. Place the pictures from **en mi mochila** in a backpack and have students take turns pulling one out and identifying it. For vocabulary for **en la sala de clases,** have students place the cards on the objects in your classroom.

Gramática·Repaso

Presentation EXPRESS GRAMMAR

Core Instruction

Resources: Voc. and Gram. Transparency 26

Suggestions: After reviewing **tener,** you might also review **venir.** Ask students to compare the two verbs. Point out that both are stem-changing verbs and have irregular **yo** forms that end in **-go.** Ask students why the **nosotros** forms of the two verbs are different. (**Venir** is an **-ir** verb.)

Bring in photos from magazines that students could describe using **tener** expressions. For example, bring in a picture of a person standing in the cold and ask: *¿Qué tiene?*

 Actividad 2 *Standards:* 1.3

Resources: Answers on Transparencies
Focus: Writing about what students have to do in their classes

Suggestions: Have students brainstorm a list of activities they do in different classes. Allow them to use the list to write their sentences.

Answers will vary but will include:

1. Yo tengo que...
2. Mi amigo *(nombre)* tiene que...
3. Nosotros tenemos que...
4. Mis amigos tienen que...
5. La profesora tiene que...
6. Tú tienes que...

Actividad 3 *Standards:* 1.2, 1.3

Resources: Answers on Transparencies
Focus: Reading and writing about descriptions of classes

Suggestions: Have students read through the entire paragraph before beginning. Remind them that when deciding on a verb to complete a question, it is helpful to read the response to the question first.

Answers:

1. hacen
2. hacemos
3. hace
4. tenemos
5. trae
6. pone
7. traen
8. Tienen
9. hacemos
10. pongo

Standards for Capítulo 1A

- To achieve the goals of the Standards, students will:

Communication

1.1 Interpersonal
- Talk: about classroom activities and school; using the verb *conocer*
- Answer questions and compare experiences about classes and subjects

1.2 Interpretive
- Read, listen to, and interpret information on: school activities, subjects, rules, and class items
- Read and interpret: a picture-based story, quotes about education, a famous poem
- Read: sayings focusing on pronunciation; descriptions using affirmative and negative words; about coats of arms; about the schools and grading system in Mexico; about good study habits and school subjects; about *Okapi*, a Spanish magazine; about Guanajuato

1.3 Presentational
- Present information about: school activities; subjects; rules; coats of arms
- Provide information about a poem
- Write about: a picture-based story, a favorite class; Mexican grades and subjects; quotes about education; write a letter about school
- Recite a poem in front of the class
- Read, complete sentences, and play a game with stem-changing verbs

Culture

2.1 Practices and Perspectives
- Describe grading systems in Mexico
- Describe teacher-student relationships in a school setting

2.2 Products and Perspectives
- Talk or write about the painter Simón Silva, the poet José Martí, and the poem *Versos sencillos*
- Talk about: *Okapi*, a Spanish magazine; coats of arms

Connections

3.1 Cross-curricular
- Describe the poet José Martí and his work; organize for success in school; make a coat of arms

3.2 Target Culture
- Read: an article from a Spanish magazine; quotes about education; about history, culture of Guanajuato

Comparisons

4.1 Language
- Interpret a reading by using cognates; practice the pronunciation of *b, v,* and *d;* describe the formality of language in student-teacher relationships
- Use affirmative and negative words

4.2 Culture
- Compare: Mexican grading systems and teacher-student relationships to those in the U.S.; *Okapi* with U.S. magazines

Communities

5.1 Beyond the School
- Identify characteristics of a good teacher

Fondo cultural ■ ◆ ● ■ ◆ ◆ ◇

Simón Silva El artista chicano Simón Silva nació *(was born)* en México en 1961 y se crió *(was raised)* en California. Con el arte, el joven artista aprende a apreciar su cultura y decide continuar su educación. En sus cuadros, celebra su biculturalismo y su bilingüismo.

- ¿Tu escuela tiene un día especial para los maestros? ¿Qué piensas de la idea?

"El día del maestro" (1990), Simón Silva
Courtesy of Simón Silva.

16 dieciséis
Tema 1 • Tu día escolar

Differentiated Instruction

STUDENTS NEEDING EXTRA HELP

Guided Practice Activities
- Vocabulary Check, Flash Cards
- Grammar
- Reading and Speaking Support

Guided Practice Audio CDs
- Disc 1, Track 1

HERITAGE LEARNERS

Realidades para hispanohablantes
- Chapter Opener, pp. 10–11
- A primera vista, p. 12
- Videohistoria, p. 13
- Manos a la obra, pp. 14–21
- ¡Adelante!, pp. 22–27
- Repaso del capítulo, pp. 28–29

ADVANCED/PRE-AP*

Pre-AP* Resource Book, pp. 96–99

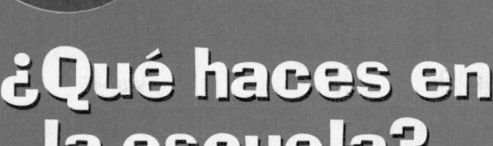

¿Qué haces en la escuela?

Chapter Objectives

- Describe classroom objects and activities
- Talk about classroom rules
- Express affirmative and negative ideas
- Compare the school rules and customs in other countries with those of your own school

Video Highlights

A primera vista: *La clase de Esteban*
GramActiva Videos: stem-changing verbs; affirmative and negative words

Country Connection

As you learn to describe what you do in school, you will make connections to these countries and places:

- España
- Illinois
- Cuba
- México
- Venezuela
- Texas
- Chile
- Argentina

Más práctica

- *Real.* para hispanohablantes, pp. 10–11

 **Go Online** PHSchool.com **For:** Online Atlas **Web Code:** jde-0002

La Plaza de la Independencia, Quito, Ecuador

diecisiete **17**
Capítulo 1A

Chapter Opener

Presentation EXPRESS ATLAS

Core Instruction

Resources: Voc. and Gram. Transparencies: Maps 12, 14–18, 20

Suggestions: Have students look at the photo of the school and point out things they notice. Explain that *Capítulo* 1A is the first of two chapters in *Tema 1, Tu día escolar.* In this chapter they will use vocabulary to discuss classroom activities and rules and will use negative and affirmative expressions. In the *Videohistoria,* they will see what happens when Esteban becomes a history teacher for a day. They will also use more stem-changing verbs to express what they do in class.

The chapter has four parts. *A primera vista* introduces vocabulary through illustrations, conversations, narratives, reading, and video. *Manos a la obra* allows students to practice vocabulary and grammar through reading, writing, speaking, and listening. *¡Adelante!* presents opportunities for reading and presentation tasks, while also giving cultural perspectives and information. *Repaso del capítulo* reviews chapter vocabulary and helps students prepare for tasks on the test.

 **Fondo cultural** *Standards:* 1.2, 2.2

Resources: Fine Art Transparencies with Teacher's Guide, p. 61; Answers on Transparencies

Suggestions: *El día del maestro* or Teacher's Day is celebrated in many cultures. In Mexico, May 15 is the official day to recognize teachers' contributions. In the United States, it took 55 years to establish an official date, but finally in 1985, May 9 was designated Teacher's Day.

Answers will vary.

Teacher-to-Teacher

Contact a Spanish teacher in another school to arrange for your classes to collaborate on a variety of projects throughout the year. For example, for this theme, have students exchange letters or e-mails to answer questions about their schools.

Teaching with Art

Resources: Fine Art Transparencies with Teacher's Guide, p. 61

Teacher Technology

TeacherEXPRESS
Plan • Teach • Assess

PLAN
Lesson Planner

 **Go Online** PHSchool.com
For: Teacher Home Page
Web Code: jdk-1001

TEACH
Teaching Resources
Interactive
Teacher's Edition
Vocabulary Clip Art

ASSESS
Chapter Quizzes and Tests

PresentationEXPRESS
Dynamic Presentations for Teachers

TEACH
Vocabulary & Grammar Powerpoints
GramActiva Video
Audio & Clip Art Activities
Transparencies and Maps
Activity Answers
Photo Gallery

ASSESS
ExamView
QuickTake Presenter

Vocabulario y gramática  *Presentation EXPRESS* VOCABULARY

Core Instruction

 Standards: 1.2

Resources: Teacher's Resource Book: Input Script, p. 24, Clip Art, pp. 36–38, Audio Script, p. 25; Voc. and Gram. Transparencies 27–28; Audio Program: Tracks 1–2

Focus: Presenting vocabulary related to school activities, classroom items, and school rules

Suggestions: The *A primera vista* presents new vocabulary in context and provides lexical examples of the grammar structures that will be explained in the chapter. The first two pages present vocabulary in visual and communicative context. The next two pages present vocabulary in the context of the *Videohistoria* reading.

Present this vocabulary in two groups: classroom tasks and items used to complete them, and classroom rules. Use the Input Script from the *Teacher's Resource Book* or the story from the *TPR Stories Book* to present the new vocabulary and grammar.

To practice new expressions, make enlarged photocopies of the images on this page, or use the Transparencies. Hold up or point to each picture as you ask students limited-response questions: for example, *¿La profesora le explica a la estudiante cómo usar el laboratorio?*

Write the rules from p. 19 on a large piece of poster board. Using non-verbal cues, pretend to break some of the rules. After each one you "break," have a volunteer come to the front of the room and point to the appropriate rule. Have students decide which rules apply to your classroom. Cut them out and display them on a bulletin board.

Variation: *Prohíbe* may be written with or without an accent mark. The written accent mark on this and a number of other words was authorized by the *Real Academia Española* in 1952 to reflect contemporary pronunciation.

Bellringer Review

Write these letters on the board and ask the students to unscramble them to create Spanish words for class items:

ihomcla; alclacurado; arcepat; lfrabogoí; roilb; lizáp

(**Answers:** mochila, calculadora, carpeta, bolígrafo, libro, lápiz)

Additional Resources

• Audio Program: Canciones CD, Disc 22

18

A primera vista *jdd-0187*

Vocabulario y gramática en contexto

Objectives

Read, listen to, and understand information about
• school activities
• school rules
• items you need for class

66 ¡Hola! Me llamo Miguel. En mi escuela siempre estamos muy ocupados. Vamos a ver **lo que** hacemos en las clases 99.

A+

Estos estudiantes **discuten** la tarea en **el laboratorio.**

sacar una buena nota

Estos estudiantes hacen **un proyecto** de arte.

Victoria **repite las palabras** nuevas para **aprender de memoria** el vocabulario.

Marcos escribe **un informe sobre** la música latinoamericana.

La profesora le **explica** a Elena cómo usar la computadora.

18 dieciocho
Tema 1 • Tu día escolar

Differentiated Instruction
Solutions for All Learners

Advanced Learners

Give students different classroom scenarios, such as taking tests, working in groups, or doing projects. Have them create a list of rules for each scenario, and post them in the classroom.

Multiple Intelligences

Bodily/Kinesthetic: Ask students to work in groups and pantomime the new words that are presented on pp. 18–19. Have them take turns acting out the vocabulary while the others in the group try to guess the word.

La profesora de español de la Escuela Benito Juárez prepara un cartel con **las reglas** de la escuela. ¿Cuáles son las reglas?

Más vocabulario

alguien someone, somebody
ningún, ninguno, -a no, none
prestar atención to pay attention
respetar to respect

Hay que . . .

Hay que llevar
el carnet de identidad.

Hay que entregar la
tarea a tiempo.

la cinta adhesiva

las tijeras

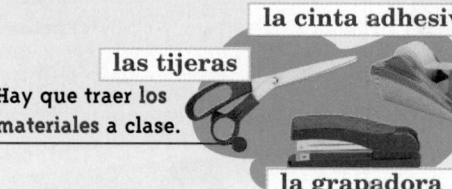

Hay que traer los
materiales a clase.

la grapadora

Hay que estar en el
asiento cuando la
clase empieza.

hacer una pregunta

Hay que pedir ayuda
si no entiendes.

contestar

Se prohíbe . . .

Se prohíbe ir al
armario durante
las clases.

Se prohíbe almorzar
en la sala de clases.

 Actividad 1 jdd-0187

🔊 **Escuchar** ─────

¿Qué hacen en la escuela?

Escucha lo que estos estudiantes hacen en la escuela y señala el dibujo apropiado.

Más práctica

- Practice Workbook, pp. 7–8: 1A-1, 1A-2
- WAV Wbk.: Writing, p. 12
- Guided Practice: Vocab. Flash Cards, pp. 17–22
- *Real*. para hispanohablantes, p. 12

Go Online PHSchool.com
For: Vocab. Practice
Web Code: jdd-0102

Actividad 2 jdd-0187

🔊 **Escuchar** ─────

¿Qué reglas tienes?

Escucha estas seis reglas. Si tienes la misma regla en tu clase de español, levanta una mano. Si no tienes la regla, levanta las dos manos.

diecinueve **19**
Capítulo 1A

Enrich Your Teaching
Resources for All Teachers

Culture Note

Many schools in Latin America do not have lockers. As a result, many students use book bags or backpacks to carry their books and personal items with them throughout the day.

Teacher-to-Teacher

Play a game of **"Las reglas tontas."** Have students use **hay que** or **se prohíbe** plus an infinitive, as in the example sentences, to make up a list of five silly classroom rules. Provide an example such as *Hay que traer a tu perro a la clase cada día.* Have students vote on the silliest list.

Actividad 1 〰 *Standards:* 1.2

Presentation EXPRESS AUDIO

Resources: Teacher's Resource Book: Audio Script, p. 25; Audio Program: Track 3; Answers on Transparencies

Focus: Listening comprehension about school-related activities

Suggestions: Throughout the program, you may choose to use the *Audio CD* or to read scripts yourself. You may wish to have students listen once and then again, stopping after each sentence. Pause to monitor that students are pointing to the correct picture.

🔊 **Script and Answers:**

1. Tengo que escribir un informe esta noche. *(boy typing on the computer)*
2. Los estudiantes van a discutir la tarea. *(students talking in laboratory)*
3. Ellos hacen un proyecto de arte. *(students doing an art project)*
4. Yo siempre repito las palabras muchas veces. *(girl repeating words)*
5. La profesora explica el programa. *(teacher helping student at the computer)*

Actividad 2 〰 *Standards:* 1.2

Presentation EXPRESS AUDIO

Resources: Teacher's Resource Book: Audio Script, p. 25; Audio Program: Track 4; Answers on Transparencies

Focus: Listening comprehension about classroom rules

Suggestions: Ask students to make a list of the rules in their own class. Have them refer to the list as you play the *Audio CD* or read the script.

🔊 **Script:**

1. Hay que llevar el carnet de identidad.
2. Hay que traer la grapadora a la clase de español.
3. Hay que estar en el asiento cuando la clase empieza.
4. Hay que ir al armario durante las clases.
5. Hay que entregar la tarea a tiempo.
6. Hay que aprender el vocabulario de memoria.

Answers will vary.

Extension: Have students identify additional rules in your class that are not mentioned in the activity.

✓ **Assessment**
- ExamView 〰 Quiz on PresEXPRESS
QuickTake Presenter

Videohistoria
Core Instruction

Standards: 1.2

Resources: Voc. and Gram. Transparencies 29–30; Audio Program: Track 5

Focus: Presenting additional vocabulary to discuss classes

Suggestions: The *Videohistoria* is a reading task that introduces additional new vocabulary and grammar in a story context, and also provides a framework for comprehension of the video.

Pre-reading: Before students open their books, show them the transparencies for panels 1–7, covering up panel 8. Have students make predictions based on what they see. Encourage them to provide supporting details for their predictions.

Reading: Play the *Audio CD* or have volunteers read the story aloud. To check comprehension, pause after panel 4 and ask students to summarize in their own words what is happening. Use the transparencies and context clues to help students with the words in blue type.

Post-reading: Ask students to point out places in the story that give clues about the outcome. Complete *Actividad 3* to check comprehension.

 Pre-AP* Support

- **Activity:** Have students work in groups of three to create a similar classroom scene as illustrated in frames 4, 5, and 7. Ask that they use real rules and content for a class in their school. As each group presents their scene, classmates can guess the teacher and class being represented.

- **Pre-AP* Resource Book:** Comprehensive guide to Pre-AP* vocabulary skill development, pp. 47–53

Videohistoria

La clase de Esteban
jdd-0187

¿Qué pasa con Esteban el primer día de clases? Lee la historia.

Estrategia

Making inferences
As you read the story, think about why such strange things are happening to Esteban.

- Why is Esteban acting like the teacher?
- Why is his mother in the class?

1 Esteban: Bienvenidos a la clase de historia. **Algunos** de Uds. me **conocen** como Esteban. Pero hoy soy el profesor.

Pedro: Esteban piensa que es el profesor. ¡Qué divertido!

Pedro Esteban Angélica Mamá Lisa

5 Esteban: ¡No! ¡Se prohíbe ir al armario durante la clase! **Nadie** tiene el libro. Es el primer día de clases.

6 Esteban: Mamá, ¿por qué estás aquí en la clase?
Mamá: No tengo idea. ¿Y qué vas a enseñar hoy?

7 Mamá: ¿Por qué no empiezas?
Esteban: Es la clase de historia. Pienso **dar un discurso** sobre algunos de los presidentes de los Estados Unidos . . . El primer presidente fue George Washington . . .

20 veinte
Tema 1 • Tu día escolar

Differentiated Instruction
Solutions for All Learners

Advanced Learners
Have volunteers pretend to be teachers of their favorite subject. Ask them to prepare a few short sentences about what they teach and what their classroom rules are. Have students act as though they were the teacher while you pretend to be a student.

Students with Learning Difficulties
If students have difficulty with inferential reasoning, ask them questions about the visual clues in the eighth panel of the *Videohistoria:* Where is Esteban? Why are Esteban's window shades drawn? Why is Esteban's mother shaking him?

2 Esteban: Señoritas, ¿saben qué hora es?

Angélica: Hola, Esteban. Son las nueve y seis.

Esteban: Y la clase empieza a las nueve y cinco. ¿Por qué **llegan tarde** Uds.?

Lisa: Pero, ¿por qué estás tú delante de la clase? ¿Dónde está la profesora?

3 Esteban: Yo soy el profesor. ¡Y hay que estar en el asiento cuando la clase empieza!

4 Lisa: Profesor . . . necesito ir al armario. No tengo el libro.

8 Mamá: Esteban. Esteban. ¡Ya es tarde!

Esteban: ¿Qué pasa? ¿Dónde estoy? ¡Ay! El primer día de clases . . .

 Escribir/Hablar

¿Comprendiste?

1. ¿Quién es el profesor de la clase?
2. ¿Quiénes llegan tarde a la clase?
3. ¿Adónde necesita ir Lisa? ¿Por qué?
4. ¿Qué enseña Esteban?
5. ¿Sobre qué da un discurso Esteban?
6. ¿Cuáles son las reglas en la clase de Esteban?

Más práctica

- Practice Workbook, pp. 9–10: 1A-3, 1A-4
- WAV Wbk.: Video, pp. 6–8
- Guided Practice: Vocab. Check, pp. 23–26
- *Real.* para hispanohablantes, p. 13

Go Online
PHSchool.com
For: Vocab. Practice
Web Code: jdd-0103

Video
Core Instruction

 Standards: 1.2

Resources: Teacher's Resource Book: Video Script, p. 28; Video Program: Cap. 1A; Video Program Teacher's Guide: Cap. 1A

Focus: Comprehension of contextualized vocabulary

Suggestions: The video is provided in two versions, one with graphic support to highlight new words, and one without. Choose whichever of the two best suits your needs.

Pre-viewing: Ask students to describe what their classroom would be like if they were the teacher. Encourage them to invent their own rules and procedures.

Viewing: The first time you show the video, pause it at points at which students might find clues to predict the outcome. Show the video a second time without stopping.

Post-viewing: Complete the Video Activities in the *Writing, Audio & Video Workbook.*

  *Standards:* 1.2
Presentation EXPRESS
ANSWERS

Resources: Answers on Transparencies

Focus: Verifying comprehension of the *Videohistoria*

Suggestions: As you review the answers, have students indicate in which panel they found the information.

Answers:

1. Esteban es el profesor.
2. Angélica y Lisa llegan tarde a la clase.
3. Lisa necesita ir al armario. No tiene su libro.
4. Esteban enseña la clase de historia.
5. Esteban da un discurso sobre los presidentes de los Estados Unidos.
6. Hay que estar en el asiento cuando la clase empieza. Se prohíbe ir al armario durante la clase.

Enrich Your Teaching
Resources for All Teachers

Teacher-to-Teacher

Have students make a cartoon sketch of themselves as teachers. They should indicate what subject they teach in their illustration. Ask them to include speech bubbles to show that they are explaining rules to the class.

Allow them to write rules that they would implement if they were in charge and encourage them to include humorous details. Compile the cartoons into a booklet or display them on a bulletin board.

Additional Resources

- WAV Wbk.: Audio Act. 5, p. 9
- Teacher's Resource Book: Audio Script, pp. 25–26
- Audio Program: Track 6

✓ **Assessment**

- **ExamView** QuickTake Presenter Quiz on PresEXPRESS
- Prueba 1A-1: Vocab. Recognition, pp. 13–14

The *Manos a la obra* provides practice with vocabulary and grammar, along with grammar explanations, cross-curricular connections, pronunciation practice, word study, cultural information, and information on Spanish in the community and in the world of work.

Actividad 4 *Standards:* 1.1, 1.3  **Presentation EXPRESS ANSWERS**

Resources: Answers on Transparencies

Focus: Writing and speaking about classroom tasks

Recycle: *tener que* + infinitive

Suggestions: To be sure students understand what is happening in each of the pictures, ask: *¿Dónde está(n)...?* In Step 2, point out that Student A should ask questions based on the activities in Step 1.

Point out that the *Para decir más...* words are not active vocabulary, and students will not be held responsible for them elsewhere.

Answers will vary but may include:

Step 1:
1. Isabel tiene que hacer la tarea en la clase de química.
2. Luis tiene que escribir un informe sobre Shakespeare en la clase de literatura (inglés).
3. Carmen tiene que repetir las palabras en el laboratorio.
4. Marta y Eva tienen que hacer un proyecto en la clase de arte.
5. David y Clara tienen que discutir la tarea en la clase de geometría.
6. Mercedes le tiene que explicar a Ana cómo usar la computadora en el laboratorio.

Step 2:
Student A answers will vary but may include:
1. ¿En qué clase tienes que hacer la tarea?
2. ¿...escribir un informe?
3. ¿...repetir las palabras?
4. ¿...hacer un proyecto?
5. ¿...discutir la tarea?
6. ¿...explicar algo?
Student B answers will vary.

Bellringer Review
Ask students to unscramble these Spanish words for classes they might be taking:

imíqacu; glinés; riastohi

(**Answers:** química, inglés, historia)

Manos a la obra
Vocabulario y gramática en uso

Objectives
- Communicate about classroom activities and rules
- Compare rules in different classes
- Learn to use affirmative and negative words
- Review stem-changing verbs

Actividad 4   **Escribir/Hablar**

¿Qué tienen que hacer?
1 Estudia los dibujos y escribe frases para describir las actividades que estos estudiantes tienen que hacer en cada clase.

Gloria

Modelo
Gloria tiene que dar un discurso en la clase de historia.

1. Isabel

2. Luis

3. Carmen

4. Marta y Eva

5. David y Clara

6. Mercedes y Ana

2 Habla con otro(a) estudiante sobre lo que ustedes tienen que hacer en sus clases.

Modelo
A —¿En qué clase tienes que dar un discurso?
B —Tengo que dar un discurso en la clase de literatura.

Para decir más . . .
el álgebra *(f.)* algebra	**la historia** history
la biología biology	**la literatura** literature
la física physics	**la química** chemistry
la geografía geography	*Para más clases, mira la página 14.*
la geometría geometry	

Differentiated Instruction
Solutions for All Learners

Advanced Learners/Pre-AP*
Have students choose two of their favorite classes and write sentences giving advice about what a student has to do to be successful in those classes. Ask students to work in pairs and agree or disagree with their partner's advice.

Students with Learning Difficulties
To help students organize the information in *Actividad 6*, have them create a chart for their classes. Have them include the subject and one or two activities students do in each class. Encourage them to list their classes in the order they attend them to make it easier to recall information.

Actividad 5 — **Hablar**

¡Tantas actividades!

Con otro(a) estudiante, habla de lo que hacen estos estudiantes en su escuela.

Modelo

A —¿Qué hace Lisa en la clase de español?
B —Repite las palabras para aprender de memoria el vocabulario.

 **Actividad 6** — **Escribir/Hablar**

Tus clases

1 Haz una lista de cinco clases que tienes. Escribe una frase para describir lo que pasa en cada clase. Usa las expresiones del recuadro.

hacer proyectos	dar discursos
hacer preguntas	escribir informes
aprender de memoria	trabajar en el laboratorio

Modelo

En la clase de inglés, la profesora da muchos discursos.

2 Trabaja con otro(a) estudiante y comparen lo que hacen en diferentes clases.

Modelo

A —En la clase de inglés, la profesora da muchos discursos.
B —En la clase de inglés, la profesora nunca da discursos.
o: —No tengo una clase de inglés.

veintitrés **23**
Capítulo 1A

 **Actividad 5**  *Standards:* 1.1

Resources: Answers on Transparencies

Focus: Speaking about school activities

Suggestions: Discuss the location of the students in the illustration. Have students use the *Para decir más...* words on p. 22. Point out that the Spanish word for cafeteria is a cognate **(cafetería).**

Answers:

Student A answers will vary but may include:
1. ¿Qué hace Miguel en la biblioteca?
2. ¿Qué hacen Pilar, Juan y Pepe en la clase de arte?
3. ¿Qué hace Isabel en la clase de álgebra?
4. ¿Qué hace Lupe en la clase de geografía?
5. ¿Qué hacen Santiago y Ricardo en la cafetería?

Student B answers will vary but may include:
1. Estudia en la biblioteca.
2. Hacen un proyecto de arte.
3. Le hace una pregunta al profesor.
4. Da un discurso.
5. Almuerzan.

 **Actividad 6** *Standards:* 1.1, 1.3

Focus: Writing and speaking about what you do in each of your classes

Suggestions: Point out that students can describe what the teacher does in their classes as well as what the students do.

Answers will vary.

Extension: Ask students to describe a class they consider challenging. Have them present their descriptions and decide who has the most difficult class.

Enrich Your Teaching
Resources for All Teachers

Culture Note

In many Spanish-speaking countries, students take between ten and twelve courses at once. These classes do not meet every day. A geography class might meet only three days a week; a music class, twice a week. As a result, student schedules vary from day to day.

Internet Search

Have students search for schools in Spanish-speaking countries to get an idea of the classes offered.

Keywords:

colegios + (Spanish-speaking country)

Resources: Answers on Transparencies

Focus: Giving advice about how to be a good student

Suggestions: Point out that **hay que** is always followed by the infinitive, and **hay** does not change according to the subject.

Answers will vary but may include:

1. ...hay que repetir las palabras muchas veces.
2. ...hay que hacerle preguntas al (a la) profesor(a).
3. ...hay que practicar a menudo.
4. ...hay que traer los materiales de arte.
5. ...hay que sacar buenas notas ahora.
6. ...hay que estudiar mucho.

Actividad 8 *Standards:* 1.1

Focus: Giving other students advice about how to solve their problems

Suggestions: Explain to students that **tener que** is directed at a specific person while **hay que** is a more generic "one must." Point out that this difference is subtle and both phrases can often be used interchangeably.

Answers:

Student A answers will vary but may include:
1. Tengo hambre.
2. No traigo ni tijeras, ni grapadora, ni cinta adhesiva.
3. No tengo mi tarea de....
4. No entiendo la tarea de....
5. No sé las reglas.
6. Muchas veces llego tarde.
7. Hablo mal de los profesores.

Student B answers will vary but may include:
1. Tienes que almorzar.
2. Tienes que traer los materiales a clase.
3. Tienes que entregar tu tarea a tiempo.
4. Hay que pedir ayuda al (a la) profesor(a).
5. Tienes que saber las reglas.
6. Hay que llegar a tiempo.
7. Tienes que respetar a los demás.

Common Errors: Students may use the infinitive of **tener.** Remind them that they need to conjugate the verb.

Bellringer Review
To review cognates, put these words on the board and ask students to be prepared to tell you what kind of words they are and to give their English equivalent: *guitarra, ritmo, sincero, romántico, instrumento, africanos, tradicional, sentimientos.*

Actividad 7 Escribir/Hablar

Para ser un(a) buen(a) estudiante

Completa las frases. Después discute tus opiniones con las de otro(a) estudiante.

Modelo

Para sacar una buena nota, . . .
Para sacar una buena nota, hay que estudiar mucho.

1. Para aprender de memoria el vocabulario, . . .
2. Para entender mejor la tarea, . . .
3. Para leer mejor en español, . . .
4. Para hacer un proyecto de arte, . . .
5. Para ir a la universidad, . . .
6. Para un examen, . . .

¿Recuerdas?

Para has a number of different meanings. Here are some you've seen:

- *in order to*
  Estudio **para** sacar buenas notas.
- *intended for*
  Estos materiales son **para** el proyecto.
- *in (my) opinion*
  Para mí, las reglas son muy buenas.

Actividad 8 Hablar

¿Qué hago?

Habla de los problemas que tienes en la escuela. Tu compañero(a) va a decirte lo que debes hacer.

Modelo

sacar malas notas
A —*Saco malas notas en la clase de inglés.*
B —*Tienes que pedir ayuda.*
o: —*Hay que pedirle ayuda a la profesora.*

Estudiante A

1. tener hambre
2. no traer ni tijeras, ni grapadora ni cinta adhesiva
3. no tener la tarea de . . .
4. no entender la tarea
5. no saber las reglas
6. muchas veces llegar tarde
7. hablar mal de los profesores

Estudiante B

saber las reglas
almorzar
entregar la tarea a tiempo
llegar a tiempo
pedir ayuda
traer los materiales a clase
respetar a los demás
prestar atención

Estas estudiantes están tomando apuntes *(taking notes)* en su clase de historia.

24 veinticuatro
Tema 1 • Tu día escolar

Differentiated Instruction
Solutions for All Learners

Advanced Learners

To review classroom objects such as **las tijeras, la cinta adhesiva,** and **el armario,** have students pretend to give advice to very young children at school. Have them write dialogues such as: *No puedo cortar el papel. ¿Qué hago? Hay que usar las tijeras.*

Multiple Intelligences

Bodily/Kinesthetic: For *Actividad* 10, have students work in pairs and invent hand motions that represent the vocabulary in the poem. Have them recite the poem to each other, incorporating the hand motions to aid in memorization.

Actividad 9

Leer/Escribir/Hablar

¿Qué aprendes de memoria?

En la escuela debes aprender muchas palabras y fechas de memoria. En casa, aprendes números de teléfono y fechas de cumpleaños. Si te gusta la música, también aprendes canciones de memoria. Aquí hay parte de un poema muy famoso, *Versos sencillos*. Lee el poema y busca los cognados para ayudarte a entenderlo mejor. Luego contesta las preguntas.

1. ¿Cuáles son los cognados que te ayudan a entender el poema?
2. ¿Qué le da el poeta a un buen amigo? ¿Y al cruel?
3. ¿Qué palabras riman *(rhyme)* en el poema?
4. ¿Te gusta el poema? ¿Por qué?

 **Conexiones La literatura**

Versos sencillos[1]
José Martí

Cultivo una rosa blanca,
en julio como en enero,
para el amigo sincero
que me da su mano franca.

Y para el cruel que me arranca[2]
el corazón[3] *con que vivo,*
cardo[4] *ni ortiga*[5] *cultivo:*
cultivo una rosa blanca.

* * *

[1]simple [2]pulls out [3]heart [4]thistle
[5]nettle *(a thorny plant)*

 Actividad 10

Leer/Hablar

¡Aprende el poema!

Lee el poema *Versos sencillos* varias veces. Luego practica con otro(a) estudiante sin mirar las palabras. Tu compañero(a) te puede ayudar. Recita el poema en grupos pequeños o para la clase. Hay que:

- hablar claramente
- expresar emoción
- comunicar los sentimientos del poeta

Estrategia

Memorizing
Repeating out loud is a good strategy for memorizing any text, such as this poem. It will also help you to remember new vocabulary and verbs.

Fondo cultural

José Martí (1853–1895) fue un poeta y patriota cubano muy famoso. Él es un símbolo de la independencia de Cuba de los españoles. Los versos que acabas de leer son sólo una pequeña parte del poema *Versos sencillos*, en el que el poeta describe su poesía y la vida *(life)* con palabras sencillas y sinceras. Muchas personas creen que este poema es lo mejor de su trabajo literario. Las palabras de la canción "Guantanamera" son de estos versos.

- ¿Qué poema o poeta es famoso por ser símbolo de la independencia de los Estados Unidos?

Una estatua de José Martí en la ciudad de Nueva York

veinticinco **25**
Capítulo 1A

 Actividad 9 *Standards: 1.2, 1.3, 2.2, 3.1, 4.1* **Pre-AP***

Resources: Answers on Transparencies

Focus: Reading and discussing a poem by Cuban poet José Martí; cross-curricular connection to literature

Suggestions: Ask students about their favorite poem. You may want to ask an English teacher at your school for a worksheet on poetry to quickly review concepts such as rhyme scheme, verse, and meter with students. After students have found the cognates, have them read items 2–3. Ask volunteers to read the poem aloud as students listen for the answers. Have students work in groups to discuss item 4.

Answers:
1. versos, cultivo, rosa, sincero, cruel
2. una rosa blanca (a los dos)
3. blanca, franca, arranca; enero, sincero; vivo, cultivo
4. Answers will vary.

Extension: José Martí is an AP* Literature author. You may want to suggest that students read additional works by this poet.

 Actividad 10 *Standards: 1.2, 1.3, 3.1*

Focus: Reciting a poem by José Martí

Suggestions: Encourage students to memorize the poem one stanza at a time. To make it easier for students to remember all of the words, have them focus on the rhyme and rhythm of the poem.

Answers will vary.

 **Fondo cultural** *Standards: 1.2, 2.2*

Suggestions: Point out that "The Star-Spangled Banner" was originally a poem written by Francis Scott Key. If students have difficulties naming poems and poets, ask them to name songs that they consider patriotic.

Enrich Your Teaching

Resources for All Teachers

Culture Note

Students in Spanish-speaking countries often wear uniforms such as those worn by the girls in the photo on p. 24. Both public and private school students wear uniforms. Girls usually wear skirts and boys wear dark slacks and a tie. Uniforms often contribute to a sense of community within a student body.

Teacher-to-Teacher

Bring in the lyrics of **"Guantanamera"** and have students read them. Have them use cognates and context clues to help with unfamiliar vocabulary. Play the song for the class and encourage students to sing along with the music.

Practice and Communicate

Bellringer Review

Have ten students stand in a row. Ask them and other students to say what position individual students are in, using ordinal numbers.

  Standards: 1.1, 1.3, 3.1

Focus: Writing and speaking about classroom rules

Suggestions: For Step 1, have students list all of their classes and time periods before writing the rules. Point out that the ordinal numbers should agree in number and gender with *hora.*

Answers will vary.

 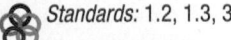 *Standards:* 1.1, 1.3

Focus: Writing and speaking about classroom activities

Suggestions: So students can talk about classes they will be taking in the future, arrange to have them use the questions to interview students in third-year Spanish.

Answers will vary.

Standards: 1.2, 1.3, 3.2

Focus: Reading and writing about authentic quotes regarding education

Suggestions: Ask students to brainstorm a list of problems society would have if education were not a priority.

Answers will vary.

Additional Resources

- WAV Wbk.: Audio Act. 6, p. 10
- Teacher's Resource Book: Audio Script, p. 26, Communicative Activity BLM, pp. 30–31
- Audio Program: Track 7

 Assessment

- Prueba 1A-2: Vocab. Production, pp. 15–16

26

 **Actividad 11** — Escribir/Hablar

Las reglas de mis clases

1 Copia esta tabla. En la tabla, escribe todas tus clases, las horas y las reglas. Luego escribe una descripción.

2 Trabaja con otro(a) estudiante y habla de las reglas en las clases. ¿Tienen las mismas reglas en las mismas clases? ¿Qué piensa tu compañero(a) de estas reglas?

Clase / Hora	Hay que . . .	Se prohíbe . . .
matemáticas /segunda	usar una calculadora	hablar con los amigos

Modelo

A —*En la clase de educación física, hay que llevar uniformes. Se prohíbe tomar refrescos. ¿Qué piensas?*

B —*En mi clase también hay que llevar uniformes y no debes tomar refrescos. ¡Estoy de acuerdo! Son buenas reglas porque . . .*

o: —*¡No estoy de acuerdo! No debemos llevar uniformes y me gustaría tomar refrescos.*

 Actividad 12 — Escribir/Hablar

Y tú, ¿qué dices?

1. ¿Qué actividades te gusta hacer en tus clases? ¿Cuáles no te gusta hacer?
2. ¿Qué proyectos haces en tus clases?
3. Piensa en las reglas de tus clases. ¿Qué regla(s) no te gusta(n)? ¿Por qué?
4. ¿Cuál es tu clase favorita este año? ¿Qué tienes que hacer en esta clase? ¿Qué se prohíbe?
5. ¿Siempre entiendes todo en tus clases? ¿Qué haces si no entiendes algo?

 Actividad 13 — Leer/Escribir

Citas sobre la educación

Lee las citas *(quotes)* sobre la educación. ¿Qué quiere decir cada persona? ¿Piensan que la educación es importante? Escoge dos citas y escribe un párrafo para compararlas. Explica lo que las citas quieren decir y da tu opinión.

"El fundamento verdadero de la felicidad: la educación". —Simón Bolívar (1783–1830), militar y político venezolano

Modelo

Las palabras de Gabriela Mistral quieren decir que hay una conexión importante entre la educación y el país. Yo estoy de acuerdo porque . . .

"Según como sea[1] la escuela, así será[2] la nación entera". —Gabriela Mistral (1889–1957), poeta y educadora chilena

"Todos los problemas son problemas de educación". —Domingo Faustino Sarmiento (1811–1888), escritor, educador y político argentino

[1]is [2]shall be

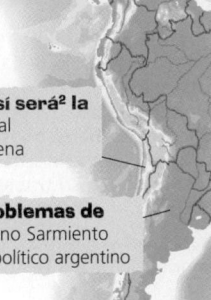

26 veintiséis
Tema 1 • Tu día escolar

Differentiated Instruction
Solutions for All Learners

Advanced Learners

Ask students to find quotes about education from thinkers in the United States. Encourage students to explain the meanings of the quotes in Spanish. Have them work in pairs to compare the quotes they found to the ones in *Actividad* 13.

Heritage Language Learners

Ask students to write an opinion essay on the topic of their favorite class. Have them use the paragraph in *Actividad* 14 as a model. Challenge them to use as many of the verbs on p. 27 as possible. Remind them to check their work for spelling, punctuation, and grammar errors.

Practice and Communicate

1A

Gramática·Repaso

Stem-changing verbs

The stem of a verb is the part of the infinitive that is left after you drop the endings -ar, -er, or -ir. For example, the stem of *empezar* is *empez-*. Stem-changing verbs have a spelling change in their stem in all forms of the present tense except the *nosotros(as)* and *vosotros(as)* forms.

There are three kinds of stem-changing verbs that you have learned. To review them, here are the present-tense forms of *poder (o → ue), empezar (e → ie),* and *pedir (e → i).*

—Si no **puedes** contestar una pregunta, ¿qué haces?
—Generalmente le **pido** ayuda a otro estudiante o al profesor.

poder (o → ue)

(yo)	**puedo**	(nosotros)(nosotras)	**podemos**
(tú)	**puedes**	(vosotros)(vosotras)	**podéis**
Ud.(él)(ella)	**puede**	Uds.(ellos)(ellas)	**pueden**

empezar (e → ie)

(yo)	**empiezo**	(nosotros)(nosotras)	**empezamos**
(tú)	**empiezas**	(vosotros)(vosotras)	**empezáis**
Ud.(él)(ella)	**empieza**	Uds.(ellos)(ellas)	**empiezan**

pedir (e → i)

(yo)	**pido**	(nosotros)(nosotras)	**pedimos**
(tú)	**pides**	(vosotros)(vosotras)	**pedís**
Ud.(él)(ella)	**pide**	Uds.(ellos)(ellas)	**piden**

GramActiva VIDEO

To learn more about stem-changing verbs, watch the **GramActiva** video.

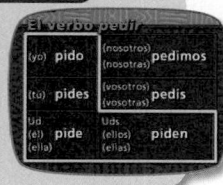

¿Recuerdas?

Here are more stem-changing verbs that follow the patterns above.

o → ue	u → ue	e → ie	e → i
almorzar	jugar	entender	servir
costar		pensar	repetir
dormir		preferir	
		querer	

Actividad 14

Leer/Escribir

Mi clase favorita

Completa las frases con la forma correcta del verbo apropiado.

Es increíble pero mi clase favorita __1.__ (empezar / entender) a las siete y media de la mañana. El profesor, el Sr. Díaz, es muy simpático y él __2.__ (pedir / entender) que todos tenemos mucho sueño en la mañana. Ningún estudiante __3.__ (dormir / querer) en esta clase porque siempre estamos muy activos. Yo creo que los estudiantes __4.__ (preferir / poder) las clases que tienen más actividades. Generalmente el Sr. Díaz __5.__ (repetir / querer) las instrucciones para las actividades dos o tres veces. A veces nosotros no __6.__ (entender / servir) los ejercicios en el libro y __7.__ (pensar / pedir) ayuda. El Sr. Díaz siempre __8.__ (jugar / poder) ayudarnos.

veintisiete 27
Capítulo 1A

Gramática·Repaso

Core Instruction

Resources: Voc. and Gram. Transparency 31; Teacher's Resource Book: Video Script, p. 28; Video Program: Cap. 1A

Suggestions: Play the *GramActiva* Video as an introduction or to reinforce your own presentation.

Have students copy the three charts on their papers and draw an outline around the forms that have stem changes. Ask them what their outlines look like. *(a boot)* Tell them to think of stem-changing verbs as "boot verbs." Point out that the stem-change only occurs in the "boot."

Direct attention to the *¿Recuerdas?* Explain to students that **jugar** follows the same pattern as **o → ue** stem-changing verbs. Have students give you forms of some of the infinitives listed.

Actividad 14

Standards: 1.2

Resources: Answers on Transparencies
Focus: Reading about a favorite class; practicing stem-changing verbs
Suggestions: Have students copy the paragraph on a sheet of paper and underline key words or phrases that help them decide which verb to choose.

Answers:
1. empieza
2. entiende
3. duerme
4. prefieren
5. repite
6. entendemos
7. pedimos
8. puede

Extension: Have students write a short paragraph describing one of their favorite classes and telling why they like it.

Enrich Your Teaching
Resources for All Teachers

Teacher-to-Teacher

Have students work in groups of three to play tic-tac-toe using stem-changing verbs. Have them make a tic-tac-toe board. To place an *X* or *O* in a square, two players must correctly write different stem-changing verbs and subjects in each square. The third student not playing judges if the verb is correct or not. If the game ends in a tie, each player must write a complete sentence using one of the verbs on the board. The one with the longest correct sentence wins.

Actividad 15 *Standards:* 1.2, 1.3

Resources: Teacher's Resource Book: GramActiva BLM, p. 35

Focus: Using a game to reinforce stem-changing verbs and to create new sentences

Recycle: Vocabulary for classes

Suggestions: Make two copies of the *GramActiva* cube template from the *Teacher's Resource Book* for each student. To save time in class, assign the first three steps for homework. Give students a minimum length for their sentences and a maximum time limit to create each one. Ask one person in each group to keep score.

Answers will vary.

 Bellringer Review

Write these sets of scrambled words on the board. Have students unscramble the words/conjugate the verbs to make logical sentences:

costar/las/calculadoras/dinero/poco

en/cafetería/la/almorzar/amigos/nuestros

(**Answers:** *Las calculadoras cuestan poco dinero. Nuestros amigos almuerzan en la cafetería.*)

Actividad 16 *Standards:* 1.1, 1.3

Focus: Writing and speaking about a typical school day

Suggestions: Before students write their sentences, have them read all the words and phrases in the box. Tell them to focus on logical ways to combine them. Remind students that when a second verb immediately follows a conjugated verb, it stays in the infinitive form.

Block Schedule

Have students work in groups and copy each word or phrase from the word box in *Actividad 16* on colored index cards, one color for each column's words. Tell them to place the cards in three piles according to the colors. Ask students to shuffle each pile before beginning. Tell them to choose one card from each pile and form a logical sentence. Allow them to add other words and phrases so that their sentences make sense. After they have written 6 sentences, have them shuffle the cards and restart.

Actividad 15 **Hablar/GramActiva**

Juego

1 Con otros(as) tres estudiantes, van a hacer dos cubos para su grupo con el modelo que les da su profesor(a).

2 Escriban un pronombre (*yo, tú, él, ella, nosotros, nosotras, Uds., ellos, ellas*) diferente en cada cara *(side)* del cubo 1. Escriban también un número diferente del 1 al 6 en cada cara.

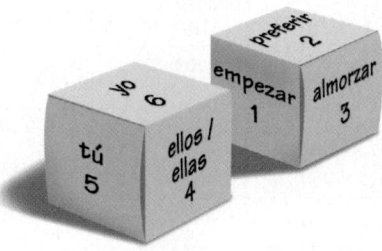

3 Escriban un infinitivo diferente en cada cara del cubo 2. Escojan entre los verbos que ves aquí. Escriban también un número diferente del 1 al 6 en cada cara.

almorzar	jugar	preferir
dormir	pedir	querer
empezar	pensar	repetir
entender	poder	servir

4 Tiren *(Roll)* los dos cubos y, según el resultado, formen una frase. Si la frase es lógica y correcta, reciben los puntos que indican los números en los cubos, pero si la frase no es ni lógica ni correcta, no reciben nada. El grupo con más puntos gana *(wins)*.

> **Modelo**
> yo (= 6 puntos) preferir (= 2 puntos)
> *Yo prefiero estudiar español y ciencias sociales.* (= 8 puntos)

Actividad 16 **Escribir/Hablar**

Un día típico

1 ¿Puedes describir tu día típico en la escuela? Usa las palabras y expresiones en el recuadro y escribe un párrafo sobre tus clases, tus compañeros, los profesores y lo que haces durante el día.

yo	almorzar	durante la clase de . . .
mi amigo(a)	empezar	en la cafetería
el (la) profesor(a)	(no) dormir	en la clase de . . .
nosotros	(no) entender	muy temprano
las clases	preferir	sacar buenas /
mis amigos	querer	malas notas

2 Ahora compara tus descripciones con las de otro(a) estudiante. Hablen de las diferencias y las semejanzas *(similarities)* en el día de cada uno de ustedes.

Estas estudiantes españolas almuerzan en la cafetería de su escuela.

28 **veintiocho**
Tema 1 • Tu día escolar

Differentiated Instruction
Solutions for All Learners

Students with Special Needs

Students who struggle with fine-motor tasks may have trouble writing on the game cubes for *Actividad 15*. Be sure to group students accordingly. Or, provide them pre-printed labels for the two cubes. Have students separate the pronoun and infinitive labels and affix them to the appropriate cube faces.

Heritage Language Learners

Students may have problems spelling words with *b* and *v*. To help them improve their spelling, have them add to the list provided in the *Pronunciación* on p. 29 and make simple crossword puzzles, along with clues. Then have students exchange puzzles and solve them.

Actividad 17 — Escribir/Hablar

Tu proyecto favorito . . .

Contesta las siguientes preguntas. Compara tus respuestas con las de otro(a) estudiante.

1. ¿En qué clases haces muchos proyectos?
2. ¿Prefieres hacer proyectos o tomar exámenes? ¿Por qué?
3. ¿Quieres hacer un proyecto en tu clase de español? ¿Qué tipo de proyecto?
4. ¿Pides ayuda cuando tienes que hacer un proyecto? ¿A quién?
5. Cuando haces un proyecto, ¿qué materiales usas?

Unos estudiantes pintan un mural en el barrio de Pilsen, Chicago, Illinois.

Pronunciación

The letters *b, v,* and *d* jdd-0188

The letters *b* and *v* are both pronounced the same. When the *b* or *v* is the first letter of a word or follows an *m* or *n*, it is pronounced like the English letter *b*. Listen to and say these words:

bien   vecinos   también   invierno

In all other positions, the letters *b* and *v* have a softer "b" sound. To produce it, put your lips close together (but not touching) and push the air through them. Listen to and say these words and sentences:

gustaba   jóvenes   árbol   devolver

Benito Vásquez era un hombre que viajaba en Brasil.

Mi novio vivía en el Caribe pero ahora vive en Buenos Aires.

Like the *b* and *v*, the Spanish *d* can have a hard or a soft sound. The *d* is hard at the beginning of a word or after *n* or *l*, like the *d* in the English word *dough*. Listen to and say these words:

donde   desfile   falda   cuando   aprender

Otherwise the *d* is soft like the English *th* in the English word *though*. Listen to the soft *d* in these words and repeat them:

ciudad   moderno   cuñado   boda   ayudar

Repeat the following *refranes*. What do you think they mean?

Un hombre que sabe dos lenguas vale por dos.

Quien mucho vive, mucho ve.

Más práctica

- Practice Workbook, p. 11: 1A-5
- WAV Wbk.: Writing, p. 13
- Guided Practice: Grammar Acts., pp. 27–28
- *Real.* para hispanohablantes, pp. 14–17

Go Online PHSchool.com
For: Stem-changing Verbs
Web Code: jdd-0104

veintinueve   **29**
Capítulo 1A

Practice and Communicate   1A

Actividad 17   *Standards:* 1.1, 1.3

Focus: Writing and speaking about favorite class projects

Suggestions: Have students talk about projects they have done for other classes in other years. Write a list on the board and have students vote on their favorite kind of project.

Answers will vary.

Extension: Have students work in groups. Ask them to choose an idea from item 3 and have them write an explanation and directions for their project. Tell them to use ordinal numbers and transition words such as *después, luego,* and *antes de.*

Pronunciación   Presentation EXPRESS AUDIO
Core Instruction

Standards: 1.2, 4.1

Resources: Teacher's Resource Book: Audio Script, p. 26; Audio Program: Track 8
Suggestions: Read the *Pronunciación* with students or play the *Audio CD.* Present the lesson in two segments: *b/v* and *d.*

Point out to students that the softer *b/v* sound is not equivalent to the *v* in English. Tell them that their upper teeth should never touch their lower lip.

Explain to students that when spelling, Spanish speakers will often say *b de burro* or *v de vaca* to differentiate between the two letters.

Tell students that when pronouncing the hard *d* sound, the tip of the tongue should be closer to the teeth than when pronouncing the English *d.*

Have students discuss the *refranes* and explain why they agree or disagree with each.

Enrich Your Teaching
Resources for All Teachers

Teacher-to-Teacher
Have students brainstorm a list of Spanish-class projects that could be done for *Tema* 1. Assign some of the projects throughout the theme. Take pictures of students doing their projects and create a bulletin board with the title: *Un hombre que sabe dos lenguas vale por dos.*

Internet Search
Have students search the Web for projects they can do for Spanish class.

Keyword: Spanish class projects

29

Standards: 1.2, 1.3

Presentation EXPRESS
ANSWERS

Resources: Voc. and Gram. Transparency 33; Answers on Transparencies

Focus: Reading and writing about the grading system in Mexico

Suggestions: Go over the *Fondo cultural* before doing *Actividad* 18. Ask students to brainstorm a list of information they expect to find on a grade report. Give students a copy of Nora's report card and have them underline the cognates and circle any unfamiliar words they cannot understand through context. After helping students understand unfamiliar vocabulary, have them work in pairs to answer the questions.

Answers:

1. La nota más alta es 10 y la nota más baja es 7.
2. Ella estudia once asignaturas.
3. Answers will vary.
4. Son para el primer semestre.

 **Fondo cultural**

Standards: 1.2, 2.1, 4.2

Suggestions: Have students compare the Mexican grading system with the one in their school. Which do they prefer? Why? To preserve student confidentiality, give each student fictitious grades to use when answering the *Fondo cultural* question.

Answers will vary.

 Pre-AP* Support

- **Activity:** Show Voc. and Gram. Transparency 33. Ask students to design a similar report card for an imaginary friend at their school. Then, have them write three true/false statements about their card to ask a partner. (You may choose to make several transparencies of the better cards and make the true/false a class activity.)

- **Pre-AP* Resource Book:** Comprehensive guide to Pre-AP* communication skill development, pp. 9–17, 36–46

Additional Resources

- WAV Wbk.: Audio Act. 7, p. 10
- Teacher's Resource Book: Audio Script, pp. 26–27
- Audio Program: Track 9

 Assessment

- **ExamView®** QuickTake Presenter Quiz on PresEXPRESS
- Prueba 1A-3: Stem-changing verbs, p. 17

30

 Actividad 18

Leer/Escribir/Hablar

¿Sacas buenas notas?

Mira las notas de Nora, una estudiante de Zacatecas, México. Observa cómo son las notas en la escuela de Nora. Observa también el número de asignaturas *(subjects)* que ella estudia.

1. ¿Cuál es la nota más alta de Nora? ¿Y la más baja?
2. ¿Cuántas asignaturas estudia Nora?
3. ¿Qué asignatura(s) estudia Nora que tú no estudias?
4. ¿Para qué semestre son las calificaciones?

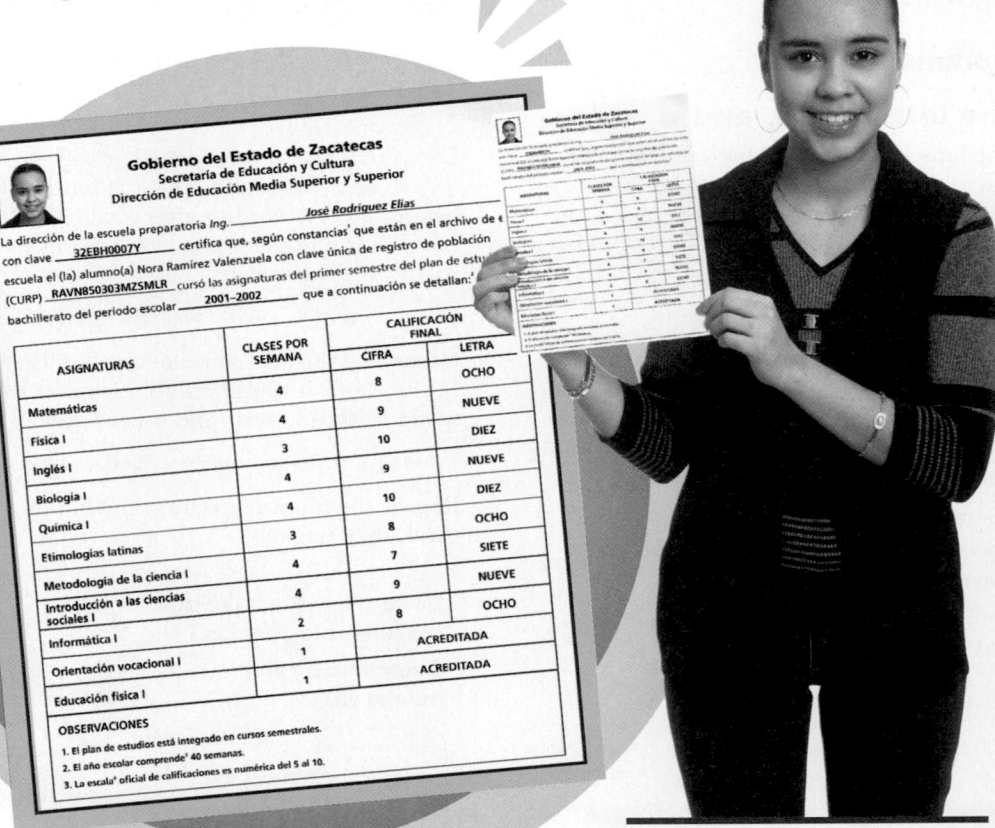

 **Fondo cultural**

Las notas El sistema de notas, o calificaciones, en México va del 1 (que es la nota más baja) al 10 (que, lógicamente, es la nota más alta). ¡Pero no todas estas notas son buenas! Para aprobar *(pass)* una asignatura necesitas una nota mínima de 6. Notas de 6 y 7 son equivalentes a una nota de "C" en los Estados Unidos. Notas de 8 son equivalentes a una "B" y las de 9 y 10 son como una "A".

- ¿Cómo son tus notas según el sistema de México?

Differentiated Instruction
Solutions for All Learners

Students with Learning Difficulties

Some students may need help interpreting information as it is presented on the report card in *Actividad* 18. Draw attention to different sections of the report card, having students underline on a photocopy the subjects in one color and the grades in a different color.

Multiple Intelligences

Visual/Spatial: Color-code students' answers for *Actividad* 19. Tell them to highlight the affirmative words in one color and the negative words in another color.

31

Gramática

Affirmative and negative words

By now you know many affirmative and negative words.

Affirmative		Negative	
alguien	*someone, anyone*	**nadie**	*no one, nobody*
algo	*something*	**nada**	*nothing*
algún, alguno(s), alguna(s)	*some, any*	**ningún, ninguno, ninguna**	*no, none, not any*
siempre	*always*	**nunca**	*never*
también	*also, too*	**tampoco**	*neither, either*

Alguno, alguna, algunos, algunas, and *ninguno, ninguna* match the number (singular or plural) and gender (masculine or feminine) of the noun to which they refer.

—¿Uds. van al laboratorio de computadoras en **algunas** clases?

—No, no vamos al laboratorio en **ninguna** clase.

When *alguno* and *ninguno* come before a masculine singular noun, they change to *algún* and *ningún.*

—¿Vas a dar **algún** discurso en la clase de inglés?

—No, no voy a dar **ningún** discurso.

¿Recuerdas?

To make a sentence negative, you usually put *no* in front of the verb.

• **No** sacamos buenas notas en la clase de álgebra.

Sometimes you can also use a negative word after the verb.

• **No** estudiamos **nunca** el sábado por la noche.

GramActiva VIDEO

Want to learn more about affirmative and negative words? Watch the **GramActiva** video.

Siempre jugamos.

Actividad 19 Leer/Escribir

Los profesores muy estrictos

Los profesores de la escuela de Hugo son muy estrictos. Completa las descripciones con la palabra apropiada.

¡La profesora de álgebra es la más estricta de la escuela! __1.__ *(Ninguno/Ningún)* estudiante quiere estudiar con ella. Hay muchas reglas en la clase __2.__ *(también/ tampoco)*. En la clase de historia, tenemos __3.__ *(ninguna/algunas)* reglas, y son muy estrictas. En nuestra escuela __4.__ *(nunca/siempre)* podemos comer __5.__ *(nada/algo)* en clase. __6.__ *(También/Tampoco)* podemos beber. En la clase de ciencias puedo trabajar con __7.__ *(nadie/alguien)* para hacer la tarea. Pero, para la clase de inglés, no podemos trabajar con __8.__ *(nadie/alguien)*. En la clase de español __9.__ *(siempre/nunca)* trabajamos en parejas o en grupos para hacer proyectos. No conozco __10.__ *(ninguna/ alguna)* escuela con tantas reglas. ¡Esta escuela tiene __11.__ *(algunos/algunas)* de los profesores más estrictos!

treinta y uno **31**
Capítulo 1A

Gramática

Presentation EXPRESS GRAMMAR

Core Instruction

 Standards: 4.1

Resources: Voc. and Gram. Transparency 32; Teacher's Resource Book: Video Script, p. 29; Video Program: Cap. 1A

Suggestions: Play the *GramActiva* Video to introduce the lesson or to reinforce your own presentation.

Direct attention to the *¿Recuerdas?* Remind students that it is acceptable and necessary to have a double negative in Spanish when a negative word follows a verb. Point out that when **alguien** and **nadie** are used as direct objects, the personal *a* is used.

On a sheet of paper, draw two stick figures side by side: one with a happy face labeled *Pablo el positivo* and the other with a frown labeled *Nano el negativo*. Tell students that they are two identical twins with opposite personalities. To help students organize negative and affirmative words, make copies of the drawings and have students list affirmative and negative words under the appropriate picture. Then work as a class to write sentences describing Pablo and Nano.

Actividad 19 *Standards:* 1.2   *Presentation EXPRESS* ANSWERS

Resources: Answers on Transparencies

Focus: Reading and writing about school rules

Suggestions: Tell students that their responses should be logical as well as grammatically correct. Have them read the paragraph once before filling in the blanks.

Answers:

1. Ningún	5. nada	9. siempre
2. también	6. Tampoco	10. ninguna
3. algunas	7. alguien	11. algunos
4. nunca	8. nadie	

Extension: Have students write several sentences about rules in their own classes, using sentences in the paragraph as models.

Teacher-to-Teacher

Have pairs of students write these words on individual cards: *alguien, nadie, algo, nada, algún, ningún, siempre, nunca, también, tampoco.* Have them shuffle their cards, place them face down, and play "Opposites Concentration" by matching pairs of opposites.

Internet Search

Nora is a student in the small town of Juchipila in the southern part of the Mexican state of Zacatecas. Have students research and write short reports about the state of Zacatecas.

Keyword: Zacatecas, Mexico

Actividad 20 Standards: 1.1   **Presentation EXPRESS** ANSWERS

Resources: Answers on Transparencies

Focus: Speaking about whom you know and what you are familiar with

Recycle: *ser;* adjectives

Suggestions: Direct students' attention to the *¿Recuerdas?* Have them identify the sentences in which the personal *a* is necessary and explain why.

Answers:
Student A:

1. ¿Conoces a algunos profesores graciosos?
2. ¿...a algunos estudiantes reservados?
3. ¿...alguna clase aburrida?
4. ¿...a alguna chica estudiosa?
5. ¿...algún libro interesante en la biblioteca?
6. ¿...algunos buenos lugares para estudiar?
7. ¿...a algunas secretarias de la escuela?

Student B answers will vary.

 **Bellringer Review**
Write these words on the board: *alguien, nadie, algo, nada, algún(o), ningún(o).* Ask students to write six sentences, using one of these words in each to tell about what is in or going on in the classroom. (Ex. *Alguien no tiene su libro. Nadie lleva un abrigo hoy.*)

 Actividad 21 Standards: 1.1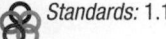

Focus: Speaking about personal experiences in school

Suggestions: Have students write notes for answering each question before they work with other students. Encourage them to ask follow-up questions to the answers they are given.

Answers will vary.

Fondo cultural Standards: 1.2, 2.1, 4.1, 4.2

■●◆●■◆●◆●■◆●■◆●■●◆●■

Suggestions: To help students answer the question, have them name two of their favorite teachers and describe them. Ask them to discuss their interactions with those teachers. Do they have the same type of relationship with their other teachers?

Answers will vary.

Actividad 20   **Hablar**

¿Qué conoces y a quién conoces?

Trabaja con otro(a) estudiante y habla de algunas personas y cosas que conoces en tu escuela.

¿Recuerdas?

Conocer means "to know" or "to be familiar with" a person, place, or thing. It is a regular *-er* verb except in the *yo* form: *conozco.* When you say that you know a person, use *a* after the verb.

• **Conozco a** Estela, la amiga de Juan.
• **¿Conoces** la escuela Benito Juárez?

When using *conocer* with *alguien* or *nadie,* use *a* after the verb, since both words refer to a person.

• **¿Conoces a** alguien en esta escuela?
• No, no **conozco a** nadie.

Modelo

estudiantes trabajadores
A —¿Conoces a <u>algunos estudiantes trabajadores</u>?
B —No, no conozco a <u>ningún estudiante trabajador</u>.
o: Sí, conozco a <u>algunos</u>. Enrique y Sara son muy <u>trabajadores</u>.

1. profesores graciosos
2. estudiantes reservados
3. clase aburrida
4. chica estudiosa
5. libro interesante en la biblioteca
6. buenos lugares para estudiar
7. secretarias de la escuela

Actividad 21   **Hablar**

¿Y en tu escuela?

Haz las siguientes preguntas a otros(as) dos estudiantes. Comparen sus experiencias en diferentes clases.

1. ¿En qué clases puedes comer? ¿En cuáles puedes beber?
2. ¿Cuándo vienes a clases los fines de semana?
3. ¿Cuándo llegas temprano a la escuela? ¿Cuándo llegas tarde a casa?
4. ¿A veces puedes trabajar con alguien en algún proyecto o alguna tarea? ¿En cuál(es)?
5. ¿Cuáles son algunas de las reglas de tu clase de español? ¿Cuáles son algunas de las reglas de tus otras clases?

 **Fondo cultural**

¿Más estrictos? En muchos países hispanohablantes *(Spanish-speaking),* las relaciones entre *(between)* los profesores y los estudiantes son más formales que en los Estados Unidos. En muchas escuelas, los estudiantes se levantan *(stand up)* cuando los profesores llegan a la sala de clases. Los estudiantes usan "usted" cuando hablan con un(a) profesor(a), y muchas veces los llaman "profesor" o "profesora" sin decir el apellido *(last name).*

• Piensa en cómo te comunicas con tus profesores. ¿En qué sentido *(way)* es similar o diferente a cómo se comunican en los países hispanohablantes? ¿Cómo afecta las relaciones entre los profesores y los estudiantes?

Differentiated Instruction
Solutions for All Learners

Advanced Learners
Give students the opportunity to be Spanish teachers. Allow time for students to present a short lesson on a topic of their choice. Would they want to be a Spanish teacher based on this experience? Why or why not?

Students with Learning Difficulties
To prepare students to write the script for *Actividad* 22, brainstorm a list of characters and vocabulary related to the situation and action. Leave the list on the board for students' reference while they write the dialogue.

Actividad 22 Escribir/Hablar

En la sala de clases

Imagina que tu clase está en un país hispanohablante. Las relaciones entre los estudiantes y los profesores son más formales. En grupos de cuatro, escriban un guión *(script)* sobre diferentes situaciones en la clase. Luego actúen su drama para la clase. Una persona es profesor(a) y los otros son estudiantes.

Modelo

La profesora entra en la sala de clases. Los estudiantes están de pie.
Clase: *Buenos días, profesora.*
La profesora: *Buenos días.*

 Actividad 23 Leer/Escribir

Y tú, ¿qué dices?

Lee lo que Joaquín te escribe por correo electrónico desde México. Luego escríbele una carta a Joaquín para contestar sus preguntas.

> ¡Hola!
>
> ¿Cómo estás? Yo estoy bien, pero tengo muchísima tarea. Tengo que escribir un informe para la clase de inglés. Quiero comparar las clases aquí en México con las clases de los Estados Unidos. ¿Me puedes ayudar? ¿Cuáles son las reglas de tus clases? ¿Qué cosas debes hacer? ¿Hay que llevar el carnet de identidad? ¿Qué se prohíbe? ¿Puedes llegar tarde a las clases? ¿Qué es lo que hay que hacer para sacar buenas notas en tus clases? Por favor, contesta mis preguntas. ¡Gracias!
>
> Joaquín

El español en el mundo del trabajo

Hace 15 años, el profesor de español, Craig Reubelt, empezó a enseñar español en la *Laboratory Schools* de la Universidad de Chicago. Empezó a estudiar español a los 13 años y vivió en México por dos años. Tiene su maestría *(master's degree)* en Literatura de la Universidad de Chicago. En los veranos, el profesor Reubelt siempre viaja a un país hispanohablante.

- ¿Qué es lo que hay que hacer para ser un(a) buen(a) profesor(a)? ¿Quieres ser profesor(a) de español?

"Me encanta enseñar español y explicar cosas sobre las culturas hispanas".

Más práctica

- Practice Workbook, pp. 12–13: 1A-6, 1A-7
- WAV Wbk.: Writing, p. 14
- Guided Practice: Grammar Acts., pp. 29–30
- *Real.* para hispanohablantes, pp. 18–21

Go Online
PHSchool.com
For: Affirmatives & Negatives
Web Code: jdd-0105

Actividad 22 *Standards:* 1.1, 1.3, 2.1, 3.2, 4.2

Focus: Writing and presenting a script about school life in a Spanish-speaking country

Suggestions: Refer students to the *Fondo cultural* on p. 32. You may wish to give them a specific situation on which to base their skits. Use a rubric for oral presentation, and review expectations before students begin.

Answers will vary.

Actividad 23 *Standards:* 1.2, 1.3 Pre-AP*

Focus: Writing about one's own school rules and policies

Suggestions: Remind students that they should include an introduction and conclusion to their response. Have them brainstorm appropriate expressions for writing a letter before they begin to write their e-mail.

Answers will vary.

El español en el mundo del trabajo
Core Instruction

 Standards: 1.2, 5.1

Suggestions: Have students discuss what they think it takes to become a Spanish teacher. What degrees do Spanish teachers need? What subjects do they need to study? Ask students to write the name of their favorite teacher and three reasons why that person is a good teacher.

Answers will vary.

Additional Resources

- WAV Wbk.: Audio Act. 8–9, p. 11
- Teacher's Resource Book: Audio Script, p. 27, Communicative Activity BLM, pp. 32–33
- Audio Program: Tracks 10–11

 Assessment

- ExamView QuickTake Presenter Quiz on PresEXPRESS
- Prueba 1A-4: Affirmative and negative words, p. 18

Enrich Your Teaching
Resources for All Teachers

Teacher-to-Teacher

Create categories for oral presentations, such as most original, funniest, and most accurate. Put a list of these categories on the board while groups are performing. After the last skit, have students vote for each category. This will not only motivate performers, it will also keep students in the audience focused.

Teacher-to-Teacher

Opportunities to study Spanish abroad exist in many Spanish-speaking countries. University students can live with host families and learn Spanish while experiencing the culture of the country.

Lectura

Core Instruction

 Standards: 1.2, 3.2

Focus: Reading about good study habits

Suggestions: The *¡Adelante!* section of the chapter provides culminating activities and high-interest information. The *Lectura* offers students authentic reading tasks drawn from many different sources.

Pre-reading: Direct attention to the *Estrategia.* Have students identify and then write the subheads on a piece of paper in three columns to use as they read.

Reading: Have volunteers read each of the three sections aloud. Stop after each section and ask students to look for at least one piece of advice to write under the appropriate subhead on their papers.

Post-reading: Ask students to share the advice they wrote for each section. Have students add their own tips to their lists. Allow them to use their lists to complete the *¿Comprendiste?* questions.

Bellringer Review
Place this chart on the board:

Un(a) estudiante bueno(a)	Un(a) estudiante malo(a)

Have students fill in the chart with the different study habits of successful and unsuccessful students.

¡Adelante!

Lectura

Para estudiar mejor . . .

Para comprender bien tus clases y sacar buenas notas, es importante estudiar bien. Pero hay muchos estudiantes que no saben estudiar. A veces no prestan atención y otras veces no piden ayuda cuando no entienden algo. Lee estos consejos *(advice)* para estudiar mejor de la revista española *Okapi.*

Objectives

- Read and understand an article about good study habits
- Make a coat of arms
- Describe what you would do if you were principal for a day
- Read about Guanajuato, Mexico

Estrategia

Using heads and subheads
Reading the heads and subheads in an article will often help you anticipate the material being presented. Before you read the magazine article below, try reading the head and subheads. What kinds of advice do you think will be in the article?

¡ENTRE NOSOTROS!

REGLAS DE ORO[1] para estudiar mejor

Silvia López, fiel lectora[2] de *Okapi,* nos da estas interesantes técnicas de estudio para los exámenes. Queremos repetirlas aquí para todos ustedes.

[1]gold   [2]faithful reader

34 treinta y cuatro
Tema 1 • Tu día escolar

Differentiated Instruction
Solutions for All Learners

Advanced Learners
Have students prioritize study habits that they use to be successful in school. Have them create posters, using words and illustrations, to hang in the classroom to remind the class about good study habits.

Students with Learning Difficulties
Help students summarize the study tips in the reading and create a flyer that lists them. Post the flyer on the bulletin board and make individual copies for students. Tell them to refer to the flyer throughout the year to help them study.

¿Comprendiste?

1. ¿Cierto o falso? No es necesario estudiar a la misma hora todos los días.
2. ¿Según el artículo, es importante ser una persona organizada?
3. ¿Qué consejos del artículo ya *(already)* practicas?
4. ¿Qué piensas de estos consejos? ¿Son fáciles de seguir *(to follow)* en tu casa?
5. ¿Qué otros consejos para estudiar mejor les puedes dar a tus compañeros?

Más práctica

- WAV Wbk.: Writing, p. 15
- Guided Practice: *Lectura*, p. 31
- *Real.* para hispanohablantes, pp. 22–23

Go Online
PHSchool.com
For: Internet Activity
Web Code: jdd-0106

 **Fondo cultural** ■◆◇◆◆◇◆■◆

Okapi es una revista publicada en España para jóvenes. Tiene artículos sobre el mundo de hoy: los estudios, la vida social, la música, la escuela. Hay secciones dedicadas a las ciencias, los deportes, la historia, la tecnología, los libros y mucho más. Las actividades y los consejos pueden interesar a todos.

- ¿Lees una revista similar a *Okapi*? ¿Qué tipo de información hay en las revistas que tú lees?

¿Qué debes hacer a la hora de estudiar?

Para estudiar mejor necesitas una buena organización del trabajo y unos hábitos saludables. Siempre debes ser positivo. Repite frases como "yo puedo hacerlo" o "soy capaz[3]". Cuida[4] tus libros y otros materiales. Generalmente una persona constante, organizada y trabajadora tiene buenos resultados en los estudios.

¿Cómo puedes organizarte para estudiar?

Establece un horario fijo para estudiar y planifica tu tiempo. Tienes que pasar suficiente tiempo para llegar al punto de máxima concentración. También

debes planear unos pequeños descansos de 5 a 10 minutos. Y si no entiendes algo, pide ayuda: ¡Tus padres o tus hermanos mayores te pueden ayudar!

¿Cómo puedes estudiar mejor y sacar buenas notas?

Tienes que cuidarte. Debes comer bien y dormir lo suficiente. Por ejemplo, no es bueno estudiar muy tarde por la noche antes de un examen. Debes estar tranquilo, sin estar ni nervioso ni ansioso. La tranquilidad emocional te ayuda a pensar mejor. También tienes que cuidar tu vista:[5] cuando lees, el libro debe estar a 35–40 cm de distancia de tus ojos y siempre debes usar una buena lámpara.

[3]capable   [4]Take care of   [5]vision

treinta y cinco **35**
Capítulo 1A

¿Comprendiste?
Presentation EXPRESS
ANSWERS

Standards: 1.2

Resources: Answers on Transparencies

Focus: Verifying reading comprehension

Suggestions: If you had students create lists as they read the *Lectura*, allow them to use these as they answer the questions. Encourage students to answer in complete sentences, even if the answer requires only a "yes" or "no" answer.

Answers:
1. Falso. Es necesario establecer un horario fijo para estudiar.
2. Sí, es importante ser una persona organizada.
3. Answers will vary.
4. Answers will vary.
5. Answers will vary.

Fondo cultural   *Standards:* 1.2, 2.2, 4.2
◆■◇■◆■◇◆■◆◇◆■◆◇■◆◇■■◆

Suggestions: If possible, bring in copies of *Okapi* or similar magazines, or find online versions on the Web. Ask students to skim the magazines and describe the types of articles they see. Have students bring in magazines they like to read to use as a reference when answering the *Fondo cultural* question.

Answers will vary.

Pre-AP* Support

- **Activity:** Divide students into groups of three. Assign each of the three students one of the subtitled sections to read silently and then write a multiple choice question about it. Finally, have each student read aloud his or her section while the group members follow along. Once all sections have been read, have them ask each other their multiple-choice questions.

- *Pre-AP* Resource Book:* Comprehensive guide to Pre-AP* reading skill development, pp.18–24

For Further Reading
Student Resources:

- Realidades para hispanohablantes: Lectura 2, pp. 24–25
- Lecturas para hispanohablantes 2: "Cuaderno de tareas," pp. 68–70
- Guided Practice: Lectura, p. 31

 AP* Literature Author: Antonio Machado, Lecturas para hispanohablantes 2, "Recuerdo infantil," p. 72

Teacher-to-Teacher

Write all of the rules mentioned in the reading on individual pieces of paper, making enough copies so that everyone in the class has one rule. Have students work in groups. Tell one student to act out a rule while the others try to guess which one it is. To encourage variety, have some students act out what not to do.

La cultura en vivo

Core Instruction

 Standards: 1.2, 1.3, 2.2, 3.1

Focus: Creating a coat of arms for the school

Suggestions: The *La cultura en vivo* sections introduce students to cultural products of the Spanish-speaking world. In alternate chapters, there is the *Perspectivas del mundo hispano,* which presents cultural perspectives.

Bring in samples of coats of arms from history books or find university logos that contain coats of arms. Ask students to point out symbols and colors and give their opinions about why they think they were chosen. If possible, bring in your own family coat of arms and explain the symbols to students. Ask interested students to research the meanings of various colors and symbols in heraldry (the study of coats of arms and emblems).

Ask the woodshop teacher at your school to make you a blank coat of arms. Have the class vote on the best coat of arms and allow the winning group to transfer their drawing onto the wood. Hang the winning coat of arms in the classroom.

Extension: Have students research their family coat of arms. Ask volunteers to present their coat of arms and explain how they symbolize the history of their family.

Teacher-to-Teacher

e-amigos: Pair students to be *e-amigos.* Have them socialize by sending each other e-mails. Ask them to introduce themselves and to exchange information about their classes. Encourage them to ask questions about their partner's classes. Have students print out their e-mails or send them to you for your review.

Additional Resources

Student Resource: Realidades para hispanohablantes, p. 26

Un nuevo escudo de armas

Los escudos de armas[1] son una manera antigua de identificar a las familias importantes o a los reyes[2]. Los escudos tienen símbolos, animales y colores que representan a la familia. Hoy, muchas familias continúan usando los escudos de armas. Muchas compañías, universidades y escuelas también usan escudos de armas que son una versión moderna de esta manera de identificación.

¡Compruébalo! ¿Tiene tu escuela un escudo de armas? Investiga si tu escuela tiene uno y cuál es su significado.

Objetivo

Haz un escudo de armas para tu escuela. Si tu escuela tiene uno, haz otro nuevo.

Figura 1 Éste es el escudo del Reino de España. En la parte de arriba está la corona *(crown)* de los reyes.

Materiales

• hojas grandes de papel
• lápices de colores

Instrucciones

Trabaja con un grupo de tres o cuatro estudiantes.

1 Piensen en los símbolos de su escuela. ¿Cómo pueden usar estos símbolos en su nuevo escudo?

2 Dibujen la forma de un escudo o hagan una copia del escudo en la Figura 2.

3 Escojan tres o más símbolos.

4 Escojan tres o más colores.

5 Escojan un lema[3] en español para la escuela, por ejemplo, *Siempre listos* o *Salud, trabajo y bienestar.*

6 Dibujen el escudo y preséntenlo a la clase.

[1]coats of arms   [2]kings   [3]slogan

Figura 2

Differentiated Instruction
Solutions for All Learners

Advanced Learners

Have students search the Web for information on the official coat of arms of Spain or of the royal family. Have them write a report explaining how the symbols reflect the history of the country.

Students with Learning Difficulties

To help students prepare for their oral presentation, encourage those with oral expression difficulties to tape-record or videotape a practice presentation. They can then play it back and make appropriate adjustments to their rate, intonation, volume, and nonverbal gestures.

Presentación oral

Director(a) por un día

Task
You have been invited to be principal for a day. Your first task is to create some new school rules and display them on a poster. Be creative! After you complete the poster, present it to the class.

1 Prepare Make a list of six new school rules. Include three things students must do and three that are not allowed. You want to create a very supportive environment where people will learn better. Then make a poster to illustrate your rules.

2 Practice Using the illustrations on your poster, go through your presentation several times. You can use your notes when you practice, but not when you present. Be sure to:
- include three things that students must do and three things that are not allowed
- use complete sentences
- speak clearly

Estrategia

Brainstorming
Before you prepare a presentation, think of all the possible ideas for your project. List *all* your ideas, without judging whether they are good or bad. Then go back and review your list. Pick the best ones for your presentation.

Modelo

Éstas son mis reglas nuevas: Todos los estudiantes deben hacer preguntas si no entienden algo. Y hay que . . . ¡Se prohíbe hablar inglés en la clase de español! Y tampoco deben . . .

3 Present Tell your classmates your new school rules, using the visuals on your poster.

4 Evaluation Your teacher may give you a rubric for how the presentation will be graded. You probably will be graded on:
- how complete your presentation is
- how easy it is to understand you
- how clearly the visuals on your poster illustrate your rules

treinta y siete **37**
Capítulo 1A

Presentación oral
Core Instruction

Standards: 1.3, 3.1

Focus: Speaking about appropriate and inappropriate school behavior

Suggestions: The *Presentación oral* helps students learn to build oral presentations of many sorts using a four-step approach. In alternate chapters, there is a parallel *Presentación escrita.*

To help students brainstorm, suggest that they think about the rules in their own school. Are there any rules that don't work? Are there some that could be improved? Also encourage students to think about problems in school that could be prevented by rules.

Review the four-step approach with students. Emphasize the importance of planning and practicing for an oral presentation. Remind students to use their visual presentation to help organize their oral presentation.

Portfolio

Record students' oral presentations on cassette or videotape for inclusion in their portfolios.

Pre-AP* Support

- *Pre-AP* Resource Book:* Comprehensive guide to Pre-AP* speaking skill development, pp. 36–46

Additional Resources
Student Resources: Realidades para hispanohablantes, p. 27; Guided Practice: Presentación oral, p. 32

✓ Assessment
- Assessment Program: Rubrics, p. T27

Give students copies of the rubric before they begin the activity. Go over the descriptions of the different levels of performance. After assessing students, help individuals understand how their performance could be improved.

Enrich Your Teaching
Resources for All Teachers

RUBRIC	Score 1	Score 3	Score 5
Completeness of your task	You provide some of the information required.	You provide most of the information required.	You provide all of the information required.
How easily you are understood	You are difficult to understand and have many grammatical errors.	You are fairly easy to understand and have occasional grammatical errors.	You are easy to understand and have very few grammatical errors.
How clearly your visuals match your rules	You provide four visuals that clearly match your rules.	You provide five visuals that clearly match your rules.	You provide six visuals that clearly match your rules.

Videomisterio

Core Instruction

Standards: 1.2, 3.2, 5.2

Resources: Voc. and Gram. Transparencies: Map 12

Focus: Reading about Guanajuato to prepare for the *Videomisterio*

Suggestions: Before reading the introductory paragraph, have students find Guanajuato on the map. Have students locate Mexico City, the Pacific Ocean, the Gulf of Mexico, and the United States. Point out that Guanajuato, the capital city of the state of Guanajuato, is bordered on the north by the Sierra Central region, which includes San Miguel de Allende and Dolores Hidalgo, two other cities students will get to know in the *Videomisterio*.

To give students perspective on the size of Guanajuato, have them research the population of their town or city, as well as various cities in their state.

Direct attention to the photo of **las estudiantinas**. Explain that these are student groups that dress in medieval attire and stroll through the streets singing and playing their music. This custom is based on the Spanish tradition of **las tunas.** The tradition was brought to Guanajuato in 1963, and today it is an important part of the culture of the city. Large groups of people follow the musicians as they tour the city's narrow streets singing songs and telling stories.

Point out the photo of the *Bocamina de la Valenciana* mine and ask students if they have ever visited a mine. If so, where? What was it like?

Ask students to look at the photo of *El Pípila*, and ask them to predict its actual size. Tell them that the statue is 26 meters (85 feet) tall. Explain that Juan Olaguíbel built it in 1939 and that it contains an interior staircase that visitors can use to climb to the top. Point out that the *Alhóndiga de Granaditas* is a fortress that was built between 1798 and 1809, and was the site of one of the first battles for Mexican independence from Spain.

Videomisterio

Preparación para . . .

En busca de la verdad

Guanajuato

Bienvenidos a Guanajuato, lugar principal del *Videomisterio*. A unos 450 kilómetros al noroeste de la Ciudad de México, Guanajuato tiene una población de más de 141,000 habitantes y es una ciudad con mucha historia. En los dos primeros Temas, van a conocer algunos lugares que tienen importancia en el video *En busca de la verdad*. Van a empezar a ver el video con el Tema 3.

Esta bella ciudad tiene una hermosa arquitectura del período colonial (siglos[1] XVI a XVIII). Esto fue posible gracias a la riqueza[2] de sus minas durante la colonización española de México. Estas minas hicieron de Guanajuato una ciudad muy importante, con costumbres y tradiciones españolas.

Hoy en día, Guanajuato todavía es una de las ciudades mexicanas más importantes en la producción de plata[3]. Sus minas, tal como la *Bocamina de la Valenciana,* son lugares de mucho valor histórico y cultural. ▶

Guanajuato es famosa por sus grandes héroes y batallas de la independencia mexicana (1810–1821). "El Pípila" es un monumento en homenaje al minero Juan José Martines de los Reyes. En 1810 él se convirtió en héroe cuando le prendió fuego[4] a la puerta de la fortificación española, llamada *Alhóndiga de Granaditas.* ▶

[1]centuries [2]riches [3]silver [4]set fire

38 treinta y ocho
Tema 1 • Tu día escolar

Las *estudiantinas* de Guanajuato son grupos de jóvenes que pasean cantando y caminando por las calles. Llevan trajes de diferentes colores y tocan instrumentos musicales. ▼

Differentiated Instruction
Solutions for All Learners

Advanced Learners
Have students search the Internet to find study-abroad programs that offer summer classes at the *Universidad de Guanajuato*. Ask them to choose a program and write a report describing what classes they would like to take and where they would like to live. Have them include information about cost, lodging, and dates.

Students with Learning Difficulties
Students may have difficulty putting the dates in Mexican history into perspective. Give them a timeline with important dates in American history and have them use a colored pencil to write in the historical dates mentioned in the reading. Encourage them to add dates to the timeline when viewing *Videomisterio* episodes.

Guanajuato es famosa por sus estrechas y empedradas[5] calles, llamadas *callejones*. También es un gran centro artístico, intelectual y cultural. Aquí nació el muralista Diego Rivera. Hay una respetada universidad en el centro. También hay una gran cantidad de museos, algunos artísticos, como el *Museo Iconográfico del Quixote*, y otros raros[6], como el *Museo de la Momia*.

Guanajuato celebra cada octubre el *Festival Cervantino*. Es en honor al escritor español Miguel de Cervantes y llegan personas de todo el mundo.

¿Sabes que . . . ?

Guanajuato tiene muchas calles subterráneas. Las calles son productos de las viejas minas y antiguos ríos. Éstas permiten que los coches pasen por la ciudad sin afectar la arquitectura colonial y estilo de vida guanajuatense.

Para pensar

La belleza colonial y la vida cultural de Guanajuato atrae a visitantes de todo el mundo. ¿Qué ciudad estadounidense conoces que hace lo mismo?

Suggestions: Direct attention to the photo of the **callejón**, a narrow street or alleyway that is typical of the city of Guanajuato. Tell students about the famous *Callejón del Beso*. Explain that when the **estudiantinas** get to the *Callejón del Beso,* they tell a story similar to that of Romeo and Juliet and encourage couples to follow the tradition of kissing at the bottom of the street.

Point out the photo of the statues of Don Quixote and Sancho Panza. Ask students if they have ever read anything written by Miguel de Cervantes. Have they ever seen the movie or play, *The Man of La Mancha?* The festival is one of the most important arts festivals held in a Spanish-speaking country. It attracts nearly 150,000 visitors annually. It has been held in Guanajuato every October since 1972.

To help students answer the *Para pensar* question, have them research colonial cities in the United States. You may prefer to list colonial cities on the board and have students who have visited them give descriptions and explanations for why they are popular among tourists.

Answers will vary.

Extension: Ask students to choose their favorite colonial city and write a tourist brochure describing the city's history and attractions. If possible, encourage them to include photos of the city that they took when they visited there, or have them download visuals from the Internet.

✓ **Assessment**
• **Exam**View ⊙ Quiz on PresEXPRESS
QuickTake Presenter

[5] narrow and cobblestoned   [6] strange

Enrich Your Teaching
Resources for All Teachers

Culture Note

Miguel de Cervantes was one of the greatest writers Spain has ever produced. His most famous work of fiction, *Don Quixote,* was published when Cervantes was already middle-aged. Prior to its publication, Cervantes had been held for a time as a slave in North Africa and had served with distinction in the Spanish Army.

Internet Search

Keywords:

Festival Cervantino + Guanajuato

Review Activities

The *Repaso del capítulo* summarizes all the active vocabulary and grammar for the chapter. It provides a useful study tool for review and test preparation. In each chapter, you will also find suggestions for review activities.

To talk about what you do in class:
Have students work in groups to copy each expression on a slip of paper. Give each group a brown paper bag to fill with the expressions. Tell students to take turns choosing a phrase, and acting it out for the others to guess.

To talk about classroom rules: Have partners use flashcards and take turns starting and finishing sentences. Student A gives an oral sentence such as *Hay que llegar a la clase ___.* Student B holds up the correct flashcard **(a tiempo).** Tell students to use the word **espacio** to indicate where the missing words belong.

To name school objects: Some objects are likely to be in the classroom, so Student A can point to an item and ask Student B *¿Qué es esto?* For words for objects not found in the classroom, have students take turns making simple drawings for their partner to identify.

Negative and affirmative words: Have Student A use one of the negatives in a sentence. Student B disagrees, and uses the corresponding affirmative word in a sentence. Partners then switch roles.

Portfolio

Invite students to review the activities they completed in this chapter, including written reports, posters or other visuals, tapes of oral presentations, or other projects. Have them select one or two items that they feel best demonstrate their achievements in Spanish to include in their portfolios, with the Chapter Checklist and Self-Assessment Worksheet.

Additional Resources

Student Resources: Realidades para hispanohablantes, p. 28

 **CD–ROM**

PuzzleView Web Code: jdd–0107

Teacher Resources:
- Teacher's Resource Book: Situation Cards, p. 34, Clip Art, pp. 36–38
- Assessment Program: Chapter Checklist and Self-Assessment Worksheet, pp. T56–T57

Repaso del capítulo

Vocabulario y gramática jdd-0189

To prepare for the test, check to see if you . . .
- know the new vocabulary and grammar
- can perform the tasks on p. 41

to talk about what you do in class

aprender de memoria	to memorize
contestar	to answer
dar un discurso	to give a speech
discutir	to discuss
explicar	to explain
hacer una pregunta	to ask a question
el informe	report
el laboratorio	laboratory
la palabra	word
pedir ayuda	to ask for help
el proyecto	project
sacar una buena nota	to get a good grade

to talk about classroom rules

a tiempo	on time
entregar	to turn in
llegar tarde	to arrive late
prestar atención	to pay attention
la regla	rule
respetar	to respect
se prohíbe . . .	it's forbidden . . .

to name school objects

el armario	locker
el asiento	seat
el carnet de identidad	I.D. card
la cinta adhesiva	transparent tape
la grapadora	stapler
los materiales	supplies, materials
las tijeras	scissors

For *Vocabulario adicional,* see pp. 498–499.

negative and affirmative words

alguien	someone, anyone
algún, alguna, algunos, -as	some, any
nadie	no one, nobody
ningún, ninguno, -a	no, none, not any

(See p. 31 for a complete chart.)

other useful words

conocer	to know
lo que	what
sobre	on, about

almorzar (o → ue) *to have lunch*

almuerzo	almorzamos
almuerzas	almorzáis
almuerza	almuerzan

empezar (e → ie) *to start, to begin*

empiezo	empezamos
empiezas	empezáis
empieza	empiezan

entender (e → ie) *to understand*

entiendo	entendemos
entiendes	entendéis
entiende	entienden

repetir (e → i) *to repeat*

repito	repetimos
repites	repetís
repite	repiten

Differentiated Instruction
Solutions for All Learners

Advanced Learners

Pair teachers with students, and ask students to conduct a survey of rules in other classes. Have them compare rules across classes and compile their results into a graph that shows similarities among rules. Ask them to write a short summary of the results.

Heritage Language Learners

Have students search the Web for the coats of arms of their heritage countries or of their families. Have them write a short paragraph about the key symbols and their significance.

Más práctica

- Practice Workbook: Puzzle, p. 14
- Practice Workbook: Organizer, p. 15

Go Online PHSchool.com
For: Test Preparation
Web Code: jdd-0107

Preparación para el examen

jdd-0189

On the exam you will be asked to . . .	Here are practice tasks similar to those you will find on the exam . . .	If you need review . . .
1 Escuchar Listen to and understand how students describe what they must do and what they cannot do in class	Listen as two students compare their Spanish classes. (a) What are two things that students do in both classes? (b) What are two things that are different? (c) Which class would you prefer? Why?	**pp. 18–21** *A primera vista*
2 Hablar Ask and respond to statements made about classroom activities	Your teacher has asked you and a partner to see which classroom activities are the most common. Each of you will make a chart with a list of your classes across the top. Then think of five or six classroom activities and write them down the side of your chart. Write an *X* next to the activities that you do in each class. Then describe how often you do these activities. *Doy discursos en las clases de historia, español e inglés. Hablo sólo español en la clase de español todos los días.*	**p. 22** Actividad 4 **p. 23** Actividades 5–6 **p. 24** Actividad 7 **p. 28** Actividades 15–16 **p. 29** Actividad 17 **p. 32** Actividad 21
3 Leer Read and understand a list of typical classroom rules	Read the rules below. Write the numbers 1–5 and then write a *P* for those statements that you think were the idea of *un(a) profesor(a)* or an *E* for those you think were written by *un(a) estudiante*. 1. Se prohíbe hacer la tarea a tiempo. 2. Hay que pedir ayuda si no entiendes. 3. Hay que prestar atención. 4. Se prohíbe traer libros a la clase de literatura. 5. Hay que dormir en las clases.	**p. 31** Actividad 19 **p. 33** Actividad 23 **p. 37** *Presentación oral*
4 Escribir Write a paragraph about your favorite class	In a short paragraph, describe your favorite class. Include: (a) what you do in the class; (b) the kind of homework you have.	**p. 26** Actividad 12 **p. 27** Actividad 14 **p. 29** Actividad 17
5 Pensar Demonstrate an understanding of coats of arms	You are researching *los escudos* before creating one for an assignment. A list of Web sites gives historical examples from Spanish-speaking countries. Based on what you have learned, what types of decoration would you expect to find on them? Where would they be displayed?	**p. 36** *La cultura en vivo*

cuarenta y uno **41**
Capítulo 1A

Differentiated Assessment
Solutions for All Learners

STUDENTS NEEDING EXTRA HELP
- **Alternate Assessment Program:** Examen del capítulo 1A
- **Audio Program CD 20:** Chap. 1A, Track 2

HERITAGE LEARNERS
- **Assessment Program: Realidades para hispanohablantes:** Examen del capítulo 1A
- **ExamView** Heritage Learner Test Bank

ADVANCED/PRE-AP*
- **ExamView** Pre-AP* Test Bank
- **Pre-AP* Resource Book,** pp. 96–99

Performance Tasks
 Standards: 1.1, 1.2, 1.3, 2.2

Presentation EXPRESS ANSWERS

Student Resource: Realidades para hispanohablantes, p. 29

Teacher Resources: Teacher's Resource Book: Audio Script, p. 27; Audio Program: Track 13; Answers on Transparencies

Suggestions: *The Preparación para el examen* provides students with performance tasks very similar to those they will encounter on the chapter test in the Assessment Program. Explain that if they can carry out these tasks, they will be able to succeed on the test.

1. Escuchar

Suggestions: Use the *Audio CD* or read the script.

 **Script:**

Girl #1: ¿Cómo es tu clase de español? En mi clase hay que entregar la tarea cada día y escribir un informe cada semana. También contestamos preguntas y hay que practicar en el laboratorio.
Girl #2: ¡Ay! ¿Mucho trabajo, no? En mi clase hay que prestar atención, pero no entregamos la tarea cada día. Practicamos y contestamos preguntas en el laboratorio. Discutimos algo de interés cada día en español y hacemos muchos proyectos.

Answers:
(a) They answer questions and they practice in the laboratory; (b) One student turns in homework every day and writes a report every week. The other student is involved in discussions in Spanish every day and does a lot of projects; (c) Answers will vary.

2. Hablar

Suggestions: Have students include expressions such as **siempre, a veces,** and **nunca** in their responses. **Answers** will vary.

3. Leer

Suggestions: Have students discuss your classroom rules before they read.

Answers: 1. E; 2. P; 3. P; 4. E; 5. E

4. Escribir

Suggestions: Before they write the paragraph, have students make a T-chart and brainstorm items for each category.

Answers will vary.

5. Pensar

Suggestions: Have students look back at the designs on p. 36 and think of other coats of arms that they have seen.

Answers will vary.

✓ Assessment
- **ExamView** QuickTake Presenter Quiz on PresEXPRESS
- Assessment Program: Examen del capítulo
- **ExamView** Test Bank: Tests A and B
- Audio Program CD 20: Chap. 1A, Track 2

41

RECYCLE
A ver si recuerdas

Vocabulary
• El tiempo libre

Grammar
• The verb *ir*

A primera vista	Manos a la obra	¡Adelante!	Repaso

Learning Sequence

INPUT	PRACTICE	APPLICATION	REVIEW
• Introduce vocabulary and grammar within an authentic context.	• Practice and develop new vocabulary. • Learn and practice new grammar structures.	• Apply vocabulary and grammar through culminating, theme-based activities. • Apply skill development.	• Review vocabulary and grammar.

Objectives

Read, listen to, and interpret information about • Extracurricular activities	• Communicate about extracurricular activities. • Compare people or things. • Talk about how long people have been doing things. • Use the verbs *saber* and *conocer*.	• Read a Web page about a dance school. • Compare schools in the United States, Mexico, and Spain. • Write a paragraph about your extracurricular activities and interests. • Read Intro: San Miguel de Allende, Mexico.	• Prepare for the chapter test.

Culture

• Antonio Berni	• *Las actividades extracurriculares* • *Los deportes más populares* • Fernando Botero • Celia Cruz	• *El ballet* • *¡A bailar!*	• Describe the role and importance of dance in Spanish-speaking cultures.

Vocabulary	Grammar	Learner Support
• Extracurricular activities • Internet activities	• *Saber* and *conocer* • *Hacer* + time expressions	

STRATEGIES
• Using visuals
• Predicting
• Personalizing

RECYCLING ♻
• Actividad 5
• Actividad 8
• Actividad 12
• Actividades 19–20
• Extracurricular activities

• Descriptive adjectives
• Comparatives
• Leisure activities
• Expressions of time

Chapter Features

Exploración del lenguaje
Nouns and Verbs

El español en la comunidad
Classes for salsa dancing

Conexiones
The Computer: Creating a Web page

Beyond the Classroom: States & Countries

Cuba
República Dominicana
Texas
Puerto Rico
México
Venezuela
Nicaragua
Colombia
Argentina

Student Resources

TECHNOLOGY

ONLINE

Interactive Textbook
• Student Edition Online plus audio, video, and flashcards

Go Online Companion Web Site
• Tutorial activities
• Self-tests
• Internet links
• Downloadable MP3 audio files
• **PuzzleView**

CD-ROM

Interactive Textbook CD-ROM
Student Edition on CD-ROM plus audio, video, and flashcards

MindPoint™ CD-ROM QUIZ SHOW

PRINT MATERIAL

CORE INSTRUCTION
Practice Workbook, pp. 16–26
• Review
• Grammar
• Organizer
• Vocabulary
• Puzzle

Writing, Audio & Video Activities, pp. 16–24
• Video
• Writing
• Audio

Grammar Study Guide 1–2 (or 3–4)

Differentiated Instruction

STUDENTS NEEDING EXTRA HELP
Guided Practice Activities, pp. 33–52
• Vocabulary Flash Cards and Vocabulary Check
• Grammar Activities
• Presentación escrita

HERITAGE LEARNERS
Realidades para hispanohablantes, pp. 30–49

Lecturas para hispanohablantes
• "Asignatura pendiente," pp. 73–74
• "AP* Literature Author: Isabel Allende, *Paula* (excerpt), pp. 76–78

ADVANCED/PRE-AP*
Pre-AP* Resource Book: Student Activity Sheet, p. 99

Teacher Resources

TECHNOLOGY

Audio Program
Video Program

Fine Art Transparencies
Vocabulary and Grammar Transparencies
Answers on Transparencies

TeacherEXPRESS™ CD-ROM
• Lesson Planner
• Web Resources
• Teacher Edition with Interactive Links
• Vocabulary Clip Art
• Teaching Resources

PresentationEXPRESS™ CD-ROM
• Vocabulary
• Grammar
• Audio
• Tranparencies and Maps
• Photo Gallery
• Clip Art

PH SuccessNet ONLINE
• Access to grades and reports from Online Interactive Textbook

ExamView® QuickTake Presenter on Presentation Express CD-ROM
• Vocabulary Quizzes
• Grammar Quizzes
• Chapter Test

TeacherEXPRESS™ CD-ROM
• Assessment Program
• **ExamView®** test generator Test Banks A and B

Go Online
PHSchool.com
For: Teacher Home Page
Web Code: jdk-1001

PRINT MATERIAL

CORE INSTRUCTION
Teacher's Resource Book, pp. 46–69
• Input Script
• Answer Keys
• Vocabulary Clip Art
• School-to-Home Connection Letters
• Communicative Activities Blackline Masters
• Video Script
• GramActiva Blackline Masters
• Chapter Resource Checklist

TPR Stories, pp. 18–23

CORE ASSESSMENT
Assessment Program, pp. 26–69
• Pruebas
  Vocabulary Recognition
  Vocabulary Production
  Making comparisons
  The verbs *saber* and *conocer*
  Hace + time expressions
• Examen del capítulo
• Speaking and Writing Rubrics
Teacher's Resource Book, p. 58
• Situation Cards
TPR Stories, pp. 18–23

Differentiated Instruction

STUDENTS NEEDING EXTRA HELP
Guided Practice Activities
Teacher's Guide, pp. T17–T26

HERITAGE LEARNERS
Realidades para hispanohablantes
Teacher's Guide, pp. 16–25
Lecturas para hispanohablantes
Teacher's Guide, pp. 28–30

ADVANCED/PRE-AP*
Pre-AP* Resource Book: Resources Chart, p. 97

Differentiated Assessment

STUDENTS NEEDING EXTRA HELP
Alternate Assessment Program
• Examen del capítulo, pp. 11–16

HERITAGE LEARNERS
Assessment Program: Realidades para hispanohablantes Teacher's Guide, pp. T96–T100
ExamView® test generator Heritage Learner Test Bank

ADVANCED/PRE-AP*
Pre-AP* Resource Book: Teacher Activity Sheet, p. 98
ExamView® test generator Pre-AP* Test Bank

Regular Schedule (50 Minutes)

Capítulo 1B Lesson Plans

For electronic lesson plans:
Teacher Express

	Warm-up / Assess	Preview Present / Practice Communicate		Wrap-up / Homework Options
DAY 1	**Warm-up (5 min.)** • Homework check • Return Examen del capítulo: Capítulo 1A	**A ver si recuerdas . . . (20 min.)** • Presentation: El tiempo libre • Actividad 1 • Presentation: The verb *ir* • Actividades 2, 3	**Chapter Opener (5 min.)** • Objectives • Fondo cultural **A primera vista (15 min.)** • Presentation: Vocabulario y gramática en contexto • Actividades 1, 2	**Wrap-up and Homework Options (5 min.)** • Practice Workbook 1B-A, 1B-B, 1B-1, 1B-2 • Go Online
DAY 2	**Warm-up (10 min.)** • Homework check	**A primera vista (35 min.)** • Presentation: Videohistoria *Después de las clases* • View: Videohistoria	• Video Activities 1, 2, 3, 4 • Actividad 3	**Wrap-up and Homework Options (5 min.)** • Practice Workbook 1B-3, 1B-4 • Go Online • Prueba 1B-1: Vocabulary recognition
DAY 3	**Warm-up (10 min.)** • Actividad 4 • Homework check ✔**Assessment (10 min.)** • Prueba 1B-1: Vocabulary recognition	**Manos a la obra (25 min.)** • Actividades 6, 7, 8 • Fondo cultural • Audio Activities 5, 6		**Wrap-up and Homework Options (5 min.)** • Actividades 5, 9 • Heritage Learner Workbook 1B-1, 1B-2 • Prueba 1B-2: Vocabulary production
DAY 4	**Warm-up (10 min.)** • Writing Activity 10 • Homework check ✔**Assessment (10 min.)** • Prueba 1B-2: Vocabulary production	**Manos a la obra (25 min.)** • Communicative Activity • Presentation: Making comparisons	• View: GramActiva video • Actividades 10, 12 • Audio Activity 7	**Wrap-up and Homework Options (5 min.)** • Practice Workbook 1B-5 • Go Online • Actividad 11
DAY 5	**Warm-up (10 min.)** • Writing Activity 11 • Homework check	**Manos a la obra (35 min.)** • Actividades 13, 14 • Fondos culturales • Presentation: The verbs *saber* and *conocer*	• View: GramActiva video • Actividades 15, 17 • Audio Activity 8	**Wrap-up and Homework Options (5 min.)** • Practice Workbook 1B-6 • Actividad 16 • Writing Activity 12 • Go Online • Heritage Learner Workbook 1B-4 • Pruebas 1B-3, 1B-4: Making comparisons; The verbs *saber* and *conocer*
DAY 6	**Warm-up (5 min.)** • Homework check ✔**Assessment (15 min.)** • Pruebas 1B-3, 1B-4: Making comparisons; *saber* and *conocer*	**Manos a la obra (25 min.)** • Presentation: *Hace* + time expressions • Actividades 18, 19, 20 • Audio Activity 9		**Wrap-up and Homework Options (5 min.)** • Practice Workbook 1B-7 • Actividades 21, 22, 23 • Writing Activity 13 • Prueba 1B-5: *Hace* + time expressions • Go Online • Heritage Learner Workbook 1B-5
DAY 7	**Warm-up (5 min.)** • Homework check ✔**Assessment (10 min.)** • Prueba 1B-4: *Hace* + time expressions	**Manos a la obra (20 min.)** • Communicative Activity • Exploración del lenguaje • El español en el mundo del trabajo **¡Adelante! (10 min.)** • Presentación escrita: Steps 1, 5		**Wrap-up and Homework Options (5 min.)** • Presentación escrita: Step 2
DAY 8	**Warm-up (5 min.)** • Homework check	**¡Adelante! (40 min.)** • Presentación escrita: Step 3 • Lectura • ¿Comprendiste?	• Fondo cultural	**Wrap-up and Homework Options (5 min.)** • Presentación escrita: Step 4 • Preparación para el examen 3, 4, 5 • Go Online: Lectura
DAY 9	**Warm-up (5 min.)** • Homework check	**¡Adelante! (25 min.)** • Videomisterio: Presentation • Perspectivas del mundo hispano	**Repaso del capítulo (15 min.)** • Vocabulario y gramática • Preparación para el examen 1, 2	**Wrap-up and Homework Options (5 min.)** • Practice Workbook 1B-8, 1B-9 • Go Online: Self-test • Examen del capítulo 1B
DAY 10	**Warm-up (5 min.)** • Homework check ✔**Assessment (40 min.)** • Examen del capítulo 1B			**Wrap-up and Homework Options (5 min.)** • A ver si recuerdas . . .: Capítulo 2A

Block Schedule (90 Minutes)

For electronic lesson plans:
Teacher Express 💿

Warm-up / Assess	Preview Present / Practice Communicate		Wrap-up / Homework Options
DAY 1 **Warm-up (5 min.)** • Homework check • Return Examen del capítulo: Capítulo 1A	**A ver si recuerdas . . .** **(20 min.)** • Presentation: El tiempo libre • Actividad 1 • Presentation: The verb *ir* • Actividades 2, 3 **Chapter Opener** **(5 min.)** • Objectives • Fondo cultural	**A primera vista** **(55 min.)** • Presentation: Vocabulario y gramática en contexto • Actividades 1, 2 • Presentation: Videohistoria *Después de las clases* • View: Videohistoria • Video Activities 1, 2, 3, 4 • Actividad 3	**Wrap-up and Homework Options (5 min.)** • Practice Workbook 1B-A, 1B-B, 1B-1, 1B-2, 1B-3, 1B-4 • Go Online • Prueba 1B-1: Vocabulary recognition
DAY 2 **Warm-up (10 min.)** • Actividad 4 • Homework check ✔**Assessment (10 min.)** • Prueba 1B-1: Vocabulary recognition	**Manos a la obra (65 min.)** • Actividades 6, 7, 8 • Fondo cultural • Audio Activities 5, 6 • Writing Activity 10 • Communicative Activity • Presentation: Making comparisons • View: GramActiva video • Actividades 10, 11, 12 • Audio Activity 7		**Wrap-up and Homework Options (5 min.)** • Practice Workbook 1B-5 • Actividad 9 • Go Online • Heritage Learner Workbook 1B-1, 1B-2 • Prueba 1B-2: Vocabulary production
DAY 3 **Warm-up (10 min.)** • Actividad 5 • Homework check ✔**Assessment (10 min.)** • Prueba 1B-2: Vocabulary production	**Manos a la obra (65 min.)** • Actividades 13, 14 • Fondos culturales • Writing Activity 11 • Presentation: The verbs *saber* and *conocer* • View: GramActiva video • Actividades 15, 16, 17 • Audio Activity 8 • Writing Activity 12 • Presentation: *Hace* + time expressions • Actividades 18, 19		**Wrap-up and Homework Options (5 min.)** • Practice Workbook 1B-6 • Go Online • Heritage Learner Workbook 1B-4 • Pruebas 1B-3, 1B-4: Making comparisons; *saber* and *conocer*
DAY 4 **Warm-up (5 min.)** • Homework check ✔**Assessment (15 min.)** • Pruebas 1B-3, 1B-4: Making comparisons; *saber* and *conocer*	**Manos a la obra** **(40 min.)** • Actividades 20, 21, 22, 23 • Audio Activity 9 • Writing Activity 13 • Exploración del lenguaje • El español en la comunidad	**¡Adelante!** **(25 min.)** • Lectura • ¿Comprendiste? • Fondo cultural • Presentación escrita: Steps 1, 5	**Wrap-up and Homework Options (5 min.)** • Practice Workbook 1B-7 • Presentación escrita: Step 2 • Go Online • Heritage Learner Workbook 1B-5 • Prueba 1B-5: *Hace* + time expressions
DAY 5 **Warm-up (5 min.)** • Homework check ✔**Assessment (10 min.)** • Prueba 1B-5: *Hace* + time expressions	**¡Adelante!** **(40 min.)** • Presentación escrita: Step 3 • Perspectives del mundo hispano	**Repaso del capítulo** **(30 min.)** • Vocabulario y gramática • Preparación para el examen 1, 2, 3, 4, 5	**Wrap-up and Homework Options (5 min.)** • Presentación escrita: Step 4 • Practice Workbook 1B-8, 1B-9 • Go Online: Self-test • Examen del capítulo 1B
DAY 6 **Warm-up (10 min.)** • Homework check • Answer questions **Repaso del capítulo (15 min.)** • Situation Cards ✔**Assessment (40 min.)** • Examen del capítulo 1B	**¡Adelante! (20 min.)** • Videomisterio: Presentation		**Wrap-up and Homework Options (5 min.)** • Go Online: Lectura • A ver si recuerdas . . .: Capítulo 2A

1B

A ver si recuerdas...

Vocabulario

El tiempo libre

los lugares

el café
el centro comercial
el cine
el gimnasio
el parque
el restaurante
el trabajo
la biblioteca
la casa
la iglesia, la mezquita,
  el templo, la sinagoga
la piscina

las actividades

caminar
dormir
escuchar música
hablar por teléfono
ir a la lección de
  (piano)
ir de compras
jugar videojuegos
leer
pasar tiempo con
  amigos
tocar (la guitarra)
trabajar
trabajar como
  voluntario, -a
usar la computadora

los deportes

correr
hacer ejercicio
ir al partido
jugar al (básquetbol,
  béisbol, fútbol, golf,
  tenis, vóleibol)
levantar pesas

Vocabulario

Core Instruction

Resources: Voc. and Gram. Transparency 34

Focus: Reviewing vocabulary about activities and places

Suggestions: Have students work in small groups to write each vocabulary word on an index card. Group members can take turns picking a card and saying a sentence using the word they chose. They might tell about a time when they performed an activity or visited a certain place. Or, they can describe how a sport is played or where a place is located in their town. Have volunteers share some of their discussions.

 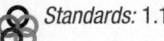

Standards: 1.1

Focus: Talking about activities that are done in different places

Suggestions: Have students brainstorm a list of places they go and activities they do at each place. If Student B answers in the negative, have Student A ask a general question: *¿Qué hace una persona en el gimnasio?*

Answers will vary.

Práctica de vocabulario • Usando el organizador gráfico

 **Escribir/Hablar**

¿Qué haces?

1 En una hoja de papel, dibuja una tabla como la que está aquí. Escoge cinco lugares de la lista de vocabulario y escríbelos en la primera columna de la tabla. Entrevista a dos compañeros(as) de clase. Pregúntales si van a los lugares de la tabla. Ellos deben contestar según el modelo, usando *todos los días, a veces* o *nunca.* Después pregúntales qué hacen en los lugares.

2 Ahora completa la tabla con información personal. Después de hacerlo, compara tu tabla con las de tus compañeros. Guarda *(Keep)* tu tabla para la Actividad 2.

nombre:			
lugares	todos los días	a veces	nunca
el gimnasio			

Modelo

A —*¿Vas al gimnasio después de las clases?*
B —*Sí, a veces voy al gimnasio.*
A —*¿Qué haces allí?*
B —*Levanto pesas y juego al básquetbol.*

42 cuarenta y dos
Tema 1 • Tu día escolar

Differentiated Instruction
Solutions for All Learners

Advanced Learners

Have students create a children's book. Ask them to write a different sentence on each page about where the main character goes at different times of the day and what he or she does at each place. Encourage them to include illustrations in their books.

Students with Special Needs

Pair students who have fine motor limitations with another student, or work with them yourself to prepare the chart for *Actividades* 1 and 2. Have them choose the locations for the chart, and allow them to do *Actividades* 2 and 3 orally.

Gramática · Repaso

The verb *ir*

Use *ir* to say where someone is going.

(yo)	voy	(nosotros) (nosotras)	vamos
(tú)	vas	(vosotros) (vosotras)	vais
Ud. (él) (ella)	va	Uds. (ellos) (ellas)	van

¿Recuerdas?

Spanish has two contractions:

$a + el = al$

$de + el = del$

• Mis amigos y yo vamos **al** café después de las clases.

• El nombre **del** café es Café Sol.

ir + *a* + infinitive

Use *ir* + *a* + infinitive to tell what someone is going to do.

Vamos a hablar por teléfono después de las clases.

Práctica de gramática

 Actividad 2 — Escribir

¿Adónde vamos?

Usa la información de la Actividad 1 para escribir frases que dicen adónde van tus compañeros y tú y qué hacen allí.

Modelo

otro(a) estudiante y tú
Después de las clases Lisa y yo vamos a casa. Usamos la computadora todos los días.

1. otros dos estudiantes
2. un(a) estudiante y tú
3. un(a) estudiante
4. otros dos estudiantes y tú
5. tú

Más práctica

• Practice Workbook, pp. 16–17: 1B-A, 1B-B
• Guided Practice Acts., p. 33: 1B-1
• *Real.* para hispanohablantes, p. 30

Go Online PHSchool.com
For: Vocab. and Grammar
Web Code: jdd-0111

 Actividad 3 — Escribir

¿Qué vas a hacer?

Di qué va a hacer cada una de estas personas. Usa los verbos en el recuadro para contestar las preguntas.

Modelo

¿Qué va a hacer Jorge en el gimnasio?
Él va a jugar al vóleibol.

beber	estudiar	leer
comprar	jugar	nadar

1. ¿Qué van a hacer Uds. en el centro comercial?
2. ¿Qué van a hacer tus hermanos en la piscina?
3. ¿Qué va a hacer Mario en el parque?
4. ¿Qué va a hacer Verónica en la biblioteca?
5. ¿Qué voy a hacer en casa?

cuarenta y tres **43**
Preparación: Vocabulario y gramática

Gramática · Repaso

 Presentation EXPRESS GRAMMAR

Core Instruction

Resources: Voc. and Gram. Transparency 35

Suggestions: Give students a variety of scenarios written on cards or slips of paper, such as: *Tengo hambre* or *Julio quiere unos zapatos nuevos.* Use the scenarios to ask volunteers what is going to be done in each situation. For example: *Si tienes hambre, ¿qué vas a hacer?* or *Si tienes hambre, ¿adónde vas?* You might also want to show the *GramActiva* Video from *Realidades* 1, *Capítulo* 4A to remind students of the verb *ir*.

 Actividad 2  *Standards:* 1.3

Resources: Answers on Transparencies

Focus: Writing about places where friends go and what they do there

Suggestions: To avoid repetition, provide students with specific times for each sentence, such as *después de las clases, los viernes,* or *los sábados por la mañana.*

Answers will vary but will include:
1. ...van...
2. ...vamos...
3. ...va...
4. ...vamos...
5. ...voy...

 Actividad 3 *Standards:* 1.3

Resources: Answers on Transparencies

Focus: Answering questions about activities done at different places

Suggestions: Encourage students to provide additional information to personalize their sentences. Point out that they should use the *tú* form when answering item 5.

Answers will vary but will include:
1. Nosotros vamos a...
2. Ellos van a...
3. Él va a...
4. Ella va a...
5. Tú vas a...

Enrich Your Teaching
Resources for All Teachers

Teacher-to-Teacher

Prepare a list of questions to review vocabulary and grammar, and have students play **Repaso** baseball. Draw a baseball diamond on the board. Put slips of paper with *hit, homerun,* and *strikeout* into a box. When each team is "at bat," the player draws a slip of paper and answers a question. For a *hit*, students can choose the level of difficulty, which should correspond to how many bases are awarded for a correct response. For example, a single is an easy question, a double is more difficult, and so on. Follow the rules of baseball, using adhesive notes to indicate who is on base. Students who answer incorrectly get an out for their team.

Standards for Capítulo 1B

- To achieve the goals of the Standards, students will:

Communication

1.1 Interpersonal
- Talk: about places, activities, and pastimes; about making comparisons and how long people have been doing things; using the verbs *saber* and *conocer*

1.2 Interpretive
- Read and interpret information about: Antonio Berni and Celia Cruz; sports and a sports club; school in Mexico, Spain, U.S.; San Miguel de Allende
- Read, watch, listen to, and compare information about activities and pastimes
- Read and listen using *saber* and *conocer*
- Read and interpret information about salsa, ballet, and a dance school

1.3 Presentational
- Present information: about going places and favorite activities and pastimes; using *saber, conocer*
- Write about and compare people's activities and how long they've been doing things

Culture

2.1 Practices and Perspectives
- Describe soccer's cultural importance
- Talk or write about: activities and favorite sports; a dance school program
- Compare differences between schools in Mexico, Spain, and the U.S.

2.2 Products and Perspectives
- Talk or write about: soccer, other sports and activities, and a sports club program; Botero and Celia Cruz; different kinds of dance

Connections

3.1 Cross-curricular
- Discuss varied activities and dances; important artists: Botero; Web pages, presentations

3.2 Target Culture
- Talk or write about: a sports club program; different kinds of dance; school in Mexico, Spain, U.S.; places; the history of San Miguel de Allende

Comparisons

4.1 Language
- Make comparisons; use nouns and verbs including *saber* and *conocer*

4.2 Culture
- Compare: activities, sports, and sports clubs of Latin America and the U.S.; Botero's work to that of U.S. artists; schools in Mexico, Spain, and the U.S.

Communities

5.1 Beyond the School
- Identify special activities in the community and places that would offer salsa classes

Fondo cultural

■◆■◆■◆■◆■◆■◆■◆■◆■◆■◆■◆■◆■◆■◆■◆■◆■

"Club Atlético Nueva Chicago" (1937), Antonio Berni
Oil on canvas, 6' ½ x 9' 10½". Inter-American fund (645.1942). The Museum of Modern Art/Licensed by Scala-Art Resource, NY. Digital Image © 2004 Museum of Modern Art, New York.

Antonio Berni (1905–1981) nació en Rosario, Argentina, y fue uno de los artistas más importantes de Argentina y de América Latina. A veces Berni pintó *(painted)* cuadros con temas populares como éste que muestra *(shows)* el equipo de fútbol del barrio. Este cuadro es un buen ejemplo del estilo realista de Berni y vemos cómo pintó a cada uno de los jugadores como individuo.

- ¿Qué importancia tiene el fútbol en la cultura latinoamericana? ¿Qué actividades extracurriculares tienen importancia en tu comunidad? ¿Por qué?

Differentiated Instruction

STUDENTS NEEDING EXTRA HELP

Guided Practice Activities
- Vocabulary Check, Flash Cards
- Grammar
- Reading and Writing Support

Guided Practice Audio CDs
- Disc 1, Track 2

HERITAGE LEARNERS

Realidades para hispanohablantes
- Chapter Opener, pp. 30–31
- A primera vista, p. 32
- Videohistoria, p. 33
- Manos a la obra, pp. 34–41
- ¡Adelante!, pp. 42–47
- Repaso del capítulo, pp. 48–49

ADVANCED/PRE-AP*

Pre-AP* Resource Book, pp. 96–99

¿Qué haces después de las clases?

Chapter Objectives

- Talk about extracurricular activities
- Compare people and things
- Say what people know or what they know how to do
- Say with whom or what people are familiar
- Ask and tell how long something has been going on
- Understand cultural perspectives on extracurricular activities

Video Highlights

A primera vista: *Después de las clases*

GramActiva Videos: making comparisons; the verbs *saber* and *conocer*

Country Connection

As you learn to talk about what you and your friends do after school, you will make connections to:

Texas
México
Nicaragua
Colombia
Cuba
República Dominicana
Puerto Rico
Venezuela
Argentina

Más práctica

● *Real. para hispanohablantes,* pp. 30–31

Go Online PHSchool.com
For: Online Atlas
Web Code: jde-0002

cuarenta y cinco **45**
Capítulo 1B

Una escuela de toreros en España

Chapter Opener

Presentation EXPRESS ATLAS

Core Instruction

Resources: Voc. and Gram. Transparencies: Maps 12–17, 20

Suggestions: Have students list popular activities at your school. Which activities that are currently not offered at your school would they like to see offered? Point out to students that they will review how to talk about who and what they know. Ask students to give you an example of something that they know how to do well, and then an example of someone they don't know. Remind students that in Spanish they will use a different verb for each of these situations.

Point out that in the *Videohistoria,* a group of friends discuss their extracurricular activities. Ask students to think about how involvement in extracurricular activities might influence the friendships they form.

Fondo cultural  *Standards:* 1.2, 2.1, 2.2, 4.2

■◆■◆■◆■◆■◆■◆■◆■◆■◆■◆

Resources: Fine Art Transparencies with Teacher's Guide, p. 6

Suggestions: To help students determine which sports are considered to be the most important, talk about attendance at sporting events. Ask students to consider activities besides sports in their answers.

Answers will vary.

Teaching with Art

Resources: Fine Art Transparencies with Teacher's Guide, p. 6

Suggestions: Point out that the *Fondo cultural* states that the painting by Antonio Berni is a reflection of the culture and the people of that time period. Ask students what the photo of the girls in a bullfighting class says about present-day Spain. Why do they think the girls are taking this class? Do students know of extracurricular activities that give people an understanding of their heritages?

Teacher Technology

TeacherEXPRESS
Plan · Teach · Assess

PLAN
Lesson Planner

Go Online PHSchool.com
For: Teacher Home Page
Web Code: jdk-1001

TEACH
Teaching Resources
Interactive Teacher's Edition
Vocabulary Clip Art

ASSESS
Chapter Quizzes and Tests

PresentationEXPRESS
Dynamic Presentations for Teachers

TEACH
Vocabulary & Grammar Powerpoints
GramActiva Video
Audio & Clip Art Activities
Transparencies and Maps
Activity Answers
Photo Gallery

ASSESS
ExamView
QuickTake Presenter

1B

Vocabulario y gramática

Presentation EXPRESS
VOCABULARY

Core Instruction

 Standards: 1.2

Resources: Teacher's Resource Book: Input Script, p. 48, Clip Art, pp. 60–63, Audio Script, p. 49; Voc. and Gram. Transparencies: 36–37; Audio Program: Tracks 1–2

Focus: Presenting vocabulary about extracurricular activities

Suggestions: Use the Input Script from the *Teacher's Resource Book* or the story from the *TPR Stories Book* to present new vocabulary. Using the transparencies, present the vocabulary in three groups: sports, the arts, and computers.

If possible, show photos either from newspapers or from a school yearbook of students participating in extracurricular activities. Ask short-answer questions about the photos that require a limited verbal response, such as: *¿Tú también eres miembro del club de computadoras? ¿Tú también practicas un deporte? ¿Participas en una actividad extracurricular?*

Bellringer Review

Distribute Clip Art (TRB pp. 60–62) for the extracurricular school activities. Have students write on the back of each picture the name of one student in the school who participates in the activity.

Additional Resources
• Audio Program: Canciones CD, Disc 22

A primera vista jdd-0197

Vocabulario y gramática en contexto

—En mi escuela los estudiantes **participan** en muchas **actividades extracurriculares.** Les gusta practicar deportes o son **miembros** de algún **club,** como el club de computadoras. Éstas son algunas de las actividades más populares **entre los jóvenes.**

el ajedrez

—¿Tienes tú **la oportunidad** de participar en muchas actividades? ¿Tiene tu escuela **tantas** actividades **como** mi escuela? **¿Cuánto tiempo hace que** participas?

jugar a los bolos

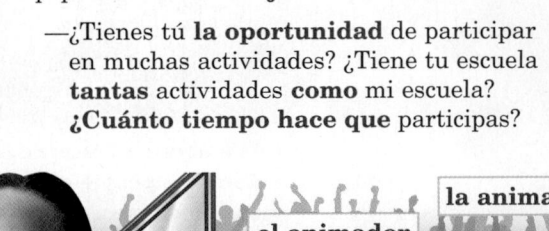

la animadora

el animador

el músico

la música

la banda

el equipo

Tienes que ir a **los ensayos** de la banda o a **las prácticas** del equipo de básquetbol para participar.

grabar una canción

la orquesta

la cantante

el coro

el cantante

El coro y la orquesta están grabando una canción.

el bailarín

la fotógrafa

la bailarina

el fotógrafo

Los dos fotógrafos son miembros del club de **fotografía. Hace dos años que son** miembros del club.

46 cuarenta y seis
Tema 1 • Tu día escolar

Differentiated Instruction
Solutions for All Learners

Advanced Learners
Ask students to make a poster to attract members to an extracurricular activity at their school. Have them write a brief description of what is involved in membership, including places and times of meetings. Promote the activities by hanging the posters in your room and asking other Spanish teachers to do the same.

Heritage Language Learners
Have students write an essay about watching their favorite sports team. They should include when, where, and with whom they watch the team's games. Remind them to begin the essay with an introductory sentence and end it with a concluding sentence.

¡Bienvenidos!

NAVEGADOR DE INTERNET

CINE
Las películas más populares

JUEGOS
Juega solo o con amigos

COMPRAS
Libros, ropa y más

MUSICA
Todo tipo de música

DEPORTES
Béisbol, fútbol, tenis

TECNOLOGÍA
Información tecnológica

... navegar en la Red.

BIENVENIDOS
a la página de Ramón

👥 Amigos
👨‍👩‍👧 Familia
📷 Fotos

... crear una página Web 99.

NAVEGADOR DE INTERNET

¡Encuéntralo aquí!

BUSCAR: [ ] IR

búsqueda avanzada

... hacer una búsqueda.

Ramón está en línea. Le gusta visitar salones de chat.

66 **Conozco** a varios miembros del club de computadoras. Creo que este club es **tan** interesante **como** los otros clubes. En el club puedo ...

66 Me gusta ir al **club atlético** 99.

las artes marciales

el hockey

hacer gimnasia

la natación

CLUB ATLÉTICO

Actividad 1
 jdd-0197 **Escuchar**

Unos estudiantes muy ocupados

Escucha a un estudiante que describe las actividades en su escuela. Señala cada actividad que él describe.

Más práctica

● Practice Workbook, pp. 18–19: 1B-1, 1B-2
● WAV Wbk.: Writing, p. 21
● Guided Practice: Vocab. Flash Cards, pp. 34–40
● *Real.* para hispanohablantes, p. 32

Go Online
PHSchool.com
For: Vocab. Practice
Web Code: jdd-0112

Actividad 2
 jdd-0197  **Escuchar**

¿Sí o no?

Escucha las frases. Si lo que escuchas es lógico, señala con el pulgar hacia arriba *(thumbs-up)*. Si la respuesta no es lógica, señala con el pulgar hacia abajo *(thumbs-down)*.

Más vocabulario
ganar to win, to earn
el pasatiempo pastime

cuarenta y siete **47**
Capítulo 1B

Enrich Your Teaching
Resources for All Teachers

Culture Note
Cuba excelled in martial arts in the 2000 Olympic Games in Sydney, Australia. Two women from the island won gold medals in judo: Legna Verdecia, who competed as a half-lightweight, and Sibelis Veranes, who won the middleweight competition. Ángel Valodía Matos Fuentes took home the gold for Cuba in the men's 80 kg taekwondo competition.

Teacher-to-Teacher
Get information from activity sponsors of different extracurricular activities in school. Have students create a bulletin board outside the classroom and post the upcoming events for various school activities. Include features about students who are involved in these activities, and post updated results such as sports or tournament scores.

Actividad 1
 Standards: 1.2  Presentation EXPRESS  AUDIO

Resources: Teacher's Resource Book: Audio Script, p. 49; Audio Program: Track 3; Answers on Transparencies

Focus: Listening comprehension about school activities

Suggestions: Play the *Audio CD* or read the script. Pause after each sentence to monitor students' identification of the pictures.

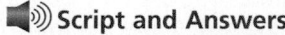 **Script and Answers:**
1. Hay dos músicos en la banda. *(band)*
2. Hay un ensayo para la obra de teatro hoy. *(dancers)*
3. Las animadoras del equipo de básquetbol son muy talentosas. *(cheerleaders)*
4. El coro va a grabar una canción esta tarde. *(chorus recording a song)*
5. Me gusta mucho navegar en la Red. *(surfing the Web)*
6. Esteban tiene una página Web muy interesante. *(creating a Web page)*
7. Los bailarines y la orquesta practican todos los días. *(dancers, orchestra)*

Actividad 2
 Standards: 1.2 Presentation EXPRESS  AUDIO

Resources: Teacher's Resource Book: Audio Script, p. 49; Audio Program: Track 4; Answers on Transparencies

Focus: Listening comprehension about extracurricular activities

Suggestions: Play the *Audio CD* or read the script at least two times. Encourage students to note words they did not understand the first time. Answer any questions they might have about those words and the script before they listen again.

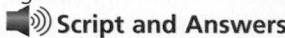 **Script and Answers:**
1. El equipo de hockey va a grabar una canción. *(down)*
2. Vamos a jugar a los bolos en el gimnasio. *(down)*
3. Los fotógrafos sacan buenas fotografías. *(up)*
4. Practicamos las artes marciales en el club atlético. *(up)*
5. Hay un ensayo para la obra de teatro esta tarde. *(up)*
6. Mis amigos van a jugar ajedrez en el salón de chat. *(down)*

Extension: Ask students to change the illogical statements to logical ones.

 Assessment
● ExamView Quiz on PresEXPRESS
QuickTake Presenter

1B Language Input

Presentation EXPRESS
VOCABULARY

 Standards: 1.2

Resources: Voc. and Gram. Transparencies 38–39; Audio Program: Track 5

Focus: Presenting additional vocabulary and grammar

Suggestions:

Pre-reading: After reviewing the *Estrategia*, have students close their books so they can't see the text. Show the transparencies and have students predict what they think the *Videohistoria* will be about.

Reading: Before reading, have students scan the text for cognates. Explain that **ganar** has two different meanings in the *Videohistoria.* Ask students to look for those meanings when they read.

Allow time for students to read the story silently. Use the transparencies and nonverbal clues to help them with the words in blue type. Ask volunteers to act out the parts of Angélica, Esteban, Lisa, and Pedro.

Post-reading: Ask students to explain the two meanings of **ganar.** Complete *Actividad* 3 to check comprehension of the story.

Pre-AP* Support

• **Activity:** Distribute Clip Art to represent the extracurricular activities presented in this chapter. Have students divide a piece of paper into four sections and write the name of each of the four students (from the Videohistoria) in each of the squares. Play the Videohistoria without showing the screen to the class. As students listen, have them place the pieces of clip art in the square for the student who would most likely be interested in each activity. Share as a class.

• *Pre-AP* Resource Book:* Comprehensive guide to Pre-AP* vocabulary skill development, pp. 47–53

Videohistoria jdd-0197

Después de las clases

¿En qué actividades extracurriculares participan Esteban y sus amigos? Vamos a ver.

Estrategia

Using visuals
Using the photographs that accompany the dialogue can help you understand what is being said.

1 **Angélica:** Hola, todos. Otro año nuevo. ¡Me encanta el primer día de clases! Hola, Lisa.

Lisa: Hola, Angélica. Esteban, ¿cómo estás?

Esteban: Estoy cansado. No dormí bien anoche.

Lisa: Lo siento. Siéntense.

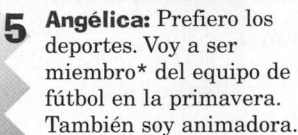

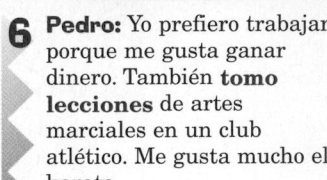

5 **Angélica:** Prefiero los deportes. Voy a ser miembro* del equipo de fútbol en la primavera. También soy animadora.

6 **Pedro:** Yo prefiero trabajar porque me gusta ganar dinero. También **tomo lecciones** de artes marciales en un club atlético. Me gusta mucho el karate.

7 **Angélica:** ¿Practicas mucho las artes marciales?

Pedro: Participo en algunas competiciones.

Lisa: ¿Ganas a veces?

Esteban: Pedro gana más que "a veces". Él tiene el cinturón negro. ¿Qué piensas de él ahora?

*The word *miembro* is used for both male and female students.

48 cuarenta y ocho
Tema 1 • Tu día escolar

Differentiated Instruction
Solutions for All Learners

Advanced Learners
Have students write a group story entitled *"Más sobre Pedro"* in which they make up more details about this character. Students could expand on his job or on his karate skills, or they could invent other talents for Pedro. Invite the group to share the story with the class.

Students with Learning Difficulties
If students have difficulty drawing inferences and reaching conclusions, ask them questions about the *Videohistoria:* From the dialogue, how do you know that Pedro is modest about his talent? What does Lisa say that shows that she is not familiar with Pedro's accomplishments?

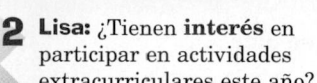

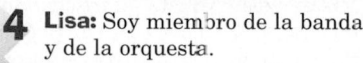

2 Lisa: ¿Tienen **interés** en participar en actividades extracurriculares este año?

3 Esteban: Hace dos años que soy miembro del club de computadoras. ¿A alguien le interesa **asistir a la reunión** conmigo esta tarde?

4 Lisa: Soy miembro de la banda y de la orquesta.

Angélica: ¿Vas a cantar en el coro también? Tienes **una voz** bonita.

Lisa: Sí, gracias. ¿Y tú? ¿Por qué no cantas en el coro? Vamos a **ensayar** hoy.

8 Angélica: Pedro, eres muy talentoso.

Pedro: Gracias.

Lisa: Pedro, ¡Eres tan misterioso! ¿Tienes más secretos?

Angélica: Bueno, hay que **volver** a clases. ¡Hasta luego!

 Actividad 3 Escribir/Hablar

¿Comprendiste?

1. ¿Dónde están los estudiantes? ¿De qué hablan?
2. ¿En qué actividad participa Esteban? ¿Cuánto tiempo hace que es miembro?
3. ¿Cuáles son las actividades extracurriculares de Lisa?
4. ¿Qué prefiere hacer Angélica?
5. ¿Por qué trabaja Pedro?
6. ¿Qué lecciones toma Pedro? ¿Dónde? ¿Es bueno?

Más práctica

- Practice Workbook, pp. 20–21: 1B-3, 1B-4
- WAV Wbk.: Video, pp. 16–17
- Guided Practice: Vocab. Check, pp. 41–44
- *Real.* para hispanohablantes, p. 33

Go Online PHSchool.com
For: Vocab. Practice
Web Code: jdd-0113

Enrich Your Teaching
Resources for All Teachers

Culture Note

Cheerleading is rare in most Spanish-speaking countries. Team mascots, however, are common in sports such as soccer. In Bogotá, Colombia, Monaguillo the lion was the living mascot for Independiente Santa Fe. When the lion died, he was immortalized in costume as Lucho Monaguillo, the current team mascot.

Teacher-to-Teacher

To reinforce new vocabulary, have students form groups and play Charades by acting out roles of participants in extracurricular activities, such as *el miembro del club de computadoras, la animadora,* or *el fotógrafo.*

Core Instruction

 Standards: 1.2

Resources: Teacher's Resource Book: Video Script, p. 52, Video Program: Cap. 1B

Focus: Comprehension of contextualized vocabulary

Suggestions:

Pre-viewing: Ask students how they feel at the beginning of a new school year. Pause the video on the first scene. Ask students how they think the characters in this story feel on their first day back at school.

Viewing: Show the video once without pausing. Then show it again, pausing along the way to check comprehension. For example, ask students: *¿Cómo está Esteban el primer día de clases? ¿Quién tiene una voz bonita? ¿Quién va a ser miembro del equipo de fútbol?*

Post-viewing: Ask students if they think these four characters would be fun to have as friends and why. Complete the Video Activities in the *Writing, Audio & Video Workbook.*

Actividad 3  *Standards:* 1.2  **Presentation EXPRESS** ANSWERS

Resources: Answers on Transparencies

Focus: Verifying comprehension of the *Videohistoria*

Suggestions: Remind students to use the photos and to search for key words to help them answer the questions.

Answers:

1. Los estudiantes están en el gimnasio. Hablan de actividades extracurriculares.
2. Esteban participa en el Club de computadoras. Hace dos años que es miembro.
3. Lisa es miembro de la banda y la orquesta y va a cantar en el coro también.
4. Angélica prefiere los deportes.
5. A Pedro le gusta ganar dinero.
6. Pedro toma lecciones de artes marciales en un club atlético. Sí, es bueno.

Additional Resources

- WAV Wbk.: Audio Act. 5, p. 18
- Teacher's Resource Book: Audio Script, p. 50
- Audio Program: Track 7

✓ **Assessment**

- **ExamView** QuickTake Presenter Quiz on PresEXPRESS
- Prueba 1B-1: Vocab. Recognition, pp. 26–27

Actividad 4 · Standards: 1.2 · Presentation EXPRESS ANSWERS

Resources: Answers on Transparencies

Focus: Reading and writing about extracurricular activities

Suggestions: Advise students to read the entire paragraph before filling in the blanks. Point out that in some cases either option might fit grammatically, but that they should choose the most logical answer.

Answers:
1. participamos
2. voz
3. el coro
4. miembro
5. un ensayo
6. Hace gimnasia
7. animadora
8. practico
9. salones de chat
10. miembros

Bellringer Review

On the board, write three or four sentences with adjectives that require gender agreement. Use the masculine singular form for the adjectives, and have students provide the correct endings.

Actividad 5 · Standards: 1.2, 1.3 · Presentation EXPRESS ANSWERS

Resources: Answers on Transparencies

Focus: Reading descriptions of people and writing sentences in response

Recycle: Extracurricular activities

Suggestions: Have students copy the descriptions on a sheet of paper and underline key words to help with comprehension.

Answers will vary but will include:
1. Es un(a) fotógrafo(a)…
2. Es un(a) músico(a)…
3. Es un(a) cantante…
4. Es un(a) bailarín / bailarina…
5. Es un(a) animador(a)…

Manos a la obra

Vocabulario y gramática en uso

Objectives
- Communicate about extracurricular activities
- Compare people or things
- Learn uses of the verbs *saber* and *conocer*
- Talk about how long people have been doing things

Actividad 4 Leer/Escribir

Las actividades de mis amigos

Completa las frases con la palabra apropiada.

Mis amigos y yo **1.** (*participamos / volvemos*) en muchas actividades extracurriculares. Mi amiga Raquel tiene una buena **2.** (*voz / reunión*). Por eso, canta en **3.** (*el coro / el ensayo*). A mi amiga Gloria le encanta el español. Ella es **4.** (*miembro / reunión*) del club de español. Raquel y Gloria también tocan un instrumento en la orquesta. Tienen **5.** (*un ensayo / el interés*) todas las tardes. María es muy deportista. **6.** (*Hace gimnasia / Estudia*) en el gimnasio y también es **7.** (*animadora / bailarina*) para el equipo de fútbol de la escuela. A mí me gustan los deportes. Por la tarde **8.** (*practico / asisto*) las artes marciales. Tengo el cinturón amarillo. También me gustan las computadoras. Con mi amigo Pedro, visitamos **9.** (*salones de chat / la práctica*). Somos **10.** (*miembros / jóvenes*) del club de computadoras. Cuando no estamos ocupados con nuestras actividades, nos gusta ir al cine o tomar un refresco en un café.

También se dice . . .

el animador, la animadora = el/la porrista (*México, Colombia*)

jugar a los bolos = jugar al boliche (*Costa Rica, México*)

Actividad 5 Leer/Escribir

¿Quién es?

Lee estas descripciones. Para cada una, escribe la palabra que corresponde a la descripción. Después escribe una frase sobre alguien que tú conoces (una persona de tu comunidad o una persona famosa) usando la palabra.

Modelo
Enseña a los estudiantes a crear páginas Web y a hacer búsquedas en la Red.
Es una profesora de la clase de tecnología. La Sra. Ramos es una profesora de tecnología fantástica.

1. Saca fotos como pasatiempo o para su trabajo.

Rubén Blades es un cantante y actor panameño muy popular.

2. Toca un instrumento en la orquesta o en la banda.
3. Canta en un coro o en otro grupo musical. A veces graba canciones también.
4. Baila en programas de la escuela o de la comunidad.
5. Apoya (*He / She supports*) a los equipos deportivos. A veces baila y hace gimnasia también.

Differentiated Instruction
Solutions for All Learners

Multiple Intelligences

Visual/Spatial: Use visuals to reinforce vocabulary. Ask students to cut out magazine pictures or create an original drawing for each item in *Actividad* 5 and use them when presenting their descriptions.

Students with Learning Difficulties

To reinforce correct word sequence for negative sentence construction, have students work in pairs. Have them copy the *Actividad* 6 model sentence (*No, no conozco a ningún miembro de la banda.*) on index cards, one word per card. Tell them to scramble the cards and reassemble the sentence.

Actividad 6 · Hablar

En tu escuela

¿A quién conoces en tu escuela que participa en actividades extracurriculares? Habla con otro(a) estudiante de estas personas.

Modelo

A —¿Conoces a un miembro de *la banda*?

B —Sí, conozco a Ryan Johnston. Es un miembro de la banda. Asiste a *los ensayos todos los días*.

o: *No, no conozco a ningún miembro de la banda.*

o: *No tenemos banda.*

Estudiante A

1. el club de
2. el equipo de
3.
4. el equipo de
5. el club de
6.

Estudiante B

las reuniones
las prácticas
los ensayos

todos los días
a menudo
a veces

¡Respuesta personal!

Actividad 7 · jdd-0198 · Escuchar/Escribir

Escucha y escribe

Escucha lo que dice una estudiante de Managua, Nicaragua, sobre las actividades extracurriculares allí. Escribe los números del 1 al 5 en una hoja de papel y escribe lo que escuchas. Después indica si estas actividades son populares entre los jóvenes de tu comunidad también.

Fondo cultural

Las actividades extracurriculares En América Latina, generalmente no hay oportunidades en las escuelas para participar en un coro, equipo deportivo, lecciones de artes marciales u otras actividades después de las clases. Los estudiantes que tienen interés en aprender algún pasatiempo como la fotografía, la música o el baile, van a centros culturales o talleres *(workshops)* en su comunidad.

• ¿Hay centros culturales en tu comunidad? ¿Qué actividades hay allí?

cincuenta y uno **51**
Capítulo 1B

Practice and Communicate 1B

Actividad 6 · Standards: 1.1

Focus: Talking about classmates and school activities

Suggestions: Before students begin their conversations, have them identify the activities in the Student A bubble and brainstorm words they could use to describe each one using the words in the Student B bubble.

Answers will vary.

Common Errors: Student may omit the personal *a* after **conocer.** Remind them that they must use *a* when the direct object is a person.

Bellringer Review

Distribute Clip Art (TRB pp. 60–62). Have students arrange the clip art in two columns representing *likes* and *dislikes.* Have them share with a partner their likes and dislikes. (Ex. *No me gusta tocar un instrumento en la orquesta.*)

Actividad 7 · Standards: 1.2, 2.1, 4.2 · Presentation EXPRESS AUDIO

Resources: Teacher's Resource Book: Audio Script, pp. 49–50; Audio Program: Track 6; Answers on Transparencies

Focus: Listening and writing from dictation about extracurricular activities

Suggestions: Play the *Audio CD* or read the script once without having students write. After completing the dictation, allow students time to revise their sentences.

Script and Answers:

1. Las clases de artes marciales son muy populares entre los jóvenes.
2. Muchos estudiantes tienen interés en el coro o la orquesta.
3. El club de ajedrez no es tan popular como el club de fotografía.
4. Visitamos salones de chat para conocer a otros jóvenes.
5. Mis amigos crean páginas Web o hacen búsquedas en la computadora.

Fondo cultural · Standards: 1.2, 2.1, 2.2, 4.2

Suggestions: Ask students to compare extracurricular activities in the United States with those in Spanish-speaking countries.

Answers will vary.

Enrich Your Teaching
Resources for All Teachers

Culture Note

Throughout Mexico, **talleres** have allowed artists and performers to share their ideas and develop their skills. *El Centro Municipal de Artes,* located in Mazatlán, Mexico, teaches classical and folkloric ballet, orchestra, jazz band, and numerous other workshops. There is also a professional theater for performances.

Teacher-to-Teacher

Writing sentences from dictation reinforces correct word order and helps students retain vocabulary. Ask students to write 2–3 sentences about their participation in extracurricular activities. Review their sentences to be sure they are error-free. Have students work in pairs dictating their own sentences and writing their partner's sentences.

51

1B Practice and Communicate

Bellringer Review

Write *caminar, comer, escribir,* and *ir* on the board. Ask students to form the present tense of each verb.

Actividad 8 *Standards:* 1.1, 1.3

Focus: Writing and speaking about after-school activities

Recycle: Extracurricular activities

Suggestions: For Step 2, have students create a T-chart with the headings **Nombres** and **Actividades.** Assign Step 3 for homework.

Answers will vary.

Actividad 9 *Standards:* 1.1, 1.3

Focus: Writing and speaking about extracurricular activities

Suggestions: Ask students to conduct a class survey about the most popular after-school activities and have them use the information to answer item 3.

Answers will vary.

Block Schedule

Have students produce a news program about extracurricular activities at their school. Assign each group one of the activities from the word bank in *Actividad 8* and have them interview someone who participates in that activity. Have them find out when the team or club meets, what activities there are, and how one can become a member.

Additional Resources

- WAV Wbk.: Audio Act. 6, p. 18
- Teacher's Resource Book: Audio Script, p. 50, Communicative Activity BLM, pp. 54–55
- Audio Program: Track 8

✓ Assessment

- Prueba 1B-2: Vocab. Production, pp. 28–29

Actividad 8 **Escribir/Hablar**

Las actividades populares

1. Escribe tres frases para describir qué actividades haces después de las clases. Usa las actividades del recuadro.

las artes marciales	la orquesta
el hockey	el béisbol
la natación	la música
la fotografía	los videojuegos
la banda	el ajedrez
el coro	

Modelo

Después de las clases yo voy a casa y navego en la Red. También tomo lecciones de piano. A veces voy a un club atlético.

2. Habla con tres estudiantes para saber qué hacen después de las clases. Escribe los nombres de los estudiantes y las actividades que hacen ellos.

Modelo

A —*¿En qué actividades extracurriculares participas después de las clases?*
B —*Ensayo con la orquesta y después voy al club atlético. También tomo clases de artes marciales.*

3. Escribe cinco frases sobre las actividades que hacen tus compañeros y tú.

Modelo

Pablo ensaya con la orquesta. Marisa va a casa y navega en la Red.

En Costa Rica

Actividad 9 **Escribir/Hablar**

Y tú, ¿qué dices?

1. ¿Qué te gusta más, ser miembro de un club o participar en un deporte? ¿Por qué?

2. ¿Usas la computadora mucho o poco en tu tiempo libre? ¿Para qué usas más la computadora? ¿Cuánto tiempo pasas en línea cada día?

3. ¿Cuáles son las actividades más populares en tu escuela? Describe por qué son populares.

4. ¿Hay suficientes actividades para jóvenes en tu comunidad? ¿Qué otras actividades debe ofrecer *(offer)*?

En Guadalajara, México

Differentiated Instruction
Solutions for All Learners

Multiple Intelligences

Logical/Mathematical: Have students poll classmates about their favorite after-school activity and then graph the results of the poll. Tell them to use their graphs to answer item 3 in *Actividad 9.*

Students with Learning Difficulties

Have students complete *Actividad 11* in three steps. First tell them to conjugate the verb so that it agrees with the given subject. Next, have them determine the form of **tanto** that agrees in gender and number with what is being compared. Finally, have them write the complete sentence.

Gramática

Making comparisons

To compare people or things that are equal to one another, you use:

tan + *adjective* + como	as + adjective + as

En mi club, levantar pesas es **tan** popular **como** correr.

To say that things are *not* equal, you can use the negative.

En el club atlético, levantar pesas **no** es **tan** popular **como** correr.

To say "as much as" or "as many as," you use:

tanto, -a + *noun* + como	as much + noun + as
tantos, -as + *noun* + como	as many + noun + as

Note that *tanto* agrees in gender and number with what is being compared.

Hay **tantas** actrices en el ensayo **como** actores.

¿Recuerdas?

You already know several ways to compare things and people.

más + *adjective* + que

menos + *adjective* + que

mayor que / **menor que**

mejor que / **peor que**

You also know how to say that someone or something is "the most" or "the least":

el / la / los / las + *noun* + más / menos + *adjective* + de

el / la / los / las + mejor(es) / peor(es) + *noun* + de

• Cecilia cree que hacer gimnasia es **la actividad más divertida de** la escuela.

GramActiva VIDEO

To learn more about making comparisons, watch the **GramActiva** video.

Mejor . . . que

Actividad 10 · Leer/Escribir

Comparaciones

Estás hablando de personas en tu escuela. Completa las siguientes frases con la palabra apropiada.

1. La canción de Mercedes es _____ (tan / tanta) buena como la de Enrique.

2. Elena no es _____ (tanta / tan) deportista como Angélica.

3. La voz de Catalina es _____ (tan / tanto) bonita como la voz de Victoria.

4. En la banda no hay _____ (tantos / tan) músicos como en la orquesta.

Actividad 11 · Leer/Escribir

En la escuela

Todos hacemos comparaciones. Ahora es tu turno. Completa las siguientes frases y usa la forma apropiada de *tanto*.

1. yo / (no) tener / amigos(as) / como Luz

2. este año nosotros / (no) tener / profesores interesantes / como el año pasado

3. el equipo de fútbol americano / (no) tener / partidos / como el equipo de básquetbol

4. los chicos / (no) tener / oportunidades para hacer gimnasia / como las chicas

5. (no) hay / interés en el club de ajedrez / como en el club de ciencias

cincuenta y tres 53
Capítulo 1B

Gramática

Presentation EXPRESS GRAMMAR

Core Instruction

Standards: 4.1

Resources: Teacher's Resource Book: Video Script, p. 53; Video Program: Cap. 1B

Suggestions: Play the *GramActiva* Video as an introduction or to reinforce your own presentation. Present the grammar in two parts: comparisons with adjectives and comparisons with nouns. Where possible, use concrete, visual examples of the comparisons to make the concept clearer.

Actividad 10 *Standards:* 1.2

Presentation EXPRESS ANSWERS

Resources: Answers on Transparencies

Focus: Choosing appropriate comparative expressions

Suggestions: Have students identify whether the word after the parenthesis is an adjective or a noun. Relate that to the information in the explanation above.

Answers:

1. tan	3. tan
2. tan	4. tantos

Actividad 11 *Standards:* 1.2, 1.3

Presentation EXPRESS ANSWERS

Resources: Answers on Transparencies

Focus: Writing sentences to compare people and things using *tanto*

Suggestions: Have students make a list of the nouns being compared and write the gender and number next to each word. Allow students to use the list to write their sentences.

Answers:

1. Yo (no) tengo tantos amigos / tantas amigas como Luz.

2. Este año nosotros (no) tenemos tantos profesores interesantes como el año pasado.

3. El equipo de fútbol americano (no) tiene tantos partidos como el equipo de básquetbol.

4. Los chicos (no) tienen tantas oportunidades para hacer gimnasia como las chicas.

5. (No) hay tanto interés en el club de ajedrez como en el club de ciencias.

Enrich Your Teaching
Resources for All Teachers

Teacher-to-Teacher

Cut out pictures of popular singers, actors or athletes. Make photocopies of the same photo twice, place them side-by-side and have students compare the "identical twins" (**gemelos idénticos**): *Juan es tan alto como su hermano. Ana está tan contenta como su hermana.* Have students create a cloze passage describing how the twins always have to have the same things. Have them exchange stories and complete the passages: *María tiene 20 discos compactos. Marta tiene _____ discos compactos _____ María. (tantos/como)* Check comprehension. Ask: *¿Cuántos discos compactos tiene Marta?*

Actividad 12 *Standards:* 1.1

Focus: Giving personal opinions to compare two things

Recycle: Descriptive adjectives; comparatives

Suggestions: Direct attention to the *¿Recuerdas?* on p. 53. To encourage variety, tell students to use a different adjective for each theme.

Answers will vary.

Actividad 13 *Standards:* 1.1, 1.3

Focus: Asking and giving opinions concerning popular activities

Recycle: Superlatives, comparisons of inequality

Suggestions: For Step 1, be sure each student has his or her own copy of the group's questions to conduct their interviews. Encourage students to use a visual such as a chart or graph when presenting the results in Step 3.

Answers will vary.

Fondo cultural *Standards:* 1.2, 2.1, 2.2

◆■◆●■◆●■◆■◆■◆■◆●■◆■◆

Suggestions: Ask students if soccer is popular at their school. Are there any Spanish-speaking players on the team? Ask students to name professional baseball players who come from Spanish-speaking countries. Have them name the countries. To help students answer the questions, tell them to refer to the models in *Actividad* 13.

Answers will vary.

Block Schedule

Post pairs of pictures of famous Spanish-speaking baseball players or soccer players throughout the classroom. Have students circulate the different photos through the room and write comparisons about the people in the pictures: *Alfonso Soriano es tan talentoso como Sammy Sosa.* Call on volunteers to share their comparisons and encourage other students to agree or disagree with the descriptions.

Actividad 12   **Hablar**

¿Qué piensas de . . . ?

Habla con otro(a) estudiante sobre lo que Uds. piensan de los siguientes temas. Usen la expresión *tan . . . como* y un adjetivo apropiado. Si prefieren, pueden usar también expresiones como *más . . . que* y *menos . . . que* para expresar sus opiniones.

Modelo
A —¿Qué piensas de *la clase de matemáticas y la clase de ciencias?*
B —Pienso que *la clase de matemáticas es tan difícil como la clase de ciencias.* ¿Y tú?
A —Pienso que *la clase de matemáticas es más interesante que la clase de ciencias.*

Estudiante A

1. la música clásica / la música rock
2. el fútbol americano / el fútbol
3. jugar a los bolos / jugar al ajedrez
4. los deportes de verano / los deportes de invierno
5. hacer gimnasia / practicar las artes marciales
6. practicar la fotografía / crear una página Web

Estudiante B

bonito, -a	fácil
emocionante	interesante
difícil	aburrido, -a

¡Respuesta personal!

Actividad 13    **Escribir/Hablar**

Las actividades más populares

1 Trabaja con otro(a) estudiante. Escriban tres preguntas que pueden hacerles a los otros estudiantes de la clase sobre diferentes categorías de actividades, pasatiempos, deportes y personas.

Modelo
Para ti, ¿cuál es la actividad extracurricular más importante?
En tu opinión, ¿quién es el (la) cantante más talentoso(a) de la escuela?

2 Cada estudiante debe hablar con otros(as) dos compañeros(as) y hacerles las preguntas. Escribe sus respuestas. Con tu compañero(a), comparen las respuestas a sus preguntas.

3 Hagan una presentación sobre las opiniones de sus compañeros de clase.

Modelo
Muchos estudiantes piensan que la actividad extracurricular más importante es el deporte en equipos. Otros estudiantes dicen que el coro y la banda son tan importantes como los deportes.

 **Fondo cultural**

Los deportes más populares El fútbol es el deporte preferido entre muchos jóvenes hispanohablantes. En la República Dominicana, Puerto Rico, Cuba, Venezuela y otros países, el béisbol es tan popular como el fútbol y muchas veces es el deporte más popular.

• ¿Cuáles son los deportes más populares en tu ciudad? Compara estos deportes con los de los jóvenes hispanohablantes. En tu opinión, ¿qué deporte es el mejor? ¿Por qué?

54 cincuenta y cuatro
Tema 1 • Tu día escolar

Differentiated Instruction
Solutions for All Learners

Heritage Language Learners
Students may use *más* when making comparisons describing something that is better, worse, older, or younger. Point out that *más* is not necessary with the adjectives *mejor, peor, mayor,* and *menor.* Have them practice comparisons using these adjectives by describing their friends and family members.

Multiple Intelligences
Naturalist: To help reinforce comparisons, have the class go outside and compare things they see. Ask them to describe what they see: *Este pajaro es más bonito que el otro.* Before leaving the classroom, have students brainstorm a list of things they might find outside. *(flores, árboles, perros, pajaros)*

Actividad 14 — Escribir/Hablar

Los músicos

Mira estos dos cuadros del gran artista colombiano Fernando Botero. ¿En qué sentido *(way)* son similares? ¿En qué sentido son diferentes?

1 Copia el diagrama de Venn y escribe Cuadro 1 y Cuadro 2 encima de los círculos según el modelo. Escribe las características diferentes de cada cuadro en el círculo apropiado y las características similares en la intersección de los círculos. Luego escribe tres frases comparando los cuadros.

"Los músicos" (1979), Fernando Botero
Oil on canvas, 74(1).75 x 85.5 in. © Fernando Botero courtesy of the Marlborough Gallery, NY.

"Tres músicos" (1983), Fernando Botero
Oil or. canvas, 64.5 x 48.5 in. © Fernando Botero courtesy of the Marlborough Gallery, NY.

Modelo

Cuadro 1   Los dos   Cuadro 2

nueve músicos — músicos grandes — tres músicos

Los músicos en el primer cuadro son tan grandes como los músicos en el segundo cuadro.

Más práctica

- Practice Workbook, p. 22: 1B-5
- WAV Wbk.: Writing, p. 22
- Guided Practice: Grammar Acts., pp. 45–46
- *Real.* para hispanohablantes, pp. 34–37

Go Online PHSchool.com
For: Comparisons
Web Code: jdd-0114

2 Trabaja con un grupo de tres. Lee una de tus frases. En grupo, escriban una comparación de los dos cuadros. Usen las ideas de todos los miembros del grupo. Presenten su comparación a la clase.

Modelo

Hay más músicos en el primer cuadro que en el segundo cuadro.

 **Fondo cultural**

Fernando Botero es conocido por su estilo de arte único *(unique)*. Es famoso tanto por sus cuadros como por sus esculturas. "El pajarru", una escultura de un pájaro, sufrió daños *(was damaged)* durante una explosión en 1995. Con el material dañado, Botero hizo una nueva escultura y la dedicó a la paz.

- Compara esta escultura con los cuadros de Botero. También compara la escultura con las esculturas en tu comunidad. ¿En qué sentido son similares y en qué sentido son diferentes?

"El Pajarru" (Little Bird or The Sparrow) (1988), Fernando Botero. Medium series, bronze sculpture. Courtesy of Jeremy Horner. © 2004 Corbis.

cincuenta y cinco **55**
Capítulo 1B

Practice and Communicate 1B

Actividad 14 — Standards: 1.3, 2.2, 3.1

Resources: Voc. and Gram. Transparency 2; Fine Art Transparencies with Teacher's Guide, pp. 9–10

Focus: Writing a comparison of two paintings and presenting the information

Suggestions: Make photocopies of a blank Venn diagram and distribute them to students. Have students brainstorm a list of adjectives and nouns they can use to describe the paintings. Write the list on the board and allow students to refer to it when completing their diagram.

Answers will vary.

Extension: Ask students to decide which of the paintings they like better, and why. Have them write their opinions. You might also use the Fine Art Transparencies reproduction of Picasso's "Trois musiciens" and compare it with Botero's "Tres músicos".

Fondo cultural — Standards: 1.2, 2.2, 3.1, 4.2

Suggestions: Explain to students that Botero's sculpture of a bird was destroyed when a terrorist bomb was detonated underneath it. The blast took place during a street festival, killing 27 people. The artist insisted that the remains of the original sculpture be left standing less than ten feet from the new sculpture. Ask students how the new sculpture represents peace.

Answers will vary.

Additional Resources

- WAV Wbk.: Audio Act. 7, p. 19
- Teacher's Resource Book: Audio Script, pp. 50–51
- Audio Program: Track 9

✓ Assessment

- ExamView Quiz on PresEXPRESS
- Prueba 1B-3: Making comparisons, p. 30

Enrich Your Teaching
Resources for All Teachers

Culture Note

Born on April 19, 1932, in Medellín, Colombia, Fernando Botero is considered to be South America's finest living artist. He has spoken out against the violence that has plagued his hometown of Medellín for decades. He considers art to be "... a spiritual, immaterial respite from the hardships of life."

Teacher-to-Teacher

Have students search the Internet for other Botero paintings or sculptures. Have them choose one and compare it to the work of one of their favorite artists. Have them use comparisons of equality as well as comparisons of inequality. Have students present their descriptions using visuals downloaded from the Internet.

1B

Core Instruction

 Standards: 4.1

Resources: Teacher's Resource Book: Video Script, p. 52; Video Program: Cap. 1B; Voc. and Gram. Transparency 40

Suggestions: Play the *GramActiva* Video as an introduction or to reinforce your own presentation. Have students practice differentiating between **saber** and **conocer** by naming facts, information, people, places, and things, and then asking them to name the verb that would be used. For example: *Madrid (conocer), ¿Dónde está Madrid? (saber), Marta (conocer), ¿Cuántos años tiene Marta? (saber).*

Actividad 15  *Standards:* 1.2
Presentation EXPRESS
AUDIO

Resources: Teacher's Resource Book: GramActiva BLM, p. 59; Answers on Transparencies

Focus: Listening to phrases and deciding whether to use **saber** or **conocer**

Suggestions: Read the script, one phrase at a time. Ask students to explain why they chose **conocer** or **saber** for each item.

Script and Answers:
1. ¿el músico talentoso en la orquesta? *(No lo conozco.)*
2. ¿la hora del ensayo esta noche? *(No lo sé.)*
3. ¿cómo grabar un disco compacto en la computadora? *(No lo sé.)*
4. ¿ese club atlético enfrente de la escuela? *(No lo conozco.)*
5. ¿el cantante colombiano con la voz bonita? *(No lo conozco.)*
6. ¿el número de personas que ensaya con la banda? *(No lo sé.)*

Block Schedule

Tell students to write a name, place, or action verb in large letters on a piece of paper. Have them sit in a circle. Ask one student to show his or her word and to call on a classmate. The student chosen says a sentence containing the word and **saber** or **conocer.** If the sentence is correct, then the student shows a word and calls on another classmate. If not, he or she leaves the circle. The last student in the circle wins.

56

The verbs *saber* and *conocer*

You already know the present-tense forms of *saber* and *conocer*. *Saber* and *conocer* both follow the pattern of regular -*er* verbs in the present tense, but each has an irregular *yo* form.

¿Recuerdas?
Use the *a personal* when you use *conocer* to say you know a person.
- Guillermo **conoce a** mi primo Tomás.

(yo)	sé	(nosotros) (nosotras)	sabemos
(tú)	sabes	(vosotros) (vosotras)	sabéis
Ud. (él) (ella)	sabe	Uds. (ellos) (ellas)	saben

(yo)	conozco	(nosotros) (nosotras)	conocemos
(tú)	conoces	(vosotros) (vosotras)	conocéis
Ud. (él) (ella)	conoce	Uds. (ellos) (ellas)	conocen

- *Saber* means to know facts and information. You can also use *saber* with the infinitive of another verb to say that you know how to do something.

  ¿Sabes si tenemos tarea para mañana?
  ¿Sabes quién es el director de la banda?
  Sé jugar al ajedrez.

- *Conocer* means to know a person or to be familiar with a place or thing.

  ¿Conoces al profesor de esta clase?
  No, no lo **conozco.**
  ¿Conoces el club atlético de la calle Ocho?

GramActiva VIDEO
To learn more about *saber* and *conocer*, watch the **GramActiva** video.

Sé mucho.

Actividad 15 Escuchar/GramActiva

Tu profesor(a) quiere saber

En una hoja de papel, escribe *No lo conozco* por un lado y *No lo sé* por el otro. Tu profesor(a) quiere saber lo que sabes y lo que conoces. Escucha sus frases y contesta cada una en el negativo. Muestra el lado apropiado del papel según lo que dice.

No lo conozco.

No lo sé.

Differentiated Instruction
Solutions for All Learners

Students with Special Needs
Provide the script for *Actividad* 15 to hearing-impaired students. Have them label one side of their paper **No lo conozco** and the other side **No lo sé.** Ask them to write each sentence on the appropriate side of the paper.

Multiple Intelligences
Bodily/Kinesthetic: Have students dramatize a conversation based on *Actividad* 16. Ask one student to play the role of an exchange student asking questions, and another to play the role of a student from the United States answering the questions.

Actividad 16

Leer/Escribir

¡Qué emocionante!

1 Imagina que un estudiante de intercambio *(exchange student)* viene a tu escuela. Completa las frases de su correo electrónico con las formas apropiadas de los verbos *saber* y *conocer*.

2 Escríbele una carta por correo electrónico a este estudiante y contesta sus preguntas.

¡Hola!

¡Hola!

Voy a ser un nuevo estudiante en tu escuela y tengo muchas preguntas. ¿Puedes ayudarme? Yo no **1.** nada de tu escuela. ¿Es grande? ¿ **2.** tú cuántos estudiantes hay? ¿ **3.** tú a muchos estudiantes? ¿Cómo son? ¿ **4.** al director de la escuela? ¿Es muy estricto? ¿ **5.** si tiene muchas reglas? ¿ **6.** qué tipo de actividades extracurriculares hay en la escuela o comunidad? Soy miembro de una banda en mi comunidad. Toco la trompeta. ¿ **7.** tocar algún instrumento musical? Me gusta salir con mis amigos después de las clases. ¿ **8.** muchos lugares bonitos adónde ir? Quiero **9.** toda la ciudad donde vives.

Escríbeme pronto.

Rogelio

Actividad 17

 Hablar/Escribir

¿Conoces a tu compañero(a)?

1 Habla con otro(a) estudiante para conocerlo(la) mejor. Usa el verbo *saber* o *conocer* y hazle preguntas. Escribe sus respuestas.

Estudiante A

muchos estudiantes en esta escuela
un buen club atlético
un buen salón de chat para visitar
navegar en la Red

otras ciudades
crear una página Web
¡Respuesta personal!

Estudiante B

¡Respuesta personal!

Modelo

A — ¿Conoces *la música de Rubén Blades?*
B — *Sí, la conozco.*
A — ¿Sabes *jugar al vóleibol?*
B — *No, no sé jugar al vóleibol, pero sé jugar al fútbol.*

2 Usa las respuestas de tu compañero(a) y escribe un párrafo sobre él (ella).

En el club de computadoras

Modelo

Mario es un chico muy talentoso. Sabe jugar al fútbol y al béisbol y sabe usar la computadora. Sabe crear páginas Web y conoce muchos salones de chat . . .

Más práctica

- Practice Workbook, p. 23: 1B-6
- WAV Wbk.: Writing, p. 23
- Guided Practice: Grammar Acts., pp. 47–48
- *Real.* para hispanohablantes, pp. 38–39

Go Online
PHSchool.com
For: *Saber* and *Conocer*
Web Code: jdd-0115

cincuenta y siete **57**
Capítulo 1B

Practice and Communicate

 1B

Actividad 16

  Standards: 1.2, 1.3

 Presentation EXPRESS
ANSWERS

Resources: Answers on Transparencies

Focus: Reading and writing e-mails

Suggestions: Have students read Rogelio's e-mail once before they fill in the blanks. Ask students to complete Step 2 on the computer either as homework or in the library and e-mail their responses to you.

Answers:

Step 1:

1. sé	4. Conoces	7. Sabes
2. Sabes	5. Sabes	8. Conoces
3. Conoces	6. Sabes	9. conocer

Step 2: Answers will vary.

Actividad 17

  Standards: 1.1, 1.3

Focus: Speaking with a classmate and writing a paragraph about him or her

Suggestions: Pair students with someone they don't know well. Before students begin, have them write several questions and use their notes during the interview.

Answers will vary.

Extension: Have your class interview students from another Spanish class either face-to-face or through e-mail.

 Pre-AP* Support

- **Activity:** Have students work in groups of four to alternate sharing with each other a descriptive sentence for one of the pictures on pages 52, 54, and 57. The group members identify which picture is being described.
- ***Pre-AP* Resource Book:*** Comprehensive guide to Pre-AP* communication skill development, pp. 9–17; 36–46

Theme Project

Students can perform Step 4 at this point. (For more information, see p. 14-a.)

Additional Resources

- WAV Wbk.: Audio Act. 8, p. 19
- Teacher's Resource Book: Audio Script, p. 51
- Audio Program: Track 10

 Assessment

- **ExamView** Quiz on PresEXPRESS
  QuickTake Presenter
- **Prueba 1B-4:** *Saber* and *conocer,* p. 31

Enrich Your Teaching
Resources for All Teachers

Teacher-to-Teacher

Have students learn about different cultures and participate in meaningful communication by writing e-mails to pen pals in a Spanish-speaking country. Reaching pen pals via e-mail has grown in popularity across the globe. Anyone with access to the Internet can join various e-mail pen pal programs. Many of

these programs emphasize cross-cultural learning and building international friendships.

Internet Search

Keywords: E-mail + pen + pals

1B Practice and Communicate

Gramática

Presentation EXPRESS — GRAMMAR

Core Instruction

Suggestions: To emphasize that each grammar structure always follows the same pattern, write on the board: *¿Cuánto tiempo hace que _____ ?* and *Hace _____ que _____ .* Have a volunteer fill in the blanks using a different color and then read the sentences. Erase the filled-in words and call on another volunteer. Continue doing this, pointing out to students that you never erase the basic structure, only the words that filled in the blanks.

 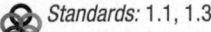 **Standards:** 1.1, 1.3

 **Presentation EXPRESS — ANSWERS**

Resources: Answers on Transparencies

Focus: Writing and speaking about how long something has been going on

Suggestions: Help students see how to integrate the activity pictured in each item with the words beneath it. Point out that the expressions of time will be at the beginning of their sentences.

Answers:

Step 1:
1. Hace diez meses que Pedro toma lecciones de artes marciales.
2. Hace muchos años que Lisa hace gimnasia.
3. Hace un año y medio que Juan y Alberto participan en el coro.
4. Hace dos años que soy miembro del club atlético.
5. Hace un año que Marta es fotógrafa.
6. Hace seis años que tú y yo jugamos al ajedrez.

Step 2:
1. ¿Cuánto tiempo hace que Pedro toma lecciones de artes marciales?
2. ¿...Lisa hace gimnasia?
3. ¿...Juan y Alberto participan en el coro?
4. ¿...eres miembro del club atlético?
5. ¿... Marta es fotógrafa?
6. ¿... tú y yo jugamos al ajedrez?

 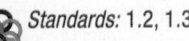 **Standards:** 1.2, 1.3

Focus: Interviewing a classmate about favorite pastimes

Recycle: Leisure activities; expressions of time

Suggestions: Encourage students to ask questions about how long their partner has done an activity. Have them take notes to use for *Actividad* 20.

Answers will vary.

Gramática

Hace + time expressions

To ask how long something has been going on, use:

¿Cuánto tiempo + hace que + present-tense verb?

¿Cuánto tiempo hace que eres miembro del club atlético?

How long have you been a member of the athletic club?

¿Cuánto tiempo hace que Uds. practican con el equipo de básquetbol?

How long have you been practicing with the basketball team?

To tell how long something has been going on, use:

Hace + period of time + que + present-tense verb

Hace más de dos años **que soy** miembro del club atlético.

I've been a member of the athletic club for more than two years.

Hace tres semanas **que practicamos** con el equipo de básquetbol.

We've been practicing with the basketball team for three weeks.

 Actividad 18 — Escribir/Hablar

Hace mucho tiempo que . . .

1 Escribe seis frases para decir cuánto tiempo hace que estos estudiantes hacen diferentes actividades.

Modelo

dos años / Esteban / ser miembro del club
Hace dos años que Esteban es miembro del club de computadoras.

1. diez meses / Pedro / tomar lecciones

2. muchos años / Lisa / hacer

3. un año y medio / Juan y Alberto / participar

4. dos años / yo / ser miembro del club

5. un año / Marta / ser

6. seis años / tú y yo / jugar

2 Trabaja con otro(a) estudiante. Pregunta y contesta sobre las actividades de los estudiantes.

Modelo

A —¿Cuánto tiempo hace que Esteban es miembro del club de computadoras?
B —Hace dos años que es miembro del club.

58 cincuenta y ocho
Tema 1 • Tu día escolar

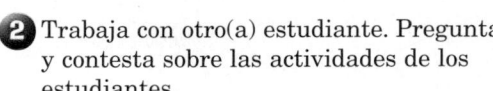

Differentiated Instruction
Solutions for All Learners

 Pre-AP*

Advanced Learners/Pre-AP*

Ask students to write descriptions of sports figures, actors, singers, or other well-known people using **hacer + time expressions.** Without saying whom they are describing, have students read their description to a partner. The partner tries to guess who is being described and asks follow-up questions if needed.

Heritage Language Learners

Students may normally use the expressions *¿Hace cuánto trabajas aquí?* or *¿Cuánto tiempo llevas trabajando aquí?* To respond, they might say: *Llevo dos años.* Point out that while these are acceptable expressions, students can vary their speech by becoming familiar with the structures taught in the *Gramática.*

 **Escribir/Hablar** ____

Actividad 19

Una entrevista

① Escribe cinco frases sobre tus actividades favoritas y tus pasatiempos.

② Entrevista a otro(a) estudiante para saber en qué actividades participa y cuándo empezó a practicarlas. Escribe las respuestas de tu compañero(a).

Modelo

A —*¿En qué actividades participas?*
B —*Me encanta esquiar en el invierno.*
A —*¿Cuánto tiempo hace que esquías?*
B —*Hace diez años que esquío.*

Actividad 20

  **Escribir/Leer/Escuchar** ____

Juego

Usa la información de la Actividad 19 y escribe una descripción de tu compañero(a). No debes incluir el nombre de tu compañero(a) en la descripción. Pon la descripción en una bolsa. Otro(a) estudiante toma una descripción y la lee delante de la clase. La clase tiene que identificar a quién describe.

Modelo

A esta persona le gusta practicar deportes. Hace diez años que . . .

Actividad 21

 **Leer/Hablar** ____

Una cantante famosa

Lee esta descripción de una cantante famosa. Después trabaja con otro(a) estudiante para contestar las preguntas.

Celia Cruz

Reina[1] de la salsa

Hace más de 50 años que el mundo[2] conoce y admira a Celia Cruz. Esta cantante y actriz cubana vivió en los Estados Unidos desde[3] los años 60 hasta[4] su muerte, en 2003. Todos la conocen por su música de "salsa". Celia grabó[5] más de 70 discos y recibió 18 nominaciones al Grammy. Recibió su primer Grammy en el año 1989. También conocemos a Celia por sus películas, como *The Mambo Kings*, una película con Antonio Banderas y Armand Assante. Ella es tan famosa que hay una estrella[6] en el Boulevard de Hollywood con su nombre. Otra cantante famosa, Gloria Estefan, dice que "Celia ejemplifica la energía y el espíritu de la música cubana y latina".

[1]Queen [2]world [3]since [4]until [5]recorded [6]star

1. ¿Por qué conoce el mundo a Celia Cruz?

2. ¿Hace cuántos años el mundo conoce a Celia Cruz?

3. ¿De dónde es Celia? ¿Cuánto tiempo hace que ella recibió su primer Grammy?

4. ¿Cómo sabemos que Celia es muy famosa?

Más práctica

- Practice Workbook, p. 24: 13-7
- Guided Practice: Grammar Acts., pp. 49–50
- *Real.* para hispanohablantes, p. 40

 **For:** *Hace* and Time Expressions
Web Code: jdd-0116

cincuenta y nueve **59**
Capítulo 1B

Enrich Your Teaching
Resources for All Teachers

 Culture Note

The roots of salsa and mambo lie in the fusion of European and African music. This combination of traditional with creative rhythms developed in the early 1800s, especially in Cuba. Salsa and mambo were introduced to the world by such famous singers as Celia Cruz and Pérez Prado.

Internet Search

Keywords:

Celia Cruz, música salsa, mambo

Practice and Communicate

 1B

Actividad 20

 Standards: 1.2, 1.3

Focus: Writing and listening to descriptions of classmates

Recycle: Leisure activities; expressions of time

Suggestions: Tell students to write their descriptions. Briefly check that the descriptions are appropriate before they are put in the bag.

Answers will vary.

Bellringer Review

Have students write two sentences telling how long they have done various activities using *"Hace que..."*. Have several students read their sentences aloud to the class.

Actividad 21

  Standards: 1.2, 2.2

 Presentation EXPRESS **ANSWERS**

Resources: Answers on Transparencies

Focus: Reading about a famous singer

Suggestions: Have students read all of the questions before starting the reading. Tell them to look for cognates and context clues to help them understand the article.

Answers:
1. La conoce por su música de "salsa".
2. Hace más de 50 años que el mundo la conoce.
3. Celia es de Cuba. Hace casi 20 años que recibió su primer Grammy.
4. Hay una estrella en el Boulevard de Hollywood con su nombre.

Additional Resources

- WAV Wbk.: Audio Act. 9, p. 20
- Teacher's Resource Book: Audio Script, p. 51, Communicative Activity BLM, pp. 56–57
- Audio Program: Track 11

 Assessment

- **Exam***View* QuickTake Presenter Quiz on PresEXPRESS
- Prueba 1B-5: *Hace* + time expressions, p. 32

59

Actividad 22

Standards: 1.3, 3.1

Pre-AP*

Focus: Cross-curricular connection to computer science

Suggestions: Brainstorm a list of terms that are useful when talking about the Internet. Explain to students that a storyboard is not just a drawing of their Web site. Tell them that it should include various panels that illustrate how visitors might be able to move around the site and show where various links will take them. You may want to provide the students with a rubric for their presentations.

Answers will vary.

Exploración del lenguaje

Presentation EXPRESS **ANSWERS**

Core Instruction

 Standards: 4.1

Resources: Answers on Transparencies

Suggestions: Students will often pronounce words with **-ción** endings like their English cognates. Point out the accent mark to students and have them practice by saying the **-ción** words in the *¡Compruébalo!* aloud. Ask them to tell you the English equivalent of the **refrán.** *(Business before pleasure.)*

Answers:

celebración	comunicar
explicación	graduar
observación	presentar
participación	repetir

  Actividad 22 · Leer/Hablar/Escribir/Dibujar

Dibuja una página Web

Trabaja con otro(a) estudiante y dibujen una página Web sobre una actividad extracurricular favorita.

Conexiones **La computación**

Para crear una página Web, pueden empezar a trabajar sin usar una computadora. Dibujen un tablero *(storyboard)* para la página principal. Decidan cómo van a ilustrar la página y qué enlaces *(links)* van a tener. Preparen una presentación de su página Web. Usen la página Web del Club de fotografía de la Escuela Secundaria Vallejo como modelo.

Club de fotografía
Escuela Secundaria Vallejo

○ Horario de reuniones
○ Lugar
○ Exposición de trabajos
○ Equipo* necesario

*Equipment

Trabaja con tu compañero(a) y comparen la página Web que Uds. dibujaron con una verdadera página Web de deportes. Luego contesta las siguientes preguntas.

1. ¿Qué información tienen las dos páginas? ¿Qué otra información tiene la verdadera página Web?
2. ¿Qué información no tiene tu página Web?
3. ¿Qué puedes cambiar para dibujar una página Web mejor?

Exploración del lenguaje

Nouns and verbs

In Spanish, you can turn some verbs into nouns by dropping the final *r* of the infinitive and adding *-ción*. The *-ción* ending is equivalent to the *-tion* ending in English. The nouns formed in this way are feminine:

decorar → la decoración

preparar → la preparación

¡Compruébalo! What are the corresponding nouns for each of the following verbs?

celebrar   explicar   observar   participar

And what are the corresponding verbs for these nouns?

comunicación	presentación
graduación	repetición

Refrán

Primero la obligación y entonces la celebración.

Differentiated Instruction
Solutions for All Learners

Heritage Language Learners

Have students prepare a written review of a Spanish-language Web site dedicated to their favorite extracurricular activity. Ask them to describe the site, to tell you what they like and don't like about the site, and to include a printout of the site's homepage.

Multiple Intelligences

Visual/Spatial: For *Actividad* 22, bring in hard copies of sample Web pages about activities mentioned in the chapter, such as martial arts or orchestra music. Point out the features, layout, and links. Ask students to use the samples to decide what they would like to highlight to attract readers to their Web page.

Un anuncio

Lee el folleto *(brochure)* del Club Deportivo Acuasol. Luego contesta las preguntas con otro(a) estudiante.

Bienvenidos

Deporte

Un estilo de vida

En el Club Deportivo Acuasol, tenemos una misión: dar a nuestra comunidad un lugar agradable para el ejercicio personal y la integración de la familia, a través del* deporte, la recreación y la cultura, con el fin de ofrecer bienestar y calidad de vida. En el Club Deportivo Acuasol hay una variedad de cursos tanto culturales como deportivos, en diferentes horarios y días de la semana.

*through

¡Club Deportivo Acuasol!

La mayor parte de nuestras actividades se ofrece sin costo adicional. También tenemos **parqueadero, cafetería** y **servicio médico.**

Por eso, empieza desde hoy a cuidar tu salud y a ampliar tus horizontes culturales y sociales aquí en el . . .

¡Club Deportivo Acuasol!

Ofrecemos:

Aeróbicos

Ballet

Cultura

Básquetbol

Danza regional

Jazz

Gimnasia reductiva

Natación

Tae Kwon Do

Tai Chi Chuan

Tenis

Recreación

Yoga

Taller de teatro

Squash

Coro

1. ¿Para qué es este folleto?
2. ¿Qué servicios hay en el Club Deportivo Acuasol?
3. ¿Te gustaría ser miembro de este club? ¿Por qué?
4. ¿Conoces un club atlético en tu comunidad? ¿Tiene ese club tantos servicios diferentes como el Club Deportivo Acuasol? Compara los dos clubes.
5. ¿Eres miembro de algún club? ¿Cómo se llama? ¿Cuánto tiempo hace que eres miembro del club?

El español en la comunidad

La salsa es uno de los bailes más populares entre los hispanohablantes. Hoy en día, muchas veces uno puede encontrar *(find)* clases que enseñan este baile en varios lugares dentro de la comunidad. Busca en el periódico o en tu comunidad o en una comunidad cerca lugares que ofrecen clases de salsa.

- ¿Te gustaría aprender a bailar salsa como actividad extracurricular? ¿Por qué?

Practice and Communicate

Resources: Voc. and Gram. Transparency 41; Answers on Transparencies

Focus: Reading and demonstrating comprehension of a brochure for a sports club

Suggestions: Remind students to use visual clues to help them understand the reading. If they are not familiar with a club and are not members of a club, have them answer items 4 and 5 using information found on the Internet about a sports club in a Spanish-speaking country.

Answers will vary but will include:

1. Este folleto es de un club deportivo.
2. En el Club Deportivo Acuasol hay muchas actividades deportivas, culturales y de recreo, y también hay parqueadero, cafetería y servicio médico.
3. Answers will vary.
4. Answers will vary.
5. Answers will vary.

Extension: Have students write responses to the following: *Imagina que eres miembro del Club Deportivo Acuasol. ¿En qué actividades te gusta participar? ¿Por qué?*

El español en la comunidad

Core Instruction

Standards: 1.2, 5.1

Suggestions: Ask students if they know how to dance salsa. If they do, ask them to demonstrate the dance. Do they know of any places in your community where people go to dance and listen to salsa music?

Answers will vary.

Theme Project

Students can perform Step 5 at this point. (For more information, see p. 14-a.)

Enrich Your Teaching
Resources for All Teachers

Culture Note

Several Spanish-language search engines exist to help Spanish-speaking surfers navigate the Web. Many popular search engines have sites that are specific to various Spanish-speaking countries. The Internet is an important tool for students studying Spanish language and culture.

Internet Search

Keywords:

español + search engines

Lectura

Core Instruction

Standards: 1.2, 2.1, 2.2, 3.1, 3.2

Focus: Reading a Web page for a dance school

Suggestions:

Pre-reading: After students read the *Estrategia,* ask a volunteer to list the predictions on the board.

Reading: Have students read the first page silently. Have students read the descriptions for each dance at the top of p. 63 silently. After each one, ask a volunteer to restate what they read in the text.

Post-reading: Have students summarize the reasons one should take dance lessons at *La Escuela Internacional de Baile.* Ask them if they are familiar with any of the dances mentioned. Can they demonstrate any steps? Have students complete the *¿Comprendiste?* questions.

 Bellringer Review
Have students express their likes and dislikes about taking a dance class and explain their reasons.

Pre-AP* Support

- **Activity:** Write the words *Tango, Merengue, Flamenco,* and *Swing* on the board and ask students to copy them on a sheet of paper. Make statements about the dances and ask students to write the number of your statements under the appropriate heading.
- **Pre-AP* Resource Book:** Comprehensive guide to reading skill development, pp. 18–24

¡Adelante!

Lectura

¡A bailar!

¿Te gusta bailar pero eres un poco tímida? ¿Piensas que bailas muy mal? ¿Necesitas aprender a bailar en seguida? ¡Haz tus sueños realidad hoy mismo! Lee la página Web de la Escuela Internacional de Baile.

Objectives

- **Read a Web page about a dance school**
- **Compare schools in the United States, Mexico, and Spain**
- **Write a paragraph about your extracurricular activities and interests**
- **Read about San Miguel de Allende, Mexico**

Estrategia

Predicting
You are going to read a page from the Web site of a dance school. What kind of information do you expect to see on the page?

La Escuela Internacional de Baile

- **TANGO**
- **MERENGUE**
- **FLAMENCO**
- **SWING**

te ofrece una gran variedad de clases de bailes tradicionales y contemporáneos.

Razones para hacerse[1] miembro hoy mismo:
- Puedes participar en una actividad sana y deportiva que te ayuda a entender las ricas tradiciones y costumbres de varios países hispanohablantes.
- Si no tienes pareja para bailar, ¡no te preocupes! Puedes conocer a otros jóvenes simpáticos de varias escuelas que vienen a aprender estos bailes.
- Puedes ir a competiciones internacionales en Francia, los Estados Unidos y el Japón, y hasta ganar muchos premios.

[1]Reasons to become

62 sesenta y dos
Tema 1 • Tu día escolar

Differentiated Instruction
Solutions for All Learners

Advanced Learners
Have students design a Web page to advertise lessons for one of the activities mentioned in this chapter. This could be done on the computer or designed on poster board. Have students tell why someone should learn how to do the activity, when and where lessons are offered, and how much they cost.

Multiple Intelligences
Rhythmic/Musical: To help students distinguish among the styles of dance, play samples of tango, merengue, flamenco, and swing music. Have students tell which type of music they like the most. Invite music learners to identify and explain some of the differences among the forms of music.

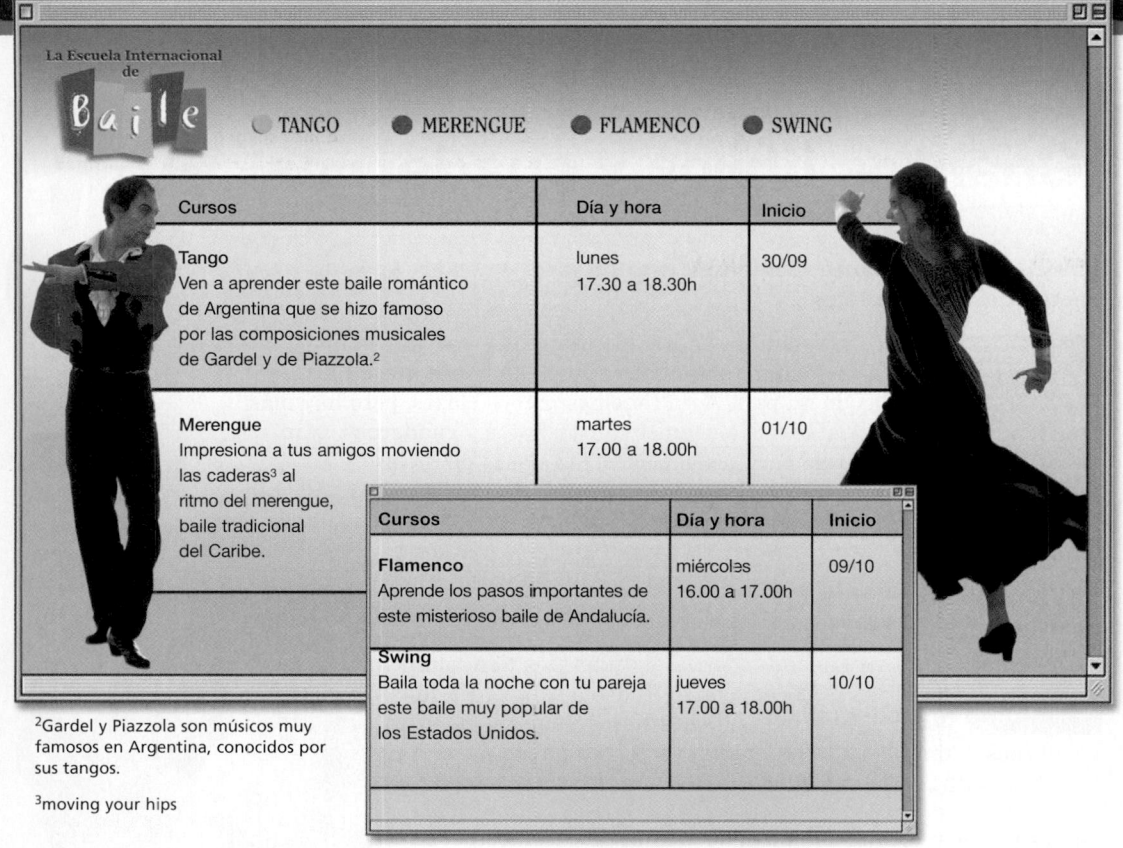

La Escuela Internacional de **Baile**

○ TANGO ● MERENGUE ● FLAMENCO ○ SWING

Cursos	Día y hora	Inicio
Tango Ven a aprender este baile romántico de Argentina que se hizo famoso por las composiciones musicales de Gardel y de Piazzola.[2]	lunes 17.30 a 18.30h	30/09
Merengue Impresiona a tus amigos moviendo las caderas[3] al ritmo del merengue, baile tradicional del Caribe.	martes 17.00 a 18.00h	01/10

Cursos	Día y hora	Inicio
Flamenco Aprende los pasos importantes de este misterioso baile de Andalucía.	miércoles 16.00 a 17.00h	09/10
Swing Baila toda la noche con tu pareja este baile muy popular de los Estados Unidos.	jueves 17.00 a 18.00h	10/10

[2]Gardel y Piazzola son músicos muy famosos en Argentina, conocidos por sus tangos.

[3]moving your hips

¿Comprendiste?

1. ¿Qué clases puedes tomar en la Escuela Internacional de Baile?

2. ¿Cuánto cuesta por mes un curso de la Escuela Internacional de Baile?

3. ¿Qué razones da la página Web para ser miembro de la escuela?

4. ¿Cuál de los bailes te interesa más? ¿Por qué?

5. ¿Te gustaría tomar una clase en esta escuela? ¿Por qué?

Más práctica

● WAV Wbk.: Writing, p. 24
● Guided Practice: *Lectura*, p. 51
● *Real.* para hispanohablantes, pp. 42–43

Go Online PHSchool.com **For:** Internet Activity **Web Code:** jdd-0117

Fondo cultural ■◆■◇■◆■■■◆■◇■◆◇■◆

El ballet El ballet clásico y el ballet folklórico tienen una larga historia en varios países hispanohablantes. Muchos países tienen un ballet nacional, como el Ballet Nacional de España o el Ballet Folklórico de México. El ballet folklórico se inspira en el folklore, la danza popular y los bailes tradicionales de un país, e interpreta estas tradiciones con técnicas de la danza clásica y moderna. Muchas compañías de ballet también tienen escuelas de baile.

Ballet Folklórico de México

• ¿El ballet es popular donde vives? ¿Hay algún baile folklórico en tu región? ¿Hay una compañía de ballet en tu ciudad?

sesenta y tres **63**
Capítulo 1B

¿Comprendiste?

Presentation EXPRESS ANSWERS

Standards: 1.2

Resources: Answers on Transparencies

Focus: Verifying comprehension of a dance school Web page

Suggestion: For each question, have students make a list of key words to help them find the information in the reading. Tell students that if they give a negative response to Items 4 and 5, they should explain why.

Answers:

1. Puedes tomar clases de tango, merengue, flamenco y swing.
2. Un curso cuesta $230.00 por mes.
3. Puedes participar en una actividad sana y deportiva; puedes entender las ricas tradiciones y costumbres de varios países hispanohablantes; puedes conocer a otros jóvenes simpáticos e ir a competencias internacionales.
4. Answers will vary.
5. Answers will vary.

Fondo cultural

Standards: 1.2, 2.2, 4.2

◆■◇■◆■■■◆■◇■◆◇■◆

Suggestions: To help students answer the question, have them list different dances that are practiced in their community. Remind them of ethnic centers in the community in which people may practice less common dances. Bring in an entertainment page from the newspaper to show students different types of dance ensembles that they could see in their community.

Answers will vary.

For Further Reading

Student Resources:

• Realidades para hispanohablantes: Lectura 2: pp. 44–45

• Lecturas para hispanohablantes 2: "Asignatura pendiente," pp. 73–74

• Guided Practice: Lectura, p. 51

AP* Literature Author: Isabel Allende, *Paula* (excerpt), Lecturas para hispanohablantes 2, pp. 76–78
Pre-AP*

Enrich Your Teaching
Resources for All Teachers

Culture Note

In Mexico, high school students can join the school of the *Ballet Folklórico.* This four-year program teaches Mexican folklore, classical ballet, and folk dances. The class size is about 110 students and some later join the *Ballet Folklórico de México.*

Teacher-to-Teacher

Show an instructional video for one of the dances mentioned in the reading. Practice with students each day to make them feel more comfortable. When they are ready, have them perform the dance in small groups for other classes. Be sensitive to students who do not dance for religious reasons.

1B Communicate: Culture

Perspectivas del mundo hispano

Core Instruction

Standards: 1.2, 2.1, 2.2, 3.2, 4.2

Focus: Reading about courses and school supplies in Spanish-speaking countries

Suggestions: Ask students to list items they take to school every day. As they read the passage, have them check off the items mentioned on their list. Have volunteers point out differences in materials that students carry in Spain and the United States. Have a volunteer summarize the courses available in your school, noting which ones are required and which are electives.

Point out the list of courses offered in Spain. Remind students that these are not representative of all Spanish-speaking countries. For example, in Mexico, most high-school students must take academic courses such as *español, matemáticas, historia universal, geografía general, civismo, biología, física y química,* and *una lengua extranjera.* They are often required to take *expresión artística, educación física,* and *educación tecnológica.*

Explain to students the various ways to refer to classes in Spanish: *clases, cursos, asignaturas,* and *materias.*

Answers will vary.

Additional Resources

Student Resource: Realidades para hispanohablantes, p. 46

Perspectivas del mundo hispano

¡Cuántos libros y cuadernos!

Marcos, un estudiante mexicano, está en una escuela estadounidense.

 "Vivo con mi familia en Estados Unidos y veo que en las escuelas estadounidenses hay menos materias que en las escuelas de mi país. Aquí tenemos menos clases, pero hay más actividades extracurriculares. No usamos tantos libros y cuadernos, pero necesitamos muchas cosas para los deportes, las clases de música y las visitas a lugares interesantes. Siempre les pregunto a mis amigos: "¿Quién me ayuda con todas estas cosas?".

Latifa, una estudiante norteamericana, está en una escuela española.

 "Aquí en España todos los estudiantes tienen muchas clases, 11 ó 12 cada curso. Todos los días hay que llevar a la escuela muchos libros y muchos cuadernos, y también el almuerzo. A veces, ¡no puedo poner todos los libros en la mochila!".

En los países hispanohablantes, los planes de estudio de la educación secundaria y el bachillerato tienen muchas asignaturas[1]. Cada plan de estudio tiene de 10 a 12 asignaturas. En los primeros años, las materias son obligatorias. En los últimos años, puedes escoger[2] algunas de las materias.

¡Compruébalo! Compara tus asignaturas con la lista de asignaturas de la escuela secundaria de España. ¿Qué clases tienes en común con las de este país? ¿Hay clases en España que no tiene tu escuela?

¿Qué te parece? ¿Tienes que llevar muchos libros y cuadernos a clase? ¿Qué otras cosas tienes que llevar? ¿Qué prefieres: tener más asignaturas y menos actividades extracurriculares o menos asignaturas y más actividades?

[1]courses [2]choose

Asignaturas de la escuela secundaria

España

Lengua y literatura castellana

Lengua y literatura de las comunidades autónomas

Lengua extranjera

Matemáticas

Ciencias sociales, Geografía e Historia

Educación física

Ciencias de la naturaleza

Educación plástica y visual

Tecnología

Música

Differentiated Instruction
Solutions for All Learners

Advanced Learners

Have students create a course description book for their school. Ask them to organize their book by subjects, and to write what supplies students will need for each course. If applicable, have students mention a club that might interest students in each course.

Students with Learning Difficulties

Provide a two-column chart labeled by country. Under *España,* list the subjects from the course list on p. 64. Ask students to list the courses they are taking under *los Estados Unidos.* Have students use the chart when completing *¡Compruébalo!*

Mis actividades extracurriculares

Task

Your school offers many extracurricular activities so that students can explore different interests. Your teacher wants to learn more about you and has asked you to write about your activities and tell why you chose them.

1 Prewrite List your activities and tell why you find them interesting or challenging. Also note how long you have been involved in doing them.

2 Draft Use your list and notes to write a first draft of your paragraph. Try to personalize it as much as possible by telling how you feel about these activities and why you do them.

3 Revise Read through your paragraph and check:

- spelling
- use of *hace* + time expressions
- verb forms

Share your paragraph with a partner. Your partner should check the following:

- Is your paragraph easy to understand?
- Does it give information about you and your activities?
- Is there anything you should add or change?
- Are there any errors?

Rewrite your paragraph, making any necessary changes. You may want to add a photo of you participating in one of the activities or some drawings that illustrate the activities.

4 Publish Make a final copy of your paragraph to give to your teacher or to add to your portfolio.

5 Evaluation Your teacher may give you a rubric for how the paragraph will be graded. You will probably be graded on:

- how much information you provide about yourself
- use of vocabulary
- accuracy and use of the writing process

Estrategia

Personalizing
To personalize your writing, think about why you enjoy certain activities and what attracts you to them.

sesenta y cinco **65**
Capítulo 1B

Presentación escrita
Expository

Standards: 1.3, 3.1

Focus: Writing about extracurricular activities

Suggestions: For Step 1, you may want to limit students to three activities. Have students brainstorm a list of adjectives that can be used to describe the different activities, and another list of adverbs that tell how students do each one. Encourage students to organize their presentation by providing one key statement, with two or three supporting details. You may wish to provide students with a checklist to use as they peer-edit their partner's work. The list can be formulated using the bulleted questions in Step 3. If possible, schedule time in the computer room for students to type their final copy. Provide a model of a top-scoring presentation for students.

Portfolio

Have students include a copy of their descriptions of their extracurricular activities in their portfolio.

Pre-AP* Support

- *Pre-AP* Resource Book:* Comprehensive guide to Pre-AP* writing skill development, pp. 25–35

Teacher-to-Teacher

e-amigos: Have students send their *e-amigos* a message describing their extracurricular activities. Encourage them to ask questions to learn more about what their *e-amigos* do in their free time.

Additional Resources

Student Resources: Realidades para hispanohablantes, p. 47; Guided Practice: Presentación escrita, p. 52

✓ Assessment

- Assessment Program: Rubrics, p. T27

Give students copies of the rubric before they begin the activity. Go over the descriptions of the different levels of performance. After assessing students, help individuals understand how their performance could be improved.

Enrich Your Teaching
Resources for All Teachers

RUBRIC	Score 1	Score 3	Score 5
How much information you communicate	You provide one activity with explanation.	You provide two activities with explanations.	You provide three or more activities with explanations.
Your use of vocabulary and grammar	You use very little variation of vocabulary and have frequent usage errors.	You use limited vocabulary and have some usage errors.	You use an extended variety of vocabulary and have very few usage errors.
Your use of the writing process	You turn in only the prewrite notes.	You turn in prewrite notes and rough draft.	You turn in prewrite notes, rough draft, and final product.

Videomisterio

Core Instruction

Standards: 1.2, 3.2, 4.2

Resources: Voc. and Gram. Transparencies: Map 12

Focus: Reading about San Miguel de Allende; building background knowledge to prepare for the *Videomisterio*

Suggestions: Ask students to locate San Miguel de Allende on a map. Point out that the city has a relatively small population today, but that it was an important colonial city. Tell them that during colonial times, in the mid-1700s, the population of San Miguel de Allende was larger than that of either New York or Boston. Point out to students that although these cities grew and changed over the years, San Miguel de Allende remained a quaint, colonial town. Point out to them that there is not even a traffic light in the entire city. Ask students if they can think of any towns in the United States that were important colonial centers but that are now considered to be small, colonial towns. Give them the example of Jamestown, Virginia, if they are unable to answer.

Have students study the large picture on pp. 66–67. Point out the large, pink, seemingly Gothic cathedral on the right-hand side of the picture. Tell students that it is the *Parroquia del Arcángel San Miguel,* a well-known landmark in the town. Explain that the cathedral is famous for its method of construction. The architect who designed the church's facade used only postcards of European churches on which to base his work. Ask students to compare the architecture of the *Parroquia* to a church or other house of worship or public building in your community. Which is more elaborate? How?

Videomisterio

Preparación para . . .

En busca de la verdad

San Miguel de Allende

Bienvenidos a San Miguel de Allende, una ciudad visitada en el videomisterio. San Miguel de Allende está a unos 92 kilómetros al sudeste de Guanajuato y tiene una población de más de 134,000 habitantes. Fue fundada por Fray Juan de San Miguel en 1542, y a él debe parte de su nombre.

El clima primaveral[1] de San Miguel de Allende la hace una de las ciudades de México más populares para visitar. La ciudad tiene un ambiente[2] cultural y artístico de muchísima variedad. Es famosa por sus restaurantes. También es un refugio para artistas y artesanos. ▶

Según la historia, San Miguel de Allende creció alrededor de un manantial[3] de agua llamado El Chorro. Este famoso manantial que da agua todo el año puede verse en el Paseo del Chorro, un parque popular al sur de la ciudad.

▲ La Plaza Allende es el corazón de la ciudad y uno de los sitios más visitados, especialmente los domingos. Tiene un quiosco y muchos jardines con flores, principalmente rosas. Desde este jardín también puedes ver la Presidencia Municipal[4], casas históricas e iglesias importantes.

[1]spring-like   [2]atmosphere   [3]spring

[4]Town Hall

66 sesenta y seis
Tema 1 • Tu día escolar

Differentiated Instruction
Solutions for All Learners

Heritage Language Learners
Have students prepare five questions that they would ask Ignacio Allende about his hometown and his involvement in the Mexican independence movement. Ask them to create a fictional interview with Allende. Encourage them to use library and Internet resources to create fact-based answers to their questions.

Advanced Learners
Have students download photographs of San Miguel de Allende from the Internet. Tell them to pretend they went there on vacation and have them share their "vacation pictures" with a group. Have students pass the photographs around and explain the significance of each.

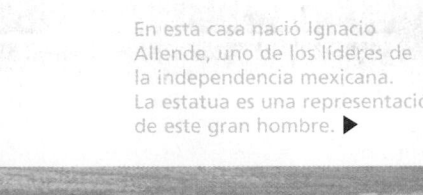

En esta casa nació Ignacio Allende, uno de los líderes de la independencia mexicana. La estatua es una representación de este gran hombre. ▶

¿Sabes que . . . ?

Ignacio Allende estudió en el colegio de San Francisco de Sales, en San Miguel de Allende. Fue aquí donde recibió la educación que lo inspiró para luchar contra[5] los españoles por la independencia. Después la ciudad tomó el apellido de este héroe.

Para pensar

San Miguel de Allende, igual que Guanajuato, se ha convertido[6] en un centro cultural e intelectual internacional sin perder su ambiente de pueblo tranquilo. ¿En Estados Unidos hay ciudades con las mismas características de San Miguel de Allende? ¿Cuáles son?

[5]to fight against   [6]has been changed

Suggestions: Direct attention to the statue of Ignacio Allende and the description of him as a *gran hombre.* Point out that the *Casa de Allende,* where the revolutionary leader was born, is one of the best examples of the architectural style of the colonial period. Explain that Ignacio Allende was a leader in the movement against Spanish control under the reign of Joseph Bonaparte, brother of the Emperor Napoleon Bonaparte. Ask students to say what the word *rebel* makes them think of. Remind students that while Ignacio Allende was considered a rebel because of his disagreement with the Spanish occupation of Mexico, he was not a radical warrior. On the contrary, Ignacio Allende was an intellectual who promoted civilized opposition. He became a prominent figure in the opposition against Spain, but was caught in an ambush in 1811 and was killed.

Tell students that San Miguel de Allende is considered an artistic and intellectual center of Mexico. Even though it is a small town, it is quite cosmopolitan. Point out to students that the *Instituto Allende,* a center for art and intellectual development, attracts many artists to the region. As a result, artwork and artisanship are primary components of the city's character. Ask students if they know of any centers in the United States that are similar to the *Instituto Allende.* Ask them to find information on the cities where these institutes are found, and compare the cities to San Miguel de Allende.

Answers will vary.

sesenta y siete **67**
Capítulo 1B

Enrich Your Teaching
Resources for All Teachers

Culture Note
The first Spanish missionaries to arrive in the Americas were the Franciscans. It is believed that the Franciscan Fray Juan de San Miguel came to Mexico towards the end of 1530. He is credited with starting the first high school in Guayangareo, Mexico. In 1542 he founded the city of San Miguel el Grande, which is now San Miguel de Allende.

Internet Search
Keywords:

Fray Juan de San Miguel

1B Review

Review Activities

 Standards: 4.1

To talk about extracurricular activities:
Have Student A say a vocabulary word from the list. Then, have Student B identify it as *Actividad* or *Persona*.

To talk about athletic activities, music, and drama: Have students look through a school yearbook. Ask Student A to name an activity to Student B, who finds a picture to match. If there is no picture, he/she should say *No tenemos* (name of activity).

To talk about actions with activities: Make grab bags of slips of paper with sentence fragments. Have students select nouns, adverbs, or direct objects to accompany fragments out of the bag. They may continue until they have a logical sentence.

To talk about and describe Internet activities: Give pairs of students a list of scenarios, such as *Estoy aburrido y quiero conocer a una persona nueva.* Have one read the sentence and the other offer advice.

To tell how long something has been going on: Give students a list of celebrities and when they began their careers. Students tell how long they are.

To make comparisons: Ask students to compare different extracurricular activities. Suggest that they talk about how long the organization has been around, how much time is involved, or which is more popular.

Portfolio

Invite students to review the activities they completed in this chapter—written reports, posters or other visuals, tapes of oral presentations, or other projects. Have them select 1 or 2 items that they feel best demonstrate their achievements in Spanish to include in their portfolios. Have them include this with the Chapter Checklist and Self-Assessment Worksheet.

Additional Resources

Student Resources: Realidades para hispanohablantes, p. 48

 **CD–ROM**

PuzzleView Web Code: jdd–0118

Teacher Resources:
- Teacher's Resource Book: Situation Cards, p. 58, Clip Art, pp. 60–63
- Assessment Program: Chapter Checklist and Self-Assessment Worksheet, pp. T56–T57

Repaso del capítulo

Vocabulario y gramática

Chapter Review

To prepare for the test, check to see if you . . .
- know the new vocabulary and grammar
- can perform the tasks on p. 69

to talk about extracurricular activities

las actividades extracurriculares	extracurricular activities
el ajedrez	chess
el club, pl. los clubes	club
el club atlético	athletic club
el equipo	team
la fotografía	photography
el fotógrafo, la fotógrafa	photographer
los jóvenes	young people
el miembro	member
ser miembro	to be a member
el pasatiempo	pastime
la práctica	practice
la reunión, pl. las reuniones	meeting

to talk about athletic activities

el animador, la animadora	cheerleader
las artes marciales	martial arts
hacer gimnasia	to do gymnastics
el hockey	hockey
jugar a los bolos	to bowl
la natación	swimming

to talk about music and drama

la banda	band
el bailarín, la bailarina	dancer
la canción, pl. las canciones	song
el (la) cantante	singer
el coro	chorus, choir
ensayar	to rehearse
el ensayo	rehearsal
el músico, la música	musician
la orquesta	orchestra
la voz, pl. las voces	voice

For Vocabulario adicional, see pp. 498–499.

to talk about actions with activities

asistir a	to attend
ganar	to win, to earn
grabar	to record
participar (en)	to participate (in)
tomar lecciones	to take lessons
volver (o → ue)	to return

to talk about and describe Internet activities

crear una página Web	to create a Web page
estar en línea	to be online
hacer una búsqueda	to do a search
navegar en la Red	to surf the Web
visitar salones de chat	to visit chat rooms

other useful words

entre	among, between
el interés	interest
la oportunidad, pl. las oportunidades	opportunity

to tell how long something has been going on

¿Cuánto tiempo hace que . . . ?	How long . . . ?
Hace + *time* + que . . .	It has been . . .

to make comparisons

tan + *adj.* + como	as + *adj.* + as
tantos(as) + *noun* + como	as much / many + *noun* + as

saber *to know (how)*

sé	sabemos
sabes	sabéis
sabe	saben

conocer *to know, to be acquainted with*

conozco	conocemos
conoces	conocéis
conoce	conocen

Differentiated Instruction
Solutions for All Learners

Students with Special Needs
As an alternative to oral work, you may want to give students time to review the vocabulary and grammar in writing. Provide a word bank for them to use to write a paragraph about the extracurricular activities in their school. Be sure to provide feedback before the exam.

Advanced Learners
Ask students to write and give an oral report about a favorite athlete. Have them include a statement telling how long that person has been involved in the sport. Ask students to include an opinion comparing some aspect of that person's skill with that of another athlete who plays the same sport.

Más práctica

- Practice Workbook: Puzzle, p. 25
- Practice Workbook: Organizer, p. 26

 Go Online
PHSchool.com
For: Test Preparation
Web Code: jdd-0118

Preparación para el examen

On the exam you will be asked to . . .	Here are practice tasks similar to those you will find on the exam . . .	If you need review . . .
jdd-0199 **1 Escuchar** Listen and understand as teenagers talk about what they do after school	Listen as two teenagers describe what they do after school. See if you can understand: (a) what they like to do; (b) why they like to do it; (c) how long they have been participating in that particular activity.	**pp. 46–49** *A primera vista* **p. 51** Actividad 7 **p. 57** Actividad 17 **p. 59** Actividad 20
2 Hablar Talk about the extracurricular activities that you are interested in doing after school and how long you have been doing these activities	Imagine that you meet a new classmate from Venezuela who is going to your school. Since you both seem to like the same types of things: (a) tell him about some of the things you do after school that you think would interest him; (b) ask him to go with you to one of your activities.	**p. 51** Actividad 6 **p. 52** Actividad 8 **p. 54** Actividad 13 **p. 58** Actividad 18 **pp. 59** Actividades 19–20
3 Leer Read and understand a letter written by a student about a problem at school	Read the following letter to an advice columnist. What problem is the writer describing? How does he compare himself to his brother? *Mi hermano mayor es muy estudioso y deportista. Pero yo . . . ¡no! A mí me interesa visitar a mis amigos en los salones de chat en la Red. Según mis amigos, soy increíble con mi computadora. ¡El problema es que todos mis profesores piensan que soy tan estudioso y deportista como mi hermano! Mis padres dicen que debo ser como mi hermano. No me gusta.* —Frustrado	**p. 53** Actividad 11 **p. 57** Actividad 16 **pp. 62–63** *Lectura*
4 Escribir Write briefly about your extracurricular activities	You're trying to get an after-school job. Most of the applications you have picked up ask the same questions: *¿En qué actividades extracurriculares participas? ¿Cómo te van a ayudar estas actividades en este trabajo?* Write a brief paragraph describing your extracurricular activities and mention why you like these activities.	**p. 50** Actividad 4 **p. 52** Actividades 8–9 **p. 57** Actividad 16 **p. 59** Actividad 19 **p. 65** *Presentación escrita*
5 Pensar Demonstrate an understanding of the differences between schools in the United States and Spain	Your friend's father is being transferred to Spain for one year, so your friend will be attending school in Madrid. Based on this chapter, what could you tell him about the differences that he will probably find in his new school there?	**p. 64** *Perspectivas del mundo hispano*

sesenta y nueve 69
Capítulo 1B

Differentiated Assessment
Solutions for All Learners

STUDENTS NEEDING EXTRA HELP
- **Alternate Assessment Program:** Examen del capítulo 1B
- **Audio Program CD 20:** Chap. 1B, Track 3

HERITAGE LEARNERS
- **Assessment Program: Realidades para hispanohablantes:** Examen del capítulo 1B
- **ExamView** Heritage Learner Test Bank

ADVANCED/PRE-AP*
- **ExamView** Pre-AP* Test Bank
- **Pre-AP* Resource Book,** pp. 96–99

Performance Tasks
 Presentation EXPRESS
ANSWERS

Standards: 1.1, 1.2, 1.3, 2.1, 2.2, 4.2

Student Resource: Realidades para hispanohablantes, p. 49

Teacher Resources: Teacher's Resource Book: Audio Script, p. 51; Audio Program: Track 13; Answers on Transparencies

1. Escuchar

Suggestions: Have students listen to the entire script once before they answer.

Script:

Person #1: No conozco a muchas personas en la escuela. Soy un nuevo estudiante aquí y soy bastante tímido. Por eso, después de las clases regreso a mi casa. Me gusta visitar salones de chat en la Red. También me gusta cantar. Hace cinco años que canto con mi hermana en una banda musical.

Person #2: ¿Te gusta cantar? ¡A mí también! ¿Quieres ir conmigo a la práctica del coro esta tarde? Hace dos años que canto en el coro. Es muy divertido.

Answers:

a) Person #1 likes to visit chat rooms and sing. Person #2 also likes to sing; b) Person #1 likes to visit chat rooms because he is new at school and shy and doesn't know many people. Person #2 likes to sing because it's fun; c) Person #1 has been singing in a band for five years. Person #2 has been singing in a chorus for two years.

2. Hablar

Suggestions: If students are not involved in extracurricular activities, ask them to answer according to which ones might appeal to a new student.

Answers will vary.

3. Leer

Suggestions: To help students relate to this letter, have them list ways they differ from their own brothers or sisters.

Answers:

a) Sus padres y profesores piensan que él debe ser tan estudioso y deportista como su hermano.
b) Él dice que no es tan estudioso y deportista como su hermano, pero usa la computadora muy bien.

4. Escribir

Suggestions: Ask students to brainstorm things they have learned from extracurricular activities. **Answers** will vary.

5. Pensar

Suggestions: Refer students to the article on p. 64 to help explain the differences. **Answers** will vary.

Assessment
- **ExamView** Quiz on PresEXPRESS
- Assessment Program: Examen del capítulo
- **ExamView** Test Bank: Tests A and B
- Audio Program CD 20: Chap. 1B, Track 3

Tema 2

Un evento especial

THEME OVERVIEW

▶ **2A ¿Cómo te preparas?**
- Getting ready for a special event

Vocabulary: daily routines; clothing

Grammar: reflexive verbs; *ser* and *estar;* possessive adjectives

Cultural Perspectives: clothing

▶ **2B ¿Qué ropa compraste?**
- Shopping for clothing

Vocabulary: clothing; fashion; shopping

Grammar: preterite of regular verbs; demonstrative adjectives; using adjectives as nouns

Cultural Perspectives: parties

Theme Project

Revista de modas

Overview: Students create two pages from a fashion magazine featuring photos of people in fashionable clothing. Students will write sentences using the preterite about what each person in the photo did to get ready, what clothing they bought, and where they went in their new outfits. They then present their magazine pages to the class.

Materials: Construction paper, markers, magazines, glue or tape, scissors

• •

Sequence: (suggestions for when to do each step are found throughout the chapters)

2A ▶ **STEP 1.** Review instructions so students know what is expected of them. Hand out the "Theme 2 Project Instructions and Rubric" from the *Teacher's Resource Book.*

STEP 2. Students submit a rough sketch of each page of their fashion magazine. Note your corrections and suggestions, then return the drafts to students. For grammar and vocabulary practice, ask students to partner and present their drafts to each other.

STEP 3. Students create layouts on different pieces of construction paper, leaving room for photos and descriptions. Encourage them to work in pencil first and to try different arrangements before gluing photos or decorations.

2B ▶ **STEP 4.** Students submit a draft of the magazine. Note your corrections and suggestions, then return drafts to students.

STEP 5. Students present their magazines to the class, explaining each page and describing selected pictures.

Options:

1. Students create a magazine about Hispanic celebrities they research.

2. Students create a Web page featuring friends or family dressed for special events.

Assessment:

Here is a detailed rubric for assessing this project:

Theme 2 Project: *Revista de modas*

RUBRIC	Score 1	Score 3	Score 5
Your evidence of planning	You provide no written draft or sketch.	Your draft was written and layout created, but not corrected.	You show evidence of corrected draft and layout.
Your use of illustrations	You include no photos or visuals.	You include very few photos or visuals.	You include several photos or visuals.
Your magazine presentation	You include little of the required information.	You include at least three photos, and describe clothing, destination, and preparations.	You include three or more photos, and describe clothing, destination, and preparations.

Bulletin Boards

Theme: *La moda*

Ask students to cut out, copy, or download photos of fashion, clothing, and clothing sale advertisements from different Spanish-speaking cultures. Cluster photos into several categories—male fashion, female fashion, children's fashion, etc.—so that similarities and differences are evident.

Bibliography

Brown, Jonathan. *Velázquez: Painter and Courtier.* Yale University Press, 1988.

Harold, Robert. *Folk Costumes of the World.* London: Cassell Academic, 1999. Folk costumes from around the world, including traditional dress from Latin America.

Hoyt-Goldsmith, Diane. *Quinceañera: A Latina's 15th Birthday Celebration.* Holiday House, 2002.

Rivera, Diego, and Gladys March. *My Art, My Life: An Autobiography.* Dover Publications, 1992.

Hands-on Culture

Recipe: *Mosaico de zanahoria* (a gelatin dessert for special events) All events have special desserts. This cool gelatin dessert is eaten in northern Mexico where it is very hot. It looks like a mosaic because of the different colors of the fruits and vegetables in the gelatin.

Ingredients:

> 4-5 carrots, peeled and grated
> 1 large can of chopped pineapple (drained)
> 1 pint of heavy whipping cream
> 1 pound of yellow American cheese, partially melted
> 2 small packages or 1 large package of lemon-flavored gelatin
> 2 cups of boiling water

Directions:

1. Grate the carrots, drain the chopped pineapple, and mix together well.

2. Add the partially melted cheese to the pineapple and carrots. Set aside.

3. Boil the two cups of water.

4. Dissolve the gelatin in the boiling water.

5. Add the pineapple, carrot, and cheese mixture to the dissolved gelatin.

6. Stir the mixture until the cheese is completely melted.

7. Fold in the cold cream to the gelatin mixture and mix well.

8. Pour into a mold, glass pan, or glass bowl.

9. Refrigerate the gelatin overnight without disturbing it.

10. Serve with additional whipped cream and/or fresh fruit as a dessert for a special event.

Game

¿Qué llevas?

Play this game during *Capítulo* 2B to review clothing and colors.

Players: Any number of students in pairs

Materials: Paper and markers, colored pencils, or crayons

Rules:

1. Give each student a piece of paper.

2. Instruct each student to write a 10-sentence clothing description. They must include colors, sizes, and fabrics. The game works best if the students include as many articles of clothing as possible. It is also important to model what you expect the students to write in addition to providing some visuals for their reference.

3. Sitting back to back, students take turns describing their clothing. Without looking at each others' descriptions, students must draw what their partner has written.

4. After both students have read their descriptions, they can turn and compare their drawings with the descriptions. For each correct detail, the student receives one point. The student with the most points wins.

Variation: You can narrow the students' possibilities by specifying a special event.

Internet Search

Use the keywords to find more information.

***2A* Keywords:**

> Diego Rivera, quinceañera, Teatro Real de Madrid

***2B* Keywords:**

> Diego Velázquez, Narciso Rodríguez, parranda

RECYCLE
A ver si recuerdas

Vocabulary
• La ropa y el cuerpo

Grammar
• Verbs and expressions that use the infinitive

A primera vista	Manos a la obra	¡Adelante!	Repaso

Learning Sequence

INPUT	PRACTICE	APPLICATION	REVIEW
• Introduce vocabulary and grammar within an authentic context.	• Practice and develop new vocabulary. • Learn and practice new grammar structures.	• Apply vocabulary and grammar through culminating, theme-based activities. • Apply skill development.	• Review vocabulary and grammar.

Objectives

Read, listen to, and interpret information about • Getting ready for an event • Daily routines	• Talk about your daily routine. • Describe yourself and others. • Use reflexive verbs. • Review differences between *ser* and *estar*. • Possession • Express possession.	• Read about the *Teatro Colón* and its programs. • Describe how to make a poncho. • Give a presentation about a special event in your life. • Read introduction: Dolores Hidalgo, Mexico.	• Prepare for the chapter test.

Culture

• Diego Rivera, *Baile en Tehuantepec*	• *La ropa de fiesta* • *La familia y los eventos especiales*	• *Los grandes teatros* • *Cómo hacer un poncho*	• Explain how to make a poncho.

Vocabulary	Grammar	Learner Support	
• Verbs to talk about getting ready • Things you need to get ready • Special events • Words to say how you feel	• Reflexive verbs • *Ser* and *estar* • Possessive adjectives	**STRATEGIES** • Relating to your own experience • Identifying the writer's attitude • Taking notes	**RECYCLING** • Actividad 5 • Actividad 10 • Actividad 13 • Actividad 8 • Actividad 21 • Formation of adverbs • Clothing items • Expressions with the infinitive • Objects in a bedroom • Prepositons of location • Possessive adjectives

Chapter Features

Pronunciación

Consonants that change their sound

El español en en la comunidad

Spanish cultural celebrations in the Unites States

Conexiones

Health: How many hours of sleep are deemed necessary

Beyond the Classroom: States & Countries

Arizona
Nueva York
Florida
México
Costa Rica
Perú
Bolivia
Argentina

Student Resources

TECHNOLOGY

ONLINE

Interactive Textbook
• Student Edition Online plus audio, video, and flashcards

Go Online Companion Web Site
• Tutorial activities   • Internet links
• Self-tests   • Downloadable MP3 audio files
• **PuzzleView**

CD-ROM

Interactive Textbook CD-ROM
Student Edition on CD-ROM plus audio, video, and flashcards

MindPoint™ CD-ROM
QUIZSHOW

PRINT MATERIAL

CORE INSTRUCTION

Practice Workbook, pp. 27–37
• Review   • Vocabu ary
• Grammar   • Puzzle
• Organizer

Writing, Audio & Video Activities, pp. 25–34
• Video   • Audio
• Writing

Grammar Study Guide 1–2 (or 3–4)

Differentiated Instruction

STUDENTS NEEDING EXTRA HELP

Guided Practice Activities, pp. 53–70
• Vocabulary Flash Cards and Vocabulary Check
• Grammar Activities
• Presentación oral

HERITAGE LEARNERS

Realidades para hispanohablantes, pp. 50–69

Lecturas para hispanohablantes
• "Las mañanitas," p. 28
• "Homenaje a los padres chicanos," p. 34

ADVANCED/PRE-AP*

Pre-AP* Resource Book: Student Activity Sheet, p. 103

PRACTICE

Teacher Resources

TECHNOLOGY

Audio Program   Fine Art Transparencies
Video Program   Vocabulary and Grammar
Transparencies
Answers on Transparencies

TeacherEXPRESS CD-ROM
• Lesson Planner   • Vocabulary Clip Art
• Web Resources   • Teaching Resources
• Teacher Edition with Interactive Links

PresentationEXPRESS CD-ROM
• Vocabulary   • Tranparencies and Maps
• Grammar   • Photo Gallery
• Audio   • Clip Art

PRINT MATERIAL

CORE INSTRUCTION

Teacher's Resource Book, pp. 74–100
• Input Script   • Video Script
• Answer Keys   • GramActiva Blackline Masters
• Vocabulary Clip Art   • Chapter Resource Checklist
• School-to-Home Connection Letters
• Communicative Activities Blackline Masters

TPR Stories, pp. 25–30

Differentiated Instruction

STUDENTS NEEDING EXTRA HELP

Guided Practice Activities Teacher's Guide, pp. T27–T35

HERITAGE LEARNERS

Realidades para hispanohablantes Teacher's Guide, pp. 26–35

Lecturas para hispanohablantes Teacher's Guide, pp. 9–11

ADVANCED/PRE-AP*

Pre-AP* Resource Book: Resources Chart, p. 100

Differentiated Assessment

STUDENTS NEEDING EXTRA HELP

Alternate Assessment Program
• Examen del capítulo, pp. 17–22

HERITAGE LEARNERS

Assessment Program: Realidades para hispanohablantes Teacher's Guide, pp. T101–T105

ExamView Heritage Learner Test Bank

ADVANCED/PRE-AP*

Pre-AP* Resource Book: Teacher Activity Sheet, p. 102

ExamView Pre-AP* Test Bank

PLAN AND TEACH

PH SuccessNet ONLINE
• Access to grades and reports from Online Interactive Textbook

ExamView on Presentation Express CD-ROM
QuickTake Presenter
• Vocabulary Quizzes   • Chapter Test
• Grammar Quizzes

TeacherEXPRESS CD-ROM
• Assessment Program
• **ExamView** Test Banks A and B
test generator

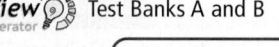

Go Online
PHSchool.com
For: Teacher Home Page
Web Code: jdk-1001

CORE ASSESSMENT

Assessment Program, pp. 41–54
• Pruebas
Vocabulary Recognition
Vocabulary Production
Reflexive verbs
Ser and *estar*
Possessive adjectives
• Examen del capítulo   • Speaking and Writing Rubrics

Teacher's Resource Book, p. 88
• Situation Cards

TPR Stories, pp. 25–30

ASSESS

Regular Schedule (50 Minutes)

For electronic lesson plans:
Teacher Express 💿

	Warm-up / Assess	Preview Present / Practice Communicate	Wrap-up / Homework Options
DAY 1	**Warm-up (5 min.)** • Homework check • Return Examen del capítulo: Capítulo 1B	**A ver si recuerdas . . . (25 min.)** • Presentation: La ropa y el cuerpo • Actividades 1, 2 • Presentation: Verbs and expressions that use the infinitive • Actividades 3, 4 **Chapter Opener (5 min.)** • Objetivos • Fondo cultural **A primera vista (10 min.)** • Presentation: Vocabulario y gramática en contexto • Actividad 1	**Wrap-up and Homework Options (5 min.)** • Practice Workbook 2A-A, 2A-B, 2A-1, 2A-2 • Go Online
DAY 2	**Warm-up (10 min.)** • Actividad 2 • Homework check	**A primera vista (35 min.)** • Presentation: Videohistoria ¿Más maquillaje? • View: Videohistoria • Video Activities 1, 2, 3, 4 • Actividad 3	**Wrap-up and Homework Options (5 min.)** • Practice Workbook 2A-3, 2A-4 • Prueba 2A-1: Vocabulary recognition • Go Online
DAY 3	**Warm-up (10 min.)** • Actividad 4 • Homework check ✔**Assessment (10 min.)** • Prueba 2A-1: Vocabulary recognition	**Manos a la obra (25 min.)** • Actividades 5, 6, 7 • Fondo cultural • Audio Activities 5, 6	**Wrap-up and Homework Options (5 min.)** • Writing Activity 10 • Heritage Learner Workbook 2A-1, 2A-2 • Prueba 2A-2: Vocabulary production
DAY 4	**Warm-up (5 min.)** • Homework check ✔**Assessment (10 min.)** • Prueba 2A-2: Vocabulary production	**Manos a la obra (30 min.)** • Communicative Activity • Presentation: Reflexive verbs • View: GramActiva video • Actividades 8, 10, 12 • Audio Activity	**Wrap-up and Homework Options (5 min.)** • Practice Workbook 2A-5 • Actividades 9, 11 • Go Online
DAY 5	**Warm-up (10 min.)** • Writing Activity 11 • Homework check	**Manos a la obra (35 min.)** • Actividades 13, 15, 16 • Fondo cultural • El español en la comunidad • Presentation: The verbs ser and estar • View: GramActiva video • Actividad 21 • Audio Activity 8	**Wrap-up and Homework Options (5 min.)** • Practice Workbook 2A-6 • Heritage Learner Workbook 2A-4 • Actividades 14, 17, 18, 20 • Writing Activity 12 • Pruebas 2A-3, 2A-4: Reflexive verbs; Ser and estar • Go Online
DAY 6	**Warm-up (10 min.)** • Actividad 19 • Homework check ✔**Assessment (15 min.)** • Pruebas 2A-3, 2A-4: Reflexive verbs; Ser and estar	**Manos a la obra (20 min.)** • Presentation: Possessive adjectives • Actividades 22, 23, 24, 25	**Wrap-up and Homework Options (5 min.)** • Practice Workbook 2A-7 • Go Online • Heritage Learner Workbook 2A-5 • Prueba 2A-5: Possessive adjectives
DAY 7	**Warm-up (10 min.)** • Writing Activity 13 • Homework check ✔**Assessment (10 min.)** (after Communicative Activity) • Prueba 2A-5: Possessive adjectives	**Manos a la obra (15 min.)** • Audio Activity 9 • Communicative Activity • Pronunciación **Adelante! (10 min.)** • Presentación oral: Steps 1, 4	**Wrap-up and Homework Options (5 min.)** • Presentación oral: Step 2
DAY 8	**Warm-up (5 min.)** • Homework check	**¡Adelante! (40 min.)** • Presentación oral: Step 3 • Videomisterio: Presentation	**Wrap-up and Homework Options (5 min.)** • Preparación para el examen 3, 4, 5 • Go Online: Self-test
DAY 9	**Warm-up (5 min.)** • Homework check	**¡Adelante! (25 min.)** • Lectura • ¿Comprendiste? • Fondo cultural • La cultura en vivo **Repaso del capítulo (15 min.)** • Vocabulario y gramática • Preparación para el examen 1, 2	**Wrap-up and Homework Options (5 min.)** • Practice Workbook 2A-8, 2A-9 • Examen del capítulo 2A • Go Online: Self-test; Lectura • La cultura en vivo
DAY 10	**Warm-up (5 min.)** • Homework check ✔**Assessment (40 min.)** • Examen del capítulo 2A		**Wrap-up and Homework Options (5 min.)** • A ver si recuerdas . . . : Capítulo 2B • La cultura en vivo

	Warm-up / Assess	Preview Present	/ Practice Communicate	Wrap-up / Homework Options
DAY 1	**Warm-up (5 min.)** • Homework check • Return Examen del capítulo: Capítulo 1B	**A ver si recuerdas . . . (25 min.)** • Presentation: La ropa y el cuerpo • Actividades 1, 2 • Presentation: Verbs and expressions that use the infinitive • Actividades 3, 4 **Chapter Opener (5 min.)** • Objectives • Fondo cultural	**A primera vista (50 min.)** • Presentation: Vocabulario y gramática en contexto • Actividades 1, 2 • Presentation: Videohistoria: ¿Más maquillaje? • View Videohistoria • Video Activities 1, 2, 3, 4 • Actividad 3	**Wrap-up and Homework Options (5 min.)** • Practice Workbook 2A-A, 2A-B, 2A-1, 2A-2, 2A-3, 2A-4 • Go Online • Prueba 2A-1: Vocabulary recognition
DAY 2	**Warm-up (10 min.)** • Actividad 4 • Homework check ✔**Assessment (10 min.)** • Prueba 2A-1: Vocabulary recognition	**Manos a la obra (65 min.)** • Actividades 5, 6, 7 • Fondo cultural • Audio Activities 5, 6 • Writing Activity 10 • Communicative Activity	• Presentation: Reflexive verbs • View: GramActiva video • Actividades 8, 9, 10, 12	**Wrap-up and Homework Options (5 min.)** • Practice Workbook 2A-5 • Actividad 14 • Go Online • Heritage Learner Workbook 2A-1, 2A-2 • Prueba 2A-2: Vocabulary production
DAY 3	**Warm-up (10 min.)** • Actividad 11 • Homework check ✔**Assessment (10 min.)** • Prueba 2A-2: Vocabulary production	**Manos a la obra (65 min.)** • Audio Activity 7 • Actividades 13, 15, 16, 18 • Fondo cultural • Writing Activity 11 • El español en la comunidad • Presentation: The verbs *ser* and *estar*	• View: GramActiva video • Actividades 19, 20, 21 • Audio Activity 8 • Writing Activity 12	**Wrap-up and Homework Options (5 min.)** • Practice Workbook 2A-6 • Actividad 17 • Go Online • Heritage Learner Workbook 2A-4 • Pruebas 2A-3, 2A-4: Reflexive verbs; *Ser* and *estar*
DAY 4	**Warm-up (5 min.)** • Homework check ✔**Assessment (15 min.)** • Pruebas 2A-3, 2A-4: Reflexive verbs; *ser* and *estar*	**Manos a la obra (40 min.)** • Presentation: Possessive Adjectives • Actividades 22, 23, 24, 25 • Audio Activity 9 • Writing Activity 13 • Pronunciación	**¡Adelante! (25 min.)** • Lectura • ¿Comprendiste? • Fondo cultural • Presentación oral: Steps 1, 4	**Wrap-up and Homework Options (5 min.)** • Practice Workbook 2A-7 • Presentación oral: Step 2 • Go Online • Heritage Learner Workbook 2A-5 • Prueba 2A-5: Possessive Adjectives
DAY 5	**Warm-up (5 min.)** • Homework check ✔**Assessment (10 min.)** • Prueba 2A-5: Possessive Adjectives	**¡Adelante! (40 min.)** • Presentación oral: Step 3 • La cultura en vivo **Repaso del capítulo (30 min.)** • Vocabulario y gramática • Preparación para el examen 1, 2, 3, 4, 5		**Wrap-up and Homework Options (5 min.)** • Practice Workbook 2A-8, 2A-9 • Go Online: Self-test • Examen del capítulo 2A
DAY 6	**Warm-up (10 min.)** • Homework check • Answer questions **Repaso del capítulo (15 min.)** • Situation Cards ✔**Assessment (40 min.)** • Examen del capítulo 2A	**¡Adelante! (20 min.)** • Videomisterio: Preparation		**Wrap-up and Homework Options (5 min.)** • Go Online: Lectura • La cultura en vivo • A ver si recuerdas . . . : Capítulo 2B

A ver si recuerdas . . .

Vocabulario   La ropa y el cuerpo

Parte superior del cuerpo

el abrigo
los anteojos de sol
la blusa
la camisa
la camiseta
la chaqueta
la corbata
la gorra
los guantes
la sudadera
el suéter
el traje
el traje be baño
el vestido

Parte inferior del cuerpo

las botas
los calcetines
la falda
los jeans
los pantalones
los pantalones cortos
los zapatos

Vocabulario

Presentation EXPRESS VOCABULARY

Core Instruction

Resources: Voc. and Gram. Transparency 42

Focus: Reinforcing vocabulary for body parts and clothing

Suggestions: Present the vocabulary using the transparencies or use pictures from old catalogs to make clothing flashcards.

To review body parts, create a large cutout of a monster with differing numbers of body parts. Give the monster a humorous name. Create true or false statements based on the picture: *(Name) tiene cuatro cabezas*. Have students give a "thumbs-up" sign if the sentence is true, or a "thumbs-down" sign if it is false. To review clothing, make paper-doll style clothes and place them on the monster.

 Actividad 1 *Standards:* 1.1, 1.3

Focus: Writing and speaking about what to wear in different situations

Suggestions: Have students include at least two articles of clothing in their answer whenever possible. Write the question *¿Qué llevas cuando hace frío?* on the board as a model to help students discuss their answers with a partner.

Answers will vary.

 Actividad 2 *Standards:* 1.2

Focus: Listening comprehension of vocabulary for body parts

Suggestions: Have students form one line facing you, so that they don't get clues from one another. Have students sit down when they make an incorrect response.

Answers will vary.

Block Schedule

Have students prepare a fashion show. Have pairs of students take turns modeling and describing clothing. Remind them to add details such as on which occasions to wear the items.

Práctica de vocabulario • Usando el organizador gráfico

 **Actividad 1** Escribir/Hablar

¿Qué llevas?

Completa las frases con la ropa que llevas en las siguientes ocasiones. Después compara tus respuestas con las de otro(a) estudiante. Habla de la ropa que los dos usan.

Modelo

Cuando hace frío, *llevo un suéter y guantes.*

1. Cuando voy a la piscina, . . .
2. Cuando voy a un partido de fútbol, . . .
3. Cuando estoy en casa, . . .
4. Cuando voy al cine, . . .
5. Cuando voy a un baile elegante, . . .
6. Cuando llueve, . . .

 Actividad 2 Escuchar

Juego

Tu profesor(a) va a ser Simón y te va a decir que toques *(touch)* una parte de tu cuerpo. Por ejemplo, si escuchas, "Simón dice . . . 'tócate la cabeza'", tienes que tocarte la cabeza. Si no escuchas "Simón dice . . ." y te tocas esa parte del cuerpo, ¡pierdes *(you lose)*!

Differentiated Instruction
Solutions for All Learners

Students with Special Needs

If students are unable to point to the various body parts for *Actividad 2*, provide them with a picture of a person. Have them point to the various body parts on the picture.

Advanced Learners

Have students create a bulletin board display to help review clothing vocabulary. Give them construction paper and have them cut out different articles of clothing. Ask them to write a sentence next to each picture to describe on which occasions they would wear each item.

Gramática·Repaso

Verbs and expressions that use the infinitive

When you use two verbs together in Spanish, the second one is usually the infinitive.

Óscar **prefiere llevar** jeans los fines de semana.
¿Vas a llevar un suéter esta noche?

- Here are some verbs and expressions that you have used that are often followed by an infinitive:

me gusta / gustaría	I like / would like	querer (e → ie)	to want
me encanta	I love	pensar (e → ie)	to plan
poder (o → ue)	to be able	necesitar	to need
deber	ought to, should	tener que	to have to
preferir (e → ie)	to prefer	ir a	to be going to

You can use the present tense of the verb *acabar* followed by *de* + the infinitive to indicate that something has just happened:

Nosotros **acabamos de escuchar** esa canción.
*We **just listened to** that song.*

Práctica de gramática

 **3** Leer/Escribir

Un mensaje electrónico

Recibes este mensaje por correo electrónico. Lee las actividades que recomienda Carlos y contéstale. Usa una combinación de dos verbos para decirle lo que te interesa hacer y lo que no te interesa hacer.

¡Hola!
¿Qué quieres hacer este fin de semana? ¿Comer en un restaurante? Todos dicen que el restaurante Las Pampas tiene comida argentina fabulosa. ¿Prefieres ir a un concierto? Hay una banda que toca música de los Andes en la plaza. ¿Jugar al tenis? Dicen que va a hacer buen tiempo todo el fin de semana. Escríbeme.

Carlos

4  Hablar

¿Qué quieres hacer?

Pregúntale a otro(a) estudiante si quiere hacer algo este fin de semana.

Modelo

A —¿Quieres *ir al parque* conmigo?
B —Sí, me gustaría *ir al parque* pero *acabo de caminar con mi amiga.*
o: —No, gracias. No puedo *ir* porque *mi primo acaba de llegar.*

1. ir al cine
2. estudiar español
3. tomar un refresco
4. jugar al béisbol
5. venir a mi casa
6. escuchar música
7. **¡Respuesta personal!**

Más práctica

- Practice Workbook, pp. 27–28: 2A-A, 2A-B
- Guided Practice Activities, pp. 53–54: 2A-1, 2A-2
- *Real.* para hispanohablantes, p. 50

Go Online PHSchool.com
For: Vocab. and Grammar
Web Code: jdd-0201

setenta y uno **71**
Preparación: Vocabulario y gramática

 **Gramática·Repaso** Presentation EXPRESS GRAMMAR

Core Instruction

Resources: Voc. and Gram. Transparency 43
Suggestions: Model each word or phrase with a sentence, and ask students follow-up questions: *Puedo cantar bien. ¿Y tú? ¿Puedes cantar o prefieres bailar?*

 3  *Standards:* 1.2, 1.3

Focus: Reading and writing a response to an e-mail about likes and dislikes
Suggestions: Point out that the message is about plans for the upcoming weekend. Ask students to brainstorm possible activities that they might see in the message. Encourage students to use a variety of verbs: *Me gustaría comer en Las Pampas. Me encanta jugar al tenis.*
Answers will vary.
Extension: Have students write Carlos a response agreeing with some suggestions that he has made and providing one or two additional suggestions.

 4  *Standards:* 1.1

Focus: Talking about plans for the weekend
Suggestions: Have students use each of the words or expressions in the *Gramática* chart at least once. Remind them that they must elaborate on their response if they agree to go, and must make an excuse if they cannot.
Answers will vary.

Enrich Your Teaching
Resources for All Teachers

Teacher-to-Teacher

If possible, borrow a skeleton from a science teacher to review body parts and clothing. Bring in clothes to put on the skeleton. Dress it with a different outfit each day for a week and have students describe the outfit as a warm-up activity. Be sure to plan humorous outfits!

Internet Search

To provide students with visuals while reviewing clothing, have them look at a Web site for a department store or mail-order company in a Spanish-speaking country.

Keywords:

comprar + ropa + online

Standards for Capítulo 2A

- To achieve the goals of the Standards, students will:

Communication

1.1 Interpersonal
- Talk: about clothing for different events, weekend plans, and daily routines; using possessive adjectives
- Describe people and things using *ser* and *estar*

1.2 Interpretive
- Listen to and interpret daily routines and choices; identify body parts
- Read and interpret possessive adjectives, sound-changing consonants, verbs that use the infinitive, and *ser* and *estar*
- Read: about getting ready for an event, preferences in attire, special events and families, traditional clothing, the *Teatro Colón,* other important theaters, the *poncho,* and Dolores Hidalgo; a picture-based story, a hair clipper ad, and about teens' sleeping patterns
- Listen to and watch a video about getting ready for an event

1.3 Presentational
- Present information about: special events, clothing for different events, getting ready for an event, *ser* and *estar* and possessive adjectives; the history of jeans
- Write and present information about daily routines
- Present a personal experience of a special event
- Write: about a clothing purchase and shopping experience; to express an interest

Culture

2.1 Practices and Perspectives
- Explain cultural perspectives on teen dress
- Talk and write about families and special events

2.2 Products and Perspectives
- Talk and write about: attire preferences, the *poncho,* traditional Mexican clothing; the *Teatro Colón,* and other important theaters; hair clippers from an ad

Connections

3.1 Cross-curricular
- Read about teens' sleeping patterns
- Describe the history of the *Teatro Colón;* how to make a *poncho;* how to make an oral presentation

3.2 Target Culture
- Describe the *Teatro Colón;* Dolores Hidalgo

Comparisons

4.1 Language
- Use reflexive verbs, infinitives after prepositions, possessive adjectives, and sound-changing consonants
- Review the verbs *ser* and *estar*

4.2 Culture
- Compare: special events in Spanish-speaking countries and the U.S.; cultural programs in Hispanic countries and the U.S.; Mexican and U.S. independence

Communities

5.1 Beyond the School
- Identify events in U.S. communities

5.2 Lifelong Learner
- Investigate events in U.S. communities

Tema 2 • Un evento especial

Fondo cultural ■◆■◆■◇■◆■◇■◆

En **"Baile en Tehuantepec"** vemos la ropa típica de los bailes de esta región de México. Las mujeres se visten con blusas y faldas tradicionales. El uso del sombrero es tradicional para los hombres del campo, no sólo en México, sino en otros países hispanohablantes como el Perú y el Ecuador.

- Compara a las personas de este cuadro con los jóvenes de la foto. ¿Qué ropa llevas cuando vas a un baile especial?

"Baile en Tehuantepec" (1935), Diego Rivera

Charcoal and watercolor. 18 15/16 x 23 7/8 in. Los Angeles County Museum of Art. Gift of Mr. and Mrs. Milton W. Lipper, from the Milton W. Lipper Estate. Photograph © 2003 Museum Associates/LACMA © Banco de México Diego Rivera & Frida Kahlo Museums Trust. Av. Cinco de Mayo No. 2, Col. Centro, Del. Cuauhtemoc 06059, México D.F. Reproduction authorized by the Instituto Nacional de Bellas Artes y Literatura.

72 setenta y dos
Tema 2 • Un evento especial

Differentiated Instruction
Solutions for All Learners

STUDENTS NEEDING EXTRA HELP

Guided Practice Activities
- Vocabulary Check, Flashcards
- Grammar
- Reading and Speaking Support

Guided Practice Audio CDs
- Disc 1, Track 3

HERITAGE LEARNERS

Realidades para hispanohablantes
- Chapter Opener, pp. 50–51
- A primera vista, p. 52
- Videohistoria, p. 53
- Manos a la obra, pp. 54–61
- ¡Adelante!, pp. 62–67
- Repaso del capítulo, pp. 68–69

ADVANCED/PRE-AP*

Pre-AP* Resource Book, pp. 100–103

Capítulo 2A

¿Cómo te preparas?

Chapter Objectives

- Describe getting ready for a special event
- Talk about daily routines
- Describe people and things
- Express possession
- Understand cultural perspectives on clothing

Video Highlights

A primera vista: ¿Más maquillaje?
GramActiva Videos: reflexive verbs; the verbs *ser* and *estar*

Country Connection

As you learn to talk about special events, you will make connections to these countries and places:

Arizona
Nueva York
La Florida
México
Costa Rica
Perú
Bolivia
Argentina

Más práctica

- *Real. para hispanohablantes*, pp. 50–51

Go Online PHSchool.com **For:** Online Atlas **Web Code:** jde-0002

Jóvenes con ropa elegante durante una quinceañera en Yuma, Arizona

setenta y tres **73**
Capítulo 2A

Chapter Opener
Core Instruction

Resources: Voc. and Gram. Transparencies: Maps 12–13, 15–17, 20

Suggestions: Bring in copies of old photos of yourself or your family members at a formal occasion such as a wedding. Have students describe what the people in the pictures are wearing. Discuss what people do to get ready for such events. Have students predict what the vocabulary will be by brainstorming a list of activities that people do to get ready, and items that they use to do them.

In the *Videohistoria*, students will see how Raúl and Tomás come to regret a favor they are doing for Gloria. Ask students if they have ever volunteered to do something for someone and later realized that it was a mistake.

 **Fondo cultural** *Standards:* 1.2, 1.3, 2.2, 4.2

Suggestions: Help students answer the question by making a three-column chart. In the first column, have students write descriptions of the clothes the people in the painting are wearing. In the second column, have them describe the clothing in the photo, and in the third column have them explain what they would wear to a special event.
Answers will vary.

Teaching with Photos

Suggestions: Point out the people's formal attire and the decorations in the photo and ask students to guess what event is being pictured. Have students compare the photo with a formal event that they have attended. Then, have students discuss what they think the people in the photo did to prepare for their event.

Culture Note

The Isthmus of Tehuantepec is located in southern Mexico between the Gulf of Mexico and the Pacific Ocean. It is the narrowest section of the country. The town of Tehuantepec is the cultural center of the Tehuana Indians. The Tehuanas are known for their beautiful clothing and distinctive gold jewelry.

Teacher Technology

PLAN	**TEACH**	**ASSESS**
Lesson Planner	Teaching Resources	Chapter Quizzes and Tests
	Interactive Teacher's Edition	
	Vocabulary Clip Art	

Go Online PHSchool.com **For:** Teacher Home Page **Web Code:** jdk-1001

PresentationEXPRESS
Dynamic Presentations for Teachers

TEACH	**ASSESS**
Vocabulary & Grammar Powerpoints	**ExamView** QuickTake Presenter
GramActiva Video	
Audio & Clip Art Activities	
Transparencies and Maps	
Activity Answers	
Photo Gallery	

Vocabulario y gramática

Presentation EXPRESS — VOCABULARY

Core Instruction

Standards: 1.2

Resources: Teacher's Resource Book: Input Script, p. 76, Clip Art, pp. 90–93, Audio Script, p. 77; Voc. and Gram. Transparencies 44–45; TPR Stories Book, pp. 24–36; Audio Program: Tracks 1–2

Focus: Presenting vocabulary for daily routines and for getting ready to go out

Suggestions: Present the vocabulary in two groups: what a boy does to get ready for an event and what a girl does. Use the Input Script from the *Teacher's Resource Book* or the story from the *TPR Stories Book* to present the new words, or use some of these suggestions.

Bring in items that students might use to get ready for an event. Have them identify each item, and ask: *¿Quién lo (la) usa? ¿Cuándo lo (la) usas?*

Point out that in Spanish, just as in English, nouns are sometimes related to the verbs associated with them. Write the words ***ducharse, cepillarse,*** and ***secarse*** on the board and have students tell the nouns that are related to each verb. Ask students to name a familiar noun that is similar to the verb ***vestirse (vestido).*** Have them guess what ***afeitadora*** (electric shaver) and ***peinarse*** (to comb one's hair) mean and ask them to explain what clues they see in the two words.

Draw two series of stick drawings on the board to illustrate two people going through their daily routines (one girl and one boy). Draw the routines in random order. Ask students to label the drawings with the infinitive form of the correct verb. Then have students tell you in what order the characters should do each activity. For example, *Primero ella debe levantarse.* Limit students to using the reflexive verbs lexically until the concept is introduced in the *Gramática* on p. 80. If needed, explain to students that reflexive verbs require a special pronoun and are used to describe actions people do to themselves. Contrast the familiar verb ***poner*** with ***ponerse.***

Additional Resources

• Audio Program: Canciones CD, Disc 22

A primera vista

 jdd-0287

Vocabulario y gramática en contexto

Objectives

Read, listen to, and understand information about
• getting ready for an event
• daily routines

" ¡Hola! Me llamo Antonio. ¿Qué hago yo **antes de** ir a **un evento especial?** Siempre **me despierto** temprano y **me levanto** de la cama. Primero **me ducho lentamente.** Generalmente estoy en la ducha unos 20 minutos.

despertarse

la ducha

ducharse

el desodorante

la toalla

el agua de colonia

el cepillo

el peine

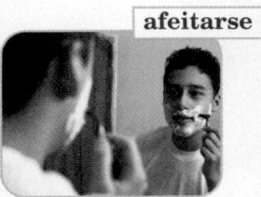

afeitarse

Después de ducharme, me afeito . . .

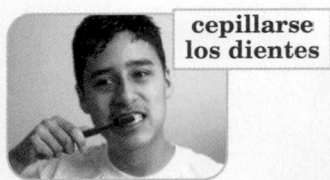

cepillarse los dientes

. . . y me cepillo los dientes.

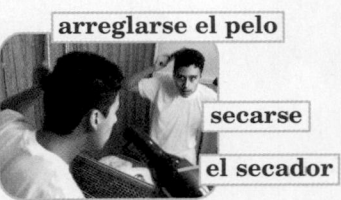

arreglarse el pelo

secarse

el secador

Luego me seco el pelo con el secador y **me arreglo** el pelo con el peine.

ponerse

vestirse

Después **me pongo** el desodorante y el agua de colonia y **me visto** ".

Más vocabulario
la audición audition
la boda wedding
el concurso contest
por ejemplo for example

74 setenta y cuatro
Tema 2 • Un evento especial

Differentiated Instruction
Solutions for All Learners

Students with Special Needs
Pair hearing-impaired students with advanced learners. Provide each hearing-impaired student with the sentences in *Actividad* 1. Write the sentences in a different order from the script. Have the advanced learners act them out while the partners identify the correct sentence.

Heritage Language Learners
Ask students to write a paragraph about their ideal evening. Have them include details such as where and with whom they would go, what they would wear, and how they would prepare. Help students to use the four-step writing process of pre-writing, drafting, editing, and revising.

—Tengo **una cita** con Rafael. ¡Vamos a un baile **elegante!**

—Debes estar muy **entusiasmada.** ¿Qué vas a hacer para **prepararte?**

—Primero **me baño, . . .**

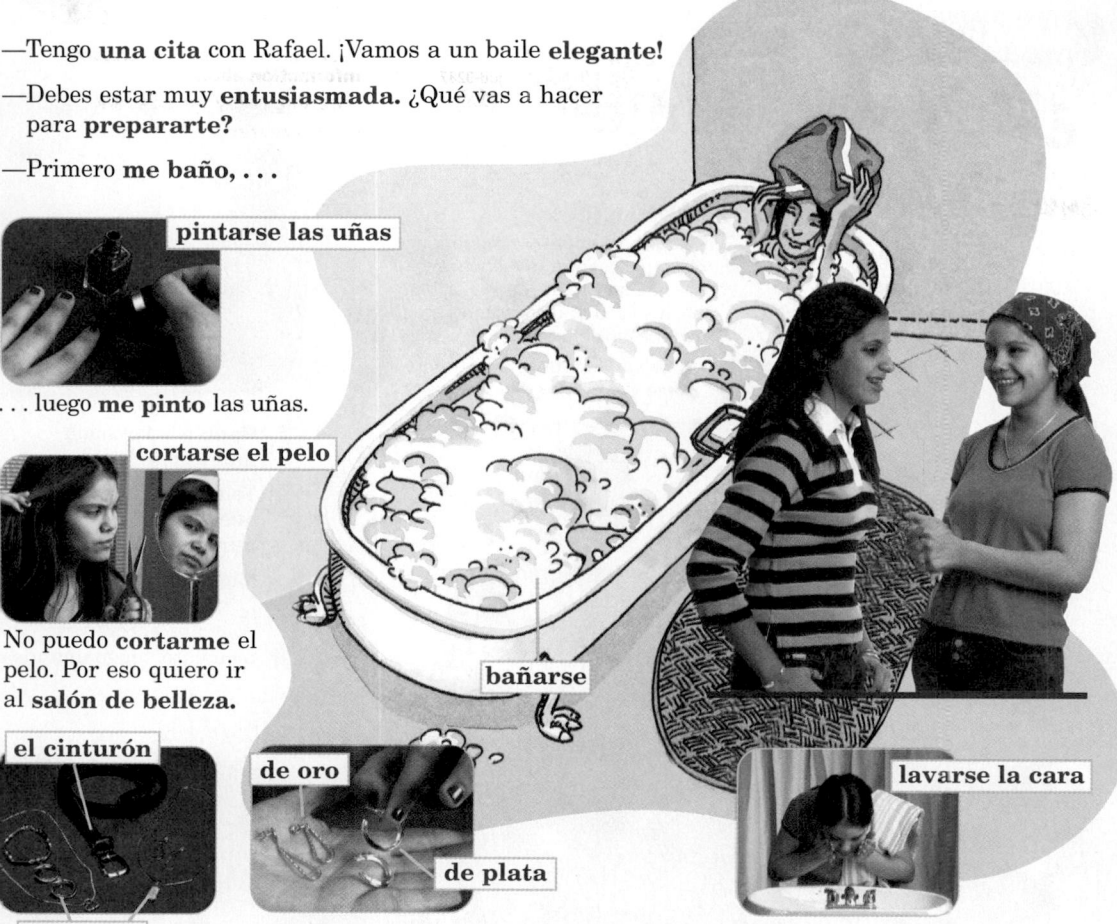

pintarse las uñas

. . . luego **me pinto** las uñas.

cortarse el pelo

No puedo **cortarme** el pelo. Por eso quiero ir al **salón de belleza.**

bañarse

el cinturón

de oro

de plata

las joyas

lavarse la cara

—¿Puedo **pedirte prestados** tus aretes?
—¿De oro o de plata?
—**Depende . . .** prefiero los aretes de plata.

Después del baile . . .
" Ahora tengo mucho sueño. Voy a **lavarme** la cara y **acostarme.** ¡Hasta mañana! **"**

 Actividad 1 jdd-0287 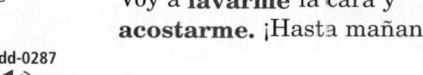 **Escuchar**

¿Qué haces por la mañana?

Vas a escuchar siete frases que describen qué hace alguien por la mañana. Representa *(Act out)* cada una de estas acciones sin hablar.

Más práctica

- Practice Workbook, pp. 29–30: 2A-1, 2A-2
- WAV Wbk.: Writing, p. 31
- Guided Practice: Vocab. Flash Cards, pp. 55–60
- *Real.* para hispanohablantes, p. 52

Go Online PHSchool.com
For: Vocab.Practice
Web Code: jdd-0202

Actividad 2 jdd-0287 **Escuchar**

¿Lógica o no?

Vas a escuchar siete frases. Algunas son lógicas y otras no. Señala con el pulgar hacia arriba si la frase es lógica y con el pulgar hacia abajo si no es lógica.

setenta y cinco **75**
Capítulo 2A

Enrich Your Teaching
Resources for All Teachers

 Culture Note
In most Spanish-speaking countries, it is more common for young people to go out in a group than on "dates." Often dance clubs will have events exclusively for teenagers. They serve soft drinks and juices instead of alcohol, and provide a safe environment for friends to get together, dance, and have a good time.

Teacher-to-Teacher
Be sure to bring in at least one each of the vocabulary items mentioned to use as visual props throughout the chapter. For toiletries, use construction paper or adhesive labels to label them in Spanish.

Actividad 1 *Standards:* 1.2  Presentation EXPRESS AUDIO

Resources: Teacher's Resource Book: Audio Script, p. 77; Audio Program: Track 3; Answers on Transparencies

Focus: Listening comprehension about daily routines

Suggestions: Establish appropriate ways to pantomime each action before beginning the activity. You may want to have students point to the picture of the appropriate activity or item on p. 74 instead of acting out the activity.

 Script and Answers
1. Me levanto a las ocho. *(wake up)*
2. Primero, me afeito. *(shave)*
3. Después me ducho. *(take a shower)*
4. Me pongo desodorante. *(put on deodorant)*
5. Me cepillo los dientes. *(brush your teeth)*
6. Me arreglo el pelo. *(fix your hair)*
7. Me visto. *(get dressed)*

★ Bellringer Review
Class brainstorm to list on the board Spanish words for special events.

Actividad 2   *Standards:* 1.2

Resources: Teacher's Resource Book: Audio Script, p. 77; Audio Program: Track 4; Answers on Transparencies

Focus: Listening comprehension about daily routines

Suggestions: Remind students that answers are not based on their personal daily routine.

 Script and Answers
1. Me levanto antes de despertarme. *(down)*
2. Me pongo los aretes en los pies. *(down)*
3. Me seco el pelo con el secador. *(up)*
4. Me lavo con el peine. *(down)*
5. Me visto después de bañarme. *(up)*
6. Me cepillo los dientes todos los días. *(up)*
7. Me pongo el desodorante antes de bañarme. *(down)*

Extension: Ask students to change the illogical statements to make them logical.

✓ Assessment
- ExamView QuickTake Presenter Quiz on PresEXPRESS

Videohistoria
Core Instruction

Presentation EXPRESS
VOCABULARY

Standards: 1.2

Resources: Voc. and Gram. Transparencies 46–47; Audio Program: Track 5

Focus: Extending the presentation of vocabulary and grammar

Suggestions:

Pre-reading: After students think of a favor that they have done for another person, ask them to tell how they felt while doing it. Point out the last three panels, and ask students to list words that describe how Tomás and Raúl might feel.

Reading: Pause after the fourth panel to have students summarize what they have read. Have them use that information to predict the outcome.

Post-reading: Complete *Actividad* 3 to check comprehension.

Pre-AP* Support

• **Activity:** Point out frame 2 to the students and ask that they imagine Gloria asks the boys to do something other than take part in a play. (Exs. Go to a party or go to a ballgame.) Have students work in groups of three to rewrite the other scenes to reflect the change and then ask for volunteers to present their scenes to the class.

• *Pre-AP* Resource Book:* Comprehensive guide to Pre-AP* vocabulary skill development, pp. 47–53

Videohistoria jdd-0287

¿Más maquillaje?

¿Qué emergencia tiene Gloria? ¿Cómo se arreglan Raúl y Tomás? Lee la historia para saber.

Estrategia

Relating to your own experience Making a connection between your own life and what you are reading will help you to understand a story better. Think about the following:

• Have you ever done a favor for someone, only to regret it later?

Gloria

Tomás

Raúl

1 Raúl: No dan nada interesante hoy.

Tomás: Tienes razón. ¿Por qué no tomamos un refresco?

Gloria: *(al teléfono)* ¡Ay, no! ¿Estás seguro? ¿Qué podemos hacer? Un momento, tengo una idea.

5 Raúl: ¡Qué idea! Mira dónde estamos.

Gloria: Primero, no es idea mía . . . ¡Tranquilos! No deben estar tan **nerviosos.**

Raúl: No estamos nerviosos. Pero no me gusta vestirme a lo ridículo.

6 Tomás: ¿Es necesario pintarse **los labios?**

Raúl: ¿Tanto **gel?** ¿Por qué tiene que ponerme tanto **maquillaje?** Dos horas así. No va a ser muy **cómodo.**

7 Tomás: Tienes razón. Pero te ves muy bien.

Raúl: ¿Tú crees? Y mira tus zapatos. ¡Qué grandes son!

Differentiated Instruction
Solutions for All Learners

Advanced Learners
Provide pictures of different Halloween disguises. Have students list two things that they would have to do to prepare each costume. Ask them to share their answers with the class and have the other students guess which disguise they are describing.

Students with Learning Difficulties
To help students use context to determine the meaning of new words, provide them with copies of sentences that contain the new words. Review the new sentences with them, in conjunction with the *Videohistoria*.

2 Gloria: ¿Les gustaría participar en una obra de teatro? Es una emergencia. Necesitamos a dos personas y tienen que venir **rápidamente.**
Raúl: ¿En qué? ¡No!

3 Tomás: Pero, ¿por qué no? Puede ser interesante.
Gloria: ¡Fantástico! Les va a gustar mucho.

4 Tomás: ¿Cómo me preparo? ¿Me arreglo el pelo?
Gloria: Tomás, **te ves** bien. Pero Raúl . . .
Raúl: Sí, voy a cepillarme los dientes, lavarme el pelo . . .
Gloria: Tienen 30 minutos.

8 Raúl: ¡Esto va a ser un desastre!

Actividad 3 · Leer/Escribir

¿Comprendiste?

Indica si las siguientes frases son *(C)* ciertas o *(F)* falsas. Si la frase es falsa, escribe la información correcta.

1. Tomás y Raúl miran un programa de televisión muy interesante.
2. Tomás quiere ayudar a Gloria con una obra de teatro.
3. Raúl no quiere ayudar a Gloria.
4. Raúl va a cepillarse los dientes y lavarse el pelo.
5. A Raúl le gusta vestirse a lo ridículo.
6. A Raúl no le gusta el maquillaje porque no es cómodo.
7. Tomás se pone zapatos muy grandes para la obra de teatro.
8. Raúl cree que todo va a ser muy divertido.

Más práctica

- Practice Workbook pp. 31–32: 2A-3, 2A-4
- WAV Wbk.: Video, pp. 25–27
- Guided Practice: Vocab. Check, pp. 61–64
- *Real.* para hispanohablantes, p. 53

Go **Online**
PHSchool.com
For: Vocab. Practice
Web Code: jdd-0203

setenta y siete **77**
Capítulo 2A

Video
Core Instruction

Standards: 1.2

Resources: Teacher's Resource Book: Video Script, p. 82; Video Program: Cap. 2A; Video Program, Teacher's Guide: Cap. 2A

Focus: Viewing and comprehending the video

Suggestions:

Pre-viewing: Remind students that they do not need to understand every word to follow the story.

Viewing: Show the video once without pausing. Show it again, pausing to point out key events and to check comprehension.

Post-viewing: Complete the Video Activities in the *Writing, Audio & Video Workbook.*

Actividad 3 · *Standards:* 1.2, 1.3

Resources: Answers on Transparencies
Focus: Verifying comprehension of the *Videohistoria*

Suggestions: As students review their answers, have them identify where they found the information in the story.

Answers:
1. falsa: No dan nada interesante hoy. *(panel 1)*
2. cierta *(panel 3)*
3. cierta *(panel 2)*
4. cierta *(panel 4)*
5. falsa: A Raúl no le gusta vestirse a lo ridículo. *(panel 5)*
6. cierta *(panel 6)*
7. cierta *(panel 7)*
8. falsa: Raúl cree que va a ser un desastre. *(panel 8)*

Additional Resources
- WAV Wbk.: Audio Act. 5, p. 28
- Teacher's Resource Book: Audio Script, pp. 77–78
- Audio Program: Track 6

Assessment
- **ExamView** QuickTake Presenter Quiz on PresEXPRESS
- Prueba 2A-1: Vocab. Recognition, pp. 41–42

Enrich Your Teaching
Resources for All Teachers

Teacher-to-Teacher
To familiarize students with the events of the *Videohistoria*, write a summary of the story on a transparency. Write each sentence on a separate line. Cut out each sentence and mix them up. Have a volunteer rearrange the sentences in the correct order on the overhead projector.

Teacher-to-Teacher
Photocopy and cut out the panels. Paste them on another sheet of paper, and make photocopies to distribute to students. Write and make copies of speech bubbles, using quotations from the reading. Ask students to place the speech bubbles next to the appropriate person.

Actividad 4 Standards: 1.3  **Presentation EXPRESS ANSWERS**

Resources: Answers on Transparencies

Focus: Writing about items you need in order to get ready to go out

Suggestions: To avoid confusion, have students write their lists first. Then, for those items that they are able to explain, ask: *¿Para qué se usa?* Have them write their answers in complete sentences.

Answers:

1. un cepillo; Margarita necesita un cepillo para arreglarse el pelo.
2. un peine; … para arreglarse el pelo.
3. el gel; para arreglarse el pelo.
4. unas joyas
5. el maquillaje
6. el perfume
7. una toalla; … para secarse.
8. un cinturón
9. un secador; … para secarse el pelo.
10. el desodorante

  Actividad 5 Standards: 1.1, 1.3

Focus: Writing and speaking about the clothes you wear to different events

Recycle: Clothing items

Suggestions: Brainstorm a list of clothing that students consider *ropa elegante* and another for *ropa cómoda.* Have students refer to the list as they complete Step 1.

Answers will vary.

Bellringer Review

Write these words on the board and ask students to give you the adverbial form to tell you how they do an action.

1. *furioso*   3. *rápido*
2. *nervioso*   4. *triste*

(**Answers:** furiosamente; nerviosamente; rápidamente; tristemente)

Additional Resources

• WAV Wbk.: Audio Act. 6, p. 28
• Teacher's Resource Book: Audio Script, p. 78, Communicative Activity BLM, p. 84
• Audio Program: Track 7

78

Manos a la obra

Vocabulario y gramática en uso

Objectives

• Talk about your daily routine
• Describe yourself and others
• Learn to use reflexive verbs
• Review differences between *ser* and *estar*
• Express possession

 Actividad 4   Escribir

¿Cómo se prepara Margarita?

Hoy Margarita va a la boda de su prima. Mira el dibujo y escribe una lista de las cosas que necesita para prepararse. Si puedes, también escribe para qué se usa cada cosa.

Modelo

un peine
Margarita necesita un peine para arreglarse el pelo.

  **Actividad 5**   Escribir/Hablar

¿Ropa elegante o ropa cómoda?

1 ¿Qué clase de ropa llevas en estas ocasiones? Haz una tabla como la que ves aquí. Escribe los eventos de la lista en la primera columna. Decide si llevas ropa elegante o ropa cómoda en esta ocasión y escribe qué llevas en la columna apropiada.

1. una boda
2. un baile elegante
3. un concurso
4. una cita para ir al cine
5. un partido de hockey
6. una fiesta en la casa de un(a) amigo(a)
7. una audición
8. **¡Respuesta personal!**

Ocasión	Ropa elegante	Ropa cómoda
la escuela		unos jeans y una camiseta
el cumpleaños de mi abuela	un traje o un vestido elegante	

2 Con otro(a) estudiante, habla de la ropa que Uds. llevan en las ocasiones del Paso 1.

Modelo

A —¿Qué llevas para el cumpleaños de tu abuela?
B —Para el cumpleaños de mi abuela llevo ropa elegante. Llevo una falda elegante y una blusa blanca.

78 setenta y ocho
Tema 2 • Un evento especial

Differentiated Instruction
Solutions for All Learners

Students with Special Needs

For *Actividad* 6, students who struggle with spatial organization tasks may have trouble designing the Venn diagram. If so, provide a full-page, lined version of the model. For each picture shown, have students write a description, cut it out, and glue it to the appropriate section of the diagram.

Advanced Learners/Pre-AP*

 Pre-AP*

Give students index cards with the names of important events in your school or community written on them. Have students discuss what type of clothing would be worn to each event, and say if it is formal or casual.

Actividad 6 · Escribir

¿Por la mañana o por la noche?

Copia el diagrama de Venn. Luego mira los dibujos y decide si haces la actividad por la mañana o por la noche. Escribe la acción en el círculo apropiado del diagrama. Si haces la actividad por la mañana *y* por la noche, escribe tu respuesta en la intersección de los círculos.

Modelo

por la mañana · por la noche
por la mañana y por la noche

Me ducho.

 1.
 2.
 3.
 4.
 5.
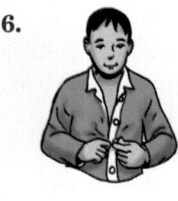 6.
 7.
 8.

Actividad 7 · Hablar

¿Rápidamente o lentamente?

¿Te preparas rápidamente para ir a la escuela? Habla con otro(a) estudiante sobre cuánto tiempo crees que es necesario para hacer las cosas de la Actividad 6.

Modelo

A —¿Cuánto tiempo necesitas para ducharte?
B —Me ducho rápidamente. Necesito sólo dos minutos.
o: —Me ducho lentamente. Necesito 20 minutos.

¿Recuerdas?

You use adverbs to tell how you do an action. In English they often end in -ly. To form adverbs in Spanish, you can often add -mente to the feminine form of the adjective.

general → generalmente
rápida → rápidamente

Fondo cultural

La ropa de fiesta En los países hispanohablantes, los jóvenes llevan ropa cómoda pero elegante a las fiestas entre amigos o para citas con amigos. Los jeans son muy populares, pero llevan jeans con camisas o blusas buenas, nunca con camisetas viejas o rotas *(torn)*. Muchos jóvenes prefieren llevar pantalones o vestidos de moda en vez de *(instead of)* jeans.

- ¿Qué llevas cuando asistes a una fiesta entre amigos?

setenta y nueve **79**
Capítulo 2A

2A Practice and Communicate

 **Gramática**
Presentation EXPRESS
GRAMMAR

Core Instruction

 Standards: 4.1

Resources: Voc. and Gram. Transparency 48; Teacher's Resource Book: Video Script, p. 82; Video Program: Cap. 2A

Suggestions: First explain what it means for a verb to be reflexive and then show students how to use reflexive pronouns.

Write two paragraphs on the board to describe what someone does on the weekend. For the first paragraph use verbs students already know, such as: *levantar pesas, lavar la ropa, poner la mesa.* For the second paragraph use the reflexive form: ***levantarse, lavarse, ponerse.*** For each verb, ask students to explain why the reflexive wasn't used in the first paragraph but was used in the second. You may also want to use the transparency or the *GramActiva* Video for reinforcement.

Point out that verbs can be reflexive in all tenses. Provide examples in the preterite.

 Bellringer Review
Review clothing by having students stand up (or raise their hands) if they are wearing the clothing item that you call out to the class.

  *Standards:* 1.2
Presentation EXPRESS
ANSWERS

Resources: Answers on Transparencies
Focus: Writing about getting ready for a party
Suggestions: Remind students that subjects are not always included in sentences. Tell them to look at the endings of the conjugated verbs to determine the reflexive pronouns. Have students write the verb along with the reflexive pronoun.

Answers:

1. se	4. me	7. te
2. nos	5. me	8. se
3. me	6. me	9. se

Gramática

Reflexive verbs

To say that people do something to or for themselves, you use reflexive verbs. For example, washing one's hands and brushing one's hair are reflexive actions because the person doing the action also receives the action.

> Antes de una cita, (yo) **me ducho** y **me arreglo** el pelo.

You know that a verb is reflexive if its infinitive form ends with the letters *se.*

> **ducharse**

The reflexive pronouns in Spanish are *me, te, se, nos,* and *os.* Each pronoun corresponds to a different subject. Here are the present-tense forms of the reflexive verb *secarse:*

(yo)	**me seco**	(nosotros) (nosotras)	**nos secamos**
(tú)	**te secas**	(vosotros) (vosotras)	**os secáis**
Ud. (él) (ella)	**se seca**	Uds. (ellos) (ellas)	**se secan**

Some verbs have both reflexive and non-reflexive forms and usages. A verb is used in its non-reflexive form if the action is being done to someone or something else.

Lavo el coche a menudo. *I wash the car often.*
Me lavo el pelo todos los días. *I wash my hair everyday.*

When you use a reflexive verb with parts of the body or clothing, use the definite article.

¿Siempre te pintas **las** uñas? *Do you always polish your nails?*
Felipe se pone **los** zapatos. *Felipe puts on his shoes.*

You can put reflexive pronouns before the conjugated verb or you can attach them to the infinitive.

Me voy a duchar.
Voy a duchar**me**.
Te tienes que vestir para la fiesta.
Tienes que vestir**te** para la fiesta.

 **GramActiva** VIDEO
Need more help with reflexive verbs? Watch the **GramActiva** video.
Me ducho.

 Actividad 8 **Leer/Escribir**

Nos preparamos para la fiesta

Isabel y Elena se preparan para ir a una fiesta de quinceañera. En una hoja de papel, escribe el pronombre reflexivo correcto para cada número para completar la historia.

Isabel y Elena son dos hermanas que __1.__ preparan para una fiesta de quinceañera. "Debemos acostar __2.__ temprano esta noche," dice Isabel. "Sí, y mañana yo __3.__ baño primero. Después __4.__ maquillo y __5.__ pinto las uñas. Me gusta preparar __6.__ lentamente," dice Elena. "Es verdad," dice Isabel. "Siempre __7.__ preparas más lentamente que yo." La noche de la fiesta Elena __8.__ arregla el pelo primero y luego ayuda a Isabel. Las dos __9.__ visten y salen para la fiesta a las seis y media.

80 ochenta
Tema 2 • Un evento especial

Differentiated Instruction
Solutions for All Learners

Students with Learning Difficulties
For *Actividad* 10, have students imagine they're preparing to attend a special event such as a wedding. Brainstorm a list of related vocabulary, eliciting reflexive verbs by asking questions about their personal routines. Leave the list on the board as reference.

Heritage Language Learners
Have students write a paragraph about what they did to get ready for a special event. Ask students to exchange papers and peer edit each other's work. For the final product, have them include a small illustration for each of the steps they describe in their paragraphs.

80

Escribir/Hablar

Una rutina lógica

¿Eres una persona lógica? Usa *antes de* o *después de* para escribir frases lógicas.

1. lavarse las manos / comer
2. despertarse / levantarse
3. vestirse / ponerse desodorante
4. acostarse / bañarse
5. ducharse / vestirse
6. cepillarse los dientes / comer

Modelo

lavarse la cara / acostarse
Me lavo la cara antes de acostarme.

> **Nota**
> Note that in Spanish you use the infinitive after a preposition even if an infinitive is not used in English.
>
> • Generalmente me pongo loción en la cara **después de afeitarme.**
> *I usually put lotion on my face after shaving.*

  Escribir/Hablar

Preparaciones

Imagina que tú y tu hermanito están preparándose para un evento especial y tienes que ayudarlo. Describe tu día según los dibujos. Usa la forma reflexiva del verbo en tu descripción si es necesario.

Modelo
Me despierto a las siete de la mañana.

Modelo
Despierto a mi hermanito a las siete y cinco.

1.

2.

3.

4.

5.
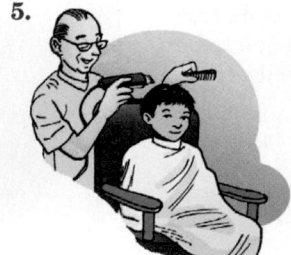

6.

 Standards: 1.3

Resources: Answers on Transparencies
Focus: Writing and speaking about logical order of daily routines
Recycle: Reflexive verbs
Suggestions: Have students form their sentences keeping the verbs in the same order in which they appear in the activity.

Answers:

1. Me lavo las manos antes de comer.
2. Me despierto antes de levantarme.
3. Me visto después de ponerme desodorante.
4. Me acuesto después de bañarme.
5. Me ducho antes de vestirme.
6. Me cepillo los dientes después de comer.

Common Errors: Students may conjugate the verb after a preposition. Remind them that verbs are always left in the infinitive after a preposition.

Extension: Have students switch the order of the infinitives and make three logical sentences and three illogical sentences. Tell them to read their sentences to a partner and have their partners decide if they are logical or not.

  Standards: 1.3

Resources: Answers on Transparencies
Focus: Writing and speaking about getting ready for a special event
Suggestions: Remind students that they need to use the personal *a* when the direct object is a person, as in item 2.

Tell students that the reflexive is always used when talking about getting a haircut unless the person who cuts the hair is specified. In most cases it is assumed that the person did not cut his or her own hair.

Answers:

1. Me visto.
2. Visto a mi hermanito.
3. Me lavo la cara.
4. Mi hermanito y yo lavamos el coche.
5. El señor le corta el pelo a mi hermanito.
6. Me corto el pelo.

Enrich Your Teaching
Resources for All Teachers

Teacher-to-Teacher

Bring in copies of authentic advertisements in Spanish for various health and hygiene products. Use appropriate reading strategies to help students understand the text. Have students write a sentence explaining how they use each item. Choose the best sentences to post on a bulletin board along with the advertisements.

Internet Search

Search the Internet for health and beauty magazines that contain advertisements that you can print and photocopy. Be careful to choose images that are appropriate for all students.

Keywords:

revistas de salud; revistas de belleza

Resources: Answers on Transparencies

Focus: Filling out a chart about your daily routine

Suggestions: Use a clock with movable hands to help students review telling at what time something happens. Say a phrase such as, *Me despierto...,* and have students supply the correct time.

Answers will include:

1. me levanto
2. me baño / me ducho
3. me cepillo los dientes
4. me arreglo el pelo
5. me visto
6. me acuesto temprano / tarde

Focus: Asking and answering questions about your daily routine

Suggestions: Encourage students to add details to their answers such as if they wash their face or hair, what they use to fix their hair, and what kind of clothes they put on.

Answers will vary.

Extension: Have students create a chart like the one in *Actividad* 11 to describe their daily routines on the weekend. Then have them work with a partner to discuss their routines.

 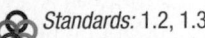

Focus: Writing and speaking about your ideal day

Recycle: Expressions that require the infinitive

Suggestions: For Step 1, have students brainstorm a list of verbs and expressions that require the infinitive. For Step 2, give a time limit for students to choose the five sentences that represent their group's ideal day. For Step 3, encourage students to explain why they think one description is better than the others.

Answers will vary.

 Escribir

Tu horario

¿Cómo es tu horario típico? Piensa en tu horario para un día de escuela. En general, ¿a qué hora haces las siguientes acciones? Usa una tabla para organizar tus respuestas.

1. levantarse
2. bañarse o ducharse
3. cepillarse los dientes
4. arreglarse el pelo
5. vestirse
6. acostarse temprano / tarde

Mi rutina	La hora
me despierto	a las 6:30

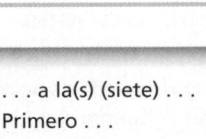

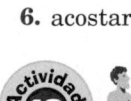 **Hablar**

Compara horarios

Ahora compara tu horario de la Actividad 11 con el de otro(a) estudiante. Hablen de las diferencias en sus rutinas.

Modelo

A —¿A qué hora te despiertas por la mañana?
B —Me despierto a las seis y media. ¿Y tú?
A —Yo me despierto a las siete. ¿Qué haces después de levantarte?
B —Siempre me ducho primero y me lavo el pelo. Y tú, ¿qué haces luego?

. . . a la(s) (siete) . . .
Primero . . .
Luego . . .
. . . después de . . .
. . . antes de . . .

   Escribir/Hablar

Mi día ideal

① Describe tu día ideal en cinco frases. Usa expresiones que necesitan un infinitivo en cada frase. También usa los verbos reflexivos.

② Ahora compara tu día ideal con el de tres estudiantes. De todas las frases que tienen, escojan *(choose)* cinco frases que describen el día ideal para todo el grupo.

③ Cada grupo debe compartir con la clase su descripción del día ideal. La clase debe votar por la mejor descripción del día ideal.

Modelo

En mi día ideal puedo levantarme muy tarde. En mi día ideal no tengo que ir a la escuela.

Differentiated Instruction
Solutions for All Learners

Students with Learning Difficulties

Have students organize the chart in *Actividad* 11 chronologically. Have students renumber the actions to reflect their morning routine and list them in that sequence in the first column. Then have them assign a starting time in the second column.

Multiple Intelligences

Logical/Mathematical: Have students prepare a survey about sleep habits for students in other Spanish classes. Ask them to compile the results and prepare a summary of students' sleep habits in your school. You may want them to prepare a visual such as a bar graph to illustrate their findings.

Actividad 14 Leer/Pensar/Escribir/Hablar

¡Quiero dormir más!

¿Es difícil despertarte temprano todas las mañanas? ¿Te gustaría dormir más? Lee el siguiente informe sobre la cantidad *(amount)* de sueño que necesita cada joven. Luego contesta las preguntas.

Conexiones | La salud

¿Necesitas dormir más?

Muchos jóvenes no pueden levantarse temprano a la hora de ir a la escuela y el 20 por ciento de ellos se duermen[1] en las clases. Nuevos estudios revelan que los jóvenes de 13 a 18 años de edad necesitan dormir 9.25 horas cada noche. Esto es 1.25 horas más que un adulto. La realidad es que muchos jóvenes duermen sólo seis o siete horas cada noche. Si un joven no duerme suficiente, puede tener problemas de concentración y de control de sus emociones.

¿Cuál es la respuesta a este problema? Pues, acuéstate temprano y sigue una rutina cada noche. Otros consejos para dormir mejor son:

➤ Toma sólo bebidas sin cafeína después de las cinco de la tarde.

➤ Evita[2] programas de televisión o películas violentas antes de acostarte. También evita usar la computadora o jugar videojuegos antes de dormir.

➤ Un baño o una ducha antes de acostarte puede ayudarte a dormir.

➤ Haz ejercicio todos los días pero no antes de acostarte.

➤ Debes acostarte y levantarte cada día a la misma hora. Si quieres acostarte tarde durante el fin de semana, es mejor no hacerlo dos noches seguidas.

[1]fall asleep [2]Avoid

1. ¿Cuántas horas duermes cada noche?
2. ¿Cuántas horas crees que debes dormir cada noche?
3. ¿Crees que estos consejos son buenos? ¿Por qué?

Actividad 15 Escribir/Hablar

¡Un día loco!

Con otro(a) estudiante, van a crear una rutina loca. Usen las ideas de abajo o piensen en otras. Luego lean su rutina a la clase. ¡La pareja con la rutina más loca gana!

Estudiante A

acostarse	afeitarse
cepillarse los dientes	vestirse
peinarse	despertarse
arreglarse el pelo	lavarse

¡Respuesta personal!

Modelo

A—*Primero nos levantamos a las tres de la mañana.*

B—*Después nos ponemos una camisa elegante y unos pantalones cortos.*

Estudiante B

¡Respuesta personal!

ochenta y tres **83**
Capítulo 2A

Enrich Your Teaching
Resources for All Teachers

Teacher-to-Teacher

Using reflexive verbs from *Actividad* 15, have students work in pairs to create and play a Concentration game. Ask students to write a list of five activities that they might do as part of their daily routine. Then have them write the name of an item associated with each activity. For example: ***vestirse/una camiseta.*** Give

students ten cards and have them write an activity or item on each card. Tell them to place all of the cards face down and mix them up. Have them take turns turning over the cards and matching the activities with the correct objects. The student with the most matches wins.

Actividad 14 *Standards:* 1.1, 1.2, 3.1

Focus: Reading comprehension; cross-curricular connection to health

Suggestions: Before beginning the reading, have students answer items 1 and 2. Write on the board *6 horas o menos, 7–8 horas, 8–9 horas,* and *9 horas o más.* Keep a tally as students tell you how many hours they sleep a night. Using the same times, survey and record what students think is the ideal amount of sleep per night. Have students read the article and ask them to compare the advice in the reading to the results of the class survey.

Answers will vary.

Bellringer Review

List these words on the board:

cama	*secador*	*jabón*
lápiz de labios	*cepillo de dientes*	

Have students write the reflexive activity they associate with each item.

Actividad 15 *Standards:* 1.1, 1.3

Focus: Writing and speaking about a crazy schedule

Suggestions: Have students create a chart like the one in *Actividad* 11 to help them organize their presentations. Encourage students to add details about when, where, and what they use as they go about their routines. After all groups have given their presentations, ask the class to vote on the strangest routine.

Answers will vary.

Extension: Ask the group that wins to write their routine on the board. Have students change the sentences so that they describe a normal routine.

Theme Project

Give students copies of the Theme Project outline and rubric from the *Teacher's Resource Book.* Explain the task to them, and have them perform Step 1. (For more information, see p. 70-a.)

Actividad 16

Standards: 1.3

Focus: Writing and speaking about preparing for school or a party

Suggestions: To encourage students to act out their routines effectively, give each team a point if it generates a correct list. Subtract one point from any team that speaks during the performances.

Answers will vary.

Actividad 17

Standards: 1.1, 1.3

Focus: Writing and speaking about daily routines

Suggestions: Use the questions to prepare an interview sheet for students. Have students speak with a different student for each of the questions.

Answers will vary.

Bellringer Review

Draw a family tree on a transparency. Point to two family members and ask students to describe how they are related. For example: *José es el primo de Lorena.*

Fondo cultural

Standards: 1.2, 2.1, 4.2

■◆■◇■◆●■◆◇■◆■◇■◆■

Suggestions: Have students brainstorm a list of special events. Ask them with whom they celebrate each event on the list. How is this similar or different from celebrations in Spanish-speaking countries?

Answers will vary.

Additional Resources
- WAV Wbk.: Audio Act. 7, p. 29
- Teacher's Resource Book: Audio Script, p. 78
- Audio Program: Track 8

Assessment
- **ExamView®** Quiz on PresEXPRESS
  QuickTake Presenter
- **Prueba 2A-3:** Reflexive verbs, p. 45

84

Actividad 16 — Escribir/Hablar

Juego

¿Cómo te preparas para la escuela o para una fiesta? Vas a presentar tu rutina sin hablar.

1 Primero cada estudiante va a escribir una lista corta de lo que hace alguien cuando se prepara para salir.

2 En grupos o equipos, cada persona tiene que representar sus acciones sin hablar. Cuando "el actor" está actuando, cada miembro del grupo debe adivinar cuáles son las actividades y debe escribirlas en una hoja de papel. Después cada estudiante lee su lista. El actor o la actriz decide si la lista tiene las acciones correctas y si están en orden.

Modelo

Primero, Marta se levanta. Luego, ella . . . Después . . .

Los resultados:

3 puntos	en orden con todos los verbos correctos
2 puntos	en orden con la mitad *(half)* de los verbos correctos
0 puntos	ni en orden ni con todos los verbos correctos

Fondo cultural ■◆◇■◆◇■◇■◆◇■◆◇■ ◆■

La familia y los eventos especiales En los países hispanohablantes, los primeros invitados a un evento especial generalmente son los miembros de la familia. Los cumpleaños, el día del santo y otros días especiales se celebran con la familia y los amigos.

- ¿Invitas a tíos y a primos a todos tus cumpleaños? ¿A quiénes invitas a tus fiestas? ¿Por qué?

Una familia de San Miguel de Allende, México, celebra un cumpleaños.

Actividad 17 — Escribir/Hablar

Y tú, ¿qué dices?

1. ¿Te gusta levantarte temprano o tarde? ¿A qué hora te acuestas generalmente? ¿A qué hora te levantas? ¿Siempre te cepillas los dientes después de comer o sólo antes de acostarte?

2. ¿Cómo te preparas para un evento especial? ¿Qué haces primero? ¿Vas al salón de belleza o te arreglas el pelo? ¿Cuánto tiempo necesitas para prepararte?

3. ¿Qué ropa u otros accesorios te pones para ir a una fiesta o un baile?

Más práctica

- Practice Workbook, p. 33: 2A-5
- WAV Wbk: Writing, p. 32
- Guided Practice: Grammar Acts., pp. 65–66
- *Real.* para hispanohablantes, pp. 54–57

Go Online
PHSchool.com
For: Reflexive Verbs
Web Code: jdd-0204

Differentiated Instruction
Solutions for All Learners

Students with Learning Difficulties
For *Actividad* 16, students with learning difficulties may be uncomfortable sharing their lists with stronger students. Monitor them closely as they are writing their lists, and offer suggestions to help them correct their errors as they write.

Heritage Language Learners
Help students organize and improve their writing by reinforcing the use of transitional words or phrases such as ***primero, entonces, pues,*** and ***por fin.*** Compile a list of transitions for students to have when they are asked to sequence events in writing.

Corte de pelo con estilo

Lee el anuncio sobre la máquina para cortar el pelo "Cortapelo" que tú puedes usar en casa. Luego contesta las preguntas.

1. ¿Por qué da un buen corte el "Cortapelo"?
2. ¿Por qué puedes crear estilos diferentes?
3. ¿Crees que es bueno pagar dinero por un corte de pelo?
4. ¿Vas a un salón de belleza o te cortas el pelo en casa? ¿Por qué?

También se dice . . .
el salón de belleza = la peluquería *(muchos países)*
el pelo = el cabello *(muchos países)*

Con el revolucionario Cortapelo puedes cortarte el pelo sin salir de casa

La profesionalidad de un buen corte de pelo

Con su exclusivo sistema puedes cortarte el pelo sin errores ya que* su peine pivotante se adapta perfectamente a la forma de tu cabeza. Su sistema de dos peines corta con precisión el corte que deseas.

Quedas siempre perfecto y con un corte de pelo verdaderamente profesional.

Cortapelo

¡Es muy fácil y muy cómodo!

*since

Actividad 18 *Standards:* 1.2, 2.2 Presentation EXPRESS ANSWERS

Resources: Answers on Transparencies

Focus: Reading comprehension of an advertisement

Suggestions: Ask students to look at the photo and guess what the advertisement is trying to sell. Have them skim the ad the first time and make a list of cognates.

Answers:
1. Porque su peine pivotante se adapta perfectamente a la forma de tu cabeza.
2. Porque tiene un sistema de dos peines.
3. Answers will vary.
4. Answers will vary.

Extension: Have students work in groups to create an ad for one of the following hair-related items: *gel, un peine, un cepillo, un secador,* or *un salón de belleza.*

El Desfile *(Parade)* Nacional Puertorriqueño en Nueva York

El español en la comunidad

En muchas regiones de los Estados Unidos donde hay una concentración de personas hispanohablantes, hay eventos especiales para la comunidad hispana. Estas comunidades se preparan durante meses para las celebraciones. Preparan comida típica, música, bailes y desfiles. La celebración puede ser internacional o de un solo país, como el festival puertorriqueño en Nueva York. Lo que estos eventos tienen en común es que siempre participan personas de todos los grupos hispanos.

• Busca un calendario de los eventos especiales de tu comunidad para saber si hay un evento hispano o internacional. Estos eventos se celebran generalmente en el verano, cuando es posible organizarlos en parques.

Festival de la calle Ocho, Miami, la Florida

El español en la comunidad

Core Instruction

Standards: 1.2, 5.1, 5.2

Suggestions: Ask students to describe how their community celebrates Independence Day. Do they have parades and music? What foods do they typically eat? How do their local Fourth of July parades compare to what they've learned about Miami's Calle Ocho celebration?

Teaching with Photos

Ask students to scan the photos of the Puerto Rican Day celebration in New York and the Calle Ocho parade in Miami to get an idea about how people might dress up to celebrate. Tell them to imagine that they are going to one of the celebrations in the photos and have them write a paragraph describing how they would get ready. Tell them to use words like **vestirse, pintarse, ponerse maquillaje,** and **ponerse joyas.**

ochenta y cinco **85**
Capítulo 2A

Enrich Your Teaching
Resources for All Teachers

Culture Note

Traditionally, Roman Catholics in Spanish-speaking countries celebrate **el día del santo.** On the feast day of a person's namesake saint, the family will gather together to celebrate. It is similar to a birthday celebration with decorations, cakes, and gifts. Sometimes the family attends Mass together.

Internet Search

Have students research the Puerto Rican Day parade in New York, or the Calle Ocho festival in Miami.

Keywords:

Desfile Puertorriqueño,
Festival Calle Ocho

Pre-AP* Support

• **Activity:** After reading the ad for *Cortapelo,* have students write an original ad for another real or imaginary hygiene product.

• *Pre-AP* Resource Book:* Comprehensive guide to Pre-AP* communication skill development, pp. 9–17, 36–46

 **Gramática**

Presentation EXPRESS
GRAMMAR

Core Instruction

 Standards: 4.1

Resources: Voc. and Gram. Transparency 49; Teacher's Resource Book: Video Script, pp. 82–83; Video Program: Cap. 2A

Suggestions: Bring in pictures of the Seven Dwarves and have students work in groups to describe them using **ser** and **estar.** Give each group a different character and tell them to create descriptions using familiar vocabulary. Remind them that they can use negatives in their descriptions: *Él es bajo y no está muy contento.* Encourage them to use their imagination to describe where each character is from, where they are located, etc. Challenge them to write sentences with all of the uses of **ser** and **estar** mentioned in the *Gramática Repaso.* Choose one of the dwarves to use as an example as you review the two verbs with students.

You may want to play the *GramActiva* Video as an introduction, or to reinforce your own presentation of **ser** and **estar.**

   *Standards:* 1.2

Presentation EXPRESS
ANSWERS

Resources: Answers on Transparencies

Focus: Reading and completing a conversation about a contest

Suggestions: For each item have students explain why they chose **ser** or **estar.**

Answers:

1. son
2. Son
3. están
4. Estás
5. estar
6. está
7. estoy
8. somos

Extension: Have students work with a partner to continue Alfredo and Juan's conversation. Ask them to write two more exchanges in which they use **ser** or **estar.** Have volunteers read their dialogues to the class.

Theme Project

Students can perform Step 2 at this point. Be sure students understand your corrections and suggestions. (For more information, see p. 70-a.)

86

Gramática·Repaso

The verbs *ser* and *estar*

You know that both *ser* and *estar* mean "to be." You have seen that their uses, however, are different.

(yo)	soy	(nosotros) (nosotras)	somos
(tú)	eres	(vosotros) (vosotras)	sois
Ud. (él) (ella)	es	Uds. (ellos) (ellas)	son

(yo)	estoy	(nosotros) (nosotras)	estamos
(tú)	estás	(vosotros) (vosotras)	estáis
Ud. (él) (ella)	está	Uds. (ellos) (ellas)	están

Use *ser* to talk about:
• what a person or thing is
• what a person or thing is like
• where a person or thing is from
• what a thing is made of
• to whom something belongs

Ricardo y Lola **son** actores.
Son muy simpáticos.
Son de Nicaragua.
Este anillo **es** de plata.
Es el anillo de Juana.

Use *estar* to talk about:
• how a person or thing is at the moment
• how someone feels
• where a person or thing is located

Mi hermana **está** muy cansada.
Alicia y Carlos **están** entusiasmados.
Alonso **está** en el baño.

GramActiva VIDEO

Need more help with *ser* and *estar?* Watch the **GramActiva** video.

 soy ≠ estoy

 Actividad 19 **Leer/Escribir**

Ellos quieren ser músicos

Alfredo y Juan tocan en la banda y van a entrar en un concurso. Escoge el verbo correcto para completar su conversación.

Alfredo y Juan **1.** *(son / están)* chicos talentosos. **2.** *(Son / Están)* miembros de la banda de su escuela. Ahora los chicos **3.** *(son / están)* en casa de Juan y se preparan para ir a un concurso de la banda.

—¿ **4.** *(Eres / Estás)* nervioso, Juan?
—Sí, un poco. Todo mi familia va a **5.** *(ser / estar)* allí. Mis padres, mis abuelos . . .
—¿Tu novia?
—No, hombre. Ella **6.** *(es / está)* enferma y no puede ir. ¿Y tú, Alfredo?
—Nervioso no. Yo **7.** *(soy / estoy)* entusiasmado. Yo sé que **8.** *(somos / estamos)* los mejores.

86 ochenta y seis
Tema 2 • Un evento especial

Differentiated Instruction
Solutions for All Learners

Heritage Language Learners

Students may already be familiar with expressions that use **ser** and **estar,** but may not understand the rules for using each verb. Have students brainstorm a list of expressions that they know. Then ask them to explain why **ser** or **estar** is used in each expression.

Students with Special Needs

For *Actividad 21,* pair advanced learners with visually impaired students. Have the advanced learner describe the illustration's details. The visually impaired student can then ask questions using **ser** and **estar.**

Actividad 20 — Leer/Escribir

¿Cómo estás?

¿Cómo están tú y las otras personas en estas situaciones? Usa adjetivos de la lista para formar frases.

1. Elena y María van a participar en un concurso.

2. Vas a un baile con el (la) chico(a) más popular de la escuela.

3. Tienes mucha tarea y también tienes que lavar el coche, cortar el césped y limpiar tu dormitorio.

4. Tu hermano va a un concierto para escuchar una banda nueva.

5. Uds. están en una clase que no les interesa y la profesora habla lentamente.

6. Tu mejor amigo(a) tiene que dar un discurso para los padres de los estudiantes de tu escuela.

Modelo
Carlos toma el sol en la playa.
Carlos está muy contento.

aburrido, -a	nervioso, -a
cansado, -a	ocupado, -a
contento, -a	tranquilo, -a
entusiasmado, -a	

Actividad 21 — Hablar/Escribir

El dormitorio de Ramona

1 Ramona tiene muchas cosas en su dormitorio. ¿Es el dormitorio típico de una chica de 16 años? Mira el dibujo y habla de Ramona y su dormitorio con otro(a) estudiante.

Modelo
A —¿Dónde están las joyas de Ramona?

B —Están encima del escritorio.

A —¿De qué son las joyas?

B —Son de oro.

2 Ahora piensa en tu dormitorio. ¿Es como el dormitorio de Ramona? Describe dónde están y cómo son las cosas en tu dormitorio.

Más práctica
- Practice Workbook, p. 34: 2A-6
- WAV Wbk.: Writing, p. 33
- Guided Practice: Grammar Acts., p. 67
- *Real.* para hispanohablantes, pp. 58–59

Go Online PHSchool.com **For:** *Ser* and *Estar* **Web Code:** jdd-0205

Practice and Communicate
 2A

Actividad 20
 Standards: 1.2, 1.3

Resources: Answers on Transparencies

Focus: Reading about events people are participating in and writing about how those people feel

Suggestions: To help guide students to a particular adjective, give them more information about the people being described in the sentences. For example, in item 1: *María y Elena no son reservadas. A ellas les encantan los concursos. Es una oportunidad muy emocionante para ellas.*

Answers will vary but may include:
1. Ellas están entusiasmadas.
2. Estoy contento(a).
3. Estoy muy ocupado(a).
4. Está contento.
5. Estamos aburridos(as).
6. Está nervioso(a).

Extension: Have students interview a partner by changing the descriptions using *tú: Tú vas a participar en un concurso. ¿Cómo estás?*

Actividad 21
  Standards: 1.1, 1.3
Pre-AP*

Focus: Describing a typical teenager's bedroom and saying where things are

Recycle: Vocabulary for objects in a bedroom; prepositions of location

Suggestions: Have students brainstorm a list of items found in their bedrooms or a typical teenager's bedroom. Ask them to look at the picture and put a checkmark next to the items on their lists that are also found in Ramona's bedroom. Have them write a separate list of items only found in the picture. Encourage them to use the lists for both Steps 1 and 2. Allow students to describe a fictitious bedroom for Step 2.

Answers will vary.

Additional Resources
- WAV Wbk.: Audio Act. 8, p. 30
- Teacher's Resource Book: Audio Script, pp. 78–79
- Audio Program: Track 9

 Assessment
- ExamView QuickTake Presenter Quiz on PresEXPRESS
- Prueba 2A-4: *Ser* and *Estar*, p. 46

Enrich Your Teaching
Resources for All Teachers

Teacher-to-Teacher

Have students bring in at least four photos from a recent family event. If students are unable to bring in photos, suggest that they find them in magazines or make illustrations. Have them prepare a presentation describing the event. For each photo, students should use the verb **ser** to describe the setting and the characteristics of the people, and **estar** to say where people and things are, and how the people feel. Record the presentations, and have students exchange photos and tapes. Their classmates should listen to the recordings and identify which photos are being described.

 Gramática

Presentation EXPRESS
GRAMMAR

Core Instruction

⊗ *Standards:* 4.1

Resources: Voc. and Gram. Transparency 50

Suggestions: Direct attention to the *¿Recuerdas?* Point out that the long forms of the possessive adjectives agree in number and gender with the noun that is being possessed. When the adjectives are used without the noun, they still must agree with the noun that is being left out. Tell students to choose the correct possessive adjective in two steps:

Step 1: Determine who is doing the possessing.

Step 2: Determine what is being possessed.

 Standards: 1.2

Presentation EXPRESS
ANSWERS

Resources: Answers on Transparencies

Focus: Reading and writing about what objects belong to whom

Suggestions: Point out to students that the second part of each question provides the clue to the correct answer.

Answers:

1. a	3. a	5. b
2. b	4. a	6. a

 Standards: 1.2

Presentation EXPRESS
AUDIO

Resources: Teacher's Resource Book: Audio Script, p. 79; Audio Program: Track 10; Answers on Transparencies

Focus: Listening and writing from dictation about a beauty salon

Suggestions: Ask students what items they expect to hear discussed in a beauty salon. Play the *Audio CD* or read the script once without having students write. Tell students to focus on correct formation of the possessive adjectives.

Script and Answers

1. El secador blanco es de Matilda; este negro no es de ella.
2. El cepillo rojo es mío; el azul es tuyo.
3. No encuentro mi gel. ¿Me pueden prestar el gel de ustedes?
4. Felipe y Carmen, estas toallas están sucias. ¿Son suyas?
5. Tenemos que comprar peines nuevos. Los nuestros son viejos.

 **Gramática**

Possessive adjectives

Spanish possessive adjectives have a long form that comes after the noun. These forms are often used for emphasis.

mío / mía míos / mías	nuestro / nuestra nuestros / nuestras
tuyo / tuya tuyos / tuyas	vuestro / vuestra vuestros / vuestras
suyo / suya suyos / suyas	suyo / suya suyos / suyas

Voy al partido con un amigo **mío**.
I'm going to the game with a friend of mine.

¿Vas al baile con unas amigas **tuyas**?
Are you going to the dance with some friends of yours?

¿Recuerdas?
You already know a different form of possessive adjectives. They agree in gender and number with the nouns they describe and always go in front of the noun. They include *mi(s), tu(s), su(s), nuestro(a), nuestros(as), vuestro(a)* and *vuestros(as)*.

• **Tus** joyas de plata son muy bonitas.
• Voy a pedirle prestado **su** cinturón.

These possessive adjectives may be used without the noun.

¿Estas chaquetas son **suyas**?
Are these jackets yours?

Sí, son **nuestras**.
Yes, they are ours.

To clarify or emphasize possession, you can use *de* + a noun or pronoun instead of a form of *suyo*.

Aquí está un collar **suyo**.
= un collar **de Ud. /él /ella /Uds. /ellos /ellas**.
Here is a necklace of yours /his /hers /theirs.

 Actividad 22 **Leer/Escribir**

¿Son suyos?

¿De quiénes son estas cosas? Escoge la mejor respuesta.

1. ¿De quién son esos zapatos elegantes? ¿De Ud.?
   a. Sí, son míos.   **b.** Sí, son mías.

2. ¿De quiénes son esos globos? ¿De los niños?
   a. Sí, son suyas.   **b.** Sí, son suyos.

3. ¿De quién es esa toalla? ¿De Uds.?
   a. Sí, es nuestra.   **b.** Sí, es mía.

4. ¿De quién son estas joyas? ¿De tu prima?
   a. Sí, son suyas.   **b.** Sí, son tuyas.

5. ¿De quién es este secador? ¿De Laura?
   a. Sí, es tuyo.   **b.** Sí, es suyo.

6. ¿De quién es esta corbata? ¿De tu hermano?
   a. Sí, es suya.   **b.** Sí, es mía.

Actividad 23 jdd-0288 **Escuchar/Escribir**

Escucha y escribe

Hoy muchos clientes están en el salón de belleza. Escucha y escribe lo que dice Felipe mientras organiza el salón.

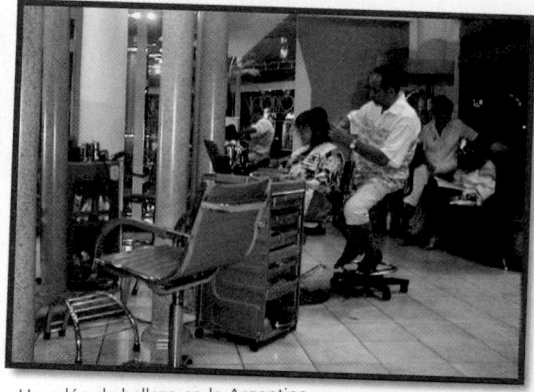

Un salón de belleza en la Argentina

Differentiated Instruction
Solutions for All Learners

Heritage Language Learners

Students whose heritage country is Spain may pronounce the *c* before a "weak" vowel like the English *th*. Be sure all students understand that for speakers whose heritage country is Spain, this pronunciation is considered correct, as opposed to the pronunciation modeled in *Pronunciación*.

Students with Learning Difficulties

Have students copy each of the questions in *Actividad* 22 on a sheet of paper and underline the noun that they will be referring to in their answer. Tell them to use the underlined words to help determine the gender and number of the possessive adjectives.

Actividad 24 Leer/Hablar

¿De quién es?

Tu hermana está arreglando su cuarto y preguntando de quién son las cosas que ella encuentra *(finds)*. Contesta sus preguntas, diciendo de quién es cada cosa.

Modelo

A —¿Es tu agua de colonia?
B —Sí, el agua de colonia es mía.
o: —No, el agua de colonia no es mía.

1. ¿Son sus toallas? (de ellos)
2. ¿Es mi peine?
3. ¿Es su gel? (de ella)
4. ¿Son nuestras joyas?
5. ¿Es tu maquillaje?
6. ¿Es su desodorante? (de él)

 **Actividad 25** Hablar

¿Es tuyo?

¿A quién le gusta pedir prestada la ropa? Pregúntale a otro(a) estudiante sobre la ropa y los accesorios que lleva. ¿Todo es de él/ella?

Modelo

A —Me gustan las joyas que llevas. ¿Son tuyas?
B —Sí, son mías.
o: —No, son de mi hermana, pero me gustan mucho.

Más práctica

- Practice Workbook, p. 35: 2A-7
- Guided Practice: Grammar Acts., p. 68
- *Real.* para hispanohablantes, p. 57

Go Online
PHSchool.com
For: Possessive Adjs.
Web Code: jdd-0206

Pronunciación

Consonants that change their sounds

jdd-0288

In Spanish, when the letter *c* combines with *a*, *o*, or *u* ("strong" vowels) it makes the sound of the letter *k*. Listen to and say these words:

expli**c**a bus**c**o **cu**chillo ¿**Có**mo? ¿**Cu**ándo?

When *c* combines with *e* or *i* ("weak" vowels) it makes the sound of the letter *s*. Listen to and say these words:*

cepillo **c**iencias cono**c**es **c**entro de re**c**iclaje

Practice saying these sentences:

Para mi **c**ita con **C**armen, voy a ponerme una corbata y un **c**inturón.

A **C**elia le gusta comer ca**c**ahuates cuando va al **c**ine.

In Spanish, the letter *g* combined with *a*, *o*, or *u* ("strong" vowels) makes a hard *g* sound. Listen to and say these words:

ganga lue**g**o al**g**ún al**g**odón yo**g**ur

In words with the letters *e* or *i* ("weak" vowels), you need to add a *u* after the *g* to keep the hard *g* sound.

Listen to and say these words:

espa**gue**tis pa**gué** **gui**sante hambur**gue**sa

Practice saying these sentences:

Gasté mucho dinero en las gangas y pagué con cheque.

Compré un regalo para Guillermo: unos guantes de algodón.

Can you figure out the meaning of the following *refranes*?

> Lo barato es caro cuando no es necesario.
>
> Peseta guardada, dos veces ganada.

*In some parts of Spain, *c* before *e* and *i* is pronounced like the *th* in *think*.

This is discussed further in *Tema 6, Capítulo 6A, Pronunciación.*

ochenta y nueve **89**
Capítulo 2A

Enrich Your Teaching
Resources for All Teachers

Teacher-to-Teacher

For *Actividad 25*, have students bring in clothing and accessories borrowed from family members and friends. Be sure that all items are appropriate before beginning the activity. Have students put on the items over their own clothes and interview their partners.

Internet Search

Refranes are an excellent way for students to practice pronunciation. Search the Internet for additional *refranes* to use in practicing other consonants.

Keyword:

refranes

  **Actividad 24** *Standards:* 1.1

Presentation EXPRESS
ANSWERS

Resources: Answers on Transparencies

Focus: Reading and answering questions about which things belong to whom

Suggestions: Bring in items (or pictures of items) mentioned in the activity as visual reinforcement. Hand an item to a student and ask the question. Tell students to answer based on who is holding the item.

Answers:

1. Sí (No), las toallas (no) son suyas.
2. Sí (No), el peine (no) es tuyo.
3. Sí (No), el gel (no) es suyo.
4. Sí (No), las joyas (no) son suyas.
5. Sí (No), el maquillaje (no) es mío.
6. Sí (No), el desodorante (no) es suyo.

  **Actividad 25** *Standards:* 1.1

Focus: Speaking about to whom the items you are wearing belong

Suggestions: To encourage a variety of responses, have students pretend that only one item they are wearing belongs to them, and that the rest was borrowed from other students in the class.

Answers will vary.

Pronunciación

Presentation EXPRESS
AUDIO

Core Instruction

 *Standards:* 1.2, 4.1

Resources: Teacher's Resource Book: Audio Script, pp. 79–80; Audio Program: Track 12

Suggestions: Read the *Pronunciación* to students or play the *Audio CD.* Emphasize that a diphthong is not formed when the *u* is preceded by a *g* and followed by a "weak" vowel.

Additional Resources

- WAV Wbk.: Audio Act. 9, p. 30
- Teacher's Resource Book: Audio Script, p. 79, Communicative Activity BLM, pp. 85–86,
- Audio Program: Track 11

✓ **Assessment**

- **ExamView** Quiz on PresEXPRESS
  QuickTake Presenter
- Prueba 2A-5: Possessive adjectives, p. 47

89

Lectura

Core Instruction

Standards: 1.2, 2.2, 3.1, 3.2

Focus: Reading about how to become involved in theater

Suggestions:

Pre-reading: Ask students if they have ever been in a theatrical production. Have them brainstorm a list of different jobs that are required to put on a show. Ask students to predict the role of the author in the production.

Reading: Point out the title and the footnote. Explain that the author writes about the **Teatro Colón** as well as how to get involved in theater. Have students summarize what he says after every paragraph.

Post-reading: If students have ever been in a production, have them relate what the author says to their own experiences.

Can they go beyond the descriptions of the different opportunities mentioned by the author, based on their own experiences with theatrical productions?

Bellringer Review

Show Voc. & Gram. Transparency 5 (word web/graphic organizer). In the center, write *eventos especiales* and in each surrounding circle write:

la iglesia   el gimnasio   el teatro   el parque

Have students complete the web with events that might take place at each location.

Pre-AP* Support

• **Activity:** Have students work with a partner to tell which classes at the *Instituto Superior de Arte* they would enjoy the most and why. Include any experiences they have already had.

• **Pre-AP* Resource Book:** Comprehensive guide to Pre-AP* reading skill development, pp. 18–24

¡Adelante!

Lectura

Asistir al teatro siempre es un evento especial. Y estar en una producción puede ser aun más especial. Vamos a ver lo que dice un joven cantante.

Objectives

• **Read about the *Teatro Colón* and its programs**

• **Learn to make a *poncho***

• **Give a presentation about a special event in your life**

• **Read about Dolores Hidalgo, Mexico**

Estrategia

Identifying the writer's attitude
As you read the *Lectura*, look for phrases that help you understand how the writer feels about the event.

El Teatro Colón: Entre bambalinas[1]

Pasar una noche en el Teatro Colón de Buenos Aires siempre es un evento especial y hoy es muy especial para mí. Vamos a presentar la ópera "La Traviata" y voy a cantar en el coro por primera vez. ¡Estoy muy nervioso! Pero, ¿qué me dices? ¿No conoces el Teatro Colón? Pues, es el teatro más importante de toda Argentina, quizás de toda América del Sur. Lleva casi 150 años ofreciendo ópera al público argentino y "La Traviata" fue la ópera que se presentó en la inauguración del teatro el 27 de abril de 1857. Por eso estamos todos muy entusiasmados.

[1] Behind the scenes

90 noventa
Tema 2 • Un evento especial

Differentiated Instruction
Solutions for All Learners

Advanced Learners

Have students use the Internet to find additional information about the theaters mentioned in the *Fondo cultural*.
Create a bulletin board displaying student work, including photos if possible. If available, add real or made-up ticket stubs and playbills in Spanish.

Multiple Intelligences

Interpersonal/Social: Have students work in groups to write and perform short skits about a person's daily routine. Encourage students to keep the dialogue simple and use their acting abilities to make themselves understood.

AUDICIONES

para jóvenes de 15 a 25 años de edad.

Si quieres ser músico, cantante o bailarín, tienes talento, eres joven y vives en Buenos Aires, tienes la oportunidad de hacer tus sueños realidad. Preséntate en el Teatro Colón para la siguiente audición.

Los interesados pueden presentarse el jueves, 22 de agosto a las 10:00 de la mañana.

Bajo el auspicio del Gobierno de la Ciudad de Buenos Aires

¿Te gustaría saber cómo ser miembro de los grupos que se presentan aquí? La mejor manera es presentarte a una audición para la escuela del teatro. Se llama el Instituto Superior de Arte y funciona dentro del teatro. En el Instituto puedes estudiar canto, danza, dirección de orquesta y otras especialidades para la ópera. Si estudias en el Instituto, puedes llegar a ser miembro del coro o del cuerpo de baile. Para músicos con talento también está la Orquesta

Académica del Teatro Colón. Esta orquesta está formada por jóvenes entre 15 y 25 años de edad. La orquesta hace sus presentaciones en el teatro o en las principales ciudades del país. Aquí en el teatro siempre buscan jóvenes con talento.

Si no te gusta actuar ni cantar, pero te encanta el teatro, puedes estudiar otra especialidad. Por ejemplo, si te gusta el arte, puedes aprender a hacer los escenarios. O si te interesa la tecnología, puedes estudiar la grabación o el video. En el teatro hay talleres[2] para todos los elementos de una presentación. Hay talleres para los decorados,[3] la ropa, los efectos especiales electromecánicos, la grabación y el video. Bueno, tengo que irme. ¡Ahora mismo empieza el "show" y tengo

que ponerme el maquillaje! ¡Nos vemos!

[2]workshops [3]scenery

Fondo cultural

Los grandes teatros son parte de la cultura de muchas ciudades hispanohablantes: el Teatro Real de Madrid (1850), el Palacio de Bellas Artes de México, D.F. (1913), el Teatro Municipal de Santiago, Chile (1857), el Teatro Nacional de San José, Costa Rica (1897). Como el Teatro Colón de Buenos Aires, ofrecen al público conciertos, óperas, ballet y otros programas culturales.

• ¿Hay un teatro o institución en tu comunidad que da programas culturales? ¿Qué tipo de programas dan?

Más práctica

• WAV Wbk.: Writing, p. 34
• Guided Practice: *Lectura*, p. 69
• *Real.* para hispanohablantes, pp. 62–63

For: Internet Activity
Web Code: jdd-0207

¿Comprendiste?

1. Según la información, ¿qué talento debes tener para participar en las audiciones? ¿Cuántos años debes tener?

2. ¿Por qué es importante el Teatro Colón?

3. Si tocas la trompeta, ¿en qué puedes participar en el Instituto?

4. Si no te gusta ni bailar ni cantar, ¿qué otras actividades puedes hacer en el teatro?

5. ¿Te gustaría ver una ópera? ¿Por qué?

6. ¿Hay presentaciones de teatro o de orquesta en tu escuela? ¿Participas en las presentaciones o te gusta verlas? ¿Por qué?

¿Comprendiste?

Standards: 1.2

Resources: Answers on Transparencies
Focus: Verifying comprehension of the *Lectura*

Suggestions: Remind students that for questions 1–4, the answers are not in the same order as the reading. Point out the newspaper clipping for the auditions, and remind students that they will need to search for answers there also.

Answers:
1. Debes saber cantar, bailar, tocar un instrumento o actuar. Debes tener de 15 a 25 años.
2. Porque lleva casi 150 años ofreciendo ópera al público.
3. Puedes participar en la Orquesta Académica.
4. Puedes estudiar otra especialidad. Por ejemplo, puedes aprender a hacer los escenarios o estudiar la grabación o el video.
5. Answers will vary.
6. Answers will vary.

Fondo cultural

Standards: 1.2, 2.2, 4.2

Suggestions: If possible, bring in pictures of these theaters to show to students. Ask students to think of different productions that they have seen to help them answer the question.

Answers will vary.

Theme Project

Students can perform Step 3 at this point. (For more information, see p. 70-a.)

For Further Reading

Student Resources: Realidades para hispanohablantes: Lectura 2, pp. 64–65; Lecturas para hispanohablantes 2: "Las mañanitas," p. 28, "Homenaje a los padres chicanos," p. 34; Guided Practice: Lectura, p. 69

Enrich Your Teaching
Resources for All Teachers

Culture Note
Spanish speakers make up the fastest-growing minority group in the United States and the entertainment industry is addressing this growth. Today, theaters are producing Spanish-language plays with greater frequency. These productions go beyond stereotypes and explore themes pertinent to Spanish-speaking cultures.

Teacher-to-Teacher
Ask students to create a playbill for an actual school production. Have them include a summary of the plot, characters' names, etc. Ask the faculty sponsor if your students can provide the Spanish playbills to spectators at the production.

2A Communicate: Culture

La cultura en vivo

Core Instruction

Standards: 1.2, 2.2, 3.1

Focus: Reading about and making a poncho

Presentation: Write the word **poncho** on the board, and have a volunteer come to the board and draw one. Have students ever worn a rain poncho? If so, ask them to describe where and when. How are those ponchos similar to or different from the **ponchos** in the photos? Point out the variety of **ponchos** pictured on the page. Can students compare any other items of clothing that they might wear to the **poncho?**

Suggestions: Remind students the day before that they should bring in a smock or wear old clothing, as they will be working with paint. Have a model **poncho** ready to share with them or bring in materials to create a **poncho** together.

Additional Resources

Student Resource: Realidades para hispanohablantes, p. 66

La cultura en vivo

Cómo hacer un poncho

Dos indígenas peruanos del Cuzco con ponchos

El poncho es ropa típica del altiplano, una zona elevada y fría, situada entre Bolivia y el Perú. El poncho también se usa en la Argentina, Chile, Colombia, el Ecuador, Guatemala y México. Estos países tienen regiones montañosas y frías. El poncho protege[1] contra el frío y está hecho de materiales como lana de llama o de oveja que son animales de estos países.

En general hay dos clases de ponchos: los ponchos de trabajo que se llevan todos los días, y los ponchos de fiesta, que se llevan en las fiestas, celebraciones y eventos especiales. Los ponchos de fiesta tienen diseños[2] más complejos y, a veces, son de colores.

Un indígena boliviano en un festival de agricultores

Objetivo

Hacer un poncho

Materiales

- una tela[3] como cobija[4] de aproximadamente 90 cm* por 120 cm
- tijeras
- hilo[5] y aguja de coser[6]
- pintura[7] para tela
- un pincel[8]

Instrucciones

1 Para hacer la parte principal del poncho, dobla la tela en diagonal como en el dibujo para hacer un cuadrado. Corta la tela que no necesitas y guárdala. *(Figura 1)*

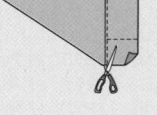

Figura 1

2 Haz un corte de unos 30 cm de largo para la cabeza. *(Figura 2)*

3 Corta un pedazo de la tela que no usaste, y cósela al poncho para hacer un bolsillo.[9] *(Figura 3)*

Figura 2

4 Decora el poncho con los colores, la mascota o el escudo de tu escuela. Si necesitas ideas, busca ejemplos de ponchos que usan los habitantes de los Andes.

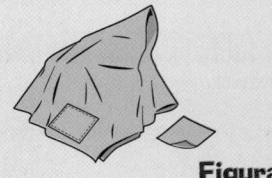

*2.54 cm = 1 in
[1] protects   [2] designs   [3] cloth   [4] blanket   [5] thread   [6] sewing needle   [7] paint
[8] paintbrush   [9] pocket

Figura 3

92 noventa y dos
Tema 2 • Un evento especial

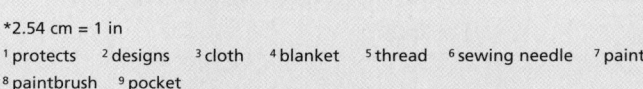
Differentiated Instruction
Solutions for All Learners

Advanced Learners

Have students search the Internet to research how **ponchos** are made in traditional Andean cultures. Have them compare the methods they read about with what they are doing in class.

Multiple Intelligences

Visual/Spatial: Have students look for symbols common in the Incan empire to reproduce on their **ponchos** in order to make them more authentic.

Presentación oral

Un evento especial

Task
You are an exchange student in Mexico. Your host family wants to know about special events in which you participate in your community. Show them photos of a typical special event you or your friends might attend.

❶ **Prepare** Bring a photo from home or a picture from a magazine of a special event that high school students might attend. Think about the process of getting ready for this event. Answer the following questions for yourself or for others:

• ¿Qué tipo de evento es? ¿Qué ropa llevas?
• ¿Qué haces para prepararte?
• ¿Cómo estás? ¿Entusiasmado(a)? ¿Nervioso(a)? ¿Contento(a)?

You might want to take notes to help you remember what you want to say.

❷ **Practice** Go through your presentation several times. Try to:

• provide as much information as you can about each point
• use complete sentences
• speak clearly

Modelo

Cuando voy a un concierto llevo ropa nueva pero no me gusta ponerme zapatos nuevos. Prefiero zapatos cómodos. Para prepararme me ducho, me peino, me pongo agua de colonia y me visto. Mis amigos y yo siempre estamos entusiasmados porque nos encanta escuchar música.

❸ **Present** Show your photo and give the information about the event.

❹ **Evaluation** Your teacher may give you a rubric for how the presentation will be graded. You will probably be graded on:

• how complete your preparation is
• how much information you communicate
• how easy it is to understand you

Estrategia

Taking notes
When preparing for a presentation, it is often helpful to take notes. These notes can help you organize your thoughts. Using index cards with your notes can help keep you on track while giving your presentation.

Standards: 1.3, 3.1

Focus: Speaking about a special event
Suggestions: Have students brainstorm a list of events that they could include in their presentations. You may want to provide students with an outline to help them organize their notes. Include details such as date and time of the event, with whom the student attended the event, what he or she wore, and how he or she prepared. If students feel uncomfortable talking about themselves, allow them to bring in a magazine photo to tell a fictional story.

Ask questions to keep students on track, should they have pauses in their presentations. Encourage students to ask their classmates for additional details.

Model a top-scoring presentation for students using a photo from your own special event.

Portfolio

Give students their grade on a copy of the grading rubric, and have them place it in their portfolio.

Pre-AP* Support

• *Pre-AP* Resource Book:* Comprehensive guide to Pre-AP* speaking skill development, pp. 36–46

Additional Resources

Student Resources: Realidades para hispanohablantes, p. 67; Guided Practice: Presentación oral, p. 70

✓ Assessment

• Assessment Program: Rubrics, p. T28

Enrich Your Teaching
Resources for All Teachers

RUBRIC	Score 1	Score 3	Score 5
Completeness of your preparation	You provide one of following: photos, answers to questions, index cards.	You provide two of the following: photos, answers to questions, index cards.	You provide all three of the following: photos, answers to questions, index cards.
How much information you communicate	You respond to only one of the questions.	You respond to two of the questions.	You respond to all of the questions.
How easily you are understood	You are difficult to understand and have many grammatical errors.	You are fairly easy to understand and have occasional grammatical errors.	You are easy to understand and have very few grammatical errors.

Core Instruction

Standards: 1.2, 3.2, 4.2, 5.2

Resources: Voc. and Gram. Transparencies: Map 12, Answers on Transparencies

Focus: Reading about Dolores Hidalgo; building background knowledge to prepare for the *Videomisterio*

Suggestions: Before reading the introductory paragraph, have students find Dolores Hidalgo on the map. Remind them that many urban areas were built near a body of water to facilitate transportation and commerce. Point out that because Dolores Hidalgo is not near water, it probably would not have become such a prominent city were it not for its historical significance.

After students have read the first paragraph, have a volunteer discuss how the city got its name. Ask students to brainstorm notable quotations from the history of the United States. Encourage them to consult their history books or a teacher to find out more about famous statements made during the colonies' struggle to gain independence from British rule.

Point out that both the garden and the monument in Dolores Hidalgo honor independence. Remind students that a country often celebrates the date that independence was declared, and not necessarily the date on which a war was won. For example, Mexicans celebrate Independence Day on September 16 because this is the date in 1810 when Miguel Hidalgo made the declaration *"¡Viva México!"* Their war for independence lasted until 1821. Likewise, the Americans signed the Declaration of Independence in 1776, but the Revolutionary War did not end until 1783. Have students list reasons why Mexico's independence from Spain was so important to them. Encourage students to consider the parallels between Mexican independence and the colonies' independence from Great Britain in the American War for Independence. Point out that historically colonists were not treated as equals by their imperial rulers.

Preparación para . . .

En busca de la verdad

Dolores Hidalgo

Bienvenidos a Dolores Hidalgo, otra ciudad visitada en el videomisterio. Está a unos 22 kilómetros al noreste de Guanajuato y tiene una población de 129,000 habitantes. Es una ciudad prominente porque allí, en la medianoche del 15 de septiembre del año 1810, el padre[1] Miguel Hidalgo y Costilla gritó:[2] "¡Viva México!". Con este histórico "Grito de la independencia", o "Grito de Dolores", empezó la independencia de México.

El Jardín de la Independencia es un lugar de gran atractivo en la ciudad de Dolores Hidalgo. El monumento principal de esta plaza es la estatua del famoso padre Hidalgo. En el jardín puedes disfrutar de[3] un agradable descanso. Si quieres, puedes probar[4] los helados tradicionales que se venden en el jardín, helados de variados y exóticos sabores como queso, aguacate, maíz y más.

◀ Este monumento honra a los héroes de la Guerra de la Independencia (1810–1821). Aproximadamente 600,000 personas murieron durante los 11 años de lucha contra España.

[1]priest [2]shouted

[3]enjoy [4]taste

Differentiated Instruction
Solutions for All Learners

Advanced Learners
Have students use the Internet to research one of the monuments or places in Dolores Hidalgo that honors Mexican independence. Encourage them to prepare a brief presentation about the place that they chose. Have them include information about what happened there, what is located there, and when it was built.

Heritage Language Learners
If appropriate, students may want to research the independence of their heritage country. Have them prepare a report to tell when their country declared independence, key events of the struggle for independence, notable people involved, and names of important places.

▲ La cerámica de Talavera es típica de Dolores Hidalgo. Muchas personas llegan a la ciudad para comprar esta cerámica de diseños originales y colores diferentes. En muchas casas de Dolores Hidalgo puedes ver a los artesanos trabajando con la cerámica en sus talleres[5].

Suggestions: Direct attention to the statue of Miguel Hidalgo on p. 95. Point out that he was one of the first intellectual revolutionaries of Mexico to take action against the Spanish Crown. Ask students to look at the details of the statue. Where else have they seen an eagle representing Mexico? How does the eagle represent the United States? What are some monuments that honor American independence?

Direct students' attention to the photo of the artisan working. Point out the details on the pottery. Ask students if they have ever watched anything being made by hand. If so, have them comment on how carefully the artist transformed the raw materials into the final product. What handicrafts, if any, are produced in your community?

You may want to have students bring their social science textbooks to class to help them answer the question.

Answers will vary but may include Boston or Philadelphia. Many of the first acts of rebellion took place in Boston, such as the Boston Tea Party. The Declaration of Independence was signed in Philadelphia.

¿Sabes que . . . ?

Cada año, el 15 y 16 de septiembre, los mexicanos celebran su independencia. En memoria del primer grito de Dolores, el presidente del país se para en el balcón del Palacio Nacional en la ciudad de México y grita tres veces "¡Viva México!".

Para pensar

Generalmente hay ciudades, como Dolores Hidalgo, que tienen una importancia histórica por los hechos que pasaron allí. ¿Qué ciudad o ciudades de los Estados Unidos tienen importancia histórica por su participación en la independencia? ¿Qué pasó en estas ciudades?

[5] workshops

Enrich Your Teaching
Resources for All Teachers

Culture Note

The *Grito de Dolores* or *Grito de la Independencia* is celebrated at the stroke of midnight on September 15 each year. Mexican Independence Day, September 16, is such an important date in Mexican history that, as for New Year's Day in the United States, most people begin celebrating the moment the great day arrives.

Internet Search

Have students use the Internet to research the Mexican war for independence.

Keywords:

guerra de independencia + México

Review Activities

To talk about getting ready: Have students write the words on index cards, and arrange the cards in the order in which they do the activities.

To talk about things you need to get ready: In pairs, have students take turns holding up an index card with an activity while the other names a related or necessary item for that activity.

To talk about a special event: Ask students to show a picture of an outfit, and have students identify to which event they would wear it.

To talk about how you feel: Have students give their partners an example of when they felt each of these emotions.

Reflexive verbs: Have students work in pairs to ask and answer questions about the daily routine of everybody in their household.

Other useful words and expressions: Provide students with a cloze passage to fill in, using these words as their word bank.

Portfolio

Invite students to review the activities they completed in this chapter, including written reports, posters or other visuals, tapes of oral presentations, or other projects. Have them select one or two items that they feel best demonstrate their achievements in Spanish to include in their portfolios. Have them include this with the Chapter Checklist and Self-Assessment Worksheet.

Additional Resources

Student Resources: Realidades para hispanohablantes, p. 68

 **CD-ROM**

PuzzleView Web Code: jdd-0208

Teacher Resources:
- Teacher's Resource Book: Situation Cards, p. 88, Clip Art, pp. 90–93
- Assessment Program: Chapter Checklist and Self-Assessment Worksheet, pp. T56–T57

Repaso del capítulo
Vocabulario y gramática jdd-0289

To prepare for the test, check to see if you . . .
- know the new vocabulary and grammar
- can perform the tasks on p. 97

to talk about getting ready

acostarse (o → ue)	to go to bed
afeitarse	to shave
arreglarse (el pelo)	to fix (one's hair)
bañarse	to take a bath
cepillarse (los dientes)	to brush (one's teeth)
cortarse el pelo	to cut one's hair
despertarse (e → ie)	to wake up
ducharse	to take a shower
levantarse	to get up
lavarse (la cara)	to wash (one's face)
pedir prestado, -a (a)	to borrow (from)
pintarse (las uñas)	to paint, to polish (one's nails)
ponerse	to put on
prepararse	to get ready
secarse	to dry
vestirse (e → i)	to get dressed

to talk about things you need to get ready

el agua de colonia	cologne
el cepillo	brush
el cinturón, pl. los cinturones	belt
el desodorante	deodorant
la ducha	shower
el gel	gel
las joyas (de oro, de plata)	(gold, silver) jewelry
los labios	lips
el maquillaje	make-up
el peine	comb
el pelo	hair
el salón de belleza, pl. los salones de belleza	beauty salon
el secador	blow dryer
la toalla	towel
las uñas	nails

For Vocabulario adicional, see pp. 498–499.

to talk about a special event

la audición, pl. las audiciones	audition
la boda	wedding
la cita	date
el concurso	contest
un evento especial	special event

to talk about how you feel

entusiasmado, -a	excited
nervioso, -a	nervous
tranquilo, -a	calm

other useful words and expressions

antes de	before
cómodo, -a	comfortable
depende	it depends
elegante	elegant
lentamente	slowly
luego	then
por ejemplo	for example
rápidamente	quickly
te ves (bien)	you look (good)

reflexive verbs

me acuesto	nos acostamos
te acuestas	os acostáis
se acuesta	se acuestan

ser *to be*

soy	somos
eres	sois
es	son

estar *to be*

estoy	estamos
estás	estáis
está	están

possessive adjectives

mío, -a, -os, -as	nuestro, -a, -os, -as
tuyo, -a, -os, -as	vuestro, -a, -os, -as
suyo, -a, -os, -as	suyo, -a, -os, -as

Differentiated Instruction
Solutions for All Learners

Students with Special Needs

Pair hearing-impaired students with advanced learners. After advanced learners have listened to the script and answered correctly, ask them to listen again and write the sentences that they hear. Then have hearing-impaired students complete the **Escuchar** task using those sentences.

Students with Learning Difficulties

To help students focus their review, distribute a photocopy of the vocabulary list and have students bring in three different-colored highlighters. Ask students to use one color to highlight words they already know, a second color for items they are somewhat familiar with, and a third for items they still need to study.

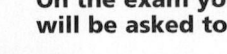 **Más práctica**

● Practice Workbook: Puzzle, p. 36
● Practice Workbook: Organizer, p. 37

Go Online
PHSchool.com

For: Test Preparation
Web Code: jdd-0208

Preparación para el examen

On the exam you will be asked to . . .	Here are practice tasks similar to those you will find on the exam . . .	If you need review . . .
jdd-0289 **① Escuchar** Listen and understand as teenagers talk about what they do on the weekend versus during the school week	Everyone does things a little differently on the weekend. Most people sleep later, dress more casually, and do things they don't have time to do during the week. As you listen to each person, decide whether you think they are talking about the weekend or a weekday. Be prepared to explain why you made your choice.	**pp. 74–77** *A primera vista* **p. 78** Actividad 5 **p. 82** Actividad 12
② Hablar Talk about your daily routine	Your parents have given you permission to go on the Spanish Club trip to Mexico this summer in which the boys share rooms and the girls share rooms. You want to share a room with a friend who wants to know if you have the same morning routine. Describe your typical routine to your friend.	**p. 78** Actividad 5 **p. 79** Actividad 7 **p. 82** Actividades 12–13 **p. 83** Actividad 15 **p. 84** Actividades 16–17
③ Leer Read and understand statements people make about typical and "not-so-typical" daily routines	Read the following statements from an online survey about people's morning routines. In your opinion, which ones would describe a typical daily routine? Which ones would be very unusual? (a) *Antes de bañarme, me pongo el maquillaje.* (b) *Después de ponerme el desodorante, me ducho.* (c) *Antes de lavarme el pelo, me seco con una toalla.* (d) *Antes de arreglarme el pelo, me ducho.*	**pp. 74–77** *A primera vista* **p. 80** Actividad 8 **p. 83** Actividad 14 **p. 85** Actividad 18 **pp. 90–91** *Lectura*
④ Escribir Write briefly about a special event that you look forward to each year	Everyone looks forward to special events during the year. Your teacher asks you to write about one of them. After writing a brief description, exchange your paragraph with a partner to see if he or she can guess what type of event it is. You might include: (a) the time of year that the event occurs; (b) how you usually feel the days before the event; (c) how you usually dress for the event. Give as many clues as you can.	**p. 78** Actividades 4–5 **p. 84** Actividad 17 **p. 86** Actividad 19
⑤ Pensar Demonstrate an understanding of the living conditions of the indigenous people of the *altiplano* in the Andes	You may have worn a *poncho* during a rainy football game or while camping. Explain where *ponchos* originated, how they are made, and why they are necessary for the people of that region.	**p. 92** *La cultura en vivo*

noventa y siete **97**
Capítulo 2A

Differentiated Assessment
Solutions for All Learners

STUDENTS NEEDING EXTRA HELP
● **Alternate Assessment Program:** Examen del capítulo 2A
● **Audio Program CD 20:** Chap. 2A, Track 4

HERITAGE LEARNERS
● **Assessment Program: Realidades para hispanohablantes:** Examen del capítulo 2A
● **ExamView** Heritage Learner Test Bank

ADVANCED/PRE-AP*
● **ExamView** Pre-AP* Test Bank
● **Pre-AP* Resource Book,** pp. 100–103

Performance Tasks

Presentation EXPRESS
ANSWERS

Standards: 1.1, 1.2, 1.3, 2.2

Student Resource: Realidades para hispanohablantes, p. 69

Teacher Resources: Teacher's Resource Book: Audio Script, p. 80; Audio Program: Track 14; Answers on Transparencies

1. Escuchar

Suggestions: Have students note differences in their own weekend routines before they listen.

 Script and Answers:

1. Generalmente, me despierto muy lentamente a las diez o diez y media. Me visto en mi ropa favorita, una sudadera vieja con mis jeans cómodos, y no me pongo maquillaje. Es mi día favorito. *(weekend)*
2. Me levanto muy temprano. Me ducho, me cepillo los dientes, y me visto. Pongo los libros en mi mochila y voy a la escuela. *(weekday)*
3. Hago la tarea y me acuesto temprano. *(weekday)*
4. Voy al cine a las 7:00 de la noche y después voy a una fiesta. Me acuesto tarde. *(weekend)*

2. Hablar

Suggestions: Encourage students to say what time they do the activities.

Answers will vary.

3. Leer

Suggestions: Point out to students that they will have to consider the sequence and the effects of each action to determine which is logical.

Answers:
1. d   2. a, b, & c

4. Escribir

Suggestions: Remind students to write about an event other than the one they spoke about for the *Presentación oral* on p. 93.

Answers will vary.

5. Pensar

Suggestions: Refer students to p. 92.

Answers will vary.

✓ **Assessment**
● **ExamView** Quiz on PresEXPRESS
    QuickTake Presenter
● Assessment Program: Examen del capítulo
● **ExamView** Test Bank: Tests A and B
    test generator
● Audio Program CD 20: Chap. 2A, Track 4

RECYCLE
A ver si recuerdas

Vocabulary
• ¿Quieres ir de compras?

Grammar
• Cardinal numbers

A primera vista	Manos a la obra	¡Adelante!	Repaso

Learning Sequence

INPUT	PRACTICE	APPLICATION	REVIEW
• Introduce vocabulary and grammar within an authentic context.	• Practice and develop new vocabulary. • Learn and practice new grammar structures.	• Apply vocabulary and grammar through culminating, theme-based activities. • Apply skill development.	• Review vocabulary and grammar.

Objectives

Read, listen to, and interpret information about • Shopping • Clothing	• Communicate about shopping, clothing, and fashion. • Talk about the past using the preterite of regular verbs. • Point out specific objects using demonstrative adjectives. • Compare things without repeating adjectives.	• Read about the history of jeans and some Spanish variations of the word. • Explain cultural perspectives about parties. • Write a letter explaining your clothing purchases. • Read: **Mexicans in WWII.**	• Prepare for the chapter test.

Culture

• *Infanta Margarita*	• *¡No sé qué talla uso!* • Narciso Rodríguez	• *La parranda*	• Describe parties held in one's home and the role they play in Spanish-speaking cultures.

Vocabulary	Grammar	Learner Support
• Shopping • Clothing • Purchases	• Preterite of regular verbs • Demonstrative adjectives • Using adjectives as nouns	**STRATEGIES** • Tolerating ambiguity • Using a chart **RECYCLING** • Clothing • Shopping • Expressions of time • Activities • Classroom objects and colors • Demonstrative adjectives *este* and *ese*

Chapter Features

Exploración del lenguaje

Origin of words from Arabic

El español en el mundo del trabajo

The growing number of employment opportunities for bilingual Spanish speakers in the United States

Conexiones

History: The evolution of weaving technology

Beyond the Classroom: States & Countries

España
Nueva York
Nueva Jersey
California
Nevada
Cuba
México
Costa Rica
Ecuador
Argentina

Student Resources

TECHNOLOGY

ONLINE

Interactive Textbook
- Student Edition Online plus audio, video, and flashcards

Go Online Companion Web Site
- Tutorial activities
- Internet links
- Self-tests
- Downloadable MP3 audio files
- **PuzzleView**

CD-ROM

Interactive Textbook CD-ROM
Student Edition on CD-ROM plus audio, video, and flashcards

MindPoint™ CD-ROM
QUIZSHOW

PRINT MATERIAL

CORE INSTRUCTION

Practice Workbook, pp. 38–48
- Review
- Vocabulary
- Grammar
- Puzzle
- Organizer

Writing, Audio & Video Activities, pp. 35–45
- Video
- Audio
- Writing

Grammar Study Guide 1–2 (or 3–4)

Differentiated Instruction

STUDENTS NEEDING EXTRA HELP

Guided Practice Activities, pp. 71–89
- Vocabulary Flash Cards and Vocabulary Check
- Grammar Activities
- Presentación escrita

HERITAGE LEARNERS

Realidades para hispanohablantes, pp. 70–89

Lecturas para hispanohablantes
- "Algo viejo, algo nuevo, algo azul y algo hispano," pp. 35–36
- "Jeans: La obsesión continúa," pp. 101–102

ADVANCED/PRE-AP*

Pre-AP* Resource Book: Student Activity Sheet, p. 103

Teacher Resources

TECHNOLOGY

Audio Program · Fine Art Transparencies
Video Program · Vocabulary and Grammar Transparencies
· Answers on Transparencies

TeacherEXPRESS CD-ROM
- Lesson Planner
- Vocabulary Clip Art
- Web Resources
- Teaching Resources
- Teacher Edition with Interactive Links

PresentationEXPRESS CD-ROM
- Vocabulary
- Transparencies and Maps
- Grammar
- Photo Gallery
- Audio
- Clip Art

PH SuccessNet ONLINE
- Access to grades and reports from Online Interactive Textbook

ExamView QuickTake Presenter on Presentation Express CD-ROM
- Vocabulary Quizzes
- Chapter Test
- Grammar Quizzes

TeacherEXPRESS CD-ROM
- Assessment Program
- **ExamView test generator** Test Banks A and B

Go Online
PHSchool.com
For: Teacher Home Page
Web Code: jdk-1001

PRINT MATERIAL

CORE INSTRUCTION

Teacher's Resource Book, pp. 102–128
- Input Script
- Video Script
- Answer Keys
- GramActiva Blackline Masters
- Vocabulary Clip Art
- Chapter Resource Checklist
- School-to-Home Connection Letters
- Communicative Activities Blackline Masters

TPR Stories, pp. 31–36

CORE ASSESSMENT

Assessment Program, pp. 55–68
- Pruebas
  - Vocabulary Recognition
  - Vocabulary Production
  - Preterite of regular verbs
  - Demonstrative adjectives
  - Using adjectives as nouns
- Examen del capítulo
- Speaking and Writing Rubrics

Teacher's Resource Book, p. 116
- Situation Cards

TPR Stories, pp. 31–36

Differentiated Instruction

STUDENTS NEEDING EXTRA HELP

Guided Practice Activities Teacher's Guide, pp. T36–T45

HERITAGE LEARNERS

Realidades para hispanohablantes Teacher's Guide, pp. 36–45

Lecturas para hispanohablantes Teacher's Guide, pp. 11–12, 39–40

ADVANCED/PRE-AP*

Pre-AP* Resource Book: Resources Chart, p. 101

Differentiated Assessment

STUDENTS NEEDING EXTRA HELP

Alternate Assessment Program
- Examen del capítulo, pp. 23–28

HERITAGE LEARNERS

Assessment Program: Realidades para hispanohablantes Teacher's Guide, pp. T106–T110

ExamView test generator Heritage Learner Test Bank

ADVANCED/PRE-AP*

Pre-AP* Resource Book: Teacher Activity Sheet, p. 102

ExamView test generator Pre-AP* Test Bank

	Warm-up / Assess	Preview Present / Practice Communicate		Wrap-up / Homework Options
DAY 1	**Warm-up (5 min.)** • Homework check • Return Examen del capítulo: Capítulo 2A	**A ver si recuerdas . . . (20 min.)** • Presentation: ¿Quieres ir de compras? • Actividad 1 • Presentation: Cardinal numbers • Actividades 2, 3	**Chapter Opener (5 min.)** • Objectives • Fondo cultual **A primera vista (15 min.)** • Presentation: Vocabulario y gramática en contexto • Actividades 1, 2	**Wrap-up and Homework Options (5 min.)** • Practice Workbook 2B-A, 2B-B, 2B-1, 2B-2 • Go Online
DAY 2	**Warm-up (10 min.)** • Homework check	**A primera vista (35 min.)** • Presentation: Videohistoria *Buscando una ganga* • View: Videohistoria • Video Activities 1, 2, 3, 4 • Actividad 3		**Wrap-up and Homework Options (5 min.)** • Practice Workbook 2B-3, 2B-4 • Go Online • Prueba 2B-1: Vocabulary recognition
DAY 3	**Warm-up (10 min.)** • Actividad 6 • Homework check ✔**Assessment (10 min.)** • Prueba 2B-1	**Manos a la obra (25 min.)** • Actividades 4, 5, 7, 8, 9 • Fondo cultural		**Wrap-up and Homework Options (5 min.)** • Actividad 12 • Writing Activity 10 • Heritage Learner Workbook 2B-1, 2B-2 • Prueba 2B-2: Vocabulary production
DAY 4	**Warm-up (10 min.)** • Actividad 11 • Homework check ✔**Assessment (10 min.)** • Prueba 2B-2	**Manos a la obra (25 min.)** • Actividad 10 • Audio Activities 5, 6 • Communicative Activity • Presentation: Preterite of regular verbs • View: GramActiva video	• Actividades 13, 14 • Audio Activity 7	**Wrap-up and Homework Options (5 min.)** • Practice Workbook 2B-5 • Go Online • Actividad 18
DAY 5	**Warm-up (10 min.)** • Actividad 15 • Homework check	**Manos a la obra (35 min.)** • Actividades 16, 17 • Exploración del lenguaje • Presentation: Demonstrative adjectives	• View: GramActiva video • Actividades 19, 20, 21 • Audio Activity 8	**Wrap-up and Homework Options (5 min.)** • Practice Workbook 2B-6 • Writing Activities 11, 12 • Go Online • Heritage Learner Workbook 2B-4 • Pruebas 2B-3, 2B-4: Preterite of regular verbs; Demonstrative adjectives
DAY 6	**Warm-up (10 min.)** • Actividad 22 • Homework check ✔**Assessment (15 min.)** • Pruebas 2B-3, 2B-4	**Manos a la obra (20 min.)** • Presentation: Using adjectives as nouns • Actividades 23, 24 • Fondo cultural		**Wrap-up and Homework Options (5 min.)** • Practice Workbook 2B-7 • Go Online • Heritage Learner Workbook 2B-5 • Prueba 2B-5: Using adjectives as nouns
DAY 7	**Warm-up (10 min.)** • Writing Activity 13 • Homework check ✔**Assessment (10 min.)** • Prueba 2B-5	**Manos a la obra (15 min.)** • Audio Activity 9 • Communicative Activity • El español en el mundo del trabajo	**¡Adelante! (10 min.)** • Presentación escrita: Steps 1, 5	**Wrap-up and Homework Options (5 min.)** • Presentación escrita: Step 2
DAY 8	**Warm-up (5 min.)** • Homework check	**¡Adelante! (40 min.)** • Presentación escrita: Step 3 • Lectura • ¿Comprendiste? / Y tú, ¿qué dices?		**Wrap-up and Homework Options (5 min.)** • Presentación escrita: Step 4 • Preparación para el examen 3, 4, 5 • Go Online: Lectura
DAY 9	**Warm-up (5 min.)** • Homework check	**¡Adelante! (40 min.)** • Videomisterio: Presentation • Perspectivas del mundo hispano	**Repaso del capítulo (15 min.)** • Vocabulario y gramática • Preparación para el examen 1, 2	**Wrap-up and Homework Options (5 min.)** • Practice Workbook 2B-8, 2B-9 • Go Online: Self-test • Examen del capítulo 2B
DAY 10	**Warm-up (5 min.)** • Homework check ✔**Assessment (40 min.)** • Examen del capítulo 2B			**Wrap-up and Homework Options (5 min.)** • A ver si recuerdas . . .: Capítulo 3A

	Warm-up / Assess	Preview Present / Practice Communicate	Wrap-up / Homework Options
DAY 1	**Warm-up (5 min.)** • Homework check • Return Examen del capítulo: Capítulo 2A	**A ver si recuerdas . . .** **(20 min.)** • Presentation: ¿Quieres ir de compras? • Actividad 1 • Presentation: Cardinal numbers • Actividades 2, 3 **Chapter Opener** **(5 min.)** • Objectives • Fondo cultural	**A primera vista** **(55 min.)** • Presentation: Vocabulario y gramática en contexto • Actividades 1, 2 • Presentation: Videohistoria *Buscando una ganga* • View: Videohistoria • Video Activities 1, 2, 3, 4 • Actividad 3	**Wrap-up and Homework Options (5 min.)** • Practice Workbook 2B-A, 2B-B, 2B-1, 2B-2, 2B-3, 2B-4 • Go Online • Prueba 2B-1: Vocabulary recognition
DAY 2	**Warm-up (10 min.)** • Actividad 6 • Homework check ✔**Assessment (10 min.)** • Prueba 2B-1: Vocabulary recognition	**Manos a la obra (65 min.)** • Actividades 4, 5, 7, 8, 9 • Fondo cultural • Actividad 10 • Audio Activities 5, 6 • Writing Activity 10 • Communicative Activity • Presentation: Preterite of regular verbs • View: GramActiva video • Actividad 14		**Wrap-up and Homework Options (5 min.)** • Practice Workbook 2B-5 • Actividad 12 • Go Online • Heritage Learner Workbook 2B-1, 2B-2 • Prueba 2B-2: Vocabulary production
DAY 3	**Warm-up (10 min.)** • Actividad 11 • Homework check ✔**Assessment (10 min.)** • Prueba 2B-2: Vocabulary production	**Manos a la obra (65 min.)** • Actividades 13, 15, 16, 17 • Audio Activity 7 • Exploración del lenguaje • Presentation: Demonstrative adjectives • View: GramActiva video • Actividades 19, 20, 21 • El español en el mundo del trabajo • Audio Activity 8 • Writing Activity 12		**Wrap-up and Homework Options (5 min.)** • Practice Workbook 2B-6 • Actividad 18 • Writing Activity 11 • Go Online • Heritage Learner Workbook 2B-4 • Pruebas 2B-3, 2B-4: Preterite of regular verbs; Demonstrative adjectives
DAY 4	**Warm-up (10 min.)** • Actividad 22 • Homework check ✔**Assessment (15 min.)** • Pruebas 2B-3, 2B-4: Preterite of regular verbs; Demonstrative adjectives	**Manos a la obra (35 min.)** • Presentation: Using adjectives as nouns • Actividades 23, 24 • Fondo cultural • Audio Activity 9 • Writing Activity 13	**¡Adelante! (25 min.)** • Lectura • ¿Comprendiste? / Y tú, ¿qué dices? • Presentación escrita: Steps 1, 5	**Wrap-up and Homework Options (5 min.)** • Practice Workbook 2B-7 • Presentación escrita: Step 2 • Go Online • Heritage Learner Workbook 2B-5 • Prueba 2B-5: Using adjectives as nouns
DAY 5	**Warm-up (5 min.)** • Homework check ✔**Assessment (10 min.)** • Prueba 2B-5: Using adjectives as nouns	**¡Adelante! (40 min.)** • Presentación escrita: Step 3 • Perspectivas del mundo hispano	**Repaso del capítulo (30 min.)** • Vocabulario y gramática • Preparación para el examen 1, 2, 3, 4, 5	**Wrap-up and Homework Options (5 min.)** • Presentación escrita: Step 4 • Practice Workbook 2B-8, 2B-9 • Go Online: Self-test • Examen del capítulo 2B
DAY 6	**Warm-up (10 min.)** • Homework check • Answer questions **Repaso del capítulo (15 min.)** • Situation Cards ✔**Assessment (40 min.)** • Examen del capítulo 2B	**¡Adelante! (20 min.)** • Videomisterio: Presentation		**Wrap-up and Homework Options (5 min.)** • Go Online: Lectura • A ver si recuerdas . . .: Capítulo 3A

2B Recycle

Vocabulario
Core Instruction

Resources: Voc. and Gram. Transparency 51

Focus: Reviewing vocabulary related to shopping

Suggestions: On a transparency, write sentences saying what you want or need to buy, leaving extra space between each one. For example, write: *Me gustaría una cartera bonita, pero barata.* Display the transparency, and on a separate transparency sheet, write a sentence suggesting where the person should go. For example, write: *Debes ir al almacén.* Cut the second sheet up into separate sentences, and give them to random students. As you read each displayed sentence, have the student with the matching sentence come to the projector and place it underneath the original sentence.

To review colors, bring in prints of paintings by well-known artists from Spanish-speaking countries. Have volunteers describe the colors in the paintings, either correctly or incorrectly. Then ask other students to express agreement by giving a "thumbs-up" sign, or disagreement by giving a "thumbs-down" sign.

Actividad 1 **Standards:** 1.1, 1.3

Focus: Writing and talking about shopping

Suggestions: Before beginning, brainstorm which items can be bought in each store. For Step 2, have pairs give points for correct guesses. For example, students can earn five points for a correct guess on the first try, three for the second try, and one for the third.

Answers will vary.

Extension: For homework, have students cut out two different pictures from a catalogue. Ask them to write a description of the products, including where they can be bought.

Preparación para 2B

A ver si recuerdas...

Vocabulario

¿Quieres ir de compras?

¿Qué vas a hacer?
buscar
comprar
ir de compras
pagar
vender

¿De qué color es?
amarillo, -a
anaranjado, -a
azul
blanco, -a
gris
marrón, *pl.* marrones
morado, -a
negro, -a
rojo, -a
rosado, -a
verde

¿Adónde vas?
el almacén,
   pl. los almacenes
el centro comercial
la joyería
la librería
la tienda de descuentos
la tienda de
   electrodomésticos
la tienda de ropa
la zapatería

¿Qué vas a comprar?
unos anteojos de sol
un bolso
una cartera
un disco compacto
un llavero
un regalo
el software
un videojuego

¿Cómo es?
barato, -a
bonito, -a
caro, -a
feo, -a
grande
nuevo, -a
pequeño, -a
viejo, -a

Práctica de vocabulario • Usando el organizador gráfico

Actividad 1   **Escribir/Hablar**

¿Qué compras?

1 Escribe tres frases para decir a qué tienda vas y qué compras. Incluye dos adjetivos para describir las cosas que compras.

> **Modelo**
> *Voy a la joyería para comprar unos aretes rojos muy elegantes.*

2 Usa las frases del Paso 1. Habla con otro(a) estudiante y trata de adivinar *(try to guess)* qué va a comprar.

> **Modelo**
> A —*¿Adónde vas de compras?*
> B —*Voy a la joyería.*
> A —*¿Qué vas a comprar?*
> B —*Algo rojo y elegante.*
> A —*¿Compras un collar?*
> B —*No, compro unos aretes.*

98 noventa y ocho
Tema 2 • Un evento especial

Differentiated Instruction
Solutions for All Learners

Multiple Intelligences

Mathematical/Logical: Provide students with a worksheet of simple addition and subtraction problems. Have them work in small groups to practice the problems aloud. Then have them solve their problems on the board, saying each number as they do so. If possible, have them present the solutions to their classmates.

Students with Learning Difficulties

To help students with *Actividad* 1, give them semantic maps like the one shown above. Write a store name in the middle, and have students list items available at each store. Encourage students to use their semantic maps to write their sentences.

Gramática · Repaso

Cardinal numbers

10 diez	90 noventa	800 ochocientos, -as
20 veinte	100 ciento (cien)	900 novecientos, -as
30 treinta	200 doscientos, -as	1,000 mil
40 cuarenta	300 trescientos, -as	2,000 dos mil
50 cincuenta	400 cuatrocientos, -as	100,000 cien mil
60 sesenta	500 quinientos, -as	200,000 doscientos, -as mil
70 setenta	600 seiscientos, -as	
80 ochenta	700 setecientos, -as	

Un is not used before *cien*, *ciento*, and *mil*.

cien personas	*a hundred* people
mil pesos	*one thousand* pesos

Un/una and numbers ending in *-cientos /-cientas* agree in gender with the nouns that follow them.

Hay **treinta y un** videojuegos en la mesa.
Esta librería tiene más de **quinientas** revistas.

• To give the date in Spanish, use:

el + *cardinal number* + **de** + *month*

el veinte **de** enero

• The year is always given using complete numbers:

mil novecientos ochenta y cuatro

Práctica de gramática

  Actividad 2 Hablar _____

¿Cuánto cuestan?

Tienes que hacer un proyecto para tu clase de economía. Con otro(a) estudiante, habla de cuántos pesos cuesta cada producto en un centro comercial en la Ciudad de México.

1. un bolso de cuero (515)
2. una cartera (325)
3. unos pantalones (250)
4. un disco compacto (179)
5. una camisa de seda (399)
6. un collar de oro (1,200)
7. una revista (35)

Más práctica

• Practice Workbook, pp. 38–39: 2B-A, 2B-B
• Guided Practice Activities, p. 71: 2B-1
• *Real.* para hispanohablantes, p. 70

Go Online
PHSchool.com
For: Vocab. and Grammar
Web Code: jdd-0211

  Actividad 3 Hablar _____

¿Cuándo fue?

Pregunta a otro(a) estudiante cuándo ocurrieron los siguientes eventos importantes.

Modelo

el Día de la Independencia en los Estados Unidos
A —¿Cuándo fue *el Día de la Independencia en los Estados Unidos?*
B —Fue *el cuatro de julio de mil setecientos setenta y seis.*

1. el primer día de clases este año
2. el año del primer viaje de Cristóbal Colón
3. el año del viaje de los peregrinos (*Pilgrims*)
4. el año del primer viaje a la Luna
5. el fin de la Segunda Guerra Mundial

Gramática · Repaso

Core Instruction

Suggestions: To model numbers for students, hold a raffle. As students enter the room, give each a different raffle ticket with a number on it. Make duplicates of each ticket, and put them into a box. (You could also use the ready-made tickets used for drawings.) Pull tickets out of the box and call out the numbers. If students have a matching number, they must accurately repeat their number aloud to win.

 Actividad 2  *Standards:* 1.1, 1.3

Resources: Answers on Transparencies
Focus: Saying how much an item costs in *pesos*
Suggestions: Model a conversation for students. Remind them to use **cuestan** with plural items.

Answers:
1. Un bolso de cuero cuesta quinientos quince pesos.
2. . . . cuesta trescientos veinticinco pesos.
3. . . . cuestan doscientos cincuenta pesos.
4. . . . cuesta ciento setenta y nueve pesos.
5. . . . cuesta trescientos noventa y nueve pesos.
6. . . . cuesta mil doscientos pesos.
7. . . . cuesta treinta y cinco pesos.

 Actividad 3  *Standards:* 1.1

Resources: Answers on Transparencies
Focus: Talking about dates of important events
Suggestions: You might review the dates of these events before students begin.

Answers:
1. Answer will vary.
2. mil cuatrocientos noventa y dos
3. mil seiscientos veinte
4. mil novecientos sesenta y nueve
5. mil novecientos cuarenta y cinco

Extension: Have students work in pairs to quiz one another on dates from their history books.

Enrich Your Teaching
Resources for All Teachers

Teacher-to-Teacher

Have students practice numbers and shopping expressions by shopping in class. Bring old school supplies or other items to class and label them with a price in **pesos.** Create play money in *pesos* and give every student the same amount, equal to what one item costs. "Pay" students for being on time, bringing their homework, or helping in class. Students can use the play money to purchase an item. "Charge" students for coming to class unprepared or late. Every few days, ask students to tell you how many **pesos** they have and how many they need to buy their desired item.

 Standards for Capítulo 2B

- To achieve the goals of the Standards, students will:

Communication

1.1 Interpersonal
- Talk: about shopping, fashion and clothes; using the preterite of verbs and cardinal numbers
- Give dates of important events
- Ask for assistance in a shopping situation
- Describe class objects

1.2 Interpretive
- Read: about royal marriage arrangements; a picture-based story; about preferences and plans; about preterites of regular verbs and about demonstrative adjectives; about native American textiles and leather and about the history of jeans; about origins of words from Arabic; about bilingual employees; about a Latin-American designer; about family parties; about Mexican involvement in WWII
- Read, watch, and listen to information about fashion, shopping, and clothes

1.3 Presentational
- Present information on: fashion, fashion shows, shopping, clothes and money; preferences, plans; the history of jeans
- Write: information based on illustrations; about a shopping purchase

Culture

2.1 Practices and Perspectives
- Talk about the economic power of Spanish-speakers
- Explain the cultural significance of parties

2.2 Products and Perspectives
- Read and talk about: the daughter of the Spanish royal family; clothing materials in the past and the history and names of jeans; designer Narciso Rodríguez
- Define and explain *la parranda*

Connections

3.1 Cross-curricular
- Discuss: conversion tables for clothing sizes; the history of textiles and clothing; how to make a written presentation

3.2 Target Culture
- Discuss: the history of jeans; Spanish-speaking participation in the U.S. army during WWII

Comparisons

4.1 Language
- Identify origin of words from Arabic
- Use: demonstrative adjectives; adjectives as nouns

Communities

5.1 Beyond the School
- Discuss the importance of being a bilingual employee in stores and shops

---

Tema 2 • Un evento especial

Fondo cultural ■◆◆◇■◆◆◇■◆

La Infanta Margarita de Austria Los reyes de España prometieron en matrimonio *(promised in marriage)* a su hija, Margarita, a su primo Leopoldo, quien luego fue emperador de Austria. Como *(Since)* Margarita y su primo no vivían *(lived)* en la misma ciudad, los reyes mandaron muchos cuadros de ella a la corte de Viena para que la familia real pudiera verla *(could see her)*. En este cuadro, Margarita tiene aproximadamente nueve años.

- ¿Qué tipo de ropa llevas tú para fotos importantes? ¿Y a quién envías estas fotos?

"La Infanta Margarita Teresa" (1659), Diego Velázquez
Oil on canvas, 120.5 x 94.5. Kunsthistorisches Museum, Vienna, Austria. Courtesy The Bridgeman Art Library International Ltd.

100 cien
Tema 2 • Un evento especial

Differentiated Instruction

STUDENTS NEEDING EXTRA HELP

Guided Practice Activities
- Vocabulary Check, Flash Cards
- Grammar
- Reading and Writing Support

Guided Practice Audio CDs
- Disk 1, Track 4

HERITAGE LEARNERS

Realidades para hispanohablantes
- Chapter Opener, pp. 70–71
- A primera vista, p. 72
- Videohistoria, p. 73
- Manos a la obra, pp. 74–81
- ¡Adelante!, pp. 82–87
- Repaso del capítulo, pp. 88–89

ADVANCED/PRE-AP*

Pre-AP* Resource Book, pp. 100–103

Capítulo 2B

¿Qué ropa compraste?

Chapter Objectives

- Describe clothing and fashion
- Talk about going shopping
- Describe events in the past
- Point out specific objects
- Avoid repetition when comparing similar things
- Understand cultural perspectives on parties

Video Highlights

A primera vista: *Buscando una ganga*
GramActiva Videos: preterite of regular verbs; demonstrative adjectives

Country Connection

As you learn to talk about shopping for clothing, you will make connections to these countries and places:

España
Nueva York
Nueva Jersey
California
Nevada
Cuba
México
Costa Rica
Ecuador
Argentina

Más práctica

- *Real.* para hispanohablantes, pp. 70–71

Go Online PHSchool.com **For:** Online Atlas **Web Code:** jde-0002

De compras en Madrid, España

ciento uno **101**
Capítulo 2B

Preview

Chapter Opener

Presentation EXPRESS ATLAS

Core Instruction

Resources: Voc. and Gram. Transparencies: Maps 13–18, 20

Suggestions: Have students describe a normal shopping trip for them. What types of stores do they go to? What do they buy? Do they pay full price, or look for bargains? Based on their discussion, have students predict what types of words and expressions they will learn in the chapter. Point out the photo. Ask students if it is common to bargain at this type of store, and tell them that they will learn how to bargain in this chapter. Have they ever had to bargain for an item? Ask them to describe their experiences. In the *Videohistoria,* they will follow a group of friends on a shopping trip. Ask students if they prefer to shop with their friends or alone. Point out that they will review talking about events in the past.

Fondo cultural *Standards:* 1.2, 2.2

Resources: Fine Art Transparencies with Teacher's Guide, p. 71

Suggestions: Brainstorm words that students might use to describe clothes. Ask students to recall an outfit they wore for their most recent family or school picture to help them answer the last question.

Teaching with Art

Resources: Fine Art Transparencies with Teacher's Guide, p. 71

Suggestions: Ask students to comment on the extravagant clothes on the nine-year-old Infanta. Explain that this painting was done during Spain's Golden Age, when the country flourished both culturally and economically.

Teacher Technology

TeacherEXPRESS Plan · Teach · Assess

PresentationEXPRESS Dynamic Presentations for Teachers

PLAN	TEACH	ASSESS
Lesson Planner	Teaching Resources	Chapter Quizzes and Tests
	Interactive Teacher's Edition	
	Vocabulary Clip Art	

Go Online PHSchool.com **For:** Teacher Home Page **Web Code:** jdk-1001

TEACH	ASSESS
Vocabulary & Grammar Powerpoints	**ExamView** QuickTake Presenter
GramActiva Video	
Audio & Clip Art Activities	
Transparencies and Maps	
Activity Answers	
Photo Gallery	

101

Vocabulario y gramática

 **Presentation EXPRESS** VOCABULARY

Core Instruction

 Standards: 1.2

Resources: Teacher's Resource Book: Input Script, p. 104, Clip Art, pp. 118–120, Audio Script, p. 105; Voc. and Gram. Transparencies 52–53; TPR Stories Book: pp. 24–36; Audio Program: Tracks 1–2

Focus: Presenting vocabulary for shopping, especially clothes shopping

Suggestions: Present the vocabulary in two groups: fashion/colors and shopping in general. Use the Input Script from the *Teacher's Resource Book* or the story from the *TPR Stories Book* to present the new words, or use some of these suggestions.

Bring in several blouses or shirts of varying colors, styles, and sizes. Add tags to them with prices ranging from extremely inexpensive to very expensive. Group the items by color and style and display them in at least two groups. Pretend to go shopping and comment on the blouses or shirts, holding up a brightly colored one, a fashionable (or unfashionable) one, etc. Comment on whether the item is a bargain or not. Hold up one that is obviously too large or too small for you and comment on its not being your size. Involve students in your shopping effort, asking questions using the vocabulary such as: *¿Te gusta el azul oscuro? ¿Está de moda esta blusa/camisa? ¿Y aquella blusa/camisa?*

Use pantomime, gestures, and signs on posterboard to indicate the store entrance, exit, and checkout. Discuss prices: *El precio es $5. ¿Es un precio bajo o alto?* Have various discount signs written on the board and point to the appropriate one as you ask: *Con un descuento de 50%, ¿cuánto voy a gastar en esta blusa / camisa?*

Display pictures of cash, a credit card, a check, and a gift certificate as you discuss payment options. Ask students how they pay for purchases.

Additional Resources

• Audio Program: Canciones CD, Disc 22

A primera vista

Vocabulario y gramática en contexto

jdd-0297

ENTRADA — la entrada

ZAPATOS

la salida — **SALIDA**

LIQUIDACIÓN de verano ¡Descuento del 70%!

LIQUIDACIÓN de verano ¡Descuento del 50%!

los colores **vivos**

los colores **pastel**

azul **oscuro**

azul **claro**

—Mira, Lupita. **Aquellas** blusas tienen un descuento del 50 por ciento. ¡Me encanta ir de compras cuando hay **una liquidación!**

—¡Es **una ganga!** Pero no me gustan los colores **tan** vivos.

—¡No importa! **Están de moda.** Con **precios** tan **bajos**, voy a **probarme** dos o tres.

—Y mira **aquellos** bolsos en la mesa. **El letrero anuncia** un descuento del 70 por ciento. ¡Vamos!

102 ciento dos
Tema 2 • Un evento especial

Differentiated Instruction
Solutions for All Learners

Advanced Learners

Ask students either to draw or to use illustrations from magazines to create their own clothing store posters. Have them add signs for sales, special bargains, discounts on certain colors/sizes/styles/brands, and payment options. Display their "stores," and use them as visual aids throughout the chapter.

Students with Special Needs

Using the script for *Actividad* 2, create a chart for hearing-impaired students. List the dictated sentences describing Lupita and her friend. Label the second column **c** for **cierta** and the third **f** for **falsa.** Have students check the column to indicate if they agree with each description.

Más vocabulario

el cheque de viajero traveler's check

el cupón de regalo gift certificate

la lana wool

el número shoe size

la seda silk

la caja

la cajera

—Es una buena **marca.** Y **encontré** mi **talla, mediana.**

—**En realidad,** no necesito estos bolsos. Pero me gusta **el estilo** y no cuestan mucho.

—Tienes razón. Y pueden ser regalos para tus amigas. Vamos a la caja para pagar.

—¿Por qué siempre pagas **en efectivo?**

—Porque no me gusta usar ni mi **tarjeta de crédito** ni **un cheque personal.**

—Yo estoy contenta. No **gasté** mucho. Con esta liquidación los precios no están muy **altos.** Compré esta blusa pero, ¿no piensas que es un poco **exagerada? ¿Qué te parece?**

—**Me parece** muy bien. Y pagaste muy poco por todas las blusas.

  jdd-0297

🔊 **Escuchar**

¿Dónde está?

Imagina que estás en la tienda de las páginas 102–103. Mira los dibujos y escucha las siguientes frases. Señala lo que escuchas.

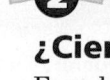 jdd-0297

🔊 **Escuchar**

¿Cierto o falso?

Escucha las siguientes frases que describen a Lupita y a su amiga. Si la frase es cierta, señala con el pulgar hacia arriba y si la frase es falsa, señala con el pulgar hacia abajo.

Más práctica

- Practice Workbook, pp. 40–41: 2B-1, 2B-2
- WAV Wbk.: Writing, p. 42
- Guided Practice: Vocab. Flash Cards, pp. 72–78
- Real. para hispanohablantes, p. 72

Go Online
PHSchool.com
For: Vocab. Practice
Web Code: jdd-0212

ciento tres **103**
Capítulo 2B

Enrich Your Teaching
Resources for All Teachers

Teacher-to-Teacher

Provide students with sales flyers or catalogs for clothing and personal accessories. Have them work in small groups to discuss the items—whether or not they are stylish, which are bargains, what colors they like. Have each group describe the items they are "buying" and how they are "paying" for the items.

Teacher-to-Teacher

Have students act out the dialogues on pp. 102–103. Encourage them to use movement, gesture, and facial expressions to convey meaning. Allow them to expand on or alter the scenario if they wish.

 Actividad 1 🌐 Standards: 1.2   Presentation EXPRESS AUDIO

Resources: Teacher's Resource Book: Audio Script, p. 105; Audio Program: Track 3; Answers on Transparencies

Focus: Listening comprehension about shopping

Suggestions: If you prefer, use the transparencies to check comprehension. As each item is read, point to any item or area shown. Have students give a "thumbs-up" sign if you have indicated the correct item or area and a "thumbs-down" sign if you haven't.

🔊 **Script and Answers:**

1. Yo te espero en la entrada. ¿Está bien? (entrance)
2. ¿Puedo pagar con mi tarjeta de crédito? (cashier)
3. ¿Dónde están los bolsos? (bags)
4. ¡Mira! Liquidación del cincuenta por ciento. (50% off sign)
5. Voy a pagar en la caja. (cash register)
6. Prefiero la blusa de color azul claro. (light blue shirt)
7. Perdón, señora. ¿Dónde está la salida? (exit)

Bellringer Review

Write these words on the board: *bolso, cartera, disco compacto, llavero, videojuego.* Beginning with *Yo recibí...,* have them write a sentence indicating one of the items that they have received as a gift in the last year.

  Actividad 2 🌐 Standards: 1.2    Presentation EXPRESS AUDIO

Resources: Teacher's Resource Book: Audio Script, p. 105; Audio Program: Track 4; Answers on Transparencies

Focus: Listening comprehension on a sale

Suggestions: After reading the directions, show the transparencies and have students scan them for details they might hear.

🔊 **Script and Answers:**

1. Las camisas en la tienda tienen un descuento de 25 por ciento. (falso)
2. A Lupita le gustan los colores vivos. (falso)
3. Según la amiga de Lupita, los colores vivos están de moda. (cierto)
4. Los bolsos en la tienda no cuestan mucho. (cierto)
5. Los bolsos pueden ser buenos regalos. (cierto)
6. Las chicas nunca pagan con dinero en efectivo. (falso)
7. Los precios en la tienda son muy bajos. (cierto)

Extension: Replay or reread the script and have students correct the false statements.

✔ **Assessment**

- ExamView QuickTake Presenter Quiz on PresEXPRESS

103

Videohistoria

Presentation EXPRESS
VOCABULARY

Core Instruction

 Standards: 1.2

Resources: Voc. and Gram. Transparencies 54–55; Audio Program: Track 5

Focus: Extending the presentation of vocabulary and grammar

Suggestions:

Pre-reading: Direct attention to the *Estrategia*. Have students examine the photos, especially the last three panels. Ask if they always end up buying what they look at.

Reading: Allow students to read silently. Ask for volunteers to take the roles of Gloria, Tomás, and Raúl. Stop students after panel 4 and ask the class to summarize the actions and the attitudes of the characters. Ask for another set of volunteers to finish the reading. Use the transparencies and non-verbal cues to help students with new words and expressions.

Post-reading: Ask if students' predictions about what the teens would buy were correct. Complete *Actividad* 3 to check comprehension.

Pre-AP* Support

• **Activity:** Give each student handouts containing Clip Art representations of twelve of the new vocabulary words presented in this chaper. Have them cut the squares apart. Then, have students work in pairs to play *"Memoria."* Pairs should mix their clip art cards and put them face down in rows on a desktop. One at a time, students turn over one picture and try to find a match by turning over a second picture. If a match is made, an extra turn is granted. A student must say they word aloud to add the pair to his/her stack.

• **Pre-AP* Resource Book:** Comprehensive guide to Pre-AP* vocabulary skill development, pp. 47–53

Videohistoria jdd-0297

Buscando una ganga

¿Qué pasó cuando Gloria fue de compras con Raúl y Tomás?

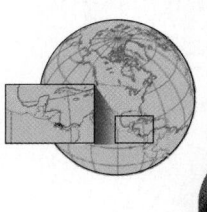

Estrategia

Scanning
By scanning the photos from the *Videohistoria* and the accompanying text, can you figure out who buys what?

Liquidación

Tomás
Gloria
Raúl

1 **Gloria:** ¡Mira **aquel** letrero!

Tomás: A ver . . . ¿qué anuncia?

Gloria: ¡Una liquidación fabulosa! ¿Qué les parece? ¿Vamos a ver qué tienen?

Raúl: No **me importa,** pero creo que los precios aquí siempre son altos.

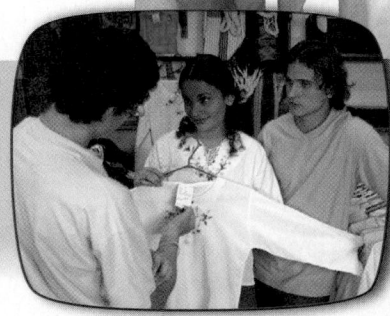

5 **Gloria:** Aquí, encontré mi talla.

Tomás: ¿Usas mediana? Es bonita. **¿De qué está hecha?**

Gloria: Está hecha de algodón. ¿Qué te parece?

Raúl: No me parece mal. Y el algodón es mejor que **las telas sintéticas.**

6 **Gloria:** ¿Cuál **escojo?** ¿Ésta o la blusa **de sólo un color?**

Raúl: No me importa. Compra algo **inmediatamente** y ¡vamos!

Gloria: ¡Qué impaciente eres! ¿Por qué no van a mirar otras cosas mientras yo me pruebo las blusas?

7 **Gloria:** Quiero comprarme esta blusa.

La dependienta: Muy bien, señorita. ¿Cómo va a pagar?

Gloria: En efectivo. Aquí está.

104 ciento cuatro
Tema 2 • Un evento especial

Differentiated Instruction
Solutions for All Learners

Advanced Learners

Ask students to rework the *Videohistoria* so that it is Gloria who is not interested in spending time shopping. They may choose to have the trio start at the market and then go to the store. Ask them to come up with other reversals in the story. Have them present the reworked story to their classmates.

Students with Learning Difficulties

Explain that scanning photos, as suggested in the *Estrategia,* provides visual clues that help comprehension. Draw attention to Raúl's crossed arms (panel 4) and ask what his body language may indicate. Then ask how the visual clues in panel 8 might indicate a change in his attitude.

2 Gloria: Compré esta blusa aquí **recientemente.** Me gusta porque me queda un poco **floja.** No me gusta la ropa **apretada.**

Raúl: Mira, no tengo dinero. ¿Cuánto tiempo pasamos aquí?

Gloria: No importa. Yo tengo dinero.

Tomás: ¿Hay **un mercado** cerca de aquí? Me gustaría visitar uno.

3 Raúl: Siempre hay buenas gangas aquí en el mercado.

Tomás: Sí, hay mucho que puedes comprar aquí. Por eso me gusta ir de compras en el mercado.

4 Gloria: ¡Mira aquellas blusas! ¡Qué estilo tan bonito tienen! ¡Y los colores son tan vivos!

Raúl: Gloria, por favor, ¿otra blusa?

8 Raúl: Estas chaquetas **de cuero** son fabulosas. ¿Cuál te gusta más?

Tomás: Te ves muy bien.

Gloria: ¿Y no tienes dinero?

3 **Escribir/Hablar**

¿Comprendiste?

1. ¿Qué anuncia el letrero que ve Gloria?
2. ¿Por qué no quiere Raúl pasar mucho tiempo en la tienda?
3. ¿Adónde van los tres jóvenes para buscar gangas?
4. ¿Qué encuentra Gloria en el mercado?
5. ¿Cómo es la ropa que compra Gloria?
6. ¿Cómo paga Gloria?
7. ¿Qué tipo de ropa se prueba Raúl?

Más práctica

- Practice Workbook, pp. 42–43: 2B-3, 2B-4
- WAV Wbk.: Video, pp. 35–37
- Guided Practice: Vocab. Check, pp. 79–82
- *Real.* para hispanohablantes, p. 73

 **Go Online**
PHSchool.com
For: Vocab. Practice
Web Code: jdd-0213

ciento cinco **105**
Capítulo 2B

Enrich Your Teaching
Resources for All Teachers

Culture Note
Some countries accept the U.S. dollar in addition to their own local currency. This is generally done to attract foreign investment and tourism, and is often limited to major cities and tourist areas.

Teacher-to-Teacher
Write out individual sentences spoken by each character and show them on the overhead projector. Have students identify which character spoke each sentence and then put the sentences in the correct order to retell the story. Add sentences that would fit each character's personality and have students incorporate them.

Core Instruction

Standards: 1.2

Resources: Teacher's Resource Book: Video Script, p. 110; Video Program: Cap. 2B; Video Program Teacher's Guide: Cap. 2B

Focus: Viewing and comprehending the video

Suggestions:

Pre-viewing: Have students brainstorm words they might use if they were shopping with friends.

Viewing: Show the video once without pausing. Show it again, pausing at key points to check for comprehension. Ask students what they would say at certain points in the video. Would their reactions differ from those of the video characters?

Post-viewing: Complete the Video Activities in the *Writing, Audio & Video Workbook.*

3 *Standards:* 1.2, 1.3  Presentation EXPRESS  ANSWERS

Resources: Answers on Transparencies

Focus: Verifying comprehension of the *Videohistoria*

Suggestions: Before doing the activity, ask students to summarize the story without looking at their books. Help them reconstruct the story as needed. If they can't remember details, have them check their books or watch the video again.

Answers:

1. El letrero anuncia una liquidación.
2. Raúl no quiere pasar mucho tiempo en la tienda porque los precios allá siempre son altos y él no tiene dinero.
3. Los tres jóvenes van al mercado para buscar gangas y porque a Tomás le gustaría visitar un mercado.
4. Gloria encuentra una blusa bonita de algodón.
5. Compra una blusa blanca y de talla mediana.
6. Paga en efectivo.
7. Raúl se prueba una chaqueta de cuero.

Additional Resources
- WAV Wbk,: Audio Act. 5, p. 38
- Teacher's Resource Book: Audio Script, pp. 105–106
- Audio Program: Track 7

✓ **Assessment**
- **ExamView** QuickTake Presenter Quiz on PresEXPRESS
- Prueba 2B-1: Vocab. Recognition, pp. 55–56

Actividad 4  *Standards:* 1.2, 1.3

Presentation EXPRESS AUDIO

Resources: Teacher's Resource Book, Audio Script, p. 105; Audio Program: Track 6; Answers on Transparencies

Focus: Listening and writing about clothing choices

Recycle: Clothing

Suggestions: Have students examine the illustration. Ask them to describe the type of clothing they would expect each character to prefer. Remind students that a verb must agree in number with its subject, even if the subject follows the verb. Provide examples with *importar: El color de la blusa no me importa. Me importa el color. Me importan los colores.* Remind students that the subject of the verb *gustar* follows the verb. Provide them with some examples: *Me gusta la ropa apretada. Me gustan las blusas de algodón.*

Script and Answers:

1. **Siempre escojo ropa de la misma marca.** *(Santiago)*
2. **La ropa floja me parece mucho más cómoda.** *(Timoteo)*
3. **En realidad, el estilo de la ropa no me importa nada.** *(Timoteo)*
4. **No me importan los precios altos si la ropa está de moda.** *(Santiago)*
5. **Me gustan mucho los colores vivos.** *(Santiago)*

Answers to Step 3 will vary but will include: *Estoy de acuerdo / No estoy de acuerdo. Para mí, ... es más importante que ....*

Extension: Have students restate their answers for Step 3 using the verb *importar* instead of *es importante. Para mí, la marca de la ropa es más importante que el precio. = La marca de la ropa me importa más que el precio.*

Actividad 5 *Standards:* 1.1, 1.3

Focus: Writing and speaking about clothing and shopping

Recycle: Shopping

Suggestions: Brainstorm a list of verbs that could be used with the boxed words. Have students refer to the list as they write their sentences.

Answers will vary.

Manos a la obra

Vocabulario y gramática en uso

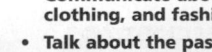

Objectives
- Communicate about shopping, clothing, and fashion
- Talk about the past using the preterite of regular verbs
- Point out specific objects using demonstrative adjectives
- Compare things without repeating adjectives

Actividad 4  jdd-0298 **Escuchar/Escribir/Hablar**

¿Quién es?

1 En una hoja de papel, escribe los números del 1 al 5. Después escucha los comentarios sobre la ropa y la moda. Escribe las frases que oyes.

2 Ahora lee los comentarios que escribiste y, según el dibujo, decide si habla Santiago o Timoteo. Escribe *Santiago* o *Timoteo* en tu papel.

3 Lee otra vez las frases sobre Timoteo y Santiago. Escoge tres y da tus opiniones. Explica por qué estás de acuerdo o no. Lee tus frases a otro(a) estudiante.

Modelo

No me importan los precios altos si la ropa está de moda.
Estoy de acuerdo. Para mí, la marca de la ropa es más importante que el precio.

Actividad 5    **Escribir/Hablar**

¿Cierta o falsa?

Escribe seis frases para describir lo que hacen Santiago y Timoteo. Usa las palabras del recuadro. Algunas frases deben ser ciertas y otras, falsas. Lee tus frases a otro(a) estudiante. Tu compañero(a) va a decir si la frase es cierta o falsa y cambiarla si es falsa para dar la información correcta.

Modelo

A —*Timoteo lleva ropa a la caja.*
B —*Falso. Santiago lleva ropa a la caja.*

color oscuro	el cajero
color claro	la talla
la salida	el descuento
la caja	la entrada

Differentiated Instruction
Solutions for All Learners

Students with Special Needs

For *Actividad 4*, make the illustration more accessible for visually impaired students by providing a magnified photocopy or enlarging it on a transparency. Point out the details before assigning the activity.

Heritage Language Learners

As an extension of *Actividad 6*, have students write a persuasive letter or e-mail to entice a friend to go shopping with them at a favorite store or shopping mall. Help students use the four-step writing process of pre-writing, drafting, editing, and revising.

Actividad 6 Leer/Escribir

Muchos descuentos

Lee el mensaje electrónico que Dolores le escribe a su amiga Marta sobre una oportunidad fantástica. Escribe la palabra apropiada para completar cada frase.

Marta:

Acabo de ver un letrero en la __1.__ *(marca / entrada)* del almacén Gutiérrez que __2.__ *(anuncia / se prueba)* una __3.__ *(salida / liquidación)* de toda su ropa de verano. ¿Quieres ir conmigo mañana? Vamos a __4.__ *(encontrar / gastar)* muchas gangas porque todo está __5.__ *(en liquidación / de moda)*: los pantalones cortos, las camisetas, los trajes de baño, ¡todo! Y, con precios tan __6.__ *(altos / bajos)*, podemos comprar muchas cosas sin __7.__ *(escoger / gastar)* mucho dinero. Escríbeme __8.__ *(inmediatamente / recientemente)* si puedes ir conmigo.

Dolores

Actividad 7 Escribir/Hablar

¿Qué compran y cómo pagan?

1 Copia y completa la tabla para indicar qué compran las diferentes personas que conoces y cómo pagan.

¿Quién?	¿Qué?	¿Cómo?
mis hermanos	discos compactos	tarjeta de crédito
mi mamá (o papá)		
yo		
mis amigos (nombre) y yo		
mi mejor amigo(a)		

2 Trabaja con otro(a) estudiante y describe lo que compra alguien de tu tabla. Tu compañero(a) debe tratar de adivinar *(try to guess)* cómo paga la persona.

Modelo

A —*Mis hermanos compran discos compactos.*

B —*¿Pagan ellos en efectivo?*

A —*No, pagan con una tarjeta de crédito.*

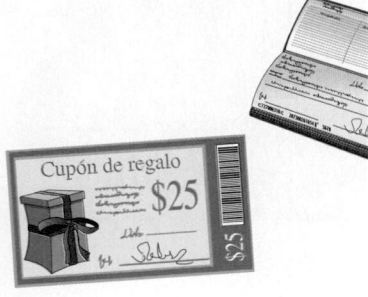

ciento siete **107**
Capítulo 2B

Enrich Your Teaching
Resources for All Teachers

 Culture Note

The currency pictured above is the euro. On January 1, 2002, twelve European countries adopted the euro as their common currency. Euro notes are the same in all twelve countries, but the coins have one common side and one national side. A portrait of King Juan Carlos I represents Spain's national side on coins of several denominations.

Teacher-to-Teacher

Divide the class into two teams. One team comes up with a question about shopping or payment. The second team works together to come up with an answer. Then the teams switch roles. Each correct question or answer earns one point.

 Actividad 6  *Standards:* 1.2

 Presentation EXPRESS
ANSWERS

Resources: Answers on Transparencies

Focus: Reading and writing about going shopping

Suggestions: Suggest that students read the entire paragraph quickly to get an idea of the subject before they begin completing the sentences.

Answers:
1. entrada
2. anuncia
3. liquidación
4. encontrar
5. en liquidación
6. bajos
7. gastar
8. inmediatamente

Extension: As a class, have students create a paragraph using the answer choices that were not used in the activity. Have a student give a sentence that uses the first unused word or expression; a second student creates a follow-on sentence using the next unused word or expression; and so on.

 Actividad 7 *Standards:* 1.1, 1.3

Resources: Teacher's Resource Book: GramActiva BLM, p. 117, Answers on Transparencies

Focus: Writing and speaking about purchases and methods of payment

Recycle: Shopping

Suggestions: Brainstorm different items that people buy and how they pay for them. Be sure students understand that they have a choice of whose purchases to list for the second, fifth, and sixth entries.

Answers will vary but will include *tarjeta de crédito, en efectivo, cheque (personal, de viajero),* and *cupón de regalo* as means of payment.

Common Errors: Students may forget to make subject-verb agreements. Ask them to determine the subject pronoun for each statement and question in Step 2. They may need help with the third item: *yo → tú* and the fifth item: *(nombre) y yo (= nosotros) → ustedes* or *vosotros.*

Extension: Put students in different pairs and have them try to guess what the people in their partner's chart (from *Actividad 7*) buy. For example: *¿Compra tu mamá una blusa?*

Actividad 8 *Standards:* 1.2, 1.3

Focus: Writing and speaking about clothing and fashion

Recycle: Clothing

Suggestions: Allow students who have difficulty drawing to use photos or illustrations from ads or catalogues.

Answers will vary.

Actividad 9 *Standards:* 1.1, 1.2

Resources: Answers on Transparencies

Focus: Speaking about fashion

Suggestions: Discuss the illustration. Ask students where they can see such jackets, where they can buy one, how much they cost, whether they like the jackets, etc. Provide the cognate **dólares** for item 2.

Answers may vary but will include:

1. Las chaquetas (no) están de moda. Son negras. Son de color oscuro.
2. Las chaquetas están hechas de cuero. Cuestan $199. Sí (No), (no) es un buen precio.
3. Son para llevar a eventos especiales (para todos los días). Voy a llevarla...

Block Schedule

Bring in a bag of old clothing and shoes. Pair students and have one play the role of a store clerk and the other the shopper. Lay out three items in front of the clerk, and give students two minutes to have an impromptu dialogue in which the shopper selects and purchases one of the items.

Pre-AP* Support

- **Activity:** Before doing *Actividad* 9, have students work in pairs. One student looks at the ad on this page. The other student has a blank sheet of paper. The student looking at the ad describes it to his or her partner while the other student tries to recreate the ad based on the description he or she hears.

- **Pre-AP* Resource Book:** Comprehensive guide to Pre-AP* communication skill development, pp. 9–17, 36–46

Additional Resources

- WAV Wbk.: Audio Act. 6, p. 38
- Teacher's Resource Book: Audio Script, p. 106, Communicative Activity BLM, pp. 112–113
- Audio Program: Track 8

108

   Dibujar/Escribir/Hablar

Muchos detalles

1 Dibuja una persona completa con diferentes prendas *(articles)* de ropa. Usa diferentes colores en tu dibujo. En una hoja de papel, escribe una descripción de la ropa de la persona. Puedes incluir información sobre:

- los colores
- el estilo
- la talla y el número
- de qué está hecha la ropa
- dónde lo compró

Tu descripción debe tener un mínimo de cuatro frases.

> **Modelo**
>
> *Esta persona usa ropa bastante exagerada. Sus pantalones son flojos y su camiseta de seda es de un color verde vivo. Su gorra roja está hecha de lana. Lleva zapatos rojos del número 11.*

2 Trabaja con un grupo de tres estudiantes. Lee tu descripción dos veces en voz alta *(aloud)*. Tus compañeros tienen que dibujar una persona según tu descripción. Deben recordar los detalles *(remember the details)* de tu descripción sin escribir lo que dices. Después van a repetir la descripción completa.

  Hablar

La moda

Con otro(a) estudiante, habla de las chaquetas de la foto.

1. ¿Cómo es el estilo de estas chaquetas? ¿De qué color son las chaquetas? ¿Son de color oscuro, claro o vivo?

2. ¿De qué están hechas las chaquetas? ¿Cuánto cuestan? ¿Es un buen precio?

3. ¿Crees que las chaquetas son para llevar a eventos especiales o para todos los días? Imagina que compraste una de estas chaquetas. ¿Adónde y cuándo vas a llevarla?

ÚLTIMA MODA

Chaquetas para hombre y mujer

Visítenos $199

de lunes a viernes, 9 A.M.–6 P.M.

Sobre Rt. 28 (al lado del Videocentro) Lawrence, MA

Differentiated Instruction
Solutions for All Learners

Heritage Language Learners

Have students write ad or catalogue copy for the leather jacket modeled on p. 108. Challenge them to use as many new vocabulary words as possible. Have them peer-edit the copy. Review the final copy with them.

Students with Learning Difficulties

For *Actividad* 8, have students use a chart to organize their ideas. In the first column list body parts on which clothing is worn: *la cabeza, el cuerpo,* and *los pies.* Label the other columns *la ropa, los colores, el estilo, la talla, de qué está hecha,* and *dónde la compró.*

Fondo cultural

¡No sé qué talla uso! Si algún día vas de compras en un país hispanohablante, debes saber que tanto la ropa como los zapatos tienen diferentes tallas. Un vestido de la talla 12, por ejemplo, puede ser 46 en España. Además, entre países, a veces las tallas son diferentes. Por ejemplo, un zapato de hombres de $9\frac{1}{2}$ es aproximadamente el 43 en España y el 27 en México. Hay sitios Web que dan las conversiones y algunas tiendas también ofrecen tablas de conversión. En España, para calcular el número de zapatos de mujer, generalmente añades *(you add)* 30, y para los de hombres añades 33.5.

- ¿Aproximadamente, qué número de zapato calzas *(do you wear)* en España?

  Hablar

Actividad 10

¿En qué puedo servirle?

Estás de compras en una zapatería en España. Necesitas comprar un par de zapatos para llevar a un evento especial y otro para usar todos los días. Pídale al dependiente (a la dependienta) lo que prefieres, indicando tu número y el color de los zapatos. Trabaja con otro(a) estudiante.

Modelo
A —¿En qué puedo servirle?
B —Necesito comprar un par de zapatos para una fiesta.
A —¿De qué número y color?
B —Soy del número . . . y prefiero zapatos de color . . .

  Hablar

Actividad 11

Juego

Describe a otro(a) estudiante la ropa de cinco estudiantes de tu clase sin decir los nombres. Menciona el color, el estilo y de qué material está hecha toda la ropa que llevan los chicos. Tu compañero(a) tiene que adivinar *(guess)* a quién describes. Por cada persona que tu compañero(a) adivina correctamente, tú recibes un punto.

Modelo
Lleva una camisa azul de tela sintética y unos pantalones cortos blancos de algodón. ¿Quién es?

 Escribir/Hablar

Actividad 12

Y tú, ¿qué dices?

1. ¿Qué colores de ropa te gusta usar? ¿Prefieres los colores claros o los oscuros? ¿Generalmente usas ropa de colores pastel o colores vivos?

2. ¿Qué ropa está de moda ahora? ¿Los estilos que están de moda te parecen exagerados o sencillos? ¿Qué marcas son más populares entre los jóvenes?

3. ¿En qué almacén o tienda puedes encontrar gangas? ¿Los precios allí siempre son bajos o sólo cuando hay una liquidación?

4. ¿Vas mucho de compras? ¿Qué compras? ¿Cómo pagas generalmente?

ciento nueve **109**
Capítulo 2B

Practice and Communicate

2B

Fondo cultural  *Standards:* 1.2, 3.1

Suggestions: Have students ask each other their shoe size in Spain: *Yo calzo número 42 en España. ¿Qué número calzas tú?*

Answers will vary but will come from the following formulas: women's sizes = U.S. size + 30; men's sizes = U.S. size + 33.5.

Actividad 10   *Standards:* 1.1

Focus: Speaking about buying shoes
Suggestions: Tell students not to use their U.S. shoe size. Direct them to the *Fondo* if you have not already read it. In the *Modelo* identify Student A as the salesperson and Student B as the customer.
Answers will vary.

Actividad 11   *Standards:* 1.1, 1.3

Focus: Describing clothing
Suggestions: Brainstorm a list of nouns and adjectives that could be used to describe the clothing of class members.
Answers will vary.

Actividad 12   *Standards:* 1.1, 1.3

Focus: Expressing personal opinions and preferences about clothing and shopping
Suggestions: Do the exercise orally, asking several students each question.
Answers will vary.

Enrich Your Teaching
Resources for All Teachers

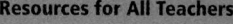

Culture Note
The Pampas of Argentina, the fertile grassland of Uruguay, and the valleys of Spain are ideal environments to raise cattle. Each country, therefore, is a substantial contributor to the world's leather market. Stylish jackets, belts, boots, and shoes are some of these countries' products.

Teacher-to-Teacher
Have students do research on the Internet and create a clothing conversion chart that compares men's and women's clothing sizes in Mexico, Spain, and the United States.

 Assessment
- Prueba 2B-2: Vocab. Production, pp. 57–58

Gramática · Repaso

Presentation EXPRESS
GRAMMAR

Core Instruction

Resources: Voc. and Gram. Transparency 56; Teacher's Resource Book: Video Script, p. 111; Video Program: Cap. 2B

Suggestions: Before reviewing the *Gramática*, write **mirar, aprender,** and **escribir** on the board and ask students to identify the stem of each verb. Ask a volunteer to explain how to identify the stem of a verb. Write present-tense forms of stem-changing verbs on the board (**se acuesta, pruebas,** etc.) and have students identify the infinitive form and the stem of each verb.

Play the *GramActiva* Video or use the transparency to review the preterite forms. Remind students that the preterite endings for **-er** and **-ir** verbs are identical.

Standards: 1.2
Presentation EXPRESS
ANSWERS

Resources: Answers on Transparencies

Focus: Using preterite forms in a letter

Suggestions: If necessary, help students logically determine the subject for items 5 (**nosotras**) and 9 (**unos aretes**). Remind them to check spelling for items 8 and 10.

Answers:

1. recibí	5. tomamos	9. gustaron
2. enviaste	6. escogí	10. llegué
3. decidí	7. compró	11. probé
4. encontramos	8. vio	

Block Schedule

Form groups of two to four students. Give each group the same list of regular verbs that could be used to describe a shopping trip (e.g., *viajar, llegar, abrir, vender, mirar, dar, pagar, decidir, comprar, contestar, salir*). Ask them to create a story using these verbs in the preterite. Have the groups present their stories to the class without using their papers.

Gramática · Repaso

Preterite of regular verbs

To talk about actions that were completed in the past, use the preterite tense. To form the preterite tense of a regular verb, add the preterite endings to the stem of the verb.

(yo)	miré aprendí escribí	(nosotros) (nosotras)	miramos aprendimos escribimos
(tú)	miraste aprendiste escribiste	(vosotros) (vosotras)	mirasteis aprendisteis escribisteis
Ud. (él) (ella)	miró aprendió escribió	Uds. (ellos) (ellas)	miraron aprendieron escribieron

Note that *-ar* and *-er* verbs that have a stem change in the present tense do not have a stem change in the preterite.

> Generalmente **me pruebo** la ropa antes de comprarla, pero ayer no **me probé** los pantalones que compré.

Ver has regular preterite endings, but unlike those of other verbs, they have no written accent marks.

> Anoche, David **vio** una camisa que le gustó mucho.

- Verbs that end in *-car, -gar,* and *-zar* have a spelling change in the *yo* form of the preterite.

buscar	c → qu	yo busqué
pagar	g → gu	yo pagué
almorzar	z → c	yo almorcé

> ¿**Pagaste** mucho por tu suéter nuevo?
> No, no **pagué** mucho. Lo encontré en una liquidación.

GramActiva VIDEO

Want more help with the preterite of regular verbs? Watch the **GramActiva** video.

aprendí

Leer/Escribir

¡Gracias por el regalo!

Elena está escribiendo una carta a su abuela. Escribe la forma apropiada del pretérito del verbo entre paréntesis para cada frase.

Cupón de regalo
0123475

Querida abuelita:

Hace tres días, yo __1.__ (recibir) el cupón de regalo que tú me __2.__ (enviar). ¡Muchas gracias! Yo __3.__ (decidir) comprarme ropa nueva. Fui de compras con mis amigas al centro comercial, pero nosotras no __4.__ (encontrar) buenas gangas. Por eso, __5.__ (tomar) el autobús al mercado. Allí, yo __6.__ (escoger) unos pantalones de cuero. ¡Están muy de moda! Mi amiga Sonia __7.__ (comprar) unos aretes que __8.__ (ver) porque le __9.__ (gustar) mucho. Cuando yo __10.__ (llegar) a casa, me __11.__ (probar) los pantalones. Son perfectos. ¡Muchísimas gracias, abuelita!

Besitos,

Elena

Differentiated Instruction
Solutions for All Learners

Heritage Language Learners

Review letter format (date, greeting, body, closing) with students. Then have them write a thank-you note to a relative for a gift, a visit, a call, or whatever is appropriate. Have them use the past tense as much as possible.

Students with Learning Difficulties

For *Actividad 15*, break the directions down into parts. For each sentence, first have students identify when the action took place. Next, have them specify who did the action. Then have them use the *Gramática • Repaso* chart to determine the correct form of the verb.

Actividad 14 · Hablar

¿Qué compraron?

Habla con otro(a) estudiante de lo que hicieron estas personas en el almacén.

Modelo

tú / encontrar
A —¿Qué encontraste en el almacén?
B —Encontré un suéter de color oscuro.

Estudiante A

1. las chicas / probarse
2. tú / comprar
3. Uds. / ver
4. Felipe / buscar
5. la madre de la novia / mirar
6. Marta / usar para pagar
7. Pedro y Félix / escoger

Estudiante B

Actividad 15 · Escribir/Hablar

La última vez

1 ¿Cuándo fue la última vez (*last time*) que alguien que tú conoces hizo estas actividades? Puede ser tú, alguien de tu familia, un(a) amigo(a) o tú y tus amigos. Usa las expresiones del recuadro para contestar. Escribe tus respuestas.

esta mañana	el mes pasado
anoche	el año pasado
ayer	hace + dos semanas,
la semana pasada	un mes . . .

Modelo

comer en un restaurante
Anoche mis amigos y yo comimos en un restaurante.

1. comprar un regalo
2. preparar la comida
3. ver una película a las dos de la tarde
4. escribir una carta por correo electrónico
5. decorar para una fiesta
6. beber un refresco
7. salir para una fiesta
8. despertarse a las diez de la mañana

2 Ahora habla con otro(a) estudiante para comparar tu lista con su lista.

3 Escribe cuatro frases para comparar lo que dijeron (*said*) los (las) dos.

Modelo

Anoche comí en un restaurante, pero Jorge comió en casa.

ciento once **111**
Capítulo 2B

Practice and Communicate

 2B

 Actividad 14 · Standards: 1.1 · Presentation EXPRESS ANSWERS

Resources: Answers on Transparencies

Focus: Speaking about shopping using the preterite

Suggestions: Have students identify each of the items depicted for *Actividad* 14 (*un vestido, una chaqueta, una camiseta, un collar, unas botas, un cupón de regalo, un disco compacto*). For item 1, you may need to help students with the placement of the reflexive pronoun since they are familiar with **me** and **te** as reflexive pronouns but not **se**.

Answers:

Student A answers will vary but will include:
1. ¿Qué se probaron las chicas en el almacén?
2. ¿Qué compraste . . . ?
3. ¿Qué vieron Uds. . . . ?
4. ¿Qué buscó Felipe . . . ?
5. ¿Qué miró la madre de la novia . . . ?
6. ¿Qué usó Marta para pagar . . . ?
7. ¿Qué escogieron Pedro y Félix . . . ?

Student B answers will vary but will include:
1. Se probaron . . . .
2. Compré . . .
3. Vimos . . .
4. Buscó . . .
5. Miró . . .
6. Usó un cupón de regalo.
7. Escogieron . . .

 Bellringer Review
Show Voc. & Gram. Transparency 56. Have students select any three verb forms from the chart and write two logical sentences.

 Actividad 15 · Standards: 1.1, 1.3

Focus: Discussing past activities

Recycle: Expressions of time

Suggestions: Write a date, time, month, etc., on the board and have students match it with one of the time expressions in the word bank. For example, if today is Tuesday, April 8, write **lunes, el 7 de abril, 17:00.** Students say, **Anoche.** Clarify that **hace** is used with a time expression (e.g., **un mes, tres días, cinco años**).

Answers will vary.

Extension: Combine two pairs of students to form groups of four. Have the students in each group peer-edit the sentences written for Step 3.

Enrich Your Teaching
Resources for All Teachers

Teacher-to-Teacher

Write stems of common regular verbs on index cards. Write the preterite endings of these verbs on different cards, one ending per card. In small groups or pairs, have students form and say preterite verb conjugations according to the subject and verb you announce.

Teacher-to-Teacher

Bring in ads from magazines or newspapers that show a product. Ask students questions in the past tense that use the product as the answer. For example:

[ad shows a soda] *¿Qué bebí ayer?*

[ad shows a car] *¿Cómo llegaron Ana y Susana a casa?*

Actividad 16 Standards: 1.1

Presentation EXPRESS ANSWERS

Resources: Answers on Transparencies

Focus: Writing and speaking about past activities

Recycle: Activities

Suggestions: Refer to the *Gramática* on p. 110 and review the spelling changes for verbs ending in *-car, -gar,* and *-zar.* Remind students that the **c** and **g** changes are needed so that the hard sounds of the letters will be pronounced. Remind students of spelling changes with **z**, using the plurals *lapiz/lápices* and *pez/peces.*

Answers:

Student A:

1. ¿Llegaste temprano a la escuela hoy?
2. ¿Tocaste un instrumento musical hoy?
3. ¿Empezaste a leer una novela hoy?
4. ¿Almorzaste con tu mejor amigo(a) hoy?
5. ¿Jugaste al ajedrez o practicaste un deporte hoy?
6. ¿Navegaste en la Red hoy?
7. ¿Buscaste un regalo para alguien hoy?

Student B answers will vary but will include:

1. Sí, llegué / No, no llegué . . .
2. Sí, toqué / No, no toqué . . .
3. Sí, empecé / No, no empecé . . .
4. Sí, almorcé / No, no almorcé . . .
5. Sí, jugué / No, no jugué . . . practiqué / no practiqué . . .
6. Sí, navegué / No, no navegué . . .
7. Sí, busqué / No, no busqué . . .

Bellringer Review

Have students write a sentence with these three verbs (*buscar, comprar,* and *pagar*) in the preterite to tell about an item they looked for, they bought, and how much they paid.

 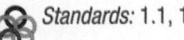

Actividad 17 Standards: 1.1, 1.3

Focus: Describing clothing for a special event; telling when, where, and how it was bought and where it was worn

Suggestions: Brainstorm with students a list of special events. Ask what different people might wear to each event. Would a rap singer wear the same clothing as a businessperson?

Answers will vary.

Actividad 16    **Escribir/Hablar**

Muchas actividades

Escribe una frase para indicar si hiciste o no cada una de las actividades de la lista. Después habla con otro(a) estudiante para saber si hizo estas actividades recientemente.

Modelo

practicar deportes

A —¿Practicaste deportes hoy?
B —Sí, practiqué deportes hoy.
o: —No, no practiqué deportes hoy.

1. llegar temprano a la escuela
2. tocar un instrumento musical
3. empezar a leer una novela
4. almorzar con tu mejor amigo(a)
5. jugar al ajedrez o practicar un deporte
6. navegar en la Red
7. buscar un regalo para alguien

Actividad 18  **Leer/Pensar/Escribir/Hablar**

Los textiles y el cuero

La lana, el algodón y el cuero son productos que los indígenas de las Américas usaban antes de la llegada de los españoles. Lee la línea cronológica *(time line)* sobre estos productos y contesta las preguntas.

Actividad 17   **Hablar**

¿Qué llevaste?

Trae una foto en que estás vestido(a) para un evento especial, o una foto de un(a) modelo de una revista. Con otro(a) estudiante, describe la ropa de la foto. Incluye el color, la tela y el estilo. Explica cuándo y dónde compraste la ropa, cómo pagaste y adónde fuiste vestido(a) así. Si traes una foto de una revista, usa tu imaginación para contestar las preguntas.

Modelo

A —Estoy vestido(a) para una fiesta. Llevo una camisa amarilla y pantalones marrones. La camisa está hecha de algodón y los pantalones están hechos de lana.
B —¿Dónde compraste la ropa?
A —La compré en . . . y pagué con . . .

Conexiones | La historia

1000
En las Américas, los indígenas precolombinos usan el telar[1]. Usan algodón y otras fibras para hacer sus telas y vestidos.

1500
Los españoles traen caballos a las Américas. Luego traen ovejas[2] y vacas[3]. Los indígenas incorporan la lana de oveja en sus telas tradicionales.

1638
Se establece la primera fábrica[4] de tela en Lowell, Massachusetts.

[1]loom [2]sheep [3]cows [4]factory

112

Differentiated Instruction
Solutions for All Learners

Advanced Learners

Ask students to describe the clothing of several centuries ago. They might look at portraits by Velázquez or El Greco to find examples. Have them describe the colors, styles, and of what materials they think the clothing is made. Have them speculate on what events the wearer might have attended dressed in this clothing.

Multiple Intelligences

Bodily/Kinesthetic: Bring in samples of cotton, wool, leather, silk, and a synthetic fabric, and have students become familiar with the feel of them. Then put the samples in a bag and have students close their eyes, choose a sample, and name the material.

Exploración del lenguaje

Origins of words from Arabic

In Spanish, words that came from Arabic often begin with the letters *al*. In Arabic, *al* means "the." Translate the following sentences, noting the words in bold borrowed from Arabic.

1. Cuando voy al **almacén** voy a comprar una **alfombra** de **algodón**.

2. También voy a comprar **azúcar**, **naranjas** y **aceitunas**.

El Patio de los Leones de La Alhambra, en Granada, España

Más práctica

- Practice Workbook, p. 44: 2B-5
- WAV Wbk.: Writing, p. 43
- Guided Practice: Grammar Acts., pp. 83–84
- *Real.* para hispanohablantes, pp. 74–77

Go Online
PHSchool.com
For: Preterite of Reg. Verbs
Web Code: jdd-0214

1793
Eli Whitney inventa la desmotadora de algodón[6] y revoluciona la industria del algodón en los Estados Unidos.

Siglo XX
Los métodos científicos, la electrónica y las computadoras permiten el desarrollo[8] de las telas sintéticas.

1760–1815
Los avances mecánicos e inventos de la Revolución Industrial aumentan[5] la producción y bajan los precios.

1900
Argentina y Brasil son grandes productores mundiales[7] de textiles y cuero.

[5]increase [6]cotton gin [7]worldwide [8]development

1. ¿Qué cosa usaron los indígenas precolombinos para hacer sus telas? ¿De qué estaban *(were)* hechas?

2. ¿Cuándo empezaron a usar los indígenas la lana de oveja en sus telas tradicionales? ¿De dónde vino esta lana?

3. ¿Quién inventó la desmotadora de algodón? ¿Cómo cambió *(changed)* esta invención la industria del algodón?

ciento trece **113**
Capítulo 2B

Enrich Your Teaching
Resources for All Teachers

Culture Note
The Patio de los Leones was built between 1354–1394 and is within the Alhambra in Granada, Spain. Construction on the Alhambra began in 1238 under the Moorish ruler Muhammed Al-Ahmar. *Alhambra* means "the Red Castle" in Arabic and is most likely related to the faded crimson stone that surrounds it.

Teacher-to-Teacher
Create a list with students of "first" events in their lives: first day of school, first recital, first rock concert, etc. Have each student choose one event and describe the clothing-related events for the day: *Mi primer día de escuela, me levanté temprano y me probé tres vestidos. Escogí ....*

Actividad 18 *Standards:* 1.2, 2.2, 3.1

Presentation EXPRESS
ANSWERS

Resources: Answers on Transparencies

Focus: Reading and writing about historical events

Suggestions: Provide a context for students' reading by asking them what their clothing is made of. What is the origin of the material? Cotton, for example, comes from a plant. Where do leather, polyester, rayon, silk, etc. come from?

Answers:
1. Los indígenas precolombinos usaron el telar para hacer sus telas. Estaban hechas de algodón y otras fibras.
2. Los indígenas empezaron a usar la lana de oveja en sus telas tradicionales después de la llegada de los españoles en 1500. La lana vino de las ovejas que trajeron los españoles a las Américas.
3. Eli Whitney inventó la desmotadora de algodón. Esta invención cambió la industria del algodón porque aumentó la producción y bajó los precios.

Exploración del lenguaje
Core Instruction

 Standards: 1.2, 4.1

Suggestions: Discuss with students why foreign words and expressions become part of a language. Have them consider occupation, conquest, immigration, and popularity of a style or fashion.

Answers:
1. When I go to the store, I'm going to buy a cotton rug.
2. I'm also going to buy sugar, oranges, and olives.

Additional Resources

- WAV Wbk.: Audio Act. 7, p. 39
- Teacher's Resource Book: Audio Script, p. 106
- Audio Program: Track 9

 Assessment
- Exam*View* Quiz on PresEXPRESS
  QuickTake Presenter
- Prueba 2B-3: Preterite of regular verbs, p. 59

113

Gramática

Core Instruction

Standards: 4.1

Resources: Voc. and Gram. Transparency 57; Teacher's Resource Book: Video Script, pp. 110–111; Video Program: Cap. 2B

Suggestions: Bring in photos of six different actors and six different actresses. Place photos of two actors and two actresses within hand's reach, photos of another two of each a few steps away, and the last photos at the other end of the room. Point at the pictures as you compare and contrast the actors and actresses.

  Standards: 1.2

Resources: Answers on Transparencies

Focus: Using *aquel* with clothing

Suggestions: Ask students what clues they might look for to help them determine gender and number (e.g., other adjectives, plural endings). Have them read through the dialogue looking for such clues before they write their answers.

Answers:

1. aquella	3. aquella	5. aquellos
2. aquel	4. aquella	6. aquellas

  Standards: 1.2

Resources: Teacher's Resource Book: Audio Script, p. 107; Audio Program: Track 10; Answers on Transparencies

Focus: Understanding demonstrative adjectives

Suggestions: Make sure students are clear on which set of demonstrative adjectives corresponds to each location description (*este = al lado de; ese = cerca de; aquel = lejos de*).

Script and Answers:

1. Me gustan esos zapatos verdes. *(cerca)*
2. Aquella corbata es horrible. *(lejos)*
3. Estas botas rojas son de cuero. *(al lado)*
4. No me gusta aquel traje azul oscuro. *(lejos)*
5. Esta blusa es de colores vivos. *(al lado)*
6. Aquellos guantes negros son grandes. *(lejos)*
7. Podemos salir por esta salida. *(al lado)*
8. Aquel cajero puede ayudarnos. *(lejos)*

Gramática

Demonstrative adjectives

To point out something or someone that is far from both you and the person you are speaking to, you use a form of *aquel*, which means "that one over there."

Here's a chart that compares the three demonstrative adjectives and their meanings.

	Singular		Plural	
este, esta	*this*	estos, estas	*these*	
ese, esa	*that*	esos, esas	*those*	
aquel, aquella	*that one over there*	aquellos, aquellas	*those over there*	

All demonstrative adjectives come before the noun and agree with the noun in gender (masculine or feminine) and number (singular or plural).

¿Recuerdas?

Do you remember this rhyme about the two demonstrative adjectives *este* and *ese*?

This and *these* both have *t*'s.
That and *those* don't.

GramActiva VIDEO

Want more help with demonstrative adjectives? Watch the **GramActiva** video.

 Leer/Escribir

¿Esta corbata o aquella corbata?

Marta y su hermano, Asís, necesitan comprar un regalo para su padre, pero nunca están de acuerdo. Completa su conversación con la forma apropiada de *aquel*.

Marta: A mí me gusta __1.__ gorra roja.

Asís: A mí no. Prefiero comprarle __2.__ disco compacto de Shakira.

Marta: ¡Asís! ¡El regalo es para papá! ¿Qué te parece __3.__ camisa azul?

Asís: Quizás, pero me gusta más __4.__ camisa roja.

Marta: ¿Qué piensas de __5.__ pantalones amarillos?

Asís: ¿Estás loca? Nuestro padre no juega al golf.

Marta: Bueno, ¿y __6.__ corbatas? Desde aquí veo dos que combinan con la camisa roja.

Asís: ¡Perfecto! Las compramos.

114 ciento catorce
Tema 2 • Un evento especial

---

jdd-0298
 **Escuchar/Escribir**

Escucha y escribe

En una hoja de papel, escribe los números del 1 al 8. Escucha y escribe las frases. Luego indica si el objeto de la frase está al lado de, cerca de o lejos de la persona que habla.

Differentiated Instruction
Solutions for All Learners

Advanced Learners

Have students bring in an illustration from a magazine or draw a scene that shows people in the foreground, middle, and background. Have them write a paragraph about the scene, using demonstrative adjectives.

Heritage Language Learners

Students may have difficulty spelling the demonstrative adjectives because of a tendency not to hear the *t* sound in the forms of *este*. Remind them that it is important to pronounce words (and hear them in their head) clearly in order to spell correctly.

Hablar

Actividad 21

¿Qué te parece?

Imagina que estás en el mercado Ipiales en Quito. Habla con otro(a) estudiante de la ropa que venden. ¿Qué te gustaría comprar?

Modelo

A —¿Qué te parece aquel suéter de colores vivos?
B —Aquel suéter es muy feo. No me gusta.
o:
A —¿Te gustan estas camisas blancas?
B —No, prefiero aquellas camisas de colores.

El mercado Ipiales en Quito, Ecuador

    Hablar

Actividad 22

Juego

1. Busca cinco objetos en la sala de clases. Unos deben estar cerca de ti, otros deben estar más lejos. Piensa en cómo puedes describirlos sin mencionar su nombre.

2. Ahora, con un grupo de tres o cuatro, describe tus objetos. Las otras personas del grupo tienen que adivinar el objeto que estás describiendo. La primera persona que identifica correctamente el objeto, y que usa el adjetivo demostrativo apropiado, recibe un punto.

Modelo

A —Es azul y negro. Es muy importante llevarlo a la clase. Lo usas para escribir.
B —Este bolígrafo.
A —No. Casi. Está lejos de mí.
B —Es aquel bolígrafo de Laura.
A —Sí. Recibes un punto.

Más práctica

- Practice Workbook, p. 45: 2B-6
- WAV Wbk.: Writing, p. 44
- Guided Practice: Grammar Acts., pp. 85–86
- *Real.* para hispanohablantes, pp. 78–79

Go Online
PHSchool.com
For: Demonstrative Adjs.
Web Code: jdd-0215

El español en el mundo del trabajo

Hoy en día, los negocios *(businesses)* quieren atraer *(attract)* a más clientes hispanohablantes, porque es el sector más creciente *(growing)* de la población. Para los hispanohablantes es importante poder comunicarse en español cuando hacen compras o abren cuentas en un banco. Por eso, las tiendas, los bancos y otros negocios emplean a personas bilingües que hablan español e inglés.

- ¿Cuáles son las tiendas o negocios en tu comunidad con empleados bilingües? ¿Por qué es importante tener empleados bilingües?

ciento quince **115**
Capítulo 2B

Practice and Communicate

2B

Actividad 21 *Standards:* 1.1

Focus: Speaking about clothing preferences
Recycle: Clothing
Suggestions: Brainstorm a list of nouns and adjectives based on the photograph. Put the list on the board as a reference.
Answers will vary.

Actividad 22   *Standards:* 1.1

Focus: Describing classroom objects
Recycle: Classroom objects and colors
Suggestions: So that they won't give away what their objects are, have students jot down notes about their objects to refer to when it is their turn.
Answers will vary.

El español en el mundo del trabajo

Core Instruction

 Standards: 1.2, 2.1, 5.1

Suggestions: Ask students what qualities they think a person who deals with the public (e.g., bank teller, sales clerk, reference librarian, police officer) should have. Why are these qualities important?
Answers will vary.

Theme Project

Students can perform Step 4 at this point. Be sure they understand your corrections and suggestions. (For more information, see p. 70-a.)

Additional Resources

- WAV Wbk.: Audio Act. 8, p. 40
- Teacher's Resource Book: Audio Script, p. 107
- Audio Program: Track 11

Assessment

- ExamView Quiz on PresEXPRESS
- Prueba 2B-4: Demonstrative adjectives, p. 60

Enrich Your Teaching

Resources for All Teachers

Culture Note

Another popular—and the largest—market in Ecuador is the Otovalo market. It is open all week and is one of the country's most popular events. Exquisite hand-woven jackets, vests, blouses, and hats are sold by indigenous artisans. Vendors usually wear their traditional clothing, which makes this market unique.

Teacher-to-Teacher

Bring in photos of open-air markets displaying clothing items and accessories, clothing stores, and catalogues that sell clothing. Have students discuss their shopping preferences, the items displayed, how they would get to the location, how they would pay, etc. Encourage them to use demonstrative adjectives.

115

 Gramática | Presentation EXPRESS GRAMMAR

Core Instruction

Standards: 4.1

Suggestions: Write several simple noun phrases on the board (for example, *una camiseta de algodón, el bolígrafo rojo, los pantalones flojos*) and show students the three elements that make up each phrase: definite or indefinite article, noun, and adjective. Cross out the noun and tell students that the expression that remains functions as a noun because of the article.

Write the following sentences on a transparency and project them. Cover up the response until students have supplied an answer.

¿Es su hermano el chico alto o el chico bajo?

El bajo (alto) es mi hermano.

¿Te gustan los zapatos negros o los zapatos azules?

Me gustan los azules (negros). Los negros (azules) me parecen feos.

 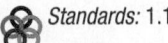 

Standards: 1.1 | Presentation EXPRESS ANSWERS

Resources: Answers on Transparencies

Focus: Expressing opinions about clothing

Suggestions: Remind students that the definite article *la* changes to *el* before a feminine noun that begins with a stressed *a* or *ha* because of the difficulty of pronouncing the two *a* sounds together. For the same reason—pronunciation—the phrase *de color* is used in the questions and answers below.

Answers:

Student A:

1. ¿Prefieres el traje claro o el oscuro?
2. ¿Prefieres la chaqueta de lana o la de cuero?
3. ¿Prefieres la camiseta verde o la de color azul?
4. ¿Prefieres la blusa de color amarilla o la blanca?
5. ¿Prefieres los pantalones morados o los grises?
6. ¿Prefieres los calcetines rosados o los blancos?

Student B answers will vary.

 Gramática

Using adjectives as nouns

When you are comparing two similar things, you can avoid repetition by dropping the noun and using an article with an adjective:

¿Cuál prefieres, la sudadera apretada o **la floja?**	Which do you prefer, the tight sweatshirt or **the loose one?**
Prefiero **la floja.**	I prefer **the loose one.**

You can also do this with expressions that use *de:*

¿Compraste una chaqueta de lana o **una de cuero?**	Did you buy a wool jacket or **a leather one?**
¿Prefieres el abrigo de Paco o **el de Juan?**	Do you prefer Paco's coat or **Juan's?**

Actividad 23 **Hablar**

¿Qué te parece?

Vas de compras con tu mejor amigo(a) que siempre tiene una opinión. Él / Ella te dice lo que prefiere.

Nota

Me parece(n) functions like *me gusta(n)* with singular and plural objects.
• **El rojo** me parece bonit**o.**
• **Los azules** me parecen feo**s.**

Modelo

A —*¿Prefieres el vestido rojo o el azul?*
B —*El rojo me parece feo. Prefiero el azul.*

Estudiante A

Estudiante B

Me parece(n) . . .
Prefiero . . .

¡Respuesta personal!

116 ciento dieciséis
Tema 2 • Un evento especial

 Differentiated Instruction
Solutions for All Learners

Advanced Learners/Pre-AP*

Pre-AP* Ask students to write a paragraph describing what they usually wear to friends' parties and why. They should use **gustar, parecer,** and adjectives as nouns. For example: *Me gusta llevar pantalones flojos porque los apretados me parecen feos.* Ask them to read their paragraphs to the class.

Heritage Language Learners

Have students research the careers of Spanish-speaking clothing designers or fashion models. Have them design a poster with a brief biography of their subject and a picture of an item of clothing associated with that person with a brief description of it. They should use the preterite in their biographical paragraphs.

Actividad 24

Pensar/Hablar/Escribir

Un desfile de modas

1 Vas a participar en un desfile de moda *(fashion show)* en tu clase. Con un grupo, tienen que decidir qué ropa va a llevar cada persona. Escriban una lista de posibilidades. Usen una tabla como ésta para organizar sus ideas:

Para un evento especial	Para todos los días
un vestido o traje elegante, color blanco	unos jeans con una sudadera roja

Un conjunto del diseñador Narciso Rodríguez

2 Usen la tabla y escriban una descripción de la ropa que va a presentar cada "modelo" en su grupo. Pueden incluir el lugar donde venden la ropa y los precios. Mientras los modelos desfilan *(model)* la ropa, un miembro del grupo va a describirla a la clase.

Modelo

Hoy Elena lleva una camisa elegante y una falda de cuero. Esta ropa es perfecta para un evento muy especial. Los colores negro y blanco siempre están de moda. Ustedes pueden comprar esta camisa por sólo 75 dólares.

3 Después del desfile de moda, vas a tener la oportunidad de "comprar" uno de los conjuntos *(outfits)* que viste. Describe el conjunto a la clase y di cómo vas a pagar.

Modelo

Yo quiero comprar la ropa de Enrique. Me gustó mucho porque es perfecta para llevar a un partido de fútbol. Él llevó unos jeans con una camiseta azul y una sudadera roja. Puedo pagar en efectivo porque no cuesta mucho: sólo 60 dólares.

 **Fondo cultural**

Narciso Rodríguez nació en Nueva Jersey, de padres cubanos y abuelos españoles. Estudió en la *Parsons School of Design* en Nueva York, y ha trabajado *(has worked)* para los diseñadores Anne Klein, Donna Karan y Calvin Klein. Presentó su primera colección independiente en 1997. Ese año también ganó el premio *(won the award)* para el mejor diseñador nuevo en los *VH1 Fashion Awards*. Diseña vestidos para muchas actrices y otras mujeres famosas.

• ¿Te gustaría ser diseñador(a)? ¿Por qué? ¿Qué talentos necesitas para este trabajo y qué debes estudiar?

Más práctica

• Practice Workbook, p. 46: 2B-7
• Guided Practice: Grammar Acts., p. 87

Go Online PHSchool.com
For: Adjs. as Nouns
Web Code: jdd-0216

ciento diecisiete **117**
Capítulo 2B

 Actividad 24 Standards: 1.3

Pre-AP*

Focus: Speaking and writing about a fashion show

Suggestions: Allow students who are uncomfortable with the idea of wearing clothing for a fashion show to participate by using a picture or illustration to depict their outfit.

Answers will vary.

 **Fondo cultural** Standards: 1.2, 2.2

Suggestions: Help students generate a list of what type of knowledge and training they think is required for being a fashion designer (e.g., art, style, mathematics, anatomy, characteristics of fabrics and other materials, etc.).

Answers will vary.

Theme Project

Students can perform Step 5 at this point. Record their presentations on cassette or videotape for inclusion in their portfolio. (For more information, see p. 70-a.)

Additional Resources

• WAV Wbk.: Audio Act. 9, p. 41
• Teacher's Resource Book: Audio Script, p. 107, Communicative Activity BLM, pp. 114–115
• Audio Program: Track 12

✓ ## Assessment

Have students write their comments for Step 3 and submit them for an informal assessment.

• **ExamView** Quiz on PresEXPRESS
• Prueba 2B-5: Using adjectives as nouns, p. 61

 Enrich Your Teaching
Resources for All Teachers

Culture Note

Each February and September, Spain hosts an international runway fashion show in Madrid. The trade fair Pasarela Cibeles showcases outstanding fashion designers from Spain and the international community. This event is considered the most prestigious fashion show in Spain.

Teacher-to-Teacher

Bring in a feltboard with a number of different items of clothing. Have students decide on outfits for different occasions and people:

—*Un cantante de rock que participa en un concierto va a llevar esos jeans.*

—*No, me parece que prefiere llevar aquellos pantalones blancos apretados.*

Lectura

Core Instruction

Standards: 1.2, 2.2, 3.2

Focus: Reading comprehension of an article on the history of jeans

Suggestions:

Pre-reading: Ask students to describe jeans. Brainstorm reasons why jeans might be popular in so many cultures. Ask them to talk about the occasions on which they wear jeans. Which brands of jeans are most popular? Remind them that thinking about what they already know about jeans will help them better understand the story.

Reading: Point out to students that there are a number of words in the article that they may not understand, but that they should focus on understanding the general content, not the meaning of every word. Provide them with a photocopy of these two pages, and suggest that they underline or highlight any areas of the reading that they find difficult to understand.

Post-reading: If students still seem unclear about segments of the story, review the meanings of unknown words and have them reread the passage. Have them complete the *¿Comprendiste?* and *Y tú ¿qué dices?*

Bellringer Review
Complete a class survey to determine the most popular brand of jeans by asking *¿Qué marca prefieres?*

Pre-AP* Support

- **Activity:** Have students work in groups of three. Assign to each student in each group either the first half of the section *Un poco de historia,* the second half of the section *Yo digo "mahones" y tú, ¿qué dices?* Rotate reading aloud the three sections in order in each group. Give students three minutes to dicuss what they read and list the main ideas. Then, have students regroup and share their main ideas/information.
- **Pre-AP* Resource Book:** Comprehensive guide to Pre-AP* reading skill development, pp. 18–24

¡Adelante!

Lectura

Objectives
- **Read about the history of jeans and some Spanish variations of the word**
- **Understand cultural perspectives on parties**
- **Write a letter explaining your clothing purchases**
- **Read about Mexican involvement in World War II**

LOS JEANS:
LOS PANTALONES MÁS POPULARES DEL MUNDO

Posiblemente tienes jeans en tu armario. Muchas personas, desde la Argentina hasta el Canadá y desde el Japón hasta España, llevan estos cómodos y prácticos pantalones. Se llevan en el trabajo, en la escuela y para salir de noche. Dicen que los jeans son ropa democrática porque los lleva gente de todas las clases sociales.

Estrategia

Tolerating ambiguity
Often when you read, you will find unfamiliar words. Don't stop, but keep on reading, since the meaning may become clear in context, or you may decide the words might not be necessary to understand the reading.

UN POCO DE HISTORIA

Levi Strauss, un joven alemán, llegó a los Estados Unidos con su familia en 1847 a la edad de 18 años. Después de trabajar algunos años con su familia, Strauss viajó a California para abrir una tienda de ropa y accesorios. Esta tienda se convirtió en un negocio[1] próspero durante los siguientes 20 años, y Strauss se hizo rico.

En el año 1872, recibió una carta de Jacob Davis, un sastre[2] de Reno, Nevada, en la que le explicó el proceso que él inventó para poner remaches en

EL REMACHE
LA ESQUINA DEL BOLSILLO
EL BOLSILLO

[1]business   [2]tailor

118 ciento dieciocho
Tema 2 • Un evento especial

Differentiated Instruction
Solutions for All Learners

Multiple Intelligences
Musical/Rhythmic: Brainstorm a list of adjectives or phrases that could describe jeans (for example, *apretado, flojo, azul, hecho de algodón, práctico, cómodo, de moda*). Ask students to create a jingle that could be part of an advertising campaign for a local store that sells jeans. Have them include details about why and where people buy them.

Heritage Language Learners
Have students choose an article of clothing specific to their heritage culture and research its history. Have students use their research to write a brief report on the item. Review the process of citing sources with students, and ask that they do so when they turn in their papers.

las esquinas de los bolsillos de los pantalones de hombres. El uso de los remaches resultó en unos pantalones bastante fuertes para aguantar[3] los rigores de un trabajo difícil y en unos bolsillos más resistentes al peso[4] del oro.

Con el dinero de Strauss y la invención de Davis, los dos decidieron pedir la patente para el proceso. En 1873 recibieron la patente para poner los remaches

en los pantalones y empezaron a fabricar "*overalls* a la cintura" o *waist overalls* (el antiguo nombre en inglés de los jeans) en San Francisco. Como dicen, "el resto es historia".

Yo digo "mahones" y tú, ¿qué dices?

Si tienes amigos que hablan español debes saber que hay varias palabras que se usan para decir "jeans." Por ejemplo, se les llaman "vaqueros"[5] porque los vaqueros del oeste de los Estados Unidos usan este tipo de pantalón. En Cuba les dicen "pitusa" mientras en México les llaman "pantalones de mezclilla." Algunas personas usan las palabras "tejanos" y "mecánicos", pero la palabra más común sigue siendo simplemente "jeans".

[3]stand up to [4]weight [5]cowboys

¿Comprendiste?

1. Haz una línea cronológica *(time line)* con las fechas mencionadas en esta lectura. Incluye las tres fechas y describe lo que pasó en cada una.

2. ¿Por qué escribió Jacob Davis una carta a Levi Strauss en 1872? ¿Qué dijo Davis en la carta?

3. Jacob Davis y Levi Strauss empezaron un nuevo negocio. ¿Qué contribuyó Davis? ¿Y Strauss?

Y tú, ¿qué dices?

1. ¿Estás de acuerdo con la expresión "los jeans son ropa democrática"? ¿Por qué?

2. ¿Llevas jeans? ¿Por qué?

3. Entre tus amigos, ¿qué ropa y colores están de moda hoy en día?

Más práctica

- WAV Wbk.: Writing, p. 45
- Guided Practice: *Lectura*, p. 88
- *Real.* para hispanohablantes, pp. 82–83

Go Online
PHSchool.com
For: Internet Activity
Web Code: jdd-0217

¿Comprendiste?

Presentation EXPRESS
ANSWERS

Standards: 1.2, 1.3, 3.1

Resources: Answers on Transparencies

Focus: Verifying reading comprehension

Suggestion: For item 1, provide students with a blank timeline and ask them to fill in the details. Encourage them to summarize what they have read in their own words instead of copying the answer directly from the reading.

Answers:

1. En 1847, Levi Strauss llegó a los Estados Unidos. En 1872, Strauss recibió una carta de Jacob Davis, un sastre de Reno, Nevada. En la carta describió su invencion. En 1873, Strauss y Davis recibieron la patente y empezaron a fabricar "waist overalls."
2. Davis le escribió a Strauss para explicarle su nuevo proceso para poner remaches en las esquinas de los bolsillos de los pantalones de hombres.
3. Davis contribuyó el proceso para poner los remaches y Strauss contribuyó el dinero.

Y tú, ¿qué dices?

Standards: 1.1, 1.3

Suggestions: If students do not agree with item 1, have them explain why not. If students answer affirmatively in item 2, have them provide examples of where it is appropriate to wear jeans, and where they must dress more formally.

Answers will vary.

For Further Reading

Student Resources: Realidades para hispanohablantes: Lectura 2, pp. 84–85; Lecturas para hispanohablantes 2: "Algo viejo, algo nuevo, algo azul y algo hispano," pp. 35–36, "Jeans: La obsesión continúa," pp. 101–102; Guided Practice: Lectura, p. 88

Enrich Your Teaching

Resources for All Teachers

Teacher-to-Teacher

Assign pairs of students to a different decade of an earlier century and have them research clothing styles in different countries for that era. Ask students to prepare a poster presentation, including illustrations and key facts. Have students present their posters to the class, and then hang them in chronological order in the room.

Internet Search

Have students find more information on the clothes of a certain period using the Internet.

Keywords:

moda en los años *(decade or century)*

Perspectivas del mundo hispano

Core Instruction

Standards: 1.2, 2.1, 2.2

Focus: Reading about a specific type of celebration

Suggestions: Have students describe a family celebration. Who was there? What did people have to eat? Was there music playing? What was being celebrated? Did they have fun? Remind students to compare celebrations they have been to with *la parranda* as they read. Encourage them to prepare answers to the questions that they will ask their classmates. In large classes, you may want to guide students through the process of collecting information to summarize the results.

Answers will vary.

Extension: Have students draw a Venn diagram comparing *la parranda* with the types of parties that they attend.

Additional Resources

Student Resource: Realidades para hispano-hablantes, p. 86

Perspectivas del mundo hispano

La parranda

Un amigo te invita a su casa. Cuando llegas, encuentras a gente de todas las edades, niños y adultos. Se oye música. Alguien te saluda. Otra persona empieza a hablar contigo. Hay varias personas bailando en pareja[1]. No ves a tu amigo. Luego alguien te invita a bailar. ¿Qué está ocurriendo aquí?

Es una parranda. Una *parranda* es una fiesta con comida, refrescos, música y baile. En las casas hispanas se celebran parrandas cuando hay algún evento especial, como una boda o alguna fiesta nacional. En estas fiestas participan los miembros de la familia y los amigos. Todos comen, bailan y se divierten. A veces, hay parranda todo el día.

En general, las casas hispanas tienen un patio y una sala grande. La sala es el cuarto que usa la familia para las grandes ocasiones. Durante las fiestas normalmente hay espacio para bailar. Frecuentemente en vez de[2] discos compactos, hay una orquesta. Muchas veces los miembros de la familia o los amigos componen[3] la orquesta y tocan música para bailar.

¡Compruébalo! Pregúntales a tus compañeros de clase si les gusta hacer fiestas con su familia. Pregúntales si bailan en pareja frecuentemente. Pregúntales cómo debe ser una buena fiesta. Según los resultados, completa las siguientes oraciones.

¿Qué te parece? ¿Qué indican las respuestas de tus compañeros sobre las fiestas familiares? En tu opinión, ¿qué debe ocurrir en una buena fiesta? Considera los diferentes tipos de fiestas. ¿Qué hay de bueno en cada una?

Modelo

Mis compañeros de clase creen que hacer una fiesta con su familia es buena idea.

1. Mis compañeros de clase creen que hacer una fiesta con su familia es . . .
2. Mis compañeros de clase bailan en pareja . . .
3. Mis compañeros de clase creen que una buena fiesta debe ser . . .

[1]in pairs [2]instead of [3]make up

Differentiated Instruction
Solutions for All Learners

Multiple Intelligences

Logical/Mathematical: Have students prepare a graph of the results of questions in the *¡Compruébalo!* Ask them to calculate the percentage of students who enjoy celebrating with their family or who dance with a partner. Have them present their graph to the class.

Heritage Language Learners

Have students write a five-paragraph essay describing a family celebration. Encourage them to include details that may make their celebration unique. Provide students with a writing rubric specific to Spanish, focusing on details such as accents and word order. Review your expectations before students begin.

Presentación escrita

Encontré unas gangas

Task
You received $200 for your birthday ($100 in cash and $100 in gift certificates) and just purchased several articles of clothing with the money. Write an e-mail to a friend describing your shopping trip.

1 Prewrite Think about what you bought. Copy and fill in the following chart.

¿Qué compraste?	¿Dónde . . . ?	¿Cuánto pagaste?	¿Por qué te gusta(n)?

2 Draft Use your answers to the questions above to write a first draft. You may want to begin your e-mail with: *¡Hola! Para mi cumpleaños recibí $200 para comprar ropa nueva. Decidí ir al centro comercial porque . . . Encontré . . . Compré . . .*

3 Revise Read through your e-mail. Check for spelling, accents, forms of the preterite, and agreement. Share the e-mail with a partner. Your partner should check the following:
- Is the e-mail easy to understand?
- Does it include all the information from your chart?
- Is there anything you should add or change?
- Are there any errors?

4 Publish Rewrite the e-mail making any necessary changes or corrections. Send it to your teacher or your friend, or print it out and add it to your portfolio.

5 Evaluation Your teacher may give you a rubric for how the e-mail will be graded. You will probably be graded on:
- how easy the message is to understand
- clearness and completeness of the information
- accuracy of verb forms, spelling, and agreement
- use of vocabulary

Estrategia

Using a chart
When writing, it is helpful to have a way to organize your thoughts. A chart or a graphic organizer is a good way to do this.

ciento veintiuno 121
Capítulo 2B

Standards: 1.1, 1.3, 3.1

Focus: Writing an e-mail about purchases during a shopping trip

Suggestions: Encourage students to be imaginative as they describe their shopping trips. Tell them to think of a store that they don't normally shop in and to name items that they don't normally buy. Remind students to include a greeting and a closing to their e-mail, and to ask questions of the recipient. After describing their trip, students might want to ask where the recipient last shopped and what he or she bought. Encourage students to focus on the use of the preterite tense as they peer edit. If possible, respond to their message as though you were the friend, and comment on what they wrote.

Portfolio

Have students include a copy of their e-mail in their portfolio.

Pre-AP* Support

- *Pre-AP* Resource Book:* Comprehensive guide to Pre-AP* writing skill development, pp. 25–35

Teacher-to-Teacher

e-amigos: Have students write their *e-amigos* and describe a recent shopping trip. Encourage them to ask at least three questions to find out where their *e-amigos* went shopping and what they bought. Have students print out their e-mails or send them to you for your review.

Additional Resources

Student Resources: Realidades para hispanohablantes, p. 87; Guided Practice: Presentación escrita, p. 89

✓ Assessment

- Assessment Program: Rubrics, p. T28

Give students copies of the rubric before they begin the activity. Go over the descriptions of the different levels of performance. After assessing students, help individuals understand how their performance could be improved.

Enrich Your Teaching
Resources for All Teachers

RUBRIC	Score 1	Score 3	Score 5
How easily your message is understood	You are difficult to understand and have many grammatical errors.	You are fairly easy to understand and have occasional grammatical errors.	You are easy to understand and have very few grammatical errors.
Completeness of your information	You provide some of the information required.	You provide most of the information required.	You provide all of the information required.
Your use of accurate spelling and grammar	You have many misspellings and grammatical errors.	You have several misspellings and grammatical errors.	You have very few misspellings and grammatical errors.

Videomisterio

Core Instruction

 Standards: 1.2, 3.2, 5.2

Resources: Voc. and Gram. Transparencies: Map 12

Focus: Reading about Mexican participation in World War II; building background knowledge to prepare for the *Videomisterio*

Suggestions: Before students read the first paragraph, ask them to list what they know about World War II. Who was involved? Why did war break out? Encourage students to ask their history teachers for specific details concerning the war. Have them discuss the effects of any war on the countries involved. Suggest that students not only focus on the effects on the soldiers, but also on the rest of the country.

Have students read the first paragraph and the captions for the photos on p. 122. Ask them to name two reasons the Mexicans were welcomed into the United States during World War II. What did they receive in exchange for helping the United States in the war? Before students read the second caption on p. 122, ask them to say who they think were the principal partici- pants in World War II. Are they surprised to learn that between 2.5% and 5% of all the people involved were Mexican? Why or why not? Point out the poster at the top of the page. Ask students to compare it to posters that they may have seen in their history books, soliciting people to join the army. Have students say whether or not they think this type of poster is an effective way to get people to enlist in the armed forces. Would they join the armed forces to fight in a war? Encourage them to provide reasons for their answers.

Direct attention to *¿Sabes que...?* Stress the importance of the Congressional Medal of Honor. Bring in a newspaper article recounting when someone won the medal. You can use the Internet or library resources to find information and a photo of one. Make photocopies of it to share with your students. Ask them to describe reasons people might receive such an honor.

Videomisterio

Preparación para...

En busca de la verdad

La participación hispana en la Segunda Guerra Mundial

La Segunda Guerra Mundial (1939–1945) cambió el destino de los hispanohablantes en los Estados Unidos. A partir de[1] diciembre de 1941, muchos estadounidenses dejaron sus trabajos para ir a luchar[2] en la guerra. Por eso, muchos mexicanos llegaron a trabajar en los Estados Unidos. En el videomisterio vas a ver algo relacionado con este tema.

En 1942, los gobiernos[3] de los Estados Unidos y de México firmaron el acuerdo[4] del programa de "braceros", que les permitió a trabajadores agrícolas mexicanos trabajar en los Estados Unidos. La mayoría de los mexicanos llegaron a trabajar en el campo y usaron sus brazos (por eso se llamaron "braceros").

Algunos braceros se enlistaron[5] en el ejército[6] de los Estados Unidos. Después de su servicio militar, ganaban la ciudadanía[7] norteamericana.

[1]From [2]to fight [3]governments
[4]pact, agreement [5]enlisted [6]army [7]citizenship

122 ciento veintidós
Tema 2 • Un evento especial

Se estima que entre 250,000 y 500,000 hispanoamericanos sirvieron en las fuerzas armadas[8] durante la Segunda Guerra Mundial. Esto representa entre el 2.5 por ciento y el 5 por ciento de todas las personas que participaron en la guerra.

COMO UN SOLO HOMBRE

▲ Braceros mostrando el signo para la victoria en 1944

[8]armed forces

Differentiated Instruction
Solutions for All Learners

Multiple Intelligences

Visual/Spatial: Have students create a poster to persuade people to enlist in the armed forces, or to suggest ways in which people can help in times of war. Encourage them to use both illus- trations and slogans.

Students with Learning Difficulties

Prepare a graphic organizer to help students comprehend each aspect of the reading. In the center, write *la Segunda Guerra Mundial.* Then write heads for three sections—*Los mexicanos en los E.E.U.U., Los soldados hispanoameri- canos,* and *La Medalla de Honor.* Have students note one or two important pieces of information under each section.

Este monumento en Los Ángeles, California, conmemora a todos los soldados del ejército de los Estados Unidos que han sido condecorados[9] por el Congreso con la Medalla de Honor.[10] Está especialmente dedicado a los 39 hispanoamericanos que han ganado ese honor. En la Segunda Guerra Mundial, doce mexicoamericanos y un cubano recibieron la medalla. ▼

▲ Algunos países hispanohablantes también participaron en la Segunda Guerra Mundial. Por ejemplo, México envió un escuadrón[11] aéreo mexicano llamado la Unidad de Caza 201. El escuadrón, llamado "Águilas Aztecas", luchó en las Filipinas y tuvo la reputación de ser feroz[12].

Suggestions: Direct attention to *Para pensar*. To help students answer the question, remind them that there are always political, economic, and social aspects of war. Have them list types of people who might be involved in or affected by each aspect. If students have difficulty answering, encourage them to consider those who are concerned with a soldier's well-being.

Answers will vary but may include medical personnel or manufacturers.

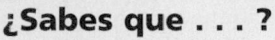

¿Sabes que . . . ?

La Medalla de Honor del Congreso es una condecoración que les dan a los soldados del ejército norteamericano por su admirable participación en la guerra. Es el honor más prestigioso que puede recibir un soldado. Más de 3,400 medallas han sido entregadas a lo largo de la historia de los Estados Unidos.

Para pensar

Aunque en las guerras siempre necesitan la colaboración de muchas personas, éstas no sólo tienen que ser soldados. ¿Qué otras personas crees que son necesarias en tiempo de guerra? ¿Para qué crees que pueden ser necesarias?

[9]decorated with honors   [10]Congressional Medal of Honor   [11]squadron
[12]had the reputation of being ferocious

ciento veintitrés **123**
Capítulo 2B

Enrich Your Teaching
Resources for All Teachers

Culture Note

The pilots of Mexican Fighter Squadron 201 flew the Republic P-47 Thunderbolt fighter plane in World War II. The squadron's pilots participated in almost 60 combat missions against Japanese forces in the Philippines as part of the U.S. Fifth Air Force. Several of the Mexican pilots were killed in action.

Internet Search

Have students learn more about the individual stories of the farm workers who came to the United States from Mexico during World War II.

Keyword:

los braceros

Review Activities

To talk about shopping: Have students draw a store and label items and areas.

To talk about colors: Provide students with crayons and have them identify the color of each crayon.

To describe what clothing is made of: Put students in pairs and provide each pair with a clothing catalogue. Have them ask each other questions about what the items are made of.

To discuss clothing purchases: Provide each group of students with a dressed doll or stuffed animal. Have students describe the doll or animal's clothing.

To discuss paying for your purchases: Put students in pairs. Provide each pair with several lists of purchases and prices (for example, *una blusa, $55* or *pantalones, $67, y un cinturón, $25*) and have them discuss the price (high, low), how much they are spending, how they will pay, and where they go to pay.

Demonstrative adjectives: Put students in groups of three. Each student displays one page of a clothing catalog and comments on at least one item in each catalog: *Me gusta esta blusa de seda, pero esos pantalones no están de moda, y aquella blusa de tela sintética es fea.*

Other useful words: Create a class story. A student begins the story with a sentence using one of the words or expressions. The next student continues the story with another sentence using a different word or expression, and so on.

Portfolio

Invite students to review the activities they completed in this chapter, including written reports, posters or other visuals, tapes of oral presentations, or other projects. Have them select one or two items that they feel best demonstrate their achievements in Spanish to include in their portfolios. Have them include this with the Chapter Checklist and Self-Assessment Worksheet.

Additional Resources

Student Resources: Realidades para hispano-hablantes, p. 88

 **CD-ROM**

PuzzleView Web Code: jdd-0218

Teacher Resources: Teacher's Resource Book: Situation Cards, p. 116, Clip Art, pp. 118–120; Assessment Program: Chapter Checklist and Self-Assessment Worksheet, pp. T56–T57

Repaso del capítulo

Vocabulario y gramática 🔊 jdd-0299

To prepare for the test, check to see if you . . .
- know the new vocabulary and grammar
- can perform the tasks on p. 125

to talk about shopping

la entrada	entrance
la ganga	bargain
el letrero	sign
la liquidación, *pl.* las liquidaciones	sale
el mercado	market
la salida	exit

to talk about colors

claro, -a	light
de sólo un color	solid-colored
oscuro, -a	dark
pastel	pastel
vivo, -a	bright

to describe what clothing is made of

¿De qué está hecho, -a?	What is it made of?
Está hecho, -a de . . .	It is made of . . .
algodón	cotton
cuero	leather
lana	wool
seda	silk
tela sintética	synthetic fabric

to discuss paying for purchases

alto, -a	high
bajo, -a	low
la caja	cash register
el cajero, la cajera	cashier
el cheque (personal)	(personal) check
el cheque de viajero	traveler's check
el cupón de regalo, *pl.* los cupones de regalo	gift certificate
en efectivo	cash
gastar	to spend
el precio	price
tan + *adjective*	so
la tarjeta de crédito	credit card

For Vocabulario adicional, see pp. 498–499.

to discuss clothing purchases

apretado, -a	tight
escoger	to choose
estar de moda	to be in fashion
el estilo	style
exagerado, -a	outrageous
flojo, -a	loose
la marca	brand
mediano, -a	medium
el número	shoe size
probarse (o → ue)	to try on
la talla	size

other useful words and expressions

anunciar	to announce
encontrar (o → ue)	to find
en realidad	really
me / te importa(n)	it matters (it's important) / they matter to me / to you
inmediatamente	immediately
me parece que	it seems to me that
¿Qué te parece?	What do you think? / How does it seem to you?
recientemente	recently

preterite of regular verbs

miré	miramos
aprendí	aprendimos
escribí	escribimos
miraste	mirasteis
aprendiste	aprendisteis
escribiste	escribisteis
miró	miraron
aprendió	aprendieron
escribió	escribieron

demonstrative adjectives

Singular		Plural	
este, esta	this	estos, estas	these
ese, esa	that	esos, esas	those
aquel, aquella that one over there		aquellos, aquellas those over there	

Differentiated Instruction
Solutions for All Learners

Advanced Learners

Have students write a review of a clothing store they have visited. They can comment on when they went, why, what kind of clothing the store offers, what the pieces are like, how shoppers can pay, etc. Have them read their reviews aloud and see if the class can identify the store.

Review **2B**

- Practice Workbook: Puzzle, p. 47
- Practice Workbook: Organizer, p. 48

¡Go Online
PHSchool.com
For: Test Preparation
Web Code: jdd-0218

Preparación para el examen

On the exam you will be asked to . . .	Here are practice tasks similar to those you will find on the exam . . .	If you need review . . .
1 Escuchar Listen and understand as people talk about why they purchased a clothing item	Listen as María explains why she bought her outfit. Was it because: (a) it was a bargain; (b) it was a good brand name; (c) it fit well; or (d) it was very "in style."	**pp. 102–105** *A primera vista* **p. 103** Actividad 2 **p. 106** Actividad 4
2 Hablar Talk about when and where you bought the clothing you are wearing today	Your partner really likes your outfit. Tell him or her: (a) where you bought it; (b) how long ago you bought it; (c) if it was very expensive or a bargain; (d) the brand, if you know it. Then reverse roles.	**p. 107** Actividad 7 **p. 108** Actividades 8–9 **p. 109** Actividades 10–11 **p. 111** Actividad 14 **p. 112** Actividad 17 **p. 115** Actividad 21 **p. 116** Actividad 23 **p. 117** Actividad 24
3 Leer Read and understand a thank-you note for a recently received gift certificate	Your Spanish class recently sent last year's exchange student from Argentina a gift certificate for her birthday. Read her note about what she bought and what she thought about her purchases. ¡Hola! Muchas gracias por el cupón de regalo para el Almacén Palete. Compré una blusa de colores pastel que me gusta mucho y está muy de moda. También encontré un cinturón de cuero muy bonito para llevar con mis pantalones favoritos. Aquí tienen mi foto. ¿Qué les parece mi nuevo estilo? Besos, Susi	**p. 107** Actividad 6 **p. 110** Actividad 13 **p. 114** Actividad 19 **pp. 118–119** *Lectura*
4 Escribir Write a short description of your most recent shopping trip for clothes, including what you bought, the brand, and how you paid for the items	Your grandmother sent you a check for your birthday and wants to know what you bought. Describe the vacation clothes that you bought and where you bought them. Include as many details as possible. You might begin by writing: Querida abuelita: Muchas gracias por el cheque que me enviaste para mi cumpleaños. Decidí comprarme ropa para las vacaciones . . .	**p. 107** Actividades 6–7 **p. 109** Actividades 10–11 **p. 110** Actividad 13 **p. 112** Actividad 16 **p. 121** *Presentación escrita*
5 Pensar Demonstrate an understanding of *la parranda* in Spanish-speaking countries	When you ask your parents if you can go to a *parranda* at the home of a Spanish-speaking friend, they have no idea what you are talking about. Explain it to them. What would you compare it to?	**p. 120** *Perspectivas del mundo hispano*

ciento veinticinco **125**
Capítulo 2B

Differentiated Assessment
Solutions for All Learners

STUDENTS NEEDING EXTRA HELP
- **Alternate Assessment Program:** Examen del capítulo 2B
- **Audio Program CD 20:** Chap. 2B, Track 5

HERITAGE LEARNERS
- **Assessment Program: Realidades para hispanohablantes:** Examen del capítulo 2B
- **ExamView Heritage Learner Test Bank**

ADVANCED/PRE-AP*
- **ExamView Pre-AP* Test Bank**
- **Pre-AP* Resource Book,** pp. 100–103

Performance Tasks
Standards: 1.1, 1.2, 1.3, 2.1

Student Resource: Realidades para hispanohablantes, p. 89

Teacher Resources: Teacher's Resource Book: Audio Script, p. 108; Audio Program: Track 14; Answers on Transparencies

1. Escuchar
Suggestions: Ask students why they might purchase a particular clothing item. If there are multiple reasons, which are the most important? Which would be the deciding factor?

Script:
Pasé mucho tiempo buscando algo perfecto para llevar al concierto. Encontré un suéter de una buena marca, pero cuando me lo probé, no me quedó bien. En realidad, no me importa mucho la marca. Después de muchas horas, compré uno de otra marca porque me quedó perfectamente.

Answer: c

2. Hablar
Suggestions: Have students review the preterite of regular *-ar, -er,* and *-ir* verbs before beginning.
Answers will vary.

3. Leer
Suggestions: Have students scan the note to find out what the exchange student bought. Then have them read for details.
Answers:
Susi bought a very fashionable pastel-colored blouse and a very pretty leather belt that she can wear with her favorite pants.

4. Escribir
Suggestions: Have students write a two-level outline for their note, with the first level answering all the questions and the second level listing details that can be included. Have them follow their outlines to write the note.
Answers will vary.

5. Pensar
Suggestions: Refer students to p. 120.
Answers:
A *parranda* is a type of party in which family members and friends of all ages participate. *Parrandas* take place to celebrate a special event. A *parranda* has food, beverages, music, and dancing and can last all day.

Assessment
- **ExamView** Quiz on PresEXPRESS
- Assessment Program: Examen del capítulo
- **ExamView** Test Bank: Tests A and B
- Audio Program CD 20: Chap. 2B, Track 5

Tema 3

Tú y tu comunidad

THEME OVERVIEW

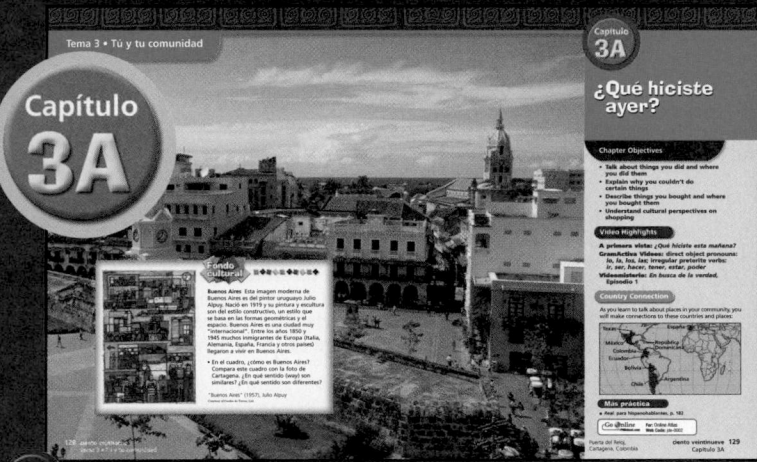

3A ¿Qué hiciste ayer?
• Running errands in the community
Vocabulary: places around town; errands
Grammar: direct object pronouns: *lo, la, los, las;*
preterite forms of *ir, ser, hacer, tener, estar, poder*
Cultural Perspectives: shopping

3B ¿Cómo se va . . .?
• Getting around town
Vocabulary: giving directions; good driving habits
Grammar: direct object pronouns *me, te, nos;* irregular
affirmative *tú* commands; present progressive: irregular forms
Cultural Perspectives: neighborhoods

Theme Project

Lugares en mi comunidad

Overview: Students write a paragraph giving directions from school to various areas around town and explaining what one can do or buy at specific locations. Assign different places (*la farmacia, el dentista,* etc.) to different students to avoid duplicate directions. Students can decorate their papers with pictures or drawings or create a map to accompany their writing. After each student has completed their paragraph, put all of the pages together in a community reference book.

Materials: Construction paper, markers, photos, glue or tape, scissors

Sequence: (suggestions for when to do each step are found throughout the chapters)

3A ▶ **STEP 1.** Review instructions so students know what is expected of them. Hand out the "Theme 3 Project Instructions and Rubric" from the *Teacher's Resource Book.*

STEP 2. Students submit a rough sketch of their page of directions. Return the drafts with your suggestions. For grammar and vocabulary practice, ask students to partner and present their drafts to each other.

STEP 3. Students create layouts on different pieces of construction paper, leaving room for photos and descriptions. Encourage them to work in pencil first and to try different arrangements before gluing photos or decorations.

3B ▶ **STEP 4.** Students submit a draft of their paragraph. Note your corrections and suggestions, then return drafts to students.

STEP 5. Students present their directions to the class, explaining each page and describing selected pictures.

Options:
1. Students research a major city in a Spanish-speaking country and give directions from one location to another.
2. Students give directions to different areas around the school.

Assessment:
Here is a detailed rubric for assessing this project:
Theme 3 Project: *Lugares en mi comunidad*

RUBRIC	Score 1	Score 3	Score 5
Your evidence of planning	You provide no written draft or sketch.	Your draft was written and layout created, but not corrected.	You show evidence of corrected draft and layout.
Your use of illustrations	You include no photos or visuals.	You include very few photos or visuals.	You include several photos or visuals.
Your presentation	You include little of the required information.	You give partially complete directions.	You give complete directions.

Bulletin Boards

Theme: *Lugares en la comunidad*

Cover the bulletin board with plain paper. Create a layout of a Spanish-speaking community including several streets, a plaza, a glorieta, and a monument or statue. Have the students decide which places they want to include in their community. Then have them draw the places, label the type of building or place, and give them a Spanish name. Students may choose to find pictures of community buildings and places from the Internet or other sources rather than draw them. The students can use their bulletin board as a means to ask for and give directions from one place to another in their *comunidad.*

Bibliography

Noble, Judith, and Jaime LaCasa. *The Hispanic Way.* Passport Books, 1995.

Rivera, Diego, and Gladys March. *My Art, My Life: An Autobiography.* Dover Publications, 1992.

Stevens, Kathryn. *Argentina.* Countries, Faces and Places Series. Chanhasse, Minn: Childs World, 2001.

DK Wilson, Anthony. *Visual Timelines of Transportation.* New York: Dorling Kindersley, 2002.

Hands-on Culture

Recipe: *Chocolate*

Chocolate is native to the American continents and is especially popular in Mexico. The hot chocolate that Mexicans drink, however, is different from that of the United States as it is made from unsweetened chocolate and contains cinnamon.

Ingredients:

1 square of unsweetened chocolate

½ teaspoon cinnamon

4 tablespoons sugar

2 cups milk

Directions:

1. Slowly heat all ingredients until chocolate is completely melted.
2. Whip mixture with a ***molinillo*** or whisk or use a blender. Continue to mix until beverage is frothy.
3. Enjoy!

Internet Search

Use the keywords to find more information.

3A Keywords:

los maya, ciudades hermanas, open air markets, mercados al aire libre

3B Keywords:

ayuntamiento, el metro

Game

¿Adónde vamos?

Play this game during *Capítulo* 3B to practice directions, *tú* commands and vocabulary.

Players: Any number of students in small groups

Materials: Street maps of cities in the Spanish-speaking world *(available online)*, paper, pens

Rules:

1. Give each each group a piece of paper and a street map.
2. Instruct each group to write directions to a certain location in the city. Be sure that students mention their starting point.
3. Collect the directions and read them aloud. Each group must follow the directions and try to find the destination.
4. Each correct destination is worth one point. The group with the most points wins.

Variations:

1. The teacher can write the directions to ensure accuracy.
2. The students can research a major city in the Spanish-speaking world and draw a map of the city.

RECYCLE
A ver si recuerdas

Vocabulary
• Los quehaceres
• La ciudad

Grammar
• Telling time

A primera vista	Manos a la obra	¡Adelante!	Repaso

Learning Sequence

INPUT	PRACTICE	APPLICATION	REVIEW
• Introduce vocabulary and grammar within an authentic context.	• Practice and develop new vocabulary. • Learn and practice new grammar structures.	• Apply vocabulary and grammar through culminating, theme-based activities. • Apply skill development.	• Review vocabulary and grammar.

Objectives

Read, listen to, and interpret information about • Running errands around town • Where people go and what they buy	• Talk about things you did and where you did them. • Explain why you weren't able to do certain things. • Discuss things you have bought and where you bought them. • Review uses of direct object pronouns.	• Read about the Sister Cities International program. • Describe open-air markets. • Talk about preparing for a trip. • Watch *En busca de la verdad, Episodio 1.*	• Prepare for the chapter test.

Culture

• Buenos Aires	• *El Palacio de Correos* • *Las farmacias* • *Los sellos, la tradición y la comunidad*	• *Intercambio cultural* • *Los mercados al aire libre*	• Describe open-air markets and the role they play in Spanish-speaking cultures.

Vocabulary
• Places in a community
• Running errands
• Items in a sporting-goods store
• Pharmacy products

Grammar
• Direct object pronouns
• Irregular preterite verbs: *ir, ser*
• Irregular preterite verbs: *hacer, tener, estar, poder*

Learner Support

STRATEGIES
• Using visuals to predict
• Using the structure of a text
• Using charts

RECYCLING
• Actividad 18
• Actividades 21–22
• *Tener que*
• Food
• Clothes

• School supplies
• Sports equipment
• Electronic equipment
• Irregular preterite verbs
• Leisure activities

Chapter Features

Pronunciación
The written accent

El español en en la comunidad
Labels and instructions in both English and Spanish

Conexiones
Mathematics: Time management
Literature: Pablo Neruda

Beyond the Classroom: States & Countries

Texas
España
México
República Dominicana
Colombia
Ecuador
Bolivia
Argentina
Chile

Student Resources

TECHNOLOGY

ONLINE
Interactive Textbook
• Student Edition Online plus audio, video, and flashcards

Go Online Companion Web Site
• Tutorial activities   • Internet links
• Self-tests   • Downloadable MP3 audio files
• **PuzzleView**

CD-ROM
Interactive Textbook CD-ROM
Student Edition on CD-ROM plus audio, video, and flashcards

MindPoint CD-ROM
QUIZSHOW

PRINT MATERIAL

CORE INSTRUCTION
Practice Workbook, pp. 49–59
• Review   • Vocabulary
• Grammar   • Puzzle
• Organizer

Writing, Audio & Video Activities,
pp. 46–55
• Video   • Audio
• Writing

Grammar Study Guide 1–2 (or 3–4)

Differentiated Instruction

STUDENTS NEEDING EXTRA HELP
Guided Practice Activities, pp. 90–107
• Vocabulary Flash Cards and Vocabulary Check
• Grammar Activities
• Presentación oral

HERITAGE LEARNERS
Realidades para hispanohablantes,
pp. 90–109

Lecturas para hispanohablantes
• "Doña Primavera," p. 61
• "Por Aventura," pp. 82–84
• "La niña sale de compras," pp. 99–100

ADVANCED/PRE-AP*
Pre-AP* Resource Book: Student Activity Sheet, p. 107

Teacher Resources

TECHNOLOGY

Audio Program Fine Art Transparencies
Video Program Vocabulary and Grammar
               Transparencies
               Answers on Transparencies

TeacherEXPRESS CD-ROM
• Lesson Planner   • Vocabulary Clip Art
• Web Resources   • Teaching Resources
• Teacher Edition with Interactive Links

PresentationEXPRESS CD-ROM
• Vocabulary   • Tranparencies and Maps
• Grammar   • Photo Gallery
• Audio   • Clip Art

PRINT MATERIAL

CORE INSTRUCTION
Teacher's Resource Book, pp. 132–157
• Input Script   • Video Script
• Answer Keys   • GramActiva Blackline Masters
• Vocabulary Clip Art • Chapter Resource Checklist
• School-to-Home Connection Letters
• Communicative Activities Blackline Masters

TPR Stories, pp. 38–43

Differentiated Instruction

STUDENTS NEEDING EXTRA HELP
Guided Practice Activities
Teacher's Guide, pp. T46–T54

HERITAGE LEARNERS
Realidades para hispanohablantes
Teacher's Guide, pp. 46–55

Lecturas para hispanohablantes
Teacher's Guide, pp. 22–23, 31–32, 38–39

ADVANCED/PRE-AP*
Pre-AP* Resource Book: Resources Chart, p. 104

Differentiated Assessment

PH SuccessNet ONLINE
• Access to grades and reports from Online Interactive Textbook

ExamView on Presentation Express
QuickTake Presenter CD-ROM
• Vocabulary Quizzes   • Chapter Test
• Grammar Quizzes

TeacherEXPRESS CD-ROM
• Assessment Program
• **ExamView** Test Banks A and B
  test generator

CORE ASSESSMENT
Assessment Program, pp. 69–82
• Pruebas
  Vocabulary Recognition
  Vocabulary Production
  Direct object pronouns
  Irregular preterite verbs: *ir, ser*
  Irregular preterite verbs: *hacer, tener, estar, poder*
• Examen del capítulo   • Speaking and Writing Rubrics
Teacher's Resource Book, p. 146
• Situation Cards
TPR Stories, pp. 38–43

STUDENTS NEEDING EXTRA HELP
Alternate Assessment Program
• Examen del capítulo, pp. 29–34

HERITAGE LEARNERS
Assessment Program: Realidades para hispanohablantes Teacher's Guide,
pp. T111–T115

ExamView Heritage Learner
test generator Test Bank

ADVANCED/PRE-AP*
Pre-AP* Resource Book: Teacher Activity Sheet, p. 106

ExamView Pre-AP* Test Bank
test generator

Go Online
PHSchool.com
For: Teacher Home Page
Web Code: jdk-1001

Lesson Plans

Regular Schedule (50 Minutes)

For electronic lesson plans:
Teacher Express 💿

	Warm-up / Assess	Preview Present / Practice Communicate		Wrap-up / Homework Options
DAY 1	**Warm-up (5 min.)** • Homework check • Return Examen del capítulo 2B	**A ver si recuerdas . . . (25 min.)** • Presentation: Los quehaceres/La ciudad • Actividades 1, 2 • Presentation: Telling time • Actividades 3, 4	**Chapter Opener (5 min.)** • Objectives • Fondo cultural **A primera vista (10 min.)** • Presentation: Vocabulario y gramática en contexto • Actividad 1	**Wrap-up and Homework Options (5 min.)** • Practice Workbook 3A-A, 3A-B, 3A-1, 3A-2 • Go Online
DAY 2	**Warm-up (10 min.)** • Actividad 2 • Homework check	**A primera vista (35 min.)** • Presentation: Videohistoria *¿Qué hiciste esta mañana?* • View: Videohistoria	• Video Activities 1, 2, 3, 4 • Actividad 3	**Wrap-up and Homework Options (5 min.)** • Practice Workbook 3A-3, 3A-4 • Go Online • Prueba 3A-1: Vocabulary recognition
DAY 3	**Warm-up (10 min.)** • Actividad 4 • Homework check ✔**Assessment (10 min.)** • Prueba 3A-1: Vocabulary recognition	**Manos a la obra (25 min.)** • Actividades 5, 6, 7 • Fondo cultural • Actividades 5, 6		**Wrap-up and Homework Options (5 min.)** • Writing Activity 10 • Actividades 9, 11 • Heritage Learner Workbook 3A-1, 3A-2 • Prueba 3A-2: Vocabulary production
DAY 4	**Warm-up (5 min.)** • Homework check ✔**Assessment (10 min.)** (after Communicative Activity) • Prueba 3A-2: Vocabulary production	**Manos a la obra (30 min.)** • Actividades 8, 10 • Fondo cultural • El español en la comunidad • Communicative Activity	• Presentation: Direct object pronouns • View: GramActiva video • Actividad 13	**Wrap-up and Homework Options (5 min.)** • Practice Workbook 3A-5 • Go Online
DAY 5	**Warm-up (10 min.)** • Writing Activity 12 • Homework check	**Manos a la obra (35 min.)** • Actividades 14 • Audio Activity 7 • Presentation: Irregular preterite verbs: *ir, ser*	• Actividades 15, 16, 17 • Audio Activity 8	**Wrap-up and Homework Options (5 min.)** • Practice Workbook 3A-6 • Actividad 18 • Writing Activities 11, 12 • Go Online • Heritage Learner Workbook 3A-4 • Pruebas 3A-3, 3A-4: Direct object pronouns; Irregular preterite verbs: *ir, ser*
DAY 6	**Warm-up (5 min.)** • Homework check ✔**Assessment (15 min.)** • Pruebas 3A-3, 3A-4: Direct pronouns; Irregular preterite verbs: *ir, ser*	**Manos a la obra (25 min.)** • Presentation: Irregular preterite verbs: *hacer, tener, estar, poder* • View: GramActiva video	• Actividades 19, 20, 21 • Fondos culturales	**Wrap-up and Homework Options (5 min.)** • Practice Workbook 3A-7 • Actividad 22 • Writing Activity 13 • Go Online • Heritage Learner Workbook 3A-5 • Prueba 3A-5: Irregular preterite verbs: *hacer, tener, estar, poder*
DAY 7	**Warm-up (10 min.)** • Actividad 23 • Homework check ✔**Assessment (10 min.)** (after Communicative Activity) • Prueba 3A-5: Irregular preterite verbs: *hacer, tener, estar, poder*	**Manos a la obra (15 min.)** • Audio Activity 9 • Communicative Activity • Pronunciación	**¡Adelante! (10 min.)** • Presentación oral: Steps 1, 4	**Wrap-up and Homework Options (5 min.)** • Presentación oral: Step 2 • Actividad 24
DAY 8	**Warm-up (5 min.)** • Homework check	**¡Adelante! (30 min.)** • Presentación oral: Step 3	**Repaso del capítulo (10 min.)** • Vocabulario y gramática • Preparación para el examen 1, 2	**Wrap-up and Homework Options (5 min.)** • Preparación para el examen 3, 4, 5 • Go Online: Self-test
DAY 9	**Warm-up (5 min.)** • Homework check	**¡Adelante! (40 min.)** • Lectura • ¿Comprendiste? / Y tú, ¿qué dices? • Videomisterio: *En busca de la verdad*, Episodio 1		**Wrap-up and Homework Options (5 min.)** • Practice Workbook 3A-8, 3A-9 • Go Online: Lectura • Videomisterio • La cultura en vivo • Examen del capítulo 3A
DAY 10	**Warm-up (5 min.)** • Homework check ✔**Assessment (40 min.)** • Examen del capítulo 3A			**Wrap-up and Homework Options (5 min.)** • A ver si recuerdas . . . : Capítulo 3B • La cultura en vivo

	Warm-up / Assess	Preview Present / Practice Communicate		Wrap-up / Homework Options
DAY 1	**Warm-up (5 min.)** • Homework check • Return Examen del capítulo: Capítulo 2B	**A ver si recuerdas . . . (25 min.)** • Presentation: Los quehaceres / La ciudad • Actividades 1, 2 • Presentation: Telling time • Actividades 3, 4 **Chapter Opener (5 min.)** • Objectives • Fondo cultural	**A primera vista (50 min.)** • Presentation: Vocabulario y gramática en contexto • Actividades 1, 2 • Presentation: Videohistoria: *¿Qué hiciste esta mañana?* • View: Videohistoria • Video Activities 1, 2, 3, 4 • Actividad 3	**Wrap-up and Homework Options (5 min.)** • Practice Workbook 3A-A, 3A-B, 3A-1, 3A-2, 3A-3, 3A-4 • Go Online • Prueba 3A-1: Vocabulary recognition
DAY 2	**Warm-up (10 min.)** • Actividad 4 • Homework check **✔Assessment (10 min.)** • Prueba 3A-1: Vocabulary recognition	**Manos a la obra (65 min.)** • Actividades 5, 6, 7, 8, 10 • Fondos culturales • Audio Activities 5, 6 • El español en la comunidad • Presentation: Direct object pronouns • View: GramActiva video • Actividades 12, 13, 14		**Wrap-up and Homework Options (5 min.)** • Practice Workbook 3A-5 • Actividad 11 • Writing Activity 10 • Go Online • Heritage Learner Workbook 3A-1, 3A-2
DAY 3	**Warm-up (10 min.)** • Actividad 9 • Homework check **✔Assessment (10 min.)** • Prueba 3A-2: Vocabulary production	**Manos a la obra (50 min.)** • Audio Activity 7 • Communicative Activity • Presentation: Irregular preterite verbs: *ir, ser* • Actividades 15, 16, 17, 18 • Audio Activity 8 • Writing Activity 12 **¡Adelante! (15 min.)** • La cultura en vivo – form groups		**Wrap-up and Homework Options (5 min.)** • Practice Workbook 3A-6 • Writing Activity 11 • Go Online • Heritage Learner Workbook 3A-4 • Pruebas 3A-3, 3A-4: Direct object pronouns; Irregular preterite verbs: *ir, ser*
DAY 4	**Warm-up (5 min.)** • Homework check **✔Assessment (15 min.)** • Pruebas 3A-3, 3A-4: Direct object pronouns; Irregular preterite verbs: *ir, ser*	**Manos a la obra (40 min.)** • Presentation: Irregular preterite verbs: *hacer, tener, estar, poder* • View: GramActiva video • Actividades 19, 20, 21, 23 • Audio Activity 9 • Pronunciación • Fondos culturales	**¡Adelante! (25 min.)** • Lectura • ¿Comprendiste? / Y tú, ¿qué dices? • Presentación oral: Steps 1, 4	**Wrap-up and Homework Options (5 min.)** • Practice Workbook 3A-7 • Presentación oral: Step 2 • Actividades 22, 24 • Writing Activity 13 • Go Online • Heritage Learner Workbook 3A-5 • Prueba 3A-5: Irregular preterite verbs: *hacer, tener, estar, poder*
DAY 5	**Warm-up (5 min.)** • Homework check **✔Assessment (10 min.)** • Prueba 3A-5: Irregular preterite verbs: *hacer, tener, estar, poder*	**¡Adelante! (45 min.)** • Presentación oral: Step 3 • La cultura en vivo **Repaso del capítulo (25 min.)** • Vocabulario y gramática • Preparación para el examen 1, 2, 3, 4, 5		**Wrap-up and Homework Options (5 min.)** • Practice Workbook 3A-8, 3A-9 • Go Online: Self-test • Examen del capítulo 3A
DAY 6	**Warm-up (10 min.)** • Homework check • Answer questions **Repaso del capítulo (15 min.)** • Situation Cards **✔Assessment (40 min.)** • Examen del capítulo 3A	**¡Adelante! (20 min.)** • Videomisterio: *En busca de la verdad,* Episodio 1		**Wrap-up and Homework Options (5 min.)** • Go Online: Lectura • La cultura en vivo • A ver si recuerdas . . . : Capítulo 3B

3A Recycle

Vocabulario

Presentation EXPRESS VOCABULARY

Core Instruction

Resources: Voc. and Gram. Transparency 58

Focus: Reviewing vocabulary related to chores and places in a community

Suggestions: To review the actions listed in the vocabulary, write the words on slips of paper and put them into a box. Invite students to choose a slip of paper and to act out the chores. Have them ask: *¿Qué hago yo?* Class members will respond with the appropriate action, for example: *Tú lavas los platos.*

To review place names, write three or four words that students would associate with the place on a flash card. For example, a card could say **coche, caminar,** and **tráfico** to elicit the word **calle.** Show the cards, and have volunteers name the place.

 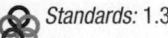

Actividad 1 *Standards:* 1.3

Focus: Writing about doing chores

Suggestions: Brainstorm expressions of frequency before beginning. Ask volunteers to personalize the model before students begin the activity.

Answers will vary.

Actividad 2 *Standards:* 1.3

Focus: Writing about the community, including points of interest

Suggestions: Remind students of the importance of pre-writing. Suggest that they make a chart listing the places they plan to write about and a few descriptive words for each place, such as what it looks like and where it is located.

Answers will vary.

Extension: Have students illustrate a map of their community. Encourage them to share their descriptions with a partner, using the map for reference.

Preparación para 3A

A ver si recuerdas...

Vocabulario   Los quehaceres   La ciudad

en el dormitorio
arreglar el cuarto
hacer la cama

en la cocina
cocinar
dar de comer al
perro/gato
lavar los platos
poner la mesa
separar (botellas,
latas, vidrio,
periódicos, cartón)

en otros cuartos
ayudar
lavar la ropa
limpiar el baño
pasar la aspiradora
quitar el polvo

fuera de la casa
cortar el césped
lavar el coche
sacar la basura
trabajar en el jardín

los lugares
el barrio
la calle
el cine
la comunidad
el estadio
el hospital
el monumento
el museo
el teatro

For additional vocabulary for the city, see *A ver si recuerdas* 1B, p. 42.

Práctica de vocabulario • Usando el organizador gráfico

Actividad 1 Escribir/Hablar

Los quehaceres

¿Quién en tu familia hizo estos quehaceres? ¿Cuándo los hizo?

Modelo

cortar el césped
El verano pasado mi hermano y yo cortamos el césped cada semana.

1. lavar los platos
2. arreglar el cuarto
3. cocinar pollo
4. limpiar el baño
5. sacar la basura
6. pasar la aspiradora
7. lavar la ropa

Actividad 2 Escribir

¿Qué hay en tu comunidad?

Imagina que alguien visita tu comunidad por primera vez. Escríbele una breve descripción. Incluye los lugares de interés y cómo son.

Modelo

Si visitas mi comunidad vas a ver muchas casas con jardines y césped. En el centro hay tiendas y restaurantes, pero no hay un cine . . .

126 ciento veintiséis
Tema 3 • Tú y tu comunidad

Differentiated Instruction
Solutions for All Learners

Multiple Intelligences

Interpersonal/Social: After completing *Actividad* 1, have students create a dialogue between a parent and a child. The parent is telling the child what chores need to be done, and the child responds that he or she needs to go somewhere and cannot do them. Have students act out each role for the class.

Students with Learning Difficulties

When students have trouble with written expression, remind them of the purpose of their writing. For *Actividad* 2, tell students that the purpose of the paragraph is to describe their community. Once they have written their paragraph, have them check to see if they have accomplished their goal.

126

Gramática · Repaso

Telling time

To ask about and tell the time of day, you usually say:

¿Qué hora es?   **Es** la una.
Son las cinco.

When you tell at what time something happens, you use *a*.

¿**A** qué hora es el concierto? **A** las ocho.

When talking about time after the hour, use *y* to express the time.

1:10	Es la una **y** diez.
3:15	Son las tres **y** cuarto.
	o: Son las tres **y** quince.
6:25	La clase empieza a las seis **y** veinticinco.
10:30	Generalmente me acuesto a las diez **y** media.

When talking about time before the hour, there are several expressions commonly used.

Son las diez **menos** veinte.
Son las nueve **y** cuarenta. ⎫ — *It's 9:40.*
Faltan veinte **para** las diez. ⎭

You know several words and expressions for talking about the time of day.

de la mañana	*in the morning,* A.M.
de la tarde	*in the afternoon,* P.M.
de la noche	*in the evening,* P.M.
temprano	*early*
tarde	*late*
a tiempo	*on time*

Práctica de gramática

 Actividad 3   Escribir

¿A qué hora?

Escribe frases para decir a qué hora . . .

Modelo

. . . te levantas durante la semana.
Me levanto a las seis.

1. . . . te acuestas los fines de semana.
2. . . . te despiertas los fines de semana.
3. . . . almuerzas durante la semana.
4. . . . regresas a casa después de las clases.
5. . . . empieza tu clase favorita.
6. . . . empieza tu programa de televisión favorito.

Más práctica

- Practice Workbook, pp. 49–50: 3A-A, 3A-B
- Guided Practice: Grammar Acts., p. 90
- *Real.* para hispanohablantes, p. 90

 **Go Online**
PHSchool.com
For: Vocab. and Grammar Review
Web Code: jdd-0301

 **Actividad 4**   Hablar

¿Quién lo hace?

Trabajen en grupos de cuatro y hagan preguntas a sus compañeros para saber quiénes del grupo hacen las siguientes actividades.

Modelo

. . . se levanta temprano todos los días
A —*Ariana, ¿te levantas temprano todos los días?*
B —*Sí, me levanto muy temprano. Me levanto a las seis de la mañana.*

¿Quién en el grupo . . .
. . . se levanta temprano los fines de semana?
. . . se levanta tarde los fines de semana?
. . . siempre llega a tiempo a la escuela?
. . . siempre llega temprano para ver a sus amigos?
. . . hace la cama antes de ir a la escuela?
. . . se acuesta antes de las diez de la noche?
. . . almuerza después de las dos de la tarde?

ciento veintisiete **127**
Preparación: Vocabulario y gramática

 Gramática · Repaso

Core Instruction

Suggestions: Write various times on index cards and distribute them to students. Say five different times, and have students who have those times hold up their index cards. Then ask students whose times were not called to say the time on their cards.

Fill in, copy, and distribute a page from an agenda book. Ask students to say at what time the person does each activity.

 Actividad 3  *Standards:* 1.3
Presentation EXPRESS™ ANSWERS

Resources: Answers on Transparencies

Focus: Writing times at which different activities are done

Suggestions: Remind students to include expressions about the time of day, as well as specific hours.

Answers will vary but will include:
1. Me acuesto a ...
2. Me despierto a ...
3. Almuerzo a ...
4. Regreso a casa a ...
5. Mi clase favorita empieza a ...
6. Mi programa de televisión favorito empieza a ...

Actividad 4  *Standards:* 1.1

Focus: Talking about what time different activities are done

Suggestions: Remind students that they need to change the statement to use the *tú* form of the verb in their questions and the *yo* form in their responses.

Answers will vary.

Enrich Your Teaching
Resources for All Teachers

Culture Note

Remind students that most Spanish-speaking countries use the 24-hour clock. On the 24-hour clock, the hours do not start over again in the afternoon but are continuous. For example, 7:00 A.M. and 7:00 P.M. would be 7:00 and 19:00 respectively on the 24-hour clock.

Teacher-to-Teacher

Using the vocabulary, create three sets of cards: activities, places and rooms, and times. Students can work in groups to take turns selecting a card from each pile and making a sentence. Some sentences may not be logical. Students will earn points for logical sentences. The student with the most points at the end of the game wins.

Block Schedule

Pass out paper plates, pipe cleaners, round-head fasteners, and markers. Have students mark the plate as if it were a clock face. Tell them to use the pipe cleaners for hands, securing them with the fasteners. Have them practice telling time.

Standards for Capítulo 3A

- To achieve the goals of the Standards, students will:

Communication

1.1 Interpersonal

- Talk about: schedules, doing errands, telling time, community stores and services, and famous people from the past
- Give information using direct object pronouns
- Talk to give and request information
- Describe using the preterite of *ir, ser, hacer, tener, estar, poder*

1.2 Interpretive

- Read: about Buenos Aires, a building in Mexico, medication labels, *barrios* in Spain and Latin America, *los sellos* in Spain, Sister Cities International, and services *farmacias* provide; a picture-based story and a newspaper ad
- Listen to and watch a video about errands
- Read, listen to, and interpret errands, schedules, and information on buying things
- Read and interpret information that uses direct object pronouns, reviewing preterite of *ir, ser, hacer, tener, estar, poder*
- View a video mystery series

1.3 Presentational

- Write: information about times, running errands, schedules, buying things, interesting places in the community; questions about famous people of the past
- Present information about: irregular preterite verbs *ir, ser, hacer, tener, estar, poder;* direct object pronouns; preparing for trips; what people did where and when; community stores and services

Culture

2.1 Practices and Perspectives

- Describe cultural characteristics of *barrios*
- Write or talk about open-air markets

2.2 Products and Perspectives

- Write or talk about painter Julio Alpuy, El Palacio de Correos, services *farmacias* provide, poet Pablo Neruda, *barrios* in Spain and Latin America, *los sellos* in Spain and the benefits of a brand of toothpaste
- Describe open-air markets

Connections

3.1 Cross-curricular

- Write or talk about Pablo Neruda, Sister Cities International, errands, and time schedules; make an oral presentation

3.2 Target Culture

- Talk about Buenos Aires and Guanajuato

Comparisons

4.1 Language

- Review: uses of direct object pronouns; rules for written accents

4.2 Culture

- Compare markets, *farmacias*, and *barrios* with those in the U.S.

Communities

5.1 Beyond the School

- Identify: medications with Spanish labels; things to do with guests

5.2 Lifelong Learner

- View a video mystery series

Fondo cultural ◼️◆◼️◆◼️◆◼️◆◼️◆

Buenos Aires Esta imagen moderna de Buenos Aires es del pintor uruguayo Julio Alpuy. Nació en 1919 y su pintura y escultura son del estilo constructivo, un estilo que se basa en las formas geométricas y el espacio. Buenos Aires es una ciudad muy "internacional". Entre los años 1850 y 1945 muchos inmigrantes de Europa (Italia, Alemania, España, Francia y otros países) llegaron a vivir en Buenos Aires.

- En el cuadro, ¿cómo es Buenos Aires? Compara este cuadro con la foto de Cartagena. ¿En qué sentido (*way*) son similares? ¿En qué sentido son diferentes?

"Buenos Aires" (1957), Julio Alpuy
Courtesy of Cecilia de Torres, Ltd.

Differentiated Instruction

STUDENTS NEEDING EXTRA HELP

Guided Practice Activities
- Vocabulary Check, Flash Cards
- Grammar
- Reading and Speaking Support

Guided Practice Audio CDs
- Disc 1, Track 5

HERITAGE LEARNERS

Realidades para hispanohablantes
- Chapter Opener, pp. 90–91
- A primera vista, p. 92
- Videohistoria, p. 93
- Manos a la obra, pp. 94–101
- ¡Adelante!, pp. 102–107
- Repaso del capítulo, pp. 108–109

ADVANCED/PRE-AP*

Pre-AP* Resource Book, pp. 104–107

¿Qué hiciste ayer?

Chapter Objectives

- Talk about things you did and where you did them
- Explain why you couldn't do certain things
- Describe things you bought and where you bought them
- Understand cultural perspectives on shopping

Video Highlights

A primera vista: *¿Qué hiciste esta mañana?*

GramActiva Videos: direct object pronouns: *lo, la, los, las;* irregular preterite verbs: *ir, ser, hacer, tener, estar, poder*

Videomisterio: *En busca de la verdad,* **Episodio 1**

Country Connection

As you learn to talk about places in your community, you will make connections to these countries and places:

Texas
España
México
República Dominicana
Colombia
Ecuador
Bolivia
Chile
Argentina

Más práctica

- *Real.* para hispanohablantes, p. 182

 **For:** Online Atlas
Web Code: jde-0002

Puerta del Reloj,
Cartagena, Colombia

ciento veintinueve **129**
Capítulo 3A

Chapter Opener

Presentation EXPRESS ATLAS

Core Instruction

Resources: Voc. and Gram. Transparencies: Maps 12, 14–18, 20

Suggestions: Ask students to imagine that their parents asked them to go into town to run errands. Have them brainstorm a list of different errands that they might need to do and places they would need to go. Have students save the list so that they can later see how much chapter vocabulary they predicted. In the *Videohistoria,* students will see the different errands that the characters have to do before they go to the movies. Ask students if their parents make them finish doing chores or errands before they go out with friends.

Tell students that they will learn additional verb forms in the preterite. Have volunteers use the preterite tense to say one thing they have done today.

Fondo cultural *Standards:* 1.2, 2.2

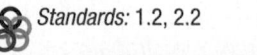

Resources: Fine Art Transparencies with Teacher's Guide, p. 4

Suggestions: Before students read the passage, show the transparency and have them describe the painting. Then have them open their books and look at the photo to make their comparison.

Answers will vary.

Teaching with Art

Resources: Fine Art Transparencies with Teacher's Guide, p. 4

Suggestions: Explain to students that the artist may have put a boat in the painting to illustrate that Buenos Aires is a port city. He also may have included people of different shapes and colors to reflect the diverse population of the city.

Culture Note

The urban design of Buenos Aires changed dramatically in the early 1900s. A need for better transportation resulted in the first subway in South America in 1913. In the 1930s more subway lines were built. In the meantime, above ground, the narrow colonial streets were expanded to become the wide avenues that make this city so distinctive.

Teacher Technology

TeacherEXPRESS
Plan • Teach • Assess

PLAN
Lesson Planner

Go Online PHSchool.com
For: Teacher Home Page
Web Code: jdk-1001

TEACH
Teaching Resources
Interactive
Teacher's Edition
Vocabulary Clip Art

ASSESS
Chapter Quizzes and Tests

PresentationEXPRESS
Dynamic Presentations for Teachers

TEACH
Vocabulary & Grammar Powerpoints
GramActiva Video
Audio & Clip Art Activities
Transparencies and Maps
Activity Answers
Photo Gallery

ASSESS
ExamView
QuickTake Presenter

Vocabulario y gramática  VOCABULARY

Core Instruction

 Standards: 1.1, 1.2

Resources: Teacher's Resource Book: Input Script, p. 134, Clip Art, pp. 148–151, Audio Script, p. 135; Voc. and Gram. Transparencies 59–60; TPR Stories Book, pp. 37–49; Audio Program: Tracks 1, 3

Focus: Presenting vocabulary for places people go, what they buy, and errands

Suggestions: Use the Input Script from the *Teacher's Resource Book* or the story from the *TPR Stories Book* to present new words. Describe a day you spent running errands, including the places you went and items you bought. As you describe the errands, have students point to pictures in their books of the places and items you mention.

Create index cards for each student. Write objects on half the cards and the places each can be found on the other half. Randomly distribute the cards and have students find their match by saying: *Busco ...* or *Trabajo en ....* When students find their match have them report to the class by saying: *Compro* (object) *de* (student) *en* (place). Or *Vendo* (object) *a* (student) *en* (place).

Bellringer Review

Have students copy these Spanish words for activities from the board and circle these activities that they did last weekend.

Comprar frutas   *Lavarse los dientes*
Escribir una carta   *Jugar al tenis*
Recibir dinero   *Leer una revista*

Then, working in pairs have them tell each other those activities that they did using the preterite tense.

Additional Resources

• Audio Program: Canciones CD, Disc 22

A primera vista jdd-0387

Vocabulario y gramática en contexto

Objectives

Read, listen to, and understand information about
• running errands around town
• where people go and what they buy

el centro
el champú
el jabón
Farmacia ORTIZ
la farmacia
el cepillo de dientes
la pasta dental
Supermercado Carranza
EL CORREO
LIQUIDACIÓN de equipo deportivo
EQUIPO DEPORTIVO
el supermercado
la tienda de equipo deportivo
el correo
la raqueta de tenis
los patines
echar una carta
la pelota
el buzón
el palo de golf
el sello
la tarjeta
la carta

—¿A qué hora **se abre** el correo en el centro? Quiero comprar unos sellos y **enviar*** una carta.

—Se abre a las nueve de la mañana y **se cierra** a las ocho de la noche.

Actividad 1 jdd-0387 ⏵)) Escuchar

¿Lógica o no?

Escucha las frases y señala con el pulgar hacia arriba si la frase es lógica y con el pulgar hacia abajo si no es lógica.

*Enviar has an accent mark on the *i* in all present-tense forms except *nosotros* and *vosotros.*

130 ciento treinta
Tema 3 • Tú y tu comunidad

Differentiated Instruction
Solutions for All Learners

Advanced Learners

Have students work in groups to create a blueprint or model for a new downtown shopping district. Encourage them to include the businesses and services that are introduced in *A primera vista.* Have them present their plan and tell what can be done or bought at each place.

Multiple Intelligences

Visual/Spatial: Have students create word webs for the buildings and stores on these pages. Ask them to write the place name in the middle, and write as many items as they can that can be found at each place. For example: ***El correo: el sello, la carta, el buzón,*** etc.

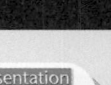

Actividad 2 jdd-0387 🔊 **Escuchar/Escribir**

¿Cómo van?

Escribe en una hoja de papel los números del 1 al 4. Escucha los diálogos y escribe la letra de la respuesta apropiada.

1. ¿Qué tiene que comprar en la farmacia?
   a. jabón y pasta dental
   b. un cepillo de dientes y champú

2. ¿Adónde va después de ir al banco?
   a. al consultorio
   b. al supermercado

3. ¿Qué necesita comprar?
   a. una tarjeta
   b. unos sellos

4. ¿Cómo van a la biblioteca?
   a. Van en coche.
   b. Van a pie.

Más práctica

- Practice Workbook, pp. 51–52: 3A-1, 3A-2
- WAV Wbk., Writing, p. 52
- Guided Practice: Vocab. Flash Cards, pp. 91–96
- *Real.* para hispanohablantes, p. 92

Go Online
PHSchool.com
For Vocab. Practice
Web Code: jdd-0302

el consultorio

CONSULTORIO

DRA. MARÍA ELENA VIVAS BLANCO MÉDICA

DR. VICENTE ROJAS CAMACHO DENTISTA

el médico, la médica

el dentista, la dentista

Biblioteca

sacar un libro

devolver un libro

BANCO NACIONAL

el banco

cobrar un cheque

BANCO NACIONAL

cuidar a los niños

💬 Ayer cuidé a Carlota y a Paco **por** cinco horas. **Fuimos a pie** al zoológico.

Nos quedamos allí **hasta** la una. Fue muy divertido.

Luego regresamos a casa. Sus padres me pagaron por cuidarlos. Me gusta cuidar niños porque puedo ganar dinero. Es importante tener mi propio dinero 💬.

ciento treinta y uno 131
Capítulo 3A

Actividad 1 Standards: 1.2  Presentation EXPRESS AUDIO

Resources: Teacher's Resource Book: Audio Script, p. 135; Audio Program: Track 2; Answers on Transparencies

Focus: Listening comprehension about errands

Suggestions: Pause after each illogical sentence and have students explain why the sentence does not make sense.

🔊 **Script and Answers:**

1. Puedo comprar jabón en el banco. *(down)*
2. Es posible comprar sellos en el correo. *(up)*
3. Busco un buzón para echar una carta. *(up)*
4. Para sacar un libro, debes ir al consultorio. *(down)*
5. Para comprar un palo de golf, debes ir a la tienda de equipo deportivo. *(up)*
6. Para cobrar un cheque, debes ir al banco. *(up)*
7. Para comprar cereal, debes ir al supermercado. *(up)*
8. Para ver al dentista, debes ir a la farmacia. *(down)*

Actividad 2 Standards: 1.2 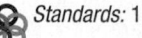 Presentation EXPRESS AUDIO

Resources: Teacher's Resource Book: Audio Script, p. 135; Audio Program: Track 4; Answers on Transparencies

Focus: Listening comprehension about where people go and what they buy

Suggestions: Before reading the script or playing the *Audio CD,* have volunteers read the questions and choices aloud. Ask students to point to the places or objects as they are mentioned.

🔊 **Script and Answers:**

1. —Necesito comprar un cepillo de dientes y champú.
   —¿Por qué no entramos en esa farmacia? *(b)*
2. —¿Qué tienes que hacer esta tarde?
   —Primero voy al banco y después al consultorio de la Dra. Sánchez. *(a)*
3. —Tengo que enviar una carta pero no tengo sellos.
   —Vamos al correo para comprarlos. Allí puedes enviarla. *(b)*
4. —Vamos a la biblioteca para devolver los libros.
   —Pero no tenemos el coche. Hay que caminar. *(b)*

✓ **Assessment**
- ExamView Quiz on PresEXPRESS
  QuickTake Presenter

Enrich Your Teaching
Resources for All Teachers

Teacher-to-Teacher

Have students create a **correo** corner in the classroom. Have the class design a sign, mailbox, and stamps. Allow students the opportunity to earn stamps by doing extra-credit work. When they have enough stamps, they can mail a letter to anyone in the room. Each day, assign different students the tasks of postmaster and mail carrier. Require students to speak to the postmaster to mail the letters: *Quiero echar una carta a ....*

Videohistoria

Presentation EXPRESS
VOCABULARY

Core Instruction

 Standards: 1.2

Resources: Voc. and Gram. Transparencies 61–62; Audio Program: Track 5

Focus: Presentation of additional vocabulary and grammar about running errands

Suggestions:

Pre-reading: Direct attention to the *Estrategia.* Using the transparencies, show each frame separately to be sure students are making logical predictions. Point out that this is a two-part story and that it will be continued in the next chapter.

Reading: Have students read the story once, using cognates and context clues to help them with unfamiliar vocabulary. Make a photocopy of the *Videohistoria* and cut out each section of dialogue. Give each student a different section of the text. Using the transparencies, show a scene and have students with the appropriate sections read the dialogue in the correct order. Pause after each scene and ask questions about the characters to check comprehension.

Post-reading: Complete *Actividad* 3 to check comprehension.

 Pre-AP* Support

• **Activity:** Distribute Clip Art for the "places around town" that are presented in this chapter. Have pairs of students recreate the dialog on p. 130 by changing *el correo* to another place and making appropriate changes. As pairs of volunteers read their new dialog to the class, classmates hold up the clip art representing the new location and name another errand that might be completed there.

• **Pre-AP* Resource Book:** Comprehensive guide to Pre-AP* vocabulary skill development, pp. 47–53

Videohistoria jdd-0387

¿Qué hiciste esta mañana?

Estrategia

Using visuals to predict
Scan the pictures to predict what will happen in the *Videohistoria.* Can you tell where the characters went and what they did there?

Ramón Manolo Claudia Teresa

1 **Teresa:** Hola, Claudia. ¿Cómo estás?

Claudia: Bien, Teresa. ¿Y tú? Oye, tenemos que darnos prisa.[1] Manolo y Ramón nos esperan[2] a las dos para ir al cine, ¿verdad?

Teresa: Sí, pero tengo que comprar **varias** cosas aquí en la farmacia. ¿Vamos a entrar?

[1]to hurry   [2]are expecting

5 **Ramón:** Primero fuimos a una tienda de equipo deportivo. Me compré una camiseta del Cruz Azul.

Claudia: ¡Genial! Es uno de mis equipos favoritos. Y después, ¿qué hicieron?

6 **Ramón:** Fuimos a **la estación de servicio** a comprar **gasolina.**

Manolo: Buenos días, señor. ¿Puede **llenar el tanque,** por favor?

Asistente: Sí señor. **En seguida.**

7 **Teresa:** ¡Ay, **caramba,** se me olvidó!

Claudia: ¿Ahora qué, Teresa?

Teresa: Mañana es el cumpleaños de mi abuela. Tengo que comprarle algo.

Claudia: Estamos cerca del Bazar San Ángel. ¿Por qué no vamos allí?

Differentiated Instruction
Solutions for All Learners

Advanced Learners

Have students work in groups to prepare their own *Videohistoria.* Assign each group a different scene. Have students use a digital camera to take pictures of themselves in poses that are logical for their scene. Ask them to present their photos as a slide show while they read their dialogue.

Multiple Intelligences

Logical/Mathematical: Have students list where each character had to go. Then have students interview their classmates to see if they regularly do the same errands. Have students determine the most common errands and draw a pie graph to illustrate what their classmates do regularly.

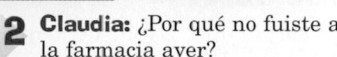

2 **Claudia:** ¿Por qué no fuiste a la farmacia ayer?

Teresa: No **pude. Tuve** que ir a la biblioteca a devolver un libro. No **estuve** allí por mucho tiempo pero tuve que hacer otras cosas también.

3 **Teresa:** Ay, **casi se me olvidó.** Tengo que enviar esta carta. Pero necesito comprar sellos . . .

Claudia: Vamos, vamos. Ramón y Manolo ya deben estar en el cine. La película empieza a las dos y media.

Teresa: Tranquila, Claudia. **Todavía** tenemos tiempo. Regreso en un momento.

4 **Claudia:** Hola, Ramón. Aquí Claudia.

Ramón: Hola, Claudia. ¿Qué tal?

Claudia: Muy bien. **Tuvimos** que ir a varios sitios, pero **pronto** vamos a ir al cine. Ya casi terminamos. Y Uds., ¿qué hicieron esta mañana?

8 **Claudia:** Ramón, vamos al Bazar San Ángel. Tenemos que comprar un regalo. ¿Por qué no nos vemos allí? Vamos al cine después.

Ramón: ¡Cómo no! Nos vemos allí.

Claudia: Adiós. **Hasta pronto.**

Hablar/Escribir

¿Comprendiste?

1. Los cuatro jóvenes tienen planes para la tarde. ¿Adónde piensan ir?
2. Antes de ver a Ramón y Manolo, ¿cuáles son las tres cosas que Teresa tuvo que hacer?
3. ¿Por qué entró Teresa en el correo?
4. ¿Qué se le olvidó a Teresa?
5. ¿Adónde fueron Ramón y Manolo por la mañana?
6. ¿Adónde decidieron ir antes de ir al cine?

Más práctica

- Practice Workbook, pp. 53–54: 3A-3, 3A-4
- WAV Wbk.: Video, pp. 46–48
- Guided Practice: Vocab. Check, pp. 97–100
- *Real.* para hispanohablantes, p. 93

Go Online
PHSchool.com
For: Vocab. Practice
Web Code: jdd-0303

ciento treinta y tres **133**
Capítulo 3A

Video

Core Instruction

Standards: 1.2, 2.1, 3.2

Resources: Teacher's Resource Book: Video Script, p. 139; Video Program: Cap. 3A

Focus: Comprehension of contextualized vocabulary

Suggestions:

Pre-viewing: Divide students into eight groups and assign each group a section of the *Videohistoria.* Have each group write a brief summary of their section on the chalkboard and allow students to refer to the summaries during the video.

Viewing: Show the video once without pausing. Then go back and show it again, stopping to check for comprehension. Pause at each place that Teresa and her friends go and ask students if they run similar errands.

Post-viewing: Complete the Video Activities in the *Writing, Audio & Video Workbook.*

 Standards: 1.2, 1.3

 Presentation EXPRESS ANSWERS

Resources: Answers on Transparencies

Focus: Verifying comprehension of the *Videohistoria*

Suggestions: For item 2, students may think Teresa has four things to do since she must buy a stamp for her letter. Explain the expression *se le olvidó* in item 4, pointing out the parallels to *se me olvidó.*

Answers:

1. Piensan ir al cine.
2. Tuvo que comprar varias cosas en la farmacia, enviar una carta y comprar un regalo.
3. Entró en el correo para comprar sellos.
4. Se le olvidó comprar un regalo de cumpleaños para su abuela.
5. Fueron a una tienda de equipo deportivo y a la estación de servicio.
6. Decidieron ir al Bazar San Ángel.

Enrich Your Teaching
Resources for All Teachers

Culture Note

Southwest of Mexico City lies San Ángel, which hosts *Bazar sábado* every Saturday. Artisans, musicians, and visitors join together and create a spirited atmosphere. Booths are set up in colonial courtyards where artists sell blown glass, ceramics, paintings, and other crafts. Mariachi music and Mexican cuisine abound in the local cafés.

Teacher-to-Teacher

Prepare multiple-choice questions about each of the characters from the *Videohistoria.* For example: *¿De qué color es el coche de Manolo?* Divide the class into two teams and play *¿Quiénes los conocen mejor?* The team that answers the most questions correctly wins.

Additional Resources

- WAV Wbk.: Audio Act. 5, p. 49
- Teacher's Resource Book: Audio Script, pp. 135–136
- Audio Program: Track 7

 Assessment

- **ExamView** Quiz on PresEXPRESS
  QuickTake Presenter
- Prueba 3A-1: Vocab. Recognition, pp. 69–70

133

Objectives

- Talk about things you did and where you did them
- Explain why you weren't able to do certain things
- Discuss things you have bought and where you bought them
- Review uses of direct object pronouns

Manos a la obra

Vocabulario y gramática en uso

Differentiated Instruction
Solutions for All Learners

Actividad 4 *Standards:* 1.3

Resources: Teacher's Resource Book: GramActiva BLM, p. 147

Focus: Writing about errands to do at different places around town

Recycle: *tener que;* food vocabulary; clothing vocabulary

Suggestions: Identify the places shown in the activity before students begin. Remind students to keep their lists for *Actividad* 5.

Answers will vary but may include:
la tienda de equipo deportivo / comprar una camiseta
la farmacia / comprar la pasta dental
el banco / cobrar un cheque
el consultorio / ver al médico
el supermercado / comprar la comida
la biblioteca / devolver un libro
el correo / comprar sellos
la estación de servicio / llenar el tanque

Common Errors: Students may try to conjugate the verbs in the second column. Point out that the expression **tener que** is followed by the infinitive.

Bellringer Review
Have students work in pairs and tell each other at what time they do the following activities: *hacer la tarea, comer la cena, mirar la tele.* Have the partner write the time as he hears them.

Actividad 5   *Standards:* 1.1

Focus: Talking about errands and hours of operation of different places around town

Recycle: Telling time

Suggestions: Remind students to use the expressions **de la mañana, de la tarde,** and **de la noche** when appropriate. Point out that **se abre** means that something opens (for example, a store or business), while **abre** is used when someone is opening something (for example, a door or a gift). Point out that **se cierra / cierra** works the same way.

Answers will vary.

Common Errors: Students may omit the **a** in **a qué hora.** Remind students that when asking at what time something happens, they must say **a qué hora,** but when they ask what time it is, they should use **qué hora.**

Actividad 4   Escribir

Muchas cosas que hacer

En una hoja de papel, escribe los lugares que ves en los dibujos. Escribe una cosa que tienes que hacer en cada lugar. Vas a usar la información para la Actividad 5.

Lugares	Tengo que . . .
el supermercado	comprar leche

Actividad 5   Hablar

¿A qué hora se abre?

Trabaja con otro(a) estudiante. Explícale lo que tienes que hacer y hablen de los horarios de cada lugar. Usen la información de la tabla de la Actividad 4.

Modelo

A —*Tengo que* comprar cereal. *¿A qué hora se abre el* supermercado?
B —*Se abre* a las ocho de la mañana.
A —*¿Y a qué hora se cierra?*
B —*Creo que se cierra* a las once de la noche.

134 ciento treinta y cuatro
Tema 3 • Tú y tu comunidad

Heritage Language Learners

Have students write an article for a newsletter published by the Chamber of Commerce in your area. Students should write about the best places for different services in your area. Have them include the address and hours of each place. Have students peer edit each other's articles before preparing a final copy.

Students with Learning Difficulties

Before assigning *Actividad 7*, which requires asking about completed errands, review the preterite of the following verbs on the board: *sacar, comprar, echar, ir, jugar, cobrar, llenar.*

Actividad 6

jdd-0388

 Escuchar/Escribir/Hablar

Escucha y escribe

1 Tu mamá necesita tu ayuda para hacer todos los quehaceres. Escucha lo que ella dice y escribe las seis frases.

2 Escoge una expresión del recuadro y escribe respuestas a las preguntas de tu mamá. Después trabaja con otro(a) estudiante y lee las conversaciones entre ustedes.

¡Caramba!	lo siento
casi	no puedo
¡Cómo no!	pronto
en seguida	se me olvidó
ir a pie	todavía

Actividad 7

 Hablar

¿Adónde fuiste?

El fin de semana pasado tus padres te dieron varios mandados (errands) que hacer. Ahora quieren saber si los hiciste. Diles adónde fuiste y cuándo hiciste todo.

Modelo

A —¿Compraste los sellos?
B —Sí, fui al correo esta mañana.

Estudiante A

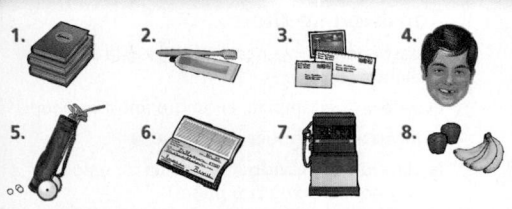

1. 2. 3. 4.
5. 6. 7. 8.

Estudiante B

esta mañana
ayer
anoche
hace . . . días
¡Respuesta personal!

Fondo cultural

El Palacio de Correos de la Ciudad de México, fue construido entre 1902 y 1907. Diseñado por el arquitecto italiano Adamo Boari, el Palacio de Correos es uno de los edificios (buildings) más famosos de la ciudad.

• El Palacio de Correos es un edificio muy conocido en México. ¿Cuáles son algunos edificios famosos de los Estados Unidos? ¿Por qué son famosos?

Interior del Palacio de Correos, Ciudad de México

Enrich Your Teaching
Resources for All Teachers

Culture Note
The *Palacio de Correos* is located in the historical center of Mexico City. More than just a post office, the *Palacio de Correos* contains government offices and a museum devoted to the history of the postal service in Mexico.

Teacher-to-Teacher
Have students create a brochure for a service that does shopping, banking, and other errands for busy people. Encourage them to include the locations that they will go and their hours of operation.

Practice and Communicate 3A

Actividad 6

  Standards: 1.1, 1.2, 1.3

AUDIO

Resources: Teacher's Resource Book: Audio Script, p. 135; Audio Program: Track 6; Answers on Transparencies

Focus: Listening, writing, and speaking about chores and errands

Suggestions: Play the *Audio CD* or read the script once. Ask students to recall the chores they heard. Allow students to listen again, this time pausing between sentences so that they may write.

Script:
1. Esta tarde necesitas quedarte en casa.
2. Necesito varias cosas de la farmacia, como jabón y champú.
3. Esta noche tienes que cuidar a tu hermanito.
4. Por favor, devuelve estos libros a la biblioteca.
5. ¿Me puedes echar esta carta en el buzón?
6. ¿Puedes ir en bicicleta al banco a cobrar un cheque?
Step 2 answers will vary.

Actividad 7

  Standards: 1.1

ANSWERS

Resources: Answers on Transparencies

Focus: Talking about completed errands

Suggestions: Encourage Student B to use expressions from *Actividad 6*.

Answers:
Student A:
1. ¿Devolviste los libros?
2. ¿Compraste la pasta dental y el cepillo de dientes?
3. ¿Echaste las cartas?
4. ¿Fuiste al dentista?
5. ¿Compraste los palos de golf?
6. ¿Cobraste el cheque?
7. ¿Llenaste el tanque?
8. ¿Compraste la fruta?
Student B answers will vary.

Fondo cultural *Standards:* 1.2, 2.2

Suggestions: Brainstorm reasons buildings are considered important. Point out elements such as their function, their style, or their historical significance.

Answers will vary but may include: The White House (it is a well-known government building); the Alamo (it played an important role in history); or the Pentagon (it has a unique shape).

135

Actividad 8  Standards: 1.1  Presentation EXPRESS ANSWERS

Resources: Answers on Transparencies

Focus: Talking about past activities

Recycle: Leisure activities

Suggestions: Brainstorm possible excuses that Student B might make. Encourage students to include details such as where they were and what time they had to be there.

Answers:

Student A:
1. ¿Fuiste al parque de atracciones el fin de semana pasado?
2. ¿Fuiste al cine...?
3. ¿Fuiste al concierto...?
4. ¿Fuiste a la playa...?
5. ¿Fuiste al lago... ?
6. ¿Fuiste a la fiesta... ?

Student B answers will vary.

Extension: Have students talk about a real event that they missed as a result of having to do an errand.

 Actividad 9 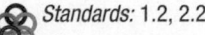 Standards: 1.2, 2.2  Presentation EXPRESS ANSWERS

Resources: Voc. and Gram. Transparency 65; Answers on Transparencies

Focus: Reading for comprehension

Suggestions: Have students predict the content of the advertisement by asking them to recall advertisements they have seen for hygiene products. Ask them to scan the questions before reading the ad.

Answers:
1. El producto se llama "Dentabrit". Es para tener los dientes más blancos.
2. Debes usar el producto todos los días.
3. El producto garantiza los dientes más blancos, más limpios y protegidos porque aporta el máximo nivel de limpieza y eficacia blanqueadora.
4. Puedes comprar el producto en las farmacias.

Actividad 8   Hablar

Un fin de semana muy aburrido

No pudiste hacer muchas cosas divertidas el fin de semana pasado. Trabaja con otro(a) estudiante y habla de las cosas que tuviste que hacer.

Modelo

A —¿Fuiste al centro el fin de semana pasado?

B —No, no pude. Tuve que cuidar a mis hermanitos.

Estudiante A

1.
2. CINE
3.
4.
5.
6.

Estudiante B

No, no pude.
Tuve que . . .
Estuve en . . . por . . . horas.
Estuve en . . . hasta las . . .
Tuve que esperar . . .
Me quedé en . . .
¡Respuesta personal!

También se dice . . .

la pasta dental = la pasta dentífrica, la pasta de dientes *(España)*

el sello = la estampilla, el timbre *(muchos países)*

la farmacia = la botica, la droguería

la estación de servicio = la bomba de gasolina, la gasolinera *(muchos países)*

Actividad 9 Leer/Escribir

Para unos dientes más blancos . . .

Lee el anuncio del periódico y contesta las preguntas.

1. ¿Cómo se llama el producto del anuncio? ¿Para qué puedes usarlo?
2. ¿Con qué frecuencia debes usar el producto, todos los días o una vez a la semana?
3. ¿Qué garantiza el producto? ¿Por qué?
4. ¿Dónde puedes comprar el producto?

¡SONRÍE! para tener los dientes más blancos

Dentabrit

DIENTES BLANCOS
ENCÍAS SANAS

Dentabrit pasta dental de uso diario[1] devuelve la blancura a los dientes. La nueva fórmula de **Dentabrit** blanqueador garantiza los dientes más blancos, más limpios y protegidos[2]. **Dentabrit** blanqueador aporta[3] el máximo nivel[4] de limpieza y eficacia blanqueadora.

¡Dentabrit blanqueador! Lo mejor en higiene, salud y belleza para los dientes.

DE VENTA EN FARMACIAS Producto de Lab. Suárez, Avda. de Loja 42 Ibarra, Ecuador

[1]daily [2]protected [3]adds [4]level

136 ciento treinta y seis
Tema 3 • Tú y tu comunidad

Differentiated Instruction
Solutions for All Learners

Multiple Intelligences

Bodily/Kinesthetic: Have students pretend they are actors trying out for a ***Dentabrit*** toothpaste commercial. Ask them to prepare a persuasive presentation of the product. Video-tape their auditions or have them perform for the class. Have other classmates decide whether or not the students get the part.

Students with Learning Difficulties

To help students organize ideas for *Actividad* 10, provide a four-column chart. Label the columns *lugar, personas, acciones,* and *otras cosas.* Make a transparency to demonstrate how the chart will help students organize their thoughts. Have students categorize the place and associated words provided in the model.

Fondo cultural

Las farmacias en los países hispanohablantes frecuentemente venden antibióticos y otras medicinas sin necesidad de receta *(prescription)* y es común consultar a un farmacéutico, y no al médico. Los horarios de servicio varían. En España, hay *Farmacias de guardia* que están abiertas las 24 horas. En otros países, se pueden encontrar *Farmacias de turno* que también dan servicio las 24 horas al día. En las farmacias uno también puede comprar productos de belleza, como perfumes y maquillaje, y de higiene personal, como champú y pasta dental.

• ¿Hay farmacias abiertas las 24 horas al día en tu comunidad? ¿Cómo son y qué productos venden?

Una farmacia en Barcelona, España

  Escribir/Hablar

Juego

❶ Vas a jugar con otro(a) estudiante. Tu profesor(a) va a decirles a todos un lugar en la ciudad. Escriban las personas, acciones u otras cosas que se asocian con este lugar. Tu profesor(a) va a indicar cuándo termina el tiempo.

Modelo

restaurante
camarero, mesa, comida, comer, servir, decoraciones, tenedor, cuchillo, ...

❷ Uds. van a trabajar con otras tres parejas. Lean la lista de palabras para un lugar. Si las otras parejas tienen una de estas palabras, ninguna pareja recibe puntos por ella. Pero si hay palabras que las otras parejas no tienen, Uds. reciben un punto por cada una.

 Escribir/Hablar

Y tú, ¿qué dices?

1. ¿Qué tipo de tiendas y servicios hay en el centro de tu comunidad? ¿A qué hora se abren? ¿A qué hora se cierran? ¿Se cierran antes o después de las seis de la tarde?

2. Cuando tu familia compra equipo deportivo, ¿dónde lo compra? ¿Y dónde compra cosas como jabón o pasta dental?

3. ¿Te gusta caminar? ¿A qué lugares puedes ir a pie fácilmente en tu comunidad?

4. ¿Qué haces para ganar dinero? ¿Te gusta cuidar a los niños? ¿Por qué?

El español en la comunidad

Hoy en día, en los Estados Unidos, muchas etiquetas *(labels)* de medicinas e instrucciones para otros productos están escritas *(written)* en inglés y en español. Para muchas personas que hablan y leen español, es más fácil y seguro *(safe)* leer las instrucciones en español.

Nodolor
Sinus pain relief without drowsiness
Calma el dolor de la sinusitis sin dar sueño

• Busca en tu casa etiquetas con instrucciones en español. ¿Qué parte de las instrucciones entiendes?

ciento treinta y siete **137**
Capítulo 3A

Practice and Communicate

 3A

Fondo cultural

Standards: 1.2, 2.2, 4.2

Suggestions: Ask students to list reasons why it is important for some medicines to be sold by prescription. What are the disadvantages of having to use prescription medicine?

Answers will vary.

Standards: 1.3

Focus: Categorizing vocabulary

Suggestions: Before beginning, write the word *restaurante* on the board and have students brainstorm words to accompany it. To model how students earn points, have them compare their results with the words in the model.

Answers will vary.

Standards: 1.1, 1.3

Focus: Writing and talking about places in the community and ways to earn money

Suggestions: Have students write short paragraphs to answer each question, adding details where applicable.

Answers will vary.

El español en la comunidad

Core Instruction

 Standards: 1.2, 5.1

Suggestions: Bring in boxes, labels, or product information sheets that include instructions in both Spanish and English to use as examples.

Enrich Your Teaching

Resources for All Teachers

Culture Note

A *farmacia de turno,* like all pharmacies, is identified by a green cross. In Central and South America, these pharmacies are designated *de turno* because they take turns staying open 24 hours to serve their customers. This system guarantees that at least one pharmacy is always open to provide assistance.

Teacher-to-Teacher

Bring in several products with labels written entirely in Spanish and place the objects around the classroom at learning stations. Prepare a list of questions about the products for students to answer at each station. Set a kitchen timer to indicate when students should change stations.

Additional Resources

• WAV Wbk.: Audio Act. 6, p. 50
• Teacher's Resource Book: Audio Script, p. 136, Communicative Activity BLM, pp. 142–143
• Audio Program: Track 8

✓ **Assessment**

• Prueba 3A-2: Vocab. Production, pp. 71–72

137

Core Instruction

 *Standards:* 4.1

Resources: Teacher's Resource Book: Video Script, p. 140; Video Program: Cap. 3A

Suggestions: Bring a bunch of seedless grapes to class as a prop to demonstrate using direct object pronouns. Review the *Gramática,* then pick up a grape and say *Voy a comer una uva. La voy a comer. Voy a comerla.* As you eat the grape, say *La como* and when you finish, say *La comí.* Repeat the process with two grapes, reinforcing the use of the plural direct object pronouns. To practice the masculine forms, you may want to bring in two hard-boiled eggs. Have students repeat the process with a partner both in the singular and in the plural. Be absolutely certain that students do not have any allergies! Use the *GramActiva* Video as an introduction or to reinforce the review.

Bellringer Review

Show Clip Art vocabulary flashcards to students and have them tell you the direct object pronoun they would use for each one. Be sure to include words from *Realidades* 1.

  *Standards:* 1.2  ANSWERS

Resources: Answers on Transparencies

Focus: Using direct object pronouns

Suggestions: Point out that the answers to all but three items (items 3, 6, and 8) are found in the sentence that comes before the blank. Tell students that in item 7 the answer would normally be written as one word, but that there is a space because of the blank.

Answers:

1. la	4. la	7. los
2. las	5. las	(lavarlos)
3. lo	6. Lo	8. lo

Extension: Compliment students on clothing or accessories they are wearing and ask when and where they bought the items.

Gramática·Repaso

Direct object pronouns

A direct object tells who or what receives the action of the verb.

> Devolví **el libro.**   *I returned **the book.** (book is the direct object)*

To avoid repeating a direct object noun, you can replace it with a direct object pronoun. In English, *him, her,* and *it* are examples of direct object pronouns. You have already used the following direct object pronouns in Spanish:

Singular	Plural
lo *it, him, you (masc. formal)*	**los** *them, you (masc.)*
la *it, her, you (fem. formal)*	**las** *them, you (fem.)*

Direct object pronouns have the same gender (masculine or feminine) and number (singular or plural) as the nouns they replace. They come right before the conjugated verb.

> ¿Devolviste **los libros** a la biblioteca? No, no **los** devolví.

> ¿Ayudaste a **tu mamá** en casa? Sí, **la** ayudé.

When an infinitive follows a verb, the direct object pronoun can be placed before the conjugated verb or attached to the infinitive.

> ¿Sacaste **el libro** sobre Simón Bolívar? No, no **lo** pude sacar. o: No, no pude sacar**lo.**

GramActiva VIDEO

Want more help with direct object pronouns? Watch the **GramActiva** video.

 *Lo veo.*

 12 Leer/Escribir

¡A lavar!

Cuando Teresa regresa a casa por la tarde, tiene esta conversación con su madre. Léela, y escribe el pronombre apropiado: *lo, la, los* o *las.*

Mamá: ¿Qué tal la película, Teresa?

Teresa: Bien, mamá. Me gustó mucho. Tú __1.__ viste anoche, ¿no?

Mamá: Sí, pero no me gustó. Oye, ¿dónde están las cosas que compraste en la farmacia? No __2.__ veo.

Teresa: El champú está sobre la mesa. ¿No __3.__ ves?

Mamá: Ah, sí, aquí está. ¿Y la pasta dental?

Teresa: Creo que __4.__ dejé (*I left*) en el baño.

Mamá: Muy bien. ¿Y enviaste las cartas?

Teresa: Sí, mamá, __5.__ envié después de ir a la farmacia.

Mamá: Gracias, hija. Ah, ¿compraste un regalo para tu abuela?

Teresa: ¡Sí, mamá! Le compré un collar muy bonito. ¿__6.__ quieres ver?

Mamá: Sí, pero más tarde. Ahora tenemos que limpiar la cocina. Tú puedes lavar los platos.

Teresa: ¡Ay! No puedo lavar __7.__ , mamá . . . ¡Se me olvidó comprar el detergente!

Mamá: No importa, Teresa. ¡Yo __8.__ compré ayer! Y ahora, ¡a lavar!

Differentiated Instruction
Solutions for All Learners

Students with Learning Difficulties

Photocopy *Actividad* 12 and present it as two tasks. For each item, have the students first identify and circle the referent for the missing direct object pronoun. Then have them write the direct object pronoun that agrees in gender and number with the circled noun it replaces.

Heritage Language Learners

When writing the direct object pronoun after an infinitive, students may separate the words. Be aware of this as students write, and encourage them to look for this as they review their work.

Actividad 13 — Hablar

De compras

Tu compañero(a) quiere saber por qué tienes varias cosas contigo. Explícale por qué las tienes.

Modelo

A —¿Por qué tienes los palos de golf?
B —Los tengo porque quiero jugar al golf esta tarde.

Estudiante A

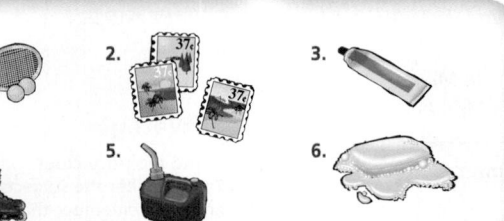

1.
2.
3.
4.
5.
6.

Estudiante B

quiero . . .
necesito . . .
voy a . . .
tengo que . . .
¡Respuesta personal!

Actividad 14 — Escribir/Hablar

¿Todavía lo usas?

A veces compramos o recibimos algo y después no lo usamos mucho.

1 Escribe cinco frases para decir qué cosas compraste tú o qué cosas te compraron otras personas.

2 Lee tus frases a tu compañero(a). Tu compañero(a) te va a preguntar si todavía tienes, usas o llevas esa cosa.

Modelo

A —Hace dos años mis padres me compraron unos palos de golf.
B —¿Todavía los usas?
A —Sí, los uso porque juego al golf mucho.
o: —No, no los uso porque no tengo tiempo para jugar al golf.

Estudiante A

Hace . . . me compraron . . .   Un día compré . . .
Hace . . . compré   **¡Respuesta personal!**

Estudiante B

¿ . . . llevas?
¿ . . . tienes?
¿ . . . usas?
¡Respuesta personal!

Más práctica

● Practice Workbook, p. 55: 3A-5
● WAV Wbk., Writing, p. 53
● Guided Practice: Grammar Acts., pp. 101–102
● *Real.* para hispanohablantes, pp. 94–97

Go Online
PHSchool.com
For: Direct Object Pronouns
Web Code: jdd-0304

Practice and Communicate — 3A

Actividad 13   Standards: 1.1

Presentation EXPRESS
ANSWERS

Resources: Answers on Transparencies
Focus: Using direct object pronouns
Suggestions: Review the objects shown and their genders before students begin their conversations.
Answers:
Student A:
1. ¿Por qué tienes una raqueta de tenis?
2. ¿ ...unos sellos?
3. ¿ ...la pasta dental?
4. ¿ ...los patines?
5. ¿ ...la gasolina?
6. ¿ ...el jabón?
Student B answers will vary.

Common Errors: If Student A uses the incorrect pronoun, Student B may follow his or her example. Remind students to monitor one another as they work in pairs.

Extension: Have partners reverse the conversation by having Student A say why he or she has an item. For example: *Lo tengo porque quiero lavarme la cara.* Student B will guess which object his or her partner is describing.

Actividad 14   Standards: 1.1, 1.3

Focus: Talking about possessions using direct object pronouns
Recycle: Clothing, sports equipment, electronic equipment, school supplies
Suggestions: Provide students with categories such as clothing, toys, electronic equipment, sports equipment, or video games. Have students brainstorm items that they have from each category to use in their conversations.
Answers will vary.

Additional Resources

● WAV Wbk.: Audio Act. 7, p. 50
● Teacher's Resource Book: Audio Script, p. 136
● Audio Program: Track 9

✓ **Assessment**

● **ExamView** QuickTake Presenter Quiz on PresEXPRESS
● Prueba 3A-3: Direct object pronouns, p. 73

Enrich Your Teaching
Resources for All Teachers

Teacher-to-Teacher

Have students work in groups of five to play a guessing game. Give each group four objects or sets of objects to elicit all four direct object pronouns. After seeing what the objects are, have one student turn around. The other students each take an item and hide it behind their backs. The fifth student uses the direct object pronouns to ask: ¿ ____ tienes? Each student answers: *Sí, ____ tengo* or *No, no ____ tengo.* Based on the pronouns, the student will guess who has which object. Once the student has identified the object each person has, another student can take a turn at guessing. Students receive a point for each match they make.

139

Gramática

Presentation EXPRESS
GRAMMAR

Core Instruction

Standards: 4.1

Resources: Voc. and Gram. Transparency 63

Suggestions: Direct attention to the *¿Recuerdas?* to remind students that they already know the forms of the verb *ir* in the preterite. Then tell students a story using the preterite forms of *ir* and *ser.* Have volunteers guess from the context whether you are using a form of *ir* or *ser.* Use the *GramActiva* Video as an introduction or to reinforce your explanation.

Bellringer Review
Have students complete these sentences from the board.

1. *Marcos fue al _____ para comprar estampillas.*
2. *Fui al _____ para cobrar un cheque.*
3. *Mis padres fueron a la _____ para comprar palos de golf.*

  Standards: 1.2

Presentation EXPRESS
ANSWERS

Resources: Answers on Transparencies

Focus: Using the preterite forms of *ir* and *ser* to complete a paragraph

Suggestions: Remind students that the forms of *ir* are usually followed by *a.*

Answers: Answers for the last question will vary.

1. fue	5. fue	9. fueron
2. fui	6. fue	10. fue
3. fuimos	7. fuimos	
4. fueron	8. fue	

Extension: Have students review the paragraph and tell which verb, *ir* or *ser,* is used in each case.

Theme Project
Give students copies of the Theme Project outline and rubric from the *Teacher's Resource Book.* Explain the task to them, and have them perform Step 1. (For more information, see p. 126–a.)

Pre-AP* Support

- **Activity:** Using *Actividad 15* as a model, have students describe aloud a similar scene with friends. Have them write two true/false statements to ask a partner (or the class).
- *Pre-AP* Resource Book:* Comprehensive guide to communication skill development, pp. 9–17, 36–46

140

Gramática

Irregular preterite verbs: *ir, ser*

In the preterite, the forms of *ser* are the same as the forms of *ir.* The context makes the meaning clear.

El cantante Jon Secada **fue** a vivir a Miami, Florida, en 1970.
*The singer Jon Secada **went** to live in Miami, Florida, in 1970.*

Después **fue** estudiante en la Universidad de Miami.
*Later he **was** a student at the University of Miami.*

(yo)	**fui**	(nosotros) (nosotras)	**fuimos**
(tú)	**fuiste**	(vosotros) (vosotras)	**fuisteis**
Ud. (él) (ella)	**fue**	Uds. (ellos) (ellas)	**fueron**

- Notice that these irregular preterite forms do not have any accents.

¿Recuerdas?
You already know the verb *ir* in the preterite.

- ¿Adónde **fueron** Uds. el verano pasado? **Fuimos** a Puerto Rico.

Estrategia

Using memory clues
To remember the subjects of *fui* and *fue,* remember that *fui,* the *yo* form, ends in *i,* while *fue,* the *él / ella* form, ends in *e.*

 Leer/Escribir

El día de Simón y sus amigos

Lee lo que hicieron Simón y sus amigos ayer. Escribe la forma correcta del verbo *ir* o *ser.* Luego contesta la pregunta sobre el día que ellos pasaron.

Ayer __1.__ un día bastante bueno para nosotros. Primero yo __2.__ a la estación de servicio para llenar el tanque con gasolina. Luego Fernando y yo __3.__ a la tienda de equipo deportivo para mirar patines. Nuestras amigas Teresa y Patricia __4.__ al almacén. Después Teresa __5.__ al correo y Patricia __6.__ al banco. En la noche todos nosotros __7.__ al cine. La película __8.__ muy cómica pero no sé quiénes __9.__ los actores principales.

En tu opinión, ¿el día de Simón y sus amigos __10.__ divertido? ¿Por qué?

Un día divertido entre amigos

Differentiated Instruction
Solutions for All Learners

Heritage Language Learners
Students may confuse direct object pronouns with third-person indirect object pronouns *(le, les).* Remind students that, with the exception of *lo,* direct object pronouns resemble the definite articles.

Students with Special Needs
If students have difficulty reading the Pablo Neruda poem, prepare a version that uses different letter forms, and distribute it to students.

Leer/Escribir
Actividad 16

Un poema de amor

Pablo Neruda (1904–1973) fue poeta chileno y ganador del Premio Nobel de Literatura en 1971. En muchos de sus poemas, Neruda escribió sobre el amor.[1] Estos versos son de su primer libro de poemas *Crepusculario,* que él publicó a los 19 años de edad. Lee los versos.

Conexiones   La literatura

Fui tuyo, fuiste mía. ¿Qué más? Juntos[2] hicimos un recodo[3] en la ruta donde el amor pasó.

1. ¿Está el poeta todavía con "su amor"? ¿Cómo lo sabes?
2. En tu opinión, ¿qué quiere decir el poeta en estos versos?

[1]love   [2]together   [3]turn

Actividad 17
 Escribir/Hablar/GramActiva

Juego

❶ Trabaja con un grupo de tres para escribir preguntas sobre quiénes fueron personas famosas del pasado. Pueden usar las ideas del recuadro o sus propias ideas. También tienen que escribir las respuestas a sus preguntas.

> el presidente en el año . . .
> los cantantes de la canción . . .
> los actores en la película . . .
> la persona que escribió el poema / libro . . .
> los campeones *(champions)* . . .
> **¡Respuesta personal!**

❷ Su profesor(a) va a formar dos grupos grandes en la clase. Un grupo lee una pregunta. Si el otro grupo contesta correctamente, recibe un punto. El grupo con más puntos al final gana.

> **Modelo**
> A —¿Quién fue el poeta que escribió Crepusculario?
> B —El poeta fue Pablo Neruda.

Actividad 18
 Escribir/Hablar

Y tú, ¿qué dices?

1. ¿Cuál fue tu día más divertido del mes pasado? ¿Por qué? ¿Adónde fuiste? ¿Con quiénes?
2. ¿Cuál fue tu viaje más interesante? ¿Adónde y con quiénes fuiste? ¿Cuáles fueron algunos de los lugares que visitaron o las actividades que hicieron?
3. ¿Cuál fue tu mejor o peor cumpleaños? ¿Por qué fue tan bueno o malo?

> **Más práctica**
> ● Practice Workbook, p. 56: 3A-6
> ● WAV Wbk., Writing, p. 56
> ● Guided Practice: Grammar Acts., pp. 103–104
> ● *Real.* para hispanohablantes, pp. 98–99

> **Go Online**
> PHSchool.com
> **For:** Irregular Preterite Verbs *Ir* and *Ser*
> **Web Code:** jdd-0305

ciento cuarenta y uno **141**
Capítulo 3A

Enrich Your Teaching
Resources for All Teachers

Teacher-to-Teacher
Have students prepare an interview about a vacation that a classmate may have taken. Ask them to write five questions to find out details about where their classmate went and what it was like. Remind them to use the preterite forms of **ser** and **ir** as they conduct their interviews.

Internet Search
Have students gather more information about the influential Chilean poet Pablo Neruda by researching his life and works on the Internet.

Keyword: Pablo Neruda

Practice and Communicate 3A

Actividad 16 *Standards:* 1.2, 2.2, 3.1
Pre-AP*

Resources: Answers on Transparencies
Focus: Understanding verses from a poem
Suggestions: Read the poem to students, and have a volunteer summarize the verse. Point out that the answers to the questions are not found in any specific spot in the poem.
Answers:
1. El poeta no está todavía con su amor. Lo sé porque está usando el pretérito.
2. Answers will vary.

Extension: Pablo Neruda is an AP* Literature author. You may want to suggest that students read additional works by this poet.

Actividad 17 *Standards:* 1.1, 1.3

Focus: Using the preterite forms of **ser** to play a game
Suggestions: As an alternative, assign Step 1 as homework so that students can research facts about famous people on the Internet or in the library. Review students' questions to be sure they are appropriate.
Answers will vary.

Actividad 18 *Standards:* 1.1, 1.3

Focus: Describing personal experiences using the preterite of *ir* and **ser**
Recycle: Leisure activities
Suggestions: Have pairs of students write their answers and then interview each other about their responses.
Answers will vary.

Additional Resources
● WAV Wbk.: Audio Act. 8, p. 51
● Teacher's Resource Book: Audio Script, p. 137
● Audio Program: Track 10

 Assessment
● **ExamView** Quiz on PresEXPRESS
  QuickTake Presenter
● Prueba 3A-4: Irregular preterite verbs: *ir, ser,* p. 74

141

 Gramática

Presentation EXPRESS GRAMMAR

Core Instruction

Standards: 4.1

Resources: Voc. and Gram. Transparency 64; Teacher's Resource Book: Video Script, pp. 139–140; Video Program: Cap. 3A

Suggestions: Ask a volunteer to write the preterite forms of **hacer** on the board as a reference. On a transparency, write the infinitives of each of the four verbs presented here. Tell students a story that uses each of the verbs. Pause when you have to use one of the verbs, and encourage a volunteer to supply it for you.

Actividad 19

Standards: 1.2

Presentation EXPRESS ANSWERS

Resources: Answers on Transparencies

Focus: Using the preterite of **tener, estar,** and **poder** in context

Suggestions: To help students fill in the passage, remind them that in this activity **poder** is followed by an infinitive, **tener** precedes **que,** and **estar** is followed by a place.

Answers:

1. estuvo
2. Tuvo
3. pudieron
4. estuvieron
5. pude
6. tuve
7. tuvimos
8. pudimos
9. estuvo

Common Errors: Students might use the right verb but the wrong ending, especially confusing the first- and third-person endings. Remind them to first be certain of the verb they should use and then decide on the ending.

Extension: Have partners act out the paragraph as a phone conversation between Rosalinda and her friend.

Gramática

Irregular preterite verbs: *hacer, tener, estar, poder*

The preterite forms of *tener, estar,* and *poder* follow a pattern similar to that of the verb *hacer.* Like *hacer,* these verbs do not have any accent marks in the preterite.

(yo)	hice tuve estuve pude	(nosotros) (nosotras)	hicimos tuvimos estuvimos pudimos
(tú)	hiciste tuviste estuviste pudiste	(vosotros) (vosotras)	hicisteis tuvisteis estuvisteis pudisteis
Ud. (él) (ella)	hizo tuvo estuvo pudo	Uds. (ellos) (ellas)	hicieron tuvieron estuvieron pudieron

¿Recuerdas?

Dar is also irregular in the preterite tense: *di, diste, dio, dimos, disteis, dieron.*

GramActiva VIDEO

Want more help with irregular preterite verbs *ir, ser, hacer, tener, estar,* and *poder?* Watch the **GramActiva** video.

hice / fui

Actividad 19 Leer/Escribir

¡Nadie pudo venir!

Rosalinda invitó a varios amigos a ver una película en su casa a las cinco, pero nadie llegó. Completa cada frase con la forma apropiada del verbo *estar, tener* o *poder* para explicar por qué no llegaron.

Fernando __1.__ en la biblioteca por tres horas. __2.__ que escribir un informe muy largo. Jorge y Pati no __3.__ venir porque __4.__ en el banco donde trabajan hasta las ocho. Yo no __5.__ ir a su casa tampoco porque __6.__ que cuidar a mi hermanito. ¡Pobre Rosalinda! Todos nosotros __7.__ que hacer otras cosas y no __8.__ ir a su casa y ella __9.__ allí sola toda la tarde.

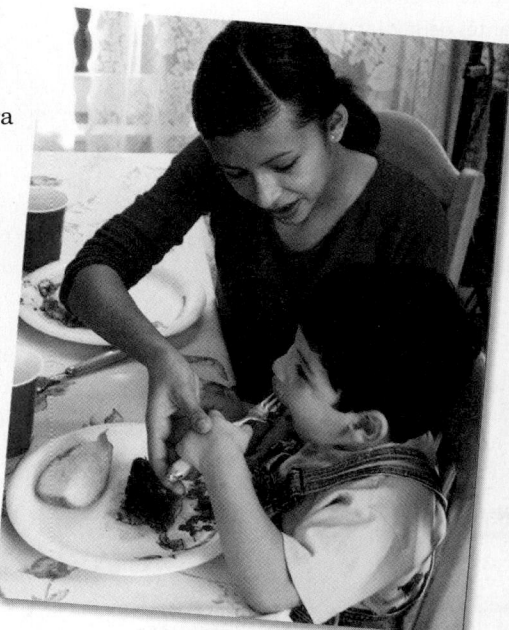

Differentiated Instruction

Solutions for All Learners

Advanced Learners/Pre-AP*

Pre-AP*

Have students work in pairs to create a skit in which one person is calling friends because he or she had a birthday party but nobody came. The other person should play the part of all of the friends, and make excuses as to what he or she had to do. Encourage students to write with humor and use exaggeration in their skit.

Students with Special Needs

Before students begin *Actividad* 21, help those who have listening difficulties by making a transparency with the questions. Circle key words and leave the transparency up to remind students of listening purpose and focus.

Actividad 20 **Hablar**

¿Por qué no hicieron sus quehaceres?

Cuando tus padres vuelven a casa después de un viaje, no entienden por qué tus hermanos y tú no hicieron los quehaceres. Trabaja con otro(a) estudiante para preguntar y contestar.

Modelo

no comprar pan
A —¿Por qué no compraron pan?
B —Porque no pudimos ir al supermercado.

Estudiante A

1. no dar de comer al perro
2. no hacer las camas
3. no ir a la farmacia para comprar champú y jabón
4. no devolver los libros a la biblioteca
5. no enviar las cartas
6. no ir al dentista

Estudiante B

tener que quedarnos en casa con el perro
no poder ir al supermercado
no tener tiempo por la mañana
no poder encontrar su comida
tener que leerlos otra vez
tener que hacer tantos quehaceres
no poder encontrar el buzón

Actividad 21 jdd-0388 **Leer/Escuchar/Escribir**

Una raqueta de tenis nueva

Santiago acaba de comprar una raqueta de tenis. Primero lee las preguntas. Después escucha la descripción dos veces y escribe respuestas a las preguntas.

1. ¿Cómo pudo tener Santiago suficiente dinero para comprar una raqueta de tenis?
2. ¿Cuándo fueron a la tienda de equipo deportivo Santiago y Héctor?
3. Para Santiago, ¿cómo fue la experiencia de buscar una raqueta nueva?
4. ¿Miraron sólo una raqueta o varias?
5. ¿Estuvieron en la tienda por mucho o por poco tiempo?
6. ¿Cuándo escogió Santiago su raqueta nueva?

Actividad 22 **Escribir**

Y tú, ¿qué dices?

Escribe un párrafo en que describes cuándo tú fuiste de compras. Usa las ideas de la experiencia de Santiago en la Actividad 21 como modelo. Puedes incluir:

- cómo conseguiste *(you obtained)* dinero para comprar algo
- si fuiste solo(a) o con otra persona
- adónde fuiste
- si tuviste que ir a diferentes tiendas
- si pudiste decidir inmediatamente
- por cuánto tiempo estuviste en la tienda
- si te gusta lo que compraste

Más práctica

- Practice Workbook, p. 57: 3A-7
- Guided Practice: Grammar Acts., p. 105
- *Real.* para hispanohablantes, pp. 98–99

 **Go Online**
PHSchool.com
For: *Hacer, Tener, Estar, and Poder*
Web Code: jdd-0306

Actividad 20 Standards: 1.1

Focus: Making excuses

Suggestions: Have partners match the most logical responses from Student B to each item for Student A.

Answers will vary.

Actividad 21 Standards: 1.2, 1.3 Presentation EXPRESS AUDIO

Resources: Teacher's Resource Book: Audio Script, p. 137; Audio Program: Track 11; Answers on Transparencies

Focus: Listening comprehension

Suggestions: Have students review the questions before listening.

 **Script:**

El verano pasado trabajé mucho para ganar dinero. Mis abuelos también me dieron dinero para comprar una raqueta de tenis nueva. La semana pasada fui a la tienda de equipo deportivo con mi amigo Héctor. Fue una experiencia divertida para mí. Héctor y yo tuvimos que mirar varias raquetas de diferentes colores y precios. No pude decidir qué raqueta comprar. Estuvimos en la tienda hasta que cerraron sus puertas. Luego escogí la raqueta que tengo. Me encanta mi raqueta.

Answers:

1. Trabajó mucho y sus abuelos le dieron dinero.
2. Fueron a la tienda de equipo deportivo la semana pasada.
3. La experiencia fue divertida.
4. Miraron varias raquetas.
5. Estuvieron en la tienda por mucho tiempo.
6. Santiago escogió su raqueta nueva cuando cerraron sus puertas.

Actividad 22   Standards: 1.3

Focus: Writing about a personal experience

Recycle: Types of stores

Suggestions: Distribute copies of the script for *Actividad 21* for students' reference as they write their paragraphs.

Answers will vary.

Enrich Your Teaching
Resources for All Teachers

Teacher-to-Teacher

Have students prepare skits about being in a support group for people who shop too much. Encourage them to use the preterite to tell what they did when they went shopping. Form groups based on the students' interests: for example, one group may buy too many clothes, another might buy too many CDs. Have students perform their skits for the class.

Teacher-to-Teacher

Have students practice irregular preterite verbs throughout the year by requiring them to give excuses in Spanish. If they miss class, ask them: *¿Por qué no estuviste en clase ayer?* If students don't complete their homework, require them to explain to you why they didn't do it. Ask them: *¿Por qué no hiciste la tarea?*

Pronunciación

Presentation EXPRESS
AUDIO

Core Instruction

 Standards: 4.1

Resources: Teacher's Resource Book: Audio Script, p. 137; Audio Program: Track 13

Suggestions: Demonstrate the importance of stressing the correct syllable by providing examples of incorrect stress in English. Write two of the words from the first list on the board without the accent marks, and have a volunteer read them. Demonstrate the difference after the reading.

Help students understand the proverb: From a fallen tree, you can make firewood. Ask what adage in English might express the same idea as this. (Every cloud has a silver lining).

 **Fondo cultural** *Standards:* 1.2, 2.1, 2.2, 4.2

Suggestions: Bring in a map of your community to help students answer the first question.

Answers will vary but may include:
Características: monumentos, tiendas, servicios y casas
Barrios famosos: Calle Ocho en Miami, Greenwich Village en Nueva York

Block Schedule

Use the Internet as a tool to allow students to visit various neighborhoods in Spanish-speaking countries. Encourage them to take a virtual tour of several cities and neighborhoods. Have them compare neighborhoods in the United States with the ones they find on the Internet.

Keywords:

virtual tours + (Spanish-speaking country)

Theme Project
Students can perform Step 2 at this point. Be sure students understand your corrections. (For more information, see p. 126–a.)

Pronunciación

The written accent jdd-0388

You already know the standard rules for stress and accent in Spanish.

- When words end in a vowel, *n*, or *s*, the stress is on the next-to-last syllable.
- When words end in a consonant (except *n* or *s*), the stress is on the last syllable.
- Words that do not follow these patterns must have a written accent (called *acento ortográfico* or *tilde*). The accent indicates that you should place the stress on this syllable as you pronounce the word.

Listen to and say these examples:

champú	olvidó	cómodo	médico
película	patín	jabón	adiós
demás	césped	fútbol	lápiz

¡Compruébalo! Here are some new words that all require accent marks. Copy the words and, as you hear them pronounced, write the accent mark over the correct vowel.

antropologo	cajon	carcel	ejercito	fosforo
lucho	nilon	util	tipico	lider

Listen to and say the following *refrán*:

Del árbol caído, todos hacen leña.

 **Fondo cultural**

Hay **barrios** *(neighborhoods)* famosos en las ciudades grandes de España y América Latina que tienen su propia identidad. Por ejemplo, el Barrio de Santa Cruz, en Sevilla, España, es el más antiguo de la ciudad y originalmente fue un barrio judío *(Jewish)*. En este barrio, las calles son muy estrechas *(narrow)* y hay monumentos históricos, como la Catedral. Las personas que viven allí se sienten muy orgullosas *(proud)* de las tradiciones, la arquitectura y la historia que existen en su barrio.

- ¿Cuáles son las características de los barrios en general? ¿Hay algún barrio famoso en tu ciudad? ¿Cómo es?

El Barrio de Santa Cruz, en Sevilla, España

Differentiated Instruction
Solutions for All Learners

Multiple Intelligences
Visual/Spatial: Have students pretend to be urban planners and design their own neighborhood. Ask them to write a paragraph describing their community. If possible, have them create a model to use as a visual as they present their neighborhood plan to the class.

Students with Learning Difficulties
For *Actividad 24*, provide a four-frame grid (comic-strip style) for students with sequencing difficulties. In the first frame have students write the starting location and time. For each of the other frames provide the prompts: *cuando llegaste* and *cuanto tiempo estuviste allí*. Have them write a related problem and illustrate it.

Actividad 23 Pensar/Hablar/Escribir

¿Por cuánto tiempo?

Es difícil encontrar el tiempo suficiente para hacer todos los quehaceres necesarios. A veces es necesario estar muy consciente del tiempo que requiere cada actividad que vas a hacer. Con otro(a) estudiante, lee y resuelve (*solve*) este problema matemático.

Conexiones Las matemáticas

1 Ayer Ángela salió de la escuela y fue a la farmacia para comprar champú y jabón. Estuvo allí por 13 minutos.

2 Después caminó al correo en diez minutos. Se quedó allí por 45 minutos mirando y comprando unos sellos bonitos e interesantes.

3 Caminó del correo a su casa en 15 minutos. Llegó a su casa a las 4:40 de la tarde.

la escuela   la farmacia   el correo   la casa

4 Si la farmacia está a dos minutos de la escuela, ¿a qué hora salió Ángela de la escuela?

5 Escribe una frase para indicar a qué hora llegó y salió Ángela de cada lugar.

Actividad 24 Hablar/Escribir

Te toca a ti

Con otro(a) estudiante, escriban un problema original similar al problema matemático de la Actividad 23. Pueden incluir una ilustración. Después cambien (*exchange*) su problema con otro grupo e intenten (*try*) resolverlo.

Fondo cultural

Los sellos, la tradición y la comunidad El tema de esta serie de sellos de España son los trajes tradicionales de las comunidades de España. Durante los festivales anuales de un pueblo o ciudad, los bailadores llevan trajes tradicionales. Los bailes, o danzas, y los trajes de cada comunidad son diferentes.

• ¿Conoces alguna serie de sellos que recuerda tradiciones regionales en los Estados Unidos? ¿Qué otros tipos de series de sellos tenemos en los Estados Unidos?

Trajes tradicionales de regiones de España: Coruña, Córdoba, Granada, Hue va y Sevilla

ciento cuarenta y cinco **145**
Capítulo 3A

Practice and Communicate

 3A

Actividad 23 — *Standards:* 1.2, 3.1 — Presentation EXPRESS ANSWERS

Resources: Answers on Transparencies
Focus: Reading comprehension; cross-curricular connection to math

Suggestions: Provide students with a photocopy of the map so that they may take notes, or have them draw a simple map on their own paper.

Answers:
3:15
Ángela llegó a la farmacia a las 3:17 y salió a las 3:30.
Ella llegó al correo a las 3:40 y salió a las 4:25.

Actividad 24 — *Standards:* 1.1, 1.3, 3.1 — Pre-AP*

Focus: Writing math problems
Suggestions: Remind students to use the preterite in their problems. Have students solve their own problems before exchanging them with another person.

Answers will vary.

Fondo cultural — *Standards:* 1.2, 2.2

Suggestions: Bring in books on stamp collecting and distribute them to groups of students. Assign each group different pages, and have them discuss the stamps' significance.

Answers will vary but may include: stamps of people who played a part in U.S. history or contributed to popular culture; special holidays and observances; history or technology.

Additional Resources

• WAV Wbk.: Audio Act. 9, p. 51
• Teacher's Resource Book: Audio Script, p. 137, Communicative Activity BLM, p. 144
• Audio Program: Track 12

✓ Assessment

• **ExamView** QuickTake Presenter Quiz on PresEXPRESS
• Prueba 3A-5: Irregular preterite verbs: *hacer, tener, estar, poder*, p. 75

Enrich Your Teaching
Resources for All Teachers

Culture Note

La Candelaria is the most notable *barrio* in Bogotá, Colombia's historical center. The city was founded in this area, and many famous writers, artists, and leaders have lived there. Many of the old, colorful buildings have been turned into museums that display artifacts from the country's history and from its struggle for independence.

Teacher-to-Teacher

Have students prepare an audio or video journal in which they narrate the events of their day. Ask them to talk about where they went, what it was like, and how long they were there. Ask students to create comprehension questions for their audience to answer as they view or listen to the tape.

145

Lectura
Core Instruction

Standards: 1.2

Resources: Voc. and Gram. Transparencies: Maps 12, 14, 18

Focus: Reading comprehension of a brochure for Sister Cities International

Suggestions:

Pre-reading: Prepare an outline of the main headings of the brochure and pass it out to students after doing the *Estrategia*. Review its format with them and tell them that they should be looking for important details for each section of the outline as they read.

Reading: Read the brochure to students, pointing out headings and subheadings. Give students time to fill in their outlines after each section.

Post-reading: Ask volunteers to provide examples of information that they included in their outline. Encourage students to add details that they did not have previously. Have students use the outline as they answer the *¿Comprendiste?* and *Y tú, ¿qué dices?* questions.

Bellringer Review
Locate these countries on the maps on pp. xvi–xxvii: *México, La República Dominicana, España*. Have students tell the nationality of two boys from each country.

Pre-AP* Support

- **Activity:** Have students work in groups of four. Assign each student in the group a specific section beginning with *¡Quiero tener una ciudad hermana!* All students should read the entire selection, but only be held responsible for their section. For each section, each student should write a brief summary of the main points, be prepared to define in Spanish any unfamiliar vocabulary, and create three multiple-choice questions to be shared with the group.
- **Pre-AP* Resource Book:** Comprehensive guide to reading skill development, pp. 18–24

¡Adelante!

Lectura

La unidad en la comunidad internacional

Objectives
- Read about the Sister Cities International program
- Learn about open-air markets
- Talk about preparations for a trip
- Watch *En busca de la verdad,* Episodio 1

Estrategia

Using the structure of a text Sometimes the way the text is structured will help you understand the main idea. Look at this brochure and read only the headings. What do you think it is about?

Ciudades Hermanas
Internacional

El programa de "Ciudades Hermanas Internacional" fue creado por el presidente de los Estados Unidos, Dwight D. Eisenhower, en el año 1956. La misión de este programa es promover[1] el intercambio y la cooperación entre los habitantes de ciudades en diferentes países. Hoy en día, más de 1,200 ciudades en los Estados Unidos tienen una ciudad hermana en casi 137 países. A través de[2] la cooperación económica, cultural y educativa, el programa de Ciudades Hermanas construye puentes[3] entre las personas y ayuda a la comprensión entre diferentes culturas.

¡Quiero tener una ciudad hermana!

Cualquier[4] ciudad de los Estados Unidos puede tener una ciudad hermana. Primero es necesario encontrar otra ciudad extranjera.[5] Esta ciudad puede tener alguna relación con la ciudad original. Por ejemplo, ciudades que tienen el mismo nombre, como Toledo,

Ohio, y Toledo, España, pueden asociarse. También las ciudades que celebran el mismo festival pueden formar relaciones de hermandad. Para tener una relación oficial, hay que llenar un formulario en la comisión del programa para las Ciudades Hermanas. La organización tiene que aprobar[6] la petición.

Intercambio económico

El programa de Ciudades Hermanas ayuda a establecer una cooperación económica entre los países. Por ejemplo, varios productos de Toledo, España, se venden en la tienda LaSalle en Toledo, Ohio. Las ciudades de Atlanta, Georgia, y de Salcedo, República Dominicana, también exploran varias posibilidades para intercambiar productos. El intercambio profesional y técnico es importante, como aprendieron los bomberos[7] y policías de la ciudad de Phoenix, Arizona, cuando tomaron clases de español en Sonora, México.

[1] to promote [2] Through [3] bridges [4] Any [5] foreign [6] approve [7] firefighters

146 ciento cuarenta y seis
Tema 3 • Tú y tu comunidad

Differentiated Instruction
Solutions for All Learners

Advanced Learners
Have students imagine that they have the opportunity to become a youth ambassador. Have them research a Spanish-speaking country and write a letter to you describing what they see and do there.

Heritage Language Learners
To help students with structured writing, have them create a magazine article about their community. Ask them to make an outline before writing. Tell them to include a topic, which they will use to write a title, and at least three subtopics to be used as headings. Encourage them to provide several supporting details under each subtopic.

·REGLAS·
para los jóvenes embajadores

Los jóvenes embajadores tienen que:

- obedecer las leyes[8] del país de la ciudad hermana
- respetar las costumbres del país
- ayudar a la familia con las tareas domésticas

- participar en muchas actividades para aprender sobre la cultura del país
- tratar de[9] hablar un poco en el idioma[10] del país

Intercambio cultural

Hay diferentes posibilidades para un intercambio cultural. Los proyectos posibles incluyen:

- un festival con bailes y comida en honor a su ciudad hermana.
- una exposición de arte. Por ejemplo, la ciudad de Phoenix, Arizona, dio una exposición de arte en Sonora, México.
- el intercambio de música, grabaciones o dramas.

Intercambio educativo

En programas de intercambio educativo, los jóvenes son embajadores[11] a las ciudades hermanas. Representan a los Estados Unidos en su viaje a otra ciudad. Se quedan con familias y así

aprenden mucho sobre la cultura de ese país. Luego un embajador del país extranjero viene a los Estados Unidos y se queda con la familia del estudiante estadounidense.

▲ *Let's All Play Together / Juguemos todos juntos* de Francisco Magano fue uno de los ganadores en el año 2001 del concurso anual de arte para jóvenes. Artistas entre 13 y 18 años de todos los países pueden enviar sus obras para competir. Se exhiben las obras de los ganadores en varias ciudades.

Let's All Play Together (2002), Francisco Magano. Sister Cities International Young Artists.

[8] laws [9] try to [10] language [11] ambassadors

¿Comprendiste?

1. ¿Por qué es importante el programa de las Ciudades Hermanas Internacional?
2. ¿Qué es necesario para tener una ciudad hermana?
3. ¿Por qué es importante el intercambio económico? ¿El intercambio cultural?
4. Si tu ciudad tiene una ciudad hermana, ¿qué puedes hacer como joven embajador?
5. ¿Cuál es la ciudad hermana de Phoenix, Arizona? ¿De Atlanta, Georgia? ¿De Toledo, Ohio?
6. En tu opinión, ¿cuál es la regla más importante para los jóvenes embajadores?

Y tú, ¿qué dices?

Imagina que los estudiantes de una clase de tu ciudad hermana vienen a tu escuela. Prepara un horario de lo que pueden hacer y ver en tu escuela y en tu comunidad.

Más práctica

- WAV Wbk., Writing, p. 55
- Guided Practice: *Lectura*, p. 106
- *Real.* para hispanohablantes, pp. 102–103

Go Online PHSchool.com
For: Internet Activity
Web Code: jdd-0307

¿Comprendiste?

Standards: 1.2

Resources: Answers on Transparencies

Focus: Verifying reading comprehension

Suggestions: Have students look for key words in each question that will guide them to the information. If students have made outlines, suggest that they highlight, underline, or make notes on their outline to help them answer the questions.

Answers may vary but will include:

1. El programa construye puentes entre las personas y ayuda a la comprensión entre diferentes culturas.
2. Es necesario encontrar otra ciudad extranjera que tiene alguna relación. También hay que llenar un formulario en la comisión del programa para las Ciudades Hermanas y la organización tiene que aprobar la petición.
3. El intercambio económico ayuda a establecer una cooperación entre los países. El intercambio cultural ayuda a aprender sobre la cultura del otro país.
4. Puedes viajar a otra ciudad para representar a los Estados Unidos. También puedes quedarte con una familia y aprender mucho sobre la cultura de la ciudad hermana.
5. La ciudad hermana de Phoenix, Arizona, es Sonora, México; la ciudad hermana de Atlanta, Georgia, es Salcedo, República Dominicana; y la ciudad hermana de Toledo, Ohio, es Toledo, España.
6. Answers will vary.

Y tú, ¿qué dices?

Standards: 1.3, 5.1

Suggestions: Have students review information they have prepared for various activities throughout the chapter to help them answer the questions.

Answers will vary.

For Further Reading

Student Resources: Realidades para hispanohablantes: Lectura 2, pp. 104–105; Lecturas para hispanohablantes 2: "Doña primavera," p. 61, "Port Aventura," pp. 82–84, "La niña sale de compras," pp. 99–100

Enrich Your Teaching
Resources for All Teachers

Teacher-to-Teacher

Have students research cities in Spanish-speaking countries to find one that might be an appropriate sister city for your town. Ask them to write a short proposal that outlines the relationship between the two cities.

Internet Search

To have students learn more about what cities participate in this organization, have them look at the Web site.

Keywords:

Sister Cities International

La cultura en vivo

Core Instruction

Standards: 1.1, 1.2, 2.1, 2.2, 4.2

Focus: Reading about outdoor markets; bargaining at an outdoor market

Suggestions: Ask students to name flea markets or outdoor markets in or near your community. Have students describe experiences that they have had at these types of markets. Did they find good prices? Did they pay full price for items? What types of goods were available at the market they visited?

If possible, bring in a travel video of one of the places mentioned to show students an outdoor market. As students watch the video, have them take notes on interactions between the vendors and the buyers.

Bring in "products" for students to sell at your market such as food, school supplies, or books. Assign some students the role of vendor, and give them items to sell. The others will be buyers. Give the buyers a fixed amount of fake money to spend at the market. If available, bring in coins from a Spanish-speaking country. Remind students that they want to bargain with the vendor, and award a prize to the buyer who can get the most items for their money. Make sure students have the opportunity to play the role of both the vendor and the buyer.

Additional Resources

Student Resource: Realidades para hispanohablantes, p. 106

La cultura en vivo

Los mercados al aire libre

En los países hispanohablantes, los mercados al aire libre son muy populares. Son lugares para comprar y vender toda clase de cosas, como comida, productos del campo, artesanías y ropa. Los vendedores ponen sus tiendas en la calle y la gente mira los productos. Estos mercados son buenos lugares para ver a los amigos, comer algo o pasear.

En México, estos mercados se llaman *tianguis,* una palabra que en náhuatl significa "el lugar del mercado." El *tianguis,* o mercado al aire libre, es una tradición antigua que viene de los aztecas.

Pero no hay mercados sólo en México. En Ecuador, el mercado de Otavalo es muy conocido por sus artesanías. En La Paz, Bolivia, un mercado popular es el mercado de las Brujas. En Madrid, España, los domingos se abre el mercado de El Rastro. Cuando los compradores pasan por las calles, los vendedores los invitan a comprar, y les preguntan, *¿Qué va a llevar?*

Objetivo

Preparar un día de mercado en tu clase

Procedimiento

Los estudiantes deben formar dos grupos. Los estudiantes en Grupo 1 (los vendedores) deben traer algo a la clase para vender y decidir el precio del objeto o producto. Los estudiantes en Grupo 2 (los compradores) deben visitar a los vendedores y, si quieren, comprar su mercancía. Pueden regatear *(bargain)* para bajar el precio. ¡Buena suerte!

El Rastro, en Madrid, España

Mercado en Zumbagua, Ecuador

Expresiones y frases útiles

Comprador
¿Cuánto cuesta(n) . . . ?
¿Cuál es el precio de . . . ?
¡Uf! Es mucho . . .
¿No me lo puede dar por . . . ?
¿Me vende esto por . . . ?
Es un buen precio. Muy bien.

Vendedor
¿Qué va a llevar?
¿Qué desea Ud.?
¡Cómprame algo!
Cuesta . . . / El precio es . . .
¡Lo siento!

Differentiated Instruction
Solutions for All Learners

Students with Special Needs

To help hearing-impaired students, have them and their partners write the bargaining expressions on flashcards. Have the partner hold up the flashcard with the message that they want to use. Be sure to demonstrate with the partner how to use non-verbal communication and flashcards.

Multiple Intelligences

Logical/Mathematical: Ask students to survey the vendors to see how much they sold. Have them write a sales report with the total of the original prices and the total of the prices at which the items were sold. Ask students to include the amount of each vendor's losses in their report, assuming that buyers were successful bargainers.

Preparándose para un viaje

Una bella playa de Cancún, México

Task
You are going to visit your best friend from Mexico for a week during summer vacation. Your friend lives in Mérida, Mexico, where it is very hot and humid during the summer. Your friend has already told you some plans: visit Mayan ruins nearby, spend time with friends, and go to the beach in Cancún for two days. Are you prepared to go? Explain what you did to prepare for the trip.

1 Prepare Make a list of ten items you need to bring for the week. Do you already have them at home? Do you need to buy them? Where do you need to go to get them? Use a chart like this one to organize your thoughts.

Cosas que necesito	¿Ya lo / la compré?	¿Dónde?
sombrero para el sol	sí, lo compré	el almacén

2 Practice Go through your presentation several times. You can use your notes in practice, but not when you present. Try to:

- talk about everything you did to get ready for the trip
- use complete sentences
- speak clearly

Estrategia
Using charts
Create a chart to help you think through the key information you will want to talk about. This will help you speak more effectively.

Modelo

Para visitar a mi amigo en Mérida necesito un sombrero para el sol, pasta dental y un cepillo de dientes. No tuve que comprar la pasta dental ni el cepillo. Pero tuve que comprar un sombrero para el sol. También tuve que ir al banco para cobrar un cheque que mi mamá me dio.

3 Present Talk about your preparation for the trip. You might want to bring in props to show some of your preparations.

4 Evaluation Your teacher may give you a rubric for how the presentation will be graded. You will probably be graded on:

- completion of task
- how you related information about things needed for the trip
- how well you were understood

Representación del dios
Quetzalcóatl, Chichén Itzá, México

Presentación oral
Core Instruction

Standards: 1.3, 3.1

Focus: Speaking about vacation preparations

Suggestions: Many students may not know much about the region of Mexico that they will be visiting. Have them research Mérida and Cancún in Mexico. Once they are familiar with these places, have them brainstorm items that they will need there and give reasons why they might need them. Two important factors to consider are weather and the activities they will do.

Review the four steps listed in the student book. Emphasize the importance of organization in the presentation. Encourage students to discuss their plans in segments—what they are already prepared for, what they need to buy, and where they need to go, for example.

Pre-AP* Support

- **Pre-AP* Resource Book:** Comprehensive guide to Pre-AP* speaking skill development, pp. 36–46

Portfolio

Record students' oral presentations on cassette or videotape for inclusion in their portfolios.

Additional Resources
Student Resources: Realidades para hispanohablantes, p. 107; Guided Practice: Presentación oral, p. 107

✓ Assessment
- Assessment Program: Rubrics, p. T28

RUBRIC	Score 1	Score 3	Score 5
Completeness of your task	You provide some of the information required.	You provide most of the information required.	You provide all of the information required.
Talking about things you need for the trip	You include up to five items.	You include up to eight items.	You include ten or more items.
How easily you are understood	You are difficult to understand and have many grammatical errors.	You are fairly easy to understand and have occasional grammatical errors.	You are easy to understand and have very few grammatical errors.

Videomisterio

Core Instruction

Standards: 1.2, 3.2, 5.2

Resources: Teacher's Resource Book: Video Script, pp. 140–141; Video Program: Cap. 3A; Video Program Teacher's Guide: Cap. 3A

Focus: Introducing the events and vocabulary of this episode; scanning and reading the episode summary

Personajes importantes

Linda Toledo, student in San Antonio
Carmen Toledo, Linda's mother; teacher
El abuelo *(flashback),* Linda's dead grandfather
El director Ruiz, principal of a bilingual school in San Antonio
El señor Balzar, travel agent in San Antonio

Synopsis: The story begins in San Antonio, Texas, where Linda Toledo attends a bilingual school. Linda's mother, Carmen, is a teacher at Linda's school, and is in charge of setting an exchange program in Guanajuato, Mexico.

Suggestions:

Pre-viewing: Review the introduction to Guanajuato in *Capítulo* 1A, and tell students that they will see this city in the video. Have a volunteer read the *Nota cultural* aloud. Ask if there are similar hotels in the United States (bed and breakfast inns, renovated mansions, etc.). Briefly discuss why they are popular.

Point out the *Palabras para comprender* to the class, giving examples in context and writing sentences on the board. Remind students that these words are used only to help them understand the episode, and that they are not otherwise responsible for learning the words as vocabulary.

Videomisterio

En busca de la verdad

Episodio 1

Antes de ver el video

"Esa noche, mi mamá, mi papá, mi hermano y yo nos reunimos y hablamos sobre el viaje".

Nota cultural En Guanajuato, muchas haciendas* antiguas ahora son hoteles para turistas. También hay hoteles nuevos que conservan el estilo colonial de México. Casi todos tienen verdes jardines con árboles y flores, fuentes de agua y patios con pisos de piedra. ¡Es como volver 300 años atrás en el tiempo!

*ranches

"Hay una escuela en Guanajuato muy interesada en un intercambio".

Resumen del episodio

La historia empieza en San Antonio, Texas. Allí vive y estudia en una escuela bilingüe Linda Toledo. Carmen, la mamá de Linda, es maestra en la misma escuela y quiere establecer un programa de intercambio con una escuela mexicana. Carmen decide visitar una escuela en Guanajuato y va con Linda a una agencia de viajes para hacer los planes del viaje. Al final del episodio Linda recuerda a su abuelo en el hospital.

Palabras para comprender
intercambio exchange
próximo next
Segunda Guerra Mundial World War II
soldado soldier
ciudadano citizen
querido, -a dear

150 ciento cincuenta
Tema 3 • Tú y tu comunidad

Differentiated Instruction
Solutions for All Learners

Advanced Learners
Ask students to write two or three sentences about Linda Toledo and her mother, Carmen. Have students describe both their physical appearances and their personalities.

Heritage Language Learners
As an ongoing project, have students prepare a poster on each city mentioned in the *Videomisterio.* They should include visuals, brief descriptions, and the importance of the city in the storyline.

"¿En qué puedo servirles?".

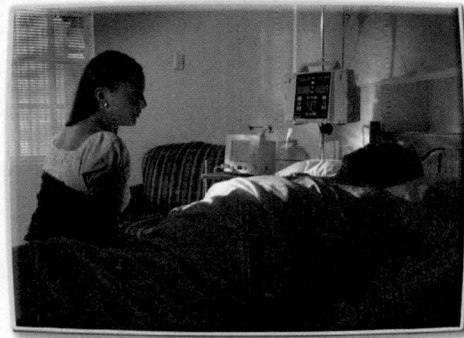

"¿Cómo estás, abuelito?".

Después de ver el video

¿Comprendiste?

A. Lee las siguientes frases y escribe quién dijo cada una: Linda, Carmen, el Sr. Balzar, el director, Berta o el abuelo.

1. "Hay una escuela en Guanajuato muy interesada en un intercambio."

2. "¿Qué le parece si me acompaña mi hija Linda?".

3. "Hay un vuelo que sale a las diez de la mañana y otro, a las seis de la tarde".

4. "Así llegamos un poco más temprano".

5. "¿Y ya tienen reservaciones de hotel en Guanajuato?".

6. "Voy a reservarles un buen hotel".

7. "Pero, ¿qué familia, abuelo?".

8. "Siempre recuerdo a mi querida familia mexicana".

B. Termina las siguientes frases explicando lo que sucede en el videomisterio:

1. El Sr. Balzar es _____.

2. Carmen y Linda quieren _____.

3. El Sr. Balzar llama a Berta Toledo en Guanajuato para _____.

4. Linda recuerda a su abuelo cuando _____.

5. El abuelo de Linda le dice que hablen otro día porque _____.

C. Mira la escena de la primera foto en la página anterior. Son el director y Carmen. Escribe un resumen de lo que hablaron.

For: More on *En busca de la verdad*
Web Code: jdd-0209

Enrich Your Teaching
Resources for All Teachers

Teacher-to-Teacher

To help students better understand the *episodios,* have them identify the basic elements of a plot for the *Videomisterio.* Review the meanings of each element: **el enredo** or **la complicación** ("set up" or "introduction"), **el punto culminante** ("climax"), and **el desenredo** or **la resolución** ("outcome"). Point out that this

formula can also be used for key events in the story. As an ongoing project, you may want to have students create posters that outline these elements for each *episodio*.

Suggestions:

Visual scanning: Direct attention to the photos. Have students read the captions and try to guess what the characters may be talking about.

Before students read the *Resumen del episodio* have them scan the text and find at least three cognates *(historia, bilingüe, mamá, establecer, programa, mexicana, visitar, agencia, planes, hospital).* Then have them read the *Resumen del episodio.* Ask one or two comprehension questions.

Viewing: Play *Episodio* 1 for the class. If there is time after viewing the full episode, go back and replay key moments that you wish to highlight. Remind students that they may not understand every word they hear in the video, but that they should listen for overall understanding.

Post-viewing: Complete the *¿Comprendiste?* in class.

¿Comprendiste?

 *Standards:* 1.2, 1.3

Resources: Answers on Transparencies
Focus: Verifying comprehension; reviewing the plot

Suggestions: List the main characters of this episode on the board. You may want to play the video (or the audio only) and stop at each of the statements to have students identify the speaker.

Answers:
A:
1. el director Ruiz
2. Carmen
3. el Sr. Balzar
4. Linda
5. el Sr. Balzar
6. Berta
7. Linda
8. el abuelo

B: Answers will vary but may include:
1. un agente de viajes
2. comprar dos boletos de avión
3. reservar una habitación de hotel para Carmen y Linda
4. pasa frente al hospital con Carmen
5. está cansado y tiene que dormir

C: Answers will vary.

Additional Resources

- *En busca de la verdad* Video Workbook, Episode 1
- *En busca de la verdad* Teacher's Video Guide: Answer Key

151

Review Activities

To talk about places in a community: Ask students to work in pairs to quiz each other. Have them take turns drawing pictures of and identifying different places in the community.

To talk about mail: Ask students to write a postcard about where they went over the weekend. Have them role-play buying stamps, mailing a letter, and locating a mailbox.

To talk about items in a sporting goods store: Show students pictures of famous athletes and ask them to name the items that each would buy at a sporting-goods store.

To talk about pharmacy products: Bring four sets of the pharmacy-related items to class. Put three of the four pharmacy-related items in each of four bags. Give the bags to students. Have them take the items out and tell what they bought and what they forgot to buy (the missing item).

To talk about errands: Provide students with pictures of places in their community, and have them describe the errands they can do at each location. Ask follow-up questions: *¿A qué hora se abre el banco? ¿Vas a la farmacia a pie?*

Portfolio

Invite students to review the activities they completed in this chapter, including written reports, posters or other visuals, tapes of oral presentations, or other projects. Have them select one or two items that they feel best demonstrate their achievements in Spanish to include in their portfolios. Have them include this with the Chapter Checklist and Self-Assessment Worksheet.

Additional Resources

Student Resources: Realidades para hispanohablantes, p. 108

 **CD-ROM**

PuzzleView Web Code: jdd-0308

Teacher Resources:
- Teacher's Resource Book: Situation Cards, p. 145, Clip Art, pp. 148–151
- Assessment Program: Chapter Checklist and Self-Assessment Worksheet, pp. T56–T57

152

Repaso del capítulo

Vocabulario y gramática

jdd-0389

To prepare for the test, check to see if you . . .
- know the new vocabulary and grammar
- can perform the tasks on p. 153

to talk about places in a community

el banco	bank
el centro	downtown
el consultorio	doctor's / dentist's office
la estación de servicio, *pl.* las estaciones de servicio	service station
la farmacia	pharmacy
el supermercado	supermarket

to talk about mail

el buzón, *pl.* los buzones	mailbox
la carta	letter
echar una carta	to mail a letter
el correo	post office
enviar *(i → í)*	to send
el sello	stamp
la tarjeta	card

to talk about items in a sporting-goods store

el equipo deportivo	sports equipment
el palo de golf	golf club
los patines	skates
la pelota	ball
la raqueta de tenis	tennis racket

to talk about pharmacy products

el cepillo de dientes	toothbrush
el champú	shampoo
el jabón	soap
la pasta dental	toothpaste

to make excuses

se me olvidó	I forgot

For *Vocabulario adicional,* see pp. 498–499.

to talk about errands

cerrar *(e → ie)*	to close
cobrar un cheque	to cash a check
cuidar a	to take care of
el dentista, la dentista	dentist
devolver *(o → ue)* (un libro)	to return (a book)
la gasolina	gasoline
ir a pie	to go on foot
llenar (el tanque)	to fill (the tank)
el médico, la médica	doctor
sacar (un libro)	to take out, to check out (a book)
se abre	opens
se cierra	closes

other useful words and expressions

caramba	good gracious
casi	almost
¡Cómo no!	Of course!
en seguida	right away
hasta	until
por	for (how long)
pronto	soon
Hasta pronto.	See you soon.
quedarse	to stay
todavía	still
varios, -as	various, several

preterite of *ir* (to go) and *ser* (to be)

fui	fuimos
fuiste	fuisteis
fue	fueron

preterite of *tener, estar,* and *poder*

tuve estuve pude	tuvimos estuvimos pudimos
tuviste estuviste pudiste	tuvisteis estuvisteis pudisteis
tuvo estuvo pudo	tuvieron estuvieron pudieron

direct object pronouns: *lo, la, los, las*

Differentiated Instruction
Solutions for All Learners

Advanced Learners

Have pairs of students interview each other to find out what each other's favorite pharmacy products and places to shop are. For example: *¿Qué supermercado te gusta más? Me gusta más King's. ¿Qué jabón te gusta más? Me gusta X.*

Students with Learning Difficulties

For additional vocabulary practice, have pairs of students make vocabulary flashcards for the vocabulary words. Tell them to put photos, postcards, or ads from an old phonebook on one side and the word on the other. Have one student show the picture while the other recalls the vocabulary word or phrase. Then have students reverse roles.

Preparación para el examen

Más práctica

● Practice Workbook: Puzzle, p. 58
● Practice Workbook: Organizer, p. 59

 **Go Online** PHSchool.com

For: Test Preparation
Web Code: jdd-C308

jdd-0389

On the exam you will be asked to . . .	Here are practice tasks similar to those you will find on the exam . . .	If you need review . . .
1 Escuchar Listen and understand as people tell where they went and what they did there	As sponsor for the school's summer trip to Mexico, the Spanish teacher has heard many excuses about why students don't return to the bus in time to depart for the next stop. Listen to the excuses to determine where the students went and why they were late.	**pp. 130–133** *A primera vista* **p. 135** Actividad 6 **p. 136** Actividad 8 **p. 143** Actividad 21
2 Hablar Ask and respond to questions about whether you did certain things that you had to do	To avoid any delays for the next day's tour, the sponsor for the Mexico City summer trip asked each student if he or she prepared the night before. She wants you to help her next time. How would you ask someone if he or she did the following: (a) cashed a check; (b) bought stamps; (c) sent postcards to friends; (d) went to the pharmacy to buy soap and toothpaste? With a partner, practice asking and answering these questions.	**p. 134** Actividad 5 **p. 135** Actividad 7 **p. 136** Actividad 8 **p. 143** Actividad 20 **p. 149** *Presentación oral*
3 Leer Read and understand what people say they received as gifts in the past	You're helping your classmate read the answers to a survey he is conducting for his Spanish project. The survey question was: *¿Cuál es el regalo más loco que recibiste este año?* Look at the first response. Can you identify what the gift was and why the person thought it was silly? *Recibí un cupón (coupon) para llenar el tanque de mi coche, pero no tengo coche. Tuve que venderlo el año pasado.*	**p. 132–133** **p. 146–147** *Lectura*
4 Escribir Write responses to questions about things you have bought in the past	You decided to answer some of the other questions on your friend's survey. What would you write for the following question: *¿Qué hiciste para ganar dinero el verano pasado y qué compraste con el dinero?*	**p. 137** Actividad 11 **p. 139** Actividad 14 **p. 143** Actividad 22
5 Pensar Demonstrate an understanding of the popularity of outdoor markets in Spanish-speaking countries	Vendors and buyers enjoy the open-air markets so popular in Spanish-speaking countries. How would both of them spend their day at the market? What might they sell and buy?	**p. 148** *La cultura en vivo*

ciento cincuenta y tres **153**
Capítulo 3A

✓ **Differentiated** Assessment
Solutions for All Learners

STUDENTS NEEDING EXTRA HELP
• **Alternate Assessment Program:**
  Examen del capítulo 3A
• **Audio Program CD 20:** Chap. 3A, Track 6

HERITAGE LEARNERS
• **Assessment Program: Realidades para hispanohablantes:** Examen del capítulo 3A
• **Exam**View **Heritage Learner Test Bank**

ADVANCED/PRE-AP*
• **Exam**View **Pre-AP* Test Bank**
• **Pre-AP* Resource Book,** pp. 104–107

Performance Tasks

Presentation EXPRESS ANSWERS

 Standards: 1.1, 1.2, 1.3, 2.2, 4.1, 4.2

Student Resource: Realidades para hispanohablantes, p. 109
Teacher Resources: Teacher's Resource Book: Audio Script, p. 138; Audio Program: Track 15; Answers on Transparencies

1. Escuchar

Suggestions: Have students make two columns on a sheet of paper: *¿Adónde fue?* and *¿Por qué llegó tarde?* Encourage them to take notes.

Script and Answers:
1. Lo siento, señora. Fui al banco a las cuatro y media para cobrar mi cheque. El banco se cierra a las cinco y tuve que ir en seguida. *(The person had to rush to the bank before it closed at 5:00.)*
2. ¡Caramba, señora! Se me olvidó regresar. Fui a la tienda de equipo deportivo y compré una pelota. *(The person was at the sporting goods store and forgot to come back.)*
3. Lo siento, señora. Fui a la farmacia para comprar un nuevo cepillo de dientes, pero la tienda no se abre hasta las dos y tuve que esperar. *(The person went to the pharmacy and had to wait because it didn't open until 2:00.)*
4. ¡Hola, señora! Fui al correo para comprar sellos. Tuve que mandar una tarjeta a mi mamá. *(The person went to the post office to buy stamps to mail a card to her mother.)*

2. Hablar

Suggestions: Have students respond negatively to two of the questions.

Answers will vary.

3. Leer

Suggestions: Have students draw a cartoon of the situation to show their understanding of the reading.

Answers:
A coupon for free gas. He didn't have a car.

4. Escribir

Suggestions: Give each person in the class the name of a different place in your community. Have students pretend that they worked at those locations.

Answers will vary.

5. Pensar

Suggestions: Refer students to the photographs on p. 148.

Answers will vary.

✓ **Assessment**
• **Exam**View **Quiz on PresEXPRESS**
• Assessment Program: Examen del capítulo
• **Exam**View **Test Bank: Tests A and B**
• Audio Program CD 20: Chap. 3A, Track 6

♻ **RECYCLE**

A ver si recuerdas

Vocabulary
• Las preposiciones y los medios de transporte

Grammar
• The verbs *salir, decir,* and *venir*

A primera vista	Manos a la obra	¡Adelante!	Repaso

Learning Sequence

INPUT	PRACTICE	APPLICATION	REVIEW
• Introduce vocabulary and grammar within an authentic context.	• Practice and develop new vocabulary. • Learn and practice new grammar structures.	• Apply vocabulary and grammar through culminating, theme-based activities. • Apply skill development.	• Review vocabulary and grammar.

Objectives

Read, listen to, and interpret information about • Places in a city or town • Driving and transportation	• Talk about getting to places in town and types of transportation. • Give directions. • Talk about good driving habits. • Give commands to other people. • Use the direct object pronouns *me, te,* and *nos.*	• Read about defensive driving. • Describe neighborhoods in Spanish-speaking countries. • Make a poster on safe driving practices. • Watch *En busca de la verdad, Episodio 2.*	• Prepare for the chapter test.

Culture

• Diego Rivera	• *La plaza mayor* • *Permiso de manejar* • *El metro de la Ciudad de México*	• *La carretera Panamericana* • *El barrio*	• Explain the concept of *barrio* and its cultural importance.

Vocabulary	Grammar	Learner Support	
• Words related to driving • Directions	• Direct object pronouns: *me, te, nos* • Irregular affirmative *tú* commands • Present progressive: Irregular forms	**STRATEGIES** • Reading for further information • Context clues • Using illustrations	**RECYCLING** ♻ • Actividades 6, 8 • Actividad 9 • Prepositions of location • *Hay* • Commands

RECYCLING (continued)
• Places in town
• Preterite verb forms
• Family vocabulary
• The present progressive
• The present tense of *estar*

Chapter Features

Exploración del lenguaje

Los gestos—gestures and body language

Conexiones

Art: *El camión,* de Frida Kahlo

El español en el mundo del trabajo

The role of Spanish speakers in the United States tourist industry

Beyond the Classroom: States & Countries

Nueva York
España
Puerto Rico
México
Costa Rica
Venezuela
Argentina

Student Resources

TECHNOLOGY

ONLINE

Interactive Textbook
• Student Edition Online plus audio, video, and flashcards

Go Online Companion Web Site
• Tutorial activities • Internet links
• Self-tests   • Downloadable MP3 audio files
• **PuzzleView**

CD-ROM

Interactive Textbook CD-ROM
Student Edition on CD-ROM plus audio, video, and flashcards

MindPoint CD-ROM
QUIZ SHOW

PRINT MATERIAL

CORE INSTRUCTION

Practice Workbook, pp. 60–70
• Review   • Vocabulary
• Grammar   • Puzzle
• Organizer

Writing, Audio & Video Activities, pp. 56–66
• Video   • Audio
• Writing

Grammar Study Guide 1–2 (or 3–4)

Differentiated Instruction

STUDENTS NEEDING EXTRA HELP

Guided Practice Activities, pp. 108–126
• Vocabulary Flash Cards and Vocabulary Check
• Grammar Activities
• Presentación escrita

HERITAGE LEARNERS

Realidades para hispanohablantes, pp. 110–129

Lecturas para hispanohablantes
• "Los problemas de la ciudad," pp. 15–16
• "Una carta a Dios," pp. 57–59

ADVANCED/PRE-AP*

Pre-AP* Resource Book: Student Activity Sheet, p. 107

Teacher Resources

TECHNOLOGY

Audio Program   Fine Art Transparencies
Video Program   Vocabulary and Grammar
                Transparencies
                Answers on Transparencies

TeacherEXPRESS CD-ROM
• Lesson Planner   • Vocabulary Clip Art
• Web Resources   • Teaching Resources
• Teacher Edition with Interactive Links

PresentationEXPRESS CD-ROM
• Vocabulary   • Tranparencies and Maps
• Grammar   • Photo Gallery
• Audio   • Clip Art

PH SuccessNet ONLINE
• Access to grades and reports from Online Interactive Textbook

ExamView on Presentation Express
QuickTake Presenter CD-ROM
• Vocabulary Quizzes   • Chapter Test
• Grammar Quizzes

TeacherEXPRESS CD-ROM
• Assessment Program
• **ExamView** Test Banks A and B
  test generator

PRINT MATERIAL

CORE INSTRUCTION

Teacher's Resource Book, pp. 158–184
• Input Script   • Video Script
• Answer Keys   • GramActiva Blackline Masters
• Vocabulary Clip Art • Chapter Resource Checklist
• School-to-Home Connection Letters
• Communicative Activities Blackline Masters

TPR Stories, pp. 44–49

CORE ASSESSMENT

Assessment Program, pp. 83–96
• Pruebas
   Vocabulary Recognition
   Vocabulary Production
   Direct object pronouns: *me, te, nos*
   Irregular affirmative *tú* commands
   Present progressive: Irregular forms
• Examen del capítulo   • Speaking and Writing Rubrics

Teacher's Resource Book, p. 172
• Situation Cards

TPR Stories, pp. 44–49

Differentiated Instruction

STUDENTS NEEDING EXTRA HELP

Guided Practice Activities Teacher's Guide, pp. T54–T63

HERITAGE LEARNERS

Realidades para hispanohablantes Teacher's Guide, pp. 56–65

Lecturas para hispanohablantes Teacher's Guide, pp. 4, 21–22

ADVANCED/PRE-AP*

Pre-AP* Resource Book: Resources Chart, p. 105

Differentiated Assessment

STUDENTS NEEDING EXTRA HELP

Alternate Assessment Program
• Examen del capítulo, pp. 35–40

HERITAGE LEARNERS

Assessment Program: Realidades para hispanohablantes Teacher's Guide, pp. T116–T120

ExamView Heritage Learner
test generator Test Bank

ADVANCED/PRE-AP*

Pre-AP* Resource Book: Teacher Activity Sheet, p. 106

ExamView Pre-AP* Test Bank
test generator

Go Online
PHSchool.com
For: Teacher Home Page
Web Code: jdk-1001

	Warm-up / Assess	Preview Present / Practice Communicate		Wrap-up / Homework Options
DAY 1	**Warm-up (5 min.)** • Homework check • Return Examen del capítulo: Capítulo 3A	**A ver si recuerdas . . . (10 min.)** • Presentation: Las preposiciones y los medios de transporte • Actividades 1, 2 • Presentation: *Salir, decir, venir* • Actividades 3, 4	**Chapter Opener (10 min.)** • Objectives • Fondo cultural **A primera vista (15 min.)** • Presentation: Vocabulario y gramática en contexto • Actividades 1, 2	**Wrap-up and Homework Options (5 min.)** • Practice Workbook 3B-A, 3B-B, 3B-1, 3B-2 • Go Online
DAY 2	**Warm-up (10 min.)** • Homework check	**A primera vista (35 min.)** • Presentation: Videohistoria *¿Cómo llegamos a la plaza?* • View: Videohistoria	• Video Activities 1, 2, 3, 4 • Actividad 3	**Wrap-up and Homework Options (5 min.)** • Practice Workbook 3B-3, 3B-4 • Go Online • Prueba 3B-1: Vocabulary recognition
DAY 3	**Warm-up (10 min.)** • Actividad 4 • Homework check ✔**Assessment (10 min.)** • Prueba 3B-1: Vocabulary recognition	**Manos a la obra (25 min.)** • Actividades 6, 7, 8, 9, 10 • Fondo cultural		**Wrap-up and Homework Options (5 min.)** • Actividades 5, 11 • Heritage Learner Workbook 3B-1, 3B-2 • Prueba 3B-2: Vocabulary production
DAY 4	**Warm-up (10 min.)** • Actividad 10 • Homework check ✔**Assessment (10 min.)** • Prueba 3B-2: Vocabulary production	**Manos a la obra (25 min.)** • Audio Activities 5, 6 • Presentation: Direct object pronouns: *me, te, nos* • Actividades 12, 13		**Wrap-up and Homework Options (5 min.)** • Practice Workbook 3B-5 • Writing Activity 11 • Go Online
DAY 5	**Warm-up (10 min.)** • Actividad 14 • Homework check	**Manos a la obra (35 min.)** • Actividad 15 • Audio Activity 7 • Presentation: Irregular affirmative *tú* commands • View: GramActiva video	• Actividades 17, 18 • Fondo cultural • Exploración del lenguaje • Audio Activity 8	**Wrap-up and Homework Options (5 min.)** • Practice Workbook 3B-6 • Writing Activity 12 • Go Online • Heritage Learner Workbook 3B-4 • Pruebas 3B-3, 3B-4: Direct object pronouns: *me, te, nos;* Irregular affirmative *tú* commands
DAY 6	**Warm-up (10 min.)** • Actividad 16 • Homework check ✔**Assessment (15 min.)** • Pruebas 3B-3, 3B-4	**Manos a la obra (20 min.)** • Presentation: Present progressive: irregular forms • View: GramActiva video • Actividades 19, 20 • Fondo cultural		**Wrap-up and Homework Options (5 min.)** • Practice Workbook 3B-7 • Writing Activity 13 • Go Online • Heritage Learner Workbook 3B-5 • Prueba 3B-5: Present progressive: irregular forms
DAY 7	**Warm-up (10 min.)** • Communicative Activity • Homework check ✔**Assessment (10 min.)** • Prueba 3B-5	**Manos a la obra (20 min.)** • Audio Activity 9 • El español en el mundo del trabajo • Actividades 21, 22	**¡Adelante! (10 min.)** • Presentación escrita: Steps 1, 5	**Wrap-up and Homework Options (5 min.)** • Presentación escrita: Step 2
DAY 8	**Warm-up (5 min.)** • Homework check	**¡Adelante! (40 min.)** • Presentación escrita: Step 3 • Lectura	• ¿Comprendiste? / Y tú, ¿qué dices? • Fondo cultural	**Wrap-up and Homework Options (5 min.)** • Presentación escrita: Step 4 • Preparación para el examen 3, 4, 5 • Go Online: Lectura
DAY 9	**Warm-up (5 min.)** • Homework check	**¡Adelante! (30 min.)** • Videomisterio: *En busca de la verdad*, Episodio 2 • Perspectivas del mundo hispano	**Repaso del capítulo (10 min.)** • Vocabulario y gramática • Preparación para el examen 1, 2	**Wrap-up and Homework Options (5 min.)** • Practice Workbook 3B-8, 3B-9 • Go Online: Self-test • Examen del capítulo 3B
DAY 10	**Warm-up (5 min.)** • Homework check ✔**Assessment (40 min.)** • Examen del capítulo 3B			**Wrap-up and Homework Options (5 min.)** • A ver si recuerdas . . .: Capítulo 4A

	Warm-up / Assess	Preview Present / Practice Communicate	Wrap-up / Homework Options
DAY 1	**Warm-up (5 min.)** • Homework check • Return Examen del capítulo: Capítulo 3A **A ver si recuerdas . . . (20 min.)** • Las preposiciones y los medios de transporte • Actividades 1, 2 • Presentation: The verbs *salir, decir,* and *venir* • Actividades 3, 4	**Chapter Opener (5 min.)** • Objetivos • Fondo cultural **A primera vista (55 min.)** • Presentation: Vocabulario y gramática en contexto • Actividades 1, 2 • Presentation: Videohistoria *¿Cómo llegamos a la plaza?* • View: Videohistoria • Video Activities 1, 2, 3, 4 • Actividad 3	**Wrap-up and Homework Options (5 min.)** • Practice Workbook 3B-A, 3B-B, 3B-1, 3B-2, 3B-3, 3B-4 • Go Online • Prueba 3B-1: Vocabulary recognition
DAY 2	**Warm-up (10 min.)** • Actividad 4 • Homework check ✔**Assessment (10 min.)** • Prueba 3B-1: Vocabulary recognition	**Manos a la obra (65 min.)** • Actividades 6, 7, 8, 9, 10 • Fondo cultural • Audio Activities 5, 6 • Writing Activity 10 • Presentation: Direct object pronouns: *me, te, nos* • Actividades 12, 13, 15	**Wrap-up and Homework Options (5 min.)** • Practice Workbook 3B-5 • Actividades 5, 11 • Go Online • Heritage Learner Workbook 3B-1, 3B-2 • Prueba 3B-2: Vocabulary production
DAY 3	**Warm-up (10 min.)** • Actividad 14 • Homework check ✔**Assessment (10 min.)** • Prueba 3B-2: Vocabulary production	**Manos a la obra (65 min.)** • Audio Activity 7 • Presentation: Irregular affirmative *tú* commands • View: GramActiva video • Actividades 16, 17 • Fondo cultural • Exploración del lenguaje • Actividad 18 • Audio Activity 8 • Writing Activity 12 • Presentation: Present progressive: irregular forms • View: GramActiva video • Actividades 19, 20	**Wrap-up and Homework Options (5 min.)** • Practice Workbook 3B-6 • Go Online • Heritage Learner Workbook 3B-4 • Pruebas 3B-3, 3B-4: Direct object pronouns: *me, te, nos;* Irregular affirmative *tú* commands
DAY 4	**Warm-up (10 min.)** • Actividad 11 • Homework check ✔**Assessment (15 min.)** • Pruebas 3B-3, 3B-4: Direct object pronouns: *me, te, nos;* Irregular affirmative tú commands	**Manos a la obra (30 min.)** • Fondo cultural • Actividades 21, 22 • El español en el mundo del trabajo • Audio Activity 9 • Writing Activity 13 **¡Adelante! (30 min.)** • Lectura • ¿Comprendiste? / Y tú, ¿qué dices? • Fondo cultural • Presentación escrita: Steps 1, 5	**Wrap-up and Homework Options (5 min.)** • Practice Workbook 3B-7 • Presentación escrita: Step 2 • Go Online • Heritage Learner Workbook 3B-5 • Pruebas 3B-5: Present progressive: irregular forms
DAY 5	**Warm-up (5 min.)** • Homework check ✔**Assessment (10 min.)** • Prueba 3B-5: Present progressive: irregular forms	**¡Adelante! (40 min.)** • Presentación escrita: Step 3 • Perspectivas del mundo hispano **Repaso del capítulo (30 min.)** • Vocabulario y gramática • Preparación para el examen 1, 2, 3, 4, 5	**Wrap-up and Homework Options (5 min.)** • Presentación escrita: Step 4 • Practice Workbook 3B-8, 3B-9 • Go Online: Self-test • Examen del capítulo 3B
DAY 6	**Warm-up (10 min.)** • Homework check • Answer questions **Repaso del capítulo (15 min.)** • Situation Cards ✔**Assessment (40 min.)** • Examen del capítulo 3B	**¡Adelante! (20 min.)** • Videomisterio: *En busca de la verdad,* Episodio 2	**Wrap-up and Homework Options (5 min.)** • Go Online: Lectura • A ver si recuerdas . . .: Capítulo 4A

A ver si recuerdas...

Vocabulario

Las preposiciones y los medios de transporte

Core Instruction

Resources: Voc. and Gram. Transparency 66

Focus: Reviewing prepositions and words for modes of transportation

Suggestions: To review prepositions, bring in a stuffed animal from home and tell the class its name. Position the animal on the desk and introduce it. For example, you could say: *Éste es Capitán. Está encima del escritorio.* Change his position in relation to the desk, narrating until you have demonstrated each of the prepositions. Call on volunteers to come to the desk and position the animal according to your instructions.

To review modes of transportation, tell students places you would like to go, and have them suggest the means of getting there.

las preposiciones

a la derecha de
a la izquierda de
al lado de
cerca de
debajo de
delante de
detrás de
encima de
entre
lejos de

los medios de transporte

el autobús, *pl.* los autobuses
el avión, *pl.* los aviones
el barco
la bicicleta
el coche
el taxi
el tren

Práctica de vocabulario • Usando el organizador gráfico

 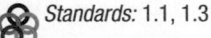 **Standards:** 1.1, 1.3

Focus: Writing and talking about the location of things in a city

Suggestions: Have students brainstorm words and phrases to describe the picture. Model true and false statements before students begin.

Answers will vary.

 **Escribir/Hablar**

¿Dónde está?

Escribe cinco frases para describir la ciudad del dibujo. Incluye cinco preposiciones y cinco medios de transporte en tu descripción. Escribe tres frases ciertas y dos falsas según el dibujo. Luego lee tus frases a otro(a) estudiante que va a repetir las frases ciertas y cambiar las frases falsas.

Modelo

A —*Hay una chica en bicicleta. Ella está a la derecha del monumento.*

B —*Sí, hay una chica en bicicleta, pero ella no está a la derecha del monumento, está a la izquierda.*

 **Dibujar/Hablar**

Completa la frase

1 Trabaja con un grupo de tres o cuatro estudiantes. Cada grupo necesita siete tarjetas. En cada tarjeta dibujen uno de los medios de transporte de la lista. Un(a) estudiante escoge una tarjeta y empieza a decir una frase.

Modelo

Muchas personas van en autobús . . .

2 El estudiante le da la tarjeta a la persona a su izquierda, que repite la frase y la completa. Si el grupo cree que la frase es correcta, el (la) estudiante que la completó escoge otra tarjeta para empezar una frase nueva.

Modelo

Muchas personas van en autobús al partido.

 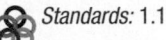 **Standards:** 1.1

Focus: Talking about how people travel

Suggestions: If you prefer, have students use the Clip Art instead of drawing the modes of transportation. Remind them that if someone in their group gives an incorrect answer, that person must correct it before choosing another card.

Answers will vary.

Extension: Have students create five cards with destinations in your community or vacation spots and have students follow the directions for *Actividad 2*.

154 ciento cincuenta y cuatro
Tema 3 • Tú y tu comunidad

Differentiated Instruction
Solutions for All Learners

Advanced Learners

Have students prepare a travel poster featuring a specific mode of transportation. Have them include the name of their company as well as rates, departure times, and destination information. Display their posters in the classroom.

Heritage Language Learners

Ask students to make a list of any other words they use to name means of transportation. For example, *una guagua, un bus, un camión, un micro* or *microbús.* Remind them that these words represent regional differences and show the richness of the Spanish language. They are not incorrect.

Gramática · Repaso

The verbs *salir, decir,* and *venir*

Salir "to leave, to go out," *decir* "to say, to tell," and *venir* "to come" are irregular *-ir* verbs. They also have a *yo* form that ends in *-go.*

(yo)	salgo digo vengo	(nosotros) (nosotras)	salimos decimos venimos
(tú)	sales dices vienes	(vosotros) (vosotras)	salís decís venís
Ud. (él) (ella)	sale dice viene	Uds. (ellos) (ellas)	salen dicen vienen

¿Recuerdas?

You already know four *-er* verbs that have a *yo* form that ends in *-go.*

tener: yo tengo   **poner:** yo pongo

hacer: yo hago   **traer:** yo traigo

Note that *salir* is irregular only in the *yo* form; *decir* follows a pattern similar to that of *e → i* stem-changing verbs; and *venir* follows a pattern similar to that of *e → ie* stem-changing verbs.

Práctica de gramática

 Actividad 3 Leer/Escribir

En la ciudad

Enrique describe lo que pasa en la ciudad. Escribe la forma apropiada del verbo correcto para completar las frases.

Muchas personas __1.__ *(poner / venir)* a la ciudad en autobús o en tren. Ellos __2.__ *(decir / salir)* que es mejor que ir en coche. Mi primo es muy deportista. Él siempre __3.__ *(decir / venir)* a la ciudad en bicicleta y __4.__ *(traer / salir)* todas sus cosas en una mochila. __5.__ *(Salir / Hacer)* de casa muy temprano porque vive bastante lejos de la ciudad. Él __6.__ *(decir / traer)* que es mejor montar en bicicleta porque __7.__ *(salir / hacer)* ejercicio al mismo tiempo. Mis hermanos y yo __8.__ *(hacer / venir)* en autobús o a veces en el coche de papá. __9.__ *(Poner / Traer)* el almuerzo porque no regresamos a casa para almorzar.

Más práctica

- Practice Workbook, pp. 60–61: 3B-A, 3B-B
- Guided Practice: Grammar Acts., p. 108
- *Real.* para hispanohablantes, p. 110

 **Go Online** PHSchool.com

For: Vocabulary and Grammar Review

Web Code: jdd-0311

 Actividad 4 Escribir/Hablar

¿Con qué frecuencia?

Escribe seis frases para decir con qué frecuencia haces las actividades del recuadro. Luego lee tus frases a otro(a) estudiante para ver si hace las mismas cosas que tú.

---

venir a la escuela en autobús

decir la verdad

traer un cuaderno a clase

salir de casa antes de las siete de la mañana

poner los libros en una mochila

hacer la tarea en casa

Modelo

salir con los amigos

A —*Siempre salgo con mis amigos los fines de semana. ¿Y tú?*

B —*Pues, salgo con ellos a veces.*

ciento cincuenta y cinco **155**
Preparación: Vocabulario y gramática

Gramática · Repaso  **Presentation EXPRESS**  GRAMMAR

Core Instruction

Resources: Voc. and Gram. Transparency 67

Suggestions: Direct attention to the *¿Recuerdas?* As you review, remind students that although all of the verbs are irregular, they do not all follow the same patterns. Before going through the *Gramática • Repaso,* show the transparency and have students identify the pattern of each irregular verb.

Actividad 3  *Standards:* 1.2

Resources: Answers on Transparencies

Focus: Reading a passage and writing present-tense forms of irregular verbs

Suggestions: Point out that the subject is not stated in every sentence in the *Actividad,* and that verb forms may correspond to a subject mentioned in a previous sentence.

Answers:

1. vienen	4. trae	7. hace
2. dicen	5. Sale	8. venimos
3. viene	6. dice	9. Traemos

Actividad 4 *Standards:* 1.1, 1.3

Resources: Answers on Transparencies

Focus: Writing and speaking about how often activities are done

Suggestions: Before beginning the activity, have students brainstorm a list of words that indicate frequency, such as **nunca, siempre, todos los días,** and **a menudo.**

Answers will vary but will include: vengo, digo, traigo, salgo, pongo, *and* hago

---

Enrich Your Teaching
Resources for All Teachers

Teacher-to-Teacher

Have students make sock puppets and put on a puppet show in which the characters are discussing what is in their town and how they get to each place. Encourage them to use the verbs from the *Gramática • Repaso.* After students have practiced, have them present their shows to the class.

Teacher-to-Teacher

Help students to group the verbs in the *Gramática • Repaso* by referring to them as the "go-go verbs." Have an artistic student draw a picture of a traffic light on green, and write each of the verbs that end in **-go** in the shape of cars. This visual will help provide a good "memory hook."

 Standards for Capítulo 3B

- To achieve the goals of the Standards, students will:

Communication

1.1 Interpersonal
- Talk: about prepositions and transportation, a telephone ad, *las glorietas,* maps, driving, traffic signs, giving directions, relationships, things people do, when and how often; using gestures to communicate

1.2 Interpretive
- Read: about city events, Diego Rivera, *la plaza mayor,* a telephone ad, the Mexico City subway, defensive driving, license requirements, the *carretera Panamericana,* Spanish-speaking employees, a picture-based story
- Read, watch, and listen to information about places, transportation, and traffic signs
- Listen to and watch a video about asking directions
- Read and interpret dialogue focusing on direct object pronouns, commands
- Observe a painting by Frida Kahlo
- View and read about the mystery series

1.3 Presentational
- Present information about: prepositions and transportation means; what, when, and how frequently people do things; driving directions, places of interest, advice, driving, and transportation; *las glorietas;* past events; using commands

Culture

2.1 Practices and Perspectives
- Tell about: the Mexico City subway; defensive driving
- Explain: communicating with gestures; driver's license requirements

2.2 Products and Perspectives
- Tell about: Diego Rivera; *la plaza mayor;* a cell phone; the Mexico City subway; driver's license requirements; Frida Kahlo; *la carretera Panamericana*

Connections

3.1 Cross-curricular
- Tell about: Mexican artist Frida Kahlo; safe driving and traffic signs

3.2 Target Culture
- Tell about driving in Costa Rica
- Recognize cultural viewpoints through viewing a video mystery series

Comparisons

4.1 Language
- Review direct object pronouns

4.2 Culture
- Compare: *plazas* of Madrid, Mexico, and the U.S.; driver's license requirements; *barrios* to U.S. neighborhoods; subways in Mexico and the U.S.

Communities

5.1 Beyond the School
- Identify tourist places in the community

5.1 Lifelong Learner
- View a video mystery series

Fondo cultural ■◆◆◆■◆▶◆■◆

Diego Rivera (1886–1957) pintó este mural en el Instituto de Arte de San Francisco en sólo cinco semanas. El artista está sentado en el centro, con sus asistentes alrededor. El mural representa la construcción de una moderna ciudad industrial e indica el entusiasmo de Rivera por el desarrollo industrial de la década de 1930.

- Compara el entusiasmo de Rivera por el desarrollo industrial con el interés que tiene la gente hoy en día en la tecnología.

271 x 357 in. The San Francisco Art Institute, California. ©2003 Museum Associates/LACMA. ©Banco de México Diego Rivera & Frida Kahlo Museums Trust. Av. Cinco de Mayo No. 2, Col. Del. Cuautehmoc 06059, México D. F. Reproduction authorized by the *Instituto Nacional de Bellas Artes y Literatura.*

"La elaboración de un fresco" (1931), Diego Rivera

Differentiated Instruction

STUDENTS NEEDING EXTRA HELP

Guided Practice Activities
- Vocabulary Check, Flash Cards
- Grammar
- Reading and Writing Support

Guided Practice Audio CDs
- Disc 1, Track 6

HERITAGE LEARNERS

Realidades para hispanohablantes
- Chapter Opener, pp. 110–111
- A primera vista, p. 112
- Videohistoria, p. 113
- Manos a la obra, pp. 114–121
- ¡Adelante!, pp. 122–127
- Repaso del capítulo, pp. 128–129

ADVANCED/PRE-AP*

Pre-AP* Resource Book, pp. 104–107

Capítulo 3B

¿Cómo se va...?

Chapter Objectives

- Give directions for getting to places
- Give a friend directions for a task
- Discuss driving and good driving habits
- Understand cultural perspectives on neighborhoods

Video Highlights

A primera vista: *¿Cómo llegamos a la plaza?*
GramActiva Videos: irregular affirmative *tú* commands; present progressive: irregular forms
Videomisterio: *En busca de la verdad,* Episodio 2

Country Connection

As you learn to talk about modes of transportation and giving directions, you will make connections to these countries and places:

Nueva York
España
Puerto Rico
México
Costa Rica
Venezuela
Argentina

Más práctica

- *Real.* para hispanohablantes, pp. 110–111

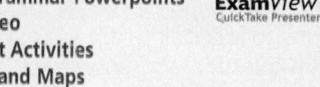
Go Online
PHSchool.com
For: Online Atlas
Web Code: jde-0002

ciento cincuenta y siete **157**
Capítulo 3B

Una vista de Buenos Aires

Teacher Technology

TeacherEXPRESS
Plan • Teach • Assess

PLAN
Lesson Planner

Go Online
PHSchool.com
For: Teacher Home Page
Web Code: jdk-1001

TEACH
Teaching Resources
Interactive
Teacher's Edition
Vocabulary Clip Art

ASSESS
Chapter Quizzes
and Tests

PresentationEXPRESS
Dynamic Presentations for Teachers

TEACH
Vocabulary & Grammar Powerpoints
GramActiva Video
Audio & Clip Art Activities
Transparencies and Maps
Activity Answers
Photo Gallery

ASSESS
ExamView
QuickTake Presenter

Preview

3B

Chapter Opener

Presentation EXPRESS
ATLAS

Core Instruction

Resources: Voc. and Gram. Transparencies: Maps 12, 14–18, 20

Suggestions: Ask students for directions to various places in your community. As they provide the directions, point out that these are the types of expressions that they will learn in this chapter. Explain that they will also learn about driving habits. What are common driving rules that they know of? If they already drive, have them discuss their driving habits. Tell students that the *Videohistoria* is about two boys who get lost on their way to meet friends at a bazaar. Ask students to describe what they would do if they got lost going somewhere. Tell students that the *GramActiva* Video will help them form and practice irregular *tú* commands so that they can give and ask for directions.

Fondo cultural

Standards: 1.2, 2.2

■◆■◆◇■◆◇◆■◆◇■◆◇◆■◆◇■◆

Resources: Fine Art Transparencies with Teacher's Guide, p. 53

Suggestions: Have students list ideas about the importance of technology in today's society. Ask volunteers to suggest possible focal points if they were creating a painting about the development of the technological era.

Answers will vary.

Teaching with Art

Resources: Fine Art Transparencies with Teacher's Guide, p. 53

Suggestions: Ask students to list advantages and disadvantages of industrial societies and agricultural societies. Point out that this mural was completed shortly after the beginning of the Great Depression in the United States. Explain that during this time, there was great excitement about industry because it represented economic prosperity.

Culture Note

Mexico City offers numerous above-ground public transportation options for its nearly 21 million inhabitants. Taxis run at all times, as do colorful yellow city buses. Green or gray vans, called **colectivos, peseros,** or **combis,** are another option.

157

Vocabulario y gramática  Presentation EXPRESS
VOCABULARY

Core Instruction

 Standards: 1.2

Resources: Teacher's Resource Book: Input Script, p. 160, Clip Art, pp. 174–177, Audio Script, p. 161; Voc. and Gram. Transparencies 68–69; TPR Stories Book, pp. 37–48; Audio Program: Tracks 1–2

Focus: Presenting vocabulary for driving, giving or following directions, and special landmarks in a city or town

Suggestions: Use the Input Script from the *Teacher's Resource Book* or the story from the *TPR Stories Book* to present new vocabulary. Separate the vocabulary into three groups: landmarks, giving directions, and words related to driving.

If possible, show a videotape of traffic scenes to the class. Pause the tape and have students describe the scene. Direct attention to traffic lights, stop signs and other items of chapter vocabulary. Ask students to identify as many objects as they can. Ask limited-response questions such as, *¿Es ancha o estrecha la carretera?* Include scenes of someone speeding and driving recklessly. Write phrases on the board such as, *Ve más despacio* and *Déjame en paz* and have students tell you what statements they would use if they were in the car with the driver.

Use the transparency of the street scene to help students practice vocabulary for directions. Make a cutout of Miguel and place him next to a landmark somewhere in the city. Ask students to describe his location. Tell them where Miguel wants to go and give directions for him to get there. Some of your directions should be incorrect. Pause after every step to have students tell you if the directions are true or false. Have them correct the false directions. Move Miguel after every step until he reaches his final destination.

Bellringer Review

Write these words for items on the board:

papel zapatos flores fruta helado

Have students write the store where one would go to get each.

Additional Resources

• Audio Program: Canciones CD, Disc 22

158

A primera vista jdd-0397

Vocabulario y gramática en contexto

Objectives

Read, listen to, and understand information about
• places in a city or town
• driving and transportation

❝Hola, me llamo Miguel. Hoy estoy en el centro y necesito ir al Banco Nacional. Voy a preguntarle a este policía **cómo se va** al banco ❞.

—Señor policía, ¿cómo se va al Banco Nacional?
—Es muy fácil.

1 —**Cruza** esta calle y **sigue derecho** hasta llegar a la señal de parada.

2 . . . Allí, **dobla** a la izquierda.

3 . . . Después de **manejar por** una cuadra, dobla a la derecha. El banco **queda** a mano izquierda **en medio de** la Avenida Juárez.

158 ciento cincuenta y ocho
Tema 3 • Tú y tu comunidad

Differentiated Instruction
Solutions for All Learners

Advanced Learners
Ask students to imagine that there is a pedestrian at the *Estás aquí* corner who is about to ask the police officer for walking directions to a certain place. Ask students to make up question-and-answer exchanges such as *¿Cómo se va a la Zapatería Dos Pies?*

Multiple Intelligences
Bodily/Kinesthetic: For *Actividad* 2, have students listen to the directions and use their finger to follow the route on the map. If you prefer, have students use game pieces or small figurines to move around the map.

Más vocabulario
hasta as far as, up to

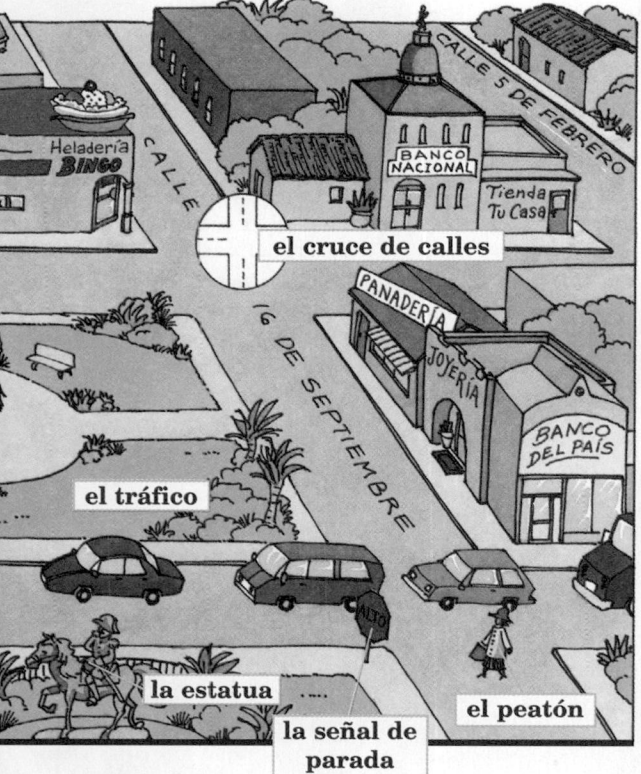

el tráfico
la estatua
la señal de parada
el peatón
el cruce de calles

CALLE 5 DE FEBRERO
CALLE 16 DE SEPTIEMBRE
Heladería Bingo
BANCO NACIONAL
Tienda Tu Casa
PANADERÍA
JOYERÍA
BANCO DEL PAÍS

el puente
estrecho, -a
ancho, -a
la carretera

—Miguel, **ten cuidado.** Es un poco **peligroso** por aquí. La carretera es ancha pero vamos a **pasar por** un puente que es bastante estrecho.

—**¡Basta! Ya** sé manejar.

el permiso de manejar
poner una multa
el conductor

—¡Hombre! **Ve** más **despacio.** La policía te va a poner una multa y a veces te **quitan** el permiso de manejar.

—**Me estás poniendo nervioso. Déjame en paz** por un momento.

Actividad 1 jdd-0397  Escuchar

¿Qué es y dónde queda?

Escucha las descripciones y busca la palabra o expresión apropiada del vocabulario en el mapa de las páginas 158–159. Señala la palabra o expresión y dila en voz alta *(say it aloud)* para indicar que la encontraste.

Más práctica

- Practice Workbook, pp. 62–63: 3B-1, 3B-2
- WAV Wbk., Writing, p. 63
- Guided Practice: Vocab. Flash Cards, pp. 109–114
- *Real.* para hispanohablantes, p. 112

Go Online
PHSchool.com
For: Vocab. Practice
Web Code: jdd-0312

Actividad 2 jdd-0397 Escuchar

¿Dónde estoy ahora?

Escucha las direcciones y síguelas en el mapa de las páginas 158–159. Empieza cada vez en las palabras *Estás aquí.* Indica adónde llegas y contesta con *Estoy delante de . . .*

ciento cincuenta y nueve **159**
Capítulo 3B

Enrich Your Teaching
Resources for All Teachers

Teacher-to-Teacher
Have students create a large picture map of an imaginary city that includes as many items of new vocabulary as possible. Nothing should be labeled. Post the map where students can practice by pointing to and identifying various items. This map can also be used in the vocabulary review at the end of the chapter.

Culture Note
International Driving Permits (IDPs) are honored in more than 150 countries outside the United States. An IDP is a legal document that translates U.S. driver's license information into 11 foreign languages. It is only needed if you are visiting a country that doesn't recognize a driver's license from the United States.

Actividad 1  Standards: 1.2 Presentation EXPRESS AUDIO

Resources: Teacher's Resource Book: Audio Script, p. 161; Audio Program: Track 3; Answers on Transparencies

Focus: Listening comprehension of descriptions of people and things found in a city or town

Suggestions: You may prefer to have students write their answers on cards and hold them up instead of saying the word aloud. Remind students to use cognates and context clues to help them with unfamiliar vocabulary.

Script and Answers:
1. Es una persona que camina al lado de una calle. *(el peatón)*
2. Tiene los colores rojo, amarillo y verde. Es importante mirarlo. *(el semáforo)*
3. Es la persona que maneja un coche. *(el conductor)*
4. Esta señal indica que es necesario parar el coche. *(la señal de parada)*
5. Es la intersección de dos calles. *(el cruce de calles)*
6. Es similar a un monumento. Generalmente es una reproducción de una persona. *(la estatua)*
7. Es similar a un parque. Es un lugar en el centro de la ciudad. *(la plaza)*

Actividad 2 Standards: 1.2 Presentation EXPRESS AUDIO

Resources: Teacher's Resource Book: Audio Script, p. 161; Audio Program: Track 4; Answers on Transparencies

Focus: Listening to and following directions

Suggestions: Ask students to imagine that they are pedestrians, beginning each time at the *Estás aquí* spot. As students listen to each set of directions, have them trace the walking route with their finger.

Script: See *Teacher's Resource Book*
Answers:
1. Estoy delante de la plaza.
2. ... del Restaurante Siglo de Oro.
3. ... la Heladería Bingo.
4. ... del Banco del País.
5. ... la Papelería Allende.
6. ... la panadería.

✓ Assessment
- **ExamView** Quiz on PresEXPRESS
  QuickTake Presenter

 **Videohistoria**

Presentation EXPRESS

VOCABULARY

Core Instruction

 Standards: 1.2

Resources: Voc. and Gram. Transparencies 70–71; Audio Program: Track 5

Focus: Presentation of additional vocabulary about giving and asking directions

Pre-reading: Ask students if they have ever gotten lost while driving. Who was driving? Did they ask for directions? Do they know anyone who refuses to ask for directions? Who? Direct attention to the *Estrategia.* Have students scan the questions in the *¿Comprendiste?* Remind them that this episode is a continuation of the one in *Capítulo* 3A.

Reading: Have students make stop signs like the one on p. 163. Ask volunteers to read the *Videohistoria* aloud while the rest of the class follows along in their books. Tell students to hold up their stop signs when they hear information that can be used to answer one of the questions. When they raise their signs, pause and ask a volunteer to tell you the number of the question for which the information can be used. Allow students to take notes and use them to complete *Actividad* 3.

Post-reading: Complete *Actividad* 3 to check comprehension.

 Pre-AP* Support

• **Activity:** Distribute Clip Art from *Capítulo* 3A representing stores and places around town. Have students draw on a sheet of paper several streets similar to the scene presented on pp. 158–159 and then place three or four of the pieces of clip art at various locations on their map. Working in pairs, have the partners tell each other how to get from one place to another so that the listener can follow the route on his or her partner's map.

• **Pre-AP* Resource Book:** Comprehensive guide to Pre-AP* vocabulary skill development, pp. 47–53

Videohistoria *jdd-0397*

¿Cómo llegamos a la plaza?

¿Cómo van los cuatro amigos al Bazar San Ángel? Lee la historia.

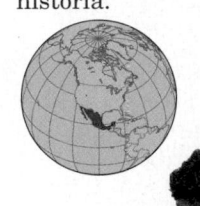

Estrategia

Reading for key information
Reading the questions at the end of the *Videohistoria* will help you focus on key information.

1 Teresa: ¿Y cómo llegamos al Bazar San Ángel?
Claudia: Vamos a tomar **el metro desde** aquí.
Teresa: Está bien. Vamos.

5 Ramón: Ahora, ¿adónde?
Manolo: Espera. Esto es **complicado.** Vamos a doblar a la derecha. No, mejor, vamos a seguir por aquí.
Ramón: ¿Estás seguro?
Manolo: Sí, sí. Yo sé por dónde vamos. Me estás poniendo nervioso.

6 Teresa: Ya son las dos y cuarto. ¿Dónde están Ramón y Manolo?
Claudia: Estoy segura que no saben dónde está . . .

7 Ramón: ¡Basta! Vamos a preguntarle a alguien. Señor, ¿cómo se va al Bazar San Ángel?
Señor: Pues, miren. En este cruce de calles van a doblar a la izquierda.
Ramón: Gracias. Vamos, rápido.

160 ciento sesenta
Tema 3 • Tú y tu comunidad

Differentiated Instruction
Solutions for All Learners

Advanced Learners
Suggest that students extend the story by making up a conversation that takes place after Ramón and Manolo finally meet up with Teresa and Claudia. It might begin with Teresa and Claudia asking why Ramón and Manolo were late.

Students with Learning Difficulties
Students may need help understanding that Ramón and Manolo get lost on their way to the bazaar. Photocopy the *Videohistoria,* and, starting with panel 4, work with students to highlight clues in the text that support this idea.

2 **Ramón:** Claudia y Teresa nos van a **esperar** en el Bazar San Ángel. Mira, aquí hay un banco. **¿Tienes prisa?**

Manolo: No, no tengo prisa. Tenemos tiempo. ¿Por qué?

Ramón: ¿Puedes **parar** por un momento, por favor? Tengo que sacar dinero.

3 **Ramón:** Doscientos pesos. Ahora, vamos a ver a Claudia y a Teresa.

Manolo: Sí. Pero no vamos a manejar el coche. Vamos a **dejarlo** en casa para ir a pie. El Bazar San Ángel queda **aproximadamente** a veinte minutos de mi casa.

Ramón: Vamos.

Manolo: De acuerdo.

4 **Ramón:** ¿Y cómo es el Bazar?

Manolo: Hace mucho tiempo que no voy por allí. Pero te va a gustar. Es muy popular.

Ramón: ¿Y **estás seguro** que sabes cómo llegar allí?

Manolo: Sí, claro. Está a* unas siete cuadras de aquí.

*Estar a is used to indicate distance.

8 **Manolo:** ¡Claudia, Teresa, aquí estamos!

Actividad 3 — Escribir/Hablar

¿Comprendiste?

1. ¿Cómo van a ir Claudia y Teresa al Bazar San Ángel?
2. Antes de ir al Bazar, ¿qué tiene que hacer Ramón?
3. ¿Cómo van a llegar Ramón y Manolo a San Ángel? ¿Por qué?
4. ¿Sabe Manolo llegar al Bazar? Según Manolo, ¿por qué?
5. ¿Tienen problemas los dos chicos en llegar al Bazar San Ángel? ¿Qué les pasa?
6. ¿Quiénes están esperándolos cuando llegan al Bazar?

Más práctica

- Practice Workbook pp. 64–65: 3B-3, 3B-4
- WAV Wbk.: Video, pp. 56–58
- Guided Practice: Vocab. Check, pp. 115–118
- *Real.* para hispanohablantes, p. 113

Go Online PHSchool.com
For: Vocab. Practice
Web Code: jdd-0313

ciento sesenta y uno **161**
Capítulo 3B

Video
Core Instruction

Standards: 1.2

Resources: Teacher's Resource Book: Video Script, p. 165; Video Program: Cap. 3B; Video Program Teacher's Guide: Cap. 3B

Focus: Comprehension of contextualized vocabulary

Suggestions:

Pre-viewing: Remind students that gestures can help them understand what is happening in the story. Have them demonstrate without talking how they would give directions to someone. Ask them to show, using body language, that they are in a hurry or frustrated.

Viewing: Show the video once without pausing; then go back and show it again, pausing along the way to check comprehension. Ask students to raise their hands at the point in which they would ask for directions if they were Manolo.

Post-viewing: Complete the Video Activities in the *Writing, Audio & Video Workbook.*

Actividad 3
Standards: 1.2, 1.3

Presentation EXPRESS ANSWERS

Resources: Answers on Transparencies

Focus: Verifying comprehension of the *Videohistoria*

Suggestions: For each item, have students list the name of the *Videohistoria* character(s) whose lines likely would contain the answer to the question. Have them scan the dialogues for the answers.

Answers:

1. Van a ir al bazar en el metro.
2. Tiene que sacar dinero.
3. Van a llegar a San Ángel a pie. El bazar queda cerca de la casa de Manolo.
4. No sabe llegar. Manolo dice que sabe, porque el bazar está cerca de su casa.
5. Sí, tienen problemas. Ellos no saben llegar al bazar. Ramón tiene que preguntarle a un señor y por fin llegan.
6. Claudia y Teresa están esperándolos.

Additional Resources
- WAV Wbk.: Audio Act. 5, p. 59
- Teacher's Resource Book: Audio Script, p. 162
- Audio Program: Track 8

Assessment
- ExamView QuickTake Presenter Quiz on PresEXPRESS
- Prueba 3B-1: Vocab. Recognition, pp. 83–84

Enrich Your Teaching
Resources for All Teachers

Teacher-to-Teacher
Discuss the benefits of public transportation. Invite students to make a poster to persuade others to take public transportation. The poster could be entitled ¡*Toma el autobús!* and perhaps could include a bus schedule along with reasons why public transportation is beneficial.

Culture Note
El Bazar San Ángel is just one of many Mexico City markets where crafts and artwork can be purchased. *Lagunilla, Mercado Insurgentes, Mercado de curiosidades mexicanas San Juan,* and *Mercado la Ciudadela* are also popular. Shoppers must be prepared to bargain for their purchases.

  **Standards:** 1.2 · Presentation EXPRESS™ ANSWERS

Resources: Answers on Transparencies

Focus: Using new vocabulary to complete a paragraph about traffic circles

Suggestions: Ask students if there are traffic circles, or rotaries, in their community. Invite students who have driven in traffic circles to share their experiences. Have them read the paragraph once before filling in the blanks. Point out that the words they choose do not have to be changed.

Answers:

1. cruces de calles
2. doblar
3. peligrosos
4. fuentes
5. estatuas
6. camiones
7. policía
8. tráfico

 **Bellringer Review**
As a class brainstorm activity, describe the picture.

 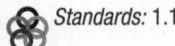 **Standards:** 1.1

Focus: Speaking and writing about local traffic situations

Suggestions: Have students review the reading in *Actividad 4* to help them respond to the questions about traffic circles. Direct attention to the *También se dice....* Remind students that they do not have to learn these words, but that it is helpful to be familiar with them.

Answers will vary.

Block Schedule

Borrow supplies from the art teacher at your school and have students recreate the road signs on p. 163. Tell them that you are the police officer and that you are going to tell them why you are giving them a traffic ticket. Have students hold up the sign that they did not obey according to your explanation. For example: *Le voy a poner una multa por manejar demasiado rápido. Ud. no respeta la velocidad máxima. Ud. sabe que es muy peligroso, ¿no?* (speed limit sign)

Objectives

- Talk about getting to places in town and types of transportation
- Give directions
- Talk about good driving habits
- Give commands to other people
- Talk about what is happening now
- Use the direct object pronouns *me*, *te*, and *nos*

 **Leer/Escribir**

Las glorietas

Lee este párrafo sobre las glorietas *(traffic circles)* y escribe las palabras correctas para completarlo.

Glorieta de Atocha, Madrid

Hace muchos años, en Europa y en América Latina, encontraron una solución al problema de accidentes en los __1.__ *(cruces de calles / peatones):* la glorieta. Las glorietas reducen el número de accidentes porque los conductores no pueden __2.__ *(tener prisa / doblar)* a la izquierda. En muchos casos, los cruces de calles con glorietas son menos __3.__ *(anchos / peligrosos)* que los que tienen semáforos. En muchas ciudades, las glorietas también son lugares de mucho interés turístico, porque hay grandes __4.__ *(fuentes / esquinas),* monumentos o __5.__ *(carreteras / estatuas)* en el centro. Frecuentemente hay muchos coches, taxis, __6.__ *(camiones / avenidas)* y autobuses que pasan por estas glorietas y es necesario tener un __7.__ *(puente / policía)* allí para ayudar a controlar el __8.__ *(tráfico / metro).* En algunas partes de los Estados Unidos, como en Nueva Jersey, también es común ver glorietas en las calles.

 Escribir/Hablar

Y tú, ¿qué dices?

1. ¿Hay una glorieta en una comunidad que tú conoces? ¿Cómo es? ¿Hay una fuente, estatua o monumento allí?

2. Para algunos conductores las glorietas parecen complicadas. ¿Qué piensas? ¿Las glorietas te parecen más o menos peligrosas que los cruces de calles con semáforos o señales de parada? ¿Por qué?

3. ¿Cómo manejan los conductores en las glorietas, despacio o con mucha prisa?

4. En tu comunidad, ¿hay mucho tráfico en los cruces de calles? ¿Los policías ayudan a controlar el tráfico? ¿Qué hacen los policías si alguien no respeta las reglas de tráfico?

También se dice . . .

el cruce de calles = la intersección *(Colombia, Ecuador)*

manejar = conducir *(España, Puerto Rico)*

doblar = dar la vuelta *(Colombia)*

la carretera = la autopista *(Colombia)*

la cuadra = la manzana *(España, Colombia)*

el permiso de manejar = la licencia de conducir *(México);* el carnet de conducir *(España)*

derecho = recto *(Ecuador, Guatemala)*

el tráfico = la circulación *(España, Uruguay, Venezuela, México);* el tránsito *(España)*

Differentiated Instruction
Solutions for All Learners

Students with Special Needs

Using the script for *Actividad 7,* create a chart for hearing-impaired students. List the dictated sentences in the first column. Label the second column *L* for *Lógica* and the third column *I* for *Ilógica.* Have students check the column that indicates whether each piece of advice is logical.

Actividad 6 — Escribir/Hablar

¿Qué hay en el mapa?

Haz una lista de ocho cosas que puedes ver en el centro de una ciudad. Trabaja con otro(a) estudiante y pregúntale si ve estas cosas en el mapa de las páginas 158–159. Si necesitas ayuda con las preposiciones ve *A ver si recuerdas* en la página 154.

> **Modelo**
> **A** —¿Hay una fuente?
> **B** —Sí. Está en medio de la plaza.

Actividad 7 — jdd-0398 — Escuchar/Escribir

Escucha y escribe

Tus parientes *(relatives)* saben que estás aprendiendo a manejar y todos tienen consejos *(advice)*. Pero algunas de sus ideas no son muy lógicas. Escucha lo que dicen y escribe las frases. Después escribe *L* si es una idea lógica o *I* si es una idea ilógica.

Actividad 8 — Leer/Hablar

¡Me estás poniendo nervioso!

Tu compañero(a) y tú están en el coche. Tú estás manejando, pero tu compañero(a) ve las señales de tráfico y te está poniendo nervioso(a) con todo lo que te dice. Hagan una conversación lógica usando las señales y frases de abajo. Las señales indican el orden de las frases que debes usar en la conversación.

> **Modelo**
>
> **A** —Ten cuidado. Hay una zona de construcción por aquí.
> **B** —Por favor. ¡Ya sé manejar!

1.    2.    3.    4.

5.    6.    7.    8. (image of train crossing sign)

Estudiante A

¡Espera! Se prohíbe entrar. No puedes seguir derecho.
Debes parar en la señal de parada.
Cuidado. Este cruce de trenes es bastante peligroso.
Si no respetas la velocidad máxima *(speed limit)*, el policía te pone una multa.
¿Estás seguro(a) que podemos cruzar este puente estrecho?
Ve más despacio. Hay muchos peatones en el cruce de calles.
En esta avenida no puedes doblar a la derecha.
Ve despacio en esta zona escolar.

Estudiante B

De acuerdo. Voy a . . .
Déjame en paz.
Ya sé manejar.
Me estás poniendo nervioso(a).
¡Basta!
Gracias, pero no necesito tu ayuda.

Enrich Your Teaching
Resources for All Teachers

Culture Note

Calle Alcalá and *Paseo de Recoletas* intersect at one of the most beautiful traffic circles in Madrid, Spain. Within the rotary is the Cibeles fountain, sculpted in 1777. The fountain depicts the Roman goddess Ceres riding a chariot drawn by two lions. Surrounding the rotary are the *Palacio de Comunicaciones* and the *Banco de España*.

Teacher-to-Teacher

Have pairs of students take turns acting out one of their own exchanges from *Actividad* 8. Encourage them to extend the conversation by saying, for example, *Pero, ¡hay que prestar atención todo el tiempo!* Have students vote for the best actors and award them special "Oscars" for their performances.

Actividad 6 — Standards: 1.1

Focus: Writing and speaking about things on a map

Recycle: Prepositions of location; *hay*

Suggestions: Ask students to list as many objects and places as they can without looking back at the labels. Suggest that students include one item that is not shown on the map.

Answers will vary.

Common Errors: Students may use *de* instead of *del.* Remind them to use the contraction when *de* comes before *el.*

Actividad 7 — Standards: 1.2 —  Presentation EXPRESS AUDIO

Resources: Teacher's Resource Book: Audio Script, pp. 162; Audio Program: Track 6; Answers on Transparencies

Focus: Listening to advice about driving

Suggestions: Play or read the entire script once before having students write the sentences. Allow students time to decide if the statements are logical or illogical.

Script: See *Teacher's Resource Book*

Answers: 1. I 2. L 3. L 4. L 5. I 6. I

Actividad 8 — Standards: 1.1, 1.2 —  Presentation EXPRESS ANSWERS

Resources: Answers on Transparencies

Focus: Reading and speaking about traffic signs

Suggestions: Have students identify each sign before they begin. Point out that speed in Spanish-speaking countries is measured in kilometers per hour.

Answers:
Student A:
1. Ve más despacio. Hay muchos …
2. ¡Espera! Se prohíbe entrar …
3. Si no respetas la velocidad …
4. ¿Estás seguro(a) que podemos …
5. Debes parar en la señal …
6. En esta avenida no puedes …
7. Ve despacio en esta zona escolar.
8. Cuidado. Este cruce de trenes …
Student B: Answers will vary.

163

Actividad 9 *Standards:* 1.2

Presentation EXPRESS
AUDIO

Resources: Voc. and Gram. Transparency 74; Teacher's Resource Book: Audio Script, p. 162; Audio Program: Track 7; Answers on Transparencies

Focus: Listening to directions and following them on a map

Recycle: Commands; places in town

Suggestions: Give students time to study the map. Have them locate the starting point, and point out some of the main attractions listed. Ask students what they think *Leyenda* means based on where it is located on the map. Students may have difficulties with perspective. Encourage them to imagine that they are actually at the places mentioned. For example, in item 3 they should imagine that they are walking out of the church heading toward the street. From that perspective they should turn right. Have students trace the route with a finger as they listen to the directions.

Script and Answers:

1. Cuando sales del Parque de las Palomas, dobla a la izquierda y sigue la calle del Cristo. Cruza la calle Fortaleza y camina por una cuadra. Dobla a la derecha. Camina por una cuadra en la calle de San Francisco. Pasa el cruce de calles. Está a mano derecha. ¿Dónde estás? *(la Plaza de Armas)*
2. Después de visitar la Plaza de Armas, sigue la calle de San Francisco hasta llegar a la calle de la Cruz. En el cruce de calles, dobla a la derecha. Sigue derecho por dos cuadras. Dobla a la izquierda. Queda a mano izquierda, en medio de la cuadra. ¿Dónde estás? *(la Iglesia de Santa Ana)*
3. Cuando sales de la Iglesia de Santa Ana, dobla a la derecha y toma la calle Tetuán. Cruza la calle de la Cruz y sigue derecho aproximadamente dos cuadras hasta llegar a la calle del Cristo. Para aquí. Queda a la izquierda. ¿Dónde estás? *(el Parque de las Palomas)*

Common Errors: Students may confuse *a la derecha* with *sigue derecho.* Point out that one means "to the right" and the other means "continue straight."

Actividad 9 jdd-0398 **Escuchar**

¿Cómo se va a . . . ?

Estás de vacaciones con tu familia en el Viejo San Juan, Puerto Rico. Empiezas tu excursión hoy en el Parque de las Palomas. (Mira ✪ en el mapa.) Escucha las direcciones que te dan tres personas y síguelas en el mapa. Escribe el nombre de cada lugar adonde llegas.

Empezaron a construir el sistema de defensas para la ciudad de San Juan en el siglo *(century)* XVI con murallas *(walls)* grandes como ésta y el famoso Castillo El Morro.

La Puerta de San Juan es la entrada a la antigua ciudad del mar.

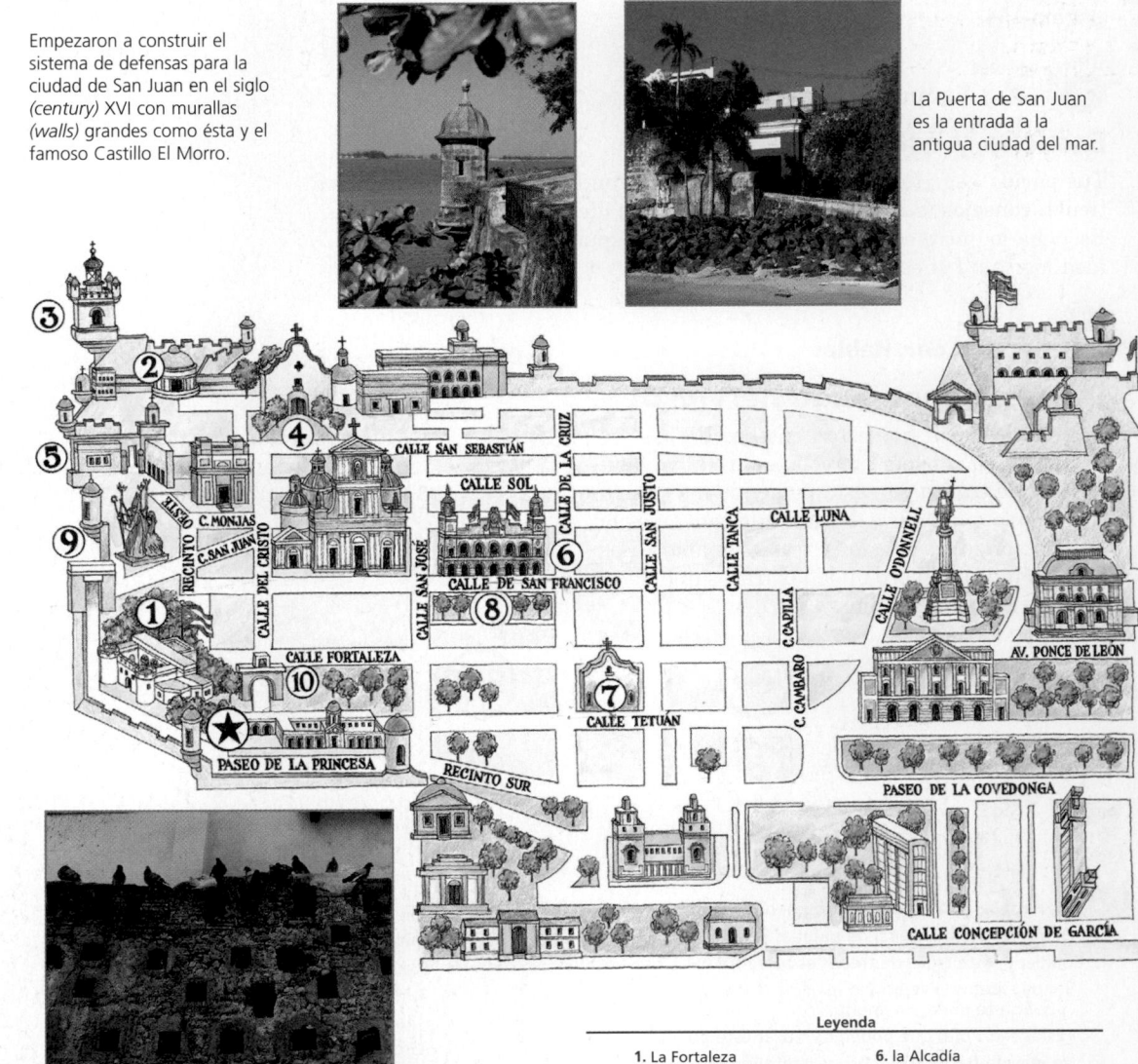

El Parque de las Palomas lleva ese nombre por la cantidad *(number)* de palomas que viven allí; es un lugar popular para visitar.

Leyenda

1. La Fortaleza
2. el Museo de las Américas
3. el Castillo El Morro
4. la Plaza Quinto Centenario
5. la Casa Blanca
6. la Alcaldía
7. la Iglesia de Santa Ana
8. la Plaza de Armas
9. la Puerta de San Juan
10. la Capilla del Cristo

164 ciento sesenta y cuatro
Tema 3 • Tú y tu comunidad

Differentiated Instruction
Solutions for All Learners

Advanced Learners/Pre-AP*

Pre-AP* Have students write a set of directions for visitors to the school. The starting point should be the school office, and the end points could be places such as the library, the gymnasium, the auditorium, and the cafeteria. Have them choose points that are on the same floor as the office if your building has more than one floor.

Students with Special Needs

Students with language processing difficulties may have difficulty following the multi-step directions required for *Actividad 9.* If so, write the directions, step by step, on a transparency to provide visual reinforcement for the vocabulary and to enable students to follow one step at a time.

Actividad 10

Hablar _____

Puntos de interés

Hoy quieres visitar otros puntos de interés en el Viejo San Juan. Empiezas tu excursión otra vez en el Parque de las Palomas. Con otro(a) estudiante, habla de cómo se va a los lugares que ven en el mapa de la página 164.

Modelo
A —*Por favor, ayúdame. ¿Cómo se va del Parque de las Palomas a la Catedral?*
B —*Camina dos cuadras por la Calle del Cristo. Queda a la derecha.*

Estudiante A

1. La Fortaleza
2. el Museo de las Américas
3. el Castillo El Morro
4. la Plaza Quinto Centenario
5. la Casa Blanca
6. la Alcaldía

Estudiante B

Camina (por) . . .
Toma . . .
Ve . . .
Sigue (derecho) . . .
Cruza . . .
Pasa (por) . . .
Dobla . . .
Para . . .

Actividad 11

Escribir/Hablar _____

Y tú, ¿qué dices?

1. En tu comunidad, ¿cómo son las calles? ¿Es fácil o es complicado ir de un lugar a otro?

2. ¿Ya tienes tu permiso de manejar? Si no, ¿cuándo lo vas a obtener? ¿Qué haces (hiciste) para aprender las reglas y señales de tráfico?

3. En una encuesta *(survey)*, les preguntaron a unos jóvenes españoles con qué frecuencia usan su coche para salir de la ciudad. Los jóvenes contestaron:

Casi todos los días	48%
Sólo el fin de semana	7%
Tres o cuatro veces a la semana	5%
Casi nunca	11%
No tengo coche	29%

¿Crees que contestarían *(would answer)* los jóvenes de tu comunidad estas preguntas de una forma similar? ¿Por qué?

Fondo cultural ■◆◆■◆■◆■◆■◆■◆■◆■◆■

La Plaza Mayor En las antiguas ciudades de España y las ciudades coloniales de América Latina, la plaza era *(was)* el centro de la ciudad. Hoy las plazas son lugares populares para pasar tiempo con los amigos. La Plaza Mayor de Madrid es una de las más bonitas de España. El Zócalo, en la Ciudad de México, es una de las más grandes del mundo.

• ¿Hay algo similar a una plaza mayor en tu comunidad? ¿Qué es? ¿Adónde vas tú para pasar tiempo con amigos?

El Zócalo, Ciudad de México

Plaza Mayor de Madrid, España

Actividad 10 *Standards:* 1.1

Focus: Asking and giving directions

Suggestions: Give students time to study the map to find the locations listed in the Student A bubble. Have them take notes on how to get to each location from *el Parque de las Palomas*. Point out that if a road doesn't go directly to a place, they can use prepositions of location to clarify. For example: *El castillo está al lado del museo.* Allow them to use their notes when they speak with their partners.

Answers will vary.

Actividad 11  *Standards:* 1.1, 1.3, 4.2

Resources: Teacher's Resource Book: GramActiva BLM, p. 173; Answers on Transparencies

Focus: Writing about and discussing various aspects of driving

Suggestions: Before students begin, have them list the requirements for getting a driver's license in your state. Photocopy the chart from the *Teacher's Resource Book* and give a copy to each student. Have them survey the class and record the results on the chart, then use it to answer item 3.

Answers will vary.

Fondo cultural *Standards:* 1.2, 2.2, 4.2

■◆■◆■◆■◆■◆■◆■◆■◆■◆■

Suggestions: Have students brainstorm a list of places where young people like to gather.

Answers will vary.

Additional Resources

• WAV Wbk.: Audio Act. 6, p. 60
• Teacher's Resource Book: Audio Script, pp. 162–163, Communicative Activity BLM, pp. 168–169
• Audio Program: Track 9

✓ **Assessment**

• ExamView QuickTake Presenter Quiz on PresEXPRESS
• Prueba 3B-2: Vocab. Production, pp. 85–86

Enrich Your Teaching
Resources for All Teachers

Culture Note

When Ponce de León established San Juan in 1511, the *Plaza de Armas* was designed to be the heart of the city. The plaza is in the center of Old San Juan, the historic seven blocks that were the foundation for modern San Juan. The *Plaza de Armas* has served as a meeting place and social hub for over 500 years.

Teacher-to-Teacher

Have students draw a map of the center of your town or city, indicating major streets, buildings, and points of interest. Then have them create sets of directions from one landmark to another to provide classmates with ¿Dónde estás? questions.

165

3B

Gramática·Repaso

Core Instruction

 Standards: 4.1

Resources: Voc. and Gram Transparency 72

Suggestions: Have students stand together in pairs. Give them a series of short oral sentences: *El policía puede ayudarnos. Te va a gustar. ¿Me ayudas, por favor? No sé qué decirte. Llámanos.* If the direct object is **me,** students point to themselves. If it is **te,** they point to their partner. For **nos,** the partners stand together and point to themselves. If you want to include **os,** students should point to another pair.

 *Standards:* 1.2

Resources: Answers on Transparencies

Focus: Writing direct object pronouns to complete a dialogue

Suggestions: Have students read the dialogue once without filling in the blanks. Point out that they will need to understand the entire dialogue to choose the correct direct object pronoun. Check for comprehension after each section to be sure students can complete the sentences appropriately.

Answers:

1. Te
2. me
3. te
4. me
5. Me
6. te
7. nos
8. te
9. me

 Standards: 1.1, 1.2, 2.2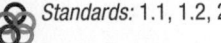

Focus: Reading and speaking about an ad

Recycle: *Communication vocabulary*

Suggestions: Ask students if they have cellular phones. What do they use their phones for? Have students use prior knowledge to help them understand the ad.

Answers will vary.

Gramática·Repaso

Direct object pronouns: *me, te, nos*

You know that direct object pronouns replace direct object nouns. The direct object pronouns *lo, la, los,* and *las* can refer to both objects and people. The pronouns *me, te, nos,* and *os* refer only to people. Here are all the direct object pronouns:

Singular		Plural	
me	me	nos	us
te	you (familiar)	os	you (familiar)
lo	him, it, you (formal)	los	them, you
la	her, it, you (formal)	las	them, you

Remember that in Spanish the subject and the verb ending tell who does the action and the direct object pronoun indicates who receives the action.

¿Me ayudas, por favor?
Can you help me please?

Direct object pronouns usually come right before the conjugated verb. When an infinitive follows a conjugated verb, the direct object pronoun can be placed before the first verb or attached to the infinitive.

¡No **te** entiendo!
Quieren llevar**nos** al centro.

 Leer/Escribir

Tarde otra vez

Hoy Manolo llegó tarde a la escuela. Completa la conversación entre él y Ramón con *me, te* o *nos.*

Ramón: Oye, Manolo, ¿por qué no tomaste el autobús a la escuela esta mañana? __1.__ esperamos en la esquina de tu calle por diez minutos.

Manolo: Lo siento. Mi padre no __2.__ despertó a tiempo.

Ramón: ¿Y cómo llegaste a la escuela? ¿Tu hermana __3.__ llevó en su coche?

Manolo: Sí, ella __4.__ llevó a la escuela.

Ramón: ¿Ya sabes que repasamos en la primera hora para el examen de mañana?

Manolo: Sí, lo sé y no entiendo la materia. ¿__5.__ ayudas a estudiar esta noche?

Ramón: Lo siento, amigo, pero no __6.__ puedo ayudar. Mi familia y yo vamos a la casa de mis tíos. Ellos __7.__ invitaron a cenar esta noche.

Manolo: Pues, entonces __8.__ veo mañana. Tengo que hablar con Claudia y Teresa. Estoy seguro que ellas __9.__ pueden ayudar.

"Perdón, señora. Nos puede decir cómo llegar a . . . ?"

Differentiated Instruction
Solutions for All Learners

Students with Learning Difficulties

For *Actividad* 14, help students with sentence structure by breaking down and rearranging the directions. Have students begin each sentence with the subject given. Then have them add the appropriate direct object pronoun. Finally, have them conjugate the verb to agree with the subject and complete the sentence.

Multiple Intelligences

Bodily/Kinesthetic: For *Actividad* 12, have students work with a partner and role-play the dialogue between Manolo and Ramón. Encourage them to use hand gestures to emphasize to whom the direct object pronouns refer. For example, tell them to point to themselves if they say: *Mi padre no me despertó a tiempo.*

 **Leer/Hablar**

Una foto y una voz

Lee el anuncio a la derecha y, con otro(a) estudiante, contesta las preguntas.

1. Si tienes este nuevo teléfono celular, ¿cuál es la ventaja (advantage) para tus amigos?

2. ¿Qué otro equipo necesitas para usar este teléfono celular?

3. ¿Te gustaría tener un teléfono celular como éste? ¿Por qué?

  Escribir

Una fiesta en el centro

Hoy es la fiesta de cumpleaños de la abuela de Teresa. La familia decidió celebrar en un restaurante del centro. Escribe lo que hicieron Teresa, su familia y los invitados (guests).

Modelo

Teresa / invitar a la fiesta de su abuela: a nosotros
Teresa nos invitó a la fiesta de su abuela.

AHORA TUS AMIGOS TE ESCUCHAN . . .

La comunicación es cada día mejor con el uso de imágenes móviles. Con la tecnología del nuevo teléfono celular de TecnoRey y nuestra cámara digital MX P-45, puedes sacar una foto a color y enviarla a tus amigos como correo electrónico.

¡Y TE VEN!

Para más información llame al 443-9876.

1. Teresa / hablar por teléfono anoche: a ti
2. mis padres / ayudar a comprar un regalo: a mí
3. mi padre / llevar en su coche a la fiesta: a mí
4. Teresa y su madre / ver: a nosotros
5. la abuela de Teresa / conocer: a ti
6. mis padres / llevar a casa a las diez: a nosotros

    Hablar

Tus relaciones con otras personas

Habla con otro(a) estudiante sobre las relaciones que tienes con otras personas.

Modelo

llevar a la escuela por la mañana
A —¿Quién te lleva a la escuela por la mañana?
B —Mis padres me llevan a la escuela.
o:—Nadie me lleva a la escuela. Voy a pie.

Estudiante A

1. invitar a su casa a menudo
2. comprender casi siempre
3. ayudar con las tareas
4. recoger de la escuela por la tarde
5. esperar mucho
6. despertar por la mañana

Estudiante B

mi mamá (papá)
mis padres
mi hermano(a)
mi mejor amigo(a)

mis amigos

¡Respuesta personal!

Más práctica

- Practice Workbook, p. 66: 3B-5
- WAV Wbk., Writing, p. 64
- Guided Practice: Grammar Acts., pp. 119–120
- *Real.* para hispanohablantes, pp. 114–117

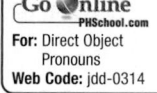
Go Online PHSchool.com
For: Direct Object Pronouns
Web Code: jdd-0314

  *Standards:* 1.3

Resources: Voc. and Gram. Transparency 75; Answers on Transparencies

Focus: Forming sentences by adding personal pronouns and correct verb forms

Recycle: Preterite verb forms

Suggestions: Remind students that direct object pronouns are placed before the conjugated verb. Point out that direct object pronouns, unlike indirect object pronouns, do not need to be clarified to be understood, so they will drop the *a ti, a nosotros,* etc., from their answers.

Answers:
1. Teresa te habló por teléfono anoche.
2. Mis padres me ayudaron a comprar un regalo.
3. Mi padre me llevó en su coche a la fiesta.
4. Teresa y su madre nos vieron.
5. La abuela de Teresa te conoció.
6. Mis padres nos llevaron a casa a las diez.

  *Standards:* 1.1

Resources: Answers on Transparencies

Focus: Speaking about who does things for you

Recycle: Family vocabulary

Suggestions: Have students brainstorm a list of family members. Point out that they will be using the present tense.

Answers:
Student A:
1. ¿Quién te invita a su casa a menudo?
2. ¿Quién te comprende casi siempre?
3. ¿Quién te ayuda con las tareas?
4. ¿Quién te recoge de la escuela por la tarde?
5. ¿Quién te espera mucho?
6. ¿Quién te despierta por la mañana?
Student B: Answers will vary.

Additional Resources

- WAV Wbk.: Audio Act. 7, p. 60
- Teacher's Resource Book: Audio Script, p. 163
- Audio Program: Track 10

 Assessment

- ExamView QuickTake Presenter Quiz on PresEXPRESS
- Prueba 3B-3: Direct object pronouns: *me, te, nos,* p. 87

Enrich Your Teaching
Resources for All Teachers

Teacher-to-Teacher

Have students write the six questions and responses from *Actividad* 15 in large letters on slips of paper. Have them cut each sentence apart word by word and clip the pieces together. To give students practice with word order and sentence construction, have them reassemble one or more of the sentences. This activity can be done when students finish an activity or a quiz early. Have students check each other's sentences for accuracy.

167

 **Gramática**

Presentation EXPRESS
GRAMMAR

Core Instruction

⊛ *Standards:* 4.1

Resources: Voc. and Gram. Transparency 73; Teacher's Resource Book: Video Script, pp. 165–166; Video Program: Cap. 3B

Suggestions: Ask volunteers to come to the front of the class and follow your instructions. Tell them what to do using irregular affirmative commands. For example: *Pon el bolígrafo encima del escritorio.* Have students decide if the volunteer is correctly following your commands or not. Students will often remember short, frequently heard commands that are used in class. List classroom expressions that include informal irregular commands on the board and be sure to use them throughout the school year. Some examples of classroom commands are: *Ten cuidado, ¡Hazlo!* or *Dime.* Use the *GramActiva* Video to introduce irregular commands or to reinforce your own presentation.

  ⊛ *Standards:* 1.2, 1.3

Presentation EXPRESS
ANSWERS

Resources: Answers on Transparencies

Focus: Reading and writing advice to a friend

Suggestions: Point out to students that some items have more than one possible answer, but that they should use each one only once. Have them read both columns before they begin.

Answers:
1. Pon el permiso de manejar . . . . *(c)*
2. Sal temprano para no encontrar . . . . *(h)*
3. Sé un buen conductor para . . . . *(e)*
4. Ten cuidado al pasar por . . . . *(a, g)*
5. Ve despacio por . . . . *(a, g)*
6. Haz un pregunta . . . . *(b)*
7. Di la verdad (¡que no sabes!) . . . . *(f, b)*
8. Ven directamente a casa . . . . *(d)*

Extension: Have students write a letter to a friend who needs directions on how to get to their school. Have students choose a starting point and use **tú** commands to give the directions.

Bellringer Review
To practice regular affirmative commands, list three regular **-ar, -er,** and **-ir** infinitives on the board and have students give the command to another classmate who will act it out.

168

Gramática

Irregular affirmative *tú* commands

Some verbs have irregular affirmative *tú* commands. To form many of these commands, take the *yo* form of the present tense and drop the *-go:*

Infinitive	yo form	command
poner	pongo	pon
tener	tengo	ten
decir	digo	di
salir	salgo	sal
venir	vengo	ven

Hacer, ser, and *ir* have irregular *tú* command forms that must be memorized.

hacer	haz
ser	sé
ir	ve

—¿Cómo se va a la carretera?

—**Sal** de aquí y sigue derecho hasta el tercer semáforo.

¿Recuerdas?
To give someone an affirmative *tú* command, use the *Ud. / él / ella* form of the verb.
• Elena, **¡maneja** con cuidado!

If you use a direct object pronoun with an affirmative command, attach the pronoun to the command. When a pronoun is added to a command of two or more syllables, a written accent mark is needed over the stressed vowel.

Josefina, **¡hazlo** ahora mismo!

Martín, **ayúdame.**

GramActiva VIDEO

Need more help with irregular affirmative *tú* commands? Watch the **GramActiva** video.

Sal del coche.

 16 **Leer/Escribir**

Los consejos de una amiga

Joaquín visita por primera vez Caracas, Venezuela, y quiere manejar al centro. Lee los consejos que le da una amiga venezolana. Empareja *(Match)* la información de las dos columnas y escribe los mandatos apropiados que ella le dice.

1. *(poner)* el permiso de manejar
2. *(salir)* temprano para no encontrar
3. *(ser)* un(a) buen(a) conductor(a) para
4. *(tener)* cuidado cuando pasas por
5. *(ir)* despacio por
6. *(hacer)* una pregunta
7. *(decir)* la verdad (¡que no sabes!)
8. *(venir)* directamente a casa

a. una zona de construcción
b. si no sabes dónde queda algo
c. en tu cartera antes de salir
d. a las cuatro de la tarde
e. no recibir multas de la policía
f. si alguien te pregunta cómo se va a algún lugar
g. las calles estrechas
h. mucho tráfico

Modelo
(ir) al banco primero
Ve al banco primero si no tienes mucho dinero.

Differentiated Instruction
Solutions for All Learners

Advanced Learners
Ask students to lead small groups in a game of *Simón dice.* Have them give affirmative commands that can be acted out. For example, students could say *Simón dice, pon la mesa,* and their classmate should pretend to set the table. If the command doesn't start with *Simón dice,* students shouldn't act it out. If they do, they must sit down.

Heritage Language Learners
Some students may omit accent marks when writing the affirmative commands. Have students practice adding accent marks to a command of two or more syllables. Give them a list of infinitives and have them write affirmative **tú** commands, adding **lo** and an accent to each one.

Actividad 17 **Hablar**

¡Toma el metro!

Mira el mapa del metro de la Ciudad de México. Habla con otro(a) estudiante sobre la mejor forma de ir de un lugar a otro usando el metro.

Para decir más . . .

bajar to get off

cambiar to change

hacia toward

Modelo

A —¿Cómo se va en el metro del Hospital General al Zócalo?

B —Pues, desde el Hospital General toma la línea 3 y ve hacia Indios Verdes. Baja en Hidalgo y cambia a la línea 2. Ten cuidado. Ve hacia Villa de Cortés y baja en la estación Zócalo. Sal del metro y estás en el Zócalo.

¿Cómo se va . . .

1. . . . del parque Chapultepec al Zócalo?
2. . . . de Santa Anita a Lázaro Cárdenas?
3. . . . del Palacio de Bellas Artes a la estación Autobuses del Norte?
4. . . . de Chabacano a San Juan de Letrán?
5. . . . de Tlatelolco a Garibaldi?
6. . . . del Colegio Militar a Insurgentes?

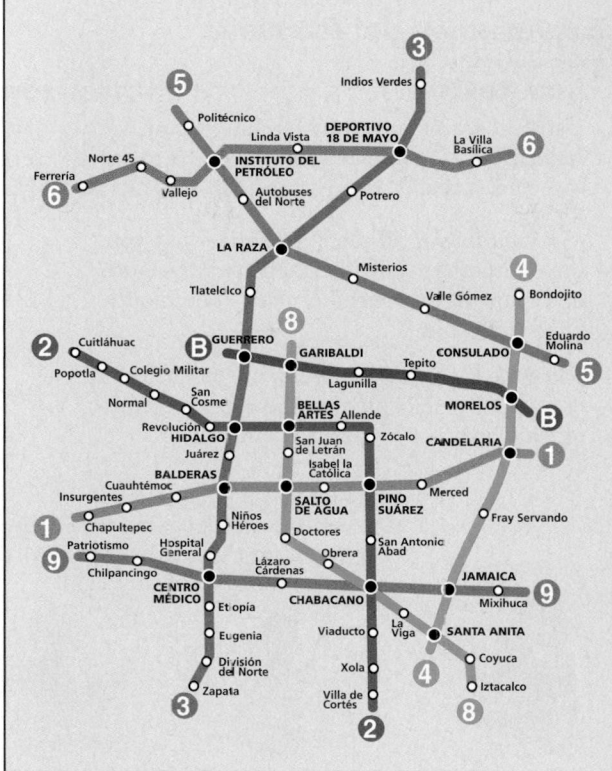

El Metro de la Ciudad de México 4.7 millones de personas usan diariamente las diez líneas del metro en la Ciudad de México. Es económico viajar por metro. Un viaje cuesta $2.00 pesos. Si usas mucho el metro, puedes comprar boletos con descuento. Durante las horas pico (rush hour) hay tantas personas que hay unos vagones (subway cars) sólo para hombres y otros vagones para mujeres y niños.

• ¿Por qué crees que el metro es un sistema de transporte tan popular en la ciudad?

La estación de metro Chapultepec, Ciudad de México

ciento sesenta y nueve **169**
Capítulo 3B

Resources: Voc. and Gram. Transparency 76; Answers on Transparencies

Focus: Giving directions on a subway map

Suggestions: Point out that some stations are located on more than one line. Where the lines intersect, you can change to a different line. Remind students to use the stations at the end of each line to indicate direction.

Answers may vary, but will include:

1. Desde Chapultepec toma la línea 1 y ve hacia Candelaria. Baja en Pino Suárez y cambia a la línea 2. Ve hacia Cuitláhuac. Baja en la estación Zócalo.
2. Desde Santa Anita toma la línea 8 hacia Garibaldi. Baja en Chabacano y cambia a la línea 9 hacia Patriotismo. Baja en la estación Lázaro Cárdenas.
3. Desde la estación Bellas Artes toma la línea 2 y ve hacia Cuitláhuac. Baja en Hidalgo y cambia a la línea 3 hacia Indios Verdes. Baja en La Raza y cambia a la línea 5 hacia Politécnico. Baja en la estación de Autobuses del Norte.
4. Desde Chabacano toma la línea 8 y ve hacia Garibaldi. Baja en la estación San Juan de Letrán.
5. Desde Tlatelolco toma la línea 3 hacia Zapata. Baja en Guerrero y cambia a la línea B hacia Morelos. Baja en la estación Garibaldi.
6. Desde el Colegio Militar toma la línea 2 y ve hacia Villa de Cortés. Baja en Hidalgo y cambia a la línea 3 hacia Zapata. Baja en Balderas y cambia a la línea 1 hacia Chapultepec. Baja en Insurgentes.

Fondo cultural  Standards: 1.2, 2.1, 2.2, 4.2

Suggestions: Have students compare public transportation in your community or in a city near you with that of Mexico City. Ask them to give reasons for taking public transportation.

Answers will vary.

 Pre-AP* Support

• **Activity:** To accompany Actividad 17, have students determine another location not already suggested and tell the class how to go from one place to another. Classmates follow the routes as given.

• **Pre-AP* Resource Book:** Comprehensive guide to Pre-AP* communication skill development, pp. 9–17, 36–46

 Enrich Your Teaching
Resources for All Teachers

Culture Note

Mexico City's metro system was the first to use colors and pictographs to identify lines and stations. A different color distinguishes each of the 10 lines and every one of the 175 stations has its own pictograph, many of them Aztec symbols. The Talismán station is symbolized by the mammoth in honor of the mammoth bones that were unearthed there during construction.

Internet Search

Keywords:

Ciudad de México, metro

Exploración del lenguaje

Presentation EXPRESS ANSWERS

Core Instruction

 Standards: 1.1, 1.2

Resources: Answers on Transparencies

Suggestions: Model the gestures and suggest that students practice them as they read the passage silently. Give students a list of contexts on which to base their skits.

Answers:
From left to right:
¡Basta!
¡Sigue derecho!
¡Vete!
¡Se me olvidó!
¡Ven aquí!

Standards: 1.2, 1.3

Presentation EXPRESS ANSWERS

Resources: Answers on Transparencies

Focus: Reading, writing, and speaking about a trip to the mall

Suggestions: When reviewing answers with students, model the correct pronunciation of the conjugated verb and direct object pronoun and have students correct accent marks when necessary.

Answers:
ANITA: Sé; llévame
ROBERTO: espérame, pregúntame
ANITA: Ayúdame, ven
ROBERTO: Escúchame
ANITA: dime

Extension: Have students work with a partner to write another dialogue between Roberto and Anita. Ask students to give directions to a store in your community.

Theme Project

Students can perform Step 4 at this point. Be sure they understand your corrections and suggestions. (For more information, see p. 126-a.)

Additional Resources

- WAV Wbk.: Audio Act. 8, p. 61
- Teacher's Resource Book: Audio Script, p. 163
- Audio Program: Track 11

 ## Assessment

- **ExamView** QuickTake Presenter **Quiz on PresEXPRESS**
- Prueba 3B-4: Irregular affirmative *tú* commands, p. 88

Exploración del lenguaje

Los gestos

Using gestures and body language is an important form of communication. Here are some gestures for expressions you know.

¡Se me olvidó! When you realize that you have forgotten something, open your mouth and slap your forehead or your open mouth with your palm.

¡Basta! If you have enough of something, cross your arms one over the other, in front of your body, with palms down.

¡Vete! If you want someone to go away, extend one arm toward the person with the palm of the open hand, as if to make a stop sign. Move the hand near and far, as if pushing something.

¡Ven aquí! If you want someone to come closer, turn the palm of your hand up and fold your fingers toward you, into your palm.

¡Sigue derecho! To help a person find the way, extend your arm ahead. Move your arm forward and back, indicating the way to go with your hand.

¡Compruébalo! Look at each drawing and write the appropriate expression for the gesture shown. Then work with a partner and use one of the gestures in a skit.

  Leer/Escribir/Hablar

Ayúdame, por favor

Anita está en casa con su hermano mayor y quiere ir al centro comercial. Primero escribe los mandatos que completan la conversación entre ellos. ¡Ojo! Si añades un pronombre a un verbo que tiene más de una sílaba, tienes que escribir un acento. Después lee la conversación con otro(a) estudiante.

ayudarme	escucharme	llevarme	ser
decirme	esperarme	preguntarme	venir

Más práctica

- Practice Workbook, p. 67: 3B-6
- WAV Wbk., Writing, p. 65
- Guided Practice: Grammar Acts., p. 105
- *Real.* para hispanohablantes, p. 118

Go Online PHSchool.com
For: Irregular Affirmative *tú* Commands
Web Code: jdd-0315

Anita: Roberto, quiero ir al centro comercial pero queda bastante lejos. __1.__ muy simpático y __2.__ en tu coche, por favor.

Roberto: No puedo. Tengo mucho que hacer. Pero __3.__ aquí un minuto. Tengo un mapa en mi coche. Estoy seguro que lo puedes encontrar. Si no entiendes algo, __4.__ .

Anita: Todavía parece complicado. __5.__ con el mapa, Roberto. O mejor, __6.__ conmigo.

Roberto: Yo sé que lo puedes hacer sola. __7.__ con atención y te explico las direcciones otra vez.

Anita: Pues, __8.__ , ¿no hay una tienda cerca de nuestra casa? Prefiero quedarme por aquí.

Differentiated Instruction
Solutions for All Learners

Students with Special Needs

If students are unable to perform the gestures from the *Exploración del lenguaje,* have them watch another pair's skit and identify the gestures that are being used. Encourage them to use the phrases given in the reading.

Advanced Learners

Have students create a bulletin board display that illustrates the accent rules introduced in this chapter. Ask them to write simple explanations for the information on poster board, and to provide models. Refer the class to the bulletin board as necessary throughout the year.

Gramática

Present progressive: Irregular forms

Some verbs have irregular present participle forms.

To form the present participle of -ir stem-changing verbs, the e in the infinitive form changes to i, and the o in the infinitive form changes to u:

decir: **diciendo**   servir: **sirviendo**
pedir: **pidiendo**   vestir: **vistiendo**
repetir: **repitiendo**   dormir: **durmiendo**
seguir: **siguiendo**

In the following -er verbs, the i of -iendo changes to y.

creer: **creyendo**
leer: **leyendo**
traer: **trayendo**

When you use object pronouns with the present progressive, you can put them before the conjugated form of estar or attach them to the present participle.

Notice that if a pronoun is attached to the present participle, an accent mark is needed. Write the accent mark over the vowel that is normally stressed in the present participle.

—¿Están Uds. esperando el autobús?

—Sí, **lo** estamos esperando.
  o: Sí, estamos esperándo**lo**.

¿Recuerdas?

To say that an action is happening right now, use the present progressive. To form the present progressive, use the present tense of estar + the present participle (-ando or -iendo).

doblar → doblando
• Ella **está doblando** a la izquierda.

aprender → aprendiendo
• **Estamos aprendiendo** a manejar.

escribir → escribiendo
• **Están escribiendo** una carta.

GramActiva VIDEO

Need more help with the present progressive? Watch the **GramActiva** video.

  **Escribir/Hablar**

Actividad 19

En la calle

Examina el cuadro del pintor español Juan Ferrer y Miró. Escribe cinco frases para decir lo que están haciendo las personas que ves. Después trabaja con otro(a) estudiante y pregúntale qué están haciendo las diferentes personas.

Modelo

A —¿Qué está haciendo el perro?
B —El perro está esperando al niño.

"Exposición de pintura" (siglo XIX), Juan Ferrer y Miró
Photo courtesy of SuperStock. © 2004 Artists Rights Society, ARS, NY.

ciento setenta y uno 171
Capítulo 3B

Gramática

Presentation EXPRESS GRAMMAR

Core Instruction

 Standards: 4.1

Resources: Teacher's Resource Book: Video Script, p. 166; Video Program: Cap. 3B

Suggestions: To reinforce the present progressive, bring in photographs and ask students to identify the actions pictured. Ask ¿Qué está haciendo en la foto?

Act out some of the verbs on the chart, and have volunteers say what you are doing. Point out that only the second **e** in **repetir** changes to **i**. Emphasize that the present progressive tense is a compound tense and must always be used with the verb **estar**. Remind students that the present participles do *not* change according to the subject. Play the *GramActiva* Video as an introduction or to reinforce your own presentation of irregular forms of the present progressive.

 Standards: 1.1, 1.3

Actividad 19

Resources: Fine Art Transparencies with Teacher's Guide, p. 21

Focus: Writing and speaking about what is happening in a painting

Recycle: Present tense of **estar**

Suggestions: Show students the transparency and have them name activities taking place in the painting.

Answers will vary.

Enrich Your Teaching
Resources for All Teachers

Teacher-to-Teacher

Have students practice irregular verb tenses by creating their own word-search activity. Give them a blank grid, and have them fill in ten irregular verb forms. Then, have them write random letters to complete the grid. Below the puzzle, have them write ten fill-in-the-blank sentences that correspond to each item in the puzzle. Have students exchange their word searches with a partner, and complete them for homework.

Actividad 20 Standards: 1.1

Presentation EXPRESS ANSWERS

Resources: Answers on Transparencies
Focus: Speaking about driving
Suggestions: Remind students that some of the verbs in the Student A list will require indirect object pronouns.

Answers:
Student A:
1. Ese señor está leyendo . . . .
2. Esos niños están diciéndole . . . .
3. Esos jóvenes están durmiendo . . . .
4. Ese perro está siguiendo . . . .
5. Esa camarera está sirviéndoles . . . .
6. Esa policía está poniéndole . . . .

Student B:
a. Para. Esos peatones están cruzando . . . .
b. Mira. Ese camión está parando . . . .
c. Ve más despacio. Nosotros estamos entrando . . . .
d. Ten cuidado. Los niños están corriendo . . . .
e. Espera. Ese conductor está doblando . . . .
f. Vuelve a la escuela. Estás poniéndome . . . .

 **Fondo cultural** Standards: 1.2, 2.1, 2.2, 4.2

Suggestions: To help students answer the question, bring in information regarding the process of obtaining a driver's license in your state. Make photocopies for students and have them refer to the information as they read the passage. Often, this information will be available in Spanish.
Answers will vary.

Additional Resources

• WAV Wbk.: Audio Act. 9, p. 62
• Teacher's Resource Book: Audio Script, p. 163, Communicative Activity BLM, pp. 170–171
• Audio Program: Track 12

 ✓ Assessment

• ExamView Quiz on PresEXPRESS
QuickTake Presenter
• Prueba 3B-5: Present progressive: Irregular forms, p. 89

 **Actividad 20** Hablar

Un(a) instructor(a) nervioso(a)

Imagina que eres un(a) estudiante que está aprendiendo a manejar. Estás poniendo nervioso(a) a tu instructor(a) porque estás mirando a la gente en vez de *(instead of)* mirar la calle. Con otro(a) estudiante que hace el papel *(plays the role)* del (de la) instructor(a), hagan una conversación.

Modelo

esa señora / pedirle ayuda al policía
mirar / el semáforo / cambiar de verde a amarillo
A —*Esa señora está pidiéndole ayuda al policía.*
B —*Mira, Catalina. El semáforo está cambiando de verde a amarillo.*

Estudiante A

1. ese señor / leer un mapa de la ciudad
2. esos niños / decirle algo a su mamá
3. esos jóvenes / dormir debajo de un árbol
4. ese perro / seguir a los niños
5. esa camarera / servirles bebidas a los clientes
6. esa policía / ponerle una multa a ese conductor

Estudiante B

a. parar / esos peatones / cruzar la calle
b. mirar / ese camión / parar
c. ir más despacio / nosotros / entrar en la plaza
d. tener cuidado / los niños / correr hacia la calle
e. esperar / ese conductor / doblar a la izquierda
f. volver a la escuela / tú / ponerme muy nervioso(a)

Fondo cultural

Permiso de manejar En los países hispanohablantes hay diferentes requisitos *(requirements)* para conseguir el permiso de manejar. En todos los países hay que presentar documentos de identidad y un certificado médico que declara que tienes buena salud física y mental. También hay que aprobar un examen. En muchos países los exámenes son de teoría (escrito) y de práctica (manejo). En Argentina puedes manejar un ciclomotor *(moped)* a los 16 años y un coche a los 17. En España puedes manejar un ciclomotor sin llevar pasajeros a los 14 años, llevar pasajeros a los 16 y manejar un coche a los 18.

• ¿Cuáles son los requisitos en tu estado para conseguir el permiso de manejar? ¿Son más fáciles o más difíciles que en los países hispanohablantes?

Una escuela para aprender a manejar en Argentina

Más práctica

• Practice Workbook, p. 68: 3B-7
• Guided Practice: Grammar Acts., pp. 123–124
• Real. para hispanohablantes, p. 119

Go Online
PHSchool.com
For: Present Progressive
Web Code: jdd-0316

Differentiated Instruction
Solutions for All Learners

Students with Learning Difficulties
For *Actividad 22*, provide students with a map of your community. Have them use colored pencils to trace the routes they take to complete errands. Allow them review their maps as they write their directions.

Multiple Intelligences
Visual/Spatial: Have students illustrate *Actividad 20* in comic-strip format. Ask them to write a title and draw the instructor and student, including speech bubbles for each exchange. Encourage them to invent an additional panel that concludes the driving lesson. Post their illustrations in the classroom.

Actividad 21 **Observar/Hablar**

El camión

La artista mexicana Frida Kahlo pintó muchos autorretratos, pero también pintó imágenes que representan la cultura popular de su país. Pintó una colorida imagen de un autobús mexicano en *El camión* (1929), que es la palabra que se usa en México para decir *el autobús*. En los viejos tiempos, los autobuses en la Ciudad de México estaban hechos de caoba *(mahogany)* por adentro. Hoy en día este estilo ya no existe.

Conexiones **El arte**

"El camión" (1929), Frida Kahlo

1. Con otro(a) estudiante, describe a las personas que viajan en el autobús del cuadro. ¿Qué tienen en común? ¿En qué sentido son diferentes? ¿Qué están haciendo?

2. ¿Las personas en el cuadro parecen ser realistas? ¿Por qué?

3. Digan cinco mandatos que la madre puede decirle al niño o al bebé.

  Actividad 22 **Dibujar/Escribir/Hablar**

En mi comunidad

Tienes un(a) amigo(a) que acaba de llegar a tu comunidad y quiere saber adónde ir para hacer sus quehaceres. Dibuja un mapa de tu comunidad con ocho lugares importantes. Marca dónde debe empezar con *Estás aquí*. Escribe tres series de instrucciones para ir de un lugar a otro. Muestra *(Show)* tu mapa a otro(a) estudiante y dile cómo se va a los diferentes lugares. Luego mira el mapa de tu compañero(a) y sigue sus instrucciones para ir de un lugar a otro en su comunidad.

El español en el mundo del trabajo

Para atraer a los turistas hispanohablantes en los Estados Unidos, es importante tener empleados *(employees)* hispanohablantes en los centros de información turística. Así pueden contestar preguntas o dar información o instrucciones a las personas hispanohablantes.

• ¿Vives en una comunidad donde llegan muchos turistas? ¿Cuáles son los lugares de interés turístico populares en tu comunidad?

 ciento setenta y tres 173
Capítulo 3B

 Actividad 21 *Standards:* 1.1, 1.2, 2.2, 3.1

Focus: Studying and speaking about a painting

Suggestions: Remind students to use prior knowledge and context clues as they read the introductions. Have students describe a typical bus ride in your community or in a nearby community. Ask them to discuss similarities and differences between what they see in the painting and their own experiences with public transportation.

Answers will vary.

 Actividad 22 *Standards:* 1.1, 1.2, 1.3  Pre-AP*

Focus: Drawing a community map and giving directions to various places

Suggestions: Provide a map of your community as a model. To avoid repetition, assign a different destination to each group of students.

Answers will vary.

El español en el mundo del trabajo
Core Instruction

 Standards: 1.2, 5.1

Suggestions: Ask students if they have ever visited another country and been helped by an English-speaking employee at a tourist information center. If so, how did that person help them? Have students list tourist attractions near your community that might be of interest to Spanish-speaking visitors.

Answers will vary.

Theme Project

Students can perform Step 5 at this point. Record their presentations on cassette or videotape for inclusion in their portfolio. (For more information, see p. 126-a.)

Enrich Your Teaching
Resources for All Teachers

Teacher-to-Teacher
Have students use local historical landmarks, restaurants, and shopping areas to create a walking tour for visitors. Ask them to prepare a flyer that outlines their tour and includes a map. Send top-scoring flyers to a local tourism office or Chamber of Commerce and ask officials if they could post them or distribute them to Spanish-speaking visitors.

Culture Note
To increase safety, new drivers in Spain are on probation for one year after receiving their licenses. A green and white "L" is placed in the rear window of cars driven by novice drivers. The maximum speed they are allowed to drive is 80 km / hr (about 50 mi / hr).

Core Instruction

 Standards: 1.2, 2.1, 3.1, 3.2

Focus: Reading comprehension of a brochure on defensive driving

Suggestions:

Pre-reading: Have students list characteristics of both good and bad drivers. Ask them what conditions might influence how people drive. Point out that they will read advice on how to be a good driver in different situations. Direct attention to the title and subtitles. Have volunteers make predictions about the content of each section.

Reading: After each paragraph, point out similarities in students' definitions of good drivers with the descriptions in the reading. If students come across a word they do not know, remind them to use context clues to help them with unfamiliar vocabulary.

Post-reading: Have volunteers summarize the article in their own words. If you have students in your class who have their licenses, ask them if they apply these practices when they drive. Are they defensive drivers? Why or why not? Complete the *¿Comprendiste?* questions.

Bellringer Review

Write the following cognates on the board and have students write the English equivalent:

defensiva	*colisiones*	*distracciones*
visibilidad	*velocidad*	*iluminación*

Pre-AP* Support

- **Activity:** As a follow-up to the reading, write the three subtitles from the article on the board and ask students to copy them on a sheet of paper. Read aloud to the class a series of "good driving suggestions" and have students place the number under the appropriate heading.
- *Pre-AP* Resource Book:** Comprehensive guide to Pre-AP* reading skill development, pp. 18–24

Additional Resources

Student Resource: Guided Practice: Lectura, p. 125

¡Adelante!

Lectura

Lee este artículo que viene de un informe de Costa Rica sobre manejar a la defensiva. La información del artículo te puede ayudar a ser un(a) buen(a) conductor(a).

¿QUÉ ES MANEJAR A LA DEFENSIVA?

Manejar a la defensiva quiere decir practicar buenos hábitos para no tener colisiones u otra clase de accidentes. También consiste en tener cuidado con todos los peligros. Se debe tener cuidado con:

- acciones peligrosas de otros conductores
- conductores que manejan muy rápido sin cuidado o sin luces en la noche
- malas condiciones del tiempo
- malas condiciones de la carretera

Distracciones al manejar

Un buen conductor siempre maneja con atención y se concentra en la carretera, sin pensar en otras cosas que pueden ser distracciones. Algunas distracciones comunes son:

- pensar en problemas personales
- leer algo en el coche o en la calle
- escuchar la radio
- conversar con amigos
- hablar por teléfono celular

8

Éstas son las reglas para estar atento:[1]

- Cuando el vehículo de se está moviendo, los ojos siempre deben estar en movimiento, pasando por los instrumentos, los espejos y especialmente la carretera.
- En la ciudad se debe mirar 100 metros adelante,[2] y en la carretera, 300 metros adelante.
- Es necesario tener buena visibilidad de los coches que vienen detrás y a los lados. Para hacerlo, deben usarse el espejo retrovisor y los espejos laterales.

Manejar de noche

Menos personas manejan de noche, pero durante la noche ocurren más accidentes que durante el día. Durante la noche ocurren aproximadamente el 80% de los accidentes registrados en un día. Para manejar a la defensiva de noche es importante pensar en lo siguiente:

- La velocidad: Debe reducirse en un 50% de la velocidad que se usa de día, y si está lloviendo debe reducirse más.

[1] attentive   [2] ahead

Tráfico en Caracas, Venezuela

174 ciento setenta y cuatro
Tema 3 • Tú y tu comunidad

Objectives

- **Read about defensive driving**
- **Learn about neighborhoods in Spanish-speaking countries**
- **Make a poster on safe driving practices**
- **Watch En busca de la verdad, Episodio 2**

Estrategia

Context clues
In this reading you may come across words you don't know. Use the context in which they are found to help you guess their meanings.

Differentiated Instruction
Solutions for All Learners

Students With Learning Difficulties

Point out that headings and bullets can help one locate specific information. Have volunteers read the *¿Comprendiste?* questions aloud. For each question, ask students which section would be most likely to contain the answer. Have them take notes and refer to them as they complete the activity.

Multiple Intelligences

Logical/Mathematical: Have students convert distances and speeds from customary units to the metric system. Ask them to research driving rules such as proper speed limits and safe following distances. Have them create a conversion chart to present the information to the class. Ask them to explain the mathematical formulas they use.

- La visibilidad: En la noche se ve el 50% menos de lo que puede verse de día. Los peatones se ven menos en la noche, especialmente si llevan ropa oscura.
- La iluminación: La iluminación del vehículo es importante. El coche siempre debe indicar su presencia en la carretera.

Manejar en carretera

Las condiciones de las carreteras no siempre son buenas, y es necesario estar muy alerta al manejar. También los conductores manejan más rápidamente en las carreteras. Se debe estar alerta a:

- La iluminación: Si la carretera no está iluminada, debe reducirse la velocidad.

10

- Obstrucciones en la carretera: La obstrucción pueden ser rocas,[3] tierra[4] u otra cosa.
- Carreteras estrechas: Muchas carreteras son estrechas, con sólo dos carriles.[5]

Recuerda . . . manejar a la defensiva hace las carreteras mejores para todos.

Carretera estrecha

11

[3] rocks   [4] soil   [5] lanes

¿Comprendiste?

1. Para manejar a la defensiva, ¿cuáles son tres peligros que debes comprender?

2. ¿Cuáles son algunas distracciones que ocurren mientras *(while)* alguien maneja? En tu opinión, ¿cuál es la distracción más común de tus amigos y familia?

3. ¿Por qué puede ser peligroso manejar de noche?

4. ¿Por qué puede ser peligroso manejar en la carretera?

5. Escribe dos cosas que aprendiste después de leer este artículo.

Y tú, ¿qué dices?

1. ¿Tienes que tomar un curso para obtener el permiso de manejar donde vives? ¿También es necesario tomar un curso de manejar a la defensiva?

2. ¿Crees que es buena idea tomar un curso de manejar? ¿Por qué?

 **Fondo cultural**

La Carretera Panamericana es una carretera que une *(links)* a los países de América del Norte, América Central y América del Sur. La idea para la carretera se originó en una conferencia de la Organización de Estados Americanos en 1923. La construcción de la carretera empezó en 1936, y hoy en día tiene aproximadamente 16,000 millas (25,750 km) de extensión.

- ¿Por dónde pasa la Carretera Panamericana en los Estados Unidos? ¿Por qué es importante esta carretera en la economía del hemisferio occidental?

Más práctica

- WAV Wbk., Writing, p. 66
- Guided Practice: *Lectura*, p. 125
- *Real.* para hispanohablantes, pp. 122–123

Go Online PHSchool.com
For: Internet Activity
Web Code: jdd-0317

Communicate: Reading   3B

¿Comprendiste?

Presentation EXPRESS ANSWERS

Standards: 1.2

Resources: Answers on Transparencies

Focus: Verifying reading comprehension

Suggestions: For each question, have students predict the heading under which the answer might be found.

Answers will vary but may include:

1. **Los peligros que debes comprender son: acciones peligrosas de otros conductores, conductores que manejan muy rápido sin cuidado o sin luces en la noche, malas condiciones del tiempo y malas condiciones de la carretera.**
2. **Algunas distracciones que ocurren mientras alguien maneja son: pensar en problemas personales, leer algo en el coche o en la calle, escuchar la radio, conversar con amigos o hablar por teléfono celular. Answers to the second part of the question will vary.**
3. **Puede ser peligroso manejar de noche porque aproximadamente el 80% de los accidentes registrados ocurren durante la noche.**
4. **Puede ser peligroso manejar en la carretera porque las condiciones no siempre son buenas y los conductores manejan más rápidamente.**
5. **Answers will vary.**

Y tú ¿qué dices?

Standards: 1.3

Focus: Writing or speaking about taking driving courses

Suggestion: Find out about courses and regulations for driving in your community. If students answer item 2 negatively, have them say why they do not think it is a good idea.

Answers will vary.

Fondo cultural   Standards: 1.2, 2.2

Suggestions: Bring in maps of the United States and Mexico and show students the Pan-American Highway.

Answers:

1. **La carretera Panamericana pasa por California, Arizona, New Mexico y Texas.**
2. **Answers will vary, but may include the transportation of products and tourism.**

For Further Reading

Student Resources: Realidades para hispanohablantes: Lectura 2, pp. 124–125; Lecturas para hispanohablantes 2: "Los problemas de la ciudad," pp. 15–16, "Una carta a Dios," pp. 57–59

Enrich Your Teaching

Resources for All Teachers

Teacher-to-Teacher

Have students map out a driving tour of part of the Pan-American Highway. Assign students different countries in North America, Central America, or South America. Ask them to list any landmarks, cities, bodies of water, or mountains that are located along their route. Have them prepare a presentation to describe their road trip.

Internet Search

Have students research the Pan-American Highway to find out about places along its route.

Keywords:

Carretera Panamericana

175

Core Instruction

Standards: 1.2, 2.1, 2.2, 4.2

Focus: Reading about close-knit communities in Spanish-speaking cultures

Suggestions: Have students write a short description of their neighborhood to share with the class. Ask volunteers to share their descriptions before reading the passage. Tell students that they will read about *el barrio,* the concept of neighborhoods in Spanish-speaking communities. As they read, have them list the characteristics of this type of neighborhood. After the reading, have them list advantages and disadvantages of living in a close-knit community. Find information on well-known Spanish-speaking communities in the United States. Share this information with students and have them identify characteristics of those communities that correspond to those described in the reading.

Answers will vary.

Additional Resources

Student Resource: Realidades para hispano-hablantes, p. 126

Perspectivas del mundo hispano

El barrio

Imagina que llegas a casa y no puedes abrir la puerta. No hay nadie en casa y no puedes entrar. Mañana tienes un examen y los libros están en la casa. No tienes dinero. No puedes llamar por teléfono. Tienes hambre y no puedes comprar comida. ¿Qué puedes hacer?

Esto no es un gran problema si vives en un barrio de un país hispanohablante. Aquí los vecinos[1] se conocen[2] bien. Son simpáticos y se ayudan. Cuando te olvidas las llaves puedes ir a casa de tus vecinos. Si pueden, ellos te ayudan a entrar en tu casa. Si tienes hambre, te dan algo de comer. Te dejan llamar por teléfono.

En los países hispanohablantes, el barrio es una institución. Las casas del barrio están cerca unas de otras y frecuentemente están cerca de una plaza. Normalmente en el barrio hay un mercado, un cine y pequeñas tiendas para comprar comida, ropa o materiales para la escuela. El barrio es como una extensión del hogar[3]—un buen lugar para la familia, donde los niños y los mayores pueden jugar y pasear.

¡Compruébalo! Compara las calles que hay cerca de tu casa con los barrios de los países hispanohablantes. ¿Conoces a los vecinos de tu comunidad? ¿Hay pequeñas tiendas familiares?[4] ¿Hay una plaza?

¿Qué te parece? ¿Cuáles son los aspectos de la organización de un barrio que más te interesan? ¿Crees que el barrio es una buena manera de organizar una comunidad? ¿Por qué?

[1]neighbors [2]know one another [3]home [4]family-run

Un barrio típico de Guanajuato, México

El Museo del Barrio en la ciudad de Nueva York. En él se pueden ver trabajos artísticos de la comunidad hispanohablante.

Uno de los muchos barrios que se encuentran en Sevilla, España

---

Differentiated Instruction

Solutions for All Learners

Heritage Language Learners

Have students interview friends or family members who have lived in their heritage country and write an essay describing the neighborhood in which they lived. Ask them to include a physical description, as well as information about the people who made the neighborhood unique. Provide a rubric for assessment.

Maneja con cuidado

Task

You and many of your classmates have recently received or will soon receive your first driver's license. Make a poster that can be displayed in the classroom that reminds everyone of safe driving practices and special traffic signs you need to recognize.

1 Prewrite Write down what you should know about driving in your state. The answers to the following questions will help you organize your information.

- ¿Qué señales son importantes y qué información dan? ¿Qué forma tienen? (cuadrados, rectángulos, triángulos, círculos, octágonos o diamantes)? ¿De qué color son? Dibújalas.
- ¿Cuáles son algunas de las zonas especiales en tu comunidad? ¿Cuál es la velocidad máxima en estas zonas?
- ¿Cómo maneja un(a) buen(a) conductor(a)? ¿Qué debes recordar *(remember)* cuando manejas un coche?

2 Draft Read through your answers to the questions in Step 1. Decide what information you want to stress in your poster. Use this information to draw a first draft of your poster.

3 Revise Reread the information on your first draft. Is it arranged in a clear and logical manner? Check spelling, verb forms, and agreement. Share the poster with a partner, who will check the following:

- Does the poster present important and accurate information?
- Is the visual presentation clear and easy to understand?
- Is there anything you should add, change, or correct?

4 Publish Prepare a final copy of your poster. Make any necessary changes or additions. Add designs or illustrations to make the poster attractive and pleasing to the eye. Display it in your classroom, the school library, or add it to your portfolio.

5 Evaluation Your teacher may give you a rubric for how the poster will be graded. You will probably be graded on:

- how complete and accurate the information is
- how clear and attractive the visuals are
- how easy it is to understand the information you present

Estrategia

Using illustrations
Photographs, designs, and colors help to draw the eye to important information.

Communicate: Writing

Presentación escrita

Expository/Persuasive

Standards: 1.3, 3.1

Focus: Communicating about safe driving

Suggestions: Have students brainstorm a list of rules that they think all good drivers need to be aware of when driving. Point out how rules may differ from area to area. Ask them to name various locations in your community, and to describe safe driving practices they would implement in those zones.

Remind students that their posters should focus on one theme. To encourage variety, assign different themes to students.

For Step 3, copy the questions on a separate sheet of paper to give to students as they evaluate each other's work. You may prefer to have students get input from more than one classmate.

Review the rubric with students so that they have clear expectations. Model a top-scoring project for them before they begin

Extension: Encourage students to include persuasive language as they create their poster to convince students of the importance to drive safely and defensively.

Pre-AP* Support

- **Pre-AP* Resource Book:** Comprehensive guide to Pre-AP* writing skill development, pp. 25–35

Portfolio

After displaying the posters, have students add them to their portfolios.

Additional Resources

Student Resources: Realidades para hispanohablantes, p. 127; Guided Practice: Presentación escrita, p. 126

✓ Assessment

- Assessment Program: Rubrics, p. T29

Review the rubric with students so that they have a clear understanding of the expectations. Model a top-scoring project for them before they begin.

RUBRIC	Score 1	Score 3	Score 5
Your completeness and accuracy of information	You provide some of the information required with many factual errors.	You provide most of the information required with some factual errors.	You provide all of the information required with very few factual errors.
Neatness and attractiveness of your presentation	You provide no visuals and your poster contains visible error corrections and smudges.	You provide few visuals and your poster contains visible error corrections and smudges.	You provide several visuals, have no error corrections and smudges, and your poster is attractive.
How easily you are understood	You are difficult to understand and have many errors.	You are fairly easy to understand and have occasional errors.	You are easy to understand and have very few errors.

Videomisterio

Videomisterio

Core Instruction

Standards: 1.2, 3.2, 5.2

Resources: Teacher's Resource Book: Video Script, pp. 166–167; Video Program: Cap. 3B; Video Program Teacher's Guide: Cap. 3B

Focus: Introducing the events and vocabulary of this episode; scanning and reading the episode summary

Personajes importantes

Carmen and Linda Toledo, from San Antonio

Roberto Toledo, resident of Guanajuato

Tomás Toledo, Roberto's father, doctor

Berta, Roberto's mother, travel agent

Daniela, Roberto's sister

Julio, Roberto's best friend

Synopsis: Carmen and Linda arrive in Guanajuato, Mexico, and go to the travel agency recommended by Sr. Balzar in *Episodio 1.* There they meet Berta Toledo, a travel agent who has made hotel reservations for them. Carmen and Linda meet Berta's family. The following day they visit the Benito Juárez school.

Suggestions:

Pre-viewing: Review the events of *Episodio* 1: The story began in San Antonio, Texas, where Linda Toledo attends a bilingual school. Linda's mother, Carmen, is a teacher at Linda's school, and is in charge of setting up an exchange program in Guanajuato, Mexico.

Have a volunteer read the *Nota cultural* aloud. Ask students how using different nouns to name schools may help distinguish a school's focus (for example, an *instituto* may be more technically oriented).

Point out the *Palabras para comprender* to the class, giving examples in context and writing sentences on the board. Remind students that these words are used only to help them understand the episode, and that they are not otherwise responsible for learning the words as vocabulary.

Videomisterio

En busca de la verdad

Episodio 2

Antes de ver el video

"Sra. Toledo . . . , y Srta. Toledo . . . Nosotros también somos Toledo".

"Volveremos en una hora, Sra. Toledo".

Resumen del episodio

Carmen y Linda llegan a Guanajuato y van directo a la agencia de viajes "Ultramar". Allí conocen a Berta Toledo, Roberto, Daniela y Julio. Al día siguiente Daniela lleva a Carmen y a Linda a la escuela.

Nota cultural En México, una *escuela* también es un "colegio" o un "instituto". A veces las escuelas tienen el nombre de personas importantes como, por ejemplo, Escuela Josefa Ortiz, Colegio Benito Juárez o Instituto Miguel Hidalgo. Los mexicanos también demuestran su admiración por personas de otros países. Algunas escuelas tienen nombres como Escuela Winston Churchill, Escuela John F. Kennedy o Escuela Abraham Lincoln.

Palabras para comprender
para nada not at all
apellido last name
acompañar to go with
mostrar to show
el idioma language

178 ciento setenta y ocho
Tema 3 • Tú y tu comunidad

Differentiated Instruction
Solutions for All Learners

Advanced Learners

As an ongoing project, have students create a visual timeline of the characters in the *Videomisterio.* For each *episodio* they should indicate: (a) the principal characters; (b) three of the most important scenes; (c) the things each person did in those scenes; and (d) with whom they interacted.

Multiple Intelligences

Bodily/Kinesthetic: Have students take the information compiled by the advanced learners and have them choose one of the scenes to reenact. You may want to give them a copy of the Video Script to rehearse with.

Después de ver el video

¿Comprendiste?

A. Decide cuáles de las siguientes frases son ciertas y cuáles son falsas:

1. Carmen y Linda llegan en avión a San Antonio.
2. Berta Toledo trabaja en una agencia de viajes.
3. La escuela Benito Juárez está muy lejos del hotel de Carmen y Linda.
4. Julio le dice a Carmen: "Mamá, necesito usar el coche."
5. Carmen y Linda van al hotel San Diego.
6. El apellido de Julio es Lobero.
7. Roberto lleva la maleta de Linda.
8. Daniela le muestra la escuela a Linda.
9. A Julio le gusta jugar al fútbol.

B. Las siguientes frases del videomisterio están incompletas. Complétalas con la palabra o palabras correctas de la lista.

ir allí	San Antonio
servirles	acompañar
aquí en Guanajuato	escuela
en común	la escuela

1. Buenas tardes. ¿En qué puedo _____?
2. Mañana tengo que _____.
3. Las señoras son de _____.
4. ¿Es el apellido de todos _____?
5. Mañana van a visitar tu _____.
6. Discúlpenme, pero no los puedo _____.
7. Daniela va a mostrarme _____.
8. Nuestras escuelas tienen mucho _____.

"Mira, allí está Julio".

Go Online
PHSchool.com
For: More on *En busca de la verdad*
Web Code: jdd-0209

Suggestions:

Visual scanning: Direct attention to the photos. Have students read the captions and try to guess what the characters may be talking about.

Before students read the *Resumen del episodio* explain that *ultramar* means "beyond the sea." Ask them if this is an appropriate name for a travel agency. Then have them read the *Resumen del episodio.* Ask one or two comprehension questions.

Viewing: Play *Episodio 2* for the class. If there is time after viewing the full episode, go back and replay key moments that you wish to highlight. Remind students that they may not understand every word they hear in the video, but that they should listen for overall understanding.

Post-viewing: Complete the *¿Comprendiste?* in class.

¿Comprendiste?

 Standards: 1.2, 1.3 Presentation EXPRESS ANSWERS

Resources: Answers on Transparencies

Focus: Verifying comprehension; reviewing the plot

Suggestions: If a statement is false, have students correct it according to the story.

Answers:

A:

1 falsa	6. cierta
2. cierta	7. falsa
3. falsa	8. cierta
4. falsa	9. cierta
5. cierta	

B:

1. servirles	5. escuela
2. ir allí	6. acompañar
3. San Antonio	7. la escuela
4. aquí en Guanajuato	8. en común

Additional Resources

- *En busca de la verdad* Video Workbook, Episode 2
- *En busca de la verdad* Teacher's Video Guide: Answer Key

Enrich Your Teaching
Resources for All Teachers

Teacher-to-Teacher

Write your own summary of the *episodio*. Make sure to include statements that are incorrect and out of order. Have students read your summary and correct it as necessary. If you use words from *Palabras para comprender,* be sure you let your students know this. You may want to turn this into a group activity by reading your summary aloud and having students call out the errors. Be sure to read slowly and pantomime if possible.

179

Review Activities

To talk about driving: Have pairs of students create a Concentration game using illustrations on one card and the corresponding word on another. Have students place the cards face down and match the words to the illustrations.

To give and receive driving advice: Have students write the words or phrases on slips of paper. Have them use one color for words that give advice, and another for receiving advice. Ask them to place the papers face down, choose two, and use them to create short dialogues.

To ask for and give directions: Give students a map of your town and a set of cards. The cards should list a starting place and a destination. Have students take turns selecting a card and asking for directions. Their partner should give them directions to the destination.

Portfolio

Invite students to review the activities they completed in this chapter, including written reports, posters or other visuals, tapes of oral presentations, or other projects. Have them select one or two items that they feel best demonstrate their achievements in Spanish to include in their portfolios. Have them include this with the Chapter Checklist and Self-Assessment Worksheet.

Additional Resources

Student Resources: Realidades para hispanohablantes, p. 128

 **CD-ROM**

PuzzleView Web Code: jdd-0318

Teacher Resources:

• Teacher's Resource Book: Situation Cards, p. 172, Clip Art, pp. 174–177

• Assessment Program: Chapter Checklist and Self-Assessment Worksheet, pp. T56–T57

Repaso del capítulo

Vocabulario y gramática jdd-0399

To prepare for the test, check to see if you . . .
• know the new vocabulary and grammar
• can perform the tasks on p. 181

to talk about driving

la avenida	avenue
el camión, *pl.* los camiones	truck
la carretera	highway
el conductor, la conductora	driver
el cruce de calles	intersection
la cuadra	block
la esquina	corner
la estatua	statue
la fuente	fountain
el peatón, *pl.* los peatones	pedestrian
el permiso de manejar	driver's license
la plaza	plaza
el policía, la policía	police officer
poner una multa	to give a ticket
el puente	bridge
el semáforo	stoplight
la señal de parada	stop sign
el tráfico	traffic

to give and receive driving advice

ancho, -a	wide
¡Basta!	Enough!
De acuerdo.	OK. Agreed.
dejar	to leave, to let
Déjame en paz.	Leave me alone.
despacio	slowly
esperar	to wait
estar seguro, -a	to be sure
estrecho, -a	narrow
Me estás poniendo nervioso, -a.	You are making me nervous.
peligroso, -a	dangerous
quitar	to take away, to remove
tener cuidado	to be careful
ya	already

For *Vocabulario adicional,* see pp. 498–499.

to ask for and give directions

aproximadamente	approximately
¿Cómo se va . . . ?	How do you go to . . . ?
complicado, -a	complicated
cruzar	to cross
derecho	straight
desde	from, since
doblar	to turn
en medio de	in the middle of
hasta	as far as, up to
manejar	to drive
el metro	subway
parar	to stop
pasar	to pass, to go
por	for, by, around, along, through
quedar	to be located
seguir (e → i)	to follow, to continue
tener prisa	to be in a hurry

present progressive: irregular forms

decir:	diciendo	vestir:	vistiendo
pedir:	pidiendo	dormir:	durmiendo
repetir:	repitiendo	creer:	creyendo
seguir:	siguiendo	leer:	leyendo
servir:	sirviendo	traer:	trayendo

irregular affirmative *tú* commands

hacer:	haz
ir:	ve
ser:	sé

See p. 168 for a more complete chart.

direct object pronouns

	Singular		Plural
me	me	nos	us
te	you (fam.)	os	you (fam.)
lo, la	him, her, it, you	los, las	them, you

Differentiated Instruction

Solutions for All Learners

Advanced Learners

Have students write a set of silly rules that only bad drivers follow. For example: *Los malos conductores siempre manejan rápidamente por las calles estrechas.* Encourage them to illustrate their rules emphasizing that these are things that one should not do when driving. Use their illustrations to make a bulletin board.

Más práctica
- Practice Workbook: Puzzle, p. 69
- Practice Workbook: Organizer, p. 70

Go Online PHSchool.com
For: Test Preparation
Web Code: jdd-0318

Preparación para el examen

On the exam you will be asked to . . .	Here are practice tasks similar to those you will find on the exam . . .	If you need review . . .
① Escuchar Listen to and understand driving advice	Gabriel's father is teaching him to drive. Listen as he cautions Gabriel about what to do. (a) Do you think they're driving on a highway or just around town? (b) Give at least two reasons why you think so.	**pp. 158–161** *A primera vista* **p. 163** *Actividades 7–8*
② Hablar Tell someone how to get from your school to a particular location near your school	You volunteered to host a student from Costa Rica who wants to see what's near your school. Can you explain to him how to get to several places? Practice by giving your partner the directions. You could begin by saying: *Sal de la escuela y toma la calle _____.*	**pp. 158–159** *A primera vista* **p. 165** *Actividad 10* **p. 169** *Actividad 17* **p. 173** *Actividad 22*
③ Leer Read and understand advice for establishing good driving habits	Take a look at some driving rules on a Web site from Mexico: 1. Ve muy *despacio* en una *zona escolar*. 2. Sigue *detrás* de otro *coche* aproximadamente el largo (length) de dos *coches*. 3. Entra con *precaución* a un *cruce de calles* con un *semáforo* amarillo. Which of the following was NOT mentioned: (a) driving through a red light; (b) driving in a school zone; or (c) being cautious at a yellow light?	**pp. 158–159** *A primera vista* **p. 168** *Actividad 16* **pp. 174–175** *Lectura*
④ Escribir Write about things that might happen as you drive that would make you nervous	Everyone occasionally gets nervous about something. What's making you nervous today? Write down at least two things for your journal entry. You could start by writing: _____ *me está poniendo nervioso(a) porque siempre está* _____ . . .	**p. 162** *Actividad 5* **p. 163** *Actividad 8* **pp. 174–175** *Lectura*
⑤ Pensar Demonstrate an understanding of the importance of one's neighborhood in Spanish-speaking communities	Your friend is going to Mexico City this summer to study Spanish and will be living with a Mexican family. What could you tell her about neighborhoods in Spanish-speaking countries? What might be different from the neighborhood she lives in now? What might be similar?	**p. 176** *Perspectivas del mundo hispano*

ciento ochenta y uno **181**
Capítulo 3B

✔ Differentiated Assessment
Solutions for All Learners

STUDENTS NEEDING EXTRA HELP
- **Alternate Assessment Program:** Examen del capítulo 3B
- **Audio Program CD 20:** Chap. 3B, Track 7

HERITAGE LEARNERS
- **Assessment Program: Realidades para hispanohablantes:** Examen del capítulo 3B
- **ExamView** Heritage Learner Test Bank

ADVANCED/PRE-AP*
- **ExamView** Pre-AP* Test Bank
- **Pre-AP* Resource Book,** pp. 104–107

Review

Performance Tasks
 **Presentation EXPRESS ANSWERS**

 Standards: 1.2, 1.3, 2.1, 2.2, 4.2

Student Resource: Realidades para hispanohablantes, p. 129
Teacher Resources: Teacher's Resource Book: Audio Script, p. 164; Audio Program: Track 14; Answers on Transparencies

1. Escuchar
Suggestions: Have students listen to the entire script before they answer the questions.

 Script: Ten cuidado, hijo. Estamos en una zona escolar. ¡Ay! ¡Espera! Hay peatones, hijo. . . ¡Más despacio, por favor! Mira el semáforo.
Answers: a) They are driving around town. b) They are in a school zone, there are pedestrians, and there is a traffic light.

2. Hablar
Suggestions: Assign one or two places to each student. Have them record their responses or share them with a partner.
Answers will vary.

3. Leer
Suggestions: Have students read the possible answers before they read the rules.
Answer: a) driving through a red light

4. Escribir
Suggestions: Provide students with a word bank to help them generate ideas.
Answers will vary.

5. Pensar
Suggestions: To help students answer the questions, refer them to the reading on p. 176.
Answers will vary.

✔ Assessment
- **ExamView** QuickTake Presenter Quiz on PresEXPRESS
- Assessment Program: Examen del capítulo
- **ExamView** test generator Test Bank: Tests A and B
- Audio Program CD 20: Chap. 3B, Track 7

Tema 4

Recuerdos del pasado

THEME OVERVIEW

4A Cuando éramos niños

• Toys and playing with other children
Vocabulary: toys, games, and childhood activities
Grammar: the imperfect tense, imperfect forms of *ir, ser,* and *ver*
Cultural Perspectives: traditional Hispanic toys and games, child care in Hispanic countries

4B Celebrando los días festivos

• Holiday celebrations and family
Vocabulary: describing family members and holiday celebrations
Grammar: the imperfect tense: describing a situation; reciprocal actions
Cultural Perspectives: different Hispanic celebrations around the world

Theme Project

Un álbum de fotos

Overview: Students create a photo album or memory book of past family holidays featuring photos of family members at different holiday celebrations and brief descriptions under each photo. Then they present their book to the class explaining each picture and holiday and describing selected family members.

El día de la independencia, mi madre, mi padre y mi hermana Lola íbamos juntos al parque para ver el desfile.

Materials: Construction paper, markers, photos, glue or tape, scissors

Sequence: (suggestions for when to do each step are found throughout the chapters)

4A ▶ **STEP 1.** Review instructions so students know what is expected of them. Hand out the "Theme 4 Project Instructions and Rubric" from the *Teacher's Resource Book.*

STEP 2. Students submit a rough sketch of each page of their photo book. Return the drafts with your suggestions. For grammar and vocabulary practice, ask students to partner and present their drafts to each other.

STEP 3. Students create layouts on different pieces of construction paper, leaving room for photos and descriptions. Encourage them to work in pencil first and to try different arrangements before gluing photos or decorations.

4B ▶ **STEP 4.** Students submit a draft of the photo captions. Note your corrections and suggestions, then return drafts to students.

STEP 5. Students complete and present their books to the class, explaining each picture and holiday and describing selected family members.

Options:

1. Students create a book about fictitious or famous families.
2. Students research and present other international holidays.

Assessment:

Here is a detailed rubric for assessing this project:

Theme 4 Project: *Un álbum de fotos*

RUBRIC	Score 1	Score 3	Score 5
Your evidence of planning	You provide no written draft or poster layout.	Your draft was written and layout created, but not corrected.	You show evidence of corrected draft and layout.
Your use of illustrations	You include no photos or visuals.	You include very few photos or visuals.	You include several photos or visuals.
Your presentation	You include little of the required information.	You describe at least three family celebrations.	You describe three or more family celebrations.

Bulletin Boards

Theme: *Recuerdos del pasado*

Ask students to cut out, copy, or download photos of traditional family celebrations from many different cultures and time periods. Cluster photos into categories of celebrations—weddings, baptisms, birthdays, bar and bat mitzvahs, graduations, etc.—so that similarities and differences are evident.

Bibliography

Ebinger, Virginia Nylander. *Niñez: Spanish Songs, Games, and Stories of Childhood.* Sunstone Press, 1995. Bilingual information and illustrations on Spanish songs and games.

Gollub, Matthew. (Leovigildo Martínez, Illustrator). *La luna se fue de fiesta/The Moon Was at a Fiesta.* Tortuga Press, 1998. Folktale about why the moon is sometimes visible during the day.

Menard, Valerie. *The Latino Holiday Book: From Cinco de Mayo to Día de los Muertos: The Celebrations and Traditions of Hispanic-Americans.* Marlowe & Co., 2000. Guide to the traditions and celebrations of Hispanic-Americans.

Wade, Mary Dodson. *The Day of the Dead (El Día de los Muertos).* Children's Press, 2002. Bilingual information and illustrations on the Day of the Dead in Mexico.

Winchester, Faith. *Hispanic Holidays: Read and Discover Ethnic Holidays.* Bridgestone Books, 1996. Introduction to Hispanic holidays.

Hands-on Culture

Craft: *Máscaras de Carnaval*

Carnaval, celebrated in most Latin American countries, is a colorful celebration where many people wear unique masks and parade through the streets. The masks can represent either animals or people, and they are always colorful!

Materials: colored card stock, scissors, glue, glitter, markers, feathers, string

Directions:

1. Draw a rough sketch of the mask on a piece of scrap paper. Create a mask that represents an animal, a person, or an imaginary creature of your choosing.

2. When you have chosen a design, cut your mask out of the card stock.

3. Add glitter, designs, or feathers to make your mask unique.

4. Tie a string from one side of the mask to the other so that you can wear it to celebrate *Carnaval!*

Internet Search

Use the keywords to find more information.

4A Keywords:

> Sir Isaac Newton, scientists, Frida Kahlo, Maya, Aztec, Leovigildo Martínez, Francisco de Goya, fábulas, Picasso

4B Keywords:

> Antonio M. Ruiz, Euskadi, el Día de la Raza, la Semana Santa, el Día de los Muertos, el Día de la Independencia, el carnaval, las Fallas, el roscón de reyes, sugar skulls

Game

¿Qué celebrábamos?

Play this game in *Capítulo* 4B, after students have learned the imperfect tense and the vocabulary for celebrations.

Players: Any number or students in small groups

Materials: blank overhead transparency pages, overhead transparency markers, an overhead projector, blank paper, pen

Rules:

1. In groups, players choose any holiday they celebrated as a child. On the overhead transparency, the students write five sentences in the imperfect describing each holiday without giving away the holiday's name.
   (Navidad)
   Recibíamos muchos regalos.
   Los regalos estaban debajo de un árbol.
   Visitábamos a nuestros abuelos y tíos.
   Comíamos juntos.
   Decorábamos la casa con luces.

2. When each team has completed their descriptions, they take turns displaying their descriptions. Using a piece of paper to cover the sentences, they can reveal one sentence at a time. The other teams guess possible holidays. The first team to guess the correct holiday gets points.

3. Points are awarded based on the number of clues that the students needed to guess the correct holiday. The team with the most points at the end of the game wins.

   one clue: 5 points
   two clues: 4 points
   three clues: 3 points
   four clues: 2 points
   five clues: 1 point

Variation: Students can include holidays from the Spanish-speaking world.

RECYCLE	Vocabulary
A ver si recuerdas	• Una celebración

A primera vista	Manos a la obra	¡Adelante!	Repaso

Learning Sequence

INPUT	PRACTICE	APPLICATION	REVIEW
• Introduce vocabulary and grammar within an authentic context.	• Practice and develop new vocabulary. • Learn and practice new grammar structures.	• Apply vocabulary and grammar through culminating, theme-based activities. • Apply skill development.	• Review vocabulary and grammar.

Objectives

Read, listen to, and interpret information about • Toys • Playing with other children	• Communicate about childhood toys and games. • Discuss past activities. • Express to whom an action is done.	• Read a fable from Mexico. • Sing traditional Spanish-language songs. • Talk about how you were as a child. • Watch *En busca de la verdad, Episodio 3*.	• Prepare for the chapter test.

Culture

• Pablo Picasso	• *Las mascotas* • *Las guarderías infantiles* • *Juguetes mayas*	• *Canciones infantiles*	• Discuss popular children's songs from Spanish-speaking countries.

Vocabulary	Grammar	Learner Support	
• Toys • Animals • Childhood activities	• The imperfect tense: Regular verbs • The imperfect tense: Irregular verbs	**STRATEGIES** • Looking ahead • Using context • Using background knowledge • Using visuals	**RECYCLING** • Family members • Leisure and sport activities • Adjectives • School activities • Clothing

Chapter Features

Pronunciación

The letters *r* and *rr*

El español en en la comunidad

The importance of learning a second language

Conexiones

Science: Sir Isaac Newton

Beyond the Classroom: States & Countries

Illinois
España
República Dominicana
México
Puerto Rico
Ecuador
Argentina

Student Resources

TECHNOLOGY

PRACTICE

ONLINE
Interactive Textbook
• Student Edition Online plus audio, video, and flashcards

Go Online Companion Web Site
• Tutorial activities
• Internet links
• Self-tests
• Downloadable MP3 audio files
• **PuzzleView**

CD-ROM
Interactive Textbook CD-ROM
Student Edition on CD-ROM plus audio, video, and flashcards

MindPoint™ CD-ROM
QUIZ SHOW

PRINT MATERIAL

CORE INSTRUCTION
Practice Workbook, pp. 71–81
• Review
• Vocabulary
• Grammar
• Puzzle
• Organizer

Writing, Audio & Video Activities, pp. 67–77
• Video
• Audio
• Writing

Grammar Study Guide 1–2 (or 3–4)

Differentiated Instruction

STUDENTS NEEDING EXTRA HELP
Guided Practice Activities, pp. 127–144
• Vocabulary Flash Cards and Vocabulary Check
• Grammar Activities
• Presentación oral

HERITAGE LEARNERS
Realidades para hispanohablantes, pp. 130–149

Lecturas para hispanohablantes
• *Cuando era puertorriqueña* (excerpt), pp. 106–108
• "Paloma Herrera: Alas en los pies," pp. 122–124

ADVANCED/PRE-AP*
Pre-AP* Resource Book: Student Activity Sheet, p. 111

Teacher Resources

TECHNOLOGY

PLAN AND TEACH

Audio Program   Fine Art Transparencies
Video Program   Vocabulary and Grammar Transparencies
                 Answers on Transparencies

TeacherEXPRESS CD-ROM
• Lesson Planner
• Vocabulary Clip Art
• Web Resources
• Teaching Resources
• Teacher Edition with Interactive Links

PresentationEXPRESS CD-ROM
• Vocabulary
• Tranparencies and Maps
• Grammar
• Photo Gallery
• Audio
• Clip Art

ASSESS

PH SuccessNet ONLINE
• Access to grades and reports from Online Interactive Textbook

ExamView on Presentation Express CD-ROM
QuickTake Presenter
• Vocabulary Quizzes
• Chapter Test
• Grammar Quizzes

TeacherEXPRESS CD-ROM
• Assessment Program
• **ExamView** Test Banks A and B
test generator

Go Online
PHSchool.com
For: Teacher Home Page
Web Code: jdk-1001

PRINT MATERIAL

CORE INSTRUCTION
Teacher's Resource Book, pp. 188–214
• Input Script
• Video Script
• Answer Keys
• GramActiva Blackline Masters
• Vocabulary Clip Art
• Chapter Resource Checklist
• School-to-Home Connection Letters
• Communicative Activities Blackline Masters

TPR Stories, pp. 52–57

CORE ASSESSMENT
Assessment Program, pp. 97–110
• Pruebas
  Vocabulary Recognition
  Vocabulary Production
  The imperfect tense: Regular verbs
  The imperfect tense: Irregular verbs
  Indirect object pronouns
• Examen del capítulo
• Speaking and Writing Rubrics

Teacher's Resource Book, p. 202
• Situation Cards

TPR Stories, pp. 52–57

Differentiated Instruction

STUDENTS NEEDING EXTRA HELP
Guided Practice Activities Teacher's Guide, pp. T64–T72

HERITAGE LEARNERS
Realidades para hispanohablantes Teacher's Guide, pp. 66–75

Lecturas para hispanohablantes Teacher's Guide, pp. 42–43, 47–48

ADVANCED/PRE-AP*
Pre-AP* Resource Book: Resources Chart, p. 108

Differentiated Assessment

STUDENTS NEEDING EXTRA HELP
Alternate Assessment Program
• Examen del capítulo, pp. 41–46

HERITAGE LEARNERS
Assessment Program: Realidades para hispanohablantes Teacher's Guide, pp. T121–T125

ExamView Heritage Learner Test Bank
test generator

ADVANCED/PRE-AP*
Pre-AP* Resource Book: Teacher Activity Sheet, p. 110

ExamView Pre-AP* Test Bank
test generator

Capítulo 4A — Lesson Plans

Regular Schedule (50 Minutes)

For electronic lesson plans:
Teacher Express

	Warm-up / Assess	Preview Present	/	Practice Communicate	Wrap-up / Homework Options
DAY 1	**Warm-up (5 min.)** • Homework check • Return Examen del capítulo 3B	**A ver si recuerdas . . .** **(20 min.)** • Presentation: Una celebración • Actividades 1, 2, 3 **Chapter Opener** **(5 min.)** • Objectives • Fondo cultural		**A primera vista** **(15 min.)** • Presentation: Vocabulario y gramática en contexto • Actividades 1, 2	**Wrap-up and Homework Options (5 min.)** • Practice Workbook 4A-A, 4A-B, 4A-1, 4A-2 • Go Online
DAY 2	**Warm-up (10 min.)** • Homework check	**A primera vista (35 min.)** • Presentation: Videohistoria: *¿Cóma era de niña?* • View: Videohistoria		• Video Activities 1, 2, 3, 4 • Actividad 3	**Wrap-up and Homework Options (5 min.)** • Practice Workbook 4A-3, 4A-4 • Prueba 4A-1: Vocabulary recognition • Go Online
DAY 3	**Warm-up (10 min.)** • Actividad 4 • Homework check ✔**Assessment (10 min.)** • Prueba 4A-1: Vocabulary recognition	**Manos a la obra (25 min.)** • Actividades 5, 6, 7, 8, 9 • Fondos culturales			**Wrap-up and Homework Options (5 min.)** • Actividades 10, 11, 12, • Writing Activity 10, • Heritage Learner Workbook 4A-1, 4A-2 • Prueba 4A-2: Vocabulary production
DAY 4	**Warm-up (10 min.)** • Communicative Activity • Homework check ✔**Assessment (10 min.)** (after Audio Activities) • Prueba 4A-2: Vocabulary production	**Manos a la obra (25 min.)** • Audio Activities 5, 6 • Pronunciación • Presentation: The imperfect tense: regular verbs • Actividad 13			**Wrap-up and Homework Options (5 min.)** • Practice Workbook 4A-5 • Writing Activity 11 • Go Online
DAY 5	**Warm-up (10 min.)** • Actividad 14 • Homework check	**Manos a la obra (35 min.)** • Actividad 15 • Audio Activity 7 • Presentation: The imperfect tense: irregular verbs		• View: GramActiva video • Actividades 16, 19, 20, 21	**Wrap-up and Homework Options (5 min.)** • Practice Workbook 4A-6 • Heritage Learner Workbook 4A-4 • Actividades 17, 18 • Pruebas 4A-3, 4A-4: The imperfect • Writing Activity 12 tense: regular and irregular verbs • Go Online
DAY 6	**Warm-up (5 min.)** • Homework check ✔**Assessment (15 min.)** (after Audio Activity) • Pruebas 4A-3, 4A-4: The imperfect tense: regular and irregular verbs	**Manos a la obra (25 min.)** • Audio Activity 8 • Presentation: Indirect object pronouns • View: GramActiva video		• Actividades 23, 25 • Fondo cultural • El español en la comunidad	**Wrap-up and Homework Options (5 min.)** • Practice Workbook 4A-7 • Prueba 4A-5: Indirect object • Actvidades 24, 26 pronouns • Writing Activity 13 • Go Online
DAY 7	**Warm-up (10 min.)** • Actividad 22 • Homework check ✔**Assessment (10 min.)** (after Communicative Activity) • Prueba 4A-5: Indirect object pronouns	**Manos a la obra (10 min.)** • Audio Activity 9 • Communicative Activity **Adelante! (5 min.)** • Presentación oral: Steps 1, 4		**Repaso del capitulo** **(10 min.)** • Vocabulario y gramática • Preparación para el examen 1, 2	**Wrap-up and Homework Options (5 min.)** • Presentación oral: Step 2
DAY 8	**Warm-up (5 min.)** • Presentación oral: Step 2	**¡Adelante! (40 min.)** • Presentación oral: Step 3 • La cultura en vivo			**Wrap-up and Homework Options (5 min.)** • Preparación para el examen 3, 4, 5 • Go Online: Self-test
DAY 9	**Warm-up (5 min.)** • Presentación oral: Step 2	**¡Adelante! (40 min.)** • Lectura • ¿Comprendiste? / Y tú, ¿qué dices?		• Videomisterio: *En busca de la verdad*, Episodio 3	**Wrap-up and Homework Options (5 min.)** • Practice Workbook 4A-8, 4A-9 • Examen del capítulo 4A • Go Online: Lectura
DAY 10	**Warm-up (5 min.)** • Homework check ✔**Assessment (40 min.)** • Examen del capítulo 4A				**Wrap-up and Homework Options (5 min.)** • Go Online: Videomisterio

	Warm-up / Assess	Preview Present / Practice Communicate	Wrap-up / Homework Options
DAY 1	**Warm-up (5 min.)** • Homework check • Return Examen del capítulo: Capítulo 3B	**A ver si recuerdas . . . (25 min.)** • Presentation: Una celebración • Actividades 1, 2, 3 **Chapter Opener (5 min.)** • Objectives • Fondo cultural **A primera vista (50 min.)** • Presentation: Vocabulario y gramática en contexto • Actividades 1, 2 • Presentation: Videohistoria: *¿Cómo era de niña?* • View Videohistoria • Video Activities 1, 2, 3, 4 • Actividad 3	**Wrap-up and Homework Options (5 min.)** • Practice Workbook 4A-A, 4A-B, 4A-1, 4A-2, 4A-3, 4A-4 • Go Online • Prueba 4A-1: Vocabulary recognition
DAY 2	**Warm-up (10 min.)** • Actividad 4 • Homework check **✔Assessment (10 min.)** • Prueba 4A-1: Vocabulary recognition	**Manos a la obra (65 min.)** • Actividades 5, 6, 7, 8, 9 • Fondos culturales • Pronunciación • Audio Activities 5, 6 • Presentation: The imperfect tense: regular verbs • Actividades 13, 14, 15	**Wrap-up and Homework Options (5 min.)** • Practice Workbook 4A-5 • Actividades 10, 11 • Writing Activities 10 • Go Online • Heritage Learner Workbook 4A-1, 4A-2 • Prueba 4A-2: Vocabulary production
DAY 3	**Warm-up (10 min.)** • Actividad 12 • Homework check **✔Assessment (10 min.)** • Prueba 4A-2: Vocabulary production	**Manos a la obra (65 min.)** • Audio Activity 7 • Writing Activity 11 • Communicative Activity • Actividades 13, 15, 16, 18 • Presentation: The imperfect tense: irregular verbs • Actividades 16, 17, 18, 19, 20, 21 • Audio Activity 8 • Writing Activity 12	**Wrap-up and Homework Options (5 min.)** • Practice Workbook 4A-6 • Go Online • Heritage Learner Workbook 4A-4 • Pruebas 4A-3, 4A-4: The imperfect tense: regular and irregular verbs
DAY 4	**Warm-up (5 min.)** • Homework check **✔Assessment (15 min.)** • Pruebas 4A-3, 4A-4: The imperfect tense: regular and irregular verbs	**Manos a la obra (45 min.)** • Presentation: Indirect object pronouns • View: GramActiva video • Actividades 22, 23, 25 • El español en la comunidad • Fondo cultural • Audio Activity 9 • Communicative Activity **¡Adelante! (30 min.)** • Lectura • ¿Comprendiste? / Y tú, ¿qué dices? • Presentación oral: Steps 1, 4	**Wrap-up and Homework Options (5 min.)** • Practice Workbook 4A-7 • Presentación oral: Step 2 • Actividades 24, 26 • Writing Activity 13 • Go Online: Indirect objects pronouns; Lectura • Heritage Learner Workbook 4A-5 • Prueba 4A-5: Indirect object pronouns
DAY 5	**Warm-up (5 min.)** • Homework check **✔Assessment (10 min.)** • Prueba 4A-5: Indirect object pronouns	**¡Adelante! (45 min.)** • Presentación oral: Step 3 • La cultura en vivo **Repaso del capítulo (25 min.)** • Vocabulario y gramática • Preparación para el examen 1, 2, 3, 4, 5	**Wrap-up and Homework Options (5 min.)** • Practice Workbook 4A-8, 4A-9 • Go Online: Self-test • Examen del capítulo 4A
DAY 6	**Warm-up (10 min.)** • Homework check • Answer questions **Repaso del capítulo (15 min.)** • Situation Cards **✔Assessment (40 min.)** • Examen del capítulo 4A	**¡Adelante! (20 min.)** • Videomisterio: *En busca de la verdad,* Episodio 3	**Wrap-up and Homework Options (5 min.)** • Go Online: Videomisterio

4A Recycle

A ver si recuerdas...

Vocabulario

Note: Starting with *Tema 4*, the *A ver si recuerdas...* feature appears only at the beginning of each theme.

Vocabulario

Presentation EXPRESS™ VOCABULARY

Core Instruction

Resources: Voc. and Gram. Transparency 77

Focus: Reviewing vocabulary for family members, food, table settings, party activities, and party decorations

Suggestions: Provide small groups of students with a photocopy of this page and photos of a family gathering, either from your own family or from magazines. Have students use a highlighter to identify the words on the paper for items that they see in the photos. Have them point out the vocabulary that they found to another group or to the class.

  *Standards:* 1.1, 1.3

Focus: Writing and talking about planning a party

Suggestions: Have students choose a theme for their party before they begin planning. Have the class vote on the party they would most like to attend.

Answers will vary.

Una celebración

las personas
los abuelos
la familia
los hermanos
los padres
los primos
los tíos

la comida
las bebidas
la galleta
la hamburguesa
el helado
el jamón
la limonada
los pasteles
el perrito caliente
la pizza
el postre
el queso
el refresco
el sándwich

la mesa
el azúcar
la cuchara
el cuchillo
la pimienta
el plato
la sal
la servilleta
el tenedor
el vaso

las decoraciones
decorar
la flor, *pl.* las flores
el globo
la luz, *pl.* las luces
el papel picado

las actividades
abrir los regalos
la celebración, *pl.* las celebraciones
celebrar
compartir
el cumpleaños
la fiesta
hacer un video
preparar
la quinceañera
romper la piñata
sacar fotos

Práctica de vocabulario • Usando el organizador gráfico

 **Hablar/Escribir/Leer/Escuchar**

Voy a dar una fiesta

1 Con otro(a) estudiante, hagan planes para dar una fiesta. Escriban una lista de:

1. las personas que van a invitar
2. la comida
3. lo que van a hacer
4. lo que van a poner en la mesa
5. las decoraciones que van a usar

2 Usen la lista y escriban una descripción de cómo va a ser la fiesta.

3 Lean sus descripciones a otros grupos. Deben decir por qué (o por qué no) les gustaría ir a las fiestas de los demás.

Modelo
Nos gustaría ir a su fiesta porque Uds....

Differentiated Instruction
Solutions for All Learners

Heritage Language Learners
Have students write a paragraph describing how they celebrate a child's birthday party, including which family members are present, the foods served, and traditional activities they participate in. If necessary, discuss spelling and grammatical errors with students before they prepare a final draft.

Advanced Learners
Have students describe a holiday celebration. Ask them to write a short paragraph about the celebration, including both logical and illogical details. Have students switch papers and make corrections to their partner's illogical phrases. Encourage humor and creativity.

Actividad 2 Escribir/Hablar

Me gustan las piñatas

Escribe cuatro frases sobre una celebración o fiesta que ya pasó. Tres de las frases deben ser ciertas y una debe ser falsa. Trabaja con un grupo de tres personas. Lee tus frases. Las otras personas del grupo tienen que decir cuál de las frases no es cierta.

Modelo

A —*Muchas personas fueron a la fiesta en el parque. Rompimos una piñata grande. Mis tíos hicieron un video de la fiesta. Comimos hamburguesas y perritos calientes.*

B —*¡No es cierto! Uds. no rompieron una piñata grande.*

A —*Correcto. No rompimos una piñata grande.*

o: —*Sí, es cierto. Rompimos una piñata grande.*

¿Recuerdas?

-ito

Add the suffix *-ito(-a, -os, -as)* to the end of nouns to mean "small" or "little." It can also be used to show affection.

• Mis primos acaban de comprar un **perrito** nuevo.

-ísimo

Add the suffix *-ísimo(-a, -os, -as)* to the end of adjectives to say that someone or something is "very . . ." or "extremely . . .".

• Esta película es **interesantísima.**

Here are a few patterns you already know:

hermano → hermanito
poco → poquito
ricas → riquísimas
popular → popularísimo

Más práctica

• Practice Workbook, pp. 71–72: 4A-A, 4A-B
• Guided Practice Acts., p. 127
• *Real.* para hispanohablantes, p. 130

 **For:** Vocab. and Grammar
Web Code: jdd-0401

Práctica de gramática

Actividad 3 Escribir

Nuevas frases

Escribe otra forma de las palabras subrayadas *(underlined)* usando *-ito(a)* o *-ísimo(a)*. Después escribe una frase usando la nueva palabra.

Modelo

Mis tíos tienen una <u>casa pequeña</u> en las montañas.
casita   Me gusta mucho ir a su casita.

Mi mamá compró un vestido <u>muy elegante</u> ayer.
elegantísimo   Va a llevar su vestido elegantísimo a la fiesta.

1. El sábado es el cumpleaños de mi <u>abuela</u>.
2. Dame un <u>plato pequeño</u>, por favor.
3. Los pasteles en ese café son <u>muy ricos</u>.
4. Quiero comprar <u>un regalo pequeño</u> para mi amiga.
5. Las fotos de la fiesta son <u>muy graciosas</u>.
6. La piñata es <u>muy grande</u>.
7. Mi <u>hermano menor</u> y yo siempre compartimos la comida.

ciento ochenta y tres 183
Preparación: Vocabulario y gramática

Actividad 2   *Standards:* 1.1, 1.3

Focus: Writing and speaking about festive occasions

Suggestions: Encourage students to use the list on p. 182 as a word bank. Review the preterite forms before they begin. Remind students to listen to all four sentences before choosing the one they think is false.

Answers will vary.

Extension: Have students draw pictures of their parties and write the descriptions below them.

Actividad 3  *Standards:* 4.1  Presentation EXPRESS ANSWERS

Resources: Answers on Transparencies
Focus: Using diminutives and superlatives
Suggestions: If necessary, review the rules for the formation of the diminutive and the superlative. Have students identify the underlined words in *Actividad* 3 as nouns, adjectives, or adverbs. Remind them that the endings must follow gender and number rules.

Answers:
1. abuelita
2. platito
3. riquísimos
4. regalito
5. graciosísimas
6. grandísima
7. hermanito

Answers will vary for sentences.

Enrich Your Teaching
Resources for All Teachers

Culture Note

The *piñata* was adopted by the Spaniards from its Italian inventors. Brought to what is today Mexico by the Spanish, the *piñata* was an instant hit. A similar ritual was already being used by the Aztecs in the celebration of the birth of their war god. Today, the *piñata* is often made of papier-maché and is usually filled with candy.

Internet Search
Keyword:

piñata

183

 Standards
for Capítulo 4A

- To achieve the goals of the Standards, students will:

Communication

1.1 Interpersonal
- Talk about: celebrations and plans for parties; toys, pets, and animals in fables; childhood and children's activities; the painting *Los niños del futuro*

1.2 Interpretive
- Listen to and interpret information about toys, play, pets, and childhood
- Read a picture-based story and fable from Mexico
- Listen to and watch a video about childhood
- Read: to interpret analogies; an advertisement and respond to questions; about nursery and elementary schools; descriptions of a person from the past; about Isaac Newton

1.3 Presentational
- Present information: about a celebration, childhood, toys, pets, and traditional songs; analogies; based on pictures
- Compose: information about childhood activities and elementary school; a description from the point of view of a person in the past
- Compare information with personal experience

Culture

2.1 Practices and Perspectives
- Describe the role of pets

2.2 Products and Perspectives
- Tell about Pablo Picasso and his art; about nursery schools and *juguetes mayas;* about *el mercado de Hidalgo* in Guanajuato
- Describe fables, nursery rhymes, and songs

Connections

3.1 Cross-curricular
- Tell about: Pablo Picasso and his work; Spanish-speaking countries; the life of Isaac Newton

3.2 Target Culture
- Listen to and sing Spanish songs
- Read a Mexican fable and think about animals portrayed in fables from different cultures

Comparisons

4.1 Language
- Explain new vocabulary by using suffixes; the pronunciation of specific Spanish letters
- Use the imperfect tense
- Review and practice the indirect object pronouns

4.2 Culture
- Compare: nursery schools, nursery rhymes and songs in Spanish-speaking countries to those in the United States; *juguetes mayas* to toys in the U.S.

Communities

5.1 Beyond the School
- Discover a nursery school that teaches Spanish to the children

---

Tema 4 • Recuerdos del pasado

Fondo cultural ■■◆■◆■◇■◆◇■◆

Pablo Picasso (1881–1973) era uno de los mejores artistas españoles del siglo XX. En este cuadro, como en muchas de sus obras, Picasso usó formas abstractas para ilustrar las dos figuras. Pintó la figura de la niña mucho más grande en proporción que la figura de la mujer y pintó las caras muy serias.

- ¿Por qué crees que pintó Picasso la figura de la niña tan grande? ¿Cómo captas tú los momentos más importantes de tu familia?

"Primeros pasos" (1943), Pablo Picasso

Oil on canvas 130.2 x 97.1 cm (51 1/4 x 38 1/4 in.) Yale University Art Gallery, gift of Stephen Carlton Clark, B.A. 1903 © 2004 Estate of Pablo Picasso/Artists Rights Society ARS, New York.

184 ciento ochenta y cuatro
Tema 4 • Recuerdos del pasado

Differentiated Instruction

STUDENTS NEEDING EXTRA HELP
Guided Practice Activities
- Vocabulary Check, Flash Cards
- Grammar
- Reading and Speaking Support

Guided Practice Audio CDs
- Disc 1, Track 7

HERITAGE LEARNERS
Realidades para hispanohablantes
- Chapter Opener, pp. 130–131
- A primera vista, p. 132
- Videohistoria, p. 133
- Manos a la obra, pp. 134–141
- ¡Adelante!, pp. 142–147
- Repaso del capítulo, pp. 148–149

ADVANCED/PRE-AP*
Pre-AP* Resource Book,
pp. 108-111

Capítulo 4A

Cuando éramos niños

Chapter Objectives

- Discuss childhood toys and games
- Describe what you were like as a child
- Talk about activities that you used to do as a child
- Discuss to or for whom something is done
- Understand cultural perspectives on childhood songs

Video Highlights

A primera vista: ¿Cómo era de niña?
GramActiva Videos: the imperfect tense; indirect object pronouns
Videomisterio: En busca de la verdad, Episodio 3

Country Connection

As you learn to talk about what you were like as a child and what you used to do, you will make connections to these countries and places:

Illinois
España
República Dominicana
México
Puerto Rico
Ecuador
Argentina

Más práctica

- *Real.* para hispanohablantes, pp. 130–131

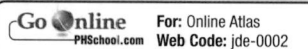

Go Online PHSchool.com **For:** Online Atlas **Web Code:** jde-0002

ciento ochenta y cinco 185
Capítulo 4A

Una familia en el parque,
Ciudad de México

Chapter Opener

Core Instruction

Resources: Voc. and Gram. Transparencies: Maps 12, 14–18, 20

Suggestions: Have students study the scene in the park. Discuss what kinds of things they did as a family or on outings. Have students brainstorm games and toys that they used to play with. Point out that in this chapter they will learn vocabulary to discuss toys and games and will learn how to describe themselves as a child. In the *Videohistoria*, they will see how embarrassed Ana is to talk about her childhood. Ask students if they like to talk about their childhood. Tell students that they will also learn a new verb tense that will allow them to express how things used to be like and what they used to do.

Fondo cultural *Standards:* 2.2, 3.1

Resources: Fine Art Transparencies with Teacher's Guide, p. 46

Suggestions: Point out that the child is the focus of the painting. Remind students that first steps can represent independence from their families. Brainstorm other milestones to help answer the second question.

Answers will vary.

Teaching with Art

Resources: Fine Art Transparencies with Teacher's Guide, p. 46

Suggestions: Have students find other works by Picasso, either in the library or on the Internet. If possible, bring in prints of paintings depicting families done by other Spanish-speaking artists, such as Botero or Goya. After students have studied the paintings, have them compare the artists' styles.

Teacher-to-Teacher

Keep in mind that some students are not comfortable talking about their families or their past. Tell all students that as they go through this chapter they may invent stories or talk about other families they know.

Teacher Technology

TeacherEXPRESS
Plan · Teach · Assess

PLAN
Lesson Planner

Go Online PHSchool.com
For: Teacher Home Page
Web Code: jdk-1001

TEACH
Teaching Resources
Interactive
Teacher's Edition
Vocabulary Clip Art

ASSESS
Chapter Quizzes
and Tests

PresentationEXPRESS
Dynamic Presentations for Teachers

TEACH
Vocabulary & Grammar Powerpoints
GramActiva Video
Audio & Clip Art Activities
Transparencies and Maps
Activity Answers
Photo Gallery

ASSESS
ExamView
QuickTake Presenter

Videohistoria

Core Instruction

Standards: 1.2

Resources: Voc. and Gram. Transparencies 80–81; Audio Program: Track 5

Focus: Presentation of additional vocabulary to discuss childhood

Suggestions:

Pre-reading: Direct attention to the *Estrategia*. Put the *¿Comprendiste?* questions on an overhead and have volunteers come to the projector to underline key words that students will need to keep in mind as they read.

Reading: Allow students time to read the story silently. Have volunteers act out the parts of Ana, Elena, Mamá, and Ignacio. Use the transparencies and non-verbal clues to help students with the words in blue type.

Post-reading: Complete *Actividad* 3 to check comprehension.

Pre-AP* Support

- **Activity:** Have students make a four-panel comic strip to illustrate the (imaginary) life of a well-known person. Have them write captions for the panels highlighting what the person might have been like as a child.

- **Pre-AP* Resource Book:** Comprehensive guide to Pre-AP* vocabulary skill development, pp. 47–53

Videohistoria   jdd-0487

¿Cómo era de niña?

¿Cómo se portaba Ana de niña? ¿Qué le gustaba a ella?

Estrategia

Looking ahead
It is often helpful to look ahead to the questions at the end of a reading. This helps you to focus on the key information you will need to understand the reading.

Elena   Ana   Mamá   Ignacio

1 **Ignacio:** Hola. ¿Qué hacéis?*

Elena: Hacemos árboles genealógicos para una clase.

Ana: Mira. Ésta soy yo, **de niña.**

Ignacio: ¿Cómo eras? **¿Obediente** o **desobediente?**

Ana: Por lo general, muy obediente y muy **tímida.**

5 **Ana:** Mamá tiene razón. Me encantaba mi oso de peluche. Era mi juguete favorito.

6 **Ignacio:** ¿También jugabas con muñecas?

Ana: Sí, y también tenía una colección de animales de peluche.

7 **Ignacio:** ¡**Tenías** tantos juguetes! Eras muy **consentida.**

Ana: Sí, un poco. ¿Y tú? ¿Cómo eras?

Ignacio: Yo era muy **bien educado** y siempre obedecía.

Elena: ¿Tú? Nunca.

* Remember that in Spain, the *vosotros(as)* form of verbs is used when speaking to a group of people you would address individually with *tú.*

188 ciento ochenta y ocho
Tema 4 • Recuerdos del pasado

Differentiated Instruction
Solutions for All Learners

Advanced Learners

If possible, have students bring in a home movie of themselves as young children. View the video to make sure that it is appropriate. Play it with the sound down, and have the students narrate the scene to their classmates, using Ana's narration as a model.

Students with Learning Difficulties

If students are confused by the imperfect forms of the verbs, explain briefly that these describe the way things used to be. Point out that to respond to the questions in *Actividad* 3, students will use the form of the verb given in the question, and not the form used in the reading.

2 Mamá: Aquí tenéis* algo para comer.

Ana: Gracias, mamá. ¿No es verdad que siempre **obedecía?**

Mamá: De vez en cuando. ¿Siempre? ¡No!

Ignacio: ¿Y quién es?

Ana: Es mi abuela. Siempre **iba** a visitarla en su casa.

3 Mamá: Aquí tengo el video de cuando eras pequeña.

Ana: ¡Ay, no, mamá!

Ignacio: ¡Vamos a verlo!

Elena: Sí. Ana, tienes que **portarte** muy **bien** mientras vemos el video. Ni una palabra.

4 Mamá: Ana era un poco tímida. Y en sus pijamas, era preciosa. Le gustaba dormir con su oso de peluche y se levantaba muy temprano.

Ignacio: Y ahora siempre llegas tarde a clase.

Ana: ¡Ignacio, **mientes!** Nunca dices **la verdad.** Yo llego a tiempo.

Ignacio: De vez en cuando.

Ana: ¡Siempre!

8 Ana: ¡No! No podemos ver más.

Ignacio: ¿Por qué no?

Ana: Nadie va a ver esto nunca.

Actividad 3 — Escribir/Hablar

¿Comprendiste?

1. ¿Qué hacen Elena y Ana para una de sus clases?
2. En la opinión de Ana, ¿cómo era ella de niña?
3. ¿Qué deciden ver los jóvenes?
4. Según su mamá, ¿cómo era Ana de niña?
5. Según Ignacio, ¿llega Ana a clase a tiempo o tarde?
6. ¿Cuáles eran los juguetes favoritos de Ana?
7. ¿Qué coleccionaba Ana?
8. ¿Cómo era Ignacio de niño?

Más práctica

- Practice Workbook, pp. 75–76: 4A-3, 4A-4
- WAV Wbk.: Video, pp. 67–68
- Guided Practice: Vocab. Check, pp. 133–136
- *Real.* para hispanohablantes, p. 133

Go Online
PHSchool.com
For: Vocab. Practice
Web Code: jdd-0403

ciento ochenta y nueve **189**
Capítulo 4A

Video
Core Instruction

Standards: 1.2

Resources: Teacher's Resource Book: Video Script, p. 194; Video Program: Cap. 4A; Video Program Teacher's Guide: Cap. 4A

Focus: Comprehension of contextualized vocabulary

Suggestions:

Pre-viewing: Brainstorm a list of key concepts from the *Videohistoria*. Write them on the board and leave them there for reference during the video.

Viewing: Show the video once without pausing, then go back and show it again, pausing along the way to check for comprehension. Ask students if they and their siblings or friends have differing views about what they were like as children.

Post-viewing: Complete the Video Activities in the *Writing, Audio & Video Workbook.*

Actividad 3 *Standards:* 1.2

Presentation EXPRESS
ANSWERS

Resources: Answers on Transparencies

Focus: Verifying comprehension of the *Videohistoria*

Suggestions: You may want to ask students the questions and have them respond without looking in their books for information.

Answers:

1. Hacen árboles genealógicos.
2. Era muy obediente y muy tímida.
3. Deciden ver el video de cuando Ana era pequeña.
4. Era un poco tímida y en sus pijamas, era preciosa.
5. Llega tarde.
6. Sus juguetes favoritos eran su oso de peluche y sus muñecas.
7. Coleccionaba animales de peluche.
8. Era bien educado.

Enrich Your Teaching
Resources for All Teachers

Teacher-to-Teacher

Have students create two characters, one who was well-behaved as a child and one who was mischievous. Have them name the characters and tell where they are from. Ask two artistic students to draw the characters on the board as the class describes them in response to your questions. Ask students: *¿Era alto(a) o bajo(a)? ¿Tenía pelo largo o corto?* etc. After the drawings are completed, have students brainstorm a list of adjectives to describe each character they created and write the words under the appropriate drawing. You may want to have students use these characters throughout the chapter to practice vocabulary and create stories using the imperfect.

Additional Resources

- WAV Wbk.: Audio Act. 5, p. 70
- Teacher's Resource Book: Audio Script, pp. 191–192
- Audio Program: Track 7

 Assessment

- **ExamView** QuickTake Presenter Quiz on PresEXPRESS
- Prueba 4A-1: Vocab. Recognition, pp. 97–98

Standards: 1.3

Presentation EXPRESS
ANSWERS

Resources: Answers on Transparencies

Focus: Writing about childhood toys

Suggestions: Point out that *cuando eras niño(a)* can go either at the beginning of a sentence or at the end.

Answers will vary but will include:

1. un pez
2. una muñeca
3. un tren eléctrico
4. un oso de peluche
5. una tortuga
6. un triciclo

 Bellringer Review
Use large Clip Art flashcards to review vocabulary for toys.

 **Standards:** 1.1

Focus: Asking and answering questions about childhood toys

Suggestions: Have students interview a different person for each item. Encourage students to use numbers and adjectives to describe their toys and pets. For example: *Tenía dos gatos amarillos cuando era niño(a).*

Answers will vary.

  **Standards:** 1.2

Presentation EXPRESS
AUDIO

Resources: Teacher's Resource Book: Audio Script, p. 191; Audio Program: Track 6; Answers on Transparencies

Focus: Listening and writing from dictation about a pet

Suggestions: Play the *Audio CD* or read the script once without having students write. Tell students to try to visualize Víctor's pet. Explain that this will help them retain important information and make it easier to write their sentences.

 **Script and Answers**

1. De niño tenía un perro muy divertido.
2. El nombre de mi perro era Julio.
3. Jugaba todos los días con Julio en el patio.
4. De vez en cuando iba al parque con Julio.
5. Julio era inteligente pero un poco travieso.

Manos a la obra

Vocabulario y gramática en uso

Objectives

- Communicate about childhood toys and games
- Discuss past activities
- Express to whom an action is done

 Escribir

¿Qué juguetes tenías?

Escribe frases para decir qué juguetes y animales tenías cuando eras niño(a).

 Modelo

Tenía un gato cuando era niño(a).
o: *Tenía muchos gatos cuando era niño(a).*
o: *No tenía un gato cuando era niño(a), pero sí tenía un perro.*

También se dice . . .

los bloques = los cubos *(muchos países)*

consentido, -a = mimado, -a *(muchos países)*

montar en triciclo = andar en triciclo *(España)*

saltar = brincar *(muchos países)*

1.    2.    3.

4.    5.   6.

  Hablar

¿Tenías lo mismo?

Lee tus frases de la Actividad 4 a otro(a) estudiante para ver si Uds. tenían las mismas cosas cuando eran niños.

Modelo

A —*Yo tenía un gato cuando era niño(a). Y tú, ¿tenías un gato?*
B —*Sí, yo tenía un gato también.*
o: —*No, yo no tenía un gato.*

 jdd-0488 **Escuchar/Escribir**

Escucha y escribe

Víctor describe un animal que tenía cuando era niño. Escucha las cinco frases y escríbelas en una hoja de papel.

Differentiated Instruction
Solutions for All Learners

Advanced Learners

Have students use their sentences from *Actividad 6* as a model to write about a childhood pet or a favorite stuffed animal they had when they were younger. Ask students to bring in the stuffed animals they wrote about or photos of their pets. Call on volunteers to present their descriptions to the class.

Multiple Intelligences

Logical/Mathematical: Have students survey the class to determine how often they played with each of the toys listed in *Actividad 7*. Ask students to display the results in a chart.

Fondo cultural

Las mascotas Generalmente en los países hispanohablantes el papel *(role)* de las mascotas *(pets)* es más que sólo ser "otro miembro de la familia". Por ejemplo, un perro protege *(protects)* la casa en la ciudad o ayuda en el campo. Por lo general, los conejillos de Indias *(Guinea pigs)* o los ratoncitos no son mascotas comunes.

- Compara el papel de las mascotas en los Estados Unidos con su papel en los países hispanohablantes.

El perro ayuda mucho a este gaucho argentino.

Actividad 7 · Hablar

¿Con qué jugabas de niño(a)?

Pregunta a otro(a) estudiante con qué juguetes jugaba de niño(a).

Modelo

A —¿Jugabas con *muñecas* de niño(a)?

B —Sí, *por lo general* jugaba con *muñecas* de niño(a).

o: —No, *nunca* jugaba con *muñecas* de niño(a).

Estudiante A

Estudiante B

nunca	a menudo
a veces	por lo general
siempre	de vez en cuando

Actividad 8 · Escribir/Hablar

¿Qué te gustaba hacer de pequeño(a)?

Escribe una lista de seis actividades que son populares entre los niños. Después pregunta a otro(a) estudiante si le gustaba hacer estas actividades de pequeño(a).

Modelo

coleccionar tarjetas de *Star Wars*

A —De pequeño(a), ¿te gustaba *coleccionar tarjetas de* Star Wars?

B —Sí, me gustaba *coleccionar tarjetas de* Star Wars.

o: —No, no me gustaba nada *coleccionar tarjetas de* Star Wars.

ciento noventa y uno **191**
Capítulo 4A

Enrich Your Teaching
Resources for All Teachers

Culture Note
The ***cimarrón uruguayo*** is a dog found only in Uruguay. This special breed evolved from hunting dogs abandoned by Spanish and Portuguese explorers. They are known for their loyalty and are often used to guard homes or to herd cattle. They are the preferred breed of the ***gauchos*** of Uruguay.

Internet Search
Keyword:

cimarrón + Uruguay

Fondo cultural · Standards: 2.1

Suggestions: Point out that this *Fondo cultural* presents general impressions of the roles that pets play in Spanish-speaking countries. Explain that people in these countries also have pets as companions. Many homes have beautiful birds, small dogs, or indoor cats. Point out that even though guinea pigs, pet mice, and hamsters are not common, they do exist in Spanish-speaking households.

Answers will vary but may include:
Pet owners in Spanish-speaking countries might appear to be less emotionally attached to their pets because their animals serve a practical use.

Actividad 7 · Standards: 1.1 · Presentation EXPRESS ANSWERS

Resources: Answers on Transparencies
Focus: Asking and answering questions about childhood toys
Suggestions: Point out that Student B should answer truthfully using any of the expressions of frequency shown.
Answers:
Student A:
¿Jugabas con dinosaurios de niño(a)?
¿Jugabas con osos de peluche de niño(a)?
¿Jugabas con pelotas de niño(a)?
¿Jugabas con bloques de niño(a)?
¿Jugabas con muñecos de niño(a)?
Student B answers will vary.

Actividad 8 · Standards: 1.1, 1.3

Focus: Writing and speaking about what you used to like to do
Suggestions: Have students brainstorm a list of activities that they used to enjoy when they were younger. Ask them to choose six activities from the list to use for *Actividad 8.*
Answers will vary.

Actividad 9 *Standards:* 1.2, 1.3

Focus: Using vocabulary to complete analogies

Suggestions: Remind students to think about the relationship between the first two words before they try to complete the analogy. Tell students to use *es* when using the infinitive of a verb as the subject. Allow varied answers if students can explain the analogy.

Answers will vary but may include:

1. mentir   4. molestar   7. permitir
2. la cuerda   5. el agua   8. el dinero
3. jugar   6. travieso(a)

Actividad 10 *Standards:* 1.2

 Presentation EXPRESS ANSWERS

Resources: Answers on Transparencies

Focus: Describing people

Suggestions: Be sure students understand the difference between *bien educado(a)* and *obediente* as well as *travieso(a)* and *desobediente.*

Answers:

1. Antonio es tímido.   4. Ricardo es bien educado.
2. Julio es travieso.   5. Ana es generosa.
3. Eugenia es obediente.

Actividad 11 *Standards:* 1.3

Focus: Writing and speaking about one's childhood

Suggestions: Have students work in pairs and interview each other using the questions.

Answers will vary.

Fondo cultural *Standards:* 2.2, 4.2

■◆■◇■◆■◆■◇■◆■◇■◆■◇

Suggestions: Before the reading, discuss the advantages and disadvantages of going to preschool or day care before starting kindergarten. After the reading, have students compare child-care programs in the United States with those in Spanish-speaking countries.

Actividad 9  **Leer/Pensar/Escribir**

Las analogías

Hay pruebas de vocabulario sobre las relaciones entre palabras, o "las analogías". Completa cada analogía según el modelo.

Modelo

los jóvenes : la escuela :: los niños : la guardería infantil

Se lee: "Los jóvenes son a la escuela como los niños son a la guardería infantil".

1. levantarse : acostarse :: decir la verdad : ____
2. montar : el triciclo :: saltar : ____
3. la piscina : nadar :: el patio de recreo : ____
4. generoso : ofrecer :: travieso : ____
5. el pájaro : el árbol :: el pez : ____
6. obedecer : obediente :: pelearse : ____
7. no : sí :: prohibir : ____
8. la blusa : la ropa :: la moneda : ____

Actividad 10 **Leer/Escribir**

La guardería infantil

Lee las descripciones de los niños en la guardería infantil y luego decide qué adjetivo del recuadro describe a cada uno. Escribe las descripciones de los niños en una hoja de papel.

bien educado, -a	generoso, -a
desobediente	tímido, -a
obediente	travieso, -a

Actividad 11 **Escribir/Hablar**

Y tú, ¿qué dices?

1. ¿Con qué juguetes te gustaba jugar de pequeño(a)?
2. De niño(a), ¿cómo eras? ¿Bien educado(a) o travieso(a)? ¿Sociable o tímido(a)?
3. De niño(a), ¿qué te gustaba coleccionar? ¿Monedas? ¿Tarjetas de algún deporte? ¿Todavía tienes tu colección?
4. De niño(a), ¿obedecías a tus padres siempre, a menudo o a veces? Y ahora, ¿los obedeces siempre? ¿Obedeces las reglas de tu escuela siempre?

192 ciento noventa y dos
Tema 4 • Recuerdos del pasado

Modelo

Los padres de Carlota le compran cada juguete que pide.
Carlota es consentida.

1. Antonio tiene miedo de hablar con otras personas.
2. Julio se porta mal y molesta a todo el mundo.
3. Eugenia no miente porque sus padres dicen que es muy malo mentir.
4. Ricardo siempre dice "gracias" y "por favor" y no se pelea con nadie.
5. Ana comparte sus juguetes con los otros niños.

Fondo cultural

Las guarderías infantiles En los países hispanohablantes hay una variedad de opciones de guarderías infantiles. Unas guarderías son del gobierno municipal *(city government)* o provincial *(provincial)*. Algunas compañías ofrecen servicio de guardería infantil para las personas que trabajan allí. También hay guarderías privadas.

• De niño(a), ¿ibas a una guardería infantil? En tu opinión, ¿cuál es la mejor opción para cuidar a los niños? ¿Por qué?

Differentiated Instruction
Solutions for All Learners

Heritage Language Learners

Students may have a little difficulty hearing the difference between the *r* and the *rr.* To help them with spelling, tell them to always use *r* if they hear a simple vibration. If they hear a multiple vibration, they should spell the word with *rr* if the sound comes between two vowels, or use *r* in all other cases.

Students with Learning Difficulties

Students may have trouble understanding the concept of analogies. Help them to visualize analogies by using pictures from magazines, bringing in objects from home, or pointing out classroom objects. For example: *El tenedor y el cuchillo son al bistec como la cuchara es a la sopa.*

Actividad 12 · Leer/Escribir/Hablar

¿Cómo cuidar al niño?

Lee este anuncio de la guardería infantil Rincón del niño en Guadalajara, México, y contesta las preguntas.

Guardería infantil Rincón del niño
Excelencia personal y escolar

Nuestros maestros tienen preparación profesional y comprenden las necesidades del niño según su edad. Ofrecemos instrucción bilingüe y varias actividades usando música y juegos.

Recibimos niños desde los 13 meses hasta los cinco años de edad. Tenemos ya 25 años de experiencia.

Cuidar a sus niños es nuestra pasión. Trabajamos todos los días para desarrollar[1] en sus niños la capacidad de:
- trabajar en grupo
- mantener una actitud positiva
- tener éxito[2] en actividades académicas
- desarrollar hábitos higiénicos y cuidados personales

Favor de llamarnos al 515-34-98
Avenida Guerrero, 48

Estrategia

Using context
Use the context of words you don't know to guess their meaning in this reading.

1. Lee la lista de características que la guardería infantil quiere desarrollar en los niños. En tu opinión, ¿cuáles son las dos más importantes? ¿Por qué?

2. ¿Esta guardería infantil es similar a las guarderías infantiles donde tú vives? ¿En qué sentido *(way)* es similar? ¿En qué sentido es diferente?

3. ¿Te gustaría trabajar en una guardería infantil como Rincón del niño? ¿Por qué?

4. En tu opinión, ¿cómo debe ser una persona que trabaja en una guardería infantil?

[1]develop [2]to be successful

Pronunciación

The letters *r* and *rr*

jdd-0488

Except at the beginning of a word or after *l* or *n*, the sound of the letter *r* is made as you raise the tip of your tongue and tap the roof of your mouth. The position of your tongue is similar to the position when you pronounce the *d* in the English word *Daddy*. The sound of the *rr* is made as you raise the tip of your tongue and tap the roof of your mouth several times very quickly. Listen to and say these pairs of words:

| pero | ahora | moro | caro |
| perro | ahorra | morro | carro |

When *r* is the first letter of a word or comes after *l* or *n,* it is pronounced like the *rr*.

¡Compruébalo! Listen to these two verses of a popular Spanish lullaby, then try to repeat them.

A la rorro[1] niño
a la rorro ya,
duérmete mi niño,
duérmete mi amor.

Señora Santa Ana,
Señor San Joaquín
Arrullen[2] al niño
que se va a dormir.

[1]sound to quiet a baby
[2]Whisper, Lull

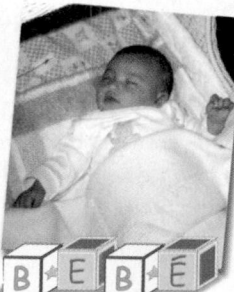

ciento noventa y tres 193
Capítulo 4A

Practice and Communicate

4A

Actividad 12
 Standards: 1.2, 4.2

Resources: Voc. and Gram. Transparency 84
Focus: Reading comprehension of an ad for a daycare facility

Suggestions: Direct attention to the *Estrategia.* Demonstrate the concept using the sentence *Recibimos niños desde los 13 meses hasta los cinco años de edad.* Have students read the questions before reading the ad.

Answers will vary.

Extension: Have students work in small groups to create a poster for their ideal kindergarten.

Pronunciación

 Presentation EXPRESS AUDIO

Core Instruction

Standards: 3.2, 4.1

Resources: Teacher's Resource Book: Audio Script, p. 192; Audio Program: Tracks 9–10

Suggestions: Read the *Pronunciación* with students or play the *Audio CD.* Trilling the *r* and *rr* is often intimidating for students. Before you have them try to say the lullaby, have them practice saying several English words that have a natural trill: *Patty, ladder, butter, batter.*

Additional Resources

- WAV Wbk.: Audio Act. 6, p. 70
- Teacher's Resource Book: Audio Script, p. 192, Communicative Activity BLM, pp. 198–199
- Audio Program: Track 8

✓ **Assessment**
- Prueba 4A-2: Vocab. Production, pp. 99–100

Enrich Your Teaching
Resources for All Teachers

Culture Note

In Spain, children under the age of six are not required to attend preschool. However, more than 80% of Spanish children between the ages of three and six take part in early childhood education. Many of the country's preschools are staffed by highly qualified early-childhood education specialists.

Teacher-to-Teacher

Some students may be apprehensive about practicing pronunciation in front of the class. To lower students' anxiety, have them work with a partner and repeat the sample words and lullaby in the *Pronunciación.* Monitor students for correct pronunciation and to be sure that everyone is participating.

193

Gramática

Presentation EXPRESS
GRAMMAR

Core Instruction

Standards: 4.1

Resources: Voc. and Gram. Transparency 82

Suggestions: Direct attention to the ¿Recuerdas? Briefly review preterite forms. This initial discussion of the imperfect is limited to habitual actions in the past. Use a time line to help students visualize the imperfect tense. Emphasize that these actions don't have a specific point in time when they start or finish. Use the time line to help students see that verbs like **tener** and **vivir** can describe actions that are ongoing, and so can be used in the imperfect. Use the transparency to help with your presentation. The *GramActiva* Video can also be used for reinforcement.

Actividad 13

Standards: 1.2

Presentation EXPRESS
AUDIO

Resources: Teacher's Resource Book: Audio Script, p. 192; Audio Program: Track 11; Answers on Transparencies

Focus: Listening comprehension

Suggestions: Use the *Audio CD* or read the script aloud. Allow students to listen several times while writing their sentences. For each sentence, have them explain why they chose **Lola, Lulú,** or **las dos.**

Script and Answers:

1. Mentía de vez en cuando. *(Lulú)*
2. Jugaban bien y nunca se peleaban. *(las dos)*
3. Por lo general se portaba bien. *(Lola)*
4. Vivían en la misma calle. *(las dos)*
5. Siempre compartía sus juguetes y muñecas. *(Lola)*
6. Molestaba a los otros niños. *(Lulú)*

Theme Project

Give students copies of the Theme Project outline and rubric from the *Teacher's Resource Book*. Explain the task to them, and have them perform Step 1. (For more information, see p. 182–a.)

Gramática

The imperfect tense: regular verbs

Another way to talk about the past is with the imperfect tense. Use the imperfect tense to talk about actions that happened repeatedly in the past.

Rafael **patinaba** y Mónica **corría.**

*Rafael **used to skate** and Monica **used to run**.*

Here are the regular forms of *-ar, -er,* and *-ir* verbs in the imperfect tense. Notice the accent mark on the *nosotros* form of *jugar:*

(yo)	jugaba	(nosotros) (nosotras)	jugábamos
(tú)	jugabas	(vosotros) (vosotras)	jugabais
Ud. (él) (ella)	jugaba	Uds. (ellos) (ellas)	jugaban

Note that *-er* and *-ir* verbs, such as *hacer* and *vivir,* have the same endings:

(yo)	hacía vivía	(nosotros) (nosotras)	hacíamos vivíamos
(tú)	hacías vivías	(vosotros) (vosotras)	hacíais vivíais
Ud. (él) (ella)	hacía vivía	Uds. (ellos) (ellas)	hacían vivían

Notice the accent mark on each ending.

> **¿Recuerdas?**
>
> You have already learned to talk about completed actions in the past using the preterite tense.
>
> • Ayer Rafael **patinó** y Mónica **corrió** en el parque.

• As you know, in Spanish you can often omit the subject of a verb because the subject is made clear in the verb ending:

> **Vivo** en Chicago. (The subject, *yo,* is included in the verb ending.)

However, since the *yo* and *Ud./él/ella* forms are the same in the imperfect for *-ar, -er,* and *-ir* verbs, speakers often use the subject pronouns to avoid confusion.

> Patricia **tenía** un triciclo rojo pero **yo tenía** uno azul.

• Expressions such as *generalmente, por lo general, a menudo, muchas veces, de vez en cuando, todos los días,* and *nunca* can cue you to use the imperfect because they imply that something happened repeatedly in the past.

Actividad 13 jdd-0488 **Escuchar/Escribir**

Escucha y escribe

Lola y Lulú eran vecinas y muy buenas amigas, pero eran muy diferentes. Lola era muy bien educada, pero Lulú era desobediente. Escucha las seis descripciones de las niñas y escribe las frases. Indica si la descripción es de Lola, de Lulú o de las dos.

Dos amigas de México

Differentiated Instruction

Solutions for All Learners

Students with Learning Difficulties

Have students draw a happy face labeled *Lola* and a mischievous face labeled *Lulú.* As students listen to each description the first time, have them point to the appropriate picture(s). Then have them write the sentences under the appropriate pictures.

Advanced Learners/Pre-AP*

Pre-AP* Have students use *Actividad* 14 as a model to write a paragraph about where they used to spend time and what they used to do there. Encourage them to use expressions such as **siempre, muchas veces,** and **de vez en cuando.**

  Actividad 14 Leer/Escribir

En la casa de nuestros abuelos

Margarita recuerda cómo, de niña, pasaba tiempo en la casa de sus abuelos. Escribe la forma apropiada del imperfecto de los verbos.

Cuando era niña mis hermanos y yo __1.__ *(pasar/pensar)* tiempo en la casa de nuestros abuelos de vez en cuando. Mi abuela __2.__ *(preparar/participar)* galletas muy ricas y nosotros las __3.__ *(correr/comer)* en el patio. Ella siempre nos __4.__ *(ofrecer/obedecer)* más galletas. Mi abuelo nos __5.__ *(estudiar/leer)* cuentos y a veces él nos __6.__ *(hacer/escribir)* pequeños juguetes de madera *(wood)*. Mis abuelos no __7.__ *(trabajar/limpiar)* y __8.__ *(decir/tener)* mucho tiempo para pasar con nosotros. Mis hermanos y yo siempre __9.__ *(regresar/bailar)* a casa muy contentos después de estar con nuestros abuelos.

Dos niños ecuatorianos

  Actividad 15 Hablar

Tus amigos y tú

Trabaja con otro(a) estudiante para hablar de lo que hacían tus amigos y tú cuando eran niños.

Modelo

jugar con los vecinos
A —¿Jugaban Uds. con los vecinos?
B —No, nunca jugábamos con los vecinos.
o: —Sí, jugábamos con los vecinos de vez en cuando.

Estudiante A

1. montar en triciclo
2. saltar a la cuerda
3. correr en el parque
4. escuchar cuentos
5. coleccionar cosas
6. compartir los juguetes

Estudiante B

No, nunca . . .
Sí, siempre . . .
De vez en cuando . . .

Más práctica

- Practice Workbook, p. 77: 4A-5
- WAV Wbk.: Writing, p. 75
- Guided Practice: Grammar Acts., pp. 137–138
- *Real.* para hispanohablantes, pp. 134-137

 **Go Online**
PHSchool.com
For: Imperfect Tense
Web Code: jdd-0404

ciento noventa y cinco **195**
Capítulo 4A

Enrich Your Teaching
Resources for All Teachers

Teacher-to-Teacher

Have students create **un párrafo loco.** Make a cloze passage using *Actividad 14* as a model. Start the paragraph with: *Cuando eran niños, mis estudiantes....* Don't allow students to see the entire paragraph. Write a list of infinitives on the board and have students randomly choose a verb for each blank and conjugate it according to the subject you give them. Hand out the paragraph and call on a volunteer to read it aloud, inserting the verbs the class has chosen. Guide your students' choices when necessary to avoid inappropriate paragraphs.

  **Actividad 14** *Standards:* 1.2, 4.1 Presentation EXPRESS ANSWERS

Resources: Answers on Transparencies
Focus: Writing about what you used to do
Recycle: Vocabulary for family members and activities
Suggestions: Before students fill in the blanks, have them read the paragraph for comprehension. Remind them that in order to conjugate the verb, they need to correctly identify the subject.
Answers:

1. pasábamos	4. ofrecía	7. trabajaban
2. preparaba	5. leía	8. tenían
3. comíamos	6. hacía	9. regresábamos

Common Errors: Students may try to use preterite- or present-tense forms of the verbs. Stress the difference in meaning.

   **Actividad 15** *Standards:* 1.1 Presentation EXPRESS ANSWERS

Resources: Answers on Transparencies
Focus: Asking and answering questions about childhood habits
Suggestions: Remind students that **tú y tus amigos** requires the **Uds.** form and that they need to use the **nosotros** form in their answers.
Answers:
Student A:
1. ¿Montaban Uds. en triciclo?
2. ¿Saltaban Uds. a la cuerda?
3. ¿Corrían Uds. en el parque?
4. ¿Escuchaban Uds. cuentos?
5. ¿Coleccionaban Uds. cosas?
6. ¿Compartían Uds. los juguetes?
Student B answers will vary.
Extension: Have students use the **tú** form of the verb when asking questions and the **yo** form when answering.

Additional Resources

- WAV Wbk.: Audio Act. 7, p. 71
- Teacher's Resource Book: Audio Script, pp. 192–193
- Audio Program: Track 12

 Assessment

- *ExamView* Quiz on PresEXPRESS
  QuickTake Presenter
- Prueba 4A-3: The imperfect tense: Regular verbs, p. 101

195

 Gramática

Presentation EXPRESS — GRAMMAR

Core Instruction

Standards: 4.1

Resources: Voc. and Gram. Transparency 83; Teacher's Resource Book: Video Script, pp. 194–195; Video Program: Cap. 4A

Suggestions: Play the *GramActiva* Video as an introduction or to reinforce your own presentation. Tell students that although *ir, ser,* and *ver* are irregular, they still follow a familiar pattern. Write *ibas, eran,* and *íbamos* on the board and ask students to identify the subject for each verb. Call on volunteers to explain the pattern. If students are confused about why *ver* is an irregular verb, explain to them that to form the stem, only the *r* is dropped from the infinitive. Regular *-er* and *-ir* endings are added to *ve-*.

 Actividad 16  **Standards:** 1.2, 4.1

Presentation EXPRESS — GRAMMAR

Resources: Answers on Transparencies

Focus: Reading comprehension; using imperfect forms of *ir, ser,* and *ver*

Recycle: Leisure and sport activities

Suggestions: Have students read the paragraph first to determine which verb to use in each sentence. Have them read a second time, focusing on conjugating the verbs.

Answers:

1. era	4. era	7. íbamos
2. íbamos	5. veía	8. veíamos
3. veíamos	6. iba	9. eran

Block Schedule

In each corner of the room, hang a picture that represents a certain season. Point out the pictures to students, and have them brainstorm a list of things that they used to do in each season when they were younger. Divide the students into four groups, and assign each group to a different season. Have them discuss what they used to do in that season. Set a timer, and when it goes off, have students move to another season and continue their discussion.

196

Gramática

The imperfect tense: irregular verbs

There are only three irregular verbs in the imperfect tense: *ir, ser,* and *ver.* Here are all the forms:

ir

(yo)	iba	(nosotros) (nosotras)	íbamos
(tú)	ibas	(vosotros) (vosotras)	ibais
Ud. (él) (ella)	iba	Uds. (ellos) (ellas)	iban

ser

(yo)	era	(nosotros) (nosotras)	éramos
(tú)	eras	(vosotros) (vosotras)	erais
Ud. (él) (ella)	era	Uds. (ellos) (ellas)	eran

• Notice the accent mark on the *nosotros* form for the verbs *ir* and *ser.*

ver

(yo)	veía	(nosotros) (nosotras)	veíamos
(tú)	veías	(vosotros) (vosotras)	veíais
Ud. (él) (ella)	veía	Uds. (ellos) (ellas)	veían

• Notice the accent mark on each form of *ver.*

GramActiva VIDEO

Want more help with the imperfect tense? Watch the **GramActiva** video.

Eran felices allí.

 Actividad 16 **Leer/Escribir**

Los veranos en Chicago

Ana María recuerda los veranos que pasaba en Chicago. Completa su descripción con las formas apropiadas del imperfecto de los verbos *ir, ser* y *ver.*

Cuando **1.** pequeña, me encantaban los veranos. Vivíamos en Chicago donde mi papá y yo **2.** al famoso estadio de béisbol de los Chicago Cubs, Wrigley Field. Cada verano nosotros **3.** a nuestros jugadores favoritos, como Sammy Sosa. Mi papá **4.** originalmente de la República Dominicana y por eso él **5.** todos los partidos cuando Sammy jugaba allí. También yo siempre **6.** al lago Michigan con mi familia. ¿Qué más? También nosotros **7.** al cine donde comíamos palomitas y **8.** las películas más populares. Los veranos en Chicago **9.** fantásticos y los recuerdo muy bien.

Sammy Sosa, cuando jugaba para los Chicago Cubs

Differentiated Instruction
Solutions for All Learners

Heritage Language Learners

Students may instinctively know when to use the imperfect and preterite, and will use both tenses when referring to past events. Allow them to use natural speech, but encourage them to explain why they are using the preterite instead of the imperfect.

Students with Learning Difficulties

Students may have trouble recognizing the subjects of the verbs they need to conjugate in cloze passages. Before they fill in the blanks, read the paragraph with them and have them identify the correct subjects. Point out that sometimes the subject comes after the verb.

Actividad 17 — Leer/Escribir

Un niño inteligente

Completa esta descripción de Isaac Newton, un famoso científico inglés, con la forma correcta del imperfecto del verbo apropiado.

Conexiones · Las ciencias

De niño

tener, ser, decir, ir

Isaac Newton nació en 1642. __1.__ un bebé tan pequeño y débil[1] que los médicos __2.__ que él no __3.__ a tener capacidad mental para hacer cosas importantes durante su vida.

En la escuela primaria

querer, ser, hacer, ver, creer

__4.__ un estudiante inteligente que nunca __5.__ sus tareas porque no le interesaba mucho lo que los profesores __6.__ enseñarle. Su madre tampoco __7.__ que era muy inteligente.

En la universidad

leer, ir, poder, trabajar

Como estudiante universitario, Newton siempre __8.__ y estaba muy metido[2] en sus experimentos físicos. No __9.__ a los restaurantes elegantes y tampoco salía con los amigos. __10.__ siempre en alguna investigación y por eso inventó el análisis matemático y descubrió que la luz blanca tiene colores.

Su fama

poder, consistir, estar, ver

Un día Newton __11.__ en casa de su madre pensando en cómo la Luna[3] __12.__ dar vueltas alrededor de[4] la Tierra,[5] cuando le cayó[6] una manzana en la cabeza. Newton empezó a pensar y recordó un juego de niños que __13.__ en llenar con agua una cubeta[7] y darle vueltas rápidamente por encima de la cabeza sin permitir caer el agua. Así se le ocurrió a Newton la idea de la gravedad y la velocidad.

[1]weak [2]involved [3]moon [4]spin around [5]Earth [6]fell [7]bucket

Actividad 18 — Escribir/Hablar

Y tú, ¿qué dices?

1. En la escuela primaria, ¿cómo eras? ¿Qué clases te interesaban más? Y ahora, ¿qué clases te interesan?

2. De pequeño(a), ¿te gustaban las ciencias? ¿Qué experimentos hacían tus compañeros de clase y tú en la escuela? Y ahora, ¿qué experimentos hacen en sus clases de ciencias?

3. De niño(a), ¿en qué pensabas más: los estudios, los libros, los deportes o los juguetes? Y ahora, ¿en qué piensas más?

ciento noventa y siete **197**
Capítulo 4A

Resources: Answers on Transparencies

Focus: Reading comprehension; cross-curricular connection to science, history

Suggestions: Before beginning, ask students to tell you who Sir Isaac Newton was. Direct attention to the photo and picture. Remind students to use footnotes and contextual clues to help with unfamiliar vocabulary.

Answers:

1. Era	8. leía
2. decían	9. iba
3. iba	10. Trabajaba
4. Era	11. estaba
5. hacía	12. podía
6. querían	13. consistía
7. creía	

Actividad 18 *Standards:* 1.3

Focus: Writing and speaking about what you did as a child

Suggestions: After students have written their answers, have them work with a partner to ask and answer the questions. When students finish the interview, have them write a short biographical paragraph about their partner.

Answers will vary.

 Pre-AP* Support

- **Activity:** Bring to class copies of two or three pages from your high school yearbook, including the page where your picture is found. Distribute one page to each student in the class. Have each student write four or more sentences using the imperfect tense to write what they imagine a particular student might have done as a young person. Share several comical "remembrances" with the class.

- **Pre-AP* Resource Book:** Comprehensive guide to Pre-AP* communication skill development, pp. 9–17, 36–46

Enrich Your Teaching
Resources for All Teachers

Teacher-to-Teacher

Have students write a paragraph about what they were like when they were younger and what they are like now. For example: *De pequeño era muy travieso, pero ahora soy obediente.* Collect the paragraphs and read them aloud. Ask students to guess the name of the person you are describing.

Internet Search

Have students research a scientist from a Spanish-speaking country. Ask them to write a brief report, using *Actividad* 17 as a model.

Keywords:

scientists + (Spanish-speaking country)

Actividad 19
Standards: 1.1, 1.3, 4.1

Resources: Answers on Transparencies

Focus: Writing and talking about childhood

Recycle: Adjectives; leisure activities

Suggestions: Encourage students to elaborate, using as many details as possible. Have them use their sentences to form a paragraph.

Answers will vary, but should include the following verbs:

| 1. era, era | 3. íbamos | 5. jugábamos |
| 2. eran | 4. iba | 6. veía |

Actividad 20
Standards: 1.2, 1.3

Focus: Writing and speaking about what people did in elementary school

Recycle: Adjectives; activities

Suggestions: Have students work in groups for the interview only. After they have taken notes, have them work individually to write their summaries.

Answers will vary.

Actividad 21
Standards: 1.2, 1.3

Focus: Describing what famous people used to be like and what they used to do

Recycle: Adjectives; activities

Suggestions: Have students brainstorm a list of famous people. Write the names on the board and ask students to choose from the people on the list. Explain that *¿Quién soy yo?* is a standard question used in riddles, just as in English. Students should write their paragraphs using the first person.

Answers will vary.

Additional Resources

- WAV Wbk.: Audio Act. 8, p. 72
- Teacher's Resource Book: Audio Script, p. 193
- Audio Program: Track 13

✔ Assessment

- **ExamView** QuickTake Presenter Quiz on PresEXPRESS
- Prueba 4A-4: The imperfect tense: Irregular verbs, p. 102

Actividad 19
  ♻ **Escribir/Hablar**

Cómo era de niño(a)

Escribe frases para hablar de tu niñez *(childhood)* usando las formas apropiadas del imperfecto de los verbos y tus propias ideas. Después trabaja con otro(a) estudiante y lean sus frases. ¿Eran similares o diferentes sus experiencias de niñez?

1. Cuando yo *(ser)* niño(a), *(ser)* muy . . .
2. Mis amigos *(ser)* . . .
3. De vez en cuando mi familia y yo *(ir)* . . .
4. A menudo yo *(ir)* a la casa de . . .
5. Mis hermanos (o amigos) y yo *(jugar)* . . .
6. Por lo general yo *(ver)* a mis primos . . .

Actividad 21
   ♻ **Escribir/Hablar**

Juego

1 Trabaja con otro(a) estudiante. Escriban una descripción del punto de vista de una persona del pasado que muchos estudiantes conocen. La descripción debe ser de cómo era, de dónde era, qué hacía para ser famoso(a), dónde vivía la persona y más.

2 Lean su descripción a otras parejas de estudiantes. Si los otros estudiantes identifican a la persona, reciben cinco puntos. Si ellos no pueden identificar a la persona, Uds. reciben cinco puntos.

> **Modelo**
>
> **A** —*Era de México. De niña a menudo estaba enferma. Cuando era mayor, era artista y pintaba mucho. Diego Rivera era mi esposo. Yo no tenía una vida muy sencilla ni feliz. ¿Quién soy yo?*
>
> **B** —*Tú eres Frida Kahlo.* (Correcto. Cinco puntos para la pareja B)

Actividad 20
   ♻ **Escribir/Hablar**

El (La) estudiante modelo

1 En una hoja de papel, escribe cuatro descripciones de cómo eras y qué hacías en la escuela primaria.

> **Modelo**
>
> *Era muy obediente. Siempre obedecía las reglas de la escuela.*

2 Trabaja con un grupo de tres. Lean sus descripciones de cómo eran en la escuela primaria. Apunten en una hoja de papel cómo responden los tres. Después escriban un resumen *(summary)* de cómo eran.

> **Modelo**
>
> *María y yo éramos muy buenos estudiantes y siempre escuchábamos a los profesores. Antonio era un poco desobediente y nunca escuchaba a los profesores.*

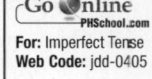

Frida Kahlo

> **Más práctica**
>
> - Practice Workbook, p. 78: 4A-6
> - WAV Wbk.: Writing, p 76
> - Guided Practice: Grammar Acts., pp. 139–140
> - *Real.* para hispanohablantes, pp. 138-139
>
> **Go Online** PHSchool.com
> **For:** Imperfect Tense
> **Web Code:** jdd-0405

Differentiated Instruction
Solutions for All Learners

Advanced Learners

Have students interview an older family member and write about where that person lived, what he or she was like as a child, and what he or she used to do. Check for spelling and grammar.

Heritage Language Learners

If you have students from Spain, they may use the indirect object pronouns **le** or **les** to replace direct objects that refer to a person or persons. This is commonly referred to as **leísmo.**

199

Gramática · Repaso

Indirect object pronouns

Remember that an indirect object tells to whom or for whom an action is performed. Indirect object pronouns are used to replace or accompany an indirect object noun.

Nuestros profesores no **nos** permitían beber refrescos en clase.

Sus abuelos siempre **les** daban regalos **a los niños.**

	Singular		Plural
me	(to / for) me	**nos**	(to / for) us
te	(to / for) you *(familiar)*	**os**	(to / for) you *(familiar)*
le	(to / for) him, her, you *(formal)*	**les**	(to / for) them, you *(formal)*

- Because *le* and *les* have more than one meaning, you can make the meaning clear by adding *a* + name, noun, or pronoun.

  Lolita siempre **les** decía la verdad **a sus padres.**

  Lolita siempre **les** decía la verdad **a ellos.**

- Like direct object pronouns and reflexive pronouns, indirect object pronouns are placed right before the verb or attached to the infinitive.

  Siempre **le** quería comprar dulces a su hija.

  Siempre quería comprar**le** dulces a su hija.

GramActiva VIDEO

Want more help with indirect object pronouns? Watch the **GramActiva** video.

Actividad 22

  Escribir

Una tía muy generosa

Mi tía era muy generosa, pero siempre nos compraba los mismos regalos. Escribe frases para decir lo que compraba ella.

Modelo
Por lo general ella le compraba una corbata a mi padre.

mi padre

1.
mi madre

2.
mis hermanitas

3.
yo

4.
su esposo

5.
mis primos

6.
nosotros

ciento noventa y nueve **199**
Capítulo 4A

Gramática · Repaso

 Presentation EXPRESS
GRAMMAR

Core Instruction

 Standards: 4.1

Resources: Teacher's Resource Book: Video Script, p. 195; Video Program: Cap. 4A

Suggestions: Play the *GramActiva* Video as an introduction or to reinforce your own presentation of indirect object pronouns. Point out that even if students use *a* + name, noun, or pronoun for clarification, they still need to use the indirect object pronoun.

Bring in a bag and have students place one item each in the bag. Take out an item and ask: *¿Quién me dio...?* Then give it to another student(s) and ask: *¿A quién le di...?* Be sure that they don't place anything of value in the bag and return all items at the end of the activity.

Bellringer Review

Show Voc. & Gram. Transparency 78 and ask student to tell how much each toy costs. *(¿Cuánto cuesta el dinosaurio?)*

Actividad 22 *Standards:* 1.3, 1.4

 Presentation EXPRESS
ANSWERS

Resources: Answers on Transparencies

Focus: Writing about what someone used to buy

Recycle: Vocabulary for clothing and family members

Suggestions: Point out that the aunt is always the subject and the names under the pictures are the people for whom she used to buy the items.

Answers:
1. Por lo general, le compraba una blusa a mi madre.
2. ...les compraba unos osos de peluche a mis hermanitas.
3. ...me compraba unos calcetines.
4. ...le compraba un reloj a su esposo.
5. ...les compraba un tren eléctrico a mis primos.
6. ...nos compraba dulces.

Enrich Your Teaching
Resources for All Teachers

Culture Note

Frida Kahlo (1907–1954) is one of the most popular Mexican painters. She had a difficult life due to an almost-fatal traffic accident that occurred when she was a teenager. Her work reflects her physical and emotional suffering. She was married to Diego Rivera, the great muralist.

Teacher-to-Teacher

Ask students to bring in toys, clothing, or classroom items. Have them make a price tag for each object. Arrange the items around the room, simulating a store. Tell students they have a certain amount of money to spend. Have them write sentences about what they are going to buy and for whom.

 *Standards:* 1.1

Focus: Asking and answering questions about rules in elementary school

Suggestions: Tell students to use **les** to refer to a general "you plural" when asking the questions. Have students answer with **nos** to refer to a general "us."

Answers will vary.

Extension: Have students describe the rules in their current school.

Fondo cultural   *Standards:* 2.2, 4.2

Suggestions: Explain to students that although the Maya were advanced thinkers and understood the concept of the wheel, they had no real use for it. Carts, wagons, and potter's wheels didn't exist. Until the Spanish arrived, there were no horses or burros to pull a cart. People transported objects on their backs, or used rafts and canoes on rivers and streams.

Answers will vary.

Actividad 24 *Standards:* 1.1

Focus: Answering questions about fine art; writing and speaking about childhood

Suggestions: Before students complete the activity, have them read the title of the painting and look at the picture. Ask them to discuss what the children are doing.

Answers will vary.

Block Schedule

Have students create a puzzle to help practice word order. Divide them into groups of four, and give each group a specific topic related to childhood activities. Have them write a four-sentence paragraph in large print, using a different subject and indirect object pronoun for each sentence. Have them cut each word out of their paragraph and put it into an envelope. Collect the envelopes, and distribute them to other groups. Have students unscramble the paragraphs, and summarize them for the rest of the class.

Actividad 23   **Hablar**

¿Qué les permitían hacer?

Trabaja con otro(a) estudiante para hablar de lo que les permitían hacer en la escuela primaria.

1. comer y beber en la sala de clases
2. tener animales en la escuela
3. jugar en el patio de recreo
4. ver películas en clase

¡Respuesta personal!

Modelo

A —¿Les permitían llevar gorras en la escuela primaria?

B —No, no nos permitían llevar gorras.

o: —Sí, nos permitían llevar gorras, pero sólo en los días especiales.

Fondo cultural

Juguetes mayas Los mayas no usaban la rueda (*wheel*) para el trabajo, pero crearon juguetes de niños en forma de animales (reales e inventados), con ruedas. Estos juguetes eran similares al *pull-toy* que se usa hoy.

• ¿Son similares los juguetes de los mayas a los juguetes con los que tú jugabas de niño(a), o son diferentes? ¿En qué sentido?

Actividad 24   **Leer/Escribir/Hablar**

Jugando con los amigos

Estudia el cuadro, lee el párrafo y luego contesta las preguntas.

1. ¿Quiénes crees que son las personas mayores del cuadro?

2. Con otro(a) estudiante, imaginen que Uds. eran unos niños del cuadro y que ya son mayores. Hablen de los juguetes que tenían cuando eran niños(as).

3. Ahora imaginen que Uds. tienen sesenta años. Piensen en los juguetes que les gustaban de niños(as). Descríbanlos para las personas que no los conocen. ¿Estos juguetes son populares hoy?

"Los niños del futuro" (1998)
© Lorenzo Armendariz/Latin Focus.com.

Leovigildo Martínez (1959–) nació en Oaxaca, México. Este cuadro es parte de un mural que pintó para el hospital que lo atendió (*treated*) cuando era niño. En el cuadro ves los juguetes tradicionales de la región.

200 doscientos
Tema 4 • Recuerdos del pasado

Differentiated Instruction
Solutions for All Learners

Advanced Learners

Have students bring in a reproduction of a painting that depicts their idea of childhood. Have them present the painting to the class and compare it to their own childhood.

Students with Special Needs

For *Actividad* 24, have advanced learners work with visually impaired students to describe the picture, using the present tense. They should describe the people as well as the toys the children are playing with. This will give visually impaired students the necessary information to answer the questions.

Actividad 25 · Hablar

¿Quiénes te compraban regalos?

Habla con otro(a) estudiante sobre quiénes hacían estas cosas para ti cuando eras niño(a).

Modelo

A —¿Quiénes te compraban regalos?
B —Mis padres me compraban regalos de vez en cuando.

1. leer cuentos
2. preparar galletas
3. enviar tarjetas de cumpleaños
4. dar dinero para comprar cosas
5. prestar (lend) juguetes
6. cantar canciones de cuna (lullabies)

Actividad 26 · Leer/Pensar/Escribir/Hablar

Los retratos

Mira el retrato (portrait) del niño y lee el párrafo. Luego contesta las preguntas.

1. ¿Qué mascotas tenías cuando eras niño(a)? ¿Cómo se llamaban?

2. Cuando te sacan fotos, ¿qué ropa te gusta llevar?

3. Hace muchos años, los artistas pintaban retratos porque las personas no tenían cámaras para sacar fotos de su familia. Compara el retrato de este niño con una foto tuya cuando eras niño(a). ¿En qué sentido son similares? ¿En qué sentido son diferentes?

El español en la comunidad

Es importante aprender otro idioma (language) a una edad muy joven. Muchas guarderías infantiles, escuelas preescolares y escuelas primarias dan clases en español o en francés. Busca en tu comunidad una guardería o escuela que enseña español. ¡Puedes visitarla para observar o para enseñarles a los niños un poco de español!

• ¿Crees que es fácil o difícil aprender otro idioma de pequeño(a)? ¿Por qué?

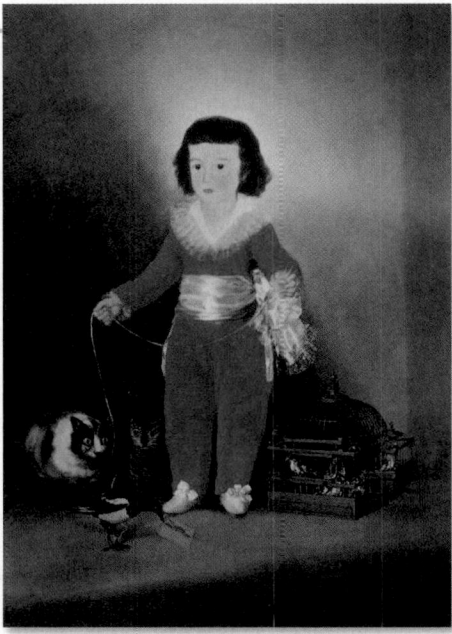

"Don Manuel Osorio Manrique de Zúñiga" (1788)
Oil on canvas, 127 x 101. Metropolitan Museum of Art, New York, USA / Bridgeman Art Library

Francisco de Goya (1746–1828) era uno de los pintores más importantes de España. Por la ropa elegante que el niño lleva en este retrato, sabemos que es de una familia aristocrática. Goya pintó al niño con sus mascotas: tres gatos y unos pájaros.

Más práctica

• Practice Workbook, p. 79: 4A-7
• WAV Wbk.: Writing, p. 120
• Guided Practice: Grammar Acts., pp. 141–142
• Real. para hispanohablantes, p. 139

Go Online PHSchool.com
For: Indirect Obj. Pronouns
Web Code: jdd-0406

Actividad 25 · Standards: 1.1

Focus: Talking about childhood using indirect object pronouns
Recycle: Activities; family vocabulary
Suggestions: Allow students to use either real or imaginary people to complete the activity. Encourage them to include expressions of frequency in their sentences.
Answers will vary.

Actividad 26 · Standards: 1.3 · Pre-AP*

Focus: Thinking about a painting and writing about childhood
Suggestions: Have students complete item 3 as homework to allow them time to find an appropriate photo.
Answers will vary.

El español en la comunidad

Core Instruction

Standards: 5.1

Suggestions: Explain to students that there are many benefits to learning a language at a young age, especially for accuracy of pronunciation and willingness to speak without fear. However, it is never too late to start learning a language.

Theme Project

Students can perform Step 2 at this point. Be sure students understand your corrections. (For more information, see p. 182–a.)

Additional Resources

• WAV Wbk.: Audio Act. 9, p. 73
• Teacher's Resource Book: Audio Script, p. 193, Communicative Activity BLM, p. 200
• Audio Program: Track 14

✓ Assessment

• ExamView ❸ Quiz on PresEXPRESS
  QuickTake Presenter
• Prueba 4A-5: Indirect object pronouns, p. 103

 Enrich Your Teaching
Resources for All Teachers

Culture Note

Leovigildo Martínez is a multi-talented Mexican artist whose work includes illustrations for children's books as well as murals. Children's books he has illustrated include *Tío Culebra, La luna se fue de fiesta,* and *Los veinticinco gatos mixtecos.* Martínez worked with the author Matthew Gollub on these books.

Teacher-to-Teacher

Have students prepare a Spanish lesson for a group of preschoolers. Have students decide on the topic, prepare flashcards, posters, and design a practice activity. If possible, allow students to present their lesson to a class.

Lectura

Core Instruction

 Standards: 1.2, 3.2

Focus: Reading comprehension of a Mexican fable

Suggestions:

Pre-reading: Have students brainstorm a list of fables they remember. What is the purpose of fables? *(To teach a moral lesson.)* Based on what students know about fables, have them predict the outcome.

Reading: Remind students that they should be reading for the main idea, not focusing on details. As they read, have students identify the following literary elements: characters, conflict, and moral.

Post-reading: Discuss the moral of the fable. Ask students to compare it with fables that they read or heard when they were children.

Bellringer Review

Have students write the correct preterite form of these verbs in the third person singluar and be prepared to pantomine each action: *salir, empezar, ver, responder, llegar.*

For Further Reading

Student Resource: Guided Practice: Lectura, p. 143

¡Adelante!

Lectura

El grillo y el jaguar
Una fábula mexicana

Objectives
- Read a fable from Mexico
- Learn traditional Spanish songs
- Talk about how you were as a child
- Watch *En busca de la verdad,* Episodio 3

Estrategia

Using background knowledge Think of fables you read as a child. Write down what you think might happen in this encounter between a cricket and a jaguar. When you finish reading, check to see how close your prediction was to the real story.

Hace ya muchísimos años, sólo vivían por el mundo los animales. Y el rey de todos era el jaguar.

Un día el jaguar salió de su casa rugiendo[1] y empezó a correr al lago porque tenía sed. Como todos los animales le tenían miedo,[2] se escondieron.[3] Todos menos el grillo, que no lo oyó[4] porque cantaba muy contento en su jardín.

El jaguar se sorprendió[5] cuando no vio a nadie, pero oyó la canción del grillo.

—¿Quién canta esa canción tan fea? —se preguntó el jaguar.

Cuando el jaguar vio al grillo, le rugió: —¡Qué mal educado eres, grillo! ¿Por qué no me saludas?[6]

—¡Ay, don Jaguar! Lo siento. ¿Me perdona?

—Sólo si eres obediente —le contestó el jaguar.

—¿Y qué tengo que hacer, don Jaguar?

—Vamos a hacer una carrera[7] hasta aquella roca enorme que está por donde empiezan las montañas. Si llegas primero, te perdono todo y puedes seguir cantando, pero si llego primero yo, te prohíbo cantar.

[1]roaring [2]were afraid [3]they hid [4]didn't hear him [5]was surprised [6]greet me [7]race

---

Differentiated Instruction
Solutions for All Learners

Heritage Language Learners

Have students research a fable from their heritage culture. Have them draw simple cartoon panels to tell the story, with captions below. The moral should be highlighted in some way. Post the stories and allow other students to read them.

Multiple Intelligences

Visual/Spatial: Have students draw scenes that illustrate the events of the fable. Hold them up as you narrate so that students can visualize the events.

El grillo no contestó inmediatamente, pero por fin dijo:
—Bien. ¿Cuándo corremos?

—¡Ahora mismo! —respondió el jaguar.

Al oír "ahora mismo" el grillo saltó a la cola[8] del jaguar y muy despacito iba saltando hasta llegar a su cabeza. Así llegaron los dos a la roca enorme. Pero en ese momento (y antes de que el jaguar lo viera[9]), el grillo saltó de la cabeza del jaguar a la roca y dijo: —¡Hola, don Jaguar! Estaba esperándolo.

El jaguar no sabía qué decir, pero perdonó al grillo, y el grillo empezó a cantar otra vez.

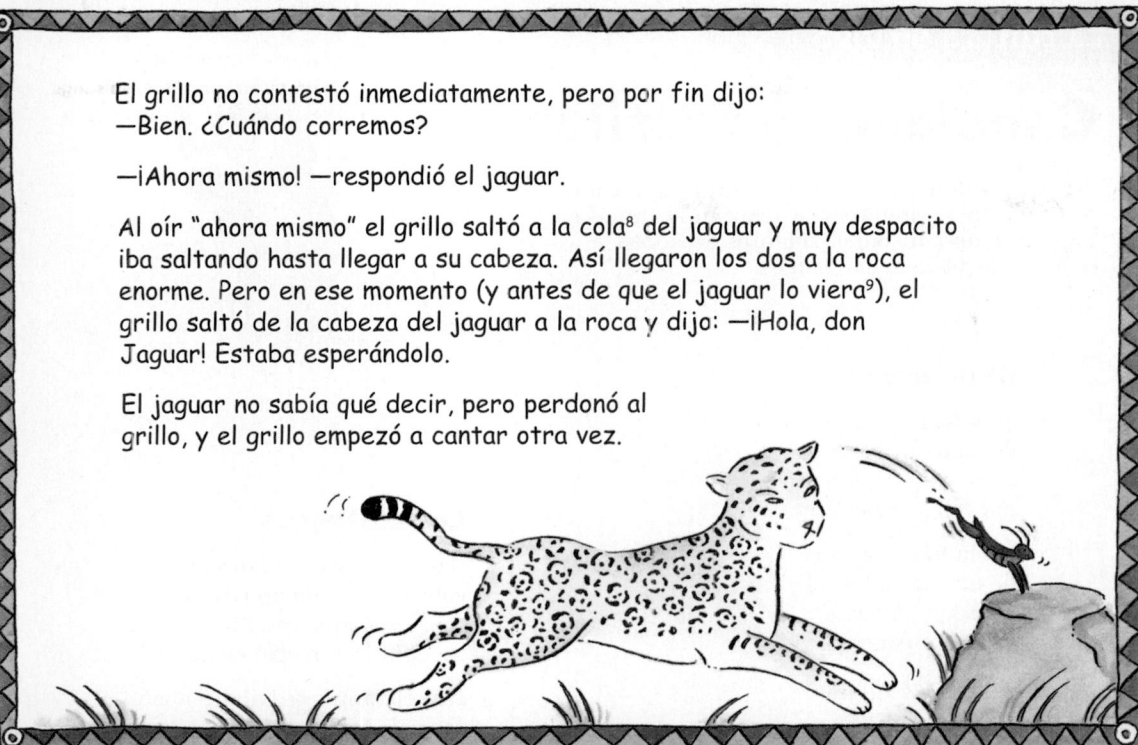

[8]tail [9]could see

¿Comprendiste?

1. Según esta leyenda, ¿quiénes vivían por el mundo hace muchos años?
2. ¿Por qué se escondieron todos los animales?
3. ¿Por qué el grillo no oyó al jaguar?
4. Según el jaguar, ¿cómo era la canción del grillo?
5. ¿Qué hizo el grillo para llegar primero a la roca?
6. Al fin, ¿quién era más inteligente, el jaguar o el grillo?

Más práctica

● WAV Wbk.: Writing, p. 77
● Guided Practice: Lectura, p. 143
● Real. para hispanohablantes, pp. 142-143

Go Online
PHSchool.com
For: Internet Activity
Web Code: jdd-0407

Y tú, ¿qué dices?

Hace muchísimos años que las fábulas son importantes en muchas culturas para enseñarles a los niños y a los adultos lecciones sobre la vida. En muchas fábulas los personajes son animales. Trabaja con otro(a) estudiante. Piensa en unas fábulas y describe a los animales en esas fábulas.

Modelo

La tortuga caminaba muy lentamente y era muy trabajadora.

Para decir más ...

el conejo rabbit
la gallina, el gallo hen, rooster
el león lion
el zorro fox

¿Comprendiste?

Presentation EXPRESS
ANSWERS

Standards: 1.2

Resources: Answers on Transparencies
Focus: Verifying reading comprehension
Suggestions: Have a volunteer summarize the events of the fable in his or her own words before discussing the questions.
Answers:
1. Sólo los animales vivían por el mundo.
2. Se escondieron porque tenían miedo del jaguar.
3. El grillo no oyó al jaguar porque cantaba muy contento en su jardín.
4. Según el jaguar, era fea la canción del grillo.
5. El grillo saltó de la cabeza del jaguar para llegar primero a la roca.
6. Al fin, el grillo era más inteligente.

Y tú, ¿qué dices?

Standards: 1.2, 2.2, 3.2

Focus: Describing animals in fables
Suggestions: To help students, divide them into groups and assign each group a different fable to summarize.
Answers will vary.
Extension: Have students illustrate their fables.

Pre-AP* Support

• **Activity:** Type five teacher-made sentences (in large font) representing a series of events that take place in this fable. Make enough copies to create one set for each pair of students in the class. Cut them into strips. Distribute the sets to the pairs of students and ask them to re-arrange the sentences on a desktop in the correct, sequential order. (You might want to make this activity a speed contest.)

• *Pre-AP* Resource Book:* Comprehensive guide to Pre-AP* reading skill development, pp. 18–24

For Further Reading

Student Resources: Realidades para hispanohablantes: Lectura 2, pp. 144–145; Lecturas para hispanohablantes 2: *Cuando era puertorriqueña* (excerpt), pp. 106–108, "Paloma Herrera: Alas en los pies," pp. 122–124

Enrich Your Teaching
Resources for All Teachers

Teacher-to-Teacher

Bring in compilations of fables to share with your students. Make them available before and after the reading. Suggest that students use them as visual aids for the *Y tú, ¿qué dices?* or have students use them as models to write their own fables.

Internet Search

Have students use the Internet to research fables from Spanish-speaking countries.

Keyword:

fábulas de + (Spanish-speaking country)

203

La cultura en vivo

Core Instruction

 Standards: 2.1, 2.2, 3.2, 4.2

Resources: Audio Program: Tracks 15–17

Focus: Becoming familiar with popular children's songs in Spanish-speaking countries

Suggestions: Play the songs using the *Audio CD.* Model the rhythm of the song for students, and have the whole class practice each before grouping them for the *¡Compruébalo!* activity.

Point out that for *Los elefantes,* once the count reaches ten, the song then counts back down to one.

Additional Resources

Student Resource: Realidades para hispano-hablantes, p. 146

La cultura en vivo jdd-0488

Canciones infantiles

A todos los niños les encanta cantar. Aquí están dos canciones populares que cantan los niños en algunos países hispanohablantes mientras *(while)* juegan con sus amigos.

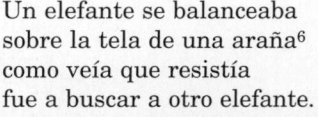

El columpio

Yo tengo un columpio[1]
de suave vaivén[2]
y en él muy contento
me vengo a mecer[3].

En la fuerte rama[4]
de un fuerte laurel[5],
mi buen papacito
lo vino a poner.

Qué suave columpio
qué rico vaivén
¿muchachos, no quieren
venirse a mecer?

[1]swing [2]swaying motion [3]to swing
[4]branch [5]laurel tree

Los elefantes

Un elefante se balanceaba
sobre la tela de una araña[6]
como veía que resistía
fue a buscar a otro elefante.

Dos elefantes se balanceaban
sobre la tela de una araña
como veían que resistía
fueron a buscar a otro elefante.

Tres elefantes se balanceaban . . .
Cuatro elefantes se balanceaban . . .
Cinco elefantes se balanceaban . . .
Seis elefantes se balanceaban . . .
Siete elefantes se balanceaban . . .
Ocho elefantes se balanceaban . . .
Nueve elefantes se balanceaban . . .

Diez elefantes se balanceaban
sobre la tela de una araña,
como veían que se rompía,
fueron a dejar a un elefante.

Nueve elefantes se balanceaban . . .

[6]spider web

¡Compruébalo! En grupos de cuatro, practiquen en voz alta *(aloud)* una de las canciones. Presten atención a la pronunciación y al ritmo de los versos. Presenten su canción a la clase.

204 doscientos cuatro
Tema 4 • Recuerdos del pasado

Differentiated Instruction
Solutions for All Learners

Multiple Intelligences

Musical/Rhythmic: Have students record their songs, or perform them live for local elementary schoolchildren. If time permits, students might spend time teaching the lyrics to the children and performing the song together.

Students with Learning Difficulties

If students have difficulty remembering information during their presentation, prompt them with questions. Be sure questions help students regain organization of the presentation. You may want to prepare a list of questions ahead of time.

Presentación oral

¿Cómo eras de niño(a)?

Task
You have a summer job at a *guardería infantil* and several students speak Spanish. They are always asking you what you were like when you were their age. Create a series of pictures that shows when you were young.

1 **Prepare** Think about your childhood: what you were like, things you used to do, and what you weren't allowed to do. Copy and complete the chart on a sheet of paper, providing at least two pieces of information about yourself in each column.

¿Cómo era?	Jugaba con . . .	Me gustaba más . . .	Tenía que . . .	No me permitían . . .
tímido(a)	mi oso de peluche	jugar con mis amigos	hacer mi cama	pelearme con mis hermanos

Create a series of drawings that illustrate all of the information on your chart. You can also bring in photos of yourself to show your childhood. You will use the visuals in your presentation. Be sure they are easy to understand and represent you when you were young!

2 **Practice** Go through your presentation several times. You can use your chart to practice, but not when you present. Use your drawings and photos when you practice to help you recall what you want to say. Try to:

- provide as much information as possible on each point
- use complete sentences
- speak clearly so that you can be understood

3 **Present** Talk about what you were like as a child. Be sure to use your drawings during your presentation.

4 **Evaluation** Your teacher may give you a rubric for how the presentation will be graded. You will probably be graded on:

- amount of information you communicate
- how easy it is to understand you
- quality of visuals

Estrategia

Using visuals
Using visuals during an oral presentation helps organize your thinking.

doscientos cinco **205**
Capítulo 4A

Presentación oral
Core Instruction

Standards: 1.3, 3.1

Resources: Teacher's Resource Book: GramActiva BLM, p. 203

Focus: Speaking about childhood in a personalized context

Suggestions: Review the task and steps with students. After reading the *Estrategia*, explain how visuals can help them remember their specific vocabulary, without having to read their charts. Give students the option of cutting out pictures from magazines.

Pre-AP* Support

- **Pre-AP* Resource Book:** Comprehensive guide to Pre-AP* speaking skill development, pp. 36–46

Portfolio
Record students' oral presentations on cassette or videotape for inclusion in their portfolios.

Additional Resources
Student Resources: Realidades para hispano-hablantes, p. 147; Guided Practice: Presentación oral, p. 144

✓ Assessment
- Assessment Program: Rubrics, p. T29

Give students copies of the rubric before they begin the activity. Go over the descriptions of the different levels of performance. After assessing students, help individuals understand how their performance could be improved. (See *Teacher's Resource Book* for suggestions and assessment.)

Enrich Your Teaching
Resources for All Teachers

RUBRIC	Score 1	Score 3	Score 5
How much information you communicate	You provide only one piece of information in each category.	You provide two pieces of information in each category.	You provide three or more pieces of information in each category.
How easily you are understood	You are difficult to understand and have many grammatical errors.	You are fairly easy to understand and have occasional grammatical errors.	You are easy to understand and have very few grammatical errors.
Quality of your visuals	You provide only one visual and it contains visible error corrections and smudges.	You provide only two visuals and they contain visible error corrections and smudges.	You provide several visuals and they contain no visible error corrections and smudges.

205

Videomisterio

Videomisterio

Core Instruction

Standards: 1.2, 3.2, 5.2

Resources: Teacher's Resource Book: Video Script, pp. 195–196; Video Program: Cap. 4A; Video Program Teacher's Guide: Cap. 4A

Focus: Reading and presenting new vocabulary needed to understand the video

Personajes importantes

Nela, Roberto's grandmother in San Miguel de Allende

Olga, friend and neighbor of Nela

Daniela y Roberto, Nela's grandchildren

Tomás, Roberto's father and Nela's son

Berta, Roberto's mother

Synopsis: Roberto and Linda make plans to visit Roberto's grandmother, Nela, who lives in San Miguel de Allende. In Guanajuato, Berta, Tomás, Roberto, and Daniela talk about the exchange program. Roberto is curious about Linda's last name. When he asks his father for more information about his grandfather, he's puzzled when told to ask his grandmother.

Suggestions:

Pre-viewing: Review the events of *Episodio* 2: Carmen and Linda arrived in Guanajuato and went to the travel agency recommended by Sr. Balzar in *Episodio* 1. There they met Berta Toledo, a travel agent who had made hotel reservations for them. Carmen and Linda met Berta's family. The following day they visited the Benito Juárez school.

Have a volunteer read the *Nota cultural* aloud. Tell students the Hidalgo market is enclosed. Have them compare it to other markets they already know (see *Mercados al aire libre, Capítulo* 3A, p. 148).

Point out the *Palabras para comprender* to the class, giving examples in context and writing sentences on the board.

Videomisterio

En busca de la verdad

Episodio 3

Antes de ver el video

"Tu abuelo se llamaba Federico Toledo. Es todo lo que puedo decirte".

"Vamos a ver . . . ¿Qué hay de nuevo en el correo electrónico?".

Nota cultural El mercado es el lugar donde la gente va a comprar comida fresca. En Guanajuato está el famoso mercado Hidalgo, donde venden frutas, verduras, carnes y muchas cosas más.

Resumen del episodio

En este episodio van a conocer a Nela, la abuela de Roberto. Él hace planes para visitarla al día siguiente. La familia Toledo almuerza en casa. Después de comer, Roberto le pregunta a su papá sobre su abuelo.

Palabras para comprender

catrina artistic rendering of a skull

una cosa más one more thing

carpintero carpenter

conocerse mejor to know each other better

a propósito by the way

Differentiated Instruction
Solutions for All Learners

Advanced Learners

Have students write a summary of a key event in this *episodio*. The summary should be divided into three sections: **Enredo, Punto culminante,** and **Desenredo** (see note, p. 151).

Heritage Language Learners

As a variation of the Advanced Learners suggestion, have students write a summary of the complete *episodio*. Students should include vocabulary from the *Palabras para comprender.*

Después de ver el video

¿Comprendiste?

A. Escoge la palabra correcta de las tres que están entre paréntesis.

1. "Me parece estupendo. Saben que ustedes siempre son (esperados/bienvenidos/queridos) en esta casa".

2. "Su mamá está aquí arreglando un programa de (juegos/televisión/intercambio) con nuestra escuela".

3. "Mañana viene el carpintero a reparar algunas (cosas/plantas/mesas) en mi casa".

4. "Hoy hablé con la maestra Toledo. Ella dice que todo está (caminando/progresando/funcionando) muy bien para el intercambio".

5. "Bueno, tengo que volver a la (escuela/clínica/casa). ¡Mis pacientes me esperan!".

6. "Dani, tengo un (mensaje/regalo/pastel) para la abuela".

7. "Ella sabe más que yo. Ahora, tengo que (vestirme/irme/dormirme)".

B. ¿Por qué crees que Roberto empieza a pensar en su abuelo con la llegada de Linda? Escribe lo que piensas.

C. Mira las fotos de Roberto y su abuela mientras hablan por teléfono. Escribe un resumen de la conversación.

Go Online
PHSchool.com

For: More on *En busca de la verdad*
Web code: jdd-0209

doscientos siete **207**
Capítulo 4A

Enrich Your Teaching
Resources for All Teachers

Culture Note
The *Mercado Hidalgo* was established in 1910 by the dictator Porfirio Díaz, Mexico's last ruler before the Mexican Revolution of the same year. The interior of this enclosed market is made of wrought iron.

Internet Seach
Keywords:

Mercado Hidalgo, Porfirio Díaz

Suggestions:

Visual scanning: Direct attention to the photos. Have students read the captions and try to guess what the characters may be talking about.

Before students read the *Resumen del episodio* have them scan the text and find the cognates. *(planes, visitar, familia, papá)* Then have them read the *Resumen del episodio.* Ask one or two comprehension questions. Can they guess where each of the characters is?

Viewing: Play *Episodio* 3 for the class. If there is time after viewing the full episode, go back and replay key moments that you wish to highlight. Remind students that they may not understand every word they hear in the video, but they should listen for overall understanding.

Post-viewing: Complete the *¿Comprendiste?* in class.

¿Comprendiste?

 Presentation EXPRESS
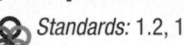 ANSWERS

Standards: 1.2, 1.3

Resources: Answers on Transparencies

Focus: Verifying comprehension; reviewing the plot

Suggestions: If there is time, play the video again so that students can check their answers for part A. For part B, you may need to point out the importance of the second surname.

Answers:
A:
1. bienvenidos
2. intercambio
3. cosas
4. progresando
5. clínica
6. pastel
7. irme

B: Answers will vary but may include: Roberto piensa en el abuelo porque quiere saber por qué Linda también tiene el apellido Toledo.

C: Answers will vary.

Additional Resources
• *En busca de la verdad* Video Workbook, Episode 3
• *En busca de la verdad* Teacher's Video Guide: Answer Key

Review Activities

To name toys and animals: Have students use flashcards or actual toys to quiz one another. They can ask, ¿Cuando eras niño(a), jugabas con…?

To discuss things you used to do and name places: Provide students with pictures of children in an early elementary school classroom, and have them ask and answer questions about what they see.

To explain your actions: Write the individual expressions on small pieces of paper, fold them, and distribute one to each pair of students. Tell students to take turns using the expression in a sentence directed at their partners. Set a timer, and have pairs exchange their slips of paper with another pair every minute.

To describe what someone was like: Provide pairs of students with pictures of children to describe to each other.

Portfolio

Invite students to review the activities they completed in this chapter, including written reports, posters or other visuals, tapes of oral presentations, or other projects. Have them select one or two items that they feel best demonstrate their achievements in Spanish to include in their portfolios. Have them include this with the Chapter Checklist and Self-Assesssment Worksheet.

Additional Resources

Student Resources: Realidades para hispanohablantes, p. 148

 **MindPoint™** QUIZ SHOW **CD-ROM**

PuzzleView Web Code: jdd-0408

Teacher Resources:
- Teacher's Resource Book: Situation Cards, p. 201, Clip Art, pp. 204–206
- Assessment Program: Chapter Checklist and Self-Assessment Worksheet, pp. T56–T57

Repaso del capítulo

Vocabulario y gramática   jdd-0489 🔊

Chapter Review

To prepare for the test, check to see if you . . .
- **know the new vocabulary and grammar**
- **can perform the tasks on p. 209**

to name toys

los bloques	blocks
la colección, *pl.* las colecciones	collection
la cuerda	rope
el dinosaurio	dinosaur
la muñeca	doll
el muñeco	action figure
el oso de peluche	teddy bear
el tren eléctrico	electric train
el triciclo	tricycle

to name animals

el pez, *pl.* los peces	fish
la tortuga	turtle

to discuss things you used to do

coleccionar	to collect
molestar	to bother
pelearse	to fight
saltar (a la cuerda)	to jump (rope)

to name places

la guardería infantil	daycare center
el patio de recreo	playground

to explain your actions

de niño, -a	as a child
de pequeño, -a	as a child
de vez en cuando	once in a while
mentir (e → ie)	to lie
obedecer (c → zc)	to obey
ofrecer (c → zc)	to offer
permitir	to permit, to allow
por lo general	in general
portarse bien / mal	to behave well / badly
todo el mundo	everyone
el vecino, la vecina	neighbor
la verdad	truth

For *Vocabulario adicional*, see pp. 498–499.

to describe what someone was like

bien educado, -a	well-behaved
consentido, -a	spoiled
desobediente	disobedient
generoso, -a	generous
obediente	obedient
tímido, -a	timid
travieso, -a	naughty, mischievous

other useful words

la moneda	coin
el mundo	world

imperfect of *ir*

iba	íbamos
ibas	ibais
iba	iban

imperfect of *jugar*

jugaba	jugábamos
jugabas	jugabais
jugaba	jugaban

imperfect of *ser*

era	éramos
eras	erais
era	eran

imperfect of *tener*

tenía	teníamos
tenías	teníais
tenía	tenían

indirect object pronouns

me	(to / for) me	nos	(to / for) us
te	(to / for) you	os	(to / for) you
le	(to / for) him, her, you *(formal)*	les	(to / for) them, you *(formal)*

Differentiated Instruction
Solutions for All Learners

Advanced Learners

Have students work in pairs to conduct an interview of a celebrity. One person should be the interviewer, and the other the celebrity. Have students create questions and fictional answers about the celebrity's childhood. If possible, have students record the conversations, and play them for the class.

Students with Learning Difficulties

You may want to review the format of the test with students. Select two or three sample questions or tasks to help students prepare. Discuss appropriate test-taking strategies necessary for performing well on the test.

Más práctica

- Practice Workbook: Puzzle, p. 80
- Practice Workbook: Organizer, p. 81

Go Online
PHSchool.com
For: Test Preparation
Web Code: jdd-0408

Preparación para el examen

On the exam you will be asked to . . .	Here are practice tasks similar to those you will find on the exam . . .	If you need review . . .
1 Escuchar Listen and understand as people describe their favorite childhood toy	You volunteer after school at the Youth Center. To get to know your kids better, you ask them about their favorite toys when they were younger. See if you can understand: (a) what the toy was; (b) how old the child was when he or she used to play with it; (c) where he or she used to play with it.	**pp. 186–189** *A primera vista* **p. 190** Actividad 6
2 Hablar Talk about what you were like as a child	Now your group at the Youth Center wants to know what you were like as a child! What could you tell them? You could start by telling them: (a) what you liked to do; (b) what your favorite toy was; (c) how you used to behave.	**pp. 188–189** *Videohistoria* **p. 190** Actividad 5 **p. 191** Actividades 7–8 **p. 192** Actividad 11 **p. 195** Actividad 15 **p. 200** Actividad 23 **p. 205** *Presentación oral*
3 Leer Read someone's recollections about their elementary school experience	Read an entry in Armando's journal about his elementary school years. As you read, see if you can determine: (a) whether he liked or disliked elementary school and (b) why or why not? *De vez en cuando yo pienso en mis amigos de la escuela primaria. ¡Ay! Jorge siempre se peleaba conmigo y Carlos me molestaba. Yo era muy tímido y no me levantaba a tiempo para la escuela porque no quería jugar con ellos.*	**p. 195** Actividad 14 **p. 196** Actividad 16 **p. 197** Actividad 17
4 Escribir Write about some of your experiences in elementary school	After reading Armando's recollection, you begin to think about your days in elementary school. What are some of the things you remember? Write a few sentences, describing what your best friend was like and what you used to do together at recess.	**p. 190** Actividad 4 **p. 191** Actividad 8 **p. 197** Actividad 18 **p. 198** Actividades 19–20
5 Pensar Demonstrate an understanding of favorite nursery rhymes and songs from Spanish-speaking countries	Children around the world love songs that are easy to remember and fun to sing. Think about the songs on p. 204. Which song do you think a child would like best? Why? Does either of them remind you of songs you sang as a child? Which ones?	**p. 193** *Pronunciación* **p. 204** *La cultura en vivo*

doscientos nueve **209**
Capítulo 4A

✓ **Differentiated Assessment**
Solutions for All Learners

STUDENTS NEEDING EXTRA HELP
- **Alternate Assessment Program:** Examen del capítulo 4A
- **Audio Program CD 20:** Chap. 4A ,Track 8

HERITAGE LEARNERS
- **Assessment Program: Realidades para hispanohablantes:** Examen del capítulo 4A
- **ExamView** test generator **Heritage Learner Test Bank**

ADVANCED/PRE-AP*
- **ExamView** test generator **Pre-AP* Test Bank**
- **Pre-AP* Resource Book,** pp. 108–111

Review

Performance Tasks

Presentation EXPRESS
ANSWERS

 Standards: 1.1, 1.2, 1.3, 2.1, 2.2, 4.2

Student Resource: Realidades para hispanohablantes p. 149

Teacher Resources: Teacher's Resource Book: Audio Script, p. 193; Audio Program: Track 19; Answers on Transparencies

1. Escuchar

Suggestions: Allow students to listen to the entire script once before they answer.

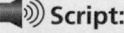 **Script:**
Mi juguete favorito era el tren eléctrico en nuestra guardería infantil. Cuando teníamos siete años, mis amigos y yo jugábamos muchas horas con aquel tren.

Answers:
a) electric train
b) seven years old
c) daycare center

2. Hablar

Suggestions: Have students make a word web for each category.

Answers will vary.

3. Leer

Suggestions: Before reading, have students scan the text once to pick out one word that might indicate whether or not Armando liked school.

Answers:
a) no
b) Porque su amigo Jorge siempre peleaba con él y su amigo Carlos le molestaba con su pistola de agua.

4. Escribir

Suggestions: Have students create a T-chart with one column for a description of their best friend, and the other for activities. Tell students to brainstorm at least three words in each column before beginning.

Answers will vary.

5. Pensar

Suggestions: To prepare students to answer the questions, refer them to the songs on p. 204 and have them brainstorm a list of songs that they used to listen to.

Answers will vary.

 Assessment
- **ExamView** QuickTake Presenter **Quiz on PresEXPRESS**
- Assessment Program: Examen del capítulo
- **ExamView** test generator **Test Bank: Tests A and B**
- Audio Program CD 20: Chap. 4A, Track 8

Chapter Overview

A primera vista	Manos a la obra	¡Adelante!	Repaso

Learning Sequence

INPUT	PRACTICE	APPLICATION	REVIEW
• Introduce vocabulary and grammar within an authentic context.	• Practice and develop new vocabulary. • Learn and practice new grammar structures.	• Apply vocabulary and grammar through culminating, theme-based activities. • Apply skill development.	• Review vocabulary and grammar.

Objectives

Read, listen to, and interpret information about • Common etiquette • Holiday celebrations	• Communicate about a social gathering involving friends and relatives. • Describe situations in the past. • Talk about how people interact. • Describe holiday celebrations.	• Read about *los Reyes Magos*. • Compare different holiday traditions. • Write about your favorite celebration. • Watch *En busca de la verdad, Episodio 4*.	• Prepare for the chapter test.

Culture

• Antonio M. Ruiz	• *Euskadi* • *El Día de la Raza* • *El Día de los Muertos* • *La ceremonia del lazo* • *El carnaval*	• *El seis de enero* - Celebration of the Three Kings	• Describe the holiday *el seis de enero* and its importance for children in Spanish-speaking cultures.

Vocabulary

• Special events
• Manners and customs

Grammar

• The imperfect tense: Describing a situation
• Reciprocal actions

Learner Support

STRATEGIES
• Using visuals
• Using background knowledge
• Using a chart

RECYCLING
• Preterite and imperfect tenses
• Family relatives
• Questions
• Leisure activities

• Reflexive verbs
• Holidays
• Descriptive adjectives

Chapter Features

Exploración del lenguaje

Prefixes

El español en el mundo del trabajo

The celebration of Hispanic holidays in the United States

Conexiones

El Día de la independencia

Beyond the Classroom: States & Countries

España
México
República Dominicana
Venezuela
Costa Rica
Colombia
Ecuador
Perú
Bolivia
Uruguay

Student Resources

TECHNOLOGY

ONLINE
Interactive Textbook
• Student Edition Online plus audio, video, and flashcards
Go Online Companion Web Site
• Tutorial activities   • Internet links
• Self-tests   • Downloadable MP3 audio files
PuzzleView

CD-ROM
Interactive Textbook CD-ROM
Student Edition on CD-ROM plus audio, video, and flashcards

MindPoint™ CD-ROM
QUIZSHOW

PRINT MATERIAL

CORE INSTRUCTION
Practice Workbook, pp. 82–90
• Review   • Vocabulary
• Grammar   • Puzzle
• Organizer
Writing, Audio & Video Activities,
pp. 78–87
• Video   • Audio
• Writing
Grammar Study Guide 1–2 (or 3–4)

Differentiated Instruction

STUDENTS NEEDING EXTRA HELP
Guided Practice Activities, pp. 145–160
• Vocabulary Flash Cards and Vocabulary Check
• Grammar Activities
• Presentación escrita

HERITAGE LEARNERS
Realidades para hispanohablantes,
pp. 150–169
Lecturas para hispanohablantes
• "Espiral," p. 39
• AP* Literature Author: Jorge Luis Borges, "Un patio," p. 41
• "Un terremoto en mi cuarto," pp. 43–44
• "Fonseca," p. 66

ADVANCED/PRE-AP*
Pre-AP* Resource Book: Student Activity Sheet, p. 111

Teacher Resources

TECHNOLOGY

Audio Program   Fine Art Transparencies
Video Program   Vocabulary and Grammar
                 Transparencies
                 Answers on Transparencies
TeacherEXPRESS™ CD-ROM
• Lesson Planner   • Vocabulary Clip Art
• Web Resources   • Teaching Resources
• Teacher Edition with Interactive Links
PresentationEXPRESS™ CD-ROM
• Vocabulary   • Transparencies and Maps
• Grammar   • Photo Gallery
• Audio   • Clip Art

PRINT MATERIAL

CORE INSTRUCTION
Teacher's Resource Book, pp. 216–241
• Input Script   • Video Script
• Answer Keys   • GramActiva Blackline Masters
• Vocabulary Clip Art • Chapter Resource Checklist
• School-to-Home Connection Letters
• Communicative Activities Blackline Masters
TPR Stories, pp. 58–63

Differentiated Instruction

STUDENTS NEEDING EXTRA HELP
Guided Practice Activities
Teacher's Guide, pp. T73–T80
HERITAGE LEARNERS
Realidades para hispanohablantes
Teacher's Guide, pp. 76–85
Lecturas para hispanohablantes
Teacher's Guide, pp. 13–16, 25–26

ADVANCED/PRE-AP*
Pre-AP* Resource Book: Resources Chart, p. 109

Differentiated Assessment

PH SuccessNet ONLINE
• Access to grades and reports from Online Interactive Textbook

ExamView® on Presentation Express
QuickTake Presenter CD-ROM
• Vocabulary Quizzes   • Chapter Test
• Grammar Quizzes
TeacherEXPRESS™ CD-ROM
• Assessment Program
• **ExamView®** Test Banks A and B
test generator

Go Online
PHSchool.com
For: Teacher Home Page
Web Code: jdk-1001

CORE ASSESSMENT
Assessment Program, pp. 111–123
• Pruebas
  Vocabulary Recognition
  Vocabulary Production
  The imperfect tense: Describing a situation
  Reciprocal actions
• Examen del capítulo   • Speaking and Writing Rubrics
Teacher's Resource Book, p. 230
• Situation Cards
TPR Stories, pp. 58–63

STUDENTS NEEDING EXTRA HELP
Alternate Assessment Program
• Examen del capítulo, pp. 47–52

HERITAGE LEARNERS
Assessment Program: Realidades para hispanohablantes Teacher's Guide, pp. T126–T130
ExamView® Heritage Learner
test generator Test Bank

ADVANCED/PRE-AP*
Pre-AP* Resource Book: Teacher Activity Sheet, p. 110
ExamView® Pre-AP* Test Bank
test generator

Regular Schedule (50 Minutes)

For electronic lesson plans:
Teacher Express 💿

	Warm-up / Assess	Preview Present / Practice Communicate		Wrap-up / Homework Options
DAY 1	**Warm Up (10 min.)** • Homework check • Return Examen del capítulo: Capítulo 4B	**Chapter Opener (10 min.)** • Objectives • Fondo cultural	**A primera vista (25 min.)** • Presentation: Vocabulario y gramática en contexto • Actividades 1, 2	**Wrap-up and Homework Options (5 min.)** • Practice Workbook 4B-A, 4B-B, 4B-1, 4B-2 • Go Online
DAY 2	**Warm-up (10 min.)** • Homework check	**A primera vista (35 min.)** • Presentation: Videohistoria *La fiesta de San Pedro* • View: Videohistoria	• Video Activities 1, 2, 3, 4 • Actividad 3	**Wrap-up and Homework Options (5 min.)** • Practice Workbook 4B-3, 4B-4 • Go Online • Prueba 4B-1: Vocabulary recognition
DAY 3	**Warm-up (10 min.)** • Actividad 4 • Homework check ✔**Assessment (10 min.)** • Prueba 4B-1: Vocabulary recognition	**Manos a la obra (25 min.)** • Actividades 5, 6, 7, 8, • Fondos culturales • Writing Activity 10		**Wrap-up and Homework Options (5 min.)** • Actividad 9 • Heritage Learner Workbook 4B-1, 4B-2 • Prueba 4B-2: Vocabulary production
DAY 4	**Warm-up (10 min.)** • Communicative Activity • Homework check ✔**Assessment (10 min.)** (after Audio Activities) • Prueba 4B-2: Vocabulary production	**Manos a la obra (25 min.)** • Audio Activities 5, 6 • Presentation: The imperfect tense: describing a situation • View: GramActiva video • Actividades 11, 12		**Wrap-up and Homework Options (5 min.)** • Practice Workbook 4B-5 • Writing Activity 10 • Actividad 15 • Go Online
DAY 5	**Warm-up (10 min.)** • Actividad 10 • Homework check	**Manos a la obra (35 min.)** • Actividades 13, 14 • Fondo cultural • Exploración del lenguaje • Audio Activity 7	• Presentation: Reciprocal actions • View: GramActiva video • Actividades 17	**Wrap-up and Homework Options (5 min.)** • Practice Workbook 4B-6 • Writing Activity 12 • Actividad 16 • Go Online • Pruebas 4B-3: The imperfect tense: describing a situation
DAY 6	**Warm-up (10 min.)** • Fondos culturales • Homework check ✔**Assessment (10 min.)** • Pruebas 4A-3: The imperfect tense: describing a situation	**Manos a la obra (25 min.)** • Actividades 18, 19 • Audio Activities 8, 9 • Writing Activity 13		**Wrap-up and Homework Options (5 min.)** • Practice Workbook 4B-7 • Go Online • Heritage Learner Workbook 4B-4 • Prueba 4B-4: Reciprocal actions
DAY 7	**Warm-up (10 min.)** • Actividad 20 • Homework check ✔**Assessment (10 min.)** • Prueba 4B-4: Reciprocal actions	**Manos a la obra (15 min.)** • Actividad 21 • El español en el mundo del trabajo	**Adelante! (10 min.)** • Presentación escrita: Steps 1, 5	**Wrap-up and Homework Options (5 min.)** • Presentación escrita: Steps 2
DAY 8	**Warm-up (5 min.)** • Homework check	**¡Adelante! (40 min.)** • Presentación escrita: Steps 3 • Lectura • ¿Comprendiste? / y tú, ¿qué dices?		**Wrap-up and Homework Options (5 min.)** • Presentación escrita: Step 4 • Presentación para el examen 3, 4, 5 • Go Online: Lectura
DAY 9	**Warm-up (5 min.)** • Homework check	**¡Adelante! (30 min.)** • Videomisterio: *En busca de la verdad*, Episodio 4 • Perspectivas del mundo hispano	**Repaso del capitulo (10 min.)** • Vocabulario y gramática • Preparación para el examen 1, 2	**Wrap-up and Homework Options (5 min.)** • Practice Workbook 4B-8, 4B-9 • Go Online: Self-test • Examen del capítulo 4B
DAY 10	**Warm-up (5 min.)** • Homework check ✔**Assessment (40 min.)** • Examen del capítulo 4B			**Wrap-up and Homework Options (5 min.)** • A ver si recuerdas . . .: Capítulo 5A

	Warm-up / Assess	Preview Present / Practice Communicate	Wrap-up / Homework Options
DAY 1	**Warm-up (10 min.)** • Homework check • Return Examen del capítulo: Capítulo 4A	**Chapter Opener (10 min.)** • Objectives • Fondo cultural **A primera vista (65 min.)** • Presentation: Vocabulario y gramática en contexto • Actividades 1, 2 • Presentation: Videohistoria: *La fiesta de San Pedro* • View: Videohistoria • Video Activities 1, 2, 3, 4 • Actividad 3	**Wrap-up and Homework Options (5 min.)** • Practice Workbook 4B-A, 4B-B, 4B-1, 4B-2, 4B-3, 4B-4 • Go Online • Prueba 4B-1: Vocabulary recognition
DAY 2	**Warm-up (10 min.)** • Actividad 4 • Homework check **✔Assessment (10 min.)** • Prueba 4B-1: Vocabulary recognition	**Manos a la obra (65 min.)** • Actividades 5, 6, 7, 8, • Fondos culturales • Audio Activities 5, 6 • Writing Activity 10 • Communicative Activity • Presentation: The imperfect tense: describing a situation • View: GramActiva video • Actividades 11, 12	**Wrap-up and Homework Options (5 min.)** • Practice Workbook 4B-5 • Actividades 9, 15 • Go Online • Heritage Learner Workbook 4B-1, 4B-2 • Prueba 4B-2: Vocabulary production
DAY 3	**Warm-up (10 min.)** • Actividad 10 • Homework check **✔Assessment (10 min.)** • Prueba 4B-2: Vocabulary production	**Manos a la obra (65 min.)** • Actividades 13, 14, • Audio Activity 7 • Fondo cultural • Exploración del lenguaje • Presentation: Reciprocal actions • View: GramActiva video • Actividades 17, 18, 19 • Audio Activities 8, 9	**Wrap-up and Homework Options (5 min.)** • Practice Workbook 4B-6, 4B-7 • Actividad 16 • Writing Activity 13 • Go Online • Heritage Learner Workbook 4B-4 • Pruebas 4B-3, 4B-4: The imperfect tense: describing a situation; Reciprocal actions
DAY 4	**Warm-up (15 min.)** • Writing Activity 11 • Homework check **✔Assessment (15 min.)** (after Writing Activities) • Pruebas 4B-3, 4B-4: The imperfect tense: describing a situation; Reciprocal actions	**Manos a la obra (25 min.)** • Writing Activity 12 • Fondo cultural • Actividades 20, 21 • El español en el mundo del trabajo **¡Adelante! (30 min.)** • Lectura • ¿Comprendiste? / Y tú, ¿qué dices? • Presentación escrita: Steps 1, 5	**Wrap-up and Homework Options (5 min.)** • Presentación escrita: Step 2 • Go Online: Lectura
DAY 5	**Warm-up (5 min.)** • Homework check	**¡Adelante! (45 min.)** • Presentación escrita: Step 3 • Perspectivas del mundo hispano **Repaso del capítulo (35 min.)** • Vocabulario y gramática • Preparación para el examen 1, 2, 3, 4, 5	**Wrap-up and Homework Options (5 min.)** • Presentación escrita: Step 4 • Practice Workbook 4B-8, 4B-9 • Go Online: Self-test • Examen del capítulo 4B
DAY 6	**Warm-up (10 min.)** • Homework check • Answer questions **Repaso del capítulo (15 min.)** • Situation Cards **✔Assessment (40 min.)** • Examen del capítulo 4B	**¡Adelante! (20 min.)** • Videomisterio: *En busca de la verdad,* Episodio 4	**Wrap-up and Homework Options (5 min.)** • Go Online: Videomisterio • A ver si recuerdas . . .: Capítulo 5A

Standards for Capítulo 4B

- To achieve the goals of the Standards, students will:

Communication

1.1 Interpersonal
- Talk about: greetings and leave-takings; celebrations; family and social occasions; family members; childhood; friendship; inappropriate behavior; the painting *Tamalada*

1.2 Interpretive
- Read: about festivals, ornaments, holidays; Independence Day observances; *el Día de la Raza; Semana Santa; el Día de los Muertos; el carnaval; la Tamborrada; las Fallas de Valencia; el Día de los Reyes Magos;* about customs of a Basque village; a picture-based story
- Read and listen to information about etiquette
- Listen to and watch a video about a *fiesta*
- Listen to information about *Tamalada*

1.3 Presentational
- Write: about *la Tamborrada* in Alsasua, family and social gatherings, celebrations; about the painting *Tamalada;* about childhood events, memories; a letter to *los Reyes Magos*
- Present information about good manners

Culture

2.1 Practices and Perspectives
- Describe celebrations: Independence Day in Mexico; the Basque celebration, *la Tamborrada; el Día de la Raza; el Día de los Muertos; el carnaval; las Fallas de Valencia; el Día de los Reyes Magos; la ceremonia del lazo*
- Interpret rules of etiquette

2.2 Products and Perspectives
- Tell about: Antonio M. Ruiz and his art; Mexico's flag; Basque language, food, and customs; celebrations: *el Día de la Raza* parade; *el Día de los Muertos* customs; *el carnaval; las Fallas de Valencia; el Día de los Reyes Magos; la ceremonia del lazo;* ornaments and decorations

Connections

3.1 Cross-curricular
- Describe Independence Days

3.2 Target Culture
- View a video mystery series

Comparisons

4.1 Language
- Describe the past with the imperfect tense
- Build antonyms using prefixes
- Explain reciprocal actions

4.2 Culture
- Compare Independence Day celebrations; wedding ceremonies

Communities

5.1 Beyond the School
- Explore ornaments used in local festivals

5.2 Lifelong Learner
- View a video mystery series

Fondo cultural

▪◆▫◈▪◆▫◈▪◆▫◈▪◆▫◈▪◆▫◈▪◆▫◈▪◆▫◈▪◆▫◈▪◆▫◈▪◆▫◈

Antonio M. Ruiz (1897–1964) pintó en este cuadro la celebración del Día de la Independencia en un pueblo de México. Es el día festivo más importante del país y todo el mundo participa. Aquí ves un desfile de estudiantes. El desfile pasa por la plaza de un pueblo mexicano. Todos los niños llevan en la mano banderas de color verde, rojo y blanco, que son los colores de la bandera mexicana. Estos colores también se ven en el centro de la plaza. Los mayores escuchan a un hombre que les habla.

- ¿Qué piensas que está diciendo el señor del cuadro? Compara este desfile con las celebraciones del Día de la Independencia en tu comunidad.

"Desfile cívico escolar" (1936), Antonio M. Ruiz

210 doscientos diez
Tema 4 • Recuerdos del pasado

Differentiated Instruction

STUDENTS NEEDING EXTRA HELP

Guided Practice Activities
- Vocabulary Check, Flash Cards
- Grammar
- Reading and Writing Support

Guided Practice Audio CDs
- Disc 1, Track 8

HERITAGE LEARNERS

Realidades para hispanohablantes
- Chapter Opener, pp. 150–151
- A primera vista, p. 152
- Videohistoria, p. 153
- Manos a la obra, pp. 154–161
- ¡Adelante!, pp. 162–167
- Repaso del capítulo, pp. 168–169

ADVANCED/PRE-AP*

Pre-AP* Resource Book, pp. 108–111

Capítulo 4B

Celebrando los días festivos

Chapter Objectives

- Describe holiday celebrations
- Talk about your family and relatives
- Describe people, places, and situations in the past
- Talk about how people interact
- Understand cultural perspectives on holidays and special events

Video Highlights

A primera vista: *La fiesta de San Pedro*

GramActiva Videos: the imperfect tense: describing a situation; reciprocal actions

Videomisterio: *En busca de la verdad,* Episodio 4

Country Connection

As you learn to talk about past events and celebrations, you will make connections to these countries and places:

España
México
República Dominicana
Venezuela
Costa Rica
Colombia
Ecuador
Perú
Bolivia
Uruguay

Más práctica

- *Real.* para hispanohablantes, pp. 150–151

Go Online PHSchool.com **For:** Online Atlas **Web Code:** jde-0002

doscientos once **211**
Capítulo 4B

Niñas vestidas para el Festival de primavera, Jerez de la Frontera, España

Chapter Opener

Presentation EXPRESS
ATLAS

Core Instruction

Resources: Voc. and Gram. Transparencies: Maps 12–18, 20

Suggestions: Tell students that this chapter focuses on celebrations. Ask them to list holidays celebrated in their family or community. What are the reasons for these celebrations? What traditions are practiced for the different celebrations? Ask students to discuss their own family celebrations or ones they are familiar with. Ask them to describe ways in which their family's traditions and customs may differ from those of other students. Explain that they will learn to discuss different customs in this chapter.

Point out that in the *Videohistoria,* they will learn about a traditional village *fiesta* in the Basque region of Spain. Point this region out on a map. Explain that people who live here have traditions unique to this part of Spain. Tell students that they will use the imperfect tense to describe a situation or to tell what used to happen.

Fondo cultural
Standards: 1.2, 2.1, 2.2, 3.1, 4.2

Suggestions: Have students use a Venn diagram to compare the painting to the Independence Day celebration in their community.

Answers will vary.

Teaching with Photos

Suggestions: The photo shows girls in Spain in the traditional dress of their region. Be sure students understand that such clothes are worn only on special occasions. Ask students to give examples of traditional dress in the United States that might be worn for special events (for example, cowboy attire, square dancing outfits, colonial dress, pioneer attire, etc.).

Teacher Technology

TeacherEXPRESS
Plan · Teach · Assess

PLAN
Lesson Planner
Go Online PHSchool.com
For: Teacher Home Page
Web Code: jdk-1001

TEACH
Teaching Resources
Interactive Teacher's Edition
Vocabulary Clip Art

ASSESS
Chapter Quizzes and Tests

PresentationEXPRESS
Dynamic Presentations for Teachers

TEACH
Vocabulary & Grammar Powerpoints
GramActiva Video
Audio & Clip Art Activities
Transparencies and Maps
Activity Answers
Photo Gallery

ASSESS
ExamView
QuickTake Presenter

211

Vocabulario y gramática

 Presentation EXPRESS — VOCABULARY

Core Instruction

 Standards: 1.2, 2.1

Resources: Teacher's Resource Book: Input Script, p. 218, Clip Art, pp. 232–234, Audio Script, p. 219; Voc. and Gram. Transparencies 85–86; TPR Stories Book, pp. 51–63; Audio Program: Tracks 1–2

Focus: Presenting vocabulary about etiquette and holiday celebrations

Suggestions: Present the vocabulary in two groups: manners and celebrations / special events. Use the Input Script from the *Teacher's Resource Book* or the story from the *TPR Stories Book* to present the new words, or use some of these suggestions.

Emphasize that good manners are extremely important in Spanish-speaking cultures, and that they will help students interact with Spanish speakers. With volunteers, act out gestures and customs for greeting and leave-taking. Ask the class to explain the relationships suggested by the exchanges. If possible, show videotapes of greetings with the sound off to the class and verbalize what the actors are doing.

Introduce the three events on p. 213 separately. Be sure students understand that you are telling about things that have already happened. Use gestures, acting, and the transparencies to help you convey meaning.

Note: This vocabulary presentation contains examples of the preterite and the imperfect tenses used in context. Students may begin to observe how the two tenses are used. You may want to refer back to these pages as you present the grammar in this chapter to your students.

Bellringer Review

Have students write one sentence to tell two activities they did at the last party they attended. Share.

Additional Resources

Audio Program: Canciones CD, Disc 22

A primera vista jdd-0497 🔊

Vocabulario y gramática en contexto

Recuerdos del pasado

sonreír

Los buenos modales

66 Mis papás me enseñaron la importancia de los buenos modales. Es importante ser sociable y sonreír cuando **te reúnes*** con las personas.

dar(se) la mano

Cuando **saludas** o **te despides** es **costumbre** siempre dar la mano.

Para saludar a los amigos, puedes decir '¡Hola!,' '¿Qué tal?' o '¿Cómo estás?'.

los mayores

Debes saludar a los mayores con una expresión como 'Buenos días, señora' o '¿Cómo está Ud.?'.

besar(se)

Cuando dos personas se conocen muy bien, generalmente se besan para **saludarse** y despedirse.

Mi papá me dijo que una persona siempre debe saludar a todas las personas en **una reunión** o una fiesta. Cuando sales, debes **despedirte** de cada persona también **99**.

**Reunirse* has an accent on the u in all present-tense forms except *nosotros* and *vosotros*: reúne, reúnes, reúne, ... reúnen.

abrazar(se)

Muchos hombres se abrazan cuando se saludan en la calle o cuando se despiden.

Differentiated Instruction
Solutions for All Learners

Students with Special Needs

Have students work together to come up with a specific physical action or pose that they can associate with the different greetings vocabulary: *saludar, sonreír, darse la mano, besarse, abrazarse.* Have the students take turns saying a word while the rest of the group shows they understand by performing the pose or action.

Multiple Intelligences

Bodily/Kinesthetic: Have students use hand puppets to demonstrate their understanding of greetings and leave-taking. Give them several situations that describe people meeting each other and saying good-bye, and have them act out the exchanges with their puppets.

Cómo celebrábamos los días festivos

66 El 10 de agosto fue el cumpleaños de mi papá. Celebramos con **una fiesta de sorpresa. Cumplió 46 años.** Durante la fiesta, mi abuela habló de cuando él **nació** y ella empezó a **llorar.** Dijo que era **un bebé** grande y guapito. ¡Mi familia y yo le **regalamos** una cámara digital!

Mis abuelos celebraron su **aniversario** el 23 de octubre. **Se casaron** hace 50 años. Todos nuestros **parientes** (mis tíos y primos) y muchos amigos asistieron para **felicitarlos.** Todos cantamos: ¡**Felicidades!** Les regalamos un reloj **antiguo** muy bonito. Durante la fiesta los niños no se pelearon; todos **se llevaban bien** porque era un día muy especial.

los fuegos artificiales

Frecuentemente, durante los veranos, nosotros íbamos a un parque **enorme** donde **hacíamos un picnic.** Mientras los mayores **charlaban,** nosotros jugábamos. Mi tío, que es muy cómico, siempre nos **contaba chistes** y todos **nos reíamos** mucho. Para días muy especiales, como el Día de la Independencia, **había** fuegos artificiales por la noche. Todas las personas **alrededor** del parque se **divertían 99.**

Actividad 1 —  Escuchar — jdd-0497

Los buenos modales

Trabaja con otro(a) estudiante. Van a escuchar ocho frases sobre los buenos modales. Tienen que representar (act out) en pareja cada una de estas acciones.

Más práctica

- Practice Workbook, pp. 82–83: 4B-1, 4B-2
- WAV Wbk.: Writing, p. 84
- Guided Practice: Vocab. Flash Cards, pp. 145–148
- *Real.* para hispanohablantes, p. 152

Go Online
PHSchool.com
For: Vocab. Practice
Web Code: jdd-0411

Actividad 2 —  Escuchar — jdd-0497

Vamos a celebrar

Escribe en una hoja de papel los números del 1 al 8. Vas a escuchar ocho frases. Escribe la letra *a*, *b* o *c* para indicar cuándo ocurrió cada actividad.

a. durante la fiesta de cumpleaños

b. durante la fiesta de aniversario

c. durante la celebración del Día de la Independencia

doscientos trece **213**
Capítulo 4B

Enrich Your Teaching
Resources for All Teachers

Culture Note

A kiss on the cheek is a common form of greeting between women or between men and women in Spanish-speaking countries. This usually involves one kiss on the right side of the person's face.

Teacher-to-Teacher

Write the words *los mayores, el picnic, el bebé, los fuegos artificiales, una fiesta, abrazarse, besarse, darse la mano, saludar, sonreír, charlar,* and *regalar* on index cards. Have a volunteer take a card and draw a picture on the board that conveys the meaning of the word on the card. The first student to identify the word is the next to draw.

Actividad 1 — Standards: 1.2 — Presentation EXPRESS AUDIO

Resources: Teacher's Resource Book: Audio Script, p. 219; Audio Program: Track 3; Answers on Transparencies

Focus: Listening comprehension about behavior and etiquette

Suggestions: Encourage students to clearly show the ages and relationships of the people they are playing through their body language.

Script and Answers:

1. Los jóvenes sonríen a sus amigos. *(teenagers smiling at friends)*
2. Los amigos se abrazan. *(friends hugging each other)*
3. Los bebés lloran mucho. *(babies crying)*
4. Los compañeros se dan la mano. *(acquaintances shaking hands)*
5. Los niños besan a sus padres y a sus abuelos. *(children kissing their parents and grandparents)*
6. La joven se despide de su amigo. *(teenager saying goodbye to a friend)*
7. Cuando escuchan los chistes, todos se ríen. *(everyone laughing at jokes)*
8. Siempre saludamos a los mayores. *(everyone greeting older adults)*

Actividad 2 — Standards: 1.2 — Presentation EXPRESS AUDIO

Resources: Teacher's Resource Book: Audio Script, p. 219; Audio Program: Track 4; Answers on Transparencies

Focus: Listening comprehension of celebration vocabulary

Suggestions: Point out that the sentences students will hear refer specifically to the information on the student text page.

Script and Answers:

1. Siempre veíamos los fuegos artificiales. *(c)*
2. Le regalamos una cámara digital. *(a)*
3. Mi tío contaba chistes y todos nos reíamos. *(c)*
4. Celebramos el día cuando mis abuelos se casaron. *(b)*
5. La celebración fue una sorpresa. *(a)*
6. Hacíamos un picnic en un parque enorme. *(c)*
7. Les regalamos un reloj antiguo. *(b)*
8. Celebramos el día en que mi papá nació. *(a)*

✓ Assessment
- ExamView QuickTake Presenter Quiz on PresEXPRESS

213

Videohistoria
Core Instruction

 Presentation EXPRESS **VOCABULARY**

 Standards: 1.2

Resources: Voc. and Gram. Transparencies 87–88; Audio Program: Track 5

Focus: Presentation of additional vocabulary about celebrations

Suggestions:

Pre-reading: Ask students to think about celebrations they have gone to and what senses were involved in enjoying the celebrations. Ask: *¿Qué ves en una fiesta? ¿Qué comes? ¿Qué cosas oyes* (hear)*?*

Reading: Have students read the story silently, then read it together as a class. Point out the words *txistu* [cheestoo] and *txistorra* [cheestora], and explain that these are words from the Basque language. Pause after the first four panels and ask students questions like those Javier asks Ignacio: *¿Adónde va Ignacio? ¿Cómo es la fiesta de San Pedro? ¿Qué es un* txistu*?* Have students read the final four panels in groups, then ask them: *¿Sabe Ignacio hablar vasco? ¿Qué comía Ignacio? ¿Qué hace la gente después de comer?*

Post-reading: Complete *Actividad* 3 to check comprehension. Have students summarize the *fiesta* activities in pairs. While one student acts out an event or activity, the other must guess what he or she is doing. Activities modeled might include the parade, playing the *tamboril* or *txistu,* eating *txistorra,* and telling jokes.

 Pre-AP* Support

- **Activity:** Have students write a brief paragraph describing a family event or local festival that they typically took part in as a child. Encourage them to highlight sights, sounds, smells, noises, and activities. Ask that each student record his or her paragraph. Select one or two of the most correct/colorful paragraphs to play to the class as a dictation activity on following class days.

- ***Pre-AP* Resource Book:*** Comprehensive guide to Pre-AP* vocabulary skill development, pp. 47–53

Videohistoria jdd-0497

La fiesta de San Pedro

¿Por qué es especial la fiesta de San Pedro?

Estrategia

Using visuals
Ignacio is describing a celebration in the Basque town of Alsasua that he visited as a child. Look at the different visuals in the *Videohistoria.* For each picture, write what you think he might say.

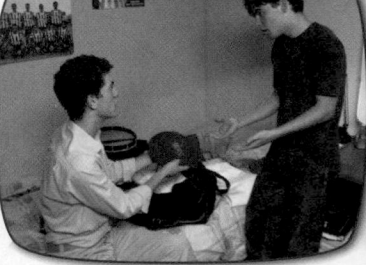

Ignacio   Javier

1 **Javier:** ¿Adónde vas, Ignacio?

Ignacio: A Alsasua para la fiesta de San Pedro. Se celebra el 29 de junio. Es **un día festivo.** De niño iba allí con mi familia todos los veranos.

5 **Ignacio:** Luego íbamos a la iglesia. Recuerdo que a veces hablaban en vasco.

Javier: ¿Sabes hablar vasco?

Ignacio: No, yo no. Mis abuelos lo hablaban.

6 **Ignacio:** Y la comida era fantástica. Comíamos paella y salchichas que se llaman en vasco *txistorra.* ¡Qué ricas!

Javier: ¡Mmm! Ya tengo hambre.

7 **Ignacio:** Después de comer, la gente charlaba, contaba chistes y se reía.

Javier: ¿Y los jóvenes?

Ignacio: Los jóvenes seguían bailando.

Differentiated Instruction
Solutions for All Learners

Multiple Intelligences
Musical: Encourage students to find out more about the *txistu* on the Internet or in the library. Suggest that they look for recordings of traditional *txistu* music online. If there is a flautist or recorder player in the group, ask them to recreate a *txistu* tune.

Students with Learning Difficulties
To help students interpret visual clues in the *Videohistoria,* draw their attention to the panels that contain smaller insets. Explain that these insets usually signal a memory or dream. Have students find words within the dialogue that reveal what the insets visualize in each case.

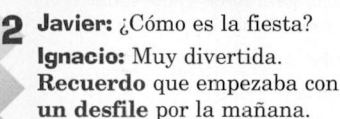

2 Javier: ¿Cómo es la fiesta?
Ignacio: Muy divertida. **Recuerdo** que empezaba con **un desfile** por la mañana.

3 Ignacio: Había bailes día y noche. Los músicos tocaban instrumentos antiguos como el *txistu* y el tamboril.[1]
Javier: ¿El *txistu*? ¿Qué es eso?

[1]El *txistu* es el instrumento característico de la música vasca. Es una flauta de madera y metal. Se usa en procesiones, serenatas y danzas. El tamboril es un tambor pequeño.

4 Ignacio: Éste es un *txistu*. Es una palabra vasca.
Javier: ¿Sabes tocarlo?
Ignacio: Sí, un poco. Mi abuelo me enseñó hace años. ¡Ay!

8 Javier: Aquí estoy. Son las siete.
Ignacio: En Alsasua tenemos que comprarte una boina[2].
Javier: Tienes razón.
Ignacio: Bueno. Vamos a la estación.

[2]beret

Actividad 3 Leer/Escribir

¿Comprendiste?

1. ¿Por qué conocía Ignacio este día festivo?
2. ¿Cómo empezaba el día?
3. ¿Qué tipo de instrumentos tocaban los músicos?
4. ¿Adónde iba Ignacio después del desfile?
5. ¿Qué otros idiomas *(languages)* hablan en Alsasua?
6. ¿Qué es la *txistorra*?
7. ¿Qué hacía la gente después de comer?
8. Según las fotos, ¿cómo se viste Ignacio para ir a la celebración?
9. ¿Qué le falta a Javier?

Más práctica

- Practice Workbook, pp. 84–85: 4B-3, 4B-4
- WAV Wbk.: Video, pp. 78–80
- Guided Practice: Vocab. Check, pp. 149–152
- *Real.* para hispanohablantes, p. 153

Go Online
PHSchool.com
For: Vocab. Practice
Web Code: jdd-0412

doscientos quince **215**
Capítulo 4B

Core Instruction

Standards: 1.2

Resources: Teacher's Resource Book: Video Script, p. 222; Video Program: Cap. 4B; Video Program Teacher's Guide: Cap. 4B

Focus: Comprehension of contextualized vocabulary

Suggestions:

Pre-viewing: Have students list the five senses. Referring to them as they watch the video will help them remember what takes place during the festival.

Viewing: Show the entire video once, then show it again, pausing while students discuss what Ignacio heard, tasted, saw, touched, or smelled.

Post-viewing: Complete the Video Activities in the *Writing, Audio & Video Workbook.*

Actividad 3 *Standards:* 1.2

Presentation EXPRESS
ANSWERS

Resources: Answers on Transparencies

Focus: Verifying comprehension of the *Videohistoria*

Suggestions: Use the transparencies to review the *Videohistoria.*

Answers:

1. De niño, Ignacio iba con su familia a celebrarlo todos los veranos.
2. Empezaba con un desfile.
3. Tocaban el *txistu* y el tamboril.
4. Iba a la iglesia.
5. Hablan vasco.
6. *La txistorra* es una salchicha vasca.
7. Charlaba, contaba chistes y se reía.
8. Lleva un traje del País Vasco.
9. Le falta una boina roja.

Additional Resources

- WAV Wbk.: Audio Act. 5, p. 81
- Teacher's Resource Book: Audio Script, p. 220
- Audio Program: Track 7

 Assessment

- ExamView QuickTake Presenter Quiz on PresEXPRESS
- Prueba 4B-1: Vocab. Recognition, pp. 111–112

Culture Note
Alsasua is in Spain's Navarra province. It is west of Pamplona and borders the País Vasco. Alsasua holds several annual celebrations, including the traditional *Fiesta de San Pedro* in June. In February a Carnival-inspired festival takes place, with a parade, costumes, and a dance, held in the center of town.

Culture Note
Explain that many regions and towns in the Spanish-speaking world hold annual celebrations that may date back hundreds of years. Some of these are unique to particular towns. Many are religious holidays that celebrate the feast days of Roman Catholic saints.

Standards: 1.2, 1.3

Resources: Answers on Transparencies

Focus: Understanding vocabulary about celebrations

Suggestions: After completing the *Actividad,* have students explain their choices. Accept different answers if they can explain their logic.

Answers:
1. recuerdo
2. hacemos un picnic
3. nací
4. los mayores
5. sonríen

Sentences will vary.

  Standards: 1.2

Resources: Teacher's Resource Book: Audio Script, p. 220; Audio Program:Track 6; Answers on Transparencies

Focus: Writing dictation sentences about a wedding and evaluating the manners described

Suggestions: Have students prepare their paper with room for six separate sentences. Review with the class their ideas of what constitutes good and bad manners.

🔊 Script and Answers:
1. Saluda y sonríe a las otras personas. *(buenos modales)*
2. Se ríe del vestido de la madre del novio. *(malos modales)*
3. Se lleva mal con los parientes de los novios. *(malos modales)*
4. Felicita y abraza a los novios. *(buenos modales)*
5. Les regala unos vasos bonitos a los novios. *(buenos modales)*
6. Cuenta chistes sobre la madre de la novia. *(malos modales)*

 Standards: 1.2, 2.1, 2.2

■◆■◆■◆■◆■◆■◆■◆■

Suggestions: Have students look at a map of Spain as you point out the regions. Explain that many of these regions were once independent kingdoms. Have students name regions in the U.S. before they answer the question.

Answers will vary.

Manos a la obra
Vocabulario y gramática en uso

Objectives
- **Communicate about social gatherings involving friends and relatives**
- **Describe situations in the past**
- **Talk about how people interact**
- **Describe holiday celebrations**

 **4** Leer/Escribir

El intruso

Identifica en cada grupo de palabras "el intruso", es decir, la palabra que no va con las otras tres. Luego escribe una frase completa con la forma apropiada del intruso.

Modelo

fiesta de sorpresa   regalo   cumplo años   me despido

Cuando me despido de mis padres, generalmente los abrazo.

1. saludo   recuerdo   le doy la mano   abrazo
2. contamos chistes   nos divertimos   hacemos un picnic   nos reímos
3. desfile   nací   día festivo   fuegos artificiales
4. los mayores   felicitan   se casan   ¡Felicidades!
5. se llevan mal   se pelean   lloran   sonríen

 **5** jdd-0498 🔊 Escuchar/Escribir

Escucha y escribe

Escucha las descripciones de diferentes personas que están presentes en la boda. Escribe las frases. Después indica si las personas tienen buenos o malos modales. *(Nota:* A las personas que acaban de casarse también se les llama "los novios").

Nota

In the present tense, these verbs have stem changes:

recordar, contar *(o → ue)*

divertirse *(e → ie)*

despedirse, reírse, sonreír *(e → i)*

In addition, *reírse* and *sonreír* have accent marks on the *i* in all present-tense forms.

 Fondo cultural

Euskadi Las diferentes regiones de España tienen su propia identidad, su comida, sus costumbres y a veces su idioma *(language)*. En el País Vasco, situado en el norte de España, se habla euskera (vasco, en español), un idioma que no tiene ninguna relación con el español. En euskera, el nombre de esta región es Euskadi. Una tradición de San Sebastián (o Donostia), una de las ciudades más grandes de Euskadi, es la Tamborrada, que se celebra el 20 de enero. Ese día, hombres tocan el tambor mientras caminan por las calles de la ciudad.

• ¿Qué diferencias de identidad hay entre las regiones de los Estados Unidos?

La Tamborrada de San Sebastián

Differentiated Instruction
Solutions for All Learners

Students with Learning Difficulties
Some students will have particular difficulty identifying which words do not belong in *Actividad* 4. For each item, ask students to name the characteristics of the words and then help them decide which things are common characteristics and which are not.

Heritage Language Learners
Have students write a list of rules for polite behavior. If there are particular customs from their heritage culture, they should make an effort to include these. They might organize the behaviors by those that should be done and those that should not be.

Actividad 6 — Leer/Escribir

Una costumbre de mi familia

Lee la historia de lo que hacía la familia de Alejandra cuando ella era niña. Completa la historia con las palabras apropiadas.

| antigua costumbre enorme reunirse |

alrededor de	había
contaban chistes	mientras
frecuentemente	nos divertíamos

Recuerdo muy bien los días festivos que celebrábamos cuando era niña. Era nuestra **1.** ir a la casa de nuestros abuelos en el campo. Ellos no vivían en una casa moderna como las casas en la ciudad. Su casa era **2.** pero también **3.** . ¡Todos mis parientes podían **4.** allí al mismo tiempo!

5. que los adultos charlaban o **6.** , nosotros jugábamos en el jardín que estaba **7.** la casa. **8.** muchos árboles en el jardín y **9.** hacíamos un picnic debajo de ellos. Siempre **10.** mucho en los días festivos en la casa de nuestros abuelos.

Actividad 7 — Hablar/Escribir

Costumbres sociales

1 ¿Cómo saludas y te despides de las personas? Habla con otro(a) estudiante y escriban sus respuestas.

| Modelo |

saludar a tus primos
A —*Generalmente, ¿cómo saludas a tus primos?*
B —*Por lo general los abrazo. ¿Y tú?*
A —*No tengo primos.*

Estudiante A

1. saludar a tus profesores
2. despedirse de tus abuelos (o tíos)
3. despedirse de los padres de tus amigos
4. saludar a tu papá (o mamá)
5. despedirse de tu mejor amigo(a)
6. saludar a un(a) amigo(a) que no has visto *(haven't seen)* recientemente

Estudiante B

hasta luego

Hola ¿Cómo estás?

2 Escribe cinco frases para decir si lo que Uds. hacen es similar o es diferente.

| Modelo |

Por lo general yo abrazo a mis primos cuando los saludo. Enrique no tiene primos, pero siempre abraza a sus abuelos cuando los saluda.

doscientos diecisiete **217**
Capítulo 4B

Enrich Your Teaching
Resources for All Teachers

Culture Note

Spain has 17 regions, 15 on the mainland and two groups of islands: the Balearic Islands and the Canary Islands. Among the better-known regions are the Basque Country in the north, Catalonia in the northeast, Galicia in the northwest, Madrid and Castile in the center, and Andalusia in the south.

Internet Search

Keyword: España + regiones

Practice and Communicate

 4B

 Standards: 1.2

Actividad 6

Resources: Answers on Transparencies

Focus: Completing a paragraph with new vocabulary

Recycle: Imperfect tense

Suggestions: Point out that there is a separate word bank for each section of the story. Remind students that knowing the part of speech required will help them fill in the blanks. If students have trouble with any words, reinforce their meanings by using them in additional sentences.

Answers:

1. costumbre
2. antigua
3. enorme
4. reunirse
5. Mientras
6. contaban chistes
7. alrededor de
8. Había
9. frecuentemente
10. nos divertíamos

 Bellringer Review

Review family vocabulary by presenting these true/false statements to the class:

1. *El hijo de mi tío es mi primo.*
2. *La madre de mi madre es mi hermana.*
3. *Mi abuelo es el padre de mi madre.*
4. *La hija de mi abuela es mi madre.*

(**Answers:** c, f, c, c)

 Standards: 1.1, 1.3

Actividad 7

Resources: Answers on Transparencies

Focus: Speaking and writing about social customs

Suggestions: Tell students that their answers for Step 1 should be based on the etiquette common to the Spanish-speaking community.

Answers:

Step 1: Student A answers will vary but will include ¿... *saludas* ...? or ¿... *te despides* ...?

Student B answers will vary but may include:

1. Les doy la mano y digo, "Buenos días. ¿Cómo están Uds.?"
2. Les beso y digo, "Nos vemos, abuelos" o "Que les vaya bien."
3. Les doy la mano y digo, "Adiós."
4. Les doy a mi mamá y a mi papá un abrazo y un beso.
5. Lo (La) abrazo y digo, "Hasta la vista, amigo(a)."
6. Lo (La) abrazo y le digo, "Hola. ¿Qué tal?"

Step 2: Answers will vary.

217

Actividad 8 **Standards:** 1.1

Resources: Answers on Transparencies

Focus: Speaking about social occasions

Recycle: Imperfect tense

Suggestions: List on the board the verbs students will need to use and have them quickly go over the imperfect forms. Pay close attention to their understanding of the reflexive verbs.

Answers:

Student A:

1. ¿Qué hacía tu familia cuando alguien cumplía años?
2. ¿... hacía un largo viaje?
3. ¿... compraba un coche nuevo?
4. ¿... celebraba un día festivo?

Student B: Answers will vary.

Actividad 9 **Standards:** 1.1, 1.3

Focus: Writing and speaking about celebrations

Suggestions: Go through the items with students before they begin and brainstorm possible answers or phrases they might include in their answers.

Answers will vary.

Fondo cultural **Standards:** 1.2, 2.1, 2.2

Suggestions: Before reading, discuss Columbus Day and what it commemorates. Ask students to consider why many people prefer celebrating it as Columbus Day, and why others prefer a different emphasis.

Answers will vary.

Additional Resources

- WAV Wbk.: Audio Act. 6, p. 81
- Teacher's Resource Book: Audio Script, p. 220, Communicative Activity BLM, pp. 226–227
- Audio Program: Track 8

 Assessment

- Prueba 4B-2: Vocab. Production, pp. 113–114

Actividad 8  **Hablar**

¿Qué hacían Uds.?

Habla con otro(a) estudiante sobre cómo celebraban diferentes ocasiones sociales cuando eran pequeños(as). Digan dos costumbres que tenían Uds. en cada ocasión.

Modelo

celebrar un aniversario

A —¿Qué hacía tu familia cuando alguien celebraba un aniversario?

B —Hacíamos una fiesta y les regalábamos cosas muy bonitas.

o: —No recuerdo lo que hacíamos.

Estudiante A

1. cumplir años
2. hacer un largo viaje
3. comprar un coche nuevo
4. celebrar un día festivo

Estudiante B

felicitar a . . .
reunirse en . . .
hacer una fiesta (de sorpresa)
hacer un picnic
comprar . . .

regalarle(s) . . .
invitar a . . .
no hacer nada
hacer una reunión de familia
despedirse

Actividad 9 **Escribir/Hablar**

Y tú, ¿qué dices?

1. Por lo general, ¿qué les dices a los padres de un bebé que nació recientemente? ¿Qué les regalas?
2. En tu comunidad, ¿en qué días festivos hay fuegos artificiales? ¿En qué días hay desfiles?
3. ¿Cuándo te reúnes con tus parientes? ¿Dónde se reúnen Uds. generalmente? ¿Con quién charlas? ¿Se llevan todos bien o a veces se llevan mal?

Fondo cultural ◆◼◆◢◆◼◆◼◆◼◆

El Día de la Raza Muchos jóvenes participan en el desfile del Día de la Raza en Costa Rica. Este día festivo conmemora la llegada de Cristóbal Colón a las Américas. Algunas personas prefieren el nombre "el Día de las Culturas" para celebrar también las contribuciones culturales de los pueblos indígenas, asiáticos y africanos del país.

- ¿Cuál de estos dos nombres prefieres tú? ¿Por qué?

Jóvenes participando en la celebración del Día de la Raza, en Costa Rica

---

Differentiated Instruction
Solutions for All Learners

Multiple Intelligences

Visual/Spatial: Encourage students to bring family photos or pictures from magazines that show people performing actions. Have them use the imperfect to describe the situations. If multiple actions are shown, they can use the preterite as well.

Students with Learning Difficulties

Before assigning *Actividad 10*, review the use of the preterite versus the imperfect. Remind students to determine tense by examining the context of each verb to be conjugated: If the action or situation happened once, or at a given moment, the preterite should be used.

Gramática

Preterite and imperfect: describing a situation

In addition to saying what someone used to do, the imperfect tense is used:

- to describe people, places, and situations in the past

  La casa de mis abuelos **era** enorme. **Tenía** cinco dormitorios.

- to talk about a past action or situation when no beginning or end is specified

  Había mucha gente en la casa para el aniversario.

- to describe the situation or background information when something else happened or interrupted the ongoing action.

  Todos mis parientes **bailaban** cuando llegamos.
  *All my relatives **were dancing** when we arrived.*

Note that the imperfect tense is used to tell what someone **was doing** when something **happened** (preterite).

> **¿Recuerdas?**
>
> Use the preterite tense to describe completed actions or events.
>
> - Mis abuelos **se casaron** hace 50 años.
> - **Celebramos** su aniversario el mes pasado.

GramActiva VIDEO

Want more help with the imperfect? Watch the **GramActiva** video.

cantaba

Actividad 10 — Leer/Escribir

La Semana Santa

Patricia, una estudiante norteamericana que está pasando un año en España, les escribe a sus padres sobre una experiencia fantástica que tuvo. Completa su descripción con las formas apropiadas del pretérito o del imperfecto.

el 30 de abril
Sevilla, España

Queridos padres:

Acabo de pasar unos días increíbles. Mi familia española __1.__ (decidir) ir a Sevilla para celebrar la Semana Santa. Nosotros __2.__ (llegar) el martes por la noche y las calles ya __3.__ (estar) llenas de personas. Había un desfile que en la Semana Santa se llama procesión. En la procesión, __4.__ (ver) pasos[1] muy grandes con flores y estatuas enormes (que se llaman imágenes) de las iglesias. Las imágenes __5.__ (ser) antiguas y muy impresionantes. Había bandas y otras personas que tocaban música durante las procesiones. Y luego ocurrió algo fantástico. Una mujer __6.__ (salir) a un balcón y __7.__ (empezar) a cantar una saeta. Una saeta es una canción del estilo flamenco que cantan aquí en Sevilla. Todas las personas en la calle escucharon con atención mientras ella cantaba. Por fin,[2] el paso __8.__ (llegar) a la entrada de la catedral y entró, como es la costumbre durante la Semana Santa. ¡Qué experiencia maravillosa!

Besos y abrazos,
Patricia

[1]floats (during Holy Week)   [2]At last

doscientos diecinueve **219**
Capítulo 4B

Enrich Your Teaching
Resources for All Teachers

Culture Note

Between Palm Sunday and Easter, many Spanish-speaking people observe *la Semana Santa* (Holy Week). Some people celebrate with parades, dances, or with *cascarones*—hollow eggs filled with confetti that are broken on someone's head as a humorous surprise. Overall, however, it is a time for religious observance and reflection.

Internet Search

Have students research the events and traditions of *la Semana Santa* in Seville.

Keywords: Sevilla + Semana Santa

Practice and Communicate

 4B

Gramática

Presentation EXPRESS
GRAMMAR

Core Instruction

 Standards: 4.1

Resources: Teacher's Resource Book: Video Script, p. 223; Video Program: Cap. 4B

Suggestions: To illustrate the third grammar point, use a timeline with a dramatic event that stops the action:

Marta se cayó

Los amigos hablaban …

Los amigos **hablaban** cuando Marta **se cayó** en la piscina.

Direct students' attention back to the vocabulary presentation on p. 213 and have them reread the three paragraphs. Ask them to describe the different ways in which the preterite and imperfect tenses are used. Ask: Where is the preterite used to describe completed actions or events?

 Bellringer Review

Write the infinitives *hablar, comer,* and *vivir* on the board, as well as the imperfect endings for *-ar* and *-er / -ir* verbs. Ask students to create silly sentences using imperfect forms of the verbs. Have them take turns sharing their sentences.

Actividad 10 — *Standards:* 1.2

Presentation EXPRESS
ANSWERS

Resources: Answers on Transparencies

Focus: Choosing preterite or imperfect tense and writing the forms

Recycle: Preterite and imperfect verb forms

Suggestions: Have students read through the letter once to get an understanding of the event. Help them with any vocabulary. Point out that *la Semana Santa* is the week before Easter, and that the celebration in Sevilla is extremely well known.

Answers:

1. decidió
2. llegamos
3. estaban
4. vimos
5. eran
6. salió
7. empezó
8. llegó

219

Actividad 11

Standards: 1.1

Presentation EXPRESS ANSWERS

Resources: Answers on Transparencies

Focus: Describing relatives using the imperfect

Recycle: Family vocabulary, personal descriptions, leisure activities

Suggestions: Brainstorm activities people do and adjectives that can describe people. Model a full interchange if necessary.

Answers will vary but will include:

1. ... era ...
2. ... se llamaba ...
3. ... era ...
4. ... vivía ...
5. ... le gustaba ...
6. ... hacía ...

Extension: For homework, have students write a paragraph with the same information they gave about a favorite relative in *Actividad* 11. Have them bring in a photograph or draw a picture of the relative to accompany the assignment.

Fondo cultural

Standards: 1.2, 2.1, 2.2

Suggestions: People in the United States often are not used to talking about death and dead family members, so the information given here may make some students uncomfortable. Be sensitive to any loss students may have experienced and to religious sensibilities in your community, presenting the information in a factual manner for cultural insight. Emphasize that this holiday provides those who observe it with an opportunity to remember and show great respect for family members.

Have students discuss why they think the bread in the photograph is in the shape of skeletons, and tell them that a variety of comical skeleton artwork is often an important part of *el Día de los Muertos* celebrations.

Answers will vary.

Block Schedule

Ask volunteers to present their *pariente favorito* to the class. This could be done immediately after the class has completed *Actividad* 11, or could be given as an overnight task for students to prepare their speech and to bring in accompanying photos.

Actividad 11  **Hablar**

Un pariente favorito

Trabaja con otro(a) estudiante para describir a un pariente favorito que recuerdas de tu niñez. Usen el imperfecto en sus preguntas y respuestas.

Modelo
¿Quién (ser) tu pariente favorito?
A —¿Quién era tu pariente favorito?
B —Mi pariente favorito era mi abuelo.

Estudiante A

1. ¿Quién (ser) tu pariente favorito?
2. ¿Cómo (llamarse)?
3. ¿Cómo (ser)?
4. ¿Dónde (vivir)?
5. ¿Qué le (gustar) hacer?
6. ¿Qué (hacer) tu pariente contigo?

Estudiante B

Mi pariente favorito era . . .
Se llamaba . . .
Era . . .
Vivía en . . .

Fondo cultural

El Día de los Muertos En México y en otros países hispanohablantes celebran el Día de los Muertos *(Day of the Dead)* el 2 de noviembre. Preparan el "pan de muertos", un pan en forma de muñecos, y dulces en forma de esqueletos y calaveras *(skulls)*. La gente hace altares en sus casas en honor a los parientes muertos. Los altares tienen fotos de los parientes muertos, flores, frutas, pan y la comida favorita del muerto. Algunas familias hacen un picnic en el cementerio donde están sus parientes muertos. Estas costumbres les permiten a las familias recordar a los parientes que ya no viven.

• Compara lo que hacen en México para recordar a los muertos con lo que hace tu familia.

El pan de muertos

Celebración del Día de los Muertos, en México

Differentiated Instruction
Solutions for All Learners

Advanced Learners

Tell students that different towns in Mexico have unique traditions that go along with *el Día de los Muertos*. In one village, families work together building kites to take to the cemetery to fly. Ask students to explore the Internet and their local library to find out more about this day. Have them bring in books and photographs to share.

Heritage Language Learners

Have students make a list of Spanish words that have the prefixes **des-, im-, in-,** and **ir-**. Have them compose five additional sentences that illustrate the prefixed words. They should carefully check their work for accents and spelling.

Actividad 12

Hablar _____

¿Cuántos años tenías?

Pregunta a otro(a) estudiante cuántos años tenía cuando hizo estas actividades por primera vez.

Modelo

recibir tu propia bicicleta

A —¿Cuántos años tenías cuando recibiste tu propia bicicleta?

B —Yo tenía seis años cuando recibí mi propia bicicleta.

Estudiante A

1. aprender a caminar
2. asistir a la escuela por primera vez
3. ir a tu primer baile
4. leer tu primer libro
5. ir al cine sin tus padres
6. ver un desfile por primera vez

Estudiante B

Yo tenía . . .

Exploración del lenguaje

Prefixes

Think about the meaning of the following Spanish words. What pattern do you notice?

obediente → desobediente
posible → imposible
formal → informal
regular → irregular

Like English, Spanish uses prefixes to extend and change the meanings of words—in this case to create a word with the opposite meaning.

¡Compruébalo! Copy the following words on a sheet of paper. Underline the prefix in each word. Then determine which word (with or without the prefix) is needed to complete the sentences about Mariana and Julieta.

desordenado   impaciente   irresponsable
injusto   impráctico

Mariana   **Julieta**

1. A Mariana no le gusta esperar a los demás. Es muy ____.

2. A Julieta le gusta tener su cuarto limpio y ____.

3. Mariana grita mucho. Es ____ llevarla al cine.

4. Julieta cree que es importante conservar agua. Cree que es ____ no hacerlo.

5. Julieta y Mariana piensan que es ____ tener que dormirse temprano.

doscientos veintiuno **221**
Capítulo 4B

Enrich Your Teaching
Resources for All Teachers

Culture Note

In Guatemala *el Día de los Muertos* often involves flying kites. The citizens of Santiago Sacatepequez gather in the cemetery to send good wishes to their ancestors via the kites. The people design kites that are vividly colored and enormous, some over 20 feet wide.

Teacher-to-Teacher

Have students play Charades. Give each group a strip of paper naming a social situation. For example: *Durante el picnic, los bebés estaban muy impacientes.* Students will play people showing impatience, irresponsibility, and disorder or the opposite. The others must guess the occasion and possible sentence.

Practice and Communicate

4B

Actividad 12 Standards: 1.2

Presentation EXPRESS
ANSWERS

Resources: Answers on Transparencies

Focus: Asking and answering questions about activities in the past

Recycle: Preterite

Suggestions: Review Student A's phrases before students begin. If some of the phrases don't apply to students, have them respond as if they were someone else.

Answers:

Student A:

1. ¿Cuántos años tenías cuando aprendiste a caminar?
2. ¿... asististe ...?
3. ¿... fuiste ...?
4. ¿ ... leíste ...?
5. ¿... fuiste ...?
6. ¿... viste ...?

Student B: Answers will vary but will include:

1. Yo tenía … años / meses cuando aprendí a caminar.
2. ... asistí ...
3. ... fui ...
4. ... leí ...
5. ... fui ...
6. ... vi ...

Extension: Have students ask the same questions of older family members and record their responses.

Exploración del lenguaje

Presentation EXPRESS
ANSWERS

Core Instruction

Standards: 4.1

Resources: Answers on Transparencies

Suggestions: Be sure students understand the meanings of the root words in the *¡Compruébalo!* They should use only the five words in the list (or a form of the word or root).

Answers:

1. impaciente   4. irresponsable
2. ordenado   5. injusto
3. impráctico

Pre-AP* Support

- **Activity:** Before students read this *Fondo cultural*, read the selection aloud to the class. Ask that they listen and concentrate on trying to remember the essential points. Read the passage aloud to students a second time and ask them to jot down, in Spanish, the main ideas and important details of the reading. Then, ask students to combine their efforts with a partner and write a brief summary of what they heard.

- *Pre-AP* Resource Book:* Comprehensive guide to Pre-AP* communication skill development, pp. 9–17, 36–46

221

Actividad 13 Standards: 1.2 | Presentation EXPRESS AUDIO

Resources: Teacher's Resource Book: Audio Script, p. 220; Audio Program: Track 9; Fine Art Transparencies with Teacher's Guide, p. 36; Answers on Transparencies

Focus: Listening to and writing about a family occasion

Recycle: Imperfect and preterite

Suggestions: Have students study the picture before they listen.

Script and Answers:
1. Entré en la cocina con mi papá.
2. Había tres personas alrededor de la mesa. (Había ocho personas ...)
3. Todos ayudaban a hacer galletas. (... a hacer tamales.)
4. Todos mis parientes tenían el pelo negro.
5. Las personas tenían diferentes trabajos.
6. Las paredes de la cocina eran amarillas (...eran azules).

Actividad 14 Standards: 1.1, 1.3

Resources: Fine Art Transparencies with Teacher's Guide, p. 36

Focus: Writing and speaking about art

Recycle: Questions; imperfect

Suggestions: Suggestions: Have students brainstorm words that are used to ask questions. Do not allow students to look at the painting as they answer. Have them check their answers against the painting once everyone has finished.

Answers will vary.

Actividad 15 Standards: 1.1, 1.3

Focus: Speaking and writing about childhood

Suggestions: Have students work in pairs to ask and answer the questions orally. Tell students that they may answer any personal questions with made-up information if they prefer.

Answers will vary.

   jdd-0498 🔊 **Escuchar/Escribir**

Actividad 13

Escucha y escribe

En el cuadro "Tamalada", la niña que está en la puerta recuerda el día, hace muchos años, cuando entró en la cocina con su padre y vio esta escena. ¿Recuerda ella la escena correctamente? Escucha las seis descripciones y escríbelas. Después, si la información es falsa, escribe la información correcta.

"Tamalada / Making tamales" (1988), Carmen Lomas Garza
Oil on linen mounted on wood, 24" x 32". © 1988 Carmen Lomas Garza. Photo credit: M. Lee Featherree. Collection of Paula Macie-Benecke and Norbert Benecke, Aptos, CA.

  **Escribir/Hablar**

Actividad 14

¿Qué había en la pared?

Usa el imperfecto y escribe tres preguntas sobre la escena que recuerda la niña del cuadro "Tamalada". Después haz tus preguntas a otro(a) estudiante y contesta las preguntas de él (ella).

Para decir más . . .

la estufa	stove
el horno	oven
las ollas	pans
el suelo	floor

Modelo
A —¿Qué había en la pared?
B —Había un cuadro de una pareja bailando flamenco en la pared.

Nota
You know that *hay* means "there is, there are." In the imperfect tense, *había* means "there was, there were." *Hay* and *había* are forms of *haber*.

 **Escribir/Hablar**

Actividad 15

Y tú, ¿qué dices?

1. ¿Siempre has vivido *(have you lived)* en la misma casa? Si no, ¿dónde vivías antes? ¿Era una casa antigua?
2. Cuando tú eras niño(a), ¿te divertías con tus amigos? ¿Charlaban? ¿Hacían picnics? ¿Contaban chistes?
3. ¿Cuántos años tenías cuando aprendiste a caminar?
4. ¿Qué te regalaban tus abuelos o tus tíos cuando eras niño(a)?

Más práctica

- Practice Workbook, p. 86: 4B-5
- WAV Wbk.: Writing, p. 85
- Guided Practice: Grammar Acts., pp. 153–157
- *Real.* para hispanohablantes, pp. 154-157

Go Online PHSchool.com
For: Imperfect Tense
Web Code: jdd-0413

Differentiated Instruction
Solutions for All Learners

Students with Learning Difficulties
Give students with spatial organization difficulties a photocopy of the *Conexiones* text. Instruct them to underline the name and date of independence for each country in a different color. Next have them number the dates chronologically and then write the events in sequence on a time line.

Heritage Language Learners
Point out that in standard Spanish the singular conjugated form of *haber* is used for both singular and plural subjects: *Hay un tamal; Había dos tamales.* In many parts of Latin America and in Catalonia, Spain, however, plural forms of *haber* are often heard and are sometimes considered a regional variant.

222

Actividad 16

El Día de la Independencia

En muchos países del mundo, la gente celebra un día para conmemorar la independencia de su país con desfiles, fuegos artificiales y bailes. Lee esta información sobre los días de la independencia en diferentes países. Luego haz una línea cronológica con las fechas de la independencia de los países mencionados abajo.

Conexiones | **La historia**

Fechas importantes

Los Estados Unidos

El 4 de julio es el Día de la Independencia en los Estados Unidos. Es el aniversario de la Declaración de la Independencia, que firmó[1] el Segundo Congreso Continental en 1776, cuando los Estados Unidos obtuvieron[2] su independencia de Gran Bretaña.

Firmando la Declaración de la Independencia

The Declaration of Independence, 4 July 1776, John Trumbull (American, 1756-1843) 1786-1820. Oil on canvas, 53 x 78.7 cm (20-7/8 x 31 in). © Corbis Bettmann.

La Revolución Francesa

Los franceses obtuvieron su independencia de la monarquía el 14 de julio de 1789. Pelearon bajo el lema[3] "Libertad, igualdad y fraternidad".

España

Los franceses invadieron España en el año 1808 y los españoles pelearon contra ellos durante la Guerra[4] de la Independencia. En 1814, los españoles obtuvieron su independencia de los franceses.

Oil on canvas, 8'6" x 11'4". © Museo Nacional del Prado, Madrid.

"Los fusilamientos del 3 de mayo, 1808 (1814)", Francisco de Goya y Lucientes

México

La independencia de los Estados Unidos y la de Francia fueron grandes ejemplos para los países de América Latina. Unos años después, el 16 de septiembre de 1810, Miguel Hidalgo comenzó la guerra de la independencia contra los españoles, que ocupaban México.

Colombia, Venezuela, Perú, Ecuador y Bolivia

Simón Bolívar comenzó el movimiento de independencia de España en muchos países hispanoamericanos. Ayudó a establecer la independencia de cinco países: Colombia (el 20 de julio de 1810), Venezuela (el 5 de julio de 1811), Perú (el 28 de julio de 1821), Ecuador (el 10 de agosto de 1809 y el 13 de mayo de 1830) y Bolivia (el 6 de agosto de 1825).

José Gil de Castro. Courtesy of Corbis Bettmann.

Simón Bolívar, El Libertador

[1]signed [2]gained [3]motto [4]War

doscientos veintitrés 223
Capítulo 4B

Enrich Your Teaching
Resources for All Teachers

Culture Note

Although preparation varies from place to place, **tamales** are usually layered. In the center is a filling (often meat or chicken) rolled in special dough (usually moist cornmeal), which is then wrapped in a corn husk. Finally, it is steamed. **Tamales** may be either salty or sweet.

Teacher-to-Teacher

Show the transparency of *Tamalada,* and have students imagine they are another person in the painting. Ask them to write about this event from that person's perspective. Display the artwork and the paragraphs for the rest of the class to see.

Actividad 16 *Standards:* 1.2, 3.1   Presentation EXPRESS ANSWERS

Resources: Fine Art Transparencies with Teacher's Guide, pp. 23, 28, 69; Answers on Transparencies

Focus: Reading and writing about Independence Day in various countries; cross-curricular connection to history

Suggestions: Have students set up their timeline before they start reading so that they can fill in information as they go along. Provide an example on the board. Encourage students to jot down notes to help discuss the reading. It might be useful to have students first complete the reading on their own and then work with another student to create a timeline.

Answers:

Línea cronológica
1776—Estados Unidos
1789—Francia
1810—Colombia
1810—México (comenzó la guerra contra los españoles)
1811—Venezuela
1814—España
1821—Perú
1809-1830—Ecuador
1825—Bolivia

Extension: Prepare and distribute the timeline with other facts from the reading placed in boxes on the same page. Have students work in groups to draw lines from the facts to the country or countries on the timeline. Examples include: *Pelearon contra los franceses* (line to *España*); *libertad, igualdad, fraternidad* (line to *Francia*); *Miguel Hidalgo* (line to *México*).

Bellringer Review

Show Fine Art Transparency 34 for thirty seconds. Cover and ask students to write one sentence using the imperfect to reflect something that was going on at the celebration. Share.

Theme Project

Students can perform Step 4 at this point. Be sure they understand your corrections and suggestions. (For more information, see p. 182-a.)

Additional Resources

• WAV Wbk.: Audio Act. 7, p. 82
• Teacher's Resource Book: Audio Script, pp. 220–221
• Audio Program: Track 10

 Assessment

• ExamView QuickTake Presenter Quiz on PresEXPRESS
• Prueba 4B-3: The imperfect tense: Describing a situation, p. 115

Gramática

Presentation EXPRESS
GRAMMAR

Core Instruction

 Standards: 4.1

Resources: Teacher's Resource Book: Video Script, p. 222; Video Program: Cap. 4B

Suggestions: Have students brainstorm a list of reflexive verbs before going over the *Gramática* and *GramActiva* Video. Remind students of the sentence patterns for reflexive verbs.

Actividad 17 *Standards:* 1.1

Presentation EXPRESS
ANSWERS

Resources: Answers on Transparencies

Focus: Asking and answering about reciprocal actions

Recycle: Leisure activities

Suggestions: Remind students that *se* is used for both third person singular and plural forms, so verb endings are very important in conveying meaning and identifying the subject of the sentence. An additional way to clarify is to use the subject pronoun. In the questions students will form, **Uds.** is the subject.

Answers:

Student A:

1. ¿Uds. se llevan bien ...?
2. ¿Uds. se ayudan con la tarea ...?
3. ¿Uds. se escriben por correo electrónico ...?
4. ¿Uds. se hablan por teléfono ...?
4. ¿Uds. se respetan ...?
6. ¿Uds. se comprenden ...?

Student B: Answers will vary but will include:

1. Sí, (No, no) nos llevamos bien....
2. Sí, (No, no) nos ayudamos....
3. Sí, (No, no) nos escribimos....
4. Sí, (No, no) nos hablamos....
5. Sí, (No, no) nos respetamos....
6. Sí, (No, no) nos comprendemos....

Extension: Have students change the questions and answers so they refer to two other people who are across the room. For example: *¿Marta y Julia se ven frecuentemente? Sí, ellas se ven todos los días.*

Gramática

Reciprocal actions

Sometimes the reflexive pronouns *se* and *nos* are used to express the idea "(to) each other." These are called reciprocal actions.

Los novios **se abrazaban** y **se besaban.**
*The bride and groom **were hugging each other** and **kissing each other.***

Por lo general **nos saludábamos** con un abrazo. También **nos dábamos la mano.**
*We usually **greeted each other** with a hug. We also **would shake hands.***

¿Recuerdas?
You already know that *Nos vemos* means "We'll see each other later."

GramActiva VIDEO

Want more help with reciprocal actions? Watch the **GramActiva** video.

Actividad 17  **Hablar**

Los buenos amigos

Habla con otro(a) estudiante sobre lo que hacen tus mejores amigos y tú.

Modelo

verse frecuentemente
A —¿Uds. se ven frecuentemente?
B —Sí, nos vemos todos los días.
o: —No, no nos vemos frecuentemente.

Unos amigos en Buenos Aires, Argentina

Estudiante A

1. llevarse bien siempre
2. ayudarse con la tarea de vez en cuando
3. escribirse por correo electrónico a menudo
4. hablarse por teléfono todos los días
5. respetarse mucho
6. comprenderse generalmente

Estudiante B

Sí, nos . . .

No, no nos . . .

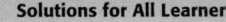 **Differentiated Instruction**
Solutions for All Learners

 Advanced Learners/Pre-AP*
Pre-AP*
For *Actividad* 18, tell students they have been hired to make a videotape of the reception that follows Carmen and Alfonso's wedding. Have them work in groups to create a narration for the videotape that describes how the guests greet each other and the newlyweds and how they spend their time at the reception.

Multiple Intelligences
Mathematical/Logical: As an extension of *Actividad* 17, have students interview classmates to see if there are differences between how girls and boys respond. Have them present their results, providing a graph to illustrate the similarities and differences.

 **Actividad 18** Hablar

Durante la boda

Durante la boda de Carmen y Alfonso algunos de los invitados (guests) se portaban mal. Usa el imperfecto para describir lo que hacían todos mientras los novios se casaban.

Modelo

Pati y Juanito
A —¿Qué hacían Pati y Juanito mientras Carmen y Alfonso se casaban?
B —Pati y Juanito se peleaban.

Roberto y Belita
el Sr. García y el Sr. Ramírez
el Sr. Vásquez
Pati y Juanito
Carmen y Alfonso
el Sr. Medina
las tías
la Sra. Fernández y la Sra. Peña
los padres de Carmen

Estudiante A

1. las tías
2. el Sr. García y el Sr. Ramírez
3. la Sra. Fernández y la Sra. Peña
4. el Sr. Vásquez y el Sr. Medina
5. Roberto y Belita
6. los padres de Carmen

Estudiante B

besar(se)
charlar
contar(se) chistes
pelear(se)
llevarse mal
hablar por teléfono
prestar atención

 **Fondo cultural**

La ceremonia del lazo En México, la ceremonia del lazo es parte de la boda y simboliza la unión entre los novios. Es cuando dicen sus promesas matrimoniales y luego el sacerdote (priest) les pone en el cuello (neck) una cuerda en forma de ocho. La expresión "atar el nudo" (to tie the knot) viene de esta tradición mexicana.

• ¿Qué piensas que significa el acto de "atar el nudo" durante la ceremonia? ¿Hay tradiciones similares en los Estados Unidos? ¿Cuáles son?

Una boda mexicana

doscientos veinticinco 225
Capítulo 4B

 Actividad 18  Standards: 1.1  Presentation EXPRESS ANSWERS

Resources: Voc. and Gram. Transparency 89; Answers on Transparencies

Focus: Describing reciprocal actions at a wedding

Recycle: Imperfect

Suggestions: Ask students to cover up the word bank for Student B. Then have them look at the picture and guess the verbs they might need for the activity. Have them uncover the words and determine if they understand their meanings. Remind them that not all verbs that express reciprocity take **se** or **nos** (i.e., **charlar**) and through usage it will become clearer which verbs use them and which do not.

Answers:

1. Las tías se llevaban mal.
2. El Sr. García y el Sr. Ramírez se contaban chistes.
3. La Sra. Fernández y la Sra. Peña charlaban.
4. El Sr. Vásquez y el Sr. Medina se hablaban por teléfono.
5. Roberto y Belita se abrazaban.
6. Los padres de Carmen se portaban bien.

 **Fondo cultural**  Standards: 1.2, 2.1, 2.2, 4.2

Suggestions: Have students work in groups to discuss wedding traditions they are familiar with in the United States or elsewhere. Have them jot down traditions and rituals they associate with weddings and then discuss them with another group in the class.

Answers will vary.

 Enrich Your Teaching
Resources for All Teachers

Culture Note

Mexico's Constitution of 1917 mandated a strict separation of Church and State. Thus, civil wedding ceremonies conducted by a judge were (and remain) required for a marriage to be official. Today, many couples in Mexico hold both church and civil wedding ceremonies.

Teacher-to-Teacher

Since the guests at Carmen and Alfonso's wedding can't behave, everyone has to change positions, even the bride and groom. Have students pair each person in *Actividad* 18 with someone different. Then have them describe how everyone gets along. For example: *El Sr. García y Carmen se abrazan.*

4B Practice and Communicate

 Fondo cultural *Standards:* 1.2, 2.1, 2.2

Suggestions: Have students close their eyes and imagine they are at a parade. Ask: What do you see? What do you hear? Who are you with? What is your strongest memory of a parade you saw as a child?

Answers will vary.

Actividad 19 *Standards:* 1.1, 1.3 **Pre-AP***

Focus: Speaking and writing about celebrations in the past

Recycle: Celebration vocabulary; imperfect

Suggestions: Have students discuss what kinds of questions might be interesting to have answered about a holiday. Encourage them to think of questions they've not asked before, such as: *¿Se disfrazaba tu mamá o papá durante* Halloween? *¿Cómo se vestía?* or *¿Tienes una memoria de* Halloween *cuando tenías muchísimo miedo?* Write key words on the board that students can use to recall the questions when they write them.

Answers will vary.

Block Schedule

Brainstorm a list of regional and local festivals that take place around the United States. Have students work in small groups to choose a festival and research the customs connected to the festival. Then have each group describe their festival to the class. Encourage students to have a visual or prop to illustrate their celebration.

Additional Resources

• WAV Wbk.: Audio Act. 8–9, pp. 82–83
• Teacher's Resource Book: Audio Script, p. 221, Communicative Activity BLM, pp. 228–229
• Audio Program: Tracks 11–12

 Assessment

• *ExamView* QuickTake Presenter Quiz on PresEXPRESS
• Prueba 4B-4: Reciprocal actions, p. 116

Fondo cultural

El carnaval es una de las celebraciones más alegres *(happy)* y animadas de América Latina. Por lo general se celebra durante tres días. Casi siempre hay desfiles de carrozas *(floats)*, grupos de personas con máscaras, bailarines y músicos. En los desfiles de la República Dominicana las personas se disfrazan *(wear costumes)* con máscaras que representan a diferentes personajes reales o imaginarios. En el Uruguay los desfiles son con música, sobre todo de tambores, llamada *candombe.* Las personas siguen a los músicos, todos bailan y algunos se disfrazan. En el Ecuador y en Venezuela no hay desfiles. La tradición es tirar *(to throw)* agua a los peatones que pasan por la calle, o entre los vecinos y miembros de la familia.

Una celebración en Venezuela

• En tu comunidad, ¿en qué festividades o celebraciones hay desfiles? ¿Participas en los desfiles? ¿Te gusta ver los desfiles?

Actividad 19  **Hablar/Escribir**

Una celebración

Habla con otro(a) estudiante sobre cómo celebraba un día festivo cuando era niño(a).

1 Pregunta a tu compañero(a) qué día festivo le gustaba celebrar.

> **Modelo**
> **A** —*¿Qué día festivo era tu favorito cuando eras niño(a)?*
> **B** —*Me encantaba Halloween.*

2 Escribe cinco preguntas que puedes hacerle a tu compañero(a) usando el imperfecto. Hazle las preguntas y escribe sus respuestas.

3 Escribe un párrafo de por lo menos *(at least)* cinco frases sobre cómo tu compañero(a) celebraba el día festivo.

> **Modelo**
> *A Carmen le encantaba Halloween cuando era niña. Siempre se vestía de princesa. Todos decían que ella era muy bonita. Iba a las casas de sus parientes y ellos le daban muchos dulces. Después se comía todos los dulces.*

Para decir más . . .

El Día de San Valentín Valentine's Day
El Día de San Patricio St. Patrick's Day
El Día de Acción de Gracias Thanksgiving Day

Más práctica

• Practice Workbook, pp. 87–88: 4B-6, 4B-7
• WAV Wbk.: Writing, p. 86
• Guided Practice: Grammar Acts., p. 158
• *Real.* para hispanohablantes, pp. 158-159

Go Online PHSchool.com
For: Reciprocal Actions
Web Code: jdd-0414

Differentiated Instruction
Solutions for All Learners

Students with Learning Difficulties
Provide a word web graphic organizer for *Actividad* 19. Label the center circle *día festivo* and the others *comidas, ropa, actividades,* and *participantes.* Have students: 1) write a question related to each topic, 2) record their partner's responses, and 3) refer to the organizer to compose the final paragraph.

Actividad 20
  Leer/Escribir

Las Fallas de Valencia

Lee el artículo sobre Las Fallas de Valencia, una de las fiestas más divertidas de España, y luego contesta las preguntas.

Las Fallas tienen origen en la celebración de San José, el santo de los carpinteros, y los valencianos conservan esta tradición tan interesante. En tiempos antiguos, los carpinteros celebraban el día de San José y la llegada de la primavera quemando¹ la madera² que ya no necesitaban. Hoy en día, durante unos seis meses, varias organizaciones en Valencia construyen unos 350 **ninots**, grandes estatuas de madera, *papier-mâché* y cartón. Estas estatuas representan los eventos del año o a personas famosas, generalmente de una forma muy cómica. Cada año escogen un ninot por voto popular y lo ponen en el Museo del Ninot. La *Cremá* (el 19 de marzo) es la última noche de la celebración, cuando ponen fuegos artificiales dentro de los otros ninots y a la medianoche los queman todos.

Un ninot en Valencia

¹burning ²wood

1. ¿Cuándo y por qué quemaban la madera en tiempos antiguos?
2. ¿Qué hacen con los ninots que construyen hoy en día?
3. ¿Te gustaría estar en Valencia la noche del 19 de marzo? ¿Por qué?

Actividad 21
  **Dibujar/Escribir/Hablar**

El mejor ninot

Con otro(a) estudiante, dibujen un ninot en color. Describan el ninot en tres o cuatro frases y expliquen por qué lo hicieron. Presenten los ninots a la clase y pongan los dibujos en la pared. Voten por el mejor ninot.

Modelo

Nuestro ninot es un jugador de básquetbol. Tiene las manos muy grandes y las piernas muy largas. Usamos los colores de la escuela en su uniforme. Hicimos este ninot porque nuestro equipo de básquetbol ganó todos los partidos el mes pasado.

El español en el mundo del trabajo

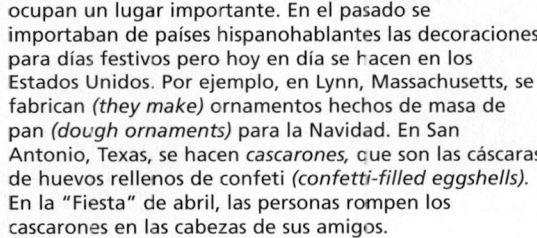

En el mercado de decoraciones y ornamentos de los Estados Unidos, los hispanohablantes ocupan un lugar importante. En el pasado se importaban de países hispanohablantes las decoraciones para días festivos pero hoy en día se hacen en los Estados Unidos. Por ejemplo, en Lynn, Massachusetts, se fabrican *(they make)* ornamentos hechos de masa de pan *(dough ornaments)* para la Navidad. En San Antonio, Texas, se hacen *cascarones,* que son las cáscaras de huevos rellenos de confeti *(confetti-filled eggshells).* En la "Fiesta" de abril, las personas rompen los cascarones en las cabezas de sus amigos.

• ¿Se usa en tu comunidad alguna decoración u ornamento en los días festivos? ¿Cómo es? ¿Dónde se fabrica? ¿Es un ornamento que se usa en otro país o región?

doscientos veintisiete 227
Capítulo 4B

Enrich Your Teaching

Resources for All Teachers

Culture Note

Valencia is the name of both a city and a region in eastern Spain. The city dates back to Roman times and is an important industrial center and seaport. The region is known for its rich agricultural output. A large percentage of oranges sold in the United States are grown in Valencia.

Teacher-to-Teacher

Have students research ornaments or decorations common to holidays celebrated in Spanish-speaking countries. Then have them make the decorations or draw pictures of them. Display their work and have students teach each other what they learned.

Actividad 20
 Standards: 1.2, 2.1, 2.2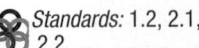
Presentation EXPRESS ANSWERS

Resources: Voc. and Gram. Transparency 90; Answers on Transparencies

Focus: Writing about a holiday

Recycle: Imperfect

Suggestions: Go over the questions before students begin the reading. Review words or phrases as necessary.

Answers may vary but will include:

1. **Para celebrar el día de San José (santo de los carpinteros) y la llegada de la primavera, los valencianos quemaban madera que no necesitaban.**
2. **Escogen un ninot por voto popular y lo ponen en el Museo del Ninot. La última noche de la celebración, ponen fuegos artificiales dentro de los demás y los queman todos.**
3. **Answers will vary.**

Actividad 21
 Standards: 1.2, 2.2, 5.1

Focus: Drawing and describing *ninots*

Recycle: Words that describe people and things

Suggestions: Remind students that *ninots* can represent events that took place during the past year or be like political cartoons, focusing on a famous person in a comical way.

Answers will vary.

El español en el mundo del trabajo

Core Instruction

 Standards: 1.2, 2.2, 5.1

Suggestions: Bring in photographs or, if possible, actual *cascarones* and dough ornaments to show students.

Theme Project

Students can perform Step 5 at this point. Record their presentations on cassette or videotape for inclusion in their portfolio. (For more information, see p. 182-a.)

Lectura

Core Instruction

Standards: 1.2, 2.1, 2.2, 3.1

Focus: Reading about Three Kings Day

Suggestions:

Pre-reading: Point out the title of the story, *El seis de enero*. Ask students if they are aware of any significance to this date. Explain that Three Kings Day, like Christmas, is a religious holiday that is now celebrated by a wide range of people. For students not familiar with the story, explain that the Three Kings or Wise Men are said to have visited Jesus as an infant, bringing him costly gifts from afar. In many cultures, January 6 is a more important day for giftgiving than is December 25.

Reading: Have students read the paragraph before reading the letters. As students read (or as you read to them), have them make notes to identify any similarities and differences that this celebration has compared with a gift-giving holiday that they celebrate.

Post-reading: Have volunteers summarize the information in the reading. Ask students who celebrate gift-giving holidays to share their comparisons. Complete the *¿Comprendiste?* questions.

Bellringer Review

Do a quick choral class review of the months of the year. As each month is mentioned, ask students who have a birthday in that month to stand so that all students are standing by the end of the activity.

Pre-AP* Support

- **Activity:** Have students read silently the two letters to the *Reyes Magos*. Then, ask that they write two statements highlighting two different pieces of information given by the children from either letter. As volunteers read their statements to the class, classmates will indicate to which letter the statement is referring.

- **Pre-AP* Resource Book:** Comprehensive guide to Pre-AP* reading skill development, pp. 18–24

¡Adelante!

Lectura

El seis de enero

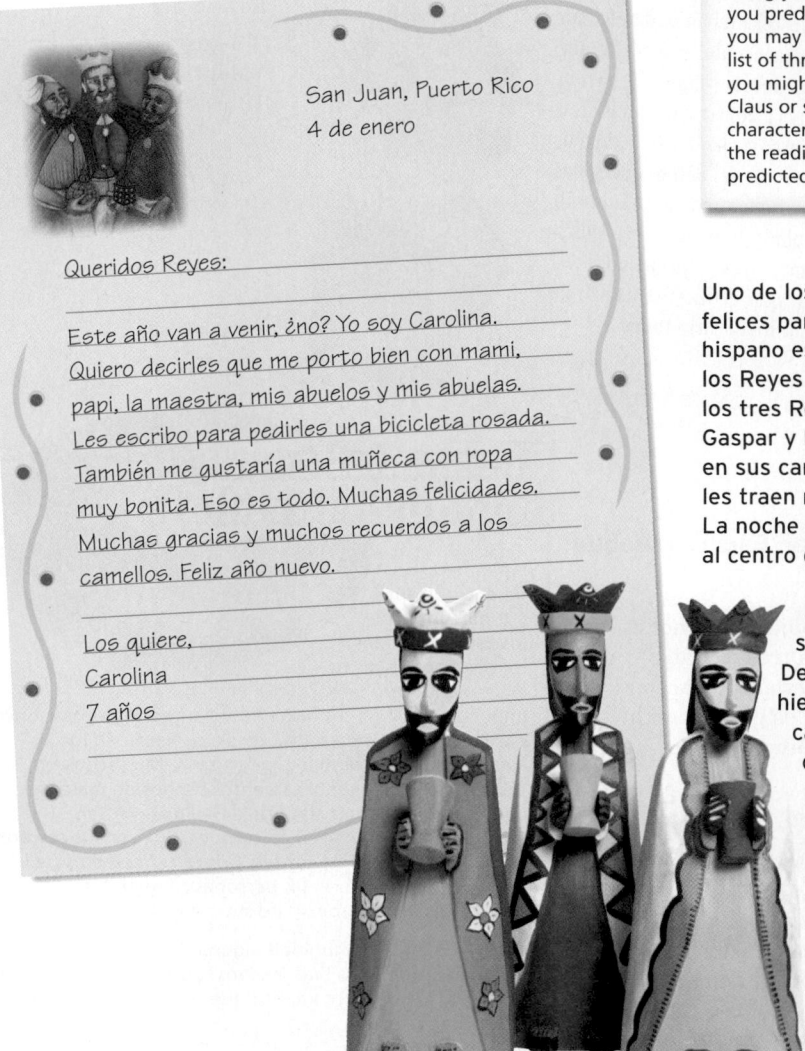

San Juan, Puerto Rico
4 de enero

Queridos Reyes:

Este año van a venir, ¿no? Yo soy Carolina.
Quiero decirles que me porto bien con mami,
papi, la maestra, mis abuelos y mis abuelas.
Les escribo para pedirles una bicicleta rosada.
También me gustaría una muñeca con ropa
muy bonita. Eso es todo. Muchas felicidades.
Muchas gracias y muchos recuerdos a los
camellos. Feliz año nuevo.

Los quiere,
Carolina
7 años

Objectives

- Read about los *Reyes Magos*
- Compare different traditional holiday foods
- Write about your favorite celebration
- Watch *En busca de la verdad,* Episodio 4

Estrategia

Using background knowledge
Using your own experience can help you predict the types of information you may find in a reading. Make a list of three types of information you might find in a letter to Santa Claus or some other fictional character. When you have finished the reading, see if what you predicted was mentioned.

Uno de los días más anticipados y felices para los niños del mundo hispano es el seis de enero, el Día de los Reyes Magos. Según la tradición, los tres Reyes Magos: Melchor, Gaspar y Baltasar, vienen montados en sus camellos[1] durante la noche y les traen regalos a todos los niños. La noche del cinco, las familias van al centro de la ciudad para ver un desfile de carrozas[2] con luces y flores y, por supuesto, los Reyes Magos. Después, los niños reúnen hierba o paja[3] para los camellos y la ponen en una caja cerca de sus zapatos. La mañana del seis, los niños se despiertan para ver qué les regalaron los Reyes Magos.

[1]camels [2]carriages [3]straw

Differentiated Instruction
Solutions for All Learners

Heritage Language Learners
If students have celebrated *el Día de los Reyes Magos,* have them write an essay describing the celebration. Encourage them to write about what they did to prepare and how they celebrated. Ask them to include details that may be unique to their heritage culture. Have students peer-edit each other's papers before preparing a final copy.

Advanced Learners
After students have written their letters, have them exchange them with a partner. Have students write a response to their partner, pretending to be one of the Three Kings.

Queridos Reyes Magos:

Me llamo José Alejandro y les escribo esta carta con mi mamá para decirles los regalos que quiero para mí y para mi hermanito, Jorge Andrés. Nos portamos bien. Yo saco muy buenas notas en la escuela y hago toda mi tarea. Yo quiero un carrito de control remoto y un videojuego de fútbol para mi computadora. Mi hermanito quiere un juguete o cualquier cosa que ustedes puedan. Gracias, y recuerden llevarles juguetes a los niños pobres y traernos paz y amor.

Los quieren,
José Alejandro y Jorge Andrés
7 y 2 años
Argentina

Antes del seis de enero, los niños les escriben cartas a los Reyes Magos pidiendo sus regalos. A veces también visitan a los Reyes Magos en los almacenes de las ciudades grandes. Antes era costumbre poner las cartas al lado de los zapatos, pero luego comenzaron a enviarlas por correo postal y hoy en día las envían por correo electrónico.

Niña con un Rey Mago, Madrid, España

Niños vestidos de Reyes Magos, en la República Dominicana

¿Comprendiste?

1. ¿Por qué es el Día de los Reyes Magos feliz para los niños?
2. ¿Qué hacen los niños antes del seis de enero?
3. ¿Qué hacen los niños el día del seis?
4. En los Estados Unidos, muchos niños creen en Santa Claus. ¿En qué sentido son similares las tradiciones de Santa Claus y de los Reyes Magos? ¿En qué sentido son diferentes?

Y tú, ¿qué dices?

Escribe una carta a los Reyes Magos. Usa una de las cartas escritas por niños del mundo hispano como modelo.

Más práctica

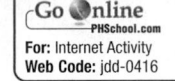

● WAV Wbk.: Writing, p. 87
● Guided Practice: *Lectura*, p. 159
● *Real.* para hispanohablantes, pp. 162-163

Go Online
PHSchool.com
For: Internet Activity
Web Code: jdd-0416

doscientos veintinueve **229**
Capítulo 4B

¿Comprendiste?

Presentation EXPRESS
ANSWERS

 Standards: 1.2

Resources: Answers on Transparencies

Focus: Verifying reading comprehension

Suggestions: Remind students that for items 1–3, they should use only the paragraph to find their answers. For item 4, have students reread both the paragraph and the letters to make their comparisons.

Answers:

1. Es un día feliz porque los Reyes Magos les traen regalos a todos los niños.
2. Los niños reúnen hierba o paja para los camellos de los Reyes Magos y la ponen en una caja cerca de sus zapatos. También les escriben cartas a los Reyes Magos y visitan a los Reyes Magos en los almacenes de las ciudades grandes.
3. Los niños se despiertan para ver qué les regalaron los Reyes Magos el 6 de enero.
4. Answers will vary.

Y tú, ¿qué dices?

 Standards: 1.3

Focus: Writing a letter to the Three Kings

Suggestions: Allow students to do an alternative activity if they prefer. Remind students to include a greeting and a farewell in their letter. Point out that they will need to include the gifts they want, and the reasons they deserve them.

Answers will vary.

Additional Resources

Student Resources: Guided Practice: Lectura, p. 159

For Further Reading

Student Resources:

● Realidades para hispanohablantes: Lectura 2, pp. 164–165

● Lecturas para hispanohablantes 2: "Espiral," p. 39, "Un terremoto en mi cuarto," pp. 43–44, "Fonseca," p. 66

 AP* Literature Author: Jorge Luis Borges, Lecturas para hispanohablantes 2: "Un Pre-AP* patio," p. 41

Enrich Your Teaching
Resources for All Teachers

Teacher-to-Teacher

It is very easy to compare Three Kings' Day to Christmas celebrations. Be careful not to assume that students celebrate Christmas or that they are familiar with the traditions. Encourage participation from students who celebrate Chanukah, Kwanzaa, or other culturally specific holidays.

Internet Search

Have students research this celebration on the Internet. Some sites are designed for Spanish-speaking children, and include activities or games.

Keyword: el Día de los Reyes Magos

Core Instruction

 Standards: 1.2, 1.3, 2.1, 2.2

Focus: Reading about *el roscón de Reyes*

Suggestions: Point out the photos to students, and explain that they will be learning about a food that is traditional is some Spanish-speaking cultures. Have students list holidays that they celebrate and specific foods that they eat for each one. Are students aware of the reasons specific foods are eaten for these celebrations? Ask students if they have ever seen a *roscón de Reyes* or similar pastry in a local grocery store or bakery. If so, ask students to compare it to the *roscones* pictured. Have students read the passage silently, or read it to them. After each paragraph, have volunteers summarize the information they learned.

Answers will vary.

Extension: Have students invent other possible traditions for the finder of the toy doll.

Additional Resources
Student Resource: Realidades para hispanohablantes, p. 166

Perspectivas del mundo hispano

El Roscón de Reyes

Es el Día de los Reyes Magos, el seis de enero, y mientras los niños juegan con sus regalos, los mayores preparan la merienda[1] de Reyes para sus amigos y familia. Esta merienda incluye un postre especial que se llama el roscón (o en México, la rosca) de Reyes. Cuando es la hora de comer el roscón, todo el mundo se acerca a la mesa y una persona empieza a cortarlo. Cada persona corta una rebanada[2] del roscón. Todos comen su porción cuando una persona grita, "¡Lo tengo!".

¿Qué es lo que tiene? Pues, dentro del roscón hay un muñequito de plástico. Según la tradición la persona que encuentra el muñequito debe pagar por la cena u otro roscón. Según otra tradición, la persona que encuentra el muñequito es el rey o la reina[3] de la fiesta.

El roscón es dulce, parecido a un pan dulce o a una torta, que se hace y se come sólo una vez al año. Está hecho con harina,[4] huevos, azúcar, mantequilla y frutas confitadas.[5] Como toda comida tradicional, la receta puede variar según la familia o la región. En ciertos países, el roscón se acompaña[6] con una taza de chocolate caliente.

¡Compruébalo! ¿Hay una tradición o celebración de tu familia en la que comen algo especial? ¿Qué es? ¿Cómo se prepara? ¿Hay algo especial que hacen mientras la preparan?

¿Qué te parece? ¿Crees que es importante mantener la tradición de preparar una comida especial? ¿Por qué?

[1]snack [2]slice [3]king or queen [4]flour
[5]candied [6]is accompanied

Un roscón de Reyes

Un vendedor de roscas de Reyes en México

Differentiated Instruction
Solutions for All Learners

Heritage Language Learners
Have students research recipes for *roscones* and write an essay explaining the steps needed to make one. Remind students that when they are writing a process essay, they should write one step as a topic sentence and have details to describe each step. Have students create a diagram to accompany their essay.

Advanced Learners
Find a recipe for students to use to prepare a *roscón de Reyes* at home. They can substitute a large lima bean for the doll. Have them explain how they made the *roscón* and share the cake with classmates. Make sure that students do not have any allergies and remind them to look for the "doll" in their slice before biting into it.

Presentación escrita

Mi celebración favorita

Task

You have an e-mail pal who wants to know about your favorite holiday or celebration. Write an e-mail message describing an event from your childhood.

1 Prewrite Think of an event you used to celebrate and want to write about. Copy the chart below on a sheet of paper. Using the questions on the top of each column as a guide, write words or expressions related to your topic.

¿Qué hacían?	¿Dónde se reunían?	¿Cómo era?	¿Quiénes estaban?	¿Por qué te gustaba?

2 Draft Use the ideas from the chart to write the first draft of your e-mail message.

Modelo

Mi celebración favorita era El Día de la Madre. Celebrábamos este día con toda la familia y, claro, con mi mamá. Íbamos a su restaurante favorito, Las Palomas. Siempre le regalábamos algo, como un collar o perfume. Ella siempre lloraba porque estaba muy contenta.

3 Revise Read your e-mail and check for correct spelling and vocabulary use. Be sure that you used the imperfect tense to describe events that used to take place. Share the e-mail with a partner, who should check the following:

- Is the e-mail easy to read and understand?
- Does it provide an interesting description of the event?
- Is there anything you should add?
- Are there any errors?

4 Publish Rewrite the e-mail, making necessary changes or corrections. Make a copy for your teacher or add it to your portfolio.

5 Evaluation Your teacher may give you a rubric for how the e-mail will be graded. You will probably be graded on:

- amount of information you provide
- accuracy in describing events in the past
- variety of vocabulary

Estrategia

Using a chart
Thinking through categories and writing down key words and expressions will give you more ideas for writing.

doscientos treinta y uno **231**
Capítulo 4B

Presentación escrita
Expository

Standards: 1.1, 1.3, 3.1

Resources: Teacher's Resource Book: Gram Activa BLM, p. 231

Focus: Writing about a favorite celebration

Suggestions: Remind students that they may create new categories for their chart if they wish to include different information. Point out that they are writing an e-mail and should include a greeting and closing in their message. Encourage students to use transitional words to describe a sequence of events. You may want to provide students with a list of words that will help them connect their sentences, such as **primero, entonces,** or **finalmente.** Point out that the model uses only the imperfect tense but that students should include the preterite where appropriate. If possible, have students e-mail you their message instead of printing it out. You may want to reply to students, asking them for further detail.

Pre-AP* Support

- *Pre-AP* Resource Book:* Comprehensive guide to Pre-AP* writing skill development, pp. 25–35

Portfolio

Have students include a copy of their e-mail in their portfolio.

Teacher-to-Teacher

e-amigos: Have students write their *e-amigos* describing their favorite childhood celebration. Encourage students to ask at least two questions about how their *e-amigos* celebrated special occasions. Have students print out their e-mails or send them to you for your review.

Additional Resources

Student Resources: Realidades para hispanohablantes, p. 167; Guided Practice: Presentación escrita, p. 160

✓ Assessment

- Assessment Program: Rubrics, p. T29

Give students copies of the rubric before they begin. Go over the different levels of performance. After assessing students, help individuals understand how they could improve their e-mails.

Enrich Your Teaching
Resources for All Teachers

RUBRIC	Score 1	Score 3	Score 5
Amount of information you provide	You respond to only two questions.	You respond to only three questions.	You respond to all five questions.
Your accuracy in describing events in the past	You use three verbs in the past with grammatical errors.	You use four verbs in the past with some grammatical errors.	You use five or more verbs in the past with very few grammatical errors.
Your use of vocabulary and grammar	You use very little variation of vocabulary and have frequent usage errors.	You use limited vocabulary and have some usage errors.	You use an extended variety of vocabulary and have very few usage errors.

Videomisterio

Core Instruction

Standards: 1.2, 3.2, 5.2

Resources: Teacher's Resource Book: Video Script, pp. 223–224; Video Program: Cap. 4B; Video Program Teacher's Guide: Cap. 4B

Focus: Reading and presenting new vocabulary needed to understand the video

Personajes importantes

Daniela y Roberto, Nela's grandchildren
Nela, grandmother
Linda, Roberto's friend
Julio, Roberto's friend
"Freddy" Toledo, Linda's grandfather

Synopsis: Roberto, Daniela, and Linda drive to San Miguel to visit Nela and have lunch at her home. While there, Linda inquires about the fact that there are no photos of Roberto's grandfather and is told that he is like a ghost to the family. Nela shows Roberto a photo that was hidden in a drawer of his grandfather and a friend. Roberto drops it and discovers names on the back. He learns that his grandfather was actually named Federico Zúñiga, not Toledo, and the friend was named Chato Montesinos, from Dolores Hidalgo. Roberto decides to find Chato. Nela then sees the image of Federico appear on her computer screen.

Suggestions:

Pre-viewing: Review the events of *Episodio 3*: Roberto and Linda made plans to visit Roberto's grandmother, Nela, who lives in San Miguel de Allende. In Guanajuato, Berta, Tomás, Roberto, and Daniela talked about the exchange program. Roberto was curious about Linda's last name. When he asked his father for more information about his grandfather, he was puzzled when told to ask his grandmother.

Have a volunteer read the *Nota cultural* aloud. Ask what U.S. dishes might be comparable to **mole.** Discuss whether students know of any festivals associated with these dishes.

Point out the *Palabras para comprender* and give examples in context.

Videomisterio

En busca de la verdad

Episodio 4

"¡Federico! Pero, ¿dónde estás?".

Antes de ver el video

"Mira, éste es tu abuelo".

Nota cultural El mole es una típica salsa mexicana. Hay muchos tipos de moles, pues en cada región de México se preparan diferentes salsas. Hay algunos moles que se hacen con unos veinte ingredientes distintos . . . ¡y a veces más de veinte! En la Ciudad de México hay una Feria Nacional del Mole todos los años en octubre. Gente de todo el país llega a la capital para participar en esta festividad.

Resumen del episodio

Linda, Roberto y Daniela van a San Miguel de Allende a visitar a Nela. Ella está contenta de conocer a Linda pero no quiere hablar de su esposo Federico. Roberto le pregunta sobre su abuelo y ella le muestra una foto antigua. Esa foto contiene la primera pista para Roberto. Al final del episodio Nela se queda sola frente a la computadora y se lleva una gran sorpresa.

Palabras para comprender
pista hint
¿Será posible? Is it possible?
No te preocupes. Don't worry.
Cuídate mucho. Take care of yourself.
Volveré lo más pronto posible. I will return as soon as possible.
No tardes. Don't be late.
apellido de soltera maiden name

232 doscientos treinta y dos
Tema 4 • Recuerdos del pasado

Differentiated Instruction
Solutions for All Learners

Heritage Language Learners
Have students reread the section on San Miguel de Allende in *Capítulo* 1B. As they watch the Videomisterio, have them identify one of the sites mentioned in *Capítulo* 1B. Have them write additional information presented in the *Videomisterio* on that site: visual details, location, and importance in the *episodio*.

Multiple Intelligences
Interpersonal/Social: Before viewing the *episodio*, have groups discuss the grandmother. What impression does she make on them? Have them talk about what they imagine the visit from Roberto and Linda will be like. Have volunteers present their findings to the class.

...

Después de ver el video

¿Comprendiste?

A. Escribe la respuesta correcta.

1. ¿Quiénes viajan en coche a San Miguel de Allende?

2. ¿Con quién habla Linda por el teléfono celular?

3. ¿Adónde invita Julio a Linda?

4. ¿Qué preparó Nela para el almuerzo?

5. ¿Cuáles fueron las últimas palabras del esposo de Nela antes de irse?

B. Contesta las siguientes preguntas.

1. ¿Qué pista obtiene *(obtain)* Roberto en este episodio?

2. ¿Cómo reacciona Roberto cuando Linda habla con Julio por teléfono? ¿Por qué?

3. ¿Por qué Roberto le pregunta a su abuela sobre el apellido de Linda?

4. En 1941, ¿con quién se fue Federico Toledo? ¿Adónde fue?

"Cuando mi esposo y yo llegamos aquí, San Miguel era un pueblo muy pequeño y muy lindo".

"Aquí estamos con la abuela".

Go Online PHSchool.com
For: More on *En busca de la verdad*
Web code: jdd-0209

doscientos treinta y tres **233**
Capítulo 4B

Suggestions:

Visual scanning: Direct attention to the photos. Have students read the captions and try to guess what the characters might be talking about.

Before students read the *Resumen del episodio* have them scan the text and find cognates *(visitar, foto, antigua, contiene)*. Remind them that they learned about San Miguel de Allende in *Capítulo* 1B. Then have them read the *Resumen del episodio*. Ask them one or two comprehension questions.

Viewing: Play *Episodio* 4 for the class. If there is time after viewing the full episode, go back and replay key moments that you wish to highlight. Remind students that they may not understand every word they hear in the video, but they should listen for overall understanding.

Post-viewing: Complete the *¿Comprendiste?* in class.

¿Comprendiste?

 Presentation EXPRESS ANSWERS

 Standards: 1.2, 1.3

Resources: Answers on Transparencies
Focus: Verifying comprehension; reviewing the plot
Suggestions: You may want to have students read the questions before watching the video or show the video again so students can verify their answers.

Answers:
A:
1. Roberto, Linda y Daniela
2. Julio
3. a almorzar
4. quesadillas y mole
5. eres lo más importante para mí

B: Answers will vary but may include:
1. Roberto encuentra el nombre de Chato Montesinos escrito en una foto del abuelo.
2. Se siente incómodo porque le gusta Linda.
3. Porque piensa que el abuelo de Linda puede ser también su abuelo Federico Zúñiga.
4. Se fue con Chato Montesinos a los Estados Unidos.

Additional Resources
• *En busca de la verdad* Video Workbook, Episode 4
• *En busca de la verdad* Teacher's Video Guide: Answer Key

Enrich Your Teaching
Resources for All Teachers

Culture Note
Movies and literature from Spanish-speaking countries sometimes include supernatural events and unexplainable occurrences, such as what Nela experiences on the computer. Magical realism is a technique made especially popular in literature by the Colombian writer Gabriel García Márquez and the Chilean author Isabel Allende. In films, Mexican directors such as Robert Rodríguez and Alfonso Arau have also used magical realism successfully.

Review Activities

To talk about manners and customs:
Prepare cards listing vocabulary for manners and customs. In groups of four, have one student hold up a word or phrase over a second student's head. The remaining students act out clues until the second student guesses the word.

To talk about people: Have pairs create a drawing in which vocabulary words are depicted and write questions to accompany their drawing. Then have pairs exchange their work, respond to the questions, and discuss the answers with the pair who created the activity.

To talk about special events: Bring in five greeting cards for different events. Give one to each group of students. Have students brainstorm as many words as they can about the event. After one minute, have groups switch cards and repeat the activity.

To discuss the past: Prepare a story in the form of a cloze passage. Have students use these vocabulary words as a word bank to complete the passage.

Portfolio

Invite students to review the activities they completed in this chapter, including written reports, posters or other visuals, tapes of oral presentations, or other projects. Have them select one or two items that they feel best demonstrate their achievements in Spanish to include in their portfolios. Have them include this with the Chapter Checklist and Self-Assessment Worksheet.

Additional Resources

Student Resources: Realidades para hispanohablantes, p. 168

 **CD-ROM**

PuzzleView Web Code: jdd-0417

Teacher Resources:
- Teacher's Resource Book: Situation Cards, p. 230, Clip Art, pp. 232–234
- Assessment Program: Chapter Checklist and Self-Assessment Worksheet, pp. T56–T57

234

Repaso del capítulo

Vocabulario y gramática

jdd-0499

To prepare for the test, check to see if you . . .
- know the new vocabulary and grammar
- can perform the tasks on p. 235

to talk about manners and customs

abrazar(se)	to hug
besar(se)	to kiss
dar(se) la mano	to shake hands
despedirse (e → i)(de)	to say good-bye (to)
los modales	manners
saludar(se)	to greet
sonreír (e → i)	to smile

to talk about people

el bebé, la bebé	baby
contar (o → ue) (chistes)	to tell (jokes)
llevarse bien / mal	to get along well / badly
llorar	to cry
los mayores	grown-ups
los parientes	relatives
reírse (e → i)	to laugh
reunirse (u → ú)	to meet

to talk about special events

alrededor de	around
el aniversario	anniversary
casarse (con)	to get married (to)
charlar	to chat
la costumbre	custom
cumplir años	to have a birthday
el desfile	parade
el día festivo	holiday
divertirse (e → ie)	to have fun
enorme	enormous
¡Felicidades!	Congratulations!
felicitar	to congratulate
la fiesta de sorpresa	surprise party
los fuegos artificiales	fireworks
hacer un picnic	to have a picnic
nacer	to be born
regalar	to give (a gift)
la reunión, pl. las reuniones	gathering

For *Vocabulario adicional*, see pp. 498–499.

to discuss the past

antiguo, -a	old, antique
frecuentemente	frequently
había	there was / there were
mientras (que)	while
recordar (o → ue)	to remember

using the preterite and imperfect to describe a situation

Use the imperfect to describe:

La casa donde **vivía estaba** al lado de un lago.

Había mucha gente en la fiesta de sorpresa.

The imperfect tense is used to tell what someone was doing when something happened:

Mis padres me **felicitaban** cuando **llegó** mi tía.

Mis tíos **se saludaban** cuando **empezaron** los fuegos artifciales.

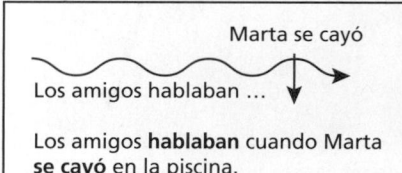

Los amigos hablaban ...

Los amigos **hablaban** cuando Marta **se cayó** en la piscina.

reciprocal actions

Los estudiantes **se saludaban** todos los días.

Nos veíamos frecuentemente cuando éramos niños.

Se escribían por correo electrónico de vez en cuando.

Differentiated Instruction
Solutions for All Learners

Students with Special Needs

Have hearing-impaired students work in pairs. Give each student 20 index cards with a word or phrase on each one. Have students draw a corresponding illustration on the blank side. Have students exchange cards and identify the words that the drawings represent.

Multiple Intelligences

Intrapersonal: Have students write a reflective essay on a celebration that they learned about in this chapter. Encourage them to incorporate facts as well as their own opinions in their essay. Have students focus on using the vocabulary words as much as possible.

- Practice Workbook Puzzle: p. 89
- Practice Workbook Organizer: p. 90

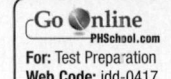
Go Online
PHSchool.com
For: Test Preparation
Web Code: jdd-0417

Preparación para el examen

jdd-0499

On the exam you will be asked to . . .	Here are practice tasks similar to those you will find on the exam . . .	If you need review . . .
1 **Escuchar** Listen and understand as people talk about their childhood memories of family celebrations	To celebrate "Grandparents' Day," your teacher invited Spanish-speakers from the community to talk about their favorite childhood memories. Listen as one of them describes one of their favorite family celebrations. See if you understand: (a) the reason for the gathering; (b) who was there; (c) what people used to do at the celebration.	**pp. 212–215** *A primera vista* **p. 218** *Actividad 8* **p. 222** *Actividad 13*
2 **Hablar** Talk about how your family used to celebrate holidays when you were a child	You have been invited to an elementary Spanish classroom to talk to the children about how you used to celebrate holidays when you were their age. What could you say? Try to include: (a) where you used to celebrate most holidays; (b) what you used to do; (c) who got together to celebrate with you.	**p. 218** *Actividad 8* **p. 222** *Actividad 14* **p. 226** *Actividad 19*
3 **Leer** Read and understand a description of activities at a special event	Read part of the notes that Miguel wrote for the wedding reception video he just finished filming for his friend, Mauricio, the groom, and the bride, Luisa. Can you determine who was having a good time and who was not without seeing the video? *Cuando Mauricio besó a Luisa, la madre de Luisa lloraba y el padre de ella sonreía. Los sobrinos pequeños se reían y jugaban con sus juguetes.*	**p. 219** *Actividad 10* **p. 227** *Actividad 20* **pp. 228–229** *Lectura*
4 **Escribir** Write about your last family celebration	A local Spanish-language radio station is asking people to send e-mails or faxes describing their best birthday. You might begin by writing: *Yo recuerdo bien mi cumpleaños de trece años . . .* Describe people who were there, where it was held, and what happened.	**p. 226** *Actividad 19* **p. 231** *Presentación escrita*
5 **Pensar** Demonstrate an understanding of how some Hispanic families celebrate special days and holidays	Describe a holiday, such as *Las Fallas* or *Carnaval,* that is of special interest to you. How is this holiday similar to one that you celebrate in your community?	**p. 210** *Fondo cultural* **pp. 214–215** *Videohistoria* **p. 220** *Fondo cultural* **p. 226** *Fondo cultural* **p. 227** *Actividad 20* **p. 230** *Perspectivas del mundo hispano*

doscientos treinta y cinco **235**
Capítulo 4B

Differentiated Assessment
Solutions for All Learners

STUDENTS NEEDING EXTRA HELP
- **Alternate Assessment Program:** Examen del capítulo 4B
- **Audio Program CD 20:** Chap. 4B, Track 9

HERITAGE LEARNERS
- **Assessment Program: Realidades para hispanohablantes:** Examen del capítulo 4B
- **ExamView** test generator **Heritage Learner Test Bank**

ADVANCED/PRE-AP*
- **ExamView** test generator **Pre-AP* Test Bank**
- **Pre-AP* Resource Book,** pp. 108–111

Review

Performance Tasks
Presentation EXPRESS ANSWERS

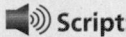 *Standards:* 1.1, 1.2, 1.3, 2.1, 2.2, 4.2

Student Resource: Realidades para hispanohablantes, p. 169

Teacher Resources: Teacher's Resource Book: Audio Script, p. 221; Audio Program: Track 14; Answers on Transparencies

1. Escuchar

Suggestions: Remind students of conversations that they have had about gatherings. Ask them to list some probable answers to the questions, and determine if their predictions were accurate.

Script:
Buenos días. Me encanta hablar con los jóvenes. Recuerdo bien los domingos con mi familia. Cada domingo nos reuníamos en la casa de nuestra abuela para comer. Cuando los mayores hablaban, los niños jugaban con el perro y el gato.

Answers:
a) They got together on Sundays to eat at their grandmother's house.
b) Grown-ups and children.
c) The grown-ups talked and the children played with the dog and cat.

2. Hablar

Suggestions: Have students brainstorm information on an index card before sharing it with a partner.

Answers will vary.

3. Leer

Answers may vary but will include:
It is possible to determine who was having a good time. The father and the nieces and nephews were having a good time. Luisa's mother may not have been having a good time.

4. Escribir

Suggestions: Have students organize the information that they want to include in a list before writing their message.

Answers will vary.

5. Pensar

Suggestions: Make a list of holidays discussed in this chapter. Have volunteers summarize the traditions of each one before students begin.

Answers will vary.

Assessment
- **ExamView** QuickTake Presenter **Quiz on PresEXPRESS**
- Assessment Program: Examen del capítulo
- **ExamView** test generator **Test Bank: Tests A and B**
- Audio Program CD 20: Chap. 4B, Track 9

235

Tema 5

En las noticias

THEME OVERVIEW

▶ **5A   Un acto heroico**
- Heroic acts

Vocabulary: emergencies, crises, rescues, and heroic acts

Grammar: imperfect tense: other uses; preterite of the verbs *oír*, *leer*, *creer*, and *destruir*

Cultural Perspectives: natural disasters

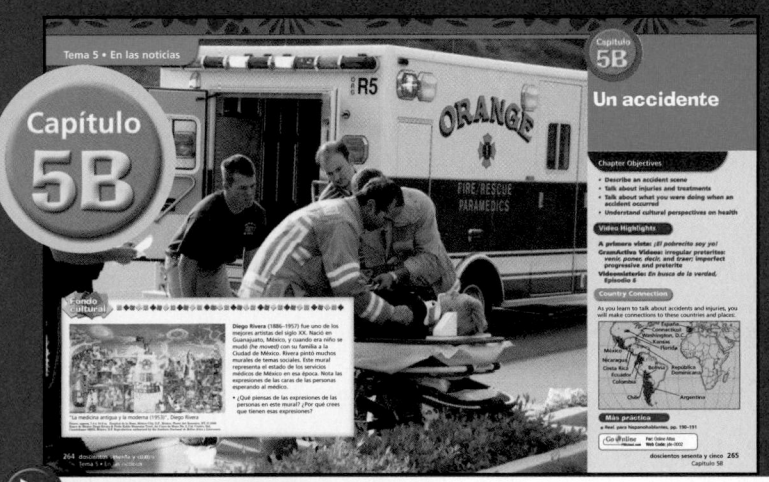

▶ **5B   Un accidente**
- Accidents

Vocabulary: accident scenes, injuries and treatments

Grammar: irregular preterites: *venir*, *poner*, *decir*, and *traer*; imperfect progressive and preterite

Cultural Perspectives: health

Theme Project

En las noticias

Overview: Students will write and present a news brief about a fictitious accident, heroic act, or natural disaster. Students must use the preterite and the imperfect and include information about:
- where, when, and how the event happened
- who was hurt and how
- who intervened to help

Students must include a poster or other visual aid to help them present their report.

Materials: poster board, markers, photos, glue or tape, scissors

Sequence: (suggestions for when to do each step are found throughout the chapters)

5A ▶ STEP 1. Review instructions so students know what is expected of them. Hand out the "Theme 5 Project Instructions and Rubric" from the *Teacher's Resource Book.*

STEP 2. Students submit a rough draft of their news brief. Return the drafts with your suggestions. For grammar and vocabulary practice, ask students to partner and present their drafts to each other.

STEP 3. Students create layouts on different pieces of poster board, leaving room for photos and descriptions. Encourage them to work in pencil first and to try different arrangements before gluing photos or decorations.

5B ▶ STEP 4. Students submit a draft of their poster. Note your corrections and suggestions, then return posters to students.

STEP 5. Students present their completed news briefs to the class.

Options:

1. Students research and present a real natural disaster or accident that occurred in a Spanish-speaking country.
2. Students work in teams to present different elements of the broadcast.

Assessment:

Here is a detailed rubric for assessing this project:

Theme 5 Project: *En las noticias*

RUBRIC	Score 1	Score 3	Score 5
Your evidence of planning	You provide no written draft or sketch.	Your draft was written and layout created, but not corrected.	You show evidence of corrected draft and layout.
Your use of illustrations	You include no photos or visuals.	You include very few photos or visuals.	You include several photos or visuals.
Your presentation	You include little of the required information.	You give two sentences about the event, the injuries, and the resolution.	You give three or more sentences about the event, the injuries, and the resolution.

Theme Support

Bulletin Boards

Theme: *Actos heroicos y desastres naturales*

Ask students to cut out, copy, or download photos of heroic acts or natural disaster relief efforts. Encourage students to find photos of police, ambulances, firefighters, military, humanitarian organizations, etc. from different Spanish-speaking cultures. Cluster photos into categories so that similarities and differences are evident.

Bibliography

DK Griffey, Harriet. *Volcanoes and Other Natural Disasters.* New York: DK Pub Merchandise, 1998. Easy-to-read discussion of natural disasters, including numerous photos.

Groman, Jeff. *The Atlas of Natural Disasters.* Friedman/Fairfax Publishing, 2002.

Rattenbury, Jeanne. *Understanding Alternative Medicine.* New York: Franklin Watts, Inc., 1999. Description of alternative medicines and therapies, such as traditional Chinese medicine, acupuncture, herbal medicine, and massage therapy.

Rivera, Diego, and Gladys March. *My Art, My Life: An Autobiography.* New York: Dover Publications, 1992. A description of the life and work of Diego Rivera that blurs the lines between fact and fiction.

Hands-on Culture

Craft: *Palo de lluvia*

The "rainstick" is a Peruvian musical instrument that makes the sound of rainfall. Its origin is a mystery, but the Incas used it in their ceremonies to summon rainfall and avoid drought. According to legend, its sound is magical and has the power to serenade the rain gods. The Diaguita people of the Elqui Valley in northern Chile still use it in their ceremonies to invoke the rain spirits.

Materials:

2 empty paper towel cardboard rolls
20 paper clips
one handful of beans (different sizes and types)
one sheet of cardboard
gift-wrap paper
wide adhesive tape

Directions:

1. Tape together the two cardboard rolls to make one long tube.
2. Straighten the paper clips.
3. Push the paper clips into one side of the cardboard tube and out the other side. Do this in a criss-cross fashion, from top to bottom (the more paper clips the better the sound). Bend in the ends of the clips so they stay in place.
4. Cut the sheet of cardboard to make ends for the tube. Cover one end, using the tape.
5. Fill the tube with different beans.
6. Cover the other end of the tube with cardboard.
7. Wrap the tube with the paper.
8. Gently turn the tube and enjoy the soothing sound of a ***palo de lluvia.***

Internet Search

Use the keywords to find more information.

5A Keywords:

Zulia Gotay de Anderson; Valdivia, Chile; Popayán, Colombia; Virtual Explorers

5B Keywords:

Diego Rivera, Ambulancia Azul, Patrulla Aérea Colombiana, jai alai, seguridad social

Game

El monstruo

Play this game during *Capítulo* 5B to practice and review parts of the body.

Players: Any number of students in small groups

Materials: overhead transparencies, overhead markers

Rules:

1. Prewrite a description of a monster. The monster can have any number of strange body parts (*dos cabezas, tres manos, una rodilla, etc.*)
2. Give each group a transparency and a transparency marker.
3. Read the description of the monster to the class. Each group must draw the monster as they hear the prompts.
4. Collect the pictures and display them on the overhead. Ask questions of the class to ensure that each monster correctly depicts the description.
El monstruo, ¿tiene dos cabezas?
5. Each correct depiction is worth one point. The group with the most points wins.

Variation: In groups, the students can write short descriptions of the monster. The teacher can then pick from the student descriptions.

 5A Preview

Standards for Capítulo 5A

• To achieve the goals of the Standards, students will:

Communication

1.1 Interpersonal
• Talk about: states of being, a building fire, emergency service personnel, natural disasters, sequences of events, past events, the Popayán quake of 1983, fire evacuation, heroes, disaster relief efforts, the home, rooms, and furnishings

1.2 Interpretive
• Read and listen to information about weather, heroism, building fires, journalism, volcanoes, the Popayán quake of 1983, the Valdivia quakes and tidal wave of 1960, volcano legends, hurricanes, disasters and preparedness
• Read: a picture-based story with a fire evacuation sign; newspaper headlines; about antonyms; Queen Sofia's relief mission to Nicaragua
• Listen to and watch a video about a fire

1.3 Presentational
• Write: about states of being, a building fire, emergency service personnel, volunteer firefighters of Chile, natural disasters, sequences of events, disaster preparedness, heroes, past events, a "disaster movie," the home, rooms, and furnishings; a legend about a local natural feature
• Present: opinions on a journalistic interview; information about states of being; past events

Culture

2.1 Practices and Perspectives
• Tell about hurricane preparedness, the volunteer firefighters of Chile, Chile's disaster awareness, volcano legends

2.2 Products and Perspectives
• Write or talk about: Zulia Gotay de Anderson and her art; Fernando Botero and his art; disaster response agencies in Chile; volcano legends

Connections

3.1 Cross-curricular
• Write or talk about: Pablo Picasso and his work; *el Reventador*, Colombian geology, meteorology, the Valdivia quakes and tidal wave of 1960
• Compose a journalistic interview

Communities

5.1 Beyond the School
• Explore local humanitarian opportunities

5.1 Lifelong Learner
• View a video mystery series

Fondo cultural ■◆■◆� ◆■◆◆◆

Zulia Gotay de Anderson nació en Ponce, Puerto Rico, y ahora vive en Port Aransas, Texas. Este cuadro ilustra un cuento de pescadores *(fishermen)* volviendo a casa durante un huracán. Sus esposas tienen miedo porque piensan que los pescadores no van a poder regresar. En 1998, más de diez mil personas murieron *(died)* en el huracán Mitch. Para reducir los efectos devastadores de los huracanes en el futuro, varios grupos trabajan en Honduras y Guatemala para mejorar los métodos de informar a la gente cuando venga *(comes)* otro huracán.

• Cuando hay un desastre en tu comunidad, por ejemplo un incendio *(fire)* o una inundación *(flood)*, ¿ayudan unas personas a otras? ¿Cómo se ayudan?

"The Storm / La tempestad" (2002), Zulia Gotay de Anderson
Oil on masonite, 24 x 30 in.

238 doscientos treinta y ocho
Tema 5 • En las noticias

Differentiated Instruction

STUDENTS NEEDING EXTRA HELP

Guided Practice Activities
• Vocabulary Check, Flash Cards
• Grammar
• Reading and Speaking Support

Guided Practice Audio CDs
• Disc 2, Track 1

HERITAGE LEARNERS

Realidades para hispanohablantes
• Chapter Opener, pp. 170–171
• A primera vista, p. 172
• Videohistoria, p. 173
• Manos a la obra, pp. 174–181
• ¡Adelante!, pp. 182–187
• Repaso del capítulo, pp. 188–189

ADVANCED/PRE-AP*

Pre-AP* Resource Book, pp. 112–115

Un acto heroico

Ayudando a las víctimas del
huracán Mitch en Nicaragua

Chapter Objectives

- **Discuss emergencies, crises, rescues, and heroic acts**
- **Describe past situations and settings**
- **Describe weather conditions**
- **Understand cultural perspectives on natural disasters and legends**

Video Highlights

A primera vista: *En el noticiero*

GramActiva Videos: the imperfect tense: other uses; the preterite of the verbs *oír, leer,* and *creer*

Videomisterio: *En busca de la verdad,* Episodio 5

Country Connection

As you learn about emergencies and disasters, you will make connections to these countries and places:

Colorado
España
México
República Dominicana
Guatemala
Puerto Rico
Nicaragua
Honduras
Costa Rica
Colombia
Ecuador
Chile

Más práctica

- *Real.* para hispanohablantes, pp. 170–171

Go **Online**
PHSchool.com
For: Online Atlas
Web Code: jde-0002

doscientos treinta y nueve **239**
Capítulo 5A

Chapter Opener

Core Instruction

Resources: Voc. and Gram. Transparencies: Maps 12–18, 20

Suggestions: Ask students to think about the news they hear or read. What kinds of stories are typically covered? Encourage students to name any Spanish-language TV, radio, or online news sources with which they are familiar. How often do students hear about natural disasters in their area? Which kinds are more likely to occur? Are there any natural disasters that are unlikely to occur in their community? Point out to students that they will learn how to talk about these events and describe weather conditions in the past. Tell students that in the *Videohistoria,* they will see how curious Tomás and Raúl are about local news coverage of a fire. Have students ever seen a fire or other disaster? If so, what was their reaction?

Standards: 1.2, 2.1, 2.2

Fondo cultural

Suggestions: Ask students to describe a hurricane. Have them discuss the effects that these events have on communities and how volunteers can help. Bring in information about the relief effort that took place after Hurricane Mitch.

Answers will vary.

Teaching with Photos

Suggestions: Have students look at the photo and describe what the volunteers are giving the children. What do they think a community hit by a hurricane would need? Ask them why they think that supplies were dropped off by helicopter.

Block Schedule

Have students identify and perhaps participate in local relief organizations that use Spanish-speaking volunteers. Many organizations can provide teens with a multitude of tasks. Have students keep a journal of their service-learning experiences. Remind them that volunteer work is a requirement for admission to many colleges and universities.

Teacher Technology

TeacherEXPRESS
Plan · Teach · Assess

Go **Online**
PHSchool.com
For: Teacher Home Page
Web Code: jdk-1001

PLAN	TEACH	ASSESS
Lesson Planner	Teaching Resources	Chapter Quizzes and Tests
	Interactive Teacher's Edition	
	Vocabulary Clip Art	

PresentationEXPRESS
Dynamic Presentations for Teachers

TEACH
Vocabulary & Grammar Powerpoints
GramActiva Video
Audio & Clip Art Activities
Transparencies and Maps
Activity Answers
Photo Gallery

ASSESS
ExamView
QuickTake Presenter

239

Vocabulario y gramática

Presentation EXPRESS
VOCABULARY

Core Instruction

Standards: 1.2

Resources: Teacher's Resource Book: Input Script, p. 6, Clip Art, pp. 20–23, Audio Script, p. 7; Voc. and Gram. Transparencies 92–93; TPR Stories Book, pp. 65–77; Audio Program: Tracks 1–2

Focus: Presenting vocabulary for natural disasters and emergencies

Suggestions: Present the vocabulary in three groups: natural disasters, fires, and news reporting. Use the Input Script from the *Teacher's Resource Book* or the story from the *TPR Stories Book* to present the new words, or use some of these suggestions.

Bring in newspaper photos of natural disasters and emergencies and show them to the class. Ask students limited-response questions about the photos: *¿Había un terremoto o un huracán en Guatemala? ¿Llovió o nevó en Argentina?*

If possible, show a videotape of television news reports or segments from a weather channel to illustrate the vocabulary. Show students the tape with the sound muted. Pause the tape and ask them to identify what they see.

Point out the reflexive *se murieron* and explain that it is an idiomatic expression.

Make photocopies of the four illustrations in the article on p. 241. Have students list words from p. 240 that they associated with each drawing and write them below the appropriate picture.

Bellringer Review
Have students complete a Word Web (See the Graphic Organizer transparencies.) to highlight weather. In the center write *El clima* and in the surrounding four circles write each of the seasons.

Additional Resources
• Audio Program: Canciones CD, Disc 22

✓ Assessment
• **ExamView** QuickTake Presenter Quiz on PresEXPRESS

A primera vista   jdd-0587

Vocabulario y gramática en contexto

Read, listen to, and understand information about
• natural disasters and crisis situations
• emergencies, rescues, and heroic acts

❝ Hoy **hubo** un incendio que **destruyó** unos apartamentos. No sabemos **la causa** del incendio, pero se cree que **comenzó** a causa de **una explosión.** Un vecino **valiente** ayudó a una señora a salir de su apartamento. **Afortunadamente,** no había más gente en el edificio. Llegaron los bomberos y **apagaron** el incendio después de unas horas. En otras noticias . . .

Tele 5 · el noticiero · la locutora · el edificio de apartamentos · quemarse · el incendio · los bomberos · la escalera · el humo

Hubo **un terremoto** en el sur de México. Dicen que más de 100 personas **se murieron** en este desastre.

Ayer **el huracán** Gabriel llegó a la costa de Honduras cerca del pueblo de La Ceiba. **Llovió** por 12 horas.

Hubo muchas **inundaciones** en Honduras a causa de **las tormentas** de **lluvia,** pero dicen que todos los habitantes están **vivos.**

En Chile, **nevó** durante tres días y las carreteras están cerradas ❞.

Differentiated Instruction
Solutions for All Learners

Students with Special Needs
For hearing-impaired students, make a photocopy of the news-story photos on p. 240 without the captions. Give them copies of the script for *Actividad* 1 and have them match the descriptions with the pictures.

Heritage Language Learners
Students may use vocabulary that is more common to their heritage countries. For example: *departamento* for *edificio de apartamentos; diario* for *periódico;* and *periodista* for *reportera.* Reassure them that the words they use are correct, but encourage them to learn the chapter vocabulary.

La Prensa

Más vocabulario
a causa de because of
de prisa in a hurry
de repente suddenly

Un héroe local
el artículo

Carlos Arroyo Medina es un héroe según sus vecinos porque le salvó la vida a una señora de 82 años. Ayer ocurrió un incendio en su edificio de apartamentos. El Sr. Arroyo le cuenta a nuestra reportera lo que pasó.

Entré corriendo y **subí** la escalera hasta llegar a su apartamento. **Traté de** abrir la puerta pero no pude. **Creí** que la Sra. Hurtado estaba **dormida** o, peor, **muerta**.

"Estaba delante del edificio y vi el humo. Pensé inmediatamente en la Sra. Hurtado, que vive en el segundo piso. Tiene 82 años y yo sabía que no podía **escaparse**. Un vecino mío **llamó** por teléfono para pedir ayuda.

Pero ella **se escondía** entre **los muebles** de su apartamento y **gritaba** '¡Socorro!'. De repente pude abrir la puerta y entré en el apartamento.

Bajamos de prisa la escalera y nos escapamos del incendio. Lo que hice no fue un acto heroico. Ayudé a mi vecina, nada más. Ella también es **heroína**."

Actividad 1 jdd-0587))) **Escuchar**

¿Quién es?

Vas a escuchar las noticias. Señala la noticia que se describe en la página 240.

Más práctica

- Practice Workbook, pp. 93–94: 5A-1, 5A-2
- WAV Wbk.: Writing, p. 94
- Guided Practice: Vocab. Flash Cards, pp. 163–170
- Real. para hispanohablantes, p. 172

Go Online
PHSchool.com
For: Vocab. Practice
Web Code: jdd-0502

Actividad 2 jdd-0587))) **Escuchar**

El noticiero de San José

Escucha las noticias y escoge la respuesta correcta.

Noticia 1
1. a. muchas personas   2. a. una escuela
   b. nadie   b. una tienda

Noticia 2
1. a. un bombero   2. a. un incendio
   b. un policía   b. un terremoto

Noticia 3
1. a. un incendio   2. a. más de 40
   b. un huracán   b. más de 50

doscientos cuarenta y uno **241**
Capítulo 5A

Enrich Your Teaching
Resources for All Teachers

Culture Note

Emergency phone numbers vary throughout the Spanish-speaking world. Dialing 9-1-1 will allow you to reach help in El Salvador and Mexico City, but it will not work in other countries. In Bogotá, Colombia, the emergency number is 1-1-2, but it is not the same in other Colombian cities. It is best to ask what the number is upon arriving in a country.

Teacher-to-Teacher

Have students use the Internet to research international weather symbols. Have them print or draw the symbols and write the words in Spanish. Students can also research and label emergency symbols for disaster vocabulary. Display symbols in the classroom.

Actividad 1  Standards: 1.2   Presentation EXPRESS AUDIO

Resources: Teacher's Resource Book: Audio Script, p. 7; Audio Program: Track 3; Voc. & Gram. Transparency 92; Answers on Transparencies

Focus: Listening comprehension about natural disasters and rescues

Suggestions: Show Transparency 92 and have volunteers point to the correct photo after the other students have had a chance to point to their own books. Be sure students understand that the sentences they hear will not match the captions on p. 240.

))) **Script and Answers**

1. Hubo un terremoto en Nicaragua. *(earthquake)*
2. El incendio destruyó una casa en el centro de la ciudad. *(fire)*
3. Tres personas se murieron en el huracán que pasó por Cuba. *(hurricane)*
4. Un bombero le salvó la vida a un niño de tres años. *(firefighter)*
5. Muchas personas dicen que vieron humo detrás de la escuela. *(smoke)*
6. Más de veinte personas se murieron en unas inundaciones en Venezuela. *(flood)*

Actividad 2  Standards: 1.2    Presentation EXPRESS AUDIO

Resources: Teacher's Resource Book: Audio Script, p. 7; Audio Program: Track 4; Answers on Transparencies

Focus: Listening comprehension of news stories

Suggestions: Have students read the possible choices for each segment before they listen to the script. Pause after each one to check comprehension.

))) **Script and Answers:**

Noticia 1: Hoy hubo un terremoto muy cerca de la Ciudad de México. Nadie se murió pero el terremoto destruyó una escuela y unos edificios de apartamentos.
1. ¿Cuántas personas se murieron en el terremoto? *(b)*
2. ¿Qué destruyó el terremoto? *(a)*

Noticia 2: Un policía le salvó la vida a un señor de ochenta años. Hubo un incendio en su casa y el policía entró en la casa y le ayudó a salir.
1. ¿Quién le salvó la vida a un señor? *(b)*
2. ¿Qué ocurrió en la casa del señor? *(a)*

Noticia 3: Hoy el huracán Miguel llegó a la costa de la República Dominicana. Hubo inundaciones a causa de la lluvia y del viento. Se murieron más de cincuenta personas.
1. ¿Qué pasó en la costa de la República Dominicana? *(b)*
2. ¿Cuántas personas se murieron? *(b)*

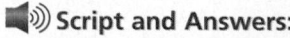

Videohistoria

Core Instruction

Standards: 1.2

Resources: Voc. and Gram. Transparencies 94–95; Audio Program: Track 5
Focus: Presentation of additional vocabulary to discuss reporting a fire

Suggestions:

Pre-reading: Direct attention to the *Estrategia.* Have students list key questions that are typically addressed in news reports *(Who? What? When? Where? Why? and How?).* Have them scan the photos and predict what event the news reporter is covering.

Reading: Ask students to read panels 1–5 and have them list answers to key questions addressed in the report. Have them read panel 6. Ask students why the reporter would want to talk with Raúl and Tomás.

Post-reading: Complete *Actividad* 3 to check comprehension.

 Pre-AP* Support

- **Activity:** Have students work in pairs to recreate the interview between the reporter and the fireman by changing the type of disaster (frames 3–5). Also ask them to write two multiple-choice questions from their new dialogue. Finally, have groups of four students (two pairs) present their dialogue to each other and then take turns reading their multiple-choice questions and answers.

- *Pre-AP* Resource Book:* Comprehensive guide to Pre-AP* vocabulary skill development, pp. 47–53

Videohistoria jdd-0587

En el noticiero

¿Qué hay en las noticias cuando Tomás y Raúl ven la televisión?

Estrategia

Scanning for key information
News reports provide important facts. Look through the dialogue before reading to find out what event happened and what connection it has with Tomás and Raúl.

el bombero

Tomás

Raúl

la reportera

1 **Raúl:** ¡Mira! Anoche hubo un incendio en una casa. ¡Caramba!

Tomás: ¿Y ahora qué?

Raúl: ¡Está a dos calles de aquí! ¡Tenemos que ir a verla! Quiero saber qué pasó.

Tomás: ¿Por qué? Yo no quiero salir ahora.

5 **Bombero:** Un vecino vio humo. Vinieron **los paramédicos.** Afortunadamente, los pudimos **rescatar** a todos.

6 **Reportera:** Y ustedes, ¿cómo se llaman?

Raúl: Pues, Raúl Padilla Salazar.

Tomás: Tomás.

Reportera: ¿Viven cerca de aquí?

Raúl: Más o menos.

7 **Reportera:** ¿**Oyeron** el incendio? ¿O vieron el humo?

Tomás: Pues, estábamos viendo la televisión en casa cuando vimos el noticiero . . .

Reportera: Entonces, ¿no saben nada del incendio?

Raúl: Pues, la verdad, no.

Differentiated Instruction
Solutions for All Learners

Advanced Learners
Have students create another scene for the *Videohistoria* in which the reporter finds actual witnesses to the fire. Students can use vocabulary to say what they saw, what time they heard the explosion, and tell where they were or what they were doing at the time of the fire. Have students incorporate as much new vocabulary as possible.

Students with Learning Difficulties
If students have difficulty with inferential reasoning, ask questions to guide them: Did Tomás and Raúl agree or disagree about going to the fire site? What must have happened between panel 1 and panel 2? What assumption do you think the reporter was making about Tomás and Raúl?

2 **Raúl:** Mira, allí está **la reportera.** Está hablando con un bombero.

Tomás: ¿Qué ocurrió?

Raúl: No sé. Vamos a **investigar.**

3 **Reportera:** ¿A qué hora comenzó el incendio?

Bombero: No estamos seguros. Sobre las dos de la mañana.

Reportera: ¿Cómo comenzó?

Bombero: Pensamos que hubo una explosión. Estamos investigando la causa.

4 **Reportera:** ¿Había personas en la casa?

Bombero: Sí. Una familia de seis personas.

Reportera: ¿Hubo algún **herido?**

Bombero: Afortunadamente, no estaban **heridos.** Pero, **sin duda,** estaban un poco **asustados.**

8 **Reportera:** Esto es todo por ahora. Laura Martínez desde Calle 21 para el canal cinco.

Actividad 3

Escribir/Hablar

¿Comprendiste?

1. ¿Qué ven Tomás y Raúl en la televisión? ¿Qué pasó?

2. ¿Adónde quiere ir Raúl? ¿Quiere ir Tomás también?

3. ¿A quiénes ven Tomás y Raúl cuando llegan a la casa? ¿Qué hacen ellos?

4. ¿A qué hora comenzó el incendio? ¿Qué lo causó?

5. ¿Había gente en la casa? ¿Cómo estaba?

6. ¿Por qué habla la reportera con Tomás y Raúl? ¿Qué le dicen los chicos?

Más práctica

- Practice Workbook, pp. 95–96: 5A-3, 5A-4
- WAV Wbk.: Video, pp. 88–90
- Guided Practice: Vocab. Check, pp. 171–174
- *Real.* para hispanohablantes, p. 173

Go Online PHSchool.com
For: Vocab. Practice
Web Code: jdd-0503

doscientos cuarenta y tres **243**
Capítulo 5A

Video

Core Instruction

Standards: 1.2

Resources: Teacher's Resource Book: Video Script, p. 11; Video Program: Cap. 5A; Video Program Teacher's Guide: Cap. 5A

Focus: Viewing and comprehending the video

Suggestions:

Pre-viewing: Remind students to look for visual clues to help with unfamiliar vocabulary. Ask what questions they would ask a firefighter if they were the reporter.

Viewing: Show the interview with the firefighter once without pausing. Show it again and pause to discuss the interview. Pause again before the reporter interviews Tomás and Raúl and ask students why they think the reporter wants to interview the two boys. Why does the reporter look surprised at the end?

Post-viewing: Complete the Video Activities in the *Writing, Audio & Video Workbook.*

Actividad 3

Standards: 1.2, 1.3

Presentation EXPRESS
ANSWERS

Resources: Answers on Transparencies
Focus: Verifying comprehension of the *Videohistoria*

Suggestions: As students review their answers, call on volunteers to act out the dialogue in which each answer is found.

Answers:

1. Raúl y Tomás ven las noticias. Hubo un incendio en una casa.
2. Raúl quiere ir a verla. Tomás no quiere ir.
3. Ven a una reportera que habla con un bombero. Ellos investigan el incendio.
4. El incendio comenzó sobre las dos de la mañana. Hubo una explosión.
5. Había una familia en la casa. Estaban asustados.
6. La reportera piensa que vieron el incendio. Los chicos no vieron nada.

Additional Resources

- WAV Wbk.: Audio Act. 5, p. 91
- Teacher's Resource Book: Audio Script, p. 8
- Audio Program: Track 7

✓ Assessment

- **ExamView** QuickTake Presenter Quiz on PresEXPRESS
- Prueba 5A-1: Vocab. Recognition, pp. 125–126

Enrich Your Teaching
Resources for All Teachers

Culture Note
On May 9, 1960, the first images were broadcast over Costa Rican television. One of Costa Rica's oldest television stations is *Teletica Canal 7.* The station broadcasts local and international news several times a day and offers a morning show as well as a variety of special news programs.

Teacher-to-Teacher
Have students work in groups of four to re-create the news report in the *Videohistoria.* Assign each student in the group a different role and have them act out the dialogues in panels 3–8. You may want to videotape their presentations and show the best performance as a quick review for *Actividad* 3.

Standards: 1.2, 1.3

 **Presentation EXPRESS ANSWERS**

Resources: Answers on Transparencies

Focus: Writing and speaking about emergencies and rescues

Suggestions: Remind students to use context clues to correctly determine number and gender.

Answers:

1. humo
2. los bomberos
3. El policía
4. una explosión
5. los muebles
6. El paramédico
7. herido
8. El héroe
9. edificio de apartamentos
10. La bombera
11. la escalera
12. el incendio

Extension: Have students rewrite the report, adding adjectives and information to make it more complete. For example: *El heroe valiente rescató a una perra asustada del edificio de apartamentos en la calle Ochoa.*

 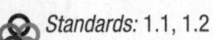 **Standards:** 1.1, 1.2

 **Presentation EXPRESS AUDIO**

Resources: Teacher's Resource Book: Audio Script. p. 8; Audio Program: Track 6; Answers on Transparencies

Focus: Listening, writing, and speaking about the correct order of an event

Suggestions: Play the *Audio CD* or read the script. Pause after each sentence and allow students time to write their answers.

Script and Answers:

1. Un paramédico ayudó al señor a bajar la escalera. *(fifth)*
2. Afortunadamente el edificio de apartamentos no se quemó completamente. *(sixth)*
3. Los vecinos oyeron la explosión y estaban asustados. *(second)*
4. El incendio comenzó en el apartamento de una anciana. *(first)*
5. Cuando entraron los bomberos, el señor se escondía en el baño. *(fourth)*
6. A causa de la explosión, muchas personas gritaban "¡Socorro!" *(third)*

Manos a la obra
Vocabulario y gramática en uso

Objectives
- Communicate about emergencies, crises, rescues, and heroic acts
- Discuss settings in the past
- Discuss weather and time in the past
- Learn the preterite forms of the verbs *oír, leer, creer,* and *destruir*

Actividad 4 — Leer/Escribir

El incendio

Escribe frases completas para explicar lo que ocurrió ayer en un barrio de la ciudad.

Modelo

 saco fotos del

El fotógrafo sacó fotos del incendio.

Una señora vio __1.__  y llamó por teléfono a __2.__  . __3.__  investigó

la causa de __4.__  en el apartamento. El incendio destruyó todos __5.__  en el

apartamento. __6.__  llevó al señor que estaba __7.__  a la ambulancia.

__8.__  rescató a una perra del __9.__  . __10.__  valiente subió

__11.__  y apagó __12.__ .

Actividad 5 jdd-0588  Escuchar/Escribir/Hablar

Escucha y escribe

Escucha las seis frases de un locutor que da las noticias del incendio que se describe en la Actividad 4. Escribe las frases. Después, con otro(a) estudiante, pongan en orden estas frases siguiendo el orden de la Actividad 4 para contar lo que ocurrió.

244 doscientos cuarenta y cuatro
Tema 5 • En las noticias

Differentiated Instruction
Solutions for All Learners

Multiple Intelligences

Verbal/Linguistic: Have students read their completed *Actividad 6* as a Spanish-language news reporter. Suggest that students create an introductory sentence, embellish their news stories with visuals, and invent eyewitness accounts.

Advanced Learners

Have students search the Internet to find articles in Spanish-language newspapers about fires. Have students describe the main events of the article and write their sentences on several strips of paper. Have students exchange their sentences with a partner and arrange the sentences in correct chronological order.

Actividad 6
Leer/Escribir

El artículo de la reportera

Una reportera, Alicia Fernández, habló con el Sr. Osorio. Lee otra vez la información del incendio en las *Actividades* 4 y 5. Escoge las palabras del recuadro y completa las notas de Alicia en preparación para escribir el artículo para el periódico.

El Sr. Osorio estaba __1.__ en su cama cuando, __2.__, su perra Blanca __3.__ a ladrar (bark). El señor salió de su cama muy __4.__ y llamó a los bomberos. __5.__ llegar a la puerta del apartamento pero no pudo.

Afortunadamente el señor y su perra __6.__ y están __7.__. Muchos dicen que Blanca es una verdadera __8.__. __9.__, Blanca ayudó a salvarle __10.__ al Sr. Osorio.

comenzó	heroína	sin duda
de prisa	muertos	trató de
de repente	se escaparon	la vida
dormido	se escondió	vivos

Actividad 7
Escribir/Hablar

Profesiones para nuestros compañeros

1 Escribe verbos y adjetivos que asocias con estas personas.

Modelo
profesor, -a
ayudar, enseñar, explicar, inteligente, simpático

1. bombero, -a
2. paramédico, -a
3. reportero, -a
4. locutor, -a
5. policía

2 Trabaja con otro(a) estudiante. Habla de las personas en tu escuela que deben tener estas profesiones.

Modelo
A —¿Quién debe ser profesor(a)?
B —*Martín Echevarría debe ser profesor de español. Es inteligente y muy simpático. Le gusta ayudar a otras personas. Explica muy bien los verbos y puede enseñar a la clase si es necesario.*

Fondo cultural

Los bomberos chilenos ¿Sabes que todos los bomberos en Chile son voluntarios? Para ser bombero, uno tiene que llenar una solicitud *(application)* en una estación de bomberos y aprobar *(pass)* un examen físico y mental. Los bomberos no tienen horarios fijos *(fixed)*. Van a la estación cuando pueden y todos tienen radios para saber cuándo los necesitan. Sirven durante el día y también durante la "guardia nocturna". Para comprar el equipo necesario, los voluntarios tienen que pagar dinero todos los meses para servir a la comunidad.

• ¿Crees que los voluntarios deben pagar sus propios gastos *(expenses)*? ¿Por qué?

Un bombero voluntario, Chile

doscientos cuarenta y cinco 245
Capítulo 5A

Practice and Communicate 5A

 Actividad 6 Standards: 1.2

Presentation EXPRESS ANSWERS

Resources: Answers on Transparencies
Focus: Reading and writing about a fire
Suggestions: Allow students to refer to their answers from *Actividades* 4 and 5. Have them read the paragraph once before filling in the blanks. Point out that the words in the box do not change.

Answers:
1. dormido
2. de repente
3. comenzó
4. de prisa
5. Trató de
6. se escaparon
7. vivos
8. heroína
9. Sin duda
10. la vida

 Actividad 7 Standards: 1.1, 1.3

Focus: Writing and speaking about professionals
Recycle: Adjectives, verbs
Suggestions: Point out to students that they should match a person with a profession based on the attributes on their lists of verbs and adjectives. Before students begin Step 2, have them share their lists with their partners. Encourage them to agree on one list to use when choosing an appropriate person for each of the professions.
Answers will vary.
Common Errors: Students may make noun and adjective agreement errors. Point out that adjectives must agree in gender and number with the person they describe.

Fondo cultural Standards: 1.2, 2.1, 2.2

Suggestions: Ask students if the firefighters in their community are volunteers. Do they know anyone who is a volunteer firefighter? In addition to city firefighters, what other types of firefighters are there?
Answers will vary.

Enrich Your Teaching
Resources for All Teachers

Culture Note

The *Corporación Nacional Forestal,* known as *CONAF,* is part of Chile's Ministry of Agriculture. It includes an elite group of professional firefighters who are responsible for controlling fires that break out in the various forests of Chile. These forests total almost one fifth of Chile's territory.

Teacher-to-Teacher

Invite a Spanish-speaking firefighter from your community to talk to students about fire safety. Provide students with a worksheet to fill out as they listen to the presentation. The day before the visit, encourage students to brainstorm questions for the firefighter.

5A Practice and Communicate

 Standards: 1.2 Presentation EXPRESS ANSWERS

Resources: Answers on Transparencies

Focus: Reading and writing using antonyms

Suggestions: Point out to students that they will need to change the adjectives to agree with the nouns they are describing.

Answers:
1. muertos
2. subir
3. comenzar
4. dormidos
5. de prisa
6. se murieron

 *Standards:* 1.1, 1.3 Presentation EXPRESS ANSWERS

Resources: Teacher's Resource Book: GramActiva BLM, p. 19; Answers on Transparencies

Focus: Writing and speaking about natural disasters

Recycle: Nouns, time references

Suggestions: First, have students identify the four drawings and enter the information on their charts. Then, have the class brainstorm a list of places where each disaster has taken place and when each happened. Write their ideas on the board and allow students to choose from the list. Encourage students to fill in the *Destrucción* section of the chart based on what they know about each type of disaster.

Answers:
Step 1 will include:
1. las tormentas (de lluvia)
2. las inundaciones
3. los terremotos
4. los huracanes
Step 2 answers will vary.

Teaching with Photos

Suggestions: Have students write a short newspaper article to accompany the photo. Ask them to answer the *Who? What? When? Where? Why?* and *How?* questions. Encourage them to add as many details as possible to make their articles more interesting.

246

 Leer/Escribir

Antónimos

Lee las frases y complétalas con el antónimo de la palabra señalada. Escoge el antónimo del recuadro y escríbelo en la forma correcta según la frase.

comenzar	muerto
de prisa	se murieron
dormido	subir

1. Sus peces no están *vivos*, están ___.
2. ¿Qué vas a hacer, ___ o *bajar* la escalera?

Estrategia

Using antonyms
Learning vocabulary through antonyms, or words of opposite meaning, can be helpful, especially in recalling the meanings of words.

3. No puede *terminar* el trabajo porque primero tiene que ___ el trabajo.
4. Los gatos no están *despiertos*. Están ___.
5. La señorita no está caminando *lentamente*. Está caminando ___.
6. En el artículo dice que tres personas *nacieron* y tres personas ___ en el hospital ayer.

  **Escribir/Hablar**

Los desastres naturales

① Mira los dibujos de los desastres naturales. Copia la tabla, escribe el nombre de los desastres y completa la información en las otras columnas. Puedes buscar información en la Red o usar tu imaginación.

Un incendio en España, 2000

Desastre	Lugar	Destrucción	Cuándo ocurrió
los incendios forestales	Colorado	árboles, animales, casas	hace dos años

1. 2. 3. 4.

② Usa la tabla para hablar con otro(a) estudiante sobre los desastres naturales.

Modelo
A — *¿Dónde ocurren frecuentemente los incendios forestales?*
B — *Creo que ocurren en Colorado.*
A — *¿Los incendios forestales destruyen* mucho?*
B — *Sí, desafortunadamente destruyen árboles, animales y a veces casas. Hace dos años hubo incendios forestales grandes en Colorado.*

*In the present tense, *destruir* adds *y* to all forms except *nosotros* and *vosotros: destruyo, destruyes, destruye, destruimos, destruís, destruyen.*

246 doscientos cuarenta y seis
Tema 5 • En las noticias

Differentiated Instruction
Solutions for All Learners

Advanced Learners
Have students research one of the disasters in *Actividad* 9 and present a detailed oral report to the class. Have them print pictures from the Internet or bring in other pictures to aid in their presentations. You may want to provide them with a rubric for their oral presentations.

Students with Learning Difficulties
Before assigning *Actividad* 10, remind students to use the preterite when sequencing events that have already occurred. List the verbs in the word bank on the board. Have students provide the third person singular and plural forms of each verb and allow them to use the list for Step 1.

Actividad 10

Escribir/Hablar/GramActiva

Juego

1 Escoge verbos del recuadro u otros verbos y escribe tres series de acciones en orden lógico, diciendo qué ocurrió primero y qué ocurrió después.

apagar	gritar	rescatar
bajar	investigar	salvar
comenzar (a)	ocurrir	subir
escaparse	quemarse	tratar de

2 Trabaja con tres estudiantes. Lee la primera frase de una de las series. Los estudiantes tienen que adivinar (guess) lo que pasó después. Si la primera persona adivina lo que pasó, gana cinco puntos. Si no puede, le toca el turno a la segunda persona. Si esta persona adivina correctamente, gana tres puntos. Si la tercera persona adivina correctamente, gana sólo un punto. Si nadie adivina correctamente, la persona que escribió la serie gana cinco puntos.

Estrategia
Sequencing of events
Putting events in a sequence helps others to understand what happened. Common expressions used to order events are *primero, luego,* and *después.*

Modelo

Primero los bomberos subieron la escalera. Luego entraron por la ventana de la casa.

Modelo

A — *Primero los bomberos subieron la escalera. ¿Qué ocurrió luego?*
B — *¿Los bomberos apagaron el incendio?*
A — *No. Lo siento. María, ¿qué ocurrió luego?*
C — *¿Entraron por la ventana?*
A — *Sí. Muy bien. Tres puntos para ti.*

Actividad 11

Escribir/Hablar

Y tú, ¿qué dices?

1. Para ti, ¿quién es un héroe o una heroína? ¿Cómo es esta persona? ¿Qué hace o hizo?

2. Mira un periódico de tu comunidad. ¿Hay información sobre algún incendio o explosión? Descríbelo.

3. ¿Qué tipo de desastres naturales afecta tu comunidad o región? ¿Qué hacen Uds. para protegerse (protect yourselves)?

 **Fondo cultural**

Los volcanes representan una amenaza (threat) para muchas comunidades de América Latina y el Caribe. En el siglo XX, de todas las personas que murieron a causa de erupciones volcánicas, el 76 por ciento murieron en esta región. El Reventador, en el Ecuador, es un volcán muy activo. El 3 de noviembre del 2002, el Reventador entró en erupción, cubriendo (covering) la capital ecuatoriana con cenizas (ashes). En 2005, hubo erupciones volcánicas en los siguientes volcanes de la región: Fuego, en Guatemala; Galeras, en Colombia; y Colima, en México.

• ¿Hay volcanes activos o dormidos cerca de tu comunidad? ¿Qué desastres naturales afectan a tu comunidad de la misma manera (in the same way) que la explosión del Reventador afectó a la ciudad de Quito? Descríbelos.

Limpiando la ciudad después de la erupción del volcán Reventador en Quito, Ecuador

doscientos cuarenta y siete 247
Capítulo 5A

Enrich Your Teaching
Resources for All Teachers

Culture Note
El Reventador is an 11,775-foot volcano located 60 miles northeast of Quito, Ecuador. The eruption of 2002 produced a 10-mile-high sulfuric cloud, causing health problems and the closure of schools and the airport. In addition to ash covering everything, burning rock rained down on the city. The tremors that followed shook the city of Quito.

Teacher-to-Teacher
Ask students to research volcanic activity in Spanish-speaking countries. To encourage variety, assign a different volcano to each group. Have them make a presentation on how the eruption affected the local community and what the people did to protect themselves. Encourage students to make a model of their volcanoes.

 Standards: 1.1, 1.3

Actividad 10

Focus: Using vocabulary in chronological order to talk about events

Suggestions: Ask students to draw a scene that illustrates their three sentences as well as various other actions. Tell them to show their pictures to help their group make their guesses. Have students prepare a scorecard to use for Step 2.

Answers will vary.

 Standards: 1.3

Actividad 11

Focus: Writing and speaking about local disasters and heroes

Suggestions: Give students newspapers or magazines. Have them base answers for items 2 and 3 on articles they read.

Answers will vary.

 *Standards:* 1.2, 3.1

Fondo cultural

Suggestions: Point out that **Reventador** means "exploder" in Spanish. Ask students why they think the men in the photo are wearing masks and sweeping the street.

Answers will vary.

Theme Project
Give students copies of the Theme Project outline and rubric from the *Teacher's Resource Book.* Explain the task to them, and have them perform Step 1. (For more information, see p. 236-a.)

Additional Resources
• WAV Wbk.: Audio Act. 6, p. 92
• Teacher's Resource Book Audio Script, p. 8, Communicative Activity BLM, pp. 14–15
• Audio Program: Track 8

 ### Assessment
• Prueba 5A-2: Vocab. Production, pp. 127–128

5A Practice and Communicate

Gramática

Core Instruction

Resources: Teacher's Resource Book: Video Script, p. 11; Video Program: Cap. 5A

Suggestions: You may want to play the *GramActiva* Video as an introduction or to reinforce your own presentation of these additional uses of the imperfect tense.

Point out that just as **hay** doesn't change in the present tense, **había** and **hubo** do not change when they mean "there was, there were."

Cut out photos from magazines that depict different weather events and different times of the day. Read descriptions to students and have them choose the picture you are describing. Distribute the remaining photos and have students work in groups to describe the pictures, using the imperfect.

Standards: 1.1

Resources: Answers on Transparencies

Focus: Speaking about what time of day a weather condition occurred

Recycle: Telling time

Suggestions: Review telling time with students. Point out that if they are telling a time that begins with **una,** as in item 4, they need to use the singular form of **ser.**

Answers:
Student A:

1. ¿Qué hora era cuando comenzó la tormenta de lluvia?
2. ¿ . . . la inundación?
3. ¿ . . . el incendio?
4. ¿ . . . el terremoto?
5. ¿ . . . la explosión?
6. ¿ . . . el huracán?

Student B:

1. Eran las seis de la tarde cuando comenzó.
2. Eran las cuatro y media de la tarde . . . .
3. Eran las dos y quince de la tarde . . . .
4. Era la una de la tarde . . . .
5. Eran las ocho menos cuarto de la noche . . . .
6. Eran las once menos diez de la noche . . . .

Gramática

Preterite and imperfect: other uses

Había and *hubo* are forms of *haber* and both mean "there was, there were." *Había* is used to describe a situation that existed in the past, while *hubo* is used to say that an event took place.

Había mucho humo en el apartamento.

Hubo un terremoto ayer a las seis de la mañana.

The preterite and imperfect tenses may both be used in a single sentence.

Use the imperfect:	Use the preterite:
• to tell what day or time it was **Eran** las cinco de la mañana cuando…	• when something happened …**empezó** a llover.
• to tell what the weather was like **Llovía** mucho cuando…	• for actions completed in the past …**salimos** de la fiesta.
• to describe the physical, mental, and emotional states of a person or thing Mucha gente **quería** ayudar cuando…	• to talk about an event …el incendio **destruyó** la casa.

These verbs are often used in the imperfect to describe states of being:

estar (triste, contento, cansado)   pensar
parecer (cansado, mal)   querer
sentirse (bien, enfermo)   saber
tener (calor, frío, hambre, sed, sueño)

¿Recuerdas?

You already know how to use the imperfect tense together with the preterite to describe a situation that existed when something else happened.

• Nadie **estaba** en la casa cuando los bomberos **entraron.**

GramActiva VIDEO

Want more help with other uses of the imperfect tense? Watch the **GramActiva** video.

Ayer, llovía.

  Hablar

¿Qué hora era?

¿Qué hora era cuando estas condiciones ocurrieron?

También se dice . . .

el **terremoto** = el sismo *(muchos países)*

4:00 P.M.

Modelo
A —¿*Qué hora era cuando comenzó la tormenta de nieve?*
B —*Eran las cuatro de la tarde cuando comenzó.*

6:00 P.M.
1.

4:30 P.M.
2.

2:15 P.M.
3.

1:00 P.M.
4.

7:45 P.M.
5.

10:50 P.M.
6.

248 doscientos cuarenta y ocho
Tema 5 • En las noticias

Differentiated Instruction
Solutions for All Learners

Heritage Language Learners

Students may use **habían** instead of **había.** While this is sometimes considered a regional variant and is commonly heard, it is not grammatically correct. Point out that just as they use only the form **hay** in the present tense to say "there was" or "there were," they should use only **había** or **hubo.**

Multiple Intelligences

Intrapersonal/Introspective: Have students describe an experience they had in which everything went wrong. Tell them to set the scene by using the imperfect and include descriptions of time, weather, and people. Remind them to use the preterite when writing about completed action. Have students illustrate their stories.

sus primos, Anita y Pepe

¡FELIZ CUMPLEAÑOS!

6:30

sus tíos

Isabel

su mamá

su papá

su hermana, Alejandra

su abuela

su primo, Federico

   **Observar/Hablar/Escribir**

El cumpleaños desastroso

Los padres de Isabel planearon una fiesta de sorpresa para su cumpleaños, pero ella llegó tarde. Con otro(a) estudiante, describan la situación usando el imperfecto de las expresiones del recuadro.

Modelo

Era el cumpleaños de Isabel. Cuando ella llegó a casa, sus parientes ya estaban allí.

estar dormido	pensar que
estar furioso	querer salir
haber	tener hambre
ir a	tener sed
llegar	tener sueño
llover	**¡Respuesta personal!**
parecer cansado	

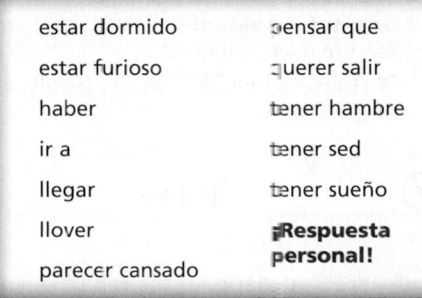

Escribir/Hablar

Y tú, ¿qué dices?

1. ¿Qué hora era cuando te despertaste hoy? ¿Tenías mucho sueño cuando te levantaste?

2. ¿Qué tiempo hacía cuando saliste de casa? ¿Alguien estaba todavía en tu casa cuando saliste?

3. ¿Qué hora era cuando llegaste a la escuela? ¿Ya había muchos estudiantes en la escuela?

4. ¿Cómo estabas cuando comenzaste a estudiar o a trabajar en tu primera clase?

Más práctica

- Practice Workbook, p. 97: 5A-5
- WAV Wbk.: Writing, p. 95
- Guided Practice: Grammar Acts. pp. 175–177
- *Real.* para hispanohablantes, pp. 174–177

Go Online PHSchool.com
For: Imperfect Tense
Web Code: jdd-0504

doscientos cuarenta y nueve **249**
Capítulo 5A

 Standards: 1.1, 1.3

Actividad 13

Focus: Writing and speaking about a surprise birthday party

Recycle: Family members

Suggestions: Have students list the names of everyone in the picture. Next to each name, have them write several adjectives to describe how each person is feeling and one verb in the infinitive to describe what each is doing. Encourage students to use their lists to write their sentences.

Answers will vary.

Extension: Have students write sentences with other words from the box and illustrate their sentences.

 Standards: 1.1, 1.3

Actividad 14

Focus: Writing and speaking about personal activities

Recycle: Telling time; physical and mental states

Suggestions: Direct attention to the *¿Recuerdas?* on p. 248. Point out that the imperfect tense often sets the scene of an event in the past. Before they answer the questions, have students copy them on a sheet of paper and circle the information in each question that sets the scene.

Answers will vary.

 Pre-AP* Support

- **Activity:** Have students work in pairs sitting with their backs to each other. One student looks at the painting, *La tempestad,* on p. 238 and the other has a blank sheet of paper on the desk. Ask the student looking at the picture to describe it so the other student can draw. Have students share with the class which drawings they believe come closest to representing the actual painting.

- ***Pre-AP* Resource Book:*** Comprehensive guide to Pre-AP* communication skill development, pp. 9–17, 36–46

Additional Resources

- WAV Wbk.: Audio Act. 7, p. 92
- Teacher's Resource Book: Audio Script, pp. 8–9
- Audio Program: Track 9

✓ **Assessment**

- **ExamView** QuickTake Presenter Quiz on PresEXPRESS

- Prueba 5A-3: The imperfect tense: Other uses, p. 129

Enrich Your Teaching
Resources for All Teachers

Teacher-to-Teacher

Have students create a children's book based on the popular story by Judith Viorst, *Alexander and the Terrible, Horrible, No Good, Very Bad Day.* Have them title their story *Umberto y el día terrible, horrible.* Explain to them that nothing goes right for Umberto during this one day. Divide the story into sections: Introduction, Umberto in the morning, Umberto in the afternoon, Umberto in the evening, and a happy ending. Have students work in groups and assign each group a different section. Tell each group to write 2–4 pages and illustrate their section. When all groups have finished, compile the sections to form a complete story. Ask volunteers to read the story to the class.

 249

Gramática

GRAMMAR

Core Instruction

Resources: Teacher's Resource Book: Video Script, pp. 11–12; Video Program: Cap. 5A; Voc. and Gram. Transparency 96

Suggestions: You may want to present the *Gramática* in two parts: the present tense of **oír** and the preterite of the verbs **oír, leer, creer,** and **destruir.**

Direct attention to the *¿Recuerdas?* If possible, play a tape of 5–10 common sounds such as a door being shut, a car, or a bird. Ask students what they hear. Have students respond using the present form of the verb **oír.**

Then have students tell what they *heard,* using the preterite.

Point out the spelling changes in the preterite of **creer** and **leer.** Explain that for -er and -ir verbs, the *i* changes to **y** between two vowels. Ask a volunteer to conjugate **destruir** on the board.

 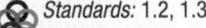 

Standards: 1.2, 1.3

AUDIO

Resources: Teacher's Resource Book: Audio Script, p. 9; Audio Program: Track 10; Answers on Transparencies

Focus: Listening and writing from dictation about an explosion

Suggestions: Play the *Audio CD* or read the script once without having students write. After the dictation, allow students time to revise their sentences. Tell them to focus on correct formation of the verbs.

Script and Answers:

Step 1:

[Male]: Cristina, ¿oíste de la explosión en la escuela?
[Female]: Sí, Pablo, oí algo en la radio pero no lo creí.
[Male]: Pues yo leí un artículo en el periódico. ¡Es increíble!
[Female]: Estoy de acuerdo. Dicen que destruyó el gimnasio y la cafetería.

Step 2:

1. Ocurrió en la escuela. Destruyó el gimnasio y la cafetería.
2. Cristina oyó de la explosión en la radio.
3. Leyó sobre la explosión en el periódico.
4. No, no la creyeron fácilmente.

Common Errors: Students may omit or add accent marks incorrectly. Suggest that they memorize the placement of accent marks along with the verb endings.

Gramática

The preterite of the verbs *oír, leer, creer* and *destruir*

In the preterite forms of *oír,* the *i* changes to *y* in the *Ud./él/ella* and *Uds./ellos/ellas* forms. There is also an accent mark over the *i* in all other forms. Here are the present and preterite forms of *oír:*

Present tense		Preterite tense	
oigo	oímos	oí	oímos
oyes	oís	oíste	oísteis
oye	oyen	oyó	oyeron

Creer and *leer* follow the same pattern in the preterite.

creer		leer	
creí	creímos	leí	leímos
creíste	creísteis	leíste	leísteis
creyó	creyeron	leyó	leyeron

—¿**Leíste** el artículo sobre el incendio en el periódico?

—No, **oí** el noticiero en la televisión.

¿Recuerdas?

You know the expression ¡*Oye!* ("Hey!"), which is used to get someone's attention. *Oye* is the affirmative *tú* command form of *oír.* It is formed from the present-tense *Ud. / él / ella* form of the verb.

- *Destruir* is conjugated like *oír, creer,* and *leer* in the preterite except that the *tú, nosotros,* and *vosotros* forms do not have accent marks.

¿**Destruiste** la carta que le mandó Raúl?

El incendio **destruyó** todos los muebles de la casa.

GramActiva VIDEO

Want more help with the preterite of *oír, leer,* and *creer?* Watch the **GramActiva** video.

 jdd-0588

Escuchar/Escribir

Escucha y escribe

1 En una hoja de papel, escribe los números del 1 al 4. Vas a oír una conversación sobre un desastre. Mientras la escuchas, escribe las frases.

2 Usa la conversación que escribiste en el Paso 1 y contesta las siguientes preguntas con frases completas.

1. ¿Dónde ocurrió la explosión? ¿Qué destruyó?
2. ¿Quién oyó de la explosión en la radio?
3. ¿Pablo leyó sobre la explosión en la Red o en el periódico?
4. ¿Los dos jóvenes creyeron la noticia fácilmente?

Differentiated Instruction

Solutions for All Learners

Students with Special Needs

Modify the first step of *Actividad 15* for hearing-impaired students. Provide a list of the four dictated sentences with blanks for students to fill in the correct verb forms. Have students write the completed sentences on a sheet of paper and continue with Step 2 of the directions.

Advanced Learners

Have students write a review of a disaster movie. Have them tell what they heard or read about the movie before seeing it, as well as what they thought the movie was going to be like and what their opinions were after seeing it. They should focus on using *oír, leer, creer,* and *destruir.*

Actividad 16

Leer/Escribir

¿Lo oíste?

La Reina Sofía de España visitó Nicaragua después del huracán. Para saber lo que José y Marcos dicen sobre el evento, completa la conversación con la forma apropiada del verbo *oír*.

José: Hoy __1.__ a la locutora del canal 5 decir que la Reina Sofía era muy simpática cuando visitó.

Marcos: Julieta, Liliana y yo también __2.__ lo mismo.

José: Recuerdo la visita muy bien. Yo __3.__ a muchas personas gritar: "¡Bienvenida!" Mamá y papá estaban con mi tío Juan y __4.__ a la reina decir cosas simpáticas.

Marcos: Mi tía Rocío __5.__ al presidente cuando le dijo a la Reina que el pueblo nicaragüense la saludaba.

José: Pero, ¿ __6.__ tú lo que dijo mi hermanito?

Marcos: Sí, __7.__ a tu hermanito cuando dijo que quería mucho a la Reina Sofía. ¡Qué gracioso tu hermanito!

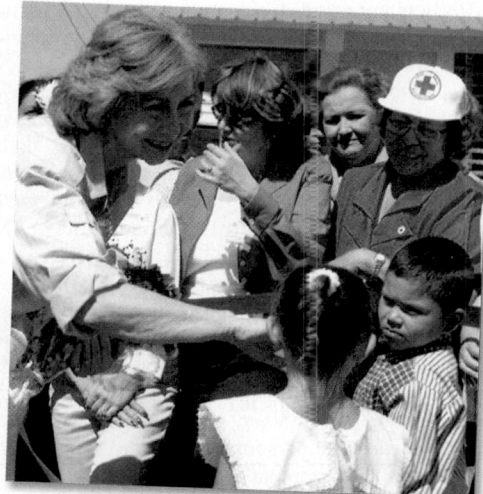

La Reina Sofía de España en Nicaragua después del huracán Mitch. Es una de las muchas oportunidades que tiene España para mantener un fuerte lazo de unión con las Américas.

Actividad 17

Escribir/Hablar

¿Qué leíste recientemente?

Habla con los estudiantes en tu clase sobre lo que leyeron recientemente.

1 En una hoja de papel, copia la tabla. En la primera línea, escribe lo que leíste tú, cuándo y cómo era.

2 Trabaja con tres estudiantes. Pregúntale a un(a) estudiante sobre lo que leyó. Este(a) estudiante contesta y los otros también deben decir lo que leyeron. Deben escribir toda la información en la tabla.

3 Cada estudiante debe usar la información en la tabla para escribir cinco frases sobre lo que leyeron los miembros del grupo y cómo eran las cosas que leyeron.

Persona	Lo que leyó	Cuándo	Descripción
yo	una revista sobre la moda	la semana pasada	fantástica

Modelo

A —Elena, ¿qué leíste tú?

B —Leí una revista sobre la moda la semana pasada. Era fantástica.

Actividad 16 *Standards:* 1.2

  Presentation EXPRESS ANSWERS

Resources: Answers on Transparencies

Focus: Using preterite forms of *oír*

Suggestions: Before students fill in the blanks, have them read the dialogue for comprehension. Have them identify the subject of each sentence before conjugating the verb.

Answers:

1. oí
2. oímos
3. oí
4. oyeron
5. oyó
6. oíste
7. oí

Actividad 17 *Standards:* 1.1, 1.3

Focus: Writing and talking about things you've read

Recycle: Time expressions, adjectives

Suggestions: Have students bring in newspaper articles, books, and magazines that they have recently read. Have them show their reading to the group while they describe what it is, when they read it, and what they thought about it.

Answers will vary.

Enrich Your Teaching
Resources for All Teachers

Culture Note

Queen Sofía of Spain serves as Honorary President of the *Centro Reina Sofía para el Estudio de la Violencia,* which is located in Valencia, Spain. The staff of this institution is dedicated to the study and prevention of violence against women and children. Queen Sofía is also a patron of the arts, especially of music. In addition, the Queen presides over the *Fundación Reina Sofía,* which is engaged primarily in worldwide humanitarian relief.

Internet Search

Keyword: Reina Sofía

251

Actividad 18 Leer/Escribir

El terremoto en Popayán

Completa la descripción de lo que ocurrió en 1983 en Popayán, Colombia, usando las formas apropiadas del pretérito o del imperfecto.

1. _(Ser)_ un día de primavera muy bonito en Popayán. **2.** _(Haber)_ muchísimas personas en la ciudad porque **3.** _(ser)_ Semana Santa.[1] Todos **4.** _(estar)_ muy alegres. De repente, **5.** _(haber)_ un terremoto de una magnitud de 5.5 en la Escala Richter que **6.** _(sacudir)_[2] la ciudad entera.[3] El terremoto **7.** _(destruir)_ el centro histórico de Popayán, donde **8.** _(haber)_ muchos edificios, iglesias y casas de arquitectura colonial. Muchas personas **9.** _(tratar de)_ salir del centro pero no **10.** _(escaparse)_. Después **11.** _(haber)_ tres incendios a causa del terremoto y una gran parte de la ciudad **12.** _(quemarse)_. Finalmente, los oficiales de la ciudad **13.** _(tener)_ que ordenar la evacuación de muchas familias. Por lo menos 120 personas se murieron en el desastre y **14.** _(haber)_ más de 1,000 personas heridas.

[1] Holy Week, the week between Palm Sunday and Easter [2] to shake [3] whole

DAÑOS EN COLOMBIA:
TERREMOTO GRADO 7 EN POPAYÁN

Una iglesia destruida por el terremoto en Popayán, Colombia

   **Actividad 19** Hablar

Un desastre natural

Con otro(a) estudiante, mira el cuadro de Botero, la foto de Popayán y la descripción del terremoto en la Actividad 18. Hablen de lo que ocurrió en Popayán y cómo la descripción, la foto y el cuadro enseñan la historia.

Modelo

En la descripción aprendemos que antes del terremoto había muchas personas en la ciudad . . . . En la foto vemos que el terremoto destruyó . . . . En el cuadro de Botero, vemos que eran las tres cuando . . . .

El pintor colombiano Fernando Botero pintó este cuadro, "Terremoto en Popayán", en 1999, 16 años después del terremoto.

Oil on canvas, 173 x 112 c. Museo Botero, Banco de la República de Colombia. Marlborough Gallery.

Actividad 18 Standards: 1.2

Presentation EXPRESS ANSWERS

Resources: Answers on Transparencies

Focus: Reading and writing about an earthquake; choosing preterite and imperfect

Suggestions: Have students make a two-column chart and label one column **pretérito** and the other **imperfecto.** Ask them to list the uses of the preterite and imperfect in the appropriate column. Allow students to use their charts to fill in the blanks.

Answers:
1. Era
2. Había
3. era
4. estaban
5. hubo
6. sacudió
7. destruyó
8. había
9. trataron de
10. se escaparon
11. hubo
12, se quemó
13. tuvieron
14. había

Common Errors: Students may conjugate **haber** in forms other than third person singular. Remind them to use only **hubo** or **había.**

Actividad 19 Standards: 1.1, 1.3, 2.2

Focus: Comparing images to discuss the effects of an earthquake

Suggestions: Before students begin, have them make a three-column chart labeled **foto, cuadro,** and **artículo.** Have them make brief notes in each column based on the information they can gather from each source. Let them use their notes as they converse.

Answers will vary.

Differentiated Instruction
Solutions for All Learners

Students with Learning Difficulties
Make a transparency with the questions from _Actividad_ 20. Highlight the key words. Direct attention to the subheadings in the reading, and ask students to predict where the pertinent information will be included for each question.

Heritage Language Learners
Students may know instinctively when to use the preterite and imperfect tenses, but may have difficulty explaining their uses. To help students verbalize the uses, ask them to explain each of their choices in _Actividad_ 18.

Actividad 20 — Leer/Hablar

En caso de un incendio . . .

Un hotel de México da información a las personas que pasan tiempo con ellos sobre cómo sobrevivir *(survive)* un incendio que puede ocurrir en el hotel. Lee la información y contesta las preguntas con otro(a) estudiante.

Estrategia

Anticipating text
Many times you can predict the kind of information you will find in a piece of text. What information would you expect to find in your hotel about how to survive a fire? Think about Spanish words that are likely to be used.

CÓMO SOBREVIVIR UN INCENDIO EN EL HOTEL

Cuando entre en el hotel, Ud. debe . . .

- **encontrar las salidas** del hotel.
- **buscar las salidas** y escaleras para incendios en el piso donde está su cuarto.
- **mirar las ventanas** de su cuarto. ¿Se abren? ¿Es posible escaparse por la ventana?

Si el incendio comienza en su cuarto, Ud. debe . . .

080

- **llamar** inmediatamente a la operadora de teléfono.
- **tratar de apagarlo.** Si no lo puede hacer, debe salir de su cuarto, cerrar la puerta y sonar[1] la alarma.

Si Ud. está en su cuarto y oye la alarma, debe . . .

- **tocar[2] la puerta** de su cuarto. Si no está caliente,[3] la puede abrir muy despacio, salir y cerrar la puerta. Si la puerta está caliente, no debe abrirla. Si es posible, debe salir por la ventana.

- **caminar a la salida** que está más cerca. Si hay mucho humo, debe gatear[4] por el corredor.[5] Si el humo esta denso en los pisos de abajo, debe subir a un piso más alto o al techo.[6] Es importante recordar que NUNCA se debe usar el elevador cuando hay un incendio.

Ud. debe recordar que muy pocas personas se queman en los incendios. La mayoría[7] de los problemas ocurren a causa del humo y del pánico. El pánico es usualmente el resultado de no saber qué hacer.

[1]sound [2]touch [3]hot [4]crawl [5]hallway [6]roof [7]majority

1. ¿Qué debes hacer primero cuando entras en el hotel?
2. ¿Debes usar el elevador o las escaleras en caso de un incendio?
3. ¿Cuáles son las cosas más importantes que debes hacer si hay un incendio en tu cuarto?
4. ¿Qué debes hacer si estás en tu cuarto y oyes la alarma?
5. ¿Cuándo es importante gatear por el corredor o por el cuarto?
6. ¿Cuáles son las causas de la mayoría de las muertes en un incendio?

Actividad 21 — Escribir/Hablar

Y tú, ¿qué dices?

¿Oíste o leíste algo recientemente sobre un incendio, una explosión o un desastre natural? Escribe un párrafo para describirlo.

- ¿Cómo lo oíste o leíste?
- ¿Qué día / hora era cuando ocurrió/comenzó?
- ¿Dónde estabas tú cuándo ocurrió?
- ¿Había personas allí cuando ocurrió?
- ¿Destruyó muchos edificios y otras cosas?
- ¿Alguien trató de ayudar en la situación?

doscientos cincuenta y tres 253
Capítulo 5A

Practice and Communicate

 5A

Actividad 20 — *Standards:* 1.2, 2.1   Pre-AP*

Resources: Voc. and Gram. Transparency 97; Answers on Transparencies

Focus: Reading comprehension of safety precautions

Suggestions: Direct attention to the *Estrategia.* Have students brainstorm a list of words. Then have them scan the text, reading only the words in boldface. Ask students why they think it would be helpful to set important information in boldface in this kind of informational material. Remind students to look at pictures for clues and to use cognates to help with unfamiliar vocabulary.

Answers:
1. Debes encontrar las salidas y las escaleras y mirar si las ventanas se abren.
2. Debes usar las escaleras.
3. Debes llamar a la operadora y tratar de apagar el incendio.
4. Tocar la puerta para saber si está caliente. Si no está caliente, debes caminar o gatear a la salida.
5. Debes gatear si hay mucho humo.
6. El humo y el pánico.

Actividad 21 — *Standards:* 1.3

Focus: Writing and speaking about a disaster

Suggestions: In case students aren't aware of events, and to encourage variety, assign each student a specific event that appeared in a newspaper article. Have them list the main ideas of what they read. Remind them to arrange events in chronological order.

Answers will vary.

Block Schedule

Have students create a pamphlet for guests at a hotel on how to survive an earthquake. Students can use the model in *Actividad* 20 as a starting point. Have students use the Internet to research safety precautions one should take when staying in an earthquake zone. Ask students to illustrate their pamphlets and to highlight important information so it can be read quickly in an emergency.

 Enrich Your Teaching
Resources for All Teachers

Culture Note

Colombia has been the scene of terrible natural disasters, including heavy rain and flooding, earthquakes, mudslides, and volcanic eruptions. This is due in part to the fact that it is located near the equator, its coastal regions are flat, and its inland territory includes the northern Andes. Cold air from the mountains combines with warm air from the coast to form volatile weather patterns. A 1985 volcanic eruption killed more than 20,000 people, and a major earthquake occurred there in 1999.

Internet Search
Keywords:

Colombia, natural disasters

253

Pronunciación

Core Instruction

 Standards: 1.2, 4.1

Resources: Teacher's Resource Book: Audio Script, p. 9; Audio Program: Track 11

Suggestions: Write the word *hacia* on the board and have students pronounce the diphthong. Then add an accent mark to make the word *hacía* and have students pronounce it aloud. Have them repeat the two words until they correctly differentiate between the two. Emphasize the importance of pronouncing diphthongs correctly by pointing out the difference in meaning of the two words *(toward* vs. *he / she / you used to make / do).*

  Standards: 1.2, 3.1

Resources: Answers on Transparencies

Focus: Reading comprehension; cross-curricular connection to geography

Suggestions: Have students scan the text and make a list of cognates. Ask if they can determine the meaning of *ciclones* and *tifones.* Have students study the map and key before answering the questions.

Answers:
1. Hay huracanes en las Américas y en el Caribe. Hay tifones y ciclones en India y en Asia. Son regiones donde hay océanos con aguas tropicales.
2. En los Estados Unidos, los huracanes ocurren en el Golfo de México y en el Atlántico.

Block Schedule

Have students work on a poster that depicts the Ring of Fire, a series of volcanic arcs and oceanic trenches around the Pacific Ocean. Have them locate major active volcanoes in different Central and South American countries. Ask them to explain what impact the volcanoes might have on Central and South America. Students might mention floods, fires, and injuries or fatalities associated with these disasters.

Pronunciación

Accent marks to separate diphthongs

jdd-0588

Remember that a single syllable called a diphthong occurs when *i* or *u* appear together or in combination with *a, e,* or *o.* Listen to and say these words:

causa	valiente	oigo
destruir	muerto	hacia

We use a written accent when the vowels that form what would otherwise be a diphthong need to be pronounced separately. Listen to and say these words:

oí	leíste	creímos
sabía	país	envío

Refrán

Explica lo que quiere decir este refrán.

Consejo* no pedido, consejo mal oído.

*advice

  Pensar/Leer/Escribir/Hablar

Conexiones La geografía

Hay tempestades[1] violentas de lluvia y vientos fuertes en varias regiones del mundo. Estas tempestades salen de un sistema de baja presión que se encuentra encima de aguas tropicales donde hay una tempestad y vientos fuertes en forma de torbellino.[2] Las tempestades con vientos de más de 39 millas por hora se llaman tormentas tropicales. Cuando los vientos superan[3] 74 millas por hora, se llaman huracán, tifón o ciclón, según la región geográfica.

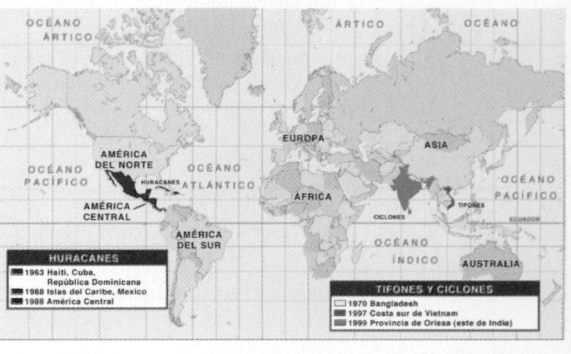

[1]storms [2]whirlwind [3]exceed

1. ¿En qué parte del mundo hay huracanes? ¿Dónde hay tifones y ciclones? ¿Qué tienen en común estas regiones?

2. ¿En qué región geográfica ocurren los huracanes en los Estados Unidos? ¿Qué estados son afectados? Compara su posición geográfica con la de las tempestades en el mapa.

Differentiated Instruction
Solutions for All Learners

Students with Special Needs

Modify *Actividad 23* for visually impaired students. Ask advanced learners to dictate detailed descriptions of the three illustrations in the present tense. Have visually-impaired students record phrases in the imperfect and preterite tenses for Step 1 according to the descriptions they hear. Have them refer to their recordings to complete Step 2.

Multiple Intelligences

Naturalist: Have students work in groups to present an extensive weather report about a hurricane, cyclone, or typhoon in a Spanish-speaking country. Encourage them to be creative. Ask them to include information on the location of the storm, its dangers, and what people in the community should do to protect themselves.

Actividad 23 Observar/Hablar/Escribir

Un bombero valiente

Mira la serie de dibujos. Trabaja con otro(a) estudiante para hablar de esta situación.

1 Primero hagan una lista de todas las partes del cuento que van a escribir usando el imperfecto. Luego hagan una lista de las acciones que van a escribir usando el pretérito.

imperfecto	pretérito
el gatito estaba en el árbol	los bomberos llegaron en su camión

2 Escriban lo que ocurrió. Usen su imaginación e incluyan detalles adicionales para hacer su cuento más interesante.

Más práctica

- Practice Workbook, pp. 98–99: 5A-6, 5A-7
- WAV Wbk.: Writing, p. 96
- Guided Practice: Grammar Acts., p. 178
- *Real.* para hispanohablantes, pp. 178–179

Go Online PHSchool.com
For: *Oír, Leer, Creer,* and *Destruir*
Web Code: jdd-0505

El español en la comunidad

Hay muchas oportunidades para ayudar a los demás en tu comunidad o en otros países. El grupo *Virtual Explorers* publica historias de "héroes" jóvenes en los Estados Unidos. Lisa es una heroína que quería ayudar a las víctimas del huracán Mitch. Vendió su colección de 100 *Beanie Babies* en una subasta (*auction*) y ganó miles de dólares que luego donó (*donated*) al esfuerzo humanitario (*relief effort*) para el huracán.

- ¿Conoces a alguien que haya ayudado (*has helped*) en un esfuerzo humanitario? ¿Hay oportunidades en tu comunidad para ayudar a personas después de algún desastre?

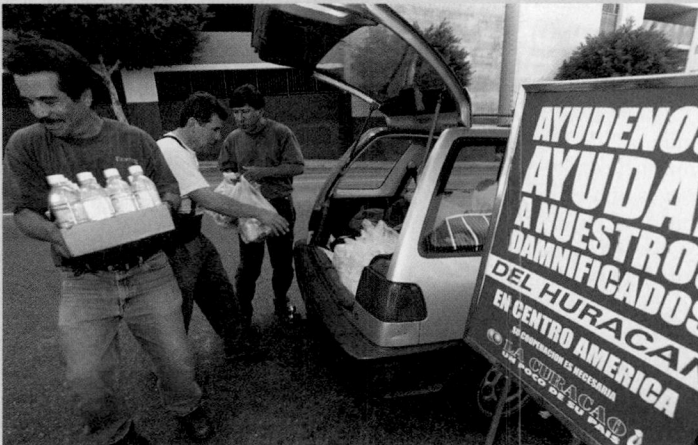

doscientos cincuenta y cinco **255**
Capítulo 5A

Actividad 23 **Standards:** 1.1, 1.3

Focus: Writing a story about a rescued cat
Suggestions: Remind students that descriptions of time, weather, and how characters are feeling will require the imperfect tense. Have students start their stories with an introductory sentence and end with a conclusion.
Answers will vary.

El español en la comunidad
Core Instruction

Standards: 1.2, 3.1

Suggestions: Have students brainstorm a list of adjectives they associate with a hero. Whom do they consider a hero? Why? Do they know of anyone in their community who is a hero?
Answers will vary.

Theme Project
Students can perform Step 2 at this point. Be sure they understand your corrections. (For more information, see p. 236-a.)

Additional Resources
- WAV Wbk.: Audio Act. 8–9, p. 93
- Teacher's Resource Book: Audio Script, pp. 9–10
- Audio Program: Tracks 12–13

✓ **Assessment**
- **ExamView** QuickTake Presenter Quiz on PresEXPRESS
- Prueba 5A-4: The preterite of the verbs *oír, leer, creer,* and *destruir*, p. 130

Enrich Your Teaching
Resources for All Teachers

Culture Note
The International Red Cross (*la Cruz Roja*) has a history of distributing emergency aid in Spanish-speaking countries in the aftermath of natural disasters. For instance, in the spring of 2003, they provided assistance to the residents of Chima, Bolivia, which was partially buried in a landslide. They also helped out in Perú during the devastating floods in 2003.

Teacher-to-Teacher
Have students create three original drawings similar to those in *Actividad 23*, but based on a natural disaster. Ask them to write a description of the drawings using the preterite and imperfect. Have them read their stories to a partner without showing their drawings. Have students draw what their partner describes and compare their pictures.

Lectura

Core Instruction

Standards: 1.2, 3.1

Resources: Voc. and Gram. Transparencies: Map 16

Focus: Reading comprehension of an article about an earthquake in Valdivia, Chile

Suggestions:

Pre-reading: Point out the *Estrategia* and have students list information that they expect to find. To help increase prior knowledge, discuss a recent earthquake that students may have read about. Before beginning the reading, review their lists with them.

Reading: After each paragraph, encourage students to refer to their lists of predictions, and add new information from the article that they did not predict.

Post-reading: Ask students if there was any information in the article that they did not expect to see. If so, what surprised them? Was there any information they expected to see but did not find? After reviewing the main ideas, have students complete the *¿Comprendiste?* questions.

 **Bellringer Review**

Write these words on the board:

un huracán	*un terremoto*
un incendio	*una inundación*

As a class, briefly brainstorm what might be consequences of these types of disasters.

(Ex. *Un huracán—no tener electricidad*)

Additional Resources

Student Resource: Guided Practice: Lectura, p. 179

¡Adelante!

Lectura

Lectura

 **Objectives**

- **Read about an earthquake in Chile**
- **Understand legends**
- **Interview a classmate about a disaster**
- **Watch *En busca de la verdad*, Episodio 5**

Después del terremoto, Valdivia, Chile

Estrategia

Using prior knowledge
Think about articles you've read about earthquakes and natural disasters. Make a list of four pieces of information you might find. After you've read the article below, refer to your list to see if the information was there.

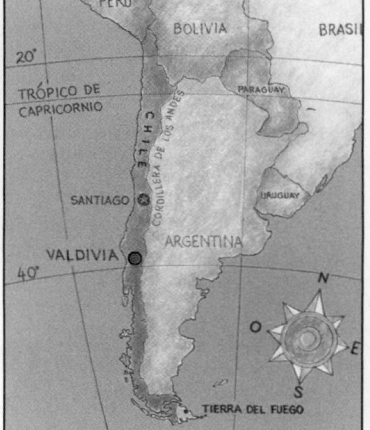

Desastre en Valdivia, Chile

Tres desastres: Dos terremotos y después un tsunami

VALDIVIA, Chile A las seis y dos minutos de la mañana, el 21 de mayo de 1960, una gran parte del país sintió el primer terremoto. El próximo día, el 22 de mayo a las tres y diez de la tarde, otro terremoto más intenso, con epicentro cerca de la ciudad de Valdivia, ocurrió. El segundo y más famoso de los terremotos registró un récord de 9.5 en la Escala Richter. Simplemente fue el terremoto de más intensidad jamás[1] registrado.

- Aproximadamente 2,000 personas murieron (de 4,000 a 5,000 en toda la región); 3,000 resultaron heridas y 2,000,000 perdieron[2] sus hogares.[3]

- Los ríos cambiaron[4] su curso. Nuevos lagos nacieron. Las montañas se movieron. La geografía cambió visiblemente.

LA ESCALA RICHTER	
Representa la energía sísmica liberada en cada terremoto y se basa en el registro sismográfico.	
MAGNITUD EN LA ESCALA RICHTER	**EFECTOS DEL TERREMOTO**
Menos de 3.5	Generalmente no se siente, pero es registrado.
3.5–5.4	A menudo se siente, pero sólo causa daños[5] menores.
5.5–6.0	Ocasiona daños a edificios.
6.1–6.9	Puede ocasionar daños graves en áreas donde vive mucha gente.
7.0–7.9	Terremoto mayor. Causa graves daños.
8 o mayor	Gran terremoto. Destrucción total de comunidades cercanas.

[1]ever [2]lost [3]homes [4]changed [5]damages

256 doscientos cincuenta y seis
Tema 5 • En las noticias

Differentiated Instruction
Solutions for All Learners

Students with Special Needs

Have students who have problems sequencing and organizing detailed information create an outline of the reading before completing the *¿Comprendiste?* questions. Tell them to read the questions first to help them determine what information to include in their outlines.

Students with Learning Difficulties

To help students activate prior knowledge, write these words on the board and ask for definitions: **terremoto, intensidad, epicentro, magnitud,** and **tsunami.** Direct attention to the photo on p. 256 and ask students if they have seen similar aftermath scenes from other earthquakes. Ask them to explain.

Revisando los daños, Valdivia, Chile

Unos minutos después del desastroso terremoto, llegó un tsunami que destruyó lo poco que quedaba en la ciudad y en las pequeñas comunidades. La gran ola[6] de agua se levantó destruyendo a su paso casas, animales, puentes, botes y, por supuesto, muchas vidas humanas. Algunos barcos fueron a quedar a kilómetros del mar, río arriba. Como consecuencia del sismo, se originaron tsunamis que llegaron a las costas del Japón, Hawai, las Islas Filipinas y la costa oeste de los Estados Unidos.

Un tsunami es una ola o serie de olas de agua producida después de ser empujada[7] violentamente. Los terremotos pueden causar tsunamis. Estos tsunamis ocurren de 10 a 20 minutos después del terremoto. El 26 de diciembre de 2004, un terremoto de magnitud 9.0, en Sumatra, causó un tsunami en Indonesia y Tailandia. La destrucción fue terrible. Hubo más de 250,000 víctimas.

¿Qué debes hacer durante un terremoto?

Dentro de un edificio

- Mantener la calma y calmar a los demás
- Mantenerse lejos de ventanas, cristales, cuadros, chimeneas y objetos que puedan caerse[8]
- Protegerse[9] debajo de los dinteles de las puertas[10] o de algún mueble sólido, como mesas, escritorios o camas; cualquier protección es mejor que ninguna
- No utilizar los elevadores

Fuera de un edificio

- Mantenerse lejos de los edificios altos, postes de energía eléctrica y otros objetos que puedan derrumbarse[11]
- Ir a un lugar abierto

En un coche

- Parar el coche y quedarse dentro del vehículo, lejos de puentes, postes de energía eléctrica y edificios dañados o zonas de desprendimientos[12]

[6]wave [7]pushed [8]fall [9]Protect yourself [10]door jams [11]collapse [12]landslides

¿Comprendiste?

1. Pon en orden de ocurrencia los tres desastres que sufrió Valdivia, Chile.

2. ¿Qué importancia tiene el segundo terremoto en los estudios sismográficos?

3. Si se registra un terremoto de 6.5 en la Escala Richter, ¿qué daños van a ocurrir?

4. ¿Cuál es una causa de los tsunamis?

5. ¿Qué debes hacer si ocurre un terremoto y estás en un coche?

Más práctica

- WAV Wbk.: Writing, p. 97
- Guided Practice: *Lectura*, p. 179
- *Real.* para hispanohablantes, pp. 178–181

Go Online PHSchool.com **For:** Internet Activity **Web Code:** jdd-0506

 **Fondo cultural**

En caso de terremoto En Chile hay un Plan Integral de Seguridad Escolar para responder ante emergencias como terremotos, incendios, inundaciones o accidentes. Este plan nacional se aplica a todas las escuelas del país. Cada escuela tiene que crear un plan que incluye a los profesores, estudiantes y trabajadores del colegio. También debe incorporar a personal especializado en emergencias como los bomberos, la Guardia Civil y la Cruz Roja. La Oficina Nacional de Emergencias quiere establecer en cada escuela una cultura de seguridad (*safety*) y prevención.

- Piensa en tu escuela. ¿Hay un plan para emergencias? ¿Qué hacen en caso de incendios, huracanes o tornados?

¿Comprendiste?

 *Standards:* 1.2

Resources: Answers on Transparencies

Focus: Verifying reading comprehension

Suggestions: Point out key words in each question that will help students determine the answer. Encourage students to use any notes that they took before and during the reading to help them answer the questions.

Answers:

1. El 21 de mayo de 1960, a las seis de la mañana, Valdivia, Chile, sufrió el primer terremoto. El 22 de mayo de 1960, a las tres y diez de la tarde, sufrió otro terremoto más intenso. Unos minutos después, llegó un tsunami.

2. Fue el terremoto de más intensidad jamás registrado.

3. Un terremoto de 6.5 en la Escala Richter puede ocasionar daños graves en áreas donde vive mucha gente.

4. Un terremoto puede causar un tsunami.

5. Se debe parar el coche y quedarse dentro del vehículo lejos de puentes, postes de energía eléctrica, edificios dañados o zonas de desprendimientos.

 *Standards:* 1.2, 2.1, 2.2

Fondo cultural

Suggestions: Have students look around the room for emergency evacuation instructions. Have them compare safety preparedness in their school with the measures described in the paragraph.

Answers will vary.

 Pre-AP* Support

- **Activity:** As a post-reading activity, have students work in pairs, one reading the information on p. 256 and the other reading the information on p. 257. Then, have them write three multiple-choice questions for their section. Finally, have each partner show their questions to the other so that they may answer them.

- *Pre-AP* Resource Book:* Comprehensive guide to Pre-AP* reading skill development, pp. 18–24

For Further Reading

Student Resources: Realidades para hispanohablantes: Lectura 2, pp. 184–185; Lecturas para hispanohablantes 2: "Qué hacer frente a un huracán," pp. 62–63, "El costo de la vida," p. 86

Enrich Your Teaching
Resources for All Teachers

Culture Note

Chile, like California, has a long, low coastal region with high mountains located a relatively short distance inland. When mountains close to the coast of a continent are formed, fault lines occur. Earthquakes are common along these fault lines. There are as many as ten major fault lines in Chile. All of them run in an overall north–south direction.

Teacher-to-Teacher

Have students organize a fundraiser to raise money for victims of a natural disaster. Have them create posters that illustrate the devastating effects of the disaster to post in school. On the day of the fundraiser, have students use a table in the cafeteria as a collection center for their relief fund. Have them prepare pamphlets to distribute at their table.

La cultura en vivo
Core Instruction

 Standards: 1.2, 1.3, 2.1, 2.2, 3.1

Focus: Reading about legends that explain natural disasters

Suggestions: Point out the photos and explain to students that they will learn about legends related to volcanoes in both Mexico and Chile. Ask students to describe what they know about volcanoes.

Have students read the passage silently or call on volunteers to read it aloud. Have them summarize the legends in their own words.

Remind students that the legend that they write is fiction and can be about any natural phenomenon. After students make a rough draft, have them peer-edit each other's work before preparing a final copy.

Answers will vary.

Extension: Have students make final corrections to their legends and compile all of them into a storybook. Make copies of the book to distribute to students. Use the stories to practice reading comprehension.

Additional Resources

Student Resource: Realidades para hispanohablantes, p. 186

La cultura en vivo

Las leyendas

Las leyendas muchas veces personifican a los fenómenos naturales o tratan de resolver misterios de fenómenos naturales. De tal manera hay muchos volcanes en México, América Central y América del Sur que llevan nombres y características humanas. Los habitantes que vivían a su alrededor contaban leyendas para explicar el origen de estos volcanes y la relación que éstos tenían con el pueblo[1].

En Chile, el volcán Parinacota lanza humo cuando trata de comunicarse con Pomerape. Según la leyenda, los novios volcanes lloran y hablan con fuego y ceniza.

También hay leyendas universales que se cuentan en muchos lugares del mundo. Por ejemplo, en México hay una famosa leyenda sobre los volcanes Popocatépetl e Iztaccíhuatl que dice que eran dos enamorados, pero su amor fue prohibido. La misma leyenda también existe en Chile sobre los volcanes Parinacota y Pomerape. Según la leyenda había un príncipe y una princesa de diferentes tribus y se enamoraron. Pero su matrimonio fue prohibido y para evitar su unión, los dos tribus mataron a los novios. Esto entristeció[2] a la Naturaleza[3] que, como castigo[4], causó una inundación que destruyó a los dos pueblos. De la inundación se formaron dos lagos, el Chungará y el Cota-Cotani. Los dos novios fueron transformados en dos hermosos volcanes cercanos, Parinacota y Pomerape. Así, siempre están juntos.

¡Compruébalo! Escoge algún lugar cerca de tu comunidad como una montaña, un lago o una formación de rocas. Escribe un cuento que explica el origen de este lugar.

[1]people, village [2]saddened [3]Nature [4]punishment

Según la leyenda, debajo del lago Chungará (que aquí se ve frente al volcán Parinacota) había una vez un pueblo.

Differentiated Instruction
Solutions for All Learners

Multiple Intelligences

Visual/Spatial: Have students illustrate one of the legends in a cartoon. Have them include speech bubbles to better tell the story. Encourage them to use humor and creativity to go beyond the legend to depict what the volcanoes might have said after they were created.

Advanced Learners

Have students research one of the volcanoes mentioned in the reading. Ask them to find out when it erupted and what the consequences were. Encourage them to use vocabulary words for telling a story. Have them present the information before the reading to provide background knowledge for all students.

Presentación oral

Y ahora, un reportaje especial...

Task
You are the anchor for a local television station and you are preparing a special report about a fire that occurred in your town. Your partner is a reporter who is at the scene of the disaster. You will interview him or her about what happened.

1 **Prepare** You will role-play this conversation with a partner. Be sure to prepare for both roles. Here's how to prepare:

Locutor(a): Make a list of questions to ask the reporter. Think of questions like "who," "what," "when," "where," and "why." You might also ask how many people were injured or died.

Reportero(a): Be prepared to report on the fire. Think of the information you'll want to provide based on the news anchor's questions.

2 **Practice** Work in groups of four in which there are two reporters and two news anchors. Work together to practice different questions and different responses. Here's how you might start the report:

Locutor(a): *Buenos días, Juan. ¿Qué pasó?*

Reportero(a): *Hubo un incendio muy grande en un edificio de apartamentos. Cinco personas se murieron y había más de diez heridos.*

Continue the conversation using your notes. Be sure to speak clearly and make your interview sound as natural as possible.

3 **Present** You will be paired with another student, and your teacher will tell you which role to play. The news anchor begins the conversation. Listen to your partner's questions or responses and keep the report going.

4 **Evaluation** Your teacher may give you a rubric for how the presentation will be graded. You will probably be graded on:
- how well you complete the task
- how well you were understood
- your ability to keep the conversation going

Estrategia

Speaking from notes
When doing an interview or reporting back as a news reporter, it is important to have thought through important questions or have notes to provide accurate answers.

El Parque de Bombas de Ponce, en Puerto Rico, es un edificio muy famoso por su arquitectura original. Era la estación de bomberos y ahora es un museo que celebra los actos heroicos de los bomberos.

doscientos cincuenta y nueve 259
Capítulo 5A

Presentación oral
Core Instruction

Standards: 1.1, 1.3, 3.1

Focus: Reporting news about a fire through an on-the-scene interview

Suggestions: If possible, videotape a segment of a local news report that covers a fire. Point out to students that the details to include are names of the people involved, the exact location of the fire, the type of building, and the time of day. Remind students that in the final presentation they may not be paired with the same student with whom they practiced. Before they present their reports, have students go around the room to interview one another. Set a timer for a minute or two, and have students change partners when it goes off.

Teaching with Photos

Suggestions: Point out the photo of *El Parque de Bombas de Ponce,* and tell students that that this museum honors the heroic acts of firefighters. Ask students why they think firefighters are considered heroes. Record their ideas on the chalkboard, and suggest that they include some of these ideas in their report.

 Pre-AP* Support

- **Pre-AP* Resource Book:** Comprehensive guide to Pre-AP* speaking skill development, pp. 36–46

Portfolio

Record students' oral presentations on cassette or videotape to be included in their portfolios.

Additional Resources

Student Resources: Realidades para hispanohablantes, p. 187; Guided Practice: Presentación oral, p. 180

✓ Assessment

- Assessment Program, Rubrics, p. T30

1. Give students a copy of the rubric for this task.

2. Model a top-scoring presentation using a current news event. After assessing students, help individuals understand how their presentations could be improved.

259

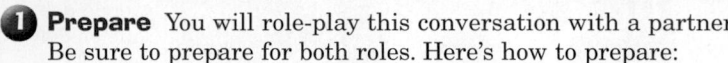

Enrich Your Teaching
Resources for All Teachers

RUBRIC	Score 1	Score 3	Score 5
Completeness of your task	You discuss up to two facts about the event.	You discuss up to four facts about the event.	You discuss six or more facts about the event.
How easily you are understood	You are difficult to understand and have many grammatical errors.	You are fairly easy to understand and have occasional grammatical errors.	You are easy to understand and have very few grammatical errors.
Ability to keep the conversation going	You do not provide a conversational response or follow-up to what your partner says.	You provide frequent responses or follow-ups to what your partner says.	You always respond to partner, listen and ask follow-up questions or volunteer additional information.

Videomisterio

Core Instruction

Standards: 1.2, 3.2, 5.2

Resources: Teacher's Resource Book: Video Script, pp. 12–13; Video Program: Cap. 5A; Video Program Teacher's Guide: Cap. 5A

Focus: Reading and presenting new vocabulary needed to understand the video

Personajes importantes

Roberto	**Carmen**
Julio	**Nela**
Linda	

Synopsis: Julio invites Linda to lunch and Roberto asks her to visit Guanajuato with him. They all visit a famous tourist site, the *Callejón del Beso.* In the meantime, Roberto keeps inquiring about his mysterious grandfather.

Suggestions:

Pre-viewing: Review the events of *Episodio* 4: Roberto, Daniela, and Linda drove to San Miguel to visit Nela and have lunch at her home. While there, Linda inquired about the fact there were no photos of Roberto's grandfather. She was told that he is like a ghost to the family. Nela showed Roberto a photo that was hidden in a drawer of his grandfather and a friend. Roberto dropped it, broke the frame, and discovered names on the back. He learned that his grandfather was actually named Federio Zúñiga, not Toledo, and the friend was named Chato Montesinos, from Dolores Hidalgo. In a flashback, we learned that Federico and Chato left to find work in the U.S. Roberto decided to find Chato. Nela saw the image of Federico appear on her computer screen.

Have a volunteer read the *Nota cultural* aloud. Ask students if they know of other cities that have narrow streets and alleys. Point out that cities built during the colonial period were not planned, and they generally expanded as necessary to accommodate a growing population.

Point out the *Palabras para comprender* to the class, giving examples in context and writing sentences on the board.

Videomisterio

En busca de la verdad

Antes de ver el video

Episodio 5

"¡Amigo, qué coincidencia!".

"Según la leyenda del Callejón del Beso, ella vivía en una casa con balcón que estaba tan cerca que podían besarse".

Nota cultural Este callejón es famoso por ser tan estrecho que una persona, asomada a la ventana de un lado, puede tocar con la mano la pared de enfrente. También es famoso por la leyenda de una bella señorita que se enamoró de un joven. Al padre de ella no le gustó nada y prohibió que su hija lo viera. Pero ella no lo obedeció y siguió viendo al joven. Un día el padre los vio besándose, el joven desde la ventana de un lado y su hija desde la otra. Se puso furioso y mató a su hija con una daga *(dagger).* El joven le dio a su enamorada el último beso en la mano, cada vez más fría. Por eso se llama El Callejón del Beso.

Resumen del episodio

Julio invita a Linda a comer. Luego llega Roberto y los tres van a pasear por Guanajuato. Van al Callejón del Beso. Al día siguiente, Roberto empieza a seguir la pista que tiene.

Palabras para comprender

amable kind

un poco antes a little earlier

dar una vuelta take a tour

la crema de elote corn soup

el pozole thick soup made with corn, meat, and vegetables

las enchiladas mineras enchiladas unique to Guanajuato, made with cheese and onion

las flautas de pollo fried tortilla dish

averiguar find out about

260 doscientos sesenta
Tema 5 • En las noticias

Differentiated Instruction
Solutions for All Learners

Advanced Learners

Have students compare the story of the *Callejón del Beso* with *Romeo and Juliet.* They should prepare a Venn diagram that compares the two stories. What do they have in common? What is unique to each one? Have them present their results to the class.

Heritage Language Learners

Have students research at least two different recipes that have corn as a main ingredient. They should be from countries other than Mexico. Then have them compare their recipes to **crema de elote** or **pozole.** Besides corn, what do they have in common? What is unique? Why is corn such a popular ingredient?

Después de ver el video

¿Comprendiste?

A. ¿Quién dijo cada una de las siguientes frases?
(Carmen / Julio / Linda / Roberto)

1. "Pues, en la Plaza San Fernando hay un buen café, la Oreja de Van Gogh".

2. "Oye, te gustaría dar una vuelta por Guanajuato?".

3. "Quiero descansar hoy. Tengo que hacer varias llamadas".

4. "Ay, no sé qué pedir. Todo parece delicioso".

5. "La comida aquí es muy buena. Aquí están los platos del día".

6. "Mejor . . . así tengo dos guías".

7. "¿Por qué no vamos al Callejón del Beso?".

B. Trabaja con otro(a) estudiante para escribir la conversación entre Linda y Julio. Luego presenten su conversación a la clase.

Go Online
PHSchool.com
For: More on *En busca de la verdad*
Web Code: jdd-C209

doscientos sesenta y uno **261**
Capítulo 5A

Suggestions:

Visual scanning: Direct attention to the photos. Have students read the captions and try to guess what the characters may be talking about.

Before students read the *Resumen del episodio* remind them that they read about **callejones** in *Capítulo* 1A. Explain that **pista** means "clue." Then have them read the *Resumen del episodio* and ask them one or two comprehension questions.

Viewing: Play *Episodio* 5 for the class. If there is time after viewing the full episode, go back and replay key moments that you wish to highlight. Remind students that they may not understand every word they hear in the video, but they should listen for overall understanding.

Post-viewing: Complete the *¿Comprendiste?* in class.

¿Comprendiste?

Presentation EXPRESS
ANSWERS

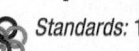
Standards: 1.1, 1.2, 1.3

Resources: Answers on Transparencies
Focus: Verifying comprehension; reviewing the plot
Suggestions: You may want to have students work in groups to answer questions in part A. For part B, you may want to allow groups extra time to discuss the questions.

Answers:
A:
1. Julio	5. Julio
2. Roberto	6. Linda
3. Carmen	7. Julio
4. Linda	

B: Answers will vary.

Additional Resources

- *En busca de la verdad* Video Workbook, Episode 5
- *En busca de la verdad* Teacher's Video Guide: Answer Key

Enrich Your Teaching
Resources for All Teachers

Teacher-to-Teacher

Help students review the major events in the *Videomisterio* with a Concentration game. Photocopy images of the characters and paste them onto index cards. Then copy or write one of the sentences from the Video Script on another card. Have students place the cards facedown on a desk and take turns matching the picture of the person with the sentence referring to them. The student with the most matches wins the game.

Review Activities

To talk about natural disasters and weather extremes: Have students use pictures from news articles to quiz one another. For example, they can ask, *¿Qué pasó en esta ciudad?*

To discuss the news: Have students use these words to write logical and illogical sentences for their partner to read and correct if necessary.

To talk about fires: Create a cloze passage and have students fill in the blanks with the appropriate word.

To discuss rescues and to tell a story: Give students a word bank to write a story about a rescue. Encourage them to write at least four sentences and share them with a partner. Pairs should ask and answer questions about each other's stories.

Portfolio

Invite students to review the activities they completed in this chapter, including written reports, posters or other visuals, tapes of oral presentations, or other projects. Have them select one or two items that they feel best demonstrate their achievements in Spanish to include in their portfolios. Have them include this with the Chapter Checklist and Self-Assessment Worksheet.

Additional Resources

Student Resources: Realidades para hispanohablantes, p. 188

 **CD–ROM**

PuzzleView Web Code: jdd–0508

Teacher Resources:
- Teacher's Resource Book: Situation Cards, p. 18, Clip Art, pp. 20–23
- Assessment Program: Chapter Checklist and Self-Assessment Worksheet, pp. T56–T57

262

Repaso del capítulo

Vocabulario y gramática jdd-0589

To prepare for the test, check to see if you . . .
- know the new vocabulary and grammar
- can perform the tasks on p. 263

to talk about natural disasters and weather extremes

el huracán, *pl.* los huracanes	hurricane
la inundación, *pl.* las inundaciones	flood
llover (o →ue)	to rain
la lluvia	rain
nevar (e →ie)	to snow
el terremoto	earthquake
la tormenta	storm

to discuss the news

el artículo	article
investigar	to investigate
el locutor, la locutora	announcer
el noticiero	newscast
ocurrir	to occur
el reportero, la reportera	reporter
tratar de	to try to

to talk about fires

apagar	to put out (fire)
bajar	to go down
el bombero, la bombera	firefighter
comenzar (e →ie)	to start
destruir (i →y)	to destroy
dormido, -a	asleep
el edificio de apartamentos	apartment building
la escalera	ladder
escaparse	to escape
esconder(se)	to hide (oneself)
la explosión, *pl.* las explosiones	explosion
el humo	smoke
el incendio	fire
los muebles	furniture
muerto, -a	dead
el paramédico, la paramédica	paramedic
quemar(se)	to burn (oneself), to burn up
se murieron	they died
subir	to go up

to discuss rescues

herido, -a	injured
el herido, la herida	injured person
el héroe	heroe
la heroína	heroine
rescatar	to rescue
salvar	to save
valiente	brave
la vida	life
vivo, -a	living, alive

to tell a story

a causa de	because of
afortunadamente	fortunately
asustado, -a	frightened
la causa	cause
de prisa	in a hurry
de repente	suddenly
gritar	to scream
hubo	there was
llamar (por teléfono)	to call (on the phone)
oír	to hear
sin duda	without a doubt
¡Socorro!	Help!

present of *oír*

oigo	oímos
oyes	oís
oye	oyen

preterite of *oír*

oí	oímos
oíste	oísteis
oyó	oyeron

preterite of *creer*

creí	creímos
creíste	creísteis
creyó	creyeron

preterite of *leer*

leí	leímos
leíste	leísteis
leyó	leyeron

preterite of *destruir*

destruí	destruimos
destruiste	destruisteis
destruyó	destruyeron

For *Vocabulario adicional,* see pp. 498–499.

Differentiated Instruction
Solutions for All Learners

Multiple Intelligences

Verbal/Linguistic: Have students create a short story and a series of comprehension questions. Remind them to include as many vocabulary words as possible. Encourage these students to guide their classmates through reading and discussion of their story.

Students with Learning Difficulties

Provide students with semantic maps that have the title of each category in the center. Encourage them to brainstorm as many words as they can. Then have them use a colored pencil or pen to fill in the rest of the words for each category. Remind them to focus on the words in color.

Preparación para el examen

Más práctica

- Practice Workbook: Puzzle, p. 100
- Practice Workbook: Organizer, p. 101

Go Online
PHSchool.com
For: Test Preparation
Web Code: jdd-0508

On the exam you will be asked to . . .	Here are practice tasks similar to those you will find on the exam . . .	If you need review . . .
1 Escuchar Listen and understand as someone talks about her experience during a tragic event	Listen as a talk-show host interviews a young woman who recently escaped from a dangerous situation. See if you can understand: (a) what happened; (b) what time it was; (c) what she was doing at the time; and (d) who she considered to be the hero of the day.	**pp. 240–243** *A primera vista* **p. 244** Actividad 5 **p. 250** Actividad 15
2 Hablar Talk about and describe how things were during certain times of the day	As part of your school's community service project, you visit an elderly man in an assisted living center. He is from Mexico and speaks little English, but he enjoys hearing about your day. Tell him what the weather was like when you woke up, how you were feeling, and what time it was when you left for school.	**p. 248** Actividad 12 **p. 249** Actividades 13–14
3 Leer Read and understand newspaper headlines	Even though you may not be able to understand an entire newspaper article in Spanish, you can get the idea by reading headlines. Read the following headline and see if you can determine if it refers to: (a) a fire; (b) a flood; or (c) an explosion. **Los bomberos salvaron a 200 personas anoche; más de 100 casas dañadas por el agua.**	**p. 241** *A primera vista* **p. 244** Actividad 4 **p. 245** Actividad 6 **p. 252** Actividad 18 **pp. 256–257** *Lectura*
4 Escribir Write about a "disaster movie"	Write a few sentences about your favorite or least favorite "disaster movie." Be sure to mention what type of disaster it was, where it took place, what people were doing before the disaster struck, and any other details that would help your classmates guess which movie it was.	**p. 246** Actividad 9 **p. 247** Actividad 11 **p. 250** Actividad 15 **p. 253** Actividad 21
5 Pensar Demonstrate an understanding of volcano names and legends that are related to them	Your friend is going sight-seeing in Chile. While there, she is going to visit the Parinacota and Pomerape volcanoes. What can you tell her about the legend behind these volcanoes? Do you know any legends about places in your community?	**p. 258** *La cultura en vivo*

Differentiated Assessment
Solutions for All Learners

STUDENTS NEEDING EXTRA HELP
- **Alternate Assessment Program:** Examen del capítulo 5A
- **Audio Program CD 21:** Chap. 5A, Track 1

HERITAGE LEARNERS
- **Assessment Program: Realidades para hispanohablantes:** Examen del capítulo 5A
- **ExamView Heritage Learner Test Bank**

ADVANCED/PRE-AP*
- **ExamView Pre-AP* Test Bank**
- **Pre-AP* Resource Book,** pp. 112–115

Performance Tasks

Presentation EXPRESS ANSWERS

Standards: 1.2, 1.3, 2.2, 3.1

Student Resource: Realidades para hispanohablantes, p. 189

Teacher's Resources: Teacher's Resource Book: Audio Script, p. 10; Audio Program: Track 15; Answers on Transparencies

1. Escuchar

Suggestions: Allow students to listen to the entire script before they answer. Have them make a chart with the following heads: ***Desastre / Hora / Actividades / Héroe.***

Script:
Era horrible. Tenía mucho miedo. Almorzaba en mi cocina en mi edificio de apartamentos. Escuchaba la radio cuando, de repente, oí una explosión muy cerca. En este instante, miré el reloj. Eran las dos de la tarde. Afortunadamente, un bombero me vio y subió hasta mi ventana. Gracias a él, estoy viva hoy.

Answers:
a. There was an explosion.
b. It was 2:00 in the afternoon.
c. She was eating lunch and listening to the radio.
d. The firefighter is her hero.

2. Hablar

Suggestions: If possible, have students tape-record their responses to share with a classmate.

Answers will vary.

3. Leer

Suggestions: Copy the passage onto a transparency to review with students. Underline key words or word roots to help them understand.

Answer: b

4. Escribir

Suggestions: Have students make a word web about the details of their movies before they begin writing.

Answers will vary.

5. Pensar

Suggestions: Refer students to p. 258. Have them ask older family members or members of the community about local legends.

Answers will vary.

Assessment
- **ExamView Quiz on PresEXPRESS**
- **Assessment Program:** Examen del capítulo
- **ExamView Test Bank:** Tests A and B
- **Audio Program CD 21:** Chap. 5A, Track 1

263

Chapter Overview

A primera vista	Manos a la obra	¡Adelante!	Repaso
INPUT	**PRACTICE**	**APPLICATION**	**REVIEW**
• Introduce vocabulary and grammar within an authentic context.	• Practice and develop new vocabulary. • Learn and practice new grammar structures.	• Apply vocabulary and grammar through culminating, theme-based activities. • Apply skill development.	• Review vocabulary and grammar.

Objectives

Read, listen to, and interpret information about • Parts of the body • Accidents • What happens in an emergency room	• Read and interpret information about medical care. • Explain injuries and emergency room procedures. • Describe what happened in the emergency room. • Describe what was taking place when an accident occurred.	• Read about a health campaign. • Read about natural disasters. • Create an injury report. • Watch *En busca de la verdad, Episodio* 6.	• Prepare for the chapter test.

Culture

• Diego Rivera	• *La Ambulancia Azul* • *Los intérpretes* (interpreters) *y traductores* (translators) *médicos* • *La Patrulla Aérea Colombiana* • *El jai alai*	• *Seguridad Social y los servicios médicos*	• Explain social security as well as public medical services.

Vocabulary	Grammar	Learner Support	
• Treatment for medical conditions • Words related to an accident • Parts of the body	• Irregular preterites: *venir, poner, decir,* and *traer* • Imperfect progressive and preterite	**STRATEGIES** • Using guiding questions • Taking notes • Using cognates	**RECYCLING** ♻ • Parts of the body • The imperfect and preterite tenses • *Hace* + length of time • The present progressive tense

Chapter Features

Exploración del lenguaje

False cognates

El español en el mundo del trabajo

The importance of translators in the medical profession in the United States

Conexiones

Health: Sport injuries

Beyond the Classroom: States & Countries

España
Connecticut
Washington, D.C.
Kansas
Florida
México
Nicaragua
Costa Rica
Ecuador
Colombia
Bolivia
República Dominicana
Chile
Argentina

Student Resources

TECHNOLOGY

ONLINE
Interactive Textbook
• Student Edition Online plus audio, video, and flashcards

Go Online Companion Web Site
• Tutorial activities
• Internet links
• Self-tests
• Downloadable MP3 audio files
• **PuzzleView**

CD-ROM
Interactive Textbook CD-ROM
Student Edition on CD-ROM plus audio, video, and flashcards

MindPoint QUIZSHOW CD-ROM

PRINT MATERIAL

CORE INSTRUCTION
Practice Workbook, pp. 102–110
• Review
• Vocabulary
• Grammar
• Puzzle
• Organizer

Writing, Audio & Video Activities, pp. 98–106
• Video
• Audio
• Writing

Grammar Study Guide 1–2 (or 3–4)

Differentiated Instruction

STUDENTS NEEDING EXTRA HELP
Guided Practice Activities, pp. 181–198
• Vocabulary Flash Cards and Vocabulary Check
• Grammar Activities
• Presentación escrita

HERITAGE LEARNERS
Realidades para hispanohablantes, pp. 190–209

Lecturas para hispanohablantes
• **AP* Literature Author:** Gabriel García Márquez, "Una resurrección en tierra extraña"(excerpt from *Relato de un náufrago*), pp. 48–49
• "Conversando con un campeón de surfing," pp. 52–54

ADVANCED/PRE-AP*
Pre-AP* Resource Book: Student Activity Sheet, p. 115

Teacher Resources

TECHNOLOGY

Audio Program
Video Program
Fine Art Transparencies
Vocabulary and Grammar Transparencies
Answers on Transparencies

TeacherEXPRESS CD-ROM
• Lesson Planner
• Vocabulary Clip Art
• Web Resources
• Teaching Resources
• Teacher Edition with Interactive Links

PresentationEXPRESS CD-ROM
• Vocabulary
• Transparencies and Maps
• Grammar
• Photo Gallery
• Audio
• Clip Art

PRINT MATERIAL

CORE INSTRUCTION
Teacher's Resource Book, pp. 30–55
• Input Script
• Video Script
• Answer Keys
• GramActiva Blackline Masters
• Vocabulary Clip Art
• Chapter Resource Checklist
• School-to-Home Connection Letters
• Communicative Activities Blackline Masters

TPR Stories, pp. 72–77

Differentiated Instruction

STUDENTS NEEDING EXTRA HELP
Guided Practice Activities Teacher's Guide, pp. T91–T99

HERITAGE LEARNERS
Realidades para hispanohablantes Teacher's Guide, pp. 96–105

Lecturas para hispanohablantes Teacher's Guide, pp. 18–20

ADVANCED/PRE-AP*
Pre-AP* Resource Book: Resources Chart, p. 113

Differentiated Assessment

PH SuccessNet ONLINE
• Access to grades and reports from Online Interactive Textbook

ExamView QuickTake Presenter on Presentation Express CD-ROM
• Vocabulary Quizzes
• Chapter Test
• Grammar Quizzes

TeacherEXPRESS CD-ROM
• Assessment Program
• **ExamView** Test Banks A and B

CORE ASSESSMENT
Assessment Program, pp. 138–150
• Pruebas
  Vocabulary Recognition
  Vocabulary Production
  Irregular preterites: *venir, poner, decir,* and *traer*
  Imperfect progressive and preterite
• Examen del capítulo
• Speaking and Writing Rubrics

Teacher's Resource Book, p. 44
• Situation Cards

TPR Stories, pp. 72–77

STUDENTS NEEDING EXTRA HELP
Alternate Assessment Program
• Examen del capítulo, pp. 59–64

HERITAGE LEARNERS
Assessment Program: Realidades para hispanohablantes Teacher's Guide, pp. T135–T139

ExamView Heritage Learner Test Bank

ADVANCED/PRE-AP*
Pre-AP* Resource Book: Teacher Activity Sheet, p. 114

ExamView Pre-AP* Test Bank

Go Online
PHSchool.com
For: Teacher Home Page
Web Code: jdk-1001

	Warm-up / Assess	Preview Present / Practice Communicate		Wrap-up / Homework Options
DAY 1	**Warm-up (10 min.)** • Homework check • Return Examen del capítulo: Capítulo 5A	**Chapter Opener (10 min.)** • Objectives • Fondo cultural	**A primera vista (25 min.)** • Presentation: Vocabulario y gramática en contexto • Actividades 1, 2	**Wrap-up and Homework Options (5 min.)** • Practice Workbook 5B-A, 5B-B, 5B-1, 5B-2 • Go Online
DAY 2	**Warm-up (10 min.)** • Homework check	**A primera vista (35 min.)** • Presentation: Videohistoria *¡El pobrecito soy yo!* • View: Videohistoria	• Video Activities 1, 2, 3, 4 • Actividad 3	**Wrap-up and Homework Options (5 min.)** • Practice Workbook 5B-3, 5B-4 • Go Online • Prueba 5B-1: Vocabulary recognition
DAY 3	**Warm-up (10 min.)** • Actividad 4 • Homework check ✔**Assessment (10 min.)** • Prueba 5B-1: Vocabulary recognition	**Manos a la obra (25 min.)** • Actividades 5, 6, 7, 8, 9 • Fondo cultural		**Wrap-up and Homework Options (5 min.)** • Actividad 11 • Writing Activity 10 • Heritage Learner Workbook 5B-1, 5B-2 • Prueba 5B-2: Vocabulary production
DAY 4	**Warm-up (10 min.)** • Actividad 10 • Homework check ✔**Assessment (10 min.)** (after Communicative Activity) • Prueba 5B-2: Vocabulary production	**Manos a la obra (25 min.)** • Audio Activities 5, 6 • Communicative Activity • Presentation: Irregular preterites: *venir, poner, decir,* and *traer* • View: GramActiva video • Actividad 12		**Wrap-up and Homework Options (5 min.)** • Practice Workbook 5B-5 • Writing Activity 11 • Actividad 14 • Go Online
DAY 5	**Warm-up (5 min.)** • Actividad 13 • Homework check	**Manos a la obra (40 min.)** • Exploración del lenguaje • Actividades 15, 16, 17 • Audio Activity 7 • Presentation: Imperfect progressive and preterite • View: GramActiva video • Actividades 18, 20		**Wrap-up and Homework Options (5 min.)** • Practice Workbook 5B-6 • Actividades 21, 22 • Go Online • Prueba 5B-3: Irregular preterites: *venir, poner, decir,* and *traer*
DAY 6	**Warm-up (10 min.)** • Actividad 19 • Homework check ✔**Assessment (10 min.)** • Prueba 5B-3: Irregular preterites: *venir, poner, decir,* and *traer*	**Manos a la obra (25 min.)** • El español en el mundo del trabajo • Actividades 23, 25, 26 • Fondos culturales		**Wrap-up and Homework Options (5 min.)** • Practice Workbook 5B-7 • Actividad 24 • Go Online • Heritage Learner Workbook 5B-4 • Prueba 5B-4: Imperfect progressive and preterite
DAY 7	**Warm-up (10 min.)** • Writing Activity 12 • Homework check ✔**Assessment (10 min.)** (after Audio Activities) • Prueba 5B-4: Imperfect progressive and preterite	**Manos a la obra (15 min.)** • Writing Activity 13 • Audio Activities 8, 9 **¡Adelante! (10 min.)** • Presentación escrita: Steps 1, 5		**Wrap-up and Homework Options (5 min.)** • Presentación escrita: Step 2
DAY 8	**Warm-up (5 min.)** • Homework check	**¡Adelante! (40 min.)** • Presentación escrita: Step 3 • Lectura • ¿Comprendiste? / Y tú, ¿qué dices?		**Wrap-up and Homework Options (5 min.)** • Presentación escrita: Step 4 • Preparación para el examen 3, 4, 5 • Go Online: Lectura
DAY 9	**Warm-up (5 min.)** • Homework check	**¡Adelante! (30 min.)** • Videomisterio: *En busca de la verdad,* Episodio 6 • Perspectivas del mundo hispano	**Repaso del capítulo (10 min.)** • Vocabulario y gramática • Preparación para el examen 1, 2	**Wrap-up and Homework Options (5 min.)** • Practice Workbook 5B-8, 5B-9 • Go Online: Self-test • Examen del capítulo 5B
DAY 10	**Warm-up (5 min.)** • Homework check ✔**Assessment (40 min.)** • Examen del capítulo 5B			**Wrap-up and Homework Options (5 min.)** • Go Online: Videomisterio • A ver si recuerdas . . .: Capítulo 6A

Warm-up / Assess	Preview Present / Practice Communicate	Wrap-up / Homework Options
DAY 1 **Warm-up (10 min.)** • Homework check • Return Examen del capítulo: Capítulo 5A	**Chapter Opener (10 min.)** • Objetivos • Fondo cultural **A primera vista (65 min.)** • Presentation: Vocabulario y gramática en contexto • Actividades 1, 2 • Presentation: Videohistoria *¡El pobrecito soy yo!* • View: Videohistoria • Video Activities 1, 2, 3, 4 • Actividades 3, 4	**Wrap-up and Homework Options (5 min.)** • Practice Workbook 5B-A, 5B-B, 5B-1, 5B-2, 5B-3, 5B-4 • Go Online • Prueba 5B-1: Vocabulary recognition
DAY 2 **Warm-up (10 min.)** • Actividad 5 • Homework check ✔**Assessment (10 min.)** • Prueba 5B-1: Vocabulary recognition	**Manos a la obra (65 min.)** • Actividades 6, 7, 8, 9 • Fondo cultural • Audio Activities 5, 6 • Writing Activity 10 • Communicative Activity • Presentation: Irregular preterites: *venir, poner, decir,* and *traer* • View: GramActiva video • Actividades 12, 13	**Wrap-up and Homework Options (5 min.)** • Practice Workbook 5B-5 • Actividad 11 • Go Online • Heritage Learner Workbook 5B-1, 5B-2 • Prueba 5B-2: Vocabulary production
DAY 3 **Warm-up (10 min.)** • Actividad 10 • Homework check ✔**Assessment (10 min.)** • Prueba 5B-2: Vocabulary production	**Manos a la obra (65 min.)** • Exploración del lenguaje • Actividades 14, 15, 16, 17 • Audio Activity 7 • El español en el mundo del trabajo • Presentation: Imperfect progressive and preterite • View: GramActiva video • Actividades 18, 20, 21 • Audio Activities 8, 9	**Wrap-up and Homework Options (5 min.)** • Practice Workbook 5B-6, 5B-7 • Actividades 23, 24 • Writing Activity 13 • Go Online • Heritage Learner Workbook 5B-4 • Pruebas 5B-3, 5B-4: Irregular preterites: *venir, poner, decir,* and *traer;* Imperfect progressive and preterite
DAY 4 **Warm-up (15 min.)** • Writing Activity 11 • Homework check ✔**Assessment (15 min.)** (after Writing Activity) • Pruebas 5B-3, 5B-4: Irregular preterites: *venir, poner, decir,* and *traer;* Imperfect progressive and preterite	**Manos a la obra (35 min.)** • Fondos culturales • Actividades 19, 22, 25, 26 • Writing Activity 12 **¡Adelante! (20 min.)** • Perspectivas del mundo hispano • Presentación escrita: Steps 1, 5	**Wrap-up and Homework Options (5 min.)** • Presentación escrita: Step 2 • Go Online: Self-test
DAY 5 **Warm-up (5 min.)** • Homework check	**¡Adelante! (50 min.)** • Presentación escrita: Steps 3, 4 • Lectura • ¿Comprendiste? / Y tú, ¿qué dices? **Repaso del capítulo (30 min.)** • Vocabulario y gramática • Preparación para el examen 1, 2, 3, 4, 5	**Wrap-up and Homework Options (5 min.)** • Presentación escrita: Step 4 • Practice Workbook 5B-8, 5B-9 • Go Online: Lectura • Examen del capítulo 5B
DAY 6 **Warm-up (10 min.)** • Homework check • Answer questions **Repaso del capítulo (15 min.)** • Situation Cards ✔**Assessment (40 min.)** • Examen del capítulo 5B	**¡Adelante! (20 min.)** • Videomisterio: *En busca de la verdad,* Episodio 6	**Wrap-up and Homework Options (5 min.)** • Go Online: Videomisterio • A ver si recuerdas . . . : Capítulo 6A

Standards for Capítulo 5B

- To achieve the goals of the Standards, students will:

Communication

1.1 Interpersonal
- Talk about: an emergency room visit; injuries; past events; medical treatment; accidents; an ambulance service; events of a party; sports injuries; a traffic accident

1.2 Interpretive
- Read and listen to information about: Diego Rivera, accidents, parts of the body, healthcare, an emergency room visit, *la Ambulancia Azul,* a television program, an ambulance service ad, medical translators, *la Patrulla Aérea Colombiana,* sports injuries, word families, Luiz Nazario da Lima
- Read about: jai alai, public information campaigns; international health organizations; social security programs and public medical care
- Listen to and watch a video about an accident
- Listen to a children's song

1.3 Presentational
- Present information about: a story plot, accidents, social security programs and public medical care
- Sing a children's song
- Write: about medical treatment, accidents, an ambulance service ad, the events of a party, sports injuries, a traffic accident; an accident report
- Play Charades

Culture

2.1 Practices and Perspectives
- Describe medical care in early 20th century Mexico; ambulance service in Spain; *la Patrulla Aérea Colombiana;* social security programs and public medical care

2.2 Products and Perspectives
- Talk or write about: Diego Rivera and his art; *la Ambulancia Azul; la Patrulla Aérea Colombiana;* jai alai; social security programs and public medical care

Connections

3.1 Cross-curricular
- Talk or write about: sports medicine; public information campaigns; international health organizations

Comparisons

4.1 Language
- Identify: false cognates, the imperfect progressive and preterite tenses; vocabulary through cognates

4.2 Culture
- Compare: local ambulance service to that of Spain; jai alai to other popular sports

Communities

5.1 Beyond the School
- Investigate local medical translator positions

5.1 Beyond the School
- View a video mystery series

264

Fondo cultural

Diego Rivera (1886–1957) fue uno de los mejores artistas del siglo XX. Nació en Guanajuato, México, y cuando era niño se mudó *(he moved)* con su familia a la Ciudad de México. Rivera pintó muchos murales de temas sociales. Este mural representa el estado de los servicios médicos de México en esa época. Nota las expresiones de las caras de las personas esperando al médico.

- ¿Qué piensas de las expresiones de las personas en este mural? ¿Por qué crees que tienen esas expresiones?

"La medicina antigua y la moderna (1953)", Diego Rivera

Fresco, approx. 7.4 x 10.8 m. Hospital de la Raza, México City, D.F., México. Photo: Art Resource, NY. © 2003 Banco de México Diego Rivera & Frida Kahlo Museums Trust. Av. Cinco de Mayo No. 2, Col. Centro, Del. Cuauhtemoc 06059, México, D.F. Reproduction authorized by the *Instituto Nacional de Bellas Artes y Literatura.*

264 doscientos sesenta y cuatro
Tema 5 • En las noticias

Differentiated Instruction

STUDENTS NEEDING EXTRA HELP

Guided Practice Activities
- Vocabulary Check, Flash Cards
- Grammar
- Reading and Writing Support

Guided Practice Audio CDs
- Disc 2, Track 2

HERITAGE LEARNERS

Realidades para hispanohablantes
- Chapter Opener, pp. 190–191
- A primera vista, p. 192
- Videohistoria, p. 193
- Manos a la obra, pp. 194–201
- ¡Adelante!, pp. 202–207
- Repaso del capítulo, pp. 208–209

ADVANCED/PRE-AP*

Pre-AP* Resource Book, pp. 112–115

Capítulo 5B

Un accidente

Chapter Objectives

- Describe an accident scene
- Talk about injuries and treatments
- Talk about what you were doing when an accident occurred
- Understand cultural perspectives on health

Video Highlights

A primera vista: *¡El pobrecito soy yo!*

GramActiva Videos: irregular preterites: *venir, poner, decir,* and *traer;* imperfect progressive and preterite

Videomisterio: *En busca de la verdad,* Episodio 6

Country Connection

As you learn to talk about accidents and injuries, you will make connections to these countries and places:

- España
- Connecticut
- Washington, D.C.
- Kansas
- Florida
- México
- Nicaragua
- Costa Rica
- Ecuador
- Colombia
- Bolivia
- República Dominicana
- Chile
- Argentina

Más práctica

- *Real.* para hispanohablantes, pp. 190–191

For: Online Atlas
Web Code: jde-0002

doscientos sesenta y cinco **265**
Capítulo 5B

Preview

Chapter Opener

Presentation EXPRESS ATLAS

Core Instruction

Resources: Voc. and Gram. Transparencies: Maps 12–18, 20

Suggestions: Ask students if they have ever witnessed an accident that required an ambulance to be called. Have them explain what happened. Explain to students that they will learn to describe various accidents that people have, injuries they sustain, and treatments they receive. They will learn more about how to describe scenarios in the past. Tell students that in the *Videohistoria,* Raúl has an accident in the middle of the night and has to go to the emergency room.

Fondo cultural
Standards: 1.2, 2.1, 2.2

◆◆■■◆◆■■◆◆■■◆◆■■◆◆

Resources: Fine Art Transparencies with Teacher's Guide, p. 54

Suggestions: Remind students that in the past, doctors were not as available to patients as they are now. Also, point out that in that era, people did not have access to the medicine and anesthetics that are widely available today.

Answers will vary.

Teaching with Art

Resources: Fine Art Transparencies with Teacher's Guide, p. 54

Suggestions: To guide discussion of the painting, ask: Who is present in the painting? What are the decorations like? What story does the picture tell? What feelings does the artist convey, and how? For more ideas, see the *Fine Art Transparencies Teacher's Guide.*

Teacher Technology

TeacherEXPRESS
Plan · Teach · Assess

PLAN
Lesson Planner

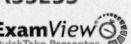
For: Teacher Home Page
Web Code: jdk-1001

TEACH
Teaching Resources
Interactive
Teacher's Edition
Vocabulary Clip Art

ASSESS
Chapter Quizzes and Tests

PresentationEXPRESS
Dynamic Presentations for Teachers

TEACH
Vocabulary & Grammar Powerpoints
GramActiva Video
Audio & Clip Art Activities
Transparencies and Maps
Activity Answers
Photo Gallery

ASSESS
ExamView
QuickTake Presenter

Vocabulario y gramática *Presentation* **EXPRESS** **VOCABULARY**

Core Instruction

Standards: 1.2

Resources: Teacher's Resource Book: Input Script, p. 32, Clip Art, pp. 46–49, Audio Script, p. 33; Voc. and Gram. Transparencies 98–99; TPR Stories Book, pp. 65–77; Audio Program: Tracks 1–2

Focus: Presenting vocabulary for body parts, accidents, and what happens in an emergency room

Suggestions: Use the Input Script from the *Teacher's Resource Book* or the story from the *TPR Stories Book* to introduce the vocabulary, or use some of these suggestions. You may want to present the vocabulary in three groups: words about accidents, body parts, and medical treatments. Borrow medical supplies such as bandages, crutches, and a wheelchair from the school nurse and use them to present the vocabulary. Ask students: *Si me rompo el tobillo, ¿qué necesito?*

Use a skeleton model from the Science Department at your school to present vocabulary for body parts. Place a bandage on various body parts and ask the class: *¿Qué le duele?* Change the bandage before each class and ask students to write a few sentences describing what happened to the skeleton. Encourage them to use their imagination.

Bellringer Review

Show Fine Art Transparency 48 and discuss what atypical body parts they see in the painting. *(Ex. A la izquierda vemos una persona con tres ojos.)*

Additional Resources

• Audio Program: Canciones CD, Disc 22

Objectives

Read, listen to, and understand information about
- **parts of the body**
- **accidents**
- **what happens in an emergency room**

A primera vista

Vocabulario y gramática en contexto

jdd-0597

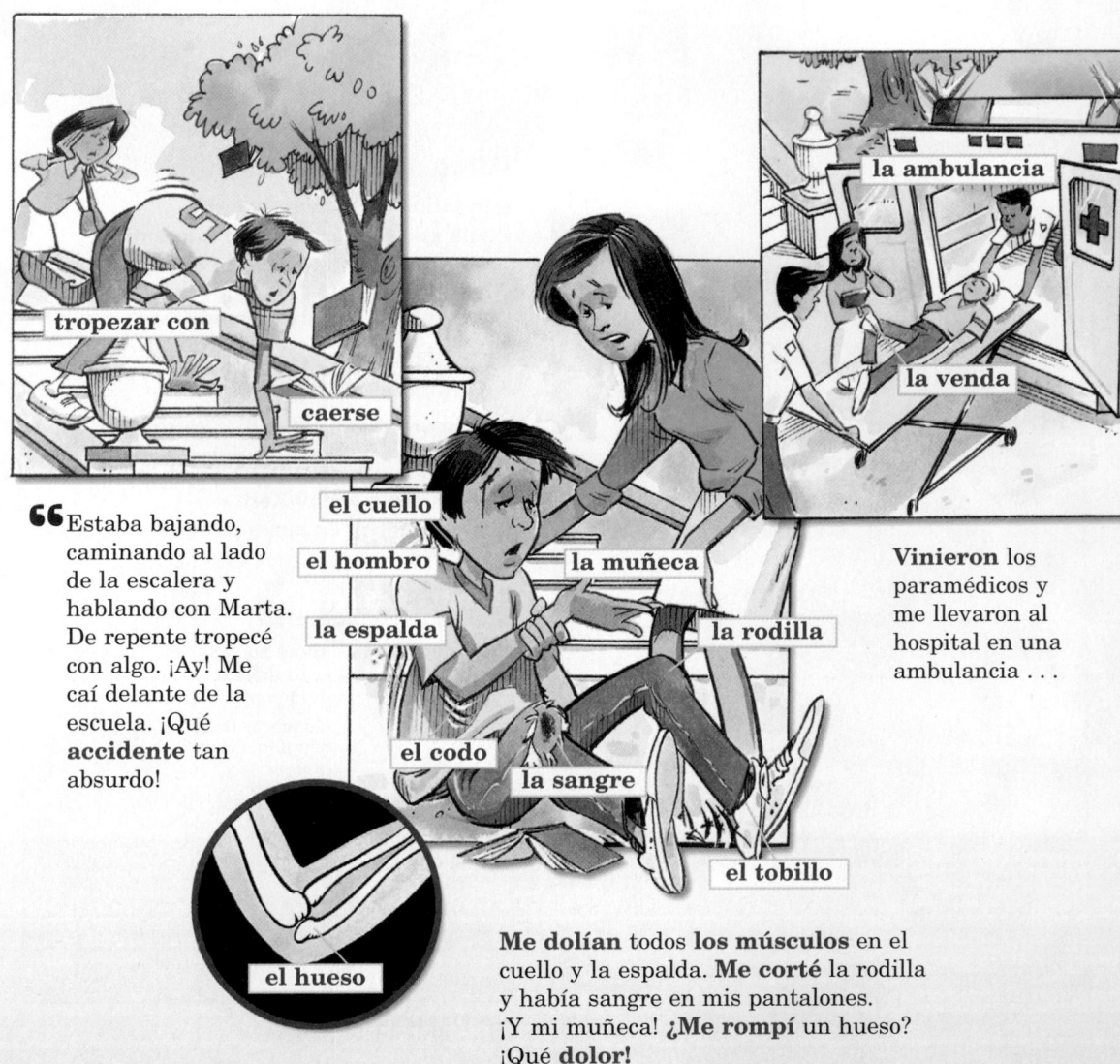

" Estaba bajando, caminando al lado de la escalera y hablando con Marta. De repente tropecé con algo. ¡Ay! Me caí delante de la escuela. ¡Qué **accidente** tan absurdo!

Vinieron los paramédicos y me llevaron al hospital en una ambulancia . . .

Me dolían todos **los músculos** en el cuello y la espalda. **Me corté** la rodilla y había sangre en mis pantalones. ¡Y mi muñeca! **¿Me rompí** un hueso? ¡Qué **dolor!**

266 doscientos sesenta y seis
Tema 5 • En las noticias

Differentiated Instruction
Solutions for All Learners

Students with Special Needs

Pair hearing-impaired students with other students for *Actividad* 1. Give them a list of the dictated sentences. Have students take turns choosing and acting out a sentence, while their partner guesses which sentence is being represented and points to it.

Multiple Intelligences

Visual: Have artistic students create story panels showing minor accidents happening to people, the results of the accidents, and the treatment. Put two of them at a time on the overhead, narrate a story, and have students identify the drawing being described.

las puntadas

la inyección

las pastillas

SALA DE EMERGENCIA

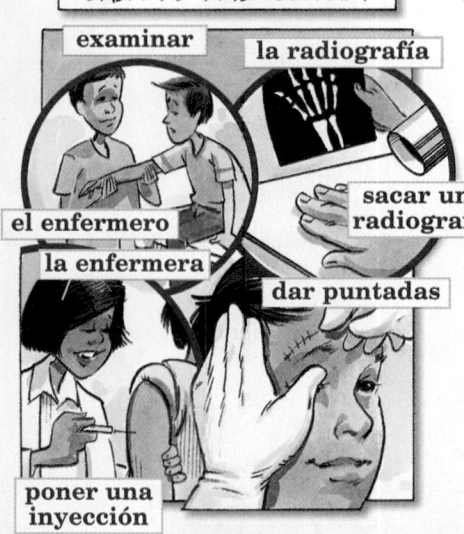
examinar
la radiografía
el enfermero
la enfermera
sacar una radiografía
dar puntadas
poner una inyección

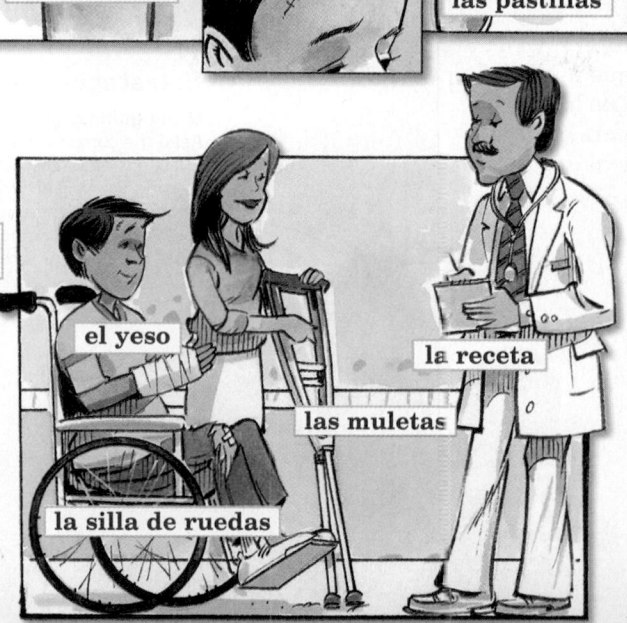
el yeso
la receta
las muletas
la silla de ruedas

Cuando entré en **la sala de emergencia,** el enfermero sacó una radiografía de mi muñeca. La enfermera me **puso** una inyección y el médico me dio puntadas.

Luego, el médico me **recetó medicina.** Sí, me rompí un hueso en la muñeca y ahora necesito llevar un yeso por unas seis semanas. Si **me siento** muy mal, el médico me dijo que puedo tomar una pastilla cada ocho horas. ¡Qué día horrible! **99**.

 Actividad 1 jdd-0597  **Escuchar**

¡Acción!

Escucha estas frases sobre varias partes del cuerpo y problemas médicos. Representa (Act out) la acción para indicar que comprendiste la frase.

Más práctica

- Practice Workbook, pp. 102–103: 5B-2
- WAV Wbk.: Writing, p. 103
- Guided Practice: Vocab. Flash Cards, pp. 181–186
- Real. para hispanohablantes, p. 192

Go Online PHSchool.com
For: Vocab. Practice
Web Code: jdd-0511

Actividad 2 jdd-0597 **Escuchar**

La sala de emergencia

Escucha las frases. Si la frase que escuchas es lógica, señala con el pulgar hacia arriba. Si la frase no es lógica, señala con el pulgar hacia abajo.

doscientos sesenta y siete **267**
Capítulo 5B

Actividad 1 Standards: 1.2 Presentation EXPRESS AUDIO

Resources: Teacher's Resource Book: Audio Script, p. 33; Audio Program: Track 3; Answers on Transparencies

Focus: Listening comprehension about body parts and medical problems

Suggestions: Establish appropriate ways to act out the medical problems before starting the activity.

Script and Answers:

1. ¡Ay! Creo que me rompí la muñeca. *(broken wrist)*
2. Siento mucho dolor en el cuello. *(hurt neck)*
3. Ayer me torcí el tobillo. *(twisted ankle)*
4. Doctora, me duele la espalda. *(back hurts)*
5. Me caí y me lastimé el codo. *(fell and hurt elbow)*
6. La enfermera me puso una inyección. *(got a shot from nurse)*
7. Tuve que usar muletas por una semana. *(use crutches)*
8. Tomé unas pastillas para el dolor. *(take pills for the pain)*

Actividad 2 Standards: 1.2 Presentation EXPRESS AUDIO

Resources: Teacher's Resource Book: Audio Script, p. 33; Audio Program: Track 4; Answers on Transparencies

Focus: Listening comprehension about accidents and body parts

Suggestions: After students indicate if the statement is logical or illogical, allow them to listen again to self-correct.

Script and Answers:

1. Necesito muletas si me rompo la muñeca. *(down)*
2. El médico me dio una inyección en la cabeza. *(down)*
3. Si me rompo el tobillo, necesito un yeso. *(up)*
4. Si no puedo caminar, necesito una silla de ruedas. *(up)*
5. Voy en ambulancia a la escuela. *(down)*
6. El codo es parte del brazo. *(up)*
7. El cuello está al lado del tobillo. *(down)*
8. Cuando hay un accidente viene una ambulancia. *(up)*

Enrich Your Teaching
Resources for All Teachers

Culture Note

Like the United States, Mexico does not have a single, government-managed, national health system. About half of the population receives health care through government social security agencies. The other half has health coverage through employers or through private health insurance.

Teacher-to-Teacher

Create a dummy to use as a prop during this lesson. Stuff old clothes with rags to form a body, and make a head out of an old T-shirt. Give the dummy a name and prop it in a corner. Use the dummy to demonstrate vocabulary for accidents and injuries.

 Assessment
- ExamView QuickTake Presenter Quiz on PresEXPRESS

Videohistoria

Presentation EXPRESS **VOCABULARY**

Core Instruction

 Standards: 1.2

Resources: Voc. and Gram. Transparencies 100–101; Audio Program: Track 5

Focus: Presentation of additional vocabulary to discuss accidents and emergency rooms

Suggestions:

Pre-reading: Direct attention to the photos. Point out that much of the story is happening in the past. Have students use visual clues to help them predict what they are going to see. Ask them to describe Raúl's injuries. Direct attention to the *Estrategia.* Have students
copy the questions in *Actividad 3* and ask them to highlight key information.

Reading: Ask volunteers to read the *Videohistoria* aloud. As students listen, have them list Raúl's injuries and recommendations for treatment as if they were his doctor. Stop students after panels 5 and 7 to check comprehension. Ask: *¿Qué le pasó a Raúl? ¿Qué recomienda Ud.?* Remind them to use context clues to help them understand unfamiliar vocabulary.

Post-reading: Complete *Actividad 3* to check comprehension.

Block Schedule

Help students become more familiar with the content of the *Videohistoria* by having them work in pairs to play a memory game. Make photocopies of each panel, cut them out, and paste them on index cards. Then write a summary for each panel on a different index card. Have students place the cards facedown on the desk and take turns looking for pairs. The partner with the most pairs wins.

Pre-AP* Support

- **Activity:** Make copies of two different pages from a children's coloring book (depicting people or animals) on the front and back of a sheet of paper and label them *Estudiante A* and *Estudiante B.* Make the two-sided copy for each student in the class. Assign one partner to be A and the other to be B and have them draw people and various medical treatments presented in this chapter (*puntadas, venda,* etc.) on their assigned coloring book. Then, have each student tell his or her partner the location of the treatment and have him or her draw appropriately on his or her copy.

- *Pre-AP* Resource Book:* Comprehensive guide to Pre-AP* vocabulary skill development, pp. 47–53

Videohistoria
 jdd-0597

¡El pobrecito soy yo!

Raúl tuvo un accidente y tuvo que ir a la sala de emergencia. Lee la historia para saber qué le pasó.

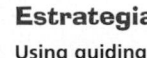

Estrategia

Using guiding questions
Read the comprehension questions on p. 269 before starting the *Videohistoria.* Knowing what the questions are beforehand can help you look for the key information as you read.

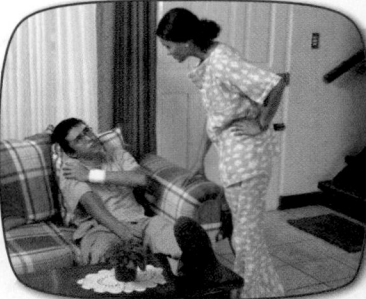

1 **Gloria:** ¡Raúl! ¿Qué te pasó?
Raúl: Pues, tuve un accidente anoche.
Gloria: Dime todo.

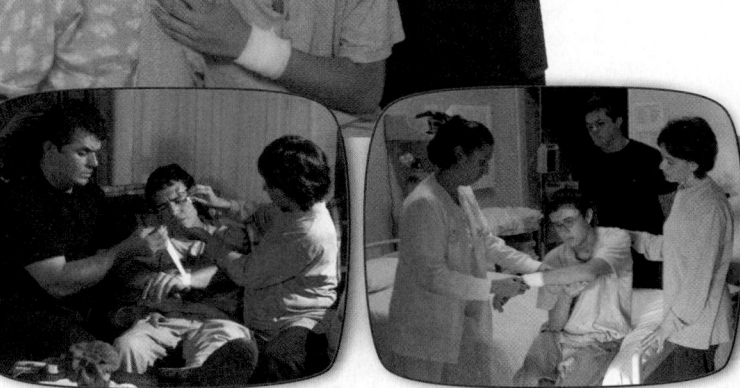

5 **Raúl:** Me sentía muy mal y me dolía mucho la muñeca. Mamá y papá me **pusieron** una venda en la muñeca y me llevaron al hospital.

6 **Raúl:** Entramos en la sala de emergencia. Me **trajeron** una silla de ruedas. Luego me dieron cinco puntadas. Me **dijeron** que no tenía el brazo **roto.**

7 **Raúl:** El médico me recetó estas pastillas para el dolor.
Gloria: ¡Qué lástima! ¿Ves, Raúl? ¡No debes despertarte tan temprano!
Raúl: Gracias.

268 doscientos sesenta y ocho
Tema 5 • En las noticias

Differentiated Instruction
Solutions for All Learners

Advanced Learners

Have students rewrite the story, making Tomás the accident victim. Ask them to use the *Videohistoria* text as a model. Provide them with a handout that has eight panels as in the format above, and ask students to illustrate their story and write their dialogue below each panel.

Students with Learning Difficulties

To help students implement the *Estrategia,* provide them with a photocopy of the *Videohistoria.* Have them use different colored highlighters to identify key words in each question. Then, as they read, have them use corresponding colors to identify words in the text that help them answer each question.

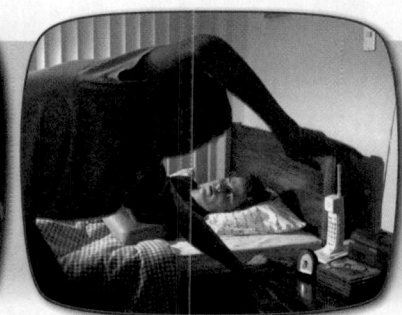

2 Raúl: Estaba durmiendo cuando de repente oí el despertador. Eran las tres. Traté de despertar a Tomás, pero no se despertó. No **se movió.** Tuve que apagar el despertador. Me levanté y empecé a caminar. Estaba muy oscuro.

3 Raúl: Tropecé con algo y **me torcí** el tobillo.

4 Raúl: Me caí al suelo. **Choqué con** la mesa y **me lastimé** el brazo. Me corté la muñeca.

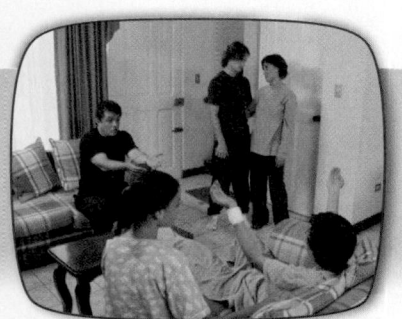

8 Mamá: ¡Pobre Tomás! ¡Nos fuimos al hospital tan de prisa que lo dejamos aquí, solo!

Raúl: ¿Tomás? ¡El **pobrecito** soy yo!

Escribir/Hablar

¿Comprendiste?

1. ¿Qué le pregunta Gloria cuando ve a Raúl?
2. ¿Qué oyó Raúl mientras dormía? ¿Qué hizo? ¿Qué hizo Tomás?
3. ¿Qué le pasó luego a Raúl?
4. ¿Cómo se sentía Raúl? ¿Qué le dolía?
5. ¿Qué hicieron los padres de Raúl?
6. ¿Qué le hicieron a Raúl en el hospital?
7. ¿Qué le dio el médico a Raúl? ¿Por qué?

Más práctica

- Practice Workbook, pp. 104–105: 5B-3, 5B-4
- WAV Wbk.: Video, pp. 98–99
- Guided Practice: Vocab. Check, pp. 187–190
- *Real.* para hispanohablantes, p. 193

Go Online
PHSchool.com
For: Vocab. Practice
Web Code: jdd-0512

doscientos sesenta y nueve **269**
Capítulo 5B

Video

Core Instruction

Standards: 1.2

Resources: Teacher's Resource Book: Video Script, p. 36; Video Program: Cap. 5B; Video Program Teacher's Guide: Cap. 5B

Focus: Comprehension of contextualized vocabulary

Suggestions:

Pre-viewing: Have each student think of two more comprehension questions like those in *Actividad* 3. Choose the five best questions and write them on the board. Have students use those questions as a guide to look for key information as they view the episode.

Viewing: Show the video once without pausing. Show it again, pausing at key points to check for comprehension.

Post-viewing: If you chose to have students write comprehension questions as a pre-viewing activity, allow them time to answer the questions on the board. Complete the Video Activities in the *Writing, Audio & Video Workbook.*

 Standards: 1.2, 1.3
Presentation EXPRESS
ANSWERS

Resources: Answers on Transparencies

Focus: Verifying comprehension of the *Videohistoria*

Suggestions: Have students answer the questions without referring to the text. Allow them to look at the photos for clues.

Answers:

1. Le pregunta qué le pasó.
2. Oyó el despertador. Trató de despertar a Tomás, pero él no se despertó y no se movió.
3. Se levantó y empezó a caminar para apagar el despertador. Se tropezó con algo.
4. Se sentía muy mal. Le dolían el tobillo, el brazo y la muñeca.
5. Le pusieron una venda en la muñeca y lo llevaron al hospital.
6. Lo pusieron en una silla de ruedas y le dieron cinco puntadas.
7. Le dio a Raúl unas pastillas para el dolor.

Enrich Your Teaching
Resources for All Teachers

Teacher-to-Teacher

Have students keep fictional dialogue journals throughout this chapter. Divide the class into four groups, and give each group a different character name. Each day, provide scenarios for each character, and have students write a short entry as though they were that person. For example, if a character were involved in an accident, each student who was assigned that character should explain what happened. At the end of the week, collect the journals and write a response to them. Include follow-up questions in your response to keep the dialogue going.

Additional Resources

- WAV Wbk.: Audio Act. 5, p. 100
- Teacher's Resource Book: Audio Script, p. 34
- Audio Program: Track 7

✓ **Assessment**

- *ExamView* Quiz on PresEXPRESS
  QuickTake Presenter
- Prueba 5B-1: Vocab. Recognition, pp. 138–139

 Standards: 1.2

Presentation EXPRESS
ANSWERS

Resources: Answers on Transparencies

Focus: Completing a story using new vocabulary

Suggestions: Remind students that their choices must fit grammatically as well as make sense contextually.

Answers:

1. enfermera
2. se torció
3. muletas
4. examinó
5. pastillas
6. se rompió
7. radiografías
8. yeso
9. roto
10. vinieron
11. ambulancia
12. Dijeron
13. sangre

 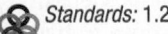 Standards: 1.2

Resources: Teacher's Resource Book: Audio Script, p. 33; Audio Program: Track 6; Answers on Transparencies

Focus: Listening and writing about accidents and injuries

Suggestions: Have students listen to the script once without pausing. Have them listen a second time. Pause after each sentence to allow them to make changes.

Script and Answers:

1. Me corté el codo y me pusieron una venda.
2. Me caí y me lastimé la espalda. Ahora me duele mucho.
3. Me pusieron una inyección y me dieron 12 puntadas en la rodilla.
4. El médico me recetó una medicina porque me sentía muy mal.
5. Cuando choqué con el árbol, me rompí la muñeca.
6. Me trajeron una silla de ruedas porque no podía mover la pierna.

  Standards: 1.3

Focus: Speaking about accidents and medical care

Suggestions: Have students make a list of the situations in *Actividades* 4–5 and ask a volunteer to write the list on the board.

Answers will vary.

Manos a la obra

Vocabulario y gramática en uso

Objectives
- Read and understand information about medical care
- Explain injuries and emergency room procedures
- Tell what happened in the emergency room
- Tell what was taking place when an accident occurred

 Leer/Escribir

En la sala de emergencia

Ana María quiere ser médica. Lee la descripción de su visita a la sala de emergencia. Escoge y escribe la palabra correcta para decir lo que pasó allí.

También se dice . . .

la radiografía = los rayos X *(muchos países)*

las puntadas = los puntos *(muchos países)*

dar puntadas = hacer puntadas, dar puntos *(muchos países)*

sala de emergencia = sala de urgencias *(muchos países)*

Ayer visité la sala de emergencia porque algún día quiero ser médica. Ayudé a una __1.__ *(receta / enfermera)* todo el día. Vi muchas cosas muy interesantes. Una chica __2.__ *(se torció / tropezó)* la rodilla esquiando, y por eso le trajeron unas __3.__ *(muletas / puntadas)*. El médico la __4.__ *(examinó / chocó)* y le recetó __5.__ *(pastillas / muletas)* para el dolor. Otra persona __6.__ *(chocó / se rompió)* el tobillo y le sacaron unas __7.__ *(radiografías / recetas)* de los huesos. Después le pusieron un __8.__ *(cuello / yeso)* porque tenía el hueso __9.__ *(roto /*

pobrecito). Unos paramédicos __10.__ *(vinieron / dijeron)* a la sala de emergencia en una __11.__ *(ambulancia / silla de ruedas)* con un señor que tuvo un accidente de coche. __12.__ *(Trajeron / Dijeron)* que tenían que hacerle una operación de emergencia porque estaba perdiendo *(losing)* mucha __13.__ *(medicina / sangre)*. A veces, durante mi visita a la sala de emergencia, tenía miedo de todo lo que estaba pasando, pero todavía quiero ser médica para ayudar a la gente.

 jdd-0598

Escuchar/Escribir

Escucha y escribe

Escucha lo que dicen unas personas que fueron a la sala de emergencia ayer. En una hoja de papel, escribe los números del 1 al 6. Escribe lo que escuchas. Vas a usar las frases para la Actividad 6.

  Dibujar/Hablar

Los accidentes

Dibuja una de las situaciones de las Actividades 4 ó 5. Muéstrales *(Show)* tu dibujo a otros(as) dos estudiantes. Traten de usar el máximo número de palabras nuevas para describir lo que les pasó a las personas que ven en los dibujos de sus compañeros(as).

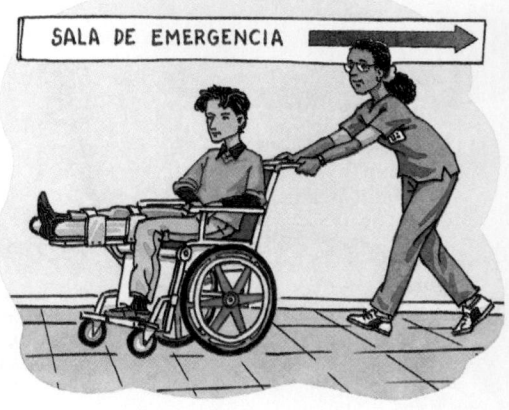

SALA DE EMERGENCIA

Differentiated Instruction
Solutions for All Learners

Students with Special Needs
Modify *Actividad* 7 for students with limited motor skills. Have students draw the basic outline of a body. Instead of standing and indicating the various body parts mentioned in the song, have them point to the corresponding body parts on their illustration.

Multiple Intelligences
Musical/Rhythmic: Have students lead small groups in doing *Actividad* 7. Encourage them to invent five different combinations of vocabulary words, and have them sing the combinations as their group performs the actions.

  **Cantar/Hablar**

Juego

Tu profesor(a) va a enseñarles una canción infantil que se usa para practicar los nombres de las partes del cuerpo.

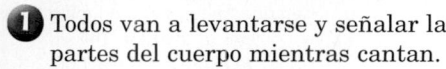

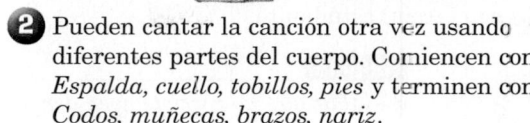
CABEZA, HOMBROS, RODILLAS, PIES
RODILLAS, PIES
RODILLAS, PIES
CABEZA, HOMBROS, RODILLAS, PIES
OJOS, OREJAS, BOCA, NARIZ

1 Todos van a levantarse y señalar las partes del cuerpo mientras cantan.

2 Pueden cantar la canción otra vez usando diferentes partes del cuerpo. Comiencen con *Espalda, cuello, tobillos, pies* y terminen con *Codos, muñecas, brazos, nariz*.

  Escribir/Hablar

En el hospital

Piensa en algunas personas que conoces que tuvieron que ir al hospital.

1 Escribe cuánto tiempo estuvieron en el hospital. Luego mira los dibujos y escribe una frase para cada uno para decir lo que le hicieron a cada persona.

Modelo

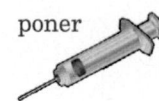
poner

Mi hermano Rafael estuvo en el hospital por tres días. Le pusieron una inyección.

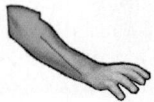
1. dar

2. llevar

3. recetar

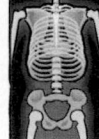
4. sacar

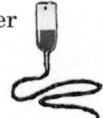
5. poner

2 Habla con otro(a) estudiante. Describan lo que les hicieron a las personas que Uds. conocen. Escribe cuatro frases para comparar lo que les hicieron.

Modelo

Mi hermano Rafael y el amigo de Carlota estuvieron en el hospital. No les pusieron sangre, pero sí les sacaron radiografías a los dos.

 **Fondo cultural**

La Ambulancia Azul es un servicio de ambulancias en España. Tiene tres niveles (*levels*) de servicio: SVA (Soporte Vital Avanzado) para pacientes en condiciones urgentes; SVB (Soporte Vital Básico) para enfermos que necesitan transporte en ambulancia, pero que no necesitan atención médica urgente; y Colectivo, una ambulancia que comparten varios pacientes.

• ¿Por qué crees que la Ambulancia Azul ofrece tres niveles de servicio? Compara este sistema al servicio de ambulancias en tu comunidad.

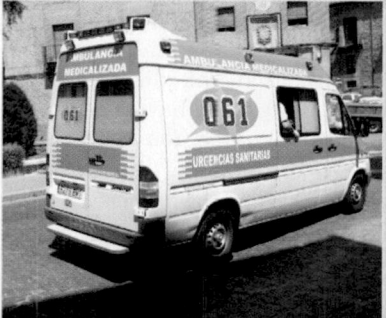

doscientos setenta y uno **271**
Capítulo 5B

 Actividad **7**  Standards: 1.2 Presentation EXPRESS ANSWERS

Resources: Answers on Transparencies

Focus: Singing a children's song about parts of the body

Recycle: Body parts vocabulary

Suggestions: Write the words to the song on the board or on a transparency and allow students to refer to it to help them learn the song.

Answers:

Step 1:
Students should point to their head, shoulders, knees, feet, knees, feet, knees, feet, head, shoulders, knees, feet, eyes, ears, mouth, and nose.

Step 2: Answers will vary.

 Actividad **8**  Standards: 1.1, 1.3 Presentation EXPRESS ANSWERS

Resources: Answers on Transparencies

Focus: Writing and speaking about going to the hospital

Suggestions: If students do not know anyone who has been in the hospital, have them use their imagination for the activity. For Step 1, tell students to answer in the negative if the people they are describing didn't experience what is depicted in the illustrations.

Answers:

Step 1: Answers may vary but will include:
1. **dieron puntadas**
2. **llevaron al hospital en una ambulancia**
3. **recetaron pastillas / medicina**
4. **sacaron una radiografía**
5. **pusieron sangre**

Step 2: Answers will vary.

 **Fondo cultural**  Standards: 1.2, 2.1, 2.2, 4.2

Suggestions: Have students interested in medical and public safety careers research the levels of paramedic assistance typically offered in the United States. Ask them to describe emergency services in your community.

Answers will vary.

Enrich Your Teaching
Resources for All Teachers

Teacher-to-Teacher

Prepare several dolls with bandages, casts, drawn-on stitches, etc., on various body parts. Arrange them in a "ward" on a table. Invite a group of "medical students" to "make rounds" with you. As you stop at each doll, ask a different "medical student" to tell you what the injury or illness was, and what the treatment was. Have the other "medical students" comment on the appropriateness of the diagnosis and treatment.

Presentation EXPRESS
ANSWERS

Actividad 9 Standards: 1.1

Resources: Answers on Transparencies

Focus: Giving excuses for not doing activities

Recycle: Imperfect and preterite tenses; activities; time expressions

Suggestions: Remind students that definite articles, not possessive adjectives, are used with body parts. Review the use of indirect object pronouns + **doler.**

Answers:

Student A:
1. ¿Por qué no jugaste al tenis el fin de semana pasado? ¿No te sentías bien?
2. ¿...esquiaste el sábado pasado?
3. ¿...hiciste gimnasia ayer?
4. ¿...levantaste pesas esta mañana?
5. ¿...patinaste anoche?
6. ¿...te moviste de la cama el domingo pasado?
7. ¿...jugaste al béisbol la semana pasada?

Student B:
1. No jugué al tenis porque me dolía la muñeca.
2. No esquié porque me dolía la rodilla.
3. No hice gimnasia porque me dolía el cuello.
4. No levanté pesas porque me dolía el codo.
5. No patiné porque me dolía la pierna / me dolían las piernas.
6. No me moví de la cama porque me dolía la espalda.
7. No jugué al béisbol porque me dolía el hombro / me dolían los hombros.

Exploración del lenguaje

Presentation EXPRESS
ANSWERS

Core Instruction

Standards: 4.1

Resources: Answers on Transparencies

Suggestions: Have students use context clues to help determine whether a word is a cognate or a false cognate.

Answers:
1. soup, not soap
2. necklace, not collar
3. bookstore, not library
4. folder, not carpet
5. glass, not vase

Pre-AP* Support

- **Activity:** Using the illustration in *Actividad* 6 on p. 270, have students write a brief, imaginary story relating what might have caused the situation. Encourage them to use both the preterite and the imperfect.
- *Pre-AP* Resource Book:* Comprehensive guide to Pre-AP* communication skill development, pp. 9–17, 36–46

Actividad 9  **Hablar**

¿Por qué no corriste?

No hiciste varias actividades la semana pasada porque te dolían diferentes partes del cuerpo. Habla de tus dolores con otro(a) estudiante.

corner / ayer
por la tarde

¿Recuerdas?

The imperfect tense is used to describe feelings and ongoing conditions in the past. The preterite expresses the actions that did or did not happen.

Modelo

A —¿Por qué no corriste ayer por la tarde? ¿No te sentías bien?

B —No corrí porque me dolía el tobillo.

Estudiante A

1. jugar al tenis / el fin de semana pasado
2. esquiar / el sábado pasado
3. hacer gimnasia / ayer
4. levantar pesas / esta mañana
5. patinar / anoche
6. moverse de la cama / el domingo pasado
7. jugar al béisbol / la semana pasada

Estudiante B

 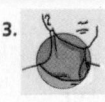 
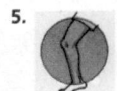

Exploración del lenguaje

False cognates

Cognates are words that look alike in both English and Spanish and have the same meaning:

bank → banco   photo → foto

But not all words that look alike in Spanish and English mean the same thing. Certain words are called **false cognates.** These are words that look alike but have different meanings. You have already learned some false cognates. You know that:

parientes means "relatives," not "parents"
recordar means "to remember," not "to record"

¡Compruébalo! Complete these sentences about other false cognates you already know:

1. **sopa** means ____, not ____
2. **collar** means ____, not ____
3. **librería** means ____, not ____
4. **carpeta** means ____, not ____
5. **vaso** means ____, not ____

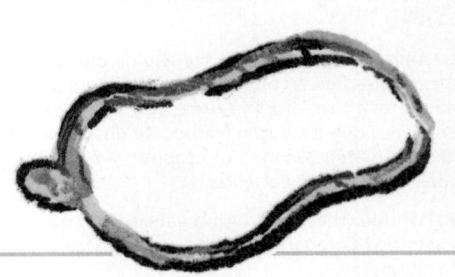

Differentiated Instruction
Solutions for All Learners

Advanced Learners/Pre-AP*

Have students write a note to their coach or physical education teacher explaining why they were unable to participate in a recent athletic event. Ask them to tell how they were injured and what treatment they received.

Students with Learning Difficulties

If students struggle to identify false cognates, provide direct instruction on how to use a bilingual Spanish-English dictionary and context to determine if a word is a false cognate. Then give them a list of phrases that contain cognates or false cognates and have them identify and categorize the words.

Actividad 10

Hablar

¿Cuánto tiempo hace . . . ?

Hace mucho tiempo que no ves a un(a) amigo(a) y no sabías que tuvo un accidente. Habla con otro(a) estudiante de lo que le pasó.

tres días

Modelo

A — Oye, ¿cuánto tiempo hace que estás en el hospital?
B — Hace <u>tres días</u>. Me rompí la pierna.
A — ¡Pobrecita! ¿Qué te pasó?
B — Me caí cuando estaba esquiando.
A — ¡Qué lástima!

Estudiante A

estar en   tener
usar   llevar

Estudiante B

romperse   ¡Respuesta
torcerse   personal!
lastimarse
cortarse

1. seis días   2. cuatro días   3. dos semanas   4. una semana

Actividad 11

 Escribir/Hablar

Y tú, ¿qué dices?

1. ¿Te gustaría ser médico(a) o enfermero(a)? ¿Te pone nervioso(a) ver sangre o huesos rotos? ¿Cómo te sientes cuando un(a) enfermero(a) te pone una inyección?

2. Cuando tienes dolor de cabeza, de estómago o de otra parte del cuerpo, ¿qué haces para sentirte mejor?

3. ¿A veces te caes* cuando practicas un deporte u otra actividad? ¿Qué te pasa cuando te caes?

*In the present tense, *caerse* is conjugated like a regular *-er* verb, except in the *yo* form: *me caigo*.

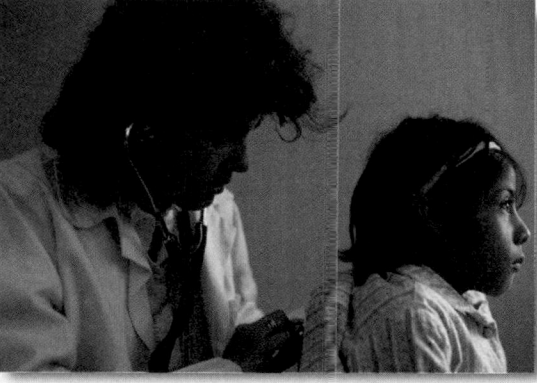

Una médica con una paciente, en México

doscientos setenta y tres **273**
Capítulo 5B

Enrich Your Teaching
Resources for All Teachers

Culture Note
Doctors in Mexico go through extensive training before receiving a license. College and medical school are combined in Mexico into either a six- or seven-year curriculum, depending on the school. After this, medical students complete two years of residency to prepare them for professional certification.

Internet Search
Have students research different medical services available in Spanish-speaking countries using the Internet.

Keywords:

servicios médicos + (name of country)

Practice and Communicate

5B

 **Bellringer Review**
Write three activities on a transparency and have students say how long they have been doing them.

Actividad 10   *Standards:* 1.1

Resources: Answers on Transparencies
Focus: Speaking about injuries and what you were doing when an injury occurred
Recycle: *hace* + length of time
Suggestions: Review the constructions using **hace** and **hace que** followed by a length of time.

Student A:
1. Oye, ¿cuánto tiempo hace que usas muletas?
2. Oye, ¿… llevas una venda?
3. Oye, ¿… estás en una silla de ruedas?
4. Oye, ¿… llevas un yeso?

Student B: Answers will vary but may include:
1. Hace seis días. Me lastimé la rodilla. Me caí cuando estaba patinando.
2. Hace cuatro días. Me lastimé el codo. Me caí … montando en bicicleta.
3. Hace dos semanas. Me rompí la pierna. Tropecé cuando estaba jugando al fútbol.
4. Hace una semana. Me rompí la muñeca. Me caí … montando en monopatín.

Actividad 11   *Standards:* 1.1, 1.3

Focus: Writing and speaking about personal experiences
Suggestions: Have students share their responses with a partner. Encourage them to ask follow-up questions about their partner's responses.
Answers will vary.

Additional Resources
- WAV Wbk.: Audio Act. 6, p. 101
- Teacher's Resource Book: Audio Script, p. 34, Communicative Activity BLM, pp. 40–41
- Audio Program: Track 8

✓ Assessment
- **ExamView** Quiz on PresEXPRESS
- Prueba 5B-2: Vocab. Production, pp. 140–141

273

Gramática

Presentation EXPRESS
GRAMMAR

Core Instruction

Standards: 4.1

Resources: Voc. and Gram. Transparency 102; Video Program: Cap. 5B; Teacher's Resource Book: Video Script, p. 36

Suggestions: Use the *GramActiva* Video as an introduction or to reinforce your own presentation. Write the verbs **estar, poder,** and **venir** on the board and have volunteers conjugate them in the preterite. Point out that **-ar, -er,** and **-ir** irregular verbs use the same endings.

 Actividad 12

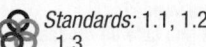 

Standards: 1.1, 1.2, 1.3

Presentation EXPRESS
AUDIO

Resources: Teacher's Resource Book: Audio Script, p. 34; Audio Program: Track 9; Answers on Transparencies

Focus: Listening, writing, and speaking about an accident

Suggestions: Ask students to listen to the script three times, the first time for overall meaning, the second to write the sentences, and the third to make corrections to spelling and word order. Be sure that students have correct sentences before moving on to the next step. Have students cut out the sentences and exchange them with a partner for Step 2.

Script and answers:

Steps 1 and 2:
1. Fui al hospital donde otro médico me puso un yeso. *(fifth)*
2. Estuve esperando en la silla de ruedas por más de una hora. *(second)*
3. Dijo que el hueso estaba roto. *(fourth)*
4. Una enfermera me trajo una silla de ruedas. *(first)*
5. Tuve que llevarlo por dos meses y no pude esquiar durante todo el invierno. *(sixth)*
6. Por fin el médico vino y me examinó el tobillo. *(third)*

Step 3:
Dos enfermeras le trajeron a Javier una silla de ruedas. Estuvo esperando en la silla de ruedas por más de una hora. Por fin dos médicos vinieron y le examinaron el tobillo. Le dijeron a Javier que el hueso estaba roto. Fue al hospital donde dos médicos le pusieron un yeso. Tuvo que llevarlo por dos meses y no pudo esquiar durante todo el invierno.

Gramática

Irregular preterites: *venir, poner, decir,* and *traer*

The verbs *venir, poner, decir,* and *traer* follow a pattern in the preterite that is similar to that of *estar, poder,* and *tener*. All these verbs have irregular stems and use the same unaccented endings.

Infinitive	Stem
decir	dij-
estar	estuv-
poder	pud-
poner	pus-
tener	tuv-
traer	traj-
venir	vin-

Irregular preterite endings	
-e	-imos
-iste	-isteis
-o	-ieron / -eron

puse	pusimos
pusiste	pusisteis
puso	pusieron

Note that verbs like *decir* and *traer,* whose irregular stems end in *j,* drop the *i* in the *Uds./ellos/ellas* form and add only *-eron.*

Me **trajeron** una silla de ruedas y me **dijeron** que no debía tratar de caminar.

GramActiva VIDEO

Want more help with the irregular preterites: *venir, poner, decir,* and *traer?* Watch the **GramActiva** video.

vine, dije

 Actividad 12

jdd-0598

🔊 **Escuchar/Escribir/Hablar**

Escucha y escribe

1 Javier fue a esquiar en las montañas. El primer día tuvo un accidente. Escucha su descripción de lo que pasó y escribe las seis frases, pero ten cuidado. Javier no está contando en orden lo que pasó.

2 Trabaja con otro(a) estudiante para poner en orden lógico el cuento de Javier.

3 Cuenten otra vez lo que le pasó a Javier, pero imaginen que dos enfermeras y dos médicos lo atendieron. Cambien las formas de los verbos apropiados.

Modelo

Dos enfermeras le trajeron a Javier una silla de ruedas.

274 doscientos setenta y cuatro
Tema 5 • En las noticias

Bariloche, Argentina, es un lugar turístico internacional. En el invierno se puede esquiar y en el verano se puede ir de pesca, montar a caballo o escalar las montañas *(go mountain climbing).*

Differentiated Instruction
Solutions for All Learners

Heritage Language Learners
Due to the similarity between the pronunciation of the Spanish *j* and the English *h,* some students may confuse the two letters in writing. Give students additional writing practice using the preterite forms of **decir** and **traer** to reinforce the use of the letter *j* in these forms.

Students with Special Needs
Give hearing-impaired students the script for *Actividad* 12. Change the verbs to the infinitive and have students conjugate them in the preterite. When students have completed their sentences, ask them to renumber them to reflect a logical sequence.

Actividad 13

Leer/Escribir

Mi programa favorito

Anoche Adela vio sólo una parte de su programa de televisión favorito, *Emergencia*. Completa el correo electrónico que ella le escribe a su amiga con las formas apropiadas de los verbos.

Tere: ¿Viste *Emergencia* anoche? Yo lo vi por media hora pero no __1.__ (poder / venir) ver más porque __2.__ (estar / tener) que llevar a mi hermana a su práctica de gimnasia. Esto es lo que vi. Una señora __3.__ (decir / venir) al hospital con mucha sangre en la mano. Ella __4.__ (decir / poner) que se cortó la mano cuando estaba cocinando. Una médica le __5.__ (poner / venir) una inyección y después le __6.__ (dar / poder) ocho puntadas. Luego los paramédicos __7.__ (decir / traer) a un anciano al hospital en una ambulancia. Ellos __8.__ (decir / venir) que el anciano __9.__ (poder / tener) un accidente en su coche. Los médicos le hicieron una operación de emergencia para salvarle la vida. Pues, dime, Tere, ¿qué __10.__ (poder / pasar) al final del programa? ¡Escríbeme pronto y dime todo!

Adela

Actividad 14

Leer/Escribir

Si necesitas ayuda . . .

Lee el siguiente anuncio sobre el servicio de ambulancias que existe para un hospital de Quito, Ecuador. Después contesta las preguntas.

Hospital de Clínicas Pichincha

Ponemos a su disposición dos ambulancias, manejadas por profesionales preparados para el transporte rápido pero seguro.*

Clínicas Pichincha AMBULANCIA

Ofrecemos:
- ambulancias equipadas para dar atención inmediata
- paramédicos entrenados para atender al paciente críticamente enfermo o herido
- equipo médico moderno
- servicio permanente, sin interrupción (disponible los 365 días del año, las 24 horas del día)
- comunicación directa con el Servicio de Emergencia

El teléfono para acceder a nuestro servicio es el 505-505 (Quito). Vamos a atender a su llamada de inmediato pues, una emergencia no espera.

*safe

1. ¿Por qué puedes tener confianza (confidence) en el servicio de estas ambulancias? Menciona tres razones (reasons).

2. ¿A qué horas puede atenderte este servicio?

3. ¿Por qué dice el servicio que va a atender rápidamente a una llamada?

Actividad 15

Escribir/Hablar

Necesitabas una ambulancia

Imagina que trabajas para el servicio de ambulancia de la Actividad 14 y quieres saber qué tipo de servicio recibieron los pacientes. Con otro(a) estudiante, entrevista (interview) a un(a) paciente y pregúntale sobre el servicio que recibió. Usa las siguientes preguntas en la entrevista:

- ¿Qué te dijeron? ¿Qué preguntas te hicieron?
- ¿Cuántos paramédicos vinieron? ¿Vinieron inmediatamente?
- ¿Qué trajeron en la ambulancia?
- ¿Te pusieron una inyección cuando llegaron?

doscientos setenta y cinco **275**
Capítulo 5B

Enrich Your Teaching
Resources for All Teachers

Culture Note

The resorts at Bariloche in Argentina rely on the services of an active and highly skilled ski patrol to enforce safety regulations and to assist or rescue injured skiers. The mountains of the Bariloche area are similar in size to the European Alps. Only the most expert of skiers can work for the Bariloche Ski Patrol.

Internet Search

Have students learn more about the resorts at Bariloche using the Internet. They might also research safety and first aid for skiers.

Keyword:

Bariloche

Actividad 13

 Standards: 1.2   Presentation EXPRESS ANSWERS

Resources: Answers on Transparencies

Focus: Completing an e-mail about the events in a television show

Suggestions: Review the verb *dar* in the preterite. Tell students to read the e-mail once and choose the appropriate verb in parentheses. Then have them read it a second time and focus on conjugating the verb correctly.

Answers:
1. pude
2. tuve
3. vino
4. dijo
5. puso
6. dio
7. trajeron
8. dijeron
9. tuvo
10. pasó

Actividad 14

 Standards: 1.2, 2.2   Presentation EXPRESS ANSWERS

Resources: Voc. and Gram. Transparency 104; Answers on Transparencies

Focus: Reading and writing about an ambulance service

Suggestions: Ask students to determine, based on the illustration and the headline, what the reading is about. Have students quickly scan the reading and identify the three sections (introduction, what is offered, contact information).

Answers:
1. Answer will vary, but will include:
   Porque son manejadas por profesionales, están equipadas para dar atención inmediata, tienen equipo médico moderno y están en comunicación directa con el Servicio de Emergencia. Los paramédicos están bien entrenados.
2. Este servicio puede atenderte los 365 días del año, las 24 horas del día.
3. Porque una emergencia no espera.

Actividad 15

  Standards: 1.1

Focus: Speaking about ambulance services and medical treatment

Suggestions: Encourage students to describe both positive and negative experiences using the ambulance service.

Answers will vary.

275

Standards: 1.1, 1.3

Presentation EXPRESS
ANSWERS

Resources: Answers on Transparencies

Focus: Speaking and writing about a party

Suggestions: You may want to have students bring in pictures to use in discussing the questions. Remind students that for Step 3 they will be writing their paragraphs in the third person.

Answers:

Step 2:

1. ¿Pusiste...?
2. ¿...vinieron...?
3. ¿...trajo...?
4. ¿...hicieron...?
5. ¿...estuvieron...?
6. ¿Pudiste...?

Step 3: Answers will vary.

Standards: 1.1, 1.3

Focus: Playing a game using irregular preterite forms

Suggestions: Have students brainstorm prepositions, conjunctions, and transitional words that might help them make longer, more creative sentences.

Answers will vary.

El español en el mundo del trabajo

Core Instruction

Standards: 1.2, 5.1

Suggestions: In order to answer the second question, provide students with contact information for local hospitals and medical facilities.

Answers will vary.

Theme Project

Students can perform Step 4 at this point. (For more information, see p. 236-a.)

Additional Resources

- WAV Wbk.: Audio Act. 7, p. 101
- Teacher's Resource Book: Audio Script, p. 34
- Audio Program: Track 10

✓ Assessment

- **ExamView** Quiz on PresEXPRESS
  QuickTake Presenter
- **Prueba 5B-3:** Irregular preterites: *venir, poner, decir,* and *traer,* p. 142

Una celebración muy especial

1 Piensa en una fiesta que muchas personas celebraron en tu casa. Vas a trabajar con otro(a) estudiante para hablar de la fiesta.

2 Completa las preguntas con los verbos en el pretérito, y hazle estas preguntas a tu compañero(a). Escribe lo que dice.

1. ¿*(Ponerse)* tú ropa elegante o ropa de todos los días para esta fiesta?

2. ¿Quiénes *(venir)* a la fiesta?

3. ¿Quién *(traer)* regalos, comida u otras cosas?

4. ¿Qué *(hacer)* todos durante la fiesta?

5. ¿Por cuánto tiempo *(estar)* las personas allí?

6. ¿*(Poder)* tú hablar con todo el mundo?

3 Escribe un resumen de la fiesta que te describió tu compañero(a).

Más práctica

- Practice Workbook, p. 106: 5B-5
- WAV Wbk.: Writing, p. 104
- Guided Practice: Grammar Acts., pp. 191–192
- *Real.* para hispanohablantes, pp. 194-197

Go Online
PHSchool.com
For: Irregular Preterites
Web Code: jdd-0513

Juego

1 Trabaja con tres estudiantes. En tarjetas o pequeñas hojas de papel, escriban las raíces *(stems)* de los verbos irregulares en el pretérito de la página 274 y pongan las tarjetas en un grupo boca abajo *(facedown).*

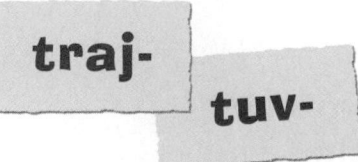
traj-
tuv-

2 Van a jugar en parejas *(pairs).* La primera pareja escoge una tarjeta y crea una frase en 30 segundos para decir lo que pasó en el hospital o en un accidente. Después leen la frase. La otra pareja tiene que decir si la frase es correcta. La primera pareja recibe un punto por cada palabra correcta en su frase.

Modelo

Anoche hubo un incendio y trajeron a varias personas heridas al hospital en una ambulancia. (15 puntos)

El español en el mundo del trabajo

Los intérpretes y traductores *(translators)* médicos son muy importantes en los hospitales de los Estados Unidos. A veces, cuando una persona que no habla inglés va al hospital, el médico y las enfermeras no pueden entender lo que dice y no pueden ayudarle. Las personas pueden morir si no reciben atención adecuada y a tiempo. Por eso los hospitales contratan a intérpretes y a traductores. Tener intérpretes en los hospitales es una necesidad y también una ley.

- ¿Crees que es importante tener intérpretes y traductores en los hospitales? ¿Hay un servicio de intérpretes en el hospital de tu comunidad?

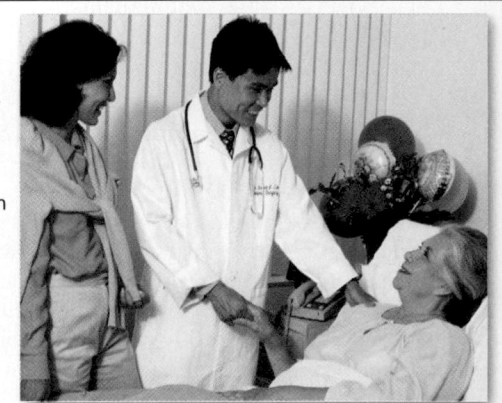

Differentiated Instruction
Solutions for All Learners

Students with Learning Difficulties

For *Actividad* 17, modify the game for students by extending the time allotted to compose the sentence. You may prefer to write the subject and the verb in the infinitive on each card and have students finish the sentence to receive points.

Multiple Intelligences

Intrapersonal/Introspective: Assign *Actividad* 16 for homework and have students do the activity with a family member. Ask them to write the questions on a sheet of paper, along with their own summary of the party. Then have them interview a family member and summarize their conversation.

Gramática

Imperfect progressive and preterite

To describe something that was taking place over a period of time in the past, use the imperfect progressive, which uses the imperfect tense of *estar* + the present participle.

Estaba esquiando cuando me caí y me torcí la rodilla.

I was skiing when I fell and sprained my knee.

The present and imperfect progressive tenses use the same present participles. Remember, to form the present participle of *-ir* stem-changing verbs, *e* changes to *i* and *o* changes to *u*:

For the following *-er* verbs, the *i* of *-iendo* changes to *y*:

e → i		o → u	i → y
decir: diciendo	seguir: siguiendo	dormir: durmiendo	creer: creyendo
pedir: pidiendo	servir: sirviendo		leer: leyendo
repetir: repitiendo	vestir: vistiendo		traer: trayendo

• When you use object pronouns with the imperfect progressive, you can put them before *estar* or attach them to the participle.

—¿Qué estabas haciendo cuando te cortaste?

—Estaba afeitándo**me. o: Me** estaba afeitando.

• Note that the imperfect progressive describes what was taking place while the preterite tells a specific occurrence in the past or interrupts the action.

Ella estaba corriendo cuando **se lastimó** el tobillo.

¿Recuerdas?

When you say that an action is happening right now, you use the present progressive tense. The present progressive uses the present tense of *estar* + the present participle.

• No puedo ir al cine. **Estoy estudiando** para el examen.

GramActiva VIDEO

Want more help with the imperfect progressive and preterite? Watch the **GramActiva** video.

Estaba hablando.

Actividad 18

Escribir

Cuando llegó la ambulancia

Mira el dibujo y escribe frases para decir lo que estaban haciendo las personas en la sala de emergencia cuando llegó la ambulancia.

Modelo

el médico

El médico estaba hablando por teléfono.

1. la médica
2. el enfermero
3. la enfermera
4. los jóvenes
5. la niña
6. los ancianos

doscientos setenta y siete **277**
Capítulo 5B

Core Instruction

Standards: 4.1

Resources: Voc. and Gram. Transparency 103; Teacher's Resource Book: Video Script, pp. 36–37; Video Program: Cap. 5B

Suggestions: Review the present progressive by writing the word **ahora** on the board, and using gestures to act out a series of actions. Model the first few actions, and then have volunteers continue your narration. Then, erase the board and write the word **antes.** Act out the same activities, but narrate them in the imperfect progressive. Remind students that the imperfect describes an ongoing action in the past, and the imperfect progressive is used to describe an ongoing action that was taking place at a specific time. Ask students what they were doing at six o'clock yesterday afternoon. Model a correct response for them.

To point out the difference between an ongoing action and a specific action in the past, use a wind-up toy. Wind up the toy, set it near the edge of your desk, and as it walks, say: *El señor estaba caminando cuando...* Pause to let it fall off the desk and say: *...se cayó.* Give additional examples and have students use the toy to create their own examples.

Actividad 18 **Standards:** 1.3
Presentation EXPRESS
ANSWERS

Resources: Answers on Transparencies

Focus: Writing about what was happening

Suggestions: Have students examine the illustration before they begin. Use the answer key to provide any necessary clarification on what is happening in the picture. Remind students that two of the items require reflexive verbs, and that they must include the appropriate pronouns and accent marks.

Answers:
1. La médica le estaba poniendo una venda a la niña.
2. El enfermero estaba leyendo.
3. La enfermera estaba pintándose las uñas.
4. Los jóvenes estaban cepillándose el pelo.
5. La niña estaba llorando.
6. Los ancianos estaban durmiendo.

Enrich Your Teaching
Resources for All Teachers

Culture Note

California hospitals handle the federal legal requirement for interpreting services in several ways. Some hospitals have interpreters on call. However, many doctors and nurses in California hospitals speak both English and Spanish. Outside interpreters are sometimes brought into conferences by speakerphone.

Teacher-to-Teacher

If possible, contact an interpreter at your local hospital. Arrange time for him or her to speak to your students about his or her career. Have students prepare questions before the visit. Encourage them to ask about training, hours, duties of interpreters, and so on.

Resources: Answers on Transparencies

Focus: Writing about what people were doing when an accident occurred

Suggestions: Have students brainstorm words for each illustration before writing.

Answers will vary but may include:

1. Yolanda estaba patinando cuando se chocó con un árbol.
2. Héctor estaba caminando cuando tropezó con un libro.
3. Juan y Anita estaban esquiando cuando se rompieron las piernas.
4. Antonio estaba jugando al básquetbol cuando se cayó y se lastimó el pie.
5. Rosa estaba preparando la cena cuando se cortó el dedo.

Extension: Ask students to describe possible treatments for each person.

Focus: Writing and speaking about what people were doing when an accident occurred

Suggestions: Have students use their imagination if they cannot think of three examples. Using a stuffed animal, model a correct dialogue with a volunteer. Have the stuffed animal sit on your desk with a book and let it fall over. Have a student make the first statement, and you can follow up with the question.

Answers will vary.

Suggestions: Discuss with students the link between population density and public services. Point out that while cities may have more than one hospital, rural areas tend to have fewer doctors and hospitals, and people have to travel farther to reach them. Provide students with a map that reflects the population density of the United States to help them answer the questions.

Answers will vary.

278

 Escribir

Tus pacientes

Tú eres enfermero(a) en una sala de emergencia y tienes que escribir una historia médica de tus pacientes. Mira los dibujos y describe qué estaban haciendo las personas y qué les pasó.

Laura

Modelo
Laura estaba cocinando cuando se quemó la mano.

1. Yolanda   2. Héctor   3. Juan y Anita   4. Antonio   5. Rosa

  Escribir/Hablar

¿Quiénes se cayeron?

Piensa en las personas que tú conoces que se cayeron alguna vez. ¿Quiénes son y cuándo se cayeron? Describe los accidentes de tres personas y describe qué estaban haciendo cuando se cayeron. Luego habla con otro(a) estudiante y compara sus respuestas.

Modelo
A —Mi hermana se cayó el mes pasado.
B —¿Qué estaba haciendo tu hermana cuando se cayó?
A —Estaba poniendo carteles en la pared.

Nota
In the preterite, *caerse* is like *leer,* with forms that change the *i* to *y* in the *Ud./él/ella* and *Uds./ellos/ellas* forms. There is also an accent mark over the *i* in all other forms.
- Cuando estaba bajando la escalera, Enrique **se cayó.**
- Cuando yo estaba subiendo la escalera, **me caí.**

 **Fondo cultural**

La Patrulla Aérea Colombiana (PAC) es un equipo de pilotos y médicos que viaja en avión a pueblos remotos que no tienen ni médicos ni hospitales. La PAC enseña programas de prevención de salud a las comunidades y ofrece servicios médicos básicos y cirugía *(surgery).* Muchos de los pueblos están en los Andes o en las regiones amazónicas y la Patrulla es el único servicio médico que llega a estas comunidades.

- ¿Conoces partes de los Estados Unidos donde no hay ni médicos ni hospitales? ¿Qué soluciones hay para esta situación en los Estados Unidos y en Colombia?

Los pilotos y médicos de la Patrulla Aérea Colombiana

Differentiated Instruction
Solutions for All Learners

Multiple Intelligences
Bodily/Kinesthetic: Reinforce the imperfect progressive for students by having them perform activities such as watching television or reading. Have volunteers exit and enter your classroom every few moments, interrupting students' activities. Ask volunteers to narrate what the others were doing when they were interrupted.

Students with Learning Difficulties
Students may need clarification of the difference between "acute" and "chronic" for *Actividad* 21. Have them list the various types of injuries in a T-chart under *aguda* and *crónica.* Help them see which ones are sudden and which are ongoing.

Actividad 21 Leer/Pensar/Hablar

Las lesiones en los deportes

¿Practicas un deporte o juegas en un equipo? Quizás patinas o montas en monopatín. ¿Sabes cuáles son las lesiones *(injuries)* que te pueden ocurrir cuando practicas deportes? Lee el artículo y luego contesta las preguntas.

Conexiones | **La salud**

Los dos tipos de lesiones deportivas

Las lesiones en los deportes son las que ocurren típicamente en los deportes organizados, los entrenamientos[1] o las actividades diarias de acondicionamiento.

⊙ **Lesión traumática aguda:**[2] causada por un golpe[3] intenso como un choque o una caída. Ejemplos son la fractura de un hueso, una torcedura (se estira[4] o se rompe un músculo o tendón) o una distensión (se estira o se rompe un ligamento). Estas lesiones afectan más las rodillas, los tobillos y las muñecas.

⊙ **Lesión crónica:** causada por el uso continuo o excesivo. Es el resultado del entrenamiento repetitivo tal como correr o lanzar[5] una pelota. Ejemplos son las fracturas de un hueso por estrés, la tendinitis (se rompen las fibras del tendón a causa de estiramientos excesivos) o la bursitis (inflamación de la bursa en el hombro, en el codo o en la rodilla).

[1]training sessions [2]acute traumatic injury [3]blow [4]pull [5]throw

En las siguientes descripciones, ¿tienen los atletas una lesión traumática aguda o crónica? Habla con otro(a) estudiante. Usen la información del artículo y den razones por su diagnóstico.

1. Lisa practicaba el golf todos los días. Siempre sentía un dolor en el codo.

2. En un partido de básquetbol, Kevin chocó con otro jugador. Se torció el tobillo y se cayó.

3. Hugo levantaba pesas todas las tarde[s] el gimnasio. Quería levantar el máxi[mo] peso. Un día trataba de levantar 300 cuando tuvo un dolor agudo en el ho[mbro] no pudo levantar la barra.

4. Sara jugaba al fútbol en el otoño y al básquetbol en el invierno. S[i]n descan[so] empezó a entrenar para el fútbol en l[a] primavera. Le dolía la rodilla despué[s de] cada práctica.

 Actividad 22 Pensar/Escribir

Familias de palabras

Si reconoces *(you recognize)* familias de palabras, entiendes mejor lo que lees. Mira las palabras de *Conexiones*. Escribe las palabras que ya conoces que te ayudan a entender las siguientes palabras nuevas.

Modelo
el uso
usar

1. una caída
2. una torcedura
3. repetitivo
4. un choque

doscientos setenta y nu[eve] **279**
Capítulo

 Actividad 21  *Standards:* 1.2, 3.1  Presentation EXPRESS ANSWERS

Resources: Answers on Transparencies

Focus: Reading and speaking about sports injuries

Suggestions: Ask students to brainstorm the types of injuries that they associate with different sports. Help them to classify the injuries into categories, based on whether they happen suddenly or gradually. Students may not be familiar with the word **bursa.** Point out that this word is a cognate for the English word "bursa," which is a small sac of fluid between the tendon and the bone. Have students point out expressions in each description (such as **un día** or **siempre**) that will help them determine whether or not it is an acute traumatic injury or a chronic injury.

Answers:
1. Lisa tiene una lesión crónica.
2. Kevin tiene una lesión traumática aguda.
3. Hugo tiene una lesión traumática aguda.
4. Sara tiene una lesión crónica.

Extension: Have students provide examples of when they or someone in their family had an acute traumatic injury or a chronic injury. Ask them to include how the injury occurred and what the treatment was.

 Actividad 22  *Standards:* 1.2  Presentation EXPRESS ANSWERS

Resources: Answers on Transparencies

Focus: Identifying new words based on their relationship with known words

Suggestions: Introduce students to the concept of word families. Write the verb **cantar** on the board and ask students to guess the meanings of the words **canción** and **cantante.** Point out that verbs often have related nouns and adjectives, and if you know one word, you can recognize the others.

Answers:
1. caer   3. repetir
2. torcer   4. chocar con

Extension: Ask students to write sentences using each of the words.

 Enrich Your Teaching
Resources for All Teachers

Culture Note

Emergency medical care in rural areas varies in Latin American countries. Many residents of remote areas are unable to obtain medical care easily. In many places, however, there are government or charitable clinics where people can have wounds treated and can obtain medication.

Teacher-to-Teacher

Have students write an artic[le] describing an injury that a well-known athlete has suffered. Have them say whether it was an acute traumatic injury or a chronic injury, describe the treatment and say how long the player was unable to play.

 Standards: 1.2, 2.1, 2.2

Presentation EXPRESS
ANSWERS

Resources: Voc. and Gram. Transparency 105; Answers on Transparencies

Focus: Reading and writing about a famous soccer player's injuries

Suggestions: To activate prior knowledge, ask students to think of a professional athlete or an athlete in your school who has overcome an injury. Have them describe the injury and the steps that the person took to recover. Have students list words that describe a person who can overcome obstacles to achieve their goals. To help them focus, suggest that they read the questions first.

Answers:
1. Sufrió una lesión en la rodilla derecha.
2. Los días que siguieron fueron tan difíciles porque no pudo jugar. Estaba tan triste que no hablaba, dormía todo el tiempo y no comía.
3. Cuando comenzó a jugar otra vez, se lastimó otra vez la misma rodilla.
4. Ronaldo pudo volver a jugar porque tenía mucha determinación y también tenía la ayuda de muchos médicos y de la fisioterapia.

 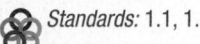 Standards: 1.1, 1.3

Focus: Writing and speaking about sports injuries

Suggestions: Have students write the answers for items 1 and 2 in a short paragraph. If students are not active in sports, invite them to write about a friend or family member.

Answers will vary.

 Fondo cultural Standards: 1.2, 2.2, 4.2

■◆◇■◆◇■◆◇■◆◇■◆◇■◆◇■◆◇■

Suggestions: Have students do an Internet search and find rules and procedures for jai alai.

Answers will vary.

 Actividad 23 Leer/Escribir/Hablar

Los días más difíciles

Lee este artículo sobre un famoso futbolista y contesta las preguntas.

1. ¿Qué le pasó a Ronaldo que cambió *(changed)* mucho su vida?
2. ¿Por qué fueron tan difíciles los días que siguieron?
3. ¿Qué le pasó cuando comenzó a jugar otra vez?
4. ¿Por qué Ronaldo pudo volver a jugar?

[1] However [2] physical therapy

 Actividad 24 Escribir/Hablar

Y tú, ¿qué dices?

1. Recientemente cuando estabas practicando un deporte o haciendo otra actividad, ¿sentiste* un dolor en algún músculo o hueso? ¿Qué hiciste para el dolor?
2. ¿Te lastimaste alguna vez cuando estabas practicando un deporte? ¿Cómo te lastimaste? ¿Qué deporte estabas practicando?
3. Piensa en alguien que conoces que se rompió un hueso o se torció un tobillo o una rodilla. ¿Qué estaba haciendo cuando ocurrió el accidente? ¿Le sacaron radiografías? ¿Tuvo que llevar un yeso o usar muletas?

* When *sentir* is followed by a noun, the non-reflexive form of the verb is used.

Fenómeno de perseverancia

Ronaldo Luiz Nazario da Lima nació en Brasil, donde empezó a jugar al fútbol. Como profesional jugó para equipos de Holanda, Italia y España. Era uno de los mejores futbolistas, pero entonces algo muy malo le pasó. Estaba jugando en un partido cuando sufrió una lesión en la rodilla derecha. Con mucho dolor, salió del partido. Primero en una silla de ruedas y después en muletas, estuvo 512 días sin jugar. Unos años después, Ronaldo dijo: "Fueron los días más difíciles de mi carrera deportiva". Ronaldo dijo que durante mucho tiempo estaba tan triste que no hablaba, dormía todo el tiempo y no comía. Finalmente volvió a jugar. Estaba jugando unos minutos cuando se lastimó otra vez la misma rodilla. Ronaldo recuerda, "gritaba y gritaba no sólo de dolor; tenía mucho miedo de la gravedad de la lesión". Sin embargo[1], Ronaldo tenía mucha determinación y con la ayuda de muchos médicos y fisioterapia[2], sí pudo volver a jugar.

 **Fondo cultural**

El jai alai ¿Sabías que el jai alai es el deporte de pelota más rápido del mundo? En este juego, ¡la pelota llega a alcanzar velocidades de 150 millas por hora! El jai alai se originó en el País Vasco, en el norte de España. Se juega en una cancha *(court)* con tres paredes y los jugadores llevan casco *(helmet)* porque este deporte puede ser peligroso y causar lesiones. Se juega en muchos países y en los Estados Unidos es muy popular en Florida y Connecticut.

• ¿En qué sentido es diferente el jai alai de los juegos que practicas tú?

Jugadores mexicanos de jai alai

280 doscientos ochenta
Tema 5 • En las noticias

Differentiated Instruction
Solutions for All Learners

Students with Special Needs

Students may feel excluded in some of these conversations if they are unable to participate in a sport or physical activity. Allow all students to make references to famous or local athletes as an alternative to personalized responses.

Heritage Language Learners

Have students write a composition about an athlete who overcame obstacles in order to achieve a goal, as did Ronaldo Luiz Nazario da Lima. Have students write multiple drafts and provide them with a checklist of things to look for as they revise their first draft.

Actividad 25

Escribir/Hablar/GramActiva

Juego

1 Trabaja con otro(a) estudiante. En pequeñas hojas de papel, escriban dos frases que describen lo que estaban haciendo una o dos personas cuando algo ocurrió. Su profesor(a) va a dividir a la clase en dos grupos. Los estudiantes en cada grupo ponen todas sus hojas de papel en una bolsa y le dan la bolsa al otro grupo.

2 Saca una hoja de papel de la bolsa y lee la frase. No puedes mostrar *(show)* la hoja a tu grupo ni puedes decirles lo que dice. Tienes un minuto para representar la situación para ver si tu grupo puede decir correctamente la frase. Si lo pueden hacer en un minuto o menos, reciben un punto. Si no lo pueden hacer en un minuto, no reciben ningún punto.

> Estabas nadando cuando chocaste con la pared de la piscina.

Actividad 26

Hablar

Un accidente en la carretera

1 Trabaja con dos estudiantes. Uno(a) de Uds. es reportero(a) y está investigando el choque de coches en el dibujo. El (La) reportero(a) está hablando con dos testigos *(witnesses)* que tienen diferentes versiones de lo que pasó en el accidente. En su dramatización, pueden incluir:

- lo que estaban haciendo los testigos cuando ocurrió el accidente
- lo que estaban haciendo los coches y los conductores cuando ocurrió
- qué hora era cuando ocurrió y qué otras condiciones existían
- qué les pasó a las personas en el accidente y si hubo muchos heridos
- quiénes vinieron a ayudar y lo que hicieron
- lo que hicieron todos después del accidente

2 Preparen su dramatización y preséntenla para la clase entera o para otro grupo.

Más práctica

- Practice Workbook, pp. 107–108: 5B-6, 5B-7
- WAV Wbk.: Writing, p. 105
- Guided Practice: Grammar Acts., pp. 192–194
- *Real.* para hispanohablantes, pp. 198-199

Go Online PHSchool.com
For: Imperfect and Preterite
Web Code: jdd-0514

doscientos ochenta y uno **281**
Capítulo 5B

 Bellringer Review
Write the infinitives for four activities that might be used in *Actividad 25* on the board, and have students change them to the imperfect progressive.

Actividad 25
Standards: 1.1, 1.3

Focus: Writing and speaking about what was happening when something else occurred

Recycle: Activities; place names

Suggestions: Have students review each other's sentences for accuracy or redundancy before giving them to the other group. Set a timer for each round to keep the game moving.

Answers will vary.

Actividad 26
Standards: 1.1, 1.3

Pre-AP*

Focus: Describing an accident

Suggestions: Have students examine the illustration and brainstorm what they think might have happened. Encourage different interpretations. You may want to videotape the presentations.

Answers will vary.

Theme Project

Students can perform Step 5 at this point. (For more information, see p. 236-a.)

Additional Resources

- WAV Wbk.: Audio Act. 8–9, p. 102
- Teacher's Resource Book: Audio Script, p. 35, Communicative Activity BLM, pp. 42–43
- Audio Program: Tracks 11–12

✓ Assessment

- ExamView QuickTake Presenter Quiz on PresEXPRESS
- Prueba 5B-4: Imperfect progressive and preterite, p. 143

Teacher-to-Teacher

Have students work in two groups to perform a mock trial. Tell students that their court case is about an injury that resulted from a car accident. Tell them that you are the judge and will keep order in the court. In their testimonies, have students describe what they were doing when the accident occurred, what happened, what the injuries were, and what the cost of treatment is going to be. After all of the testimonies are heard, have the other students in the class act as the jury and determine the verdict. If possible, videotape the performance and view it as a class.

281

5B

Videomisterio

Core Instruction

Standards: 1.2, 3.2, 5.2

Resources: Teacher's Resource Book: Video Script, pp. 37–38; Video Program: Cap. 5B; Video Program Teacher's Guide: Cap. 5B

Focus: Reading and presenting new vocabulary needed to understand the video

Personajes importantes

Roberto

Linda

Chato Montesinos, an old friend of Roberto's grandfather

El Sr. De León, bank employee

El Sr. Turrón, an acquaintance of De León

Synopsis: Roberto and Linda go to Dolores Hidalgo to inquire about the missing grandfather, Federico Zúñiga. They meet with Chato in his home. Chato tells them that Federico entered the U.S. Army when the two of them went to San Antonio. He gives them the name of a bank in Texas where they both opened accounts. Roberto calls the bank and speaks with Sr. De León in the Closed Accounts department. De León tells Roberto that there is an account, but that it must be claimed in person by an adult relative of Federico Zúñiga. De León calls the mysterious Sr. Turrón to tell him that someone has been making inquiries.

Suggestions:

Pre-viewing: Review the events of *Episodio* 5: Julio invited Linda to lunch, while Roberto offered to show her Guanajuato. They visited the *Callejón del Beso.* Roberto continued inquiring about his mysterious grandfather.

Have a volunteer read the *Nota cultural* aloud. Remind students that they learned about the *Grito de la Independencia (¡Viva México!)* in *Capítulo* 1A, when they read about Dolores Hidalgo. Ask them to name a few slogans that we associate with independence *(Land of the free, home of the brave; Liberty and justice for all).*

Point out the *Palabras para comprender* and help students familiarize themselves with them.

Videomisterio

En busca de la verdad

Antes de ver el video

Episodio 6

"Déjelo en mis manos. Y no hable con nadie".

"Cuando Federico y yo entramos en el ejército, abrimos cuentas en este banco, el Banco de la Frontera, en San Antonio".

Nota cultural Cada 15 de septiembre, a medianoche, los mexicanos se reúnen en ciudades y pueblos para conmemorar su independencia de España y recordar a sus héroes nacionales. Todos los mexicanos saben de memoria los famosos "vivas": "¡Vivan los héroes que nos dieron Patria y Libertad! ¡Viva Miguel Hidalgo! ¡Viva Allende! ¡Viva la Independencia de México! ¡Viva México! ¡Viva México! ¡Viva México!".

Resumen del episodio

Roberto empieza a buscar la verdad sobre su abuelo. Él y Linda van a Dolores Hidalgo para hablar con Chato Montesinos. Allí descubren otra pista sobre el misterio del abuelo. El episodio termina con una llamada misteriosa.

Palabras para comprender

movimiento movement

Yo he estado varias veces. I have been many times.

nadie ha visto nobody has seen

Se casó. He / She got married.

nieto grandson

desapareció disappeared

ejército army

cuenta de banco bank account

286 doscientos ochenta y seis
Tema 5 • En las noticias

Differentiated Instruction
Solutions for All Learners

Advanced Learners

Ask students to prepare questions to test the class's comprehension of the *episodio.* Have them work in pairs or small groups to ask *Who?, What?, When?, Where?,* and *Why?* questions. Provide them with a model. You may want to have volunteers call out questions while the class answers.

Multiple Intelligences

Bodily/Kinesthetic: Have students choose a scene to act out in class. Be sure they have enough time to practice. Ask them to summarize briefly what happened in that scene and why they chose it. If possible, videotape their presentation and include it in their portfolios.

Después de ver el video

¿Comprendiste?

A. Decide cuáles de las siguientes frases son ciertas y cuáles son falsas:

1. Roberto obtiene la dirección de Chato Montesinos en San Miguel de Allende.
2. Linda va con Roberto a Dolores Hidalgo.
3. Cuando llegan a Dolores Hidalgo, Roberto y Linda compran un pastel.
4. Linda no sabe quién era el padre Hidalgo.
5. Roberto conoce bastante bien Dolores Hidalgo.
6. Chato Montesinos sabe dónde está Federico Zúñiga.
7. Después de visitar a Chato Montesinos, Roberto llama a una agencia de viajes en San Antonio.
8. Federico Zúñiga y Chato Montesinos se fueron juntos para México.
9. Roberto llama al Banco de la Frontera para obtener información sobre su abuelo Federico Zúñiga.

B. Contesta las siguientes preguntas.

1. Escribe un resumen de todo lo que Roberto sabe hasta ahora sobre su abuelo.
2. Haz una predicción. ¿Quién es el hombre misterioso? ¿Dónde está? ¿Por qué tiene tanto interés en el abuelo de Roberto? Lee tus predicciones y discútelas con el resto de la clase. Tu profesor(a) va a guardar las predicciones hasta el final del video. Entonces vas a saber si estabas cerca de la verdad.

Go Online
PHSchool.com
For: More on *En busca de la verdad*
Web Code: jdd-0209

doscientos ochenta y siete **287**
Capítulo 5B

Enrich Your Teaching
Resources for All Teachers

Teacher-to-Teacher

Have students read the photo captions and continue the conversations based both on what they know so far about the *Videomisterio* and on their answers to *Actividad* B, item 2. Have students work in pairs to practice their dialogues. Call on volunteers to present their dialogues to the class. If possible, videotape students' presentations and include them in their portfolios.

Suggestions:

Visual scanning: Direct attention to the photos. Have students read the captions and try to guess what the characters might be talking about. Have students read the *Resumen del episodio,* then ask them one or two comprehension questions. Call attention to the *llamada misteriosa* and have students brainstorm what this mysterious phone call might be about.

Viewing: Play *Episodio* 6 for the class. If there is time after viewing the full episode, go back and replay key moments that you wish to highlight. Remind students that they may not understand every word they hear in the video, but they should listen for overall understanding.

Post-viewing: Complete the *¿Comprendiste?* in class.

¿Comprendiste?

 Standards: 1.2, 1.3

Resources: Answers on Transparencies
Focus: Verifying comprehension; reviewing the plot

Suggestions: Have students provide the correct answer for the false statements in part A. For part B, students may need to go back and review the *Resumen del episodio* summaries. You may want to assign this as homework.

Answers:

A:
1. **falsa; Roberto obtiene la dirección de Chato Montesinos en Dolores Hidalgo.**
2. **cierta**
3. **falsa; Al llegar a Dolores Hidalgo, Roberto y Linda pasean por el centro.**
4. **falsa; Linda sabe quién era el padre Hidalgo.**
5. **cierta**
6. **falsa; Chato Montesinos no sabe dónde está Federico Zúñiga.**
7. **falsa; Después de visitar a Chato Montesinos, Roberto llama a un banco.**
8. **falsa; Federico Zúñiga y Chato Montesinos se fueron juntos para los Estados Unidos.**
9. **cierta**

B:
1. **Answers will vary.**
2. **Answers will vary, but may include: Turrón; en San Antonio; tiene algo que le pertenecía a Federico Zúñiga**

Additional Resources
- *En busca de la verdad* Video Workbook, Episode 6
- *En busca de la verdad* Teacher's Video Guide: Answer Key

Review Activities

To talk about treatments for medical conditions: Write the words for different injuries on a piece of paper and put them in a box. Have students work in pairs to choose an injury from the box and present it to their partner, who will recommend a treatment.

To explain how accidents occurred: Create two sets of cards. One set contains the infinitives from this vocabulary section. The other set states a tense and person. Students draw one card from each set and must create a sentence using the verb in the tense and person indicated.

To name parts of the body: Give each student a baseball card with the player's whole body shown. Have students take turns pointing to different body parts while their partner names them.

Portfolio

Invite students to review the activities they completed in this chapter, including written reports, posters or other visuals, tapes of oral presentations, or other projects. Have them select one or two items that they feel best demonstrate their achievements in Spanish to include in their portfolios. Have them include this with the Chapter Checklist and Self-Assessment Worksheet.

Additional Resources

Student Resources: Realidades para hispanohablantes, p. 208

 **CD-ROM**

PuzzleView Web Code: jdd-0517

Teacher Resources:
- Teacher's Resource Book: Situation Cards, p. 44, Clip Art, pp. 46–49
- Assessment Program: Chapter Checklist and Self-Assessment Worksheet, pp. T56–T57

288

Repaso del capítulo

Vocabulario y gramática jdd-0599

Chapter Review

To prepare for the test, check to see if you . . .
- know the new vocabulary and grammar
- can perform the tasks on p. 289

to talk about treatments for medical conditions

doler (o → ue)	to hurt
el dolor	pain
el enfermero, la enfermera	nurse
examinar	to examine, to check
la inyección, pl. las inyecciones	injection, shot
poner una inyección	to give an injection
la medicina	medicine
las muletas	crutches
las pastillas	pills
las puntadas	stitches
dar puntadas	to stitch (surgically)
la radiografía	X-ray
sacar una radiografía	to take an X-ray
la receta	prescription
recetar	to prescribe
roto, -a	broken
la sala de emergencia	emergency room
la sangre	blood
la silla de ruedas	wheelchair
la venda	bandage
el yeso	cast

to explain how an accident occurred

el accidente	accident
la ambulancia	ambulance
caerse	to fall
me caigo	I fall
te caes	you fall
se cayó	he / she fell
se cayeron	they / you fell
chocar con	to crash into, to collide with
cortarse	to cut oneself
lastimarse	to hurt oneself
¿Qué te pasó?	What happened to you?
romperse	to break, to tear
torcerse (o → ue)	to twist, to sprain
tropezar (e → ie) (con)	to trip (over)

For *Vocabulario adicional*, see pp. 498–499.

to name parts of the body

el codo	elbow
el cuello	neck
la espalda	back
el hombro	shoulder
el hueso	bone
la muñeca	wrist
el músculo	muscle
la rodilla	knee
el tobillo	ankle

other useful words and expressions

moverse (o → ue)	to move
pobrecito, -a	poor thing
¡Qué lástima!	What a shame!
sentirse (e → ie)	to feel

preterite of *venir*

vine	vinimos
viniste	vinisteis
vino	vinieron

preterite of *decir* and *traer*

dije	traje	dijimos	trajimos
dijiste	trajiste	dijisteis	trajisteis
dijo	trajo	dijeron	trajeron

preterite of *poner*

puse	pusimos
pusiste	pusisteis
puso	pusieron

imperfect progressive tense

Use the imperfect-tense forms of *estar* + the present participle to say that something was taking place over a period of time in the past.

present participles:

-ar	stem + -ando → caminando
-er	stem + -iendo → corriendo
-ir	stem + -iendo → escribiendo

Differentiated Instruction
Solutions for All Learners

Advanced Learners

Have students host a quiz show for the class. Ask them to write definitions for the vocabulary on paper squares and tape them up backwards on the board. Classmates will choose a square, read the definition, and respond. If students wrote *Es una parte del cuerpo entre la rodilla y el pie,* the player should say *el tobillo.*

Students with Special Needs

Be sensitive to students who need special test-taking arrangements as they may be self-conscious about their needs. If students' needs are significant, it may be easier to test them individually. Give them practice test questions or review activities to work on while their classmates are taking the test.

Preparación para el examen

Más práctica
- Practice Workbook: Puzzle, p. 109
- Practice Workbook: Organizer, p. 110

Go Online
PHSchool.com
For: Test Preparation
Web Code: jdd-0517

jdd-0599

On the exam you will be asked to . . .	Here are practice tasks similar to those you will find on the exam . . .	If you need review . . .
1 Escuchar Listen and understand as someone talks about what has happened at an accident	Listen as a 911 operator takes a call from someone who is at the scene of an accident. See if you can understand: (a) what the victim was doing before the accident occurred; (b) what caused the accident; and (c) what the injury appears to be.	pp. 266–269 *A primera vista* p. 270 *Actividad 5* p. 274 *Actividad 12*
2 Hablar Ask and answer questions about how someone was injured	You would like to get some training in emergency room questioning techniques. With a partner, practice what you learned by role-playing a situation in which one person asks: (a) what time the patient came to the emergency room and how he / she got there; (b) what caused the injury; and (c) what the person was doing at the time of the injury. Then switch roles.	p. 270 *Actividad 6* p. 271 *Actividad 8* p. 272 *Actividad 9* p. 273 *Actividad 10* p. 275 *Actividad 15* p. 278 *Actividad 20* p. 281 *Actividad 26*
3 Leer Read and understand an account of an accident	In the newspaper, you see an account of an accident. See if you can understand what happened, as well as what medical treatment the victims received. *Ayer, dos niños se chocaron cuando estaban montando en bicicleta en la calle Suárez. La ambulancia llegó rápidamente para llevarlos a la sala de emergencia. Los paramédicos dijeron que uno de los niños tenía la muñeca rota y el otro necesitaba diez puntadas en la rodilla.*	pp. 266–269 *A primera vista* p. 270 *Actividad 4* p. 275 *Actividad 13* p. 279 *Actividad 21* p. 280 *Actividad 23* pp. 282–283 *Lectura*
4 Escribir Write an account of what medical treatment was given to injured people	Several children that you were supervising were injured on the playground and you took them to the emergency room. Write a summary, in Spanish, describing the medical treatment each child received.	p. 270 *Actividad 4* p. 274 *Actividad 12* p. 275 *Actividades 13, 15* p. 285 *Presentación escrita*
5 Pensar Demonstrate an understanding of emergency medical services in different countries	Imagine that you've been injured. Where would you go? How would you get there? What type of emergency medical services are available in your community? How are they similar to or different from those in Spanish-speaking countries?	p. 271 *Fondo cultural* p. 278 *Fondo cultural* pp. 282–283 *Lectura* p. 284 *Perspectivas del mundo hispano*

doscientos ochenta y nueve **289**
Capítulo 5B

✓ **Differentiated Assessment**
Solutions for All Learners

STUDENTS NEEDING EXTRA HELP
- Alternate Assessment Program: Examen del capítulo 5B
- Audio Program CD 21: Chap. 5B, Track 2

HERITAGE LEARNERS
- Assessment Program: Realidades para hispanohablantes: Examen del capítulo 5B
- **ExamView** test generator **Heritage Learner Test Bank**

ADVANCED/PRE-AP*
- **ExamView** test generator **Pre-AP* Test Bank**
- **Pre-AP* Resource Book,** pp. 112–115

Performance Tasks

Presentation EXPRESS
ANSWERS

 Standards: 1.1, 1.2, 1.3, 2.1, 2.2, 4.2

Student Resource: Realidades para hispanohablantes, p. 209

Teacher Resources: Teacher's Resource Book: Audio Script, p. 35; Audio Program: Track 14; Answers on Transparencies

1. Escuchar

Suggestions: You may have students write what they hear as a dictation.

🔊 **Script:**
Mi hermano tuvo un accidente. Él estaba corriendo con sus amigos cuando, de repente, tropezó con una bicicleta. Creo que se torció su rodilla.

Answers:
a. He was running with his friends.
b. He tripped over a bicycle.
c. He seems to have sprained his knee.

2. Hablar

Suggestions: Give students a scenario to discuss for each dialogue.

Answers will vary but may include:
a. ¿A qué hora vino la paciente a la sala de emergencia? ¿Cómo llegó aquí?
b. ¿Qué causó el accidente?
c. ¿Qué estaba haciendo cuando se lastimó?

3. Leer

Suggestions: Have students scan the text for key words before they begin.

Answers:
Two children who were riding bicycles collided. An ambulance came quickly and took them to the emergency room. One child had a broken wrist and the other needed ten stitches in his knee.

4. Escribir

Suggestions: Have students create a chart that shows each child's name, what the child was doing, what happened, and what medical treatment was received. The students can then create sentences using the information from the chart.

Answers will vary.

5. Pensar

Suggestions: For information on emergency medical services in Spanish-speaking countries, refer students to p. 284.

Answers will vary.

✓ **Assessment**
- **ExamView** QuickTake Presenter **Quiz on PresEXPRESS**
- Assessment Program: Examen del capítulo
- **ExamView** test generator **Test Bank: Tests A and B**
- Audio Program CD 21: Chap. 5B, Track 2

289

Tema 6

La televisión y el cine

THEME OVERVIEW

▶ **6A** **¿Viste el partido en la televisión?**
- Watching television
Vocabulary: televised sporting events; game shows; beauty contests
Grammar: preterite of *-ir* stem-changing verbs; other reflexive verbs
Cultural Perspectives: television programs in Spanish-speaking countries

▶ **6B** **¿Qué película has visto?**
- Movies
Vocabulary: movie plots and characters; opinions
Grammar: verbs that use indirect object pronouns; the present perfect
Cultural Perspectives: Spanish-language movies

Theme Project

Las películas y la televisión: un juego de mesa

Overview: Students will create a board game in which they ask questions in Spanish about their favorite movies and television shows. Students can choose the type of game they would like to recreate. Students must ask and answer questions about:
- actors, actresses, directors, celebrities, sports figures
- kinds of television programs and movies
- plots and characters

On the gameboard, students should include photos or drawings of the movies or shows they ask questions about.

Materials: Poster board, markers, photos, glue or tape, scissors, game pieces (buttons, pennies, etc.)

Sequence: (suggestions for when to do each step are found throughout the chapters)

6A ▶ **STEP 1.** Review instructions so students know what is expected of them. Hand out the "Theme 6 Project Instructions and Rubric" from the *Teacher's Resource Book*.

STEP 2. Students submit a rough draft of their questions. Return the drafts with your suggestions. For grammar and vocabulary practice, ask students to partner and present their drafts to each other.

STEP 3. Students create layouts of their game boards on pieces of poster board, leaving room for photos or drawings. Encourage them to work in pencil first and to try different arrangements before gluing photos or drawing in marker.

6B ▶ **STEP 4.** Students submit a draft of the instructions to their game. Note your corrections and suggestions, then return them to students.

STEP 5. Students play their games in small groups.

Options:
1. Students research movies and television shows in a Spanish-speaking country. Their questions can reflect their research.
2. Students present their games to the class. The class votes on their favorite game.

Assessment:

Here is a detailed rubric for assessing this project:

Theme 6 Project: *Las películas y la televisión: un juego de mesa*

RUBRIC	Score 1	Score 3	Score 5
Your evidence of planning	You provide no written draft or gameboard layout.	Your draft was written and layout created, but not corrected.	You show evidence of corrected draft and layout.
Your use of illustrations	You include no photos or visuals.	You include very few photos or visuals.	You include several photos or visuals.
Your presentation	You include little of the required information.	You include a gameboard and some questions.	You include a gameboard and enough questions to play the game.

Bulletin Boards

Theme: *El cine y la televisión*

Ask students to cut out, copy, or download photos of television programs or movies. Cluster photos into categories—sports, game shows, beauty pageants, cartoons, dramas, comedies, etc.—so that similarities and differences are evident.

Bibliography

Hershfield, Joanne. *Mexico's Cinema: A Century of Film and Filmmakers.* Wilmington, Del.: Scholarly Resources, 1999. A look at Mexico's cinema industry.

DK Hornby, Hugh. *Soccer.* DK Eyewitness Books. New York: Dorling Kindersley, 2000. The inside story of soccer, from its origins to the lastest World Cup finals.

Stone, Rob. *Spanish Cinema: Inside Film.* New York: Longman, 2001. An exploration of Spanish cinema.

Venezia, Mike. *Salvador Dalí: Getting to Know the World's Greatest Artists.* Chicago: Children's Press, 1994. The life and art of Salvador Dalí.

Hands-on Culture

Craft: *Bark Painting*

A traditional craft in Mexico and in South America is bark painting. Artisans paint brightly colored traditional designs on unfinished thick paper made from the bark of trees.

Materials:
- brown paper bags
- brightly colored paint
- paintbrushes
- pencils

Directions:

1. Rip a square section of the paper bag so that the edges are rough.

2. Research and select a traditional design to reproduce. Common designs are animals and plants.

3. Draw a rough sketch of the design in pencil. Fill in the drawing with the paint.

4. Let the painting dry and hang it up.

Internet Search

Use the keywords to find more information.

6A Keywords:

béisbol, Pasapalabra, Saber y ganar, los Juegos Panamericanos

6B Keywords:

Mario Moreno, Cantinflas, Salma Hayek-Jiménez, los premios ALMA, premios Goya

Game

¡Dibuja y gana!

Play this game after *Capítulo* 6B to practice Tema 6 vocabulary.

Players: Any number of students in three large groups

Materials: Blackboard, chalk, index cards

Rules:

1. Before the game, create index cards with *Tema 6* vocabulary words on them. Shuffle the deck.

2. One student from each group comes up to the board. Show only those students the card with the word on it.

3. All students at the board will attempt to draw the vocabulary word. Students in the groups raise their hands to guess the word. Choose one group at a time.

4. If a student correctly identifies the word, his or her team gets one point. They must then use that word in a sentence. If they can do this correctly, they get another point. If their sentence is not correct, the other groups get a chance to use the word correctly for a point.

5. The group with the most points wins.

RECYCLE
A ver si recuerdas

Vocabulary
• Los programas y las películas

Grammar
• Verbs like *gustar*

A primera vista	Manos a la obra	¡Adelante!	Repaso

Learning Sequence

INPUT	PRACTICE	APPLICATION	REVIEW
• Introduce vocabulary and grammar within an authentic context.	• Practice and develop new vocabulary. • Learn and practice new grammar structures.	• Apply vocabulary and grammar through culminating, theme-based activities. • Apply skill development.	• Review vocabulary and grammar.

Objectives

Read, listen to, and interpret information about • Television programs • Sporting events	• Talk about televised sporting events and programs. • Describe past televised events. • Express your feelings about watching television.	• Read about the PanAmerican Games. • Talk about sporting competitions. • Create a television guide. • Review a television program. • Watch *En busca de la verdad*, *Episodio 7*.	• Prepare for the chapter test.

Culture

• Salvador Dalí	• *Latinoamericanos en el béisbol* • *Concursomanía*	• *La guía de la tele*	• Explain a Spanish-language television guide.

Vocabulary	Grammar	Learner Support		
• Sporting events • Contests • Emotions	• Preterite of *-ir* stem-changing verbs • Other reflexive verbs	**STRATEGIES** • Using visuals • Using prior knowledge • Note taking	**RECYCLING** • Television programs • Present tense of stem-changing verbs • Indirect object pronouns • Restaurant vocabulary • Reflexive verbs	• Imperfect tense • Sports vocabulary

Chapter Features

Pronunciación

Regional variations of *ll/y* and *c/z*

Conexiones

Social Sciences: Important events in the history of television

El español en la comunidad

The television station Univisión and the important role it plays in the Spanish-speaking community

Beyond the Classroom: States & Countries

España
Nueva York
Indiana
Cuba
México
Puerto Rico
República Dominicana
El Salvador
Venezuela
Costa Rica
Ecuador
Colombia
Argentina
Chile

Student Resources

TECHNOLOGY

ONLINE

Interactive Textbook
• Student Edition Online plus audio, video, and flashcards

Go Online Companion Web Site
• Tutorial activities   • Internet links
• Self-tests   • Downloadable MP3 audio files
PuzzleView

CD-ROM

Interactive Textbook CD-ROM
Student Edition on CD-ROM plus audio, video, and flashcards

MindPoint™ CD-ROM
QUIZSHOW

PRINT MATERIAL

CORE INSTRUCTION
Practice Workbook, pp. 111–121
• Review   • Vocabulary
• Grammar   • Puzzle
• Organizer

Writing, Audio & Video Activities, pp. 107–115
• Video   • Audio
• Writing

Grammar Study Guide 1–2 (or 3–4)

Differentiated Instruction

STUDENTS NEEDING EXTRA HELP
Guided Practice Activities, pp. 199–217
• Vocabulary Flash Cards and Vocabulary Check
• Grammar Activities
• Presentación oral

HERITAGE LEARNERS
Realidades para hispanohablantes, pp. 210–229

Lecturas para hispanohablantes
• "Ficción," pp. 88–89
• "Los chicos del fin del mundo," pp. 111–114

ADVANCED/PRE-AP*
Pre-AP* Resource Book: Student Activity Sheet, p. 119

Teacher Resources

TECHNOLOGY

Audio Program   Fine Art Transparencies
Video Program   Vocabulary and Grammar
Transparencies
Answers on Transparencies

TeacherEXPRESS CD-ROM
• Lesson Planner   • Vocabulary Clip Art
• Web Resources   • Teaching Resources
• Teacher Edition with Interactive Links

PresentationEXPRESS CD-ROM
• Vocabulary   • Transparencies and Maps
• Grammar   • Photo Gallery
• Audio   • Clip Art

PH SuccessNet ONLINE
• Access to grades and reports from Online Interactive Textbook

ExamView on Presentation Express CD-ROM
QuickTake Presenter
• Vocabulary Quizzes   • Chapter Test
• Grammar Quizzes

TeacherEXPRESS CD-ROM
• Assessment Program
• **ExamView** Test Banks A and B
test generator

Go Online
PHSchool.com
For: Teacher Home Page
Web Code: jdk-1001

PRINT MATERIAL

CORE INSTRUCTION
Teacher's Resource Book, pp. 60–85
• Input Script   • Video Script
• Answer Keys   • GramActiva Blackline Masters
• Vocabulary Clip Art   • Chapter Resource Checklist
• School-to-Home Connection Letters
• Communicative Activities Blackline Masters

TPR Stories, pp. 80–84

CORE ASSESSMENT
Assessment Program, pp. 151–163
• Pruebas
Vocabulary Recognition
Vocabulary Production
Preterite of -ir stem-changing verbs
Other reflexive verbs

• Examen del capítulo   • Speaking and Writing Rubrics
Teacher's Resource Book, p. 74
• Situation Cards
TPR Stories, pp. 80–84

Differentiated Instruction

STUDENTS NEEDING EXTRA HELP
Guided Practice Activities
Teacher's Guide, pp. T100–T109

HERITAGE LEARNERS
Realidades para hispanohablantes
Teacher's Guide, pp. 106–115

Lecturas para hispanohablantes
Teacher's Guide, pp. 34, 43–44

ADVANCED/PRE-AP*
Pre-AP* Resource Book: Resources Chart, p. 116

Differentiated Assessment

STUDENTS NEEDING EXTRA HELP
Alternate Assessment Program
• Examen del capítulo, pp. 65–70

HERITAGE LEARNERS
Assessment Program: Realidades para hispanohablantes Teacher's Guide, pp. T139–T143

ExamView Heritage Learner
test generator **Test Bank**

ADVANCED/PRE-AP*
Pre-AP* Resource Book: Teacher Activity Sheet, p. 118

ExamView Pre-AP* Test Bank
test generator

Regular Schedule (50 Minutes)

For electronic lesson plans:
Teacher Express 💿

	Warm-up / Assess	Preview / Present	Practice / Communicate	Wrap-up / Homework Options
DAY 1	**Warm-up (5 min.)** • Homework check • Return Examen del capítulo 5B	**A ver si recuerdas . . . (20 min.)** • Presentation: Los programas y las películas • Actividad 1 • Presentation: Verbs like *gustar* • Actividades 2, 3	**Chapter Opener (5 min.)** • Objectives • Fondo cultural **A primera vista (15 min.)** • Presentation: Vocabulario y gramática en contexto • Actividad 1, 2	**Wrap-up and Homework Options (5 min.)** • Practice Workbook 6A-A, 6A-B, 6A-1, 6A-2 • Go Online
DAY 2	**Warm-up (10 min.)** • Homework check	**A primera vista (35 min.)** • Presentation: Videohistoria *El partido final* • View: Videohistoria	• Video Activities 1, 2, 3, 4 • Actividad 3	**Wrap-up and Homework Options (5 min.)** • Practice Workbook 6A-3, 6A-4 • Go Online • Prueba 6A-1: Vocabulary recognition
DAY 3	**Warm-up (10 min.)** • Actividad 4 • Homework check ✔**Assessment (10 min.)** • Prueba 6A-1: Vocabulary recognition	**Manos a la obra (25 min.)** • Actividades 5, 6, 7, 8, 9 • Fondo cultural		**Wrap-up and Homework Options (5 min.)** • Actividades 10, 11 • Writing Activity 10 • Heritage Learner Workbook 6A-1, 6A-2 • Prueba 6A-2: Vocabulary production
DAY 4	**Warm-up (10 min.)** • Communicative Activity • Homework check ✔**Assessment (10 min.)** (after Audio Activities) • Prueba 6A-2: Vocabulary production	**Manos a la obra (25 min.)** • Audio Activities 5, 6 • Presentation: Preterite of *-ir* stem-changing verbs	• View: GramActiva video • Actividades 12, 13	**Wrap-up and Homework Options (5 min.)** • Practice Workbook 6A-5 • Actividades 15, 16 • Writing Activity 11 • Go Online
DAY 5	**Warm-up (10 min.)** • Writing Activity 14 • Homework check	**Manos a la obra (35 min.)** • Audio Activity 7 • Presentation: Other reflexive verbs • View: GramActiva video • Actividades 17, 18, 19	• El español en la comunidad • Fondo cultural	**Wrap-up and Homework Options (5 min.)** • Practice Workbook 6A-6 • Actividades 20, 21 • Go Online • Prueba 6A-3: Preterite of *-ir* stem-changing verbs
DAY 6	**Warm-up (5 min.)** • Homework check ✔**Assessment (10 min.)** • Prueba 6A-3: Preterite of *-ir* stem-changing verbs	**Manos a la obra (30 min.)** • Audio Activities 8, 9 • Pronunciación • Actividades 22, 23		**Wrap-up and Homework Options (5 min.)** • Practice Workbook 6A-7 • Writing Activity 13 • Go Online • Heritage Learner Workbook 6A-4 • Prueba 6A-4: Other reflexive verbs
DAY 7	**Warm-up (10 min.)** • Writing Activity 12 • Homework check ✔**Assessment (10 min.)** • Prueba 6A-4: Other reflexive verbs	**¡Adelante! (10 min.)** • Presentación oral: Steps 1, 4	**Repaso del capítulo (15 min.)** • Vocabulario y gramática • Preparación para el examen 1, 2	**Wrap-up and Homework Options (5 min.)** • Presentación oral: Step 2
DAY 8	**Warm-up (5 min.)** • Presentación oral: Step 2	**¡Adelante! (40 min.)** • Presentación oral: Step 3 • La cultura en vivo		**Wrap-up and Homework Options (5 min.)** • Preparación para el examen 3, 4, 5 • Go Online: Self-test • La cultura en vivo
DAY 9	**Warm-up (5 min.)** • Homework check	**¡Adelante! (40 min.)** • Lectura • ¿Comprendiste? / Y tú ¿que dices? • Videomisterio: *En busca de la verdad*, Episodio 7		**Wrap-up and Homework Options (5 min.)** • Practice Workbook 6A-8, 6A-9 • Go Online: Lectura • Examen del capítulo 6A
DAY 10	**Warm-up (5 min.)** • Homework check ✔**Assessment (40 min.)** • Examen del capítulo 6A			**Wrap-up and Homework Options (5 min.)** • Go Online: Videomisterio

Block Schedule (90 Minutes)

For electronic lesson plans:
Teacher Express

	Warm-up / Assess	Preview Present / Practice Communicate	Wrap-up / Homework Options
DAY 1	**Warm-up (5 min.)** • Homework check • Return Examen del capítulo: Capítulo 5B	**A ver si recuerdas . . . (25 min.)** • Presentation: Los programas y las películas • Actividad 1 • Presentation: Verbs like *gustar* • Actividades 2, 3 **Chapter Opener (5 min.)** • Objectives • Fondo cultural	**A primera vista (50 min.)** • Presentation: Vocabulario y gramática en contexto • Actividades 1, 2 • Presentation: Videohistoria *El partido final* • View: Videohistoria • Video Activities 1, 2, 3, 4 • Actividad 3	**Wrap-up and Homework Options (5 min.)** • Practice Workbook 6A-A, 6A-B, 6A-1, 6A-2, 6A-3, 6A-4 • Go Online • Prueba 6A-1: Vocabulary recognition
DAY 2	**Warm-up (10 min.)** • Actividad 4 • Homework check ✔**Assessment (10 min.)** • Prueba 6A-1: Vocabulary recognition	**Manos a la obra (65 min.)** • Actividades 5, 6, 7, 8, 9 • Fondo cultural • Audio Activities 5, 6 • Communicative Activity • Presentation: Preterite of -*ir* stem-changing verbs	• View: GramActiva video • Actividades 12, 13	**Wrap-up and Homework Options (5 min.)** • Practice Workbook 6A-5 • Actividad 10, 11 • Go Online • Heritage Learner Workbook 6A-1, 6A-2 • Prueba 6A-2: Vocabulary production
DAY 3	**Warm-up (10 min.)** • Writing Activity 10 • Homework check ✔**Assessment (10 min.)** • Prueba 6A-2: Vocabulary production	**Manos a la obra (65 min.)** • Actividades 14, 15, 16 • Audio Activity 7 • Writing Activity 11 • Presentation: Other reflexive verbs • View: GramActiva video • Actividades 17, 18, 19 • Audio Activities 8, 9 • Writing Activity 12		**Wrap-up and Homework Options (5 min.)** • Practice Workbook 6A-6 • Go Online • Heritage Learner Workbook 6A-4 • Prueba 6A-3: Preterite of -*ir* stem-changing verbs
DAY 4	**Warm-up (5 min.)** • Homework check ✔**Assessment (10 min.)** • Prueba 6A-3: Preterite of -*ir* stem-changing verbs	**Manos a la obra (40 min.)** • Actividades 20, 21, 22, 23 • El español en la comunidad • Pronunciación • Fundo cultural • Writing Activity 13 **¡Adelante! (30 min.)** • Lectura • ¿Comprendiste? / Y tú ¿que dicés? • Presentación oral: Steps 1, 4		**Wrap-up and Homework Options (5 min.)** • Practice Workbook 6A-7 • Presentación oral: Step 2 • Go Online: Reflexive verbs; Lectura • Prueba 6A-4: Other reflexive verbs
DAY 5	**Warm-up (5 min.)** • Homework check ✔**Assessment (10 min.)** • Prueba 6A-5: Other reflexive verbs	**¡Adelante! (45 min.)** • Presentación oral: Step 3 • La cultura en vivo **Repaso de capítulo (25 min.)** • Vocabulario y gramática • Preparación para el examen 1, 2, 3, 4, 5		**Wrap-up and Homework Options (5 min.)** • Practice Workbook 6A-8, 6A-9 • Go Online: Self-test • Examen del capítulo 6A
DAY 6	**Warm-up (5 min.)** • Homework check **Repaso del capítulo (20 min.)** • Situation Cards • La cultura en vivo ✔**Assessment (40 min.)** • Examen del capítulo 6A	**¡Adelante! (20 min.)** • Videomisterio: *En busca de la verdad,* Episodio 7		**Wrap-up and Homework Options (5 min.)** • Go Online: Videomisterio • La cultura en vivo

Note: Starting with *Tema 4*, the *A ver si recuerdas . . .* feature appears only at the beginning of each theme.

Vocabulario

Core Instruction

Resources: Voc. & Gram. Transparency 106

Focus: Reviewing vocabulary for television programs and movies

Suggestions: Lead a discussion about movies and television. Mention different types of television programs, and ask students to give examples of television programs that fit into each category.

Have students name their favorite and least favorite television programs and describe each using adjectives from the list.

Make photocopies of local movie listings and ask students to describe current movies. Who are the actors and actresses? How long does each movie last? In which theaters are the movies being shown?

Actividad 1

Standards: 1.1, 1.3

Focus: Writing and talking about favorite programs and movies

Suggestions: To help students choose a variety of programs, distribute copies of television programming guides to them. If they have difficulty guessing the name of the program, have their partners tell them what day of the week and time of day the show is aired.

Answers will vary.

Extension: Have students select one of the programs from the charts they made and ask them to write a brief description of an episode.

A ver si recuerdas . . .

Vocabulario

Los programas y las películas

la televisión
el canal
la comedia
el drama
el programa de
  concursos
el programa de
  dibujos animados
el programa deportivo
el programa educativo
el programa de
  entrevistas
el programa de la
  vida real
el programa de
  noticias
el programa musical
la telenovela
¿Qué clase de . . . ?

el cine
el actor
la actriz, *pl.* las actrices
dar
durar
la película de ciencia
  ficción
la película de horror
la película policíaca
la película romántica

opiniones
cómico, -a
emocionante
fascinante
infantil
interesante
realista
tonto, -a
triste
violento, -a

Práctica de vocabulario • Usando el organizador gráfico

Actividad 1  Escribir/Hablar

Los programas que te gustan

1 Piensa en cuatro programas de televisión o películas que te gustan. Haz una copia de la tabla en una hoja de papel y úsala para describir los programas.

programa / película	descripción	canal / cine	actor / actriz
Planeta de los animales	un programa educativo fascinante	canal 14	Ramón Fernández

2 Trabaja con otro(a) estudiante. Lee sólo la descripción de un programa o película en tu tabla. Tu compañero(a) va a hacerte dos preguntas para identificarlo.

Modelo
A —*Es un programa educativo fascinante.*
B —*¿En qué canal / cine lo (la) dan?*
o:—*¿Quiénes son los actores principales?*

Differentiated Instruction
Solutions for All Learners

Students with Learning Difficulties
Write sentences using the four example verbs in the *Gramática • Repaso*. Diagram the sentences with the students. Ask them to point out the subject, verb, and indirect object pronoun in each sentence. Then have them help you write new sentences. Ask them to first give you a subject, then a verb, and then an indirect object.

Multiple Intelligences
Mathematical/Logical: Have students create a poll to see what types of TV shows students like best and least. Have them graph the results. If possible, ask them to compare the results to the preferences of another Spanish class. Ask: Do preferences vary between the classes? How?

Gramática · Repaso

Verbs like *gustar*

You already know several verbs that are always used with indirect objects:

encantar	to love, to delight
gustar	to be pleasing
importar	to be important
interesar	to interest

These verbs all use a similar construction: indirect object pronoun + verb + subject.

Me **gusta** el béisbol.

Literally: *Baseball is **pleasing to me.***

The two forms of these verbs that are most commonly used are the *Ud. / él / ella* and *Uds. / ellos / ellas* forms.

¿Te **interesan** los deportes?

Literally: *Are sports **interesting to you?***

Remember that, in the sentences above, the subjects are *béisbol* and *deportes,* and *me* and *te* are indirect object pronouns.

Práctica de gramática

  **Actividad 2** Hablar

Tu programa favorito

¿Cuál es tu programa de televisión favorito? Pregúntale a otro(a) estudiante sus opiniones usando las palabras del recuadro.

Modelo

gustar / las telenovelas
A —¿Te gustan las telenovelas?
B —Sí, me encantan.

encantar	los programas educativos
gustar	
interesar	los programas de la vida real
la comedia	
el drama	las telenovelas
los programas de dibujos animados	

 Actividad 3 Escribir/Hablar

Expresa tu opinión

¿Qué piensas del cine? Usa la lista de actividades y el verbo *importar* o *interesar* para expresar tu opinión.

Modelo

las comedias
A mí me interesan las comedias.
o: *No me interesan las comedias; me aburren.*

1. las películas de ciencia ficción
2. las películas de horror
3. las películas policíacas
4. las películas románticas
5. el drama
6. las películas realistas

Más práctica

- Practice Workbook, pp. 111–112: 6A-A, 6A-B
- Guided Practice: Grammar Acts., pp. 199–200
- *Real.* para hispanohablantes, p. 210

Go Online
PHSchool.com
For: Vocab. and Grammar
Web Code: jdd-0601

doscientos noventa y uno **291**
Preparación: Vocabulario y gramática

Gramática · Repaso

Core Instruction

Standards: 4.1

Suggestions: Direct attention to the literal translations of the example sentences. Point out that the true meanings are "I like baseball" and "Are you interested in sports?" Emphasize that the subjects are the items you like or the things you are interested in.

Actividad 2 *Standards:* 1.1

Focus: Speaking about favorite television programs
Recycle: Vocabulary for television shows
Suggestions: Have students make a three-column chart and label the columns *Indirect objects, Verbs,* and *Subjects.* Have them fill in the first column with the correct indirect object pronouns for questions and answers and the remaining columns with words from the box.
Answers will vary.

Actividad 3 *Standards:* 1.1, 1.3

Presentation EXPRESS
ANSWERS

Resources: Answers on Transparencies
Focus: Writing and talking about your opinions on different kinds of movies
Suggestions: Have students encourage their partners to give reasons for their opinions by asking: ¿Por qué?

Answers will vary but may include:
1. (No) me importan / interesan …
2. (No) me importan / interesan …
3. (No) me importan / interesan …
4. (No) me importan / interesan …
5. (No) me importa / interesa …
6. (No) me importan / interesan …

Enrich Your Teaching
Resources for All Teachers

Culture Note

Univisión is one of the most popular Spanish-language networks in the United States. Another is Telemundo, which is the older of the two. Both networks feature news, drama, variety shows, and movies.

Teacher-to-Teacher

Ask your local movie rental store for movie posters. Show them to your students and model verbs like **gustar** by telling them what you think of each movie. Have students work in groups. Give each group a different poster and have them discuss the movie: ¿Te interesa la película ...? ¿Te gustan los actores ...?

Standards for Capítulo 6A

• To achieve the goals of the Standards, students will:

Communication

1.1 Interpersonal

• Talk about: a beauty pageant; attitudes toward television; emotions; sports; competitions; television programming and viewing habits; entertainment; the painting *Pantallas*

1.2 Interpretive

• Read and listen to information about: Salvador Dalí; sporting events, competitions, and game shows; María Isabela Fernández Melgarejo; preferences and attitudes about television; *la Serie de Béisbol del Caribe;* past events; television programming; the Pan-American Games; Jefferson Pérez; television guides

• Read a picture-based story

• Listen to and watch a video about sports

1.3 Presentational

• Present information about: a story plot; an article about a beauty pageant; emotions; preferences and attitudes about television; sporting events; television programs; the painting *"Pantallas"*

• Create a television guide

Culture

2.1 Practices and Perspectives

• Describe: beauty pageants; *la Serie de Béisbol del Caribe*

2.2 Products and Perspectives

• Write or talk about: Salvador Dalí and his art; *la Serie de Béisbol del Caribe;* the Pan-American Games

• Read a riddle from Mexico

Connections

3.1 Cross-curricular

• Write or talk about the Pan-American Games

3.2 Target Culture

• View a video mystery series

Comparisons

4.1 Language

• Practice regional pronunciations of *ll/y* and *c/z*

4.2 Culture

• Compare game shows

Communities

5.1 Beyond the School

• Talk about a Spanish-language television network

5.2 Lifelong Learner

• View a video mystery series

Fondo cultural ■◆◆◆■◆◇■◆

Salvador Dalí Salvador Felipe Jacinto Dalí (1904–1989) nació en la provincia de Cataluña, España, cerca de Barcelona. Dalí estudió pintura y experimentó con varios estilos. Después de la Guerra Civil Española *(Spanish Civil War)*, Dalí vivió en los Estados Unidos por unos años. Este cuadro es titulado "El futbolista".

• ¿Qué tipo de fútbol crees que juegan en este cuadro? ¿Por qué? ¿Hay elementos del cuadro que crees que son típicos de España? ¿En qué otros países crees que el cuadro puede estar situado?

292 doscientos noventa y dos
Tema 6 • La televisión y el cine

Differentiated Instruction

STUDENTS NEEDING EXTRA HELP

Guided Practice Activities
• Vocabulary Check, Flash Cards
• Grammar
• Reading and Speaking Support

Guided Practice Audio CDs
• Disc 2, Track 3

HERITAGE LEARNERS

Realidades para hispanohablantes
• Chapter Opener, pp. 210–211
• A primera vista, p. 212
• Videohistoria, p. 213
• Manos a la obra, pp. 214–221
• ¡Adelante!, pp. 222–227
• Repaso del capítulo, pp. 228–229

ADVANCED/PRE-AP*

Pre-AP* Resource Book, pp. 116–119

Capítulo 6A

¿Viste el partido en la televisión?

Chapter Objectives

- Talk about what you saw on television
- Explain how you feel about watching television
- Understand cultural perspectives on television programs in Spanish-speaking countries

Video Highlights

A primera vista: *El partido final*

GramActiva Videos: the preterite of *-ir* stem-changing verbs; other reflexive verbs

Videomisterio: *En busca de la verdad,* Episodio 7

Country Connection

As you learn to talk about television, you will make connections to these countries and places:

España
Nueva York
Indiana
Cuba
Puerto Rico
México
República Dominicana
El Salvador
Venezuela
Costa Rica
Ecuador
Colombia
Argentina
Chile

El Bus es un programa de televisión español.

Más práctica

- *Real.* para hispanohablantes, pp. 210–211

Go Online
PHSchool.com
For: Online Atlas
Web Code: jde-0002

doscientos noventa y tres 293
Capítulo 6A

Preview

Chapter Opener

Presentation EXPRESS ATLAS

Core Instruction

Resources: Voc. and Gram. Transparencies: Maps 12–18, 20

Suggestions: Have students discuss the last sporting event they attended. What teams were playing? What was the score? Bring in pictures from sport magazines of crowds at soccer matches and ask students to describe the people.

Ask students to guess what kind of show is shown in the photo. *(un concurso)* Tell students that they will be learning how to talk about television programs, sporting events, and beauty pageants in this chapter.

In the *Videohistoria* students will read about an interview with a soccer player. Ask students whom they would choose to interview if they could interview any athlete they wanted. Why?

Standards: 1.2, 2.2

Fondo cultural

◆■◆■◆■◆□■◆■◆□◆■◆□◆■◆

Resources: Fine Art Transparencies with Teacher's Guide, p. 15; Answers on Transparencies

Suggestions: Ask students to describe a soccer field and a football field. How are they similar? How are they different? Have students name the countries where football is played. Ask students to describe soccer uniforms and football uniforms.

Answers will vary but may include:

Juegan al fútbol americano porque llevan uniformes de ese deporte.

Puede ser en los Estados Unidos o en Canadá.

Teaching with Photos

Resources: Fine Art Transparencies with Teacher's Guide, p. 15

Suggestions: Have students imagine that they are directors for the game show *El Bus*. What would the contestants have to do to win? What would they win? Have them write an introduction for each contestant. For example: *Buenos días. Me llamo Esmeralda. Soy de Madrid. Me encanta bailar, leer y bucear.* Ask students to write an introduction for themselves and read it aloud.

Teacher Technology

TeacherEXPRESS
Plan · Teach · Assess

PLAN
Lesson Planner

Go Online
PHSchool.com
For: Teacher Home Page
Web Code: jdk-1001

TEACH
Teaching Resources
Interactive Teacher's Edition
Vocabulary Clip Art

ASSESS
Chapter Quizzes and Tests

PresentationEXPRESS
Dynamic Presentations for Teachers

TEACH
Vocabulary & Grammar Powerpoints
GramActiva Video
Audio & Clip Art Activities
Transparencies and Maps
Activity Answers
Photo Gallery

ASSESS
ExamView
QuickTake Presenter

293

Vocabulario y gramática  Presentation EXPRESS VOCABULARY

Core Instruction

 Standards: 1.2

Resources: Teacher's Resource Book: Input Script, p. 62, Clip Art, pp. 76-79, Audio Script, p. 63; Voc. and Gram. Transparencies 107-108; TPR Stories Book, pp. 79-90; Audio Program: Tracks 1-2

Focus: Presenting vocabulary for television programs and sporting events

Suggestions: Use the Input Script from the *Teacher's Resource Book* or the story from the *TPR Stories Book* to present the new vocabulary, or use some of these suggestions. Present the vocabulary in three groups: sporting events, beauty pageants, and game shows.

You may want to wear a T-shirt with your favorite team's logo. Place the transparency on the screen and tell students about the latest game you saw your team play. As you mention new vocabulary, point to the images in the *A primera vista.* Cut out photos from sports magazines to illustrate the sports commentator's report. For example, find photos of a soccer team that is celebrating a win and of angry or ecstatic sports fans. Show the photos as you have volunteers read the text.

To present vocabulary for beauty pageants, search the Internet for various beauty pageant contestants from your state and download photos. Tell where the finals were held in your state, who the presenter was and the name of the beauty queen.

Have students brainstorm a list of their favorite game shows and tell you what prizes can be won for each.

Block Schedule

Tell students that throughout the chapter you will be playing a trivia game show called *¿Quién quiere un millón de pesos?* Choose topics from previous chapters as well as *Capítulo* 6A. Divide students into teams and assign each team a chapter. Have them prepare questions for upcoming episodes of the game show. Assign a different student to be the game show host or hostess for each episode. You may want to have groups prepare commercials for the show.

Additional Resources

• Audio Program: Canciones CD, Disc 22

A primera vista

Vocabulario y gramática en contexto

jdd-0687 🔊

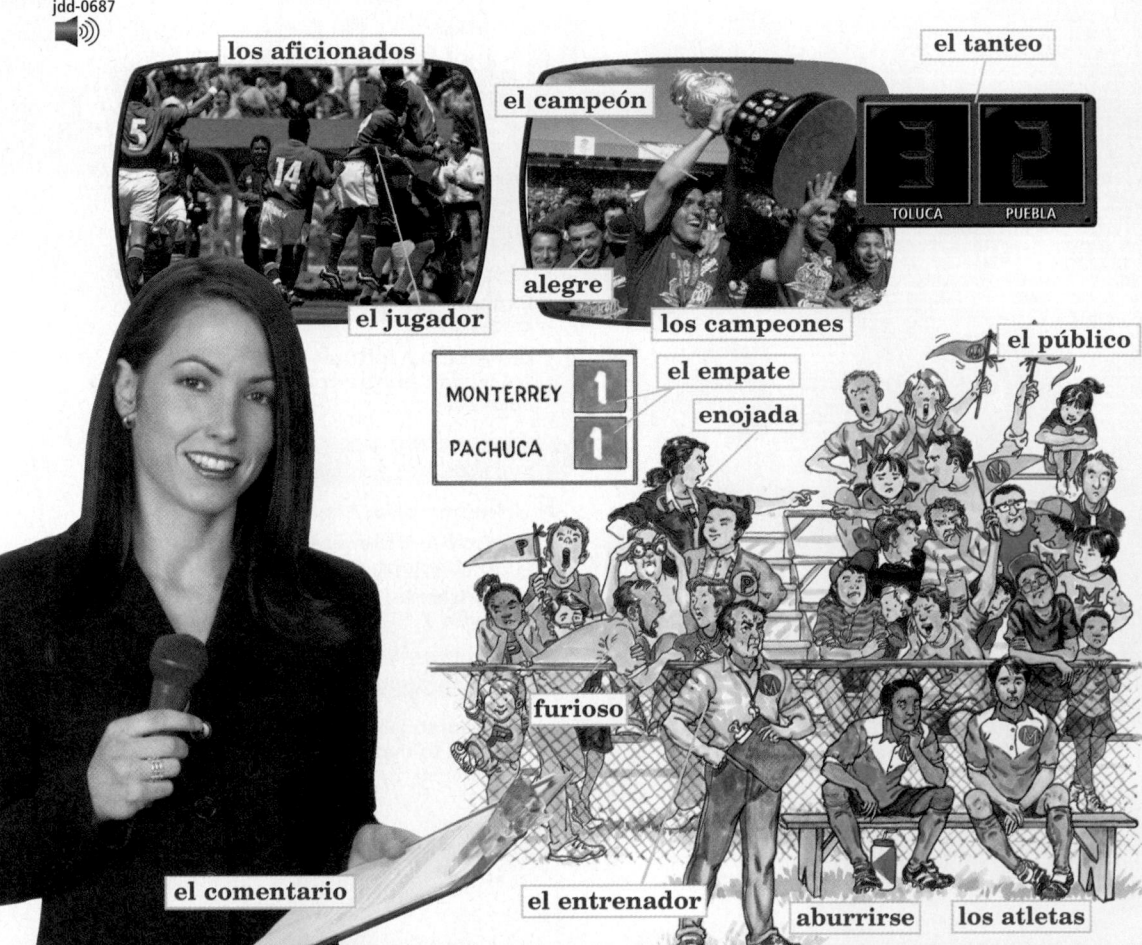

los aficionados · el jugador · el campeón · alegre · los campeones · el tanteo · TOLUCA · PUEBLA · el empate · enojada · el público · MONTERREY 1 · PACHUCA 1 · furioso · el comentario · el entrenador · aburrirse · los atletas

❝ Los aficionados del equipo de Toluca se pusieron **alegres** y muy **emocionados** cuando su equipo ganó **el campeonato** de **la Liga** Mexicana **por tercera vez.** El equipo de Puebla **perdió** el partido final con un tanteo de 3 a 2. **La competencia** entre estos dos equipos siempre **resulta** muy intensa.

El partido entre Monterrey y Pachuca terminó en un empate, 1 a 1. **Al final** del partido el entrenador de Monterrey dijo: 'Pareció que nos aburrimos y **nos dormimos** mientras jugábamos. Tenemos que **competir** con más emoción. También hubo problemas entre **el público.** Los aficionados se pusieron muy **agitados. Se enojaron** y empezaron a pelearse. En mi opinión, pueden **aplaudir** y gritar, pero nunca deben **volverse locos**' **❞**

294 doscientos noventa y cuatro
Tema 6 • La televisión y el cine

Differentiated Instruction
Solutions for All Learners

Students with Special Needs

Modify *Actividad* 2 for physically impaired students. Give them two index cards: one labeled **belleza** and the other labeled **concurso.** Have students indicate whether each dictated sentence refers to a beauty contest or to a game show by pointing to the corresponding index card.

Advanced Learners

If students have access to a digital camera, have them attend a sports competition at your school and take pictures of the coaches, athletes, and fans. Ask them to print out the photos and label them using the new vocabulary. They could also create a slide show using presentation software.

NOTICIAS

Concurso de Carnaval ayer

FELICIDADES a Rosalinda Pérez Urcillo. Anoche en **el Auditorio** Nacional fue escogida Reina del Carnaval. En **el concurso de belleza** participaron 30 jóvenes talentosas, pero Rosalinda fascinó al público con su presentación de guitarra. La presentadora le entregó un cheque para pagar por su primer año de estudios en la universidad.

la reina   la presentadora

Rosalinda Pérez Urcillo, Reina del Carnaval 2003

13 DE MARZO

¡Número uno!

NUESTRA comunidad tiene una ganadora en la profesora Cecilia Mendoza. La semana pasada participó y ganó en el programa de concursos "¿Quién lo sabe?" Cecilia es profesora de historia en el Colegio Andrés Bello. Como premio, Cecilia recibió un coche nuevo y el presentador del programa le entregó un cheque por **un millón de pesos.**

el presentador
¿QUIÉN LO SABE?

Cecilia Mendoza, profesora y ganadora

el premio

Actividad 1 jdd-0687 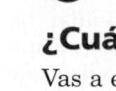 Escuchar

¿Cierta o falsa?

En una hoja de papel, escribe los números del 1 al 8. Escucha las siguientes frases sobre las noticias deportivas de la página 294 y escribe *C* si la frase es cierta o *F* si es falsa.

Más práctica

- Practice Workbook, pp. 113–114: 6A-1, 6A-2
- WAV Wbk.: Writing, p. 112
- Guided Practice: Vocab. Flash Cards, pp. 201–206
- *Real.* para hispanohablantes, p. 212

Go Online PHSchool.com
For: Vocab. Practice
Web Code: jdd-0602

Actividad 2 jdd-0687 Escuchar

¿Cuál es el concurso?

Vas a escuchar seis frases. Si la frase describe un concurso de belleza, levanta una mano. Si describe un programa de concursos, levanta las dos manos.

doscientos noventa y cinco **295**
Capítulo 6A

Enrich Your Teaching
Resources for All Teachers

Culture Note

The Azteca stadium in Mexico City holds 106,000 soccer fans. It is the largest soccer stadium in the Spanish-speaking world, and one of the largest in the world. By contrast, 78,741 fans can fit into Giants Stadium, a large American football stadium in New Jersey.

Teacher-to-Teacher

Have students choose two of their favorite game shows and ask them to write sentences that are typically heard on those shows. You may want to have them read the *¡Número uno!* article again and make a list of words they could use. Ask them to work with a partner and take turns reading their sentences and guessing the names of the shows.

 Actividad 1 *Standards:* 1.2   Presentation EXPRESS AUDIO

Resources: Teacher's Resource Book: Audio Script, p. 63; Audio Program: Track 3; Answers on Transparencies

Focus: Listening comprehension of a sports commentary

Suggestions: Ask students to summarize the information given in the sports commentator's report on p. 294 before they listen.

Script and Answers:

1. El equipo de Toluca ganó el partido contra el equipo de Puebla. *(C)*
2. El tanteo del partido entre Toluca y Puebla fue de 3 a 1. *(F)*
3. El partido de Monterrey y Pachuca terminó con un tanteo de 2 a 1. *(F)*
4. Pareció que los atletas del equipo de Monterrey se durmieron durante el partido. *(C)*
5. Para competir el equipo de Monterrey necesita un nuevo entrenador. *(F)*
6. Hubo problemas con los aficionados de los dos equipos. *(C)*
7. Según la locutora, es mejor aplaudir y gritar que pelearse. *(C)*

 Actividad 2 *Standards:* 1.2  Presentation EXPRESS AUDIO

Resources: Teacher's Resource Book: Audio Script, p. 63; Audio Program: Track 4; Answers on Transparencies

Focus: Listening comprehension of phrases from beauty contests and game shows

Suggestions: Have students brainstorm statements they would expect to hear at beauty contests and game shows.

Script and Answers:

1. ¡Si puedes decirme el precio de esta caja de cereal, vas a ganar el coche nuevo! *(two)*
2. Marta, ¿por qué quieres ser Miss Carnaval? *(one)*
3. ¡Pablo, quiero comprar dos letras, por favor! *(two)*
4. ¡Lo siento! No es la respuesta correcta. Pierdes el turno. *(two)*
5. ¡Aquí está la señorita más talentosa de toda la ciudad! ¡Felicidades! *(one)*
6. ¡Bienvenidos amigos al programa donde pueden ganar un millón de pesos! *(two)*

 Assessment
- **ExamView** Quiz on PresEXPRESS
QuickTake Presenter

Videohistoria

Core Instruction

 Standards: 1.2

Resources: Voc. & Gram. Transparencies 109–110; Audio Program: Track 5

Focus: Presentation of additional vocabulary to discuss sporting events

Suggestions:

Pre-reading: Have students discuss the differences between watching a sporting event on TV and watching it in person. Then direct attention to the *Estrategia* and ask students to look at photos in panels 1 and 8. Ask them what they think Ramón and his friends are holding in panel 8 *(tickets)*. Why do Ramón and Manolo look more excited in panel 8 than in panel 1? Encourage students to read the *¿Comprendiste?* questions before beginning the reading.

Reading: To help students answer the *¿Comprendiste?* questions, have them number their papers 1–6 and take notes as they read. Pause after panel 6 and ask comprehension questions to be sure students understand with whom Claudia is speaking on the telephone.

Post-reading: Complete *Actividad* 3 to check comprehension.

Pre-AP* Support

- **Activity:** Have students bring to class a picture from a magazine or newspaper illustrating a sporting event or contest. Allow students two minutes to write a description of their illustration. Then form groups of five students and ask that they redistribute the illustrations to other members in their group. Have students identify the appropriate illustration as each group member reads his or her description.

- **Pre-AP* Resource Book:** Comprehensive guide to Pre-AP* vocabulary skill development, pp. 47–53

Videohistoria
jdd-0687

El partido final

Ramón y Manolo están viendo la entrevista con un jugador de fútbol. ¿Qué sorpresa les da Claudia?

Estrategia
Using visuals
Look at the images as you read to help you understand the story. What do you predict happens at the end of the story? Why?

1 **Locutor:** ¡Gol! Y con este gol **fenomenal**, el equipo de los Lobos de Madero le ganó a las Águilas del América y llegó al partido final del campeonato mexicano de fútbol.

5 **Claudia:** Oye, Manolo, ¿a quién están entrevistando?
Manolo: Es Luis Campos. Claudia, esta entrevista nos interesa mucho. ¿Por qué no te vas a hablar al otro cuarto?
Claudia: ¡Uy! Manolo está un poco enojado. Sí . . . a ver.

6 **Claudia:** Oigan, Teresa dice que su tío trabaja en el estadio y que si queremos podemos ir a ver el partido allí.

7 **Claudia:** Creo que no quieren ir.
Ramón: ¿Ir adónde?
Claudia: Al estadio, a ver el partido allí.
Manolo y Ramón: ¿Qué?
Claudia: Ahora creo que quieren ir. Están gritando. Están muy alegres. **Se mueren** de emoción.

296 **doscientos noventa y seis**
Tema 6 • La televisión y el cine

Differentiated Instruction
Solutions for All Learners

Students with Learning Difficulties
Have students make cards with the numbers 1–8. Make copies of the *¿Comprendiste?* questions for students and have them underline key words for each item that will help them find the answer. Then have a volunteer read each question aloud and have students hold up the number of the panel in which the answer can be found.

Heritage Language Learners
Have students write three additional panels to continue the *Videohistoria*. Ask them to explain what happens when Ramón and his friends go to the soccer game. Give them guidance on how to write a dialogue. Direct attention to panels 2, 3, and 5 and explain the use of ellipses.

2 **Locutor:** Hoy vamos a **entrevistar** al jugador que **metió el gol,** Luis Campos, "la Pantera." Luis, gracias por estar aquí.

Luis: Gracias por invitarme.

Locutor: Este año tuvimos un campeonato muy interesante.

Luis: Así es. Competimos con equipos muy buenos . . .

3 **Claudia:** Sí, podemos ir al cine. O de compras . . . ¿Ahora? Estamos viendo la televisión. No sé, parece una **entrevista.**

4 **Locutor:** Luis, ¿qué nos puedes decir del **último** partido que ganaron contra las Águilas?

Luis: Bueno, fue un partido muy duro. Ellos metieron el primer gol, pero cinco minutos después nosotros empatamos. Luego, en el segundo tiempo,* metimos dos goles más y ganamos.
*second half

8 **Manolo:** ¡No puedo creer que vamos a ver el partido en el estadio!

Ramón: Vamos a divertirnos mucho.

Claudia: ¿Por qué no entramos ahora?

Actividad 3 — Escribir/Hablar

¿Comprendiste?

1. ¿Qué están viendo Ramón y Manolo? ¿Por qué no están contentos?
2. ¿Qué hizo Luis Campos durante el partido?
3. ¿Por qué es importante el partido que los Lobos de Madero van a jugar hoy?
4. ¿A Claudia le interesa la entrevista?
5. ¿Qué quiere preguntarles Teresa?
6. ¿Cuál es la reacción de Ramón y Manolo?

Más práctica

- Practice Workbook, pp. 115–116: 6A-3, 6A-4
- WAV Wbk.: Video, pp. 107–108
- Guided Practice: Vocab. Check, pp. 207–210
- *Real.* para hispanohablantes, p. 213

Go Online PHSchool.com
For: Vocab. Practice
Web Code: jdd-0603

doscientos noventa y siete **297**
Capítulo 6A

Video
Core Instruction

Standards: 1.2

Resources: Teacher's Resource Book: Video Script, p. 67; Video Program: Cap. 6A; Video Program Teacher's Guide: Cap. 6A

Focus: Comprehension of contextualized vocabulary

Suggestions:

Pre-viewing: Review the *Videohistoria* with students and have them list the key ideas. Play a video excerpt with the sound muted, and ask students to tell you what is occurring.

Viewing: Tell students to use words they already know to help them understand the context of a story. Show the video once without pausing. Show it a second time and have students raise their hands when they hear key words such as **partido.**

Post-viewing: Complete the Video Activities in the *Writing, Audio & Video Workbook.*

Actividad 3

Standards: 1.2 · Presentation EXPRESS · ANSWERS

Resources: Answers on Transparencies

Focus: Verifying comprehension of the *Videohistoria*

Suggestions: Have students point out which questions can be answered by using visuals. *(items 4 and 6)* Ask them to explain how the photos help them.

Answers:
1. Ramón y Manolo están viendo una entrevista. No están contentos porque quieren escuchar la entrevista y Claudia les habla.
2. Luis Campos metió el gol que ganó el partido.
3. El partido es importante porque es el último partido del campeonato.
4. A Claudia no le interesa la entrevista.
5. Teresa quiere preguntarles si quieren ir a ver el partido en el estadio.
6. Ramón y Manolo están muy alegres.

Enrich Your Teaching
Resources for All Teachers

Culture Note
Television broadcasts of soccer games have been greatly enlivened by the colorful commentary of Andrés Cantor, who is famous for shouting *"Goool"* when a team scores. At times Cantor seems to be even more excited than the fans who are watching. Cantor has written a book about soccer entitled *Goool.*

Internet Search
Keyword:

fútbol + (Spanish-speaking country)

Additional Resources
- WAV Wbk.: Audio Act. 5, p. 109
- Teacher's Resource Book: Audio Script, p. 64
- Audio Program: Track 7

✓ Assessment
- ExamView QuickTake Presenter Quiz on PresEXPRESS
- Prueba 6A-1: Vocab. Recognition, pp. 151–152

 Standards: 1.2

Resources: Answers on Transparencies

Focus: Reading and writing about a championship soccer game

Suggestions: Remind students to read the entire sentence before filling in the blank. Tell them that their choices must make sense within the context of the entire dialogue.

Answers:

1. aficionados	7. tanteo
2. resultó	8. atleta
3. el campeonato	9. entrevistaron
4. empate	10. premio
5. últimos	11. entrenadores
6. metió un gol	12. público

Extension: Have students work with a partner and read the completed dialogue aloud. Ask them to add two sentences, using the words that they did not choose as answers.

Bellringer Review

Have students work with a partner and look at the photo on this page. Have them alternate telling each other as many descriptive sentences as they can in one minute.

 Standards: 1.2

Resources: Answers on Transparencies

Focus: Completing definitions for soccer, game show, and beauty pageant vocabulary

Suggestions: Have students identify and tell you the meaning of the verb in each item before completing the sentences.

Answers:

1. el (la) jugador(a)
2. el (la) presentador(a)
3. el campeón / la campeona
4. la reina
5. el público
6. el (la) entrenador(a)
7. el auditorio
8. la liga

Common Errors: Students may want to complete sentences that begin with *la persona* with only feminine nouns and those that begin with *el grupo* with only masculine nouns. Explain that both words refer to men and women.

298

Objectives
- Talk about televised sporting events and programs
- Discuss past televised events
- Express your feelings about watching television

 Leer/Escribir

Un día malísimo

Lee la conversación entre dos amigos que no están muy contentos con el resultado del campeonato de fútbol. Escribe las palabras apropiadas.

Un partido de fútbol entre Colombia y Bolivia

A —¿Viste el partido ayer en la televisión?

B —Sí, unos amigos míos vinieron a mi casa a verlo. Todos somos __1.__ *(atletas / aficionados)* a los Tigres y por eso __2.__ *(resultó / perdió)* ser un día malísimo.

A —Fue horrible, ¿no te parece? No puedo creer que los Tigres perdieron __3.__ *(el campeonato / el campeón)* por segunda vez.

B —Por unos minutos, pensábamos que el partido iba a terminar en un __4.__ *(empate / tanteo)* pero en los __5.__ *(últimos / primeros)* segundos el jugador de los Osos __6.__ *(metió un gol / compitió)* y ellos ganaron. Al final, el __7.__ *(tanteo / concurso)* fue 4 a 3. ¡Qué horror!

A —Ese jugador es un __8.__ *(atleta / entrenador)* fenomenal. Lo __9.__ *(entrevistaron / empataron)* anoche en la tele después de que le dieron el __10.__ *(tanteo / premio)* por ser el mejor jugador del partido.

B —Sí, vi la entrevista también. Parece ser un hombre muy bueno. Dijo que ganaron a causa de los esfuerzos *(efforts)* de todos los jugadores en el equipo y de sus __11.__ *(entrenadores / presentadores)*. También le dio las gracias a su familia y al __12.__ *(comentario / público)* que siempre lo apoyan *(support)*.

 Leer/Escribir

¿Quién lo hace?

Escribe la persona, el lugar o la cosa apropiada que corresponde a cada una de estas descripciones.

1. La persona que mete un gol es ____.
2. La persona que da los premios en un programa de concursos es ____.
3. La persona que gana el campeonato es ____.
4. La persona que gana el concurso de belleza es ____.
5. El grupo de personas que ven una competencia o un concurso es ____.
6. La persona que les dice a los jugadores lo que deben hacer es ____.
7. El lugar donde ocurre el concurso de belleza es ____.
8. El grupo de equipos que compiten unos contra otros es ____.

También se dice . . .

la competencia = la competición
(muchos países)

298 doscientos noventa y ocho
Tema 6 • Le televisión y el cine

Differentiated Instruction
Solutions for All Learners

Students with Learning Difficulties

For *Actividad 6*, photocopy the reading to help students with comprehension. Have them underline words that are unfamiliar. Encourage them to think of cognates or words with similar roots that may contribute to their understanding of the meaning of these words. Then demonstrate the use of context clues to confirm the meaning.

Multiple Intelligences

Bodily/Kinesthetic: Have students work in groups to play Charades. Tell them to use two words from *Actividad 5* and two other words from *Capítulo 6A*. Have them get together with another group and act out their words. Ask students to indicate if the word is a person, place, or thing. The team with the most correct guesses wins.

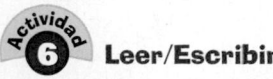

Actividad 6 · Leer/Escribir

La nueva reina

Lee este artículo de las páginas sociales de un periódico sobre un evento muy especial. Después contesta las preguntas.

Felicitaciones a la Señorita Centroamérica

María Isabel Fernández Melgarejo

Anoche, en todas las ciudades y pueblos de El Salvador, la gente se volvía loca. Por primera vez en la historia de esta pequeña nación, pueden proclamar que la reina del Concurso de belleza, la Señorita Centroamérica, es una joven salvadoreña. La nueva reina es María Isabel Fernández Melgarejo, nativa de Zacatecoluca, Departamento de La Paz. La señorita Melgarejo, una joven talentosa y bonita de 19 años, participó en la competencia de talento con una voz fenomenal,

cantando "Mi último recuerdo eres tú." Momentos antes de anunciar a la nueva reina había un silencio increíble en el auditorio. Cuando el presentador Mario Montero anunció el nombre de la joven salvadoreña, el público comenzó a gritar y a aplaudir. Después, en una entrevista, la nueva Señorita Centroamérica habló de sus planes como reina en el año que viene: visitar a personas enfermas y heridas en los hospitales de su país.

1. ¿Qué evento ocurrió anoche? ¿Cómo resultó el evento?

2. ¿Por qué es tan especial el resultado del evento?

3. ¿Qué hizo la nueva reina en la competencia de talento?

4. ¿Quién es Mario Montero y qué hizo en el concurso?

5. ¿El público se puso alegre o agitado cuando oyó el nombre de la nueva reina? ¿Por qué?

6. ¿Qué quiere hacer la nueva reina para ayudar a los demás?

Actividad 7 · Escribir/Hablar

¿Qué dices . . . ?

Imagina que no leíste bien el artículo de la Actividad 6 sobre la nueva reina. Escribe cuatro frases con información incorrecta sobre lo que ocurrió. Lee tus frases a otro(a) estudiante. Tu compañero(a) tiene que corregir *(correct)* tu información.

> **Modelo**
>
> **A** —*Es la segunda vez que la reina es de El Salvador, ¿no?*
>
> **B** —*No, no tienes razón. Es la primera vez que ella es de El Salvador.*

doscientos noventa y nueve **299**
Capítulo 6A

Enrich Your Teaching
Resources for All Teachers

Culture Note

Women from the Spanish-speaking world participate in the Miss América Latina pageant. This event is hosted by a different country each year and is seen on television by more than 100 million people. Young *latinas* from the U.S. compete in the Miss Latina U.S. pageant to represent the country in the Miss América Latina event.

Teacher-to-Teacher

Research the names and e-mail addresses of reigning beauty queens in Spanish-speaking countries and have students write to them. Have them ask questions about where the women live, what they are currently doing, and how winning the contest has changed their lives. Have them ask general questions about pageants as well.

Actividad 6 *Standards:* 1.2, 2.1

Resources: Voc. and Gram. Transparency 113; Answers on Transparencies

Focus: Reading and writing about a beauty pageant

Suggestions: To activate prior knowledge, ask students if they have ever seen a beauty pageant on television. What do the contestants do? What is the role of the presenter? How does the audience usually react when the winner is announced?

Answers:

1. Anoche ocurrió un concurso de belleza. María Isabel Fernández ganó.
2. Es la primera vez que una salvadoreña ganó el concurso.
3. La nueva reina cantó la canción "Mi último recuerdo eres tú."
4. Fue el presentador y anunció el nombre de la nueva reina.
5. El público se puso alegre porque por primera vez una salvadoreña ganó.
6. Quiere visitar a personas enfermas y heridas en los hospitales.

Actividad 7 *Standards:* 1.1, 1.3

Focus: Writing and speaking about a beauty pageant

Suggestions: Ask students to focus on information that is not mentioned in their answers to *Actividad* 6. To encourage students to discuss the entire reading, have them write questions from the beginning, middle, and end of the article.

Answers will vary.

Extension: Have students write two correct statements and two incorrect statements about the article in *Actividad* 6. Ask them to exchange their papers with a partner and indicate which of their partner's sentences are true and which are false. Have them correct the false statements.

6A Practice and Communicate

Actividad 8 · *Standards:* 1.1, 1.2 · Presentation EXPRESS AUDIO

Resources: Teacher's Resource Book: Audio Script, pp. 63–64; Audio Program: Track 6; Answers on Transparencies

Focus: Listening comprehension about emotions

Suggestions: Have students listen to the script once without pausing. Have them listen a second time and pause after each sentence to ask students to identify the emotion mentioned. Allow students time to complete their sentences before moving on to Step 2.

🔊 Script and Answers:

1. Me pongo enojado cuando mi equipo favorito pierde el campeonato.
2. Me aburro cuando tengo que ver una competencia de golf en la tele.
3. Me enojo cuando no puedo ver una entrevista con mi cantante favorita.
4. Me vuelvo loca cuando anuncian el nombre de la reina del concurso de belleza.
5. Me duermo durante los comentarios sobre los desastres naturales.

Answers will vary.

Actividad 9 · *Standards:* 1.1, 1.3

Focus: Writing and speaking about emotions

Suggestions: To help students focus on specific situations, have them first write where they experience each emotion and then go back and tell why they feel that way in that particular place.

Answers will vary.

Actividad 10 · *Standards:* 1.1, 1.3

Focus: Writing and speaking about television programs and sporting events

Suggestions: To help students answer item 4, bring in a school yearbook and have them find the names of coaches.

Answers will vary.

300

Actividad 8 · jdd-0688 · 🔊 **Escuchar/Escribir/Hablar**

Escucha y escribe

1 Unos jóvenes hablan de cómo se sienten cuando ven diferentes programas de televisión. Escribe las cinco frases que escuchas.

2 Habla con otro(a) estudiante. ¿Cuál de las reacciones es más similar a la tuya? ¿Cuál es más diferente? ¿Por qué?

Actividad 9 · **Escribir/Hablar**

¿Cuándo te sientes así?

Escribe una frase para decir en qué situaciones te sientes así *(this way)*. Lee tus frases a otro(a) estudiante para ver si se siente lo mismo.

1. me aburro
2. me enojo
3. me pongo emocionado, -a
4. me vuelvo loco, -a
5. me pongo agitado, -a
6. me pongo alegre

Modelo

me pongo furioso, -a

A —*Me pongo furiosa cuando mi hermana usa mis cosas sin mi permiso. ¿Y tú?*

B —*Pues, no tengo hermanos. Pero me pongo furioso cuando un amigo me miente. ¿Y tú?*

A —*Sí, me pongo muy furiosa cuando alguien me miente.*

Actividad 10 ·  **Escribir/Hablar**

Y tú, ¿qué dices?

1. ¿Qué clase de programa te gusta ver en la televisión, un programa de premios o un programa de entrevistas? ¿Por qué?

2. ¿Cuál es tu programa de concursos favorito? ¿Quién es el (la) presentador(a)? ¿Qué clase de premios dan?

3. ¿Quién es tu jugador(a) profesional favorito(a)? ¿Compitió recientemente en un campeonato? ¿Ganó o perdió?

4. ¿Conoces a algún (alguna) entrenador(a) profesional o de tu comunidad? ¿Con qué deportes o equipos trabaja él (ella)? ¿Cómo es?

Sergio García, de España, participa en un campeonato de golf.

Rafael Nadal, jugador español

300 trescientos
Tema 6 • Le televisión y el cine

Differentiated Instruction
Solutions for All Learners

Multiple Intelligences

Visual/Spatial: Have students illustrate each of the emotions in *Actividad* 9. Ask them to work with a partner, who will describe the emotions depicted in each illustration. Have students ask their partner: *¿Cómo se siente?*

Advanced Learners

Ask students to choose one of the emotions in *Actividad* 9 and create a poster depicting the top ten situations that make them feel that way. Have them write a caption for each situation. To encourage variety, you may want to write all the emotions on strips of paper and have students randomly draw a strip out of a hat.

Actividad 11 — Leer/Hablar

La Serie del Caribe

¿Eres aficionado(a) al béisbol? Lee la información y contesta las preguntas.

Campeones del Caribe

Miguel Tejada de las Águilas de la República Dominicana batea contra México en la Serie de Béisbol del Caribe, 2003.

Si te gusta el béisbol, la Serie de Béisbol del Caribe es una de las mejores competencias después de la Serie Mundial de las Ligas Mayores.

Equipos de México, Venezuela, la República Dominicana y Puerto Rico participan en esta Serie. Cada equipo tiene cientos y hasta miles de aficionados que lo apoyan[1] durante el campeonato. La gente se reúne para disfrutar de[2] una semana del béisbol extraordinaria.

Como ejemplo de la emoción de esta serie, podemos tomar los tres partidos del final de la Serie de 1999, en la que jugaron Puerto Rico y a República Dominicana. El primer partido lo ganó la República Dominicana y los aficionados se volvieron locos. El segundo partido lo ganó Puerto Rico en una dramática y emocionante recuperación en la novena entrada.[3]

El último partido entre estos dos rivales fue lo que todo el mundo esperaba, una batalla[4] hasta el final. Puerto Rico anotó la primera carrera,[5] pero más adelante perdió su ventaja,[6] se recuperó en las últimas entradas y al final perdió por una carrera, en la segunda mitad de la entrada 12.

Después de ver un partido como éste, se puede decir que ningún aficionado perdió. Por tercera vez consecutiva la República Dominicana obtuvo el primer puesto en el campeonato de la Serie de Béisbol del Caribe. Sin embargo ¡los verdaderos campeones fueron todos los equipos y aficionados caribeños!

[1]support [2]enjoy [3]inning [4]battle [5]scored the first run [6]advantage

1. ¿Qué países compiten en la Serie?
2. ¿Qué hacen los aficionados durante el campeonato?
3. ¿Qué equipos compitieron en el final de la Serie?
4. ¿Qué fue el tanteo después de dos partidos?
5. ¿Cómo fue el último partido? ¿Quién ganó?

Fondo cultural

Latinoamericanos en el béisbol Hoy en día hay más de 200 jugadores de América Latina en las Ligas Mayores. Se dice que el béisbol caribeño "empezó" en Cuba en el año 1874, con una competencia entre dos equipos cubanos. Luego la popularidad del deporte pasó a algunos países latinoamericanos. En julio de 1895 se estableció el primer club venezolano, y en 1943 empezó la Federación Mexicana de Béisbol. El club atlético Licey, el club más antiguo de béisbol dominicano, se fundó en 1907.

• ¿Crees que el béisbol es tan popular en América Latina como en los Estados Unidos? Explica.

Francisco Rodríguez, de los Angels of Anaheim

trescientos uno **301**
Capítulo 6A

Actividad 11

 Standards: 1.2, 2.1, 2.2  Presentation EXPRESS ANSWERS

Resources: Voc. and Gram. Transparency 114; Answers on Transparencies

Focus: Reading comprehension about baseball in the Caribbean

Suggestions: Show students a map of the Caribbean. Point out that item 4 is asking for the score of the series.

Answers:
1. México, Venezuela, la República Dominicana y Puerto Rico compiten en la Serie.
2. Apoyan a los equipos.
3. Puerto Rico y la República Dominicana compitieron en la final.
4. Después de dos partidos el tanteo fue de 1 a 1.
5. El último partido fue muy emocionante. La República Dominicana ganó.

Common Errors: Students may make comprehension errors due to difficulties understanding word order. Help them by explaining the sentence construction of *El primer partido lo ganó la República Dominicana ....*

Fondo cultural

 Standards: 1.2, 2.1, 2.2

Suggestions: Have students brainstorm a list of professional baseball players from Spanish-speaking countries. What does the number of players in Major League Baseball say about the sport's popularity in Spanish-speaking countries?

Answers will vary.

Additional Resources
• WAV Wbk.: Audio Act. 6, p. 109
• Teacher's Resource Book: Audio Script, p. 64, Communicative Activity BLM, pp. 70–71
• Audio Program: Track 8

 Assessment
• Prueba 6A-2: Vocab. Production, pp. 153–154

Enrich Your Teaching
Resources for All Teachers

Culture Note
Sergio García is a rising star in golf's PGA tour. Born and raised in Spain, García has won several major golf tournaments. Another well-known Spanish athlete is tennis player Carlos Moya. Born in Majorca, Moya turned pro in 1995. He has won tournaments around the world, including in Spain, Argentina, Mexico, and the United States.

Gramática

Presentation EXPRESS GRAMMAR

Core Instruction

Resources: Voc. and Gram. Transparency 111; Teacher's Resource Book: Video Script, pp. 67–68; Video Program: Cap. 6A

Suggestions: Point out that ***-ar*** and ***-er*** verbs do not have stem changes in the preterite tense.

Direct attention to the *¿Recuerdas?* Give students blank verb charts. Have them fill in the charts with the present tense of the verbs ***preferir, pedir,*** and ***dormir.*** In each chart, have students draw an outline around the forms that have stem changes and point out that they form the shape of a boot. Then have students copy the preterite stem-changing verbs from the charts in the *Gramática.* In each chart, have them draw an outline around the forms that have stem changes and point out that the outline looks like a sandal.

Bellringer Review

Write the words ***almorzar, preferir,*** and ***servir*** on the board and have students tell you what time they eat lunch on the weekends, what they prefer to eat, and which restaurants serve that kind of food.

Actividad 12

Standards: 1.2

Presentation EXPRESS ANSWERS

Resources: Answers on Transparencies

Focus: Completing sentences with correct forms of verbs

Recycle: Present tense of stem-changing verbs

Suggestions: Ask students to scan the sentences and find the word that indicates the use of the preterite tense. ***(ayer)***

Answers:

1. prefiere, prefirió
2. se sintió, se siente
3. se duerme, se durmió
4. se ríen, se rieron

Common Errors: Students may have difficulty with item 4. Remind them that the reflexive pronoun goes in front of the conjugated form of the verb.

Gramática

Preterite of *-ir* stem-changing verbs

In the preterite, *-ir* verbs like *preferir, pedir,* and *dormir* also have stem changes but only in the *Ud. / él / ella* and *Uds. / ellos / ellas* forms. In these forms *e* changes to *i* and *o* changes to *u.*

Mi mamá se aburrió y **se durmió** durante la película.
Mis padres **prefirieron** ver el concurso de belleza.
En la liga **compitieron** los mejores equipos de México.

¿Recuerdas?

You know that stem changes in the present tense take place in all forms except *nosotros* and *vosotros.*

preferir *(e → ie)*
- **Prefiero** ver programas deportivos.

pedir *(e → i)*
- **Pedimos** los espaguetis.

dormir *(o → ue)*
- Los hermanos **duermen** tarde.

preferir (e → i)		pedir (e → i)		dormir (o → u)	
preferí	preferimos	pedí	pedimos	dormí	dormimos
preferiste	preferisteis	pediste	pedisteis	dormiste	dormisteis
prefirió	**prefirieron**	**pidió**	**pidieron**	**durmió**	**durmieron**

- Note the special spelling of the preterite forms of *reír: reí, reíste, rió, reímos, reísteis, rieron*

Here are other *-ir* verbs with stem changes in the preterite tense.

- Verbs like *preferir: divertirse, mentir, sentirse*
- Verbs like *pedir: competir, despedirse, repetir, seguir, servir, vestirse*
- Verbs like *dormir: morir*
- Verbs like *reír: sonreír*

GramActiva VIDEO

Want more help with the preterite of *-ir* stem-changing verbs? Watch the **GramActiva** video.

Actividad 12 — Leer/Escribir

Ayer fue diferente

La familia Sánchez ve los mismos programas de televisión todos los días y tiene la misma reacción, pero ayer fue diferente. Completa las frases con las formas de los verbos en el presente y en el pretérito.

Modelo

(divertirse) *Pablito casi siempre* se divierte *cuando juega videojuegos en la tele, pero ayer no* se divirtió.

1. *(preferir)* Generalmente el Sr. Sánchez ____ ver los partidos en la tele, pero ayer ____ ver un programa de entrevistas.
2. *(sentirse)* Ayer la abuela ____ bastante triste después de ver su telenovela favorita, pero por lo general ella ____ muy entusiasmada después de verla.
3. *(dormirse)* La Sra. Sánchez casi siempre ____ durante uno de los comentarios en la tele, pero ayer no ____. Vio el comentario completo.
4. *(reírse)* A menudo los miembros de la familia ____ cuando escuchan al presentador en el programa de concursos. Ayer no ____ tanto.

Differentiated Instruction

Solutions for All Learners

Multiple Intelligences

Musical/Rhythmic: Have students practice the preterite of ***-ir*** stem-changing verbs by creating a rhythmic chant. For example, start off with *dormir bien* and say *yo.* The class will chant *Yo dormí bien.* Then say *tú* and students repeat the first phrase and add *Tú dormiste bien,* and so on. Add a percussion accompaniment.

Advanced Learners/Pre-AP*

Pre-AP*

Have students create crossword puzzles using the preterite of ***-ir*** stem-changing verbs as well as present-tense stem-changing verbs. Ask them to create cloze sentences like the ones in *Actividad* 12 as clues. Collect the puzzles and photocopy the best ones for students to use for review throughout this chapter.

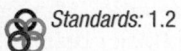

Actividad 13

Escribir _____

Los Juegos Olímpicos

En los Juegos Olímpicos del 2000 en Sydney, Australia, atletas de varios países hispanohablantes ganaron medallas. Aquí hay algunos de los campeones con información sobre el evento y las medallas que ganaron. Forma frases para decir en qué evento compitió cada atleta y qué medalla ganó.

Nicolás Massu, de Chile, gana la medalla de oro en tenis en las Olimpíadas de Atenas en 2004.

Modelo

Milton Wyants, Uruguay, ciclismo, plata
Milton Wyants compitió en el ciclismo y ganó una medalla de plata.

1. Soraya Jiménez Mendivil, México, oro, y María Isabel Urrutia, Colombia, oro, levantamiento de pesas
2. Juan Llaneras, España, ciclismo, oro
3. Jorge Gutiérrez y Félix Savón, Cuba, boxeo, oro
4. los españoles, fútbol, plata
5. las cubanas, vóleibol, oro
6. Claudia Poll, Costa Rica, natación, bronce

Mabel Mosquera, de Colombia, gana la medalla de bronce en levantamiento de pesas en las Olimpíadas de Atenas en 2004.

Actividad 14

Leer/Escribir _____

Un camarero distraído

Ayer Úrsula fue al restaurante Cancún con su mamá, y el camarero no les sirvió lo que pidieron. Lee su diálogo con su amigo Raúl y escribe las formas correctas de los verbos.

Raúl: ¿Cómo fue tu visita al restaurante ayer?
Úrsula: ¡Terrible! El camarero no nos __1.__ *(servir)* lo que nosotras __2.__ *(pedir)*.
Raúl: ¿De veras? ¿Qué __3.__ *(pedir)* Uds.?
Úrsula: Primero, yo __4.__ *(pedir)* una hamburguesa con queso, pero el camarero me __5.__ *(servir)* arroz con pollo.
Raúl: ¿Y qué pasó con tu mamá?
Úrsula: Ella __6.__ *(pedir)* una ensalada y una sopa. ¡Luego nuestro camarero y otro camarero también le __7.__ *(servir)* bistec con papas fritas! Mi mamá le __8.__ *(repetir)* lo que nosotras __9.__ *(pedir)*.

Raúl: ¿Qué hizo él?
Úrsula: Pues, él __10.__ *(sonreír)* y todos nosotros __11.__ *(reír)*. Pero, ¿sabes? Quizás él __12.__ *(divertirse)* anoche, pero nosotras no __13.__ *(divertirse)* mucho. No pensamos regresar a ese restaurante.

Enrich Your Teaching
Resources for All Teachers

Culture Note

Only seven Spanish-speaking nations sent athletes to the 2002 Winter Olympics in Salt Lake City. However, 17 Spanish-speaking nations participated in the 2000 Sydney Summer Olympics. Athletes from Cuba, Uruguay, Chile, Argentina, Mexico, Costa Rica, Colombia, and Spain won medals.

Internet Search

Keyword: Olympic Games

Actividad 13 **Standards: 1.3** **Presentation EXPRESS ANSWERS**

Resources: Answers on Transparencies

Focus: Using the preterite to discuss sports competition results

Suggestions: Have students scan each item and determine if they need to use the third person singular or plural form of *competir*.

Answers:
1. Soraya Jiménez Mendivil y María Isabel Urrutia compitieron en el levantamiento de pesas y ganaron unas medallas de oro.
2. Juan Llaneras compitió en el ciclismo y ganó una medalla de oro.
3. Jorge Gutiérrez y Félix Savon compitieron en el boxeo y ganaron unas medallas de oro.
4. Los españoles compitieron en el fútbol y ganaron una medalla de plata.
5. Las cubanas compitieron en el vóleibol y ganaron una medalla de oro.
6. Claudia Poll compitió en la natación y ganó una medalla de bronce.

Common Errors: Students may use *oro, plata,* and *bronce* as adjectives. Tell them that to say what something is made of they must use *de* + the material.

Bellringer Review

Have students complete these sentences to reflect what took place yesterday in class:
1. *Mariela y Elena___(repetir) las palabras.*
2. *José Antonio___(pedir) un bistec.*
3. *Esteban y Claudia___(discutir) el proyecto.*

(**Answers:** repiten; pide; discuten)

Actividad 14 **Standards: 1.2** **Presentation EXPRESS ANSWERS**

Resources: Answers on Transparencies

Focus: Reading and writing about eating in a restaurant

Recycle: Restaurant vocabulary; indirect object pronouns

Suggestions: Have students read the paragraph once before filling in the blanks. Point out that all verbs will be conjugated in the preterite.

Answers:

1. sirvió	8. repitió
2. pedimos	9. pedimos
3. pidieron	10. sonrió
4. pedí	11. reímos
5. sirvió	12. se divirtió
6. pidió	13. nos divertimos
7. sirvieron	

Actividad 15

Standards: 1.2, 1.3

Presentation EXPRESS
ANSWERS

Resources: Answers on Transparencies

Focus: Reading a timeline and using the preterite to discuss events

Focus: Reading comprehension; cross-curricular connection to social sciences

Suggestions: Remind students to use prior knowledge, cognates, and visual clues as reading strategies when completing this activity. Have them look at the dates in the television icons and the photos that are connected to them and predict what events will be mentioned.

Answers:

1. Neil Armstrong caminó en la Luna en 1969.
2. Martin Luther King, Jr., se murió en 1968.
3. En 1991 el mundo vio una guerra transmitida en directo por primera vez.
4. Answers will vary.
5. Answers will vary.
6. Answers will vary.

Extension: Have students choose a recent news event and interview three students about how they felt when the event occurred.

Actividad 16

Standards: 1.3

Focus: Writing and talking about television viewing

Suggestions: Have students review the vocabulary on p. 290 to help them discuss the types of television programs they have seen recently.

Answers will vary.

Theme Project

Give students copies of the Theme Project outline and rubric from the *Teacher's Resource Book*. Explain the task to them, and have them perform Step 1. (For more information, see p. 290-a.)

Additional Resources

- WAV Wbk.: Audio Act. 7, p. 110
- Teacher's Resource Book: Audio Script, pp. 64–65
- Audio Program: Track 9

✓ ## Assessment

- **ExamView** QuickTake Presenter Quiz on PresEXPRESS
- Prueba 6A-3: Preterite of *-ir* stem-changing verbs, p. 155

Actividad 15 Leer/Escribir/Hablar

Eventos importantes en la televisión

El invento de la televisión trajo muchos eventos importantes al hogar *(home)*. Lee la información sobre las noticias transmitidas por televisión y contesta las preguntas.

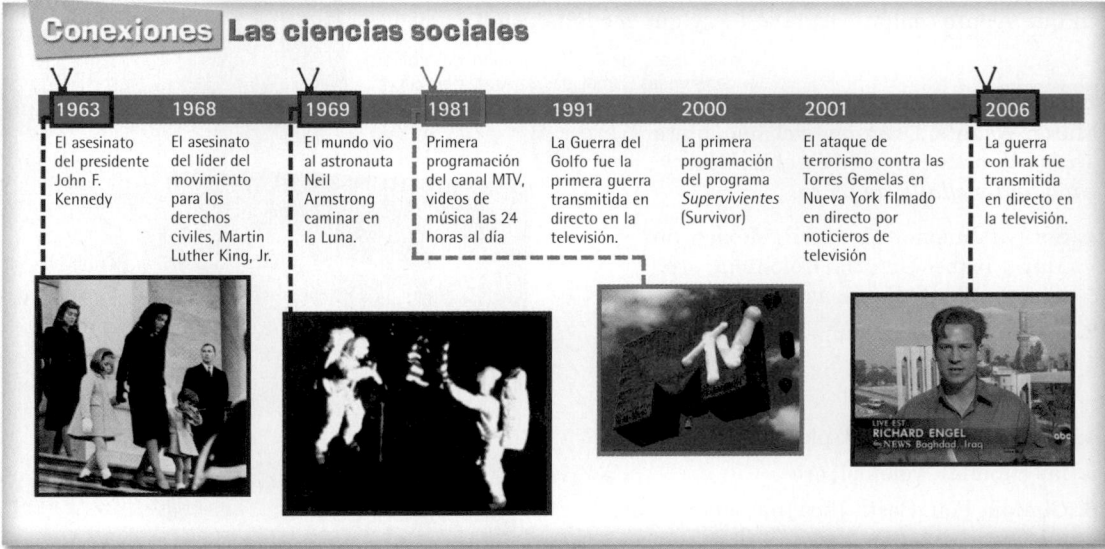

Conexiones Las ciencias sociales

| 1963 | 1968 | 1969 | 1981 | 1991 | 2000 | 2001 | 2006 |

El asesinato del presidente John F. Kennedy

El asesinato del líder del movimiento para los derechos civiles, Martin Luther King, Jr.

El mundo vio al astronauta Neil Armstrong caminar en la Luna.

Primera programación del canal MTV, videos de música las 24 horas al día

La Guerra del Golfo fue la primera guerra transmitida en directo en la televisión.

La primera programación del programa *Supervivientes* (Survivor)

El ataque de terrorismo contra las Torres Gemelas en Nueva York filmado en directo por noticieros de televisión

La guerra con Irak fue transmitida en directo en la televisión.

1. ¿Cuándo caminó en la Luna Neil Armstrong?
2. ¿Quién se murió en 1968?
3. ¿Qué se vio por primera vez en 1991?
4. ¿Cuál de estos eventos tuvo el mayor impacto en tu vida?
5. Piensa en una noticia importante que viste en la televisión. ¿Cómo te sentiste cuando lo viste?
6. Piensa en algún evento histórico que viste en la televisión con otras personas. ¿Cómo se sintieron?

Actividad 16 Escribir/Hablar

Y tú, ¿qué dices?

1. ¿Qué viste recientemente en la televisión? ¿Los miembros de tu familia también lo vieron o prefirieron ver otro programa?

2. ¿Te dormiste recientemente cuando estabas viendo la tele? ¿Te dormiste porque estabas muy cansado(a) o porque te aburriste mucho?

Más práctica

- Practice Workbook, p. 117: 6A-5
- WAV Wbk.: Writing, p. 113
- Guided Practice: Grammar Acts., pp. 211–213
- *Real.* para hispanohablantes, pp. 214–217

Go Online
PHSchool.com
For: Preterite of *-ir* Verbs
Web Code: jdd-0604

Differentiated Instruction
Solutions for All Learners

Students with Learning Difficulties

Use a transparency to help students understand the timeline in *Actividad* 15. Explain that the dates go from earliest to most recent and represent events of historical significance. Have students categorize each event as politics or entertainment. Highlight each event, using two colors to indicate category.

Heritage Language Learners

To help students practice communicating about complex topics, have them research two or three news events to add to the timeline in *Actividad* 15. Remind them to use the four-step writing process of pre-writing, drafting, editing, and revising. You may want to require them to hand in a preliminary draft for you to review.

Gramática

Other reflexive verbs

Other reflexive verbs use reflexive pronouns and verb forms but do not have the meaning of a person doing an action to or for himself or herself. These reflexive verbs often describe a change in mental, emotional, or physical state, and can express the idea that someone "gets" or "becomes."

Examples of these verbs are:

aburrirse	to get bored	enojarse	to become angry
casarse	to get married	ponerse (furioso, -a; alegre; . . .)	to become (furious, happy, . .)
divertirse	to have fun		
dormirse	to fall asleep	volverse loco, -a	to go crazy

Se durmieron durante la película.

Se puso alegre después de ganar.

¿Recuerdas?

You know that you use reflexive verbs to say that people do something to or for themselves.

• Felipe **se afeitaba** mientras yo **me cepillaba** los dientes.

GramActiva VIDEO

Want more help with other reflexive verbs? Watch the **GramActiva** video.

Se aburre.

  Actividad 17   **Leer/Escribir**

En la casa de mi novia

A Lorenzo le gusta ir a la casa de su novia, pero ¡no es nada divertido ver la tele con sus padres! Completa su descripción con las formas apropiadas de *aburrirse, divertirse, dormirse* y *ponerse*.

No me gusta ver la tele con los padres de mi novia. Les gusta ver los programas educativos. No me gustan estos programas y __1.__ viéndolos. Y lo malo es que su papá casi siempre __2.__ durante los programas y nunca los ve hasta el final. Pero si yo quiero ver otra cosa y cambio *(I change)* de canales, él siempre se despierta. Entonces __3.__ un poco agitado porque su programa no está en la pantalla. Ellos también __4.__ viendo los programas de concursos que a mí me parecen muy tontos. Su mamá __5.__ emocionada cuando sabe la respuesta correcta o el precio correcto de algún objeto. Me encanta visitar a mi novia pero si veo la tele, __6.__ más cuando estoy en mi propia casa.

"Operación Triunfo", un programa de concursos de España

trescientos cinco 305
Capítulo 6A

Gramática

Presentation EXPRESS
GRAMMAR

Core Instruction

Resources: Voc. and Gram. Transparency 112; Teacher's Resource Book: Video Script, p. 68; Video Program: Cap. 6A

Suggestions: Direct attention to the *¿Recuerdas?* and remind students that the reflexive pronouns go before the conjugated verb or are attached to the infinitive.

Pantomime the reflexive verbs in the *Gramática* and have students guess which word you are demonstrating. Tell students to raise their hands and tell you their guesses using the *Ud.* form.

Bring in pictures from magazines that will elicit the use of the new reflexive verbs: a couple getting married, people having fun, or someone going crazy. Have students work in groups to create sentences describing the photos.

 Bellringer Review
Have students complete a mini-timeline using the preterite to highlight three important events in their life.

 Actividad 17 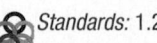 *Standards:* 1.2 
Presentation EXPRESS
ANSWERS

Resources: Answers on Transparencies

Focus: Using reflexive verbs to complete a paragraph

Recycle: Television vocabulary

Suggestions: Read the paragraph aloud with exaggerated expressions and gestures to convey to students the gist of the text before they begin writing their answers. Stop when you come to a blank and have students tell you which verb to use.

Answers:

1. me aburro
2. se duerme
3. se pone
4. se divierten
5. se pone
6. me divierto

Common Errors: Students may forget that some of the verbs have stem changes. Remind them that *divertirse* is an *e → ie* stem-changing verb and *dormirse* is an *o → ue* stem-changing verb.

Enrich Your Teaching
Resources for All Teachers

Culture Note

Many U.S. cable television channels offer Spanish-language programming that is created for viewers in Spanish-speaking countries. Examples include CNN en Español, MTV Latin America, HBO Latino, ESPN International and Spanish television, and TNT Latin America.

Teacher-to-Teacher

Have students choose one of the reflexive verbs from the *Gramática* and create a smiley-face-style icon that illustrates their verb. Have them use the verb they chose to write a sentence to describe themselves. You may want to have students create T-shirts with their design on the front and their sentence on the back.

305

6A Practice and Communicate

Standards: 1.1

Presentation EXPRESS
ANSWERS

Resources: Answers on Transparencies

Focus: Speaking about television programs

Recycle: Television programs; descriptive adjectives

Suggestions: Review the pictures with students to be sure that they understand which television programs they represent. Have students brainstorm a list of adjectives to describe each program.

Answers:

Student A:

1. ¿Qué piensas de los programas musicales?
2. ¿...los programas de entrevistas?
3. ¿...los concursos de belleza?
4. ¿...los programas de concursos?
5. ¿...las telenovelas?
6. ¿...los programas deportivos?

Student B: Answers will vary.

Standards: 1.1

Presentation EXPRESS
ANSWERS

Resources: Answers on Transparencies

Focus: Speaking about reactions to a sporting event

Suggestions: Point out that students should use the verbs in the *Gramática* on p. 305 to describe the people at the game.

Have students brainstorm a list of verbs for each person in the illustration before working with a partner.

Answers:

Student A:

¿Cómo estuvo Ramón durante el partido?
¿Cómo estuvo Guillermo ...?
¿Cómo estuvieron Carlota y Miguel ...?
¿Cómo estuvo Paco ...?
¿Cómo estuvieron Juanita y su hija ...?
¿Cómo estuvieron Pepe y Luisa ...?
¿Cómo estuviste tú ...?

Student B answers will vary.

Extension: Have students choose two people from the activity and write a dialogue of what they said after the game.

Block Schedule

Have students view segments of various Spanish-language television programs. Ask them to describe each program and to write a few sentences telling what they thought of each one.

306

Actividad 18 — Hablar

Los programas

¿Cómo te sientes cuando ves cada clase de programa? Con otro(a) estudiante, pregunta y contesta según el modelo.

Modelo

A —¿Qué piensas de <u>los programas deportivos</u>?

B —Creo que son muy <u>divertidos</u>. Me pongo <u>emocionado(a)</u> cuando los veo.

Estudiante A

1. 2. 3.
4. 5. 6.

Estudiante B

aburrirse	ponerse agitado, -a
divertirse	alegre
dormirse	emocionado, -a
	enojado, -a
	furioso, -a

¡Respuesta personal!

Actividad 19 — Hablar/Escribir

Un empate

¿Qué pasó cuando el partido resultó en un empate? ¿Cómo estuvieron los aficionados? Trabaja con otro(a) estudiante para describirlos. Usa los verbos de la Actividad 18. Luego imagina que tú estabas en el estadio durante el partido. ¿Cómo te sentiste tú cuando el partido resultó en un empate?

Modelo

David

A —¿Cómo estuvo David durante el partido?

B —Se puso agitado.

306 trescientos seis
Tema 6 • La televisión y el cine

Differentiated Instruction
Solutions for All Learners

Students with Special Needs

For *Actividad* 19, make the illustration more accessible to visually impaired students. Provide an enlarged photocopy of each person or group of people in the drawing. Draw attention to visual clues such as body language and facial expressions to be sure that students understand the emotions that are being illustrated.

Advanced Learners

Have students work in groups to make a silent movie about fan reactions at a sporting event. Encourage them to demonstrate a variety of emotions as they portray the fans. Have them make cards to hold up with descriptions of people's reactions. Allow them to present their videos to the class.

Actividad 20 — Escribir/Hablar

Y tú, ¿qué dices?

Escoge un verbo del recuadro y escribe tres o cuatro frases describiendo cuándo y por qué te sentiste así.

Modelo

Mis amigos y yo queríamos ir al cine el sábado a ver una nueva película. Mi mamá me dijo que tenía que ir con mi familia a la casa de mis tíos. Me puse furioso.

aburrirse	ponerse agitado, -a
divertirse	alegre
enojarse	emocionado, -a
	furioso, -a

¿Recuerdas?

Remember that when telling a story in the past, the preterite tense describes actions that began and ended at a specific time. The imperfect tense, however . . .

- provides background information such as time and weather conditions.
- describes the existing physical, mental, and emotional states of a person or thing.
- says what was happening when something else took place.

Actividad 21 — Escribir/Hablar

Las pantallas

Mira el cuadro de Mariano Sapia, un artista argentino. Luego contesta las preguntas.

1. En "Pantallas", ¿dónde está la gente?
2. ¿Qué hace la gente? ¿Qué ve en los televisores? ¿Hay una diferencia entre los televisores y las ventanas de las tiendas?
3. ¿Por qué crees que tanta gente mira la cancha de fútbol donde nadie juega y tan poca gente mira el otro televisor? ¿Cómo piensas que se siente la gente?

"Pantallas" (2002), Mariano Sapia
Oil on canvas, 120 x 170 cm. Photo courtesy of Praxis International Art, New York.

El español en la comunidad

La cadena de televisión número uno en Nueva York, Los Ángeles y Chicago para ver las noticias entre adultos de 18 a 34 años no es ni ABC, ni CBS, ni NBC, ni Fox, ni CNN. Es Univisión, la cadena en español más grande y más vista de los Estados Unidos. Muchos profesores de español en los Estados Unidos recomiendan Univisión para sus estudiantes.

- ¿Tienes canal de Univisión en tu comunidad? ¿Por qué puede ser bueno ver algunos programas en Univisión?

trescientos siete **307**
Capítulo 6A

Enrich Your Teaching
Resources for All Teachers

Culture Note

Born in 1964 in Buenos Aires, Mariano Sapia grew up in a household that placed importance on art and education. His art expresses the emotions of daily life in an urban environment. His paintings have been shown in exhibits throughout the world, including one at the Metropolitan Museum of Art in New York City.

Teacher-to-Teacher

Tell students about the SAP feature on televisions. Explain that it enables viewers to get a translated version of English-language television programs by simply pressing a button on their remote. If it is a feature available in your community, encourage students to use it to practice listening comprehension.

Practice and Communicate

Actividad 20
 Standards: 1.3

Focus: Writing and speaking about personal experiences

Recycle: Imperfect tense

Suggestions: Direct attention to the *¿Recuerdas?* Have students identify the imperfect and preterite verbs in the model and say why each tense was used. Point out that **Me puse furioso.** ("I became furious.") is a completed action. Even though the phrase describes an emotional state, the preterite is used.

Answers will vary.

Extension: Have students keep a daily journal for one week and record the emotions they experienced each day and the events that made them feel that way.

Actividad 21
 Standards: 1.2, 5.1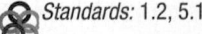

Resources: Answers on Transparencies

Focus: Speaking and writing about a painting by Mariano Sapia

Suggestions: Help students answer item 3 by asking if they believe people should be more active participants in sports rather than watching events on television. What about in other aspects of life?

Answers:

1. La gente está en un centro comercial.
2. La gente mira un televisor. Ve una cancha de fútbol. No hay mucha diferencia entre los televisores y las ventanas de las tiendas.
3. Answers will vary.

Common Errors: Students may not know the meaning of **cancha.** Have them use the painting as a visual clue to help them understand the meaning of the word.

El español en la comunidad
Core Instruction

 Standards: 1.2, 5.1

Suggestions: Show students segments of various programs and commercials aired on Univisión or another Spanish-language network.

Answers will vary.

307

Pronunciación

Core Instruction

 Standards: 1.2, 2.2, 4.1

Resources: Teacher's Resource Book: Audio Script, pp. 65–66, Audio Program: Track 12

Suggestions: To help students understand the concept of regional variations within a language, ask them to give examples of variations in the way letters and words are pronounced in different English-speaking countries: "schedule" is pronounced in British English with a *sh* sound. Point out that there are also regional differences in pronunciation within the United States. Southerners generally lengthen vowel sounds more than speakers in the North.

Fondo cultural  *Standards:* 1.2, 2.2, 4.2

Suggestions: Ask students to brainstorm a list of popular game shows in the United States. Have them look at a Spanish-language television guide and see if they can identify any game shows, especially those that are versions of U.S. programs.
Answers will vary.

Pre-AP* Support

- **Activity:** Have students bring to class a picture from a magazine, etc., illustrating one of the verbs or adjectives found in the box in *Actividad* 20. Then ask that they write a mini-story using the picture as an illustration, but without using the verb or adjective. Finally, working in pairs, have students show their picture to their partner and read the mini-story. The partner summarizes the story by using the appropriate verb or adjective.
- *Pre-AP* Resource Book:* Comprehensive guide to Pre-AP* communication skill development, pp. 9–17, 36–46

Additional Resources
- WAV Wbk.: Audio Act. 8-9, pp. 110–111
- Teacher's Resource Book: Audio Script, p. 65, Communicative Activity BLM, pp. 72–73
- Audio Program: Tracks 10–11

Pronunciación

Regional variations of *ll / y* and *c / z*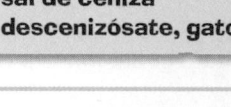

jdd-0688

The majority of Spanish speakers do not distinguish between *ll* and *y*, pronouncing both like *y* in the English word *yes*. Listen to and say these words and sentences as the majority of Spanish speakers would:

rodilla	joyas	cepillo	rayas
llamar	sellos		

Tiene que llevar un yeso.

La calle está cerca de la playa.

Note, however, that the pronunciation of *ll* and *y* varies around the Spanish-speaking world. In Argentina and Uruguay, *ll* and *y* are pronounced like the *s* in the English word *measure*. In other countries, the *ll* is pronounced with a hint of an *l*, much like the English word *million*, but a bit softer.

Listen to and say the words and sentences above again, first as a speaker from Argentina or Uruguay would pronounce them, and then as many other Spanish speakers would.

Enjoy this children's riddle from Mexico:

> A ver tú chiquitillo,
> cara de pillo,
> si sabes contestar.
> Es muy grande y muy feo
> fuerte y fiero
> y vive por el mar.

In Latin America and parts of Spain, *c* before *e* and *i*, and *z* before a vowel are pronounced like the *s* in *sink*. In some parts of Spain, however, these letters are pronounced like the *th* in *think*.

Listen to and say the following words as most Spaniards would pronounce them:

cierto dice bronce ciclismo concierto

belleza abrazo azúcar buzón comenzar

¡Compruébalo! Try this tongue twister about a cat:

> Gato cenizoso,
> sal de ceniza
> descenizósate, gato.

Fondo cultural

Concursomanía En España, durante los últimos años, se han estrenado *(have premiered)* muchos programas de concursos donde los participantes compiten contestando preguntas de cultura general. Programas como "Pasapalabra" o "Saber y ganar" son divertidos y dan muchos premios como dinero, coches y viajes. Recientemente, los concursos de supervivencia *(survival)* están de moda. Con frecuencia, los concursantes se convierten en personajes muy populares, conocidos en todo el país.

- Compara la popularidad de los programas de concursos y de supervivencia en España y en los Estados Unidos. ¿Son similares estos programas o son diferentes?

Participantes en el programa "Gran Hermano", en España

Differentiated Instruction
Solutions for All Learners

Students with Learning Difficulties
For *Actividad* 23, help students with difficulties in written expression by reviewing words related to sequencing. Explain that these words can provide transition and structure to a story. Write **primero, luego, de repente,** and **finalmente** on the board. Discuss the meanings of each word and allow students to use them to complete the activity.

Heritage Language Learners
Students who do not pronounce the **c** and **z** before an **e** or **i** as a **th** may confuse the **c, z,** and **s** when writing. Use the words in the *Pronunciación* as a dictation. Have students close their books and write the words they hear. Have them correct their answers and keep a list of those vocabulary words in which they often confuse the **c, z,** and **s**.

Escribir/Hablar/GramActiva

Juego

❶ Trabaja con un grupo de tres. En pequeñas hojas de papel o tarjetas, escriban palabras que conocen de este capítulo y otros capítulos que pueden usar para contar lo que pasó en los dibujos.

❷ Pongan todas las tarjetas en un grupo boca abajo *(facedown)*. Un(a) estudiante toma una tarjeta y forma una frase usando la palabra para contar lo que pasó.

> **Modelo**
> *Los aficionados se pusieron muy alegres.*

el tanteo

alegres

los aficionados

   Escribir/Hablar

El cuento

Usen las ideas de la Actividad 22 y preparen el cuento de lo que pasó en las ilustraciones. Vean la nota *¿Recuerdas?* en la página 307 para recordar cómo usar el pretérito y el imperfecto juntos en un cuento. Presenten su cuento a otro grupo, a su profesor(a) o a la clase.

Más práctica

- Practice Workbook, pp. 118–119: 6A-6, 6A-7
- WAV Wbk.: Writing, p. 114
- Guided Practice: Grammar Acts., pp. 214–215
- *Real.* para hispanohablantes, pp. 218–221

Go Online PHSchool.com
For: Reflexive Verbs
Web Code: jdd-0605

trescientos nueve **309**
Capítulo 6A

Actividad 22 *Standards:* 1.3 **Pre-AP***

Focus: Describing illustrations in the context of a game

Recycle: Sports vocabulary

Suggestions: Before students work with a group, ask them to brainstorm a list of words to describe each of the illustrations. Have them share their lists with the other members of the group and choose the most appropriate vocabulary words to write on their cards. Bring in a timer and give students a time limit for forming their sentences.

Answers will vary.

Extension: Bring in magazine photos of sporting events, distribute them to students, and have them continue the game.

Actividad 23 *Standards:* 1.3

Focus: Preterite and imperfect

Recycle: Sports vocabulary

Suggestions: Have students invent names for the people in the illustrations to use in their stories. Tell them to describe each person's emotional state as well as the events they observe in the images.

Answers will vary.

Common Errors: Students may confuse the imperfect and the preterite. Remind them of the uses of the two tenses.

Extension: Have students create a fifth drawing showing events either before or after the ones pictured in *Actividad* 22. Ask them to exchange their drawing with a partner and write a description of their partner's illustration.

Theme Project

Students can perform Step 2 at this point. Be sure students understand your corrections. (For more information, see p. 290-a.)

 Assessment

- **Exam**View QuickTake Presenter Quiz on PresEXPRESS
- Prueba 6A-4: Other reflexive verbs, p. 156

Enrich Your Teaching
Resources for All Teachers

Teacher-to-Teacher

Ask your local library for sports magazines that are going to be discarded. Distribute them to students and have them look for a photo of a sporting event that interests them. Tell them to cut out the photo and write a radio broadcast–style description of the event. Encourage them to give a description of the players, coaches, and fans, along with play-by-play coverage of the sporting event. Have students work with a partner to practice their broadcast. Ask them to present their photo and description to the class without reading it word-for-word. You may want to record the presentation to include in students' portfolios.

309

6A

Lectura

Core Instruction

Standards: 1.2, 2.2, 3.1

Focus: Reading comprehension of an article about the Pan-American Games

Suggestions:

Pre-reading: Direct attention to the *Estrategia* and ask students what they know about the Olympic Games. Have them brainstorm a list of topics they might expect to find in an article about international sports competitions. Present the reading in three parts: *Los Juegos Panamericanos, Logos y mascotas,* and *Jefferson Pérez.* Encourage students to use visual clues to help them with the reading.

Ask them to describe the photo on p. 310. Who are the people in the photo? How are they feeling? Have students look at the drawing at the bottom of the same page. What is it? Have them name the colors and ask them to compare it to the symbol for the Olympic Games. Direct attention to the illustrations on p. 311. What do students think that part of the article is going to discuss? Point out the photo of Jefferson Pérez and ask students if they think he won or lost. Have them look at the flag below the photo and predict where Pérez is from.

Reading: Have students read the article once, relying on cognates and context clues to help them with unfamiliar vocabulary. Then have them skim the article to look for the answers to the *¿Comprendiste?* questions.

Post-reading: Have students complete the *¿Comprendiste?* and *Y tú, ¿qué dices?* questions.

Bellringer Review
Conduct a class brainstorm of sports activities available to students at your school.

Additional Resources
Student Resource: Guided Practice: Lectura, p. 216

¡Adelante!

Lectura

Objectives
- **Read about the Pan-American Games**
- **Create a TV guide**
- **Review a television program**
- **Watch** *En busca de la verdad,* **Episodio 7**

Atletas en la ceremonia de inauguración en Winnipeg, Canadá

Los Juegos Panamericanos

Estrategia

Using prior knowledge
When reading a text in Spanish, use your knowledge of the subject in English to help you understand the context of the reading. The following piece is about the Pan-American Games, an event similar to the Summer Olympics. What would you expect to find in a reading about a major sporting event?

LOS JUEGOS PANAMERICANOS se establecieron para promover la comprensión entre las naciones del continente americano. Los primeros Juegos se inauguraron el 25 de febrero de 1951 en Buenos Aires, con 2,513 atletas de 22 países. El lema[1] de los Juegos —"América, Espirito, Sport, Fraternité"— incorpora cuatro de los idiomas más importantes de las Américas: el español, el portugués, el inglés y el francés. Todos los países de las Américas pueden mandar atletas a competir. Aproximadamente el 80 por ciento de los deportes de los Juegos Panamericanos se juegan en las Olimpíadas. Los Juegos Panamericanos se celebran cada cuatro años durante el verano previo a los Juegos Olímpicos.

 **EL EMBLEMA DE LOS JUEGOS** es una antorcha sobre cinco círculos concéntricos con los colores amarillo, verde, blanco, rojo y azul. Aparece por lo menos[2] uno de estos colores en cada bandera nacional de los países de las Américas.

[1] motto [2] at least

310 trescientos diez
Tema 6 • La televisión y el cine

Differentiated Instruction
Solutions for All Learners

Students with Learning Difficulties
To help students with the *Estrategia,* have them make three-column charts on their papers. Ask them to label the columns *Nouns, Adjectives,* and *Verbs.* Have students brainstorm a list of vocabulary related to international sports competitions and to write each word in the appropriate column.

Multiple Intelligences
Visual/Spatial: Have students create the poster that they describe in item 2 in the *Y tú, ¿qué dices?* section. Encourage them to research significant cultural and historical events in their community to better create an appropriate mascot. Ask them to present their poster to the class and explain why it represents their community.

LOGOS Y MASCOTAS

Para conmemorar los Juegos Panamericanos, cada cuatro años el país anfitrión[3] crea una mascota que representa algo histórico o cultural del país.

Indianápolis, Estados Unidos, 1987
Amigo—Un papagayo[4] lleno de colores fue la mascota oficial de los Juegos porque el papagayo es un ave[5] típica de las Américas, y el nombre Amigo fue inspirado en el espíritu de amistad y unidad de la gente del continente.

La Habana, Cuba, 1991
Tocopan—El nombre de la mascota oficial de los Juegos Panamericanos en la Habana proviene de la combinación de la palabra Tocororo (considerado el ave nacional de Cuba por poseer los colores de la bandera nacional) con la palabra *Panamericanos*.

Mar del Plata, Argentina, 1995
Lobi—El león marino es un habitante tradicional del mar cerca de la ciudad de Mar del Plata. Sonriendo con brazos abiertos, Lobi da cordiales saludos de bienvenida a la familia panamericana.

Santo Domingo, República Dominicana, 2003
Tito—El manatí es una especie en peligro de extinción. Tito, la mascota, simboliza el deseo que tienen los dominicanos de proteger su medio ambiente.

JEFFERSON PÉREZ: UN HÉROE NACIONAL

Muchos de los atletas que participan en los Juegos Panamericanos participan también en las Olimpíadas. El ecuatoriano Jefferson Pérez, por ejemplo, ganó la medalla de oro en la marcha[6] de 20 km durante los Juegos Panamericanos de Mar del Plata, Argentina, en el año 1995. Se convirtió en un héroe nacional de Ecuador cuando ganó otra vez la medalla de oro en 1996, en Atlanta, Estados Unidos, durante los Juegos Olímpicos. Fue la primera vez que un atleta de Ecuador ganó una medalla de oro en las Olimpíadas. Jefferson Pérez vino de un barrio muy pobre de Cuenca, Ecuador, y llegó a ser un símbolo de lo que uno puede alcanzar[7] con mucho trabajo y esfuerzo.

El ecuatoriano Jefferson Pérez ganó otra vez la medalla de oro en 1996.

La bandera de Ecuador

[3]host country [4]parrot [5]bird [6]cycling [7]accomplish

¿Comprendiste?

1. ¿Cómo representan el lema y el símbolo de los Juegos Panamericanos los diferentes países del continente?

2. ¿Por qué son importantes los Juegos Panamericanos para un(a) atleta que quiere competir en las Olimpíadas?

3. ¿Qué representan las mascotas de los Juegos? ¿Qué representa el papagayo?

4. ¿Por qué llegó a ser un héroe nacional Jefferson Pérez?

Y tú, ¿qué dices?

1. ¿Crees que un(a) atleta puede ser un(a) héroe (heroína) nacional? ¿Por qué?

2. Tienes que crear una mascota y un cartel para una celebración para unos juegos deportivos internacionales en tu comunidad. ¿Qué pones en el cartel? ¿Cómo es la mascota?

Más práctica

- WAV Wbk.: Writing, p. 115
- Guided Practice: *Lectura*, p. 216
- *Real.* para hispanohablantes, pp. 222–223

 Go **O**nline
PHSchool.com
For: Internet Activity
Web Code: jdd-0606

trescientos once **311**
Capítulo 6A

Enrich Your Teaching
Resources for All Teachers

Culture Note

Starting with the first Paralympics Games in Rome in 1960, the International Paralympics Committee has organized international competitions that follow the regular summer Olympic Games. More than 160 nations participate in this nonprofit event, with over 6,000 physically challenged participants worldwide.

Internet Search

Keyword: Paralympics Games

¿Comprendiste?
Standards: 1.2

Resources: Answers on Transparencies
Focus: Verifying comprehension of reading about the Pan-American Games
Suggestions: Ask students to read all the questions before answering them. For each one, have them predict which section of the article is most likely to include the answer. Tell them to skim the appropriate section for the answer.

Answers:
1. El lema representa los cuatro idiomas más importantes de las Américas (el español, el portugués, el inglés y el francés). En el emblema, o símbolo, aparece por lo menos uno de los colores en cada bandera nacional de los países de las Américas.
2. Aproximadamente el 80 por ciento de los deportes de los Juegos Panamericanos se juegan en las Olimpíadas. Muchos de los atletas en los Juegos Panamericanos también participan en las Olimpíadas.
3. Las mascotas representan algo histórico o cultural del país. El papagayo es un ave llena de colores y típica de las Américas.
4. Porque ganó una medalla de oro en los Juegos Panamericanos de Santo Domingo.

Y tú, ¿qué dices?
Standards: 1.3

Suggestions: Have students brainstorm qualities they associate with a hero. Then ask them to brainstorm a list of qualities they associate with an athlete. Which are the same? Which are different?
Answers will vary.

Pre-AP* Support

- **Activity:** Have students work with a partner. Assign one student to read the section *Los Juegos Panamericanos* (p. 310) and the other read *Logos y mascotas* (p. 311). Then have each write four true/false statements. Next, with textbooks closed, read the article aloud to the class. Finally, read the article a second time and ask students to indicate *cierta/falsa* to the statements they received from their partner.
- *Pre-AP* Resource Book:* Comprehensive guide to Pre-AP* reading skill development, pp. 18–24

For Further Reading

Student Resources: Realidades para hispanohablantes: Lectura 2, pp. 224–225; Lecturas para hispanohablantes 2: "Ficción," pp. 88–89, "Los chicos del fin del mundo," pp. 111–114

311

La cultura en vivo
Core Instruction

Standards: 1.2, 1.3, 2.2

Focus: Reading about and making a television programming guide

Suggestions: Bring in television guides from your community to distribute to each group. You may prefer to have students search the Internet for television guides from various Spanish-speaking countries. Have students use the guides as models to help them develop ideas. Remind them to include a variety of programs, not only those that are of interest to them.

Give students examples of television guides that use the 24-hour clock. Have them practice converting times in U.S. guides.

Encourage students to be creative when naming their programs. Give them examples of Spanish translations for names of popular television shows and movies in the United States.

Have students use Steps 2–4 as a checklist to make sure they have covered everything before turning in their guides.

Extension: Have students create a television guide crossword puzzle. Encourage them to use the new vocabulary in their clues. Tell them to include some clues about information included in the descriptions of the programs in their guide.

Additional Resources

Student Resource: Realidades para hispano-hablantes, p. 226

La cultura en vivo

La guía de la tele

¿Sabías que las guías *(guides)* de televisión son las revistas más leídas en muchos países hispanohablantes? A la gente le gusta informarse de lo que hay en la televisión y por eso consulta las guías. Muchos periódicos publican la programación en sus ediciones diarias y, los fines de semana, publican una guía para toda la semana.

Preparar una buena programación no es fácil. La programación debe tener variedad e interés para muchas personas. Tiene que ser divertida, ofrecer noticias informativas y tener programas culturales también.

Los locutores del programa de Univisión, *Despierta América*

Objetivo

Hacer una guía de programas de televisión

Materiales

• papel, marcadores y lápices de colores

Instrucciones

Formen grupos de dos o tres estudiantes.

1 Van a planear la programación en un canal para un día de la semana desde las cuatro de la tarde hasta medianoche.

2 Escojan la clase de programas que quieren ofrecer (informativos, culturales, cine, concursos, deportivos y más) y las horas en que se dan. ¡Cuidado! En los países hispanohablantes se usa un horario de programación de 24 horas. ¡No se olviden de dar un nombre a cada programa!

3 Preparen la guía. Usen colores diferentes para las diferentes clases de programas.

4 Al final de la guía, escriban una recomendación para el mejor programa del día.

312 trescientos doce
Tema 6 • La televisión y el cine

HORA	Canal 2	Canal 3	Canal 4	Canal 7
06:30	Noticias	El tiempo	Dibujos animados	Música
07:00	¡Hagamos ejercicio!	Programa escolar	Mundo animal	
07:30	Grandes viajes			Actualidad deportiva
08:00				El tiempo
08:30	La buena cocina	Las aventuras de Simón	Tú y yo	Pueblos de América
09:00	Noticias			
09:30	Cine clásico	Medicina y salud	Fútbol mundial	Película
10:00				
10:30		Siglo XXI		
11:00				Vida en el mar
11:30	Telenovela	Película infantil	Noticias	
12:00				

Programación de televisión para el martes (table title)

Differentiated Instruction
Solutions for All Learners

Advanced Learners

Tell students to work in groups to create a television guide for their community. Assign each group a different one-hour time slot. Be sure to assign late-afternoon and early-evening times. Have each student in the group choose a different television show, watch it, and write a synopsis of the show to include in their guide.

Multiple Intelligences

Bodily/Kinesthetic: Have students present their television guides in the format of an entertainment news show. Tell them to play the role of the hosts, and ask them to talk about what is on television and to give a synopsis of each show in their guide. Videotape their presentations and include them in students' portfolios.

Un programa de televisión

Task

Choose your favorite television program and prepare a review of it to present to your class.

1 Prepare Look at a TV guide and find a program you like to watch and other people might like to watch as well. What essential facts would your listeners need to know in order to decide which TV show to watch? Make a list and then fill in the facts about the program you have chosen. Include the following:

- nombre del programa
- descripción
- día, hora y canal
- para quién (niños, adolescentes, mayores o todos)
- actores / presentadores
- lo que ocurrió en un episodio reciente
- un adjetivo que describe el programa
- cómo te sentiste cuando viste el programa
- por qué te gustó o no te gustó

2 Practice Go through your presentation several times. You can use your notes in practice, but not when you present. Try to:

- present a persuasive and interesting review
- provide all the information on the program
- use complete sentences and speak clearly

Modelo

Mi programa de televisión favorito es Survivor. *Lo dan en el canal seis a las nueve de la noche los jueves . . .*

3 Present Make your presentation about the TV program.

4 Evaluation Your teacher may give you a rubric for how the presentation will be graded. You will probably be graded on:

- how persuasive your review is
- how much information you communicate
- how easy it is to understand you

Estrategia

Note-taking

Taking notes can help you prepare for an oral or written presentation. As you watch the show you are reviewing, take notes to help you remember details. What do you like about the show? What happens in the particular episode?

trescientos trece **313**
Capítulo 6A

Presentación oral
Core Instruction

Standards: 1.3, 3.1

Focus: Describing and giving opinions about a favorite television program

Suggestions: Have students brainstorm a list of programs that they could use for their presentations. Be sure to eliminate any inappropriate television shows from the list.

Direct attention to the *Estrategia* and provide students with an outline to help them organize their notes. Include the points listed under Step 1.

If there are long pauses in students' presentations, encourage them to stay on track by asking them questions.

Portfolio

Record students' oral presentations on cassette or videotape for inclusion in their portfolios.

Pre-AP* Support

- *Pre-AP* Resource Book:* Comprehensive guide to Pre-AP* speaking skill development, pp. 36–46

Additional Resources

Student Resources: Realidades para hispano-hablantes, p. 227; Guided Practice: Presentación oral, p. 217

✓ Assessment

- Assessment Program: Rubrics, p. T30

Give students copies of the rubric before they begin the activity. Go over the descriptions of the different levels of performance. After assessing students, help individuals understand how their performance could be improved.

Enrich Your Teaching
Resources for All Teachers

RUBRIC	Score 1	Score 3	Score 5
Persuasiveness of your review	You are ineffective in persuading the audience.	You are somewhat effective in persuading the audience.	You are very effective in persuading the audience.
How much information you communicate	You provide up to three facts to your audience.	You provide up to six facts to your audience.	You provide all nine facts to your audience.
How easily you are understood	You are difficult to understand and have many grammatical errors.	You are fairly easy to understand and have occasional grammatical errors.	You are easy to understand and have very few grammatical errors.

Videomisterio

Core Instruction

Standards: 1.2, 3.2, 5.2

Resources: Teacher's Resource Book: Video Script, pp. 68–69; Video Program: Cap. 6A; Video Program Teacher's Guide: Cap. 6A

Focus: Reading and presenting new vocabulary needed to understand the video

Personajes importantes

Roberto	**Tomás**
Linda	**Berta**
Julio	**Daniela**

Synopsis: After Linda and Julio finish lunch, Roberto meets them and the three of them visit tourist sites in Guanajuato. Roberto speaks to his father about the bank account that Federico Zúñiga opened in San Antonio and says that he wants to go to Texas to claim it. Meanwhile, a mysterious man, Turrón, has appeared in Guanajuato and is asking questions about the Toledo family.

Suggestions:

Pre-viewing: Review the events of *Episodio* 6: Roberto and Linda went to Dolores Hidalgo to inquire about the missing grandfather, Federico Zúñiga. They met with Chato Montesinos in his home. Chato told them that Federico entered the U.S. Army when the two of them went to San Antonio. He gave them the name of a bank where they both opened accounts. Roberto called the bank and spoke with Sr. De León in the Closed Accounts department. De León told Roberto that there is an account, but that it must be claimed in person by an adult relative of Federico Zúñiga. De León then called the mysterious Sr. Turrón to tell him that someone has been making inquiries.

Have a volunteer read the *Notas culturales* aloud. Remind students that they read about **estudiantinas** and the *Jardín de la Unión* in the introduction to the *Videomisterio, Capítulo* 1A. Ask what traditions similar to **estudiantinas** exist in the United States (*Christmas caroling*).

Point out the *Palabras para comprender*. Give students sentences to help them understand the words in context.

Videomisterio

En busca de la verdad

Episodio 7

Antes de ver el video

"Señor, no podemos darle tal información".

"Papá, creo que tengo una pista para saber lo que pasó con el abuelo".

Nota cultural La palabra "estudiantina" se usa para hablar de un grupo musical de estudiantes universitarios. Su origen es muy antiguo, y viene de los músicos cantores llamados trovadores. Los trovadores cantaban en las calles, y hoy las estudiantinas cantan en los parques y en las plazas. En México hay más de 200 estudiantinas. Algunas se presentan en Guanajuato durante el festival de teatro que se celebra todos los años.

Resumen del episodio

Roberto, Linda y Julio pasan el día paseando por Guanajuato. Por la tarde, Roberto y Linda van al Jardín de la Unión y escuchan una estudiantina. Al día siguiente, Roberto habla con la familia de lo que sabe sobre el abuelo. El misterioso hombre del episodio anterior llega a Guanajuato.

Palabras para comprender
mensaje message
si me permites if you allow me
a eso de las 9 around 9 o'clock
Están de acuerdo. They agree.
pasado past
pronto soon
pista clue

314 trescientos catorce
Tema 6 • La televisión y el cine

Differentiated Instruction
Solutions for All Learners

Multiple Intelligences
Musical/Rhythmic: Have students research *estudiantinas* in Mexico and other Spanish-speaking countries. Have them investigate clothing, instruments, and type of music played. Have them replicate these as best as possible and lead the class in an *estudiantina* singalong.

Heritage Language Learners
Have students write a creative continuation of the *episodio*. Have them use the *Palabras para comprender*. Tell them to include what happens to each character in the video. Be sure to correct spelling and grammar.

Después de ver el video

¿Comprendiste?

A. Escoge la palabra correcta entre paréntesis y di quién dice cada frase. (Roberto, Linda, Julio o Tomás Toledo)

a. "No olvides el de Diego Rivera. Fue su _____ casa". (última / primera / bella)

b. "Luego Julio tuvo que _____". (acostarse / irse / salir)

c. "¿Quieres comer o _____ algo mientras esperamos?". (jugar / tomar / ponerte)

d. "El abuelo _____ una cuenta en un banco de los Estados Unidos". (cambió / cerró / abrió)

e. "Por eso en el Banco de San Antonio estaban _____". (confundidos / bravos / asustados)

f. "Hijo, a veces es mejor no tocar el _____". (teléfono / dolor / pasado)

B. Habla de los planes de Roberto. ¿Adónde va a ir para seguir las pistas? ¿Con quién? ¿Qué quiere el hombre misterioso?

Nota cultural El Jardín de la Unión es el parque más importante de Guanajuato. Está sembrado de árboles llamados *Laureles de la India* y tiene la forma de un triángulo. Por eso los habitantes de la ciudad llaman este parque "pedazo de queso." Allí hay un quiosco donde toca la banda del estado. Los parques y las plazas siempre han sido lugares de reunión para los mexicanos. Son espacios públicos que todos pueden disfrutar.

"¡Tú vas con nosotras!".

Go Online
PHSchool.com
For: More on *En busca de la verdad*
Web Code: jdd-0209

trescientos quince **315**
Capítulo 6A

Suggestions:

Visual scanning: Direct attention to the photos. Have students read the captions and try to guess what the characters might be talking about. Then have them read the *Resumen del episodio* and ask them one or two comprehension questions.

Viewing: Play *Episodio* 7 for the class. If there is time after viewing the full episode, go back and replay key moments that you wish to highlight. Remind students that they may not understand every word they hear in the video, but they should listen for overall understanding.

Post-viewing: Complete the *¿Comprendiste?* in class.

¿Comprendiste?

Presentation EXPRESS
ANSWERS

 *Standards:* 1.2, 1.3

Resources: Answers on Transparencies

Focus: Verifying comprehension; reviewing the plot

Suggestions: For part A, challenge students to remember as much as possible. For part B, you may want to replay scenes 4–6 of the *episodio*.

Answers:

A:
a. primera; Roberto
b. irse; Roberto
c. tomar; Roberto
d. abrió; Roberto
e. confundidos; Roberto
f. pasado; Tomás

B: Answers will vary.

Additional Resources

• *En busca de la verdad* Video Workbook, Episode 7
• *En busca de la verdad* Teacher's Video Guide: Answer Key

Culture Note

In 1988, the United Nations Educational, Scientific, and Cultural Organization (UNESCO) declared Guanajuato and its surrounding mines a World Heritage Site. As such, they promised to preserve and protect this historical treasure from natural or intentional destruction. Other colonial cities in Mexico that share this distinction are Oaxaca, Puebla, Mexico City, Morelia, Zacatecas, and Querétaro.

Review Activities

To talk about a sporting event: Give pairs of students an envelope containing pictures cut out of sports pages. Ask students to use the vocabulary to describe each of the athletes or sporting events in the pictures. Students may invent their descriptions.

To talk about a contest: Write a short paragraph about a recent beauty contest, leaving out vocabulary words. Write a definition of each word where it would be found in the paragraph. Have students fill in the correct term.

To talk about how you feel: Ask students to write five scenarios on a piece of paper, and cut them into individual strips. Collect all of the sentences and put them in a box. Redistribute five scenarios to each student, and have them give an appropriate word to describe how they would feel.

Portfolio

Invite students to review the activities they completed in this chapter, including written reports, posters or other visuals, tapes of oral presentations, or other projects. Have them select one or two items that they feel best demonstrate their achievements in Spanish to include in their portfolios. Have them include this with the Chapter Checklist and Self-Assessment Worksheet.

Additional Resources

Student Resources: Realidades para hispanohablantes, p. 228

 **CD-ROM**

PuzzleView Web Code: jdd-0608

Teacher Resources:
- Teacher's Resource Book: Situation Cards, p. 74, Clip Art, pp. 76–79
- Assessment Program: Chapter Checklist and Self-Assessment Worksheet, pp. T56–T57

316

Repaso del capítulo

Vocabulario y gramática jdd-0689 🔊))

To prepare for the test, check to see if you . . .
- know the new vocabulary and grammar
- can perform the tasks on p. 317

to talk about a sporting event

el aficionado, la aficionada	fan
al final	at the end
aplaudir	to applaud
el/la atleta	athlete
el campeón, la campeona, *pl.* los campeones	champion
el campeonato	championship
la competencia	competition
competir (e → i)	to compete
el empate	tie
el entrenador, la entrenadora	coach, trainer
fenomenal	phenomenal
el jugador, la jugadora	player
la liga	league
meter un gol	to score a goal
perder (e → ie)	to lose
por . . . vez	for the . . . time
resultar	to result, to turn out
el tanteo	score
último, -a	last, final

to talk about a contest

el auditorio	auditorium
el comentario	commentary
el concurso de belleza	beauty contest
la entrevista	interview
entrevistar	to interview
un millón de/ millones de	a million/ millions of
el premio	prize
el presentador, la presentadora	presenter
el público	audience
la reina	queen

to talk about how you feel

aburrirse	to get bored
agitado, -a	agitated
alegre	happy
emocionado, -a	excited, emotional
enojado, -a	angry
enojarse	to get angry
furioso, -a	furious
ponerse + adjective	to become
volverse (o → ue) loco, -a	to go crazy

other useful words

dormirse (o → ue, o → u)	to fall asleep
morirse (o → ue, o → u)	to die

preterite of *-ir* stem-changing verbs

preferir

preferí	preferimos
preferiste	preferisteis
prefirió	prefirieron

pedir

pedí	pedimos
pediste	pedisteis
pidió	pidieron

dormir

dormí	dormimos
dormiste	dormisteis
durmió	durmieron

For *Vocabulario adicional,* see pp. 498–499.

Differentiated Instruction
Solutions for All Learners

Advanced Learners

Have students create a practice test. Remind them to consider the content and structure of previous tests when writing their own. Have them provide an answer key. Make copies of each test so students can lead small groups in reviewing with their practice tests.

Students with Learning Difficulties

Give students large pieces of paper with one of the categories of vocabulary written at the top of each. Have students brainstorm as many words from the vocabulary list as they can remember without looking at the book. Then have them used a colored pencil to fill in the rest of the words. Encourage them to focus on the words in color while studying.

Preparación para el examen

Más práctica

- Practice Workbook: Puzzle, p. 120
- Practice Workbook: Organizer, p. 121

Go Online PHSchool.com
For: Test Preparation
Web Code: jdd-0608

On the exam you will be asked to . . .	Here are practice tasks similar to those you will find on the exam . . .	If you need review . . .
1 Escuchar Listen and understand as people talk about a television program they saw	Listen as people talk about an awards show they saw on television. Try to identify their reactions to this type of show. Did they become angry? Emotional? Excited? Bored? Nervous?	**pp. 294–297** *A primera vista* **p. 300** *Actividades 8–9*
2 Hablar Talk about a recent television program you saw and describe your reactions to it	As part of a class project, you may be interviewed about a television program you saw. Practice what you might say by telling a partner: (a) what type of program you saw; (b) when you saw it; (c) how you reacted to the program.	**p. 300** *Actividad 10* **p. 304** *Actividad 16* **p. 306** *Actividad 18* **p. 313** *Presentación oral*
3 Leer Read and understand a description of a soccer game	Your friend just returned from a trip to Spain. He brought a newspaper clipping from a soccer game he saw. As you read, see if you can understand what happened.	**pp. 294–297** *A primera vista* **p. 298** *Actividad 4* **p. 299** *Actividad 6* **p. 301** *Actividad 11* **pp. 310–311** *Lectura*

MADRID CONOCE A BARCELONA
Ayer fue una competencia fenomenal. Millones de madrileños vieron el partido en la tele. En los primeros tres minutos del partido, el Real Madrid metió un gol. Treinta minutos más tarde, Morales de Barcelona también metió un gol. Un empate. Todos los aficionados se pusieron muy alegres durante el partido, pero el público se volvió loco cuando Madrid metió otro gol en los últimos dos minutos. Al final, un tanteo de Madrid 2 y Barcelona 1.

4 Escribir Write about an occasion when you became angry	You may have heard that rather than acting out your anger, it is better to write about it to get it out of your system. Write about a recent event or situation that caused you to feel angry. Describe what happened and why you became angry.	**p. 300** *Actividad 9* **p. 303** *Actividad 14* **p. 306** *Actividad 19* **p. 307** *Actividad 20*
5 Pensar Demonstrate an understanding of television shows on Spanish-speaking channels	Think about the popularity of soap operas, game shows, and sporting events on television stations in the United States. Do you think they would be popular choices on Spanish-language television stations too? Give examples from the chapter to support your answer.	**p. 308** *Fondo cultural* **p. 312** *La cultura en vivo*

trescientos diecisiete **317**
Capítulo 6A

Differentiated Assessment
Solutions for All Learners

STUDENTS NEEDING EXTRA HELP
- **Alternate Assessment Program:** Examen del capítulo 6A
- **Audio Program CD 21:** Chap. 6A, Track 3

HERITAGE LEARNERS
- **Assessment Program: Realidades para hispanohablantes:** Examen del capítulo 6A
- **ExamView** Heritage Learner Test Bank

ADVANCED/PRE-AP*
- **ExamView** Pre-AP* Test Bank
- **Pre-AP* Resource Book**, pp. 116–119

Performance Tasks

Standards: 1.1, 1.2, 1.3, 2.1, 2.2, 4.2

Student Resource: Realidades para hispanohablantes, p. 229

Teacher Resources: Teacher's Resource Book: Audio Script, p. 66; Audio Program: Track 14; Answers on Transparencies

1. Escuchar

Suggestions: Allow students to listen to the script more than once.

 Script:

Female #1: Me puse loca anoche cuando vi el programa de Premios Velásquez. ¡Lupe Lazo ganó el premio para la actriz del año! Yo grité a la televisión.
Female #2: Yo, no. Me aburrí y me dormí durante el programa. No puedo soportar esos programas ridículos.

Answers:
The first woman got very excited, but the second was bored.

2. Hablar

Suggestions: Assign students types of television programs to talk about, such as sporting events, sitcoms, or interviews.

Answers will vary.

3. Leer

Suggestions: Distribute copies of the news article or make an overhead transparency. Have students identify the times in the game when each of the three goals occurred.

Answers:
Ayer el Madrid le ganó al Barcelona en un partido de fútbol.

4. Escribir

Suggestions: Remind students to provide some background information using verbs in the imperfect.

Answers will vary.

5. Pensar

Suggestions: Remind students to be specific in their examples. Refer students to p. 312 for information on programming for Spanish-language television stations.

Answers will vary.

Assessment

- **ExamView** Quiz on PresEXPRESS
- Assessment Program: Examen del capítulo
- **ExamView** Test Bank: Tests A and B
- Audio Program CD 21: Chap. 6A, Track 3

Chapter Overview

A primera vista	Manos a la obra	¡Adelante!	Repaso
Learning Sequence			
INPUT	**PRACTICE**	**APPLICATION**	**REVIEW**
• Introduce vocabulary and grammar within an authentic context.	• Practice and develop new vocabulary. • Learn and practice new grammar structures.	• Apply vocabulary and grammar through culminating, theme-based activities. • Apply skill development.	• Review vocabulary and grammar.
Objectives			
Read, listen to, and interpret information about: • Movies • Making a movie	• Express your opinion with verbs that use indirect objects. • Use the present perfect tense to talk about what you have done. • Read movie reviews and a movie schedule in Spanish.	• Read movie reviews and compare movie ratings in different countries. • Define subtitling and dubbing. • Write a film script. • Watch *En busca de la verdad, Episodio* 8.	• Prepare for the chapter test.
Culture			
• *El centenario del cine mexicano*	• *La época de oro del cine mexicano* • Selma Hayek-Jiménez • *El cine en el mundo hispano*	• *Las clasificaciones de las películas* • *Películas en otros idiomas*	• Explain foreign language films, dubbing, and subtitles.

Vocabulary	Grammar	Learner Support	
• Movies • Movie production	• Verbs that use indirect object pronouns • The present perfect	**STRATEGIES** • Predicting meaning • Reading for details • Outlining your ideas • Drawing a scene	**RECYCLING** ♻ • *Gustar* and related-verbs; adjectives • Leisure activities, sports, music, and clothes • Clothing and food
			• Vocabulary for accidents and injuries • Reflexive and indirect object pronouns • Numbers

Chapter Features

Exploración del lenguaje

The suffixes **-oso(a)** and **-dor(a)**

Conexiones

Mathematics: Create a table showing movie-going habits

El español en el mundo del trabajo

Opportunities for Spanish speakers in the film industry of the United States

Beyond the Classroom: States & Countries

España
Cuba
Puerto Rico
California
Panamá
México
Costa Rica
Argentina

Student Resources

TECHNOLOGY

PRACTICE

ONLINE

Interactive Textbook
• Student Edition Online plus audio, video, and flashcards

Go Online Companion Web Site
• Tutorial activities • Internet links
• Self-tests • Downloadable MP3 audio files
• **PuzzleView**

CD-ROM

Interactive Textbook CD-ROM
Student Edition on CD-ROM plus audio, video, and flashcards

MindPoint CD-ROM
QUIZSHOW

PRINT MATERIAL

CORE INSTRUCTION

Practice Workbook, pp. 122–130
• Review • Vocabulary
• Grammar • Puzzle
• Organizer

Writing, Audio & Video Activities,
pp. 116–125
• Video • Audio
• Writing

Grammar Study Guide 1–2 (or 3–4)

Differentiated Instruction

STUDENTS NEEDING EXTRA HELP

Guided Practice Activities, pp. 218–234
• Vocabulary Flash Cards and Vocabulary Check
• Grammar Activities
• Presentación escrita

HERITAGE LEARNERS

Realidades para hispanohablantes,
pp. 230–249

Lecturas para hispanohablantes
• "La casa de los azulejos," pp. 10–11
• "La navidad de Miguelito," pp. 30–32
• "Lo hispano es bello," pp. 92–94

ADVANCED/PRE-AP*

Pre-AP* Resource Book: Student Activity Sheet, p. 119

Teacher Resources

TECHNOLOGY

PLAN AND TEACH

Audio Program Fine Art Transparencies
Video Program Vocabulary and Grammar
Transparencies
Answers on Transparencies

TeacherEXPRESS CD-ROM
• Lesson Planner • Vocabulary Clip Art
• Web Resources • Teaching Resources
• Teacher Edition with Interactive Links

PresentationEXPRESS CD-ROM
• Vocabulary • Transparencies and Maps
• Grammar • Photo Gallery
• Audio • Clip Art

PRINT MATERIAL

CORE INSTRUCTION

Teacher's Resource Book, pp. 86–111
• Input Script • Video Script
• Answer Keys • GramActiva Blackline Masters
• Vocabulary Clip Art • Chapter Resource Checklist
• School-to-Home Connection Letters
• Communicative Activities Blackline Masters

TPR Stories, pp. 85–90

Differentiated Instruction

STUDENTS NEEDING EXTRA HELP

Guided Practice Activities
Teacher's Guide, pp. T110–T115

HERITAGE LEARNERS

Realidades para hispanohablantes
Teacher's Guide, pp. 116–125

Lecturas para hispanohablantes
Teacher's Guide, pp. 2, 10, 35–36

ADVANCED/PRE-AP*

Pre-AP* Resource Book: Resources Chart,
p. 117

✓ Differentiated Assessment

ASSESS

PH SuccessNet ONLINE
• Access to grades and reports from Online Interactive Textbook

ExamView on **Presentation Express**
QuickTake Presenter **CD-ROM**
• Vocabulary Quizzes • Chapter Test
• Grammar Quizzes

TeacherEXPRESS CD-ROM
• Assessment Program
• **ExamView** Test Banks A and B
test generator

CORE ASSESSMENT

Assessment Program, pp. 164–176
• Pruebas
  Vocabulary Recognition
  Vocabulary Production
  Verbs that use indirect object pronouns
  The present perfect
• Examen del capítulo • Speaking and Writing Rubrics

Teacher's Resource Book, p. 100
• Situation Cards

TPR Stories, pp. 85–90

STUDENTS NEEDING EXTRA HELP

Alternate Assessment Program
• Examen del capítulo, pp. 71–75

HERITAGE LEARNERS

Assessment Program: Realidades para hispanohablantes Teacher's Guide,
pp. T144–T148

ExamView Heritage Learner
test generator **Test Bank**

ADVANCED/PRE-AP*

Pre-AP* Resource Book: Teacher Activity Sheet, p. 118

ExamView Pre-AP* Test Bank
test generator

Go Online
PHSchool.com
For: Teacher Home Page
Web Code: jdk-1001

Lesson Plans

Regular Schedule (50 Minutes)

For electronic lesson plans:
Teacher Express 💿

	Warm-up / Assess	Preview Present / Practice Communicate	Wrap-up / Homework Options
DAY 1	**Warm-up (10 min.)** • Homework check • Return Examen del capítulo: Capítulo 6A	**Chapter Opener (10 min.) A primera vista (25 min.)** • Objetives • Fondo cultural • Presentation: Vocabulario y gramática en contexto • Actividades 1, 2	**Wrap-up and Homework Options (5 min.)** • Practice Workbook 6B-A, 6B-B, 6B-1, 6B-2 • Go Online
DAY 2	**Warm-up (10 min.)** • Homework check	**A primera vista (35 min.)** • Presentation: Videohistoria *El mosquito* • View: Videohistoria • Video Activities 1, 2, 3, 4 • Actividad 3	**Wrap-up and Homework Options (5 min.)** • Practice Workbook 6B-3, 6B-4 • Go Online • Prueba 6B-1: Vocabulary recognition
DAY 3	**Warm-up (10 min.)** • Actividad 5 • Homework check **✔Assessment (10 min.)** • Prueba 6B-1: Vocabulary recognition	**Manos a la obra (25 min.)** • Actividades 4, 6, 7, 8 • Fondos culturales	**Wrap-up and Homework Options (5 min.)** • Actividad 10 • Writing Activity 10 • Heritage Learner Workbook 6B-1, 6B-2 • Prueba 6B-2: Vocabulary production
DAY 4	**Warm-up (10 min.)** • Actividad 9 • Homework check **✔Assessment (10 min.)** (after Communicative Activity) • Prueba 6B-2: Vocabulary production	**Manos a la obra (25 min.)** • Audio Activities 5, 6 • Communicative Activity • Presentation: Verbs that use indirect object pronouns • View: GramActiva video • Actividad 11	**Wrap-up and Homework Options (5 min.)** • Practice Workbook 6B-5 • Actividad 15 • Go Online
DAY 5	**Warm-up (5 min.)** • Actividad 16 • Homework check	**Manos a la obra (40 min.)** • Exploración del lenguaje • Actividades 12, 13, 14 • Audio Activity 7 • Presentation: The present perfect • View: GramActiva video • Actividades 18, 19	**Wrap-up and Homework Options (5 min.)** • Practice Workbook 6B-6 • Writing Activity 11 • Go Online • Pruebas 6B-3: Verbs that use indirect object pronouns
DAY 6	**Warm-up (10 min.)** • Actividad 17 • Homework check **✔Assessment (10 min.)** • Prueba 6B-3: Verbs that use indirect object pronouns	**Manos a la obra (25 min.)** • El español en el mundo del trabajo • Actividades 21, 22, 24, 25 • Fondos culturales	**Wrap-up and Homework Options (5 min.)** • Practice Workbook 6B-7 • Actividades 20, 23 • Go Online • Heritage Learner Workbook 6B-4 • Prueba 6B-4: The present perfect
DAY 7	**Warm-up (10 min.)** • Writing Activity 12 • Homework check **✔Assessment (10 min.)** (after Audio Activities) • Prueba 6B-4: The present perfect	**Manos a la obra (15 min.)** • Writing Activity 13 • Audio Activities 8, 9 **¡Adelante! (10 min.)** • Presentación escrita: Steps 1, 5	**Wrap-up and Homework Options (5 min.)** • Presentación escrita: Step 2
DAY 8	**Warm-up (5 min.)** • Homework check	**¡Adelante! (40 min.)** • Presentación escrita: Step 3 • Lectura • ¿Comprendiste? / Y tú, ¿qué dices? • Fondo cultural	**Wrap-up and Homework Options (5 min.)** • Presentación escrita: Step 4 • Preparación para el examen 3, 4, 5 • Go Online: Lectura
DAY 9	**Warm-up (5 min.)** • Homework check	**¡Adelante! (30 min.)** • Videomisterio: *En busca de la verdad*, Episodio 8 • Perspectivas del mundo hispano **Repaso del capítulo (10 min.)** • Vocabulario y gramática • Preparación para el examen 1, 2	**Wrap-up and Homework Options (5 min.)** • Practice Workbook 6B-8, 6B-9 • Go Online: Self-test • Examen del capítulo 6B
DAY 10	**Warm-up (5 min.)** • Homework check **✔Assessment (40 min.)** • Examen del capítulo 6B		**Wrap-up and Homework Options (5 min.)** • Go Online: Videomisterio • A ver si recuerdas . . .: Capítulo 7A

	Warm-up / Assess	Preview Present / Practice Communicate	Wrap-up / Homework Options
DAY 1	**Warm-up (10 min.)** • Homework check • Return Examen del capítulo: Capítulo 6A	**Chapter Opener (10 min.)** • Objectives • Fondo cultural **A primera vista (65 min.)** • Presentation: Vocabulario y gramática en contexto • Actividades 1, 2 • Presentation: Videohistoria *El mosquito* • View: Videohistoria • Video Activities 1, 2, 3, 4 • Actividades 3, 4	**Wrap-up and Homework Options (5 min.)** • Practice Workbook 6B-A, 6B-B, 6B-1, 6B-2, 6B-3, 6B-4 • Go Online • Prueba 6B-1: Vocabulary recognition
DAY 2	**Warm-up (10 min.)** • Actividad 5 • Homework check **✔Assessment (10 min.)** • Prueba 6B-1: Vocabulary recognition	**Manos a la obra (65 min.)** • Actividades 6, 7, 8, 9 • Fondos culturales • Audio Activities 5, 6 • Writing Activity 10 • Communicative Activity • Presentation: Verbs that use indirect object pronouns • View: GramActiva video • Actividades 11, 12	**Wrap-up and Homework Options (5 min.)** • Practice Workbook 6B-5 • Actividad 15 • Go Online • Heritage Learner Workbook 6B-1, 6B-2 • Prueba 6B-2: Vocabulary production
DAY 3	**Warm-up (10 min.)** • Actividad 10 • Homework check **✔Assessment (10 min.)** • Prueba 6B-2: Vocabulary production	**Manos a la obra (65 min.)** • Exploración del lenguaje • Actividades 13, 14, 16 • Audio Activity 7 • Presentation: The present perfect • View: GramActiva video • Actividades 17, 18, 19 • El español en el mundo del trabajo • Audio Activities 8, 9	**Wrap-up and Homework Options (5 min.)** • Practice Workbook 6B-6, 6B-7 • Actividades 20, 23 • Writing Activity 13 • Go Online • Heritage Learner Workbook 6B-4 • Pruebas 6B-3, 6B-4: Verbs that use indirect object pronouns; The present perfect
DAY 4	**Warm-up (15 min.)** • Writing Activity 11 • Homework check **✔Assessment (15 min.)** (after Writing Activity) • Pruebas 6B-3, 6B-4: Verbs that use indirect object pronouns; The present perfect	**Manos a la obra (35 min.)** • Fondos culturales • Actividades 21, 22, 24, 25 • Writing Activity 12 **¡Adelante! (20 min.)** • Perspectivas del mundo hispano • Presentación escrita: Steps 1, 5	**Wrap-up and Homework Options (5 min.)** • Presentación escrita: Step 2 • Go Online: Self-test
DAY 5	**Warm-up (5 min.)** • Homework check	**¡Adelante! (50 min.)** • Presentación escrita: Steps 3, 4 • Lectura • ¿Comprendiste? / Y tú, ¿qué dices? • Fondo cultural **Repaso del capítulo (30 min.)** • Vocabulario y gramática • Preparación para el examen 1, 2, 3, 4, 5	**Wrap-up and Homework Options (5 min.)** • Presentación escrita: Step 4 • Practice Workbook 6B-8, 6B-9 • Go Online: Lectura • Examen del capítulo 6B
DAY 6	**Warm-up (10 min.)** • Homework check • Answer questions **Repaso del capítulo (15 min.)** • Situation Cards **✔Assessment (40 min.)** • Examen del capítulo 6B	**¡Adelante! (20 min.)** • Videomisterio: *En busca de la verdad*, Episodio 8	**Wrap-up and Homework Options (5 min.)** • Go Online: Videomisterio • A ver si recuerdas . . .: Capítulo 7A

 **Standards
for Capítulo 6B**

- To achieve the goals of the Standards, students will:

Communication

1.1 Interpersonal
- Talk about: movies and filmmaking; movie genres, plots, and preferences; a movie poster; actors and actresses; leisure activities; recent events in the news

1.2 Interpretive
- Read and listen to information about: Mexican cinema; filmmaking; movies genres, plots, and preferences; the Spanish-language film and video industries; Salma Hayek-Jiménez; the American Latino Media Arts Awards; plans to go out; the actor Chayanne; film ratings systems; subtitles
- Read a picture-based story; film reviews; a movie poster
- Listen to and watch a video about filmmaking

1.3 Presentational
- Present information about: a story plot; movies and filmmaking; movie genres, plots, and preferences; actors and actresses; leisure activities; plans to go out; recent events in the news
- Write: advertisements for businesses; a brief screenplay

Culture

2.1 Practices and Perspectives
- Write or talk about: the American Latino Media Arts Awards; the Spanish-language film industry

2.2 Products and Perspectives
- Write or talk about: Pablo Picasso and his art; the golden age of, and the 100th anniversary of, Mexican cinema; Salma Hayek-Jiménez; the American Latino Media Arts Awards; the Spanish-language video market; film ratings systems

3.1 Cross-curricular
- Reinforce mathematics skills

3.2 Target Culture
- View a video mystery series

Comparisons

4.1 Language
- Use the suffixes –oso(a) and –dor(a)
- Use the present perfect tense

4.2 Culture
- Compare film ratings systems

Communities

5.1 Beyond the School
- Talk about opportunities for Spanish-speakers in the motion picture industry

5.2 Lifelong Learner
- View a video mystery series

Fondo cultural

◼◆◼◆◼◆◼◆◼◆◼◆◼◆◼◆◼◆◼◆◼◆◼◆◼◆◼◆◼◆◼◆◼◼◆

El centenario del cine mexicano se celebró en 1996, el mismo año que se emitió *(issued)* este sello, que representa a algunas de las estrellas más famosas del cine mexicano. La primera película mexicana, "El Presidente de la República paseando a caballo en el Bosque de Chapultepec", se filmó en 1896. Hoy en día, la moderna industria del cine mexicano produce películas que compiten en los Óscares de Hollywood.

- Imagina un sello para el centenario de la industria del cine en los Estados Unidos. ¿Qué películas se representan? ¿En qué sentido es similar al sello mexicano? ¿En qué sentido es diferente?

Centenario del Cine en México (1996), César Fernández de la Reguera y Patricia Mitre

Differentiated Instruction

STUDENTS NEEDING EXTRA HELP
Guided Practice Activities
- Vocabulary Check, Flash Cards
- Grammar
- Reading and Writing Support
Guided Practice Audio CDs
- Disc 2, Track 4

HERITAGE LEARNERS
Realidades para hispanohablantes
- Chapter Opener, pp. 230–231
- A primera vista, p. 232
- Videohistoria, p. 233
- Manos a la obra, pp. 234–241
- ¡Adelante!, pp. 242–247
- Repaso del capítulo, pp. 248–249

ADVANCED/PRE-AP*
Pre-AP* Resource Book, pp. 116–119

Capítulo 6B

¿Qué película has visto?

Chapter Objectives

- Discuss movie plots and characters
- Give opinions about movies
- Talk about activities you have done
- Understand cultural perspectives on movies

Video Highlights

A primera vista: *El mosquito*
GramActiva Videos: verbs that use indirect object pronouns; the present perfect
Videomisterio: *En busca de la verdad,* Episodio 8

Country Connection

As you learn about movies you will make connections to these countries and places:

Cuba
España
Puerto Rico
California
Panamá
México
Costa Rica
Argentina

Más práctica

- *Real.* para hispanohablantes, pp. 230–231

 **Go Online** PHSchool.com **For:** Online Atlas **Web Code:** jde-0002

Los premios Goya, en Barcelona

trescientos diecinueve 319
Capítulo 6B

 **Teacher Technology**

Chapter Opener

Presentation EXPRESS ATLAS

Core Instruction

Resources: Voc. and Gram. Transparencies: Maps 12–14, 16–18, 20

Suggestions: Have students describe the types of films that they like to watch. Write a list of current films on the board. Make sure that various genres are included in the list. Have students brainstorm words that they would associate with each film. Point out to students that they will learn to describe movies and filmmaking. Bring in a movie review from a local paper, and have students underline the words that they think they might learn in this chapter.

Tell students that in the *Videohistoria* they will see the film that Manolo has made for his class. Ask students how often video technology is used for instruction in their classes.

Fondo cultural  *Standards:* 1.2, 2.2

■◆■◆■◆■◆■◆■◆■◆■◆■◆■◆

Suggestions: Ask students to brainstorm popular films and movie stars of the twentieth century. Bring in books on the history of movies in the United States to provide students with more information on older movies.

Answers will vary.

Teaching with Photos

Suggestions: Point out that the people in this picture are at the Goya Film Awards. Like the Academy Awards, the Goya Film Awards honor achievement in acting and filmmaking. Have students comment on similarities between the two ceremonies, based on what they see in the photo.

PLAN
Lesson Planner

Go Online PHSchool.com
For: Teacher Home Page
Web Code: jdk-1001

TEACH
Teaching Resources
Interactive
Teacher's Edition
Vocabulary Clip Art

ASSESS
Chapter Quizzes
and Tests

PresentationEXPRESS
Dynamic Presentations for Teachers

TEACH
Vocabulary & Grammar Powerpoints
GramActiva Video
Audio & Clip Art Activities
Transparencies and Maps
Activity Answers
Photo Gallery

ASSESS
ExamView
QuickTake Presenter

Vocabulario y gramática

Presentation EXPRESS
VOCABULARY

Core Instruction

 Standards: 1.2

Resources: Teacher's Resource Book: Input Script, p. 88, Clip Art, pp. 102–104, Audio Script, p. 89; Voc. and Gram. Transparencies 115–116; TPR Stories Book, pp. 79–90; Audio Program: Tracks 1–2

Focus: Understanding information about movie plots and characters

Suggestions: Use the Input Script from the *Teacher's Resource Book* or the story from the *TPR Stories Book* to present the new vocablary, or use these suggestions.

Hang two or three movie posters representing various film genres on the wall. Point out details in the posters that will help students' comprehension as you describe the film. Tell them whether or not you have seen each movie and what the critics have said about it. Ask students short-answer questions about each movie, such as: *¿Has visto …? ¿Te gustó?*

Be sure to include genres taught in *Realidades 1,* as well.

For the short article on *En busca de la verdad,* have students read silently, then go through it with the class. Can they identify cognates and false cognates? Can they guess the meaning of *hace el papel de* from context? Prepare similar paragraphs about other movies.

Bellringer Review

Show Voc. and Gram. Transparency 115. Ask students to mention each type of movie illustrated and name one current movie that fits into each category.

Block Schedule

Hold a Spanish-language film festival. Bring in one or two movies during the chapter for students to watch. Be sure to get the films approved by an administrator before screening them. Look for films that will provide students with historical or cultural information about a particular Spanish-speaking country.

Additional Resources

• Audio Program: Canciones CD, Disc 22

320

Objectives

Read, listen to, and understand information about
• movies
• making a movie

A primera vista

Vocabulario y gramática en contexto

jdd-0697

—**¿Has visto** la película *2050?* **¿Qué tal es?**

—Pues, **me fascinan** las películas de ciencia ficción, pero **no he visto** esa película **todavía. Los críticos** han escrito varios artículos sobre la película y todos la **recomiendan.** Creo que la película **será** muy popular con el público.

—Bueno. ¿Se puede alquilar ya el video o el DVD?

—No. Todavía no.

*Note that la víctima is always feminine.

320 trescientos veinte
Tema 6 • La televisión y el cine

Differentiated Instruction
Solutions for All Learners

Students with Special Needs

Using the script for *Actividad* 1, provide hearing-impaired students with a list of the dictated sentences and a photocopy of the signs on pp. 320–321. Have students cut out the individual sentences and place them with the corresponding signs.

Advanced Learners

Have students choose a movie from one of the posters on pp. 320–321 and invent a summary of the movie. Ask them to create names for the characters and create a plot. Have students who chose the same movies compare their summaries.

LAS CALLES CRUELES

capturar

arrestar

el criminal

la criminal

el galán

EL AMOR ETERNO

El galán **está enamorado de** la mujer, pero ella **no se enamora de** él hasta el final de la película.

Detrás de *En busca de la verdad*

En busca de la verdad tiene **un argumento** muy básico. Se trata de tres generaciones de una familia mexicana. Roberto le pregunta a su abuela dónde está su abuelo, Federico, pero nadie sabe qué le pasó. Roberto decide buscar la verdad.

los personajes principales

la directora

la escena

Dora Guzmán Trujillo, como directora, está en control de **la dirección** de la película. Roberto Castañeda **hace el papel de** Roberto. Él vive en la ciudad de Querétaro y ha participado en muchas obras de teatro. Elia González hace el papel de Linda. Ella también vive en Querétaro y hace muchos años que es actriz. A los dos jóvenes les gusta **la actuación** y desean tener **papeles** cada vez más importantes en el cine, el teatro y la televisión.

Actividad 1  Standards: 1.2, 2.2

Resources: Teacher's Resource Book: Audio Script, p. 89; Audio Program: Track 3; Answers on Transparencies

Focus: Understanding lines from movies

Suggestions: Before they listen, ask students what classic lines might be appropriate for each type of movie.

Script and Answers:
1. Carmen, mi amor. No puedo vivir sin ti. Te quiero. *(El amor eterno)*
2. ¡Vamos, rápido! Viene la policía. Toma las joyas ahora. *(El robo perfecto)*
3. Mira, a la izquierda. ¡Hay tres extraterrestres con dos cabezas! *(2050)*
4. ¿Cómo murió la víctima? *(Violencia en la ciudad)*
5. Carlos. ¡Claro! Voy a casarme contigo. Eres el amor de mi vida. *(El amor eterno)*
6. Parece que es el crimen perfecto. No sabemos cómo ocurrió. *(El robo perfecto)*
7. ¡Policía! Pongan las manos sobre la cabeza. ¡Rápido! *(Las calles crueles)*

Actividad 1 jdd-0697 **Escuchar**

¿Qué película es?

Mira los carteles de las películas que hay en las páginas 320 y 321. Escucha las frases y señala el cartel de la película que corresponde a cada frase.

Más práctica

- Practice Workbook, pp. 122–123: 6B-1, 6B-2
- WAV Wbk.: Writing, p. 122
- Guided Practice: Vocab. Flash Cards, pp. 218–222
- *Real.* para hispanohablantes, p. 232

Go Online PHSchool.com
For: Vocab. Practice
Web Code: jdd-0611

Actividad 2 jdd-0697 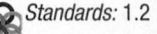 **Escuchar**

¿Cuánto sabes de las películas?

Escucha las frases y contesta las preguntas.

1. a. el personaje principal
   b. el director

2. a. la directora
   b. el actor

3. a. los extraterrestres
   b. los efectos especiales

4. a. se enamoran de ellos
   b. los capturan

Más vocabulario

la estrella (del cine)   star, (movie) star

tratarse de   to be about

trescientos veintiuno **321**
Capítulo 6B

Actividad 2  Standards: 1.2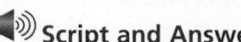

Resources: Teacher's Resource Book: Audio Script, p. 89; Audio Program: Track 4; Answers on Transparencies

Focus: Understanding information about movies

Suggestions: Pause after each statement for students to write key words that will help them choose the correct response.

Script and Answers:
1. En la película *Violencia en la ciudad*, Manuel Farol hace el papel del detective. ¿Es Manuel el personaje principal o el director? *(a. el personaje principal)*
2. En una película, ¿la persona que está en control de todos los aspectos de la actuación es la directora o el actor? *(a. la directora)*
3. En la película *2050*, ¿los personajes que vienen de otro planeta son los extraterrestres o los efectos especiales? *(a. los extraterrestres)*
4. Cuando los detectives llegan a la escena de un crimen, ¿qué hacen con los criminales? ¿Se enamoran de ellos o los capturan? *(b. los capturan)*

Enrich Your Teaching
Resources for All Teachers

Teacher-to-Teacher

Have students create their own video rental store. Have each student bring in an old VHS tape from home. Ask students to remake the cover with a Spanish title and a summary. Keep the movies in a safe place. Give students a video card and invite them to "rent" the videos. When renting, students will ask you for a particular type of movie. As the video store

"clerk," you can offer suggestions based on your collection. Make sure that the movies in your rental store are appropriate for viewing. After students see the movies, pair them with someone else who has seen their movie and have them summarize the movie and discuss their opinions.

Assessment

- *ExamView* Quiz on PresEXPRESS
  QuickTake Presenter

Core Instruction

 Standards: 1.2

Resources: Voc. and Gram. Transparencies 117–118; Audio Program: Track 5

Focus: Extending the presentation of vocabulary related to movies

Suggestions:

Pre-reading: To help students with the *Estrategia,* give them a photocopy of each panel without the corresponding dialogue.

Reading: Have students read the *Videohistoria* silently, or have them listen to the *Audio CD.* Ask volunteers to summarize what they have read after panels 4 and 8.

Post-reading: Complete *Actividad 3* to check comprehension.

 Pre-AP* Support

- **Activity:** Distribute Clip Art representing different types of movies presented in this chapter. Have students form circles of four students. Ask that each student select three pieces of clip art representing the types of movies. Then, ask each student to show one piece of clip art to each member of his or her group and ask that they identify the type of movie, a current movie of this type, and the lead actor or actress.
- **Pre-AP* Resource Book:** Comprehensive guide to Pre-AP* vocabulary skill development, pp. 47–53

Videohistoria jdd-0697

El mosquito

¿Qué pasa en la película que hace Manolo para su clase? ¿Quién es "el mosquito"?

Estrategia

Predicting meaning
The images of a movie can tell a story, even if you don't hear the audio. Look at the images from Manolo's movie. What happens to Ramón? Will he get a good grade on the test?

1 Profesor: Buenos días. ¿Qué película vamos a ver primero? A ver . . . ¿Manolo?
Manolo: Bien. **Está basada en** la historia de un mosquito y un estudiante.

Director: Manolo
Estudiante: Ramón
El mosquito: Claudia
Amiga: Teresa

5 Ramón: ¿Lees? ¿Qué dice este libro?
Claudia: Se trata de la historia de los Estados Unidos. Tú puedes dormirte mientras que yo leo el libro. Mañana puedo decirte las respuestas durante el examen.
Ramón: Muy bien. Me voy a dormir.

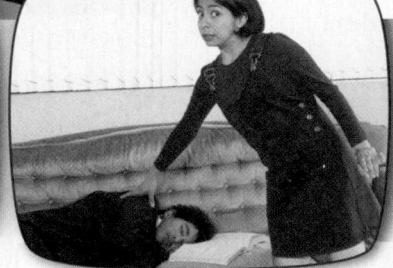

6 Teresa: ¡Ramón, despiértate! ¿Has estudiado para el examen?

7 Teresa: ¿Qué es esto?
Ramón: ¡Mi libro! ¡Teresa! ¡Déjalo! ¡Lo necesito!
Claudia: ¡NOOOOO!

Differentiated Instruction
Solutions for All Learners

Students with Learning Difficulties
For *Actividad 3,* have students make a three-column chart. In the first column, they can write the item numbers for events that came early in the video. The second column can be used for sentences in the middle, and the third column for the end of the video. Students can focus on the smaller groups before combining them in order.

Multiple Intelligences
Bodily/Kinesthetic: Have students perform a version of the story in the *Videohistoria* in small groups. Give each group a different way to rewrite the story. For example, tell one group to rewrite it so that the mosquito lives, while another group has Ramón declining help from the mosquito.

2 **Ramón:** Mañana tengo un examen y no he estudiado. No sé nada. ¿Qué puedo hacer?

3 **Claudia:** No vas a **matar**me, ¿verdad? ¡No quiero morirme!

Ramón: ¿Qué has dicho? ¿Tú hablas?

Claudia: Sí. Puedo hablar inglés y español.

4 **Claudia:** Yo puedo leer también.

Ramón: ¿Cómo? Yo tengo que estudiar y tú me molestas.

Claudia: ¿Quieres **tener éxito** en el examen? Yo puedo ayudarte a estudiar.

8 **Ramón:** ¡Teresa! ¡No! ¿Qué has hecho? Mi libro . . . El examen . . . ¿Qué voy a hacer? ¡Qué **fracaso**!

Actividad 3 **Leer/Escribir**

¿Comprendiste?

En una hoja de papel escribe las frases de abajo, poniéndolas en orden cronológico.

1. Los dos deciden que el mosquito va a estudiar para el examen de historia.

2. Ramón le grita y ahora no sabe qué va a hacer.

3. Teresa cierra el libro.

4. Teresa entra en el cuarto para despertar a Ramón.

5. Ramón está nervioso porque tiene un examen y no ha estudiado.

6. El mosquito le dice a Ramón que puede hablar inglés y español.

7. Manolo le va a presentar su película a la clase.

8. Ramón va a matar al mosquito.

Más práctica

- Practice Workbook, pp. 124–125: 6B-3, 6B-4
- WAV Wbk.: Video, pp. 116–118
- Guided Practice: Vocab. Check, pp. 223–226
- *Real.* para hispanohablantes, p. 233

Go Online PHSchool.com
For: Vocab. Practice
Web Code: jdd-0612

trescientos veintitrés 323
Capítulo 6B

Enrich Your Teaching
Resources for All Teachers

Teacher-to-Teacher

Have students write a paragraph summarizing the events of a popular movie. Ask them to cut out each sentence of their summary individually and put the papers in an envelope with that movie's title written on it. Collect the envelopes and redistribute them, allowing students to choose a movie that they have seen. You may want to include your own summaries of classic films that students most likely have seen, in case you have a student who has not seen any of the films. Have students use the sentences to reconstruct the summaries. When they finish, have the authors of the summaries verify the responses.

Video
Core Instruction

Standards: 1.2

Resources: Teacher's Resource Book: Video Script, p. 93; Video Program: Cap. 6B; Video Program Teacher's Guide: Cap. 6B

Focus: Viewing and comprehending the video with contextualized vocabulary

Suggestions:

Pre-viewing: Have students review important concepts and terms from the *Videohistoria*. Remind them to use the context to identify and understand new vocabulary.

Viewing: Show the video once without pausing. Show it again, pausing at key points to ask students what is happening. Encourage them to ask for clarification about parts that they may not understand.

Post-viewing: Complete the Video Activities in the *Writing, Audio & Video Workbook.*

Actividad 3 *Standards:* 1.2

 Presentation EXPRESS ANSWERS

Resources: Answers on Transparencies

Focus: Verifying comprehension of the *Videohistoria*

Suggestions: Give each student an adhesive paper note. Have them tear it into eight small strips, and place one next to each sentence. Then, as students read the sentences, have them write the corresponding panel number on the adhesive paper.

Answers:
The correct order is 7, 5, 8, 6, 1, 4, 3, 2.

Additional Resources

- WAV Wbk.: Audio Act. 5, p. 119
- Teacher's Resource Book: Audio Script, p. 90
- Audio Program: Track 7

 Assessment

- **ExamView** QuickTake Presenter Quiz on PresEXPRESS
- Prueba 6B–1: Vocab. Recognition, pp. 164–165

323

6B Practice and Communicate

Standards: 1.1

Presentation EXPRESS
ANSWERS

Resources: Answers on Transparencies

Focus: Speaking about movies and movie characters

Suggestions: Have students list movies in which they have seen each type of character before having them work in pairs.

Answers:

Student A:

1. ¿En qué película has visto a un galán?
2. ¿... unos extraterrestres?
3. ¿... un detective?
4. ¿... una mujer bonita?
5. ¿... una ladrona?
6. ¿... una víctima?

Student B: Answers will vary.

Common Errors: Students may forget that *víctima* is always feminine. Remind them that there are several nouns that end in **–ma** that are masculine. Do they remember *programa*?

Bellringer Review

Have students unscramble these letters for words that represent characters found in movies:

roldna   retatrxrserest   lanag

(**Answers:** *ladrona; extraterrestre; galán*)

 Standards: 1.2

Resources: Answers on Transparencies

Focus: Reading a movie review and filling in missing words

Suggestions: Remind students of the elements of a movie review, such as a plot summary and commentary on the acting and directing. Encourage them to consider the structure as they read. Have students scan the entire passage before filling in the correct words.

Answers:

1. ¿Qué tal es
2. director
3. fracaso
4. El argumento
5. se trata
6. enamorado
7. actuación
8. dirección
9. capturan
10. arrestar
11. has visto
12. Alquila

Manos a la obra

Vocabulario y gramática en uso

Objectives

- Express your opinion with verbs that use indirect objects
- Use the present perfect tense to talk about what you have done
- Read movie reviews in Spanish

 **Hablar**

¿En qué película . . . ?

Trabaja con otro(a) estudiante para hablar de las películas en que has visto a estas personas o cosas. ¿Qué clase de película es cada una? Si necesitas repasar *(review)* las diferentes clases de películas, ve las páginas 320 y 321.

Modelo

un criminal

A —¿En qué película has visto a <u>un criminal</u>?
B —He visto a <u>un criminal en El hombre araña</u>. *Es una película de acción.*
o:—No he visto a <u>un criminal</u> en ninguna película.

1.   2.   3.   4.   5.   6.

Leer/Escribir

El crítico nos recomienda . . .

Lee el siguiente artículo que escribió el crítico de películas del periódico. Escribe en una hoja de papel la palabra apropiada.

Muchos me preguntan, __1.__ *(¿Qué tal es / ¿Cómo estás)* la nueva película del __2.__ *(director / criminal)* Antonio Sánchez? Pues, en mi opinión, esta película va a ser un(a) __3.__ *(fracaso / escena)* total. __4.__ *(Los efectos especiales / El argumento)* de la película está(n) basado(s) en una novela de amor, pero esta película no es nada romántica: es una película de acción. ¡La película __5.__ *(se trata / hace el papel)* de la violencia, no del amor! En la novela, el personaje principal está __6.__ *(basado / enamorado)* de una joven bonita

pero en la película él sólo trata de arrestar a los criminales. La __7.__ *(actuación / acción)* del actor que hace el papel del galán es terrible también. Y la __8.__ *(actuación / dirección)* del director Sánchez es peor. Por ejemplo, en la escena final, la víctima inocente se muere cuando los criminales la __9.__ *(capturan / fascinan)*. Y el detective no puede __10.__ *(arrestar / robar)* a los criminales. Si no __11.__ *(has visto / he visto)* esta película todavía, ¡no la recomiendo! __12.__ *(Alquila / Roba)* un video y quédate en casa.

324   trescientos veinticuatro
Tema 6 • La televisión y el cine

Differentiated Instruction
Solutions for All Learners

Heritage Language Learners

Have students determine a Golden Age of film for their heritage culture. Encourage them to ask older family members for assistance. Have them prepare a review of the era, including the most popular films and names of successful directors. Remind them to use the writing process of pre-writing, drafting, editing, and publishing.

 Pre-AP*

Advanced Learners/Pre-AP*

Have students work in groups to publish an entertainment magazine. Have them include at least two movie reviews, as well as articles featuring famous actors and actresses. Photocopy students' completed magazines and distribute them to the class. Use them for additional reading practice.

Actividad 6

jdd-0698

  Escuchar/Escribir

Escucha y escribe

Escucha las siguientes descripciones y escríbelas en una hoja de papel. Luego decide quién del recuadro hace cada acción y escribe su nombre al lado de la frase.

el (la) criminal	el ladrón, la ladrona
el crítico, la crítica	el director, la directora
el galán	el (la) detective
el (la) extraterrestre	

También se dice . . .

el (la) extraterrestre = el marciano, la marciana (muchos países)

el ladrón, la ladrona = el bandido, la bandida; el malo, la mala (muchos países)

Actividad 7

Observar/Leer/Hablar

Las películas clásicas

¿Te gusta ver las películas clásicas? Mira el cartel de cine de una película mexicana de los años 40. Luego, con otro(a) estudiante, contesta las preguntas.

1. ¿Qué clase de película es?
2. ¿Quién es la estrella de la película? ¿Pueden decir qué papel hace?
3. ¿Cómo se llama el director?
4. Según lo que ves en el cartel, ¿te gustaría ver esta película? ¿Por qué?

"Romeo y Julieta" (1943), director Miguel M. Delgado

 **Fondo cultural**

La época de oro del cine mexicano Entre 1930 y 1950, el cine mexicano tuvo una época de oro, produciendo muchas películas y compitiendo con Hollywood. Uno de los actores más famosos de esta época fue Mario Moreno, mejor conocido como Cantinflas. Cantinflas era un cómico que hizo reír a muchos espectadores desde España hasta Argentina. En los años 60 el cine mexicano no pudo competir con la televisión y la época de oro se terminó.

• ¿Qué películas producidas en otros países conoces? ¿En qué sentido son similares a las películas producidas en los Estados Unidos? ¿En qué sentido son diferentes?

Mario Moreno, famoso actor mexicano

trescientos veinticinco 325
Capítulo 6B

 Enrich Your Teaching
Resources for All Teachers

Culture Note

Born in 1911, in Mexico City, Mario Moreno gained popularity as an acrobatic, fast-talking comic known as Cantinflas. He starred in more than 50 feature films. After retiring, Cantinflas championed causes for Mexican actors and impoverished children. In 1988, he received a lifetime achievement award from the *Entrega del Ariel*.

Teacher-to-Teacher

Have students work in groups to describe current movies. Ask local movie theaters for popcorn buckets. Make photocopies of current film ads, fold them, and place three or four of them in each bucket. Give one to each group and have members take turns choosing a movie to describe.

Practice and Communicate

 6B

Actividad 6

Standards: 1.2
Presentation EXPRESS
AUDIO

Resources: Teacher's Resource Book: Audio Script, p. 90; Audio Program: Track: 6; Answers on Transparencies

Focus: Listening and writing about people in movies

Suggestions: Pause after each sentence to give students time to write. Let them listen again without pausing so they can check their answers.

 Script and Answers:

1. Se enamora de la mujer bonita. *(el galán)*
2. Viene de otro planeta. *(el [la] extraterrestre)*
3. Captura y arresta a los criminales. *(el [la] detective)*
4. Habla con los actores sobre sus papeles. *(el director / la directora)*
5. Dice que la película es un fracaso o un éxito. *(el crítico / la crítica)*
6. Roba el banco o la joyería. *(el ladrón / la ladrona)*
7. Mata a alguien o hace otro crimen. *(el [la] criminal)*

Actividad 7

 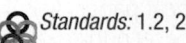 
Standards: 1.2, 2.2
Presentation EXPRESS
ANSWERS

Resources: Answers on Transparencies

Focus: Reading a movie poster and talking about the movie

Suggestions: Ask a student volunteer to summarize the story of Romeo and Juliet to help students make predictions about the movie.

Answers:

1. Es una película de amor / una comedia.
2. La estrella de la película es Cantinflas. Hace el papel de Romeo.
3. El director se llama Miguel M. Delgado.
4. Answers will vary.

Fondo cultural

 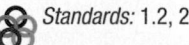
Standards: 1.2, 2.2

Suggestions: If you have shown students a film from a Spanish-speaking country, make reference to it when discussing the question.

Answers will vary.

325

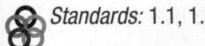 **Bellringer Review**
Write the names of three popular movies on the board, and have students list adjectives that they would use to describe each one.

 **Actividad 8** *Standards:* 1.1, 1.3

Focus: Expressing opinions about movies

Recycle: *gustar* and related verbs; adjectives

Suggestions: Point out that students do not need to describe all of the aspects for each movie. Have them brainstorm movies for each category and base their conversations on this list.

Answers will vary.

Fondo cultural *Standards:* 1.2, 2.2

■◆◇◆■◆◇◆■◆◇◆■◆□◇◆□◇◆

Suggestions: Have students scan the movie ads in the local paper. Ask if they see any names they recognize of actors from Spanish-speaking countries.

Answers will vary.

Block Schedule

To extend *Actividad* 9, have students create and play a movie trivia board game. Make them a game board by drawing connected blocks on a sheet of paper. Photocopy the board and distribute it to groups of students. Have students write at least 15 questions in addition to those from *Actividad* 9 about current and past movies, such as who directed the films or where it took place. Have groups exchange their questions with another group to play. Students can use coins as pawns. For each correct answer, they can move ahead one block. The player who reaches the end of the board first wins.

326

Actividad 8   **Escribir/Hablar**

Los diferentes aspectos de una película

Habla con otro(a) estudiante sobre los diferentes aspectos de una película que ayudan a determinar si la película va a tener éxito o si será un fracaso.

1 Copia la tabla en una hoja de papel. Escribe el título de las películas en que has observado estos aspectos. Escribe una descripción de los aspectos.

la película	la música	los efectos especiales	los personajes	la actuación	el argumento
Chicago	estupenda				

2 Habla con otro(a) estudiante sobre tus opiniones de diferentes películas usando la tabla que llenaste.

Modelo

la música

A —*La música en la película* Chicago *me pareció estupenda*

B —*Estoy de acuerdo. Me fascinó la música en esa película.*

o: *No estoy de acuerdo. No me gustó nada la música en esa película.*

o: *¿De veras? No he visto todavía esa película.*

Estudiante A

fantástico, -a
tremendo, -a
increíble
interesante

complicado, -a
aburrido, -a
horrible
malo / malísimo, -a

tonto, -a
realista
¡Respuesta personal!

Estudiante B

me fascinó / me fascinaron
me gustó / me gustaron
me encantó / me encantaron

Fondo cultural

■◆◇◆□◆◇■◆◇◆■◆□◆◇◆□◆◇◆

Salma Hayek-Jiménez, la primera actriz mexicana en hacerse estrella de Hollywood después de Dolores del Río (1904–1983), nació en el sureste de México el 2 de septiembre de 1966. Empezó su carrera como actriz en las telenovelas mexicanas. Después viajó a California a buscar papeles en Hollywood. En el año 2002, Salma hizo el papel de la famosa pintora Frida Kahlo en la película *Frida.*

• ¿Crees que es más fácil o más difícil para un actor o actriz hacer el papel de alguien famoso? ¿Por qué?

La actriz mexicana Salma Hayek

326 trescientos veintiséis
Tema 6 • La televisión y el cine

Differentiated Instruction
Solutions for All Learners

Multiple Intelligences

Intrapersonal/Introspective: Have students choose a well-known actor or actress from a Spanish-speaking country about whom they can write a biography. Ask them to include details about that person's life, as well as names of movies that he or she starred in. Encourage them to include a photo of the movie star with their final product.

Students with Learning Difficulties

To help students write questions for *Actividad* 9, give them the name of a film or movie star to base their question upon.

Actividad 9 Escribir/Hablar

Juego

1 Usa las palabras del recuadro y trabaja con otro(a) estudiante para escribir cuatro preguntas sobre los actores o las actrices que salieron en diferentes películas. Después compitan contra otro grupo.

hacer el papel de	matar
enamorarse de	morirse
capturar y arrestar	robar

¡Respuesta personal!

2 Hagan sus preguntas para ver si el otro grupo puede identificar al actor o a la actriz. Si pueden, ellos ganan un punto. Si no, Uds. ganan un punto.

Modelo

A —¿Quién es el actor que hizo el papel del médico en la película *Antwone Fisher*?

B —*Es Denzel Washington.*

 Actividad 10 Escribir/Hablar

Y tú, ¿qué dices?

1. ¿Qué es más importante en una película: mucha acción o personajes interesantes? ¿La actuación o los efectos especiales?
2. ¿Hay demasiada violencia en las películas? ¿Por qué piensas así?
3. ¿Prestas atención a lo que dicen los críticos? Si dicen que una película es un fracaso, ¿la vas a ver? ¿Por qué?
4. ¿Qué película en el cine ahora será un fracaso? ¿Qué película va a tener mucho éxito?

Exploración del lenguaje

The suffixes *-oso(a)* and *-dor(a)*

Spanish adjectives that end in *-oso(a)* often have English cognates ending in *-ous*:

famoso → *famous*
nervioso → *nervous*

¡Compruébalo! Write the Spanish adjective for these English words and use the correct form to complete the sentences.

studious   furious   generous

Una chica que estudia mucho es _____.

Él se pone _____ cuando le mentimos.

Ella siempre está dándome regalos. Es _____.

Words ending in *-dor(a)* indicate people who do different actions. Words ending in *-dor(a)* are either nouns or adjectives. Look at these verbs and related nouns and adjectives.

jugar → jugador / jugadora
trabajar → trabajador / trabajadora

Una chica que **anima** a otros durante un partido es una animadora.

Un niño que **habla** mucho es muy hablador.

¡Compruébalo! Look at the drawing and answer the questions.

¿Qué hizo el **ganador**?

¿Qué hizo el **perdedor**?

trescientos veintisiete **327**
Capítulo 6B

 Enrich Your Teaching
Resources for All Teachers

Culture Note
There have been a number of Spanish-speaking actors and actresses who have gained fame in Hollywood. Anthony Quinn, born in Mexico, won Best Supporting Actor Oscars in 1952 and 1956 for his roles in *Viva Zapata!* and *Zorba the Greek*. Rita Moreno, raised in Puerto Rico, earned the Oscar for Best Supporting Actress in 1961 for her role in *West Side Story*.

Internet Search
Have students use the Internet to find out more about the history of Spanish-speaking actors and actresses in Hollywood.

Keywords:

hispanohablantes + Hollywood

Practice and Communicate

 Standards: 1.1, 1.3

Actividad 9

Focus: Writing and speaking about actors and actresses
Suggestions: Remind students to write specific questions that have only one answer.
Answers will vary.

  Standards: 1.1, 1.3

Actividad 10

Focus: Expressing opinions about movies
Suggestions: Have students discuss their answers in small groups. Walk around the room to monitor and participate in discussions. Encourage students to give examples to support their answers.
Answers will vary.

Exploración del lenguaje

Core Instruction

 Standards: 4.1

Resources: Answers on Transparencies
Suggestions: Remind students that not all words ending in **-oso** are cognates, even though they might have the same suffixes. Give them the example of **dangerous** and **peligroso**.

Answers:
estudioso, furioso, generoso
estudiosa, furioso, generosa
El ganador ganó.
El perdedor perdió.

Additional Resources
- WAV Wbk.: Audio Act. 6, p. 119
- Teacher's Resource Book: Audio Script, p. 90, Communicative Activity BLM, pp. 96–97
- Audio Program: Track 8

 Assessment
- Prueba 6B–2: Vocab. Production, pp. 166–167

327

Core Instruction

 *Standards:* 4.1

Resources: Voc. and Gram. Transparency 119; Teacher's Resource Book: Video Script, p. 93; Video Program: Cap. 6B

Suggestions: Use the *GramActiva* video to review the verbs that use indirect object pronouns. Then write the name of a popular movie on the board and ask students a series of questions about the movie. For example: *¿Les fascinan películas de acción? ¿A quién le aburre esta película? ¿Cómo les parece el actor?*

After providing the model, give pairs of students movie titles and have them create questions to discuss the film using a verb that uses an indirect object pronoun. Have students use the **nosotros** and third-person forms to report their discussions to the class.

 Bellringer Review

Say **a** + a noun or pronoun and have students give the indirect object pronoun. For example: **a tus profesores,** and students reply with **les.**

 *Standards:* 1.2 Presentation EXPRESS ANSWERS

Resources: Answers on Transparencies
Focus: Indirect object pronouns
Suggestions: Point out that the noun that corresponds to the indirect object pronoun does not always come directly before the blank.

1. nos	6. le
2. me	7. le
3. le	8. me
4. le	9. te
5. les	

Verbs that use indirect object pronouns

Here are some verbs that you've already learned that use indirect object pronouns.

aburrir	*to bore*
doler	*to ache*
encantar	*to love*
fascinar	*to fascinate*
gustar	*to like*
importar	*to matter*
interesar	*to interest*
molestar	*to bother*
parecer	*to seem*
quedar	*to fit*

These verbs all use a similar construction: indirect object pronoun + verb + subject.

> **Les encantan los efectos especiales** en esa película.
>
> **Nos aburre** mucho **esa película.**

A + a noun or a pronoun is often used with these verbs for emphasis or clarification. The pronouns agree with and clarify the indirect object pronoun.

(A mí)	me	(A nosotros) (A nosotras)	nos
(A ti)	te	(A vosotros) (A vosotras)	os
(A Ud.) (A él) (A ella)	le	(A Uds.) (A ellos) (A ellas)	les

A mí me importan mucho los efectos especiales en una película.

A Juanita le fascinan las películas de terror.

¿A Uds. les parece realista la película de acción?

GramActiva VIDEO

Want more help with verbs that use indirect object pronouns? Watch the **GramActiva** video.

Me trajo el café.

 Actividad 11 Leer/Escribir

Nos gustan las películas

En una hoja de papel, escribe el complemento indirecto *(indirect object pronoun)* apropiado.

A nosotros __1.__ gusta mucho el cine. A mí __2.__ encantan las películas biográficas, como *Selena,* pero a mi novio __3.__ aburren. Esta película __4.__ parece demasiado triste a él. A mis padres __5.__ interesan los dramas o las comedias. A mi mamá __6.__ fascina *Lo que el viento se llevó (Gone with the Wind)* con Clark Gable y Vivien Leigh, porque es muy romántica y a ella __7.__ encantan los vestidos que llevaban las actrices. ¡A mí no __8.__ interesa nada esa clase de película! ¿Qué clase de película __9.__ interesa a ti?

Jennifer López, en el papel de Selena

Differentiated Instruction
Solutions for All Learners

Students with Learning Difficulties

Because indirect object pronouns and direct object pronouns do not differ in English, students may forget to make the distinction in Spanish. Remind students that they need to differentiate between **lo,** the direct object pronoun, and **le,** the indirect object pronoun. Create sentences that require the distinction.

Multiple Intelligences

Mathematical/Logical: Have students make a bar graph of the results of *Actividad* 13. Have them write the categories on the left side. On the bottom, have them write the numbers 1–10. Have them choose the most common responses, such as **les encanta(n)** or **les aburre(n),** and make a color-coded graph key.

Actividad 12 **Escribir/Hablar** _____

¿Te molesta o te fascina?

¿Cuáles son las cosas que te molestan o te fascinan de las películas, del cine o de la televisión? Escribe cuatro frases. Puedes usar las ideas del recuadro o tus propias ideas. Después lee tus frases a otro(a) estudiante para ver si tu compañero(a) reacciona de la misma manera *(in the same way)*.

| la actuación |
| el argumento |
| los efectos especiales |
| las películas . . . |
| los personajes |
| las personas . . . |
| las telenovelas |
| la violencia |

Modelo
A —*Me fascina un argumento muy complicado en una película. ¿Y a ti?*

B —*No, me gusta más un argumento sencillo.*

Estudiante A

me aburre(n)   me gusta(n) (más)

me encanta(n)   me interesa(n)

me fascina(n)   me molesta(n)

Estudiante B

¡Respuesta personal!

   Actividad 13 **Escribir/Hablar** _____

Una encuesta entre tres

Trabaja con un grupo de tres estudiantes. Primero lee la lista de temas y escribe tus opiniones. Luego cada persona va a expresar su opinión sobre una categoría y preguntarle a otro(a) estudiante su opinión. En una hoja de papel, anoten las opiniones de su grupo para cada categoría en una tabla.

1. las películas de acción
2. las telenovelas
3. la música
4. los deportes
5. los videojuegos
6. la ropa
7. la computadora

Modelo
las películas de acción

A —*A mí me encantan las películas de acción. ¿Y a ti, Isabel?*

B —*No me interesan mucho. ¿Y a ti, Roberto?*

C —*A mí también me encantan las películas de acción.*

  Actividad 14 **Escribir** _____

¿Qué les interesa más?

Usa la información de la Actividad 13 y escribe una o dos frases sobre las opiniones de tu grupo para cada categoría.

Modelo
A Roberto y a mí nos encantan las películas de acción, pero a Isabel no le interesan mucho.

trescientos veintinueve 329
Capítulo 6B

 Actividad 12 *Standards:* 1.1, 1.3

Focus: Expressing personal opinions about movies

Suggestions: Have students write a sentence for each item in the Student A bubble. Encourage them to support their statements with examples from movies that they have seen.

Answers will vary.

  Actividad 13 *Standards:* 1.1, 1.3

Focus: Expressing personal opinions

Recycle: Pastimes, sports, music, and clothes

Suggestions: Remind students that they will not always express a general opinion. For example, for item 6, they will talk about what kinds of clothing they prefer or dislike.

Answers will vary.

Extension: Have students ask their partners follow-up questions.

  Actividad 14 *Standards:* 1.3

Focus: Writing about personal opinions

Recycle: Leisure activities, sports, music, and clothes

Suggestions: Encourage students to use all the indirect object pronouns, if possible, when reporting their answers.

Answers will vary.

Enrich Your Teaching
Resources for All Teachers

Culture Note
Point out that the movie *Selena* is a biography of the famous Mexican American singer of the same name. The Grammy-winning artist quickly gained popularity throughout Mexico and the United States. Her success was cut short, however, when in 1995, Selena was tragically killed by the president of her fan club. Her music is still heard on many Mexican and U.S. radio stations.

Actividad 15 *Standards:* 1.3

Focus: Writing radio advertisements

Recycle: Clothing and food

Suggestions: For each illustration, have students brainstorm what each establishment offers, what type of people would be attracted to it, and why it is unique.

Answers will vary.

Extension: If possible, have students rehearse their ads and then record them. Play them for the class and ask students comprehension questions as they listen.

Actividad 16 *Standards:* 1.2, 2.1, 2.2   **Pre-AP***

Resources: Voc. and Gram. Transparency 121; Answers on Transparencies

Focus: Reading about entertainment industry awards

Suggestions: Ask students to describe awards ceremonies that they are familiar with. Have them list reasons why people receive awards in these ceremonies. As students read the passage, point out direct comparisons that can be made based on students' prior knowledge.

Answers:
1. cierta
2. falsa (Los premios reconocen a los artistas latinos.)
3. falsa (Les dan premios a los latinos que producen películas en inglés para el público en los Estados Unidos.)
4. cierta

Theme Project

Students can perform Step 4 at this point. Be sure they understand your corrections and suggestions. (For more information, see p. 290–a.)

Additional Resources

• WAV Wbk.: Audio Act. 7, p. 120
• Teacher's Resource Book: Audio Script, pp. 90–91
• Audio Program: Track 9

✓ Assessment

• **ExamView** Quiz on PresEXPRESS
• Prueba 6B–3: Verbs that use indirect object pronouns, p. 168

Actividad 15 ♻ **Escribir**

Los anuncios

Trabajas para una compañía de publicidad. Tienes que escribir un anuncio de radio para cada producto o lugar que ves abajo.

Modelo

¿Te fascinan los libros? ¿Te aburren los programas de televisión? ¿Por qué no visitas la Librería Ricardo? Tenemos miles de libros para toda la familia.

 1.  2.  3.  4.

Actividad 16 Leer

Los premios ALMA

Lee este artículo sobre los premios ALMA. Después lee las frases que siguen y decide si cada una es *C* (cierta) o *F* (falsa) según el artículo. Si la frase es falsa, escribe la información correcta.

En 1995 se establecieron los premios ALMA[1] para ayudar a promover[2] la representación justa y balanceada de los latinos en la televisión, el cine y la música. Los premios reconocen[3] a los artistas latinos por sus éxitos y su impacto positivo en la imagen del latino en los Estados Unidos. En la categoría del cine, le dan premios a los directores, actores y actrices latinos que producen películas en inglés para el público en los Estados Unidos. Hay premios también para diferentes clases de programas de televisión y los actores y actrices que aparecen en ellos. Otra categoría es la música: los videos, los álbumes, los cantantes y los grupos musicales. Algunas de las estrellas que han recibido premios en años recientes incluyen a Benjamin Bratt, Laura Elena Harring, Andy García, Esai Morales, Rita Moreno, Salma Hayek, Antonio Banderas, Marc Anthony, Jennifer López, Ricky Martin y Shakira.

Benjamin Bratt ganó por su papel en *Piñero*.

[1]soul, spirit [2]promote [3]recognize

1. Un actor latino puede ganar un premio ALMA por su papel en un programa de televisión dramático.
2. Una cantante que no es latina puede ganar un premio ALMA si canta en español.
3. Una actriz latina tiene que hablar español en la película para recibir el premio ALMA.
4. Tratan de usar los premios ALMA para dar una imagen positiva de los latinos en la televisión, el cine y la música.

Más práctica

• Practice Workbook, p. 126: 6B-5
• WAV Wbk.: Writing, p. 123
• Guided Practice: Grammar Acts., pp. 227–228
• *Real.* para hispanohablantes, pp. 234–237

Go Online PHSchool.com **For:** Indirect Obj. Pronouns **Web Code:** jdd-0613

Differentiated Instruction
Solutions for All Learners

Advanced Learners
Have students use magazine and Internet resources to collect additional information on the ALMA awards. Encourage them to find out when and where the awards ceremony takes place and who has won or is being considered for awards this year.

Multiple Intelligences
Musical/Rhythmic: Have students create jingles for the establishments in *Actividad 15.* Encourage students to perform their jingles for the class.

Gramática

The present perfect

The present perfect tense is used to say what a person *has done*.

Recientemente **hemos alquilado** muchos videos.
*Recently **we have rented** a lot of videos.*

To form the present perfect tense, use present-tense forms of *haber* + the past participle.

he alquilado	hemos alquilado
has alquilado	habéis alquilado
ha alquilado	han alquilado

To form the past participle of a verb, drop the ending of the infinitive and add *-ado* for *-ar* verbs and *-ido* for *-er* and *-ir* verbs.

hablar → **hablado**

comer → **comido**

vivir → **vivido**

Most verbs that have two vowels together in the infinitive have a written accent on the *í* of the past participle.

caer → **caído**   oír → **oído**

leer → **leído**   traer → **traído**

Some verbs have irregular past participles.

decir → **dicho**   poner → **puesto**

devolver → **devuelto**   romper → **roto**

escribir → **escrito**   ver → **visto**

hacer → **hecho**   volver → **vuelto**

morir → **muerto**

When you use object or reflexive pronouns with the present perfect, the pronoun goes immediately before the form of *haber*.

— ¿Has visto la nueva película de Ramón Guevara?

— No, **no la he visto**.

GramActiva VIDEO

Want more help with the present perfect? Watch the **GramActiva** video.

Lo has preparado.

17

Leer/Escribir

Un informe

En una hoja de papel, escribe la forma correcta del presente perfecto. Después di qué película has visto recientemente.

Sofía: ¿Paco, **1.** *(oír)* recientemente de algunas películas buenas?

Paco: Pues, no, y tampoco **2.** *(ir)* al cine, pero **3.** *(alquilar)* una película aburrida sobre dos personas que **4.** *(enamorarse)* en un barco en el Atlántico.

Sofía: Sí, sí, la conozco. Entonces, ¿ **5.** *(escribir)* tu informe para la clase de inglés?

Paco: ¿Qué informe? Yo **6.** *(estar)* enfermo y todavía no **7.** *(hacer)* ninguna tarea de ayer.

Sofía: Tenemos que escribir un informe sobre una película que nosotros **8.** *(ver)* recientemente. La profesora nos **9.** *(decir)* que no quiere leer sobre ninguna película aburrida.

Paco: Pues, ya **10.** *(devolver)* esa película aburrida que alquilé. ¡Voy a buscar otra película esta noche!

trescientos treinta y uno **331**
Capítulo 6B

Gramática

Presentation EXPRESS
GRAMMAR

Core Instruction

 Standards: 4.1

Resources: Voc. and Gram. Transparency 120; Teacher's Resource Book: Video Script, p. 94; Video Program: Cap. 6B

Suggestions: Point out that students are already familiar with the concept of a compound verb structure, having learned the present and imperfect progressive. Remind them that the present perfect is also formed by a helping verb and a participle. However, warn them not to confuse the two participles. Explain that the participle used in the progressive tenses is not the same as the past participle. Provide examples of both participles on flashcards, and have students practice making distinctions. Point out that they will only be conjugating the helping verb ***haber.*** Use the *GramActiva* Video as an introduction or reinforcement to your own grammar presentation.

17 *Standards:* 1.2
Presentation EXPRESS
ANSWERS

Resources: Answers on Transparencies

Focus: Reading and writing using the present perfect

Suggestions: Remind students to look for clues such as other verb forms or possessive adjectives to decide what forms to put in the blanks. Point out that in item 2 the present participle is ***ido.*** The verb *ir* follows the same rule as *-er* and *-ir* verbs even though it doesn't have a stem.

Answers:
1. has oído
2. he ido
3. he alquilado
4. se han enamorado
5. has escrito
6. he estado
7. he hecho
8. hemos visto
9. ha dicho
10. he devuelto

Enrich Your Teaching
Resources for All Teachers

Culture Note

Media companies are looking for ways to reach out to the rapidly growing Spanish-speaking population in the United States. An increase in the release of Spanish-speaking films and of music CDs demonstrates ways in which these companies target their audience. Additionally, a number of television networks now broadcast entirely in Spanish.

Teacher-to-Teacher

Have students develop dialogue journals to write about activities that they have participated in and television shows or movies that they have seen recently. After students write their entries, have them exchange them with a partner who will read and respond by making comments or asking follow-up questions.

Resources: Teacher's Resource Book: Audio Script, p. 91; Audio Program: Track 10; Answers on Transparencies

Focus: Listening to and writing sentences describing a crime scene

Recycle: Vocabulary for injuries and disasters

Suggestions: Have students use the pictures to help them brainstorm words that they should listen for.

 **Script and Answers:**

a. Los médicos le han puesto una venda a la víctima en el hospital. (3)
b. Nadie ha muerto, pero los paramédicos han tenido que ayudar a una víctima. (2)
c. Los detectives han capturado y arrestado a los criminales. (4)
d. Los ladrones han hecho una explosión y han robado el banco. (1)

Resources: Answers on Transparencies
Focus: Saying who did various actions
Recycle: Vocabulary for injuries and disasters; object pronouns

Suggestions: Have students say the direct object pronoun for each item that appears in the Student A bubble before beginning.

Answers:
Student A:
1. ¿Quién ha tratado de apagar el incendio?
2. ¿... ha visto el crimen?
3. ¿... ha capturado a los criminales?
4. ¿... ha llevado a los heridos al hospital?
5. ¿... ha puesto una venda en la cabeza de la víctima?
6. ¿... ha manejado el coche de los ladrones?
Student B: Answers will vary.

Suggestions: Explain that the popularity of Spanish-language films not only results from the increased number of Spanish speakers living in the United States, but also from U.S. interest in the cultures coexisting within the country.

Answers will vary.

  jdd-0698 **Escuchar/Escribir**

Escucha y escribe

Tus amigos están viendo una película, pero tú llegaste tarde. Ahora te están diciendo lo que ha pasado. Escribe lo que te dijeron. Después pon las frases en orden según los dibujos.

  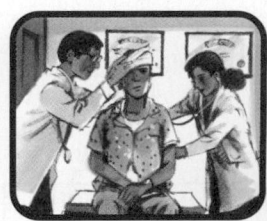 

  **Hablar**

¿Quién lo ha hecho . . . ?

Trabaja con otro(a) estudiante. Habla de lo que han hecho las diferentes personas en la película de la Actividad 18.

Modelo
robar las joyas
A —¿Quién ha robado las joyas?
B —Los ladrones las han robado.

Estudiante A

1. tratar de apagar el incendio
2. ver el crimen
3. capturar a los criminales
4. llevar a los heridos al hospital
5. poner una venda en la cabeza de la víctima
6. manejar el coche de los ladrones

Estudiante B

¡Respuesta personal!

 **Fondo cultural**

El cine en el mundo hispano España, México y Argentina tienen industrias cinematográficas importantes, y son los principales productores de películas para el público hispanohablante. Las películas compiten en festivales internacionales como los premios Goya en España, el Festival de Cine de la Habana en Cuba y el Festival de Cine Hispano de Miami. Las películas más populares de estos países se muestran con frecuencia en los Estados Unidos. Además de *(Besides)* competir en festivales internacionales, muchas películas de América Latina compiten y ganan premios Óscar en los Estados Unidos.

• ¿Por qué crees que las películas del mundo hispano son tan populares aquí?

El actor mexicano Gael García Bernal, en una escena de la película *Diarios de motocicleta*

Differentiated Instruction
Solutions for All Learners

Advanced Learners
Have students research and create a movie poster for a Spanish-language film. Have them include the title, director, leading actors and actresses, year of release, and country of origin. Display students' work in the classroom.

Students with Special Needs
For hearing-impaired students, modify *Actividad 21*. Instead of having pairs describe the movie aloud, have them write descriptions on the board. If the team guesses the movie title after one statement, one point is earned, after two statements, two points, and so on. The team that guesses three titles with the fewest points wins.

Actividad 20 · Escribir

Preparaciones para el cine

Cristina quiere ir al cine con sus amigos, pero sus padres no están en casa. Di lo que ella ha hecho antes de salir. Escoge los verbos apropiados de la lista y escribe las formas correctas del presente perfecto para completar las frases.

cepillarse	decirle	escribirles	hacer
leer	llamarles	pedirle	ponerse

1. ___ todos sus quehaceres.
2. ___ el pelo y los dientes.
3. ___ jeans y su suéter favorito.
4. ___ un comentario sobre la película de un crítico en el periódico.
5. ___ a su hermana mayor adónde va.

6. ___ dinero a su hermana para comprar la entrada al cine.
7. ___ una nota a sus padres diciéndoles cuándo va a regresar.
8. ___ por teléfono a sus amigos para decirles cuándo va a llegar al cine.

Modelo
___ una película a sus amigos.
Les ha recomendado una película a sus amigos.

Actividad 21 · Hablar/GramActiva

Juego

1 Van a jugar en dos equipos. Una persona del equipo A escoge una tarjeta del (de la) profesor(a) que tiene el título de una película. Con otro(a) estudiante describan la película a su equipo sin decir el nombre. Pueden indicar:

• si han visto la película y si les ha gustado
• si la película ha tenido éxito o no
• qué papeles han hecho los actores
• cómo ha sido el argumento

2 Si alguien del equipo A puede adivinar *(guess)* el nombre de la película en menos de un minuto, este equipo gana un punto. Si al final del minuto, el equipo A no ha adivinado el título, el equipo B tiene una sola oportunidad de decirlo. Si lo pueden hacer, ellos ganan el punto. Después los equipos cambian *(change)* de papel. El primer equipo que gana tres puntos gana el juego.

El español en el mundo del trabajo

¿Te interesa una carrera en la industria cinematográfica? Hay muchas compañías en los Estados Unidos que filman películas y videos en los países hispanohablantes. Puedes trabajar con ellos en varios aspectos de la producción de la película: director, asistente del director, técnica de sonido *(sound)*, técnica de luz y otros trabajos. ¿Los requisitos? Talento en filmación, tener una visión del proyecto, capacidad de trabajar en equipo y habilidad de comunicarse en español.

• ¿Por qué crees que es importante poder comunicarse en español durante la filmación en Costa Rica, por ejemplo? ¿En qué aspectos de la producción vas a usar el español?

trescientos treinta y tres **333**
Capítulo 6B

Enrich Your Teaching
Resources for All Teachers

Culture Note
Spanish-language films that have won Oscars as Best Foreign Film are: *Volver a empezar,* Spain (1982); *The Official Story (La historia oficial),* Argentina (1985); *Belle Epoque,* Spain (1993); and *All About My Mother (Todo sobre mi madre),* Spain (1999).

Internet Search
Have students use the Internet to learn more about the filmmaking industry in Spanish-speaking countries.

Keywords:
cinematografía de + (name of Spanish-speaking country)	

Actividad 20 Standards: 1.2  Presentation EXPRESS ANSWERS

Resources: Answers on Transparencies

Focus: Using the present perfect tense with personal pronouns

Recycle: Reflexive and indirect object pronouns

Suggestions: Have students match the appropriate infinitive to the sentence before changing the form of the verb.

Answers:
1. Ha hecho
2. Se ha cepillado
3. Se ha puesto
4. Ha leído
5. Le ha dicho
6. Le ha pedido
7. Les ha escrito
8. Les ha llamado

Common Errors: Students may confuse reflexive pronouns with indirect object pronouns. Point out that they can find the forms at the ends of the infinitives in the word bank.

Actividad 21 Standards: 1.1, 1.3

Focus: Talking about movies

Suggestions: After each team earns a point, make the game more difficult by giving students less time. Limit them to 45 seconds on the second round and 30 seconds on the third.

Answers will vary.

El español en el mundo del trabajo
Core Instruction

 Standards: 1.2, 5.1

Suggestions: Point out that movie scenes often take a long time to film. If a crew goes to a Spanish-speaking country, they will be living in that area, and will have to communicate in order to meet their everyday needs—as well as to benefit from getting to know new people.

Answers will vary.

333

Actividad 22 **Standards:** 1.1, 1.3, 3.1

Resources: Teacher's Resource Book: GramActiva BLM, p. 101; Answers on Transparencies

Focus: Discussing types of movies and how often people see them; cross-curricular connection to mathematics and statistics

Recycle: Numbers

Suggestions: You may want to make photocopies of each group's results to help students compile them. Remind students that to find the percentage, they should take the number of students who gave a certain answer and divide it by the total number of students in the class. Have students check their work by making sure that the percentages for all the categories add up to 100.

Answers will vary.

Fondo cultural **Standards:** 1.2, 2.2

■◆◈◆◈■◆◈◈■◆◈◈◆◈◈■◆◈■

Suggestions: Ask students if they have seen Spanish-language videos of films that were originally in English. Remind students of the rapid increase in the number of Spanish speakers in the United States. Point out that companies are always ready to adapt to such trends, since doing so will help the company thrive and grow.

Answers will vary.

Pre-AP* Support

- **Activity:** Write the answers to questions 1–5 from *Actividad* 23 on long strips of paper and distribute sets to pairs of students. With textbooks closed, read the article to the class. Next, have pairs of students open their textbooks, look at the questions, and arrange the strips of answers in the correct order. (Make this a timed activity.) Confirm as a class.
- **Pre-AP* Resource Book:** Comprehensive guide to Pre-AP* communication skill development, pp. 9–17, 36–46

   Actividad 22 **Escribir/Hablar**

Las películas que hemos visto

En grupos de cuatro estudiantes, hagan preguntas sobre las películas que han visto en el último mes.

Modelo
A —¿Cuántas películas has visto en el último mes?
B —He visto dos películas.
o:— No he visto ninguna película.

Conexiones **Las matemáticas**

1 Escriban en una tabla el número de películas, la clase de película (acción, comedia, drama) y los lugares donde las vieron (casa, cine o casa de amigos o familiares).

	Total para el grupo	Total para la clase
¿Cuántas películas han visto?		
¿Qué clase de películas?		
¿Dónde las han visto?		

2 Ahora compartan sus resultados con la clase y sumen el total para el número de películas, la clase de película y los lugares. Hagan dos gráficas circulares como las que se ven aquí para indicar qué clase de películas han visto más todos los estudiantes y dónde las han visto.

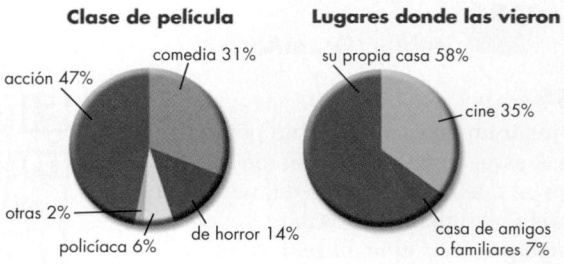

Clase de película
acción 47%
comedia 31%
otras 2%
policíaca 6%
de horror 14%

Lugares donde las vieron
su propia casa 58%
cine 35%
casa de amigos o familiares 7%

Fondo cultural

■◆◈■◆◈■◆◈■◆◈■◆◈■◆◈■

Videos en español Las compañías que producen y distribuyen los videos de películas se han dado cuenta *(have realized)* en los últimos años del poder económico del mercado hispanohablante. Algunas han empezado a ofrecer películas clásicas, originalmente en inglés, ya dobladas al español. Otras compañías, como Disney, ofrecen sus principales películas animadas en versiones en español.

- ¿Por qué crees que hay más demanda de videos en español?

En una tienda de videos en la Ciudad de México, México

Differentiated Instruction
Solutions for All Learners

Advanced Learners

Have students perform a skit in which one person is a talk show host and another is an actor or actress who is trying to promote the recent release of his or her movie on video.

Have students ask and answer questions that will help them summarize the plot, comment on the characters, and say where the film is available to rent or buy.

Actividad 23 — Leer/Escribir/Hablar

Una estrella de cine herida

Lee el artículo de una revista sobre una estrella de cine y contesta las preguntas.

1. ¿Qué ha aprendido Chayanne sobre ser estrella del cine?

2. ¿Cómo se ha lastimado el actor durante la filmación de la película?

3. ¿Qué han hecho los médicos? ¿Qué le han dado? ¿Por qué?

4. ¿Qué más le ha pasado al actor?

5. ¿Qué ha hecho el público para decirle a Chayanne que están pensando en él?

6. ¿Se lastimó otra estrella del cine? ¿Qué le ha pasado?

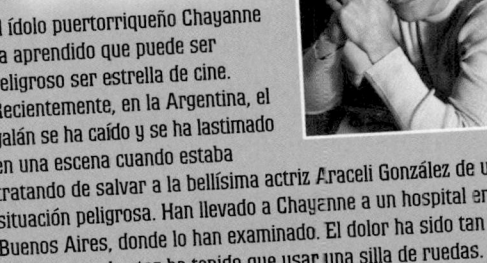

¡Un trabajo peligroso!

El ídolo puertorriqueño Chayanne ha aprendido que puede ser peligroso ser estrella de cine. Recientemente, en la Argentina, el galán se ha caído y se ha lastimado en una escena cuando estaba tratando de salvar a la bellísima actriz Araceli González de una situación peligrosa. Han llevado a Chayanne a un hospital en Buenos Aires, donde lo han examinado. El dolor ha sido tan intenso que el actor ha tenido que usar una silla de ruedas. Además, una inundación ha destruido una parte de su casa en la Argentina. Sus admiradores le han escrito y le han enviado un montón de cartas, tarjetas y mensajes electrónicos.

Actividad 24 — Escribir/Hablar

En las noticias

¿Cuáles son las noticias que han ocurrido recientemente en tu comunidad y en el mundo? Trabaja con otro(a) estudiante. Piensen en una noticia que han oído en el noticiero o que han leído en el periódico. Escriban un artículo de cinco frases sobre lo que ha pasado. Usen el modelo y el artículo de la Actividad 23 para escribirlo. Diseñen (Design) su artículo para el periódico, incluyendo una ilustración o foto. Van a usar su artículo para la Actividad 25.

Modelo

La atleta panameña, Yolanda Salazar, ha ganado un premio en la competencia de natación en Costa Rica. Los aficionados y su entrenador se han vuelto locos porque ella ha terminado en primer lugar en este campeonato. Esta competencia ha sido la mejor para Panamá en los últimos años. En una entrevista, Yolanda se ha sentido muy emocionada. Ha dicho que su familia y su público son muy importantes para ella.

Actividad 25 — Leer/Hablar

Leyendo las noticias

Lean los artículos que crearon para la Actividad 24 con otros grupos y hablen de ellos.

Modelo

A —¿Has leído el artículo sobre Yolanda Salazar?
B —Sí, dice que ella ha ganado un premio en la competencia de natación en Costa Rica.

Más práctica

- Practice Workbook, pp. 127–128: 6B-6, 6B-7
- WAV Wbk.: Writing, p. 124
- Guided Practice: Grammar Acts., pp. 229–232
- Real. para hispanohablantes, pp. 238–241

Go Online PHSchool.com
For: Present Perfect
Web Code: jdd-0614

trescientos treinta y cinco **335**
Capítulo 6B

Enrich Your Teaching
Resources for All Teachers

Culture Note

DVD technology can currently create individual disks with the capability of switching between Spanish and English. Viewers may be able to choose subtitles or dubbing with specific movies. Future technology is being explored in order to design a DVD player that can play any disk in any language the viewer prefers.

Internet Search

Have students use the Internet to find out more about the availability of Spanish-language products from U.S. entertainment companies.

Keywords:

(name of company) + en español

Practice and Communicate

6B

Actividad 23
Standards: 1.2, 2.1, 2.2
Presentation EXPRESS ANSWERS

Resources: Voc. and Gram. Transparency 122; Answers on Transparencies

Focus: Reading and writing about an injured movie star

Recycle: Vocabulary for accidents and injuries

Suggestions: Have students use the title of the article to predict what it is about.

Answers:

1. Ha aprendido que puede ser peligroso ser estrella del cine.

2. Se ha lastimado cuando estaba tratando de salvar a una actriz.

3. Los médicos lo han examinado. Le han dado una silla de ruedas porque el dolor ha sido tan intenso.

4. Una inundación ha destruido una parte de su casa en Argentina.

5. Sus admiradores le han escrito.

6. Answers will vary.

Actividad 24
Standards: 1.3

Focus: Writing a news article

Recycle: Activities, adjectives

Suggestions: Encourage students to write about an event from a Spanish-speaking country. Bring in Spanish-language newspapers, magazines, or Internet pages that would help students find a story.

Answers will vary.

Actividad 25
Standards: 1.1, 1.2

Focus: Reading and speaking about current events

Recycle: Activities, adjectives

Suggestions: Compile the articles into a class newspaper to give to each student.

Answers will vary.

Additional Resources

- WAV Wbk.: Audio Act. 8–9, pp. 120–121
- Teacher's Resource Book: Audio Script, p. 91, Communicative Activity BLM, p. 98
- Audio Program: Tracks 11–12

✔ Assessment

- ExamView QuickTake Presenter Quiz on PresEXPRESS
- Prueba 6B-4: The present perfect, p. 169

335

Lectura

Core Instruction

Standards: 1.2, 3.1

Focus: Reading comprehension of film reviews

Suggestions:

Pre-reading: Ask students to look at the pictures to identify the movies. If students have seen the movies, have them describe the characters and summarize the plot. Ask students who have seen the movies to give their opinions of them. Have students scan the elements of each review, pointing out the titles and subtitles. Have students list other elements of movie reviews that they have read and identify those elements in these reviews.

Reading: Read each review to students, and have a volunteer summarize the critic's review. Ask students who have seen the movie if they agree or disagree with the review.

Post-reading: Ask students who have seen the films to give them a rating from 1–10. Complete the *¿Comprendiste?* questions.

 Bellringer Review

Have students complete these sentences to express their opinions of current movies:

1. *Me encanta la película___.*
2. *No me gusta nada la película___.*
3. *A mis padres les gusta mucho la película___.*

Pre-AP* Support

- **Activity:** Assign pairs of students one of the movie reviews found on pp. 336–337. Have the pairs write two sets of two multiple-choice questions for their particular review. Then combine pairs of students to form groups of six with each review being represented. Each pair will distribute their questions to the others in the group and then read aloud their review. (The other students' textbooks should be closed.) The group members will then respond to the multiple-choice questions that they have received.

- **Pre-AP* Resource Book:** Comprehensive guide to Pre-AP* reading skill development, pp. 18–24

Theme Project

Students can perform Step 5 at this point. Record their presentations on cassette or videotape for inclusion in their portfolio. (For more information, see p. 290–a.)

336

¡Adelante!

Lectura

La cartelera del cine

Lee las siguientes críticas de una revista mexicana. ¿Qué película te gustaría ver?

Objectives

- **Read movie reviews and compare ratings in different countries**
- **Learn about subtitling and dubbing**
- **Write a film script**
- **Watch *En busca de la verdad*, Episodio 8**

Estrategia

Reading for details
When you read a text for specific information, you may need to read it more than once. First, you might read for the "big picture," and then reread for additional details. Read the text below to find out which film(s) you might be interested in watching.

★ ESTRENOS DE HOY ★

EL HOMBRE ARAÑA[1]
EE.UU., 2002 | CLASIFICACIÓN: B | DIRECTOR: SAM RAIMI | ACTORES: TOBEY MAGUIRE, WILLEM DAFOE, KIRSTEN DUNST

SINOPSIS
La historia del hombre araña cuenta la transformación de Peter Parker. Una araña genéticamente alterada lo muerde[2] y el joven comienza a notar cambios[3] físicos: es más fuerte[4] y ágil. Cuando una tragedia le enseña[5] la realidad de sus poderes,[6] decide pelear contra el crimen para ayudar a los demás.

CRÍTICA
El hombre araña es una película fenomenal. La historia es interesante y los actores son muy buenos. Los efectos especiales son espectaculares, especialmente cuando el hombre araña va por el aire de un edificio a otro. Le recomiendo esta película a todo el mundo.

CALIFICACIÓN: 10/10

EL SEÑOR DE LOS ANILLOS 2: LAS DOS TORRES
EE.UU., NUEVA ZELANDIA 2002 | CLASIFICACIÓN: B | DIRECTOR: PETER JACKSON | ACTORES: ELIJAH WOOD, IAN MCKELLEN, VIGGO MORTENSEN, LIV TYLER, CATE BLANCHETT

SINOPSIS
Los *Hobbits* Frodo y Sam continúan su viaje hacia Mordor, con la misión de destruir el Anillo Único, pero se dan cuenta[7] de que los sigue Gollum. Al mismo tiempo, el resto de la comunidad —Aragorn, Legolas, Gimli, Merry y Pippin—hacen nuevas alianzas con el pueblo de Rohan. La comunidad va a tener que pelearse contra las fuerzas que salen de las dos torres.

CRÍTICA
Las dos torres es espectacular. La historia, los personajes y la cinematografía son excelentes, sobre todo los efectos especiales. Los actores actúan muy bien, y me encantó el personaje digital Gollum. ¡Ojo! ¡La película es muy larga! Compre dulces y refrescos antes de sentarse.

CALIFICACIÓN: 10/10

[1]spider [2]bites [3]changes [4]stronger [5]shows [6]powers [7]realize

336 trescientos treinta y seis
Tema 6 • La televisión y el cine

Differentiated Instruction
Solutions for All Learners

Students with Learning Difficulties
To aid reading comprehension, make a transparency of the *Lectura*. As you read, ask students to note terms used by the critic to express opinions. Underline positive ones in blue and negative ones in red. Leave the transparency up for students' reference as they answer the questions.

Multiple Intelligences
Bodily/Kinesthetic: Have students prepare a skit in which one of them is the movie critic and the other is the director. The critic should comment on the film and ask the director for details. The director can comment on the review and answer questions. Students may choose one of the movies above, or base their skit on another movie.

EL ATAQUE DE LOS CLONES

EE.UU., 2002 | CLASIFICACIÓN: B | DIRECTOR: GEORGE LUCAS |
ACTORES: EWAN MCGREGOR, HAYDEN CHRISTENSEN, NATALIE PORTMAN

SINOPSIS

La película comienza diez años después de los eventos de *La amenaza fantasma.* La Reina Amidala es ahora una senadora del gobierno del planeta Naboo. Cuando tratan de matarla, el Concilio Jedi le da de guardaespaldas[8] al Caballero Jedi Obi Wan Kenobi y a su estudiante, Anakin Skywalker. Un segundo ataque provoca que la senadora y Anakin regresen a Naboo. Obi Wan investiga los ataques contra Amidala. Así, cada "equipo" por su parte descubre una conspiración política y militar.

CRÍTICA

Esta película es muy comercial. Lo más interesante es el uso de los efectos especiales. El argumento es horrible. Es muy difícil de entender y no es muy lógica. Por los efectos especiales, le doy 10/10. Por el argumento, sólo le doy 5/10.

CALIFICACIÓN: 5/10

[8]bodyguard

¿Comprendiste?

1. ¿Es positiva o negativa la crítica de *El hombre araña?* ¿Qué palabras indican la opinión del crítico?

2. ¿Por qué le gustó al crítico la película *Las dos torres?*

3. ¿Por qué el crítico le da 5 / 10 al argumento de *El ataque de los clones?*

4. ¿Quién descubre una conspiración política y militar?

5. Según las recomendaciones, ¿cuál(es) de las películas quieres ver? ¿Por qué?

Y tú, ¿qué dices?

1. ¿Has visto algunas de estas películas? ¿Cuáles? ¿Estás de acuerdo con la crítica de estas películas?

2. ¿Qué prefieres, los efectos especiales o un buen argumento?

3. ¿Cómo decides qué películas vas a ver? ¿Has visto alguna película hispana? ¿En qué sentido *(way)* son diferentes de las películas americanas?

Más práctica

- WAV Wbk.: Writing, p. 125
- Guided Practice: *Lectura,* p. 233
- *Real.* para hispanohablantes, pp. 242–243

Go Online PHSchool.com
For: Internet Activity
Web Code: jdd-0615

 **Fondo cultural**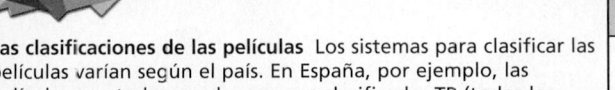

Las clasificaciones de las películas Los sistemas para clasificar las películas varían según el país. En España, por ejemplo, las películas que todos pueden ver son clasificadas TP (todos los públicos). También existe allí la clasificación –7 (los menores de siete años no deben ver esta película). En México, usan las letras A, B y C para clasificar las películas. La letra A corresponde a todos los públicos mientras que la B es para los mayores de 15 años y la C sólo para los mayores de 18 años.

- ¿Qué sistema de clasificación se usa en los Estados Unidos? ¿En qué sentido es diferente del sistema de España o de México?

Película	España	México	Estados Unidos
"El rey león"	TP	A	G
"El señor de los anillos 2: Las dos torres"	–13	B	PG-13
"Titanic"	–13	B	PG-13
"Matrix"	–18	C	R

Enrich Your Teaching
Resources for All Teachers

Teacher-to-Teacher

Give students a list of American-made movies. Have them use the Internet to find their ratings and, if possible, the Spanish translation of the title. Have students use the chart on p. 337 to convert the ratings for either Spain or Mexico. Ask students to create a movie-theater listing that includes the titles and ratings.

Internet Search

Have students use the Internet to search for movie ratings.

Keyword:

clasificaciones de películas

¿Comprendiste?

 Presentation EXPRESS ANSWERS

 Standards: 1.2

Resources: Answers on Transparencies

Focus: Verifying comprehension of film reviews

Suggestions: Write a two-column chart on the board and label the columns *Palabras positivas* and *Palabras negativas.* Write the names of the movies on the left-hand side of the chart. Classify words from each review in the appropriate column.

Answers will vary but may include:

1. La crítica es positiva. Las palabras positivas son *fenomenal, interesante, buenos* y *espectaculares.*

2. Al crítico le gusta porque la historia, los personajes y la cinematografía son excelentes, sobre todo los efectos especiales. También, los actores actúan bien.

3. El argumento es horrible. Es muy difícil de entender y no es muy lógico.

4. Cada "equipo" descubre una conspiración política y militar.

5. Answers will vary.

Y tú, ¿qué dices?

 Standards: 1.1, 1.3

Focus: Expressing opinions about movies

Suggestions: For item 1, if students have not seen any of the movies, have them tell whether or not they plan to see them, based on the critics' reviews. Have them include reasons to support their answer.

Answers will vary.

 **Fondo cultural** *Standards:* 1.2, 2.2, 4.2

Suggestions: To help students answer the question, have them give the meanings of G *(general public),* PG-13 *(parental guidance for children under 13),* and R *(restricted).* Have them use the chart to make their comparisons.

Answers will vary.

For Further Reading

Student Resources: Realidades para hispanohablantes: Lectura 2, pp. 244–245; Lecturas para hispanohablantes 2: "La casa de los azulejos, pp. 10–11, "La navidad de Miguelito," pp. 30–32, "Lo hispano es bello," pp. 92– 94

Additional Resources

Student Resource: Guided Practice: Lectura, p. 233

337

Perspectivas del mundo hispano

Core Instruction

Standards: 1.1, 1.2, 1.3, 2.1

Focus: Reading about and discussing preferences regarding foreign films

Suggestions: Ask students to list any foreign films that they may have seen. What language were the movies in? Did students understand what the characters were saying? If not, how were they able to understand the meaning of the movie?

Read the passage to students, pausing after each paragraph to check for comprehension. Ask students how many of them have seen films with subtitles or dubbing. If they have not, bring in an example of each. Show students a segment and ask: Which method did they prefer? What are the advantages and disadvantages of each? Have students list their responses before discussing the *¡Compruébalo!* with a partner. To help students answer the *¿Qué te parece?* questions, list five movies and have students give examples of how they reflect aspects of U.S. culture.

Answers will vary.

Additional Resources

Student Resource: Realidades para hispanohablantes, p. 246

Perspectivas del mundo hispano

Películas en otros idiomas

¿Has visto una película de otro país en que los actores hablan un idioma[1] que no es inglés? Por ejemplo, las películas de Francia y México son muy populares en los Estados Unidos. ¡Si no entiendes ni el francés ni el español, son difíciles de comprender!

Pero eso no es un problema. En muchas películas de otros países el diálogo de la película aparece en inglés en la parte de abajo de la pantalla. Con estos subtítulos es más fácil comprender el argumento de la película. Cuando hay subtítulos, es importante concentrarse un poco más y observar las expresiones y movimientos de los actores. Lo bueno es que es más interesante ver la película en versión original con subtítulos.

Otra solución para que el público pueda comprender una película es sustituir el diálogo original por una nueva grabación del diálogo en el idioma del país. Esto se llama doblaje.[2] Por ejemplo, uno puede ver una película italiana en que se oye el diálogo en inglés.

¡Compruébalo! Algunas personas prefieren ver las películas en versión original, con subtítulos, porque comprenden el idioma de la película y pueden escuchar la voz verdadera de los actores y los sonidos de la ambientación. A otras personas les gusta leer los subtítulos porque, cuando los leen, pueden aprender un poco del idioma original de la película. Y otras dicen que no les gusta el doblaje porque pierden el tono de la voz y la entonación de los actores. Si has visto una película de un país extranjero, piensa en lo que prefieres. Pregúntales a otras personas qué prefieren y por qué.

¿Qué te parece? Cuando vemos una película producida en otro país, podemos aprender algo de la cultura y del idioma de ese país. ¿Qué más puedes aprender? ¿Crees que es más fácil aprender de una película con doblaje o con subtítulos? ¿Qué crees que la gente de otros países aprende de nosotros cuando ve las películas de Hollywood?

[1]language [2]dubbing

Differentiated Instruction
Solutions for All Learners

Advanced Learners

Have students report on foreign films playing in your community or in nearby cities. Ask them to contact theaters or look in the newspaper. Have them present each film that is playing by giving a summary of its plot, saying who is in it, and telling what country it is from. Also, have students say whether the film will be shown with subtitles or dubbing.

Multiple Intelligences

Visual/Spatial: Have artistic students draw a storyboard of a scene from a well-known film. Then have them label each section with subtitles of the dialogue. Ask students to present their storyboards. Have other students in the class guess what movie is being depicted.

Luces, cámara, acción

Task

Your class is having a contest to produce exciting or humorous new movie ideas. For this contest you will need to produce a brief description of the plot and the main characters. You also will need to plan the details of one scene to provide a preview of your movie.

1 Prewrite Use the chart below to help you focus on "the big picture." Think about the type of movie you want to write: a mystery, a comedy, science fiction, or a romance. What is the plot? Who are the main characters? Which scene would provide a good feel for your movie?

Clase de película	Argumento	Actores principales	Escena

2 Draft Use the notes from your chart to write a short synopsis of the movie. Then write a script for the scene you've chosen. Include the dialog and directions to the actors. You might want to use the storyboard method to show how the scene progresses.

3 Revise Read through your synopsis and scene and check for spelling, agreement, correct verb usage, and vocabulary. Share your review with a partner, who will check for errors and to see that the synopsis is complete, the story is presented in a logical order, and the scene is easy to understand.

4 Publish Rewrite your summary and scene, making any necessary changes or corrections. Give a copy to your teacher or put one in your portfolio. The class can select the winner of the contest from all entries.

5 Evaluation Your teacher may give you a rubric for how the contest entry will be graded. You will probably be graded on:
- completeness of information in the synopsis
- clarity and logical presentation of ideas in the synopsis
- appropriateness of short scene to present the plot

Estrategia

Outlining your ideas
Many filmwriters do extensive outlining of key ideas before they begin to write. They focus on "big picture" vision: type of movie, plot, and description of the characters. This skill will be helpful as you write your contest entry.

Estrategia

Drawing a scene
A common tool in movie writing is to draw the scene. This is called storyboarding. You might sketch the scene you will be writing about.

Standards: 1.3, 3.1

Focus: Writing a synopsis of a movie script

Suggestions: Point out that the task asks for a brief description of the plot and main characters. Suggest that students also consider which of these elements will be the driving force for the type of movie they choose to write about. For example, mystery movies center around the plot, whereas romantic movies tend to focus more on the characters. Encourage students to focus on meaningful details according to the type of movie they choose as they develop their descriptions. As students are drafting, remind them to not reveal too much about the movie. The readers should be interested, so that they will still want to see more.

The second *Estrategia* talks about drawing out a scene, or storyboarding. Students may want to expand on this by using photographs, props, or other visuals.

Portfolio

Have students include a copy of their storyboard and synopsis in their portfolio.

 Pre-AP* Support

- **Pre-AP* Resource Book:** Comprehensive guide to Pre-AP* writing skill development, pp. 25–35

Teacher-to-Teacher

e-amigos: Have students send their *e-amigos* a written summary of the movie plot that they described in the *Presentación escrita*. Encourage students to ask each other questions about the movies and give their opinions. Have students print out their e-mails or send them to you.

Additional Resources

Student Resources: Realidades para hispanohablantes, p. 247; Guided Practice: Presentación escrita, p. 234

✓ Assessment

- Assessment Program: Rubrics, p. T31

Model a top-scoring description for students. Provide students with a copy of the rubric you will use for evaluation to help in the revision and publishing stages.

Enrich Your Teaching
Resources for All Teachers

RUBRIC	Score 1	Score 3	Score 5
Completeness of your information	You provide two pieces of information in your synopsis.	You provide three pieces of information in your synopsis.	You provide all pieces of information in your synopsis.
Logical presentation of ideas	Your ideas do not have a logical sequence and are difficult to understand.	Your ideas have a somewhat logical sequence and are somewhat understandable.	Your ideas have a logical sequence and are understandable.
Presentation of plot in scene	You present the plot poorly and not all aspects are evident.	You present the plot somewhat clearly and most aspects are evident.	You present the plot clearly and all aspects are evident.

Videomisterio

Core Instruction

Standards: 1.2, 3.2, 5.2

Resources: Teacher's Resource Book: Video Script, pp. 94–95; Video Program: Cap. 6B; Video Program Teacher's Guide: Cap. 6B

Focus: Reading and presenting new vocabulary needed to understand the video

Personajes importantes

Roberto	**Carmen**
Tomás	**Turrón**
Linda	**El Sr. Tos,** a strange man

Synopsis: Turrón continues asking questions around town about Dr. Tomás Toledo. A patient, Sr. Tos, tells Dr. Toledo about Turrón. Roberto makes plans to go to San Antonio with Carmen and Linda, and Roberto's family takes them out for a farewell dinner.

Suggestions:

Pre-viewing: Review the events of *Episodio 7:* Linda, Roberto, and Julio visited various tourist sites in Guanajuato. Roberto spoke to his father about the bank account in San Antonio, and told him that he wanted to go to Texas to claim it. Meanwhile, Turrón appeared in Guanajuato and was asking questions about the Toledo family.

Have a volunteer read the *Nota cultural* aloud. Point out that the **mariachi** are an institution in Mexico and can be found everywhere. Ask students to compare what they know about the **mariachi** and the **estudiantinas.**

Help students understand the words in the *Palabras para comprender*.

Videomisterio

En busca de la verdad

Episodio 8

Antes de ver el video

"Espero que puedas encontrar la respuesta a este misterio de tantos años".

"¿Sabe que por ahí anda un hombre haciendo preguntas sobre Ud.?".

Resumen del episodio

El hombre misterioso sigue haciendo preguntas en Guanajuato sobre la familia Toledo. Nadie sabe quién es ni por qué está allí. La familia Toledo invita a Carmen y a Linda a una cena de despedida.

Nota cultural El Mariachi, una tradición típica mexicana, surgió en el estado de Jalisco en el siglo XIX. Es un grupo de músicos vestidos de ropa tradicional de la época de la Revolución Mexicana. Sus instrumentos incluyen el violín, la guitarra, el bajo y la trompeta, y sus canciones tratan de temas como la traición, el amor y la Revolución. Hoy en día se pueden oír Mariachi en fiestas, celebraciones y hasta en restaurantes.

Palabras para comprender
sigue tosiendo keep coughing
cena de despedida farewell dinner
he disfrutado I have enjoyed
agradecer to thank

Después de ver el video

¿Comprendiste?

A. Lee las siguientes frases. Di cuáles son ciertas y cuáles son falsas.

1. El hombre misterioso averigua muchas cosas sobre la familia Toledo.

2. A Tomás no le importa que un hombre extraño pregunte por él.

3. Linda no disfrutó de su viaje a México.

4. Roberto va a viajar a San Antonio para investigar qué pasó con el abuelo.

5. A Berta le gusta la idea del viaje de Roberto a San Antonio.

6. Linda dice que va a regresar a Guanajuato en el invierno.

7. Julio no puede acompañar a Roberto y a Linda porque tiene que ir a ver a Josefina.

B. Imagina que eres un(a) amigo(a) de Roberto. Descríbele todo lo que ha hecho el hombre misterioso en Guanajuato. ¿Con quién habló? ¿Qué quería saber?

Go Online
PHSchool.com
For: More on *En busca de la verdad*
Web Code: jdd-0209

trescientos cuarenta y uno **341**
Capítulo 6B

Enrich Your Teaching
Resources for All Teachers

Culture Note

Though ***mariachi*** is very popular and internationally recognized as symbolizing Mexican music, it is one of a number of musical forms found in Mexico. Among many others, in the northern states there is the rambunctious ***música norteña;*** in the Southeast mountain area is the ***música huasteca*** with its country feel; in the Southeast coastal area is the ***música de trio,*** soft and melodic.

Suggestions:

Visual scanning: Direct attention to the photos. Have students read the captions and try to guess what the characters might be talking about.

Before students read the *Resumen del episodio* have them consider what they think the mysterious man wants. Then have them read the *Resumen del episodio* and ask them one or two comprehension questions.

Viewing: Play *Episodio* 8 for the class. If there is time after viewing the full episode, go back and replay key moments that you wish to highlight. Remind students that they may not understand every word they hear in the video, but they should listen for overall understanding.

Post-viewing: Complete the *¿Comprendiste?* in class.

¿Comprendiste?

 Standards: 1.2, 3.1

Resources: Answers on Transparencies
Focus: Verifying comprehension; reviewing the plot
Suggestions: For part A, have students correct false statements to make them true. For part B, you may want to have students brainstorm in groups.

Answers:

A:
1. cierta
2. falsa
3. falsa
4. cierta
5. falsa
6. falsa
7. cierta

B: Answers will vary.

Additional Resources

- *En busca de la verdad* Video Workbook, Episode 8
- *En busca de la verdad* Teacher's Video Guide: Answer Key

341

Review Activities

To talk about movies: Have students work in pairs. One person will say a word, and another will name the movie genre(s) to which it applies.

To talk about making movies: Use these words as sentence starters. Have students choose a movie that they are familiar with and fill in the rest of the information for each sentence. For example, start the sentence with: *Mi película favorita está basada* en … Have students share the results with a partner.

Present perfect, past participles, and irregular past participles: Give students a dictation describing a movie that you saw recently. Use the present tense in the dictation. Have students rewrite the dictation using the present perfect. Have students work in pairs to check each other's work.

Portfolio

Invite students to review the activities they completed in this chapter, including written reports, posters or other visuals, tapes of oral presentations, or other projects. Have them select one or two items that they feel best demonstrate their achievements in Spanish to include in their portfolios. Have them include this with the Chapter Checklist and Self-Assessment Worksheet.

Additional Resources

Student Resources: Realidades para hispanohablantes, p. 248

 **CD-ROM**

PuzzleView Web Code: jdd-0617

Teacher Resources:

• Teacher's Resource Book: Situation Cards, p. 100, Clip Art, pp. 102–104

• Assessment Program: Chapter Checklist and Self-Assessment Worksheet, pp. T56–T57

Repaso del capítulo

Vocabulario y gramática

jdd-0699

To prepare for the test, check to see if you . . .
• know the new vocabulary and grammar
• can perform the tasks on p. 343

to talk about movies

alquilar	to rent
el amor	love
arrestar	to arrest
capturar	to capture
el crimen	crime
el (la) criminal	criminal
el crítico, la crítica	critic
el (la) detective	detective
enamorarse (de)	to fall in love (with)
(estar) enamorado, -a de	(to be) in love with
la estrella (del cine)	(movie) star
el (la) extraterrestre	alien
fascinar	to fascinate
el fracaso	failure
el galán	leading man
he visto	I have seen
has visto	you have seen
el ladrón, la ladrona, *pl.* los ladrones	thief
matar	to kill
la película de acción	action film
¿Qué tal es . . . ?	How is (it) . . . ?
recomendar *(e → ie)*	to recommend
robar	to rob, to steal
será	he / she / it will be
tener éxito	to succeed, to be successful
tratarse de	to be about
la víctima	victim
la violencia	violence

to talk about making movies

la actuación	acting
el argumento	plot
la dirección	direction
el director, la directora	director
los efectos especiales	special effects
la escena	scene
estar basado, -a en	to be based on
el papel	role
hacer el papel de	to play the role of
el personaje principal	main character

other useful words

no . . . todavía	not yet

indirect object pronouns

me	nos
te	os
le	les

present perfect
haber + past participle

he estudiado	hemos estudiado
has estudiado	habéis estudiado
ha estudiado	han estudiado

past participles

hablar → hablado
comer → comido
vivir → vivido

irregular past participles

decir: dicho
devolver: devuelto
escribir: escrito
hacer: hecho
morir: muerto
poner: puesto
romper: roto
ver: visto
volver: vuelto

For *Vocabulario adicional*, see pp. 498–499.

Differentiated Instruction
Solutions for All Learners

Advanced Learners

Have students create true and false sentences based on movies they have seen. For example: *En la película* El hombre araña, *el galán mató a los extraterrestres.* Collect their sentences and put them on a transparency. Have the entire class read them, say whether they are true or false, and correct false statements.

Students with Special Needs

To reinforce vocabulary, pair advanced learners with visually impaired students. Using the vocabulary list on p. 342, have the advanced learners give clues for each word. For example, students can say a word's definition or its opposite. Have the visually impaired student guess the vocabulary word or phrase and use it in a sentence.

Preparación para el examen

Más práctica
- Practice Workbook: Puzzle, p. 129
- Practice Workbook: Organizer, p. 130

Go Online PHSchool.com
For: Test Preparation
Web Code: jdd-0617

On the exam you will be asked to . . .	Here are practice tasks similar to those you will find on the exam . . .	If you need review . . .
1 Escuchar Listen and understand as people talk about a movie they have seen	Listen as you hear a film critic interview people as they leave the movie *Mil secretos.* What did they think of: (a) the actors; (b) the director; (c) the special effects; (d) the theme; and (e) future award possibilities.	**pp. 320–323** *A primera vista* **p. 325** Actividad 6 **p. 332** Actividad 18
2 Hablar Talk about a recent film you have seen at the movies or at home	You discover that you and an exchange student from Spain share a love of movies. What could you say about a recent movie that you saw? Practice the conversation with a classmate and include: (a) the type of film it was; (b) what the movie was about; (c) who the principal actors were; and (d) why you liked or disliked the movie.	**p. 324** Actividad 4 **p. 325** Actividad 7 **p. 326** Actividad 8 **p. 329** Actividades 12–13 **p. 332** Actividad 19
3 Leer Read and understand a movie review	Read this review by a popular Spanish movie critic. Do you think he likes the movie? Why or why not? *Esta película, "Nuestra familia", nos cuenta la historia de una "familia" de criminales violentos. ¡Es un producto de Hollywood y nosotros somos las víctimas! Sin duda, la película ha capturado la sociedad mala que nos fascina. Está basada en una familia de la vida real y se trata de la vida diaria de ellos. El actor Ramón Robles hace el papel del galán. Él es un hombre físicamente atractivo y talentoso y sólo su participación vale el precio de la entrada. La película tiene una clasificación de prohibida para menores. ¡Debe ser prohibida para TODOS!*	**p. 324** Actividad 5 **p. 328** Actividad 11 **p. 330** Actividad 16 **pp. 336–337** *Lectura*
4 Escribir Write about a movie that you would like to produce	While searching the Internet for movie reviews in Spanish, you come upon a survey that you decide to answer. You are asked to write a few sentences about: (a) movies that you have seen within the past month; (b) whether or not you liked them; and (c) what the critics have said about these movies.	**p. 326** Actividad 8 **p. 327** Actividades 9–10 **p. 329** Actividades 12–14 **p. 334** Actividad 22 **p. 339** *Presentación escrita*
5 Pensar Demonstrate an understanding of how movies can reflect the language and culture of the country where they are produced	Your Spanish teacher assigns a Mexican movie to the class as homework. When you rent the movie at your local video store and bring it home, your family wants to know why it is subtitled or dubbed. How could you explain the process to them? What do you think they would be surprised to learn?	**p. 338** *Perspectivas del mundo hispano*

trescientos cuarenta y tres 343
Capítulo 6B

jdd-0699

Review

Performance Tasks — Presentation EXPRESS ANSWERS

Standards: 1.1, 1.2, 1.3, 2.2, 4.2

Student Resource: Realidades para hispanohablantes, p. 249

Teacher Resources: Teacher's Resource Book: Audio Script, p. 92; Audio Program: Track 14; Answers on Transparencies

1. Escuchar

Suggestions: Tell students that they will hear interviews with a man and a woman. Ask students to predict who might like the movie more based on its title.

Script:

EL CRÍTICO: Buenas tardes, señorita. ¿Qué piensa de Mil secretos?

LA MUJER: Me fascina el argumento de la película—el de una chica que se enamora de un criminal. Marco Antonio hace el papel del galán. La escena con ella y Marco en el restaurante fue fantástica.

EL CRÍTICO: Gracias. ¿Y Ud., señor? ¿Qué piensa?

EL HOMBRE: Fue un fracaso. No va a tener mucho éxito. El director fue horrible. ¡Nunca he visto efectos especiales tan malos! ¡Yo busqué la salida a los diez minutos!

Answers:
a) The woman liked the actors.
b) The man thinks the director was horrible.
c) The man found the special effects to be the worst he had ever seen.
d) The woman loved the theme.
e) According to the man, it was a failure.

2. Hablar

Suggestions: Encourage students to refer to summaries of movies that they did in this chapter to use as models.

Answers will vary.

3. Leer

Suggestions: Have students point out words that indicate the critic's opinion.

Answers:
The critic doesn't like the movie. He says it should be prohibited.

4. Escribir

Suggestions: Prepare the questions in the format of a questionnaire.

Answers will vary.

5. Pensar

Suggestions: For information on foreign films, refer students to p. 338.

Answers will vary.

Assessment
- ExamView QuickTake Presenter Quiz on PresEXPRESS
- Assessment Program: Examen del capítulo
- ExamView Test Bank: Tests A and B
- Audio Program CD 21: Chap. 6B, Track 4

Differentiated Assessment
Solutions for All Learners

STUDENTS NEEDING EXTRA HELP
- **Alternate Assessment Program:** Examen del capítulo 6B
- **Audio Program CD 21:** Chap. 6B, Track 4

HERITAGE LEARNERS
- **Assessment Program: Realidades para hispanohablantes:** Examen del capítulo 6B
- **ExamView** Heritage Learner Test Bank

ADVANCED/PRE-AP*
- **ExamView** Pre-AP* Test Bank
- **Pre-AP* Resource Book,** pp. 116–119

Buen provecho

THEME OVERVIEW

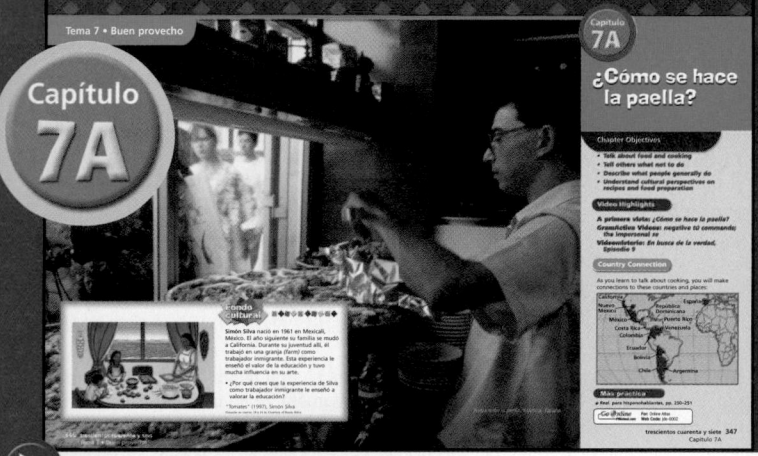

7A ¿Cómo se hace la paella?

• Food and cooking

Vocabulary: food and cooking; following recipes; giving instructions in the kitchen

Grammar: negative *tú* commands; the impersonal *se*

Cultural Perspectives: recipes and food preparation

7B ¿Te gusta comer al aire libre?

• Food and outdoor cooking

Vocabulary: food and outdoor cooking; outdoor activities

Grammar: *Usted* and *ustedes* commands; uses of *por*

Cultural Perspectives: special foods and outdoor food vendors

Theme Project

Una comida especial

Overview: Students plan a menu for a special meal. They should include ingredients for an appetizer, a salad, a main dish, and a dessert, at least one of which needs to be from a Spanish-speaking country. Students will present their menus to the class.

Materials: Poster board, markers, photos, glue or tape, scissors

· ·

Sequence: (suggestions for when to do each step are found throughout the chapters)

STEP 1. Review instructions so students know what is expected of them. Hand out the "Theme 7 Project Instructions and Rubric" from the *Teacher's Resource Book.*

STEP 2. Students submit a rough draft of their proposed menus. Return the drafts with your suggestions. For grammar and vocabulary practice, ask students to partner and present their drafts to each other.

STEP 3. Students create layouts of their menus on poster board, leaving room for photos or drawings. Encourage them to work in pencil first and to try different arrangements before gluing photos or drawing in marker.

STEP 4. Students submit a draft of the menu. Note your corrections and suggestions, then return them to students.

STEP 5. Students present their special meal to the class.

Options: Students research and present traditional Hispanic dishes.

Assessment:

Here is a detailed rubric for assessing this project:

Theme 7 Project: *Una comida especial*

RUBRIC	Score 1	Score 3	Score 5
Your evidence of planning	You provide no written draft or sketch.	Your draft was written and layout created, but not corrected.	You show evidence of corrected draft and layout.
Your use of illustrations	You include no photos or visuals.	You include very few photos or visuals.	You include several photos or visuals.
Your presentation	You include little of the required information.	You include a partial list of courses and their ingredients.	You include a complete list of courses and their ingredients.

Theme Support

Bulletin Boards

Theme: *La comida*

Ask students to cut out, copy, or download photos of foods and meals from different Hispanic cultures. Cluster photos into categories—desserts, breakfast foods, fruits, vegetables etc.—so that similarities and differences are evident.

Bibliography

Downs, Cynthia, and Terry Becker. *Bienvenidos: A Monthly Bilingual/Bicultural Teacher's Resource Guide to Mexico & Hispanic Culture.* McGraw-Hill Children's Publishing, 1991.

Lomas Garza, Carmen. *En mi familia/In My Family.* Children's Book Press, 1996.

Parnell, Helga. *Cooking the South American Way: Revised and Expanded to Include New Low-Fat and Vegetarian Recipes.* Minneapolis: Lerner Publications, 2002.

Step-by-Step Cooking Series. *Spanish Cooking.* Murdoch Books, 1993.

Hands-on Culture

Recipe: *Churros*

Churros, a pastry similar to a donut, originated in Spain. In Sevilla, people often go to cafés in the early morning hours during the week of the *Feria de abril* (the week following *Semana Santa*) to eat *churros y chocolate,* or *churros* dipped in hot chocolate.

Ingredients:

1 cup water
$\frac{1}{2}$ cup butter
1 cup flour
dash salt
3 or 4 eggs
oil for frying
powdered sugar or
cinnamon sugar

Directions:

(Tell students to seek adult supervision when frying the *churros.*)

1. Boil water and add butter.

2. As soon as the butter melts, add the flour and salt. Stir until the mixture forms a single mass. Remove from heat and let cool slightly.

3. Beat in the eggs one at a time.

4. Put dough into a pastry bag and squeeze 6-inch strips into hot oil.

5. Fry until golden brown. Sprinkle with powdered sugar or cinnamon sugar. Enjoy!

Internet Search

Use the keywords to find more information.

7A Keywords:

Simón Silva, arepa, plátano, paella, Pablo Neruda, poetas hispanos, comida mexicana

7B Keywords:

Carmen Lomas Garza, parrillada mixta, El Parque de la Familia, San Salvador, El Yunque, coquí

Game

Categorías

Play this game to review food vocabulary.

Players: The entire class

Materials: Paper, pens

Rules:

1. Arrange students' desks in five rows. Ask students to clear their desks. Give the first student in each row a sheet of paper and a pen.

2. Call out one of the following categories: ***desayuno, almuerzo, cena, bebida, al aire libre.*** Tell students that they have one minute to write as many words from the category as they can on their row's piece of paper.

3. After you say ***empiecen,*** the first student in each row writes a word, then passes the paper and pen to the next student. That student writes another word, then passes it to the third student, and so on until the paper reaches the end of the row. The last student brings the paper to the first student, and the relay begins again until you call time.

4. Rows exchange papers for correction. The team with the most correctly spelled words wins a point.

5. Continue playing until all categories have been completed. If there is a tie at the end, have students define each word on their list. The winner is the first row to define all of the words correctly.

Variation: Have a relay spelling bee. Call out a vocabulary word or expression and have each student in a row write one letter at a time.

♻ RECYCLE	Vocabulary	Grammar
A ver si recuerdas	• La comida	• Verbs with irregular *yo* forms

A primera vista	Manos a la obra	¡Adelante!	Repaso
Learning Sequence			
INPUT	**PRACTICE**	**APPLICATION**	**REVIEW**
• Introduce vocabulary and grammar within an authentic context.	• Practice and develop new vocabulary. • Learn and practice new grammar structures.	• Apply vocabulary and grammar through culminating, theme-based activities. • Apply skill development.	• Review vocabulary and grammar.
Objectives			
Read, listen to, and interpret information about: • Cooking expressions • Foods and appliances • Following a recipe • Giving directions in the kitchen	• Communicate about food and cooking. • Give and receive instructions for making a recipe. • Write rules to promote safety in the kitchen. • Use negative *tú* commands. • Use the impersonal *se*.	• Read poems about two common foods. • Discuss regional foods. • Exchange information about tropical fruits. • Describe how to prepare your favorite dish. • Watch *En busca de la verdad, Episodio* 9.	• Prepare for the chapter test.
Culture			
• Simón Silva	• *La paella* • *El plátano* • *La arepa*	• *¡Tortillas y tacos!*	• Explain the significance of tortillas in Spanish-speaking cultures. • Making tacos

Vocabulary	Grammar	Learner Support		
• The kitchen • Recipes • Cooking	• Negative *tú* commands • The impersonal *se*	**STRATEGIES** • Using prior experience • Reading and rereading • Using background knowledge	**RECYCLING** ♻ • Regular affirmative *tú* commands • Cooking terms and utensils • Food • Direct object pronouns	• Use of pronouns with commands • *Se prohíbe* • Vocabulary related to school

Chapter Features

Conexiones

Science: Table of minerals and the foods that contain them

Pronunciación

Dividing words into syllables

El español en la comunidad

Advertisements and advertising in Spanish

Beyond the Classroom: States & Countries

California
Nuevo México
México
Costa Rica
Colombia
Ecuador
Bolivia
Chile
Argentina
España
República Dominicana
Puerto Rico
Venezuela

Student Resources

TECHNOLOGY

ONLINE

Interactive Textbook
• Student Edition Online plus audio, video, and flashcards

Go Online Companion Web Site
• Tutorial activities
• Internet links
• Self-tests
• Downloadable MP3 audio files
PuzzleView

CD-ROM

Interactive Textbook CD-ROM
Student Edition on CD-ROM plus audio, video, and flashcards

MindPoint™ CD-ROM
QUIZ SHOW

PRINT MATERIAL

CORE INSTRUCTION

Practice Workbook, pp.131–141
• Review
• Vocabulary
• Grammar
• Puzzle
• Organizer

Writing, Audio & Video Activities, pp. 126–135
• Video
• Audio
• Writing

Grammar Study Guide 1–2 (or 3–4)

Differentiated Instruction

STUDENTS NEEDING EXTRA HELP

Guided Practice Activities, pp. 235–254
• Vocabulary Flash Cards and Vocabulary Check
• Grammar Activities
• Presentación oral

HERITAGE LEARNERS

Realidades para hispanohablantes, pp. 250–269

Lecturas para hispanohablantes
• "Obatalá y Oruda," pp. 19–20
• "Frutos del paraíso," pp. 25–26

ADVANCED/PRE-AP*

Pre-AP* Resource Book: Student Activity Sheet, p. 123

Teacher Resources

TECHNOLOGY

Audio Program
Video Program

Fine Art Transparencies
Vocabulary and Grammar Transparencies
Answers on Transparencies

TeacherEXPRESS CD-ROM
• Lesson Planner
• Vocabulary Clip Art
• Web Resources
• Teaching Resources
• Teacher Edition with Interactive Links

PresentationEXPRESS CD-ROM
• Vocabulary
• Transparencies and Maps
• Grammar
• Photo Gallery
• Audio
• Clip Art

PRINT MATERIAL

CORE INSTRUCTION

Teacher's Resource Book, pp. 116–141
• Input Script
• Video Script
• Answer Keys
• GramActiva Blackline Masters
• Vocabulary Clip Art
• Chapter Resource Checklist
• School-to-Home Connection Letters
• Communicative Activities Blackline Masters

TPR Stories, pp. 92–97

Differentiated Instruction

STUDENTS NEEDING EXTRA HELP

Guided Practice Activities Teacher's Guide, pp. T118–T127

HERITAGE LEARNERS

Realidades para hispanohablantes Teacher's Guide, pp. 126–135

Lecturas para hispanohablantes Teacher's Guide, pp. 5–8

ADVANCED/PRE-AP*

Pre-AP* Resource Book: Resource Chart, p. 120

Differentiated Assessment

PH SuccessNet ONLINE
• Access to grades and reports from Online Interactive Textbook

ExamView on Presentation Express CD-ROM
QuickTake Presenter
• Vocabulary Quizzes
• Chapter Test
• Grammar Quizzes

TeacherEXPRESS CD-ROM
• Assessment Program
• **ExamView** Test Banks A and B
test generator

Go Online
PHSchool.com
For: Teacher Home Page
Web Code: jdk-1001

CORE ASSESSMENT

Assessment Program, pp. 177–189
• Pruebas
  Vocabulary Recognition
  Vocabulary Production
  Negative *tú* commands
  The impersonal *se*
• Examen del capítulo
• Speaking and Writing Rubrics

Teacher's Resource Book, p. 130
• Situation Cards

TPR Stories, pp. 92–97

STUDENTS NEEDING EXTRA HELP

Alternate Assessment Program
• Examen del capítulo, pp. 77–82

HERITAGE LEARNERS

Assessment Program: Realidades para hispanohablantes Teacher's Guide, pp. T148–T152

ExamView Heritage Learner Test Bank
test generator

ADVANCED/PRE-AP*

Pre-AP* Resource Book: Teacher Activity Sheet, p. 122

ExamView Pre-AP* Test Bank
test generator

Regular Schedule (50 Minutes)

For electronic lesson plans:
Teacher Express 💿

	Warm-up / Assess	Preview Present /	Practice Communicate	Wrap-up / Homework Options
DAY 1	**Warm-up (5 min.)** • Homework check • Return Examen del capítulo 6B	**A ver si recuerdas . . . (20 min.)** • Presentation: La comida • Actividad 1 • Presentation: Verbs with irregular *yo* forms • Actividades 2, 3	**Chapter Opener (5 min.)** • Objectives • Fondo cultural **A primera vista (15 min.)** • Presentation: Vocabulario y gramática en contexto • Actividades 1, 2	**Wrap-up and Homework Options (5 min.)** • Practice Workbook 7A-A, 7A-B, 7A-1, 7A-2 • Go Online
DAY 2	**Warm-up (10 min.)** • Homework check	**A primera vista (35 min.)** • Presentation: Videohistoria *¿Cómo se hace la paella?* • View: Videohistoria	• Video Activities 1, 2, 3, 4 • Actividad 3	**Wrap-up and Homework Options (5 min.)** • Practice Workbook 7A-3, 7A-4 • Go Online • Prueba 7A-1: Vocabulary recognition
DAY 3	**Warm-up (10 min.)** • Actividad 6 • Homework check ✔**Assessment (10 min.)** • Prueba 7A-1: Vocabulary recognition	**Manos a la obra (25 min.)** • Actividades 4, 5, 7, 8, 9 • Fondos culturales		**Wrap-up and Homework Options (5 min.)** • Actividades 10, 11 • Writing Activity 10 • Heritage Learner Workbook 7A-1, 7A-2 • Prueba 7A-2: Vocabulary production
DAY 4	**Warm-up (10 min.)** • Actividad 10 • Homework check ✔**Assessment (10 min.)** (after Communicative Activity) • Prueba 7A-2: Vocabulary production	**Manos a la obra (25 min.)** • Audio Activities 5, 6 • Communicative Activity • Presentation: Negative *tú* commands	• View: GramActiva video • Actividad 12	**Wrap-up and Homework Options (5 min.)** • Practice Workbook 7A-5 • Actividad 13 • Writing Activity 11 • Go Online
DAY 5	**Warm-up (10 min.)** • Actividad 14 • Homework check	**Manos a la obra (35 min.)** • Actividades 15, 16 • Fondo cultural • Pronunciación • Audio Activity 7	• Presentation: The impersonal *se* • View: GramActiva video • Actividad 17	**Wrap-up and Homework Options (5 min.)** • Practice Workbook 7A-6 • Actividades 16, 21 • Go Online • Prueba 7A-3: Negative *tú* commands
DAY 6	**Warm-up (5 min.)** • Homework check ✔**Assessment (10 min.)** • Prueba 7A-3: Negative *tú* commands	**Manos a la obra (30 min.)** • Actividades 18, 20, 22, 23 • Audio Activity 8 • El español en la comunidad		**Wrap-up and Homework Options (5 min.)** • Practice Workbook 7A-7 • Prueba 7A-4: The • Writing Activity 12 impersonal *se* • Go Online • Heritage Learner Workbook 7A-4
DAY 7	**Warm-up (10 min.)** • Actividad 20 • Homework check ✔**Assessment (10 min.)** • Prueba 7A-4: The impersonal *se*	**¡Adelante! (10 min.)** • Presentación oral: Steps 1, 4 **Repaso del capítulo (15 min.)** • Vocabulario y gramática • Preparación para el examen 1, 2		**Wrap-up and Homework Options (5 min.)** • Presentación oral: Step 2
DAY 8	**Warm-up (5 min.)** • Presentación oral: Step 2	**¡Adelante! (40 min.)** • Presentación oral: Step 3 • La cultura en vivo		**Wrap-up and Homework Options (5 min.)** • Preparación para el examen 3, 4, 5 • Go Online: Self-test • La cultura en vivo
DAY 9	**Warm-up (5 min.)** • Homework check	**¡Adelante! (40 min.)** • Lectura • ¿Comprendiste? / Y tú, ¿qué dices? • Videomisterio: *En busca de la verdad*, Episodio 9		**Wrap-up and Homework Options (5 min.)** • Practice Workbook 7A-8, 7A-9 • Go Online: Lectura • Examen del capítulo 7A
DAY 10	**Warm-up (5 min.)** • Homework check ✔**Assessment (40 min.)** • Examen del capítulo 7A			**Wrap-up and Homework Options (5 min.)** • Go Online: Videomisterio

Warm-up / Assess	Preview Present / Practice Communicate		Wrap-up / Homework Options
DAY 1 **Warm-up (5 min.)** • Homework check • Return Examen del capítulo: Capítulo 6B	**A ver si recuerdas . . . (25 min.)** • Presentation: La comida • Actividad 1 • Presentation: Verbs with irregular *yo* forms • Actividades 2, 3 **Chapter Opener (5 min.)** • Objectives • Fondo cultural	**A primera vista (50 min.)** • Presentation: Vocabulario y gramática en contexto • Actividades 1, 2 • Presentation: Videohistoria: *¿Cómo se hace la paella?* • View: Videohistoria • Video Activities 1, 2, 3, 4 • Actividad 3	**Wrap-up and Homework Options (5 min.)** • Practice Workbook 7A-A, 7A-B, 7A-1, 7A-2, 7A-3, 7A-4 • Go Online • Prueba 7A-1: Vocabulary recognition
DAY 2 **Warm-up (10 min.)** • Actividad 6 • Homework check ✔**Assessment (10 min.)** • Prueba 7A-1: Vocabulary recognition	**Manos a la obra (65 min.)** • Actividades 4, 5, 7, 8, 9 • Fondos culturales • Audio Activities 5, 6 • Communicative Activity • Presentation: Negative *tú* commands • View: GramActiva video • Actividades 12, 13		**Wrap-up and Homework Options (5 min.)** • Practice Workbook 7A-5 • Actividad 10, 11 • Go Online • Heritage Learner Workbook 7A-1, 7A-2 • Prueba 7A-2: Vocabulary production
DAY 3 **Warm-up (10 min.)** • Writing Activity 10 • Homework check ✔**Assessment (10 min.)** • Prueba 7A-2: Vocabulary production	**Manos a la obra (65 min.)** • Actividades 14, 15, 16 • Fondo cultural • Pronunciación • Audio Activity 7 • Writing Activity 11 • Presentation: The impersonal *se* • View: GramActiva video • Actividades 17, 18, 19 • Audio Activity 8		**Wrap-up and Homework Options (5 min.)** • Practice Workbook 7A-6 • Go Online • Heritage Learner Workbook 7A-4 • Pruebas 7A-3: Negative *tú* commands
DAY 4 **Warm-up (5 min.)** • Homework check ✔**Assessment (10 min.)** • Pruebas 7A-3: Negative *tú* commands	**Manos a la obra (35 min.)** • Actividades 20, 21, 22, 23 • El español en la comunidad • Writing Activity 12 **¡Adelante! (35 min.)** • Lectura • ¿Comprendiste? / Y tú, ¿qué dices? • Presentación oral: Steps 1, 4		**Wrap-up and Homework Options (5 min.)** • Practice Workbook 7A-7 • Presentación oral: Step 2 • Go Online: The impersonal *se*; Lectura • Prueba 7A-4: The impersonal *se*
DAY 5 **Warm-up (5 min.)** • Homework check ✔**Assessment (10 min.)** • Prueba 7A-4: The impersonal *se*	**¡Adelante! (40 min.)** • Presentación oral: Step 3 • La cultura en vivo **Repaso del capítulo (30 min.)** • Vocabulario y gramática • Preparación para el examen 1, 2, 3, 4, 5		**Wrap-up and Homework Options (5 min.)** • Practice Workbook 7A-8, 7A-9 • Go Online: Self-test • Examen del capítulo 7A
DAY 6 **Warm-up (5 min.)** • Homework check **Repaso del capítulo (20 min.)** • Situation Cards ✔**Assessment (40 min.)** • Examen del capítulo 7A	**¡Adelante! (20 min.)** • Videomisterio: *En busca de la verdad*, Episodio 9		**Wrap-up and Homework Options (5 min.)** • Go Online: Videomisterio • La cultura en vivo

7A Recycle

Note: Starting with *Tema 4*, the *A ver si recuerdas...* feature appears only at the beginning of each theme.

Vocabulario

Core Instruction

Resources: Voc. and Gram. Transparency 123

Focus: Reviewing vocabulary related to food and meals

Suggestions: Provide a blank Food Guide Pyramid for each student. Have them sort the foods named under **comida** and **bebidas** according to the categories on the pyramid. Ask students to name foods that are **bueno para la salud** and **malo para la salud.**

Standards: 1.1

Resources: Answers on Transparencies

Focus: Writing and speaking about healthy eating habits

Suggestions: Encourage students to further discuss healthy eating habits. Explain that the U.S. Department of Agriculture has developed guidelines for a healthy diet. Spanish-language versions *(Guía Pirámide de alimentos)* available on the Internet show suggested servings per day of each food group. Provide this information for students to use as they evaluate their diets.

Answers will vary.

Extension: Have students create meal plans in Spanish for several days that comply with U.S.D.A. recommendations.

A ver si recuerdas...
Vocabulario **La comida**

hablando de las comidas y la salud

el almuerzo
bueno / malo para
  la salud
la cena
las comidas
el desayuno
mantener la salud
rico, -a
sabroso, -a

la comida

el arroz	las judías	el plátano
el bistec	verdes	el pollo
la cebolla	la lechuga	las salchichas
el cereal	la mantequilla	la sopa
la ensalada	la manzana	el tocino
los espaguetis	la naranja	los tomates
las fresas	el pan	las uvas
las frutas	el pan tostado	las verduras
los guisantes	las papas fritas	el yogur
los huevos	el pescado	las zanahorias

las bebidas

el agua *f.*
el café
el jugo
la leche
el té
el té helado

Práctica de vocabulario • Usando el organizador gráfico

Escribir/Hablar

¿Cómo comes?

Comer bien para mantener la salud puede ser difícil. ¿Comes tú bien?

1 Piensa en lo que comes en un día típico en el desayuno, en el almuerzo y en la cena. Usa una tabla como ésta para organizar tus ideas.

el desayuno	el almuerzo	la cena
huevos	arroz con pollo	bistec

2 Ahora compara tu tabla con la de otro(a) estudiante. ¿Comen cosas similares? ¿Pueden comer mejor para mantener la salud? Discútelo con tu compañero(a) y escribe unas frases sobre lo que comen y cómo pueden comer mejor.

Modelo

Normalmente en el desayuno como huevos, tocino y salchichas. Carla come cereal y fruta con yogur. Yo debo comer mejor. Por ejemplo, no debo comer salchichas con huevos, pero sí puedo comer fresas o una manzana.

344 trescientos cuarenta y cuatro
Tema 7 • Buen provecho

Differentiated Instruction
Solutions for All Learners

Advanced Learners
Have students name the food guide categories in Spanish: *el pan, el arroz y la pasta; verduras; frutas; productos de leche; carnes, pescado y huevos; grasas* (fats). Have them keep a food journal for one week, after which they will work in pairs to evaluate how healthy their diet was that week.

Students with Special Needs
Modify *Actividad 3* for hearing-impaired students. Pair students, having each student write three true sentences and one false one. Then, rather than having students read their statements aloud, have them exchange papers and guess which of their partner's statements is false.

Gramática · Repaso

Verbs with irregular *yo* forms

Remember that some verbs are irregular in the *yo* form in the present tense.

Verbs with irregular *-go* forms			
caer:	caigo	poner:	pongo
decir:	digo	salir:	salgo
hacer:	hago	tener:	tengo
oír:	oigo	venir:	vengo

Verbs with irregular *-zco* forms	
conocer:	conozco
obedecer:	obedezco
ofrecer:	ofrezco
parecer:	parezco

Práctica de gramática

 Actividad **2** Escribir

¿De acuerdo o no?

Lee las siguientes frases y decide si estás de acuerdo o no. Si no estás de acuerdo, explica por qué.

Modelo

Cuando saludas a una persona que no conoces, le dices: ¿Cómo estás tú?
No estoy de acuerdo. Le digo: ¿Cómo está Ud.?

1. Normalmente haces ejercicio a las seis de la mañana.
2. Nunca obedeces a tus padres.
3. Tienes tarea todas las noches.
4. No conoces a muchas personas de tu escuela.
5. Los sábados sales con tus amigos.
6. Cuando uno de tus amigos no tiene el almuerzo, le ofreces parte de tu almuerzo.
7. Eres muy ordenado(a). Siempre pones tus cosas en su lugar.

 Actividad **3**   Escribir/Hablar

No te creo . . .

1 Escribe cuatro frases usando los verbos con formas irregulares de *-go* y *-zco*. Tres de tus frases deben ser ciertas y una debe ser falsa.

2 Ahora trabaja con un grupo de cuatro estudiantes y lee tus frases al grupo. Los otros tienen que adivinar cuál de tus frases es falsa.

Modelo

A —*Yo siempre salgo de la escuela a las diez de la noche.*
B —*¡No te creo! ¡Nunca sales de la escuela a las diez de la noche!*

Más práctica

- Practice Workbook, pp. 131–132: 7A-A, 7A-B
- Guided Practice Activities, pp. 235–236
- *Real.* para hispanohablantes, p. 250

Go Online PHSchool.com
For: Vocab. and Grammar
Web Code: jdd-0701

trescientos cuarenta y cinco **345**
Preparación: Vocabulario y gramática

Gramática · Repaso  GRAMMAR

Core Instruction

Resources: Answers on Transparencies
Suggestions: Ask volunteers to use each verb in a sentence.

 Actividad **2**  *Standards:* 1.2  ANSWERS

Resources: Answers on Transparencies
Focus: Writing to show agreement or disagreement with a statement
Suggestions: Remind students to respond using the *yo* form of the verbs.
Answers will vary but will include:
1. hago
2. obedezco
3. tengo
4. conozco
5. salgo
6. ofrezco
7. pongo

 Actividad **3** *Standards:* 1.1

Focus: Writing and reading aloud true and false statements
Suggestions: To help students generate ideas, suggest that they think about things they do every day, things they never do, and things they do once in a while (**de vez en cuando**).
Answers will vary.

Enrich Your Teaching
Resources for All Teachers

Culture Note
Both Europe and the Americas benefited from the exchange of produce between the continents. Europe received corn, beans, squash, potatoes, turkeys, and chocolate. The Americas were introduced to chicken, beef, milk, sugar, and wheat.

Teacher-to-Teacher
Have students promote healthy eating along with the Spanish language at school by creating a list of tips in Spanish. Suggestions can include which foods should be eaten daily as well as foods to limit or avoid. Tips can be made into one or many posters, illustrated, and displayed in health classes or the school cafeteria.

7A Preview

Standards for Capítulo 7A

• To achieve the goals of the Standards, students will:

Communication

1.1 Interpersonal
• Talk about: meals, food, and cooking; traditional dishes; recipes; school policies; nutrition; a restaurant advertisement

1.2 Interpretive
• Read and listen to information about: meals, food, and cooking; *paella;* kitchen items and appliances; traditional dishes; *plátanos;* neatness and kitchen rules; *arepa;* nutrition; Spanish-language signs
• Read: a picture-based story; recipes; an ode to *papas fritas;* a restaurant advertisement
• Listen to and watch a video about *paella*

1.3 Presentational
• Write about: meals, food, and cooking; kitchen rules; school policies; nutrition
• Present information about: a story plot; traditional dishes; restaurant dining
• Create a restaurant advertisement
• Explain in the style of a cooking show how to make a favorite dish

Culture

2.1 Practices and Perspectives
• Read about the impact of migrant farm work as a youth on artist Simón Silva

2.2 Products and Perspectives
• Describe: Simón Silva and his art; Pablo Neruda and his poetry; *paella;* traditional dishes of Spanish-speaking countries; *plátanos; arepa; papas fritas*

Connections

3.1 Cross-curricular
• Talk about: nutrition; artist Simon Silva and his work; Pablo Neruda and his poetry

3.2 Target Culture
• Read two poems by Pablo Neruda
• View a video mystery series

Comparisons

4.1 Language
• Use the impersonal *se*

4.2 Culture
• Compare traditional dishes and foods

Communities

5.1 Beyond the School
• Identify local Spanish-language signs in restaurants and retail shops

5.2 Lifelong Learner
• View a video mystery series

Tema 7 • Buen provecho

Fondo cultural ■◆■◇■◆■◇■◆

Simón Silva nació en 1961 en Mexicali, México. El año siguiente su familia se mudó a California. Durante su juventud allí, él trabajó en una granja *(farm)* como trabajador inmigrante. Esta experiencia le enseñó el valor de la educación y tuvo mucha influencia en su arte.

• ¿Por qué crees que la experiencia de Silva como trabajador inmigrante le enseñó a valorar la educación?

"Tomates" (1997), Simón Silva
Gouache on canvas, 18 x 24 in. Courtesy of Simón Silva.

Differentiated Instruction

STUDENTS NEEDING EXTRA HELP

Guided Practice Activities
• Vocabulary Check, Flash Cards
• Grammar
• Reading and Speaking Support

Guided Practice Audio CDs
• Disc 2, Track 5

HERITAGE LEARNERS

Realidades para hispanohablantes
• Chapter Opener, pp. 250–251
• A primera vista, p. 252
• Videohistoria, p. 253
• Manos a la obra, pp. 254–261
• ¡Adelante!, pp. 262–267
• Repaso del capítulo, pp. 268–269

ADVANCED/PRE-AP*

Pre-AP* Resource Book,
pp. 120–123

Capítulo 7A

¿Cómo se hace la paella?

Chapter Objectives

- Talk about food and cooking
- Tell others what not to do
- Describe what people generally do
- Understand cultural perspectives on recipes and food preparation

Video Highlights

A primera vista: *¿Cómo se hace la paella?*
GramActiva Videos: negative *tú* commands; the impersonal *se*
Videomisterio: *En busca de la verdad,* Episodio 9

Country Connection

As you learn to talk about cooking, you will make connections to these countries and places:

California
Nuevo México
México
Costa Rica
Colombia
Ecuador
Bolivia
Chile
España
República Dominicana
Puerto Rico
Venezuela
Argentina

Más práctica

- *Real. para hispanohablantes,* pp. 250–251

Go Online
PHSchool.com
For: Online Atlas
Web Code: jde-0002

trescientos cuarenta y siete **347**
Capítulo 7A

Preparando la paella, Valencia, España

Chapter Opener
Presentation EXPRESS
ATLAS

Core Instruction

Resources: Voc. and Gram. Transparencies: Maps 12–18, 20

Suggestions: Have students discuss the foods from Spanish-speaking countries that are available in your community. Make a class list on the board. As homework, you may wish to ask students to go to a market to find more examples of foods from Spain and the Americas to add to the list. In the *Videohistoria*, students will learn how to make *paella.* They will see a variety of recipes throughout the chapter. They will also use the impersonal *se* and negative *tú* commands that will help them describe how to make favorite meals.

Fondo cultural  *Standards:* 1.2, 2.1, 2.2

Resources: Fine Art Transparencies with Teacher's Guide, p. 62

Suggestions: Remind students that *el tomate* originated in the Americas. Its name is derived from *náhuatl,* an ancient language spoken by the Aztecs in Central Mexico. Words derived from *náhuatl* are distinguished by their *-te* (formerly *-tl*) ending. Can students think of other foods with *-te* endings? *(chocolate, aguacate, cacahuate)* Students will read an ode to the tomato on p. 364.

Answers will vary.

Teaching with Art

 Standards: 1.2, 2.1, 2.2

Resources: Fine Art Transparencies with Teacher's Guide, p. 62

Suggestions: What clues can students find about Mexican culture in the painting? Point out that the mortar and pestle here is used for grinding the garlic and peppers that are hanging on the wall for easy access. Ask: *¿Qué están preparando?*

TeacherEXPRESS
Plan · Teach · Assess

PresentationEXPRESS
Dynamic Presentations for Teachers

PLAN	TEACH	ASSESS
Lesson Planner	Teaching Resources	Chapter Quizzes and Tests
	Interactive Teacher's Edition	
	Vocabulary Clip Art	

Go Online
PHSchool.com
For: Teacher Home Page
Web Code: jdk-1001

TEACH
Vocabulary & Grammar Powerpoints
GramActiva Video
Audio & Clip Art Activities
Transparencies and Maps
Activity Answers
Photo Gallery

ASSESS
ExamView
QuickTake Presenter

347

Vocabulario y gramática

Presentation EXPRESS
VOCABULARY

Core Instruction

 Standards: 1.2

Resources: Teacher's Resource Book: Input Script, p. 118, Clip Art, pp. 132–135, Audio Script, p. 119; Voc. and Gram. Transparencies 125–126; TPR Stories Book, pp. 91–103; Audio Program: Tracks 1–2

Focus: Presenting vocabulary for cooking, foods, and appliances

Suggestions: Use the Input Script from the *Teacher's Resource* Book or the story from the *TPR Stories Book* to present the new vocabulary, or use one of these suggestions.

Have students brainstorm a list of their favorite dishes. Ask students what ingredients are needed to make the dishes. Have them think of verbs they would find in a recipe: *add, chop, peel, mix, beat.*

Present the vocabulary in three groups: cooking expressions, foods, and appliances.

Gather recipe card pictures or photos of different dishes and their preparation from magazines. Using the new vocabulary, ask students yes / no questions about the pictures. Then ask where certain foods are stored or cooked: *¿Pongo la mantequilla en el horno? ¿Cocinas el tocino en la sartén?*

Write three column labels on the board: *enlatado, congelado, fresco.* As you name different foods, ask students in which column they should be placed. Then ask students to raise their hands if they agree with you on which foods taste better, using sentences such as: *Las frutas frescas son más sabrosas que las frutas congeladas.*

Bellringer Review

Have students copy these words for rooms of a house and write next to them two activities that they might do there:

sala   cocina   comedor

Additional Resources

• Audio Program: Canciones CD, Disc 22

348

A primera vista jdd-0787

Vocabulario y gramática en contexto

Objectives

Read, listen to, and understand information about
• cooking expressions
• foods and appliances
• following a recipe
• giving directions in the kitchen

enlatado, -a

congelado, -a

el refrigerador

el microondas

fresco, -a

el horno

el fregadero

probar

al horno

la estufa

la olla

calentar

batir   mezclar

la sartén

pelar   picar   el pedazo

el fuego

frito, -a

añadir   freír   hervir

348 trescientos cuarenta y ocho
Tema 7 • Buen provecho

Differentiated Instruction

Solutions for All Learners

Advanced Learners

Have students create an advertisement for a cooking show. They should include the name of the show, the dishes that will be made, and pictures with labels of ingredients and utensils that the viewers will need: *una olla para mezclar.* Post their ads in the classroom.

Heritage Language Learners

Have students choose one of their favorite dishes that is typical of their heritage country and write the recipe in Spanish. Over the course of the chapter, have them prepare a script and make a how-to video of their dish. Review the script with them, and have them present the video to the class, sharing the script with viewers.

—¿Qué vamos a preparar? —**Una receta** que aprendí de mi abuela que vivía en Valencia. Se llama arroz a banda. Es un arroz típico de la provincia de Alicante y ha sido el favorito de mi familia. Aquí está la lista de **los ingredientes** que necesitamos.

el caldo
el vinagre
el ajo
el aceite
la salsa
la cucharada

los camarones

los mariscos

Arroz a banda

Ingredientes (8 personas)

unos 3 litros
de caldo de pescado

100 gr de camarones

½ kg de sepia[1]

1 tomate grande bien cortado

1 cucharada de pimentón dulce[2]

1 kg de arroz

azafrán[3]

aceite de oliva

ajoaceite (una salsa de ajo y aceite)

[1]cuttlefish [2]paprika [3]saffron
(Saffron is an expensive spice used for its bright orange-yellow color, intense flavor, and aroma.)

Actividad 1 jdd-0787 Escuchar

La cocina típica

¿Qué hay en tu cocina? Escucha mientras Ignacio describe una cocina típica. Mira los dibujos y las fotos, y señala el objeto (o los objetos) que menciona.

Más práctica

- Practice Workbook, pp. 133–134: 7A-1, 7A-2
- WAV Wbk.: Writing, p. 132
- Guided Practice: Vocab. Flash Cards, pp. 237–242
- *Real.* para hispanohablantes, p. 252

Go Online
PHSchool.com
For: Vocab. Practice
Web Code: jdd-0702

Actividad 2 jdd-0787 Escuchar

¿Lógico o no?

¿Sabes cocinar? Levanta una mano si lo que oyes es lógico y levanta las dos manos si no es lógico.

trescientos cuarenta y nueve **349**
Capítulo 7A

Enrich Your Teaching
Resources for All Teachers

Culture Note

The Spanish town of Valencia is located on the Mediterranean Sea. Since it first became a town in 138 B.C., **los valencianos** have fished for their food. Bass, bream, squid, mussels, and prawns are still an important part of Valencia's cuisine.

Teacher-to-Teacher

Have small groups research foods and cooking techniques of one country. Is there a variety of ways to prepare foods that are in abundance? Have students write instructions in command form for making one dish. They should include a picture of the dish.

Actividad 1 *Standards:* 1.2 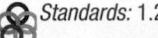 Presentation EXPRESS AUDIO

Resources: Teacher's Resource Book: Audio Script, p. 119; Audio Program: Track 3; Answers on Transparencies

Focus: Listening comprehension about items in the kitchen

Suggestions: If you prefer, use the transparency to check comprehension. As each item is read, point to any object. Have students give a "thumbs-up" sign if you have indicated the correct object, and a "thumbs-down" sign if you haven't.

 **Script and Answers:**

1. En la cocina hay comida enlatada. *(cans)*
2. Siempre hay aceite y vinagre. *(oil and vinegar)*
3. Debes lavar las verduras en el fregadero antes de cocinarlas. *(sink)*
4. Todas las cocinas tienen una sartén y una olla. *(frying pan and pot)*
5. Mucha gente no tiene un microondas. *(microwave)*
6. Muchas personas prefieren comer la comida fresca. *(fresh vegetables)*
7. Necesito una cucharada de sal. *(measuring spoons)*

Actividad 2 *Standards:* 1.2  Presentation EXPRESS AUDIO

Resources: Teacher's Resource Book: Audio Script, p. 119; Audio Program: Track 4; Answers on Transparencies

Focus: Listening comprehension about cooking

Suggestions: Explain some basic cooking techniques: *batir, freír, picar.*

 **Script and Answers:**

1. A veces hay que cortar el pollo en pedazos pequeños. *(one hand)*
2. Es importante picar el caldo. *(two hands)*
3. Vamos a beber el aceite. *(two hands)*
4. A muchas personas les gusta freír el pollo. *(one hand)*
5. Es importante abrir la lata antes de usar las zanahorias enlatadas. *(one hand)*
6. Normalmente se usa leche congelada para cocinar. *(two hands)*
7. Las verduras frescas son mejores para la salud que las verduras enlatadas. *(one hand)*
8. Normalmente se mezclan con las manos los ingredientes de una receta. *(two hands)*

 Assessment
- **ExamView** QuickTake Presenter Quiz on PresEXPRESS

Videohistoria

 Presentation EXPRESS VOCABULARY

Core Instruction

 Standards: 1.2

Resources: Voc. and Gram. Transparencies 127–128; Audio Program: Track 5

Focus: Presentation of additional vocabulary to discuss cooking

Pre-reading: Direct attention to the *Estrategia.* Conduct a survey to find out who likes to cook or bake and who thinks cooking consists of popping food in the microwave. Have both groups discuss how they "feel" about cooking. Scan the photos and decide which boy is a cook: Javier or Ignacio. Have students turn to p. 352 for more information on **paella.**

Reading: Pause after the second panel and discuss Javier's approach to cooking *(Le gusta cocinar con ingredientes frescos).* Pause after panel 6 and discuss how Javier and Ignacio are feeling and if students can understand each one's frustration. Have volunteers act out the dialogue.

Post-reading: After reading, have students predict whether or not Ana will like her surprise dinner. Complete *Actividad* 3 to check comprehension.

 Pre-AP* Support

- **Activity:** Make flashcards to represent the nine new verbs presented on p. 348. Divide the class in two groups. Alternate bringing to the front of the room one member from each group. Hold the large flashcards up above the student's head so that he or she cannot see it (but his or her group can) and have group members pantomime the activity to him or her to identify. Allow 5 seconds. If the student does not guess the word in the time allowed, show the card to the other group for an instant point if called out appropriately. Continue until all flashcards have been used.

- ***Pre-AP* Resource Book:*** Comprehensive guide to Pre-AP* vocabulary skill development, pp. 47–53

Teacher-to-Teacher

If your school allows it, have students prepare a variety of dishes from Spanish-speaking countries to share with another class. Have them label the dishes in Spanish and write a list of the ingredients for others to read. Be sure students are aware of the ingredients in each dish, in case of food allergies or other dietary restrictions. Encourage them to be food critics and write notes about every dish they sample. Volunteers may share their reviews with the class.

350

Videohistoria jdd-0787

¿Cómo se hace la paella?

Ignacio y Javier van a hacer paella. ¿Qué les pasa en la cocina?

Estrategia

Using prior experience
What do you know about cooking? Are you "at home" in the kitchen or do you feel uncomfortable? Look at the photos and guess how Javier and Ignacio feel.

1 **Ignacio:** Javier, **¿cómo se hace** la paella? Quiero preparar una comida especial para Ana.

Javier: Bueno, está bien. Vamos a necesitar camarones y mariscos. No uso ingredientes ni congelados ni enlatados. Queremos todo bien fresco.

Javier Ignacio

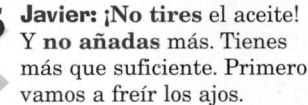

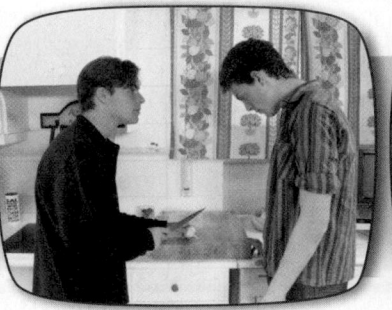

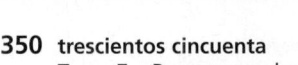

5 **Javier:** ¡No tires el aceite! Y **no añadas** más. Tienes más que suficiente. Primero vamos a freír los ajos.

6 **Javier:** ¡No, Ignacio! Tienes que picar los ajos primero.

Ignacio: ¿Picar?

Javier: Sí, cortar los ajos en pedazos muy pequeños.

7 **Ignacio:** Voy a encender la cocina . . .

Javier: A ver . . . el aceite tiene que estar bien **caliente.** No, todavía no está . . . Yo preparo los mariscos. Tú **no te olvides del** aceite. **No dejes** que se caliente demasiado.

También se dice . . .

los camarones = las gambas *(España)*

la cocina = la estufa *(España)*

350 **trescientos cincuenta**
Tema 7 • Buen provecho

Differentiated Instruction

Solutions for All Learners

Advanced Learners

Have students create the scene in which Ana arrives for dinner. How does Ana react? Does Ignacio take all the credit? Perhaps Ana can inquire how the dish was made and Ignacio does not know how to respond. Encourage students to use humor. Remind them to include the new vocabulary.

Students with Learning Difficulties

Draw attention to the *Estrategia.* Before students begin reading the *Videohistoria,* ask questions to build on their prior experience: Have you prepared a favorite dish so many times that the recipe is committed to memory? When you are attempting an unfamiliar task, do you ask questions of someone more experienced?

2 **Ignacio:** ¿Con qué se sirve la paella? ¿Con papas fritas?

Javier: No, no, no . . . Se sirve con una ensalada.

3 **Ignacio:** Bueno, ¿enciendo el horno ya?

Javier: ¡No! No se puede usar el horno para hacer la paella. Se prepara la paella encima de la cocina.

4 **Ignacio:** ¿Pongo el aceite en la olla?

Javier: Deja esa olla y escucha bien. Primero tienes que calentar el aceite en una sartén grande.

8 **Javier:** ¡Ignacio! ¡Apaga la cocina! ¿En qué estabas pensando?

Ignacio: Bueno, en la sorpresa de Ana cuando . . .

Javier: Pues, así, creo que va a recibir una gran sorpresa, pero no va a ser buena . . . Vamos a seguir . . .

Actividad 3 — Escribir/Hablar

¿Comprendiste?

1. ¿Qué le pregunta Ignacio a Javier? ¿Por qué?
2. ¿Qué necesitan los chicos?
3. Según Javier, ¿se puede servir la paella con papas fritas? ¿Con qué se sirve?
4. ¿Qué quiere hacer Ignacio primero en la cocina? ¿Está bien? ¿Qué le dice Javier?
5. ¿Qué quiere hacer Ignacio luego? ¿Qué le dice Javier?
6. ¿Qué le pasó a Ignacio al final? ¿En qué estaba pensando?

Más práctica

- Practice Workbook, pp. 135–136: 7A-3, 7A-4
- WAV Wbk.: Video, pp. 126–128
- Guided Practice: Vocab. Check, pp. 243–246
- Real. para hispanohablantes, p. 253

Go Online
PHSchool.com
For: Vocab. Practice
Web Code: jdd-0703

Enrich Your Teaching
Resources for All Teachers

Culture Note

La paella originated in the eighth century in Valencia after the Moors introduced rice to the Iberian peninsula. The rice was grown in marshy wetlands that were also home to rabbits, snails, and ducks. These items, plus beans, were added to the rice to make the original *paella* *valenciana.* Each area of Spain adds its own regional ingredients. In Costa del Sol mussels, squid, and shrimp are used. In Seville, they also use seafood, including lobster, garnished with lemon wedges.

Language Input

Video
Core Instruction

 Standards: 1.2

Resources: Teacher's Resource Book: Video Script, p. 122; Video Program: Cap. 7A; Video Program Teacher's Guide: Cap. 7A

Focus: Comprehension of contextualized vocabulary

Suggestions:

Pre-viewing: Have students review the *Videohistoria* and write a list of ingredients for **paella** and the initial steps, according to Javier. Have students brainstorm a list of ingredients that Javier would use to make a salad.

Viewing: Show the video once without pausing, then show it again, pausing to discuss why Javier's **paella** tastes so good. Discuss the steps Ignacio wants to take to prepare **paella.** Ask students how they can tell that Javier and Ignacio are both getting frustrated.

Post-viewing: Complete the Video Activities in the *Writing, Audio & Video Workbook.*

Actividad 3

 *Standards:* 1.2
Presentation EXPRESS
ANSWERS

Resources: Answers on Transparencies

Focus: Verifying comprehension of the *Videohistoria*

Suggestions: Read the questions and have students look at their lists. Have students identify where they found the answers in the story.

Answers:

1. Ignacio quiere saber cómo se hace la paella porque quiere preparar una comida especial para Ana. (1)
2. Necesitan camarones y mariscos frescos (y aceite y ajo). (1, 4, and 5)
3. No. Se sirve la paella con una ensalada. (2)
4. Quiere encender el horno. No está bien porque se prepara la paella encima de la cocina. (3)
5. Quiere poner el aceite en una olla. Javier dice que debe calentar el aceite en una sartén grande. (4)
6. Se olvidó del aceite y lo quemó. Estaba pensando en Ana. (8)

Additional Resources

- WAV Wbk.: Audio Act. 5, p. 129
- Teacher's Resource Book: Audio Script, pp. 119–120
- Audio Program: Track 7

✓ **Assessment**

- *ExamView* Quiz on PresEXPRESS
  QuickTake Presenter
- Prueba 7A-1: Vocab. Recognition, pp. 177–178

351

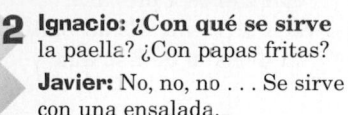

Actividad 4 Standards: 1.2

Presentation EXPRESS ANSWERS

Resources: Answers on Transparencies

Focus: Completing a dialogue about making *paella*

Suggestions: Have students read the entire conversation before they answer. Point out that the impersonal *se* is used as a reference to "you" or "one."

Answers:

1. ingredientes
2. mariscos
3. se hace
4. el aceite
5. sartén
6. Se puede
7. fuego
8. pedazos
9. ajo
10. se sirve
11. vinagre

Extension: Have students work in pairs and ask each other to list two ingredients for a dish (*¿Qué ingredientes hay en ___?*) or what to serve with a dish (*¿Con qué se sirve ___?*).

Bellringer Review

Use large Clip Art flashcards to review these actions:

pelar picar añadir freír hervir

 **Fondo cultural** Standards: 1.2, 2.2, 4.2

Suggestions: Many people believe the secret to great-tasting *paella* is in the pan. A *paellera* is a wide, round, shallow pan with two looped handles. It does not have a lid. The pan's shape, dipped in the middle so that oil can pool, is designed to cook the rice a certain way. If a *paellera* is used, the rice at the bottom of the pan will form a caramelized crust, yielding *paella* perfection!

Make a list of the different rice dishes students eat. Compare the ingredients and how the dishes are prepared.

Answers will vary.

Manos a la obra

Vocabulario y gramática en uso

Objectives

- Communicate about food and cooking
- Give and receive instructions for making a recipe
- Write rules to promote safety in the kitchen
- Learn to use negative *tú* commands
- Learn to use the impersonal *se*

Actividad 4  **Escribir/Leer/Hablar**

¡Ignacio lo sabe todo!

Después de ver a Ignacio en la cocina preparando una paella, ya sabes cómo hacerla. Trabaja con otro(a) estudiante. Completen las preguntas con expresiones y palabras del recuadro y completen las respuestas según los dibujos. Después lean la conversación.

Estudiante A

ingredientes	se hace	se puede
pedazos	se llama	se sirve

A —¿Qué __1.__ hay en la paella?

B —Arroz, pollo y __2.__ .

A —¿Cómo __3.__ la paella?

B —Pues, primero hay que calentar __4.__ en una __5.__ .

A —¿ __6.__ usar el microondas para prepararla paella?

B —¡No, en absoluto! Hay que prepararla sobre un __7.__ lento en la estufa.

A —¿Corto la cebolla en __8.__ grandes?

B —No, pica la cebolla y el __9.__ .

A —¿Con qué __10.__ la paella?

B —Con una ensalada de lechuga y tomate con aceite y __11.__ .

Modelo

A —Ignacio, ¿cómo <u>se llama</u> lo que vamos a preparar?

B —Es una *paella*. Es un plato tradicional de España.

Estudiante B

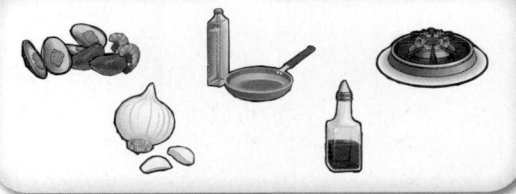

Fondo cultural ■◆■◆■◆■◆■◆■◆■◆■◆

La paella es el plato más popular de la cocina española. El nombre *paella* viene de la paellera, la sartén especial que se usa para cocinarla. Su ingrediente principal es el arroz. La paella tradicional se hace sólo con mariscos, pero también se puede añadir pollo y salchichas. En la costa, ponen los mariscos frescos del día. La paella se come en muchos países. En América Latina preparan platos similares, como el arroz con frijoles y el arroz con pollo.

- Compara la paella con la comida típica que comes. ¿Comes muchas comidas hechas con arroz? ¿Son similares a la paella, o diferentes?

También se dice . . .

el refrigerador = la nevera, el frigorífico (*España, muchos países*); la heladera (*Argentina, Uruguay*)

el fregadero = el lavaplatos (*Colombia*); la pileta (*Argentina*)

Differentiated Instruction

Solutions for All Learners

Heritage Language Learners

Have students write a sensory poem about their favorite person's cooking. *(Nombre) es el (la) mejor cocinero(a). Prepara un(a) ___ (adjetivo). Huele a ___ ; Parece a ___ ; La textura es ___ ; El sabor es ___ ; ¡Qué ___!*

Students with Special Needs

Students who struggle with spatial organization may have difficulty drawing the kitchen described in *Actividad* 5. Provide illustrations of the kitchen items instead. Have students cut out the items, paste them on a piece of paper according to the description, and label them.

Actividad 5 jdd-0788 **Escuchar/Dibujar/Escribir/Hablar**

La cocina de mi tía

Escucha mientras la tía de Juanita describe su cocina. Dibuja y escribe los nombres de las cosas que menciona. Luego compara tu dibujo con el de otro(a) estudiante.

¿Recuerdas?

Regular affirmative *tú* commands use the present-tense *Ud./él/ella* form of the verb. Some verbs, like *tener* and *poner*, have irregular command forms.

Actividad 6 **Leer/Escribir**

Los huevos revueltos

Hoy es sábado y tu madre tiene que trabajar. Ha dejado para ti unas instrucciones para hacer huevos revueltos *(scrambled)*. Usa los verbos en el recuadro y escribe el mandato apropiado para cada número.

Modelo

preparar
Por favor, *prepara* huevos revueltos para la familia.

añadir	hervir
apagar	mezclar
batir	poner
dejar	probar
encender	servir
freír	tener

En el desayuno

1. los huevos con un tenedor y 2. sal y pimienta.
3. los huevos con un poquito de leche y queso rallado *(shredded)*.
4. la estufa pero 5. cuidado. No necesitas un fuego muy alto.
6. el tocino.
7. los huevos batidos en una sartén y cocínalos.
8. cocinar los huevos por unos minutos.
9. agua para hacer café.
10. los huevos para ver si tienen suficiente sal y pimienta.
11. la estufa y 12. el desayuno.

Actividad 7 **Leer/Hablar**

¿Qué has probado?

Lee estas descripciones de unos platos típicos de diferentes países hispanohablantes. Después habla con otro(a) estudiante sobre los platos que han probado y sobre los que les gustaría probar.

Modelo

A —¿Has probado el ceviche?
B —Sí, lo he probado.
 (No) Me gusta mucho porque . . .

 **Camarones al ajillo** Fríen los camarones muy frescos con aceite y ajo en una pequeña sartén y los sirven muy calientes.

 **Pescado frito** Fríen el pescado en aceite caliente. Añaden sal, pimienta y otras especias *(spices)*. Es popular en muchos países, desde España hasta Puerto Rico.

 **Gazpacho** Sirven fría esta sopa de tomate, aceite y ajo que también puede contener verduras como apio *(celery)* y chiles.

 **Ceviche** Mezclan el pescado con tomate, cebolla, vinagre, chile y jugo de limón. Hay diferentes variaciones de ceviche.

trescientos cincuenta y tres **353**
Capítulo 7A

Enrich Your Teaching
Resources for All Teachers

Culture Note

The most expensive of spices, **azafrán** (saffron) is gathered by hand-picking dried red stigmas of the purple saffron crocus. One pound of saffron requires anywhere from 70,000 to 250,000 flowers! This flower is found predominantly in Spain, Iran, and India. Saffron is a major export of Spain.

Teacher-to-Teacher

Have students write the steps needed to make a grilled cheese sandwich or a soup, modeling their directions on the steps in *Actividad 6*.

 Actividad 5  *Standards:* 1.2  Presentation EXPRESS AUDIO

Resources: Teacher's Resource Book: Audio Script, p. 119; Audio Program: Track 6; Answers on Transparencies

Focus: Listening, drawing, writing, and speaking about kitchen appliances

Suggestions: Allow the students to listen several times so they can make and label their drawings.

 **Script:**
1. En mi cocina hay un refrigerador nuevo.
2. Al lado del refrigerador hay un fregadero.
3. Al otro lado del refrigerador están la estufa y el horno.
4. Encima de la estufa hay una sartén y una olla.
5. Delante del fregadero hay una mesa con un microondas.
6. Al lado del microondas hay un libro de recetas.

Answers: In the drawing there is a refrigerator with a sink on one side and a stove and oven on the other side. On top of the stove there are a frying pan and a pot. In front of the sink there is a table with a microwave. Next to the microwave there is a recipe book.

 Actividad 6 *Standards:* 1.2  Presentation EXPRESS ANSWERS

Resources: Answers on Transparencies

Focus: Reading and writing about preparing breakfast

Suggestions: Review *tú* commands. Point out verbs that require spelling changes.

Answers:

1. Bate	5. ten	9. Hierve
2. añade	6. Fríe	10. Prueba
3. Mezcla	7. Pon	11. Apaga
4. Enciende	8. Deja	12. sirve

 **Actividad 7** *Standards:* 1.1, 1.2, 2.2

Focus: Reading and speaking about different dishes
Recycle: Vocabulary for different foods
Suggestions: Point out the use of the plural command form.
Answers will vary.

Bellringer Review
Review prepositions (*al lado de, encima de, delante de*) and commands by asking students to place their books in various spots.

Actividad 8 Standards: 1.1 — Presentation EXPRESS ANSWERS

Resources: Answers on Transparencies

Focus: Speaking about food preferences

Recycle: Food; negative constructions

Suggestions: Preview the illustrations.

Answers:

Student A:
1. ¿Qué prefieres, las verduras frescas o las verduras congeladas?
2. ¿... el té helado o el té caliente?
3. ¿... las frutas enlatadas o las frutas frescas?
4. ¿... el pollo al horno o el pollo frito?
5. ¿... las verduras congeladas o las verduras enlatadas?

Student B: Answers will vary.

Actividad 9 Standards: 1.1 — Presentation EXPRESS ANSWERS

Resources: Answers on Transparencies

Focus: Speaking about where things go in the kitchen

Recycle: Direct object pronouns

Suggestions: Go over the illustrations with students before they begin.

Answers:

Student A:
1. ¿Dónde pongo el aceite?
2. ¿... las papas congeladas?
3. ¿... las verduras frescas?
4. ¿... las ollas y las sartenes sucias?
5. ¿... la sartén?
6. ¿... las latas?

Student B:
1. Ponlo en la sartén.
2. Ponlas en el refrigerador.
3. Ponlas en el microondas.
4. Ponlas en el fregadero.
5. Ponla en la estufa.
6. Ponlas en el estante.

Actividad 10 Standards: 1.2, 1.3 — Presentation EXPRESS ANSWERS

Resources: Answers on Transparencies

Focus: Reading, writing, listening, and speaking about cooking tips

Recycle: Food vocabulary

Suggestions: Have students read the sentences before they answer.

Answers:

1. frescas	3. olla	5. el microondas
2. no tires	4. No te olvides de	6. caldo

  Hablar

¿Qué prefieres?

Con otro(a) estudiante, habla de sus preferencias.

Modelo
A —¿Qué prefieres, <u>las papas fritas</u> o <u>las papas al horno</u>?
B —Prefiero <u>las papas al horno</u>.
o:—No me <u>gustan</u> ni <u>las papas fritas</u> ni <u>las papas al horno</u>.

1.    2.    3.

4.    5.

  Hablar

¿Dónde los pongo?

Con otro(a) estudiante, habla de dónde se ponen las cosas en la cocina.

Modelo
A —¿Dónde pongo <u>los pedazos de tomate</u>?
B —<u>Ponlos</u> en <u>la ensalada</u>.

Estudiante A

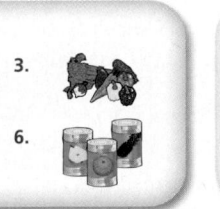

1. 2. 3.
4. 5. 6.

Estudiante B

1. 2. 3.
4. 5. 6.

  Leer/Escribir/Escuchar/Hablar

Recomendaciones para cocinar

Lee las recomendaciones para cocinar y escoge la mejor palabra o expresión para completar cada una. Luego usa estas frases como modelo y escribe cuatro más con tus propias recomendaciones. Lee tus frases a otro(a) estudiante, quien tiene que completarlas.

1. En una ensalada, las verduras ___ *(frescas / enlatadas)* son más sabrosas.

2. Mientras fríes algo, ___ *(no tires / prueba)* el aceite caliente.

3. Es mejor hervir agua para los espaguetis en una ___ *(olla / sartén)*.

4. ___ *(Deja / No te olvides de)* apagar la estufa después de usarla.

5. Usa ___ *(el microondas / el horno)* para preparar algo rápidamente.

6. Para algunas recetas de arroz necesitas un ___ *(caldo / ajo)* de pescado o pollo.

354 trescientos cincuenta y cuatro
Tema 7 • Buen provecho

Differentiated Instruction
Solutions for All Learners

Multiple Intelligences

Bodily/Kinesthetic: For *Actividad* 9, bring in a play kitchen with toy foods and dishes for the class to manipulate. Student A holds up a tomato and asks where to put it. Student B points to the bowl and says to put it there. Student A puts the tomato in the bowl.

Advanced Learners

Have students take turns calling out a letter of the alphabet and giving the rest of the group 30 seconds to write down as many food-and kitchen-related words as they can that begin with that letter. Have the group compare lists. Any student who has a word that no one else has earns a point.

Actividad 11 — Leer/Escribir/Hablar

Tostones isleños

Lee este artículo de una revista de cocina. Luego trabaja con otro(a) estudiante para contestar las preguntas.

TOSTONES

¡No tienes que esperar un viaje a la fantástica isla de Puerto Rico para disfrutar de[1] este riquísimo plato tropical! Puedes seguir esta receta fácil y preparar tostones con mojito (¡esa salsa deliciosa de aceite y ajo!) en tu propia casa.

Ingredientes

Tostones
6 plátanos verdes
agua
sal
aceite

Mojito
8 dientes[2] de ajo
½ taza de aceite
    de oliva
perejil[3]

Preparación

Tostones
Pela los plátanos y córtalos en pedazos medianos. Ponlos en una olla con agua y sal por 15 minutos. Luego ponlos a secar en una toalla de papel. Calienta aceite en una sartén. Fríe los plátanos dos minutos por cada lado. Pon los plátanos sobre una toalla de papel para escurrirles[4] el aceite y aplasta[5] los pedazos. Fríelos otra vez. Escúrrelos y añade sal.

Mojito
Pela los dientes de ajo y machácalos[6]. Pica el perejil. Calienta el aceite de oliva y añade el ajo. Caliéntalo a fuego lento hasta que el ajo esté dorado[7]. Añade el perejil picado. Pon la mezcla caliente al lado de los tostones y sírvelos.

¡Buen provecho!

[1] enjoy [2] cloves [3] parsley [4] drain them [5] flatten [6] crush them [7] 's golden

1. En una hoja de papel, hagan dos columnas. Escriban las cosas que necesitan para preparar los tostones con mojito en una columna y escriban para qué las necesitan en la otra.

Necesitamos	Para
un cuchillo	pelar el ajo

2. ¿Has probado tostones con mojito? Si ya los has probado, ¿te gustaron? Si todavía no los has probado, ¿te gustaría probarlos?
3. Dicen que los tostones son similares a las papitas (*potato chips*). ¿En qué sentido son similares o diferentes?

 Fondo cultural

El plátano es uno de los alimentos más populares de los países tropicales de América Latina. Se cree que el plátano es originario del sudeste asiático. Los plátanos amarillos que ves en los supermercados son sólo un tipo de la gran diversidad de plátanos que hay. Hay pequeños plátanos amarillos y plátanos grandes, como los verdes y los rojos. Con los plátanos verdes se preparan los tostones. Otras recetas con plátanos verdes son sopa de plátano verde y bolas de verde (Ecuador y Colombia).

• ¿Qué relación crees que hay entre la popularidad del plátano como comida y su abundancia?

trescientos cincuenta y cinco **355**
Capítulo 7A

Practice and Communicate 7A

Actividad 11 Standards: 1.2, 2.2, 4.2

Resources: Voc. and Gram. Transparency 129; Answers on Transparencies

Focus: Reading, writing, and speaking about *tostones*

Suggestions: Have students scan the recipe and look at the picture. Ask if they are reminded of any food they have had before.

Answers will vary but may include:

Necesitamos	Para
una olla	poner los plátanos
una toalla de papel	secar y escurrir los plátanos
un cuchillo	picar el perejil
una cuchara	mezclar el perejil con el ajo
una sartén	calentar el aceite
un tenedor	freír los plátanos
un plato	servir los tostones

Extension: Have students make a list of the unique command forms found in the recipe and use them in new sentences.

Fondo cultural  Standards: 1.2, 2.2, 4.2

Suggestions: Point out that *un plátano* is similar to a banana. When green, plantains are considered a starch, much like potatoes, and can be boiled, mashed, stuffed, or fried. However, when *plátanos* are ripe and black, they are sweet and are often used for desserts. Despite their similarity to bananas, people do not peel and eat *plátanos* whole because they are so sweet.

Answers will vary.

Additional Resources

• WAV Wbk.: Audio Act. 6 p. 129
• Teacher's Resource Book: Audio Script, p. 120, Communicative Activity BLM, pp. 126–127
• Audio Program: Track 8

✓ Assessment

• Prueba 7A-2: Vocab. Production, pp. 179–180

Enrich Your Teaching
Resources for All Teachers

Culture Note

The *plátano* is essential for *tostones.* Plantains can be easily found in tropical areas, which is one reason *tostones* are often served throughout the Caribbean and Central America. *Tostones* usually accompany a main dish, often fish, during lunch or dinner, although they are also a popular appetizer.

Teacher-to-Teacher

Play "Name That Dish" by having small groups create recipe cards for familiar soups, main dishes, and appetizers. Cards will include a list of ingredients and four or five steps, but not the name of the dish. Each step should begin with a command. Students will exchange recipe cards and guess the recipe.

355

 Gramática

 Presentation EXPRESS
GRAMMAR

Core Instruction

Resources: Teacher's Resource Book: Video Script, pp. 122–123; Video Program: Cap. 7A

Suggestions: Before reading, review the present-tense **yo** form of several verbs. After reading, have students make a chart that shows the negative **tú** commands for regular **-ar, -er,** and **-ir** verbs. Use the transparency and *GramActiva* Video to help with your presentation.

Have students brainstorm a list of verbs, including **-car, -gar,** and **-zar** verbs. *(practicar, sacar, apagar, jugar, llegar, empezar)* Have students use the verbs to write five classroom rules that include both positive and negative commands. Try to write as many rules as possible, using a variety of verbs. As a class, decide on the five most useful rules.

 **Actividad 12** Standards: 1.2

Presentation EXPRESS
ANSWERS

Resources: Answers on Transparencies

Focus: Writing negative commands

Suggestions: Point out that verbs whose present-tense **yo** form ends in **-go** *(decir, salir, hacer, poner, tener, traer)* form their negative **tú** commands according to the regular rule. Suggest that students first choose the correct verb, then work on forming the negative **tú** command.

Answers:

1. No dejes ollas sucias en el fregadero.
2. No comas en tu cama.
3. No uses la estufa sin limpiarla después.
4. No pongas pollo frito encima del sofá.
5. No hagas espaguetis en el microondas.
6. No des de comer al perro en la sala.
7. No seas egoísta. Piensa en los otros miembros de la familia.

Extension: Have students write sentences giving advice to younger children concerning good behavior.

Gramática

Negative *tú* commands

To tell someone what *not* to do, use a negative command. To form negative *tú* commands, drop the *-o* of the present-tense *yo* form and add:

- *-es* for *-ar* verbs.

  usar   uso: **No uses** el microondas.

- *-as* for *-er* and *-ir* verbs.

  encender enciendo: **No enciendas** el horno.
  añadir   añado: **No añadas** demasiada sal.
  poner   pongo: **No pongas** los camarones en la sartén todavía.

Verbs ending in *-car, -gar,* or *-zar* have spelling changes: *c* changes to *qu*, *g* changes to *gu*, and *z* changes to *c*.

  picar   pico: **No piques** los tomates.
  pagar   pago: **No pagues** demasiado.
  empezar   empiezo: **No empieces** a cocinar ahora.

These verbs have irregular negative *tú* commands:

dar	no des	ir	no vayas
estar	no estés	ser	no seas

Remember that pronouns are attached to affirmative commands. If the pronoun is added to a command form that has two or more syllables, write an accent mark on the syllable stressed in the present tense.

—¿Pico las cebollas?

—Sí, pícalas.

With negative commands, pronouns always go right before the conjugated verb.

—¿Pico los tomates también?

—No, no **los** piques.

 **GramActiva** VIDEO

Want more help with negative *tú* commands? Watch the **GramActiva** video.

No corras.

 Actividad 12 **Escribir**

¡Así no!

Tu hermano mayor acaba de limpiar la casa y no quiere limpiarla otra vez. Te escribe una nota diciendo las cosas que no debes hacer. Completa lo que dice él con los mandatos negativos correctos.

Modelo

(picar/tirar) leche en el suelo
No tires leche en el suelo.

1. *(mezclar / dejar)* ollas sucias en el fregadero
2. *(comer / añadir)* en tu cama
3. *(pelar / usar)* la estufa sin limpiarla después
4. *(salir / poner)* pollo frito encima del sofá
5. *(hacer / probar)* espaguetis en el microondas
6. *(dar de comer / ver)* al perro en la sala
7. *(ir / ser)* egoísta*. Piensa en los otros miembros de la familia.

*selfish

 Differentiated Instruction
Solutions for All Learners

Advanced Learners/Pre-AP*

Pre-AP*

Have students think of a well-known fairy tale, legend, or story, and give the main character advice on things not to do or say, or places not to go. Students can write their advice on a poster and present it to the class or display it on a bulletin board. Can other students identify the character?

Multiple Intelligences

Verbal/Linguistic: Draw attention to the verbs with irregular negative **tú** commands in the *Gramática (dar, ir, estar, ser).* Ask: What do these infinitives have in common in the present tense? *(the **yo** form ends in **-oy**)*

Actividad 13

Leer/Escribir _____

Para tener empanadas exquisitas

① A Manolo le gusta hacer las empanadas y ha escrito unas instrucciones para hacerlas. Escoge verbos del recuadro y completa las instrucciones con el mandato negativo.

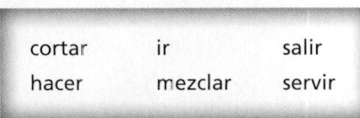

cortar	ir	salir
hacer	mezclar	servir

1. ___ al supermercado por los ingredientes sin llevar una lista.
2. ___ la masa *(dough)* si no te has lavado las manos.
3. ___ las empanadas sin añadir la sal.
4. ___ la carne y las verduras con el mismo cuchillo sin lavarlo.
5. ___ de la cocina cuando las empanadas están en el horno.
6. ___ las empanadas sin probar una primero.

② Ayuda a Manolo a escribir cuatro reglas adicionales sobre cómo tener éxito en la cocina. Usa mandatos negativos.

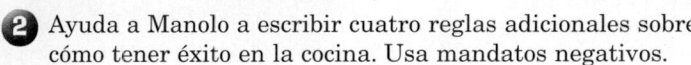 **Modelo**

comenzar

___ a cocinar sin leer la receta.
No comiences a cocinar sin leer la receta.

 Actividad 14

Escribir _____

Un mundo negativo

Imagina que eres el (la) director(a) de la cafetería de tu escuela. Escribe mandatos negativos para dar instrucciones en la cocina.

1. venir a la cocina con las manos sucias
2. tirar el almuerzo a la basura
3. ofrecer demasiado café
4. hacer muchas tortillas
5. ¡Respuesta personal!

 **Modelo**

dejar la sartén en el fuego
No dejes la sartén en el fuego.

Más práctica

- Practice Workbook, p. 137: 7A-5
- WAV Wbk.: Writing, p. 133
- Guided Practice: Grammar Acts., pp. 247–250
- *Real.* para hispanohablantes, pp. 254–257

Go Online PHSchool.com
For: Neg. *Tú* Commands
Web Code: jdd-0704

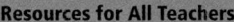

trescientos cincuenta y siete **357**
Capítulo 7A

Practice and Communicate 7A

 Actividad 13  *Standards:* 1.2, 1.3 Presentation EXPRESS ANSWERS

Resources: Answers on Transparencies

Focus: Reading and writing about cooking rules

Suggestions: Have students read all the sentences first to decide which verb will fit in each sentence. Remind students that all verbs will be in the negative *tú* command form.

Answers:
Step 1:
1. No vayas
2. No mezcles
3. No hagas
4. No cortes
5. No salgas
6. No sirvas
Step 2: Answers will vary.

Extension: A new student has arrived at school. Write six school rules in the negative that he or she should follow. *(No traigas tus refrescos a la clase.)*

 Actividad 14  *Standards:* 1.3  Presentation EXPRESS ANSWERS

Resources: Answers on Transparencies

Focus: Writing rules for cafeteria workers

Recycle: Food; health

Suggestions: Point out that most of the verbs in this activity are irregular or will have a spelling change. Commands should be in the familiar *tú* form.

Answers:
1. No vengas a la cocina con las manos sucias.
2. No tires el almuerzo a la basura.
3. No ofrezcas demasiado café.
4. No hagas muchas tortillas.
5. Answers will vary.

Extension: Have students compose **un párrafo loco** about cooking. They should write at least four nonsensical statements using negative and affirmative commands.

Additional Resources

- WAV Wbk.: Audio Act. 7, p. 130
- Teacher's Resource Book: Audio Script, p. 120
- Audio Program: Track 9

 Assessment

- **Exam***View* Quiz on PresEXPRESS
QuickTake Presenter
- Prueba 7A-3: Negative *tú* commands, p.181

Enrich Your Teaching
Resources for All Teachers

Culture Note

Derived from **empanar,** meaning "to bread," **empanadas** are pastries filled with meat and/or vegetables. All Spanish-speaking countries have some variation. Chile has an **empanada de pino** made with beef and a black olive. The Spanish region of Galicia uses pork.

Teacher-to-Teacher

Tell students they are going to eat in a very expensive restaurant and must use proper manners (letting the host or hostess seat you, using the right utensils, ordering, paying the check). Have groups write five affirmative commands and five negative commands, each using a different verb, and present their lists to the rest of the class.

357

Actividad 15 Standards: 1.1, 1.2, 2.2

Presentation EXPRESS ANSWERS

Resources: Voc. and Gram. Transparency 130; Answers on Transparencies

Focus: Asking and answering questions on how to prepare *arepas*

Suggestions: Have students read the recipe card and write down the verbs that are used. Point out the verb constructions used in the question and the answer.

Answers:
Student A: Answers will vary, but may include:
¿Añado la harina con el agua rápidamente?
¿Amaso la masa ya?
¿Añado la mantequilla ya?
¿Formo bolas de masa?
¿Caliento una plancha?
¿Aplasto las bolas?
¿Pongo las bolas en la plancha de cocina?
Student B: Answers will vary, but may include:
No, no la añadas rápidamente.
No, no la amases todavía.
No, no la añadas.
No, no las formes.
No, no las calientes.
No, no las aplastes.
No, no las pongas en la plancha todavía.

Fondo cultural Standards: 1.2, 2.2, 4.2

■◆■◆■◆■◆■◆■◆■◆■◆■◆■◆■◆■◆■

Suggestions: *Arepas* were originally made from moistened maize that had been ground between two stones. Later, they were formed in round disks on earthenware called **aripo,** whence the name. Many Venezuelans eat **arepas** for breakfast, but they are also prepared with a variety of fillings, including papaya, chopped meat, avocado, or cheese.

Answers will vary but may include the fact that the variety is due to people trying new ideas and adding their favorite ingredients. Some dishes that vary in the United States include rice and beans, pancakes, potatoes, biscuits, and chili.

Assessment
• Have students tape their question and answer session in *Actividad* 15 for an informal evaluation.

Actividad 15 👥 **Hablar**

¡No lo hagas todavía!

Imagina que estás en Venezuela y quieres ayudar a la madre (o al padre) de tu familia venezolana en la cocina. Lee la receta para arepas que está abajo. Con otro(a) estudiante, haz preguntas para ver si puedes comenzar a hacer las arepas. Tu compañero(a) no está listo(a) todavía.

Modelo
mezclar el agua con la sal
A —¿Mezclo el agua con la sal ya?
B —No, no las mezcles todavía.

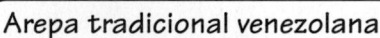
Arepa tradicional venezolana

Ingredientes:
1 taza de harina de maíz[1] precocida[2]
2 tazas de agua
$\frac{1}{2}$ cucharadita de sal
$\frac{1}{2}$ cucharadita de mantequilla

Preparación:
1. Mezcla las dos tazas de agua con la sal.
2. Añade la harina de maíz poco a poco y amasa[3] hasta tener una masa[4] bien mezclada y sin grumos[5].
3. Añade la mantequilla y forma bolas de masa.
4. Calienta una plancha[6] de cocina, aplasta[7] las bolas de masa un poco y ponlas en la plancha hasta que estén doradas[8] por los dos lados. Si prefieres, puedes ponerlas al horno después para hacerlas más abombadas[9].

Se venden arepas en la playa de Miami, Florida.

[1]corn flour [2]precooked [3]knead [4]dough [5]lumps [6]griddle [7]flatten [8]they are golden [9]dome-shaped

Fondo cultural ■◆■◆■◆■◆■◆■◆■◆■◆■◆■

La arepa es una comida tradicional que se come casi todos los días en Venezuela. Blancas o amarillas, las arepas siempre han sido el desayuno o la cena perfecta para muchas familias venezolanas. Hay diferentes variedades de arepa: algunas están hechas con papas y otras con queso. En cada región de Venezuela se preparan las arepas de manera diferente. Muchas veces las arepas están rellenas de *(filled with)* pollo, jamón, huevos y otras cosas.

• ¿Por qué crees que hay tantas variedades de arepas venezolanas? ¿Qué platos de los Estados Unidos se preparan de varias maneras según la región del país?

Haciendo arepas en Mérida, Venezuela

Differentiated Instruction
Solutions for All Learners

Advanced Learners
Have students make a poster of safe cooking practices for the stove or microwave. Use drawings to show the correct way to use the appliance, putting an **X** or the international symbol of the red circle and slash over a drawing to indicate incorrect usage. Students should include text for each point.

Multiple Intelligences
Musical: To help students with the *Pronunciación,* slowly pronounce the example words and suggest that students clap or tap with a pencil as they divide the words into syllables.

 **Escribir/Dibujar**

En la guardería infantil

Una guardería infantil cerca de tu casa necesita personas para trabajar con los niños que sólo hablan español. Otro(a) estudiante y tú van a trabajar allí. Su primera responsabilidad: la comida saludable para los niños.

1 En una hoja de papel, escriban cinco mandatos afirmativos y cinco negativos para los niños, usando la forma *tú*.

2 Hagan un cartel usando los mandatos afirmativos y negativos. Hagan dibujos o corten ilustraciones para hacerlo más interesante. Muestren *(Show)* el cartel en la clase.

Modelo

comer/jugar

Afirmativo	Negativo
come despacio	no juegues con la comida

Pronunciación

Dividing words into syllables

jdd-0788

In Spanish, you divide words into syllables after a vowel sound or between most double consonants. Listen to and say these words:

ca-ma-ro-nes	fres-co	her-vir
ma-ris-cos	en-cien-do	con-ge-la-do

However, you do not separate most combinations of a consonant followed by *l* or *r*. Listen to and say these words:

do-**bl**e	in-**gre**-dien-tes	**fre**-ga-de-ro
re-**fres**-cos	vi-na-**gre**	re-**fri**-ge-ra-dor

When two strong vowels *(a, e, o)* appear together, each is pronounced individually, forming two syllables. Listen to and say these words:

pa-e-lla	tra-e-mos	to-a-lla
mi-cro-on-das	fe-o	hé-ro-e

¡Compruébalo! Lee estos versos del poema "Oda a las papas fritas", del famoso poeta chileno, Pablo Neruda (1904–1973), quien ganó el Premio Nobel de Literatura en 1971.

"Oda a las papas fritas"

Chisporrotea[1]
en el aceite
hirviendo
la alegría
del mundo:
las papas
fritas
entran
en la sartén
como nevadas
plumas
de cisne matutino[2]
y salen
semidoradas por el crepitante[3]
ámbar[4] de las olivas.

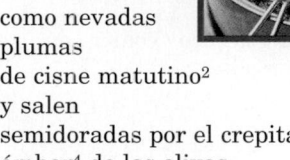

[1] Hissing [2] snowy feathers of a morning swan [3] crackling [4] amber

Escribe estas palabras del poema y divídelas en sílabas:

chisporrotea	aceite	hirviendo
alegría	sartén	semidoradas

trescientos cincuenta y nueve **359**
Capítulo 7A

Practice and Communicate

7A

 Standards: 1.3

Actividad 16

Focus: Writing and drawing posters about healthy eating

Suggestions: Discuss the kinds of foods children typically like to eat, the foods they don't like, and which of these foods are healthy. Discuss some of the things children tend to do when eating, such as eating with dirty hands; sharing food, utensils, and straws; and running and playing during or immediately after meals.

Answers will vary.

Pronunciación

Presentation EXPRESS AUDIO

Core Instruction

 Standards: 1.2, 2.2

Resources: Teacher's Resource Book: Audio Script, p. 120; Audio Program: Track 10

Suggestions: Write several familiar polysyllabic Spanish words on the board: for example, **comida, frutas, salchichas.** Have students say them aloud. Point out that without thinking about it, they knew how to pronounce the words and where to put the stress. Read the first section of the *Pronunciación* to students or play the *Audio CD*. Using the words on the board, have the class decide how the words should be divided into syllables.

Discuss the differences between diphthongs and strong vowels. Demonstrate the division of the following words: *causa (cau-sa), limpio (lim-pio), río (rí-o), sueño (sue-ño), ideal (i-de-al)*. Read "Oda a las papas fritas" to students. The poem is not recorded on the Audio CD.

Theme Project

Give students copies of the Theme Project outline and rubric from the *Teacher's Resource Book*. Explain the task to them, and have them perform Step 1. (For more information, see p. 344-a.)

Enrich Your Teaching
Resources for All Teachers

Culture Note

A traditional meal in Venezuela is **pabellón criollo,** spicy shredded meat accompanied by black beans and rice. A popular Venezuelan dessert is sponge cake soaked in a coconut cream sauce. Venezuelans call it **bienmesabe,** which means "it tastes good to me."

Teacher-to-Teacher

Have groups write and perform skits in which a customer asks the waiter and chef how certain dishes are prepared. Give students a list of verbs to include in their skits. Students should use both affirmative and negative commands, and also incorporate chapter vocabulary.

7A Practice and Communicate

Gramática

Core Instruction

Standards: 4.1

Resources: Teacher's Resource Book: Video Script, p. 123; Video Program: Cap. 7A

Suggestions: Ask students to recall any phrases they have learned that use **se** (**se abre, se cierra, se prohíbe**) or any signs they have seen in the community that use **se** (**se habla, se vende**).

After reading the *Gramática,* write a few sentences on the board: *Se venden libros. Se usa leche. Se sirven frutas.* Ask: Who is performing the action in these sentences? *(people in general)* Point out that it is the word that follows the verb that determines whether the verb is singular or plural. Use the transparency and the *GramActiva* Video to help with your presentation.

Bellringer Review

Write this sentence on the board.

Se prohíbe _____ en la cocina.

Brainstorm as a class a set of rules for the kitchen.

  **Standards:** 1.3, 2.2

Resources: Answers on Transparencies

Focus: Writing about regional foods

Suggestions: Provide a plural example before students begin the activity: *En España se usan siempre los mariscos.* Make sure students are familiar with the foods shown in the photos.

Answers will vary but may include:
1. En México se sirve a menudo la fruta fresca.
2. En Puerto Rico se comen tostones con mojito.
3. En España se preparan camarones con ajo.
4. En Argentina se come mucho la carne de res.
5. En Bolivia se preparan las papas de maneras diferentes.
6. En la República Dominicana se sirven los mariscos bien frescos.
7. En Costa Rica se come arroz con frijoles.
8. En Nuevo México se sirven las enchiladas con chiles.

Extension: Have students write sentences telling where in your community different foods are sold, served, or prepared.

Gramática

The impersonal *se*

In English, you use *they, you, one,* or *people* in an impersonal or indefinite sense to mean "people in general." In Spanish, you use *se* + the *Ud. / él / ella* or *Uds. / ellos / ellas* form of the verb.

A menudo **se sirve** pan con la paella.
*Bread **is** often **served** with paella.*
Se usan otros mariscos también para hacer paella.
***They** also **use** other shellfish to make paella.*

¿Recuerdas?

Remember that you use *se prohíbe* to tell that something is prohibited.

• **Se prohíbe** comer en clase.

GramActiva VIDEO

Want more help with the impersonal *se*? Watch the **GramActiva** video.

Se habla español.

 Actividad 17

Escribir

Comidas populares

Para cada foto, escribe una frase diciendo cuál es una de las comidas populares del país o de la región.

Modelo

España / preparar frecuentemente
En España se prepara frecuentemente la paella.

1.  México / servir a menudo

2. Puerto Rico / comer con mojito

3. España / preparar con ajo

4.  Argentina / comer mucho

5.  Bolivia / preparar de maneras diferentes

6.  la República Dominicana / servir bien frescos

7.  Costa Rica / comer con frijoles

8.  Nuevo México / servir con chiles

360 trescientos sesenta
Tema 7 • Buen provecho

Differentiated Instruction
Solutions for All Learners

Advanced Learners

Have students work in groups to play a food version of "Twenty Questions." Example:
A—Estoy pensando en un restaurante.
B—¿Se venden papas fritas allí?
A—No, no se venden papas fritas allí.
C—¿Se sirve jugo fresco allí?

Students with Learning Difficulties

For *Actividad 17,* it may be difficult for some students to recall the names of the dishes pictured. Provide a word bank with the names of the dishes in scrambled order.

Actividad 18 — Escribir/Hablar

¿Se puede . . . ?

Imagina que un estudiante nuevo llega a tu comunidad y quiere saber qué se puede hacer en tu escuela.

1 Escribe cinco preguntas sobre las cosas que se pueden, se permiten o se prohíben hacer en tu escuela.

> **Modelo**
>
> *En el gimnasio, ¿se puede levantar pesas?*

2 Pregúntale a otro(a) estudiante si se pueden hacer las actividades.

> **Modelo**
>
> A —*En el gimnasio, ¿se puede levantar pesas?*
>
> B —*Claro, se puede levantar pesas.*

Actividad 19 — Pensar/Escribir/Hablar

La dieta ideal

Comer bien es muy importante para todos. ¿Cómo se decide qué comer cada día? Se debe prestar atención a la buena nutrición.

Conexiones | Las ciencias

Lee esta tabla sobre los minerales y las comidas en las que se encuentran.

Mineral	Comidas
Calcio	Leche, queso y verduras
Fósforo	Huevos, pescado, granos integrales (trigo,[1] maíz,[2] arroz, y más), leche, hígado,[3] brócoli y frijoles[4]
Hierro[5]	Hígado, huevos, carnes, verduras, guisantes y melaza[6]
Yodo[7]	Mariscos y sal que contiene yodo

[1] wheat　[2] corn　[3] liver　[4] beans　[5] Iron　[6] molasses　[7] Iodine

1 Trabaja con otro(a) estudiante y busquen en la tabla los minerales que tiene:

1. una paella hecha con arroz, pollo, pescado y mariscos
2. una pizza con salsa de tomate, queso y salchicha

Escriban una lista de los minerales que tienen estas dos comidas. Compárenlas. ¿Cuál de las dos tiene más minerales? ¿Cuál es la comida más saludable?

2 En un grupo de cuatro estudiantes, escojan una comida y busquen en la tabla los minerales que contienen los ingredientes. Lean la descripción de los ingredientes y los minerales a la clase sin decir qué comida es. Los demás deben adivinar la comida.

trescientos sesenta y uno **361**
Capítulo 7A

Actividad 18 — *Standards: 1.1* — Pre-AP*

Focus: Writing and telling what things are allowed at school

Suggestions: Begin a class discussion about school-wide rules and rules in certain areas of your school. To help with their writing, have students write two headings: *Se puede* and *No se puede*.

Answers will vary.

Actividad 19 — *Standards: 1.3, 3.1* — Presentation EXPRESS ANSWERS

Resources: Answers on Transparencies

Focus: Reading comprehension; cross-curricular connection to science and health

Suggestions: Bring in books on nutrition and healthy eating, and ask students to find out what each mineral is used for by the body. Or have students do an Internet search to find out the benefits of each mineral in the chart.

Answers:

Step 1:
1. fósforo, hierro y yodo
2. calcio, fósforo y hierro

Tienen el mismo número de minerales.
La paella es más saludable porque no tiene tanta grasa.

Step 2: Answers will vary.

Block Schedule

Have groups of students invent a recipe for a healthy prepared food. Have them decide on a catchy name that will make children ask for it in the grocery store. Assign different students to the tasks of designing attractive packaging, researching information for the nutrition label, and writing the copy in Spanish.

Enrich Your Teaching
Resources for All Teachers

Culture Note

Approximately one fourth of Argentina's 1,068,300 square miles is in the Pampas. These fertile grasslands sustain large numbers of cattle. Most Argentine beef is consumed domestically. About 400,000 tons of beef are available for export annually.

Teacher-to-Teacher

Discuss healthy food choices with the class. Have small groups each create a poster explaining the benefits of healthy choices and how to make healthy eating easier—for example, by keeping cut-up fruit in the refrigerator. The posters should include negative and affirmative commands.

Actividad 20

Standards: 1.1, 1.2, 2.2

Presentation EXPRESS ANSWERS

Resources: Voc. and Gram. Transparency 131; Answers on Transparencies

Focus: Reading and speaking about a restaurant advertisement

Suggestions: Begin a discussion of unique restaurants or cafés in or near your community, such as Internet cafés or restaurants with live music. Have students read the questions before reading the ad and skim the ad for cognates. List the cognates on the board. Pause after each paragraph to discuss the main idea. Discuss item 7 as a group.

Answers:

1. Se recomiendan mariscos, la pesca del día y las sopas y los guisados de la comida mexicana moderna.
2. Se puede disfrutar de las obras de arte regional más contemporáneas.
3. Se encuentran influencias española y francesa.
4. Se prepara la comida mexicana moderna con técnicas e ingredientes usados por los pueblos originales—fuego lento, salsas sabrosas e ingredientes frescos.
5. No se puede almorzar en el Café de los Artistas porque se abre a las 18:00 h.
6. Se debe hacer reservaciones.
7. Answers will vary.

Actividad 21

Standards: 1.1, 1.3

Focus: Writing and speaking about restaurants

Suggestions: Have students discuss their favorite restaurants before they begin writing. Remind them to use the impersonal *se* in their answers. Tell students to save their responses for *Actividad* 22.

Answers will vary.

Additional Resources

- WAV Wbk.: Audio Act. 8–9, pp. 130–131
- Teacher's Resource Book: Audio Script, pp. 120–121, Communicative Activity BLM, pp. 128–129
- Audio Program: Tracks 11–12

✓ Assessment

- **ExamView** QuickTake Presenter Quiz on PresEXPRESS
- Prueba 7A-4: The impersonal *se*, p. 182

Actividad 20

Leer/Hablar

¡Se come bien aquí!

Lee este anuncio sobre un restaurante en Puerto Vallarta, México. Trabaja con otro(a) estudiante y contesta las preguntas.

1. ¿Qué comidas se recomiendan en este restaurante?
2. ¿Qué se puede hacer mientras se cena allí?
3. ¿Qué influencias diferentes se encuentran en la comida mexicana moderna?
4. ¿Cómo se prepara la comida mexicana moderna?
5. ¿Se puede almorzar en este restaurante?
6. ¿Qué se debe hacer si se quiere cenar allí?
7. ¿Te gustaría comer en el Café de los Artistas? ¿Por qué?

Actividad 21

Escribir/Hablar

Y tú, ¿qué dices?

1. Piensa en un restaurante donde comes a menudo. ¿Qué comidas se sirven allí? ¿Con qué se sirven estas comidas?
2. ¿Cuál de las comidas de este restaurante es tu favorita? ¿Con qué se hace esta comida?
3. ¿Cuándo se abre el restaurante? ¿Cuándo se cierra? ¿Se recomienda reservar una mesa?

Más práctica

- Practice Workbook, pp. 138–139: 7A-6, 7A-7
- WAV Wbk.: Writing, p. 134
- Guided Practice: Grammar Acts., pp. 251–252
- *Real.* para hispanohablantes, pp. 258–261

Go Online PHSchool.com
For: Impersonal *se*
Web Code: jdd-0705

Café de los Artistas

LA MÁXIMA EXPRESIÓN DE COMIDA Y ARTE

Mientras Ud. está en Puerto Vallarta, se le recomienda cenar en el Café de los Artistas. ¡Se come bien aquí! En este restaurante elegante, se puede disfrutar de[1] la mejor comida de la ciudad y al mismo tiempo de las obras de arte regionales más contemporáneas.

En la cena, se deben probar los fresquísimos mariscos y la pesca[2] del día. También se recomienda la comida mexicana moderna, el resultado de las influencias española y francesa con técnicas e ingredientes usados por los pueblos prehispánicos.

Esta comida se caracteriza por sus sopas y guisados[3] cocinados a fuego lento, sus salsas sabrosas y sus ingredientes frescos. Una vez terminada la comida, se quiere prolongar la visita para tomar un café y uno de los riquísimos postres mientras contempla el arte más nuevo y bello de Jalisco.

¡No se pierda[4] la mejor experiencia de comida y arte en Puerto Vallarta! Coma esta noche en el Café de los Artistas.

Se abre diariamente a las 18:00 h.

Se recomienda hacer reservaciones al 225-01-61.
Calle Guerrero 215
Centro

[1] enjoy [2] catch [3] dishes [4] Don't miss

Differentiated Instruction
Solutions for All Learners

Multiple Intelligences

Naturalist: Ask students to think of ways a restaurant can make the most of nature (views through the windows, outdoor seating, plants, vegetarian dishes). Have them make a list of recommendations for restaurant owners.

Students with Special Needs

Modify *Actividad* 23 for hearing-impaired students. Have student pairs create a poster or Web page, providing as much detail as possible about a restaurant without naming it. The other pairs then read the advertisement and guess which restaurant it represents.

Escribir/Hablar/Dibujar

Un anuncio para un restaurante

Trabaja con otro(a) estudiante para crear un anuncio de un restaurante. El restaurante puede ser uno que conocen en su comunidad o en otro lugar, uno que encuentran en la Red o uno que Uds. mismos inventan. Van a crear un cartel o página Web con ilustraciones en las que dan información sobre:

• por qué se debe comer allí
• cómo se preparan diferentes platos
• con qué se sirven estos platos
• qué ingredientes se usan

Incluyan también por lo menos *(at least)* un mandato afirmativo y un mandato negativo en el anuncio. Pueden usar el anuncio de la Actividad 20 como modelo y usar algunas ideas suyas de la Actividad 21 para escribir su anuncio.

El español en la comunidad

En muchas comunidades de los Estados Unidos, en las tiendas, los restaurantes, las bibliotecas y otros lugares públicos, se ven frecuentemente anuncios en español que comienzan con la palabra *se*. Los anuncios más comunes dan información, como "Se habla español"; ofrecen servicios o productos, como "Se alquila . . ." o "Se vende . . ."; anuncian un trabajo o una necesidad, como "Se busca . . .", o "Se necesita . . ." o prohíben algo, como "Se prohíbe . . .".

• ¿Has visto anuncios similares en tu comunidad? ¿Cuáles has visto? ¿Puedes escribir algunos anuncios en español?

Anuncios para clientes hispanohablantes

 **Escuchar/Hablar**

¡Nos gustaría visitar ese restaurante!

Presenten su anuncio de la Actividad 22 a otros dos grupos. Luego hablen de por qué les gustaría o no les gustaría visitar los restaurantes que se describen. Pueden hacer preguntas para recibir más información.

Modelo

Nos gustaría visitar ese restaurante porque . . . ¿Se recomienda reservar una mesa? ¿A qué hora se abre?

Un restaurante popular en México

trescientos sesenta y tres **363**
Capítulo 7A

Practice and Communicate **7A**

 Standards: 1.3

Focus: Creating an advertisement for a restaurant

Suggestions: Encourage students to be creative and include possibilities such as musical entertainment or poetry reading. After students finish their posters or Web pages, have them present them. The class can vote on the restaurant most likely to succeed, the most original, the most traditional, and so on.

Answers will vary.

 Standards: 1.1, 1.3

Focus: Speaking about liking restaurants

Suggestions: Once all of the restaurant ads have been presented, break students into groups. Students' questions should focus on the food served and other facts depicted on their posters. Remind them to construct questions with the impersonal *se*.

Answers will vary.

El español en la comunidad

Core Instruction

 Standards: 1.2, 5.1

Suggestions: Discuss the advantage of speaking Spanish or other languages in a business. Have students brainstorm a list of local businesses that advertise in Spanish or in another language.

Answers will vary.

 Pre-AP* Support

• **Activity:** Have students work with a partner. First, have one student refer to the picture of the restaurant in Mexico on p. 363. Allow this student twenty seconds to describe it to the partner. Then ask the second student to refer to the picture on p. 362 and allow twenty seconds to describe the picture to the partner. You may want to have a few students in the class describe their picture aloud for the rest of the class.

• **Pre-AP* Resource Book:** Comprehensive guide to Pre-AP* communication skill development, pp. 9–17, 36–46

Theme Project

Students can perform Step 2 at this point. Be sure students understand your corrections. (For more information, see p. 344-a.)

363

Enrich Your Teaching
Resources for All Teachers

Teacher-to-Teacher

Ask students to make a list of services available for speakers of other languages in your community. They should include other services they feel are lacking. Have groups of students brainstorm the services that would be provided in a "model community." Each group could work on a separate area: business, services (child care, healthcare), education, transportation, communication, residential areas, recreational facilities. Groups can present their ideas as an oral or written report. Students may want to draw a map to illustrate how all the features work together.

Lectura

Pre-AP*

Core Instruction

 Standards: 1.2, 2.2, 3.1

Focus: Reading comprehension of Pablo Neruda poetry excerpts

Suggestions:

Pre-reading: Ask students to think of their absolute favorite thing to eat. How do they feel when they imagine this food? Assign the poems for homework, telling students to imagine the scenes described by the poet as they read.

Reading: *"Oda al tomate"*: Bring a tomato, onion, knife, and olive oil to class. Read the poem aloud. Read it again, stopping after each action (cutting, "union" with onion, pouring of oil) and using your props to demonstrate the image. Then read the poem together with the students.

"Oda a la cebolla": Read the excerpt aloud. Have volunteers suggest ways to demonstrate the images in *"Oda a la cebolla"*.

Post-reading: Encourage students to give their reactions to the poems. Ask students to find a clue in *"Oda al tomate"* as to Neruda's nationality. What words in *"Oda a la cebolla"* could make you think that the onion is a very common food?

Refer students to Neruda's *"Oda a las papas fritas"* (p. 359). Have them compare it to *"Oda al tomate"*. What do they have in common?

Extension: Pablo Neruda is an AP* Literature author. You may want to suggest that students read additional works by this poet.

Bellringer Review

As a class brainstorm activity, ask students to suggest ingredients that might go into 1. *una ensalada de frutas* and 2. *una ensalada de verduras*. (Be sure that *tomate, aceite de oliva,* and *cebolla* are mentioned.)

Block Schedule

Have students create a collage illustrating one of the poems. Or have them create a collage about another food, using sensory images. They should then present their collages to the class. Ask the class to describe what they see and feel.

¡Adelante!

Lectura

Objectives

- **Read poems about two common foods**
- **Learn how to make tacos**
- **Describe how to prepare your favorite dish**
- **Watch *En busca de la verdad*, Episodio 9**

"ODA AL TOMATE"

La calle
Se llenó de tomates,
mediodía,
verano,
5 la luz
se parte
en dos
mitades
de tomate,
10 corre
por las calles
el jugo.
En diciembre
se desata[1]
15 el tomate,
invade
las cocinas,
entra por los almuerzos,
se sienta
20 reposado[2]
en los aparadores,[3]
entre los vasos,
las mantequilleras,
los saleros[4] azules.
25 Tiene
luz propia,
majestad benigna.[5]

Debemos, por desgracia,[6]
asesinarlo;
30 se hunde[7]
el cuchillo
en su pulpa viviente,
en una roja
víscera,[8]
35 un sol
fresco,
profundo,[9]
inagotable,[10]
llena las ensaladas
40 de Chile,
se casa alegremente
con la clara cebolla,
y para celebrarlo
se deja
45 caer
aceite,
hijo
esencial del olivo,[11]
sobre sus hemisferios
50 entreabiertos[12]
agrega
la pimienta
su fragancia,
la sal su magnetismo (. . .)

Estrategia

Reading and rereading

Poetry is meant to be read several times for a deeper understanding. Remember to pause at the punctuation, not at the end of a line. Read each of Neruda's poems aloud so that you can hear the language. Jot down the descriptive language used to describe the tomato and the onion. Focusing on these words will help you understand the poem better.

[1] is let loose
[2] rested
[3] cupboards
[4] salt shakers
[5] mild
[6] unfortunately
[7] sinks
[8] guts
[9] deep
[10] tireless
[11] olive tree
[12] half-open

Differentiated Instruction

Solutions for All Learners

Advanced Learners

Have students research a Spanish-speaking poet, select one poem, create a lesson plan, and present it to the class. Some suggested books are Neruda's *Veinte poemas de amor* and *Odes to Opposites,* or José Martí's *Versos sencillos.* Other poets: César Vallejo, Federico García Lorca, Sor Juana Inés de la Cruz, Gabriela Mistral.

**PABLO NERUDA
(1904–1973),**
un poeta chileno, es
considerado uno de los
poetas más importantes del
siglo XX. En 1971 recibió el
Premio Nobel de Literatura y
el Premio Lenin de la Paz.

"Oda a la cebolla"

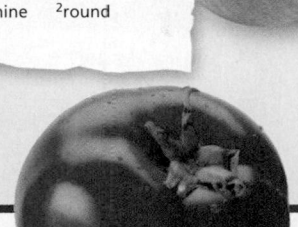

(...) cebolla,

clara como un planeta,

y destinada

a relucir,[1]

constelación constante,

redonda[2] rosa de agua,

sobre la mesa

de las pobres gentes.

[1]shine [2]round

¿Comprendiste?

"Oda al tomate"

1. ¿Por qué crees que Neruda usa el verbo *asesinar*? ¿Qué está describiendo?

2. El poeta no se refiere al tomate como un objeto. ¿Cómo describe el poeta el tomate?

3. ¿Qué quiere decir el poeta con la frase "se casa alegremente con la clara cebolla . . ."?

4. ¿A qué se refiere Neruda con la frase "hijo esencial del olivo"?

5. Lee el poema otra vez. Piensa en cuatro imágenes del poema y dibújalas.

"Oda a la cebolla"

En este poema, Neruda compara la cebolla con varias cosas. ¿Cuáles son?

Y tú, ¿qué dices?

Piensa en algo que comes o bebes, por ejemplo: el pan, el chocolate, las fresas, una tortilla, el cereal o la leche. Escribe un poema de cuatro a seis versos como éstos de Neruda.

Más práctica

- WAV Wbk.: *Writing*, p. 135
- Guided Practice: *Lectura*, p. 253
- *Real.* para hispanohablantes, pp. 262–263

Go Online
PHSchool.com
For: Internet Activity
Web Code: jdd-0706

Resources: Answers on Transparencies

Focus: Verifying comprehension of Neruda's poems

Suggestions: Answer questions as part of post-reading process or as homework.

Answers will vary but may include:

"Oda al tomate":
1. El tomate está vivo y por eso cortarlo es como asesinarlo.
2. Neruda lo describe como la luz y también algo vivo que invade, entra, se sienta y se casa.
3. Se casan el tomate y la cebolla como una mujer y un hombre. Se mezclan bien.
4. Se refiere al aceite que viene del olivo, como un hijo.
5. Answers will vary but may include: *la calle se llenó de tomates, el jugo que corre por las calles, el tomate invade las cocinas, el tomate se sienta reposado, el cuchillo que se hunde en su pulpa viviente, la unión del tomate y de la cebolla.*

"Oda a la cebolla":

Neruda compara la cebolla con un planeta, una constelación constante y una rosa de agua.

Extension: Pablo Neruda is an AP* Literature author. Have students read more works by this author.

Y tú, ¿qué dices?
 Standards: 1.3

Focus: Writing a poem

Suggestions: To help students, model writing a food poem. Remind students that poems can be very funny. Suggest that they work in pairs. Ask partners to decide on one food. Have them write a word list about the food, using adjectives and verbs that have to do with the senses: sight, sound, smell, and taste. Then have them write the poem together, focusing on their word list. Display poems in the classroom or add them to a class poetry book.

 Pre-AP* Support

- **Activity:** Have pairs of students prepare a crossword puzzle using 10–15 vocabulary words from the two poems presented on these pages. Redistribute the puzzles to pairs of classmates for completion.

- **Pre-AP* Resource Book:** Comprehensive guide to Pre-AP* reading skill development, pp. 18–24

Additional Resources

Student Resources: Realidades para hispanohablantes: Lectura 2, pp. 264–265; Lecturas para hispanohablantes 2: "Obatalá y Oruda," pp. 19–20, "Frutos del paraíso," pp. 25–26; Guided Practice: Lectura, p. 253

Culture Note

Neruda's poetry ranges from the whimsical to strong social and political commentary. *Cien sonetos de amor* (1959) was dedicated to his wife. *España en el corazón* (1937) expressed his sentiments regarding the Spanish Civil War. Not everyone agreed with Neruda, but nearly all respected his style.

Teacher-to-Teacher

Introduce the cinquain: Line 1 is a noun (subject); line 2 has two adjectives describing line 1; line 3 as three action verbs related to line 1; line 4 is four feelings or a complete sentence related to line 1; and line 5 is a synonym of line 1 or a summary word. Work with students to write a cinquain.

La cultura en vivo

Core Instruction

 Standards: 1.2, 2.2, 4.2

Focus: How to make tacos

Suggestions: Begin a class discussion by eliciting a description of a sandwich: usually two pieces of bread with ingredients between the bread. Make sure students include meat, cheese, and vegetables as possible ingredients. Then ask what main ingredient is used in making bread. *(flour)* Tell students that in the United States wheat is a major crop and from it we get flour that is used in preparing a variety of foods, among them bread and pasta.

When students are done reading, ask for a description of a taco. Have students compare it to a sandwich. If necessary, point out the similarities.

Review with students the ingredients needed to make tacos. Point out that these items are easily found in Central and South America. Have students hypothesize why tortillas are most often made of corn. If necessary, mention that corn is a major product of the region and, therefore, it is natural to find it used in abundance. Guide students to understand that people make dishes out of the foods most readily available to them, and some of these dishes become traditional in that region.

Extension: Gather cookbooks from countries in Central and South America. These may be available from the local library, or you can find recipes on the Internet. Have students use them to find dishes in which corn is used. Of special interest will be dishes not often found in the United States. Create a bulletin board illustrating some of the dishes. Recipes may be included if you wish.

Additional Resources

Student Resource: Realidades para hispanohablantes, p. 266

La cultura en vivo

¡Tortillas y tacos!

La tortilla es la comida fundamental de México y de toda América Central. La tortilla se hace con maíz y también con harina[1]. Los tacos son tortillas con carne o pollo, verduras, queso y chile. El maíz es una planta originaria de las Américas y su nombre azteca fue *toconayao*.

Hoy en día, las tortillas son populares en los Estados Unidos. Las tortillas se pueden comprar frescas o congeladas en los supermercados en casi todas partes del país.

La preparación de los tacos es fácil. Aquí están los ingredientes y la receta.

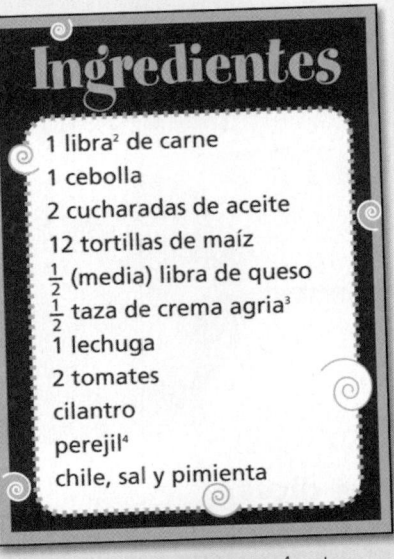

Ingredientes

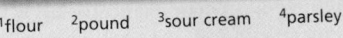

1 libra[2] de carne
1 cebolla
2 cucharadas de aceite
12 tortillas de maíz
$\frac{1}{2}$ (media) libra de queso
$\frac{1}{2}$ taza de crema agria[3]
1 lechuga
2 tomates
cilantro
perejil[4]
chile, sal y pimienta

[1]flour   [2]pound   [3]sour cream   [4]parsley

1. Para preparar la salsa: poner los tomates, la cebolla, el cilantro, el perejil, el chile, la sal y la pimienta en la licuadora por unos minutos.

2. Para preparar la carne: freír la carne en aceite con sal y pimienta. Después mezclar un poco de salsa con la carne.

3. Para hacer los tacos: poner una cucharada de carne en cada tortilla.

4. Para hacer más sabrosos los tacos: poner la crema agria primero, y después la salsa, la lechuga y el queso.

Differentiated Instruction
Solutions for All Learners

Advanced Learners

Explain to students that there was a time when people had access only to local foods. Modern modes of transportation allow people to transport food all over the world. Have students make a list of foods from other places that are found in their local grocery store, then identify a dish that could *not* be made without one of those foods.

Multiple Intelligences

Mathematical/Logical: Assume that the taco recipe serves four. Have students calculate the ingredient measurements to increase the recipe to serve 12 people.

Cómo preparar un plato favorito

Task
You are a guest on a television cooking show and will be explaining to the audience how to prepare your favorite dish. Explain what the ingredients are, the main steps for preparing it, and what utensils you need.

Estrategia

Using background knowledge
Think about cooking shows you have seen. How does the chef present the ingredients? How does he or she explain how to prepare and cook the dish? Use these techniques in your presentation.

① Prepare Bring in samples of the main ingredients and utensils you need to prepare your dish. (You might want to select a recipe that isn't too complicated!) If you prefer, you may bring in pictures instead. If possible, prepare the dish ahead of time and bring in a sample for the class. Make a recipe card like the one to the right to help you organize your presentation.

② Practice Go through your presentation several times. You can use your recipe card in practice, but not when you present. Try to:

- include the ingredients and utensils needed
- describe and show the preparation in clear steps
- speak clearly

Modelo

Para hacer una quesadilla se necesitan una tortilla, frijoles refritos y queso. Primero se calienta la sartén . . .

③ Present Tell and show the class how to prepare the dish. Use the materials (ingredients and utensils) or visuals as part of your presentation. You may serve the sample of the dish that you prepared ahead of time.

④ Evaluation Your teacher may give you a rubric for how the presentation will be graded. You will probably be graded on:

- how complete your preparation is
- how much information you communicate
- how easy it is to understand you

Quesadillas

Ingredientes que
se necesitan
tortillas de harina
queso
frijoles refritos

Cosas que se usan
un cuchillo
una sartén

Preparación
1. Primero se extiende $\frac{1}{4}$ taza de frijoles refritos sobre
   la mitad de cada tortilla.
2. Luego se ponen dos cucharadas de queso . . .

trescientos sesenta y siete 367
Capítulo 7A

Presentación oral

Core Instruction

 Standards: 1.3, 3.1

Focus: Presenting a favorite recipe
Suggestions: Review the task and have a discussion with students about cooking shows they have watched. Read Step 1 of the procedure. Provide suggestions of simple recipes, for example, sandwiches, crackers with toppings, fruit salad, or dips. Explain that students do not actually have to prepare the dish during the presentation. They can display the finished product (or picture) and act out the preparation with utensils or other props.

During the practice stage, remind students to speak slowly. Viewers of a real cooking show may want to take notes. You may wish to have students practice in small groups to allow for audience feedback.

Hand out copies of the rubric for students to review before giving their presentations. Encourage them to think of ways to make their presentations lively. For example, presenters might invite volunteers from the audience to perform the steps in the recipe or distribute samples to the class.

Portfolio

Record students' oral presentations on cassette or videotape for inclusion in their portfolios.

Pre-AP* Support

- *Pre-AP* Resource Book:* Comprehensive guide to Pre-AP* speaking skill development, pp. 36–46

Additional Resources

Student Resources: Realidades para hispanohablantes, p. 267; Guided Practice: Presentación oral, p. 254

✓ Assessment

- Assessment Program: Rubrics, p. T31

Give students copies of the rubric before they begin the activity. Go over the descriptions of the different levels of performance. After assessing students, help individuals understand how their performance could be improved.

Enrich Your Teaching
Resources for All Teachers

RUBRIC	Score 1	Score 3	Score 5
How complete your preparation is	You provide one of the following: utensils, pictures, recipe card.	You provide two of the following: utensils, pictures, recipe card.	You provide all three of the following: utensils, pictures, recipe card.
Amount of information given	Your presentation includes one of the following: ingredients, utensils, and steps for preparation.	Your presentation includes two of the following: ingredients, utensils, and steps for preparation.	Your presentation includes all three of the following: ingredients, utensils, and steps for preparation.
How easily you are understood	You are difficult to understand and make many errors.	You are fairly easy to understand and make occasional errors.	You are easy to understand and make very few errors.

Videomisterio

Core Instruction

Standards: 1.2, 3.2, 5.2

Resources: Teacher's Resource Book: Video
Script, pp. 123–124; Video Program: Cap. 7A; Video
Program Teacher's Guide: Cap. 7A

Focus: Reading and presenting new
vocabulary needed to understand the video

Personajes importantes

Roberto	**Tomás**	**De León**
Linda	**Carmen**	**Turrón**
Berta		

Synopsis: Roberto, Linda, and Carmen fly
to San Antonio. Tomás gives Roberto
important documents to present at the
bank to prove his identity. Roberto and
Linda visit De León at the bank, and he
sends them to Austin. There, they meet
none other than the mysterious Turrón,
who tells them that he has some very
important things to tell them about
Federico Zúñiga.

Suggestions:

Pre-viewing: Review the events of *Episodio*
8: Turrón continued asking questions
around town about Dr. Toledo. A patient,
Sr. Tos, told Dr. Toledo about it. Roberto
decided to go to San Antonio with
Carmen and Linda.

Have a volunteer read the *Nota cultural*
aloud. Ask what expressions or gestures of
polite familiarity exist in the United States.
*(allowing guests to serve themselves,
allowing them to roam around the house
during a party, receiving guests without an
appointment)*

Point out the *Palabras para comprender*
and give examples in context.

Videomisterio

En busca de la verdad

Episodio 9

Antes de ver el video

"Este archivo contiene las respuestas a todas sus preguntas".

Nota cultural Cuando haces nuevos amigos en México y ellos ya te tienen confianza, es muy común que te digan "Mi casa es tu casa" o "Siéntete como en tu casa". Son expresiones de cortesía.

"Estamos buscando a mi abuelo, Federico Zúñiga. Ésta es su cuenta".

Resumen del episodio

Antes de salir para el aeropuerto, Tomás le da a Roberto unos documentos muy importantes. Carmen, Linda y Roberto llegan a San Antonio. Al día siguiente, Roberto y Linda van al Banco de la Frontera y conocen al Sr. De León. Él les da la última pista para descubrir la verdad sobre el abuelo de Roberto.

Palabras para comprender

certificado de nacimiento birth certificate

tarjeta de estudiante student ID

puede que it may be that

heredero heir

Estoy a cargo del caso. I am in charge of the case.

368 trescientos sesenta y ocho
Tema 7 • Buen provecho

Differentiated Instruction
Solutions for All Learners

Advanced Learners
Have students summarize what happened in the previous episode for the class. They may need to write down their thoughts ahead of time. Allow them to look at the Video Script if necessary.

Heritage Language Learners
Have students write a creative ending to the *Videomisterio* once they finish watching this *episodio*. Tell them to include information on what happens to each character in the video. Do they end up happy or sad? Why? After watching the final *episodio* in the next chapter, have them compare their ending with the real one.

Después de ver el video

¿Comprendiste?

A. Completa las siguientes frases.

1. Antes de salir para San Antonio, el padre de Roberto le da _____.

2. Enrique es _____.

3. Linda quiere ir primero a su escuela porque _____.

4. Roberto le dice a De León que su familia no usa el apellido Zúñiga porque _____.

5. De León no puede darle a Roberto más información sobre su abuelo porque _____.

6. De León le dice a Roberto que le pueden dar más información en _____.

7. El hombre misterioso viajó a Guanajuato para _____.

8. Roberto descubre que el hombre misterioso es _____.

B. Escribe un resumen de la conversación entre Roberto y De León.

"Buenas tardes, señor. Me llamo Roberto Toledo".

Go Online
PHSchool.com
For: More on *En busca de la verdad*
Web Code: jdd-0209

Visual scanning: Direct attention to the photos. Have students read the captions and try to guess what the characters may be talking about. Point out that **archivo** in this case means "folder." Then have them read the *Resumen del episodio* and ask them one or two comprehension questions.

Viewing: Play *Episodio* 9 for the class. If there is time after viewing the full episode, go back and replay key moments that you wish to highlight. Remind students that they may not understand every word they hear in the video, but they should listen for overall understanding.

Post-viewing: Complete the *¿Comprendiste?* in class.

¿Comprendiste?

Presentation EXPRESS
ANSWERS

 Standards: 1.2, 1.3

Resources: Answers on Transparencies
Focus: Verifying comprehension; reviewing the plot
Suggestions: For part B, have students exchange their summaries and comment on each other's work. You may want to have partners present their conversations to the class.

Answers:
A:
1. unos documentos
2. el esposo de Carmen
3. ha perdido cuatro días de clases
4. su papá (Tomás) nunca conoció a su padre
5. la cuenta es muy antigua
6. Austin
7. hacer una pequeña investigación sobre la familia Toledo
8. Turrón

B: Answers will vary.

Enrich Your Teaching
Resources for All Teachers

Teacher-to-Teacher

If your class has kept a visual timeline of the most important events in the *Videohistoria* (see Advanced Learners note on p. 178), now may be a good time to quickly review it. Have groups or pairs focus on summarizing the events in each of the *episodios*. Be sure students focus on the most important ideas and encourage them to use words from the *Palabras para comprender*.

Additional Resources
- *En busca de la verdad* Video Workbook, Episode 9
- *En busca de la verdad* Teacher's Video Guide: Answer Key

369

Review Activities

To name foods and items in the kitchen:
Have students create word searches or crossword puzzles with the new vocabulary, then pass their puzzle to a partner to complete.

To follow a recipe: Have students play "What's My Recipe?" One group will tell what ingredients are needed and the steps to be followed. The other group has to guess what dish is being prepared. Students can use simple recipes for dips or sandwiches, or recipes they have shared over the course of the chapter.

To use negative *tú* commands and talk about food preparation: Have students prepare a list of dos and don'ts for safe and delicious cooking. Have students use irregular commands as well as other vocabulary from the chapter.

Portfolio

Invite students to review the activities they completed in this chapter, including written reports, posters or other visuals, tapes of oral presentations, or other projects. Have them select one or two items that they feel best demonstrate their achievements in Spanish to include in their portfolios. Have them include this with the Chapter Checklist and Self-Assessment Worksheet.

Additional Resources

Student Resources: Realidades para hispanohablantes, p. 268

 **CD-ROM**

PuzzleView Web Code: jdd-0707

Teacher Resources:
- Teacher's Resource Book: Situation Cards, p. 130, Clip Art, pp. 132–135
- Assessment Program: Chapter Checklist and Self-Assessment Worksheet, pp. T56–T57

370

Repaso del capítulo

Vocabulario y gramática

jdd-0789

To prepare for the test, check to see if you . . .
- know the new vocabulary and grammar
- can perform the tasks on p. 371

to name foods and items in the kitchen

el aceite	cooking oil
el ajo	garlic
el caldo	broth
el camarón, *pl.* los camarones	shrimp
la estufa	stove
el fregadero	sink
el fuego	fire, heat
el horno	oven
los mariscos	shellfish
el microondas, *pl.* los microondas	microwave
la olla	pot
el pedazo	piece, slice
el refrigerador	refrigerator
la salsa	salsa, sauce
la sartén, *pl.* las sartenes	frying pan
el vinagre	vinegar

to follow a recipe

añadir	to add
no añadas	don't add
batir	to beat
calentar *(e → ie)*	to heat
la cucharada	tablespoon(ful)
freír *(e → i)*	to fry
hervir *(e → ie) (e → i)*	to boil
el ingrediente	ingredient
mezclar	to mix
pelar	to peel
picar	to chop
probar *(o → ue)*	to taste, to try
la receta	recipe

to talk about food preparation

al horno	baked
apagar	to turn off
caliente	hot
¿Cómo se hace . . . ?	How do you make . . . ?
¿Con qué se sirve?	What do you serve it with?
congelado, -a	frozen
dejar	to leave, to let
no dejes	don't leave, don't let
encender *(e → ie)*	to turn on, to light
enlatado, -a	canned
fresco, -a	fresh
frito, -a	fried
olvidarse de	to forget about / to
no te olvides de	don't forget about / to
tirar	to spill, to throw away
no tires	don't spill, don't throw away

another useful expression

se puede	you can

negative *tú* commands

No hables.	Don't speak.
No comas.	Don't eat.
No escribas.	Don't write.

irregular negative *tú* commands

dar	no des
estar	no estés
ir	no vayas
ser	no seas

For *Vocabulario adicional*, see pp. 498–499.

Differentiated Instruction
Solutions for All Learners

Multiple Intelligences

Bodily/Kinesthetic: Write several theme-related scenarios on index cards (for example, eating in a restaurant or preparing baked fish). As a group, students pantomime the scene and the class guesses what is on the card.

Students with Learning Difficulties

Play a game to reinforce the chapter's vocabulary and grammar. Have students write five positive and five negative commands, incorporating as many vocabulary words as possible. The students receive one point per vocabulary word used.

 **7A**

Preparación para el examen

Más práctica
- Practice Workbook: Puzzle, p. 140
- Practice Workbook: Organizer, p. 141

 **Go Online** PHSchool.com
For: Test Preparation
Web Code: jdd-0707

jdd-0789

On the exam you will be asked to . . .	Here are practice tasks similar to those you will find on the exam . . .	If you need review . . .
❶ Escuchar Listen to and understand someone giving instructions for cooking a meal	Listen as Gabriel's sister Valeria gives him cooking instructions over the phone. See if you can identify: (a) what he wants to cook; (b) what ingredients he still needs to buy; and (c) the first few steps in the recipe.	**pp. 348–351** *A primera vista* **p. 354** Actividades 9–10 **p. 358** Actividad 15
❷ Hablar Tell someone the first steps in making a particular recipe	Based on the illustrations below, tell someone the first three steps in preparing paella. 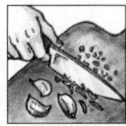	**pp. 350–351** *Videohistoria* **p. 355** Actividad 11 **p. 358** Actividad 15 **p. 367** *Presentación oral*
❸ Leer Read and understand as someone gives general advice on cooking	You are reading an article about cooking in a Spanish magazine. Tell which of the following suggestions are focused on: (a) things to do before cooking; (b) things to do while cooking; and (c) things to do after cooking. 1. Apaga el horno cuando terminas de cocinar. 2. Lee primero la receta para saber si tienes todos los ingredientes. 3. No salgas nunca de la cocina mientras algo está hirviendo.	**pp. 350–351** *Videohistoria* **p. 353** Actividad 6 **p. 354** Actividad 10 **p. 357** Actividad 13 **pp. 364–365** *Lectura*
❹ Escribir Write rules to promote safety in the kitchen	The home economics teacher asks you to write down a list of five rules for cooking safely for her Spanish-speaking students. You might begin with something like: *Ten cuidado cuando picas las verduras.*	**p. 356** Actividad 12 **p. 357** Actividad 13 **p. 359** Actividad 16
❺ Pensar Demonstrate an understanding of how certain foods from one culture are incorporated into another culture	You would like to prepare dinner for your family using some recipes from a Mexican cookbook, but your little brother and sister are very picky eaters. What could you tell them about food(s) from another country that they have eaten before and liked? What might be the best American food or dish to introduce to teenagers from other countries? Why?	**p. 366** *La cultura en vivo*

trescientos setenta y uno **371**
Capítulo 7A

Differentiated Assessment
Solutions for All Learners

STUDENTS NEEDING EXTRA HELP
- **Alternate Assessment Program:** Examen del capítulo 7A
- **Audio Program CD 21:** Chap. 7A, Track 5

HERITAGE LEARNERS
- **Assessment Program: Realidades para hispanohablantes:** Examen del capítulo 7A
- **ExamView** Heritage Learner Test Bank

ADVANCED/PRE-AP*
- **ExamView** Pre-AP* Test Bank
- **Pre-AP* Resource Book,** pp. 120–123

Performance Tasks
Presentation EXPRESS ANSWERS

Standards: 1.2, 1.3, 2.1, 2.2, 4.2

Student Resource: Realidades para hispanohablantes, p. 269

Teacher Resources: Teacher's Resource Book: Audio Script, p. 121; Audio Program: Track 14; Answers on Transparencies

1. Escuchar

Suggestions: Allow students to listen several times before they answer. Suggest they use a chart with the following heads: *¿Qué hace?, Ingredientes, Los pasos.*

 **Script:**

VALERIA: Diga.
GABRIEL: Valeria, soy yo, Gabriel. Tengo una cebolla, un ajo, unos tomates y unos mariscos. ¿Es bastante para hacer una paella? ¿Cómo se hace?
VALERIA: Necesitas comprar un pollo y unas verduras, como guisantes.
GABRIEL: ¿Qué hago primero?
VALERIA: Primero pica la cebolla y el ajo. Luego corta los tomates en pedazos.
GABRIEL: Un momento. Necesito un lápiz para escribir.

Answers: a. paella; b. pollo y verduras (guisantes); c. Primero pica la cebolla y el ajo. Luego corta los tomates en pedazos.

2. Hablar

Suggestions: Remind students to use commands to describe the steps.
Answers:
a. Pica la cebolla (el ajo).
b. Hierve los camarones.
c. Calienta el aceite en una sartén grande.

3. Leer

Suggestions: Have students read the tips first and look for words that will provide clues. *(terminas, primero, mientras)*
Answers: a. Lee primero la receta para saber si tienes todos los ingredientes. b. No salgas nunca de la cocina mientras algo está hirviendo. c. Apaga el horno cuando terminas de cocinar.

4. Escribir

Suggestions: Encourage students to use both affirmative and negative commands for their rules. **Answers** will vary.

5. Pensar

Suggestions: Have students look back at p. 366. Brainstorm a list of Mexican foods students have eaten. Point out that some children do not like spicy foods, so you could make the recipe using less chile.
Answers will vary.

✓ Assessment
- **ExamView** Quiz on PresEXPRESS QuickTake Presenter
- Assessment Program: Examen del capítulo
- **ExamView** Test Bank: Tests A and B
- Audio Program CD 21: Chap. 7A, Track 5

Chapter Overview

A primera vista	Manos a la obra	¡Adelante!	Repaso

Learning Sequence

INPUT	PRACTICE	APPLICATION	REVIEW
• Introduce vocabulary and grammar within an authentic context.	• Practice and develop new vocabulary. • Learn and practice new grammar structures.	• Apply vocabulary and grammar through culminating, theme-based activities. • Apply skill development.	• Review vocabulary and grammar.

Objectives

Read, listen to, and interpret information about • Camping and cookouts • Foods	• Communicate about what you like or dislike about outdoor camping. • Give instructions to a group on how to get ready for a cookout. • Read and interpret signs in a park or campground. • Use *usted* and *ustedes* commands. • Use *por*.	• Read about a forest in Puerto Rico. • Read about eating outside in Spanish-speaking countries. • Plan a special meal. • Watch *En busca de la verdad, Episodio* 10.	• Prepare for the chapter test.

Culture

• Carmen Lomas Garza	• *La parillada mixta* • *La comida picante* • *Las vacaciones de verano* • *El Parque de la Familia*	• *El coquí* • *La comida al aire libre*	• Describe customs involving both cooking and eating outdoors in Spanish-speaking cultures.

Vocabulary / Grammar / Learner Support

Vocabulary	Grammar	Learner Support	
• Foods • The outdoors • Eating outdoors	• *Usted* and *ustedes* commands • Uses of *por*	**STRATEGIES** • Using visuals • Circumlocution • Anticipating meaning • Brainstorming	**RECYCLING** • Outdoor activities • Food vocabulary • Adjectives • Negative *tú* commands • Uses of *por*

Chapter Features

Exploración del lenguaje

Compound Words

Conexiones

Art: Still life and a painting of Elena Climent

El español en el mundo del trabajo

Employment opportunities working in the outdoors in the United States for the National Parks Service

Beyond the Classroom: States & Countries

España, Texas, Puerto Rico, El Salvador, México, Guatemala, Ecuador, Perú, Bolivia, Chile, Argentina, Uruguay

Student Resources

TECHNOLOGY

ONLINE

Interactive Textbook
- Student Edition Online plus audio, video, and flashcards

Go Online Companion Web Site
- Tutorial activities
- Internet links
- Self-tests
- Downloadable MP3 audio files
- **PuzzleView**

CD-ROM

Interactive Textbook CD-ROM
Student Edition on CD-ROM plus audio, video, and flashcards

MindPoint CD-ROM
QUIZ SHOW

PRINT MATERIAL

CORE INSTRUCTION
Practice Workbook, pp. 142–150
- Review
- Vocabulary
- Grammar
- Puzzle
- Organizer

Writing, Audio & Video Activities,
pp. 136–145
- Video
- Audio
- Writing

Grammar Study Guide 1–2 (or 3–4)

Differentiated Instruction

STUDENTS NEEDING EXTRA HELP
Guided Practice Activities, pp. 255–270
- Vocabulary Flash Cards and Vocabulary Check
- Grammar Activities
- Presentación escrita

HERITAGE LEARNERS
Realidades para hispanohablantes,
pp. 270–289
Lecturas para hispanohablantes
- AP* Literature Author: Pablo Neruda, "Oda a las papas fritas," p. 23
- "Buenos Hot Dogs," pp. 80–81

ADVANCED/PRE-AP*
Pre-AP* Resource Book: Student Activity Sheet, p. 123

Teacher Resources

TECHNOLOGY

Audio Program   Fine Art Transparencies
Video Program   Vocabulary and Grammar
                 Transparencies
                 Answers on Transparencies

TeacherEXPRESS CD-ROM
- Lesson Planner
- Vocabulary Clip Art
- Web Resources
- Teaching Resources
- Teacher Edition with Interactive Links

PresentationEXPRESS CD-ROM
- Vocabulary
- Transparencies and Maps
- Grammar
- Photo Gallery
- Audio
- Clip Art

PH SuccessNet ONLINE
- Access to grades and reports from Online Interactive Textbook

ExamView on Presentation Express CD-ROM
QuickTake Presenter
- Vocabulary Quizzes
- Chapter Test
- Grammar Quizzes

TeacherEXPRESS CD-ROM
- Assessment Program
- **ExamView** Test Banks A and B
  test generator

Go Online
PHSchool.com
For: Teacher Home Page
Web Code: jdk-1001

PRINT MATERIAL

CORE INSTRUCTION
Teacher's Resource Book, pp. 142–168
- Input Script
- Video Script
- Answer Keys
- GramActiva Blackline Masters
- Vocabulary Clip Art
- Chapter Resource Checklist
- School-to-Home Connection Letters
- Communicative Activities Blackline Masters

TPR Stories, pp. 98–103

CORE ASSESSMENT
Assessment Program, pp. 190–202
- Pruebas
  Vocabulary Recognition
  Vocabulary Production
  Usted and *ustedes* commands
  Uses of *por*
- Examen del capítulo
- Speaking and Writing Rubrics

Teacher's Resource Book, p. 156
- Situation Cards

TPR Stories, pp. 98–103

Differentiated Instruction

STUDENTS NEEDING EXTRA HELP
Guided Practice Activities
Teacher's Guide, pp. T128–T135

HERITAGE LEARNERS
Realidades para hispanohablantes
Teacher's Guide, pp. 136–145
Lecturas para hispanohablantes
Teacher's Guide, pp. 6–7, 30–31

ADVANCED/PRE-AP*
Pre-AP* Resource Book: Resources Chart,
p. 121

Differentiated Assessment

STUDENTS NEEDING EXTRA HELP
Alternate Assessment Program
- Examen del capítulo, pp. 83–87

HERITAGE LEARNERS
Assessment Program: Realidades para hispanohablantes Teacher's Guide,
pp. T153–T157
ExamView Heritage Learner
test generator **Test Bank**

ADVANCED/PRE-AP*
Pre-AP* Resource Book: Teacher Activity Sheet, p. 122
ExamView Pre-AP* Test Bank
test generator

Regular Schedule (50 Minutes)

For electronic lesson plans:
Teacher Express

	Warm-up / Assess	Preview Present / Practice Communicate		Wrap-up / Homework Options
DAY 1	**Warm-up (10 min.)** • Homework check • Return Examen del capítulo: Capítulo 7A	**Chapter Opener (10 min.)** • Objetivos • Fondo cultural	**A primera vista (25 min.)** • Presentation: Vocabulario y gramática en contexto • Actividades 1, 2	**Wrap-up and Homework Options (5 min.)** • Practice Workbook 7B-A, 7B-B, 7B-1, 7B-2 • Go Online
DAY 2	**Warm-up (10 min.)** • Homework check	**A primera vista (35 min.)** • Presentation: Videohistoria *Un día al aire libre* • View: Videohistoria	• Video Activities 1, 2, 3, 4 • Actividad 3	**Wrap-up and Homework Options (5 min.)** • Practice Workbook 7B-3, 7B-4 • Go Online • Prueba 8B-1: Vocabulary recognition
DAY 3	**Warm-up (10 min.)** • Actividad 4 • Homework check ✔**Assessment (10 min.)** • Prueba 7B-1: Vocabulary recognition	**Manos a la obra (25 min.)** • Actividades 5, 7, 8, 9, 11 • Fondos culturales		**Wrap-up and Homework Options (5 min.)** • Actividades 10, 12 • Writing Activity 10 • Heritage Learner Workbook 7B-1, 7B-2 • Prueba 7B-2: Vocabulary production
DAY 4	**Warm-up (10 min.)** • Actividad 6 • Homework check ✔**Assessment (10 min.)** (after Communicative Activity) • Prueba 7B-2: Vocabulary production	**Manos a la obra (25 min.)** • Audio Activities 5, 6 • Communicative Activity • Presentation: *Usted* and *ustedes* commands • View: GramActiva video • Actividad 13		**Wrap-up and Homework Options (5 min.)** • Practice Workbook 7B-5 • Actividad 15 • Go Online
DAY 5	**Warm-up (5 min.)** • Actividad 17 • Homework check	**Manos a la obra (40 min.)** • Exploración del lenguaje • Actividades 14, 16 • Fondo cultural • Audio Activity 7 • Presentation: Uses of *por*	• View: GramActiva video • Actividades 19	**Wrap-up and Homework Options (5 min.)** • Practice Workbook 7B-6 • Actividades 18, 20 • Writing Activity 11 • Go Online • Prueba 7B-3: *Usted* and *ustedes* commands
DAY 6	**Warm-up (10 min.)** • Actividad 21 • Homework check ✔**Assessment (10 min.)** • Prueba 7B-3: *Usted* and *ustedes* commands	**Manos a la obra (25 min.)** • Actividades 22, 23, 24, 25 • Fondo cultural • El español en el mundo del trabajo		**Wrap-up and Homework Options (5 min.)** • Practice Workbook 7B-7 • Go Online • Heritage Learner Workbook 7B-4 • Prueba 7B-4: Uses of *por*
DAY 7	**Warm-up (10 min.)** • Writing Activity 12 • Homework check ✔**Assessment (10 min.)** (after Audio Activities) • Pruebas 7B-4: Uses of *por*	**Manos a la obra (15 min.)** • Writing Activity 13 • Audio Activities 8, 9 **¡Adelante! (10 min.)** • Presentación escrita: Steps 1, 5		**Wrap-up and Homework Options (5 min.)** • Presentación escrita: Step 2
DAY 8	**Warm-up (5 min.)** • Homework check	**¡Adelante! (40 min.)** • Presentación escrita: Step 3 • Lectura • ¿Comprendiste?	• Fondo cultural	**Wrap-up and Homework Options (5 min.)** • Presentación escrita: Step 4 • Preparación para el examen 3, 4, 5 • Go Online: Lectura
DAY 9	**Warm-up (5 min.)** • Homework check	**¡Adelante! (30 min.)** • Videomisterio: *En busca de la verdad*, Episodio 10 • Perspectivas del mundo hispano	**Repaso del capítulo (10 min.)** • Vocabulario y gramática • Preparación para el examen 1, 2	**Wrap-up and Homework Options (5 min.)** • Practice Workbook 7B-8, 7B-9 • Go Online: Self-test • Examen del capítulo 7B
DAY 10	**Warm-up (5 min.)** • Homework check ✔**Assessment (40 min.)** • Examen del capítulo 7B			**Wrap-up and Homework Options (5 min.)** • Go Online: Videomisterio • A ver si recuerdas . . .: Capítulo 8A

	Warm-up / Assess	Preview Present / Practice Communicate	Wrap-up / Homework Options
DAY 1	**Warm-up (10 min.)** • Homework check • Return Examen del capítulo: Capítulo 7A	**Chapter Opener (10 min.)** • Objectives • Fondo cultural **A primera vista (65 min.)** • Presentation: Vocabulario y gramática en contexto • Actividades 1, 2 • Presentation: Videohistoria *Un día al aire libre* • View: Videohistoria • Video Activities 1, 2, 3, 4 • Actividades 3, 4	**Wrap-up and Homework Options (5 min.)** • Practice Workbook 7B-A, 7B-B, 7B-1, 7B-2, 7B-3, 7B-4 • Go Online • Prueba 7B-1: Vocabulary recognition
DAY 2	**Warm-up (10 min.)** • Actividad 5 • Homework check ✔**Assessment (10 min.)** • Prueba 7B-1: Vocabulary recognition	**Manos a la obra (65 min.)** • Actividades 7, 8, 9, 11 • Fondos culturales • Audio Activities 5, 6 • Writing Activity 10 • Communicative Activity • Presentation: *Usted* and *ustedes* commands • View: GramActiva video • Actividades 13, 14	**Wrap-up and Homework Options (5 min.)** • Practice Workbook 7B-5 • Actividades 10, 12 • Go Online • Heritage Learner Workbook 7B-1, 7B-2 • Prueba 7B-2: Vocabulary production
DAY 3	**Warm-up (10 min.)** • Actividad 6 • Homework check ✔**Assessment (10 min.)** • Prueba 7B-2: Vocabulary production	**Manos a la obra (65 min.)** • Exploración del lenguaje • Actividades 15, 16, 17 • Audio Activity 7 • Presentation: Uses of *por* • View: GramActiva video • Actividades 19, 21, 22 • El español en el mundo del trabajo • Audio Activities 8, 9	**Wrap-up and Homework Options (5 min.)** • Practice Workbook 7B-6, 7B-7 • Actividad 18 • Writing Activity 13 • Go Online • Heritage Learner Workbook 7B-4 • Pruebas 7B-3, 7B-4: *Usted* and *ustedes* commands; Uses of *por*
DAY 4	**Warm-up (15 min.)** • Writing Activity 11 • Homework check ✔**Assessment (15 min.)** (after Writing Activity) • Pruebas 7B-3, 7B-4: *Usted* and *ustedes* commands; Uses of *por*	**Manos a la obra (30 min.)** • Fondo cultural • Actividades 20, 23, 24, 25 • Writing Activity 12 **¡Adelante! (25 min.)** • Perspectivas del mundo hispano • Presentación escrita: Steps 1, 5	**Wrap-up and Homework Options (5 min.)** • Presentación escrita: Step 2 • Go Online: Self-test
DAY 5	**Warm-up (5 min.)** • Homework check	**¡Adelante! (50 min.)** • Presentación escrita: Steps 3, 4 • Lectura • ¿Comprendiste? • Fondo cultural **Repaso del capítulo (30 min.)** • Vocabulario y gramática • Preparación para el examen 1, 2, 3, 4, 5	**Wrap-up and Homework Options (5 min.)** • Presentación escrita: Step 4 • Practice Workbook 7B-8, 7B-9 • Go Online: Lectura • Examen del capítulo 7B
DAY 6	**Warm-up (10 min.)** • Homework check • Answer questions **Repaso del capítulo (15 min.)** • Situation Cards ✔**Assessment (40 min.)** • Examen del capítulo 7B	**¡Adelante! (20 min.)** • Videomisterio: *En busca de la verdad*, Episodio 10	**Wrap-up and Homework Options (5 min.)** • Go Online: Videomisterio • A ver si recuerdas . . .: Capítulo 8A

Standards for Capítulo 7B

• To achieve the goals of the Standards, students will:

Communication
1.1 Interpersonal
• Talk: about camping, cookouts, food, weather, the outdoors, outdoor activities, details of a party and other activities; using the preposition *por* in various ways

1.2 Interpretive
• Read, listen to, and understand information about: the outdoors, camping, cookouts, food, weather
• Read: about Carmen Lomas Garza, *la parrillada mixta*, *el parque de la familia*, U.S. parks, *El Yunque* in Puerto Rico, summer vacation preferences in Spain, Mexican food, and regional spicy foods; information requiring understanding of uses of preposition *por*; a picture-based story
• Listen to and watch: a video about outdoor activities; a video mystery series
• Read and understand information about *senderismo* and *el coquí*

1.3 Presentational
• Present information about: camping; outdoor cookouts; food; weather; safety; preferences in food and outdoor activities; Mexican food; a party

Culture
2.1 Practices and Perspectives
• Describe: *la parrillada mixta; senderismo;* paintings of artists Carmen Lomas Garza and Elena Climent; spicy food; Mexican food; *el coquí*
• Talk about: summer vacation preferences in Spain; a park in El Salvador; a forest in Puerto Rico

2.2 Products and Perspectives
• Describe: painters Carmen Lomas Garza and Elena Climent and their works; regional spicy foods and kinds of foods in Mexico; a recreational park in El Salvador; *senderismo;* a forest in Puerto Rico; *la parrillada mixta;* and *el coquí*

Connections
3.1 Cross-curricular
• Describe Mexican artist Elena Climent; a forest in Puerto Rico; prepare a written presentation

3.2 Target Culture
• Recognize cultural viewpoints by viewing a video mystery series

Comparisons
4.1 Language
• Identify compound words

4.2 Culture
• Compare: a painting of a family reunion to one's own family gatherings; a park in San Salvador to U.S. parks; *la parrillada mixta* to a U.S. tradition

Communities
5.1 Beyond the School
• Read information on workers who use Spanish at national parks or monuments

5.2 Lifelong Learner
• View a video mystery series

372

"Sandía / Watermelon" (1986), Carmen Lomas Garza

Gouache painting on paper, 20 x 28 in. Photo Credit: Wolfgang Dietze Collection of Dudley D. Brooks and Tomas Ybarra-Frausto, New York, NY.

Fondo cultural

Carmen Lomas Garza nació en Kingsville, Texas, en 1948. Ella empezó a pintar cuando tenía 13 años. Los cuadros de Lomas Garza muestran *(show)* escenas familiares de la vida diaria y fiestas y actividades de la comunidad hispana. En este cuadro, titulado "Sandía", una familia hispana se reúne a comer esa fruta al aire libre.

• ¿Se reúne tu familia o algunos amigos o vecinos en tu casa frecuentemente? ¿En qué sentido *(way)* son similares las reuniones de tu familia a la que se ve en el cuadro? ¿En qué sentido son diferentes?

372 trescientos setenta y dos
Tema 7 • Buen provecho

Differentiated Instruction

STUDENTS NEEDING EXTRA HELP

Guided Practice Activities
• Vocabulary Check, Flash Cards
• Grammar
• Reading and Writing Support

Guided Practice Audio CDs
• Disc 2, Track 6

HERITAGE LEARNERS
Realidades para hispanohablantes
• Chapter Opener, pp. 270–271
• A primera vista, p. 272
• Videohistoria, p. 273
• Manos a la obra, pp. 274–281
• ¡Adelante!, pp. 282–287
• Repaso del capítulo, pp. 288–289

ADVANCED/PRE-AP*
Pre-AP* Resource Book, pp. 120–123

¿Te gusta comer al aire libre?

Chapter Objectives

- Discuss food and outdoor cooking
- Tell people what to do or not to do
- Indicate duration, exchange, reason, and other expressions
- Understand cultural perspectives on special foods and outdoor food vendors

Video Highlights

A primera vista: *Un día al aire libre*
GramActiva Videos: *usted* and *ustedes* commands; uses of *por*
Videomisterio: *En busca de la verdad,* Episodio 10

Country Connection

As you learn to talk about outdoor cooking, you will make connections to these countries and places:

España
Texas
Puerto Rico
El Salvador
México
Guatemala
Ecuador
Perú
Bolivia
Chile
Argentina
Uruguay

Más práctica

- *Real.* para hispanohablantes, p. 270

Go Online PHSchool.com **For:** Online Atlas **Web Code:** jde-0002

Una celebración al aire libre

trescientos setenta y tres **373**
Capítulo 7B

Chapter Opener

Core Instruction

Resources: Voc. and Gram. Transparencies: Maps 12–18, 20

Suggestions: Ask students to describe when and where they eat meals outside. Have them brainstorm lists of food that are typically served at a barbecue or from a street vendor. How are these foods typically prepared? Have students predict the vocabulary words by preparing a shopping list of foods that they would need to buy if they were having a picnic. Ask them to refer to their list later in the chapter to see how accurate their predictions were.

Tell students that they will learn how to give commands. Ask them to give examples of when they give commands and reasons why they give them. Tell students that in the *Videohistoria,* they will see how a group of friends goes to a park for a picnic and runs into a problem. Ask students if they ever prepare picnics with their friends. If so, where do they go for picnics in their community?

 **Fondo cultural** *Standards:* 1.2, 2.1, 2.2, 4.2

Suggestions: Ask students to bring in a picture from a family picnic to compare with the painting.
Answers will vary.

Teaching with Art

Suggestions: Point out to students that members of the extended family are in the painting. It is not uncommon in Spanish-speaking cultures for members of the extended family to live together or to spend a good deal of time together.

Teacher-to-Teacher

Prepare picnic baskets to use as props in this chapter. Go to a discount store for baskets and plastic toy foods. Assemble the baskets and distribute them to groups of students for appropriate activities in this chapter.

Teacher Technology

TeacherEXPRESS
Plan · Teach · Assess

PLAN
Lesson Planner
Go Online PHSchool.com
For: Teacher Home Page
Web Code: jdk-1001

TEACH
Teaching Resources
Interactive Teacher's Edition
Vocabulary Clip Art

ASSESS
Chapter Quizzes and Tests

PresentationEXPRESS
Dynamic Presentations for Teachers

TEACH
Vocabulary & Grammar Powerpoints
GramActiva Video
Audio & Clip Art Activities
Transparencies and Maps
Activity Answers
Photo Gallery

ASSESS
ExamView
QuickTake Presenter

374

Vocabulario y gramática

Presentation **EXPRESS**
VOCABULARY

Core Instruction

 Standards: 1.2

Resources: Teacher's Resource Book: Input Script, p. 144, Clip Art, pp. 158–161, Audio Script, p. 145; Voc. and Gram. Transparencies 132–133; TPR Stories Book, pp. 91–103; Audio Program: Tracks 1–2

Focus: Presenting vocabulary for camping, cookouts, and foods

Suggestions: Present the vocabulary in three groups: fruits, meats and grilling, and camping words. Use the Input Script from the *Teacher's Resource Book* or the story from the *TPR Stories Book* to present the new words, or use some of these suggestions.

Have students brainstorm a list of what they like to do on camping trips. Find out who your experienced campers are and use them as resources during the chapter. Ask students what kinds of foods they eat while camping or at a cookout.

Create a T-chart to list the advantages and disadvantages of going on a camping vacation. Ask students to tell you whether the sentences you say show an advantage or a disadvantage. Use sentences such as: *Hacemos una fogata. Puedo comer al aire libre. Hay hormigas. No hay electricidad.* Be prepared for differences of opinion.

Have students make two lists: *Lo que es necesario llevar* and *Lo que está en la naturaleza.* Tell students to place the new vocabulary under the appropriate heading. Encourage them to add words they already know for the *naturaleza* category.

Bellringer Review

Have students unscramble these letters for fruits and be prepared to tell which they like best:

amnazan   najaran   refsa   noáptal

(**Answers:** *manzana naranja fresa plátano*)

Additional Resources

• Audio Program: Canciones CD, Disc 22

Objectives

Read, listen to, and understand information about
• camping and cookouts
• foods

A primera vista jdd-0797

Vocabulario y gramática en contexto

—Voy a encender el fuego ahora. ¿Me puedes dar los fósforos?

—Claro. ¿Qué vamos a comer?

—Carne de res a la parrilla, tortillas de **maíz** y guacamole. También tengo una salsa que está hecha con chiles verdes y es bien **picante.** Y de postre, piña y sandía. Las dos son muy **dulces.**

—¡Fabuloso! Gracias por hacer todas las preparaciones.

—De nada. Me encanta comer **al aire libre.**

374 trescientos setenta y cuatro
Tema 7 • Buen provecho

Differentiated Instruction
Solutions for All Learners

Advanced Learners

Have students plan a camping trip or a day hike. Have them refer to the vocabulary here and use other vocabulary they know to make a list of what they might need, including food, supplies, and clothing. Have them share and compare lists.

Students with Special Needs

It may be difficult for students to understand who speaks which lines of dialogue. Point out in the illustration that the girl's outstretched hand is a visual clue that she is asking for the matches and is, therefore, the first speaker in the dialogue.

las nubes
el cielo
dar una caminata
el sendero
la fogata
la leña

la hormiga   la mosca

—¡Ay! No me gustan nada los mosquitos. Hay muchos por aquí.

—Sí, y hay moscas y hormigas también. ¡Qué problema!

—Pedro y Roberto, **traigan** más leña para la fogata. Si no, la fogata se va a apagar. **Pongan**la aquí muy cerca.

—Ahora, no. Vamos a dar una caminata por una hora.

—**Tengan** cuidado. Dicen que va a llover.

—Gracias. ¡Hasta pronto!

secos

mojados

Una hora después . . .

—No **entren** en la cabaña.* Están mojados. Aquí, **dentro de** la cabaña, todo está seco. ¡Y dejen las botas sucias **fuera!**

—¿Qué dicen? **¡Abran** la puerta ahora!

*cabin

  jdd-0797   Escuchar

¿Cierta o falsa?

Escucha las siguientes frases. Según la información de la escena de la página 374, indica si son ciertas o falsas. Señala con el pulgar hacia arriba si la frase es cierta y con el pulgar hacia abajo si es falsa.

Más práctica

● Practice Workbook, pp. 142–143: 7B-1, 7B-2
● WAV Wbk.: Writing, p. 142
● Guided Practice: Vocab. Flash Cards, pp. 255–260
● *Real.* para hispanohablantes, p. 272

Go Online
PHSchool.com
For: Vocab. Practice
Web Code: jdd-0711

 jdd-0797 Escuchar

Al aire libre

Escucha las frases y preguntas sobre un día al aire libre. Escoge la respuesta correcta para cada pregunta.

1. **a.** la piedra   **b.** el fósforo
2. **a.** unas nubes   **b.** un pavo
3. **a.** mojada   **b.** seca
4. **a.** la piña   **b.** la chuleta de cerdo
5. **a.** el durazno   **b.** la carne de res
6. **a.** la mostaza   **b.** la sandía

 *Standards:* 1.2   Presentation EXPRESS AUDIO

Resources: Teacher's Resource Book: Audio Script, p. 145; Audio Program: Track 3; Answers on Transparencies

Focus: Listening comprehension about a cookout

Suggestions: Have students look at the details of the picture and reread the text on p. 374 before they listen to the script.

 **Script and Answers:**

1. Los dos van a comer al aire libre. *(cierta)*
2. Van a apagar la fogata con los fósforos. *(falsa)*
3. Los dos van a comer pollo asado. *(falsa)*
4. De postre, van a comer fruta. *(cierta)*
5. El pavo es un pollo grande. *(falsa)*
6. El aguacate es carne. *(falsa)*
7. El chico preparó toda la comida. *(falsa)*

 *Standards:* 1.2   Presentation EXPRESS AUDIO

Resources: Teacher's Resource Book: Audio Script, p. 145; Audio Program: Track 4; Answers on Transparencies

Focus: Listening comprehension about a camping trip

Suggestions: Play the *Audio CD* or read the script once. Then allow students to listen again so they can answer the questions.

 **Script and Answers:**

1. Ramón, ¿puedes encender el fuego?
   ¿Qué necesita Ramón, la piedra o el fósforo? *(b)*
2. Creo que va a llover. Mira el cielo.
   ¿Qué se ve en el cielo, unas nubes o un pavo? *(a)*
3. —Mira. Está lloviendo y la leña está fuera.
   —¡Ay! ¿Cómo vamos a encender la fogata?
   ¿Cómo está la leña, mojada o seca? *(a)*
4. Voy a preparar una ensalada de frutas.
   ¿Qué necesitas, la piña o la chuleta de cerdo? *(a)*
5. Vamos a cocinar a la parrilla esta noche.
   ¿Qué van a comer, el durazno o la carne de res? *(b)*
6. Las hamburguesas están listas para comer.
   ¿Qué necesitamos para ellas, la mostaza o la sandía? *(a)*

 Enrich Your Teaching
Resources for All Teachers

Culture Note

Two universal and versatile condiments that add an extra touch of spiciness to many meals in Mexico are chili sauce and fresh limes. The chili sauce can be made fresh from green peppers or bought ready made. Many Mexicans enjoy chili and lime on a wide variety of foods.

Teacher-to-Teacher

Have students make a poster or collage that reflects what they like to do on camping trips or at cookouts. They can use photos, illustrations, or pictures from magazines to show what they like best about camping and what they typically do and eat at cookouts. Allow students to present their posters in class.

 Assessment
● ExamView QuickTake Presenter Quiz on PresEXPRESS

375

Core Instruction

Standards: 1.2

Resources: Voc. and Gram. Transparencies 134–135; Audio Program: Track 5

Focus: Presentation of additional vocabulary to discuss a picnic

Suggestions:

Pre-reading: Direct attention to the *Estrategia*. After students study the pictures and make their predictions, ask volunteers to share what they think the problem is. What clues did they use to make the prediction?

Reading: Pause after panel 1 and discuss who doesn't like eating outside and why. Pause again after panel 5 and discuss what else they learn about Manolo. Discuss whether any of the text is supporting their predictions about what the problem is.

Post-reading: Have students review their predictions. Discuss how the visuals helped them understand the story. Complete *Actividad* 3 to check comprehension.

 Pre-AP* Support

- **Activity:** Have students draw a scene similar to the top frame on p. 375, placing drawings for new vocabulary from this chapter around the scene. Redistribute the drawings among the students. Then have students work with a partner to take turns asking where various items are located. (¿Dónde está la mostaza?)

- **Pre-AP* Resource Book:** Comprehensive guide to Pre-AP* vocabulary skill development, pp. 47–53

Videohistoria  jdd-0797

Un día al aire libre

Claudia, Teresa, Manolo y Ramón van a pasar el día en el parque Desierto de los Leones. Todos tienen hambre, pero hay un problema. Lee para saber qué pasa.

Estrategia

Using visuals
Using visuals can help you understand the story. Look at the pictures and write what you think the problem is. Then read to see if your prediction was correct.

Ramón   Claudia Manolo Teresa

1 Claudia: Me encanta ir al parque y comer al aire libre.
Teresa: A mí también.
Manolo: A mí no me gusta. No me gustan ni las moscas ni los mosquitos.

5 Ramón: ¡Uumm, chuletas de cerdo! ¡Qué **olor** tan bueno!
Manolo: Sí. Un poco **grasosas,** pero muy ricas. ¡Ahora tengo sed y hambre!

6 Teresa: ¿Me pasas las tortillas?
Claudia: Pues, no están aquí. Tampoco está la carne de res. Esta mañana tenía tanta prisa . . . que dejé la comida en la mesa.
Teresa: Pues, ¿qué vamos a comer?

7 Manolo: Tenemos hambre. ¡Vamos a comer!
Claudia: Tenemos un problema . . . Toda la comida que preparé . . .
Manolo: Bien. Podemos comprar la comida en uno de **los puestos.** Vamos a comer allí.

Differentiated Instruction
Solutions for All Learners

Advanced Learners
Have students create a skit similar to the *Videohistoria:* a group of students is planning to go on a picnic and one person is never happy with the arrangements. Have them refer to the vocabulary to decide what they will take in their picnic basket to eat and drink.

Students with Learning Difficulties
To demonstrate the *Estrategia*, explain that visual clues such as body language can significantly aid comprehension. Have students identify the nonverbal clues such as gestures and facial expressions within the *Videohistoria* panels.

2 **Teresa:** Oye, ¿y qué traes en la cesta?

Claudia: Carne de res, tortillas de **harina, frijoles** y guacamole.

Teresa: ¡Qué rico! Ya tengo mucha hambre.

3 **Teresa:** Miren, aquí lo podemos poner.

Claudia: Pero **el suelo** está mojado. Vamos a buscar un lugar seco.

4 **Ramón:** Manolo, ¿quieres dar una caminata?

Manolo: ¿Dar una caminata? Tengo sed. Quiero un refresco.

Ramón: Sí, podemos comprar un refresco también. ¿Quieren **acompañar**nos?

Claudia: Gracias, pero vamos a quedarnos aquí, a charlar.

8 **Manolo:** ¡Qué bien! Claudia no puede cocinar muy bien. Su comida no tiene mucho **sabor.** Será mucho mejor comer la comida de aquí, del parque.

Claudia: ¿Qué dicen?

Manolo: Nada . . .

También se dice . . .

la cesta = la canasta *(muchos países)*

 Actividad 3

Escribir/Hablar

¿Comprendiste?

1. ¿Adónde van los chicos y qué van a hacer?
2. ¿A Manolo le gusta comer al aire libre? ¿Por qué?
3. ¿Qué dice Claudia que trae en la cesta?
4. ¿Adónde van Manolo y Ramón? ¿Qué ven?
5. ¿Qué le pide Teresa a Claudia? ¿Qué le dice Claudia?
6. ¿Qué deciden hacer los chicos? ¿Qué le dice Manolo a Ramón? ¿Lo oye Claudia?

Más práctica

- Practice Workbook, pp. 144–145: 7B-3, 7B-4
- WAV Wbk.: Video, pp. 136–138
- Guided Practice: Vocab. Check, pp. 261–264
- *Real.* para hispanohablantes, p. 273

Go Online PHSchool.com
For: Vocab. Practice
Web Code: jdd-0712

trescientos setenta y siete **377**
Capítulo 7B

Video

Core Instruction

Standards: 1.2

Resources: Teacher's Resource Book: Video Script, p. 148; Video Program: Cap. 7B; Video Program Teacher's Guide: Cap. 7B

Focus: Comprehension of contextualized vocabulary

Suggestions:

Pre-viewing: Have students list the main characters from the *Videohistoria* and write one thing about each person. Discuss whom they would choose to spend time with and why.

Viewing: Show the video, pausing to discuss the things Manolo complains about. Then show it again without pausing. After viewing, ask students if they know anyone like Manolo. How would they respond to Manolo?

Post-viewing: Complete the Video Activities in the *Writing, Audio & Video Workbook.*

 Actividad 3 *Standards:* 1.2
Presentation EXPRESS
ANSWERS

Resources: Answers on Transparencies
Focus: Verifying comprehension of the *Videohistoria*

Suggestions: Have students create a plot chart before they begin answering the questions. The chart should include a list of characters, the setting, the problem, and how the problem is solved.

Answers:

1. Los chicos van al parque para comer al aire libre.
2. A Manolo no le gusta comer al aire libre porque hay moscas y mosquitos.
3. Claudia dice que trae carne de res, tortillas de harina, frijoles y guacamole.
4. Van a dar una caminata. Ven a otras personas asando chuletas de cerdo.
5. Teresa le pide las tortillas. Claudia le dice que no están en la cesta porque dejó la comida en la mesa.
6. Los chicos deciden comer en uno de los puestos. Manolo le dice a Ramón que Claudia no sabe cocinar bien, pero no lo oye Claudia.

Enrich Your Teaching
Resources for All Teachers

Culture Note

El Parque Desierto de los Leones is in Mexico City. The desert in its title does not refer to geology but rather to a cloistered convent that was established there over 300 years ago. Covering close to six square miles, the park offers both historical interest and natural beauty. A coniferous forest surrounds much of the park area.

Teacher-to-Teacher

Have students plan a picnic in small groups. They should plan what foods they will make beforehand, what foods they will grill, and if they will bring or buy drinks from vendors. Their presentation should include a drawing of their picnic table. Place all drawings on the wall to create a mural of picnics at a park.

Additional Resources

- WAV Wbk.: Audio Act. 5, p. 139
- Teacher's Resource Book: Audio Script, p. 146
- Audio Program: Track 7

 Assessment

- **ExamView** QuickTake Presenter Quiz on PresEXPRESS
- Prueba 7B-1: Vocab. Recognition, pp. 190–191

Resources: Answers on Transparencies

Focus: Reading and writing to identify common objects

Suggestions: Have students identify the classification category for items in each group to help them decide which word does not belong.

Answers will vary but will include:

1. el flan
2. la harina
3. la cereza
4. el fósforo
5. la piedra
6. el maíz

Extension: Have partners follow the model and create their own word lists. Have them exchange lists with another pair.

Resources: Teacher's Resource Book: Audio Script, p. 146; Audio Program: Track 6; Answers on Transparencies

Focus: Listening comprehension about cookouts

Suggestions: Play the *Audio CD* or read the script several times. Have students focus on the details of the dictation and later identify whether the statement reflects someone who likes to cook outdoors or not. After students discuss which statements they agree with, conduct a class survey.

Audio Script: See the *Teacher's Resource Book.*

Answers will vary but will include:

1. Sí, le gusta.
2. No, no le gusta.
3. Sí, le gusta.
4. Sí, le gusta.
5. No, no le gusta.
6. No, no le gusta.

Fondo cultural Standards: 1.2, 2.1, 2.2, 4.2

Suggestions: Point out that the *parrillada mixta* is in a way a continuation of the gaucho tradition. The lives of the gauchos revolved around cattle and the outdoors, and the *parrillada mixta* is a meat-heavy meal consumed outdoors. Thus, it is no accident that the *parrillada mixta* is common in what were the gaucho homelands—Uruguay and Argentina.

Answers will vary but may include the weekend barbecue or grill.

378

Manos a la obra

Vocabulario y gramática en uso

Objetives

- Say what you like or dislike about outdoor cooking
- Give instructions to a group on how to get ready for a cookout
- Read and understand signs in a park or campground
- Learn to make and use *Ud.* and *Uds.* commands
- Learn the uses of *por*

Leer/Escribir

Una parrillada bien organizada

Tú y tus amigos van a hacer una parrillada en el parque. Tus amigos te traen las cosas que necesitan y tú tienes que organizarlas. Lee las listas y escoge cuál de las cosas no debe estar con las demás. Escribe esta palabra y otra palabra que asocias con ella.

1. la carne de res, el pavo, las chuletas de cerdo, el flan
2. la sandía, la harina, la piña, el melón
3. la cereza, la cesta, la leña, la piedra

Modelo

la parrilla, la leña, el fósforo, el durazno
el durazno, la manzana

4. el fósforo, el melón, el maíz, las cerezas
5. los frijoles, el maíz, la piedra, los aguacates
6. la mayonesa, la salsa de tomate, la mostaza, el maíz

 jdd-0798

Escuchar/Escribir

Escucha y escribe

Seis personas van a hablar de comer al aire libre.

1 Escribe lo que dicen. Después indica si a la persona le gusta o no le gusta comer al aire libre.

2 Habla con otro(a) estudiante. ¿Estás de acuerdo con las seis opiniones? ¿Por qué? Escriban tres razones *(reasons)* para comer o no comer al aire libre.

 **Fondo cultural**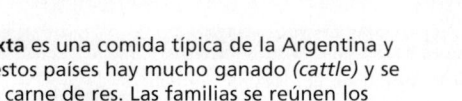

La parrillada mixta es una comida típica de la Argentina y el Uruguay. En estos países hay mucho ganado *(cattle)* y se consume mucha carne de res. Las familias se reúnen los domingos para hacer parrilladas mixtas al aire libre. La parrillada mixta puede incluir varios cortes de carne, una variedad de chorizos, salchichas y más.

• ¿Qué tradición en los Estados Unidos es similar a la parrillada? ¿Cuál es el origen de esta tradición? ¿Qué comidas son típicas de esta tradición?

Una parrillada típica de la Argentina y el Uruguay

Differentiated Instruction
Solutions for All Learners

Heritage Language Learners

Names for many foods vary from region to region in Central and South America. Have students list any words in addition to those in the *También se dice...* that they say in a different way. Can students explain why words often vary? Explain that this is partly due to the different languages and dialects spoken in the regions before the Spanish conquest.

Students with Learning Difficulties

For Actividad 8, have each student divide the barbecue foods into **Me gusta(n)** and **No me gusta(n)** lists. Then have student pairs create Venn diagrams to show comparisons. Expand the discussion by asking them to also talk about the outer circles that include foods about which they disagree.

Actividad 6 — **Leer/Escribir**

Mi hermano Luis

Lee lo que pasó cuando un joven fue al parque con su hermano. Completa su historia con las palabras apropiadas del recuadro.

El sábado pasado, fuimos al parque para __1.__ y pasar el día __2.__ casa. A mí me encanta hacer muchas actividades al aire libre, pero Luis no quería ir. Mientras __3.__, él decía que el __4.__ estaba demasiado mojado y que no quería tener los zapatos sucios. Luego Luis no podía encontrar un lugar __5.__ para comer. Pero cuando empezamos a __6.__ las hamburguesas, Luis dijo que le gustaba el olor de la carne __7.__ y que tenía un __8.__ increíble. ¡Comió cuatro hamburguesas! Luego él no podía caminar rápidamente porque no se sentía bien. Creo que si hacemos otra parrillada, Luis no nos va a __9.__.

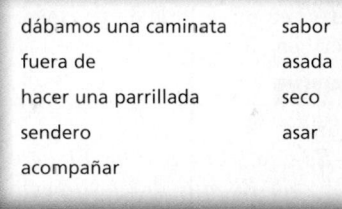

dábamos una caminata	sabor
fuera de	asada
hacer una parrillada	seco
sendero	asar
acompañar	

 Actividad 7 — **Escribir/Hablar**

¿Cómo son las comidas?

1 Haz una lista de tres comidas para cada una de las siguientes categorías de comidas: *dulces, grasosas, picantes.*

2 Compara tu lista con la de otro(a) estudiante. ¿Cuántas comidas pueden poner en la lista para cada categoría?

También se dice . . .

la parrillada = el asado, la barbacoa *(muchos países)*

el fósforo = el cerillo *(países andinos, México);* la cerilla *(España)*

el durazno = el melocotón *(España)*

los frijoles = las habichuelas *(Puerto Rico);* las judías *(España);* las caraotas *(Venezuela)*

el pavo = el guajolote *(México)*

   **Actividad 8** — **Hablar**

¿Qué vamos a servir?

Un(a) amigo(a) y tú quieren decidir qué comidas van a servir en la parrillada. Hablen de las comidas que les gustan y de las que no les gustan. Digan por qué.

Modelo
A —¿Te gusta *la sandía*?
B —¡Sí, claro! *Me encanta* porque es *muy dulce*.
o: —No, no *me gusta nada*. *Es demasiado dulce.*

Estudiante A

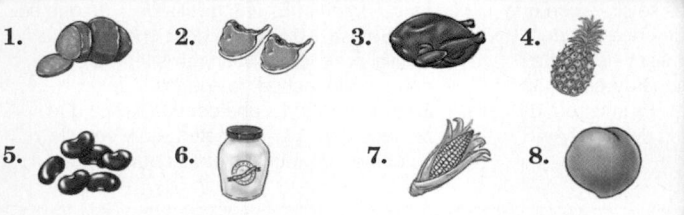

Estudiante B

muy	seco, -a
bastante	picante
demasiado	dulce
	grasoso, -a
	sabroso, -a
	delicioso, -a
	riquísimo, -a
	horrible

trescientos setenta y nueve **379**
Capítulo 7B

 Enrich Your Teaching
Resources for All Teachers

Culture Note

The meat at a **parrillada mixta** is often served with lemon wedges and a sauce made from vinegar and oil mixed with spices and garlic. Often the meat is marinated beforehand. Side dishes are usually simple, such as salad, **papas fritas,** or guacamole. In Mexico, expect to eat beans and tortillas at a **parrillada.**

Teacher-to-Teacher

Have students create invitations to a cookout. They should include the following details: when, where, what activities there will be, and what foods will be served.

  Standards: 1.2

Resources: Answers on Transparencies
Focus: Reading and writing about a day in the park
Recycle: Outdoor activities
Suggestions: Have students read the entire passage first. Remind them that they are looking for the correct phrase and do not need to change the form.
Answers:

1. hacer una parrillada
2. fuera de
3. dábamos una caminata
4. sendero
5. seco
6. asar
7. asada
8. sabor
9. acompañar

  Standards: 1.1, 1.3

Focus: Categorizing foods
Recycle: Food vocabulary
Suggestions: Have students brainstorm a long list for each category and then choose three favorites. After they discuss their choices with a partner, compare class lists to see if people agree or disagree.
Answers will vary.

  Standards: 1.1

Resources: Answers on Transparencies
Focus: Discussing cookout foods
Recycle: Foods; adjectives
Suggestions: Point out that Student B must provide the reason for his or her preference. Have students reverse roles.
Answers:
Student A:

1. ¿Te gusta la carne de res?
2. ¿Te gustan las chuletas de cerdo?
3. ¿Te gusta el pavo asado?
4. ¿Te gusta la piña?
5. ¿Te gustan los frijoles?
6. ¿Te gusta la mostaza?
7. ¿Te gusta el maíz?
8. ¿Te gusta el durazno?

Student B: Answers will vary.

Common Errors: Students may forget about agreement between nouns and adjectives. Review plural endings.

 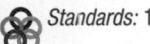

7B Practice and Communicate

 Standards: 1.1

Focus: Writing and speaking using circumlocutory words to describe an object

Recycle: Foods; classroom objects; colors; sizes

Suggestions: After discussing the *Estrategia*, brainstorm a list of adjectives and write them on the board for reference.

Answers will vary.

 **Standards:** 1.2, 2.2

Resources: Answers on Transparencies

Focus: Reading and writing about Mexican cuisine

Recycle: Foods; food preparation

Suggestions: Bring in recipes for the dishes from a Spanish-language cookbook, and review the ingredients and directions with students. Work together as a class to do this activity.

Answers:
1. maíz
2. harina
3. carne de res
4. queso
5. harina
6. carne de res
7. frijoles
8. salsa
9. maíz / harina
10. queso
11. aguacate

Block Schedule

Have students create a set of flashcards for some of the chapter vocabulary. Have them write a noun on one side of an index card and the description of it on the other side. Ask them to read their descriptions with the card facedown and identify the word. This can be played as a game with points awarded to the person or group with the most correct answers.

Actividad 9 **Escribir/Hablar**

No recuerdo la palabra

No recuerdas o no sabes la palabra en español para una cosa y tienes que usar otras palabras para describirla. Piensa en un objeto o una comida. Escribe tres descripciones. Luego léelas a diferentes miembros de tu clase. Ellos tienen que decir lo que describes.

Estrategia

Circumlocution
When you don't know or can't remember a word, use other words you know to describe what it looks like, is used for, or is similar to.

| Modelo |

sandía

A —*Es una fruta grande. El color de la fruta es verde y rojo. Es muy dulce y la comemos en el verano.*

B —*Es una sandía.*

Actividad 10 **Leer/Escribir**

La cocina mexicana

¿Conoces bien la cocina[1] mexicana? Hay muchas variaciones regionales, pero por lo general se usa mucho el ajo, la cebolla, el aceite y el cilantro. Casi todas las comidas se sirven con arroz. Lee las descripciones y complétalas con las palabras apropiadas del recuadro. Se puede usar una palabra más de una vez.

aguacate	maíz
carne de res	queso
frijoles	salsa
harina	

El taco: Es una tortilla de __1.__ o de __2.__ . Dentro de la tortilla, hay, por lo general, __3.__ , pollo o __4.__ .

El chile relleno: Es un chile, que generalmente está relleno de[2] queso. Se cubre[3] el chile con la parte blanca del huevo y se fríe.

El burrito: Esta comida viene del norte de México y el suroeste de los Estados Unidos. Se hace con una tortilla de __5.__ . Dentro de la tortilla se pone __6.__ , pollo o __7.__ . A veces se sirve con una __8.__ picante hecha de chiles verdes.

El tamal: Es una masa[4] hecha de harina de maíz rellena de carne de res o cerdo y chiles. Es una comida muy popular para los días festivos, como la Navidad.

La enchilada: Generalmente está hecha de una tortilla de maíz con diferentes ingredientes dentro de la tortilla, como pollo, carne de res o queso. Se sirve con una salsa hecha de chiles rojos o a veces de crema.

El mole: Es una salsa que se hace de chiles rojos y chocolate. Puede ser bastante picante. Muchas veces se come con pollo.

La quesadilla: Es una tortilla de __9.__ que se fríe. Se usa __10.__ dentro de o encima de la tortilla. A veces se usan otros ingredientes, como pollo y chiles jalapeños.

El guacamole: Es una comida fresca que se hace con __11.__ , tomates, ajo y cebolla y se come con muchas otras comidas.

[1]cuisine   [2]stuffed with   [3]Is covered   [4]dough

380 trescientos ochenta
Tema 7 • Buen provecho

Differentiated Instruction
Solutions for All Learners

Students with Learning Difficulties
For *Actividad 9*, help students by writing these headings on the board: ***clase, color, sabor,*** and ***tiempos especiales cuando se comen.*** Have students use the headings as prompts to recall vocabulary needed to write descriptions of foods.

Heritage Language Learners
Have students write an "Ode to the Chile", similar to the odes on pp. 359 and 365. Review their first drafts with them and post their final odes in the classroom.

Actividad 11 **Escribir/Hablar**

¿Adentro o al aire libre?

❶ ¿Has ido a una fiesta de familia o de amigos en casa de alguien? ¿Y una fiesta al aire libre? Hay diferencias, ¿verdad? Prepara un diagrama de Venn indicando lo que te gustó de las fiestas dentro de la casa y lo que fue bueno de las fiestas al aire libre. Indica también lo que te gustó hacer adentro y al aire libre. Piensa en los olores, el sabor de la comida, el tiempo que hacía, las personas que vinieron y las actividades que hicieron.

❷ Después describe tus experiencias a otro(a) estudiante, comparando lo bueno de las fiestas.

Modelo

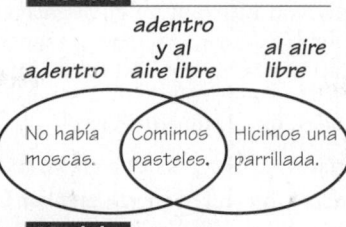

adentro   adentro y al aire libre   al aire libre

No había moscas.   Comimos pasteles.   Hicimos una parrillada.

Modelo

Me gustó la fiesta en casa de mi primo porque no había moscas.
o: Prefiero estar al aire libre.
Me encantan las parrilladas.

 Actividad 12 **Escribir/Hablar**

Y tú, ¿qué dices?

1. ¿Te gusta la comida picante? ¿Cuáles son algunas comidas picantes que tú u otras personas en tu comunidad comen?

2. ¿Qué comidas son grasosas? ¿Qué comidas son dulces? ¿Comes estas comidas a menudo?

3. ¿Cuándo y dónde hicieron Uds. una parrillada la última vez? ¿Qué asaron a la parrilla? ¿Qué otras cosas comieron? ¿Cómo estuvo la comida?

4. Cuando estás al aire libre, ¿qué te gusta hacer? ¿Dar una caminata? ¿Mirar el cielo y las nubes? ¿Encender una fogata?

5. ¿Cuál fue la última comida que compraste en un puesto? ¿Dónde estaba el puesto? ¿Te gustó la comida? ¿Qué otras cosas vendían?

Fondo cultural

La comida picante Muchas personas creen que todos los platos de la cocina de los países hispanohablantes son picantes. Esto no es cierto. El chile, ají o pimiento picante es originario de las Américas. Se han encontrado semillas *(seeds)* en el Perú y Bolivia, que tienen más de 7,000 años de antigüedad. En países como el Ecuador o México el picante es muy popular, pero en la mayoría de los países hispanohablantes, la gente usa el picante con moderación. Se puede decir que el picante es más popular en las regiones cálidas porque el picante hace sudar *(sweat)* y el sudor refresca la piel. Sin embargo, también hay platos picantes en regiones donde hace frío, como en los Andes, en Bolivia y el Perú.

• ¿Conoces un plato picante de los Estados Unidos? ¿Se comen en tu casa platos picantes? ¿Por qué crees que a algunas personas les gusta la comida picante?

Enrich Your Teaching
Resources for All Teachers

Teacher-to-Teacher

There are more than 140 varieties of peppers grown in Mexico, such as *chile de árbol,* *habaneros,* and *chipotle chiles.* Have students research the chili pepper and create a chart or poster listing peppers on a scale from the hottest to the mildest. Have them research the Scoville rating scale for rating the "heat" of peppers. What makes the chili hot? What should you eat or drink if your mouth feels too hot after eating a chili? What other facts can they find? Before students present their posters to the class, suggest that they give a true / false quiz about the chili.

Practice and Communicate **7B**

 Actividad 11 *Standards:* 1.1, 1.3

Resources: Voc. and Gram. Transparency 2; Teacher's Resource Book: GramActiva BLM, p. 157

Focus: Writing and speaking about indoor and outdoor parties

Recycle: Celebrations; food; weather; leisure activities

Suggestions: Use the Venn diagram transparency to begin brainstorming a few ideas as a class.

Answers will vary.

✓ **Assessment**
• For Step 2, have students tape-record their conversations for evaluation.

 Actividad 12 *Standards:* 1.1, 1.3

Focus: Writing and speaking about food and activity preferences

Suggestions: Have students work in pairs to brainstorm a list of foods and a list of outdoor activities. Then have them write their answers in complete sentences. Allow students to use their notes to discuss the questions with the class.

Answers will vary.

Fondo cultural  *Standards:* 1.2, 2.1, 2.2

Suggestions: In addition to spicy food from the United States, encourage students to think of other ethnic foods that can be spicy, such as Thai, Szechuan, and Indian.

Answers will vary.

Additional Resources
• WAV Wbk.: Audio Act. 6, p. 140
• Teacher's Resource Book: Audio Script, p. 146, Communicative Activity BLM, pp. 152–153
• Audio Program: Track 8

✓ **Assessment**
• Prueba 7B-2: Vocab. Production, pp. 192–193

Gramática

Presentation EXPRESS
GRAMMAR

Core Instruction

Resources: Voc. and Gram. Transparency 136; Teacher's Resource Book: Video Script, pp. 148–149; Video Program: Cap. 7B

Suggestions: After reading the *Gramática,* ask students to write on the board the present tense **yo** forms of several **-car, -gar,** and **-zar** verbs and verbs whose present tense **yo** forms end in **-go.** Ask them what they would use as a stem to form the **Ud.** and **Uds.** commands.

Use the transparency and *GramActiva* Video to help with your presentation.

Bellringer Review
Show Fine Art Transparency 36. Point to various adults and ask students to make up a sentence asking that each adult do certain logical actions. (Ex. *Señor, entre con su niña.*)

  Standards: 1.3

Presentation EXPRESS
ANSWERS

Resources: Answers on Transparencies

Focus: Writing commands for a cookout

Suggestions: For each verb in the word bank, have students write the stem they will use to form the plural command.

Answers:

Step 1:
1. Primero pongan las cestas en el suelo.
2. Segundo recojan leña y piedras.
3. Después saquen los fósforos.
4. Luego enciendan la fogata.
5. Ahora asen la carne.
6. Apaguen la fogata.
7. No dejen la comida al aire libre.

Step 2:
1. Primero pónganlas en el suelo.
2. Segundo recójanlas.
3. Después sáquenlos.
4. Luego enciéndanla.
5. Ahora ásenla.
6. Apáguenla.
7. No la dejen al aire libre.

Gramática

Usted and *ustedes* commands

To give an affirmative or negative command in the *Ud.* or *Uds.* form, use the present-tense *yo* form as the stem just as you did for negative *tú* commands.

- Add *-e* or *-en* for *-ar* verbs.

| cortar | corto | Señor, **corte** las chuletas de cerdo. |
| probar | pruebo | Señores, **prueben** la carne asada. |

- Add *-a* or *-an* for *-er* and *-ir* verbs.

| perder | pierdo | **No pierdan** Uds. los fósforos. |
| servir | sirvo | Señorita, **sirva** la ensalada. |

Affirmative and negative *Ud.* and *Uds.* commands have the same spelling changes and irregular forms as negative *tú* commands.

The same rules you know for *tú* commands regarding pronouns apply to *Ud.* and *Uds.* commands as well.

Attach pronouns to affirmative commands.

—¿Dónde ponemos la leña?

—**Póngan**la en un lugar seco.

With negative commands, pronouns go right before the verb.

—¿Encendemos la fogata ahora?

—No, no **la** enciendan todavía.

¿Recuerdas?
You already know how to give negative *tú* commands.
- **No prepares** los frijoles todavía.
- **No enciendas** la fogata.
- **No salgas** de este sendero.

negative *tú* command	*Ud.* command	*Uds.* command
no busques	(no) busque	(no) busquen
no hagas	(no) haga	(no) hagan
no des	(no) dé	(no) den
no vayas	(no) vaya	(no) vayan
no seas	(no) sea	(no) sean

GramActiva VIDEO

Want more help with *usted* and *ustedes* commands? Watch the **GramActiva** video.

Lave el coche.

 Escribir

¿Qué hacemos ahora?

1 Pon en orden las cosas que las personas deben hacer para una parrillada. Usa mandatos e incluye expresiones como *primero, segundo, luego, después* y *entonces*.

sacar los fósforos	poner las cestas en el suelo
apagar la fogata	asar la carne
recoger leña y piedras	no dejar la comida al aire libre
encender la fogata	

2 Luego escribe cada frase del Paso 1 con sólo el pronombre *(pronoun)*.

Modelo

buscar un lugar seco
Primero busquen un lugar seco.
Primero búsquenlo.

Differentiated Instruction
Solutions for All Learners

Advanced Learners/Pre-AP*
Have students write out a list of recommendations they would give to campers who are camping during different seasons. They can include what clothes to bring, a list of dos and don'ts, and rules about camping.

Pre-AP*

Multiple Intelligences
Mathematical/Logical: Students might benefit from writing out the rules in the *Gramática* in equation form, for example:

Ud. command = **-ar** verb − **o** in **yo** form + **e.**

 **Actividad 14**  **Observar/Hablar/Escribir**

La naturaleza muerta

Este cuadro es de la artista mexicana Elena Climent. Sus cuadros representan escenas de la vida diaria. Observa el cuadro con otro(a) estudiante y contesten las preguntas.

Conexiones **El arte**

En el estilo de arte que se llama naturaleza muerta *(still life)*, un(a) artista trata de pintar unos objetos como frutas y verduras, con realismo.

"Tienda de legumbres" (1992), Elena Climent
Oil on canvas, 36 x 44-1/8 in. Courtesy of Mary-Anne Martin/Fine Art, New York.

1. ¿Qué objetos se ven?
2. ¿Qué colores ha escogido la artista para representar los objetos? ¿Por qué crees que usó estos colores?
3. ¿Cuál fue la belleza que la artista vio en esta escena? ¿Qué hizo ella para pintar el cuadro con un estilo realista?

 Actividad 15 **Observar/Hablar/Escribir**

Para ayudar a tu mamá

Imagina que estás en México con un(a) amigo(a) y tu mamá necesita varias cosas de la tienda que se ve en el cuadro de Elena Climent. Trabaja con otro(a) estudiante y escriban mandatos con *Uds.* que ella les puede dar.

Modelo

no comprar
No compren juguetes en la tienda.

1. ir
2. pedir
3. traerme
4. escoger
5. preguntar si
6. tener prisa

Exploración del lenguaje

Compound words

Spanish, like English, sometimes combines two existing words to create new vocabulary. The invention of a new type of oven led to the English "micro" + "wave" and the Spanish *micro* + *ondas*. Like *el microondas,* compound words formed this way are masculine and singular. In the plural, the noun does not change: *los microondas.*

¡Compruébalo! Create a compound word by combining the action (verb) in the orange box with the object (noun) in the blue box. Write a command using each compound word.

abre		latas
corta		césped
lava	**+**	platos
saca		puntas
salva		vidas

Modelo

el microondas
Señor, use el microondas para preparar la comida rápidamente.

Enrich Your Teaching
Resources for All Teachers

Culture Note

Early in his career, Spanish-born Pablo Picasso painted a still-life portrait entitled "Carafe, Jug, and Fruit Bowl." Other great Spanish still-life artists include Sanchez Cotán ("Fruit Still Life"), Juan van der Hamen y León ("Still Life with Sweets and Pottery"), and Juan de Zurbarán ("Baskets of Apples and Quinces").

Teacher-to-Teacher

Tell students they are going to share a room with a roommate during summer camp. To avoid conflicts, they will create a list of rules. Brainstorm possible situations to get students started, such as leaving on lights, losing keys, sharing belongings, playing the radio, etc.

Practice and Communicate

 7B

 Actividad 14  *Standards:* 2.1, 2.2, 3.1 **Presentation EXPRESS ANSWERS**

Resources: Answers on Transparencies
Focus: Speaking and writing about art
Suggestions: Ask students how they feel when they look at the painting. Is the scene a familiar one?

Answers will vary but may include:

1. plátanos, aguacates, manzanas, tomates, piñas, naranjas, dulces
2. amarillo, verde, rojo, anaranjado
3. Answers will vary.

Teaching with Art

Suggestions: Have students bring in a copy of a still life they like and explain why it is a still life and why it appeals to them. Have them compare it to the Elena Climent picture.

 Actividad 15  *Standards:* 2.1, 2.2, 3.1 **Presentation EXPRESS ANSWERS**

Resources: Answers on Transparencies
Focus: Writing about shopping
Suggestions: Have students refer to their answers to *Actividad 14* to help them construct sentences.

Answers will vary but will include:

1. vayan
2. pidan
3. tráiganme
4. escojan
5. pregunten si
6. tengan prisa

Exploración del lenguaje **Presentation EXPRESS ANSWERS**
Core Instruction

 Standards: 1.3

Resources: Answers on Transparencies
Suggestions: Review the meanings of the words in each box. Students may need help with the compound word *sacapuntas.*

Answers will vary but will include:

el abrelatas
el cortacésped
el lavaplatos
el sacapuntas
el salvavidas

383

Actividad 16 Standards: 1.1 Presentation EXPRESS ANSWERS

Resources: Answers on Transparencies

Focus: Discussing how to prepare for a cookout

Recycle: Food vocabulary

Suggestions: Review the vocabulary for the illustrations and the stems of the verbs. Allow student to take notes to use in their conversations.

Answers:

Student A:
1. ¿Qué jugo compro?
2. ¿Qué comida preparo?
3. ¿Qué pongo en la ensalada?
4. ¿Qué pastel hago?
5. ¿Qué fruta sirvo?
6. Answers will vary.

Student B: Answers will vary but may include:
1. Compre jugo de piña (manzana).
2. Prepare arroz (papas fritas).
3. Ponga aguacate (frijoles).
4. Haga un pastel de cerezas (durazno).
5. Sirva melón (sandía).
6. Answers will vary.

Pre-AP* Support

- **Activity:** Vary the Advanced Learners activity presented on this page. Have students record their advertisement. Pair the students and have them trade recordings. Have them write one content question from the ad and pose the question to the partner who recorded the ad.

- **Pre-AP* Resource Book:** Comprehensive guide to Pre-AP* communication skill development, pp. 9–17, 36–46

 **Fondo cultural** Standards: 1.2, 2.1

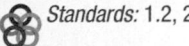

Suggestions: Each year millions of people flock to the island of Mallorca to enjoy the beautiful beaches and the deep-blue water. Discuss why people like to go on vacation. What kinds of vacation trips do your students like? Do they prefer going to the beach, the mountains, or the desert?

Answers will vary but may include: People vacation in July and August because schools are closed and those are months with good weather. Camping is popular because it is inexpensive.

Block Schedule

Have students write a paragraph about a recent camping trip or day hike. Have them name the foods they ate and what they did. They should describe what they liked best and what they didn't like using new vocabulary.

384

Actividad 16   **Hablar**

Una nueva vecina

Con otro(a) estudiante, haz planes para una parrillada. Decide qué comida van a servir y cómo prepararla. Haz preguntas y contéstalas con mandatos con *Ud*.

Modelo

asar a la parrilla / carne
A —¿*Qué carne aso a la parrilla?*
B —*Ase el pavo.*

Estudiante A

1. comprar / jugo
2. preparar / comida
3. poner / en la ensalada
4. hacer / pastel
5. servir / fruta
6. **¡Respuesta personal!**

Estudiante B

  1.  2.   3.

 4.   5. 6. **¡Respuesta personal!**

 **Fondo cultural**

Las vacaciones de verano La mayoría de las familias españolas van de vacaciones en los meses de julio y agosto. Los lugares favoritos son la playa (40 por ciento) y la montaña (30 por ciento). Muchas familias van de vacaciones a una casa de pueblo, otras alquilan un apartamento y otras van a un hotel o a una pensión (*guesthouse*). Algunas visitan otros países. Los "campings" también son populares porque son baratos.

- ¿Por qué crees que muchos españoles van de vacaciones en julio y agosto? ¿Por qué son populares los "campings"? ¿Cuándo y adónde van de vacaciones las familias de tu comunidad?

Mallorca, España

Differentiated Instruction
Solutions for All Learners

Advanced Learners

Have students design an advertisement for a summer camp. The goal is to convince parents to send their children there. The ad should provide some of the rules the campers are expected to follow.

Multiple Intelligences

Naturalist: As an extension to *Actividades* 17 and 18, have students create a flyer that advertises a special hike. Students should write why the hike is so special.

Actividad 17

Leer/Escribir

El club de senderismo

A los miembros del club "Aire puro" de Santiago, Chile, les encanta dar caminatas largas por los bosques *(forests)* y por las montañas. Este pasatiempo se llama *senderismo*. Lee el artículo y contesta las preguntas.

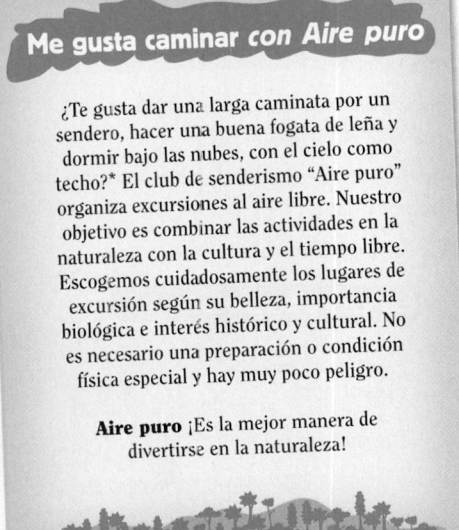

Me gusta caminar *con Aire puro*

¿Te gusta dar una larga caminata por un sendero, hacer una buena fogata de leña y dormir bajo las nubes, con el cielo como techo?* El club de senderismo "Aire puro" organiza excursiones al aire libre. Nuestro objetivo es combinar las actividades en la naturaleza con la cultura y el tiempo libre. Escogemos cuidadosamente los lugares de excursión según su belleza, importancia biológica e interés histórico y cultural. No es necesario una preparación o condición física especial y hay muy poco peligro.

Aire puro ¡Es la mejor manera de divertirse en la naturaleza!

*roof

1. ¿Cuál es el objetivo del club "Aire puro"? ¿Qué hace el club?

2. ¿Quién puede dar una caminata en una excursión del club? ¿Se necesita algo especial para participar?

3. ¿De qué cosas puedes disfrutar *(enjoy)* en las excursiones del club?

En los Andes, Chile

  Actividad 18

Hablar

Las reglas de la caminata

Antes de dar una caminata, los miembros tienen que conocer bien las reglas del senderismo. Trabaja con otro(a) estudiante y dile las reglas que los miembros deben seguir. Tu compañero(a) te va a responder.

1. usar / una mochila para llevar sus cosas

2. no jugar / con los fósforos

3. traer / un mapa de los senderos

4. salir / en grupos, nunca solos

5. no dar caminatas / sin compañero(a)

6. no dejar / la basura en las cestas

Modelo

llevar / zapatos adecuados

A —*Lleven zapatos adecuados.*

B —*Tienes razón. Es difícil caminar por los senderos.*

Más práctica

- Practice Workbook, p. 146: 7B-5
- WAV Wbk.: Writing, p. 143
- Guided Practice: Grammar Acts., pp. 265–267
- *Real.* para hispanohablantes, pp. 274–277

 **Go Online** PHSchool.com
For: *Ud.* and *Uds.* Commands
Web Code: jdd-0713

 Actividad 17  *Standards:* 1.2, 2.1, 2.2 | **Presentation EXPRESS ANSWERS**

Resources: Voc. and Gram. Transparency 137; Answers on Transparencies

Focus: Reading comprehension about a hiking club

Suggestions: Show the transparency of the article and have students highlight the cognates. Then have them read the questions. After reading, discuss any unfamiliar words. Ask to whom the club would appeal.

Answers:

1. El objetivo es combinar las actividades en la naturaleza con la cultura y el tiempo libre. Organiza excursiones al aire libre.
2. Las personas que quieren dar una caminata pueden. No es necesaria una preparación o condición física especial.
3. Pueden disfrutar de una caminata larga y una buena fogata y pueden dormir al aire libre, bajo las nubes.

 Actividad 18  *Standards:* 1.1 | **Presentation EXPRESS ANSWERS**

Resources: Answers on Transparencies

Focus: Discussing hiking rules

Suggestions: Bring in magazines or park brochures that discuss proper hiking behavior or have an experienced camper discuss why general rules are needed.

Answers will vary but will include:

1. usen
2. no jueguen
3. traigan
4. salgan
5. no den
6. no dejen

Theme Project

Students can perform Step 4 at this point. Be sure they understand your corrections and suggestions. (For more information, see p. 344-a.)

Additional Resources

- WAV Wbk.: Audio Act. 7, p. 140
- Teacher's Resource Book: Audio Script, p. 146
- Audio Program: Track 9

 Assessment

- *ExamView* Quiz on PresEXPRESS QuickTake Presenter
- Prueba 7B–3: *Usted* and *ustedes* commands, p. 194

Enrich Your Teaching

Resources for All Teachers

Teacher-to-Teacher

Have students write a poem using new vocabulary. The first and last lines are nouns: antonyms or related words. The second line has two adjectives describing the first noun. The third line has four gerunds: two that relate to the first noun and two that refer to the last noun. The fourth line has two adjectives describing the last noun.

Sandía
Dulce, sabrosa
Cortando, comiendo, asando, sirviendo
Salada, grasosa
Chuleta de cerdo

 Gramática

Core Instruction

Resources: Teacher's Resource Book: Video Script, p, 149; Video Program: Cap. 7B

Suggestions: Take time to explain each use of **por**. Have students think of other sentences for each use, and write them on the board. Use the transparency and *GramActiva* Video to help with your presentation.

 Bellringer Review

Have students choose one of these expressions and write one logical sentence with it to share with the class:

por lo general	*por la tarde*
por supuesto	*por eso*
por primera vez	

 **Standards:** 1.2

 **ANSWERS**

Resources: Answers on Transparencies

Focus: Reading and writing about a trip to Guatemala

Suggestions: Have students read the postcard in its entirety before answering. If they have trouble choosing the correct expression, have them read the sentence aloud, using both options.

Answers:

1. por la mañana
2. Por eso
3. Por supuesto
4. Por ejemplo
5. por primera vez
6. Por lo general
7. por la noche

Extension: Have students write original sentences using expressions from the activity.

Block Schedule

Have students create a bulletin board or poster board display that lists expressions using **por**. Have them add to the lists as they learn new expressions, and keep it posted for class reference.

 Gramática

Uses of *por*

The preposition *por* is used in several ways. You already know many of its uses.

To indicate length of time or distance:

> Dejen el pollo en la parrilla **por** unos minutos más.

To indicate movement through, along, or around:

> Vamos a dar una caminata **por** ese sendero.
>
> Hay un buen lugar **por** allí.

To indicate an exchange of one thing for another:

> No pague Ud. demasiado **por** esos melones.

To indicate reason or motive:

> Las chuletas de cerdo no son muy saludables **por** ser bastante grasosas.

¿Recuerdas?

You know several expressions that use *por*. See if you can remember them all.

por ejemplo	por la mañana, tarde, noche
por eso	
por favor	por primera, segunda, . . . vez
por lo general	por supuesto

To indicate a substitution or action on someone's behalf:

> Felipe y Marcos, traigan esa leña al fuego **por** su papá.

To indicate means of communication or transportation:

> Nos hablamos **por** teléfono ayer.

GramActiva VIDEO

Want more help with uses of *por*? Watch the **GramActiva** video.

 ¿Cuánto por . . . ?

 **Leer/Escribir**

Un viaje a Guatemala

Raquel le está escribiendo una tarjeta postal a su amiga, Anita, en Washington. Lee lo que le dice y escribe las expresiones apropiadas con *por*.

> Querida Anita:
>
> ¡Qué bonito país es Guatemala! Ayer, __1.__ (por lo general / por la mañana), fuimos a la ciudad de Tikal, unas ruinas mayas bellísimas. Tikal está en medio de una selva tropical.* __2.__ (Por eso / Por lo general) vimos pájaros en muchos árboles. __3.__ (Por supuesto / Por eso) hemos probado la comida guatemalteca. El maíz es importante en la comida aquí. __4.__ (Por favor / Por ejemplo), comen tortillas, tamales y enchiladas. También he probado los postres guatemaltecos. Ayer, __5.__ (por primera vez / por lo general), comí buñuelos—un tipo de postre frito riquísimo. __6.__ (Por lo general / Por favor) los guatemaltecos comen postres __7.__ (por la noche / por supuesto). Mañana visitamos Chichicastenango.
> Raquel
>
> *rain forest

 ¡Guatemala!

Differentiated Instruction

Solutions for All Learners

Advanced Learners

Have students conduct an Internet search on outdoor activities for tourists in Guatemala. Suggest they focus on water activities at the beach or lakes, climbing and hiking volcanoes, or visiting Mayan ruins. Have them present an illustrated postcard to the class about their virtual tour to Guatemala, *al aire libre.*

Multiple Learners

Bodily/Kinesthetic: Have volunteers act out some of the examples with **por** in the *Gramática.*

Actividad 20

Escribir

¿Cuál es?

Completa las siguientes frases con la expresión correcta de *por*.

1. Fuimos al concierto ___.

2. Omar quiere visitar a su familia en Perú. Va ___.

3. En la ciudad había mucha gente ___.

4. El profesor de español está enfermo hoy. ¿Quién va a enseñar ___?

5. Pagué 200 dólares ___ de avión.

a. por un mes en verano

b. por él

c. por los boletos

d. por la música

e. por todas partes

Actividad 21

Hablar

Voy al mercado

Imagina que encuentras a un(a) amigo(a). Habla con él (ella) sobre qué va a hacer.

Modelo

A —*¡Hola! ¿Adónde vas?*

B —*Necesito ir al mercado. ¿Quieres ir conmigo?*

A —*¿Por cuánto tiempo vas?*

B —*Voy por una hora, más o menos.*

Estudiante A

¿Cómo vas?

¿Por qué vas?

¿A qué mercado vas?

Estudiante B

la calle principal

duraznos frescos

. . . para no pagar mucho por ellos

¡Respuesta personal!

Fondo cultural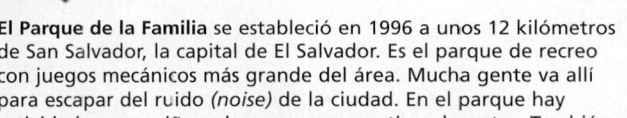

El Parque de la Familia se estableció en 1996 a unos 12 kilómetros de San Salvador, la capital de El Salvador. Es el parque de recreo con juegos mecánicos más grande del área. Mucha gente va allí para escapar del ruido *(noise)* de la ciudad. En el parque hay actividades para niños y lugares para practicar deportes. También hay peces y pájaros, un anfiteatro, un mirador panorámico, puestos de artesanías *(handicrafts)*, un área de piñatas, cafetines *(small cafés)* y un parqueadero amplio.

• ¿Hay un parque en tu comunidad similar al Parque de la Familia? ¿En qué sentido es similar? ¿Por qué es tan popular este tipo de parque?

Leyendo en el Parque de la Familia, en El Salvador

trescientos ochenta y siete **387**
Capítulo 7B

Enrich Your Teaching

Resources for All Teachers

Culture Note

Visitors can appreciate the impressive history of the Mayan people at the ruins of Tikal in Guatemala. The site includes pyramids, plazas, and temples. Visitors can also enjoy current Mayan culture at the market in the hill town of Chichicastenango, where the Maya gather to sell their wares.

Teacher-to-Teacher

Have students create postcards, telling where they went on vacation and describing the places they visited. They may also recommend places to stay and things to do. Encourage them to use expressions with **por.** To avoid embarrassing students whose families do not take vacations, stress that students may make up the information.

Actividad 20 Standards: 1.2

Resources: Answers on Transparencies

Focus: Writing sentences using **por**

Suggestions: Have students read both columns before beginning. As they work through the activity, remind them to look for words that are clues. After students complete the assignment, discuss what clues they used to help them with the answers.

Answers:

1. d   2. a   3. e   4. b   5. c

Extension: Have small groups create their own matching activity. Review the activities before you distribute them to the class.

Actividad 21 Standards: 1.1

Resources: Answers on Transparencies

Focus: Talking about shopping using **por** expressions

Suggestions: Point out that this is a single, continuous conversation between students.

Answers will vary but may include:

Student A:

1. ¿Cómo vas al mercado?
2. ¿Por qué vas al mercado?
3. ¿A qué mercado vas? ¿Por qué?

Student B:

1. Voy por la calle principal.
2. Voy por duraznos frescos.
3. Voy al mercado. . . .

Fondo cultural Standards: 1.2, 2.1, 2.2, 4.2

Suggestions: Ask students if they go to parks in the community, and ask why they go and what they do. Explain that the park in this photograph was constructed by the government. Like many parks all over the world, its main focus is on children. However, there are also features for teens and adults. Discuss parks in your area that cater to the entire family.

Answers will vary.

Actividad 22 Standards: 1.1

Resources: Answers on Transparencies

Focus: Speaking about how much time different activities take

Suggestions: Review the construction *se debe* with students, reminding them that it is followed by an infinitive and that it means "one should."

Answers:
Student A:
1. ¿Por cuánto tiempo se debe asar hamburguesas a la parrilla?
2. ¿... estudiar para un examen de español?
3. ¿... usar la computadora sin descansar?
4. ¿... hacer ejercicio sin beber agua?
5. ¿... dormir un chico de 15 años?
6. ¿... hablar por teléfono celular con un(a) amigo(a)?
Student B: Answers will vary.

Extension: Have students make four recommendations on how long they should spend on different activities, such as watching TV or reading a book.

Actividad 23 Standards: 1.3

Focus: Creating a brochure

Recycle: Places; activities; clothing; food; time

Suggestions: Bring in brochures from your local travel agency or chamber of commerce to use as models. Study the brochures to see if recommendations are written in the imperative. Have students find out if your local travel agencies have any brochures in Spanish.

Answers will vary.

El español en el mundo del trabajo

Core Instruction

 Standards: 1.2, 5.1

Suggestions: Have students work in small groups and choose two national parks. Have them find out if the parks have literature or offer tours in Spanish or another language. If possible, have students request the Spanish-language literature to share with the class.

Answers will vary.

Actividad 22 Hablar

¿Por cuánto tiempo?

Habla con otro(a) estudiante sobre cuánto tiempo se debe hacer diferentes cosas en la cocina, en los estudios y en los deportes.

Modelo

dejar la leche en el refrigerador
A —¿Por cuánto tiempo se debe dejar la leche en el refrigerador?
B —Por una semana, más o menos.

1. asar hamburguesas a la parrilla
2. estudiar para un examen de español
3. usar la computadora sin descansar
4. hacer ejercicio sin beber agua
5. dormir un chico de 15 años
6. hablar por teléfono celular con un(a) amigo(a)

Actividad 23 Escribir/Dibujar/Hablar

Nuestras recomendaciones

Imagina que un grupo de jóvenes que no conocen la región donde vives vienen a visitarte. Sabes que les encanta hacer actividades al aire libre.

1 Escribe cinco recomendaciones, usando mandatos en la forma *Uds.*, que puedes darles. Puedes incluir:

• adónde deben ir y qué deben hacer al aire libre
• por dónde deben pasar y cuánto tiempo deben pasar en diferentes lugares
• qué cosas y ropa deben llevar
• qué pueden comer y dónde
• reglas que necesitan seguir
• si deben tener cuidado con algo

2 Trabaja con un grupo de tres estudiantes. Hagan un cartel o folleto (*brochure*) usando visuales. Preséntenlo a la clase.

El español en el mundo del trabajo

¿Te gusta trabajar al aire libre? Las agencias federales de los Estados Unidos tienen más de 300 millones de hectáreas (*aproximadamente 1,214,575 acres*) de bosques (*forests*), parques y reservas nacionales. El Servicio de Parques Nacionales, formado en 1916, es muy conocido ya que (*since*) administra 48 parques nacionales. El Sistema de Parques Nacionales incluye más de 32 millones de hectáreas y cerca de 340 unidades que incluyen desde Monumentos Nacionales hasta Áreas Nacionales de Recreación. Cada año vienen más turistas hispanohablantes a los Estados Unidos y se necesitan empleados bilingües para ayudarlos. También hay que escribir folletos de turismo, crear programas educativos y escribir información en los sitios Web.

• Piensa en un parque nacional o monumento nacional cerca de tu comunidad. ¿Hablan español los empleados del parque? ¿Hay información en español para los visitantes?

388 trescientos ochenta y ocho
Tema 7 • Buen provecho

Differentiated Instruction
Solutions for All Learners

Advanced Learners
Have students research the responsibilities of a park ranger. If possible, have them conduct a personal interview and obtain a copy of the park's rules. Have students create a chart that indicates how much time is spent outdoors and the different activities the park ranger has to do. Students can present their results to the class.

Multiple Intelligences
Bodily/Kinesthetic: Give students the option of drawing posters, filming commercials, singing jingles, building a set, or acting out the ad in *Actividad* 25.

  Actividad 24 jdd-0798 🔊 **Leer/Escuchar** _____

Supermercado El Ranchero

Lee las preguntas sobre un anuncio. Luego escucha el anuncio para el supermercado El Ranchero. Escribe la letra correcta para cada pregunta.

1. ¿Cuándo empiezan los precios especiales?
   a. mañana por la tarde
   b. mañana por la mañana
   c. hoy por la mañana

2. ¿Qué se vende en la carnicería?
   a. carne de res, pollo y chuletas de cerdo
   b. pescado, chuletas de cerdo y bistec
   c. carne de res, verduras y frutas

3. ¿Cuánto cuesta la carne de res para asar?
   a. $2.99 por libra[1]
   b. $3.49 por libra
   c. $2.49 por libra

4. ¿Qué ofrecen en la taquería?
   a. carne de res con arroz
   b. pedazos de pollo con tortillas
   c. un pollo gratis[2] si compra un pollo entero

5. ¿Con qué vienen los pollos enteros?
   a. arroz, frijoles, salsa y tortillas
   b. refrescos y verduras con tortillas
   c. sólo tortillas de maíz

[1] pound   [2] free

 Actividad 25 👥 **Escribir/Hablar** _____

Un producto delicioso

La compañía Productos NOEL quiere crear un anuncio de radio para uno de sus productos, las galletas Festival. La compañía también va a ofrecer precios especiales para las galletas Festival por un tiempo limitado.

① Trabaja con otro(a) estudiante y escriban un anuncio para la radio.

Modelo

Con galletas Festival, tus niños estarán* más contentos. No compren otras galletas . . .

② Presenten su anuncio a la clase.

*To say "they will be," use _estarán_.

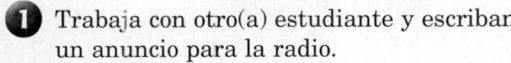

NUEVO PRODUCTO:
GALLETA FESTIVAL
- Galleta dulce con crema, tipo sándwich
- Posicionada como una marca divertida, moderna y dirigida a los niños entre los ocho y los 12 años de edad
- Consumidas por los niños fuera de la casa, preferiblemente en la escuela
- Vienen en deliciosos sabores a fresa, vainilla, chocolate, choco-choco y limón
- Adultos también las buscan para calmar el hambre

Más práctica

- Practice Workbook, pp. 147–148: 7B-6, 7B-7
- WAV Wbk.: Writing, p. 144
- Guided Practice: Grammar Acts., p. 268
- Real. para hispanohablantes, pp. 278–281

Go Online PHSchool.com
For: Uses of _por_
Web Code: jdd-0714

trescientos ochenta y nueve **389**
Capítulo 7B

Actividad 24 Standards: 1.2, 2..2
Presentation EXPRESS AUDIO

Resources: Teacher's Resource Book: Audio Script, pp. 146–147; Audio Program: Track: 10; Answers on Transparencies

Focus: Listening comprehension about a supermarket advertisement

Suggestions: Tell students they will be listening to an advertisement for a supermarket. Ask them what they would expect to hear. Then have them read all the questions and answer choices. Tell students they should listen for the main idea the first time they listen. Have them listen again, and have them take notes about the details asked in the questions.

🔊 **Script:** See the _Teacher's Resource Book._

Answers:
1. b   2. a   3. c   4. c   5. a

Actividad 25 Standards: 1.3
Pre-AP*

Resources: Voc. and Gram. Transparency 138; Answers on Transparencies

Focus: Writing and presenting ad copy

Suggestions: After students read the ad, have them make a list of important ideas they want to endorse. Listen to Spanish-language radio announcements or tape TV commercials to provide students with examples of how to inflect their voices. Some students may feel more comfortable tape-recording their radio announcements.

Answers will vary.

Theme Project

Students can perform Step 5 at this point. Record their presentations on cassette or videotape for inclusion in their portfolios. (For more information, see p. 344-a.)

Additional Resources

- WAV Wbk.: Audio Act. 8–9, p. 141
- Teacher's Resource Book: Audio Script, p. 147, Communicative Activity BLM, pp. 154–155
- Audio Program: Tracks 11–12

✓ **Assessment**
- ExamView Quiz on PresEXPRESS
- Prueba 7B-4: Uses of _por_, p. 195

Enrich Your Teaching
Resources for All Teachers

Culture Note

The U.S. National Park Service administers the San Juan National Historic Site in Puerto Rico. This is a large coastal fortification built in the seventeenth century when Puerto Rico was still a Spanish possession. The fortress was armed with cannons to protect San Juan harbor.

Teacher-to-Teacher

Have students look at local newspaper flyers and create one of their own. The flyer should have a theme, such as a Fourth of July cookout or _Cinco de Mayo_ barbecue. The flyer may also include recipes to use with products they sell. Students should use expressions with **por.**

389

Core Instruction

🔆 *Standards:* 1.2, 2.1, 2.2, 3.1

Focus: Reading comprehension of an article about El Yunque national forest in Puerto Rico

Suggestions:

Pre-reading: Gather material and books about national parks in the United States and Spanish-speaking countries. Ask students whether they have ever visited any of the national parks or historic sites, and have them describe what they did and saw. Have them preview the materials you bring in, and discuss what information they might receive at a park information center, such as rules, maps, and trail guides. Point out that this is a nonfiction article, and ask students to predict the kind of information they would expect.

Reading: Ask student volunteers to read the article aloud. After each paragraph, ask students to take notes and write down key information from the paragraph.

Post-reading: Give students time to review their notes before completing the *¿Comprendiste?* questions. Ask them if the article had the kind of information they were expecting.

Bellringer Review

Refer to the Map Transparency on pp. xx–xxi and discuss weather and possible activities one might do on these islands. *(En Cuba hace calor y se puede bucear.)*

Additional Resources

Student Resource: Guided Practice: Lectura, p. 269

¡Adelante!

Objectives

- Read about a forest in Puerto Rico
- Read about eating outside in Spanish-speaking countries
- Plan a special meal
- Watch *En busca de la verdad,* Episodio 10

El Yunque

Estrategia

Anticipating meaning
What kind of information would you expect to receive at the information center of a major national park? Look through the reading and see if you find the information you listed.

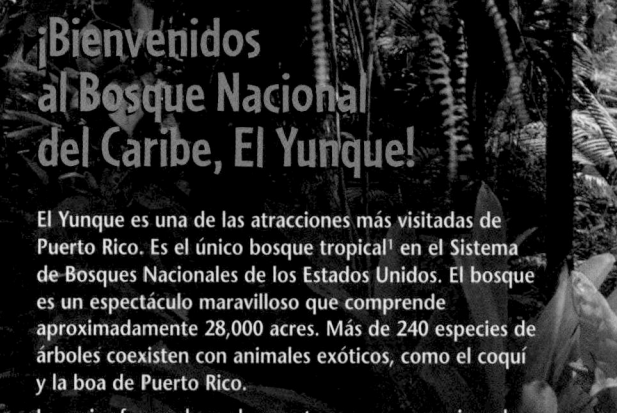

¡Bienvenidos al Bosque Nacional del Caribe, El Yunque!

El Yunque es una de las atracciones más visitadas de Puerto Rico. Es el único bosque tropical[1] en el Sistema de Bosques Nacionales de los Estados Unidos. El bosque es un espectáculo maravilloso que comprende aproximadamente 28,000 acres. Más de 240 especies de árboles coexisten con animales exóticos, como el coquí y la boa de Puerto Rico.

La mejor forma de explorar este parque es caminando por las varias veredas[2] que pasan por el bosque. Hay más de 13 millas de veredas recreativas que sólo se pueden recorrer a pie (no se permiten ni caballos ni motocicletas ni bicicletas de montaña). También hay varias áreas de recreación con comodidades para hacer picnics y parrilladas y está permitido acampar en muchas áreas del bosque. ¡Venga y disfrute del parque!

La cotorra puertorriqueña es un ave en peligro de extinción.

Vereda la Mina

La Vereda la Mina es la más popular del parque. Tiene una longitud de 0.7 millas (1.2 kilómetros) y se tarda entre 30 y 45 minutos en recorrer solamente el camino de ida.[3] Empiece a caminar en el Centro de Información y el área de recreación Palo Colorado. Este camino va al lado del río de la Mina y se termina en la magnífica Cascada la Mina, un salto de agua[4] de 35 pies de altura que forma una bonita piscina, donde puede usted bañarse para refrescarse después de una larga caminata. Tenga los ojos bien abiertos para ver la cotorra[5] puertorriqueña, una de las diez aves[6] en mayor peligro de extinción[7] en el mundo. En El Yunque sólo hay aproximadamente 70 cotorras.

[1] rain forest [2] paths [3] one way [4] waterfall [5] parrot [6] birds [7] endangered

---

Differentiated Instruction
Solutions for All Learners

Advanced Learners
Have students use the Internet to plan a hike in a national park in a Spanish-speaking country. Have them find a map and outline an itinerary, including what to pack, where to stop along the way, and the length of the trip. Ask them to include a description of what they will see and any difficulties they might encounter.

Students with Learning Difficulties
Make a transparency with the key vocabulary from the *Lectura* text. Discuss the meanings of the words and then reread the selection aloud as a group. After every few sentences, ask specific comprehension questions that require attentive listening.

Consejos para el caminante

1. Nunca camine solo. Siempre vaya acompañado.
2. Traiga agua y algo para comer.
3. Use repelente para insectos.
4. No abandone las veredas para no perderse[8].
5. No toque[9] las plantas del bosque.
6. No moleste ni alimente[10] a los animales.
7. ¡No tire basura en el parque! Por favor, ¡ayúdenos a mantener limpio este parque!

La boa puertorriqueña está en peligro de extinción.

Cascada la Mina

[8] to get lost   [9] touch   [10] feed

Fondo cultural

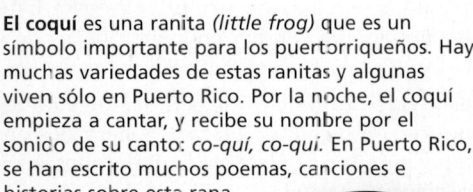

El coquí es una ranita *(little frog)* que es un símbolo importante para los puertorriqueños. Hay muchas variedades de estas ranitas y algunas viven sólo en Puerto Rico. Por la noche, el coquí empieza a cantar, y recibe su nombre por el sonido de su canto: *co-quí, co-quí.* En Puerto Rico, se han escrito muchos poemas, canciones e historias sobre esta rana misteriosa y encantadora.

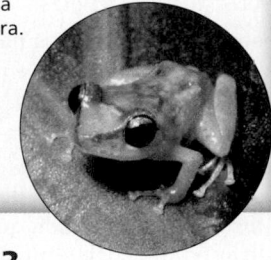

• ¿Hay algún animal tan importante como el coquí en tu región? ¿Y en los Estados Unidos?

¿Comprendiste?

Escribe *C* si la frase es cierta o *F* si la frase es falsa.

1. Casi nadie visita El Yunque.
2. No hay animales exóticos en el bosque.
3. Las veredas del bosque se pueden recorrer en bicicleta de montaña.
4. Se puede hacer una parrillada en el parque.
5. Se puede alimentar a los animales del parque.
6. Si quieres caminar la Vereda la Mina, para caminar desde el Centro de Información hasta la Cascada y volver tardas *(you take)* una hora y media.

Más práctica

- WAV Wbk.: Writing, p. 145
- Guided Practice: *Lectura*, p. 269
- *Real.* para hispanohablantes, pp. 282–283

Go Online PHSchool.com
For: Internet Activity
Web Code: jdd-0716

trescientos noventa y uno **391**
Capítulo 7B

¿Comprendiste?

Presentation EXPRESS ANSWERS

 Standards: 1.2

Resources: Answers on Transparencies

Focus: Verifying comprehension of an article on El Yunque

Suggestions: Answers questions aloud. If an answer is false, have students correct the sentence.

Answers:
1. F. El Yunque es una de las atracciones más visitadas de Puerto Rico.
2. F. Sí, hay animales exóticos en el bosque.
3. F. No se pueden recorrer en bicicleta.
4. C
5. F. No se puede alimentar a los animales.
6. C

Fondo cultural

 *Standards:* 1.2, 2.1, 2.2

Suggestions: Have students read about the **coquí** in *Song of El Coquí and other Tales of Puerto Rico* by Nicholasa Mohr and Antonio Martorell. Discuss why an animal becomes a symbol and find out if there is an animal symbol for your community or region. If not, have students suggest one.

Answers will vary.

Pre-AP* Support

- **Activity:** Have students work in pairs to write eight multiple-choice questions about the selection *El Yunque.* Collect and redistribute the questions to other pairs of students. With textbooks closed, read the article aloud to the class. Read the article a second time so that students can respond to the multiple-choice questions that they received.

- *Pre-AP* Resource Book:* Comprehensive guide to Pre-AP* reading skill development, pp. 18–24

For Further Reading

Student Resources:

- Realidades para hispanohablantes: Lectura 2, pp. 284–285
- Lecturas para hispanohablantes 2: "Buenos Hot Dogs," pp. 80–81

 AP* Literature Author: Pablo Neruda, Lecturas para hispanohablantes 2: "Oda a las papas fritas," p. 23

Enrich Your Teaching
Resources for All Teachers

Culture Note
King Alfonso XII of Spain proclaimed El Yunque a protected area in 1876, making it the oldest park in the Western Hemisphere. There are 88 unique tree species found nowhere else in the world and more than 50 rare orchid species.

Teacher-to-Teacher
Spanish-language children's books provide an enjoyable way to use Spanish and learn culture. Tales, myths, and fables about the origin of animals, plants, and geographical features enrich learning by involving students in meaningful reading. Acting out or illustrating stories provides entertaining oral or written practice.

Perspectivas del mundo hispano
Core Instruction

Standards: 1.2, 1.3, 2.1, 2.2

Focus: Reading about Mexican foods and outdoor eating customs

Suggestions: Ask students to describe Mexican food that they have eaten. How is it served? Point out to students that some Mexican dishes are wrapped in either a tortilla or banana leaves, and therefore are easy to eat anywhere. As they read, ask students to list foods that sound appealing to them. Have students identify places in their community where food is sold outdoors by street vendors. What types of food are sold? How do they compare with the foods mentioned in the reading? To help students answer the *¿Qué te parece?* question, have them identify how their eating habits change from winter to summer (if you live in a climate with varied seasons).

Answers will vary.

For Further Reading
Student Resource: Realidades para hispanohablantes, p. 286

Perspectivas del mundo hispano

La comida mexicana al aire libre

Has salido a caminar con unas amigas. Después de unas horas Uds. tienen hambre. Están cerca de una calle en la que hay muchos puestos de comida o comedores al aire libre. En algunos de los comedores hay tortillas amarillas y delgadas. Se pone la comida dentro de la tortilla, se enrolla[1] y ya está listo el taco. Unos vendedores venden pollo y chuletas de cerdo a la parrilla.

Haciendo tortillas de maíz

Otros venden tamales, que son pasteles de maíz envueltos[2] en hojas[3] de plátano y hervidos en agua. Para acompañar al plato principal, todos los vendedores ofrecen arroz y frijoles.

Los refrescos son jugos naturales de frutas tropicales: mango, piña, papaya. De postre hay quesos de varias clases, dulces y más frutas. ¡Ummm! Todo está recién hecho.[4] ¿Comemos?

En muchos países hispanohablantes es muy popular pasear y comer con familia y amigos en los comedores al aire libre. La comida que se puede comprar es deliciosa y no cuesta mucho. También se puede descansar y divertirse.

Preparando la comida al aire libre

¡Compruébalo! ¿Donde se vende comida al aire libre en los Estados Unidos? ¿Cuáles son algunos lugares en tu comunidad? (Piensa, por ejemplo, en el béisbol.) ¿Hay algunos en tu barrio? ¿Qué clase de comida venden? ¿Cuál es la comida al aire libre favorita de tus compañeros(as) de clase?

¿Qué te parece? ¿Por qué es popular la comida al aire libre? ¿Qué influencia tiene el clima en la popularidad de los lugares donde se vende la comida al aire libre?

Comprando helados de frutas frescas

[1] rolled up   [2] wrapped   [3] leaves   [4] freshly made

Differentiated Instruction
Solutions for All Learners

Heritage Language Learners
Have students write an article for a food magazine, describing outdoor eating in their heritage country. Ask them to recommend popular foods and street vendors. Invite students to invent details when necessary. After students have revised their work, compile and publish the works in a magazine format.

Students with Learning Difficulties
To help students answer the *¡Compruébalo!* questions, make photocopies of a family restaurant menu and have students underline items that are commonly sold by outdoor vendors. Have them ask their classmates what their favorite food is among those they've underlined, and make a mark next to that item on the menu.

Presentación escrita

Comiendo al aire libre

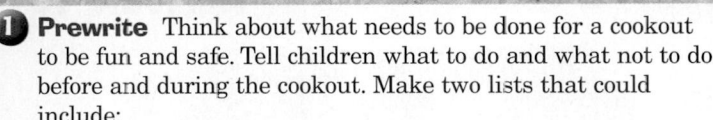

Task
An elementary school that many Spanish-speaking children attend is preparing its students for summer activities. You have been asked to prepare a poster on safety and fun at outdoor cookouts. Prepare a poster that provides directions for what to do and not to do.

1 Prewrite Think about what needs to be done for a cookout to be fun and safe. Tell children what to do and what not to do before and during the cookout. Make two lists that could include:

Antes de la parrillada
- la comida que deben comprar
- otras cosas que deben traer
- el lugar que van a escoger

Durante la parrillada
- cómo deben preparar el lugar
- qué van a hacer para preparar la comida
- cómo van a limpiar el lugar antes de salir

2 Draft Choose what you will write from the information in the lists you have brainstormed. Present the information in a logical sequence and in an attractive format.

Modelo
Antes de la parrillada
Decidan qué quieren comer.
Escojan un lugar seco.

3 Revise Review the spelling, vocabulary, and the commands. Compare your ideas with those of a classmate, who should review the following:

- Is what you have written easy to understand?
- Have you included appropriate commands?
- Should you change or add anything?

4 Publish Make any necessary changes. Add artwork that conveys the meaning of the commands.

5 Evaluation Your teacher may give you a rubric for how the poster will be graded. You will probably be graded on:

- how easy it is to understand your poster
- whether you have presented the information in a clear and attractive format
- your use of appropriate vocabulary and grammatical forms

Estrategia

Brainstorming
Brainstorming can help you come up with ideas that you may not have otherwise thought of. When listing items for your poster, write down all the tasks you could possibly suggest. Then, when your list is complete, select the best items.

trescientos noventa y tres **393**
Capítulo 7B

Presentación escrita
Expository

Standards: 1.3, 3.1

Focus: Making a poster about summer activities

Suggestions: Review the five-step procedure with students. They may find it helpful to brainstorm in small groups. Provide some ideas for groups to think about in the planning stages. They will need to plan what will be on the menu for food and drinks. If there are children invited, recreation and games should be part of the preparation. Suggest that students look at the photo on the student text page for more ideas.

To think about the safety aspect of the poster, remind students of possible concerns, such as hot barbecue grills. If the cookout takes place near a lake or other body of water, water safety needs to be a consideration. Other summer hazards include the heat and sun and insects that might sting or bite.

Once students have brainstormed ideas, suggest that they narrow the focus for their poster. For example, they might choose to emphasize only preparation or safety during the cookout.

Portfolio

Have students include their poster in their portfolio.

Pre-AP* Support

- *Pre-AP* Resource Book:* Comprehensive guide to Pre-AP* writing skill development, pp. 25–35

Additional Resources

Student Resources: Realidades para hispanohablantes, p. 287; Guided Practice: Presentación escrita, p. 270

✓ Assessment

- Assessment Program: Rubrics, p. T31

Before students begin the revision process, provide them with a copy of the rubric you will use for evaluation.

Enrich Your Teaching
Resources for All Teachers

RUBRIC	Score 1	Score 3	Score 5
How easy it is to understand your poster	You have few visuals to support your information.	You have some visuals to support your information.	You have many visuals to support your information.
Attractiveness and clarity of your poster	Your layout is confusing and contains visible error corrections and smudges.	Your layout is somewhat clear and contains visible error corrections and smudges.	Your layout is clear and attractive, and contains no error corrections and smudges.
Your use of vocabulary and grammar	You use very little variation of vocabulary and have frequent grammatical errors.	You use limited vocabulary and have some grammatical errors.	You use an extended variety of vocabulary and have very few grammatical errors.

Videomisterio

Videomisterio

Core Instruction

Standards: 1.2, 3.2, 5.2

Resources: Teacher's Resource Book: Video Script, pp. 149–150; Video Program: Cap. 7B; Video Program Teacher's Guide: Cap. 7B

Focus: Reading and presenting new vocabulary needed to understand the video

Personajes importantes

Roberto   Turrón

Linda   Nela

Synopsis: Roberto learns from Sr. Turrón that Federico Zúñiga, his grandfather, died a hero in WWII. Among his belongings is a Congressional Medal of Honor that was awarded to him posthumously. Roberto, now proud of his grandfather, returns to Mexico, where the family has a party to celebrate. Nela Toledo, once ashamed of her husband, now proudly announces that she is to be called Sra. Zúñiga.

Suggestions:

Pre-viewing: Review the events of *Episodio 9*: Roberto, Linda, and Carmen flew to San Antonio. Roberto and Linda visited De León at the bank, and he sent them to Austin. There, they met none other than the mysterious Turrón, who said that he had some very important things to tell them about Federico Zúñiga.

Have a volunteer read the *Nota cultural* aloud. Ask what special occasions, besides birthdays and holidays, warrant a large family gathering in the United States *(anniversaries, a new baby, housewarming parties).*

Point out the *Palabras para comprender* giving examples in context and writing sentences on the board.

Videomisterio

En busca de la verdad

Episodio 10

Antes de ver el video

"Aquí traigo las respuestas a todas nuestras preguntas sobre el abuelo".

"Por fin se ha resuelto el misterio de mi vida".

Nota cultural En América Latina las celebraciones familiares son muy importantes. Cualquier evento agradable es motivo de celebración. Todos los miembros de la familia se reúnen y siempre invitan a los amigos más cercanos para estar juntos. Normalmente se preparan comidas, se toca música, se canta o se baila. ¡En este videomisterio, la noticia sobre el abuelo es un buen motivo para celebrar!

Resumen del episodio

En este episodio Roberto finalmente descubre la verdad sobre su abuelo Federico. Regresa a Guanajuato y toda la familia se reúne para celebrar la noticia sobre el abuelo.

Palabras para comprender

pertenece belongs to

cuenta de ahorros savings account

póliza de seguro insurance policy

sobreviviente survivor

Has tenido razón. You were right.

Differentiated Instruction
Solutions for All Learners

Multiple Intelligences

Interpersonal/Social: After viewing the *episodio*, have groups of students discuss the meaning of the caption for the second photo: *Por fin se ha resuelto el misterio de mi vida.*

How was the mystery solved? Who were the key players in getting it solved? Why did it have to be solved? Then have a volunteer group share its findings with the class.

"¡Y ahora hay que celebrar!".

Después de ver el video

¿Comprendiste?

A. ¿Qué personaje dice cada una de las siguientes frases?

(Tomás Toledo / Roberto / Nela / Federico / Linda)

1. "Tengo que regresar a Guanajuato con mi familia".

2. "Qué bien que por fin se resolvió este misterio".

3. "Nunca me ha gustado tocar el pasado".

4. "Nunca me imaginé todo esto. Tanto tiempo . . . tanto tiempo".

5. "Por fin se ha resuelto el misterio de mi vida".

6. "Ahora ya sabes la verdad. No me olvides".

7. "Hola. ¿Cómo estás?".

B. Contesta las siguientes preguntas.

1. ¿Cuál ha sido tu personaje favorito de *En busca de la verdad*? ¿Por qué?

2. ¿Cuál ha sido tu escena favorita? ¿Por qué?

3. ¿Qué va a pasar cuando Linda regrese a Guanajuato en la primavera con el programa de intercambio?

Go Online
PHSchool.com
For: More on *En busca de la verdad*
Web Code: jdd-0209

trescientos noventa y cinco **395**
Capítulo 7B

Enrich Your Teaching
Resources for All Teachers

Teacher-to-Teacher

As an extension to the Multiple Intelligences suggestion on p. 394, you may want to have the same groups of students brainstorm alternate endings to the story. Then encourage one group to write a skit for it and present it to the class. If possible, videotape their presentation and include it in their portfolios.

Suggestions:

Visual scanning: Direct attention to the photos. Have students read the captions and try to guess what the characters might be talking about. Call attention to the second photo on p. 394. Ask students to predict the ending to the story; after the viewing, see if they guessed correctly. Then have them read the *Resumen del episodio* and ask them one or two comprehension questions.

Viewing: Play *Episodio* 10 for the class. If there is time after viewing the full episode, go back and replay key moments that you wish to highlight. Remind students that they may not understand every word they hear in the video, but that they should listen for overall understanding.

Post-viewing: Remind students that in *Capítulo* 2B they read about Hispanic participation in WWII. You may want to quickly review that section. Complete the *¿Comprendiste?* in class.

¿Comprendiste?

 Standards: 1.2, 1.3

Resources: Answers on Transparencies

Focus: Verifying comprehension; reviewing the plot

Suggestions: You may want to replay key points in the video so that students have a chance to listen carefully for the statements in part A. For part B, question 3, you may want to have students brainstorm in groups.

Answers:

A:
1. Roberto
2. Linda
3. Tomás
4. Nela
5. Nela
6. Federico
7. Roberto

B: Answers will vary.

Additional Resources

• *En busca de la verdad* Video Workbook, Episode 10

• *En busca de la verdad* Teacher's Video Guide: Answer Key

395

Cómo ser un buen turista

THEME OVERVIEW

Capítulo 8A

▶ **8A   Un viaje en avión**
• Taking a trip by plane
Vocabulary: visiting an airport; taking a trip to a foreign country; safe travel
Grammar: the present subjunctive; irregular verbs *dar, estar, ir, saber,* and *ser* in the subjunctive
Cultural Perspectives: traveling

Capítulo 8B

▶ **8B   Quiero que disfrutes de tu viaje**
• Traveling in a foreign city
Vocabulary: staying in a hotel; traveling in a foreign city; being a good tourist
Grammar: present subjunctive with impersonal expressions; present subjunctive of stem-changing verbs
Cultural Perspectives: traveling in Spanish-speaking countries

Theme Project

Cómo ser un buen turista

Overview: Ask students to create a poster that displays good travel habits. Have students write the letters in the words *Cómo ser un buen turista* in bold, block letters down the center of the poster. Each piece of advice that the student gives must be written in smaller handwriting and must incorporate one of the letters of the phrase. After the students write their lists of travel habits, they should decorate their posters with photos or drawings.

Es importante que	Cambies el dinero en la casa de cambio.
Es necesario que no	Olvides tu pasaporte.
Es importante que	Mandes tarjetas postales a tu familia.
Es necesario que no	Ofendas a la gente.

Materials: Poster board, markers

Sequence: (suggestions for when to do each step are found throughout the chapters)

8A ▶ **STEP 1.** Review instructions so students know what is expected of them. Hand out the "Theme 8 Project Instructions and Rubric" from the *Teacher's Resource Book.*

STEP 2. Students submit a rough draft of their acrostic list of rules. Return the drafts with your suggestions. For grammar and vocabulary practice, ask students to partner and present their drafts to each other.

STEP 3. Students create layouts on different pieces of poster board, leaving room for photos and descriptions. Encourage them to work in pencil first and to try different arrangements before gluing photos or decorations.

8B ▶ **STEP 4.** Students submit a draft of their poster. Note your corrections and suggestions, then return drafts to students.

STEP 5. Students present their posters to the class, explaining each rule and describing selected pictures.

Options:

1. Students research a popular tourist location in the Spanish-speaking world and present advice to travelers who are interested in vacationing there.
2. Students create a travel brochure catering to students on a limited budget.

Assessment:

Here is a detailed rubric for assessing this project:

Theme 8 Project: *Cómo ser un buen turista*

RUBRIC	Score 1	Score 3	Score 5
Your evidence of planning	You provide no written draft or poster layout.	Your draft was written and layout created, but not corrected.	You show evidence of corrected draft and layout.
Your use of illustrations	You include no photos or visuals.	You include very few photos or visuals.	You include several photos or visuals.
Your poster presentation	You include little of the required information.	You give a partially complete list of advice (some letters used).	You give a complete list of advice (all letters used).

Bulletin Boards

Theme: *De viaje*

Ask students to cut out, copy, or download photos of airports, train stations, bus stations, and foreign travel destinations. Cluster photos into categories—modes of transportation, tropical zones, mountainous areas, beaches, etc.—so that similarities and differences are evident.

Bibliography

Day, Nancy. *Your Travel Guide to Ancient Mayan Civilization.* Runestone Press, 2002.

DK DK Travel Writers. *Spain: Eyewitness Travel Guides.* Dorling Kindersley, 2003.

Mason Crest Publishers. *Healthy Traveler: Answers on Staying Well Away from Home.* Mason Crest Publishers, 2002.

Young, Brian, and Mike Buckby. *Destination Spanish: Illustrated Phrasebook & Travel Information.* Passport Books, 1995.

Hands-on Culture

Craft: *Yarn Painting*

Traditional designs filled in with gradually decreasing circles of yarn are very popular art forms among indigenous peoples of Latin America.

Materials:

> yarn in varied colors and lengths
> card stock
> researched traditional Latin American designs
> glue
> pencil

Directions:

1. Research traditional Latin American designs. Animals and plant designs work the best.

2. Trace the design in pencil onto a piece of card stock.

3. Squeeze some glue in a line onto part of the outline. Lay a strand of black yarn onto the outline. Continue until the entire design is outlined.

4. Fill in the inside of the design with colored yarn and glue. Wrap the yarn around in circles, starting at the outside, until you reach the center of the design.

5. Fill in the background.

Internet Search

Use the keywords to find more information.

8A Keywords:

> códices, Oaxaca, Valencia García, office of tourism + (Spanish-speaking country)

8B Keywords:

> Oaxaca; Punta del Este, Uruguay; Cartagena; REMAJ; paradores; RENFE

Game

Frases en pedazos

Play this game after *Capítulo* 8B to review subjunctive and vocabulary.

Players: Any number of students in small groups

Materials: Index cards, paper, pen, markers

Rules:

1. On the board, write the phrase *Para ser un buen turista....*

2. Give each group a stack of index cards, a piece of paper, and a marker.

3. Instruct each group to finish the phrase on the board by writing as many phrases as they can using the subjunctive and an impersonal expression. Make sure that the verbs are in the *tú* form. Check the sentences for accuracy.

4. Using the markers, have each group write their sentences, one word at a time, on the index cards. Collect and shuffle the decks.

5. Give the groups a new deck of cards. Ask them to use the words on the cards to make as many sentences as they can until you call time.

6. Each correct sentence is worth one point. The team with the most points wins.

Variation: The teacher can give various beginning phrases such as *Para ser cortés...*, *Para hacer un viaje...*, or *Para visitar un aeropuerto.*

♻ RECYCLE	**Vocabulary**	**Grammar**
A ver si recuerdas	• Las vacaciones	• The infinitive in verbal expressions

A primera vista	**Manos a la obra**	**¡Adelante!**	**Repaso**
		Learning Sequence	
INPUT	**PRACTICE**	**APPLICATION**	**REVIEW**
• Introduce vocabulary and grammar within an authentic context.	• Practice and develop new vocabulary. • Learn and practice new grammar structures.	• Apply vocabulary and grammar through culminating, theme-based activities. • Apply skill development.	• Review vocabulary and grammar.
		Objectives	
Read, listen to, and explain information about • visiting an airport • planning a trip • traveling safely	• Communicate about traveling by plane. • Discuss travel plans. • Make recommendations about traveling.	• Read a travel article about Ecuador. • Identify historic travel chronicles. • Research and talk about taking a trip to a Spanish-speaking country.	• Prepare for the chapter test.
		Culture	
• Valencia García	• *Los nombres de los aeropuertos* • *El transporte* • *Los programas de intercambio*	• *Ecuador, país de maravillas* • *Los códices*	• Explain the importance of historical record-keeping.

Vocabulary	**Grammar**	**Learner Support**	
• Making travel plans • Airports	• The present subjunctive • Irregular verbs in the subjunctive	**STRATEGIES** • Scanning for basic understanding • Previewing • Brainstorming with a flow chart	**RECYCLING** ♻ • Words related to airports, airlines, and flights • Verbs in the indicative • Verbs with *que* + **subjunctive** • Activities; use of *gustar* • Parts of the body • Vacation vocabulary

Chapter Features

Beyond the Classroom: States & Countries

Conexiones

Health: Stretching and movement exercises recommended during air travel

Pronunciación

Linking sounds

El español en la comunidad

The roles that consulates serve for Spanish-speaking visitors to the United States

España
República Dominicana
México
Honduras
Puerto Rico
Nicaragua
Colombia
Ecuador
Perú
Bolivia
Argentina

Student Resources

TECHNOLOGY

ONLINE

Interactive Textbook
- Student Edition Online plus audio, video, and flashcards

Go Online Companion Web Site
- Tutorial activities
- Internet links
- Self-tests
- Downloadable MP3 audio files
- **PuzzleView**

CD-ROM

Interactive Textbook CD-ROM
Student Edition on CD-ROM plus audio, video, and flashcards

MindPoint™ CD-ROM
QUIZSHOW

PRINT MATERIAL

CORE INSTRUCTION

Practice Workbook, pp. 151–161
- Review
- Vocabulary
- Grammar
- Puzzle
- Organizer

Writing, Audio & Video Activities, pp. 146–155
- Video
- Audio
- Writing

Grammar Study Guide 1–2 (or 3–4)

Differentiated Instruction

STUDENTS NEEDING EXTRA HELP

Guided Practice Activities, pp. 271–290
- Vocabulary Flash Cards and Vocabulary Check
- Grammar Activities
- Presentación oral

HERITAGE LEARNERS

Realidades para hispanohablantes, pp. 290–309

Lecturas para hispanohablantes
- "Aprender el inglés," p. 91
- "Canción con todos," p. 104
- "Ansia," pp. 109–110

ADVANCED/PRE-AP*

Pre-AP* Resource Book: Student Activity Sheet, p. 127

Teacher Resources

TECHNOLOGY

Audio Program
Video Program

Fine Art Transparencies
Vocabulary and Grammar Transparencies
Answers on Transparencies

TeacherEXPRESS CD-ROM
- Lesson Planner
- Vocabulary Clip Art
- Web Resources
- Teaching Resources
- Teacher Edition with Interactive Links

PresentationEXPRESS CD-ROM
- Vocabulary
- Tranparencies and Maps
- Grammar
- Photo Gallery
- Audio
- Clip Art

PH SuccessNet ONLINE
- Access to grades and reports from Online Interactive Textbook

ExamView® on Presentation Express CD-ROM
QuickTake Presenter
- Vocabulary Quizzes
- Chapter Test
- Grammar Quizzes

TeacherEXPRESS CD-ROM
- Assessment Program
- **ExamView®** Test Banks A and B
test generator

Go Online
PHSchool.com
For: Teacher Home Page
Web Code: jdk-1001

PRINT MATERIAL

CORE INSTRUCTION

Teacher's Resource Book, pp. 172–197
- Input Script
- Video Script
- Answer Keys
- GramActiva Blackline Masters
- Vocabulary Clip Art
- Chapter Resource Checklist
- School-to-Home Connection Letters
- Communicative Activities Blackline Masters

TPR Stories, pp. 106–111

CORE ASSESSMENT

Assessment Program, pp. 203–215
- Pruebas
  Vocabulary Recognition
  Vocabulary Production
  The present subjunctive
  Irregular verbs in the subjunctive
- Examen del capítulo
- Speaking and Writing Rubrics

Teacher's Resource Book, p. 186
- Situation Cards

TPR Stories, pp. 106–111

Differentiated Instruction

STUDENTS NEEDING EXTRA HELP

Guided Practice Activities Teacher's Guide, pp. T136–T145

HERITAGE LEARNERS

Realidades para hispanohablantes Teacher's Guide, pp. 146–155

Lecturas para hispanohablantes Teacher's Guide, pp. 35, 41–43

ADVANCED/PRE-AP*

Pre-AP* Resource Book: Resources Chart, p. 124

Differentiated Assessment

STUDENTS NEEDING EXTRA HELP

Alternate Assessment Program
- Examen del capítulo, pp. 89–94

HERITAGE LEARNERS

Assessment Program: Realidades para hispanohablantes Teacher's Guide, pp. T157–T161

ExamView® Heritage Learner Test Bank
test generator

ADVANCED/PRE-AP*

Pre-AP* Resource Book: Teacher Activity Sheet, p. 126

ExamView® Pre-AP* Test Bank
test generator

	Warm-up / Assess	Preview Present / Practice Communicate		Wrap-up / Homework Options
DAY 1	**Warm-up (5 min.)** • Homework check • Return Examen del capítulo 7B	**A ver si recuerdas . . . (20 min.)** • Presentation: Las vacaciones • Actividades 1, 2 • Presentation: The infinitive in verbal expressions • Actividades 3, 4	**Chapter Opener (5 min.)** • Objectives • Fondo cultural **A primera vista (15 min.)** • Presentation: Vocabulario y gramática en contexto • Actividades 1, 2	**Wrap-up and Homework Options (5 min.)** • Practice Workbook 8A-A, 8A-B, 8A-1, 8A-2 • Go Online
DAY 2	**Warm-up (10 min.)** • Homework check	**A primera vista (35 min.)** • Presentation: Videohistoria ¡Buen viaje! • View: Videohistoria	• Video Activities 1, 2, 3, 4 • Actividad 3	**Wrap-up and Homework Options (5 min.)** • Practice Workbook 8A-3, 8A-4 • Go Online • Prueba 8A-1: Vocabulary recognition
DAY 3	**Warm-up (10 min.)** • Actividad 4 • Homework check ✔**Assessment (10 min.)** • Prueba 8A-1: Vocabulary recognition	**Manos a la obra (25 min.)** • Actividades 5, 6, 7, 8, 9 • Fondo culturales		**Wrap-up and Homework Options (5 min.)** • Writing Activity 10 • Heritage Learner Workbook 8A-1, 8A-2 • Prueba 8A-2: Vocabulary production
DAY 4	**Warm-up (10 min.)** • Actividad 10 • Homework check ✔**Assessment (10 min.)** (after Communicative Activity) • Prueba 8A-2: Vocabulary production	**Manos a la obra (25 min.)** • Audio Activities 5, 6 • Communicative Activity • Presentation: The present subjunctive	• View: GramActiva video • Actividad 11	**Wrap-up and Homework Options (5 min.)** • Practice Workbook 8A-5 • Actividad 13 • Writing Activity 11 • Go Online
DAY 5	**Warm-up (10 min.)** • Actividad 14 • Homework check	**Manos a la obra (35 min.)** • Actividades 12, 15, 16 • Fondo cultural • Audio Activity 7	• Presentation: Irregular verbs in the subjunctive • View: GramActiva video • Actividad 17	**Wrap-up and Homework Options (5 min.)** • Practice Workbook 8A-6 • Actividades 19, 24 • Go Online • Prueba 8A-3: The present subjunctive
DAY 6	**Warm-up (5 min.)** • Homework check ✔**Assessment (10 min.)** • Pruebas 8A-3: The present subjunctive	**Manos a la obra (30 min.)** • Actividades 18, 20, 22, 23 • Audio Activity 8		**Wrap-up and Homework Options (5 min.)** • Practice Workbook 8A-7 • Writing Activity 12 • Go Online • Heritage Learner Workbook 8A-4 • Prueba 8A-4: Irregular verbs in the subjunctive
DAY 7	**Warm-up (10 min.)** • Actividad 21 • Homework check ✔**Assessment (10 min.)** • Prueba 8A-4: Irregular verbs in the subjunctive	**¡Adelante! (10 min.)** • Presentación oral: Steps 1, 4 **Repaso del capítulo (15 min.)** • Vocabulario y gramática • Preparación para el examen 1, 2		**Wrap-up and Homework Options (5 min.)** • Presentación oral: Step 2
DAY 8	**Warm-up (5 min.)** • Presentación oral: Step 2	**Manos a la obra (10 min.)** • Pronunciación • El español en la comunidad	**¡Adelante! (30 min.)** • Presentación oral: Step 3	**Wrap-up and Homework Options (5 min.)** • Preparación para el examen 3, 4, 5 • Go Online: Self-test
DAY 9	**Warm-up (5 min.)** • Homework check	**¡Adelante! (40 min.)** • Lectura • ¿Comprendiste? / Y tú, ¿qué dices? • La cultura en vivo		**Wrap-up and Homework Options (5 min.)** • Practice Workbook 8A-8, 8A-9 • Go Online: Lectura • Examen del capítulo 8A
DAY 10	**Warm-up (5 min.)** • Homework check ✔**Assessment (40 min.)** • Examen del capítulo 8A			**Wrap-up and Homework Options (5 min.)** • La cultura en vivo

	Warm-up / Assess	Preview Present / Practice Communicate	Wrap-up / Homework Options
DAY 1	**Warm-up (5 min.)** • Homework check • Return Examen del capítulo: Capítulo 7B	**A ver si recuerdas . . . (25 min.)** • Presentation: Las vacaciones • Actividades 1, 2 • Presentation: The infinitive in verbal expressions • Actividades 3, 4 **Chapter Opener (5 min.)** • Objectives • Fondo cultural **A primera vista (50 min.)** • Presentation: Vocabulario y gramática en contexto • Actividades 1, 2 • Presentation: Videohistoria: ¡Buen viaje! • View: Videohistoria • Video Activities 1, 2, 3, 4 • Actividad 3	**Wrap-up and Homework Options (5 min.)** • Practice Workbook 8A-A, 8A-B, 8A-1, 8A-2, 8A-3, 8A-4 • Go Online • Prueba 8A-1: Vocabulary recognition
DAY 2	**Warm-up (10 min.)** • Actividad 4 • Homework check ✔**Assessment (10 min.)** • Prueba 8A-1: Vocabulary recognition	**Manos a la obra (65 min.)** • Actividades 5, 6, 7, 8, 9 • Fondo culturales • Audio Activities 5, 6 • Communicative Activity • Presentation: The present subjunctive • View: GramActiva video • Actividades 11, 12	**Wrap-up and Homework Options (5 min.)** • Practice Workbook 8A-5 • Writing Activity 10 • Go Online • Heritage Learner Workbook 8A-1, 8A-2 • Prueba 8A-2: Vocabulary production
DAY 3	**Warm-up (10 min.)** • Actividad 10 • Homework check ✔**Assessment (10 min.)** • Prueba 8A-2: Vocabulary production	**Manos a la obra (65 min.)** • Actividades 13, 14, 15, 16 • Fondo cultural • Audio Activity 7 • Presentation: Irregular verbs in the subjunctive • View: GramActiva video • Actividades 17, 18, 19, 20 • Audio Activity 8	**Wrap-up and Homework Options (5 min.)** • Practice Workbook 8A-6 • Go Online • Heritage Learner Workbook 8A-4 • Pruebas 8A-3: The present subjunctive
DAY 4	**Warm-up (10 min.)** • Writing Activity 11 • Homework check ✔**Assessment (10 min.)** • Pruebas 8A-3: The present subjunctive	**Manos a la obra (35 min.)** • Actividades 21, 22, 23, 24 • Pronunciación • El español en la comunidad • Writing Activity 12 **¡Adelante! (30 min.)** • Lectura • ¿Comprendiste? / Y tú, ¿qué dices? • Presentación oral: Steps 1, 4	**Wrap-up and Homework Options (5 min.)** • Practice Workbook 8A-7 • Presentación oral: Step 2 • Go Online: Irregular subjunctives; Lectura • Prueba 8A-4: Irregular verbs in the subjunctive
DAY 5	**Warm-up (5 min.)** • Homework check ✔**Assessment (10 min.)** • Prueba 8A-4: Irregular verbs in the subjunctive	**¡Adelante! (35 min.)** • Presentación oral: Step 3 **Repaso del capítulo (35 min.)** • Vocabulario y gramática • Preparación para el examen 1, 2, 3, 4, 5	**Wrap-up and Homework Options (5 min.)** • Practice Workbook 8A-8, 8A-9 • Go Online: Self-test • Examen del capítulo 8A
DAY 6	**Warm-up (5 min.)** • Homework check **Repaso del capítulo (20 min.)** • Situation Cards ✔**Assessment (45 min.)** • Examen del capítulo 8A	**¡Adelante! (15 min.)** • La cultura en vivo	**Wrap-up and Homework Options (5 min.)** • La cultura en vivo

8A Recycle

Note: Starting with *Tema 4*, the *A ver si recuerdas...* feature appears only at the beginning of each theme.

Vocabulario

Core Instruction

Resources: Voc. and Gram. Transparency 139

Focus: Reviewing vocabulary for vacations

Suggestions: Get travel brochures and vacation posters from a local travel agency or from a tourism office. Try to obtain visuals from a variety of locations and seasons: country, city, beach, ski slopes, and so on. Have students identify the type of location and say what activities can be done at each place, and when.

Actividad 1 — *Standards:* 1.3

Focus: Writing about vacation spots and activities

Suggestions: Be sure students understand that they cannot simply write down the first eight items from the graphic organizer. Explain that they need to read the whole list and choose, because some of the words listed are not places you can go on vacation.

Answers will vary.

Extension: Have students select one place from their list and write two or three sentences to describe it.

Actividad 2 — *Standards:* 1.1

Focus: Speaking about activities students have done on vacation

Suggestions: Review the present perfect tense with students and point out that the verb *ir* is not irregular. Allow students to use their imagination when describing their vacation experiences.

Answers will vary.

Block Schedule

Have students work in groups to create a travel brochure for your state. Tell them to choose several attractions and write a description of each, including available activities. Encourage them to include photos of their locations.

A ver si recuerdas...

Vocabulario

Las vacaciones

lugares y atracciones

el campo
la ciudad
el estadio
el hotel
el lago
el lugar
el mar
el mercado
las montañas
el museo
la obra de teatro
el país
el parque de diversiones
el parque nacional
el partido
la piscina
la playa
el teatro
el zoológico

actividades

bucear
comprar recuerdos
dar una caminata
descansar
esquiar
ir de cámping
ir de compras
ir de pesca
ir de vacaciones
montar a caballo
montar en bicicleta
pasar tiempo
pasear en bote
regresar
salir
viajar
visitar
tomar el sol

Práctica de vocabulario • Usando el organizador gráfico

Actividad 1 Escribir

¿Qué puedo hacer allí?

En una hoja de papel, haz dos columnas. En la columna a la izquierda, escribe una lista de ocho lugares adonde se puede ir de vacaciones. En la columna a la derecha, escribe una actividad que se puede hacer en cada lugar. Trata de variar las actividades en la segunda columna.

Modelo

Lugares	Actividades
las montañas	*esquiar*

Actividad 2   Hablar

Lugares y actividades

Usa las listas de la Actividad 1 y pregúntale a otro(a) estudiante si ha ido a estos lugares de vacaciones y si ha hecho las diferentes actividades.

Modelo

A —¿*Has ido de vacaciones a las montañas alguna vez?*

B —*Sí, he ido a las montañas varias veces.*

A —¿*Has esquiado en las montañas?*

B —*No, hemos ido allí en el verano. Hemos dado caminatas en las montañas.*

Differentiated Instruction
Solutions for All Learners

Students with Special Needs

Modify *Actividad 4* for hearing-impaired students. Have students write their recommendations on postcards and exchange them with a partner. Then ask them to respond to the postcard by e-mail. If possible, reserve the computer room at your school and have students exchange e-mail addresses.

Advanced Learners

Have students make a picture album of an imaginary vacation. Ask them to research a Spanish-speaking country on the Internet and download photos of places and attractions. Tell them to paste photos of themselves on the pictures they found. Have them write captions about where they went and what they did.

Gramática·Repaso

The infinitive in verbal expressions

Remember that the infinitive is used in many types of expressions with verbs.

To express plans, desires, and wishes:

desear	pensar
encantar	preferir
gustar	querer
ir + a	

Este verano mis padres **quieren ir** a las montañas, pero mis hermanos y yo **preferimos pasar** tiempo en la playa.

To express obligation:

deber	tener que
necesitar	

Cuando vas a un país latinoamericano, **debes visitar** un mercado al aire libre.

In impersonal expressions:

es divertido	es necesario
es importante	hay que
es interesante	

En Chile **es divertido ir** de cámping y **dar** caminatas en los parques nacionales.

Práctica de gramática

  Actividad 3 Escribir/Hablar

Tus intereses

Piensa en las vacaciones que te interesan. Escribe cinco frases usando los verbos de *Gramática* para decir cuándo y dónde prefieres ir y qué te gusta hacer. Lee tus frases a otro(a) estudiante para ver si Uds. tienen los mismos intereses.

Modelo
preferir
A —En el invierno mi familia y yo preferimos ir a Utah para esquiar.
B —¿De veras? Nosotros preferimos ir a un lugar donde hace calor, como la Florida.

Más práctica
- Practice Workbook, pp. 151–152: 8A-A, 8A-B
- Guided Practice Acts., pp. 271–272
- *Real.* para hispanohablantes, p. 290

Go Online PHSchool.com
For: Vocab. and Grammar
Web Code: jdd-0801

  Actividad 4 Escribir/Hablar

Recomendaciones para turistas

Escoge un lugar turístico y escribe un párrafo con recomendaciones para lo que se debe hacer allí. Usa las expresiones de *Gramática* en tu párrafo. Luego, con otro(a) estudiante, intercambien *(exchange)* papeles y haz comentarios o preguntas sobre el lugar.

Modelo
Cuando vas a Puerto Rico, es muy divertido visitar el Viejo San Juan. Es interesante ver los edificios antiguos. También debes . . .
A —Me gustaría mucho visitar Puerto Rico. ¿Cuándo debo ir?
B —Pues, el clima es fantástico durante todo el año, pero hay muchos turistas en el invierno. Creo que debes ir en el verano.

trescientos noventa y nueve **399**
Preparación: Vocabulario y gramática

Enrich Your Teaching
Resources for All Teachers

Culture Note
The geography and climate of many Spanish-speaking countries make them ideal vacation spots. Activities include snow skiing in Bariloche, Argentina; hiking to the ruins in Machu Picchu, Peru; scuba diving in Cozumel, Mexico; and sunbathing on the Costa del Sol in Spain.

Teacher-to-Teacher
Ask students to make travel posters to present their vacation spot activities from *Actividad* 4 to the class. After all presentations have been given, have the class vote on their favorite locations. Make a bulletin board entitled *Destinación del día* and post a different winning presentation every day during this chapter.

Gramática·Repaso

Core Instruction

Suggestions: Remind students that infinitives are verbs that are not conjugated. When they stand alone, they do not have a subject assigned to them. Remind them that infinitives in English usually start with to: *to run, to sleep, to eat,* etc.

Point out that the verbs *gustar* and *encantar* always use indirect object pronouns. Explain that the form of those verbs does not change if you have multiple infinitives following it: *Me gusta bucear, esquiar y pasear en bote.*

Divide the class into groups. Give each group two sets of prepared index cards. On the first set, on each card write a verb or expression that is followed by the infinitive. On the other set, write a different infinitive on each card. Have students take turns drawing a card from each pile and making a sentence using the two words. When students have each had two or three chances, have the group vote on the best sentence.

 Actividad 3  *Standards:* 1.1, 1.3

Focus: Writing about preferences for where and when to take vacations
Suggestions: You may have students who have never taken vacations. Encourage students to write about places they have never been to but would love to visit.
Answers will vary.

 Actividad 4 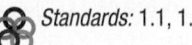 *Standards:* 1.1, 1.3

Focus: Writing and speaking about recommendations for vacation activities
Suggestions: To encourage variety, assign each student a different vacation spot in a Spanish-speaking country. Have students search the Internet to find information on activities available at their location.
Answers will vary.

Standards for Capítulo 8A

• To achieve the goals of the Standards, students will:

Communication

1.1 Interpersonal

• Talk about: travel; international flights; vacation plans, advice, and activities; a student exchange program; leisure activities

1.2 Interpretive

• Read: about painter Valencia García; a picture-based story and a magazine article; information about airport names; about a student exchange program, consulates in the U.S., and *los codices*

• Read, listen to, and interpret information about: travel and vacation plans, advice, and activities

• Listen to and watch a video about travel

• Read and interpret a travel article about Ecuador

1.3 Presentational

• Present information: about travel and vacation plans, recommendations and activities, airline rules, international travel; on magazine advice

• Write: about buses and other means of transportation in Latin American countries; opinions on tourism in Ecuador

Culture

2.1 Practices and Perspectives

• Talk about: painter Valencia García; buses and other means of transportation in Latin American countries; *los codices;* travel chronicles

• Discuss exchange student programs

2.2 Products and Perspectives

• Talk about: painter Valencia García; the names of airports in Spanish-speaking countries; buses and other means of transportation in Latin American countries; exchange student programs; places in Ecuador; *codices;* and historical records

Connections

3.1 Cross-curricular

• Talk: about consulates and their purpose, and the history and geography of Ecuador; make a *códice;* prepare an oral presentation

Comparisons

4.1 Language

• Use: the present subjunctive; irregular verbs in the subjunctive; pronunciation links

4.2 Culture

• Compare: Oaxacan tourist sites with those in the U.S.; airport names; exchange student programs

Communities

5.1 Beyond the School

• Identify services available to Spanish speakers at their country's consulates

---

AU 2824 MAR DEL PLATA 09:20
AR 0974 VILLA GESELL 09:45
AR 1402 CORDOBA 10:00
AR 1852 SALTA 10:10
AR 1258 PUNTA DEL ESTE 10:15
AR 1874 SGO DEL ESTERO/ JUJUY 10:20

Fondo cultural ■◆■◆◇■◆■◆□■◆

Valencia García nació en México en 1963 y ahora vive en California. A los 12 años empezó a pintar paisajes *(landscapes)*, especialmente de playas y lugares relacionados con el mar. Este cuadro es de una playa del estado de Oaxaca. Las playas del estado de Oaxaca no están cerca de la ciudad de Oaxaca. Para llegar a ellas, los turistas deben viajar varias horas por una carretera entre las montañas. Muchas personas van de vacaciones a estas playas.

• ¿Qué te gusta de las playas a donde van muchos turistas? ¿Hay playas turísticas en tu comunidad?

"Playas de Oaxaca" (2000), Valencia García
Oil on canvas, 36 x 48 in. Courtesy of Dragon Aleksic.

400 cuatrocientos
Tema 8 • Cómo ser un buen turista

Differentiated Instruction

STUDENTS NEEDING EXTRA HELP

Guided Practice Activities
• Vocabulary Check, Flash Cards
• Grammar
• Reading and Speaking Support

Guided Practice Audio CDs
• Disc 2, Track 7

HERITAGE LEARNERS

Realidades para hispanohablantes
• Chapter Opener, pp. 290–291
• A primera vista, p. 292
• Videohistoria, p. 293
• Manos a la obra, pp. 294–301
• ¡Adelante!, pp. 302–307
• Repaso del capítulo, pp. 308–309

ADVANCED/PRE-AP*

Pre-AP* Resource Book, pp. 124–127

Un viaje en avión

Chapter Objectives

- Talk about visiting an airport
- Plan for a trip to a foreign country
- Make suggestions about safe travel
- Read about travel destinations in Spanish-speaking countries
- Understand cultural perspectives on traveling

Video Highlights

A primera vista: *¡Buen viaje!*
GramActiva Videos: the present subjunctive; irregular verbs in the subjunctive

Country Connection

As you learn to talk about planning a trip, you will make connections to these countries and places:

España
República Dominicana
México
Honduras
Puerto Rico
Nicaragua
Ecuador
Colombia
Perú
Bolivia
Argentina

Más práctica

- *Real.* para hispanohablantes, pp. 290–291

Go Online PHSchool.com
For: Online Atlas
Web Code: jde-0002

cuatrocientos uno 401
Capítulo 8A

El viaje empieza en el aeropuerto.

Preview

Chapter Opener
Core Instruction

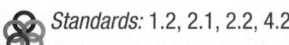

Resources: Voc. and Gram. Transparencies: Maps 12–18

Suggestions: Have students study the scene in the photo. Where do they think it was taken? What do they think the people at the counter are doing? If possible, bring in photos of vacations you've taken abroad and talk about where you went, how you got there, and what you saw. Tell students that in the *Videohistoria,* they will see Ana and Elena making plans for a trip. Tell them that they will learn a new verb tense to allow them to make recommendations and to influence the actions of others.

 **Fondo cultural** *Standards:* 1.2, 2.1, 2.2, 4.2

Resources: Fine Art Transparencies with Teacher's Guide, p. 22

Suggestions: Share with students the information in the Culture Note below. Ask if they have ever driven long distances to see a tourist attraction. Have them consider that the things that make places attractive to tourists may also cause them to become overcrowded and thus unpleasant. If your community is far from beaches, have students think of other places such as the mountains, a national or state park, historical villages, etc., when they answer the questions.

Answers will vary.

Teaching with Art

Resources: Fine Art Transparencies with Teacher's Guide, p. 22

Suggestions: Ask students if they would like to go to Oaxaca based on what they see in the painting. Have them describe the scene and tell what they would like to do if they had the opportunity to visit the beaches of Oaxaca.

 Culture Note
With 342 miles of coastline, beautiful white sand beaches are easy to find in the Mexican state of Oaxaca. The trip from the capital city to the coast is more than 100 miles, through the Sierra Madre, and can take up to eight hours by car. Popular Oaxacan beaches are Zicatela for its surfing, Puerto Ángel for its beauty, and Escobilla for the rare turtles.

Teacher Technology

TeacherEXPRESS
Plan · Teach · Assess

PLAN
Lesson Planner

Go Online PHSchool.com
For: Teacher Home Page
Web Code: jck-1001

TEACH
Teaching Resources
Interactive
Teacher's Edition
Vocabulary Clip Art

ASSESS
Chapter Quizzes
and Tests

PresentationEXPRESS
Dynamic Presentations for Teachers

TEACH
Vocabulary & Grammar Powerpoints
GramActiva Video
Audio & Clip Art Activities
Transparencies and Maps
Activity Answers
Photo Gallery

ASSESS
ExamView
QuickTake Presenter

Vocabulario y gramática

Presentation EXPRESS VOCABULARY

🔖 *Standards:* 1.2

Resources: Teacher's Resource Book: Input Script, p. 174. Clip Art, pp. 188–191, Audio Script, p. 175; Voc. and Gram. Transparencies 140–141; TPR Stories Book, pp. 105–118; Audio Program: Tracks 1–2

Focus: Presenting vocabulary for traveling

Suggestions: Present the vocabulary in two groups: travel preparations, and flights, airports, and customs inspections. Use the Input Script from the *Teacher's Resource Book* or the story from the *TPR Stories Book* to present the new words, or use some of these suggestions.

Have students look at the drawings to predict what topics the dialogue will cover. Ask students to skim the reading and use cognates and context clues to help them understand the meaning of unfamiliar vocabulary. If students have not traveled before, you may need to explain some of the situations.

Bring in a boarding pass from a past flight and a passport. Tell the students you are going on a trip. Point to a place on the map and demonstrate the concept of round trip, direct flight, and stopover.

Bring in several suitcases and narrate as you pack your bags for your trip.

Give students boarding passes with numbers on them. Make some of the passes for a flight to Buenos Aires and the other half for Panama City. Play the role of gate agent and make flight announcements. Write two gate numbers on the board and have students come to the front of the room when their flight is called.

Play the role of flight attendant and have students pretend that they are seated in an airplane. Welcome students to the flight and point out the different sections of the plane.

Play the role of customs officer and ask volunteers to come to the front of the class and pass through customs. Allow them to use your passport and suitcases.

Additional Resources
• Audio Program: Canciones CD, Disc 22

✔ **Assessment**
• **ExamView** QuickTake Presenter Quiz on PresEXPRESS

402

A primera vista
Vocabulario y gramática en contexto

jdd-0887
🔊

Objectives

Read, listen to, and understand information about
• visiting an airport
• planning a trip
• traveling safely

hacer la maleta

❝ Mi hermano Antonio y yo vamos a **hacer un viaje** a Nicaragua para visitar a nuestros abuelos. Para **planear** el viaje, fuimos con nuestros padres a una agencia de viajes ❞.

la tarjeta de embarque

la agencia de viajes

Viajes INTERNACIONALES

los turistas

la maleta

el equipaje

el agente de viajes

el pasaporte

—Les he hecho **las reservaciones.** Tienen dos boletos **de ida y vuelta** entre Miami y Managua. Aquí están sus boletos electrónicos. Van a recibir sus tarjetas de embarque en **el aeropuerto.** Ya tienen los asientos 8D y 8F. Antes de llegar a Managua van a **hacer escala** en Tegucigalpa, Honduras, porque no hay **vuelo directo** a Managua.

—Muchas gracias, Sr. Salazar. ¿Y qué más necesitamos?

—Necesitan sus pasaportes. **Las líneas aéreas** sugieren que **lleguen** al aeropuerto dos horas antes de **la salida** del vuelo para **facturar** el equipaje. También **insisten en** que **pasen** por **la inspección de seguridad.**

Más vocabulario
sugerir *(e→ie)* to suggest

402 cuatrocientos dos
Tema 8 • Cómo ser un buen turista

Differentiated Instruction
Solutions for All Learners

Students with Learning Difficulties
Have students make a four-column chart with the headings *pasajera, agente, auxiliar de vuelo,* and *aduanera.* Ask them to brainstorm a list of vocabulary words for each column. Allow students to use their charts to complete *Actividad 2.*

Heritage Language Learners
Throughout this theme, students may talk about time using different constructions from those in the book. For example, students might use *a las cinco y cincuenta* instead of *a las seis menos diez.* Point out that this is an acceptable way of talking about time, but also encourage them to learn the other method.

la piloto   el piloto   la ventanilla   el auxiliar de vuelo

VUELO: 342
DESTINO A: TEGUCIGALPA
SALIDA: 2:10
LLEGADA: 3:35

la puerta de embarque   el pasajero   la auxiliar de vuelo   registrar   la aduanera

la empleada   la pasajera

el anuncio   el pasillo   el aduanero

la aduana

66 Lo sentimos mucho. Hay un pequeño **retraso** en la salida del vuelo 342 **con destino a** Tegucigalpa, Honduras. Dentro de 20 minutos **tendremos** más información sobre la salida del vuelo 342 99.

66 El vuelo 342 con destino a Tegucigalpa está **listo**. En unos minutos vamos a **abordar**. Favor de pasar a la puerta número 17 de la Terminal A 99.

—**Bienvenid** a Managua. ¿Qué tiene?

—Una maleta y una mochila.

—Pase a la izquierda. Tendremos que ver qué cosas tiene dentro de su equipaje. Ese señor va a registrar el equipaje. Aquí está su pasaporte.

Actividad 1  Escuchar — jdd-0887

En el aeropuerto

Estás en un aeropuerto esperando tu vuelo. Oyes muchas conversaciones entre los pasajeros y muchos anuncios. Si escuchas buenas noticias, señala con el pulgar hacia arriba. Si escuchas malas noticias, señala con el pulgar hacia abajo.

Actividad 2 Escuchar — jdd-0887

¿Quién lo dice?

Escucha cada frase, y en una hoja de papel escribe quién lo dijo: una pasajera, una agente de viajes, una auxiliar de vuelo o una aduanera.

Más práctica

- Practice Workbook, pp. 153–154: 8A-1, 8A-2
- WAV Wbk.: Writing, p. 152
- Guided Practice: Vocab. Flash Cards, pp. 273–278
- *Real.* para hispanohablantes, p. 292

Go Online
PHSchool.com
For: Vocab. Practice
Web Code: jdd-0802

cuatrocientos tres **403**
Capítulo 8A

Enrich Your Teaching
Resources for All Teachers

Teacher-to-Teacher

Set up a travel agency in a corner of your room. Have students research attractions in Spanish-speaking countries on the Internet and contribute pictures, brochures, and other information to the travel agency. Assign each student a specific day to visit the agency. As the agent, ask students where they want to go,

how they want to travel, and other questions that will allow them to practice theme vocabulary.

Internet Search
Keyword:

tourism + (Spanish-speaking country)

Actividad 1 Standards: 1.2   Presentation EXPRESS AUDIO

Resources: Teacher's Resource Book: Audio Script, p. 175; Audio Program: Track 3; Answers on Transparencies

Focus: Listening comprehension about air travel

Suggestions: To activate students' prior knowledge, ask them if they have ever been to an airport. What kind of announcements do gate agents and flight attendants make? Which announcements would they consider good news and which ones would they consider bad news? What kind of information might the pilot give to the passengers?

Script: See *Teacher's Resource Book,* Audio Script

Answers:

1. down   5. down
2. up   6. down
3. down   7. up
4. up   8. up

Bellringer Review
Have students brainstorm a list of items they might want to take on a trip to a beach resort in Mexico.

Actividad 2 Standards: 1.2   Presentation EXPRESS AUDIO

Resources: Teacher's Resource Book: Audio Script, pp. 175–176; Audio Program: Track 4; Answers on Transparencies

Focus: Listening comprehension about air travel

Suggestions: Pause after each statement to give students time to write the answer. You may prefer to have students respond by pointing to the picture of the appropriate person on pp. 402–403.

Script and Answers:

1. Bienvenidos a bordo. ¿Sabe Ud. dónde está su asiento? *(flight attendant)*
2. Muy bien. Aquí en la computadora dice que hay un vuelo directo entre Chicago y la Ciudad de México. *(travel agent)*
3. Señor, ¿puede Ud. abrir la mochila? Tengo que registrarla a mano. *(customs officer)*
4. Señorita, ¿a qué hora va a salir el avión? *(passenger)*
5. ¿Quisiera Ud. un refresco, café o jugo? *(flight attendant)*
6. ¿Por cuánto tiempo quiere Ud. quedarse en Guatemala? *(customs officer or travel agent)*
7. Es importante llegar al aeropuerto dos horas antes de la salida de un vuelo internacional. *(travel agent)*
8. Bienvenidos a Montevideo. Necesito ver su pasaporte. *(customs officer)*

Videohistoria

Core Instruction

 Standards: 1.2

Resources: Voc. and Gram. Transparencies 142–143; Audio Program: Track 5

Focus: Presenting additional vocabulary to discuss planning a trip

Suggestions:

Pre-reading: Direct attention to the *Estrategia*. Have students scan the reading for cognates and unfamiliar vocabulary. Remind them to use context clues as they read to help them figure out the meaning of the words.

Reading: Allow time for students to read the story silently. Have volunteers act out the roles of Ana, Elena, and the travel agent. Tell students to use visual cues in panels 1 and 8 to help them with the words in blue type. Pause after panel 7 to have students summarize what they have read and predict the outcome.

Post-reading: Complete *Actividad* 3 to check comprehension.

Pre-AP* Support

- **Activity:** Have students write four sentences describing what a typical tourist might do to prepare for a trip. Then have them cut the sentences into four strips. Ask students to work with a partner and rearrange the strips in a logical order on their desktops. Compare and share with the class.
- **Pre-AP* Resource Book:** Comprehensive guide to Pre-AP* vocabulary skill development, pp. 47–53

Videohistoria jdd-0887

¡Buen viaje!

Ana y Elena van a Londres para estudiar inglés. Compran los boletos para el viaje en una agencia de viajes, pero hay un problema. Lee para saber qué pasa.

Estrategia

Scanning for basic understanding
Reading a new text can be easier if you already know what the story is about. Before reading the *Videohistoria*, scan it for cognates and words you already know. Based on the words you find, predict what the story is about.

1 Ana: ¿Dónde puede estar Elena? Siempre llega tarde.

Agente: Ten paciencia, señorita. Seguramente llega pronto. Nuestra agencia está **abierta** hasta la una y media.

5 Elena: ¿Cuánto **dura** el viaje?

Agente: Un poco más de 14 horas.

Elena: Es muy largo.

Ana: Puedes dormir en el tren.

Agente: Te va a gustar. Es muy divertido.

6 Elena: Muy bien. Vamos a hacer las reservaciones.

Agente: Aquí tenéis* los boletos. ¡Buen viaje!

7 Elena: ¡Caramba! Vamos a mirar los boletos.

Ana: A ver. ¿Dónde están? ¿No los tienes tú?

Elena: No. ¿Los dejamos en la agencia de viajes?

* Remember that in Spain, the *vosotros(as)* form is used when speaking to a group of people you would address individually with *tú.*

404 cuatrocientos cuatro
Tema 8 • Cómo ser un buen turista

Differentiated Instruction
Solutions for All Learners

Multiple Intelligences

Mathematical/Logical: Have students research the exchange rate of the euro to the U.S. dollar as well as monetary units from other Spanish-speaking countries. Ask them to write out the formula that would be used to convert the price of the flight from Madrid to London as quoted by the travel agent.

Advanced Learners

Have students extend the story by writing what they think will happen next. What will Ana and Elena say to the travel agent once the agency reopens? Ask them to have Ana and Elena explain their situation to the agent and have the agent respond. Encourage volunteers to present the scene to the class.

2 **Ana:** Elena, ¿por qué no llegas a tiempo?

Elena: Eres tan impaciente. Tenemos mucho tiempo.

3 **Ana:** Queremos hacer reservaciones para ir de Madrid a Londres.

Agente: ¿En avión?

Ana: Creo que sí.

Agente: Hay un vuelo directo que cuesta 92 euros.

Ana: ¿Qué más hay?

4 **Agente:** Hay un tren.

Elena: ¿Un tren?

Ana: ¿Por qué no? ¿Cuánto cuesta?

Agente: El boleto para estudiantes es muy barato. Muchos estudiantes **extranjeros** toman el tren.

8 **Ana:** Está **cerrada.** ¿Qué hacemos?

Elena: Mira. Allí están nuestros boletos.

Ana: ¿A qué hora abren otra vez?

Elena: A las cuatro y media. Ten paciencia, Ana. Tenemos que esperar.

 Escribir

Más vocabulario
extranjero, -a foreign

¿Comprendiste?

Usa cada palabra de la lista en una frase completa para indicar lo que pasó en la *Videohistoria.*

Modelo

tarde
Ana está enojada porque Elena llega tarde.

1. impaciente
2. Madrid a Londres
3. 92 euros
4. el tren
5. la agencia de viajes
6. cerrado, -a
7. a las cuatro y media

Más práctica

- Practice Workbook, pp. 155–156: 8A-3, 8A-4
- WAV Wbk.: Video, pp. 146–148
- Guided Practice: Vocab. Check, pp. 279–282
- *Real.* para hispanohablantes, p. 293

Go Online
PHSchool.com
For: Vocab. Practice
Web Code: jdd-0803

cuatrocientos cinco **405**
Capítulo 8A

Language Input

Video

Core Instruction

Standards: 1.2

Resources: Teacher's Resource Book: Video Script, p. 179; Video Program: Cap. 8A; Video Program Teacher's Guide: Cap. 8A

Focus: Comprehension of contextualized vocabulary for planning a trip

Suggestions:

Pre-viewing: Ask students if they have ever planned a trip. Ask them to predict the topics that will be discussed at the travel agency.

Viewing: Show the video once without pausing. Show it again, pausing at the moment Elena shows up at the travel agency. Ask students to tell how Ana is feeling and why.

Post-viewing: Complete the Video Activities in the *Writing, Audio & Video Workbook.*

Standards: 1.2, 1.3

Resources: Answers on Transparencies
Focus: Verifying comprehension of the *Videohistoria*

Suggestions: Have students first identify which panel could be related to each item. Encourage students to tie their sentences together into a paragraph that retells the main ideas of the *Videohistoria.*

Answers will vary but may include:
1. Elena llega tarde y Ana está impaciente porque la está esperando.
2. Ana y Elena van de Madrid a Londres.
3. El vuelo directo cuesta 92 euros.
4. El tren es más barato que el vuelo.
5. Ana y Elena regresan a la agencia de viajes.
6. La agencia de viajes está cerrada por unas horas.
7. Abren otra vez a las cuatro y media.

Additional Resources
- WAV Wbk.: Audio Act. 5 p. 149
- Teacher's Resource Book: Audio Script, p. 176
- Audio Program: Track 7

Assessment
- ExamView Quiz on PresEXPRESS
- Prueba 8A-1: Vocab. Recognition, pp. 203–204

Enrich Your Teaching
Resources for All Teachers

Culture Note
Railways crisscross Spain and all of Europe, with national systems coordinating with and feeding into international systems. Both systems offer discounts to young people. *RENFE,* Spain's national train carrier, offers the **carnet joven** for people between ages 12 and 26. The tickets usually allow travelers to stop in multiple cities.

Internet Search
Keyword: RENFE + España

405

Manos a la obra

Vocabulario y gramática en uso

Objetives
- Communicate about traveling by plane
- Discuss travel plans
- Make recommendations about traveling

 Actividad **4** 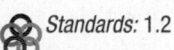 Standards: 1.2  Presentation EXPRESS ANSWERS

Resources: Answers on Transparencies

Focus: Reading and writing about travel advice

Suggestions: Tell students that although some choices may make sense grammatically, only one choice makes sense within the context of the sentence. Encourage them to focus on the roots of the verbs in items 1 and 3 to help them recognize the verbs in the subjunctive.

Answers:

1. extranjero
2. agencia de viajes; cerrada
3. escala
4. pasillo; ventanilla
5. aeropuerto; salida
6. listos; anuncio
7. la puerta de embarque
8. retraso; paciencia

Bellringer Review

Show Voc. and Gram. Transparency 144, the second frame only. Have students write a sentence describing what might be taking place in this scene. Share.

Actividad **5** 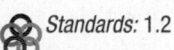 Standards: 1.2 Presentation EXPRESS AUDIO

Resources: Teacher's Resource Book: Audio Script; p. 176; Audio Program: Track 6; Answers on Transparencies

Focus: Listening to identify what is being talked about

Suggestions: Divide the activity into three steps. First, have students listen and jot down notes about what they hear in each item. Have them listen again to confirm what they have heard. Finally, have them listen again and write down the words that are being defined.

Script and Answers:

1. Cuando viajas a un país extranjero, lo necesitas como identificación. *(el pasaporte)*
2. La haces antes de salir de casa. Pones tu ropa y otras cosas dentro de ella. *(la maleta)*
3. La recibes en el aeropuerto y la necesitas para abordar el avión. *(la tarjeta de embarque)*
4. Es el boleto que necesitas para ir a un lugar y volver al aeropuerto de donde sales. *(el boleto de ida y vuelta)*
5. Es el vuelo que prefieres si no quieres hacer escala durante el viaje. *(el vuelo directo)*
6. Lo facturas cuando llegas al aeropuerto. *(el equipaje)*

 Actividad **4** Leer/Escribir

Unos consejos

Cuando viajas por primera vez, vas a tener muchas preguntas. Lee los consejos *(advice)* y escribe la palabra apropiada para completar cada frase.

1. Si vas a un país *(extranjero/pasajero)* insisten en que tengas un pasaporte.
2. Puedes recibir información sobre los vuelos en una *(agente de viajes/agencia de viajes)*. Si está *(cerrada/llegada)*, puedes hacer una búsqueda en la Red.
3. Si no quieres hacer *(reservación/escala)*, sugiero que busques un vuelo directo.
4. Es más cómodo tener un asiento en el *(pasillo/retraso)* o al lado de la *(llegada/ventanilla)*.
5. Debes llegar al *(aeropuerto/pasillo)* dos horas antes de la *(salida/llegada)* de un vuelo internacional.
6. Cuando los empleados de la línea aérea están *(listos/abiertos)* para abordar el vuelo, hacen un *(directo/anuncio)*.
7. Antes de abordar el avión vas a pasar por *(la tarjeta de embarque/la puerta de embarque)*.
8. A veces hay un *(retraso/vuelo)* a causa del mal tiempo o problemas mecánicos. Hay que tener *(paciencia/equipaje)* y no enojarse con los empleados.

Actividad **5** jdd-0888 Escuchar/Escribir

Escucha y escribe

Hay cosas que vas a necesitar para tu viaje. Escucha estos consejos y escribe la cosa que necesitas.

Modelo

(escuchas) La necesitas hacer con la línea aérea antes de comenzar el viaje.
(escribes) *la reservación*

También se dice . . .

la maleta = la valija *(Argentina)*; la petaca *(México)*

el boleto = el billete *(España)*; el pasaje *(Bolivia)*

Debes llegar temprano al aeropuerto.

Differentiated Instruction

Solutions for All Learners

Students with Special Needs

To help visually impaired students recognize details that will help them complete *Actividad* 6, enlarge the drawings using transparencies. Direct attention to visual clues that are specific to each worker's role. Use the transparencies throughout the chapter to reinforce vocabulary.

Advanced Learners/Pre-AP*

Have students choose one of the workers from the Student B list in *Actividad* 6 and write a description of a typical day at work. Ask them to read their descriptions to the class and have the class guess which worker they are describing.

Actividad 6 **Hablar**

¿Quién hace qué?

Una persona que no ha viajado mucho tiene muchas preguntas sobre quiénes hacen diferentes cosas durante el viaje y la preparación para el viaje. Trabaja con otro(a) estudiante para hacer preguntas y contestarlas.

Modelo

pasar por el pasillo con bebidas

A —¿Quién pasa por el pasillo con bebidas?

B —*La auxiliar de vuelo pasa por el pasillo con bebidas.*

Estudiante A

1. sugerir los vuelos y hacer las reservaciones
2. llevar su pasaporte y tarjeta de embarque
3. facturarles el equipaje a los pasajeros
4. ayudar al pasajero a planear el viaje
5. pasar por la inspección de seguridad
6. registrar las maletas en la aduana
7. decir cuánto dura el vuelo
8. hacer un anuncio sobre la llegada de un vuelo
9. decir "Bienvenidos" a la ciudad adonde llegas

Estudiante B

Fondo cultural

Los nombres de los aeropuertos tienen un significado histórico. Por ejemplo, el aeropuerto de San Juan, Puerto Rico, se llama Luis Muñoz Marín, el nombre del gobernador de la isla entre 1949 y 1965. Para muchos puertorriqueños, Luis Muñoz Marín es un héroe porque ayudó a desarrollar la economía de la isla. El aeropuerto de Lima, Perú, se llama Jorge Chávez para conmemorar al gran aviador peruano que murió cuando intentó volar sobre los Alpes en 1910. El aeropuerto de Buenos Aires se llama Ministro Pistarini, por un político que empezó la construcción del aeropuerto. De esta forma, los aeropuertos son parte de la cultura del país porque los nombres reconocen a las personas importantes de su historia.

• ¿Cómo se llama el aeropuerto más cercano a tu ciudad? ¿Por qué tiene ese nombre?

El aeropuerto de San Juan, Puerto Rico

cuatrocientos siete **407**
Capítulo 8A

Actividad 6 *Standards: 1.1* Presentation EXPRESS ANSWERS

Resources: Answers on Transparencies

Focus: Speaking about people in the travel industry and what they do

Suggestions: Have students identify the pictures before they begin. Point out that they may refer either to the passenger or the employee in the first picture.

Answers:
Student A:
1. ¿Quién sugiere ...?
2. ¿... lleva ...?
3. ¿... les factura ...?
4. ¿... ayuda ...?
5. ¿... pasa ...?
6. ¿... registra ...?
7. ¿... dice ...?
8. ¿... hace ...?
9. ¿... dice ...?
Student B:
1. El agente de viajes sugiere los vuelos y hace las reservaciones.
2. El pasajero lleva su pasaporte y tarjeta de embarque.
3. El empleado les factura el equipaje a los pasajeros.
4. El agente de viajes ayuda al pasajero a planear el viaje.
5. El pasajero pasa por la inspección de seguridad.
6. El aduanero registra las maletas en la aduana.
7. La piloto dice cuánto dura el vuelo.
8. La empleada hace un anuncio sobre la llegada de un vuelo.
9. El aduanero dice "Bienvenidos a la ciudad".

Fondo cultural *Standards: 2.1, 4.1*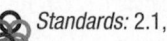

Suggestions: Point out to students that when people arrive somewhere by plane, their first impression of the location is often the airport. Ask them how an airport named after a historical figure might give them insight into the character of a place.

Answers will vary.

Enrich Your Teaching
Resources for All Teachers

Culture Note

Miami International Airport services 55 airlines, 17 of which are from Spanish-speaking countries. This is more than any other major U.S. airport, giving it the nickname "the hub of Latin America." From Miami International Airport, travelers can fly nonstop to nearly all Spanish-speaking countries and many of the larger Caribbean islands.

Teacher-to-Teacher

Have students work in groups to write a paragraph explaining the names of airports in Spanish-speaking countries. Ask them to research airports with historical names. Assign each group a different country and have them describe the location of the airport, as well as the historical significance of its name.

8A Practice and Communicate

Bellringer Review

Hold up flashcards with various numbers from 100 to 1,000. Have students say the numbers aloud.

 Standards: 1.1

Resources: Voc. and Gram. Transparency 146; Answers on Transparencies

Focus: Speaking about flight arrivals and departures

Recycle: Telling time; numbers

Suggestions: Remind students to use *a* when talking about the time that something happens. Have them do the calculations for delayed flights before they get together with a partner.

Answers:
Student A:
1. Perdone, señor (señorita), ¿a qué hora sale el vuelo 486 para Montevideo?
2. ¿... sale el vuelo 199 para Santiago?
3. ¿... llega el vuelo 564 de Miami?
4. ¿... sale el vuelo 927 para Asunción?
5. ¿... llega el vuelo 731 de La Paz?
6. ¿... sale el vuelo 872 para Río de Janeiro?

Student B: Answers will vary but will include:
1. debe salir a las 2:05   4. sale a las 12:45
2. sale a las 6:05   5. llega a las 6:20
3. el vuelo está cancelado   6. sale a las 4:15

 Standards: 1.1, 1.2, 1.3

Focus: Reading and understanding a magazine article about airline rules

Suggestions: Have students use cognates and context clues to help them.

Answers will vary.

Pre-AP* Support

- **Activity:** Have students write the following on a sheet of paper: *Destino:; Número de vuelo:; Puerta:; Hora:.* Assign any one of four Spanish-speaking cities to each student in the class. Create flight information for each destination and read it aloud to the class. Have each student listen for the destination and write down the appropriate infomation. **Model:** *Buenas tardes, pasajeros. Iberia anuncia la salida del vuelo #305 con destino a Buenos Aires. Sale de la puerta #9 a las 13:05.*
- **Pre-AP* Resource Book:** Comprehensive guide to Pre-AP* communication skill development, pp. 9–17, 36–46

408

   Hablar

Los vuelos internacionales

En el aeropuerto de Buenos Aires, Argentina, los pasajeros tienen muchas preguntas sobre los vuelos internacionales. Trabaja con otro(a) estudiante. Hagan y contesten las preguntas según la información en el letrero electrónico.

> **Para decir más . . .**
> procedente de   arriving from

Vuelo	Ciudad	Llegada	Salida	Observaciones
927	Asunción		12:45	a tiempo
358	Lima	1:50		retraso de 40 minutos
486	Montevideo		2:05	más información pronto
564	Miami	3:30		vuelo cancelado
872	Río de Janeiro		4:15	a tiempo
199	Santiago		5:35	retraso de 30 minutos
731	La Paz	6:20		a tiempo

Modelo

llegar de / Lima
A —*Perdone, señor (señorita), ¿a qué hora llega el vuelo 358 de Lima?*
B —*Un momento, por favor. El avión llega de Lima a la 1:50. Tiene un retraso de 40 minutos.*

Estudiante A
1. salir para / Montevideo
2. salir para / Santiago
3. llegar de / Miami
4. salir para / Asunción
5. llegar de / La Paz
6. salir para / Río de Janeiro

Estudiante B
Un momento, por favor.
Lo siento.
con destino a
procedente de
Sale / Llega a tiempo.

Tiene un retraso de . . .
Tuvieron que cancelar el vuelo.
Tendremos más información muy pronto.
Tenga paciencia, por favor.

  Leer/Dibujar/Hablar

En la revista de la línea aérea

Muchas líneas aéreas tienen su propia revista, que generalmente está en tu asiento en el avión. Las revistas tienen una sección que se llama *A bordo*. Esta sección les da a los pasajeros reglas sobre los vuelos.

1 Lee las reglas. Para cada regla, haz un dibujo que se puede usar para explicar la idea principal de la regla.

2 Muéstrale *(Show)* el dibujo para una de las reglas a otro(a) estudiante. Tu compañero(a) tiene que decir, en sus propias palabras, la regla que se representa con el dibujo.

- **El abordaje** Las reservaciones se pueden cancelar si usted se presenta en la puerta de embarque menos de diez minutos antes del despegue[1] en vuelos domésticos.

- **Equipaje de mano** Las piezas de equipaje de mano deben ponerse debajo del asiento del pasajero o en un compartimiento arriba. Los perros y animales domésticos a bordo deben quedarse en todo momento en sus receptáculos correspondientes.

- **Dispositivos[2] electrónicos portátiles** Algunos dispositivos electrónicos portátiles pueden interferir con los equipos de navegación de los aviones. Se permite el uso de estos dispositivos mientras el avión está en tierra[3] con la puerta de abordaje abierta y durante el vuelo cuando los auxiliares de vuelo así lo permitan.

- **Teléfonos celulares** Se permite el uso de los teléfonos celulares sólo cuando el avión está en la puerta de embarque y la puerta del avión está abierta.

- **Tabaco** Se prohíbe fumar[4] y usar tabaco sin humo en todos los vuelos de esta línea aérea. Se le puede poner una multa de hasta US $2,200 por obstruir los detectores de humo de los servicios.[5]

[1]take off [2]devices [3]ground [4]to smoke [5]rest rooms

408 cuatrocientos ocho
Tema 8 • Cómo ser un buen turista

Differentiated Instruction
Solutions for All Learners

Students with Learning Difficulties

Provide a formula to students who have difficulty calculating departure and arrival times due to delays: *scheduled time + delay = actual time.* You may want to give students a worksheet that lists all of the flights in *Actividad* 7 and blank spaces for them to fill in the times. Remind students to write *0* if the flight is not delayed.

Multiple Intelligences

Mathematical/Logical: Have students figure out word problems based on the information in *Actividad* 7. Vary the flight schedules by telling students that there has been a delay or an unplanned stopover and have them calculate the new arrival time. For example: *Está lloviendo en Asunción y el vuelo 927 tiene un retraso de 50 minutos. (1:35)*

 Actividad 9 Observar/Escribir/Hablar

El autobús latinoamericano

El autobús es un medio (means) de transporte común en América Latina. Observa el autobús que es arte folklórico de Colombia. Luego contesta las preguntas.

1. ¿Qué llevan los pasajeros en el autobús? ¿Qué crees que indican estas cosas sobre sus vidas?

2. ¿Adónde crees que van las personas en el autobús? ¿Piensas que sus viajes duran mucho o poco tiempo? ¿Por qué?

 **Fondo cultural**

El transporte más usado en los países hispanohablantes es el autobús. Hay autobuses de lujo (luxury), de primera clase y de segunda clase. Llevan pasajeros, maletas y hasta animales. En algunos países los autobuses de segunda clase no tienen rutas fijas (fixed) y sirven más como taxis. Hay varios nombres para los autobuses. En Colombia y Ecuador, los autobuses se llaman flotas y se usan para viajar entre provincias. En España, se llaman autocares y en los países del Caribe son guaguas. En México y Bolivia los autobuses también se llaman camiones.

• ¿Por qué crees que los autobuses son populares en muchos países hispanohablantes?

Una flota de Montecristi, Ecuador

  Actividad 10 Pensar/Comparar/Hablar/Escribir

Dos medios de transporte

El avión y el autobús son dos medios de transporte populares. Trabaja con otro(a) estudiante para comparar estos dos medios.

1 Copien el diagrama de Venn en una hoja de papel y escriban palabras y expresiones para describir los dos medios de transporte.

2 Escriban un resumen de los dos medios de transporte. Pueden incluir impresiones de cómo se viaja en los países hispanohablantes y en los Estados Unidos.

viajes cortos | boletos de ida y vuelta | viajes largos

el autobús   el avión

Modelo

Las personas que hacen viajes cortos frecuentemente van en autobús, especialmente en los países hispanohablantes. Si hacen un viaje largo, por ejemplo a un país extranjero, muchas veces van en avión. Para los dos medios de transporte se puede comprar boletos de ida y vuelta ...

cuatrocientos nueve 409
Capítulo 8A

Enrich Your Teaching
Resources for All Teachers

Teacher-to-Teacher

Have students plan a bus trip around Mexico. Ask them to do an Internet search for destinations, schedules, and prices. Tell them that their departure city is Mexico City and that they should choose three places in Mexico to visit. Ask them to write a travel itinerary that lists travel dates, departure and arrival times, ticket price, and destination. Encourage them to add other information to make their itinerary more complete, such as stopovers and names of bus companies.

Internet Search

Keyword:

terminal de autobuses – México D.F.

 Actividad 9 *Standards:* 1.3, 2.2

Resources: Answers on Transparencies
Focus: Writing and speaking about a piece of folk art and relating it to real-life situations
Suggestions: Have students brainstorm a list of items they see on the bus and write them on the board. Point out that they are looking at a piece of folk art and that it doesn't represent real-life situations.
Answers will vary but may include:
1. Los pasajeros llevan los animales, las verduras y las frutas. Probablemente los pasajeros viven en el campo.
2. Answers will vary.

 **Fondo cultural** 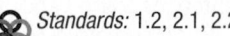 *Standards:* 1.2, 2.1, 2.2

Suggestions: Ask students if they have ever taken a long trip by bus. Have them discuss the advantages of taking a bus rather than other modes of transportation.
Answers will vary.

 Actividad 10 *Standards:* 1.1, 1.3

Resources: Voc. and Gram. Transparency 2 and Teacher's Resource Book: GramActiva BLM, p. 187
Focus: Writing and speaking about bus and air travel
Suggestions: Have students brainstorm a list of words they associate with bus travel and a list of words they associate with air travel. Allow them to use their lists to complete their Venn diagram. Assign Step 2 for homework.
Answers will vary.

Additional Resources

• WAV Wbk.: Audio Act. 6, p. 149
• Teacher's Resource Book: Audio Script, pp. 176–177, Communicative Activity BLM, pp. 182–183
• Audio Program: Track 8

 Assessment

• Prueba 8A-2: Vocab. Production, pp. 205–206

409

Gramática

Core Instruction

 Standards: 4.1

Resources: Voc. and Gram. Transparency 145; Teacher's Resource Book: Video Script, pp. 179–180; Video Program: Cap. 8A

Suggestions: Direct attention to the *¿Recuerdas?* Explain to students that the indicative and subjunctive are considered moods and not tenses because, by themselves, they do not indicate a time period such as the present, preterite, and future tenses do.

Draw a cartoon-style picture of a drill sergeant and write **Sargento Simón sugiere** under the drawing. Write a list of infinitives on the board. Give students sample sentences using various subjects: *Sargento Simón sugiere que Uds. hagan la tarea.* Ask volunteers to play the role of the sergeant and use different verbs of influence to tell students what to do.

Use the *GramActiva* Video to present the present subjunctive or to reinforce your own presentation.

  *Standards:* 1.2

Resources: Teacher's Resource Book: Audio Script, p. 177; Audio Program: Track 9; Answers on Transparencies

Focus: Listening and writing about travel recommendations

Suggestions: Review the script with students to be sure they have correct sentences when they underline and circle the verbs.

 Script and Answers:

Circled words are indicated by parentheses.
1. Les <u>sugiero</u> que (compren) un boleto de ida y vuelta.
2. <u>Insisten</u> en que (pasen) por la inspección de seguridad.
3. Les <u>prohíben</u> que (lleven) tijeras o cuchillos en el avión.
4. Les <u>recomiendo</u> que no (facturen) la maleta que tiene sus medicinas.
5. <u>Prefieren</u> que (lleguen) al aeropuerto dos horas antes de la salida del vuelo.
6. <u>Quieren</u> que (tengan) su pasaporte siempre durante el viaje.

Gramática

The present subjunctive

The subjunctive mood is used to say that one person influences the actions of another.

> Recomendamos **que Uds. hablen** con un agente de viajes.
>
> *We recommend **that you speak** with a travel agent.*
>
> ¿Quiere Ud. **que escribamos** nuestros nombres en las maletas?
>
> *Do you want **us to write** our names on our suitcases?*

Note that the subjunctive sentences have two parts, each with a different subject, connected by the word *que:*

Ella sugiere que yo aprenda francés.

The first part uses the present indicative verb (recommendation, suggestion, prohibition, and so on) + *que,* and the second part uses the present subjunctive verb (what should happen).

Verbs that are often followed by *que* + subjunctive:

decir	prohibir
insistir en	querer *(e → ie)*
necesitar	recomendar *(e → ie)*
permitir	sugerir *(e → ie)*
preferir *(e → ie)*	

¿Recuerdas?

Until now you have used verbs in the indicative mood, used to talk about facts or actual events.

• **Aprendo** francés para mi viaje.

The present subjunctive is formed in the same way as negative *tú* commands and all *Ud. / Uds.* commands. You drop the *-o* of the present-tense indicative *yo* form and add present-tense subjunctive endings.

hablar

hable	hablemos
hables	habléis
hable	hablen

aprender / escribir

aprenda escriba	aprendamos escribamos
aprendas escribas	aprendáis escribáis
aprenda escriba	aprendan escriban

The present subjunctive has the same spelling changes and irregular *yo* form changes used with the negative *tú* commands and *Ud. / Uds.* commands.

llegar

llegue	lleguemos
llegues	lleguéis
llegue	lleguen

hacer

haga	hagamos
hagas	hagáis
haga	hagan

GramActiva VIDEO

Want more help with the present subjunctive? Watch the **GramActiva** video.

Actividad 11 jdd-0888  Escuchar/Escribir

Escucha y escribe

Escucha a una persona que viaja mucho dar recomendaciones sobre su viaje. Escribe sus seis recomendaciones. Después subraya *(underline)* el verbo en la expresión de recomendación y traza *(draw)* un círculo alrededor del verbo que indica lo que debes hacer.

Modelo
Les <u>recomiendo</u> que ⓗⓐⓖⓐⓝ las reservaciones temprano.

410 cuatrocientos diez
Tema 8 • Cómo ser un buen turista

Differentiated Instruction
Solutions for All Learners

Heritage Language Learners
Students may know instinctively when to use the present subjunctive tense, but they may not know what it is or why they are using it. Provide students with five to ten sentences in the subjunctive and indicative moods. For each sentence, have students identify the verbs as either subjunctive or indicative and explain why each was used.

Multiple Intelligences
Bodily/Kinesthetic: Have students work in groups to play "I'm the Boss." Give each group ten index cards and tell them to write a different action verb on each. Tell them to take turns drawing cards and telling someone else in the group to do something. Ask them to use verbs of influence and the subjunctive. Monitor groups to ensure that requests are appropriate.

Actividad 12

Escribir/GramActiva

Juego

1 En el pizarrón *(chalkboard)*, tu profesor(a) va a dibujar dos triángulos. Cada uno tiene cinco secciones y representa una montaña.

2 La clase se divide en dos equipos. Una persona de cada equipo va al pizarrón. Tu profesor(a) les da un verbo. Los estudiantes deben conjugar el verbo en el presente del subjuntivo, empezando con la forma *yo* en la base de la "montaña". Si cometen un error, su profesor(a) dice *avalancha* y tienen que borrar *(erase)* las palabras y empezar otra vez. El equipo que escribe todas las formas primero gana un punto.

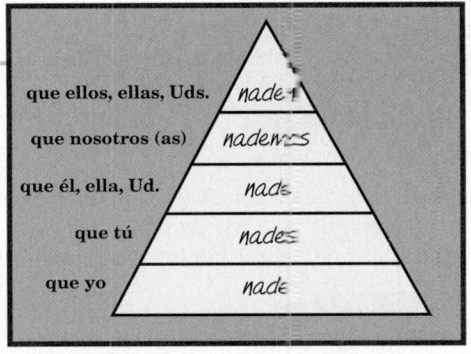

que ellos, ellas, Uds.	nade**n**
que nosotros (as)	nade**mos**
que él, ella, Ud.	nade
que tú	nade**s**
que yo	nade

Actividad 13

Leer/Escribir

Un programa de intercambio

Lee el anuncio sobre un programa de intercambio en Tegucigalpa, Honduras, y contesta las preguntas.

1. ¿Cuáles son las ventajas *(advantages)* de asistir a un programa como éste?
2. ¿Por cuánto tiempo puedes quedarte allí?
3. ¿Cómo dan la bienvenida a los estudiantes que vienen al programa?
4. ¿Te gustaría participar en un programa como éste? ¿Por qué?

¡Vive con una familia en Tegucigalpa, Honduras!

JÓVENES DE LAS AMÉRICAS

Clases de español diarias • Discursos sobre la cultura e historia hondureña • Excursiones dentro y fuera de la ciudad • Vuelos directos desde los Estados Unidos • Programas que duran de tres semanas a tres meses

Nuestros empleados bilingües te esperan en el aeropuerto y te ayudan a pasar por la aduana. Luego te llevan a la casa de tu familia hondureña.

Llama al 525-8357

Actividad 14

Hablar

Tres semanas en Honduras

El programa de intercambio en Tegucigalpa les envía una carta con recomendaciones a los estudiantes que van a participar. ¿Cuáles son las recomendaciones? Habla con otro(a) estudiante sobre ellas.

Modelo

recomendar
A —¿Qué recomiendan?
B —Recomiendan que llevemos ropa cómoda de algodón.

Estudiante A

1. sugerir
2. recomendar
3. prohibir
4. querer
5. insistir en
6. decirnos

Estudiante B

usar el teléfono de la familia
comprar un regalo para la familia
sacar fotos
traer sólo una maleta y una mochila

llevar ropa cómoda de algodón
tener un diccionario
sólo beber agua en botellas
¡Respuesta personal!

cuatrocientos once **411**
Capítulo 8A

Enrich Your Teaching

Resources for All Teachers

Culture Note

Tegucigalpa was established in 1578 when it became an important silver-mining center. The city grew, adding a cathedral and a university. Today, it is an active metropolis. The name *Tegucigalpa* means "silver hill" in the indigenous language. Locals now call it simply *Tegus*.

Teacher-to-Teacher

Using the advertisement in *Actividad* 13 as a model, have students create an ad promoting an exchange program that invites students from Spanish-speaking countries to come to their city or town to learn English and stay with local families. Have them brainstorm ideas for excursions that reflect the culture and history of their community.

Actividad 12

 Standards: 1.3

Focus: Conjugating verbs in the present subjunctive in the context of a game

Suggestions: To save time, make your list of verbs in advance and be sure that verbs with *-ar*, *-er*, and *-ir* endings are relatively equally represented. Use only verbs that are regular in the subjunctive.

Answers will vary.

Actividad 13

 Standards: 1.2, 2.2

Resources: Answers on Transparencies
Focus: Reading and writing about an exchange program

Suggestions: Have students read the questions before reading the ad. Ask students to brainstorm a list of topics they would expect to see mentioned in an ad for an exchange program.

Answers will vary but may include:

1. Son: clases de español diarias, discursos sobre la cultura e historia hondureña y excursiones.
2. Puedes quedarte de tres semanas a tres meses.
3. Les esperan en el aeropuerto, les ayudan a pasar por la aduana y les llevan a las casas de las familias hondureñas.
4. Answers will vary.

Actividad 14

 Standards: 1.1

Resources: Answers on Transparencies
Focus: Speaking about recommendations
Suggestions: Point out that Student A should ask questions using *they* and Student B should answer using *we* in the dependent clause.

Answers:

Student A:
1. ¿Qué sugieren?
2. ¿Qué recomiendan?
3. ¿Qué prohíben?
4. ¿Qué quieren?
5. ¿En qué insisten?
6. ¿Qué nos dicen?
Student B: Answers will vary.

411

Actividad **15**  Standards: 1.1, 1.2, 1.3

Presentation EXPRESS **ANSWERS**

Resources: Voc. and Gram Transparency 147; Answers on Transparencies

Focus: Reading a magazine article and writing suggestions based on the text

Suggestions: Show the transparency and have students highlight sentences that give recommendations.

Answers:

Step 1: Answers will vary but may include:
1. Recomiendan que encuentres el lugar perfecto para estudiar.
2. Sugieren que busques un lugar sin distracciones.
3. Sugieren que encuentres un lugar cerca de una ventana.
4. Pero recomiendan que no mires directamente la ventana.
5. Recomiendan que uses un escritorio con sólo los materiales necesarios.

Step 2: Answers will vary.

 Actividad **16** Standards: 1.1, 1.3

Focus: Writing and speaking about rules

Recycle: Household chores

Suggestions: Have students brainstorm a list of things parents commonly want and don't want their children to do.

Answers will vary.

 Fondo cultural Standards: 1.2, 2.1, 2.2, 4.2

■◆■◇■◆◇■◆■◇◆■◇■◆■◇■◆■◇■

Suggestions: Have students list cultural differences they might find while living in Spanish-speaking countries and suggest ways of dealing with those differences.

Answers will vary.

Additional Resources

• WAV Wbk.: Audio Act. 7, p. 150
• Teacher's Resource Book: Audio Script, p. 177
• Audio Program: Track 10

 ## Assessment

• **ExamView** QuickTake Presenter Quiz on PresEXPRESS
• Prueba 8A-3: The present subjunctive, p. 207

 Actividad **15** **Leer/Escribir/Hablar**

Estudia mejor

Lee el artículo de una revista para jóvenes.

1 Escribe cinco frases usando las expresiones *recomiendan que* y *sugieren que* para hablar de las recomendaciones del artículo.

> **Modelo**
> *Recomiendan que no estudies ni en el dormitorio ni en la cocina.*

2 Escribe tres frases adicionales en que das tus propias recomendaciones sobre cómo puedes prepararte para un examen difícil.

> **Modelo**
> *Sugiero que escojas un lugar lejos del televisor.*

3 Lee tus frases a otro(a) estudiante. ¿Está de acuerdo con tus recomendaciones? ¿Por qué?

¡Puedes sacarte un diez!

Seguramente te ha pasado que justo cuando tienes el examen más difícil de tu vida no puedes concentrarte para estudiar. El secreto está en encontrar el lugar perfecto para estudiar, y créelo o no, tu dormitorio y la cocina no son buenas opciones. El lugar ideal tiene una ventana porque la luz natural te ayuda a desestresarte*. Pero, ¡cuidado! Se recomienda no mirar directamente la ventana porque siempre hay distracciones en el exterior. En el lugar ideal, también hay un escritorio con sólo los materiales necesarios para estudiar. Con este sistema de estudio, será posible sacarse un diez y con él puedes impresionar a tus padres y a tus profesores.

*relax, release stress

 Actividad **16**   **Escribir/Hablar**

Reglas de la casa

Probablemente hay muchas cosas que tus padres quieren o no quieren que hagas.

1 Escribe frases sobre cinco cosas que quieren (o no quieren) que hagas. Usa las expresiones *quieren que, insisten en que, necesitan que, me dicen que* y *me prohíben que.*

> **Modelo**
> *Mis padres me prohíben que gaste mucho dinero en la ropa.*

2 Trabaja con otros dos estudiantes. Comparen sus listas. Escriban una lista para su grupo de las cosas en que insisten los padres en general. Presenten sus listas a la clase.

 **Fondo cultural**

Los programas de intercambio ofrecen la oportunidad de vivir con una familia anfitriona *(host)*. Es la mejor manera de aprender el idioma y conocer la cultura del país. Los estudiantes de intercambio deben respetar las diferencias culturales y las reglas de la familia. Sobre todo, hay que mantener una actitud positiva y abierta.

• ¿Qué consejos te gustaría dar a un(a) estudiante de intercambio que llega a tu comunidad? ¿Qué sería *(would be)* lo más difícil para él (ella)?

Más práctica

• Practice Workbook, p. 157: 8A-5
• WAV Wbk.: Writing, p. 153
• Guided Practice: Grammar Acts., pp. 283–287
• *Real.* para hispanohablantes, pp. 294–297

Go Online PHSchool.com **For:** Present Subjunctive **Web Code:** jdd-0804

Differentiated Instruction

Solutions for All Learners

Multiple Intelligences

Verbal/Linguistic: Have students study their completed sentences in *Actividad* 17 to try to find common elements in the sentences that require the subjunctive. Prompt students by asking about the subjects of the two verbs *(different)*, the one word that is in every sentence *(que)*, and the type of verb found in the first clause *(influence).*

Advanced Learners

Ask students to write a skit about an ordinary student living in a household run by circus clowns *(payasos).* Have them mention silly rules that have to be followed by those who live there. Tell them to describe the household rules by using verbs of influence: *Los payasos insisten en que monte en bicicleta en casa.*

Gramática

Irregular verbs in the subjunctive

Verbs that have irregular negative *tú* and *Ud. / Uds.* commands also have irregular subjunctive forms.

dar

dé	demos
des	deis
dé	den

estar

esté	estemos
estés	estéis
esté	estén

ir

vaya	vayamos
vayas	vayáis
vaya	vayan

saber

sepa	sepamos
sepas	sepáis
sepa	sepan

ser

sea	seamos
seas	seáis
sea	sean

El agente sugiere que **vayamos** a la puerta de embarque.

*The agent suggests that **we go** to the boarding gate.*

GramActiva VIDEO

Want more help with irregular verbs in the subjunctive? Watch the **GramActiva** Video.

 Actividad 17 Escribir

Un viaje con la profesora

Unos estudiantes acaban de llegar al aeropuerto para hacer un viaje al extranjero *(abroad)*. Completa lo que dice su profesora sobre lo que quiere que todos hagan. Usa una forma de los verbos *dar, estar, ir, saber o ser* en cada frase.

1. Quiero que Uds. ____ dónde están sus pasaportes.
2. El empleado necesita que nosotros le ____ los pasaportes antes de facturar el equipaje.
3. Les prohíbo que ____ fuera del aeropuerto.
4. Insisto en que todos ____ cerca de la puerta de embarque media hora antes de la salida del vuelo.
5. Necesito que todos Uds. ____ responsables.
6. Insisto en que todos Uds. ____ listos para abordar el avión.
7. Quiero que el viaje ____ una buena experiencia.

Un aeropuerto mexicano

Enrich Your Teaching
Resources for All Teachers

Culture Note

Interested students can find summer programs in which they can live with a host family, participate in cultural activities, and refine their Spanish-language skills. Generally, students must be between 16 and 18 years of age. The cost usually includes class fees, health coverage, and support networks in the host country.

Internet Search
Keyword:

> study abroad + (Spanish-speaking country)

Gramática 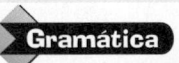 GRAMMAR

Core Instruction

 Standards: 4.1

Resources: Voc. and Gram. Transparency 145; Teacher's Resource Book: Video Script, p. 180; Video Program: Cap. 8A

Suggestions: Use the *GramActiva* Video to introduce irregular verbs in the subjunctive or to reinforce your own presentation.

Emphasize the importance of the accent marks on **dé** and **esté** by pointing out that if they are left off, the meanings change to "of" *(de)* and "this" or "east" *(este).*

Have students review the negative *tú* commands. Give students index cards with sentences that describe people doing things they shouldn't be doing: *Yo llego tarde al aeropuerto.* Ask them to read their sentences aloud and call on volunteers to use negative *tú* commands to tell them what not to do. Have students exchange index cards with a partner and write two sentences of advice using verbs of influence and irregular verbs in the subjunctive.

Actividad 17 *Standards:* 1.2  ANSWERS

Resources: Answers on Transparencies
Focus: Using irregular subjunctive verbs in context

Suggestions: To reinforce the pattern of sentences that use the subjunctive, have students highlight the verbs. Tell them to write the sentences on a sheet of paper and highlight the indicative verbs in one color and subjunctive verbs in another color. For item 3, direct attention to the indirect object pronoun.

Answers:

1. sepan	4. estén	6. estén
2. demos	5. sean	7. sea
3. vayan		

Theme Project

Give students copies of the Theme Project outline and rubric from the *Teacher's Resource Book.* Explain the task to them, and have them perform Step 1. (For more information, see p. 398-a.)

Actividad 18 Standards: 1.1

Presentation EXPRESS ANSWERS

Resources: Answers on Transparencies

Focus: Speaking about suggestions for traveling abroad

Suggestions: Point out to students that Student A is speaking for himself / herself and a group of friends by using **nosotros.** Student B will answer using **Uds.**

Answers:

Student A:
1. ¿Qué debemos saber ...?
2. ¿Qué debemos darles ...?
3. ¿... debemos tener?
4. ¿Qué debemos decir ...?
5. ¿Cómo debemos ir ...?

Student B:
1. Les sugiero que sepan todas las reglas sobre lo que no puedes llevar en el avión.
2. Les recomiendo que les den un número de teléfono donde van a estar.
3. Les sugiero que tengan un pasaporte y un permiso de manejar.
4. Les recomiendo que digan que son estudiantes y turistas norteamericanos.
5. Les sugiero que vayan en taxi porque no van a conocer la ciudad todavía.

Actividad 19 Standards: 1.2

Pre-AP*

Resources: Voc. and Gram. Transparency 148; Answers on Transparencies

Focus: Reading, writing, and speaking about financial advice for traveling abroad

Suggestions: Have students identify key words in the questions that will help direct them to the appropriate section of the article. Then have them skim those sections for the answers.

Answers:

1. Te sugieren que la lleves en un lugar seguro muy cerca de tu cuerpo.
2. Te recomiendan que sepas el teléfono del banco.
3. Te recomiendan que los firmes y escribas sus números antes de salir del banco.
4. Muchos lugares insisten en que muestres una forma de identificación.
5. Te sugieren que pongas tu dinero en efectivo en diferentes bolsillos.
6. Te dicen que vayas a una casa de cambio.

Actividad 18  Hablar

Algunas sugerencias

Unos amigos están planeando un viaje al extranjero. Tú acabas de regresar de un viaje similar y tienes muchas sugerencias para darles. Trabaja con otro(a) estudiante para dar tus recomendaciones.

Modelo
A —¿Cuándo debemos estar en el aeropuerto?
B —*Les sugiero que lleguen dos horas antes de la salida del vuelo.*

Estudiante A

1. qué / saber sobre la inspección de seguridad
2. qué / darles a los empleados de la línea aérea
3. qué forma de identificación / tener
4. qué / decir en la aduana
5. cómo / ir al hotel

Estudiante B

todas las reglas sobre lo que no puedes llevar en el avión
en taxi porque no van a conocer la ciudad todavía
un número de teléfono donde van a estar en el extranjero
que son estudiantes y turistas norteamericanos
un pasaporte y un permiso de manejar

Actividad 19 Leer/Escribir/Hablar

¡No viajes sin leer esto!

¿Qué recomiendan los expertos que hagas para no tener problemas financieros durante un viaje al extranjero? Lee el artículo y contesta las preguntas según el modelo.

Modelo
¿Qué recomiendan para no tener problemas financieros cuando viajas al extranjero?
Te recomiendan que tomes precauciones.

Para no tener problemas financieros en un viaje al extranjero, toma precauciones.

◆ **Tarjeta de crédito**
Con ella puedes pagar las compras, comidas y otros gastos, y sacar dinero de cajeros automáticos, pero hay que tener cuidado de no perderla. Por eso se debe llevarla en un lugar seguro[1] muy cerca de tu cuerpo y saber el teléfono del banco para informar de su pérdida.

◆ **Cheques de viajero**
Se aceptan exactamente como el dinero en efectivo y se reembolsan[2] en menos de 24 horas si los pierdes o te los roban. Se deben firmar y escribir sus números antes de salir del banco, así otra persona no los puede usar. En muchos lugares hay que mostrar[3] una forma de identificación para usarlos.

◆ **"Cash"**
Si traes dinero en efectivo, ponlo en diferentes bolsillos.[4] Cuando llegues a tu destino, pregunta en el hotel por un lugar donde se puede obtener moneda local. En muchos países las casas de cambio[5] son más accesibles para efectuar esta transacción que los bancos.

[1]safe [2]they are refunded [3]show [4]pockets [5]currency exchange offices

1. ¿Qué sugieren para no perder la tarjeta de crédito?
2. ¿Qué recomiendan saber si pierdes la tarjeta de crédito?
3. ¿Qué recomiendan hacer con los cheques de viajero?
4. ¿En qué insisten muchos lugares para usar los cheques de viajero?
5. ¿Dónde sugieren poner el dinero en efectivo?
6. ¿Adónde dicen ir para cambiar *(exchange)* el dinero?

414 cuatrocientos catorce
Tema 8 • Cómo ser un buen turista

Differentiated Instruction
Solutions for All Learners

Advanced Learners
Ask students to research vacation spots in Spanish-speaking countries. Tell them to work with a partner and take turns playing the role of the travel agent in *Actividad* 21. Have them give recommendations based on information they found about their locations: *Si a tu madre le gusta bucear, recomiendo que vayan a las aguas azules de Cozumel.*

Heritage Language Learners
Have students make a travel brochure for their heritage country or for another Spanish-speaking country. Tell them to use the reading in *Actividad* 21 as a model. Remind them to use the four-step writing process of pre-writing, drafting, editing, and revising. You may want to require them to hand in a preliminary draft.

Actividad 20 Escribir/Hablar

Un viaje sin estrés

1 Dos amigos tuyos planean un viaje al extranjero. Escribe seis frases para ayudarles a hacer las preparaciones, pasar por el aeropuerto y abordar el avión. Usa expresiones como *sugiero que* y *recomiendo que*.

2 Lean las recomendaciones de otros dos estudiantes, decidan cuáles son las tres mejores y preséntenlas a la clase.

| Modelo |
Sugiero que vayan a una agencia de viajes para planear su viaje.

| Modelo |
Recomendamos que siempre lleven los pasaportes durante el viaje.

  Actividad 21 Leer/Hablar

La República Dominicana

Vas de vacaciones con tu familia. Imagina que otro(a) estudiante es el (la) agente de viajes. Hablen sobre lo que le gustaría a tu familia hacer allí.

| Modelo |
a mí / sacar fotos
A —*A mí me gusta sacar fotos.*
B —*Recomiendo que vaya a la zona colonial.*

Pasándolo bien en la República Dominicana

Zona Colonial
Es uno de los lugares favoritos de los jóvenes, por sus cafés y sus tiendas al aire libre. Aquí hay muchos edificios históricos, como la catedral.

Las Terrenas
En la costa norte de la isla, se encuentra la playa más larga y bonita de todo el país. Aquí se puede tomar el sol o bucear en las tranquilas aguas.

Los Haitises
Es un parque nacional formado por un grupo de islas cubiertas de selva tropical.* Aquí se pueden apreciar diferentes especies de plantas, pájaros y animales exóticos.

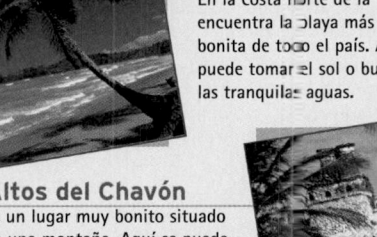

Altos del Chavón
Es un lugar muy bonito situado en una montaña. Aquí se puede estudiar en la escuela de arte, visitar el museo arqueológico, o escuchar conciertos y festivales de jazz en el gran anfiteatro.

*covered with rain forests

1. a nosotros / visitar playas bonitas
2. a mí / tomar lecciones de arte
3. a mis hermanos / observar los pájaros
4. a mi madre / bucear
5. a mi hermana / ir de compras
6. a mis padres / escuchar música

cuatrocientos quince **415**
Capítulo 8A

 Actividad 20 Standards: 1.1, 1.3

Focus: Writing and speaking about recommendations for traveling

Suggestions: Ask students to brainstorm a list of situations that might be stressful to a person traveling to a foreign country for the first time. Write the list on the board and allow students to refer to it in Step 1.

Answers will vary.

Extension: Have students agree or disagree with the recommendations. Encourage them to explain their position and if they disagree, to offer another suggestion.

 Actividad 21 Standards: 1.1, 1.2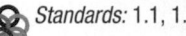

Resources: Answers on Transparencies
Focus: Reading and speaking about recommendations for things to do in the Dominican Republic

Suggestions: Have students work with their partners to identify the infinitives in each item. For each infinitive, have them scan the reading to determine where that activity could be performed. Have them take turns being the travel agent.

Answers:
Student A:
1. A nosotros nos gusta visitar playas bonitas.
2. A mí me gusta tomar lecciones de arte.
3. A mis hermanos les gusta observar los pájaros.
4. A mi madre le gusta bucear.
5. A mi hermana le gusta ir de compras.
6. A mis padres les gusta escuchar música.
Student B:
1. Recomiendo que vayan a Las Terrenas.
2. Sugiero que visite Los Altos del Chavón.
3. Recomiendo que vayan al parque nacional Los Haitises.
4. Sugiero que ella vaya a Las Terrenas.
5. Recomiendo que vaya a la zona colonial.
6. Sugiero que visiten Los Altos del Chavón.

Enrich Your Teaching
Resources for All Teachers

Culture Note
Santo Domingo, the capital of the Dominican Republic, was founded by Bartholomeo Columbus in 1496. Its *zona colonial* includes buildings of great historical importance, such as the Alcazár de Colón. Columbus, Ponce de León, and Cortés all passed through Santo Domingo at one time or another.

Standards: 1.2, 1.3, 3.1

Presentation EXPRESS — ANSWERS

Resources: Answers on Transparencies

Focus: Reading, writing, and speaking about suggestions for passengers on long flights

Recycle: Parts of the body

Suggestions: Activate students' prior knowledge by asking them how they feel when they have to sit for a long time without moving, on a long flight, car ride, or even during a long movie. Encourage students to look for cognates to help them with unfamiliar vocabulary.

Answers:

Step 1:
1. tercer dibujo
2. cuarto dibujo
3. primer dibujo
4. segundo dibujo

Step 2: Answers will vary.
Step 3: Answers will vary.

Pronunciación

Presentation EXPRESS — AUDIO

Core Instruction

 Standards: 1.2, 4.1

Resources: Answers on Transparencies

Suggestions: Have students copy the example words on a sheet of paper. As they listen and pronounce the words, have them draw linking symbols in a different color under the words.

Answer: el avión

Block Schedule

Have students write other suggestions for good health, such as correct posture when sitting at a computer, stress-relieving techniques while studying, or stretching muscles before exercising. Ask them to present their recommendations to the class and encourage the class to try them out.

   Leer/Hablar/Escribir

Viajar y sentirse bien

Estos ejercicios se recomiendan a los pasajeros de vuelos largos para estimular y estirar *(stretch)* los músculos.

 Lee las instrucciones con otro(a) estudiante. Luego observen los diagramas y decidan qué diagrama corresponde a cada ejercicio.

Conexiones | La salud

1. **Círculos de tobillo**
   Levantar los pies del piso. Hacer un círculo con las puntas de los pies moviéndolas en direcciones contrarias.

2. **Flexiones de pie**
   Tres pasos: Con los talones *(heels)* en el piso, llevar las puntas de los pies hacia arriba. Poner luego los dos pies en el piso. Levantar después los talones y dejar las puntas en el piso.

3. **Elevaciones de rodilla**
   Levantar la pierna con la rodilla doblada. Alternar las piernas. Repetir 20 a 30 veces con cada pierna.

   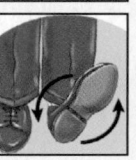

4. **Rotación de hombros**
   Mover los hombros hacia adelante, luego moverlos hacia arriba, hacia atrás y hacia abajo con un movimiento circular.

   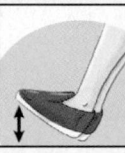

2 Escojan dos de los ejercicios y escriban las recomendaciones que les pueden hacer a los pasajeros.

Modelo

Les recomendamos que muevan los hombros hacia adelante . . .

3 Lean sus recomendaciones a otro grupo. Ellos van a seguir sus instrucciones.

416 cuatrocientos dieciséis
Tema 8 • Cómo ser un buen turista

Pronunciación

Linking sounds

When people speak a language fluently, they run words together rather than pausing in between them. This is done in English when the five-word question *Do you want to go?* comes out sounding like *Jawanna go?* Here are ways sounds are linked in Spanish.

Two identical sounds are pronounced together as one sound. Listen and repeat:

tarjeta_de_embarque
línea_aérea
va_a_hacer la maleta

Two vowels are usually run together. Listen and repeat:

de_ida_y_vuelta
la_empleada
su_equipaje_amarillo

The consonant at the end of a word is linked with the next word. Listen and repeat:

país_extranjero
hablar_al_agente
insisten_en

¡Compruébalo! Practice reading this riddle as a poem, connecting the sounds. Then figure out its meaning.

Sin ser ángel tengo alas,[1]
sin ser auto tengo motor,
y viajo sobre las aguas,
sin ser yate ni vapor.[2]
¿Quién soy yo?

[1]wings [2]steamship

Differentiated Instruction
Solutions for All Learners

Students with Special Needs

Modify Step 3 of *Actividad* 22 for students who have gross motor restrictions. As students read their recommendations to another group, have any students with physical limitations assess whether the dictated instructions have been followed and provide advice to those needing correction.

Multiple Intelligences

Bodily/Kinesthetic: Have students write recommendations for people who have to sit through long classes. Ask them to suggest exercises that can done while sitting at a desk. Encourage them to be creative in their exercises: *Recomiendo que levanten las dos manos para contestar preguntas.* Have students act out their suggestions as they present them.

Hablar/Escribir

Actividad 23

Para una visita divertida

Unos amigos de un país hispanohablante vienen a tu ciudad para pasar el verano.

1 Trabaja con otro(a) estudiante y escriban seis recomendaciones de lo que deben hacer y ver mientras estén allí. Pueden comenzar sus frases con *recomendar que, sugerir que, querer que* y *preferir que.* Pueden incluir estas ideas u otras:

- adónde ir
- dónde y qué comer
- qué partidos, espectáculos y más ver
- dónde dar una caminata o hacer otras actividades al aire libre
- cómo pasar el tiempo libre
- cómo viajar o llegar

2 Trabajen con otra pareja. Lean sus recomendaciones. ¿Están de acuerdo con sus ideas? Presenten sus ideas a la clase y hagan una lista completa de ideas para visitantes.

Un punto de encuentro en El Aeropuerto de Oaxaca-Xoxocotlan, México

 Escribir/Hablar

Actividad 24

Y tú, ¿qué dices?

1. ¿Adónde has viajado? ¿Qué hiciste para planear el viaje? ¿Qué le sugieres a un(a) amigo(a) para planear un viaje?

2. Escoge tres lugares interesantes para visitar en los Estados Unidos. ¿Cómo sugieres que alguien viaje de tu ciudad a estos lugares? ¿Por qué?

3. ¿Qué recomiendas que una persona lleve en su maleta o mochila para no aburrirse en un vuelo largo?

Más práctica

- Practice Workbook, pp. 158–159: 8A-6, 8A-7
- WAV Wbk.: Writing, p. 154
- Guided Practice: Grammar Acts. p. 288
- *Real.* para hispanohablantes, pp. 298–301

Go Online PHSchool.com
For: Irregular Subj. Verbs
Web Code: jdd-0805

El español en la comunidad

Las personas de los países hispanohablantes que visitan los Estados Unidos a veces necesitan ayuda porque han perdido su pasaporte o tienen otro problema. Los países hispanohablantes tienen representantes en los Estados Unidos para ayudar a sus ciudadanos *(citizens)*. Uno de éstos es el cónsul, un diplomático que tiene funciones políticas y económicas en un país extranjero. Ayuda al turista de su país y también ofrece información cultural sobre su propio país y, a veces, hace presentaciones culturales para grupos de estudiantes o adultos.

- Busca información sobre un consulado o embajada *(embassy)* de un país hispanohablante que está cerca de tu comunidad. Pide información sobre cómo se puede visitar el consulado o invitar a un representante a tu escuela.

cuatrocientos diecisiete 417
Capítulo 8A

Actividad 23
 Standards: 1.1, 1.3

Focus: Speaking and writing about recommendations for summer visitors
Recycle: Leisure activities
Suggestions: If possible, obtain copies of brochures on attractions and places of interest in or near your community from a Chamber of Commerce or tourism office, and distribute them to students. If you prefer, bring in several copies of the local phone book for students to use as a reference.
Answers will vary.

Actividad 24
  Standards: 1.1, 1.3

Focus: Writing and speaking about traveling
Suggestions: Point out that traveling doesn't always mean that you go far away. It might be a trip to the closest big city or to a rural area nearby.
Answers will vary.

El español en la comunidad
Core Instruction
 Standards: 1.3, 3.1, 5.1

Suggestions: Have students choose a Spanish-speaking country and write to the embassy or consulate requesting information about the country and places to visit. Tell them that they can find the e-mail address of the embassy of their chosen country by conducting an Internet search.

Additional Resources
- WAV Wbk.: Audio Act. 8–9, pp. 150–151
- Teacher's Resource Book: Audio Script, pp. 177–178, Communicative Activity BLM: pp. 184–185
- Audio Program: Tracks 11–12

 ### Assessment
- **Exam**View Quick Take Presenter Quiz on PresEXPRESS
- Prueba 8A-4: Irregular verbs in the subjunctive, p. 208

 Enrich Your Teaching
Resources for All Teachers

Culture Note
Each of the Spanish-speaking countries has a single embassy in the United States, located in Washington, D.C. Countries may have consulates in other large cities. An embassy is distinguished from a consulate by the presence of an ambassador. Otherwise, embassies and consulates offer the same services.

Internet Search
Keyword:

> embassy, consulate + (Spanish-speaking country)

Lectura

Core Instruction

Standards: 1.2, 2.1, 2.2, 3.1

Focus: Reading comprehension of an article about Ecuador

Suggestions:

Pre-reading: Write three or four personalized questions that require students to use their prior knowledge, visuals, or titles to answer. Design the questions so that students make predictions about the reading. For example: *Según las fotos, ¿qué lugares puedes visitar?* Review students' responses before they begin.

Reading: Read the article to students or have them read it silently. Pause after each section to check comprehension. Ask students to take notes on places to visit in Ecuador as they are reading.

Post-reading: Complete the *¿Comprendiste?* questions to check comprehension.

Bellringer Review

Write these questions about Ecuador on the board and have students consult the information found on p. xxii to find the answers:

1) *¿Cómo se llama la capital?*
2) *¿Es más grande que Bolivia?*
3) *¿Cómo se llama su dinero?*

(**Answers: 1.** Quito; **2.** No. Es más pequeña que Bolivia; **3.** Dólar)

Theme Project

Students can perform Step 2 at this point. Be sure they understand your corrections and suggestions. (For more information, see p. 398-a.)

Additional Resources

Student Resource: Guided Practice: Lectura, p. 289

¡Adelante!

Lectura

ECUADOR
país de maravillas

El Ecuador está en la costa Pacífica del norte de América del Sur y representa un país típico de la zona andina. Es un país pequeño, pero tiene paisajes para todos los gustos[1]. Desde playas tropicales hasta montañas nevadas, desde ciudades coloniales hasta parques naturales, el Ecuador es una joya que deleita[2] al visitante. Le invitamos a descubrir este país de maravillas.

La iglesia la Compañía de Jesús, Quito

Quito

Quito, la capital del Ecuador, es una ciudad cosmopolita situada en un valle rodeado por las cimas[3] nevadas de Pichincha y de Cotopaxi. La ciudad está a 9,200 pies de altura. Para el visitante que no está acostumbrado a la altitud, le puede resultar difícil respirar y puede sentirse cansado.

Declarada parte del patrimonio mundial por la UNESCO en 1978, Quito mantiene el centro histórico colonial mejor preservado de América Latina. La iglesia La Compañía de Jesús, con un interior muy rico en oro, representa el estilo barroco típico de Quito. Otras iglesias interesantes para el turista son La iglesia de San Francisco y la Catedral.

Mitad del Mundo

A 30 minutos al norte de Quito está el monumento a la Mitad del Mundo. Se llama así porque la Línea Ecuatorial que divide al planeta en dos hemisferios pasa por este lugar. Los turistas se divierten tomando fotos con un pie en el hemisferio norte y el otro en el hemisferio sur. ¡De un lado, es invierno, y del otro, verano! Durante los equinoccios del 21 de marzo y del 23 de septiembre, las personas y los objetos no tienen sombra[4].

La Mitad del Mundo

[1]tastes   [2]delights   [3]peaks   [4]shadow

418 cuatrocientos dieciocho
Tema 8 • Cómo ser un buen turista

Objectives

- Read a travel article about Ecuador
- Learn about historic travel chronicles
- Research and talk about taking a trip to a Spanish-speaking country

Estrategia

Previewing
Before you read a magazine article, look at the photos and read the title, subheads, and photo captions. This will help you determine what type of information you will be reading. What do the title and subheads of this article tell you about the information it's likely to contain? What types of places are featured in the photos?

Differentiated Instruction
Solutions for All Learners

Multiple Intelligences

Visual/Spatial: Have students draw postcards for tourist attractions in Ecuador. Encourage them to use the reading or images from other resources to help them with their drawings. Photocopy and distribute the postcards to the class. Have students use the information in the reading to write the postcard they've been given and send it to a partner.

Haciendo tejidos en un mercado Otavalo, Ecuador

Dentro del monumento hay un museo que celebra las distintas culturas indígenas del Ecuador. De hecho, el 25 por ciento de la población del país es de origen indígena. Entre los grupos más conocidos están los salasacas, los shuars y los otavalos. Cada grupo se viste de una manera diferente, habla su propio idioma y se especializa en algún tipo de artesanía, como los tejidos, los sombreros, las joyas o las canastas[5].

El Ecuador le ofrece al visitante un viaje inolvidable por su gran riqueza cultural y natural. Como dijo el científico Humboldt[6], "Un viaje por el Ecuador se puede comparar con un viaje desde la Línea Ecuatorial casi hasta el Polo Sur"[7].

Islas Galápagos

Las Islas Galápagos representan una de las atracciones turísticas más importantes del Ecuador. Estas islas, así llamadas por las gigantescas tortugas galápagos que viven allí, están en el océano Pacífico a más de 600 millas de la costa del Ecuador. El archipiélago tiene 125 islas e islotes. Para proteger las especies de animales que viven en las islas, como las iguanas, los leones marinos[8] y la gran variedad de pájaros, los turistas no pueden visitar las islas por su cuenta[9]. Tienen que tomar una excursión organizada dirigida por un guía naturalista.

La mejor manera de llegar a las islas es por avión desde el aeropuerto de Quito o de Guayaquil. Vuelos diarios[10] salen hacia la isla de Baltra. De ahí, se llega a la Isla de Santa Cruz, donde está la Estación Científica Charles Darwin. El científico inglés visitó las islas en el siglo XIX y su teoría de la evolución

Las Islas Galápagos

se basa en los estudios que hizo durante su viaje. Desde la Isla de Santa Cruz salen barcos para explorar el archipiélago. La mejor época del año para visitar las islas es entre los meses de enero y mayo porque las temperaturas son más cálidas. Los turistas pueden disfrutar de[11] actividades al aire libre, como el buceo y las caminatas que les permite entrar en contacto con la inmaculada naturaleza de estas bellas islas.

[5]baskets   [6]German scientist who traveled extensively in Latin America   [7]South Pole   [8]sea lions   [9]on their own   [10]daily   [11]enjoy

¿Comprendiste?

1. ¿Por qué crees que el Ecuador es una destinación turística tan popular?
2. ¿Por qué puede ser difícil un viaje al Ecuador?
3. ¿Por qué es tan importante el centro histórico de Quito?
4. ¿Por qué se llama así el monumento a la Mitad del Mundo?
5. ¿Por qué son importantes las culturas indígenas en el Ecuador?
6. ¿Qué hace el gobierno del Ecuador para preservar las Islas Galápagos?

Y tú, ¿qué dices?

1. ¿Qué partes del Ecuador te gustaría visitar? ¿Por qué?
2. ¿Crees que el turismo es bueno para las Islas Galápagos? ¿Por qué?

Más práctica

- WAV Wbk.: Writing, p. 155
- Guided Practice: *Lectura*, p. 289
- *Real.* para hispanohablantes, pp. 302–303

Go Online
PHSchool.com
For: Internet Activity
Web Code: jdd-0806

Enrich Your Teaching
Resources for All Teachers

Culture Note

The *otavaleños* were in Ecuador before the Incas and have maintained their cultural identity. They wear traditional clothing, such as ponchos for the men and colorful skirts and glass jewelry for women. Many *otavaleños* speak Quechua, an indigenous Andean language.

Teacher-to-Teacher

Have students work in groups to write a proposal to the school board and principal for a class trip to Ecuador. In their proposal, they must include an itinerary of places they want to visit, with a reason for wanting to go to each one. Remind students that they must persuade their audience that their reasons are justified.

¿Comprendiste?

Presentation EXPRESS ANSWERS

Standards: 1.2

Resources: Answers on Transparencies

Focus: Verifying reading comprehension of an article about Ecuador

Suggestions: Make a transparency of the reading. As you review the answers, highlight where they are found in the reading.

Answers:

1. Es popular porque tiene paisajes para todos los gustos. Hay playas tropicales, montañas nevadas, ciudades coloniales y parques naturales.
2. Quito está a 9,200 pies de altura. Para el visitante que no está acostumbrado a la altitud, le puede resultar difícil respirar y puede sentirse cansado.
3. Porque es el centro histórico colonial mejor preservado de América Latina.
4. Se llama así porque la Línea Ecuatorial que divide al planeta en dos hemisferios pasa por este lugar.
5. Son importantes porque el 25 por ciento de la población del país es de origen indígena.
6. Para proteger las especies de animales que viven en las Galápagos, los turistas no pueden visitar las islas por su cuenta. Tienen que tomar una excursión dirigida por un guía naturalista.

Pre-AP* Support

- **Activity:** Have students read *Islas Galápagos* silently, one sentence at a time, looking up after they finish each sentence. Pose a content question after each sentence and ask that everyone respond aloud with the answer. Continue reading and questioning in this way through the end of the selection.
- *Pre-AP* Resource Book:* Comprehensive guide to Pre-AP* reading skill development, pp. 18–24

Y tú, ¿qué dices?

Standards: 1.3

Suggestions: Have students cite specific examples from the reading to support their answers.

Answers will vary.

For Further Reading

Student Resources: Realidades para hispanohablantes: Lectura 2, pp. 304–305; Lecturas para hispanohablantes 2: "Aprender el inglés," p. 91, "Canción con todos," p. 104, "Ansia," pp. 109–110

419

8A Communicate:
Culture

Core Instruction

✿ *Standards:* 1.2, 2.1, 2.2, 3.1

Focus: Using *códices* to tell a story about a voyage

Suggestions: Display library books that show different examples of pictorial representations, such as those in the caves at Altamira or on the Bayeux tapestry. Ask students if they have seen any examples in the United States, such as the pictographs in the Southwest. Have students look at the examples of *códices* in their texts.

Divide the class into two groups. Have each group analyze one of the *códices* and create a story of what is happening. Model for students how to make a *códice* using stick figures on a transparency. Narrate your story for students, pointing out what each representation means.

Before students begin their own *códices,* have them make a list of events that they wish to include. Have them use sketches to prepare a rough draft. Point out that their *códices* will not be in separate panels but in one illustration. Encourage students to work from the top to the bottom and left to right to organize the representation of their sequence of events. After students have completed drafting their *códice,* give them materials for working on their final draft. You may want to borrow painting supplies from the art teacher. If students are painting, remind them to bring a smock to cover their clothing.

Extension: Make a "museum" in your classroom to exhibit students' work. Have students use cardboard to cut out frames for their *códices,* and hang them in the room. Use the computer to create labels with the students' names and the titles of their works.

Additional Resources

Student Resource: Realidades para hispano-hablantes, p. 306

Los códices

Antiguamente los indígenas americanos viajaban de un sitio a otro para explorar nuevos lugares, comunicarse con otros grupos indígenas y buscar rutas para el transporte de sus productos. A veces, los viajes eran largos, y cuando se alejaban mucho[1] necesitaban anotar el camino para poder regresar a sus casas. Para recordar el camino de regreso, las cosas que veían y los resultados de sus intercambios comerciales, anotaban sus observaciones en unos libros llamados *códices*.

Los antiguos indígenas americanos anotaban sus observaciones en códices.

Objetivo

• Contar un viaje imitando un códice

Materiales

• papel para dibujar (sirven las bolsas de papel)
• marcadores o pinturas acuarelas[2]
• pinceles[3] y lápices

Instrucciones

1 Piensa en un viaje que quieres contar en tu códice. Incluye entre cuatro a seis eventos.

2 Escoge los momentos importantes y represéntalos siguiendo una secuencia lógica. Haz una esquema[4] en una hoja de papel para planear el códice. Piensa en cómo vas a representar con dibujos y símbolos los lugares, medios de transporte, actividades y otros detalles importantes.

3 Dibuja el códice usando una variedad de colores. Lo más importante es que el lector pueda leer la historia de tu viaje por medio del códice. El códice debe ser un dibujo continuo.

4 Cuando termines los dibujos, dobla[5] el códice como lo hacían los aztecas.

Algunos códices famosos: Códice Florentino, Códice Borgia, Códice de Tlaxcala, Códice Mendocino, Códice Madrid

Algunos códices muestran el contacto entre los indígenas americanos y los europeos.

[1]traveled far from home [2]water colors [3]brushes [4]outline [5]fold

420 cuatrocientos veinte
Tema 8 • Cómo ser un buen turista

Differentiated Instruction
Solutions for All Learners

Students with Special Needs

Point out to visually impaired students that another traditional way of recounting events was by the spoken word. Have students retell the story of their voyage in the form of a folk tale. Give them a folk tale to use as a model, and encourage them to exaggerate the details of their trip.

Advanced Learners

Ask students to use the Internet or library resources to research one of the specific *códices* mentioned in the reading. Have them present the image, as well as a real or possible story of what the illustrations represent.

Presentación oral

Un viaje al extranjero

Task
You have a job at a travel agency. A client wants to take her family on a summer trip to a Spanish-speaking country. She wants to spend a few days in a nice city, a day or two visiting ruins or historical sites, and a few days at the beach. Recommend a country and provide key travel information.

❶ Prepare Choose a country that meets the client's criteria. Be sure to look at several countries before deciding which one to select. Research the following information for your client:

- **Lugar**

  ¿Qué país, ciudad, lugares históricos y playas recomiendas que visiten? ¿Qué itinerario sugieres?

- **Documentos**

  ¿Necesitan un pasaporte u otro documento?

- **Transporte y equipaje**

  ¿Cómo recomiendan que viajen? ¿Cuánto cuesta el boleto? ¿Cuánto equipaje pueden llevar? ¿Qué ropa deben levar?

❷ Practice Go through your presentation. You can use your notes in practice, but not when you present. Try to:

- provide all the information on each point
- present the information in a logical sequence
- speak clearly

Modelo

Recomiendo que Uds. viajen a Puerto Rico. Allí pueden ver muchos lugares interesantísimos. La ciudad de San Juan es muy grande y les ofrece mucho a los turistas . . .

❸ Present Present the trip you've planned to your client. You may want to include a map or visuals to assist with your presentation.

❹ Evaluation Your teacher may give you a rubric for how the presentation will be graded. You will probably be graded on:

- how complete your research is
- how much information you communicate
- how easy it is to understand you

Estrategia

Brainstorming with a word web
To make sure you have all the information you need for your presentation, start by making a word web. Begin by writing the country you choose in the center of a piece of paper. Around the country name, write the words *lugar, documentos,* and *transporte y equipaje.* For each topic, write as many related ideas as you can. This way, you will have your ideas on paper in an organized format.

lugar · documentos · Puerto Rico · transporte y equipaje

Core Instruction

 Standards: 1.3, 3.1

Focus: Making recommendations for a vacation destination

Suggestions: Direct attention to the *Estrategia.* Make photocopies of a semantic map to help students organize their ideas for each category. Remind students that the trip will be in the summer (for North Americans) and that they should plan their destinations and advice around the weather. Point out that it will be winter for any destination south of the Equator. Encourage students to use the Internet, travel magazines, or books to find additional information about their destination. Students may want to contact a travel agent for detailed information. When students practice their presentations, remind them that they are trying to sell a product. They need to be confident about what they are saying, as well as persuasive. Have students practice with a partner, who can pretend to be the client. Have students who are pretending to be the client ask questions and provide feedback that will help students refine their final presentation.

Portfolio
Record students' oral presentations on cassette or videotape for inclusion in their portfolios.

 Pre-AP* Support

- *Pre-AP* Resource Book:* Comprehensive guide to Pre-AP* speaking skill development, pp. 36–46

Additional Resources
Student Resources: Realidades para hispanohablantes, p. 307; Guided Practice: Presentación oral, p. 290

 Assessment

- Assessment Program: Rubrics, p. T32

Give students copies of the rubric before they begin. Model a top-scoring presentation for them. After assessment, help individual students understand how their performance could be improved.

Enrich Your Teaching
Resources for All Teachers

RUBRIC	Score 1	Score 3	Score 5
Your completeness of research	You consulted one source for information and cited the source.	You consulted two sources for information and cited sources.	You consulted three or more sources and cited sources.
Amount of information you communicated	You included one of the following: place, documents needed, travel directions, and luggage.	You included two of the following: place, documents needed, travel directions, and luggage.	You included all of the following: place, documents needed, travel directions, and luggage.
How easily you are understood	You are difficult to understand and make many grammatical errors.	You are fairly easy to understand and make occasional grammatical errors.	You are easy to understand and make very few grammatical errors.

Review Activities

To talk about making travel plans: Have students work in small groups and give each group a word list. Have the group spontaneously make up a skit that includes all the vocabulary. Tell them to check off each phrase as it is used.

To talk about airports: Have students make a large diagram of the inside of an airport or airplane. Ask students to work with a partner and use coins as game pieces. Tell them to read sentences about different locations while their partners move the coin based on what they hear.

Other useful words and expressions: Ask students to make flashcards for each word. Have Student A say a sentence with a word missing and have Student B hold up the word that completes each sentence.

Portfolio

Invite students to review the activities they completed in this chapter, including written reports, posters or other visuals, tapes of oral presentations, or other projects. Have them select one or two items that they feel best demonstrate their achievements in Spanish to include in their portfolios. Have them include this with the Chapter Checklist and Self-Assessment Worksheet.

Teacher-to-Teacher

e-amigos: Have students write their *e-amigos* and recommend a place to go on vacation. Encourage them to ask each other questions to find out more about the recommended travel locations. Have students print out their e-mails or send them to you for review.

Additional Resources

Student Resources: Realidades para hispanohablantes, p. 308

 **CD-ROM**

PuzzleView Web Code: jdd-0808

Teacher Resources:
- Teacher's Resource Book: Situation Cards, p. 186, Clip Art, pp. 188–191
- Assessment Program: Chapter Checklist and Self-Assessment Worksheet, pp. T56–T57

Repaso del capítulo

Vocabulario y gramática

jdd-0889

To prepare for the test, check to see if you . . .
- **know the new vocabulary and grammar**
- **can perform the tasks on p. 423**

to talk about making travel plans

la agencia de viajes	travel agency
el / la agente de viajes	travel agent
el equipaje	luggage
extranjero, -a	foreign
hacer un viaje	to take a trip
la maleta	suitcase
hacer la maleta	to pack the suitcase
el pasaporte	passport
planear	to plan
la reservación, *pl.* las reservaciones	reservation
la tarjeta de embarque	boarding pass
el / la turista	tourist

to talk about airports

abordar	to board
la aduana	customs
el aduanero, la aduanera	customs officer
el aeropuerto	airport
el anuncio	announcement
el / la auxiliar de vuelo	flight attendant
con destino a	going to
de ida y vuelta	round-trip
directo, -a	direct
durar	to last
el empleado, la empleada	employee
facturar	to check (*luggage*)
hacer escala	to stop over
la inspección, *pl.* las inspecciones de seguridad	security checkpoint
la línea aérea	airline
la llegada	arrival
el pasajero, la pasajera	passenger
el pasillo	aisle
el / la piloto	pilot
la puerta de embarque	departure gate
registrar	to inspect, to search (*luggage*)

el retraso	delay
la salida	departure
la ventanilla	(*airplane*) window
el vuelo	flight

other useful words and expressions

abierto, -a	open
bienvenido, -a	welcome
cerrado, -a	closed
insistir en	to insist
listo, -a	ready
sugerir (e → ie)	to suggest
tendremos	we will have
tener paciencia	to be patient

verbs often followed by *que* + subjunctive

decir	prohibir
insistir en	querer (e → ie)
necesitar	recomendar (e → ie)
permitir	sugerir (e → ie)
preferir (e → ie)	

present subjunctive

hablar

hable	hablemos
hables	habléis
hable	hablen

aprender / escribir

aprenda	aprendamos
escriba	escribamos
aprendas	aprendáis
escribas	escribáis
aprenda	aprendan
escriba	escriban

irregular verbs in the subjunctive

dar	hacer	llegar	ser
estar	ir	saber	

(To see these verbs fully conjugated in the present subjunctive, refer to pp. 410 and 413.)

For *Vocabulario adicional,* see pp. 498–499.

Differentiated Instruction
Solutions for All Learners

Advanced Learners

Have students create an airline ticket for travel to a Spanish-speaking country. Bring in a ticket for students to use as a model. Have them include the date and time of the flight, the flight number, the airline, the gate, and the type of seat. Tell them to work with a partner and ask and answer questions about their flights.

Students with Learning Difficulties

Select several questions from the *Examen del capítulo,* modify them slightly, and use them as practice questions. Encourage students to share personal test-taking strategies by having them work in groups and explain how they arrived at various answers. Ask groups to share the most effective strategies with the class.

Preparación para el examen

Más práctica
- Practice Workbook: Puzzle, p. 160
- Practice Workbook: Organizer, p. 161

 **Go Online** PHSchool.com
For: Test Preparation
Web Code: jdd-0808

On the exam you will be asked to . . .	Here are practice tasks similar to those you will find on the exam . . .	If you need review . . .
jdd-0889 **2 Escuchar** Listen and understand as someone gives travel recommendations	A student from Spain gives travel tips to students who are thinking of traveling there this summer. Decide if the suggestion includes: (a) planning tips; (b) packing tips; (c) airport arrival tips; or (d) in-flight tips.	**pp. 402–405** *A primera vista* **p. 406** Actividad 5 **p. 410** Actividad 11
2 Hablar Make recommendations for planning a stress-free trip	Your teacher asks you to give the class travel tips. You might talk about (a) getting to the airport; (b) checking in at the airline desk; (c) going through security checks; and (d) things to do on the plane. Begin with: *Sugiero que llegues al aeropuerto dos horas antes de la salida de tu vuelo.*	**p. 407** Actividad 6 **p. 411** Actividad 14 **p. 414** Actividades 18–19 **p. 415** Actividades 20–21 **p. 417** Actividad 24 **p. 421** *Presentación oral*
3 Leer Read and understand a pamphlet about air travel	While at a travel agency, you pick up the pamphlet *Sugerencias para viajar a España.* Look at their suggestions and place them in order, starting with the planning stages and ending with your arrival in Madrid. Label them from A–D. 1. Recomendamos que hagas una reservación seis meses antes de su viaje. 2. Sugerimos que duermas durante el vuelo. 3. Recomendamos que bebas mucha agua antes de abordar el vuelo. 4. Sugerimos que pases por la aduana con todos los documentos necesarios.	**pp. 402–403** *A primera vista* **p. 406** Actividad 4 **p. 408** Actividad 8 **p. 414** Actividad 19 **p. 416** Actividad 22
4 Escribir Write suggestions for a safe and enjoyable vacation	A travel agency asked your class to design a Web page for its Spanish-speaking clients. You are writing the section *Sugerencias para un buen viaje.* Write four suggestions or more. Include advice about such things as planning your trip through a travel agent vs. on the Internet, packing your suitcase, or asking for a particular seat on the plane.	**p. 410** Actividad 11 **p. 413** Actividad 17 **p. 414** Actividad 19 **p. 415** Actividades 20–21 **p. 417** Actividad 24
5 Pensar Demonstrate an understanding of historical record-keeping	Explain how accounts of travel and trade were recorded by the indigenous peoples and Spaniards in Latin America. What information was recorded? What purpose did the documents serve? Who used the documents? What modern documents perform a similar function?	**p. 420** *La cultura en vivo*

cuatrocientos veintitrés **423**
Capítulo 8A

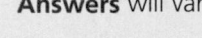

Differentiated Assessment

Solutions for All Learners

STUDENTS NEEDING EXTRA HELP
- **Alternate Assessment Program:** Examen del capítulo 8A
- **Audio Program CD 21:** Chap. 8A, Track 7

HERITAGE LEARNERS
- **Assessment Program: Realidades para hispanohablantes:** Examen del capítulo 8A
- **ExamView** Heritage Learner Test Bank test generator

ADVANCED/PRE-AP*
- **ExamView** Pre-AP* Test Bank test generator
- **Pre-AP* Resource Book,** pp. 124–127

Performance Tasks

 Presentation EXPRESS ANSWERS

Standards: 1.2, 1.3, 2.1, 2.2

Student Resource: Realidades para hispanohablantes, p. 309

Teachers Resources: Teacher's Resource Book: Audio Script, p. 178; Audio Program: Track 14; Answers on Transparencies

1. Escuchar

Suggestions: Ask students to name one or two words that could be clues for each answer choice. Have students listen to the entire script before answering.

Script:
Hola. Soy Marisol, de Barcelona. Sugiero que llames a tu agente de viajes muy pronto. En el verano muchos turistas quieren viajar a España. ¡Es muy popular! Recomiendo que viajes en el mes de junio. Hace mucho calor en julio y agosto.

Answer: (a)

2. Hablar

Suggestions: Give students specific situations on which to base their advice.

Answers will vary.

3. Leer

Suggestions: Remind students to pay particular attention to words like *antes* or *durante* as they sequence the sentences.

Answers:
1. A
2. C
3. B
4. D

4. Escribir

Suggestions: Have students make their final product look like a Web page. Encourage them to use illustrations and design elements such as bullets and headings to organize the page and make it more realistic.

Answers will vary.

5. Pensar

Suggestions: Refer students to p. 420.

Answers will vary.

✓ **Assessment**

- **ExamView** Quiz on PresEXPRESS QuickTake Presenter
- Assessment Program: Examen del capítulo
- **ExamView** Test Bank: Tests A and B test generator
- Audio Program CD 21: Chap. 8A, Track 7

Chapter Overview

A primera vista	Manos a la obra	¡Adelante!	Repaso

Learning Sequence

INPUT	PRACTICE	APPLICATION	REVIEW
• Introduce vocabulary and grammar within an authentic context.	• Practice and develop new vocabulary. • Learn and practice new grammar structures.	• Apply vocabulary and grammar through culminating, theme-based activities. • Apply skill development.	• Review vocabulary and grammar.

Objectives

Read, listen to, and interpret information about: • Staying in a hotel • Appropriate tourist behaviors • Traveling in a foreign city	• Talk about being a tourist in a foreign city. • Use the subjunctive with impersonal expressions. • Use stem-changing verbs in the subjunctive.	• Read about the historic city of Antigua, Guatemala. • Describe train transportation in Spain. • Write and illustrate a travel brochure.	• Prepare for the chapter test.

Culture

• *Artesanía de Oaxaca*	• *Regatear* • *Cinco estrellas* • *REMAJ* • *El parador de Sigüenza*	• *La Red Nacional de Ferrocarriles Españoles (RENFE)*	• Explain cultural practices related to travel in Spanish-speaking countries.

Vocabulary	Grammar	Learner Support	
• Tourist sites • Staying in a hotel • Tourist behaviors and activities	• Present subjunctive with impersonal expressions • Present subjunctive of stem-changing verbs	**STRATEGIES** • Using prior experiences • Using heads and subheads • Using key questions	**RECYCLING** ♲ • Place names; adjectives • Sports; adjectives • Using the subjunctive to express desires

Chapter Features

Exploración del lenguaje

The suffix *-ero(a)*

Conexiones

Mathematics: Creating survey graphs

El español en el mundo del trabajo

Employment opportunities for Spanish-speakers in the tourist industry

Beyond the Classroom: States & Countries

España
República Dominicana
México
Guatemala
Puerto Rico
Panamá
Colombia
Ecuador
Uruguay

Student Resources

PRACTICE

TECHNOLOGY

ONLINE

Interactive Textbook
• Student Edition Online plus audio, video, and flashcards

Go Online Companion Web Site
• Tutorial activities   • Internet links
• Self-tests   • Downloadable MP3 audio files

PuzzleView

CD-ROM

Interactive Textbook CD-ROM
Student Edition on CD-ROM plus audio, video, and flashcards

MindPoint™ CD-ROM
QUIZSHOW

PRINT MATERIAL

CORE INSTRUCTION
Practice Workbook, pp.162–170
• Review   • Vocabulary
• Grammar   • Puzzle
• Organizer

Writing, Audio & Video Activities,
pp. 156–165
• Video   • Audio
• Writing

Grammar Study Guide 1–2 (or 3–4)

Differentiated Instruction

STUDENTS NEEDING EXTRA HELP

Guided Practice Activities, pp. 291–306
• Vocabulary Flash Cards and Vocabulary Check
• Grammar Activities
• Presentación escrita

HERITAGE LEARNERS

Realidades para hispanohablantes,
pp. 310–329

Lecturas para hispanohablantes
• "México lindo," p. 8
• "Verdeluz," p. 46
• **AP* Literature Author:** Julia de Burgos, "Cantar marinero," p. 51

ADVANCED/PRE-AP*

Pre-AP* Resource Book; Student Activity Sheet, p. 127

Teacher Resources

PLAN AND TEACH

TECHNOLOGY

Audio Program   Fine Art Transparencies
Video Program   Vocabulary and Grammar
                 Transparencies
                 Answers on Transparencies

TeacherEXPRESS **CD-ROM**
• Lesson Planner   • Vocabulary Clip Art
• Web Resources   • Teaching Resources
• Teacher Edition with Interactive Links

PresentationEXPRESS **CD-ROM**
• Vocabulary   • Tranparencies and Maps
• Grammar   • Photo Gallery
• Audio   • Clip Art

PRINT MATERIAL

CORE INSTRUCTION
Teacher's Resource Book, pp. 198–223
• Input Script   • Video Script
• Answer Keys   • GramActiva Blackline Masters
• Vocabulary Clip Art • Chapter Resource Checklist
• School-to-Home Connection Letters
• Communicative Activities Blackline Masters

TPR Stories, pp. 112–113

Differentiated Instruction

STUDENTS NEEDING EXTRA HELP

**Guided Practice Activities
Teacher's Guide,** pp. T146–T153

HERITAGE LEARNERS

**Realidades para hispanohablantes
Teacher's Guide,** pp. 156–165

**Lecturas para hispanohablantes
Teacher's Guide,** pp. 1–2, 17–19

ADVANCED/PRE-AP*

Pre-AP* Resource Book Resources Chart,
p. 125

Differentiated Assessment

ASSESS

PH SuccessNet **ONLINE**
• Access to grades and reports from Online Interactive Textbook

ExamView **on Presentation Express
CD-ROM**
QuickTake Presenter
• Vocabulary Quizzes   • Chapter Test
• Grammar Quizzes

TeacherEXPRESS **CD-ROM**
• Assessment Program
• **ExamView** Test Banks A and B
test generator

CORE ASSESSMENT
Assessment Program, pp. 216–228
• Pruebas
    Vocabulary Recognition
    Vocabulary Production
    Present subjunctive with impersonal expressions
    Present subjunctive of stem-changing verbs
• Examen del capítulo   • Speaking and Writing Rubrics

Teacher's Resource Book, p. 212
• Situation Cards

TPR Stories, pp. 112–113

STUDENTS NEEDING EXTRA HELP

Alternate Assessment Program
• Examen del capítulo, pp. 95–99

HERITAGE LEARNERS

Assessment Program: Realidades para hispanohablantes Teacher's Guide,
pp. T162–T166

ExamView **Heritage Learner
Test Bank**
test generator

ADVANCED/PRE-AP*

Pre-AP* Resource Book: Teacher Activity Sheet, p. 126

ExamView **Pre-AP* Test Bank**
test generator

Go Online
PHSchool.com
For: Teacher Home Page
Web Code: jdk-1001

Regular Schedule (50 Minutes)

For electronic lesson plans:
Teacher Express 💿

	Warm-up / Assess	Preview Present / Practice Communicate		Wrap-up / Homework Options
DAY 1	**Warm-up (10 min.)** • Homework check • Return Examen del capítulo: Capítulo 8A	**Chapter Opener (10 min.)** • Objectives • Fondo cultural	**A primera vista (25 min.)** • Presentation: Vocabulario y gramática en contexto • Actividades 1, 2	**Wrap-up and Homework Options (5 min.)** • Practice Workbook 8B-A, 8B-B, 8B-1, 8B-2 • Go Online
DAY 2	**Warm-up (10 min.)** • Homework check	**A primera vista (35 min.)** • Presentation: Videohistoria *Un día en Toledo* • View: Videohistoria	• Video Activities 1, 2, 3, 4 • Actividad 3	**Wrap-up and Homework Options (5 min.)** • Practice Workbook 8B-3, 8B-4 • Go Online • Prueba 8B-1: Vocabulary recognition
DAY 3	**Warm-up (10 min.)** • Actividad 5 • Homework check ✔**Assessment (10 min.)** • Prueba 8B-1: Vocabulary recognition	**Manos a la obra (25 min.)** • Actividades 4, 7, 8, 9 • Fondos culturales		**Wrap-up and Homework Options (5 min.)** • Writing Activity 10 • Heritage Learner Workbook 8B-1, 8B-2 • Prueba 8B-2: Vocabulary production
DAY 4	**Warm-up (10 min.)** • Actividad 6 • Homework check ✔**Assessment (10 min.)** (after Communicative Activity) • Prueba 8B-2: Vocabulary production	**Manos a la obra (25 min.)** • Audio Activities 5, 6 • Communicative Activity • Presentation: Present subjunctive with impersonal expressions	• View: GramActiva video • Actividad 10	**Wrap-up and Homework Options (5 min.)** • Practice Workbook 8B-5 • Actividad 12 • Go Online
DAY 5	**Warm-up (5 min.)** • Actividad 11 • Homework check	**Manos a la obra (40 min.)** • Exploración del lenguaje • Actividad 13 • Fondo cultural • Audio Activity 7	• Presentation: Present subjunctive of stem-changing verbs • View: GramActiva video • Actividades 14, 16, 18	**Wrap-up and Homework Options (5 min.)** • Practice Workbook 8B-6 • Actividad 17 • Writing Activity 11 • Go Online • Prueba 8B-3: Present subjunctive with impersonal expressions
DAY 6	**Warm-up (10 min.)** • Actividad 15 • Homework check ✔**Assessment (10 min.)** • Prueba 8B-3: Present subjunctive with impersonal expressions	**Manos a la obra (25 min.)** • Actividades 19, 20, 21 • Fondo cultural • El español en el mundo del trabajo		**Wrap-up and Homework Options (5 min.)** • Practice Workbook 8B-7 • Go Online • Heritage Learner Workbook 8B-4 • Prueba 8B-4: Present subjunctive of stem-changing verbs
DAY 7	**Warm-up (15 min.)** • Writing Activity 12 • Homework check ✔**Assessment (10 min.)** (after Audio Activity) • Pruebas 8B-4: Present subjunctive of stem-changing verbs	**Manos a la obra (10 min.)** • Actividad 22 • Audio Activity 8 **¡Adelante! (10 min.)** • Presentación escrita: Steps 1, 5		**Wrap-up and Homework Options (5 min.)** • Presentación escrita: Step 2
DAY 8	**Warm-up (5 min.)** • Homework check	**¡Adelante! (40 min.)** • Presentación escrita: Step 3 • Lectura • ¿Comprendiste?		**Wrap-up and Homework Options (5 min.)** • Presentación escrita: Step 4 • Go Online: Lectura
DAY 9	**Warm-up (5 min.)** • Homework check	**¡Adelante! (10 min.)** • Perspectivas del mundo hispano	**Repaso del capítulo (30 min.)** • Vocabulario y gramática • Preparación para el examen 1, 2, 3, 4, 5 • Situation Cards	**Wrap-up and Homework Options (5 min.)** • Practice Workbook 8B-8, 8B-9 • Go Online: Self-test • Examen del capítulo 8B
DAY 10	**Warm-up (5 min.)** • Homework check ✔**Assessment (40 min.)** • Examen del capítulo 8B			**Wrap-up and Homework Options (5 min.)** • A ver si recuerdas . . .: Capítulo 9A

	Warm-up / Assess	Preview Present / Practice Communicate	Wrap-up / Homework Options
DAY 1	**Warm-up (10 min.)** • Homework check • Return Examen del capítulo: Capítulo 8A	**Chapter Opener (10 min.)** • Objectives • Fondo cultural **A primera vista (65 min.)** • Presentation: Vocabulario y gramática en contexto • Actividades 1, 2 • Presentation: Videohistoria *Un día en Toledo* • View: Videohistoria • Video Activities 1, 2, 3, 4 • Actividades 3, 4	**Wrap-up and Homework Options (5 min.)** • Practice Workbook 8B-A, 8B-B, 8B-1, 8B-2, 8B-3, 8B-4 • Go Online • Prueba 8B-1: Vocabulary recognition
DAY 2	**Warm-up (10 min.)** • Actividad 5 • Homework check ✔**Assessment (10 min.)** • Prueba 8B-1: Vocabulary recognition	**Manos a la obra (65 min.)** • Actividades 6, 7, 8, 9 • Fondos culturales • Audio Activities 5, 6 • Writing Activity 10 • Communicative Activity • Presentation: Present subjunctive with impersonal expressions • View: GramActiva video • Actividades 10, 13	**Wrap-up and Homework Options (5 min.)** • Practice Workbook 8B-5 • Go Online • Heritage Learner Workbook 8B-1, 8B-2 • Prueba 8B-2: Vocabulary production
DAY 3	**Warm-up (10 min.)** • Actividad 11 • Homework check ✔**Assessment (10 min.)** • Prueba 8B-2: Vocabulary production	**Manos a la obra (65 min.)** • Exploración del lenguaje • Fondo cultural • Audio Activity 7 • Presentation: Present subjunctive of stem-changing verbs • View: GramActiva video • Actividades 14, 15, 16, 18, 19, 20 • El español en el mundo del trabajo • Fondo cultural • Audio Activity 8	**Wrap-up and Homework Options (5 min.)** • Practice Workbook 8B-6, 8B-7 • Go Online • Heritage Learner Workbook 8B-4 • Pruebas 8B-3, 8B-4: Present subjunctive with impersonal expressions; Present subjunctive of stem-changing verbs
DAY 4	**Warm-up (15 min.)** • Writing Activity 11 • Homework check ✔**Assessment (15 min.)** (after Writing Activity) • Pruebas 8B-3, 8B-4: Present subjunctive with impersonal expressions; Present subjunctive of stem-changing verbs	**Manos a la obra (30 min.)** • Actividades 12, 17, 21, 22 • Writing Activity 12 **¡Adelante! (25 min.)** • Perspectivas del mundo hispano • Presentación escrita: Steps 1, 5	**Wrap-up and Homework Options (5 min.)** • Presentación escrita: Step 2 • Go Online: Self-test
DAY 5	**Warm-up (5 min.)** • Homework check	**¡Adelante! (50 min.)** • Presentación escrita: Steps 3, 4 • Lectura • ¿Comprendiste? **Repaso del capítulo (30 min.)** • Vocabulario y gramática • Preparación para el examen 1, 2, 3, 4, 5	**Wrap-up and Homework Options (5 min.)** • Presentación escrita: Step 4 • Practice Workbook 8B-8, 8B-9 • Go Online: Lectura • Examen del capítulo 8B
DAY 6	**Warm-up (15 min.)** • Homework check • Answer questions **Repaso del capítulo (25 min.)** • Situation Cards • Communicative Activities ✔**Assessment (45 min.)** • Examen del capítulo 8B		**Wrap-up and Homework Options (5 min.)** • A ver si recuerdas . . .: Capítulo 9A

 **Standards for Capítulo 8B**

- To achieve the goals of the Standards, students will:

Communication

1.1 Interpersonal
- Talk about: travel and vacation plans, recommendations, and activities; giving advice to a sport trainer

1.2 Interpretive
- Read about: crafts from Oaxaca; the custom of *regatear;* international systems to evaluate hotels; hostels in Mexico; *el parador de Sigüenza* in Spain; the city of Antigua, Guatemala; the railroad system in Spain (*RENFE);* the tourism industry in Latin America and the need for Spanish-speaking guides; Punta del Este, Uruguay; use of Spanish suffix *-ero*
- Read, listen to, and understand information about: tourist travel to a foreign city; itineraries, hotels; and rules and behavior; recommendations for foreign travel
- Listen to and watch a video about a trip to a foreign city

1.3 Presentational
- Present: information on travel to a foreign city, itineraries, hotels, and rules and behavior; suggestions for foreign travel; information to promote tourism in the community

Culture

2.1 Practices and Perspectives
- Talk about: *regatear;* hostels in Mexico; rail system in Spain; Antigua, Guatemala
- Describe the international star system for hotels
- Explain cultural practices related to travel in Spanish-speaking countries

2.2 Products and Perspectives
- Talk about: wood carving from Oaxaca; international star system hotels; hostels in Mexico; *el parador de Sigüenza* in Spain; Antigua, Guatemala; the rail system in Spain; customs related to foreign travel

Connections

3.1 Cross-curricular
- Review and analyze information in a graph
- Talk about Antigua, Guatemala; prepare a written presentation

Comparisons

4.1 Language
- Use the present subjunctive with impersonal expressions

4.2 Culture
- Compare Oaxacan crafts with U.S. crafts; Spanish and U.S. perspectives on spending money on vacation

Communities

5.1 Beyond the School
- Use Spanish in tourism

Fondo cultural ■◆■◆□■◆□◆■□■□◆□◆

Artesanía de Oaxaca En Oaxaca, México, el tallado de madera *(wood carving)* es una tradición de los indígenas zapotecas. Los tallados más famosos se llaman alebrijes. Son figuras de animalitos como gatos, caballos, iguanas y vacas, y de animales fantásticos como dragones y monstruos míticos. Hoy en día, en Oaxaca hay alrededor de 200 familias que tallan madera.

- ¿Cuáles son algunos ejemplos de artesanía típica de la región donde vives? ¿En qué sentido *(way)* son similares a los alebrijes de Oaxaca? ¿En qué sentido son diferentes?

Alebrije *(Oaxacan wood carving)* de un armadillo

424 cuatrocientos veinticuatro
Tema 8 • Cómo ser un buen turista

Differentiated Instruction

STUDENTS NEEDING EXTRA HELP

Guided Practice Activities
- Vocabulary Check, Flash Cards
- Grammar
- Reading and Writing Support

Guided Practice Audio CDs
- Disc 2, Track 8

HERITAGE LEARNERS

Realidades para hispanohablantes
- Chapter Opener, pp. 310–311
- A primera vista, p. 312
- Videohistoria, p. 313
- Manos a la obra, pp. 314–321
- ¡Adelante!, pp. 322–327
- Repaso del capítulo, pp. 328–329

ADVANCED/PRE-AP*

Pre-AP* Resource Book, pp. 124–127

Capítulo 8B

Quiero que disfrutes de tu viaje

Chapter Objectives

- Discuss traveling in a foreign city
- Talk about staying in a hotel
- Explain how to be a good tourist
- Make recommendations for sightseeing
- Understand cultural perspectives on traveling in Spanish-speaking countries

Video Highlights

A primera vista: *Un día en Toledo*

GramActiva Videos: present subjunctive with impersonal expressions; present subjunctive of stem-changing verbs

Country Connection

As you learn about traveling, you will make connections to these countries and places:

España
República Dominicana
Puerto Rico
México
Guatemala
Colombia
Panamá
Ecuador
Uruguay

Más práctica

- *Real.* para hispanohablantes, pp. 310–311

 **For:** Online Atlas
PHSchool.com **Web Code:** jde-0002

La pirámide de Kukulcán, Chichén Itzá, México

cuatrocientos veinticinco **425**
Capítulo 8B

Teacher Technology

TeacherEXPRESS
Plan · Teach · Assess

PLAN
Lesson Planner

Go Online
PHSchool.com
For: Teacher Home Page
Web Code: jdk-1001

TEACH
Teaching Resources
Interactive
Teacher's Edition
Vocabulary Clip Art

ASSESS
Chapter Quizzes
and Tests

PresentationEXPRESS
Dynamic Presentations for Teachers

TEACH
Vocabulary & Grammar Powerpoints
GramActiva Video
Audio & Clip Art Activities
Transparencies and Maps
Activity Answers
Photo Gallery

ASSESS
ExamView
QuickTake Presenter

Chapter Opener

 Presentation EXPRESS
ATLAS

Core Instruction

Resources: Voc. and Gram. Transparencies Maps 12–18

Suggestions: Ask students if they have ever traveled outside of the United States. If so, have them talk about where they went and how it compared to their own community. How long was their trip? Did they follow an itinerary? If so, have them describe it. Were there things students had to do outside of the country that are not done the same way here? Ask students if they have ever gone on a class trip with a teacher. If so, what were some things that they were taught before they went? Did their teachers give them rules for appropriate behaviors while traveling? If so, what were those rules?

Tell students that in the *Videohistoria*, Ignacio and Javier visit the Spanish city of Toledo. Have students visited historical sites in the United States or abroad? If so, what types of places have they visited?

 **Fondo cultural** *Standards:* 1.2, 2.2, 4.2

◆■◆◆■◆◆■◆◆■◆◆■◆◆■◆◆■◆

Suggestions: Students may not be familiar with local artisanship in your area. Look in your community's newspaper for features on local artisans, to share with students.

Answers will vary.

Teaching with Photos

Suggestions: Explain to students that Kukulcán was one of the gods of the Maya and was represented as a feathered serpent. Share with them the information in the Culture Note below. Ask them to guess the uses of the pyramid in the photo. Have individuals research the topic, then have them report back to the class to see whether their suppositions were correct.

Culture Note

Sculptures of the head of Kukulcán, the feathered serpent, surround the pyramid in a very precise arrangement. On the days of the equinox, the sun casts a shadow on the side of the pyramid in such a way that it appears that a serpent is descending the pyramid. The statue of the serpent's head at the bottom completes the effect.

425

Language Input

Presentation EXPRESS VOCABULARY

Core Instruction

Standards: 1.2

Resources: Teacher's Resource Book: Input Script, p. 200, Clip Art, pp. 214–217, Audio Script, p. 201; Voc. and Gram. Transparencies 149–150; TPR Stories Book, pp. 105–118; Audio Program Tracks 1–2.

Focus: Presenting vocabulary for traveling abroad, tourist behavior, and hotel stays

Suggestions: Have students brainstorm words about traveling with which they are already familiar. Have them scan the itinerary for this vocabulary. Use the Input Script from the *Teacher's Resource Book* or the story from the *TPR Stories Book* to present the new words, or use some of these suggestions. Divide the vocabulary into two categories: *itinerario* and *reglas para el viaje.* Before looking at the *reglas para el viaje,* have students talk about what it means to be a good tourist and predict what some of the rules might be. If possible, use tourist and museum brochures from Madrid or Valencia. You may want to supplement the itinerary on this page with a detailed map of Madrid to point out the location of the airport, *el Palacio Real, la Plaza Mayor,* and *el Parque del Retiro.*

Bellringer Review

 Write these three sentences on the board and have students consult the map on p. xxvii to complete them:

Valencia queda en el _____ de España.
Madrid está en el _____ del país.
El Mar _____ está al este del país.

(**Answers:** este; centro; Mediterráneo)

Additional Resources

• Audio Program: Canciones CD, Disc 22

A primera vista jdd-0897 🔊

Vocabulario y gramática en contexto

❝ Aquí tienen nuestro **itinerario.** Vamos a pasar diez días visitando Madrid, la capital de España, la ciudad **histórica** de Toledo y la ciudad de Valencia ❞.

El Palacio Real en Madrid

El Escorial

Ciudad de las Artes y las Ciencias, Valencia

426 cuatrocientos veintiséis
Tema 8 • Cómo ser un buen turista

Objectives

Read, listen to, and understand information about
• staying in a hotel
• appropriate tourist behavior
• traveling in a foreign city

ITINERARIO
para el grupo de la Sra. Guzmán

Día 1	Llegada al Aeropuerto de Barajas en Madrid. Transporte en autobús al hotel en Madrid.
Días 2 a 4	Primero vamos a **hacer una gira** de la capital y en los días **siguientes** vamos a regresar a los lugares más **famosos** de la ciudad.

• La Plaza Mayor: un lugar histórico con tiendas y cafés al aire libre
• **El Palacio** Real: palacio ceremonial de **los reyes**
• El Parque del Buen Retiro: un parque **bello,** originalmente lugar privado de los reyes
• El Museo del Prado: uno de los museos de arte más grandes y famosos del mundo

Día 5	Lugares cerca de Madrid. El autobús sale a las 8:00 A.M. **en punto;** no vamos a salir tarde.

• El Escorial: palacio impresionante de Felipe II, **el rey** de España entre los años 1556 y 1598
• El Valle de los Caídos: monumento a los españoles que murieron en la Guerra Civil (1936–1939)

Día 6	**Excursión** a Toledo. El autobús sale a las 7:30 A.M. y regresa a las 5:00 P.M.

• El Alcázar: originalmente un palacio árabe y después palacio del rey Carlos V en 1545
• La Iglesia de Santo Tomé: para ver el famoso cuadro de El Greco, "El entierro del conde de Orgaz" (1586–88)
• **La Catedral:** un buen ejemplo de la arquitectura gótica y una de las catedrales más **estupendas** del mundo

Más práctica

• Practice Workbook, pp. 162–163: 8B-1, 8B-2
• WAV Wbk.: Writing, p. 162
• Guided Practice: Vocab. Flash Cards, pp. 291–296
• *Real.* para hispanohablantes, p. 312

 **Go Online** PHSchool.com **For:** Vocab. Practice **Web Code:** jdd-0811

Differentiated Instruction
Solutions for All Learners

Students with Special Needs
Using the script for *Actividad* 1, create a chart for hearing-impaired students. In the first column, list the dictated descriptions of places in Spain. Label the second column *Madrid,* the third column *Toledo,* and the fourth column *Valencia.* Have students make a check mark in the column that identifies which city is being described.

Advanced Learners
Have students research one of the attractions listed in the itinerary. Ask them to find out information such as when it was built, its purpose, how many people visit it each year, or what is contained within the building. Suggest that students present their information on a poster and include additional photographs of the attraction.

Madrid • Toledo • Valencia

Días 7 a 8 Viaje en tren a Valencia. Dos días de excursiones en Valencia.
- Ciudad de las Artes y las Ciencias: un lugar con un poco de todo
- Museo Nacional de Cerámica: una colección de cerámica en un edificio histórico

Día 9 Descansar en la playa cerca de Valencia. Con el permiso de sus padres, pueden hacer surf de vela, esquí acuático y moto acuática. También podemos ir con nuestro **guía** a **navegar** en un bote de vela.

el surf de vela

la moto acuática

el esquí acuático

el bote de vela

Día 10 Regresamos a los Estados Unidos en el vuelo 519.

REGLAS PARA EL VIAJE

Para **disfrutar de** este viaje a España, tenemos que ser buenos turistas. Por eso necesitamos prestar atención a las siguientes reglas.

Durante el viaje hay que . . .

- Ser **cortés.** Los buenos modales siempre son importantes.

- Estar en **la habitación** a las 11:00 en punto. No debes **hacer ruido** en las habitaciones.

- Darle **una propina** al hombre que lleva el equipaje. Es una costumbre que debes **observar.**

- Estar muy **atento.** Prestar atención a los (las) guías cuando hacemos excursiones y giras.

- Quedarse en grupos y ser **puntual.** Es necesario llegar a tiempo.

- Usar el tiempo libre para **cambiar** dinero. Se puede ir a **una casa de cambio,** al banco o se puede usar **el cajero automático.**

Language Input
8B

Actividad 1  *Standards:* 1.2 · Presentation EXPRESS AUDIO

Resources: Teacher's Resource Book: Audio Script, pp. 201–202; Audio Program: Track 3; Answers on Transparencies
Focus: Listening to descriptions of cities
Suggestions: Photocopy the itinerary so students can take notes as they listen.

Script and Answers:

1. En este lugar hay muchas tiendas y cafés al aire libre. *(Madrid)*
2. Los turistas vienen de todas partes del mundo para ver esta catedral estupenda. *(Toledo)*
3. Vamos a la playa para hacer surf de vela o el esquí acuático. *(Valencia)*
4. Vamos a ver un cuadro muy famoso del artista El Greco en esta iglesia. *(Toledo)*
5. Vamos a hacer una gira en este museo enorme, que es famoso por sus colecciones importantes de arte. *(Madrid)*
6. En una de nuestras excursiones, vamos a este parque grande y bello. *(Madrid)*
7. Hay una bella colección de cerámica en este lugar. *(Valencia)*

Actividad 2  *Standards:* 1.2 · Presentation EXPRESS  AUDIO

Resources: Teacher's Resource Book: Audio Script, p. 202; Audio Program: Track 4; Answers on Transparencies
Focus: Listening to good travel advice
Suggestions: Have students listen to the entire activity once before responding.

Script and Answers:

1. Se puede hacer mucho ruido en la habitación a la una de la mañana. *(down)*
2. Hay que dejar una propina después de comer en un restaurante. *(up)*
3. Hay que estar atento a lo que dice el guía. *(up)*
4. Se pueden cambiar cheques o dinero en una casa de cambio. *(up)*
5. Ser cortés y puntual no será tan importante en este viaje. *(down)*
6. Se puede salir solo para hacer una gira en la ciudad. *(down)*
7. No es necesario observar las horas de salida en el itinerario. *(down)*
8. Se puede sacar dinero del banco usando el cajero automático. *(up)*

Actividad 1 jdd-0897 🔊 **Escuchar**

¿Madrid, Toledo o Valencia?

Vas a escuchar varias descripciones de lugares en España. En una hoja de papel, escribe el nombre de la ciudad (Madrid, Toledo o Valencia) donde se encuentra cada lugar.

Actividad 2 jdd-0897 🔊 **Escuchar**

¿Es buena idea o no?

Imagina que eres turista en España con tu clase de español. Escucha lo que dicen tus compañeros y si es buena idea, señala con el pulgar hacia arriba. Si es mala idea, señala con el pulgar hacia abajo.

cuatrocientos veintisiete **427**
Capítulo 8B

Enrich Your Teaching
Resources for All Teachers

Culture Note
The *Ciudad de las Artes y las Ciencias* in Valencia is a vast complex that features a museum, an aquarium, a botanical garden, and a theater. Perhaps the most interesting aspects are the buildings that house these facilities. They represent stunning examples of modern architecture and are themselves part of the exhibits.

Teacher-to-Teacher
Contact local travel agencies to gather Spanish-language travel brochures and itineraries. Keep them on display in the room for students to refer to throughout the chapter.

Videohistoria

Core Instruction

Presentation EXPRESS VOCABULARY

Standards: 1.2

Resources: Voc. and Gram. Transparencies 151–152; Audio Program: Track 5

Focus: Extending presentation of vocabulary for traveling

Suggestions:

Pre-reading: Show students the transparencies. Give students some background of the story, and ask them to predict the events based on the story. As they view each panel, have them guess the causes and effects that link each scene.

Reading: Have students read the story silently once. Ask them to look up after they finish panels 4 and 8, and ask volunteers to summarize the reading. Then have students work in small groups to read it aloud, taking the parts of Javier, Ignacio, and the hotel employee.

Post-reading: Complete *Actividad* 3 to check comprehension.

 Pre-AP* Support

• **Activity:** Have students use the Internet to research points of interest in other capital cities in the Spanish-speaking world. Each student will prepare a visual to include at least four of the points of interest and then create an itinerary similar to the one found on p. 426. Finally, working in pairs, students will read their itinerary to a partner so that the partner can indicate on the visual which point of interest is being described.

• **Pre-AP* Resource Book:** Comprehensive guide to Pre-AP* vocabulary skill development, pp. 47–53

 Videohistoria jdd-0897

Un día en Toledo

¡Acompaña a Ignacio y a Javier durante su visita a la ciudad de Toledo!

Estrategia

Using prior experience
Have you ever taken a trip to a historical site or seen a movie about one? Think about experiences such as checking into the hotel, reading a guide book, walking to various destinations, and buying a souvenir. Prior to reading, look at the visuals to see if Javier's experience is similar.

1 Ignacio: Me dijeron que nuestro hotel queda muy cerca de aquí. ¿Dejamos nuestras cosas y vamos a caminar por la ciudad? ¿Quieres conocerla?

Javier: Sí, me gustaría mucho y **tal vez** comprar recuerdos, como **artesanía** de la ciudad.

Javier   Ignacio

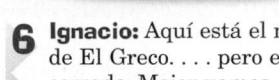

5 Javier: Hay mucho que ver aquí en Toledo.

Ignacio: Sí, la catedral, **el castillo,** el museo de El Greco . . .

Javier: Y no te olvides que quiero comprar algo **típico.**

Ignacio: Sí, después de ver los museos buscamos una tienda de artesanía.

6 Ignacio: Aquí está el museo de El Greco. . . . pero está cerrado. Mejor vamos a una tienda.

Javier: Sí, buena idea.

Ignacio: Entonces vamos a buscar una tienda de artesanía.

7 Ignacio: ¡Qué grande es esta espada!

Javier: Sí, debe ser muy cara. ¿Podemos ofrecerle menos dinero?

Ignacio: No, hombre. No se puede **regatear** aquí. No estamos en un mercado. Vas a **ofender** al **vendedor.**

Javier: Entonces creo que sólo voy a comprar **unas tarjetas postales.**

Differentiated Instruction
Solutions for All Learners

Multiple Intelligences

Verbal/Linguistic: Ask students to create a bulletin board with new vocabulary. Have them write the words on large pieces of paper. Ask students to use the words in an example in a different context. Refer to the display when students have trouble understanding a word.

Students with Learning Difficulties

Help students to comprehend the reading by pointing out the cause / effect relationships that guide the story's action. Give students the causes and have them state the effects. For example, say: *Javier y Ignacio necesitan conseguir un libro sobre la ciudad.* Students respond: *Van a un quiosco.*

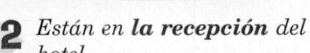 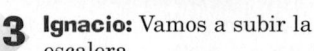

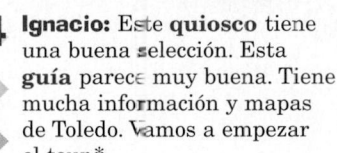

2 *Están en **la recepción** del hotel.*

Empleado: ¿Queréis* **una habitación doble** o dos **habitaciones individuales?**

Ignacio: Una habitación doble, por favor.

Empleado: Bien, pues aquí está **la llave.**

3 **Ignacio:** Vamos a subir la escalera.

Javier: De acuerdo. No me gusta esperar **el ascensor.**

Javier: ¿Adónde vamos primero?

Ignacio: Necesitamos **conseguir** un libro sobre la ciudad.

4 **Ignacio:** Este **quiosco** tiene una buena selección. Esta **guía** parece muy buena. Tiene mucha información y mapas de Toledo. Vamos a empezar el tour.*

*Hacer una gira is common usage for planning to take a tour of a city, but el tour is also used in many Spanish-speaking countries.

8 **Javier:** Es mejor. No cuestan tanto. Toledo sí que es una ciudad muy bella.

Ignacio: Tienes razón. Hemos visto muchas cosas interesantes e históricas. Pero ahora debemos descansar un poco. Mañana tenemos un partido de fútbol muy importante.

*Remember that in Spain, the vosotros(as) form of verbs is used when speaking to a group of people you would address individually with tú.

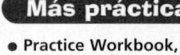 Actividad **3** Escribir/Hablar

¿Comprendiste?

1. ¿Por qué están Javier e Ignacio en Toledo?
2. ¿Adónde van primero después de llegar a Toledo?
3. ¿Qué les da el empleado del hotel?
4. ¿Qué compra Ignacio después de salir del hotel?
5. ¿Qué visitan los dos jóvenes en Toledo?
6. ¿Por qué no entran en el museo de El Greco?
7. ¿Por qué no compra Javier la espada?
8. ¿Qué decide comprar Javier? ¿Por qué?
9. ¿Qué van a hacer los dos después de salir de la tienda?

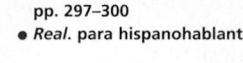 **Más práctica**

- Practice Workbook, pp. 164–165: 8B-3, 8B-4
- WAV Wbk.: Video, pp. 156–158
- Guided Practice: Vocab. Check, pp. 297–300
- *Real.* para hispanohablantes, p. 313

Go Online
PHSchool.com
For: Vocab. Practice
Web Code: jdd-0812

cuatrocientos veintinueve **429**
Capítulo 8B

Video

Core Instruction

Standards: 1.2

Resources: Teacher's Resource Book: Video Script, p. 205; Video Program: Cap. 8B; Video Program Teacher's Guide: Cap. 8B

Focus: Listening comprehension of contextualized vocabulary

Suggestions:

Pre-viewing: Summarize the *Videohistoria,* using the transparencies as a guide. Remind students that they do not need to understand every word of the video to comprehend the main idea.

Viewing: Show the video once without pausing, then show it again, pausing along the way to check comprehension.

Post-viewing: Complete the Video Activities in the *Writing, Audio & Video Workbook.*

Actividad **3** *Standards:* 1.2
Presentation EXPRESS
ANSWERS

Resources: Answers on Transparencies

Focus: Verifying comprehension of the *Videohistoria*

Suggestions: Point out that the answers are not found in order in the story. Have students read the questions and reread the entire story before answering them. Have them tell which panel gave them the information for each answer.

Answers:

1. Van a participar en un partido de fútbol. *(8)*
2. Van al hotel. *(1)*
3. El empleado les da la llave. *(2)*
4. Ignacio compra un libro sobre la ciudad. *(4)*
5. Visitan la catedral, un castillo y una tienda de artesanía. *(5–7)*
6. Porque el museo está cerrado. *(6)*
7. Porque piensa que debe ser muy cara. *(7)*
8. Decide comprar tarjetas postales porque no cuestan tanto. *(7–8)*
9. Van a descansar porque tienen un partido de fútbol el próximo día. *(8)*

Additional Resources

- WAV Wbk.: Audio Act. 5, p. 159
- Teacher's Resource Book: Audio Script, pp. 202–203
- Audio Program: Track 8

✓ **Assessment**

- *ExamView* Quiz on PresEXPRESS
  QuickTake Presenter
- Prueba 8B-1: Vocab. Recognition, pp. 216–217

429

Enrich Your Teaching
Resources for All Teachers

Culture Note

The city of Toledo reflects the history of various cultures that existed there. Part of the Roman Empire for some 600 years, Toledo still has traces of Roman architecture. Several buildings also survive from the Moorish period in Spanish history. The tradition of manufacturing fine steel in Toledo dates to Roman times.

Internet Search

Have students search the Internet for more information about the historic city of Toledo.

Keyword: Toledo, España

 Standards: 1.1, 1.2

Presentation EXPRESS
ANSWERS

Resources: Answers on Transparencies

Focus: Reading and talking about appropriate tourist behavior

Suggestions: Encourage students to read each sentence before choosing the appropriate word. If you have students who have not traveled much, you may want to give them an index card describing a fictional person. For example, if the card says *Eres una persona muy generosa, pero nunca eres puntual,* students may choose their answers from this point of view.

Answers:
Part 1:
1. haces ruido
2. observar
3. itinerario / puntual
4. atento
5. propina
6. artesanía / vendedores
7. históricos
8. cortés

Parts 2 and 3: Answers will vary.

 Standards: 1.1

Presentation EXPRESS
ANSWERS

Resources: Answers on Transparencies

Focus: Talking about foreign travel

Suggestions: Have students identify the items in each illustration before beginning.

Student A: Answers:
1. ¿Dónde pido la llave?
2. ¿Dónde consigo una guía de Madrid?
3. ¿Dónde cambio mi dinero?
4. ¿Dónde regateo con los vendedores sobre la artesanía?
5. ¿Dónde veo la residencia de los reyes?
6. ¿Dónde saco dinero?
7. ¿Cómo subo a mi habitación?

Student B: Answers will vary but may include:
1. Debes ir a la recepción del hotel.
2. Debes buscar un quiosco.
3. Debes buscar una casa de cambio.
4. Debes ir a un mercado.
5. Debes visitar el palacio.
6. Debes buscar un cajero automático.
7. Debes usar el ascensor.

Bellringer Review
Write the following on the board and have students match the associated word(s) from these two columns:
1) *hacer ruido*   a. *bien conocido*
2) *famoso*   b. *lugar histórico*
3) *propina*   c. *molestar*
4) *castillos*   d. *buenos modales*
5) *cortés*   e. *dinero*

Manos a la obra
Vocabulario y gramática en uso

Objetivos
- Talk about being a tourist in a foreign country
- Use the subjunctive with impersonal expressions
- Learn to use stem-changing verbs in the subjunctive

 Actividad 4   **Leer/Escribir/Hablar**

¿Qué clase de turista eres?

Piensa en lo que hace un(a) turista bueno(a) en un país extranjero.

Nota
La guía is both a book you refer to when you travel and a female tour guide. *El guía* always refers to a male tour guide.

1 Lee las frases y escribe las palabras correctas para completarlas.

1. Cuando llegas a tu habitación, no *(haces ruido / disfrutas)* porque no quieres molestar a las otras personas en el hotel.

2. Tratas de *(ofender / observar)* a las personas en un país extranjero para aprender más de su cultura.

3. Consultas tu *(itinerario / llave)* para saber las horas de salida de las excursiones y los vuelos para no llegar tarde. Eres una persona muy *(bella / puntual)*.

4. Estás muy *(famoso / atento)*. Prestas atención al guía durante una gira.

5. Le dejas una *(propina / recepción)* para la persona que te sirvió en un restaurante.

6. Compras la *(artesanía / habitación)* típica del país que visitas y les preguntas a los *(castillos / vendedores)* sobre quiénes la han hecho.

7. Haces una gira de los lugares *(siguientes / históricos)* para saber más de la historia del lugar que visitas.

8. Tienes buenos modales y eres *(típico / cortés)*. Siempre les dices *por favor* y *gracias* a los demás.

2 En otra hoja escribe los números del 1 al 8 y lee las frases de arriba otra vez. Usa los siguientes números para indicar con qué frecuencia haces cada cosa.

⑤ siempre   ② a veces
④ casi siempre   ① casi nunca
③ a menudo

3 Suma *(Add up)* tus puntos. Luego explícale a otro(a) estudiante qué clase de turista eres.

40–32 Eres un(a) turista estupendo(a). Sabes lo que debes hacer en el extranjero *(abroad)*.

31–23 Eres un(a) turista bueno(a). Vas a disfrutar de tus viajes si observas las costumbres del país que visitas.

22–14 Eres un(a) turista típico(a). Debes estar más atento(a) a las costumbres y la cultura del país que visitas.

13–0 Eres el (la) típico(a) turista feo(a). Debes leer otra vez y aprender de memoria todos los *Fondos culturales* en *REALIDADES* 1 y 2.

▼ Turistas en un mercado en Ixtapa, México

Differentiated Instruction
Solutions for All Learners

Multiple Intelligences
Bodily/Kinesthetic: Have students demonstrate bargaining at a market. Give them an item to bargain over and have them prepare a skit. Encourage them to exaggerate and use humor. For example, have the vendor ask an unreasonable price for an item, and have the seller offer him or her a minimal amount.

Students with Special Needs
Help hearing-impaired students with *Actividad* 6 by preparing an index card for each of the sentences in the script. Have students copy the columns on a sheet of paper and arrange the appropriate index cards under each title.

Actividad 5

Hablar

Recomendaciones para los turistas

Habla con otro(a) estudiante y hagan recomendaciones para los turistas.

dejar

Modelo

A —¿Dónde dejo el equipaje?
B —Debes ir a la habitación.

Estudiante A

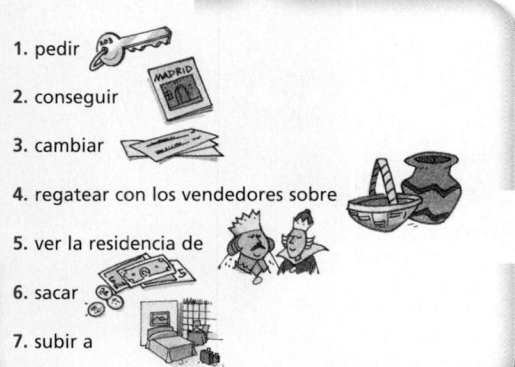

1. pedir
2. conseguir
3. cambiar
4. regatear con los vendedores sobre
5. ver la residencia de
6. sacar
7. subir a

Estudiante B

usar   buscar
ir a   visitar

Actividad 6

jdd-0898

Escuchar/Escribir

Escucha y escribe

Vas a escuchar lo que puede hacer un(a) turista en un país extranjero. En una hoja de papel, haz dos columnas. Sobre una columna, escribe *cortés*. Sobre la otra columna, escribe *descortés (impolite)*. Escribe cada acción que escuchas en la columna correcta.

cortés	descortés

Fondo cultural

 ◼◆◻◆◻◆◻◆◻◆◻◆◻◆◻

Regatear es una costumbre de negociar precios, y es muy común en los mercados de los países hispanohablantes. En cambio, es una costumbre menos común en las tiendas. Si quieres comprar algo en un mercado, le pides el precio al vendedor. El vendedor y el cliente ofrecen y piden precios hasta acordar *(agree)* un precio final. Si no sabes si debes regatear o no, puedes preguntar: "¿Son precios fijos *(fixed)*?".

• Imagina que eres vendedor(a) en un mercado. ¿Te gustaría regatear con los clientes para vender tus cosas? ¿Por qué?

En el mercado de Otavalo, en el Ecuador

cuatrocientos treinta y uno **431**
Capítulo 8B

Actividad 6

Standards: 1.2

Presentation EXPRESS AUDIO

Resources: Teacher's Resource Book: Audio Script, p. 202, GramActiva BLM, p. 213; Audio Program: Track 6; Answers on Transparencies

Focus: Listening to and demonstrating comprehension of information about tourist behavior

Suggestions: Have students listen once and then again. Give them time to write their answers.

Script and Answers:

1. Hacer mucho ruido en la habitación del hotel. *(descortés)*
2. Regatear en un almacén grande. *(descortés)*
3. Estar atento cuando el guía está hablando. *(cortés)*
4. Observar las costumbres del país extranjero. *(cortés)*
5. Darle una propina a la persona que lleva tu maleta a tu habitación. *(cortés)*
6. Decir "Buenos días," "por favor" y "gracias." *(cortés)*
7. Reírse de la artesanía que tienen los vendedores. *(descortés)*

Fondo cultural

Standards: 1.2, 2.1

◼◆◻◆◻◆◻◆◻◆◻◆◻◆◻◆◻

Suggestions: Have students give examples of when they have bargained for an item. Ask them to brainstorm possible motives that vendors have for bargaining with customers.

Answers will vary.

Enrich Your Teaching

Resources for All Teachers

Culture Note

One common bargaining strategy at markets is to offer half the stated price for the item; buyer and seller will eventually meet in the middle. When bargaining, it is important to remain polite and friendly. A rushed, rude, or demanding attitude may be perceived as insulting by the vendor.

Teacher-to-Teacher

Have students prepare a travel itinerary and advice for an exchange student visiting your town. Ask them to include historical sites and places of interest as well as helpful tips for where to stay, dine, and shop.

Actividad 7  Standards: 1.2

Presentation EXPRESS ANSWERS

Resources: Voc. and Gram. Transparency 154; Answers on Transparencies

Focus: Comprehending written information about water activities

Suggestions: Have students use the pictures to predict what this article is about. Ask them to brainstorm a list of water sports. Have them scan the reading once to determine what sports are discussed.

Answers will vary but may include:
1. Puedes navegar en botes de vela, practicar la moto acuática, el surf de vela o el esquí acuático.
2. actividades náuticas, bello, escuelas de surf, tranquilidad, estupendo
3. Sí, porque hay escuelas e instructores para ayudarles a aprender. También hay otras actividades, como la moto acuática o navegar en botes de vela.
4. Puedes alquilarlo allí.

Actividad 8 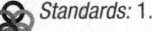 Standards: 1.1

Focus: Talking about water sports

Recycle: Sports; place names

Suggestions: Write the names of the sports on transparency sheets. Show the word that students should be discussing. Allow them two or three minutes to discuss each sport before posting a different one.

Answers will vary.

Actividad 7 **Leer/Escribir/Hablar**

Vacaciones en Punta del Este

Lee el siguiente anuncio para Punta del Este, Uruguay. Luego contesta las preguntas.

Punta del Este:
Destino acuático

EL CLUB NÁUTICO PUNTA DEL ESTE, FAMOSO A NIVEL[1] NACIONAL Y LOCAL, TIENE MUCHAS ACTIVIDADES NÁUTICAS PARA LOS TURISTAS EN, TAL VEZ, EL LUGAR MÁS BELLO DE URUGUAY.

Tanto en el puerto[2] como en la playa se encuentran lugares que alquilan pequeños botes de vela para navegar dentro de la bahía[3] o para llegar hasta la isla Gorriti.

Para los aficionados de la moto acuática, también se puede alquilarlas en la playa. Infórmese de los lugares designados para el deporte porque no se permite su práctica en todas partes.

El surf de vela es un deporte muy popular en Punta del Este. Se puede encontrar escuelas de surf de vela y hay la posibilidad de alquilar tablas[4] en el arroyo[5] Maldonado y en la laguna del Diario. En los días de mucho viento siempre es posible ver la habilidad de los navegantes con sus tablas de salto.

Gracias a la tranquilidad de las aguas del área, Punta del Este es un lugar estupendo para hacer esquí acuático. Hay varias escuelas aquí donde se puede encontrar un gran número de expertos que ofrecen sus servicios de instructor en el arroyo Maldonado y en la laguna del Diario.

[1]level [2]port [3]bay [4]surfboards [5]stream

1. ¿Qué deportes puedes practicar en Punta del Este?

2. ¿Qué palabras indican que Punta del Este es un buen lugar para los turistas?

3. Si no sabes hacer ni el surf de vela ni el esquí acuático, ¿puedes disfrutar de unas vacaciones en Punta del Este? ¿Por qué?

4. Imagina que no puedes llevar tu propio equipo para practicar los deportes acuáticos en Punta del Este. ¿Qué puedes hacer?

Actividad 8  **Hablar**

Los deportes acuáticos

Habla con otro(a) estudiante sobre los deportes acuáticos que se mencionan en el anuncio de Punta del Este. Puedes hacer preguntas como:

- ¿Has hecho . . . alguna vez?
- ¿Dónde lo (la) practicas (practicaste)?
- ¿Te diviertes (divertiste) mucho practicando . . . ?

- ¿Te gustaría practicarlo(la) alguna vez?
- ¿Cuál de los deportes te parece más interesante?

Differentiated Instruction
Solutions for All Learners

Multiple Intelligences

Intrapersonal/Introspective: Have students write a travel journal entry about a real or an imagined vacation. Have them describe the hotel they stayed in and the activities they participated in while they were there. If students choose to describe a real vacation, have them include a photo with their entry.

Heritage Language Learners

Have students create an advertisement for a hotel. Ask them to describe its location, amenities, and prices. Point out that the goal of the ad is to persuade travelers to stay there. Post students' work and have other students vote on the best ad by placing a sticker on the hotel they would choose.

Actividad 9 · Leer/Escuchar · jdd-0898

Los mejores hoteles

Imagina que eres agente de viajes y puedes recomendarles a tus clientes uno de los hoteles en estos anuncios. Lee los anuncios. Después escucha las preferencias de las personas y escribe *Hotel Real, Hotel Canarias* o *los dos hoteles* según la información en los anuncios.

El centro turístico de Cancún, el **Hotel Real** está sobre una de las más bellas playas de arena[1] blanca y frente a la Laguna Nichupté. Su arquitectura moderna y servicios de primera clase, hacen el hotel ideal para cualquier[2] vacacionista.

Habitaciones: Tenemos 300 habitaciones que están perfectamente equipadas con aire acondicionado, televisión a color vía satélite, teléfono directo, balcón privado, tina de baño[3] y secadora de pelo.

Servicios adicionales:
• Restaurantes (3)
• Piscina y gran Jacuzzi
• Salones de reuniones

De enero hasta abril:
Habitación individual
o doble: $146
De abril hasta diciembre:
Habitación individual
o doble: $78

Tel: 289-06-59

Hotel Real

¹sand ²any ³bathtub

El Hotel Canarias, en la República Dominicana, es uno de los más bellos y exclusivos destinos turísticos / vacacionales del Caribe. Este centro turístico se extiende sobre unos 7,000 acres con árboles tropicales y ofrece villas, habitaciones hoteleras, campos de golf (3), canchas de tenis (13), piscinas (19), así como la playa Minitas.

También ofrecemos:
• Restaurantes (9: desde gourmet hasta informal)
• Tiendas de regalo
• Salones de belleza
• Aeropuerto privado
• Oficina de aerolínea
• Gimnasio
• Banco

Tel: 59-28-59

Villas de 2 a 6 habitaciones: $136 hasta $615

 **Fondo cultural**

Cinco estrellas Un sistema internacional de evaluar un hotel es el sistema de estrellas: cinco estrellas es el mejor. ¿Qué necesita tener un hotel de cinco estrellas? En España, el hotel necesita tener aire acondicionado y calefacción *(heating)*, salones sociales, garaje y salón de belleza. En México, tiene que tener un restaurante, cafetería, discoteca y seguridad.

• ¿Prefieres un hotel con muchos servicios?, ¿una habitación de gran lujo? Si vas a un país extranjero, ¿es mejor gastar tu dinero en un hotel de cinco estrellas, en restaurantes caros o en comprar recuerdos?

cuatrocientos treinta y tres **433**
Capítulo 8B

Practice and Communicate

8B

Actividad 9 · Standards: 1.2 · Presentation EXPRESS AUDIO

Resources: Voc. & Gram. Transparency 155; Teacher's Resource Book: Audio Script, p. 202; Audio Program: Track 7; Answers on Transparencies

Focus: Comprehending information about hotels

Recycle: Place names; adjectives

Suggestions: Before listening to the script, have students read the hotel ads and create a chart to compare and contrast the major attractions, activities, location, and amenities.

Script and Answers:

1. A nosotros nos encanta nadar, tomar el sol y hacer deportes acuáticos. *(los dos hoteles)*
2. Vamos a viajar al hotel en un avión privado pequeño. *(Hotel Canarias)*
3. No puedo pasar una semana sin ver mis telenovelas favoritas. *(Hotel Real)*
4. Mi esposa tiene que llamar por teléfono cada día a la tienda en Nueva York donde trabaja. *(Hotel Real)*
5. Tenemos cuatro hijos de 10 a 19 años; por eso, necesitamos una pequeña casa privada. *(Hotel Canarias)*
6. Mi esposo va a trabajar durante el viaje. Tiene que reunirse con otros empleados de su compañía. *(Hotel Real)*
7. Siempre compramos recuerdos para nuestros amigos cuando vamos de vacaciones. *(Hotel Canarias)*
8. A mis hijos les gusta jugar al golf, pero mi esposa y yo preferimos el tenis. *(Hotel Canarias)*
9. A mis hijos les importa mucho bañarse y arreglarse el pelo antes de salir por la noche. *(los dos hoteles)*

 **Fondo cultural** · Standards: 1.2, 2.1, 2.2

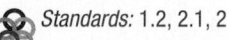

Suggestions: Have students describe their ideal hotel before reading.

Answers will vary.

Additional Resources

• WAV Wbk.: Audio Act. 6, p. 160
• Teacher's Resource Book: Audio Script, p. 203, Communicative Activity BLM, pp. 208–209
• Audio Program, Track 9

✓ **Assessment**
• Prueba 8B-2: Vocab. Production, pp. 218–219

Enrich Your Teaching
Resources for All Teachers

Teacher-to-Teacher
Have students contact hotels in your area to find out what types of rooms and amenities are available. Ask students to use the information to prepare an advertisement for one of the hotels, using *Actividad 9* as a model. Upon completion, give students cards with different scenarios, and have them choose the best hotel for their situation.

Internet Search
Have students use the Internet to learn more about the ratings different hotels have.

Keywords:

hoteles + (name of Spanish-speaking country)

433

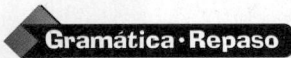 
 Gramática · Repaso — Presentation EXPRESS GRAMMAR

Core Instruction

Standards: 4.1

Resources: Teacher's Resource Book: Video Script, p. 205; Video Program: Cap. 8B

Suggestions: Give each student a piece of paper with appropriate or inappropriate travel advice written on it. Have students act out what they see on the paper, and narrate their actions using the subjunctive. For example, if you tell a student to make noise, say: *¿Es bueno que haga ruido?* Have students respond with **sí** or **no,** and reinforce their response by repeating the phrase: *Es importante que no haga ruido.*

Use the *GramActiva* Video as an introduction or to reinforce your own grammar explanation.

 Actividad 10 — 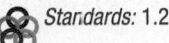 *Standards:* 1.2 — Presentation EXPRESS ANSWERS

Resources: Answers on Transparencies

Focus: Using the subjunctive mood with impersonal expressions

Suggestions: Give students additional practice by having them write the forms of both verbs in the subjunctive and underline the correct word to fill in the blank.

Answers:

1. lleves
2. des
3. seas
4. ofrezcas
5. te pongas
6. observes

Common Errors: If students have difficulty with items 4 and 5, remind them that they need to use the **yo** form of the verb as their stem when forming the subjunctive.

Block Schedule

Create a board game to practice the subjunctive. Write an infinitive on each square, and write six numbered sentence starters (such as *Es importante que él…*) on the board. Have students roll number cubes and form a sentence with the verb and the starter that corresponds to the numbers rolled. Students who answer correctly can take another turn. The player who reaches the end of the board first wins.

434

 **Gramática**

Present subjunctive with impersonal expressions

Sometimes you use an impersonal expression to express how you influence another person's actions.

Here are some impersonal expressions that are often followed by *que* + subjunctive:

es importante   es necesario   es mejor   es bueno

Es necesario que Uds. tengan buenos modales.
It's necessary that you have good manners.

Es mejor que consigamos una habitación doble.
It's better that we get a double room.

- Note that in the examples above, a specific person is mentioned in the second half of the sentence. If no person is specified, the infinitive is used without *que*. Compare the following sentences.

Para ser un buen turista, **es importante ser** muy cortés.
To be a good tourist, it's important to be very polite.

Es importante que seas un turista cortés.
It's important that you be a polite tourist.

> **¿Recuerdas?**
> You know that the subjunctive mood is used to say that one person influences the actions of another.

 **GramActiva** VIDEO

Need more help with the present subjunctive with impersonal expressions? Watch the **GramActiva** video.

Es importante que salga . . .

 Actividad 10 — **Leer/Escribir**

Para ser cortés . . .

Para ser cortés en un país extranjero, ¿qué debes hacer? Completa las frases con la forma apropiada del verbo.

Modelo

Es importante que no *(hacer / ser)* mucho ruido en la habitación del hotel.
Es importante que no hagas mucho ruido en la habitación del hotel.

1. Es mejor que no *(llegar / llevar)* pantalones cortos si visitas la catedral.

2. Es importante que le *(dar / ir)* una propina al hombre que te ayuda con el equipaje.

3. Es necesario que *(ser / ver)* puntual para no enojar a los otros miembros de tu grupo.

4. Es bueno que les *(ofender / ofrecer)* a los ancianos tu asiento en el autobús.

5. Es mejor que *(poder / ponerse)* algo sobre tu traje de baño cuando entras en el hotel.

6. Es importante que *(observar / asistir)* las costumbres de las personas que viven allí.

El Viejo San Juan, Puerto Rico

Differentiated Instruction
Solutions for All Learners

Heritage Language Learners

Remind students not to forget spelling changes when using the subjunctive form of verbs ending in **-gar** or **-car.** Point out that both types of verbs retain the hard consonant sound. Verbs that end in **-gar** add a **u,** changing the ending to **-gue.** When verbs end in **-car,** they change to **-que.**

Multiple Intelligences

Verbal/Linguistic: Have students write a list of guidelines that tourists should consider when visiting specific places. Assign a different destination to each student, making sure that students have some prior knowledge of the place. Have them use the impersonal expressions to say what is good to bring, see, and do while visiting.

Actividad 11 Leer/Escribir

Debes visitar Cartagena

Lee el correo electrónico de un joven, Isidoro, que visitó Cartagena, Colombia. Completa sus recomendaciones a Daniela con la forma apropiada de uno de los verbos del recuadro.

acompañar	pasar
buscar	usar
decir	ver
ir	

Querida Daniela:

Me preguntaste sobre qué lugares en América del Sur les recomiendo para pasar unas vacaciones estupendas. Pues, en mi opinión, es necesario que Uds. __1.__ a Cartagena, Colombia. Es una combinación de lugares históricos y de playas bellas. Es mejor que un guía local los __2.__ a Uds. Es importante que Uds. __3.__ los servicios de un guía profesional licenciado. Es necesario que Uds. le __4.__ al guía que quieren hacer una gira por el castillo, la catedral y la antigua universidad. También es importante que __5.__ el Museo del Oro—un museo impresionante. Es bueno también que __6.__ por los barrios coloniales para ver las casas históricas. Para más información, es mejor que __7.__ en la Red, porque hay unos sitios Web muy buenos sobre Cartagena.

Tu amigo,
Isidoro

Actividad 12 Leer/Escribir

En la Red

Lee la información que Daniela encuentra en la Red sobre Cartagena, Colombia. Daniela quiere que su familia vaya allí. Completa las frases usando la información del artículo y otras ideas.

Modelo

es bueno / los policías (*estar*) en las playas porque . . .
Es bueno que los policías estén en las playas porque así no hay ningún problema para los turistas.

1. es importante / nosotros (*planear*) ir a las playas porque . . .
2. es bueno / los turistas (*tomar*) el autobús a las playas porque . . .
3. es mejor / nosotros (*ir*) a una de las playas populares porque . . .
4. es mejor / nosotros (*mirar*) la artesanía de los vendedores porque . . .
5. es necesario / Uds. (*hablar*) con un agente de viajes sobre Cartagena porque . . .

Cartagena

Cartagena está rodeada[1] por el Mar Caribe. Sus bellas playas se encuentran a pocos metros del centro histórico. A menos de 35 minutos en autobús desde la Ciudad Vieja, se pueden encontrar las playas llamadas La Boquilla y Manzanillo. Para que los turistas disfruten de estas playas, el gobierno local las limpia todas las noches. Además, las playas son patrulladas[2] por la policía para evitar cualquier problema. Aquí los vendedores se acercan a los turistas para ofrecerles artesanías.

La gente de Cartagena es muy sociable y está acostumbrada a tratar a los turistas. Todas las playas de Cartagena se consideran seguras[3] para bañarse. Estas playas no tienen corrientes fuertes[4]. Las playas más frecuentadas tienen banderas de seguridad que informan a los bañistas sobre el estado del tiempo.

¡Cartagena lo tiene TODO!

[1]surrounded [2]patrolled [3]safe [4]strong currents

cuatrocientos treinta y cinco **435**
Capítulo 8B

Enrich Your Teaching
Resources for All Teachers

Culture Note

Cartegena is important to Colombia as a historical and commercial center, as well as a coastal resort. A fortress in the old city has cannons dating back to the early nineteenth century, when Cartegena was attacked by Spanish forces. The nearby Rosary Islands are accessible by boat and feature pristine beaches.

Internet Search:

Have students use the Internet to research more information about tourism in Cartagena.

Keywords:

Cartagena, Colombia

Actividad 11 Standards: 1.2

Resources: Answers on Transparencies

Focus: Reading and completing an e-mail about a visit to Cartagena, Colombia

Suggestions: Have students choose which words to fill in each blank before they conjugate them. Point out that item 2 is the only one not in the **ustedes** form.

Answers:
1. vayan   5. vean
2. acompañe   6. pasen
3. usen   7. busquen
4. digan

Common Errors: Students may forget which verbs are irregular or have spelling changes. Double-check for the correct spelling of **buscar** and **decir**.

Bellringer Review

Have students unscramble the words and conjugate the verbs to make logical sentences.
1) querer/nosotros/el guía/estar a la entrada/a tiempo/que
2) desear/nuestra profesora/nosotros/nuestras experiencias/disfrutar de

(**Answers: 1)** Nosotros queremos que el guía esté a la entrada a tiempo.
2) Nuestra profesora desea que nosotros disfrutemas de nuestras experiencias.)

Actividad 12 Standards: 1.2, 1.3

Resources: Voc. and Gram. Transparency 156; Answers on Transparencies

Focus: Reading and writing information about visiting Cartagena, Colombia

Suggestions: Before beginning, ask students one or two questions to review the reasons for visiting Cartagena, discussed in *Actividad* 11. Have students read each item. Then, as they read the Web site about Cartagena, have them take notes that will help them answer each question. After they have all of their information, have them form their sentences.

Answers may vary but will include:
1. Es importante que nosotros planeemos ir a las playas porque ...
2. Es bueno que los turistas tomen el autobús ...
3. Es mejor que nosotros vayamos ...
4. Es mejor que nosotros miremos la artesanía ...
5. Es necesario que Uds. hablen con un agente ...

Resources: Answers on Transparencies

Focus: Talking about personal preferences when on vacation

Suggestions: Point out to students that although they are beginning their sentence with **Para mí,** they must use the **nosotros** form in the subjunctive.

Answers will vary but will include:
1. … nos quedemos …
2. … comamos …
3. … saquemos …
4. … practiquemos …
5. … hagamos …
6. … observemos …

Exploración del lenguaje

Core Instruction

 Standards: 1.2

Resources: Answers on Transparencies

Suggestions: Point out that the same phenomenon occurs in English with the suffixes **-er** and **-or.**

Answers:
1. aduanero(a)   4. flores
2. noticiero   5. banco
3. cocina

Fondo cultural *Standards:* 1.2, 2.1, 2.2

◆■◆■□◆●■◆■◆■◆■◆■◆■□■

Suggestions: Point out that hostels are an inexpensive alternative to hotels. Ask students if they know anyone who has ever stayed in a hostel.

Answers will vary.

Additional Resources
• WAV Wbk.: Audio Act. 7, p. 160
• Teacher's Resource Book: Audio Script, p. 203
• Audio Program: Track 10

 Assessment
• ExamView Quiz on PresEXPRESS
• Prueba 8B-3: Present subjunctive with impersonal expressions, p. 220

  Hablar

Para disfrutar de las vacaciones

Con otro(a) estudiante, habla de lo que es necesario que hagan tu familia y tú para disfrutar de las vacaciones. Usen las expresiones *es importante, es necesario, es mejor* y *es bueno.*

1. quedarse en un hotel elegante
2. comer comidas típicas del país
3. sacar fotos de todo

Modelo

ver edificios históricos
A —*Para mí, es importante que veamos los edificios históricos de una ciudad.*
B —*Para mí, no. No es importante que veamos edificios históricos. Prefiero ir a un cine.*

4. practicar deportes acuáticos
5. hacer una gira de una ciudad principal
6. observar con cuidado el itinerario

Exploración del lenguaje

The suffix *-ero(a)*

The Spanish suffix *-ero(a)* indicates *someone* or *something* that performs an action:

Alguien que **viaja** es un(a) **viajero(a).**

Algo que muestra *(shows)* **letras** es un **letrero.**

¡Compruébalo! Here are some words that you have learned so far. Complete each sentence with the logical word to tell what the people do or where they work.

1. Alguien que trabaja en la **aduana** es un(a) ___.
2. Algo que te trae **noticias** es un ___.
3. Esa señora es **cocinera.** Ella ___ bien.
4. Mi tía es **florera.** Es artística y trabaja con ___.
5. Cuando fui al ___ hablé con una **banquera** sobre cómo conseguir cheques de viajero.

Refrán

Zapatero, a tus zapatos.

Fondo cultural

REMAJ es la Red Mexicana de Albergues *(Hostels)* para Jóvenes. Los jóvenes turistas pueden visitar el campo y las ciudades de México y sentirse seguros y cómodos sin gastar mucho dinero. En los albergues, los jóvenes también pueden conocer a otros turistas jóvenes de todo el mundo.

• ¿Por qué crees que los albergues son tan populares entre los jóvenes?

Muchos jóvenes se alojan *(stay)* en albergues.

Más práctica

• Practice Workbook, p. 166: 8B-5
• WAV Wbk.: Writing, p. 163
• Guided Practice: Grammar Acts., pp. 301–302
• *Real.* para hispanohablantes, pp. 314–317

Go Online PHSchool.com
For: Impersonal Expressions
Web Code: jdd-0813

Differentiated Instruction
Solutions for All Learners

Multiple Intelligences
Verbal/Linguistic: Give students a list of verbs that have corresponding nouns with the suffix **-ero.** Have students use a Spanish-language dictionary to look for the noun. Ask them to present the word and definition to the class and use the word in a sentence.

Students with Learning Difficulties
Help students focus on types of irregularities in the subjunctive. Give them a yellow highlighter, and have them use it each time they write a verb with an irregular ending formed in the subjunctive. Then have them use a blue highlighter for verbs with irregular stems. Have students do this on all writing activities until they master the irregularities.

Gramática

Present subjunctive of stem-changing verbs

Stem-changing verbs ending in *-ar* and *-er* have the same stem changes in the subjunctive as in the indicative.

¿Recuerdas?
You know that stem-changing verbs in the present indicative have a stem change in all forms except *nosotros* and *vosotros*.

recordar (o → ue)	
recuerde	recordemos
recuerdes	recordéis
recuerde	recuerden

perder (e → ie)	
pierda	perdamos
pierdas	perdáis
pierda	pierdan

Es importante que **recordemos** los buenos modales.
Es mejor que no te **pierdas** en el centro. Cómprate una guía.

Stem-changing verbs ending in *-ir* have changes in all forms of the present subjunctive.

pedir (e → i)	
pida	pidamos
pidas	pidáis
pida	pidan

divertirse (e → ie), (e → i)	
me divierta	nos divirtamos
te diviertas	os divirtáis
se divierta	se diviertan

dormir (o → ue), (o → u)	
duerma	durmamos
duermas	durmáis
duerma	duerman

Es necesario que **pidas** la llave.
Queremos que **se diviertan**.
Es bueno que **duermas** durante el vuelo.

GramActiva VIDEO

Need help with the present subjunctive of stem-changing verbs? Watch the **GramActiva** video.

Quieren que empiecen ...

Actividad 14

Escribir

¿Qué debemos hacer?

Si vas a otro país con un grupo de estudiantes, ¿qué deben y no deben hacer Uds.? Escribe frases usando *es importante, es necesario, es mejor* y *(no) es bueno*.

Modelo

conseguir cheques de viajero antes de salir
Es importante que consigamos cheques de viajero antes de salir.

1. sentirse superiores a los demás
2. reírse de las costumbres de otras personas
3. seguir las instrucciones de los líderes
4. mentir en la aduana
5. dormir durante el vuelo muy largo
6. divertirse mucho en el viaje

cuatrocientos treinta y siete 437
Capítulo 8B

Enrich Your Teaching
Resources for All Teachers

Culture Note
There are many options for students who wish to find youth hostels in which to stay while traveling in South America. Hostels can be found in big cities such as Santiago, Chile, or high in the Peruvian Andes. There are even hostels in parts of the Amazonian rain forest.

Internet Search
Have students use the Internet to find out more about the availability of youth hostels in Spanish-speaking countries.

Keywords:

albergues de + (name of Spanish-speaking country)

Gramática

GRAMMAR

Core Instruction

Resources: Voc. and Gram. Transparency 153; Teacher's Resource Book: Video Script, pp. 205–206; Video Program: Cap. 8B

Suggestions: Before going over the *Gramática,* have students brainstorm a list of the stem-changing verbs they have studied. Have volunteers write examples of each on the board. Point out the verbs' irregularities by highlighting them on the transparencies. Use the *GramActiva* Video as an introduction or to reinforce your own grammar presentation.

Actividad 14 *Standards:* 1.3

ANSWERS

Resources: Answers on Transparencies

Focus: Writing about what you should do when traveling, using stem-changing verbs

Suggestions: Point out to students that some of the sentences will be written in the negative. Remind them that the verbs ending in **-ir** will have stem changes in the **nosotros** form.

Answers may vary but will include:
1. ... no nos sintamos ...
2. ... no nos riamos ...
3. ... sigamos ...
4. ... no mintamos ...
5. ... durmamos ...
6. ... nos divirtamos ...

Extension: Have students use **-ar** and **-er** stem-changing verbs to create additional recommendations.

Theme Project

Students can perform Step 4 at this point. Be sure they understand your corrections and suggestions. (For more information, see p. 398-a.)

 Pre-AP* Support

- **Activity:** After reading the *Fondo cultural* on p. 436, ask students to write five suggestons that would make staying at an *albergue* an enjoyable experience. Ask them to use impersonal expressions and make some of the statements logical and others illogical. Then have students read their statements to a partner to decide if the statements are logical or not.

- **Pre-AP* Resource Book:** Comprehensive guide to Pre-AP* communication skill development, pp. 9–17, 36–46

Actividad 15  *Standards:* 1.2  Presentation EXPRESS ANSWERS

Resources: Answers on Transparencies

Focus: Reading and completing a description of an excursion in Ponce, Puerto Rico

Recycle: Using the subjunctive to express a wish or a request

Suggestions: Have students choose the correct verbs to fill in the blank before they form the subjunctive for each. Point out to students that there is one item in which they do not need to use the subjunctive. Can they identify it? *(item 5)*

Answers:

1. entiendan	6. se sienten
2. sigan	7. cierre
3. pidan	8. vuelvan
4. repita	9. consigan
5. recordar	

Common Errors: Students may have difficulty determining who is being encouraged to do the action. Ask students to reread the whole sentence or groups of sentences to determine which subject is given or implied.

 Actividad 16  *Standards:* 1.1  Presentation EXPRESS ANSWERS

Resources: Answers on Transparencies

Focus: Talking about what players on a sports team should do to perform better

Recycle: Sports; adjectives

Suggestions: As you monitor students' responses, be sure to listen for the subjunctive. Students may be tempted to use the impersonal expressions followed by an infinitive.

Answers:

Student A:

1. Las jugadoras están cansadas durante las prácticas.
2. ... parecen estar aburridas.
3. ... no saben qué hacer durante un partido.
4. ... juegan como personas que no se conocen.
5. ... no llegan a las prácticas a tiempo.

Student B: Answers will vary.

 Actividad 15 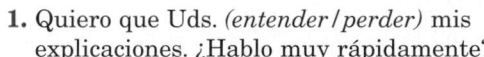 Leer/Escribir

Una excursión en Ponce

En Ponce, Puerto Rico, en medio de la zona histórica turística, está el Museo Castillo Serralles. Completa las reglas del guía de una gira del castillo.

El castillo Serralles originalmente fue la casa de la familia Serralles, una familia que ganó mucho dinero con la producción de azúcar en los años 30.

1. Quiero que Uds. *(entender / perder)* mis explicaciones. ¿Hablo muy rápidamente?

2. Es necesario que me *(seguir / conseguir)* siempre. No pueden ir solos a otras partes del castillo.

3. Si tienen preguntas sobre algún aspecto del castillo, prefiero que me *(poder / pedir)* que se lo explique.

4. Si Uds. quieren que yo *(repetir / reír)* algo, sólo tienen que decírmelo.

5. Es importante *(pensar / recordar)* que muchos de los objetos en el comedor son de los años 30.

6. En la Sala doña Mercedes, no permitimos que *(sentirse / sentarse)* en las sillas ni en los sofás.

7. Por favor, le pido a la última persona que entra en la sala que *(despertar / cerrar)* la puerta.

8. Después de la gira, recomiendo que *(volver / competir)* a los jardines para disfrutar de las vistas impresionantes de la ciudad y del mar.

9. Si quieren hacer otra gira, es necesario que *(conseguir / despedirse)* otro boleto para entrar.

 Actividad 16   Hablar

Una entrenadora frustrada

Una entrenadora está bastante frustrada con las jugadoras en su equipo. Trabaja con otro(a) estudiante para describir el problema y dar recomendaciones.

Modelo

no tener energía durante las prácticas
A —*Las jugadoras no tienen energía durante las prácticas.*
B —*Es importante que almuercen comida que es buena para la salud.*

Estudiante A

1. estar cansadas durante las prácticas
2. parecer estar aburridas durante los partidos
3. no saber qué hacer durante un partido
4. jugar como personas que no se conocen
5. no llegar a las prácticas a tiempo

Estudiante B

es importante	jugar con entusiasmo
es necesario	empezar a jugar como un equipo unido
les pido	acostarse a las 11:00 de la noche en punto
les recomiendo	seguir mis instrucciones
insisto en	vestirse 15 minutos antes de la práctica
sugiero	

Differentiated Instruction
Solutions for All Learners

Students with Special Needs

Modify *Actividad 18* for students with language-expression difficulties who may have trouble spontaneously responding to the game questions. Allow them to write their responses prior to orally expressing them.

 Advanced Learners/Pre-AP*

Pre-AP* Have one group of students pretend they are advice columnists for parents of teenagers. A second group will write letters about the problems they are having with their children. Tell students that they must use the subjunctive in their responses. Publish students' work to share with the class.

Actividad 17

Leer/Escribir

Una carta de Pablo

Pablo aprendió mucho durante su viaje a Panamá. Lee su carta a su madre y, según las experiencias de Pablo, escribe seis recomendaciones para los viajeros al extranjero.

Modelo

Es importante que no pierdas tu pasaporte.

Querida mamá:

He aprendido mucho aquí en Panamá. Por ejemplo, mi maleta era demasiado grande y tuve que facturarla. No sabía que aquí hace tanto calor y tuve que comprar más ropa.

Compré unos recuerdos en el mercado, pero probablemente pagué demasiado porque no regateé con los vendedores. Aprendí que en Panamá ahora se aceptan los dólares estadounidenses.

En el hotel tuve algunos problemas. Olvidé el número de mi habitación y perdí mi llave y tuve que conseguir otra. Pero afortunadamente no he perdido mi pasaporte. Las habitaciones aquí son muy cómodas, pero es difícil dormir porque a veces algunos estudiantes hacen ruido en el hotel.

Un abrazo,
Pablo

   Actividad 18

Escribir/Hablar/GramActiva

Juego

1. Trabajen en grupos de tres. En pequeñas hojas de papel o tarjetas, escriban tres preguntas sobre el tema de viajar. Pongan todas las preguntas en una bolsa para cada equipo.

2. El (La) profesor(a) divide a la clase en dos equipos, "México" y "España".

3. Una persona del equipo "México" lee una de las preguntas que está en la bolsa a una persona del equipo "España." Si esta persona puede contestar correctamente usando el subjuntivo y la información apropiada, gana una letra de su país, "España," para su equipo. ¡El primer equipo que gana todas las letras de su país gana el juego!

Modelo

México: *¿Adónde voy para cambiar un cheque de viajero?*

España: *Recomiendo que vayas a una casa de cambio.*

¿Adónde voy para cambiar un cheque de viajero?

¿Qué tengo que conseguir antes de ir a un país extranjero?

¿Dónde se puede regatear por la artesanía?

El español en el mundo del trabajo

Hoy en día el turismo en los países hispanohablantes es más popular que nunca. Los turistas de todo el mundo están descubriendo la riqueza histórica y cultural del mundo hispano. Muchas compañías de turismo ofrecen giras a varios países y necesitan empleados que hablan español, conocen la cultura hispana y tienen interés en ayudar a sus clientes.

• ¿Cómo puedes usar el español trabajando para una compañía de turismo o una agencia de viajes? ¿Qué le recomiendas a alguien que quiere hacer este tipo de trabajo?

cuatrocientos treinta y nueve 439
Capítulo 8B

 Actividad 17 *Standards:* 1.2, 1.3

Focus: Writing recommendations for tourists
Suggestions: Have students list the problems they are going to focus on before they write their recommendations.
Answers will vary.

 Actividad 18 *Standards:* 1.1

Focus: Asking and answering questions about travel
Recycle: Place names; activities
Suggestions: Point out that students' questions must be specific. There should be only one correct response. Cut out the letters for each country and post one whenever a team member answers correctly.
Answers will vary.

El español en el mundo del trabajo

Core Instruction

 Standards: 1.2, 5.1

Suggestions: Ask students to list possible job descriptions for tour guides and travel agents before answering the question.
Answers will vary.

Enrich Your Teaching
Resources for All Teachers

Culture Note

Tourism is important for the economy both on the continent of South America and in the surrounding areas. For example, adventurous Chileans and Argentineans can apply for jobs as tour guides or as members of ships' crews for cruises to Antarctica, an increasingly popular vacation destination.

Teacher-to-Teacher

Invite an international tour guide to your class to talk about his or her job responsibilities. Have the visitor stress the importance of speaking another language in his or her job. Encourage students to prepare questions for the tour guide before the discussion.

8B Practice and Communicate

  Actividad 19 *Standards:* 1.1, 1.3

Focus: Writing and talking about travel recommendat ons

Suggestions: Suggest a tourist spot for students to focus on if they're having diffi-culties when writing questions. Have them brainstorm a list of all the ways to spend money when on vacation, such as for hotels, transportation, dining, or enter-tainment.

Answers will vary.

 **Actividad 20** *Standards:* 1.1, 1.3

Focus: Making recommendations

Suggestions: Form small groups that can each focus on one of the questions. Have students share their recommendations with the class. Have classmates indicate if they agree or disagree with each recommen-dation.

Answers will vary.

 Fondo cultural *Standards:* 1.2, 2.2

■◆✕■◆✕■◆✕■◆✕■◆✕■◆✕■◆

Suggestions: To help students answer the second quest on, direct attention to the *Fondos culturales* on pp. 433 and 436.

Answers wil vary but may include:
Para forma parte de la palabra *parador.*
Un parador es un lugar donde una persona para por la noche.

Additional Resources

- WAV Wbk.: Au jio Act. 8–9, p. 161
- Teacher's Resource Book: Audio Script, pp. 203–204, Communicative Activity BLM, pp. 208–211
- Audio Program: Tracks 11– 12

✓ **Assessment**
- **Exam***View* Quiz on PresEXPRESS
- *Prueba* 8B-4: Present subjunctive of stem-changing verbs, p. 22

  Actividad 19 Hablar/Pensar/Escribir

Recomendaciones

Trabajen en grupos de cuatro estudiantes y hagan recomendaciones sobre las vacaciones. Dos estudiantes van a escribir cinco recomendaciones para las personas que no gastan mucho en las vacaciones y dos van a escribir cinco recomendaciones para las personas que gastan demasiado. Compartan sus recomendaciones con las del otro grupo. Preparen reacciones a las recomendaciones y explíquenselas al otro grupo.

> **Modelo**
> Grupo 1: *Para no gastar tanto en las vacaciones, es importante que viajen en coche y no en avión.*
> Grupo 2: *Muchas veces no es posible viajar en coche. Queremos ir de vacaciones a Puerto Rico.*

 Actividad 20 Escribir/Hablar

Y tú, ¿qué dices?

1. Para aprender a hablar español muy bien, ¿qué es importante que haga un(a) estudiante?

2. ¿Qué es muy importante que una persona haga para indicar que es cortés?

3. ¿Qué recomiendas que haga un(a) turista cuando acaba de llegar a un país extranjero?

> **Más práctica**
> - Practice Workbook, pp. 167–168: 8B-6, 8B-7
> - WAV Wbk.: Writing, p. 164
> - Guided Practice: Grammar Acts., pp. 303–304
> - *Real.* para hispanohablantes, pp. 318–319

 **Go Online** PHSchool.com
For: Stem-changing Verbs
Web Code: jdd-0814

Fondo cultural  ■◆✕■◆✕■◆✕■◆✕■◆✕■◆✕■◆✕■◆✕■◆✕■◆✕■◆

El Parador de Sigüenza es uno de los muchos paradores que hay en España. Estos edificios históricos fueron restaurados y convertidos en alojamientos *(lodgings)* por el gobierno español. Aunque son lujosos *(luxurious)*, quedarse en un parador no es muy caro, y es una manera muy conveniente de conocer España.

- ¿Por qué crees que estos edificios se llaman paradores? ¿Qué palabra que ya sabes forma parte de la palabra *parador*? ¿Qué prefieres tú, una habitación en un albergue juvenil, en un hotel de cinco estrellas o en un parador? ¿Por qué?

El Parador de Sigüenza, España

Differentiated Instruction
Solutions for All Learners

Multiple Intelligences

Mathematical/Logical: Post student work for *Actividad 22*, and have students tally up the most popular answers for each category. Encourage them to prepare a presentation on the class's results. Tell them to include the percentage of students who made a particular suggestion.

Students with Learning Difficulties

It may be helpful for students if you bring in a guidebook or directory for your community or state. Your local chamber of commerce or municipal government may publish a directory or welcome brochure for new residents. Have students scan the guide before developing their advertisement for *Actividad 22*.

 **Actividad 21** Hablar/Leer/Pensar/Escribir

Las vacaciones

¿Crees que los estadounidenses y los españoles piensan lo mismo sobre la importancia de gastar dinero en las vacaciones?

Conexiones | Las matemáticas

- Pregúntales a tres adultos si creen que los estadounidenses gastan demasiado en las vacaciones. Escribe el nombre de la persona y su respuesta.

- Compartan y sumen (add up) las respuestas a la pregunta con tres estudiantes. Calculen el porcentaje de personas que contestaron afirmativamente y de las que contestaron negativamente.

- Estudia la gráfica que representa cómo contestó un grupo de adultos españoles la misma pregunta. Copia la gráfica y añade la información de tu clase. Luego contesta las siguientes preguntas.

¿Cree Ud. que las personas gastan demasiado de lo que ganan en las vacaciones?		
NO	Uno trabaja 11 de cada 12 meses, al menos,[1] para disfrutar del mes que le queda.	**66%**
SÍ	Gastarlo todo en vacaciones y no ahorrar[2] es un error muy extendido.	**34%**

[1]at least [2]to not save

1. ¿En qué sentido son similares las respuestas de los estadounidenses y de los españoles? ¿En qué sentido son diferentes?
2. Para tu familia y las familias de tus amigos ¿es importante pasar tiempo de vacaciones? ¿Adónde van y qué hacen durante las vacaciones?

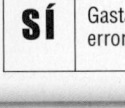  **Actividad 22** Escribir/Hablar

Mi ciudad

1 Tienes que crear un anuncio para promocionar el turismo en tu comunidad. Escribe sobre cuatro o cinco lugares que recomiendas que visiten los turistas. Usa las expresiones *es mejor que, es importante que, es necesario que, sugiero que* y *recomiendo que*. Incluye consejos (advice) sobre lo siguiente:

- la mejor estación para visitar tu ciudad
- lugares para comer, atracciones culturales, los horarios y los precios
- lugares para ir de compras y lo que se puede comprar allí
- consejos sobre las costumbres y los modales
- puntos de interés y actividades divertidas

2 Compara tus recomendaciones con las de otro(a) estudiante y hablen de ellas.

cuatrocientos cuarenta y uno **441**
Capítulo 8B

 **Actividad 21** Standards: 1.2, 3.1, 4.2 **Pre-AP***

Focus: Researching and writing about vacation spending

Suggestions: Direct attention to the question and the answers of the Spanish adults. Point out to students that they need to find out this information from adults in their community. Remind them that their survey results will reflect only those people interviewed by their group members. Have all groups post their results to check for variations.

Answers will vary.

Extension: Have students ask their friends the same question and report their findings to the class. After the student responses are tallied and graphed, have them compare and contrast these responses to those of the adults in both cultures.

 Actividad 22 Standards: 1.1, 1.3

Focus: Writing and talking about tourist attractions in your community

Suggestions: Have students scan their partner's advertisement and write five follow-up questions that can be used for discussion.

Answers will vary.

Theme Project

Students can perform Step 5 at this point. Record their presentations on cassette or videotape for inclusion in their portfolio. (For more information, see p. 398-a.)

Enrich Your Teaching
Resources for All Teachers

Culture Note
Paradores provide a pleasant alternative to the private hotels in Spain and give an additional boost to tourism. Staff members of *paradores* are government employees who pride themselves on giving exceptional service. *Paradores* are quite comfortable and are often located in scenic areas.

Teacher-to-Teacher
Contact your community's visitors bureau or Chamber of Commerce. Ask if you can arrange to post on a bulletin board students' advertisements for visiting the community.

---

cultura maya

Si le interesan las ruinas, le recomendamos que haga planes para visitar Tikal, una de las ciudades más

gente es tan simpática que usted va a sentirse como en su propia casa. ¡Visite Antigua, lo(a) esperamos con anticipación![4]

[3]City hall [4]We hope

◄ El Ayuntamiento, Antigua

Más práctica

- WAV Wbk.: Writing, p. 165
- Guided Practice: *Lectura*, p. 305
- *Real.* para hispanohablantes, pp. 322–323

 Online
PHSchool.com
For: Internet Activity
Web Code: jdd-0816

cuatrocientos cuarenta y tres **443**
Capítulo 8B

Enrich Your Teaching
Resources for All Teachers

Culture Note
Tikal, in present-day Guatemala, was a major center of Mayan civilization. The city of Tikal probably had 10,000 inhabitants in the year 750 A.D. *El Templo I de la Gran Plaza* is one of five large pyramids built there. The monuments at Tikal are popular with both tourists and historians.

Teacher-to-Teacher
Have students pretend they are visiting Antigua and are writing a postcard to a friend or family member. Ask them to use a photo or illustration of an important monument on the front. On the back, have students describe what they have seen, what their hotel is like, and where they ate. Have them use the Internet and the reading as resources.

- **Activity:** Have students work in groups of three and assign each group member one of the three segments of the article found on this page. Ask the group to create one listening activity and one multiple-choice question for each assigned segment. Collect and redistribute the recordings and questions. Then have each new group complete the listening and comprehension activity without consulting their textbooks. For variety, you may choose to read the information on p. 443 and ask similar teacher-made questions.
- **Pre-AP* Resource Book:** Comprehensive guide to Pre-AP* reading skill development, pp. 18–24

For Further Reading
Student Resources:
- Realidades para hispanohablantes: Lectura 2, pp. 324–325
- Lecturas para hispanohablantes 2: "México Lindo," p. 8, "Verdeluz," p. 46.

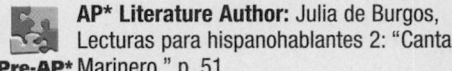 **AP* Literature Author:** Julia de Burgos, Lecturas para hispanohablantes 2: "Cantar **Pre-AP*** Marinero," p. 51

Lectura

Core Instruction

Standards: 1.2, 2.1, 2.2, 3.1

Focus: Reading comprehension of tourist information for Antigua, Guatemala

Suggestions:

Pre-reading: Point out that the purpose of the reading is to inform readers about the city and to persuade them to visit it. Ask students what they would include in a description of their community if they had the same purpose. Point out that the term **colonial** refers to a period when Guatemala was a colony of Spain, before it gained independence in 1821. Ask students to compare the photos on this page to pictures of Spanish cities in other parts of this chapter. Refer students to pp. 426 and 428 to make comparisons. Can students see examples of Spanish influence in the city of Antigua? Point out similarities.

Reading: Read the passage aloud. Pause after each segment and ask students to identify its purpose. As they read each section, have them take notes on things in the city that might interest them.

Post-reading: Ask students if they would

 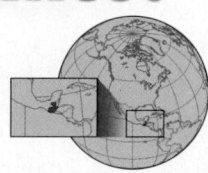

¡Adelante!

Lectura

Objectives
- Read about the historical city of Antigua, Guatemala
- Learn about train transportation in Spain
- Write and illustrate a travel brochure

Antigua, una ciudad colonial

Estrategia

Using heads and subheads Heads and subheads help to organize information. Before you read each section, use its subhead to think about the information you're likely to read.

S ITUADA a 45 minutos de la Ciudad de Guatemala, Antigua le fascina al turista por sus calles de piedras, su arquitectura colonial y sus ruinas de iglesias y monasterios. El español Francisco de la Cueva fundó la ciudad el 10 de marzo de 1543. La "Ciudad de las Perpetuas Rosas," nombrada así por sus jardines con flores, tiene un clima muy agradable y preserva un sabor colonial único. Caminar por sus calles es como visitar el pasado y descubrir una ciudad típica española del siglo[1] XVII. ¡Los invitamos a venir y a disfrutar de esta ciudad!

¡Bienvenidos a la hermosa ciudad de Antigua!

HOTELES
Antigua ofrece una gran variedad de hoteles. Los precios pueden variar entre $35.00 y $300.00 la noche. El mejor hotel de Antigua es la Casa de Santo Domingo. Este hotel de cinco estrellas,

y varios jacuzzis. Las ruinas del convento están todavía en el hotel y así el visitante puede apreciar lo moderno con lo antiguo.

RESTAURANTES
La ciudad de Antigua tiene

 Perspectivas del mundo hispano

Core Instruction

Standards: 1.2, 2.1, 2.2

Presentation EXPRESS ANSWERS

Resources: Voc. and Gram. Transparencies: Map 18

Focus: Reading about the *RENFE*

Suggestions: Ask students if they have ever traveled by train. If so, have them describe their experiences. Go to your local travel agent or use the Internet to obtain information on the *RENFE* system. Use the information you find to share schedules, ticket prices, and routes with students. Have students compare these aspects of the *RENFE* system with means of transportation to which they are accustomed. Point out that train travel is not very common in the United States, unlike in Europe. Ask students to offer possible explanations for this phenomenon, and point out that the United States is large but not densely populated in much of the central part of the country. Europe, however, has more urban areas in close proximity to one another, making train travel a more logical option. Encourage students to research the options for train travel in and out of your community.

Answers will vary.

For Further Reading

Student Resource: Realidades para hispano-hablantes: Lectura 2, p. 326

Perspectivas del mundo hispano

La Red Nacional de Ferrocarriles Españoles

¿Te gustaría viajar por un país hispanohablante en un vehículo moderno, cómodo, rápido, seguro, limpio y económico? Puedes hacerlo en España si viajas en los trenes de la Red Nacional de Ferrocarriles Españoles (RENFE). El ferrocarril, o tren, es un medio de transporte muy popular en España y en toda Europa. El tren es una buena alternativa al automóvil porque transporta a muchos pasajeros y mercancías. Consume menos energía y por eso es más limpio y contamina menos.

La red[1] ferroviaria española tiene más de 12,000 kilómetros y se extiende por todo el país. Hay servicios de metro[2] en Madrid, Barcelona, Valencia y Bilbao y trenes que comunican la ciudad con los suburbios, con otras ciudades de la región y con ciudades lejanas en el país y en otros países. RENFE ofrece billetes[3] más baratos para jóvenes y personas mayores.

Recientemente, RENFE ha introducido los trenes de alta velocidad, o AVE, que viajan a velocidades superiores a los 200 kilómetros por hora y recorren largas distancias. Con estos servicios tan rápidos, mucha gente prefiere viajar en tren en vez de en avión.

¡Compruébalo! ¿Hay metro en tu ciudad? ¿Tiene tu estado un sistema de ferrocarriles? ¿Qué servicios ofrece? ¿Lo has usado alguna vez? ¿Lo usa algún miembro de tu familia?

¿Qué te parece? ¿Qué te parece el transporte por ferrocarril? ¿Cuáles son algunas de sus ventajas[4] y desventajas?[5]

El AVE, España

---

[1]system [2]subway [3]tickets [4]advantages [5]disadvantages

---

Differentiated Instruction
Solutions for All Learners

Multiple Intelligences
Mathematical/Logical: Have students research prices and schedules of train and air travel to and from your town or a nearby city. Have them choose two destinations on which to base their research. Ask them to choose the most practical and economical method of travel. Have them support their choice with details about convenience and price.

Advanced Learners
Give students an origin and a destination and have them plan an itinerary for travel within Spain on the *RENFE*. Direct students to the company's Web site that allows potential passengers to view schedules specific to their travel plans.

8B

Presentación escrita

Viajemos juntos

La Plaza de Armas en Lima, Perú

Task
You are part of a group of students who are going with your teacher to a Spanish-speaking country. Prepare an illustrated brochure for your group.

1 Prewrite Think of the preparations you must make before your trip. Answer the following questions to organize the information for your brochure.

- ¿Qué país van a visitar y cómo van a viajar?
- ¿Qué deben llevar? ¿Una cámara? ¿Unos anteojos de sol?
- ¿Qué lugares van a visitar? ¿Qué excursiones o giras van a hacer? ¿Qué actividades van a hacer?
- ¿Cómo deben vestirse? ¿Hay restricciones de vestido?

2 Draft Use your responses to develop a brochure that will help your classmates to prepare thoroughly. Include photos or drawings in your brochure.

3 Revise Reread your draft and check the spelling, vocabulary, verb usage, and agreement. Share what you've written with a classmate, who will check the following:

- Is the information clear and well organized?
- Have you included all the necessary information?
- Are the visuals useful?
- Is there anything you should add or change?
- Are there any errors?

4 Publish Make a new version of the brochure with the necessary changes and corrections. Make a final copy for your teacher or include it in your portfolio.

5 Evaluation Your teacher may give you a rubric for how the brochure will be graded. You will probably be graded on:

- how much information you provide
- how clear and attractive the brochure is
- appropriate use of vocabulary and grammar

Estrategia

Using key questions
Key questions are a good way to brainstorm. Jot down answers to a wide range of questions and you will have many ideas to help you with your writing.

Ruinas de una misión, en la Argentina

cuatrocientos cuarenta y cinco 445
Capítulo 8B

Presentación escrita
Persuasive

Standards: 1.3, 3.1

Focus: Preparing a brochure for a Spanish-speaking country

Suggestions: Collect travel brochures to use as models. Go to your local library and ask for old editions of travel magazines that may have photos for students to cut out and informational articles that will provide students with background information. Assign a different Spanish-speaking country to each student to avoid repetition. Have students divide their brochures into sections, such as how to travel, what to see, and what to bring. Point out the format of a brochure. For each section of their brochure, they should provide a short paragraph, along with bulleted items to highlight the main points for the reader. You may want to have students write one or two comprehension questions about their own brochure. After students have prepared a final copy, they can exchange brochures and questions with a partner to practice reading comprehension.

Portfolio

Have students include a copy of their brochure in their portfolio.

Pre-AP* Support

- *Pre-AP* Resource Book:* Comprehensive guide to Pre-AP* writing skill development, pp. 25–35

Additional Resources

Student Resources: Realidades para hispanohablantes, p. 327; Guided Practice: Presentación escrita, p. 306

✓ Assessment

- Assessment Program: Rubrics, p. T32

Before students prepare their brochures, give them a copy of the rubric you will use for evaluation.

Enrich Your Teaching
Resources for All Teachers

RUBRIC	Score 1	Score 3	Score 5
Amount of information you provided	You only address some of the questions in your brochure.	You address most of the questions in your brochure.	You address all of the questions in your brochure.
Attractiveness and clarity of your brochure	Your layout is confusing and contains visible error corrections and smudges.	Your layout is somewhat clear but contains visible error corrections and smudges.	Your layout is clear and attractive and contains no error corrections or smudges.
Your use of vocabulary and grammar	You use very little variation of vocabulary and make frequent usage errors.	You use limited vocabulary and make some usage errors.	You use an extended variety of vocabulary and make very few usage errors.

Review Activities

To talk about places to visit in a city:
Make a simple map of a city with arrows pointing to representations of the different places. Have students write the words on adhesive paper and place them either correctly or incorrectly on the map. Their partners should arrange the words so that they are correct.

To talk about staying in a hotel: Have students role-play the parts of a hotel reception clerk and a tourist. Give students scenarios on which to base their dialogue.

To talk about appropriate tourist behaviors: Give students a cloze version of a list of rules from a resort. Each blank should represent one of the vocabulary words. Have them supply the missing words.

To talk about tourist activities: Give students four or five pictures taken during a vacation. Have them describe what is happening in each photograph.

Portfolio

Invite students to review the activities they completed in this chapter, including written reports, posters or other visuals, tapes of oral presentations, or other projects. Have them select one or two items that they feel best demonstrate their achievements in Spanish to include in their portfolios. Have them include this with the Chapter Checklist and Self-Assessment Worksheet.

Additional Resources

Student Resources: Realidades para hispanohablantes, p. 328

 **CD-ROM**

PuzzleView Web Code: jdd-0817

Teacher Resources:
- Teacher's Resource Book: Situation Cards, p. 212, Clip Art, pp. 214–217
- Assessment Program: Chapter Checklist and Self-Assessment Worksheet, pp. T56–T57

Repaso del capítulo

Vocabulario y gramática 🔊

Chapter Review

To prepare for the test, check to see if you . . .
- know the new vocabulary and grammar
- can perform the tasks on p. 447

jdd-0899

to talk about places to visit in a city

el cajero automático	ATM
la casa de cambio	currency exchange
el castillo	castle
la catedral	cathedral
histórico, -a	historical
el palacio	palace
el quiosco	newsstand

to talk about staying in a hotel

el ascensor	elevator
conseguir (e → i)	to obtain
la habitación, pl. las habitaciones	room
la habitación doble	double room
la habitación individual	single room
la llave	key
la recepción	reception desk

to talk about appropriate tourist behaviors

atento, -a	attentive
cortés	polite
hacer ruido	to make noise
observar	to observe
ofender	to offend
la propina	tip
puntual	punctual

For *Vocabulario adicional*, see pp. 498–499.

to talk about tourist activities

la artesanía	handicrafts
el bote de vela	sailboat
cambiar	to change, to exchange
disfrutar de	to enjoy
el esquí acuático	waterskiing
la excursión, pl. las excursiones	excursion, short trip
el guía, la guía	guide
la guía	guidebook
hacer una gira	to take a tour
el itinerario	itinerary
la moto acuática	personal watercraft
navegar	to sail, to navigate
regatear	to bargain
el surf de vela	windsurfing
la tarjeta postal	postcard
el vendedor, la vendedora	vendor

other useful words and expressions

bello, -a	beautiful
en punto	exactly (time)
estupendo, -a	stupendous, wonderful
famoso, -a	famous
el rey, pl. los reyes	king, king and queen
siguiente	next, following
tal vez	maybe, perhaps
típico, -a	typical

present subjunctive with impersonal expressions

Es bueno que los estudiantes **hagan** la tarea.
Es importante que comas un buen desayuno.
Es mejor que no **vayamos** al museo hoy.
Es necesario que hagas una gira de la ciudad.

present subjunctive of stem-changing verbs

recordar (o → ue)	divertirse (e → ie), (e → i)
perder (e → ie)	
pedir (e → i)	dormir (o → ue), (o → u)

(To see these verbs fully conjugated in the present subjunctive, see p. 437.)

Differentiated Instruction
Solutions for All Learners

Heritage Language Learners

Have students use the subjunctive to make a list of ten rules for how a tourist should not behave. For example, students can write: *Es importante que hagas mucho ruido en el hotel por la noche.* Have students peer-edit each other's work before posting their rules. Ask the rest of the class to offer suggestions to make the rules more logical.

Multiple Intelligences

Bodily/Kinesthetic: Have students prepare a skit in which one person is a television talk-show host and the other person is an etiquette expert. The topic of the show is travel advice. Have the "expert" give bad advice. The host should point out the errors and offer better suggestions. Encourage students to be creative and humorous.

Más práctica

- Practice Workbook: Puzzle, p. 169
- Practice Workbook: Organizer, p. 170

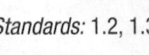 **PHSchool.com**
For: Test Preparation
Web Code: jdd-0817

Preparación para el examen

On the exam you will be asked to . . .	Here are practice tasks similar to those you will find on the exam . . .	If you need review . . .
jdd-0899 **1 Escuchar** Listen and understand as people make recommendations for travel	You need some advice for your trip to Mexico. Listen to these recommendations and determine what is the most important thing to do when you get there. What is the best thing to do there?	**pp. 426–429** *A primera vista* **p. 431** Actividad 6 **p. 433** Actividad 9
2 Hablar Talk about ways to have an enjoyable vacation when you travel away from home	Give a group at a Spanish Club meeting some advice about travel in Mexico. How can they be "good" tourists? What is the best way to get to know the city they visit?	**p. 430** Actividad 4 **p. 431** Actividad 5 **p. 432** Actividad 7 **p. 436** Actividad 13 **p. 440** Actividades 19–20
3 Leer Read and understand vacation postcards from friends and family	Read a postcard from a classmate in Mexico. Is the person: (a) having a good or bad trip; (b) using Spanish; and (c) learning about Mexico? *Querido Juan:* *Estoy aquí en Cancún. Es muy divertido pasar tiempo en la playa y luego ir al mercado. Me encanta hablar español para regatear. Es importante que no ofendas a los vendedores cuando regateas por el mejor precio.*	**p. 432** Actividad 7 **p. 433** Actividad 9 **p. 434** Actividad 10 **p. 435** Actividades 11–12 **p. 439** Actividad 17 **pp. 442–443** *Lectura*
4 Escribir Write a "tip sheet" for students planning to travel to a foreign country	You are developing a Web site for teen travelers. Complete the following sentences with at least three suggestions per topic: (a) Para ser un(a) turista bueno(a), es importante que . . . ; (b) Para disfrutar mucho de tu viaje, te recomiendo que . . .	**p. 430** Actividad 4 **p. 434** Actividad 10 **p. 435** Actividades 11–12 **p. 437** Actividad 14 **p. 439** Actividad 17 **p. 445** *Presentación escrita*
5 Pensar Demonstrate an understanding of cultural practices related to travel in Spanish-speaking countries	Think about how American tourists would most likely travel within a Spanish-speaking country. To get from one city to another, what kind of transportation would they use? How would this compare with how tourists would travel while visiting the United States?	**pp. 442–443** *Lectura* **p. 444** *Perspectivas del mundo hispano*

cuatrocientos cuarenta y siete **447**
Capítulo 8B

Differentiated Assessment
Solutions for All Learners

STUDENTS NEEDING EXTRA HELP
- **Alternate Assessment Program:** Examen del capítulo 8B
- **Audio Program CD 21:** Chap. 8B, Track 8

HERITAGE LEARNERS
- **Assessment Program: Realidades para hispanohablantes:** Examen del capítulo 8B
- **ExamView Heritage Learner Test Bank**

ADVANCED/PRE-AP*
- **Pre-AP* Test Bank**
- **Pre-AP* Resource Book,** pp. 124–127

Performance Tasks

 **Presentation EXPRESS ANSWERS**

Standards: 1.2, 1.3, 2.1, 2.2

Student Resource: Realidades para hispanohablantes, p. 329

Teacher Resources: Teacher's Resource Book: Audio Script, p. 204; Audio Program: Track 14; Answers on Transparencies

1. Escuchar

Suggestions: Have students brainstorm a list of travel tips that they should listen for.

 **Script:**

FEMALE: Para ser un buen turista, es importante que Uds. aprendan español antes de salir y que practiquen cada día.
MALE: Así es. Si hablen con la gente del lugar, pueden disfrutar más de su visita al país.

Answers:
Students should learn Spanish and talk to the people native to the area when they get there.

2. Hablar

Suggestions: Have students work in small groups and provide their tips as if the rest of the class were the Spanish Club.

Answers will vary.

3. Leer

Suggestions: Have students discuss what information is typically found in postcards.

Answers may vary but will include:
1. He is having a good trip.
2. He is using Spanish while bargaining with vendors.
3. He is learning about how to bargain in Mexico without insulting the vendor.

4. Escribir

Suggestions: Remind students that their audience is teenagers. They should form their advice accordingly.

Answers will vary.

5. Pensar

Suggestions: Refer students to p. 444.

Answers will vary.

✓ Assessment

- **ExamView** Quiz on PresEXPRESS
- **Assessment Program:** Examen del capítulo
- **ExamView** Test Bank: Tests A and B
- **Audio Program CD 21:** Chap. 8B, Track 8

¿Cómo será el futuro?

THEME OVERVIEW

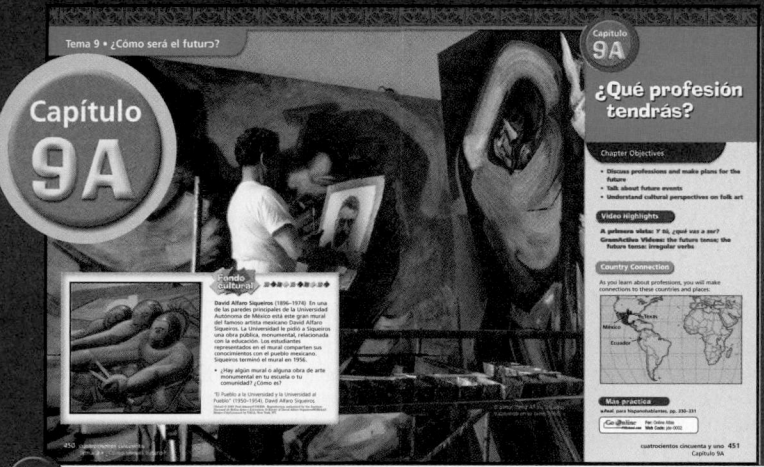

▶ **9A ¿Qué profesión tendrás?**
• Future plans
Vocabulary: professions; making plans for the future
Grammar: the future tense; the verbs *hacer, poder, saber, tener,* and *haber* in the future tense
Cultural Perspectives: folk art

▶ **9B ¿Qué haremos para mejorar el mundo?**
• Environmental issues
Vocabulary: predictions for the future; ecological issues; environmental problems and solutions
Grammar: *decir, poner, querer, salir,* and *venir* in the future; the present subjunctive with expressions of doubt
Cultural Perspectives: ecological problems and solutions

Theme Project

La exposición de carreras

Overview: Tell students that they are in charge of planning a job fair for high school students. They must make and present a poster advertising five different jobs and the responsibilities that each job will entail. Students must use the future tense. At least one of the jobs must deal with the environment. Pictures or drawings on the poster should serve as visual aids.

Materials: Poster board, markers, glue or tape, scissors, photos

Sequence: (suggestions for when to do each step are found throughout the chapters)

STEP 1. Review instructions so students know what is expected of them. Hand out the "Theme 9 Project Instructions and Rubric" from the *Teacher's Resource Book.*

9A ▶

STEP 2. Students submit a rough draft of their list of job requirements. Return the drafts with your suggestions. For grammar and vocabulary practice, ask students to partner and present their drafts to each other.

STEP 3. Students create layouts on poster board, leaving room for photos or drawings. Encourage them to work in pencil first and to try different arrangements before gluing photos or decorations.

STEP 4. Students submit a draft of their poster. Note your corrections and suggestions, then return drafts to students.

9B ▶

STEP 5. Students present their posters to the class, explaining each job description and describing selected pictures.

Options:

1. Students research and present jobs that deal with Spanish usage outside of the classroom.

2. Students research and present actual jobs in environmental science or with national or international service organizations.

Assessment:
Here is a detailed rubric for assessing this project:
Theme 9 Project: *La exposición de carreras*

RUBRIC	Score 1	Score 3	Score 5
Your evidence of planning	You provide no written draft or sketch.	Your draft was written and layout created, but not corrected.	You show evidence of corrected draft and layout.
Your use of illustrations	You include no photos or visuals.	You include very few photos or visuals.	You include several photos or visuals.
Your poster presentation	You include little of the required information.	You include two or three jobs and descriptions.	You include five or more jobs and descriptions.

Bulletin Boards

Theme: *Las profesiones y el medio ambiente*

Ask students to cut out, copy, or download photos of the environment and of different professions around the world. Cluster photos into categories so that similarities and differences are evident.

Bibliography

Earthworks Group. *Fifty Simple Things Kids Can Do to Save the Earth.* Scott, Foresman, 1990.

Madonna Flood Williams, Colleen. *Ecuador: Discovering Latin America.* Mason Crest Publishers, 2003.

Murdico, Suzanne. *Volunteering to Help the Environment.* Children's Press, 2000.

Wolfe, Joan, and Peter A. A. Berle. *Making Things Happen: How to Be an Effective Volunteer.* Island Press, 1991.

Hands-on Culture

Project: *Environmental Poster*

There is a Central American consortium of environmental agencies called PACA (Proyecto ambiental para Centro América), whose mission is to protect endangered species from extinction. A *paca* is a spotted rodent that has become endangered because people prize its meat. There are many endangered species throughout Latin America and Spain. In this project students identify these endangered species and design posters to inform the general public of the dangers of their extinction.

Materials:
- poster boards
- markers
- access to the Internet

Directions:

1. Research which animals are on the endangered species lists in Latin America and Spain. Examples might include *la cotorra caribeña, la tortuga tinglar, el lince ibérico,* and *la cabra montés pirenaica.*

2. Choose an animal and draft a sketch of it on the poster board.

3. Label the animal and list the country or countries where it exists. Draft one or two sentences that explain why it is important to save this animal from extinction; be sure to use the subjunctive with impersonal expressions.

4. Exchange drafts with a partner for editing and proofreading before using markers in different colors to illustrate your environmental poster.

Internet Search

Use the keywords to find more information.

9A Keywords:

> David Alfaro Siquieros, Celina Hinojosa, Programa del Muchacho Trabajador

9B Keywords:

> Alfredo Arreguín, El Parque Nacional Darién, Ecuador

Game

Buscapalabras

Play this game after *Capítulo* 9B to review vocabulary.

Players: The entire class

Materials: Paper printed with a grid of small squares, approximately 15 squares by 15 squares, pen

Rules:

1. Give each student a blank grid. Have students "hide" Spanish words from the chapter in the grid by writing them forwards, backwards, diagonally, horizontally, and vertically. Words can share letters.

2. As the students write Spanish words in the grid, have them write the English equivalents in a list below the grid.

3. When the students have written 15–20 words in the grid, have them fill in the blank spaces with random letters.

4. Have students exchange their word searches. The student who can find the most words in a given time period is the winner.

Variation: Instead of using English clues, students can define words in Spanish.

RECYCLE	Vocabulary	Grammar
A ver si recuerdas	• El mundo natural	• Verbs with spelling changes in the present tense

A primera vista	Manos a la obra	¡Adelante!	Repaso

Learning Sequence

INPUT	PRACTICE	APPLICATION	REVIEW
• Introduce vocabulary and grammar within an authentic context.	• Practice and develop new vocabulary. • Learn and practice new grammar structures.	• Apply vocabulary and grammar through culminating, theme-based activities. • Apply skill development.	• Review vocabulary and grammar.

Objectives

Read, listen to, and interpret information about • Professions • Making plans for the future • Earning a living	• Communicate about future plans. • Talk about professions. • Tell others what things will be like in the future. • Use the future tense.	• Read about languages and careers. • Make a work of folk art. • Give a presentation about your future career plans.	• Prepare for the chapter test.

Culture

• David Alfaro Siqueiros	• *La educación básica* • Celina Hinojosa • *Los centros de educación superior*	• *Los centros de carreras* • *Los artistas naif*	• Identify and describe folk art from Spanish-speaking countries.

Vocabulary	Grammar	Learner Support	
• Professions in science and technology • Professions in business • Professions in the arts • Professions in law and politics	• The future tense • The future tense: Irregular verbs	**STRATEGIES** • Activating background knowledge • Using memory cues • Using heads and subheads • Using charts	**RECYCLING** • Professions • School vocabulary • Television vocabulary • The future tense

Learner Support (continued):
• Talk about future events using the present tense
• Talk about future events using *ir* + *a* + **infinitive**

Chapter Features

Pronunciación

Diéresis - the dieresis

Conexiones

Mathematics: Create a table showing different industries and the number of students who might work in them

El español en la comunidad

The ability to speak Spanish is an important skill to have in many of the career fields in the United States.

Beyond the Classroom: States & Countries

Texas
México
Ecuador

Student Resources

PRACTICE

TECHNOLOGY

ONLINE
Interactive Textbook
- Student Edition Online plus audio, video, and flashcards

Go Online Companion Web Site
- Tutorial activities
- Internet links
- Self-tests
- Downloadable MP3 audio files
- **PuzzleView**

CD-ROM
Interactive Textbook CD-ROM
Student Edition on CD-ROM plus audio, video, and flashcards

MindPoint™ CD-ROM
QUIZSHOW

PRINT MATERIAL

CORE INSTRUCTION
Practice Workbook, pp. 171–181
- Review
- Vocabulary
- Grammar
- Puzzle
- Organizer

Writing, Audio & Video Activities, pp. 166–175
- Video
- Audio
- Writing

Grammar Study Guide 1–2 (or 3–4)

Differentiated Instruction

STUDENTS NEEDING EXTRA HELP
Guided Practice Activities, pp. 307–326
- Vocabulary Flash Cards and Vocabulary Check
- Grammar Activities
- Presentación oral

HERITAGE LEARNERS
Realidades para hispanohablantes, pp. 330–349

Lecturas para hispanohablantes
- "El tío Lucho" (excerpt from *El pez en agua*), pp. 117–118
- "Paloma Herrera: Alas en los pies," pp. 122–124

ADVANCED/PRE-AP*
Pre-AP* Resource Book: Student Activity Sheet, p. 131

Teacher Resources

PLAN AND TEACH

TECHNOLOGY

Audio Program   Fine Art Transparencies
Video Program   Vocabulary and Grammar
                Transparencies
                Answers on Transparencies

TeacherEXPRESS CD-ROM
- Lesson Planner
- Vocabulary Clip Art
- Web Resources
- Teaching Resources
- Teacher Edition with Interactive Links

PresentationEXPRESS CD-ROM
- Vocabulary
- Transparencies and Maps
- Grammar
- Photo Gallery
- Audio
- Clip Art

PRINT MATERIAL

CORE INSTRUCTION
Teacher's Resource Book, pp. 228–255
- Input Script
- Video Script
- Answer Keys
- GramActiva Blackline Masters
- Vocabulary Clip Art
- Chapter Resource Checklist
- School-to-Home Connection Letters
- Communicative Activities Blackline Masters

TPR Stories, pp. 120–126

Differentiated Instruction

STUDENTS NEEDING EXTRA HELP
Guided Practice Activities Teacher's Guide, pp. T154–T163

HERITAGE LEARNERS
Realidades para hispanohablantes Teacher's Guide, pp. 166–175

Lecturas para hispanohablantes Teacher's Guide, pp. 45–48

ADVANCED/PRE-AP*
Pre-AP* Resource Book: Resources Chart, p. 128

Differentiated Assessment

ASSESS

PH SuccessNet ONLINE
- Access to grades and reports from Online Interactive Textbook

ExamView© on Presentation Express CD-ROM
QuickTake Presenter
- Vocabulary Quizzes
- Chapter Test
- Grammar Quizzes

TeacherEXPRESS CD-ROM
- Assessment Program
- **ExamView©** Test Banks A and B
test generator

Go Online
PHSchool.com
For: Teacher Home Page
Web Code: jdk-1001

CORE ASSESSMENT
Assessment Program, pp. 229–241
- Pruebas
  Vocabulary Recognition
  Vocabulary Production
  The future tense
  The future tense: Irregular verbs
- Examen del capítulo
- Speaking and Writing Rubrics

Teacher's Resource Book, p. 242
- Situation Cards

TPR Stories, pp. 120–126

STUDENTS NEEDING EXTRA HELP
Alternate Assessment Program
- Examen del capítulo, pp. 101–105

HERITAGE LEARNERS
Assessment Program: Realidades para hispanohablantes Teacher's Guide, pp. T166–T170

ExamView© Heritage Learner
test generator   **Test Bank**

ADVANCED/PRE-AP*
Pre-AP* Resource Book: Teacher Activity Sheet, p. 130

ExamView© Pre-AP* Test Bank
test generator

	Warm-up / Assess	Preview Present / Practice Communicate	Wrap-up / Homework Options
DAY 1	**Warm-up (5 min.)** • Homework check • Return Examen del capítulo 8B	**A ver si recuerdas . . .** **(20 min.)** • Presentation: El mundo natural • Actividades 1, 2 • Presentation: Verbs with spelling changes in the present tense • Actividades 3, 4 **Chapter Opener (5 min.)** • Objetives • Fondo cultural **A primera vista (15 min.)** • Presentation: Vocabulario y gramática en contexto • Actividades 1, 2	**Wrap-up and Homework Options (5 min.)** • Practice Workbook 9A-A, 9A-B, 9A-1, 9A-2 • Go Online
DAY 2	**Warm-up (10 min.)** • Homework check	**A primera vista (35 min.)** • Presentation: Videohistoria Y tú, ¿qué vas a ser? • View: Videohistoria • Video Activities 1, 2, 3, 4 • Actividad 3	**Wrap-up and Homework Options (5 min.)** • Practice Workbook 9A-3, 9A-4 • Go Online • Prueba 9A-1: Vocabulary recognition
DAY 3	**Warm-up (10 min.)** • Actividad 4 • Homework check ✔**Assessment (10 min.)** • Prueba 9A-1: Vocabulary recognition	**Manos a la obra (25 min.)** • Actividades 5, 7, 8, 9, 10 • Fondo cultural	**Wrap-up and Homework Options (5 min.)** • Writing Activity 10 • Actividad 11 • Heritage Learner Workbook 9A-1, 9A-2 • Prueba 9A-2: Vocabulary production
DAY 4	**Warm-up (10 min.)** • Actividad 6 • Homework check ✔**Assessment (10 min.)** (after Communicative Activity) • Prueba 9A-2: Vocabulary production	**Manos a la obra (25 min.)** • Audio Activities 5, 6 • Communicative Activity • Presentation: The future tense • View: GramActiva video • Actividad 12	**Wrap-up and Homework Options (5 min.)** • Practice Workbook 9A-5 • Actividad 15 • Writing Activity 11 • Go Online
DAY 5	**Warm-up (10 min.)** • Actividad 14 • Homework check	**Manos a la obra (35 min.)** • Pronunciación • Actividad 13 • Audio Activity 7 • Presentation: The future tense: irregular verbs • View: GramActiva video • Actividades 16, 18, 19	**Wrap-up and Homework Options (5 min.)** • Practice Workbook 9A-6 • Actividades 17, 22 • Go Online • Prueba 9A-3: The future tense
DAY 6	**Warm-up (5 min.)** • Homework check ✔**Assessment (10 min.)** • Pruebas 9A-3: The future tense	**Manos a la obra (30 min.)** • Actividades 20, 21, 23, 24 • Audio Activity 8	**Wrap-up and Homework Options (5 min.)** • Practice Workbook 9A-7 • Heritage Learner • Writing Activity 12 Workbook 9A-4 • Actividad 26 • Prueba 9A-4: The future • Go Online tense: irregular verbs
DAY 7	**Warm-up (10 min.)** • Actividad 25 • Homework check ✔**Assessment (10 min.)** • Prueba 9A-4: The future tense: irregular verbs	**¡Adelante! (10 min.)** • Presentación oral: Steps 1, 4 **Repaso del capítulo (15 min.)** • Vocabulario y gramática • Preparación para el examen 1, 2	**Wrap-up and Homework Options (5 min.)** • Presentación oral: Step 2
DAY 8	**Warm-up (5 min.)** • Presentación oral: Step 2	**Manos a la obra (10 min.)** **¡Adelante! (30 min.)** • Fondos culturales • Presentación oral: Step 3 • El español en la comunidad	**Wrap-up and Homework Options (5 min.)** • Preparación para el examen 3, 4, 5 • Go Online: Self-test
DAY 9	**Warm-up (5 min.)** • Homework check	**¡Adelante! (40 min.)** • Lectura • ¿Comprendiste? / Y tú, ¿qué dices? • La cultura en vivo	**Wrap-up and Homework Options (5 min.)** • Practice Workbook 9A-8, 9A-9 • Go Online: Lectura • Examen del capítulo 9A
DAY 10	**Warm-up (5 min.)** • Homework check ✔**Assessment (40 min.)** • Examen del capítulo 9A		**Wrap-up and Homework Options (5 min.)** • La cultura en vivo

	Warm-up / Assess	Preview Present / Practice Communicate		Wrap-up / Homework Options
DAY 1	**Warm-up** (5 min.) • Homework check • Return Examen del capítulo: Capítulo 8B	**A ver si recuerdas . . .** **(25 min.)** • Presentation: El mundo natural • Actividades 1, 2 • Presentation: Verbs with spelling changes in the present tense • Actividades 3, 4 **Chapter Opener** **(5 min.)** • Objectives • Fondo cultural	**A primera vista** **(50 min.)** • Presentation: Vocabulario y gramática en contexto • Actividades 1, 2 • Presentation: Videohistoria: *Y tú, ¿qué vas a ser?* • View: Videohistoria • Video Activities 1, 2, 3, 4 • Actividad 3	**Wrap-up and Homework Options** (5 min.) • Practice Workbook 9A-A, 9A-B, 9A-1, 9A-2, 9A-3, 9A-4 • Go Online • Prueba 9A-1: Vocabulary recognition
DAY 2	**Warm-up** (10 min.) • Actividad 4 • Homework check ✔**Assessment** (10 min.) • Prueba 9A-1: Vocabulary recognition	**Manos a la obra** (65 min.) • Actividades 5, 7, 8, 9, 10, 11 • Fondo cultural • Pronunciación • Audio Activities 5, 6 • Communicative Activity • Presentation: The future tense • View: GramActiva video • Actividad 12		**Wrap-up and Homework Options** (5 min.) • Practice Workbook 9A-5 • Writing Activity 10 • Go Online • Heritage Learner Workbook 9A-1, 9A-2 • Prueba 9A-2: Vocabulary production
DAY 3	**Warm-up** (10 min.) • Actividad 6 • Homework check ✔**Assessment** (10 min.) • Prueba 9A-2: Vocabulary production	**Manos a la obra** (65 min.) • Actividades 13, 14, 15 • Audio Activity 7 • Presentation: The future tense: irregular verbs • View: GramActiva video • Actividades 16, 17, 18, 19, 20, 21 • Fondo cultural • Audio Activity 8		**Wrap-up and Homework Options** (5 min.) • Practice Workbook 9A-6 • Go Online • Heritage Learner Workbook 9A-4 • Pruebas 9A-3: The future tense
DAY 4	**Warm-up** (10 min.) • Writing Activity 11 • Homework check ✔**Assessment** (10 min.) • Pruebas 9A-3: The future tense	**Manos a la obra** (35 min.) • Actividades 22, 23, 24, 25, 26 • El español en la comunidad • Writing Activity 12 **¡Adelante!** (30 min.) • Lectura • ¿Comprendiste? / Y tú, ¿qué dices? • Presentación oral: Steps 1, 4		**Wrap-up and Homework Options** (5 min.) • Practice Workbook 9A-7 • Presentación oral: Step 2 • Go Online: Irregular future; Lectura • Prueba 9A-4: The future tense: irregular verbs
DAY 5	**Warm-up** (5 min.) • Homework check ✔**Assessment** (10 min.) • Prueba 9A-4: The future tense: irregular verbs	**¡Adelante!** (35 min.) • Presentación oral: Step 3 **Repaso del capítulo** (35 min.) • Vocabulario y gramática • Preparación para el examen 1, 2, 3, 4, 5		**Wrap-up and Homework Options** (5 min.) • Practice Workbook 9A-8, 9A-9 • Go Online: Self-test • Examen del capítulo 9A
DAY 6	**Warm-up** (5 min.) • Homework check **Repaso del capítulo** (20 min.) • Situation Cards ✔**Assessment** (45 min.) • Examen del capítulo 9A	**¡Adelante!** (15 min.) • La cultura en vivo		**Wrap-up and Homework Options** (5 min.) • La cultura en vivo

 **9A Recycle**

Vocabulario · Presentation EXPRESS VOCABULARY

Core Instruction

Resources: Voc. and Gram. Transparency 157

Focus: Review vocabulary related to nature and recycling

Suggestions: Before class, find pictures of the plants and animals on the list. As you show the pictures, have students say the Spanish name, tell if it is *una planta* or *un animal,* and name a place where it can be found.

To review the words in the *el reciclaje* and *los materiales* boxes, bring in a recycling container with an example of each kind of material. Show an item, have students name the material, and talk about how they recycle at home or at school.

 Actividad 1  *Standards:* 1.2  Presentation EXPRESS ANSWERS

Resources: Answers on Transparencies

Focus: Matching vocabulary words to definitions

Suggestions: Tell students that instead of writing three definitions for Step 2, they may choose to use clue words, riddles, or fill-in-the-blank sentences.

Answers:

Step 1:
1. el zoológico
2. el mono
3. el periódico
4. el cartón
5. las flores

Step 2: Answers will vary.

 Actividad 2 *Standards:* 1.3

Focus: Answering questions using vocabulary words

Suggestions: You may want to tell students not to answer *no* to any of the questions. They can provide fictitious answers, if necessary, or talk about other people or places.

Answers will vary.

A ver si recuerdas...

Vocabulario

El mundo natural

las plantas y los animales

el árbol, *pl.* los árboles
la flor, *pl.* las flores
el mono
el oso
el pájaro
el pez, *pl.* los peces
el tigre

los lugares

al aire libre
el jardín, *pl.* los jardines
el lago
el mar
las montañas
el mundo
el parque nacional
el río
el zoológico

el reciclaje

el centro de reciclaje
reciclar
recoger
separar
tirar
trabajar como voluntario, -a
usar

los materiales

la botella
el cartón
la lata
el papel
el periódico
el plástico
la revista
el vidrio

Práctica de vocabulario • Usando el organizador gráfico

 **Actividad 1** Escribir/Hablar _____

¿Qué es?

1 Lee las siguientes definiciones y escribe la palabra que se define.

1. lugar donde se ven los animales
2. animal que come plátanos
3. publicación que da las noticias
4. material usado para hacer cajas
5. rosa, tulipán, orquídea

2 Ahora escribe tres definiciones más. Léelas a otro(a) estudiante para ver si puede decir la palabra que se define.

Actividad 2 Escribir/Hablar _____

Lugares interesantes

Contesta las siguientes preguntas.

1. ¿Cuál es el zoológico más impresionante que has visitado? ¿Por qué te pareció tan fantástico?
2. ¿En tu comunidad hay parques o jardines públicos? Describe uno.
3. ¿Has ido alguna vez a un parque nacional? ¿Cómo era? ¿Qué había? ¿Qué hiciste allí?
4. ¿Has trabajado como voluntario(a) en un centro de reciclaje alguna vez? ¿Qué hacen los voluntarios allí?

448 cuatrocientos cuarenta y ocho
Tema 9 • ¿Cómo será el futuro?

Differentiated Instruction
Solutions for All Learners

Heritage Language Learners

Students may recognize exceptions to the *g/gu* spelling rules in the *Gramática • Repaso.* If they point out words like **güiro, Camagüey,** and **bilingüe,** tell them that these words are written with a dieresis to allow for a change in pronunciation. Tell them that they will learn more about the dieresis later on in this chapter.

Multiple Intelligences

Naturalist: Have students write a paragraph about the importance of recycling. They should explain the benefits recycling offers for plants, animals, people, and the environment. Invite students to share their ideas with others.

Gramática · Repaso

Verbs with spelling changes in the present tense

Remember that some verbs have spelling changes in the present tense to preserve the pronunciation of the infinitive in the conjugated forms.

Remember that *g* has a hard or soft sound depending on the vowel that follows it. To maintain the soft consonant sound before the vowel *o*, verbs that end in *-ger*, like *escoger* and *recoger*, change from *g* to *j* in the present-tense *yo* form.

> **Recojo** basura en la calle y la tiro en el basurero. Otras personas no la **recogen**.

In the present-tense *yo* form of verbs like *seguir* and *conseguir*, the silent *u* used in the infinitive and other forms in which the *g* is followed by *e* or *i* is dropped to preserve the sound of *g* as in *get*.

> En el jardín botánico, algunos turistas **siguen** a una guía por los senderos. Yo no la **sigo**; prefiero caminar solo.

Verbs like *enviar* and *esquiar* have an accent mark on the *i* in all present-tense forms except *nosotros* and *vosotros*.

> **Enviamos** cartas a las compañías que destruyen los árboles. Yo también **envío** información por correo electrónico.

Práctica de gramática

 Leer/Escribir _____

Una semana de vacaciones

Lee lo que dice una muchacha sobre sus vacaciones. Completa su historia con las formas apropiadas de los verbos *escoger*, *esquiar* y *seguir*.

Cada año mi familia y yo vamos a las montañas para esquiar. Yo __1.__ muy bien porque hace cinco años que tomo lecciones de esquí. Mis padres me dicen, "Amalia, __2.__ o esquías con nosotros o tomas una lección". Yo siempre __3.__ un día de lecciones porque los instructores __4.__ estupendamente. Escucho con atención y __5.__ sus instrucciones. Algunos chicos en las lecciones son demasiado atrevidos y no __6.__ instrucciones.

Más práctica

- Practice Workbook, pp. 171–172: 9A-A, 9A-B
- Guided Practice: AVSR, pp. 307–308
- *Real.* para hispanohablantes, p. 330

 **Go Online**
PHSchool.com
For: Vocab. and Grammar
Web Code: jdd-0901

 Escribir _____

Un proyecto en la comunidad

Un grupo de personas de una escuela decide ayudar a limpiar su comunidad. Escribe frases para decir qué hacen.

Modelo

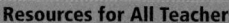

mi profesor de ciencias / conseguir permiso para . . .
Mi profesor de ciencias consigue permiso para hacer el proyecto.

1. yo
2. mis amigos
3. mi mejor amigo(a)
4. nosotros
5. nuestros profesores

enviar cartas a la comunidad para . . .
recoger basura en . . .
seguir las instrucciones de . . .
escoger el lugar donde . . .
conseguir bolsas de plástico para . . .

Enrich Your Teaching
Resources for All Teachers

Culture Note

Tourism is essential to Costa Rica's economy. The government encourages ecotourism (visiting nature and wildlife without disturbing either). Large tracts of land have been designated as national parks where visitors can observe an amazing variety of flora and fauna.

Teacher-to-Teacher

Set up a classroom recycling center. Include separate bins for paper, plastic, glass, and metal. Have students label the bins and also display posters with instructions for proper recycling.

Gramática · Repaso

 **Presentation EXPRESS GRAMMAR**

Core Instruction

Suggestions: Review letter combinations that make the hard **g** and soft **g** sounds with each of the five vowels.

Hard g	Soft g
ganar	jardín
sigue	gente
guía	gira
hago	joven
gusta	jugar

 3 **Standards:** 1.2  **Presentation EXPRESS ANSWERS**

Resources: Answers on Transparencies

Focus: Completing sentences with correct verb forms

Suggestions: Use the first sentence of the paragraph as a model. Read the sentence aloud and ask a volunteer to select the correct infinitive. Have another volunteer provide the correct conjugated form.

Answers:
1. esquío
2. escoge
3. escojo
4. esquían
5. sigo
6. siguen

4 **Standards:** 1.3

Focus: Writing sentences with verbs with spelling changes

Suggestions: To be sure students write sentences with verb forms that require spelling changes, assign a subject to each verb phrase. For example: *(mi mejor amigo) enviar cartas a la comunidad para …* and *(yo) recoger basura en …*

Answers will vary.

Vocabulario y gramática

Presentation EXPRESS
VOCABULARY

Core Instruction

Standards: 1.2

Resources: Teacher's Resource Book: Input Script, p. 230, Clip Art, pp. 244–248, Audio Script, p. 231; Voc. and Gram. Transparencies 158–159; TPR Stories Book, pp. 119–130; Audio Program: Tracks 1–2

Focus: Presenting vocabulary for professions

Suggestions: Use the Input Script from the *Teacher's Resource Book* or the story from the *TPR Stories Book* to present the vocabulary, or use some of the following suggestions.

Distribute copies of the Vocabulary Clip Art and present the vocabulary on p. 452 by telling a story (real or fictional) about all the careers you had before you became a teacher. Use pantomime to convey meaning. Give humorous reasons why you quit the different careers. Have students hold up the Clip Art images as you mention each career.

Present the vocabulary on p. 453 by drawing pictures of the careers in large thought bubbles toward the top of the board. Name and describe each career as you draw it. Then call out the careers one by one. Call on volunteers to stand under the correct image and strike a thoughtful pose like the ones shown by the teens on p. 453.

Bellringer Review

Write these professions on the board:

profesor médico dependiente

Have students work in pairs to write one word describing a personality trait and a phrase to describe an ability that would be important for each. (Ex. *locutor— sociable/saber hablar claramente*)

Additional Resources

• Audio Program: Canciones CD, Disc 22

✓ Assessment

• **ExamView** Quiz on PresEXPRESS
QuickTake Presenter

A primera vista jdd-0987 🔊

Vocabulario y gramática en contexto

Objectives

Read, listen to, and understand information about
• professions
• making plans for the future
• earning a living

Exposición de carreras

❝Bienvenidos a la Exposición de **carreras.** Hoy les vamos a hablar sobre las posibilidades que hay para Uds. después de **graduarse** del **colegio.** Después de **la graduación** de la escuela secundaria, algunos de Uds. asistirán a **la universidad** y estudiarán para **una profesión.** Otros irán a **una escuela técnica,** y otros conseguirán un trabajo inmediatamente. Tenemos información para todos ❞

el hombre de negocios
la mujer de negocios

la oficina — el (la) secretario(a) — el (la) contador(a)

En el mundo de **los negocios** es importante tener a personas **bilingües.** En **el futuro** hablar dos **idiomas,** como el inglés y el español, será más importante.

el (la) arquitecto(a) — el (la) diseñador(a) — el (la) técnico(a)

Habrá carreras importantes en la tecnología: arquitectos para la construcción de casas y edificios y diseñadores para sitios Web y juegos de computadoras.

el juez, la jueza — el (la) abogado(a)

Algunos de Uds. **seguirán** la carrera de **derecho** y tendrán **un programa de estudios** muy interesante. Para ser abogado o juez hay que ir a la universidad y estudiar **leyes** seis u ocho años.

el (la) agricultor(a) — el (la) cartero(a) — el (la) mecánico(a)

Hay muchas otras oportunidades de trabajo: carreras de agricultor, mecánico, bombero o cartero, por ejemplo. Tal vez algunos seguirán una carrera **militar.**

Differentiated Instruction
Solutions for All Learners

Advanced Learners

Have students brainstorm a list of courses they would have to study to pursue the careers and professions introduced in this chapter. Ask them to choose one of the professions and recommend a list of courses. For example: *Para ser político(a), recomiendo que estudies inglés, español, historia y ciencias sociales.*

Students with Special Needs

Modify *Actividad* 1 for hearing-impaired students. Using the script for the activity, provide a list of the dictated descriptions. Have students add a second column listing the professions illustrated on pp. 452–453. Then have them draw a line matching each profession to its description.

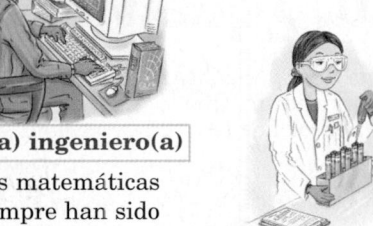

el (la) político(a)

el (la) ingeniero(a)

el (la) científico(a)

" Me gusta estudiar ciencias sociales. Creo que seguiré una carrera en **la política** ".

" Las matemáticas siempre han sido fáciles para mí. Me gustaría ser ingeniero ".

" A mí me encantan las ciencias. Seré científica y trabajaré en un laboratorio ".

el (la) gerente

el (la) veterinario(a)

" Hace dos años que trabajo como dependiente en una tienda de ropa. Quisiera ser gerente de la tienda ".

" Me interesa el estudio de la medicina, pero también me gustan los animales. Estudiaré para ser veterinaria ".

Actividad 1

 Escuchar — jdd-0987

Las profesiones

Escucha las descripciones de diferentes profesiones. Mira los dibujos y las fotos y señala la profesión que se describe en cada frase.

Más práctica

• Practice Workbook, pp. 173–174: 9A-1, 9A-2
• WAV Wbk.: Writing, p. 172
• Guided Practice: Vocab. Flash Cards, pp. 309–316
• *Real.* para hispanohablantes, p. 332

Go Online PHSchool.com
For: Vocab. Practice
Web Code: jdd-0902

Actividad 2

 Escuchar — jdd-0987

¿Lógico o no?

¿Qué sabes sobre las profesiones y las carreras? Levanta una mano si lo que escuchas es lógico y levanta las dos manos si no es lógico.

cuatrocientos cincuenta y tres **453**
Capítulo 9A

 9A

Language Input

Actividad 1

Standards: 1.2 — Presentation EXPRESS AUDIO

Resources: Teacher's Resource Book: Audio Script, p. 231; Audio Program: Track 3; Answers on Transparencies

Focus: Listening comprehension about professions

Suggestions: If you prefer, distribute copies of the Clip Art and have students arrange careers in the order they hear them.

Script and Answers:

1. El diseñador puede imaginar cómo será algo antes de crearlo. *(designer)*
2. Los carteros son importantes porque nos traen el correo. *(mail carrier)*
3. Mi vecina vende casas. Es una mujer de negocios. *(businesswoman)*
4. Mi hermano siempre ha dibujado bien. Ahora estudia para ser arquitecto. *(architect)*
5. Una jueza tiene que conocer muy bien el derecho. *(judge)*
6. Seguiré un programa de estudios para ser abogado. *(lawyer)*
7. El gerente en la tienda donde trabajo es muy simpático. *(manager)*

Actividad 2

Standards: 1.2 — Presentation EXPRESS AUDIO

Resources: Teacher's Resource Book: Audio Script, p. 231–232; Audio Program: Track 4; Answers on Transparencies

Focus: Listening comprehension about professions

Suggestions:

Have students listen once and hold up Clip Art of the careers they hear. Have them listen again and have them decide if the statements are logical or illogical.

Script and Answers:

1. No me gusta trabajar con las manos. Voy a ser mecánica. *(two hands)*
2. Hablo dos idiomas. Puedo ser un hombre de negocios para una compañía norteamericana en España o en México. *(one hand)*
3. Un contador tiene que trabajar mucho con los números. *(one hand)*
4. Me gustaría ser agricultor porque me gusta trabajar en el campo al aire libre. *(one hand)*
5. Los científicos hacen experimentos e investigaciones interesantes. *(one hand)*
6. No me gustan los animales. Por eso quiero ser veterinario. *(two hands)*
7. Es necesario ir a la universidad antes de tener una carrera militar. *(two hands)*

Enrich Your Teaching
Resources for All Teachers

Teacher-to-Teacher

Have professionals who work in the careers presented in the *A primera vista* speak to your class about how learning Spanish would be helpful to someone considering a career in their profession. Invite parents, school staff members, and other members from your community. Have students take notes and write a short paragraph on the advantages of being bilingual. Create a bulletin board with the title: *Ser bilingüe me ayuda ...* Post students' paragraphs along with photos of the guest speakers.

453

9A Language Input

Videohistoria
Core Instruction

 Standards: 1.2

Resources: Voc. and Gram. Transparencies 160–161; Audio Program: Track 5

Focus: Presenting additional vocabulary for professions

Suggestions:

Pre-reading: Have students use the images to guess which careers will be discussed in the *Videohistoria*. Then review the *Estrategia*.

Reading: Play the *Audio CD* and have students follow along in their books. Stop the *Audio CD* after each segment and ask questions to check for comprehension. Discuss what a person needs to do to work as an artist, a businesswoman, an engineer, or an architect.

Post-reading: Encourage students to share whether they think they would prefer creative careers, technical careers, or business careers. Have them answer the questions in *Actividad* 3.

Pre-AP* Support

- **Activity:** As a variation of the Advanced Learners activity on p. 452, write several of the professions and careers introduced in this chapter on the board. Then call on volunteers to offer personality types, interests, goals, etc., that might be related to one of the professions without actually naming the profession. Have the class identify the profession associated with the comment and discuss.

- **Pre-AP* Resource Book:** Comprehensive guide to Pre-AP* vocabulary skill development, pp. 47–53

Videohistoria

Y tú, ¿qué vas a ser?

¿Qué van a ser Angélica, Esteban y Pedro? ¿Qué le pasa a Pedro? Lee la historia.

Estrategia

Activating background knowledge
As you read the *Videohistoria*, think about what you already know about the professions being discussed.

- What do the characters need to do in order to work in their chosen professions?

Angélica   Lisa   Pedro   Esteban

1 **Angélica:** Hola, Pedro, ¿qué tal?

Pedro: Hola. Muy bien, ¿y tú? ¿Está Esteban?

Angélica: ¿Adónde van?

Esteban: A la escuela. Hay un concurso de arte, de dibujos. Y Pedro va a participar.

5 **Pedro:** No sé. Es difícil ganarse la vida como **artista.** Quizás podré ser **escritor.** Sabes que también me gusta mucho escribir. Y tú, ¿qué piensas hacer?

6 **Esteban:** Pues a mí me gustan las profesiones técnicas. Quiero estudiar para ingeniero o arquitecto . . .

7 **Directora:** Todos los trabajos son excelentes, pero uno de ellos es el mejor . . . ¡Pedro Ríos! ¡Felicidades!

Differentiated Instruction
Solutions for All Learners

Advanced Learners
Have students research the salaries of different careers. Have them present the information in a chart or graph.

Students with Learning Difficulties
To elaborate on the *Estrategia*, draw attention to panels 3–6 of the *Videohistoria*. Ask students to point out the text that shows the characters are thinking about factors that affect career choices (salary, benefits, talent, interest).

2 **Pedro:** Y bien, ¿qué te parece?

Esteban: ¡Genial!

Angélica: A mí no me gusta.

Esteban: Porque tú no comprendes el mundo de **las artes.**

Angélica: Sí, lo comprendo, pero . . .

3 **Angélica:** **Algún día** prefiero **ganarme la vida** como mujer de negocios. Tendré **un salario** decente y **beneficios.**

Esteban: Sí, y querrás ser **dueña** de tu negocio . . .

Pedro: Mejor vamos o llegaremos tarde al concurso.

4 **Esteban:** Oye, creo que eres muy talentoso. Algún día podrás ser **pintor . . .**

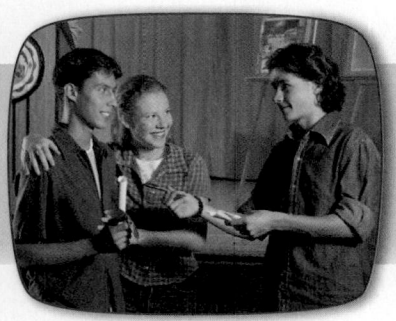

8 **Lisa:** ¡Felicidades, Pedro!

Pedro: Gracias, Lisa. Es un momento muy importante para mí.

Esteban: ¿Un autógrafo, por favor?

Pedro: ¿Cómo? Ah, sí, por supuesto. Voy a ser un pintor muy famoso.

 Actividad 3

Escribir/Hablar

¿Comprendiste?

1. ¿Adónde van Pedro y Esteban? ¿Por qué?
2. ¿Qué más piensa hacer Angélica en el futuro? ¿Por qué?
3. ¿Qué más le gusta hacer a Pedro? ¿Qué profesión piensa seguir?
4. ¿Qué profesión le gustaría seguir a Esteban?
5. ¿Quién ganó el concurso? ¿Qué le pide Esteban a Pedro?

Más práctica

- Practice Workbook, pp. 175–176: 9A-3, 9A-4
- WAV Wbk.: Video, pp. 166–168
- Guided Practice: Vocab. Check, pp. 317–320
- *Real.* para hispanohablantes, p. 333

 **Go Online** PHSchool.com

For: Vocab. Practice
Web Code: jdd-0903

cuatrocientos cincuenta y cinco **455**
Capítulo 9A

Video
Core Instruction

 Standards: 1.2

Resources: Teacher's Resource Book: Video Script, p. 235; Video Program: Cap. 9A; Video Program Teacher's Guide: Cap. 9A

Focus: Checking comprehension of contextualized vocabulary

Suggestions:

Pre-viewing: Have eight volunteers write a summary on the board of one panel from the *Videohistoria.* Review the summaries with the rest of the class.

Viewing: Play the video once. Play it again and have students raise their hands whenever a career is mentioned.

Post-viewing: Discuss the positive and negative aspects of the career ideas of Angélica, Pedro, and Esteban.

Actividad 3 *Standards:* 1.2 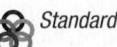 Presentation EXPRESS  ANSWERS

Resources: Answers on Transparencies

Focus: Verifying comprehension of the *Videohistoria*

Suggestions: Divide the class into two groups. Have Group 1 read the first question aloud to the other group. After Group 2 responds, Group 1 will decide if the response is correct. Group 2 will ask the next question, and so on.

Answers:

1. Pedro y Esteban van a la escuela porque hay un concurso de arte y Pedro va a participar.
2. Angélica piensa ser mujer de negocios porque quiere tener un salario decente y beneficios.
3. A Pedro también le gusta escribir. Piensa ser escritor.
4. A Esteban le gustaría seguir una profesión técnica como de ingeniero o de arquitecto.
5. Pedro ganó el concurso. Esteban le pide a Pedro un autógrafo.

Enrich Your Teaching
Resources for All Teachers

Culture Note

In Spain the *Oposición-Concurso* is a two-part test (akin to a Civil Service Examination in the United States) that enables people to get government jobs. The *Oposición* is a written test and carries more weight than the *Concurso,* which is an evaluation of a person's qualification as a whole. Many Spaniards go through the *Oposición-Concurso* because some of the highest paying and most prestigious jobs in the country are with the government. Government jobs in general are coveted because they are very stable.

Internet Search

Keywords:

oposiciones + España

Additional Resources

- WAV Wbk.: Audio Act. 5, p. 169
- Teacher's Resource Book: Audio Script, p. 232
- Audio Program: Track 8

✓ **Assessment**

- **ExamView** Quiz on PresEXPRESS QuickTake Presenter
- Prueba 9A-1: Vocab. Recognition, pp. 229–230

9A

 Actividad 4 Standards: 1.2 — Presentation EXPRESS ANSWERS

Resources: Answers on Transparencies

Focus: Writing career vocabulary

Suggestions: Be certain students understand the categories of careers before they begin.

Answers:

1. mecánica
2. cartero
3. agricultor
4. juez
5. mujer de negocios
6. cantante

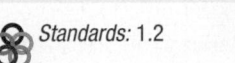 **Bellringer Review**
Have students match the profession in Column A with a logical association from Column B.

A	B
1. mecánico	a. edificio
2. escritor	b. carro
3. arquitecto	c. caballo
4. científico	d. experimento
5. veterinario	e. novela

Actividad 5 Standards: 1.2 — Presentation EXPRESS AUDIO

Resources: Teacher's Resource Book: Audio Script, p. 232; Audio Program: Track 6; Answers on Transparencies

Focus: Listening and writing about careers

Suggestions: Have students identify the careers in the images before they listen.

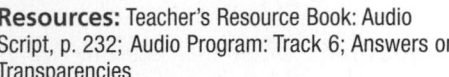 **Script and Answers:**

1. En la universidad, estudié los negocios. Me gustan mucho las matemáticas y los números. En mi trabajo, uso mucho la computadora y una calculadora. *(mujer de negocios)*
2. En mi trabajo les reparo los coches a otras personas. A veces uso una computadora. Asistí a una escuela técnica por dos años para prepararme para este trabajo. *(mecánico)*
3. Cuando me gradué del colegio, fui a una escuela técnica. Después de la graduación empecé a trabajar en el correo. Conozco a todas las personas que viven en el barrio donde entrego las cartas a sus casas. *(cartera)*
4. Cada día paso muchas horas dibujando o pintando. A veces estoy en casa y otros días voy al campo o a la playa. Asistí a una escuela para las artes. *(artista)*
5. En la universidad yo estudié derecho. Antes era abogada, pero ahora escucho lo que dicen los abogados y tengo que tomar unas decisiones muy importantes. *(jueza)*
6. Después de graduarme del colegio, asistí a la universidad para estudiar ciencias. Siempre me han gustado los animales. Ahora trabajo en una clínica médica donde cuido a los animales enfermos o heridos. *(veterinario)*

Manos a la obra

Vocabulario y gramática en uso

Objectives

- Communicate about future plans
- Talk about professions
- Tell others what things will be like in the future
- Learn the future tense

 Actividad 4 Escribir

¡A trabajar en el periódico!

Un joven trabaja en un periódico y tiene que organizar los anuncios clasificados. Escribe la profesión que no corresponde a cada una de estas categorías.

Modelo
la tecnología: arquitecta, contador, diseñador, técnica
contador

1. los negocios: contadora, secretario, gerente, mecánica
2. las artes: pintora, artista, escritor, cartero
3. la política y el derecho: agricultor, jueza, político, abogada
4. la tecnología: diseñadora, arquitecta, juez, ingeniero
5. las ciencias: veterinario, científico, médica, mujer de negocios
6. el servicio público: policía, cartera, política, cantante

 **Actividad 5** jdd-0988 Escuchar/Escribir

Así es mi trabajo

Copia la tabla en una hoja de papel. Vas a escuchar a seis personas hablar de su trabajo. Escribe lo que escuchas sobre los estudios de cada persona, lo que hace en su trabajo y cuál es su profesión.

los estudios	lo que hace	su profesión

Differentiated Instruction
Solutions for All Learners

Students with Special Needs

Students with language-processing difficulties may have trouble listening, processing, and encoding the information by category in *Actividad* 5 within the allotted time. Visually reinforce the dialogue with a written script from which they can extract information.

 Actividad 6 — Leer/Escribir

Una carrera en negocios internacionales

Lee la historia de un hombre que ahora tiene una carrera en los negocios internacionales. Escoge y escribe las palabras apropiadas para completar la descripción de su preparación profesional y de su trabajo ahora.

colegio	programa de estudios
idioma	universidad
me gradué	

Hace nueve años __1.__ del colegio. Decidí asistir a la __2.__ para seguir un __3.__ en los negocios. Durante mis años en el __4.__, estudié español y quería seguir estudiando este __5.__ en la universidad también. Por eso tomé clases avanzadas de español.

beneficio	me gano la vida
bilingüe	oficinas
hombre de negocios	salario

Soy __6.__ ahora y por eso conseguí un trabajo como __7.__ con una compañía internacional después de graduarme de la universidad. Uno de los buenos aspectos de mi carrera en los negocios internacionales es que __8.__ viajando a varios países de América del Sur durante el año. Otro __9.__ es que recibo un __10.__ muy bueno porque puedo comunicarme con los empleados que trabajan en nuestras __11.__ en estos países.

  Actividad 7 — Hablar

Los planes para el futuro

Con otro(a) estudiante, hablen de sus planes para el futuro.

Modelo

A —¿Piensas seguir una carrera en el mundo de _las artes_ después de graduarte del colegio?

B —Posiblemente. Algún día me gustaría ser _pintor(a)_.

o: —No, no quiero ser _pintor(a)_. Quisiera ganarme la vida como _ingeniero(a)_ en el futuro.

1.

2.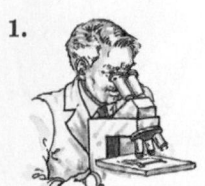

3.

4.

5.

cuatrocientos cincuenta y siete **457**
Capítulo 9A

 Actividad 6  — _Standards:_ 1.2 Presentation EXPRESS ANSWERS

Resources: Answers on Transparencies

Focus: Reading and writing a description of a career

Suggestions: Have students read the entire selection for general comprehension before they begin to fill in the blanks. Remind them to use context, verb tenses, and definite and indefinite articles as clues. If students have difficulty deciding where some words belong, tell them to first complete the items they are sure of, then try out the words that are left over in the other blanks.

Answers:

1. me gradué
2. universidad
3. programa de estudios
4. colegio
5. idioma
6. bilingüe
7. hombre de negocios
8. me gano la vida
9. beneficio
10. salario
11. oficinas

Extension: Have students write a paragraph about a career they are interested in and then turn it into a cloze activity for a partner to complete.

 Actividad 7  — _Standards:_ 1.1 Presentation EXPRESS ANSWERS

Resources: Answers on Transparencies

Focus: Speaking about career domains and plans

Suggestions: Have students identify the career domains represented by each picture before they begin. Be sure they understand that they are to use the forms of the nouns that match their own gender.

Answers will vary, but will include:

1. las ciencias / científico(a)
2. la política / político(a)
3. el derecho / juez(a)
4. la tecnología / técnico(a)
5. los negocios / contador(a), hombre / mujer de negocios

Extension: Have students extend the conversation by having Student A ask why Student B wishes or does not wish to pursue a particular career.

Enrich Your Teaching
Resources for All Teachers

Culture Note

Like their counterparts in the United States, many young people in Spanish-speaking countries are seeking jobs in the fields of computers and technology. Because English remains the most commonly used language on the Internet, speaking English is an asset to those pursuing a career in technology.

Teacher-to-Teacher

Have pairs of students act out a scene between a school counselor and a student who does not find any career appealing.

 9A

Practice and Communicate

  **Actividad 8** Standards: 1.1, 1.3 **Presentation EXPRESS** ANSWERS

Resources: Answers on Transparencies

Focus: Writing and speaking about others' career plans

Suggestions: Students may not know what people in the careers pictured like to do. Discuss what is involved in the careers before they begin. Practice the model by having students identify classmates who would be likely to pursue a career as an engineer. Discourage negative comments about any of the jobs or about classmates.

Answers will vary, but will include:

1. agricultor(a)
2. arquitecto(a)
3. escritor(a)
4. ingeniero(a)
5. secretario(a)
6. gerente

Extension: Have students repeat the activity, this time telling the *least* likely careers for people they know and why.

  Actividad 9 Standards: 1.1, 1.3

Focus: Identifying categories of careers in the context of a game

Suggestions: Students may limit themselves to the careers they've learned in this chapter. Suggest that they look in previous chapters for other careers *(bombero, entrenador, director, etc.)*. To be sure all students participate, have each student write at least two careers on flashcards. During the game, have the students hold up and state the careers on their cards.

Answers will vary.

 **Fondo cultural** Standards: 1.2, 2.1, 2.2, 4.2

■◆◇◆■◆◇■◆◇◆■◇◆■◆◇■

Suggestions: Have students form groups. Assign each group a sentence from the reading to write a comprehension question about on the board. Answer the questions as a class.

Answers will vary.

  Actividad 8 **Escribir/Hablar**

Las profesiones de mis amigos

Piensa en las personas a quienes conoces. ¿Qué profesión tendrán ellos en el futuro?

1 Para cada dibujo, escribe la profesión de la persona. Luego escribe el nombre de una persona a quien conoces que puede tener esta profesión en el futuro.

2 Trabaja con otro(a) estudiante. Usen lo que escribieron y hablen sobre quiénes tendrán estas profesiones en el futuro.

Modelo
A —¿Quién será *ingeniero* algún día?
B —*Mi primo Alejandro* será *ingeniero*. Le gusta mucho estudiar *matemáticas*.

1. 　2. 　3.

4. 　5. 　6.

   **Actividad 9** ♻ **Escribir/Hablar**

Juego

1 Tu profesor(a) va a dividir a la clase en grupos de cuatro o cinco estudiantes. Va a decir una categoría de trabajo y cada grupo va a escribir diferentes carreras y profesiones para esta categoría.

2 Cuando tu profesor(a) indica que no hay más tiempo, un grupo lee su lista en voz alta. El grupo recibe un punto por cada carrera o profesión que tiene y que otro grupo no tiene. Luego otro grupo lee las carreras o profesiones que no leyó el primer grupo. Van a seguir hasta no tener más carreras o profesiones diferentes.

3 Luego el (la) profesor(a) les da otra categoría. El grupo con más puntos al final gana. Van a usar las listas de carreras y profesiones en la Actividad 10.

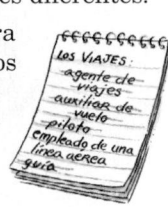
LOS VIAJES:
- agente de viajes
- auxiliar de vuelo
- piloto
- empleado de una línea aérea
- guía

Fondo cultural ■◆◇◆■◆◇◆■◆

La educación básica en los países hispanohablantes incluye *(includes)* la educación preescolar, la primaria y la secundaria. Todos los jóvenes tienen que completarla; es decir, es obligatoria. La educación secundaria dura tres años (de los 13 a los 15 años). Luego sigue el bachillerato y los estudios medios profesionales. En la secundaria, muchos jóvenes aprenden un oficio *(trade)* relacionado con los servicios o la educación tecnológica.

• ¿Te parece similar o diferente la educación básica en los países hispanohablantes a cómo es en los Estados Unidos?

Differentiated Instruction
Solutions for All Learners

Advanced Learners
Have students establish a "sister school" relationship with a school in a Spanish-speaking country. Have them create a video letter about their school to send to the sister school.

Students with Learning Difficulties
For *Actividad 10*, help students prepare to write and discuss their classified ads by providing a graphic organizer. Label the first column *Carrera,* the second column *Requisitos,* and the last column *Beneficios.*

 **Hablar/Escribir/Escuchar**

Se busca . . .

Usa las listas de carreras y profesiones de la Actividad 9 para crear anuncios clasificados de un periódico.

1 Trabaja con otro(a) estudiante y escriban tres anuncios. Cada anuncio debe indicar el trabajo, describir lo que necesita hacer o saber la persona e indicar un beneficio del trabajo.

2 Lean los anuncios clasificados a otro grupo, sin decir el trabajo que se busca. El otro grupo tiene que escuchar y decirles a Uds. la persona que se busca, según la descripción.

Modelo

Se busca secretario bilingüe. Debe tener experiencia trabajando en una oficina. Es necesario que hable inglés y español y que sepa usar la computadora. No hay que trabajar los fines de semana.

 Escribir/Hablar

Y tú, ¿qué dices?

1. Describe a un adulto a quien conoces bien. ¿Qué profesión tiene? ¿Se preparó para su carrera en la universidad? ¿En una escuela técnica? ¿Qué programa de estudios siguió?

2. ¿Qué vas a hacer después de graduarte del colegio? ¿Piensas asistir a la universidad o a una escuela técnica, o comenzar a trabajar?

3. ¿Te gustaría seguir una carrera militar? ¿Crees que hay beneficios de una carrera militar? ¿Cuáles son?

4. ¿Te interesa ser dueño(a) de tu propio negocio algún día? ¿Por qué?

Pronunciación

Diéresis

As you have seen, when *gu* is used before *e* and *i*, the *u* is silent. To indicate that the *u* is pronounced, it is written with a *diéresis* (*ü*). Listen to and say the following sentences:

Ramón **Gue**vara es bilin**güe**. Quiere se**gui**r una carrera como **guí**a para los turistas extranjeros.

¡Compruébalo! Listen to the sentences as they are read. Complete the spelling of the words by adding *güe* or *güi*. ¡Ojo! In one case, you will also have to add a written accent mark to the *e* or *i*.

1. Un ave *(bird)* graciosa de la Antártida es el pin___no.
2. Si hablas sólo un idioma, eres monolin___.
3. El estudio de lenguaje *(language)* se llama la lin___stica.

¡Trabalenguas!

Gárgaras
Gla-gle-gli-glo-glu-güe-güi,
¡qué difícil es así!
Güi, güe, glu, glo, gli, gle, gla,
¡qué trabajo igual me da!

Practice and Communicate 9A

Standards: 1.2, 1.3

Actividad 10

Focus: Write and discuss "help wanted" ads

Recycle: Subjunctive

Suggestions: To ensure that students write ads for a variety of jobs, write careers on slips of paper and have each student draw three slips. Point out that **sepa** is an irregular subjunctive form of **saber.**

Answers will vary.

Extension: Have students write interview questions for the job applicants who respond to the ads.

 Standards: 1.1, 1.3

Actividad 11

Focus: Writing and speaking about career choices

Suggestions: Assign *Actividad* 11 as homework to give students time to write thoughtful responses to the questions. Then have them discuss their answers with you in one-on-one interviews.

Students who are not sure what they would like to do after high school may make up an answer or write about careers they know they would *not* like to pursue.

Answers will vary.

Pronunciación Presentation EXPRESS AUDIO

Core Instruction

Standards: 1.2

Resources: Audio Program: Track 7; Answers on Transparencies

Suggestions: Point out that the **diéresis** does not change a word's stress pattern.

Answers:
1. pingüino   2. monolingüe   3. lingüística

Additional Resources

• WAV Wbk.: Audio Act. 6, p. 170
• Teacher's Resource Book: Audio Script, pp. 232–233, Communicative Activity BLM, pp. 238–239
• Audio Program: Track 9

 Assessment

• Prueba 9A-2: Vocab. Production, pp. 231–232

 Enrich Your Teaching

Resources for All Teachers

Culture Note

After completing their secondary education, students in Spain who wish to go on to a university must pass the *Selectividad,* a very demanding written test. To prepare students for the *Selectividad,* secondary schools in Spain provide rigorous training in many different subjects, including economics, philosophy, calculus, and history.

Internet Search

Keywords:

Selectividad + España

9A Practice and Communicate

Gramática

Presentation EXPRESS
GRAMMAR

Core Instruction

⊗ *Standards:* 4.1

Resources: Voc.and Gram. Transparency 162; Teacher's Resource Book: Video Script, p. 235; Video Program: Cap. 9A

Suggestions: Review the *¿Recuerdas?*. Present the future tense by describing a friend who has big dreams for the future. The *GramActiva* Video can be used for initial presentation or as reinforcement.

Bellringer Review

Have students complete these sentences logically using the words from this word bank.

    pintar   anunciar   reparar

1. *Mañana el artista va a ___ la escena del océano.*
2. *Mañana el juez va a ___ una decisión muy importante.*
3. *Mañana el mecánico va a ___ el carro de mi papá.*

  Standards: 1.2

Presentation EXPRESS
AUDIO

Resources: Teacher's Resource Book: Audio Script, p. 233; Audio Program: Track 10; Answers on Transparencies

Focus: Listening and writing the future tense

Suggestions: Have students listen and write down the subject(s) and verb of each sentence. Have them listen again and write the complete sentences in the future tense.

Script and Answers:

1. Mi mejor amigo va a seguir una carrera militar. *(... seguirá)*
2. Tú vas a trabajar en una tienda de equipo deportivo para ganar dinero. *(Trabajarás)*
3. Dos de mis amigos van a asistir a una escuela técnica. *(... asistirán)*
4. Vamos a pasar tiempo con nuestros amigos antes de salir para la universidad. *(Pasaremos)*
5. Varios atletas van a participar en una liga de béisbol de verano. *(... participarán)*
6. Mi amiga y yo vamos a aprender a hacer surf de vela. *(... aprenderemos)*

Common Errors: Students may add an accent mark to **nosotros/nosotras** future forms. Remind them that the **nosotros/nosotras** future forms are the only ones that do *not* have an accent.

Extension: Have students write a sentence about their plans for after school today. Have them circulate around the room and ask each other about their plans.

Gramática

The future tense

Another way to talk about future events is to use the future tense. The future tense expresses what will happen. To form the future tense of regular *-ar, -er,* and *-ir* verbs, use the same set of endings for all verbs and add them to the infinitive.

-é	-emos
-ás	-éis
-á	-án

(yo)	trabajaré seré viviré	(nosotros) (nosotras)	trabajaremos seremos viviremos
(tú)	trabajarás serás vivirás	(vosotros) (vosotras)	trabajaréis seréis viviréis
Ud. (él) (ella)	trabajará será vivirá	Uds. (ellos) (ellas)	trabajarán serán vivirán

¿Recuerdas?

You already know two ways to talk about future events.

Using the present tense:

• Mañana **comenzamos** el trabajo.
Tomorrow we begin work.

Using *ir + a +* infinitive:

• El futuro **va a ser** mejor.
The future is going to be better.

Note that all forms have a written accent mark except *nosotros(as).*

Mañana **comenzaremos** el trabajo.
Tomorrow we will begin work.

El futuro **será** mejor.
The future will be better.

GramActiva VIDEO

Want more help with regular verbs in the future tense? Watch the **GramActiva** video.

Seré . . .

 jdd-0988
🔊 Escuchar/Escribir

Escucha y escribe

Un estudiante va a escribir un artículo para el periódico de su escuela sobre los planes de los estudiantes que se graduarán del colegio este año. Escucha los planes de sus compañeros y escríbelas según el modelo.

Modelo

Escuchas: Voy a ir de vacaciones a Costa Rica.
Escribes: *Iré de vacaciones a Costa Rica.*

Estrategia

Using memory cues
To learn the endings for the future tense, remember the present-tense forms of *haber (he, has, ha, hemos, habéis, han).* The sound of these is identical for all forms except *vosotros(as).*

460 cuatrocientos sesenta
Tema 9 • ¿Cómo será el futuro?

Differentiated Instruction
Solutions for All Learners

 Advanced Learners/Pre-AP*
Pre-AP*

Have students write fictional plans for a dream vacation. Using the future tense, have them review the things they will and will not do during the vacation. Read the plans aloud and have the class vote on the most exciting ideas.

Students with Learning Difficulties

Break down the steps for *Actividad 12.* First have students write the dictated sentences verbatim. Then have them underline the verb phrase in each sentence. Finally, have them rewrite the sentence, replacing the underlined words with the correct form of the verb in the future tense.

 **Actividad 13** **Escribir/Hablar** _____

Haciendo deportes en las playas de Miami

¿Y ustedes?

En la Actividad 12 Uds. escucharon los planes de unos estudiantes después de terminar el año escolar. Ahora van a hablar sobre los planes de otras personas para el verano.

1 Escribe frases sobre qué van a hacer estas personas.

> **Modelo**
>
> mi profesor(a) de . . .
> *Mi profesora de matemáticas tomará cursos en la universidad.*

1. yo
2. mis amigos(as) y yo
3. muchos estudiantes
4. mi mejor amigo(a)

2 Trabaja con otro(a) estudiante. Comparen sus ideas para el verano.

> **Modelo**
>
> A —*Mi profesora de matemáticas tomará cursos en la universidad.*
> B —*¿De veras? Mi profesor de español viajará por América Central.*

 Standards: 1.1, 1.3

Focus: Writing about and discussing future plans

Suggestions: Encourage students to come up with imaginative plans for the people in the activity if they do not know their real plans.

Answers will vary.

 Actividad 14 **Leer/Escribir** _____

Las profesiones del futuro

Lee el artículo del periódico y escribe qué van a hacer las personas en las profesiones del futuro.

> **Modelo**
>
> trabajar
> *Los técnicos médicos trabajarán en consultorios y hospitales.*

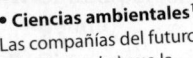

• **Ciencias ambientales**[1] Las compañías del futuro __1.__ *(entender)* que la planificación[2] y la conservación de nuestro planeta __2.__ *(ser)* esenciales.

• **Experto en turismo** La gran demanda de turismo pronto __3.__ *(resultar)* que no exista ninguna parte del planeta sin ser visitada. Los expertos en turismo __4.__ *(ayudar)* a los clientes a escoger las vacaciones apropiadas.

• **Ingeniero de robots** Los robots __5.__ *(estar)* en nuestras casas y lugares de trabajo con más frecuencia. Por eso (nosotros) __6.__ *(necesitar)* miles de diseñadores y técnicos para crear y reparar las máquinas.[3]

• **Médico** Los ancianos __7.__ *(visitar)* a sus médicos con más frecuencia. Y los científicos __8.__ *(tratar)* de encontrar nuevas curas para las enfermedades que existen hoy en día.

[1]environmental [2]planning [3]machines

 Standards: 1.2  Presentation EXPRESS ANSWERS

Resources: Answers on Transparencies

Focus: Reading and writing about careers of the future

Suggestions: Have volunteers read each sentence and supply the verb in the future tense.

Answers:

1. entenderán	4. ayudarán	7. visitarán
2. serán	5. estarán	8. tratarán
3. resultará	6. necesitaremos	

 Actividad 15 **Escribir/Hablar** _____

Y tú, ¿qué dices?

1. En tu opinión, de los cuatro grupos de profesiones mencionados en el artículo, ¿cuál será más importante? ¿Por qué?

2. Escoge uno de los cuatro grupos y escribe tres frases diciendo lo que las personas van a hacer en el futuro en estas carreras.

3. ¿Qué serás tú algún día? ¿Crees que tu profesión será tan importante en el futuro como es ahora? ¿Por qué?

Más práctica

- Practice Workbook, p. 177: 9A-5
- WAV Wbk.: Writing, p. 173
- Guided Practice: Grammar Acts., pp. 321–322
- *Real.* para hispanohablantes, pp. 334–337

Go Online PHSchool.com
For: Future Tense
Web Code: jdd-0904

 Standards: 1.1, 1.3

Focus: Writing and talking about professions

Suggestions: Help students answer item 1 by having them first decide what makes a career important.

Answers will vary.

Extension: Have students write a sentence about another aspect of their future (where they will live, will they be married, will they have children).

Additional Resources

- WAV Wbk.: Audio Act. 7, p. 170
- Teacher's Resource Book: Audio Script, p. 233
- Audio Program: Track 11

✓ Assessment

- *ExamView* QuickTake Presenter Quiz on PresEXPRESS
- Prueba 9A-3: The future tense, p. 233

 Enrich Your Teaching
Resources for All Teachers

Culture Note

Education and training have always been assets in obtaining a job, but more and more they are becoming part of the job itself. In nearly all jobs, workers are required to update and sometimes replace their skills multiple times, as their jobs change to meet the demands of an increasingly global, diverse, and technology-driven world.

Teacher-to-Teacher

Have students write a *Back to the Future*–style skit in which they travel back to the 1950s and tell people about technological developments such as personal computers, cell phones, and CDs.

9A Practice and Communicate

Actividad 24 · *Standards:* 1.1, 1.3, 3.1

Focus: Using the future tense to conduct and report research; cross-curricular connection to math and statistics

Suggestions: To be sure students progress smoothly through the steps of the activity, provide a checklist of the steps for each group. Have students raise their hands for you to check their work when they have finished each step.

Suggest that each student do an individual pie chart if you think that some students will allow others in their group to do all the work. Encourage students to use spreadsheet and presentation software to make professional-quality charts.

Answers will vary.

Extension: Have each student make a small cutout doll of themselves in their future profession and attach it to the appropriate category on the pie chart.

Fondo cultural · *Standards:* 1.2, 2.1, 2.2, 4.2

■◆◇■◆◇■■◇◆◇■◇◆◇■■◆◇■■

Suggestions: Bring materials from universities, community colleges, and technical schools to class and set up learning stations around the room. Have small groups of students circulate from station to station to get information to answer the question.

Answers will vary.

Theme Project

Students can perform Step 2 at this point. Be sure they understand your corrections and suggestions. (For more information, see p. 448-a.)

Additional Resources

- WAV Wbk.: Audio Act. 8–9, p. 171
- Teacher's Resource Book: Audio Script, pp. 233–234, Communicative Activity BLM, pp. 240–241
- Audio Program: Tracks 12–13

Actividad 24   Hablar/Pensar/Escribir

¿Qué harás en el futuro?

¿Qué profesión tendrás en el futuro? Haz una encuesta en la clase y suma los resultados para determinar cuáles son las profesiones más populares.

Conexiones | **Las matemáticas**

1 Trabaja con un grupo de cuatro o cinco personas. Hagan una tabla con las profesiones indicadas. Indiquen el número de estudiantes del grupo que trabajará en cada profesión.

2 Escriban una o dos frases sobre la tabla y compartan la información con la clase.

> **Modelo**
> *Dos personas de nuestro grupo trabajarán en el mundo de la tecnología . . . y una persona es indecisa* (undecided).

3 Reúnan las tablas de la clase y sumen entre todos el número de estudiantes que trabajará en cada profesión.

4 Hagan entre todos una gráfica circular *(pie chart)* para indicar el porcentaje *(percentage)* de estudiantes que trabajará en cada profesión. Expliquen la gráfica circular.

> **Modelo**
> *El 33 por ciento de los estudiantes en la clase seguirán una carrera en la tecnología. Asistirán a la universidad o a una escuela técnica para ser ingenieros o diseñadores.*

Profesiones	Número de estudiantes
Tecnología	✓✓
Técnica/Mecánica	
Artes	✓
Ciencias	
Negocios	✓
Derecho	
Música/Drama	
Servicio público	
Política	
Indecisos/Otros	✓

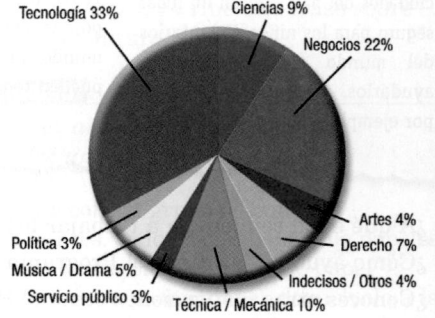

Fondo cultural

Los centros de educación superior en América Latina y España están muy diversificados. Después de graduarse del colegio, los estudiantes pueden continuar sus estudios en la universidad para graduarse como abogados, arquitectos, ingenieros o médicos. Los estudiantes que desean ser maestros pueden continuar sus estudios en las Escuelas Normales o de Magisterio y los que quieren ser técnicos en computación o enfermería asisten a las Escuelas Politécnicas. Los que quieren ser artistas pueden estudiar en los conservatorios y las escuelas de drama.

- Si quieres continuar los estudios después de graduarte del colegio, ¿qué opciones hay en la región donde vives?

Differentiated Instruction
Solutions for All Learners

Heritage Language Learners
Have students write a formal letter requesting information from a university in a Spanish-speaking country. They should specify what area of study they hope to pursue, and inquire about what courses will be offered for that specialty. Encourage them to use the future tense. Share with them models of formal letter writing in Spanish.

Advanced Learners
Have students use the future tense to write a paragraph predicting which career will disappear in the future. They should include supporting details for why they believe this profession will not be needed. Students could use humor or a science-fiction approach to the subject.

Actividad 25 — Escribir/Hablar

En la exposición de carreras

Imaginen que Uds. asisten a la exposición de carreras.

1 Con otro(a) estudiante, escriban preguntas que los jóvenes pueden hacerles a los adultos sobre la universidad o las escuelas técnicas, las carreras, el salario y otra información.

Modelo

¿Tendremos que asistir a la universidad si queremos seguir una carrera en la música?

2 Formen un grupo de cuatro estudiantes. Una pareja de los jóvenes hace las preguntas y los adultos tienen que contestarlas. Después cambien papeles.

Una exposición de carreras en una escuela secundaria

Actividad 26 — Escribir/Hablar

Y tú, ¿qué dices?

1. ¿Qué clases tienes ahora? ¿Crees que estudiarás estas materias en la universidad? ¿Por qué?

2. ¿Has pensado en qué profesión tendrás en el futuro? ¿Cómo será? ¿Podrás ganar un buen salario? ¿Qué otros beneficios habrá?

3. ¿Qué cosas hay hoy en día que no habrá en el futuro? ¿Qué cosas habrá que no existen ahora?

El español en la comunidad

Ya sabes la importancia de poder comunicarse en español en una variedad de trabajos y profesiones. En muchísimas comunidades en los Estados Unidos, se necesitan empleados bilingües: que hablen inglés y español, u otros idiomas e inglés.

• ¿En qué trabajos o profesiones en tu comunidad es necesario ser bilingüe? ¿Qué idiomas se hablan en tu comunidad?

Más práctica

• Practice Workbook, pp. 178–179; 9A-6, 9A-7
• WAV Wbk.: Writing, p. 174
• Guided Practice: Grammar Acts., pp. 323–324
• *Real* para hispanohablantes, pp. 338–341

Go Online
PHSchool.com
For: Future Irreg. Verbs
Web Code: jdd-0905

Enrich Your Teaching
Resources for All Teachers

Culture Note

Bilingualism and multilingualism, although still somewhat remarkable in the U.S., have been the norm in many countries where children are encouraged to learn a second language, usually English. Encourage students to reflect on how knowing another language may have an impact on their future.

Teacher-to-Teacher

Have students write a letter to themselves describing their future. Have students seal their letters in an envelope and write "Do not open until *(today's date, five years in the future)*." Instruct them to keep the letter in a safe place until that date when they can open it and see if their predictions came true.

Practice and Communicate

 9A

Actividad 25   *Standards:* 1.1, 1.3   Pre-AP*

Focus: Using the future tense to get information

Suggestions: Describe to students some of the differences between high school and college to help them think of ideas for questions. Remind them to ask questions about both technical schools and universities. You may wish to invite former students to class to play the adults in Step 2 and to discuss college life or the working world.

Answers will vary.

Actividad 26   *Standards:* 1.1, 1.3

Focus: Discussing the future

Suggestions: For item 1, if students do not plan to attend a university, ask them to write whether they believe the classes they take now will help them in whatever work they plan to do in the future.

For item 2, explain what is meant by "benefits" (health insurance, paid vacation and sick time, bonuses, retirement plans, employee discounts).

Answers will vary.

Extension: Have students create a poster depicting the future as they described it in item 3.

El español en la comunidad

Core Instruction

 Standards: 1.2, 5.1

Suggestions: Encourage students to think of professions in which people come in contact with members of the Spanish-speaking community. Assign the second question as homework to give students a chance to research the languages spoken in your community.

✓ **Assessment**

• **ExamView** Quiz on PresEXPRESS
• Prueba 9A-3: The future tense, p. 233

467

Core Instruction

Focus: Reading comprehension of an article about a career center

Suggestions:

Pre-reading: Create **un expediente personal** for the class, using the form shown in the reading and adding **características personales** y **carreras interesantes.** Have students complete the form and discuss their answers before reading.

Reading: As you read the brochure with students, focus on heads and subheads, stopping to ask volunteers: *¿Qué información vamos a encontrar?*

Post-reading: Ask students to list all new vocabulary words from the reading, and have them make a final draft of their **expedientes personales.**

Bellringer Review

Working in pairs, have studnets write and share with their partner three extracurricular activities in which they participate or have an interest.

Additional Resources

Student Resource: Guided Practice: Lectura, p. 325

¡Adelante!

Lectura

¿Qué vas a hacer después de graduarte?
Visita un centro de carreras para decidir.

Objectives

- **Read about careers**
- **Make a work of folk art**
- **Give a presentation about your future career plans**

Estrategia

Using heads and subheads
You can quickly learn what an article or brochure is about by reading the heads and subheads. Quickly read the heads in the following brochure to find out what information is provided.

¡Bienvenidos al Centro de Carreras!

El Centro de Carreras es un servicio de información para los colegios de nuestro estado. Creemos que todas las personas que desean ir a la universidad deben tener la oportunidad de hacerlo, y podemos ayudarles a alcanzar este objetivo.

En nuestro centro, pueden . . .

* buscar carreras
* buscar y conectar con más de 100 universidades
* crear y asegurar un expediente[1] privado para mantenerse informado(a) de las notas y actividades
* encontrar toda la información necesaria para financiar los estudios
* buscar y solicitar becas,[2] ayuda financiera y préstamos[3]
* informarse sobre el plan de ahorros[4] para la universidad
* reunirse con consejeros[5] que hablan español

El expediente personal te permite crear una carpeta con toda tu información académica del colegio. Cuando termines una clase y tengas una nota, escribe la información en tu expediente. El expediente te ayudará cuando llenes solicitudes[6] para las universidades.

```
Nombre: _____

Dirección: _____

Clases y Notas

Grado:

    9 _____

   10 _____

   11 _____

   12 _____

Intereses extracurriculares: _____

_____

_____

Universidades que me interesan: _____

_____

_____
```

[1]record [2]scholarships [3]loans [4]savings [5]counselors [6]fill out applications

---

Differentiated Instruction
Solutions for All Learners

Multiple Intelligences

Logical/Mathematical: Before taking the quiz in the *Lectura,* have students poll classmates to find out what careers they want to pursue. Have them display their findings in a graph. After students have completed the quiz, have them repeat the survey of the results and create another graph. Ask them to compare the two graphs.

Multiple Intelligences

Interpersonal/Social: Have students interview a counselor at your school about determining career choices based on personal interests. Ask students to obtain an interest inventory from the counselor, and encourage them to redesign it as a **prueba de aptitud** to give to the class.

Una prueba de aptitud puede ayudarte a encontrar la mejor profesión para ti. Lo primero que debes hacer es determinar tu personalidad. Lee las siguientes descripciones. ¿Cuál te describe?

✱ **Personalidad**

a. realista
b. investigadora
c. artística
d. sociable
e. emprendedora[7]
f. analítica

✱ **Te gusta ...**

a. trabajar con animales, máquinas[8] y herramientas.[9]
b. estudiar y resolver problemas de ciencias o de matemáticas.
c. participar en actividades creativas como el arte, el teatro y la música.
d. hacer cosas con otras personas.
e. ser el líder.
f. trabajar con números y máquinas de manera ordenada.

✱ **Prefieres ...**

a. cosas prácticas que se pueden tocar y ver.
b. las ciencias.
c. actividades creativas.
d. enseñar o ayudar a otras personas.
e. la política y los negocios.
f. el éxito en los negocios.

✱ **Evitas[10] ...**

a. situaciones sociales.
b. ser el líder.
c. actividades repetitivas.
d. las máquinas, los animales y las herramientas.
e. actividades científicas.
f. actividades desordenadas.

Profesiones

Para saber la carrera más relacionada a tus gustos e intereses, revisa tus respuestas. Haz la suma para ver qué letra marcaste más y compara este resultado con la siguiente información. Si marcaste dos letras diferentes o más, puede ser que tengas aptitud para varias carreras.

✱ Si marcaste más la letra *a*, debes ser ingeniero(a) o arquitecto(a).
✱ Si marcaste más la letra *b*, debes ser científico(a) o médico(a).
✱ Si marcaste más la letra *c*, debes ser actor o actriz o diseñador(a) de ropa.
✱ Si marcaste más la letra *d*, debes ser profesor(a) o enfermero(a).
✱ Si marcaste más la letra *e*, debes ser vendedor(a) o abogado(a).
✱ Si marcaste más la letra *f*, debes ser contador(a) o cajero(a).

[7]enterprising [8]machines [9]tools [10]You avoid

¿Comprendiste?

1. ¿Qué es un centro de carreras? ¿Qué servicios ofrece?
2. ¿Qué información debes incluir en tu expediente personal?
3. ¿Para qué sirve una prueba de aptitud?

Más práctica

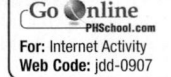
- WAV Wbk.: Writing, p. 175
- Guided Practice: *Lectura*, p. 325
- *Real.* para hispanohablantes, pp. 342-343

Go Online PHSchool.com
For: Internet Activity
Web Code: jdd-0907

Y tú, ¿qué dices?

1. ¿Crees que una visita a un centro de carreras sería útil *(would be useful)* para ti? ¿Por qué?
2. ¿Cuál es tu profesión ideal según la prueba? ¿Crees que tiene razón la prueba? Si no, ¿qué te gustaría cambiar para mejorarla?

¿Comprendiste? Presentation EXPRESS ANSWERS

Standards: 1.2

Resources: Answers on Transparencies
Focus: Verifying reading comprehension
Suggestions: Ask students to exchange their final drafts of the *expedientes personales.* Have the class guess who wrote each summary, based on the answers.

Answers:
1. Es un servicio de información sobre carreras. Se puede buscar carreras, universidades, becas, ayuda financiera y préstamos. También se puede crear un expediente privado y reunirse con consejeros que hablan español.
2. Debo incluir nombre, dirección, clases y notas, grado, intereses extracurriculares y universidades que me interesan.
3. Una prueba de aptitud puede ayudarte a encontrar la mejor profesión para ti.

 Pre-AP* Support

- **Activity:** Working in pairs, have students create a *Memoria* game using Clip Art for professions to match with statements about aptitudes, personality traits, preferences, etc., as mentioned in *Una prueba de aptitud* found on this page. Have students exchange games and play.
- *Pre-AP* Resource Book:* Comprehensive guide to Pre-AP* reading skill development, pp. 18–24

Y tú, ¿qué dices?
Standards: 1.2, 1.3

Suggestions: Have students review their answers to item 1 of the *¿Comprendiste?* to help them answer item 1 of *Y tú, ¿qué dices?* You may prefer to handle item 2 as a class or to use it with advanced learners only.
Answers will vary.

Enrich Your Teaching
Resources for All Teachers

Culture Note
Fulbright Scholarships are administered by the U.S. Department of State, and are often awarded to graduate students to encourage international study. There are many Fulbright Scholarships and programs, with different requirements for each. Any student applying for a Fulbright Scholarship needs strong recommendations from his or her teachers.

Internet Search
Keywords:

Fulbright, study abroad + (Spanish-speaking country)

For Further Reading
Student Resources: Realidades para hispanohablantes: Lectura 2, pp. 344–345; Lecturas para hispanohablantes 2: "El tío Lucho" (excerpt from *El pez en el agua*), pp. 117–118, "Paloma Herrera: Alas en Los pies," pp. 122–124

469

La cultura en vivo
Core Instruction

Standards: 1.2, 2.2, 3.1

Resources: Fine Art Transparencies with Teacher's Guide, p. 68

Focus: Creating folk art

Suggestions: Before you do the activity, have students bring in small, simple objects from their everyday lives to include in their works of art. These items may be from nature, such as leaves, seeds, sticks, tree bark, pebbles or sand, or manufactured objects such as buttons, keys, jewelry, erasers, pencils, game pieces, and so on. Emphasize that the items should be simple and should not be valuable or irreplaceable. You might also provide a small selection yourself.

On the day you do the activity, begin by having students read the paragraph. Ask students to name any art they have seen that they think is folk art. Point out that some wall paintings on buildings, often in cities, depict everyday scenes that could be called folk art. Some works of folk art incorporate everyday objects that are attached to them. These objects are relevant to the theme depicted.

Brainstorm some appropriate ideas to depict in a work of folk art. List these on the board so students can refer to them as they think of their own topic.

Review the instructions with the class, making sure students complete Step 4 before beginning their actual piece of work. Remind students to plan a work that they can successfully complete. Distribute materials to the class. You may need glue or yarn for attaching objects.

Theme Project

Students can perform Step 3 at this point. (For more information, see p. 448-a.)

Additional Resources

Student Resource: Realidades para hispanohablantes, p. 346

La cultura en vivo

Los artistas *naif*

Hay un grupo de artistas en los países hispanohablantes que producen arte de origen campesino[1]. Este estilo se conoce como arte *naif*, arte ingenuo o arte campesino. Generalmente los artistas *naif* no tienen una educación artística académica. Sus obras están relacionadas con escenas de la vida rural y los trabajos del campo. Las imágenes son sencillas, espontáneas y llenas de fantasía. Algunas veces los artistas y artesanos añaden los materiales que usan en su trabajo o también productos de la naturaleza, como flores secas, piedras, conchas[2] y pedazos de madera[3].

"Targelia, Christmas Eve" (1990), Julio Toaquiza
Photo courtesy of the Art Archive / Picture Desk, Kobal Collection.

Objetivo

Hacer una pintura[4] imitando el estilo de los artistas *naif*.

Materiales

Busca materiales sencillos, objetos de la naturaleza o cosas que usas en tus actividades diarias. Quizás necesites pintura y pincel[5].

Instrucciones

1 Estudia los cuadros de las artesanías en esta página. Piensa en sus características.

2 Escoge una escena que quieres pintar.

3 ¡Recuerda! Los artistas naif usan ideas sencillas.

4 Antes de empezar el trabajo, haz un dibujo del proyecto.

Opciones

Puedes mostrar el trabajo en clase y explicar qué características del arte *naif* has usado, qué representa tu trabajo y por qué escogiste ese tema.

"Xochimilco, San Miguel de Allende, Guanajuato, México", E. Louis

[1]peasant   [2]shells   [3]wood   [4]painting   [5]paintbrush

Differentiated Instruction
Solutions for All Learners

Advanced Learners

Have students research one of the artists whose work is shown here. Have students look for other works by the same artist and prepare a report, including information on where the works are displayed and the subjects depicted.

Students with Learning Difficulties

Rather than writing notes for their oral presentation, some students would benefit from writing out their entire paragraph. Rehearsing by reading the paragraph numerous times will aid memorization. It may also be helpful to have students exchange paragraphs to check for content and grammar errors.

Presentación oral

Mi vida hoy y en el futuro

Task
It is increasingly common for people to have more than one job in a lifetime. Prepare a presentation in which you talk about the jobs you expect to have in the future, based on your current hobbies and pursuits.

❶ Prepare Think about what your life is like today. What are your favorite subjects in school? What do you do for fun? Which jobs appeal to you? Then think about how these things might influence your future job choices. Make a chart to organize the things you want to include in your presentation.

	Ahora	En el futuro
cursos favoritos	las matemáticas y el arte	diseñadora en una escuela técnica
diversiones	trabajo en la computadora	crearé diseños nuevos

Estrategia

Using charts
Create a chart to help you think through the key information you want to talk about. This will help you speak more effectively.

❷ Practice Go through your presentation several times. You can use your notes in practice, but not when you present. Try to:

- provide as much information as you can
- use complete sentences
- speak clearly

Modelo
Ahora mis cursos favoritos en la escuela son las matemáticas y el arte. Estudiaré para ser diseñadora en una escuela técnica.

❸ Present Tell the audience about your interests today and how they will impact your job choices in the future.

❹ Evaluation Your teacher may give you a rubric for how the presentation will be graded. You will probably be graded on:

- how complete your preparation was
- how much information you communicated
- how easy it was to understand you

cuatrocientos setenta y uno **471**
Capítulo 9A

Presentación oral
Core Instruction

 Standards: 1.3, 3.1

Focus: Communicating about expected future jobs

Suggestions: Help students brainstorm some possible fields or careers based on preferences and performances in different subjects. Some suggestions are listed below.

Math: engineer, accountant, financial services, computer programmer

Science: research, biochemistry, medicine, physical therapy

English: newspaper reporter, magazine editor

Physical Education: personal trainer, coach

Encourage students to add as many ideas as possible to this list. Perhaps a school guidance counselor can lend you resources that will help with this activity, such as college handbooks or books that focus on careers and vocations. Such resources are often available in Spanish.

Have students discuss their ideas with a partner. Suggest that they include more than one current interest, preferred class subject, or hobby in their presentation.

 Pre-AP* Support

- *Pre-AP* Resource Book:* Comprehensive guide to Pre-AP* speaking skill development, pp. 36–46

Portfolio

Record students' oral presentations on cassette or videotape to include in their portfolios.

Additional Resources

Student Resource: Realidades para hispanohablantes, p. 347; Guided Practice: Presentación oral, p. 326

✓ **Assessment**
- Assessment Program: Rubrics, p. T32

Provide students with copies of the rubric that you will use for assessment before they begin the task. Be sure they understand the levels of performance and what is expected of them. Model a presentation for them. After assessing the presentations, give individual students feedback on how they might improve their performance.

Enrich Your Teaching
Resources for All Teachers

RUBRIC	Score 1	Score 3	Score 5
How complete your preparation is	You provide the Information but not the chart.	You provide the information but the chart is only partially completed.	You provide the information and a completed chart.
Amount of information communicated	You include one of the following: classes, leisure activities, potential jobs.	You include two of the following: classes, leisure activities, potential jobs.	You include all of the following: classes, leisure activities, potential jobs.
How easily you are understood	You are difficult to understand and make many grammatical errors.	You are fairly easy to understand and make occasional grammatical errors.	You are easy to understand and make very few grammatical errors.

471

Review Activities

To talk about professions in science and technology: Have groups of students take turns describing what each professional does. The others in the group must guess the name of that profession.

To talk about professions in business: Have groups of students create and perform skits about a mail carrier who must deliver mail to an office where all of the employees are named either Juan Sánchez or Juanita Sánchez. One student plays the office manager and must explain who each person is by stating their profession.

To talk about professions in the arts: Say the names of well-known people in the arts and have students tell you whether they are artists, writers, or painters.

To talk about professions in law and politics and about the future: Have students write game show-style clues about words to talk about professions in law and politics and about the future. Use their clues to quiz the entire class.

Portfolio

Invite students to review the activities they completed in this chapter, including written reports, posters or other visuals, tapes of oral presentations, or other projects. Have them select one or two items that they feel best demonstrate their achievements in Spanish to include in their portfolios. Have them include this with the Chapter Checklist and Self-Assessment Worksheet.

Additional Resources

Student Resources: Realidades para hispanohablantes, p. 348

 **MindPoint QUIZSHOW CD-ROM**

PuzzleView Web Code: jdd-0908

Teacher Resources:
- Teacher's Resource Book: Situation Cards, p. 242, Clip Art, pp. 244–248
- Assessment Program: Chapter Checklist and Self-Assessment Worksheet, pp. T56–T57

Repaso del capítulo

Vocabulario y gramática jdd-0989 🔊

Chapter Review

To prepare for the test, check to see if you . . .
- know the new vocabulary and grammar
- can perform the tasks on p. 473

to talk about professions in science and technology

el agricultor, la agricultora	farmer
el arquitecto, la arquitecta	architect
el científico, la científica	scientist
el diseñador, la diseñadora	designer
el ingeniero, la ingeniera	engineer
el mecánico, la mecánica	mechanic
el técnico, la técnica	technician
el veterinario, la veterinaria	veterinarian

to talk about professions in business

el cartero, la cartera	mail carrier
el contador, la contadora	accountant
el dueño, la dueña	owner
el / la gerente	manager
el hombre de negocios	businessman
la mujer de negocios	businesswoman
los negocios	business
el secretario, la secretaria	secretary

to talk about professions in the arts

las artes	the arts
el / la artista	artist
el escritor, la escritora	writer
el pintor, la pintora	painter

For *Vocabulario adicional,* see pp. 498–499.

to talk about professions in law and politics

el abogado, la abogada	lawyer
el derecho	*(study of)* law
el juez, la jueza, *pl.* los jueces	judge
la ley	law
la política	politics
el político, la política	politician

to talk about the future

algún día	some day
los beneficios	benefits
bilingüe	bilingual
la carrera	career
el colegio	high school
la escuela técnica	technical school
el futuro	future
ganarse la vida	to make a living
la graduación	graduation
graduarse $(u \rightarrow ú)$	to graduate
habrá	there will be
el idioma	language
militar	military
la oficina	office
la profesión, *pl.* las profesiones	profession
el programa de estudios	course of studies
el salario	salary
seguir $(e \rightarrow i)$ (una carrera)	to pursue (a career)
la universidad	university

the future tense: irregular verbs

haber	habr-
hacer	har-
poder	podr-
saber	sabr-
tener	tendr-

future-tense endings

-é	-emos
-ás	-éis
-á	-án

Differentiated Instruction
Solutions for All Learners

Multiple Intelligences

Visual/Spatial: Have students prepare illustrated flashcards for the professions and use them to review with their classmates.

Students with Learning Difficulties

Play a game: Have each student write a sentence including a profession and a future-tense verb. The sentence can be logical or illogical. *(El pintor pintará con las tortugas.)* Split the class into two groups. One group member reads his or her sentence aloud. The members of the other group raise one hand if the statement is logical and two hands if it is illogical, earning one point if correct.

Más práctica

- Practice Workbook: Puzzle, p. 180
- Practice Workbook: Organizer, p. 181

Go Online
PHSchool.com
For: Test Preparation
Web Code: jdd-0908

Preparación para el examen

On the exam you will be asked to . . .	Here are practice tasks similar to those you will find on the exam . . .	If you need review . . .
1 Escuchar Listen and understand as people talk about their future plans	At the Senior Send-off Assembly, some graduating seniors are asked what they will do after they graduate. Listen and identify: (a) what they will do next year; (b) what professions they will pursue; and (c) what they think their salary will be.	**pp. 452–455** *A primera vista* **p. 456** Actividad 5 **p. 459** Actividad 10 **p. 460** Actividad 12
2 Hablar Talk to incoming students about what high school will be like in your school	You volunteer to help incoming Spanish-speaking students enroll for classes. How would you describe what high school will be like for them? You could talk about: (a) classes; (b) extracurricular activities; and (c) advice on how to meet new people. Give as many details as you can.	**p. 458** Actividad 8 **p. 459** Actividad 11 **p. 464** Actividades 19–21 **p. 466** Actividad 24 **p. 467** Actividad 25 **p. 471** *Presentación oral*
3 Leer Read and understand notes sent to graduating seniors about their future	On the inside of Miguel's graduation card is a note from his mother. As you read it, determine what she predicts college will be like for him. *Querido hijo:* *El año que viene irás a la universidad. Tú y tus amigos comenzarán una vida nueva en la universidad y tendrán oportunidades de conocer a gente interesante. Tu padre y yo sabemos que sacarás buenas notas.* *Con mucho amor,* *Mamá*	**p. 461** Actividad 14 **p. 462** Actividad 16 **pp. 468–469** *Lectura*
4 Escribir Write about your future plans	As part of an application for a summer job, you are asked to write a short paragraph about your future career plans. For example, you might include: *Estudiaré en la universidad por seis años para prepararme para ser veterinario(a).*	**p. 458** Actividad 8 **p. 460** Actividad 12 **p. 461** Actividades 13–14 **p. 462** Actividad 16 **p. 463** Actividades 17–18 **p. 467** Actividades 25–26
5 Pensar Demonstrate an understanding of folk art from Spanish-speaking countries	A classmate is going on a trip to South America. Your teacher asks the student to bring back typical handicrafts from the countries she visits. Based on what you have learned in this chapter, what would you expect the student to bring back?	**p. 470** *La cultura en vivo*

jdd-0989

cuatrocientos setenta y tres **473**
Capítulo 9A

Differentiated Assessment
Solutions for All Learners

STUDENTS NEEDING EXTRA HELP
- **Alternate Assessment Program:** Examen del capítulo 9A
- **Audio Program CD 21:** Chap. 9A, Track 9

HERITAGE LEARNERS
- **Assessment Program: Realidades para hispanohablantes:** Examen del capítulo 9A
- **ExamView** Heritage Learner Test Bank

ADVANCED/PRE-AP*
- **ExamView** Pre-AP* Test Bank
- **Pre-AP* Resource Book,** pp. 128–131

Performance Tasks
Presentation EXPRESS
ANSWERS
Standards: 1.2, 1.3, 2.2

Student Resource: Realidades para hispanohablantes, p. 349

Teacher Resources: Teacher's Resource Book: Audio Script, p. 234: Audio Program: Track 15; Answers on Transparencies

1. Escuchar

Suggestions: Have students make a chart with the headings: *Next Year, Profession,* and *Salary.* Tell them they will hear the activity three times. Each time they should listen for information to complete just one of the columns.

Script:
1. Después de la graduación, iré a la universidad. Quiero seguir una carrera de arquitecto. Creo que el salario de un buen arquitecto es más de cien mil dólares.
2. No sé cuánto es el salario ni me importa, pero estudiaré para ser veterinaria en la universidad. Me gustan mucho los animales y quiero ayudarlos.

Answers:
1. (a) Irá a la universidad.
   (b) Seguirá una carrera de arquitecto.
   (c) Ganará más de cien mil dólares.
2. (a) Irá a la universidad.
   (b) Estudiará para ser veterinaria.
   (c) No sabe cuánto ganará.

2. Hablar

Suggestions: Pretend to be an incoming Spanish-speaking student. Ask questions to prompt students' responses.

Answers will vary.

3. Leer

Suggestions: Have students identify the predictions by writing a short letter as Miguel indicating whether the predictions came true or not.

Answers: Miguel's mother predicts that he will begin a new life, that he will have the opportunity to meet interesting people, and that he will get good grades.

4. Escribir

Suggestions: Bring in copies of an actual application for students to fill out to make the activity even more authentic.

Answers will vary.

5. Pensar

Suggestions: Have partners work together to brainstorm different kinds of folk art they have seen in this chapter or previous ones.

Answers will vary.

Assessment
- **ExamView** QuickTake Presenter Quiz on PresEXPRESS
- Assessment Program: Examen del capítulo
- **ExamView** test generator Test Bank: Tests A and B
- Audio Program CD 21: Chap. 9A, Track 9

Chapter Overview

A primera vista	Manos a la obra	¡Adelante!	Repaso

Learning Sequence

INPUT	PRACTICE	APPLICATION	REVIEW
• Introduce vocabulary and grammar within an authentic context.	• Practice and develop new vocabulary. • Learn and practice new grammar structures.	• Apply vocabulary and grammar through culminating, theme-based activities. • Apply skill development.	• Review vocabulary and grammar.

Objectives

Read, listen to, and interpret information about • What the world may be like in the future • Problems facing the environment • Solutions for facing the problems in our environment	• Communicate about protecting the environment. • Talk about the future of the world. • Use more irregular future-tense verbs. • Use the subjunctive to express doubts and uncertainty.	• Read and interpret information about the Antarctic and Tierra del Fuego. • Read about rain forests. • Write a presentation on community service.	• Prepare for the chapter test.

Culture

• Alfredo Arrecuín	• *Los pingüinos* • *El Parque Nacional Darién* • *El ecoturismo en Ecuador*	• *La deforestación de los bosques tropicales*	• Describe efforts to protect natural resources in the Spanish-speaking world.

Vocabulary

• Earth
• Energy
• The environment

Grammar

• The future: Other irregular verbs
• The present subjunctive with expressions of doubt

Learner Support

STRATEGIES
• Recognizing cognates
• Detecting point of view
• Key questions

RECYCLING
• Verbs, seasons
• Vocabulary about recycling
• Items in a recycling center
• Vocabulary for leisure activities and weather conditions
• Irregular verbs in the future tense

Chapter Features

Exploración del lenguaje

Antonyms

Conexiones

Ecology: Ways that you can conserve water

El español en el mundo del trabajo

A company that hires employees to work on ecological projects in Central and South American countries

Beyond the Classroom: States & Countries

España
Texas
México
Honduras
Costa Rica
Panamá
Ecuador
Uruguay
Chile
Argentina

Student Resources

PRACTICE

TECHNOLOGY

ONLINE

Interactive Textbook
• Student Edition Online plus audio, video, and flashcards

Go Online Companion Web Site
• Tutorial activities   • Internet links
• Self-tests   • Downloadable MP3 audio files

PuzzleView

CD-ROM

Interactive Textbook CD-ROM
Student Edition on CD-ROM plus audio, video, and flashcards

MindPoint™ CD-ROM
QUIZ SHOW

PRINT MATERIAL

CORE INSTRUCTION

Practice Workbook, pp. 182–190
• Review   • Vocabulary
• Grammar   • Puzzle
• Organizer

Writing, Audio & Video Activities, pp. 176–184
• Video   • Audio
• Writing

Grammar Study Guide 1–2 (or 3–4)

Differentiated Instruction

STUDENTS NEEDING EXTRA HELP

Guided Practice Activities, pp. 327–343
• Vocabulary Flash Cards and Vocabulary Check
• Grammar Activities
• Presentación escrita

HERITAGE LEARNERS

Realidades para hispanohablantes, pp. 350–369

Lecturas para hispanohablantes
• "Los problemas de la ciudad," pp. 15–16
• "Los chicos del fin del mundo," pp. 111–114

ADVANCED/PRE-AP*

Pre-AP* Resource Book: Student Activity Sheet, p. 131

Teacher Resources

PLAN AND TEACH

TECHNOLOGY

Audio Program   Fine Art Transparencies
Video Program   Vocabulary and Grammar Transparencies
Answers on Transparencies

TeacherEXPRESS CD-ROM
• Lesson Planner   • Vocabulary Clip Art
• Web Resources   • Teaching Resources
• Teacher Edition with Interactive Links

PresentationEXPRESS CD-ROM
• Vocabulary   • Transparencies and Maps
• Grammar   • Photo Gallery
• Audio   • Clip Art

PRINT MATERIAL

CORE INSTRUCTION

Teacher's Resource Book, pp. 256–278
• Input Script   • Video Script
• Answer Keys   • GramActiva Blackline Masters
• Vocabulary Clip Art   • Chapter Resource Checklist
• School-to-Home Connection Letters
• Communicative Activities Blackline Masters

TPR Stories, pp. 127–130

Differentiated Instruction

STUDENTS NEEDING EXTRA HELP

Guided Practice Activities Teacher's Guide, pp. T164–T172

HERITAGE LEARNERS

Realidades para hispanohablantes Teacher's Guide, pp. 176–185

Lecturas para hispanohablantes Teacher's Guide, pp. 4, 43–44

ADVANCED/PRE-AP*

Pre-AP* Resource Book: Resources Chart, p. 129

Differentiated Assessment

ASSESS

PH SuccessNet ONLINE
• Access to grades and reports from Online Interactive Textbook

ExamView on Presentation Express CD-ROM
QuickTake Presenter
• Vocabulary Quizzes   • Chapter Test
• Grammar Quizzes

TeacherEXPRESS CD-ROM
• Assessment Program
• **ExamView** Test Banks A and B
test generator

Go Online
PHSchool.com
For: Teacher Home Page
Web Code: jdk-1001

CORE ASSESSMENT

Assessment Program, pp. 242–254
• Pruebas
  Vocabulary Recognition
  Vocabulary Production
  The future tense: Irregular verbs
  The present subjunctive with expressions of doubt
• Examen del capítulo   • Speaking and Writing Rubrics

Teacher's Resource Book, p. 268
• Situation Cards

TPR Stories, pp. 127–130

STUDENTS NEEDING EXTRA HELP

Alternate Assessment Program
• Examen del capítulo, pp. 107–111

HERITAGE LEARNERS

Assessment Program: Realidades para hispanohablantes Teacher's Guide, pp. T171–T175

ExamView Heritage Learner Test Bank
test generator

ADVANCED/PRE-AP*

Pre-AP* Resource Book: Teacher Activity Sheet, p. 130

ExamView Pre-AP* Test Bank
test generator

	Warm-up / Assess	Preview Present / Practice Communicate		Wrap-up / Homework Options
DAY 1	**Warm-up (10 min.)** • Homework check • Return Examen del capítulo: Capítulo 9A	**Chapter Opener (10 min.)** • Objectives • Fondo cultural	**A primera vista (25 min.)** • Presentation: Vocabulario y gramática en contexto • Actividades 1, 2	**Wrap-up and Homework Options (5 min.)** • Practice Workbook 9B-A, 9B-B, 9B-1, 9B-2 • Go Online
DAY 2	**Warm-up (10 min.)** • Homework check	**A primera vista (35 min.)** • Presentation: Videohistoria ¡Caramba, qué calor! • View: Videohistoria	• Video Activities 1, 2, 3, 4 • Actividad 3	**Wrap-up and Homework Options (5 min.)** • Practice Workbook 9B-3, 9B-4 • Go Online • Prueba 9B-1: Vocabulary recognition
DAY 3	**Warm-up (10 min.)** • Actividad 6 • Homework check ✔**Assessment (10 min.)** • Prueba 9B-1: Vocabulary recognition	**Manos a la obra (25 min.)** • Actividades 4, 5, 8, 9, 10 • Fondos culturales		**Wrap-up and Homework Options (5 min.)** • Writing Activity 10 • Actividad 11 • Heritage Learner Workbook 9B-1, 9B-2 • Prueba 9B-2: Vocabulary production
DAY 4	**Warm-up (10 min.)** • Actividad 7 • Homework check ✔**Assessment (10 min.)** (after Communicative Activity) • Prueba 9B-2: Vocabulary production	**Manos a la obra (25 min.)** • Audio Activities 5, 6 • Communicative Activity • Presentation: The future tense: other irregular verbs	• View: GramActiva video • Actividad 12	**Wrap-up and Homework Options (5 min.)** • Practice Workbook 9B-5 • Actividad 13 • Go Online
DAY 5	**Warm-up (5 min.)** • Actividad 14 • Homework check	**Manos a la obra (40 min.)** • Exploración del lenguaje • Actividades 15, 16 • Fondo cultural • Audio Activity 7	• Presentation: The present subjunctive with expressions of doubt • View: GramActiva video • Actividades 17, 18	**Wrap-up and Homework Options (5 min.)** • Practice Workbook 9B-6 • Actividad 20 • Go Online • Prueba 9B-3: The future tense: other irregular verbs
DAY 6	**Warm-up (10 min.)** • Actividad 11 • Homework check ✔**Assessment (10 min.)** • Prueba 9B-3: The future tense: other irregular verbs	**Manos a la obra (25 min.)** • Actividades 19, 21, 23, 24 • Fondo cultural • El español en el mundo del trabajo		**Wrap-up and Homework Options (5 min.)** • Practice Workbook 9B-7 • Prueba 9B-4: The present • Actividad 22 subjunctive with • Writing Activity 13 expressions of doubt • Go Online • Heritage Learner Workbook 9B-4
DAY 7	**Warm-up (10 min.)** • Writing Activity 12 • Homework check ✔**Assessment (10 min.)** (after Audio Activities) • Prueba 9B-4: The present subjunctive with expressions of doubt	**Manos a la obra (15 min.)** • Actividad 25 • Audio Activities 8, 9 **¡Adelante! (10 min.)** • Presentación escrita: Steps 1, 5		**Wrap-up and Homework Options (5 min.)** • Presentación escrita: Step 2
DAY 8	**Warm-up (5 min.)** • Homework check	**¡Adelante! (40 min.)** • Presentación escrita: Step 3 • Lectura • ¿Comprendiste? / Y tú, ¿qué dices?		**Wrap-up and Homework Options (5 min.)** • Presentación escrita: Step 4 • Go Online: Lectura
DAY 9	**Warm-up (5 min.)** • Homework check	**¡Adelante! (10 min.)** • Perspectivas del mundo hispano	**Repaso del capítulo (30 min.)** • Vocabulario y gramática • Preparación para el examen 1, 2, 3, 4, 5	**Wrap-up and Homework Options (5 min.)** • Practice Workbook 9B-8, 9B-9 • Go Online: Self-test • Examen del capítulo 9B
DAY 10	**Warm-up (5 min.)** • Homework check ✔**Assessment (45 min.)** • Examen del capítulo 9B			

Warm-up / Assess	Preview Present / Practice Communicate	Wrap-up / Homework Options
DAY 1 **Warm-up (10 min.)** • Homework check • Return Examen del capítulo: Capítulo 9A	**Chapter Opener (10 min.)** • Objectives • Fondo cultural **A primera vista (65 min.)** • Presentation: Vocabulario y gramática en contexto • Actividades 1, 2 • Presentation: Videohistoria ¡Caramba, qué calor! • View: Videohistoria • Video Activities 1, 2, 3, 4 • Actividades 3, 4	**Wrap-up and Homework Options (5 min.)** • Practice Workbook 9B-A, 9B-B, 9B-1, 9B-2, 9B-3, 9B-4 • Go Online • Prueba 9B-1: Vocabulary recognition
DAY 2 **Warm-up (10 min.)** • Actividad 6 • Homework check ✔**Assessment (10 min.)** • Prueba 9B-1: Vocabulary recognition	**Manos a la obra (65 min.)** • Actividades 5, 7, 8, 9 • Fondo cultural • Audio Activities 5, 6 • Writing Activity 10 • Communicative Activity • Presentation: The future tense: other irregular verbs • View: GramActiva video • Actividades 12, 14	**Wrap-up and Homework Options (5 min.)** • Practice Workbook 9B-5 • Actividades 11, 13 • Go Online • Heritage Learner Workbook 9B-1, 9B-2 • Prueba 9B-2: Vocabulary production
DAY 3 **Warm-up (10 min.)** • Actividad 10 • Homework check ✔**Assessment (10 min.)** • Prueba 9B-2: Vocabulary production	**Manos a la obra (65 min.)** • Exploración del lenguaje • Fondo cultural • Actividades 15, 16 • Audio Activity 7 • Presentation: Present subjunctive of stem-changing verbs • View: GramActiva video • Actividades 17, 18, 19, 21, 23 • Writing Activity 12	**Wrap-up and Homework Options (5 min.)** • Practice Workbook 9B-6, 9B-7 • Actividades 20, 22 • Go Online • Heritage Learner Workbook 9B-4 • Pruebas 9B-3, 9B-4: The future tense: other irregular verbs; Present subjunctive of stem-changing verbs
DAY 4 **Warm-up (15 min.)** • Writing Activity 11 • Homework check ✔**Assessment (15 min.)** (after Writing Activity) • Pruebas 9B-3, 9B-4: The future tense: other irregular verbs; Present subjunctive of stem-changing verbs	**Manos a la obra (30 min.)** • Actividades 24, 25 • Audio Activities 8, 9 • Writing Activity 13 • El español en el mundo del trabajo **¡Adelante! (25 min.)** • Perspectivas del mundo hispano • Presentación escrita: Steps 1, 5	**Wrap-up and Homework Options (5 min.)** • Presentación escrita: Step 2 • Go Online: Self-test
DAY 5 **Warm-up (5 min.)** • Homework check	**¡Adelante! (50 min.)** • Presentación escrita: Steps 3, 4 • Lectura • ¿Comprendiste? / Y tú, ¿qué dices? **Repaso del capítulo (30 min.)** • Vocabulario y gramática • Preparación para el examen 1, 2, 3, 4, 5	**Wrap-up and Homework Options (5 min.)** • Presentación escrita: Step 4 • Practice Workbook 9B-8, 9B-9 • Go Online: Lectura • Examen del capítulo 9B
DAY 6 **Warm-up (15 min.)** • Homework check • Answer questions **Repaso del capítulo (25 min.)** • Situation Cards • Communicative Activities ✔**Assessment (45 min.)** • Examen del capítulo 9B		

Vocabulario y gramática

Presentation EXPRESS
VOCABULARY

Core Instruction

 Standards: 1.2

Resources: Teacher's Resource Book: Input Script, p. 258, Clip Art, pp. 270–271, Audio Script, p. 259; Voc. and Gram. Transparencies 165–166; TPR Stories Book, pp. 119–130; Audio Program: Tracks 1–2

Focus: Presenting vocabulary for nature and the environment

Suggestions: Present the vocabulary in three groups: problems facing the environment, nature, and energy. Use the Input Script from the *Teacher's Resource Book* or the story from the *TPR Stories Book* to present the new words, or use some of these suggestions.

Bring in magazine photos from nature magazines that show images of forests, jungles, hills, and valleys and have students identify the pictures. Have students identify symbols that are associated with peace (handshake, dove, people laughing) and those that are associated with war (tanks, bombs, aircraft carriers).

Ask students to brainstorm a list of vocabulary they have already learned for recycling and the environment and relate it to the new vocabulary.

Bellringer Review

Have students refer to pp. 390–391 and complete this matching activity from the board:

1. *La boa*
2. *La cotorra*
3. *La cascada La Mina*
4. *El coquí*

a. *aguas que caen muy rápidamente*
b. *un símbolo importante para los puertorriqueños*
c. *serpiente en peligro de extinción*
d. *pájaro en peligro de extinción*

(**Answers: 1.** c; **2.** d; **3.** a; **4.** b)

Block Schedule

Create nature murals depicting the desert, the mountains, outer space, and the rain forest. Have students label plants, animals, or objects and describe the environment: *seco, mucha lluvia, poco ruido,* and so on.

Additional Resources

• Audio Program: Canciones CD, Disc 22

476

Objectives

Read, listen to, and understand information about
• **what the world may be like in the future**
• **problems facing the environment**
• **solutions for the problems in our environment**

A primera vista

Vocabulario y gramática en contexto

jdd-0997

66 **La destrucción** de nuestro **medio ambiente** afecta a cada persona. Tenemos que **luchar contra** este problema **grave.**

Para la salud de la gente de nuestro pueblo, hay que **eliminar** la contaminación del aire y del agua.

la contaminación

el aire **contaminado**

el pueblo

el agua **contaminada**

la calefacción solar

Tenemos que **reducir** el uso de **la electricidad** y usar otras **fuentes** de **energía.**

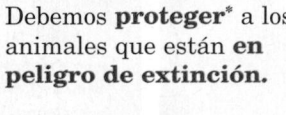

Debemos **proteger*** a los animales que están **en peligro de extinción.**

Proteger is a regular *-er* verb with a spelling change in the *yo* form of the present tense: *protejo.*

la paz

Para **mejorar** la situación del mundo es necesario **resolver** los problemas entre los países. Es importante que **haya** paz y que no haya **guerra 99.**

476 cuatrocientos setenta y seis
Tema 9 • ¿Cómo será el futuro?

Differentiated Instruction
Solutions for All Learners

Students with Special Needs

Using the script for *Actividad* 1, create a chart for hearing-impaired students. List the dictated dialogue in the first column and label the other columns *la Luna, la Tierra, la colina, el valle,* and *la planta.* Have students check the column that indicates which part of the scene each sentence describes.

Multiple Intelligences

Naturalist: Have students look through Spanish-language magazines or on the Internet to locate articles about environmental problems and solutions. Ask them simply to identify the problem or solution addressed in each article. Ask: *¿Cuál es el problema?* or *¿Cuál es la solución?* Have students give you short answers: *el agua contaminada, el reciclaje,* etc.

¡Hay MUCHAS **MANERAS** EN QUE UDS. PUEDEN AYUDAR A PROTEGER LA BELLEZA DE NUESTRA **NATURALEZA** . . .

• • • EN **EL ESPACIO!**

EN **LAS SELVAS TROPICALES!**

EN **LOS BOSQUES!**

• • • EN **LOS DESIERTOS!**

la Luna

la planta

la colina

la Tierra

el valle

❝Júntense con amigos y participen en uno de los grupos **ecológicos** de nuestra comunidad hoy **❞**

 **Escuchar** jdd-0997

En las noticias

Escucha lo que dice el señor del grupo ecológico en la página 476. Señala con el dedo qué parte de la escena se describe.

Más práctica

- Practice Workbook, pp. 182–183; 9B-1, 9B-2
- WAV Wbk.: Writing, p. 181
- Guided Practice: Vocab. Flash Cards, pp. 327–332
- *Real.* para hispanohablantes, p. 352

Go Online PHSchool.com
For: Vocab. Practice
Web Code: jdd-0911

 **Escuchar** jdd-0997

¿Cierta o falsa?

En una hoja de papel, escribe los números del 1 al 7. Si la frase que escuchas es cierta, escribe *C.* Si es falsa, escribe *F.*

cuatrocientos setenta y siete **477**
Capítulo 9B

Actividad 1 *Standards:* 1.2 | **Presentation EXPRESS** AUDIO

Resources: Teacher's Resource Book: Audio Script, p. 259; Audio Program: Track 3; Voc. and Gram. Transparency 165; Answers on Transparencies

Focus: Listening comprehension of new vocabulary in sentence context

Suggestions: Leave Transparency 165 on the screen as students listen. Encourage students not to react to the prompts until the second time they listen. Have them listen a third time and confirm the answers by pointing to the appropriate pictures on the transparency.

Script and Answers:
1. Los coches producen mucha de esta contaminación. *(polluted air)*
2. Si continuamos la destrucción del medio ambiente, habrá más animales en peligro de extinción. *(endangered animals)*
3. Usar la calefacción solar es buena idea para reducir el uso de la electricidad. *(solar heating)*
4. Un pueblo es más pequeño que una ciudad. *(town)*
5. Las naciones deben luchar por la paz. *(peace)*
6. Hay que eliminar las fuentes de contaminación del agua. *(polluted water)*

Actividad 2  *Standards:* 1.2 | **Presentation EXPRESS** AUDIO

Resources: Teacher's Resource Book: Audio Script, p. 259; Audio Program: Track 4; Answers on Transparencies

Focus: Listening comprehension about nature

Suggestions: Before listening, have students name features of the climate and the environment of the desert, the forest, and the rain forest. After listening, have volunteers correct the false statements.

Script and Answers:
1. Nosotros vivimos en la Luna. *(F)*
2. Hay muchos lagos y océanos en el desierto. *(F)*
3. Hace mucho calor en la selva tropical. *(C)*
4. Hay muchos árboles diferentes en el bosque. *(C)*
5. Una colina es más alta que una montaña. *(F)*
6. La naturaleza de la Tierra está en peligro. *(C)*
7. Los valles se encuentran entre las montañas. *(C)*

✓ **Assessment**
- *ExamView* Quiz on PresEXPRESS
  QuickTake Presenter

Enrich Your Teaching
Resources for All Teachers

Teacher-to-Teacher

Have students research endangered species in Spanish-speaking countries. Tell them to choose an animal from the desert, the ocean, the forest, or the rain forest. Ask them to make posters about protecting the species. Hang the posters in the classroom and refer to them throughout the chapter.

Internet Search

Keyword:
endangered species + (Spanish-speaking country)

Videohistoria

Core Instruction

 **Standards:** 1.2, 4.1

Resources: Voc. and Gram. Transparencies 167–168; Audio Program: Track 5

Focus: Presenting additional contextualized vocabulary

Suggestions:

Pre-reading: Help students activate prior knowledge by asking them about what they have done to cool off on a really hot day. Then review the photos and have students predict what Esteban and Pedro try to do to escape the heat.

Reading: Have students pause after the third panel and identify Esteban and Pedro's problem. Direct attention to the photo for panel 7 and ask students to predict Esteban's and Pedro's solution to the problem. Tell students to pause again after they read the text for panel 7. Ask if their predictions were correct.

Post-reading: Have students complete *Actividad* 3 to check comprehension.

Pre-AP* Support

• **Activity:** Distribute Clip Art for the vocabulary in this chapter and have students cut out the squares and arrange them on their desktop. Working in pairs, have students tell their partners one practice that might improve the environment so that the partners can identify which illustration is being described. When a student identifies the correct illustrations, he or she collects them in a stack. The winner is the student who has identified the most illustrations by the end of a teacher-selected time limit.

• ***Pre-AP* Resource Book:*** Comprehensive guide to Pre-AP* vocabulary skill development, pp. 47–53

¡Caramba, qué calor!

Hoy hace mucho calor en San Antonio. Lee la historia para saber qué hacen Esteban y Pedro.

Estrategia

Recognizing cognates
Before you read the *Videohistoria*, focus on the boldfaced words.

• Which of these words are cognates? Can you find other cognates that have not been boldfaced?

1 **Esteban:** ¿Qué pasa?

Pedro: No sé, pero creo que no tenemos **aire acondicionado.**

Esteban: ¿Cómo? ¿Con este calor? Imposible. Mamá, ¿qué pasa con el aire acondicionado?

Esteban   Angélica   Pedro

5 **Pedro:** Esteban, ¿no te gustaría tener el aire acondicionado solar?

Esteban: ¿Por qué?

Pedro: Pues, **conserva** energía y reduce el uso de la electricidad. Debemos usar mejor lo que ya tenemos. ¿Ves? El autobús es muy **eficiente.**

Esteban: Sí, **es cierto.** También es **económico.**

6 **Pedro:** El aire contaminado es un problema grave. Para tener aire más **puro** debemos montar en bicicleta.

Esteban: Sí, pero con tanto calor el coche es más cómodo y más rápido.

Pedro: ¡Ay, Esteban, pero así podemos **ahorrar** energía y dinero al mismo tiempo!

7 **Esteban:** ¿No **funciona** el aire acondicionado?

Cajera: No, y dudo que funcione mañana tampoco.

478 cuatrocientos setenta y ocho
Tema 9 • ¿Cómo será el futuro?

Differentiated Instruction
Solutions for All Learners

Students with Learning Difficulties
Help students with inferential reasoning by asking them questions about the *Videohistoria:* What clue signaled Esteban that the air conditioning wasn't working? Who is more bothered by the heat, Angélica or Pedro? Why does Esteban suggest going to the movies? Who is more concerned about conservation, Esteban or Pedro?

Multiple Intelligences
Bodily/Kinesthetic: Have volunteers act out the *Videohistoria* or the longer script of the video itself. Encourage them to personalize the story in some way, using their own names, places in your community, or details more appropriate to the climate of your community.

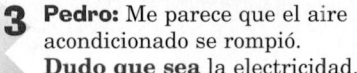

2 **Angélica:** ¿Qué necesitas, Esteban? Mamá no está.

Esteban: Pues, parece que el aire acondicionado está mal. No lo oigo. ¿Puedes ver lo que pasa?

Angélica: ¡Por supuesto que no! Hazlo tú. **Además, ¡**no hace tanto calor!

Pedro: ¡Silencio! Yo mismo voy a ver lo que pasa.

3 **Pedro:** Me parece que el aire acondicionado se rompió. **Dudo que sea** la electricidad.

4 **Esteban:** No podemos quedarnos aquí. ¿Por qué no vamos al cine? Angélica, ¿nos puedes llevar en el coche?

Angélica: Bueno, pero tendrán que esperar media hora. Tengo que terminar algo.

Pedro: ¿Por qué no caminamos? El cine no está muy lejos.

Escribir/Hablar

¿Comprendiste?

1. ¿Dónde están los jóvenes? ¿Cuál es el problema?
2. ¿Quién piensa que hace mucho calor, Angélica o Esteban?
3. ¿Adónde deciden ir Pedro y Esteban? ¿Cómo van a ir?
4. Según Pedro, ¿por qué es bueno usar el aire acondicionado solar?
5. Según Pedro, ¿qué pueden hacer para no crear más contaminación del aire?
6. ¿Qué pasa cuando Pedro y Esteban llegan al cine? ¿Qué solución tiene Esteban?

8 **Esteban:** Sí, Angélica. Aquí, Esteban. Oye, ¿nos puedes venir a recoger en tu coche?

Angélica: ¡Esteban!

Más práctica

- Practice Workbook, pp. 184–185: 9B-3, 9B-4
- WAV Wbk.: Video, pp. 176–178
- Guided Practice: Vocab. Check, pp. 333–336
- *Real.* para hispanohablantes, p. 353

Go Online
PHSchool.com
For: Vocab. Practice
Web Code: jdd-0912

cuatrocientos setenta y nueve **479**
Capítulo 9B

Video

Core Instruction

 Standards: 1.2

Resources: Teacher's Resource Book: Video Script, p. 262; Video Program: Cap. 9B; Video Program Teacher's Guide: Cap. 9B

Focus: Comprehension of contextualized vocabulary

Suggestions:

Pre-viewing: Have students brainstorm a list of words and phrases to describe how Pedro, Esteban, and Angélica are feeling. Ask them to say why they are feeling that way.

Viewing: Show the video once without pausing. Then show it again and pause to discuss the environmental problems Pedro identifies and some solutions mentioned in the video.

Post-viewing: Complete the Video Activities in the *Writing, Audio & Video Workbook.*

Actividad 3  *Standards:* 1.2
Presentation EXPRESS
ANSWERS

Resources: Answers on Transparencies

Focus: Verifying comprehension of the *Videohistoria*

Suggestions: Have students read all of the questions first and then skim the *Videohistoria* for the answers. Point out that when *según* is followed by a name, students should look for the answer in that person's dialogue.

Answers:

1. Están en la casa de Esteban y el aire acondicionado no funciona.
2. Esteban piensa que hace mucho calor.
3. Deciden ir al cine. Esteban quiere ir en coche, pero Pedro quiere caminar.
4. Porque conserva energía y reduce el uso de la electricidad.
5. Se puede tomar el autobús o montar en bicicleta.
6. El aire acondicionado no funciona en el cine tampoco. Esteban quiere que Angélica venga a recogerlos en su coche.

Additional Resources

- WAV Wbk.: Audio Act. 5, p. 179
- Teacher's Resource Book: Audio Script, pp. 259–260
- Audio Program: Track 7

✓ **Assessment**

- **ExamView** Quiz on PresEXPRESS
  QuickTake Presenter
- Prueba 9B-1: Vocab. Recognition, pp. 242–243

479

Enrich Your Teaching
Resources for All Teachers

Culture Note

In many urban locations in Spanish-speaking countries and throughout the United States, major changes are being implemented to reduce air pollution. In Mexico City, for example, automobile owners are required to leave their cars at home one day a week. The last digit of the car's license plate determines which day of the week is prohibited. When the air pollution level is extremely high, cars must stay off the road twice a week. Industries in the city have begun to use cleaner fuels and several studies have been made to identify other ways to cut down on pollution.

 **Standards:** 1.2

Resources: Teacher's Resource Book: Audio Script, p. 259; Audio Program: Track 6; Answers on Transparencies

Focus: Listening comprehension about the environment

Suggestions: Before listening, have students brainstorm a list of words to describe each picture.

 Script and Answers:

1. Es un lugar donde hay muchos árboles y donde viven los osos. *(el bosque)*
2. Es algo que vemos en el cielo de noche. *(la Luna)*
3. Es similar a un árbol pero más pequeño. *(la planta)*
4. Es el lugar en el espacio donde vivimos. *(la Tierra)*
5. Es un lugar entre dos montañas. *(el valle)*
6. Es similar a una montaña pero no es tan alta. *(la colina)*
7. Es el lugar donde están el Sol, la Luna y las estrellas. *(el espacio)*
8. Es un lugar donde hay poca lluvia. *(el desierto)*

 Bellringer Review
Write these words on the board and then have students write two associated words under each:

el espacio   las selvas tropicales   los desiertos

  Standards: 1.1

Focus: Speaking about different environments and their locations

Suggestions: Bring in a map that shows desert regions, mountainous areas, and rain forests. Encourage students to identify these environments in Spanish-speaking countries.

Answers will vary.

Have students create a collage to illustrate an environment from *Actividad* 5. Bring in magazines with photos of different environments. Have students present their collages to the class. Encourage them to describe the locations shown in the photos and any unique features of their chosen environment.

Manos a la obra
Vocabulario y gramática en uso

Objectives
- Communicate about what you and others can do to protect the environment
- Talk about the future of the world
- Learn to use more irregular future-tense verbs
- Learn to use the present subjunctive to express doubt and uncertainty

 jdd-0998
Escuchar/Escribir

Descripciones del medio ambiente

Escucha las descripciones del medio ambiente. En una hoja de papel, escribe los números del 1 al 8. Escribe el nombre de lo que está describiendo.

Modelo
 Escuchas: Es un lugar donde llueve mucho y donde hay muchos árboles y plantas. Escribes: *la selva tropical*

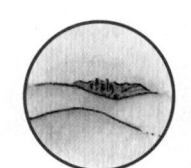   

  Hablar

¿Dónde se encuentra . . . ?

Para cada dibujo de la Actividad 4, piensa en dónde se encuentra este aspecto del medio ambiente. Puede estar cerca de tu comunidad, en un país hispanohablante que has estudiado o en el espacio. Habla con otro(a) estudiante sobre los lugares.

Modelo
A —¿Dónde se encuentran <u>desiertos</u>?   B —Hay <u>desiertos</u> en <u>Chile</u>.

El desierto de Atacama, en Chile

Differentiated Instruction
Solutions for All Learners

Advanced Learners
Have students write more analogies related to the environment, using *Actividad* 6 as a model. Make copies of the best ones and distribute them to the class to review chapter vocabulary.

Multiple Intelligences
Interpersonal/Social: Have students find out what kinds of environmental organizations or programs exist in your school or community. They can attend a meeting or visit the appropriate department in the local government. Students should take notes on their experiences and write a paragraph to present later to the class.

Actividad 6 **Leer/Pensar/Escribir**

Las analogías

Completa cada analogía según el modelo. Usa las palabras del recuadro.

Modelo

flor : jardín :: árbol : *bosque*

ahorrar	económico	guerra
calefacción	energía	luchar
dudar	espacio	

1. resolver : problema :: conservar _____
2. volver : regresar :: pelear : _____
3. llegar : salir :: gastar : _____
4. verano : aire acondicionado :: invierno : _____
5. puro : contaminado :: paz : _____
6. añadir : eliminar :: creer : _____
7. océano : la Tierra :: la Luna : _____
8. quizás : tal vez :: barato : _____

 Actividad 7 **Leer/Escribir**

Una reunión del club de ecología

Un estudiante asistió a una reunión del club de ecología. Tomó apuntes *(notes)* para después escribir un artículo para el periódico. Escribe los verbos que completan las frases.

Modelo

 Para <u>resolver</u> los problemas ecológicos, hay que tener leyes estrictas.

1. Tendremos que hacer leyes más estrictas para _____ *(luchar / mejorar)* el medio ambiente.
2. Si reciclamos las latas, los periódicos y el cartón, podemos _____ *(reducir / conservar)* la basura que está en el mundo.
3. Si queremos vivir en un mundo limpio, debemos _____ *(eliminar / mejorar)* la destrucción de medio ambiente.
4. Es importante _____ *(luchar / mejorar)* contra la destrucción de las selvas tropicales.
5. Las leyes que protegen la naturaleza no pueden _____ *(reducir / funcionar)* si no las obedecemos.
6. Todos deben _____ *(juntarse / dudar)* con otras personas para participar en una organización que trabaja por la protección del medio ambiente.

Fondo cultural

Los pingüinos *(penguins)* de la Patagonia, una región al sur de Argentina y Chile, comen peces. Están amenazados *(threatened)* por la pesca excesiva y la contaminación de la industria petrolera. Antes los buques petroleros *(oil tankers)* descargaban *(unloaded)* en el mar el agua de lastre *(ballast)* sucia, y la contaminación petrolera causó la muerte de más de 40,000 pingüinos al año. Ahora, para proteger a los pingüinos, los buques petroleros pasan por rutas más alejadas de la costa.

• ¿Qué impacto tienen las industrias de tu comunidad en el medio ambiente?

Pingüinos magallánicos, Argentina

cuatrocientos ochenta y uno **481**
Capítulo 9B

Practice and Communicate **9B**

 Actividad 6 *Standards:* 1.2, 3.1 **Presentation EXPRESS ANSWERS**

Resources: Answers on Transparencies

Focus: Using vocabulary to complete analogies

Recycle: Seasons

Suggestions: Discuss the relationship of the two words in the model *(object / location)*. Remind students of how analogies work. Have students read all three words first, then determine the relationship between the first two words to solve the analogy.

Answers:

1. energía
2. luchar
3. ahorrar
4. calefacción
5. guerra
6. dudar
7. el espacio
8. económico

 Actividad 7 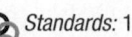 *Standards:* 1.1  **Presentation EXPRESS ANSWERS**

Resources: Answers on Transparencies

Focus: Reading comprehension about ecology; using verbs about the environment

Recycle: Recycling

Suggestions: Point out to students that they do not need to conjugate the verbs. Before students complete the activity, have them read all the sentences for the main idea.

Answers:

1. mejorar
2. reducir
3. eliminar
4. luchar
5. funcionar
6. juntarse

Fondo cultural 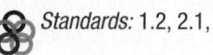 *Standards:* 1.2, 2.1, 2.2, 3.1

Suggestions: Explain that oil tankers carry seawater in holding tanks as ballast. The seawater is taken in or discharged as necessary to balance the boat and its cargo. Sometimes oil from the cargo tanks leaks into the ballast tanks and mixes with the seawater. The contaminated seawater is then discharged into the ocean.

Answers will vary.

Enrich Your Teaching

Resources for All Teachers

Culture Note

Stretching 2,666 miles from north to south, Chile contains a wide range of environments. At its northern tip lies the Atacama Desert, covering over 600 miles. This arid expanse is the driest on Earth. Some parts have never recorded any rainfall. The dusty landscape is bereft of vegetation but is rich in minerals.

Culture Note

Oil spills are devastating to penguins. When they swim in contaminated water, they become coated in oil and can no longer control their body temperature. The oil coating also affects the bird's ability to float and consequently it becomes unable to fish and feed itself.

 **Standards:** 1.2

Presentation EXPRESS ANSWERS

Resources: Answers on Transparencies

Focus: Reading comprehension of a news article; using adjectives

Suggestions: Have students read the paragraph once before filling in the blanks.

Answers:

1. grave
2. contaminados
3. pura
4. eficiente
5. solar
6. económico
7. ecológica
8. cierto

 Standards: 1.1

Presentation EXPRESS ANSWERS

Resources: Answers on Transparencies

Focus: Talking about ways to improve the environment

Suggestions: Before students converse in pairs, go through the options for Student B responses with the class as a whole.

Answers:

Student A:
1. ¿Cómo se puede proteger el medio ambiente?
2. ¿... resolver el problema de la contaminación del agua?
3. ¿... conservar energía?
4. ¿... mejorar la condición de la Tierra?
5. ¿... ahorrar la electricidad?
6. ¿... salvar a los animales en peligro de extinción?

Student B: Answers will vary.

Exploración del lenguaje

Presentation EXPRESS ANSWERS

Core Instruction

 **Standards:** 1.2

Resources: Answers on Transparencies

Suggestions: Provide students with a list of words from previous chapters and have them give an antonym for each.

Answers:

contaminado   calefacción
cierto   destrucción

1. guerra
2. después
3. nada
4. muerto

  **Leer/Escribir**

Un artículo para el periódico

cierto	eficiente
contaminado	grave
ecológico	puro
económico	solar

El estudiante de la Actividad 7 ha comenzado a escribir su artículo. Completa el párrafo con las formas apropiadas de los adjetivos en el recuadro.

Tenemos una situación __1.__ en nuestro pueblo. Los ríos y lagos están __2.__ y cada día mueren más peces. Si no reducimos la contaminación, no habrá ni agua __3.__ para beber ni aire para respirar. ¿Cómo podemos resolver estos problemas? Primero, los científicos deben buscar otras fuentes de energía __4.__, como la calefacción __5.__. Segundo, debemos usar nuestros coches menos y usar el transporte público más. Es mejor para el medio ambiente y más __6.__. Tercero, podemos trabajar en alguna organización __7.__ que trata de conservar el medio ambiente. Es __8.__ que nuestra comunidad tiene un problema, pero si luchamos juntos, podemos resolverlo.

 **Hablar**

¿Cómo se puede . . . ?

Habla con otro(a) estudiante sobre lo que se puede hacer para conservar el medio ambiente.

Modelo
A —¿Cómo se puede _reducir la basura?_
B —_Se puede reciclar las botellas de vidrio y de plástico._

Estudiante A

1. proteger   la electricidad
2. resolver   el medio ambiente
3. conservar   a los animales en peligro de extinción
4. mejorar   energía
5. ahorrar   el problema de la contaminación del agua
6. salvar   la condición de la Tierra

Estudiante B

luchar contra la destrucción de . . .
reciclar . . .
no usar el coche y . . .
apagar . . .

no tirar basura en . . .
buscar . . .
juntarse con . . .
eliminar . . .

Exploración del lenguaje

Antonyms

You have learned many ways to increase your vocabulary. One of these is learning words as antonym, or opposite, pairs. Write the antonyms for the following words:

puro ≠ __?__   aire acondicionado ≠ __?__

falso ≠ __?__   construcción ≠ __?__

¡Compruébalo! Here is a series of popular _refranes_ using _Más vale_ ("It's better, worth more"). Complete each _refrán_ with the antonym of the word in bold type.

Más vale uno en **paz** que ciento en _____.

Más vale **antes** que _____.

Más vale **algo** que _____.

Más vale perro **vivo** que león _____.

Differentiated Instruction
Solutions for All Learners

Students with Learning Difficulties

To help students understand the _Exploración de lenguaje,_ bring in visuals to illustrate the concept of antonyms. Bring in photos of tall and short people, big and small cars, war and peace, and so on. Show students four pictures at a time and have them say the words and pair up the antonyms.

 Advanced Learners/Pre-AP*

Pre-AP*

Have students use vocabulary from previous chapters to make a crossword puzzle. Tell them to give clues using antonyms. Ask students to exchange puzzles and work with a partner. If you prefer, collect the crossword puzzles, choose the best ones, and distribute them to the class as a vocabulary review.

Actividad 10 Leer/Escribir/Hablar

Animales en peligro de extinción

Según los científicos en México, más del 20 por ciento de los animales del país están en peligro de extinción. A causa de la contaminación, la destrucción de su hábitat y la caza *(hunting)*, animales como el oso negro, la ballena *(whale)* gris, la tortuga marina y muchos más podrán desaparecer si no se encuentran soluciones a este grave problema ecológico.[1] En 2002, el Banco de México anunció un programa que podrá ayudar a los animales. Lee el anuncio y contesta las preguntas.

1. Según los científicos, ¿por qué están en peligro de extinción algunos animales en México?

2. ¿Qué programa ofrece el Banco de México? ¿Qué piensas del programa?

3. ¿Te gustaría comprar una moneda? ¿Por qué?

[1]Fuente: *El Universal*, 25 de agosto de 2002

El Parque Nacional Darién, en el Panamá, es el parque nacional más grande de América Central. Fue creado en 1980 para proteger la gran selva tropical del Darién, que se encuentra en la frontera entre el Panamá y Colombia. Hay siete especies de mamíferos y cinco especies de pájaros que sólo viven en esta selva. Además, tres grupos indígenas precolombinos todavía viven en el Darién: los kunas, los emberá y los wounaan.

• ¿Hay un parque cerca de tu comunidad creado para proteger y conservar la naturaleza? Descríbelo.

Un águila arpía, ave nacional del Panamá

¡Tú puedes ayudar a evitar su extinción!
Monedas y especies

El Banco de México pone a su disposición una colección de diez monedas de plata pura con motivos de animales en peligro de extinción en México. Con la compra de cada moneda, se destinarán recursos[2] para ayudar los proyectos de conservación de especies y su hábitat.

De venta en:
Banamex
Bital
Bancomer
BanRegio

[2]money will be donated

 Actividad 11 Escribir/Hablar

Y tú, ¿qué dices?

1. Describe la naturaleza que existe cerca de tu comunidad. ¿Te gusta estar afuera?

2. ¿Dónde prefieres pasar tiempo: en un bosque, en una selva tropical o en un desierto? Explica por qué.

3. ¿Cuáles son los peores problemas ecológicos de tu región? ¿Cómo se puede mejorar la situación?

4. Además de la electricidad, ¿qué otras fuentes de energía se usan en tu región? ¿Son eficientes y económicas? ¿El uso de estas fuentes de energía conserva o destruye el medio ambiente?

 Actividad 10  Standards: 1.2, 2.1, 2.2

Resources: Voc. and Gram. Transparency 170; Answers on Transparencies

Focus: Reading and writing about endangered species

Suggestions: Have students read the questions before reading the ad. Encourage them to look for cognates to help them with unfamiliar vocabulary. Point out that they should base their answers on the reading that precedes the questions, as well as on the ad.

Answers:
1. Están en peligro por la contaminación, la destrucción de su hábitat y la caza.
2. El Banco de México vende monedas para ayudar los proyectos de conservación de especies y su hábitat.
3. Answers will vary.

  Standards: 1.2, 2.2, 3.1, 4.2

Suggestions: Encourage students to describe protected lands, wetlands, and conservation areas, as well as state or national parks.

Answers will vary.

 Actividad 11 Standards: 1.3, 3.1

Focus: Writing and speaking about environmental issues

Suggestions: Bring in information from a park or environmental group in your area. Photocopy the information for students to reference when answering the questions.

Answers will vary.

Additional Resources
• WAV Wbk.: Audio Act. 6, p. 179
• Teacher's Resource Book: Audio Script, p. 260, Communicative Activity BLM, pp. 264–265
• Audio Program: Track 8

 Assessment
Prueba 9B-2: Vocab. Production, pp. 244–245

Enrich Your Teaching
Resources for All Teachers

Culture Note
Darién National Park, in Panama, is a bird-watcher's paradise. More than 450 bird species inhabit the park, with the most numerous being the treerunner, the green-naped tanager, the varied solitaire, the Pirre warbler, and the rufous-cheeked hummingbird. Also present is the harpy eagle, one of the largest raptors of its family and Panama's national bird.

Teacher-to-Teacher
Ask students to identify the endangered species shown on the coins in *Actividad* 10. Have them work in groups and choose one animal to research. Have them search the Internet to find out what has caused the animal to become endangered and solutions to help preserve the species. Have students present their findings to the class.

483

Gramática

Presentation EXPRESS
GRAMMAR

Core Instruction

 Standards: 4.1

Resources: Voc. and Gram. Transparency 169; Teacher's Resource Book: Video Script, p. 262; Video Program: Cap. 9B

Suggestions: Direct attention to the *¿Recuerdas?* Have students practice conjugating the verbs they already know by asking them questions about what the world will be like when they graduate college. Write the future endings on the board and have students identify the subject pronoun to which each refers.

Use the transparency and the *GramActiva* Video to introduce the new irregular verbs in the future tense, or to reinforce your own presentation.

Give students unlikely scenarios in the future and have them correct you: *El próximo viernes saldrás de la escuela a las once de la noche. Mañana vendrás a las seis de la mañana.*

  *Standards:* 1.2

Presentation EXPRESS
AUDIO

Resources: Teacher's Resource Book: Audio Script, p. 260; Audio Program: Track 9; Answers on Transparencies

Focus: Listening comprehension about a recycling center

Recycle: Items in a recycling center

Suggestions: Have students listen once without writing. Tell them to concentrate on the context of the sentences. Have them listen a second time, pausing after each sentence to give students time to write. Be sure students have correct sentences before they determine if they refer to the present or future.

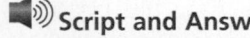 **Script and Answers:**
1. **¿A qué hora saldremos para el centro de reciclaje?** *(futuro)*
2. **Mis hermanos vendrán conmigo esta vez.** *(futuro)*
3. **¿Qué haremos para ayudarlos?** *(futuro)*
4. **Siempre nos dicen que somos muy trabajadores.** *(presente)*
5. **Pondré el plástico y el vidrio en cajas diferentes.** *(futuro)*
6. **Generalmente quieren darnos refrescos.** *(presente)*

Gramática

The future tense: Other irregular verbs

Other verbs that have irregular stems in the future tense are:

decir	dir-
poner	pondr-
querer	querr-
salir	saldr-
venir	vendr-

En el futuro **dirán** que la destrucción de las selvas tropicales causó muchos problemas ecológicos.
*In the future **they will say** that the destruction of the rain forests caused many ecological problems.*

Pondremos más plantas en nuestra casa.
We will put more plants in our house.

Querremos luchar contra la guerra y por la paz.
We will want to fight against war and for peace.

Saldré muy temprano por la mañana. **¿Vendrás** conmigo?
*I will leave very early in the morning. **Will you come** with me?*

¿Recuerdas?
You know how to form irregular verbs in the future using the same endings that you use for regular verbs *(-é, -ás, -á, -emos, -éis, -án)*. You already know these irregular verbs:

haber	**habr-**
hacer	**har-**
poder	**podr-**
saber	**sabr-**
tener	**tendr-**

GramActiva VIDEO

Want more help with other verbs that are irregular in the future tense? Watch the **GramActiva** video.

Querrá jugar.

---

 12 jdd-0998 **Escuchar/Escribir**

Escucha y escribe

Unos jóvenes hablan de sus experiencias como voluntarios en un centro de reciclaje. Hablan de lo que ocurre siempre y de lo que ocurrirá en el futuro. Escucha las seis frases y escríbelas. Después escribe *presente* si ocurre ahora o *futuro* si ocurrirá en el futuro.

484 cuatrocientos ochenta y cuatro
Tema 9 • ¿Cómo será el futuro?

Un centro de reciclaje

Differentiated Instruction
Solutions for All Learners

Students with Special Needs

Modify *Actividad* 12 for hearing-impaired students by providing them with the sentences from the script in scrambled order. Tell them to unscramble the sentences and then write **futuro** if the sentence talks about the future, or **presente** if it refers to the present.

Multiple Intelligences

Intrapersonal/Introspective: Have students write a description of what they will be like and what they will do at their ten-year high school reunion: *Yo seré muy rico. Me pondré un traje nuevo y saludaré a todos mis amigos.* Encourage them to use their imagination and to use both regular and irregular verbs.

Actividad 13

Leer/Escribir

Vamos al centro de reciclaje

Lee la conversación entre dos jóvenes que van a trabajar en el centro de reciclaje. Escribe la forma correcta de los verbos en el futuro.

Angélica: Oye, Pedro. El sábado voy al centro de reciclaje. ¿ __1.__ *(Venir)* tú conmigo?

Pedro: Está bien. __2.__ *(Ir)* contigo pero sólo tengo dos horas. ¿Qué __3.__ *(hacer)* nosotros?

Angélica: Primero nosotros __4.__ *(tener)* que llevar estas cajas al centro. Luego __5.__ *(poner)* los periódicos, el cartón y el vidrio en sus cajas.

Pedro: Y si no podemos quedarnos por más de dos horas, ¿qué les __6.__ *(decir)?*

Angélica: La verdad. Yo les __7.__ *(decir)* que tengo que estudiar. Y tú __8.__ *(poder)* salir al mismo tiempo. No __9.__ *(haber)* ningún problema.

Fondo cultural

El ecoturismo en el Ecuador Hay varias compañías de ecoturismo que ofrecen excursiones que benefician al medio ambiente y a las comunidades que los turistas visitan. Por ejemplo, en el Ecuador los turistas visitan la región del Amazonas y se quedan en casas típicas de la región. Esto no causa problemas para el medio ambiente. Además, los guías son indígenas de la región y con las excursiones ganan dinero para sus comunidades.

- ¿Cómo pueden causar problemas los turistas y el turismo en una región de mucha belleza ecológica? Compara las excursiones ecológicas que puedes hacer en Ecuador con las que puedes hacer en los Estados Unidos.

Selva tropical en la región amazónica del Ecuador

Actividad 14

Hablar

El turismo

Unos amigos tratan de decidir adónde irán de vacaciones, pero es difícil decidir porque no están de acuerdo. Con otro(a) estudiante, pregunta y contesta según el modelo.

Estudiante A

1. junio
2. octubre
3. agosto
4. julio

Modelo

julio

A —*Saldremos en julio. Iremos a la ciudad. ¿De acuerdo?*
B —*Pero nos dirán que no hay habitaciones libres.*

Estudiante B

a. Miles de turistas *(estar)* allí. Todos *(ponerse)* los trajes de baño y *(venir)* a la playa.

b. Las plantas y los árboles *(ser)* muy bonitos pero *(haber)* muchos mosquitos y moscas y *(llover)* todos los días.

c. *(Hacer)* demasiado calor. Además el aire *(ser)* muy seco. *(Querer)* encontrar un lugar con aire acondicionado.

d. No *(saber)* si *(hacer)* frío o calor. *(Querer)* dar caminatas pero no *(poder)* si hay mucha nieve en los valles.

cuatrocientos ochenta y cinco **485**
Capítulo 9B

Enrich Your Teaching
Resources for All Teachers

Culture Note

The Amazon is the world's second longest river, running 4,080 miles east from the Andes in Peru to the Atlantic Ocean. It drains 2,750,000 square miles—nearly half the South American landmass—and its basin, which lies in Brazil, Colombia, Ecuador, Peru, and Bolivia, contains 30% of all known plant and animal species.

Practice and Communicate

 9B

Actividad 13

  *Standards: 1.2*

 Presentation EXPRESS ANSWERS

Resources: Answers on Transparencies

Focus: Reading and writing about recycling

Suggestions: Remind students that although the verb *ir* is considered an irregular verb in many tenses, it is a regular verb in the future tense.

Answers:
1. Vendrás
2. Iré
3. haremos
4. tendremos
5. pondremos
6. diremos
7. diré
8. podrás
9. habrá

Bellringer Review

Write these sentences on the board and ask students to complete them with the correct verb in the future:

1. *De esa manera nosotros (tener/poder) conservar energía.* (**podremos**)

2. *Todos los habitantes (saber/poner) proteger a los animales.* (**sabremos**)

3. *Los pueblos (tener/haber) que reducir el uso de la electricidad.* (**tendremos**)

Fondo cultural

 *Standards: 1.2, 2.1, 2.2, 3.1, 4.2*

Suggestions: Have students brainstorm a list of different ecological areas in the United States (Florida Everglades, Smoky Mountains, redwood forests in California). Have them think of the ways uncontrolled tourism can negatively impact those areas.

Answers will vary.

Actividad 14

 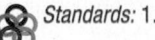 *Standards: 1.1*

 Presentation EXPRESS ANSWERS

Resources: Answers on Transparencies

Focus: Speaking about vacation plans

Recycle: Leisure activities; weather

Suggestions: Have students first identify the locations pictured and tell what each place is like during the month noted.

Answers:
Student A:
1. Saldremos en junio. Iremos a la selva tropical.
2. Saldremos en octubre. Iremos a las montañas.
3. Saldremos en agosto. Iremos a la playa.
4. Saldremos en julio. Iremos al desierto.
Student B:
1. b. serán; habrá; lloverá
2. d. sabremos; hará; Querremos; podremos
3. a. estarán; se pondrán; vendrán
4. c. Hará; será; Querremos

485

Actividad 15 *Standards:* 1.1, 1.3

Presentation EXPRESS ANSWERS

Resources: Teacher's Resource Book: GramActiva BLM, p. 269; Answers on Transparencies

Focus: Writing and talking about life now and in the future

Suggestions: Before completing the chart, discuss how students see themselves in the future: What do they want to do? Where do they want to live? What will they worry about?

Answers:
Step 1: Answers will vary but will include:
quiero / querré
sé / sabré
salgo / saldré
tengo / tendré/
vivo / viviré
Step 2: Answers will vary.

 Actividad 16 *Standards:* 1.1, 1.3

Focus: Writing and talking about environmental causes and effects

Suggestions: Have students work in pairs to brainstorm some of the possible results.

Answers will vary.

Extension: Have students make predictions about what their community will be like in the future: *Habrá menos árboles y más casas en el futuro.*

Theme Project
Students can perform Step 4 at this point. Be sure they understand your corrections and suggestions. (For more information, see p. 448-a.)

Additional Resources
- WAV Wbk.: Audio Act. 7, p. 180
- Teacher's Resource Book: Audio Script, p. 260
- Audio Program: Track 10

 Assessment
- *ExamView* Quiz on PresEXPRESS
- Prueba 9B-3: The future tense: Other irregular verbs, p. 246

 **Actividad 15** **Hablar/Escribir**

En el presente y en el futuro

¿Crees que tu vida en el futuro será muy diferente de tu vida ahora?

yo (ahora)	yo (futuro)	mi compañero(a) (ahora)	mi compañero(a) (futuro)
en una tienda de descuentos	en una oficina de abogados		

1 Trabaja con otro(a) estudiante. Copia la tabla en una hoja de papel. Para cada verbo del recuadro, escribe la información que describe tu vida ahora y cómo crees que será en el futuro. Después escribe las respuestas de tu compañero(a).

querer
saber (+ *infinitive*)
salir con
tener que
vivir

¡Respuesta personal!

> **Modelo**
> A —*Ahora trabajo en una tienda de descuentos. En el futuro, trabajaré en una oficina de abogados. ¿Y tú?*
> B —*Ahora trabajo . . .*

2 Escribe cinco frases para describir las semejanzas *(similarities)* o diferencias entre la vida de tu compañero(a) ahora y su vida en el futuro.

 Actividad 16 **Escribir/Hablar**

¿Qué resultará?

¿Qué resultará de las situaciones que existen ahora? Usa los verbos del recuadro para escribir un posible resultado para cada situación. Luego, con otro(a) estudiante, compara los resultados que han escrito. ¿Son muy similares o muy diferentes sus ideas sobre el futuro?

decir	poder	salir
haber	poner	ser
hacer	querer	tener
ir	saber	venir

> **Modelo**
> Cada día se destruyen las selvas tropicales.
> *Habrá más animales en peligro de extinción.*

1. Mis padres quieren usar la energía de una manera más eficiente en la casa.
2. Vamos a recoger la basura en el parque.
3. Tratamos de ahorrar la electricidad en la escuela.
4. Los científicos quieren explorar el espacio.
5. La contaminación del aire en la ciudad es muy grave.
6. Hay muchos grupos ecológicos que tratan de conservar el medio ambiente.

Más práctica
- Practice Workbook, p. 186: 9B-5
- WAV Wbk.: Writing, p. 182
- Guided Practice: Grammar Acts., pp. 337–338
- *Real.* para hispanohablantes, pp. 354-357

 **Go Online**
PHSchool.com
For: Irreg. Future Verbs
Web Code: jdd-0913

Differentiated Instruction
Solutions for All Learners

Students with Special Needs
Students with language processing difficulties may need help following the multi-step directions required for *Actividad* 15. If so, divide Step 1 into several steps. Write the steps on a transparency to provide visual reinforcement.

Advanced Learners
Have students interview a family member or friend who is not in the class to find out what that person thinks the future will be like: *¿Dónde trabajarás? ¿Quién será tu mejor amigo(a)? ¿Dónde vivirás?* If necessary, they may conduct the interview in English, but have them report back to the class in Spanish.

Gramática

The present subjunctive with expressions of doubt

You have used the subjunctive to say that one person tries to persuade another to do something. It is also used after verbs and expressions that indicate doubt or uncertainty.

Dudamos que puedan resolver todos los problemas.
We doubt that they can solve all the problems.

No es cierto que protejan las selvas tropicales.
It is not certain that they will protect rain forests.

Other expressions that indicate doubt or uncertainty are:

no creer que	*to not believe*
no estar seguro, -a de que	*to be unsure*
es imposible que	*it is impossible*
es posible que	*it is possible*

When the verb or expression indicates certainty, use the indicative, *not* the subjunctive.

Estoy seguro de que destruyen los bosques.
I'm sure that they are destroying the forests.

Creemos que es importante proteger la naturaleza.
We believe that it is important to protect nature.

• The subjunctive form of *hay* is *haya*, from *haber*.

Es posible que **haya** suficiente electricidad.
*It is possible that **there is** enough electricity.*

GramActiva VIDEO

Want more help with the subjunctive with expressions of doubt? Watch the **GramActiva** video.

Actividad 17

Leer/Escribir

¿Cierto o no?

Lee lo que dicen estas personas sobre el futuro y decide si es necesario usar el subjuntivo o el indicativo. Luego escribe la forma apropiada del verbo.

1. No creo que _____ *(haber)* soluciones fáciles para los problemas ecológicos en la Tierra.

2. Dudamos que la contaminación del medio ambiente se _____ *(mejorar)* pronto.

3. Es posible que las leyes estrictas _____ *(poder)* ayudar a reducir la contaminación.

4. Es cierto que muchos animales _____ *(estar)* en peligro de extinción.

5. Estoy seguro de que el reciclaje _____ *(eliminar)* la destrucción de las selvas tropicales.

Modelo

Es imposible que sólo las leyes protejan los bosques de la contaminación.

6. El profesor no cree que las guerras _____ *(ir)* a terminar nunca.

7. No estoy seguro de que las leyes para proteger el medio ambiente _____ *(funcionar)* muy bien.

8. Es verdad que la calefacción solar _____ *(ser)* mejor para el medio ambiente que la electricidad.

cuatrocientos ochenta y siete 487
Capítulo 9B

Enrich Your Teaching

Resources for All Teachers

Teacher-to-Teacher

Have students work in groups to play *Sabelotodo*. Tell them to write four sentences using expressions of certainty, three false and one true. Encourage students to write sentences that are not easily identified as true or false. Have them read their sentences aloud while the other members of the group respond with expressions of doubt to the false sentences or expressions of certainty to the true ones. Students earn one point for each correct response. The first person to determine the true sentence gets two bonus points.

 Bellringer Review

Review the formation of the present subjunctive. Ask students to write three recommendations for maintaining good health using the verbs **caminar, comer,** and **dormir.**

Gramática

Core Instruction

Resources: Teacher's Resource Book: Video Script, pp. 262–263; Video Program: Cap. 9B

Suggestions: Use the *GramActiva* Video as an introduction or to reinforce your own presentation.

Before presenting the *Gramática,* remind students that the subjunctive is used in sentences with two parts that are connected by the word **que.** Write sample sentence starters on the board and have volunteers complete the sentences orally. For example: *Es necesario que ...; Quiero que ...; Insisto en que ...; Es importante que ....*

After reading the *Gramática,* have students make flashcards of the expressions of doubt that trigger the present subjunctive and the expressions of certainty that trigger the use of the indicative. In pairs, have them review the cards and decide if the phrase expresses doubt or certainty and whether it requires the subjunctive or the indicative.

Actividad 17  *Standards:* 1.2

Resources: Answers on Transparencies

Focus: Reading about the future; choosing between the present subjunctive and the indicative

Suggestions: If students have difficulty determining when to use the subjunctive or indicative, have them use their flashcards as they complete the exercise.

Answers:

1.	haya	5.	elimina
2.	mejore	6.	vayan
3.	puedan	7.	funcionen
4.	están	8.	es

Common Errors: In item 1, students may conjugate the verb **haber** and want to use **hayan.** Point out that just as **hay** is used to mean "there is" and "there are," so **haya** is used with both singular and plural complements.

Actividad 18  *Standards:* 1.1

 **ANSWERS**

Resources: Answers on Transparencies

Focus: Expressing beliefs or doubts using the subjunctive and indicative

Suggestions: Review the *Nota*. Point out that students will use the subjunctive in the questions since they don't know much about the future. If their answer expresses doubt, it should be in the subjunctive. If their answer is affirmative, it should be in the indicative.

Answers:

Student A:
1. ¿Crees que haya más guerras?
2. ¿... funcionen los coches con energía solar?
3. ¿... viajen a otros planetas?
4. ¿... encuentren nuevas fuentes de energía?
5. ¿... tengan a una mujer como presidente?
6. ¿... todos sean bilingües?

Student B answers will vary but may include:
1. haya *OR* hay
2. funcionen *OR* funcionan
3. viajen *OR* viajan
4. encuentren *OR* encuentran
5. tengan *OR* tienen
6. sean *OR* son

 Actividad 19  *Standards:* 1.1, 1.3

Focus: Expressing beliefs or doubts using the subjunctive and indicative

Suggestions: Have students look at the word box and brainstorm a list of possible verbs, both regular and irregular, they could use in their opinions.

Answers will vary.

Actividad 18  **Hablar**

En 15 años

Imagina que otro(a) estudiante y tú van a filmar una película sobre qué pasará en el mundo en 15 años. Hablen de si están seguros de que las cosas ocurrirán.

> **Nota**
>
> In a question, *creer que* is followed by the subjunctive if the speaker has doubts about, or suggests the possibility of, the action.

Modelo

A —¿*Crees que haya paz en la Tierra en 15 años?*
B —*No, no creo que haya paz.*
o: —*Sí, estoy seguro(a) de que habrá paz.*

Estudiante A

1. haber guerras
2. funcionar los coches con energía solar
3. viajar a otros planetas
4. encontrar nuevas fuentes de energía
5. tener una mujer como Presidenta
6. todos ser bilingües

Estudiante B

(no) dudar que
es (im)posible que
(no) creer que
(no) estar seguro, -a de que
(no) es cierto que

Actividad 19 **Escribir/Hablar**

Y ahora, tu opinión

¿Será posible resolver los problemas ecológicos de hoy? Escribe tus opiniones sobre lo que van a hacer las personas de la lista en el futuro. Luego trabaja con otro(a) estudiante y di si Uds. están de acuerdo o no en sus opiniones.

Modelo

Creo que viviremos en la Luna algún día.
o: *Es imposible que vivamos algún día en la Luna.*

los científicos	los problemas ecológicos
nosotros	el aire acondicionado solar
yo	por la paz y contra la guerra
el Presidente	a los animales en peligro de extinción
toda la gente	la destrucción de las selvas tropicales
¡Respuesta personal!	**¡Respuesta personal!**

Differentiated Instruction
Solutions for All Learners

Heritage Language Learners

Review the *Nota* with students, emphasizing that it is the speaker who chooses the subjunctive or the indicative after ***creer que,*** depending on the degree of certainty he or she wishes to express. Ask students to write four sentences using ***creer que*** followed by the subjunctive and the indicative. Have them explain why they used each.

Actividad 20 Leer/Escribir/Hablar

La contaminación acústica

Cuando pensamos en la contaminación, casi siempre pensamos en el aire y el agua. Pero la contaminación acústica *(noise)* es también un gran problema, especialmente en las ciudades grandes. La ciudad de Madrid, España, tiene una campaña *(campaign)* que se llama "Controla tu ruido", para reducir la contaminación acústica. Lee la siguiente información de su página Web y contesta las preguntas.

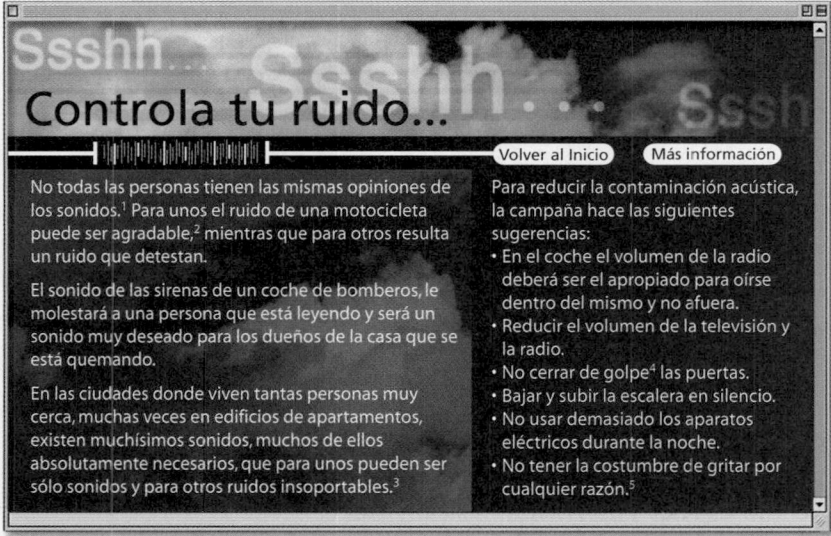

Controla tu ruido...

No todas las personas tienen las mismas opiniones de los sonidos.[1] Para unos el ruido de una motocicleta puede ser agradable,[2] mientras que para otros resulta un ruido que detestan.

El sonido de las sirenas de un coche de bomberos, le molestará a una persona que está leyendo y será un sonido muy deseado para los dueños de la casa que se está quemando.

En las ciudades donde viven tantas personas muy cerca, muchas veces en edificios de apartamentos, existen muchísimos sonidos, muchos de ellos absolutamente necesarios, que para unos pueden ser sólo sonidos y para otros ruidos insoportables.[3]

Volver al Inicio — Más información

Para reducir la contaminación acústica, la campaña hace las siguientes sugerencias:
• En el coche el volumen de la radio deberá ser el apropiado para oírse dentro del mismo y no afuera.
• Reducir el volumen de la televisión y la radio.
• No cerrar de golpe[4] las puertas.
• Bajar y subir la escalera en silencio.
• No usar demasiado los aparatos eléctricos durante la noche.
• No tener la costumbre de gritar por cualquier razón.[5]

[1]sounds [2]pleasant [3]unbearable [4]slam [5]any reason

1. ¿Estás de acuerdo de que un sonido puede ser agradable para una persona y no para otra? Da otro ejemplo de esto.

2. ¿Crees que la contaminación acústica es un gran problema donde vives? ¿Por qué? ¿Qué recomendaciones resolverían *(would solve)* problemas acústicos en tu comunidad?

3. ¿Qué leyes o reglas hay en tu escuela o comunidad para reducir la contaminación acústica? ¿Crees que funcionan?

4. Escribe otras dos sugerencias que puedan ayudar a reducir la contaminación acústica.

  Actividad 21 Hablar

¿La campaña puede tener éxito?

¿Crees que sea posible reducir la contaminación acústica? Usa ideas de la página Web de "Controla tu ruido" y tus propias ideas de la Actividad 20 para decirle a otro(a) estudiante si crees que la campaña pueda tener éxito. Usa también las expresiones de la Actividad 18 de la página 488.

Modelo
Dudo que muchas personas reduzcan el volumen de su televisor o radio.

cuatrocientos ochenta y nueve **489**
Capítulo 9B

Practice and Communicate **9B**

Actividad 20 *Standards:* 1.2, 1.3, 3.1

Resources: Voc. and Gram. Transparency 171; Answers on Transparencies

Focus: Reading comprehension about noise pollution

Suggestions: Write the word **contaminación** on the board and have students say what words come to mind (*aire, agua, basura*). Then add **acústica** and explain that it is a cognate. Call on a volunteer to explain what the term could mean. Ask students if they have heard the term *noise pollution* and what they think it means. What are some examples?

Read the introduction aloud and discuss how noise pollution can be a problem in large cities. Have students read the Web page silently and take notes, highlighting the main points.

Remind students to use the subjunctive when making recommendations in items 2 and 4.

Answers will vary.

Actividad 21 *Standards:* 1.1

Focus: Expressing belief or doubt about outcomes, based on a reading

Suggestions: Review the main points of the campaign and discuss which suggestions seem realistic or enforceable. Have students tape their conversations for evaluation.

Answers will vary.

Enrich Your Teaching
Resources for All Teachers

Culture Note

The city government of Madrid began its formal campaign against noise pollution in September 2002 after hosting the International Meeting on Acoustic Pollution in Cities in April of the same year. Authorities planned a lengthy campaign, knowing that its success depends on educating the public.

Teacher-to-Teacher

Have students work in groups to create a poster with recommendations for reducing noise pollution in their community, school, or home. Tell students to first think about noise pollution in their own lives. They should brainstorm a list of places where noise pollution is a concern and then think about ways to reduce the problem.

Actividad 22 Standards: 1.2, 2.2, 3.1
Pre-AP*

Focus: Answering questions about fine art

Suggestions: Point out that José Antonio Velásquez's painting depicts the calm of a town from a distance, while Joaquín Torres-García's painting represents a more distorted view of a city. Have students read the introductory paragraph with these interpretations in mind. You may want to share the Culture Note on p. 491 with students before beginning.

Answers will vary.

Actividad 23 Standards: 1.1, 1.2, 1.3

Focus: Reading comprehension; cross-curricular connection to ecology, science

Suggestions: Remind students to use visuals, footnotes, and contextual clues to help with unfamiliar vocabulary. Point out that the word **regar** is a verb meaning "to water," and should not be confused with the noun **agua.**

Answers will vary.

Block Schedule

Have students work in groups to use the suggestions in *Actividad* 23 and add some of their own to prepare announcements to promote water conservation in your school. Have them post their announcements near sinks for students and staff to see.

 Pre-AP* Support

• **Activity:** Display in the classroom several ecology/environmental promotion posters captioned in English or without captions. Ask that students write possible captions in Spanish for the posters to read aloud to the class. Class members then determine for which poster each caption might apply.

• *Pre-AP* Resource Book:* Comprehensive guide to Pre-AP* communication skill development, pp. 9–17, 36–46

 Actividad 22 Pensar/Escribir

Dos lugares muy distintos

Joaquín Torres-García nació en Uruguay, un país urbano y moderno. José Antonio Velásquez nació en Honduras, un país más rural y menos moderno que Uruguay. En los cuadros de estos dos artistas, vemos dos mundos diferentes.

"Paisaje hondureño de San Antonio de Oriente" (1972), José Antonio Velásquez
Oil on canvas, 47 1/4" x 60 1/2". Museum of Modern Art of Latin America, Washington D.C.

1. Describe el primer cuadro. ¿Qué cosas puedes identificar? ¿Ves algún elemento de la naturaleza? ¿Cómo te hace sentir?

2. Describe el segundo cuadro. ¿Qué elementos de la naturaleza ves? ¿Qué cosas hechas por personas hay? ¿Cómo te hace sentir?

3. Compara los cuadros. ¿Qué crees que los artistas están tratando de decirnos sobre la gente y su relación con la naturaleza? ¿Con cuál estás de acuerdo? ¿Por qué?

"Nueva York a vista de pájaro" (1920), Joaquín Torres-García
Gouache and watercolor on cardboard, 33.8 x 48.5. Yale University Art Gallery, Gift of Collection Societé Anonyme.

 **Actividad 23** Leer/Pensar/Escribir/Hablar

El uso y abuso del agua

Trabajen en grupos de cuatro y observen los dibujos. Túrnense para leer las sugerencias para ahorrar el agua. Luego contesta las preguntas.

Conexiones La ecología

1. Tomar duchas más cortas. Si se usa la bañera,[1] llenarla sólo hasta la mitad.[2]

2. Lavar las verduras en un recipiente y no bajo el grifo.[3]

3. Cerrar el grifo cuando se cepilla los dientes.

4. Regar[4] el jardín por la mañana o al anochecer[5] para que el sol no evapore el agua.

5. Usar la lavadora sólo cuando esté llena de ropa.

[1]bathtub [2]halfway [3]faucet [4]Water [5]dusk

1. ¿En tu comunidad hay restricciones sobre el uso del agua? ¿Cuáles son?

2. Trabaja con otro(a) estudiante. Escriban cuatro frases para decir qué sugerencias darán más resultado en sus casas y qué sugerencias dudan que tengan resultado.

490 cuatrocientos noventa
Tema 9 • ¿Cómo será el futuro?

Differentiated Instruction
Solutions for All Learners

Students with Special Needs

Describe the paintings in *Actividad* 22 to visually impaired students. Then have them write a short paragraph about what a city or town is like. Encourage them to use different viewpoints in their writing. For example, have them describe the city for someone who has lived there their whole life, as well as for someone who was raised in the country.

Multiple Intelligences

Interpersonal/Social: Have students interview someone associated with a conservation organization via e-mail. Ask them to prepare five questions. Have them find the organization's contact information and write an introductory e-mail, explaining that they are conducting research for school.

Actividad 24 — Leer/Escribir/Hablar

El Día de la Tierra

Lee el lema (slogan) que usó Costa Rica en 1998 para su Día de la Tierra y contesta las preguntas.

1. ¿Qué aspectos del medio ambiente y qué problemas ecológicos se incluyen en el lema?

2. Usa lo que has aprendido sobre Costa Rica y explica por qué se preocupan (worry) los costarricenses.

3. Explica lo que entiendes de "entenderemos que no se puede comer el dinero".

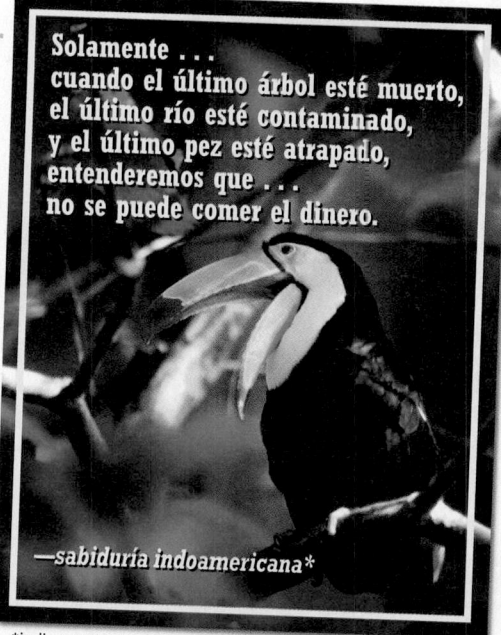

Solamente . . .
cuando el último árbol esté muerto,
el último río esté contaminado,
y el último pez esté atrapado,
entenderemos que . . .
no se puede comer el dinero.

—sabiduría indoamericana*

*indigenous saying

Actividad 25 — Escribir/Dibujar/Hablar

La conservación

Trabaja con otro(a) estudiante. Creen su propio lema para animar (encourage) a otras personas a pensar en la conservación.

1. Hagan una lista de los problemas ecológicos que quieren mencionar y escriban un lema basado en la lista.

2. Pon su lema en un cartel o una camiseta. Añadan dibujos o fotos. Preséntenlo a la clase.

Más práctica

- Practice Workbook, pp. 187–188: 9B-6, 9B-7
- WAV Wbk.: Writing, p. 183
- Guided Practice: Grammar Acts., pp. 339–341
- Real. para hispanohablantes, pp. 358–361

 Go Online
PHSchool.com
For: Present Subjunctive and Doubt
Web Code: jdd-0914

El español en el mundo del trabajo

Conservation International (CI) es una de varias organizaciones sin fines de lucro (nonprofit) cuya misión es proteger el medio ambiente. Tiene sus oficinas principales en Washington, D.C., pero muchos de sus empleados hablan español o portugués. Gran parte de sus esfuerzos (efforts) ecológicos se centran en los países de América Central y América del Sur. Por eso, también tiene empleados en México, Costa Rica, Panamá, Ecuador, Bolivia y Perú.

- Además de hablar español, ¿cómo debe ser la persona que trabajará para Conservation International? ¿Qué le interesará a esta persona?

Homero Aridjis, famoso escritor y naturalista mexicano

cuatrocientos noventa y uno **491**
Capítulo 9B

Practice and Communicate

 9B

 Actividad 24  Standards: 1.2, 1.3 Presentation EXPRESS ANSWERS

Resources: Voc. and Gram. Transparency 172; Answers on Transparencies

Focus: Reading, writing, and talking about ecology

Suggestions: To answer item 2, have students make a list of what they know about Costa Rica and its policies on conservation of natural resources.

Answers:

1. Se incluyen la destrucción de los árboles, la contaminación del agua y la extinción de especies.

Answers to items 2 and 3 will vary.

 Actividad 25 Standards: 1.3

Focus: Creating an environmental slogan and poster

Suggestions: Encourage students to focus on two or three problems in their slogan. Remind students that the image they use should support the text.

Answers will vary.

El español en el mundo del trabajo

Core Instruction

 Standards: 1.2, 5.1

Suggestions: Have students brainstorm some reasons why it is important to speak various languages when you work for an international organization.

Answers will vary.

Theme Project

Students can perform Step 5 at this point. Record their presentations on cassette or videotape for inclusion in their portfolio. (For more information, see p. 448-a.)

Additional Resources

- WAV Wbk.: Audio Act. 8–9, p. 180
- Teacher's Resource Book: Audio Script, pp. 260–261, Communicative Activity BLM, pp. 266–267
- Audio Program: Tracks 11–12

 Assessment

- ExamView QuickTake Presenter Quiz on PresEXPRESS
- Prueba 9B-4: The present subjunctive with expressions of doubt, p. 247

491

Enrich Your Teaching
Resources for All Teachers

Culture Note

San Antonio de Oriente, Honduras, is located in a valley southeast of the capital, Tegucigalpa. In the 1960s and 1970s, the village was a favorite subject of artist José Antonio Velásquez, who did several landscapes of the lovely scenery in and around the town.

Teacher-to-Teacher

Have students keep track of how much water they use in a week. They should chart the number of times they shower, wash their hands, or do laundry, for example. Ask students if they became more conscious of water consumption as they charted their use. Have them write guidelines explaining how they can save water in their daily routine.

Lectura

Core Instruction

Focus: Reading an article about Antarctica and Tierra del Fuego

Suggestions:

Pre-reading: Point out Chile, Argentina, and Antarctica on the map. Have students make a list of words that come to mind when they think of Antarctica. Have a volunteer read the title. Ask students to list possible reasons Antarctica needs to be protected. Have them use the photos to help them develop their list.

Reading: Have the students read the article silently or read it to them. Ask a volunteer to summarize the information for each subhead. Because there are various themes discussed in the reading, you may want to provide students with a graphic organizer to complete as they read.

Post-reading: Ask students to identify examples of when the author expressed an opinion instead of providing factual information. Have students complete the *¿Comprendiste?* questions.

Bellringer Review

Have students refer to the picture accompanying the *Fondo cultural* on p. 481. As a class brainstorm what weather conditions and geographical areas these penguins might prefer.

Block Schedule

Ask students to work in groups to make a list of six guidelines for visitors to Antarctica. Have them use the information in the reading to develop their guidelines. Encourage them to present their guidelines using the sign in the photo on p. 493 as a model. You may want to supplement the reading with travel videos about visiting Antarctica.

Addidtional Resources

Student Resource: Guided Practice: Lectura, p. 342

¡Adelante!

Lectura

Objectives

- **Learn about the Antarctic and Tierra del Fuego**
- **Read about rain forests**
- **Write a presentation on community service**

Estrategia

Detecting point of view
When reading an article, you need to be aware that the author might have strong opinions about certain issues. While you read this article, try to identify those passages and sentences that support the point of view of the author. Do you agree or disagree?

Protegemos la Antártida

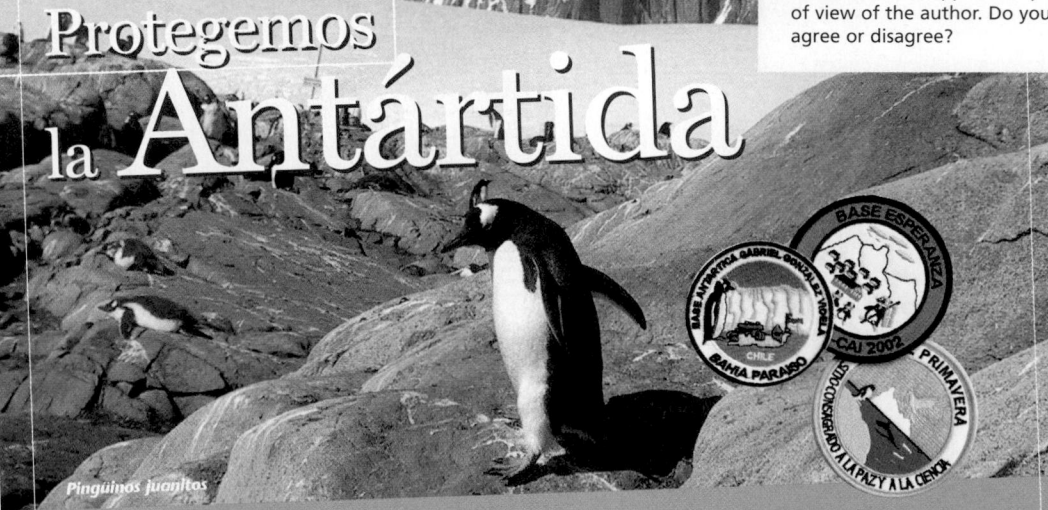

Pingüinos juanitos

Con un área de 16.5 millones de kilómetros cuadrados, la Antártida es un continente de hielo, y es el quinto en tamaño de la Tierra. El 90 por ciento del hielo de la Tierra se encuentra en la Antártida. Es un desierto frígido donde casi nunca llueve. El continente está rodeado por islas que tienen un clima menos frío y por esto hay una variedad de plantas. Estas plantas mantienen un gran número de pájaros y animales. La existencia de especies está limitada por el clima y el hielo, pero existe una abundancia de vida en el agua: plancton, coral, esponjas, peces, focas,[1] ballenas y pingüinos.

¡Estamos en peligro!

Las regiones polares son muy importantes para la supervivencia[2] de la Tierra entera. Los casquetes de hielo[3] en las zonas polares reflejan luz solar y así regularizan la temperatura de la Tierra. Cuando se destruyen estos casquetes, hay menos luz solar que se refleja y la Tierra se convierte en un receptor termal. Esto se llama el efecto de invernadero.[4] Es en la Antártida que en 1985 se reportaron por primera vez los hoyos[5] en la capa[6] del ozono y aquí es donde hoy día se trata de encontrar una solución.

El Tratado Antártico

A través de los años, muchos países han declarado soberanía de derechos[7] sobre la Antártida y esto ha producido problemas, especialmente en la Argentina y Chile. Pero el 1ro de diciembre de 1959, los problemas se acabaron con el Tratado[8] Antártico.

[1]seals [2]survival [3]ice caps [4]greenhouse effect [5]holes [6]layer [7]sovereign land rights [8]Treaty

---

Differentiated Instruction
Solutions for All Learners

Multiple Intelligences

Naturalist: Ask students to research more about plant and animal life in Antarctica. Have them write a fictional postcard describing all of the plants and animals that they have seen on their recent trip to Antarctica.

Advanced Learners

Have students contact a travel agency to find out more about ways to travel to Antarctica. Ask them to find specific places in Chile and Argentina, such as Ushuaia, that have cruises to Antarctica. Have students use the information to create a flier advertising a vacation package to Antarctica.

Ushuaia, Argentina

proteger el medio ambiente de la Antártida. La región de Tierra del Fuego dividida entre Chile y la Argentina es hoy un centro de investigación científica polar. La ciudad de Ushuaia se ha convertido en el punto de partida[10] para los que visitan la Antártida.

por científicos especializados en el medio ambiente de la región. Los barcos tardan dos días en llegar a la Antártida y los visitantes pueden quedarse en las bases de actividad científica que se encuentran en el continente.

El tratado estableció reglas para el uso de la región. Las dos más importantes son el uso pacífico del continente para objetivos científicos y la prohibición de la explotación minera. La Argentina y Chile, entre otros, han tomado medidas[9] para

Ushuaia

Es la ciudad más al sur del mundo. Desde aquí salen equipos científicos a la Antártida para estudiar el clima, la naturaleza, el hielo y la roca. También salen excursiones turísticas dirigidas

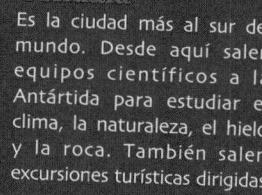

Base científica de la Argentina, Antártida

Un crucero, la Antártida

⁹have taken steps   ¹⁰departure

¿Comprendiste?

1. Según el artículo, ¿cómo afectan las regiones polares al medio ambiente?

2. ¿Por qué se considera la Antártida un desierto?

3. ¿Por qué fue importante el Tratado Antártico?

Y tú, ¿qué dices?

¿Te gustaría visitar la Antártida? ¿Por qué?

Más práctica

- WAV Wbk.: Writing, p. 184
- Guided Practice: *Lectura*, p. 342
- *Real.* para hispanohablantes, pp. 362–363

Go Online
PHSchool.com
For: Internet Activity
Web Code: jdd-0915

Enrich Your Teaching
Resources for All Teachers

Culture Note

Tierra del Fuego—literally meaning "Land of Fire"—is a group of islands separated from South America between the Strait of Magellan and divided politically between Chile and Argentina. The largest town on the islands is Ushuaia, Argentina. It is less than 620 miles from Antarctica and is recognized as the southernmost town in the world.

Internet Search

Encourage students to find out more about Tierra del Fuego using the Internet.

Keyword: Tierra del Fuego

¿Comprendiste?

 *Standards:* 1.2

Presentation EXPRESS
ANSWERS

Resources: Answers on Transparencies

Focus: Verifying comprehension of the *Lectura*

Suggestions: Point out that students will find the answer for item 2 first. Have students point out the place in the reading where they found their information. Encourage them to provide supporting details for each answer.

Answers:

1. El hielo refleja la luz solar y así regulariza la temperatura de la Tierra.
2. Se considera un desierto porque casi nunca llueve.
3. El tratado estableció reglas para el uso de la región. Las dos más importantes son el uso pacífico del continente para objetivos científicos y la prohibición de la explotación minera.

Y tú, ¿qué dices?

 Standards: 1.1, 1.3

Suggestions: Have students prepare their response in the form of a paragraph, with a topic sentence and supporting details.

Answers will vary.

Pre-AP* Support

- **Activity:** Have students work together in groups of three. Read aloud to the class the introductory paragraph to this article. Then ask one student to read aloud the first subtitled paragraph to the group. The student to his or her right writes or asks a content question about the paragraph that has just been read and the third student answers it. Continue around the circle in this way to complete the reading.

- *Pre-AP* Resource Book:* Comprehensive guide to Pre-AP* reading skill development, pp. 18–24

For Further Reading

Student Resources: Realidades para hispanohablantes: Lectura 2, pp. 364–365; Lecturas para hispanohablantes 2: "Los problemas de la ciudad," pp. 15–16, "Los chicos del fin del mundo," pp. 111–114

Core Instruction

Standards: 1.2, 1.3, 2.1, 3.1

Focus: Reading about deforestation

Suggestions: Ask students to give a definition of the word *deforestation*. If they are unsure, instruct them on how to use word parts to determine the meaning of a word. Have students predict possible effects of deforestation on the affected areas. Refer them to the map to determine in which parts of the world deforestation is taking place.

Have students read the passage silently or aloud. Ask them to name two reasons deforestation is occurring. Can they think of possible alternatives for solving these problems?

To help students obtain information for the *¡Compruébalo!*, contact the parks and recreation department in your community or state. Ask the employees to send you information about deforestation in your area. Photocopy the information to share with your students. You may want to have students use a Venn diagram to make their comparisons.

Answers will vary.

Block Schedule

Invite an expert on environmental studies to your classroom to discuss the problems associated with deforestation. Encourage students to prepare questions specific to the effects of deforestation on the environment of Spanish-speaking countries in the affected areas. Allow time for students to ask their questions of the guest speaker.

Additional Resources

Student Resource: Realidades para hispanohablantes, p. 366

Perspectivas del mundo hispano

La deforestación de los bosques tropicales

La selva tropical y el río Amazonas

La selva o el bosque tropical son bosques con una vegetación rica y abundante, situados alrededor de la zona de la línea ecuatorial. En América Latina y el Caribe, los bosques cubren[1] el 47 por ciento del área total, y la región del río Amazonas tiene el 33 por ciento de todos los bosques tropicales del mundo.

Hace tres o cuatro mil años, los bosques tropicales cubrían el 14 por ciento de la Tierra. Hoy en día los bosques tropicales sólo cubren el dos por ciento de la Tierra. La mayoría de la deforestación ha ocurrido en los últimos 250 años, producida por el aumento[2] de la producción industrial y de la población. El 84 por ciento de la deforestación en América Latina es causada por la expansión de áreas para la agricultura, el 12.5 por ciento se debe a la tala[3] de árboles y el 3.5 por ciento a la construcción de carreteras, puentes y otras obras públicas.

Es importante proteger los bosques porque en ellos viven personas y animales que están perdiendo sus hogares.[4] Además, los bosques tropicales son una fuente muy importante de recursos naturales y medicinas.

¡Compruébalo! Busca información en Internet sobre el porcentaje[5] de bosques en tu estado.[6] ¿Ha aumentado[7] o bajado en los últimos 50 años? ¿Hay programas para proteger los bosques? Descríbelos.

¿Qué te parece? Compara el problema de la deforestación de los bosques tropicales con la situación que existe en tu estado. ¿En qué sentido es similar? ¿En qué sentido es diferente?

La deforestación en la zona amazónica, Brasil

[1]cover [2]increase [3]logging [4]homes
[5]percentage [6]state [7]increased

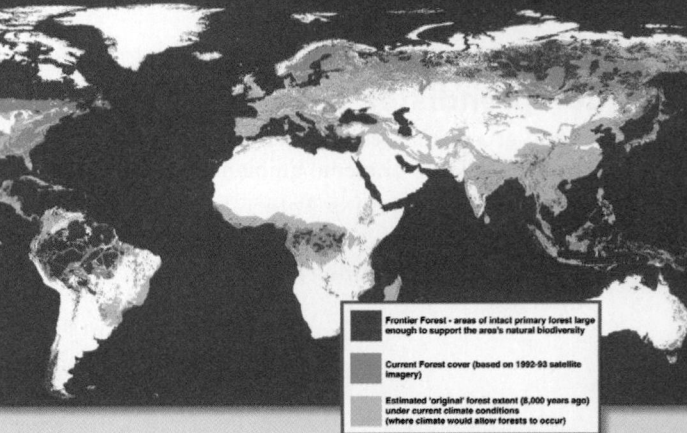

Frontier Forest - areas of intact primary forest large enough to support the area's natural biodiversity

Current Forest cover (based on 1992-93 satellite imagery)

Estimated 'original' forest extent (8,000 years ago) under current climate conditions (where climate would allow forests to occur)

Differentiated Instruction
Solutions for All Learners

Students with Learning Difficulties
Explain to students that they must consider the target audience when deciding which information to include in a persuasive article. Instruct students to think about to whom their project would appeal, whom they would like to recruit, and in what ways companies or individuals in the community could contribute.

Multiple Intelligences
Mathematical/Logical: Have students prepare a graph that represents the increase or decrease of forested land in your state, using the information that they gathered for the *¡Compruébalo!* questions.

Prestemos servicio

Task
Summer vacation is a good time to do something to improve your community. You are organizing a volunteer project and have been asked to write an article for the daily paper explaining your project.

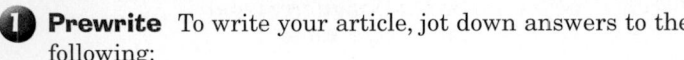

1 Prewrite To write your article, jot down answers to the following:

- ¿Qué . . . ?
- ¿Quién(es) . . . ?
- ¿Por qué . . . ?
- ¿Dónde . . . ?
- ¿Cuándo . . . ?
- Para más información . . .

2 Draft Using the answers to the key questions, write the first draft of your article. Try to use a title that captures the interest of your readers. It is important to present your ideas in a logical, concise, and interesting format so that others will want to participate.

3 Revise Read your article and correct the spelling, agreement, verb forms, and use of vocabulary. Have a classmate check the following:

- Did you present your plan in a logical, concise format?
- Did you include all the necessary information?
- Should you add or change anything?
- Are there errors in spelling, verb forms, or agreement?

4 Publish Rewrite the article, making the necessary corrections and changes. Make a copy for your teacher and include another in your portfolio.

5 Evaluation Your teacher may give you a rubric for how the article will be graded. You will probably be graded on:

- how logical and concise the article is
- how complete the information is
- accuracy in the use of the future and the present subjunctive

Estrategia
Key questions
Before writing an article, it's always a good idea to organize the information you will need. Questions such as Who?, What?, When?, Where?, and Why? are useful in planning your article.

Proyecto

¿Qué?	
¿Quién?	
¿Por qué?	
¿Dónde?	
¿Cuándo?	

Communicate: Writing

9B

Presentación escrita
Expository/Persuasive

Standards: 1.3, 3.1

Focus: Writing a newspaper article about a project to improve the community

Suggestions: To help students determine a topic for their article, have them brainstorm a list of people or places in need of volunteer work in your community.

Bring in recent copies of local newspapers to help students determine issues in your community that need to be addressed.

You will also want to have them refer to the newspaper as a model for writing style. Remind students that they must be persuasive, as they are looking for people to contribute to their project. Encourage them to give specific examples of how their idea will help the community.

Give each student an evaluation checklist to use as they peer-edit each other's work. The checklist should be a simplified version of the questions listed under Step 3.

Compile the final version of each student's paper into a newspaper. Make copies of the paper to share with other Spanish teachers. Ask them to have their classes read the articles and determine which project they would most like to be involved in.

Extension: Have students add a concluding paragraph designed to persuade the reader to volunteer for their summer projects.

Portfolio
Have students include a copy of their article in their portfolio.

Pre-AP* Support
- **Pre-AP* Resource Book:** Comprehensive guide to Pre-AP* writing skill development, pp. 25–35

Additional Resources
Student Resources: Realidades para hispanohablantes, p. 367; Guided Practice: Presentación escrita, p. 343

✓ Assessment
- Assessment Program: Cap. 9B, Rubrics, p. T33

Give students a copy of the rubric you will use for evaluation before they begin.

495

Enrich Your Teaching
Resources for All Teachers

RUBRIC	Score 1	Score 3	Score 5
Logical presentation of your ideas	Your ideas do not have a logical sequence and your writing is not concise.	Your ideas have a somewhat logical sequence and your writing is somewhat concise.	Your ideas have a logical sequence and your writing is concise
Completeness of your information	You answer two key questions in the article.	You answer four key questions in the article.	You answer all key questions in the article.
Your accuracy in using the future and present subjunctive	You use one verb in each tense with grammatical errors.	You use two verbs in each tense with some grammatical errors.	You use three or more verbs in each tense with very few grammatical errors.

Review Activities

To talk about Earth: Have students use postcards or magazine pictures to quiz one another using logical or illogical questions. For example, they may ask, *¿Es cierto que no hay árboles en el bosque?* or *¿Llueve mucho en el desierto?*

To talk about the environment and energy: Have students work in pairs and create a T-chart. On one side, have them list some of the environmental problems in their community or state. On the other side, have them list solutions to the problems. Have students use the words in their T-charts to create a crossword puzzle. Ask them to write five fill-in-the-blank sentences, and give them a grid in which to write their puzzle. Collect their puzzles and redistribute them throughout the class.

Portfolio

Invite students to review the activities they completed in this chapter, including written reports, posters or other visuals, tapes of oral presentations, or other projects. Have them select one or two items that they feel best demonstrate their achievements in Spanish to include in their portfolios. Have them include this with the Chapter Checklist and Self-Assessment Worksheet.

Additional Resources

Student Resources: Realidades para hispanohablantes, p. 368

 **CD-ROM**

PuzzleView Web Code: jed-0916

Teacher Resources:

- Teacher's Resource Book: Situation Cards, p. 268, Clip Art, pp. 270–271

- Assessment Program: Chapter Checklist and Self-Assessment Worksheet, pp. T56–T57

Repaso del capítulo

Vocabulario y gramática jdd-0999

Chapter Review

To prepare for the test, check to see if you . . .
- know the new vocabulary and grammar
- can perform the tasks on p. 497

to talk about Earth

el bosque	forest
la colina	hill
el desierto	desert
el espacio	(outer) space
la Luna	the moon
la naturaleza	nature
la planta	plant
el pueblo	town
la selva tropical	rain forest
la Tierra	Earth
el valle	valley

to talk about energy

ahorrar	to save
el aire acondicionado	air conditioning
la calefacción	heat
económico, -a	economical
eficiente	efficient
la electricidad	electricity
la energía	energy
solar	solar

to talk about the environment

conservar	to conserve
la contaminación	pollution
contaminado, -a	polluted
contra	against
la destrucción	destruction
ecológico, -a	ecological
eliminar	to eliminate
en peligro de extinción	endangered, in danger of extinction
la fuente	source
funcionar	to function, to work
grave	serious
la guerra	war
juntarse	to join
luchar	to fight
la manera	way, manner
el medio ambiente	environment
mejorar	to improve
la paz	peace
proteger	to protect
puro, -a	pure
reducir	to reduce
resolver (o→ue)	to solve

other useful words and expressions

además (de)	in addition (to), besides
dudar	to doubt
es cierto	it is certain
haya	there is, there are (subjunctive)

other verbs that have irregular stems in the future tense

decir	dir-
poner	pondr-
querer	querr-
salir	saldr-
venir	vendr-

the present subjunctive with expressions of doubt

No creo que los estudiantes **lleguen** a tiempo.

Dudamos que el aire acondicionado **funcione.**

Ramón **no está seguro de que** el concierto **empiece** a las siete.

Es posible que veamos al Presidente.

Es imposible que la gente **viva** en el espacio.

No es cierto que el agua del río **sea** pura.

For *Vocabulario adicional,* see pp. 498–499.

Differentiated Instruction

Solutions for All Learners

Students with Learning Difficulties

Have students prepare color-coded flashcards to help them organize their vocabulary. Give them green paper for words about Earth, red paper for words about energy, and blue paper to talk about the environment.

Multiple Intelligences

Bodily/Kinesthetic: Have students prepare a public service announcement for environmental issues. Ask them first to prepare a short outline for their announcement. When they've written their announcement, have them share it with the class. They should present it as though it were being broadcast either on radio or TV.

Preparación para el examen

Más práctica
● Practice Workbook: Puzzle, p. 189
● Practice Workbook: Organizer, p. 190

Go Online PHSchool.com
For: Test Preparation
Web Code: jdd-0916

On the exam you will be asked to . . .	Here are practice tasks similar to those you will find on the exam . . .	If you need review . . .
1 Escuchar Listen and understand as students talk about people's actions with respect to the environment	In honor of *"Día de la Tierra"*, a class is discussing what people currently do or will do to improve the environment. Listen to their comments, and write *presente* if their statements deal with the present or *futuro* if they deal with the future.	**pp. 476–479** *A primera vista* **p. 480** Actividad 4 **p. 484** Actividad 12
2 Hablar Tell what you will do personally to save the environment	The director from the Hispanic Youth Center asks you to talk to a group about five things that *you* will do this year to make a positive impact on the environment. For example, you might say: *Trabajaré en un centro de reciclaje.*	**p. 482** Actividad 9 **p. 483** Actividad 10 **p. 486** Actividad 16 **p. 488** Actividad 19 **p. 489** Actividades 20–21 **p. 490** Actividad 23 **p. 491** Actividad 25
3 Leer Read and understand a description of the future	Read a description of a film director's portrayal of how the world will be in 30 years. Where will people live? What will we use for energy? Does he include anything you consider impossible? En el futuro, habrá apartamentos debajo del océano o en las estaciones del espacio. Dudo que usemos la gasolina para los coches. Será necesario usar la energía solar. Para conservar la energía, no tendremos más que una computadora y un televisor en cada apartamento.	**p. 481** Actividad 7 **p. 482** Actividad 8 **p. 485** Actividad 13 **p. 487** Actividad 17 **p. 490** Actividad 23 **p. 491** Actividad 24
4 Escribir Write information to include on a *"Proteger nuestro medio ambiente"* poster	Your science teacher asks you to write a Spanish version of an environmental poster. What recommendations would you include on the poster? For example, you might write: *Sugerimos que reciclen los periódicos.*	**p. 481** Actividad 7 **p. 482** Actividad 8 **p. 487** Actividad 17 **p. 488** Actividad 19 **p. 491** Actividades 24–25 **p. 495** *Presentación escrita*
5 Pensar Demonstrate an understanding of efforts to protect natural resources in the Spanish-speaking world	Think about what you have learned in this chapter about how the people and governments in Spanish-speaking countries address environmental problems. Compare these efforts to those in the United States. Does this seem to be a regional or a worldwide problem?	**p. 481** *Fondo cultural* **p. 483** Actividad 10, *Fondo cultural* **p. 485** *Fondo cultural* **p. 494** *Perspectivas del mundo hispano*

cuatrocientos noventa y siete **497**
Capítulo 9B

Differentiated Assessment
Solutions for All Learners

STUDENTS NEEDING EXTRA HELP
● **Alternate Assessment Program:** Examen del capítulo 9B
● **Audio Program CD 21:** Chap. 9B, Track 10

HERITAGE LEARNERS
● **Assessment Program: Realidades para hispanohablantes:** Examen del capítulo 9B
● **ExamView Heritage Learner Test Bank**

ADVANCED/PRE-AP*
● **ExamView Pre-AP* Test Bank**
test generator
● **Pre-AP* Resource Book,** pp. 128–131

Review

Performance Tasks
Presentation EXPRESS
ANSWERS

Standards: 1.2, 1.3, 2.1, 2.2, 3.1, 4.2

Student Resource: Realidades para hispanohablantes, p. 369
Teacher Resources: Teacher's Resource Book: Audio Script, p. 261; Audio Program: Track 14; Answers on Transparencies

1. Escuchar
Suggestions: Allow students to listen to the entire script once before they answer.

Script and Answers:
MALE: Mi familia usa el aire acondicionado solar para conservar la electricidad. *(presente)*
FEMALE: Viviremos en el espacio. *(futuro)*
MALE: Limpiamos los lagos contaminados. *(presente)*

2. Hablar
Suggestions: Have students make an outline of their talk. Ask them to list their five main ideas and add two details to support each idea.
Answers will vary.

3. Leer
Suggestions: Have students identify key words to answer each question. Point out that the last question asks for students' opinions. Have students support their answer.
Answers:
People will live in apartments below the ocean or in space stations. We will use solar energy for cars and will not have anything but a computer and a television in each apartment.
Answers for question 3 will vary.

4. Escribir
Suggestions: Have students pick a theme for their poster.
Answers will vary.

5. Pensar
Suggestions: Refer students to pp. 481, 483, 485, and 494. Ask students to list environmental protection efforts in the United States.
Answers will vary.

Assessment
● **ExamView Quiz on PresEXPRESS**
QuickTake Presenter
● Assessment Program: Examen del capítulo
● **ExamView Test Bank: Tests A and B**
test generator
● Audio Program CD 21: Chap. 9B, Track 10

Vocabulario adicional

Tema 1

Las actividades en la clase

anotar to take notes

el ensayo essay

reflexionar to reflect on, to think about

responder (a) to respond

el resumen, *pl.* **los resúmenes** summary

Las cosas de la escuela

el borrador, *pl.* **los borradores** eraser

el marcador, *pl.* **los marcadores** marker

el pisapapeles, *pl.* **los pisapapeles** paperweight

el pizarrón *pl.* **los pizarrones** blackboard

el sujetapapeles, *pl.* **los sujetapapeles,** paper clip

la tiza chalk

Tema 2

Las cosas para arreglarse

el esmalte de uñas nail polish

la espuma de afeitar shaving foam

el fijador hair spray

el lápiz de labios, *pl.* **los lápices de labios** lipstick

la loción, *pl.* **las lociones** lotion

la loción astringente astringent

la loción humectante moisturizing lotion

la loción para después de afeitarse aftershave lotion

la maquinilla de afeitar razor

la sombra de ojos eye shadow

Las compras de ropa

estar pasado, -a de moda to be out of style

Los precios

accesible affordable

Tema 3

Los lugares en la comunidad

el asilo para ancianos senior citizen home

el ayuntamiento city hall

el centro cultural cultural center

el centro de salud health center

Las cosas en la tienda deportiva

los anteojos de esquí / de natación goggles

el balón, *pl.* **los balones** ball (football, soccer, and so on)

el bate de béisbol baseball bat

el casco helmet

el guante de béisbol baseball glove

el uniforme del equipo team uniform

Las cosas relacionadas con el banco

el billete bill

el cambio change

la cuenta corriente checking account

depositar un cheque to deposit a check

Las expresiones para el correo

el correo aéreo air mail

el correo urgente express mail

el sobre envelope

Las expresiones para manejar

la acera sidewalk

el bache pothole

Las expresiones para el metro

bajar de to get off

hacia toward

la parada (del autobús, del metro, . . .) (bus, metro, . . .) stop

subir a to get on

Tema 4

Las expresiones para los eventos especiales

agradecer *(c → zc)* to be grateful for, to be appreciative of

el bautizo baptism

brindar to propose a toast

el Día de Acción de Gracias Thanksgiving

el Día de San Valentín Saint Valentine's Day

la Nochebuena Christmas Eve

la Víspera del Año Nuevo New Year's Eve

Los miembros de la familia

el bisabuelo great-grandfather

la bisabuela great-grandmother

el cuñado brother-in-law

la cuñada sister-in-law

el nieto grandson

la nieta granddaughter

el padrino godfather

la madrina godmother

el sobrino nephew

la sobrina niece

Las expresiones para describir cómo era de niño(a)

creativo, -a creative

inquieto, -a restless

juguetón, juguetona playful

mentiroso, -a fibber

prudente prudent, sensible

El equipo para niños

el cajón de arena sandbox

el carrusel merry-go-round

el columpio swing

el patio de recreo playground

la subibaja seesaw

el tobogán, *pl.* **los toboganes** slide

Los animales en las fábulas

el águila, *pl.* **las águilas** *f.* eagle

el conejo rabbit

el cuervo raven

la gallina hen

el gallo rooster

la oveja sheep

la rana frog

el toro bull

la vaca cow

el zorro, la zorra fox

Tema 5

Las expresiones para las emergencias

la alergia allergy

el análisis, *pl.* **los análisis** medical test

el antibiótico antibiotic

la aspirina aspirin

la camilla stretcher

el cirujano, la cirujana surgeon

estar resfriado to have a cold

estornudar to sneeze

la fiebre fever

la fractura fracture

la gripe flu

la hinchazón swelling

el jarabe cough syrup

la lesión, *pl.* las lesiones injury

el oído ear (inner)

la operación, *pl.* las operaciones operation

el pecho chest

la picadura sting

sufrir to suffer

la tos cough

Las expresiones para hablar sobre los desastres naturales

el ciclón, *pl.* los ciclones cyclone

el daño damage

el derrumbe landslide

la erupción volcánica volcanic eruption

huir *(i → y)* to flee

el maremoto tidal wave

seguro, -a safe

sobrevivir to survive

la tempestad storm

el tifón, *pl.* los tifones typhoon

el tornado tornado, twister

Las expresiones para hablar sobre las noticias

los detalles details

en vivo live

el / la periodista journalist, reporter

el titular headline

Los eventos deportivos

el atletismo track and field

la carrera race

la corona crown

empatar to tie

la meta finish line (in a race)

el resultado score

el torneo tournament

el trofeo trophy

vencer *(c → z)* to defeat, to conquer

Los sentimientos

alegrarse to be happy

estar conmovido, -a to be moved

Las expresiones para el cine

el bandido, la bandida bandit

el / la culpable guilty person

el / la delincuente delinquent

el documental documentary

el festival de cine film festival

filmar to shoot, film

el monstruo monster

Las cosas de la cocina

la cafetera coffee maker

el cucharón, *pl.* los cucharones ladle

la licuadora blender

el molde baking pan

las tazas para medir measuring cups

Las comidas al aire libre

el aceite de oliva olive oil

el ají pepper; hot sauce made with this pepper

el apio celery

los calamares squid

el chorizo sausage

la ciruela plum

el cordero lamb

los espárragos asparagus

las espinacas spinach

la fruta de estación seasonal fruit

el hígado liver

la langosta lobster

el pepino cucumber

la ternera veal

la toronja grapefruit

Las expresiones para describir comidas

agrio, -a bitter

cocido, -a cooked

crudo, -a raw

jugoso, -a juicy

salado, -a salty

Los viajes

acampar to camp

el / la excursionista excursionist

la expedición, *pl.* las expediciones expedition

el explorador, la exploradora explorer

ir al extranjero to go abroad

el paisaje landscape

el paseo trip

el recorrido route

la tienda de acampar tent

el / la trotamundos globe-trotter, world traveler

Las expresiones para el avión

abrocharse el cinturón to fasten one's seat belt

la almohada pillow

aterrizar *(z → c)* to land

el compartimiento sobre la cabeza overhead compartment

despegar to take off

procedente de arriving from

la tripulación crew

la turbulencia turbulence

la salida de emergencia emergency exit

la señal de no fumar no smoking sign

Expresiones y palabras

asombroso, -a amazing

extraordinario, -a extraordinary

glorioso, -a glorious

maravilloso, -a wonderful

tradicional traditional

único, -a unique, special

Más expresiones sobre trabajos

el / la electricista electrician

el horario fijo regular schedule

el / la intérprete interpreter

el plomero, la plomera plumber

el programador, la programadora computer programmer

el puesto job position

el tiempo completo full time

el tiempo parcial part time

el título universitario college degree

el trabajador social, la trabajadora social social worker

el traductor, la traductora translator

El medio ambiente

el aluminio aluminum

prevenir to prevent

la reserva natural nature reserve

Resumen de gramática

Grammar Terms

Adjectives describe nouns: *a red car.*

Adverbs usually describe verbs; they tell when, where, or how an action happens: *He read it quickly.* Adverbs can also describe adjectives or other adverbs: *very tall, quite well.*

Articles are words in Spanish that can tell you whether a noun is masculine, feminine, singular, or plural. In English, the articles are *the, a,* and *an.*

Commands are verb forms that tell people to do something: *Study!, Work!*

Comparatives compare people or things.

Conjugations are verb forms that add endings to the stem in order to tell who the subject is and what tense is being used: *escribo, escribiste.*

Conjunctions join words or groups of words. The most common ones are *and, but,* and *or.*

Direct objects are nouns or pronouns that receive the action of a verb: *I read the book. I read it.*

Future tense is used to talk about actions in the future and to express what will happen: *Tomorrow we will begin working.*

Gender in Spanish tells you whether a noun, pronoun, or article is masculine or feminine.

Imperfect tense is used to talk about actions that happened repeatedly in the past; to describe people, places, and situations in the past; to talk about a past action or situation where no beginning or end is specified; and to describe an ongoing action in the past. The imperfect tense may also be used to tell what time it was or to describe weather in the past and to describe the past physical, mental, and emotional states of a person or thing.

Imperfect progressive tense is used to describe something that was taking place over a period of time in the past: *He was skiing when he broke his leg.*

Indirect objects are nouns or pronouns that tell you to whom / what or for whom / what something is done: *I gave him the book.*

Infinitives are the basic forms of verbs. In English, infinitives have the word "to" in front of them: *to walk.*

Interrogatives are words that ask questions: *What is that? Who are you?*

Nouns name people, places, or things: *students, Mexico City, books.*

Number tells you if a noun, pronoun, article, or verb is singular or plural.

Prepositions show relationship between their objects and another word in the sentence: *He is in the classroom.*

Present tense is used to talk about actions that always take place, or that are happening now: *I always take the bus; I study Spanish.*

Present perfect tense is used to say what a person *had done: We have seen the new movie.*

Present progressive tense is used to emphasize that an action is happening *right now: I am doing my homework; he is finishing dinner.*

Preterite tense is used to talk about actions that were completed in the past: *I took the train yesterday; I studied for the test.*

Pronouns are words that take the place of nouns: *She is my friend.*

Reflexive verbs are used to say that people do something to or for themselves: *I wash my hair.* Other reflexive verbs often describe a change in mental, emotional, or physical state, and can express the idea that someone "gets" or "becomes": *They became angry.*

Subjects are the nouns or pronouns that perform the action in a sentence: *John sings.*

Subjunctive mood is used to say that one person influences the actions of another: *I recommend that you speak with your doctor; it is important that she have good manners.* It is also used after verbs and expressions that indicate doubt or uncertainty: *It's possible that there's enough food.*

Superlatives describe which things have the most or least of a given quality: *She is the best student.*

Verbs show action or link the subject with a word or words in the predicate (what the subject does or is): *Ana writes; Ana is my sister.*

Nouns, Number, and Gender

Nouns refer to people, animals, places, things, and ideas. Nouns are singular or plural. In Spanish, nouns have gender, which means that they are either masculine or feminine.

Singular Nouns	
Masculine	**Feminine**
libro	carpeta
pupitre	casa
profesor	noche
lápiz	ciudad

Plural Nouns	
Masculine	**Feminine**
libros	carpetas
pupitres	casas
profesores	noches
lápices	ciudades

Definite Articles

El, *la*, *los*, and *las* are definite articles and are the equivalent of "the" in English. *El* is used with masculine singular nouns; *los* with masculine plural nouns. *La* is used with feminine singular nouns; *las* with feminine plural nouns. When you use the words *a* or *de* before *el*, you form the contractions *al* and *del*: *Voy **al** centro; Es el libro **del** profesor.*

Masculine	
Singular	Plural
el libro	los libros
el pupitre	los pupitres
el profesor	los profesores
el lápiz	los lápices

Feminine	
Singular	Plural
la carpeta	las carpetas
la casa	las casas
la noche	las noches
la ciudad	las ciudades

Indefinite Articles

Un and *una* are indefinite articles and are the equivalent of "a" and "an" in English. *Un* is used with singular masculine nouns; *una* is used with singular feminine nouns. The plural indefinite articles are *unos* and *unas*.

Masculine	
Singular	Plural
un libro	unos libros
un baile	unos bailes

Feminine	
Singular	Plural
una revista	unas revistas
una mochila	unas mochilas

Pronouns

Subject pronouns tell who is doing the action. They replace nouns or names in a sentence. Subject pronouns are often used for emphasis or clarification: *Gregorio escucha música. **Él** escucha música.*

A *direct object* tells who or what receives the action of the verb. To avoid repeating a direct object noun, you can replace it with a *direct object pronoun*. Direct object pronouns have the same gender and number as the nouns they replace: *¿Cuándo compraste **el libro?** **Lo** compré ayer.*

An *indirect object* tells to whom or for whom an action is performed. *Indirect object pronouns* are used to replace an indirect object noun: ***Les** doy dinero. (I give money to them.)* Because *le* and *les* have more than one meaning, you can make the meaning clear, or show emphasis, by adding *a* + the corresponding name, noun, or pronoun: ***Les** doy el dinero a **ellos.***

A *reflexive pronoun* is used to show that someone does an action to or for herself or himself. Each reflexive pronoun corresponds to a different subject and always agrees with the subject pronoun: *Todos los días **me ducho** y **me arreglo** el pelo.* You know that a verb is reflexive if its infinitive form ends with the letters *se: ducharse, arreglarse.*

After most prepositions, you use *mí* and *ti* for "me" and "you." The forms change with the preposition *con: conmigo, contigo.* For all other persons, you use subject pronouns after prepositions.

The personal a

When the direct object is a person, a group of people, or a pet, use the word *a* before the object. This is called the "personal *a*": *Visité **a** mi abuela. Busco **a** mi perro, Capitán.*

Subject Pronouns		Direct Object Pronouns		Indirect Object Pronouns		Reflexive Pronouns		Objects of Prepositions	
Singular	Plural	Singular	Plural	Singular	Plural	Singular	Plural	Singular	Plural
yo	nosotros, nosotras	me	nos	me	nos	me	nos	(para) mí, conmigo	nosotros, nosotras
tú	vosotros, vosotras	te	os	te	os	te	os	(para) ti, contigo	vosotros, vosotras
usted (Ud.), él, ella	ustedes (Uds.), ellos, ellas	lo, la	los, las	le	les	se	se	Ud., él, ella	Uds., ellos, ellas

Adjectives

Words that describe people and things are called adjectives. In Spanish, most adjectives have both masculine and feminine forms, as well as singular and plural forms. Adjectives must agree with the nouns they describe in both gender and number. When an adjective describes a group including both masculine and feminine nouns, use the masculine plural form.

Masculine	
Singular	**Plural**
alto	altos
inteligente	inteligentes
trabajador	trabajadores
fácil	fáciles

Feminine	
Singular	**Plural**
alta	altas
inteligente	inteligentes
trabajadora	trabajadoras
fácil	fáciles

Shortened Forms of Adjectives

When placed before masculine singular nouns, some adjectives change into a shortened form.

bueno	→	buen chico
malo	→	mal día
primero	→	primer trabajo
tercero	→	tercer plato
grande	→	gran señor

One adjective, **grande,** changes to a shortened form before any singular noun: *una* **gran** *señora, un* **gran** *libro.*

Possessive Adjectives

Possessive adjectives are used to tell what belongs to someone or to show relationships. Like other adjectives, possessive adjectives agree in number with the nouns that follow them.

Only *nuestro* and *vuestro* have different masculine and feminine endings. *Su* and *sus* can have many different meanings: *his, her, its, your,* or *their.*

The long forms of possessive adjectives are used for emphasis and come *after* the noun. They may also be used without a noun: *Esta chaqueta es* **tuya?** *Sí, es* **mía.**

Singular	**Plural**
mi	mis
tu	tus
su	sus
nuestro, -a	nuestros, -as
vuestro, -a	vuestros, -as
su	sus

Singular	**Plural**
mío/mía	míos/mías
tuyo/tuya	tuyos/tuyas
suyo/suya	suyos/suyas
nuestro/nuestra	nuestros/nuestras
vuestro/vuestra	vuestros/vuestras
suyo/suya	suyos/suyas

Demonstrative Adjectives

Like other adjectives, demonstrative adjectives agree in gender and number with the nouns that follow them. Use *este, esta, estos, estas* ("this" / "these") before nouns that name people or things that are close to you. Use *ese, esa, esos, esas* ("that" / "those") before nouns that name people or things that are at some distance from you.

Use *aquel, aquella, aquellos,* or *aquellas* ("that [those] over there") before nouns that name people or things that are far from both you and the person to whom you are speaking.

Singular	**Plural**
este libro	estos libros
esta casa	estas casas
ese niño	esos niños
esa manzana	esas manzanas
aquel bolso	aquellos bolsos
aquella blusa	aquellas blusas

Interrogative Words

You use interrogative words to ask questions. When you ask a question with an interrogative word, you put the verb before the subject. All interrogative words have a written accent mark.

¿Adónde?	¿Cuándo?	¿Dónde?
¿Cómo?	¿Cuánto, -a?	¿Por qué?
¿Con quién?	¿Cuántos, -as?	¿Qué?
¿Cuál?	¿De dónde?	¿Quién?

Comparatives and Superlatives

Comparatives Use *más . . . que* or *menos . . . que* to compare people or things: *más interesante que . . . , menos alta que . . .*

When talking about number, use *de* instead of *que: Tengo más de cien monedas en mi colección.*

To compare people or things that are equal, use *tan . . . como:* **tan** *popular* **como** *. . . Tanto i tanta . . . como* is used to say *"as much as"* and *tantos / tantas . . . como* is used to say "as many as": **tanto** *dinero* **como** *. . .* **tantas** *amigas*

como . . . Tanto and *tanta* match the number and gender of the noun to which they refer.

Superlatives Use this pattern to express the idea of "most" or "least."

el
la   + *noun* + más / menos + *adjective*
los
las

Es **el programa de televisión** **más interesante.**
Son **los perritos más pequeños.**

Several adjectives are irregular when used with comparisons and superlatives.

older	mayor
younger	menor
better	mejor
worse	peor

To say that something is "the most," "the least," "the best," or "the worst" in a group or category, use *de*.

Es **la chica más seria de** *la clase.*
Es **la mejor película del** *festival de cine.*

Affirmative and Negative Words

To make a sentence negative in Spanish, *no* usually goes in front of the verb or expression. To show that you do not like either of two choices, use *ni . . . ni.*

Alguno, alguna, algunos, algunas and *ninguno, ninguna* match the number and gender of the noun to which they refer. When *alguno* and *ninguno* come before a masculine singular noun, they change to *algún* and *ningún*.

Affirmative	Negative
algo	nada
alguien	nadie
algún	ningún
alguno, -a, -os, -as	ninguno, -a
siempre	nunca
también	tampoco

Adverbs

To form an adverb in Spanish, *-mente* is added to the feminine singular form of an adjective. This *-mente* ending is equivalent to the "-ly" ending in English. If the adjective has a written accent, such as *rápida, fácil,* and *práctica,* the accent appears in the same place in the adverb form.

general	→ generalmente
especial	→ especialmente
fácil	→ fácilmente
feliz	→ felizmente
rápida	→ rápidamente
práctica	→ prácticamente

Verbos

Regular Present, Preterite, Imperfect, Future, and Subjunctive

Here are the conjugations for regular -ar, -er, and -ir verbs in the present, preterite, imperfect, future, and subjunctive tenses.

Infinitive	Present		Preterite		Imperfect		Future		Subjunctive	
estudiar	estudio	estudiamos	estudié	estudiamos	estudiaba	estudiábamos	estudiaré	estudiaremos	estudie	estudiemos
	estudias	estudiáis	estudiaste	estudiasteis	estudiabas	estudiabais	estudiarás	estudiaréis	estudies	estudiéis
	estudia	estudian	estudió	estudiaron	estudiaba	estudiaban	estudiará	estudiarán	estudie	estudien
correr	corro	corremos	corrí	corrimos	corría	corríamos	correré	correremos	corra	corramos
	corres	corréis	corriste	corristeis	corrías	corríais	correrás	correréis	corras	corráis
	corre	corren	corrió	corrieron	corría	corrían	correrá	correrán	corra	corran
vivir	vivo	vivimos	viví	vivimos	vivía	vivíamos	viviré	viviremos	viva	vivamos
	vives	vivís	viviste	vivisteis	vivías	vivíais	vivirás	viviréis	vivas	viváis
	vive	viven	vivió	vivieron	vivía	vivían	vivirá	vivirán	viva	vivan

Present Progressive and Imperfect Progressive

When you want to emphasize that an action is happening *right now,* you use the present progressive tense.

To describe something that was taking place over a period of time *in the past,* use the imperfect progressive.

Infinitive	Present Progressive				Imperfect Progressive	
estudiar	estoy	estudiando	estamos	estudiando	estaba estudiando	estábamos estudiando
	estás	estudiando	estáis	estudiando	estabas estudiando	estabais estudiando
	está	estudiando	están	estudiando	estaba estudiando	estaban estudiando
correr	estoy	corriendo	estamos	corriendo	estaba corriendo	estábamos corriendo
	estás	corriendo	estáis	corriendo	estabas corriendo	estabais corriendo
	está	corriendo	están	corriendo	estaba corriendo	estaban corriendo
vivir	estoy viviendo		estamos viviendo		estaba viviendo	estábamos viviendo
	estás viviendo		estáis viviendo		estabas viviendo	estabais viviendo
	está viviendo		están viviendo		estaba viviendo	estaban viviendo

Present Perfect Tense

When you want to say what a person *has done,* use the present perfect tense.

Infinitive	Present Perfect	
estudiar	he estudiado	hemos estudiado
	has estudiado	habéis estudiado
	ha estudiado	han estudiado
correr	he corrido	hemos corrido
	has corrido	habéis corrido
	ha corrido	han corrido
vivir	he vivido	hemos vivido
	has vivido	habéis vivido
	ha vivido	han vivido

Commands

When telling a friend, a family member, or a young person to do something, use an affirmative *tú* command. To give these commands for most verbs, use the same present-tense forms that are used for *Ud., él, ella.* Some verbs have an irregular affirmative *tú* command.

When telling a friend, a family member, or a young person *not* to do something, use a negative *tú* command. To give these commands for most verbs, drop the *-o* of the present-tense *yo* form and add *-es* for *-ar* verbs and *-as* for *-er* and *-ir* verbs. Some verbs have an irregular negative *tú* command.

To give affirmative or negative commands in the *Ud.* or *Uds.* form, drop the *-o* of the present-tense *yo* form and add *-e* or *-en* for *-ar* verbs and *-a* or *-an* for *-er* and *-ir* verbs. Some verbs have an irregular *Ud.* or *Uds.* command.

For stem-changing and spelling-changing verbs see the tables on pages 506–509.

Infinitive	Tú	Negative *tú*	Usted	Ustedes
estudiar	estudia	no estudies	(no) estudie	(no) estudien
correr	corre	no corras	(no) corra	(no) corran
vivir	vive	no vivas	(no) viva	(no) vivan

Infinitive	Tú	Negative *tú*	Usted	Ustedes
dar	da	no des	(no) dé	(no) den
decir	di	no digas	(no) diga	(no) digan
estar	está	no estés	(no) esté	(no) estén
hacer	haz	no hagas	(no) haga	(no) hagan
ir	ve	no vayas	(no) vaya	(no) vayan
poner	pon	no pongas	(no) ponga	(no) pongan
salir	sal	no salgas	(no) salga	(no) salgan
ser	sé	no seas	(no) sea	(no) sean
tener	ten	no tengas	(no) tenga	(no) tengan
venir	ven	no vengas	(no) venga	(no) vengan

Stem-changing Verbs

Here is a list of the stem-changing verbs. Only conjugations with changes are shown.

Infinitive in *-ar*

Infinitive	Present Indicative		Present Subjunctive	
pensar (e→ie)	pienso	pensamos	piense	pensemos
	piensas	penséis	pienses	penséis
	piensa	piensan	piense	piensen
Verbs like **pensar:** calentar, comenzar,[1] despertar(se), recomendar, tropezar				
contar (o→ue)	cuento	contamos	cuente	contemos
	cuentas	contáis	cuentes	contéis
	cuenta	cuentan	cuente	cuenten
Verbs like **contar:** acostar(se), almorzar, costar, encontrar(se), probar(se), recordar				
jugar (u→ue)	juego	jugamos	juegue	juguemos
	juegas	jugáis	juegues	juguéis
	juega	juegan	juegue	jueguen

Infinitive in *-er*

	Present Indicative		Present Subjunctive	
entender (e→ie)	entiendo	entendemos	entienda	entendamos
	entiendes	entendéis	entiendas	entendáis
	entiende	entienden	entienda	entiendan
Verbs like **entender:** encender, perder				
devolver (o→ue) past participle: devuelto	devuelvo	devolvemos	devuelva	devolvamos
	devuelves	devolvéis	devuelvas	devolváis
	devuelve	devuelven	devuelva	devuelvan
Verbs like **devolver:** mover(se), resolver, torcer(se),[2] volver (past participle: **vuelto**)				

[1]Remember that verbs like *comenzar* and *tropezar* also have a spelling change *(z → c)* in all forms of the present subjunctive. See p. 508 for a complete conjugation of *empezar*.

[2]Verbs like *torcer(se)* also have a spelling change *(c → z)* in all forms of the present subjunctive. See p. 509 for a complete conjugation of *torcer(se)*.

Stem-changing Verbs (continued)

Infinitive in -ir

	Indicative				Subjunctive	
	Present		Preterite		Present	
pedir (e→i) (e→i)	pido	pedimos	pedí	pedimos	pida	pidamos
present participle: pidiendo	pides	pedís	pediste	pedisteis	pidas	pidáis
	pide	piden	pidió	pidieron	pida	pidan

Verbs like **pedir**: conseguir,* despedir(se), repetir, seguir, vestir(se)

preferir (e→ie) (e→i)	prefiero	preferimos	preferí	preferimos	prefiera	prefiramos
present participle:	prefieres	preferís	preferiste	preferisteis	prefieras	prefiráis
prefiriendo	prefiere	prefieren	prefirió	prefirieron	prefiera	prefieran

Verbs like **preferir**: divertir(se), hervir, mentir, sugerir,

dormir (o→ue) (o→u)	duermo	dormimos	dormí	dormimos	duerma	durmamos
present participle:	duermes	dormís	dormiste	dormisteis	duermas	durmáis
durmiendo	duerme	duermen	durmió	durmieron	duerma	duerman

Verbs like **dormir**: morir(se) (past participle: **muerto**)

*Verbs like *conseguir* and *seguir* also have a spelling change *(gu → g)* in all forms of the present subjunctive. See p. 509 for a complete conjugation of *seguir*.

Spelling-changing Verbs

These verbs have spelling changes in the present, preterite, and/or subjunctive. The spelling changes are indicated in boldface blue type.

Infinitive, Present Participle, Past Participle	Present		Preterite		Subjunctive	
almorzar (z → c) almorzando almorzado	See regular *-ar* verbs		**almorcé** almorzaste almorzó	almorzamos almorzasteis almorzaron	**almuerce** **almuerces** **almuerce**	**almorcemos** **almorcéis** **almuercen**
buscar (c → qu) buscando buscado	See regular *-ar* verbs		**busqué** buscaste buscó	buscamos buscasteis buscaron	**busque** **busques** **busque**	**busquemos** **busquéis** **busquen**
comunicarse (c → qu) comunicándose comunicado	See reflexive verbs		See reflexive verbs and **buscar**		See reflexive verbs and **buscar**	
conocer (c → zc) conociendo conocido	**conozco** conoces conoce	conocemos conocéis conocen	See regular *-er* verbs		**conozca** **conozcas** **conozca**	**conozcamos** **conozcáis** **conozcan**
creer (i → y) creyendo creído	See regular *-er* verbs		creí creíste **creyó**	creímos creísteis **creyeron**	See regular *-er* verbs	
destruir (i → y) destruyendo destruido	**destruyo** **destruyes** **destruye**	destruimos destruis **destruyen**	destruí destruiste **destruyó**	destruimos destruisteis **destruyeron**	**destruya** **destruyas** **destruya**	**destruyamos** **destruyáis** **destruyan**
empezar (z → c) empezando empezado	See stem-changing verbs		**empecé** empezaste empezó	empezamos empezasteis empezaron	**empiece** **empieces** **empiece**	**empecemos** **empecéis** **empiecen**
enviar (i → í) enviando enviado	**envío** **envías** **envía**	enviamos enviáis **envían**	See regular *-ar* verbs		**envíe** **envíes** **envíe**	enviemos enviéis **envíen**
escoger (g → j) escogiendo escogido	**escojo** escoges escoge	escogemos escogéis escogen	See regular *-er* verbs		**escoja** **escojas** **escoja**	**escojamos** **escojáis** **escojan**
esquiar (i → í) esquiando esquiado	See **enviar**		See regular *-ar* verbs		See **enviar**	
jugar (g → gu) jugando jugado	See stem-changing verbs		**jugué** jugaste jugó	jugamos jugasteis jugaron	See stem-changing verbs	
leer (i → y) leyendo leído	See regular *-er* verbs		See **creer**		See **creer**	
obedecer (c → zc) obedeciendo obedecido	See **conocer**		See regular *-er* verbs		See **conocer**	

Spelling-changing Verbs (continued)

Infinitive, Present Participle Past Participle	Present		Preterite		Subjunctive	
ofrecer (c → zc) ofreciendo ofrecido	See **conocer**		See regular -er verbs		See **conocer**	
pagar (g → gu) pagando pagado	See regular -ar verbs		See **jugar**		**pague** **pagues** **pague**	**paguemos** **paguéis** **paguen**
parecer (c → zc) pareciendo parecido	See **conocer**		See regular -er verbs		See **conocer**	
practicar (c → qu) practicando practicado	See regular -ar verbs		See **buscar**		See **buscar**	
recoger (g → j) recogiendo recogido	See **escoger**		See regular -er verbs		See **escoger**	
reir(se) (e → i)* riendo (riéndose) reído	**me río** **te ríes** **se ríe**	**nos reímos** **os reís** **se ríen**	**me reí** **te reíste** **se rió**	**nos reímos** **os reísteis** **se rieron**	**me ría** **te rías** **se ría**	**nos riamos** **os riáis** **se rían**
reunirse (u → ú)* reuniéndose reunido	**me reúno** **te reúnes** **se reúne**	**nos reunimos** **os reunís** **se reúnen**	See preterite regular -ir verbs		**me reúna** **te reúnas** **se reúna**	**nos reunamos** **os reunáis** **se reúnan**
sacar (c → qu) sacando sacado	See regular -ar verbs		See **buscar**		See **buscar**	
seguir (e → i) (gu → g)* siguiendo seguido	**sigo** **sigues** **sigue**	**seguimos** **seguís** **siguen**	See **pedir**		**siga** **sigas** **siga**	**sigamos** **sigáis** **sigan**
tocar (c → qu) tocando tocado	See regular -ar verbs		See **buscar**		See **buscar**	
torcer(se) (o → ue) (c → z) torciendo torcido	**me tuerzo** **te tuerces** **se tuerce**	**nos torcemos** **os torcéis** **se tuercen**	See **conocer**		**me tuerza** **te tuerzas** **se tuerza**	**nos torzamos** **os torzáis** **se tuerzan**

*Verbs like **reír(se)**: sonreír, freír (past participle: frito)
*Verbs like **reunirse**: graduarse (present: *me gradúo, te gradúas, se gradúa, nos graduamos, os graduáis, se gradúan*; preterite: see preterite of regualr -ar verbs; subjunctive: *me gradúe, te gradúes, se gradúe, nos graduemos, os graduéis, se gradúen)*
*Verbs like **seguir**: conseguir

Irregular Verbs

These verbs have irregular patterns.

1 Infinitive Present Participle Past Participle	2 Present		3 Preterite	
dar dando dado	doy das da	damos dais dan	di diste dio	dimos disteis dieron
decir diciendo dicho	digo dices dice	decimos decís dicen	dije dijiste dijo	dijimos dijisteis dijeron
estar estando estado	estoy estás está	estamos estáis están	estuve estuviste estuvo	estuvimos estuvisteis estuvieron
haber habiendo habido	he has ha	hemos habéis han	hube hubiste hubo	hubimos hubisteis hubieron
hacer haciendo hecho	hago haces hace	hacemos hacéis hacen	hice hiciste hizo	hicimos hicisteis hicieron
ir yendo ido	voy vas va	vamos vais van	fui fuiste fue	fuimos fuisteis fueron
oír* oyendo oído	oigo oyes oye	oímos oís oyen	oí oíste oyó	oímos oísteis oyeron
poder pudiendo podido	puedo puedes puede	podemos podéis pueden	pude pudiste pudo	pudimos pudisteis pudieron
poner poniendo puesto	pongo pones pone	ponemos ponéis ponen	puse pusiste puso	pusimos pusisteis pusieron

*Verbs like **oír**: caerse

Irregular Verbs (continued)

4 Imperfect		5 Future		6 Subjunctive	
daba	dábamos	daré	daremos	dé	demos
dabas	dabais	darás	dareis	des	deis
daba	daban	dará	darán	dé	den
decía	decíamos	diré	diremos	diga	digamos
decías	decíais	dirás	diréis	digas	digáis
decía	decían	dirá	dirán	diga	digan
estaba	estábamos	estaré	estaremos	esté	estemos
estabas	estabais	estarás	estaréis	estés	estéis
estaba	estaban	estará	estarán	esté	estén
había	habíamos	habré	habremos	haya	hayamos
habías	habíais	habrás	habréis	hayas	hayáis
había	habían	habrá	habrán	haya	hayan
hacía	hacíamos	haré	haremos	haga	hagamos
hacías	hacíais	harás	haréis	hagas	hagáis
hacía	hacían	hará	harán	haga	hagan
iba	íbamos	iré	iremos	vaya	vayamos
ibas	ibais	irás	iréis	vayas	vayáis
iba	iban	irá	irán	vaya	vayan
oía	oíamos	oiré	oiremos	oiga	oigamos
oías	oíais	oirás	oiréis	oigas	oigáis
oía	oían	oirá	oirán	oiga	oigan
podía	podíamos	podré	podremos	pueda	podamos
podías	podíais	podrás	podréis	puedas	podáis
podía	podían	podrá	podrán	pueda	puedan
ponía	poníamos	pondré	pondremos	ponga	pongamos
ponías	poníais	pondrás	pondréis	pongas	pongáis
ponía	ponían	pondrá	pondrán	ponga	pongan

Irregular Verbs (continued)

Infinitive Present Participle Past Participle	Present		Preterite	
1	2		3	
querer queriendo querido	quiero quieres quiere	queremos queréis quieren	quise quisiste quiso	quisimos quisisteis quisieron
saber sabiendo sabido	sé sabes sabe	sabemos sabéis saben	supe supiste supo	supimos supisteis supieron
salir saliendo salido	salgo sales sale	salimos salís salen	salí saliste salió	salimos salisteis salieron
ser siendo sido	soy eres es	somos sois son	fui fuiste fue	fuimos fuisteis fueron
tener teniendo tenido	tengo tienes tiene	tenemos tenéis tienen	tuve tuviste tuvo	tuvimos tuvisteis tuvieron
traer trayendo traído	traigo traes trae	traemos traéis traen	traje trajiste trajo	trajimos trajisteis trajeron
venir viniendo venido	vengo vienes viene	venimos venís vienen	vine viniste vino	vinimos vinisteis vinieron
ver viendo visto	veo ves ve	vemos veis ven	vi viste vio	vimos visteis vieron

Irregular Verbs (continued)

	4		5		6
Imperfect		**Future**		**Subjunctive**	
quería	queríamos	querré	querremos	quiera	queramos
querías	queríais	querrás	querréis	quieras	queráis
quería	querían	querrá	querrán	quiera	quieran
sabía	sabíamos	sabré	sabremos	sepa	sepamos
sabías	sabíais	sabrás	sabréis	sepas	sepáis
sabía	sabían	sabrá	sabrán	sepa	sepan
salía	salíamos	saldré	saldremos	salga	salgamos
salías	salíais	saldrás	saldréis	salgas	salgáis
salía	salían	saldrá	saldrán	salga	salgan
era	éramos	seré	seremos	sea	seamos
eras	erais	serás	seréis	seas	seáis
era	eran	será	serán	sea	sean
tenía	teníamos	tendré	tendremos	tenga	tengamos
tenías	teníais	tendrás	tendréis	tengas	tengáis
tenía	tenían	tendrá	tendrán	tenga	tengan
traía	traíamos	traeré	traeremos	traiga	traigamos
traías	traíais	traerás	traeréis	traigas	traigáis
traía	traían	traerá	traerán	traiga	traigan
venía	veníamos	vendré	vendremos	venga	vengamos
venías	veníais	vendrás	vendréis	vengas	vengáis
venía	venían	vendrá	vendrán	venga	vengan
veía	veíamos	veré	veremos	vea	veamos
veías	veíais	verás	veréis	veas	veáis
veía	veían	verá	verán	vea	vean

Reflexive Verbs

Infinitive and Present Participle	Present	
lavarse lavándose	me lavo te lavas se lava	nos lavamos os laváis se lavan
	Preterite	
	me lavé te lavaste se lavó	nos lavamos os lavasteis se lavaron
	Subjunctive	
	me lave te laves se lave	nos lavemos os lavéis se laven

Familiar *(tú)* Commands
lávate no te laves

Formal *(Ud. and Uds.)* Commands
lávese no se lave

Sometimes the reflexive pronouns *se* and *nos* are used to express the idea "(to) each other." These are called reciprocal actions: ***Nos** dábamos la mano.*

Vocabulario español-inglés

The *Vocabulario español-inglés* contains all active vocabulary from the text, including vocabulary presented in the grammar sections.

A dash (—) represents the main entry word. For example, **pasar la —** after **la aspiradora** means **pasar la aspiradora.**

The number following each entry indicates the chapter in which the word or expression is presented. A Roman numeral (I) indicates that the word was presented in REALIDADES 1.

The following abbreviations are used in this list: *adj.* (adjective), *dir. obj.* (direct object), *f.* (feminine), *fam.* (familiar), *ind. obj.* (indirect object), *inf.* (infinitive), *m.* (masculine), *pl.* (plural), *prep.* (preposition), *pron.* (pronoun), *sing.* (singular).

A

a to *(prep.)* (I)

— **…le gusta(n)** he/she likes (I)

— **…le encanta(n)** he/she loves (I)

— **casa** (to) home (I)

— **causa de** because of (5A)

— **la derecha (de)** to the right (of) (5A)

— **la izquierda (de)** to the left (of) (I)

— **la una de la tarde** at one (o'clock) in the afternoon (I)

— **las ocho de la mañana** at eight (o'clock) in the morning (I)

— **las ocho de la noche** at eight (o'clock) in the evening / at night (I)

— **menudo** often (I)

— **mí también** I do (like to) too (I)

— **mí tampoco** I don't (like to) either (I)

¿— **qué hora?** (At) what time? (I)

— **tiempo** on time (1A)

— **veces** sometimes (I)

— **ver.** Let's see. (I)

al (a + el), a la to the (I)

abierto, -a open (8A)

el **abogado, la abogada** lawyer (9A)

abordar to board (8A)

abrazar(se) to hug (4B)

el **abrigo** coat (I)

abril April (I)

abrir to open (I)

el **abuelo, la abuela** grandfather, grandmother (I)

los **abuelos** grandparents (I)

aburrido, -a boring (I)

aburrir to bore (I)

aburrirse to get bored (6A)

me aburre(n) it bores me (they bore me) (I)

acabar de + inf. to have just … (I)

el **accidente** accident (5B)

acción: película de — action film (6B)

el **aceite** cooking oil (7A)

acompañar to accompany (7B)

acostarse (o →ue) to go to bed (2A)

las **actividades extracurriculares** extracurricular activities (1B)

el **actor** actor (I)

la **actriz,** *pl.* **las actrices** actress (I)

la **actuación** acting (6B)

acuerdo:

Estoy de —. I agree. (I)

No estoy de —. I don't agree. (I)

además (de) in addition (to), besides (9B)

adhesiva: la cinta — transparent tape (1A)

¡Adiós! Good-bye! (I)

¿Adónde? (To) where? (I)

la **aduana** customs (8A)

el **aduanero, la aduanera** customs officer (8A)

el **aeropuerto** airport (8A)

afeitarse to shave (2A)

el **aficionado, la aficionada** fan (6A)

afortunadamente fortunately (5A)

la **agencia de viajes** travel agency (8A)

el / la **agente de viajes** travel agent (8A)

agitado, -a agitated (6A)

agosto August (I)

el **agricultor, la agricultora** farmer (9A)

el **agua** *f.* water (I)

el **— de colonia** cologne (2A)

el **aguacate** avocado (7B)

ahora now (I)

ahorrar to save (9B)

aire: al — libre outdoors (7B)

el **aire acondicionado** air conditioning (9B)

el **ajedrez** chess (1B)

el **ajo** garlic (7A)

al *(a + el),* **a la** to the (I)

— **aire libre** outdoors (7B)

— **final** at the end (6A)

— **horno** baked (7A)

— **lado de** next to (I)

alegre happy (6A)

la **alfombra** rug (I)

algo something (I)

¿— **más?** Anything else? (I)

el **algodón** cotton (2B)

alguien someone, anyone (1A)

algún, alguno, -a some (1A)

— **día** some day (9A)

algunos, as some, any (1A)

allí there (I)

el **almacén,** *pl.* **los almacenes** department store (I)

almorzar (o→ue) (z→c) to have lunch (1A)

el **almuerzo** lunch (I)

en el — for lunch (I)

alquilar to rent (6B)

alrededor de around (4B)

alto, -a tall (I); high (2B)

amarillo, -a yellow (I)

la **ambulancia** ambulance (5B)

el **amor** love (6B)

anaranjado, -a orange (I)

ancho, -a wide (3B)

el **anciano, la anciana** older man, older woman (I)

los **ancianos** older people (I)

el **anillo** ring (I)

el **animador, la animadora** cheerleader (1B)

el **animal** animal (I)

el **aniversario** anniversary (4B)

anoche last night (I)

los **anteojos de sol** sunglasses (I)

antes de before (I, 2A)

antiguo, -a old, antique (4B)

anunciar to announce (2B)

el **anuncio** announcement (8A)

añadir to add (7A)

no añadas don't add (7A)

el **año** year (I)

   el **— pasado** last year (I)

   ¿Cuántos —s tiene(n)...? How old is / are ...? (I)

   Tiene(n)...—s. He / She is / They are ...(years old). (I)

apagar (g → gu) to put out *(fire)* (5A); to turn off (7A)

el **apartamento** apartment (I)

aplaudir to applaud (6A)

aprender (a) to learn (I)

   — de memoria to memorize (1A)

apretado, -a tight (2B)

aproximadamente approximately (3B)

aquel, aquella that (over there) (2B)

aquellos, aquellas those (over there) (2B)

aquí here (I)

el **árbol** tree (I)

los **aretes** earrings (I)

el **argumento** plot (6B)

el **armario** closet, locker (I, 1A)

el **arquitecto, la arquitecta** architect (9A)

arreglar (el cuarto) to straighten up (the room) (I)

arreglarse (el pelo) to fix (one's hair) (2A)

arrestar to arrest (6B)

el **arroz** rice (I)

el **arte: la clase de —** art class (I)

las **artes** the arts (9A)

   las — marciales martial arts (1B)

la **artesanía** handicrafts (8B)

el **artículo** article (5A)

el **artista, la artista** artist (9A)

artístico, -a artistic (I)

asado, -a grilled (7B)

asar to grill, to roast (7B)

el **ascensor** elevator (8B)

asco: ¡Qué —! How awful! (I)

el **asiento** seat (1A)

asistir a to attend (1B)

asustado, -a frightened (5A)

atención: prestar to pay attention (1A)

atento, -a attentive (8B)

el / la **atleta** athlete (6A)

la **atracción,** *pl.* **las atracciones** attraction (I)

atrevido, -a daring (I)

la **audición,** *pl.* **las audiciones** audition (2A)

el **auditorio** auditorium (6A)

el **autobús,** *pl.* **los autobuses** bus (I)

el / la **auxiliar de vuelo** flight attendant (8A)

la **avenida** avenue (3B)

el **avión** airplane (I)

   ¡Ay! ¡Qué pena! Oh! What a shame / pity! (I)

ayer yesterday (I)

la **ayuda** help (1A)

ayudar to help (I)

el **azúcar** sugar (I)

azul blue (I)

B

bailar to dance (I)

el **bailarín, la bailarina,** *pl.* **los bailarines** dancer (1B)

el **baile** dance (I)

bajar to go down (5A)

bajar (información) to download (I)

bajo, -a short *(stature)* (I); low (2B)

el **banco** bank (3A)

la **banda** (musical) band (1B)

la **bandera** flag (I)

bañarse to take a bath (2A)

el **baño** bathroom (I)

   el traje de — swimsuit (I)

barato, -a inexpensive, cheap (I)

el **barco** boat, ship (I)

el **barrio** neighborhood (I)

basado, -a: estar — en to be based on (6B)

el **básquetbol: jugar al —** to play basketball (I)

¡Basta! Enough! (3B)

bastante enough, rather (I)

batir to beat (7A)

el **bebé, la bebé** baby (4B)

beber to drink (I)

las **bebidas** drinks (I)

béisbol: jugar al — to play baseball (I)

bello, -a beautiful (8B)

los **beneficios** benefits (9A)

besar(se) to kiss (4B)

la **biblioteca** library (I)

bien well (I)

   — educado, -a well-behaved (4A)

bienvenido, -a welcome (8A)

bilingüe bilingual (9A)

el **bistec** beefsteak (I)

blanco, -a white (I)

los **bloques** blocks (4A)

la **blusa** blouse (I)

la **boca** mouth (I)

la **boda** wedding (2A)

el **boleto** ticket (I)

el **bolígrafo** pen (I)

los **bolos: jugar a los —** to bowl (1B)

la **bolsa** bag, sack (I)

el **bolso** purse (I)

el **bombero, la bombera** firefighter (5A)

bonito, -a pretty (I)

el **bosque** forest (9B)

las **botas** boots (I)

el **bote:**

    pasear en — to go boating (I)

    el **— de vela** sailboat (8B)

la **botella** bottle (I)

el **brazo** arm (I)

bucear to scuba dive, to snorkel (I)

bueno (buen), -a good (I)

    Buenas noches. Good evening. (I)

    Buenas tardes. Good afternoon. (I)

    Buenos días. Good morning. (I)

buscar (c→qu) to look for, to search (for) (I)

la **búsqueda** search (1B)

    hacer una — to do a search (1B)

el **buzón,** *pl.* **los buzones** mailbox (3A)

C

el **caballo: montar a —** to ride horseback (I)

la **cabeza** head (I)

cada día every day (I)

la **cadena** chain (I)

caerse to fall (5B)

    (yo) me caigo I fall (5B)

    (tú) te caes you fall (5B)

    se cayó he/she fell (5B)

    se cayeron they/you fell (5B)

el **café** coffee, café (I)

la **caja** box (I); cash register (2B)

el **cajero, la cajera** cashier (2B)

el **— automático** ATM (8B)

los **calcetines** socks (I)

la **calculadora** calculator (I)

el **caldo** broth (7A)

la **calefacción** heat (9B)

calentar (e→ie) to heat (7A)

caliente hot (7A)

la **calle** street, road (I)

calor:

    Hace —. It's hot. (I)

    tener — to be warm (I)

la **cama** bed (I)

    hacer la — to make the bed (I)

la **cámara** camera (I)

    la — digital digital camera (I)

el **camarero, la camarera** waiter, waitress (I)

el **camarón,** *pl.* **los camarones** shrimp (7A)

cambiar to change, to exchange (8B)

caminar to walk (I)

la **caminata** walk (7B)

    dar una — take a walk (7B)

el **camión,** *pl.* **los camiones** truck (3B)

la **camisa** shirt (I)

la **camiseta** T-shirt (I)

el **campamento** camp (I)

el **campeón, la campeona,** *pl.* **los campeones** champion (6A)

el **campeonato** championship (6A)

el **campo** countryside (I)

el **canal** (TV) channel (I)

la **canción,** *pl.* **las canciones** song (I, 1B)

canoso: pelo — gray hair (I)

cansado, -a tired (I)

el / la **cantante** singer (1B)

cantar to sing (I)

capturar to capture (6B)

la **cara** face (2A)

cara a cara face-to-face (I)

caramba good gracious (3A)

la **carne** meat (I)

    la — de res steak (7B)

el **carnet de identidad** ID card (1A)

caro, -a expensive (I)

la **carpeta** folder (I)

    la — de argollas three-ring binder (I)

la **carrera** career (9A)

la **carretera** highway (3B)

la **carta** letter (I, 3A)

    echar una — to mail a letter (3A)

el **cartel** poster (I)

la **cartera** wallet (I)

el **cartero, la cartera** mail carrier (9A)

el **cartón** cardboard (I)

la **casa** home, house (I)

    a — (to) home (I)

    en — at home (I)

    — de cambio currency exchange (8B)

casarse (con) to get married (to) (4B)

casi almost (I, 3A)

castaño: pelo — brown (chestnut) hair (I)

el **castillo** castle (8B)

la **catedral** cathedral (8B)

catorce fourteen (I)

la **causa** cause (5A)

    a — de because of (5A)

la **cebolla** onion (I)

celebrar to celebrate (I)

la **cena** dinner (I)

el **centro** center, downtown (I, 3A)

    el — comercial mall (I)

    el — de reciclaje recycling center (I)

cepillarse (los dientes) to brush (one's teeth) (2A)

el **cepillo** brush (2A)

    el — de dientes toothbrush (3A)

cerca (de) close (to), near (I)

el **cerdo** pork (7B)

 la **chuleta de —** pork chop (7B)

el **cereal** cereal (I)

la **cereza** cherry (7B)

cero zero (I)

cerrado, -a closed (8A)

cerrar to close (3A)

la **cesta** basket (7B)

el **champú** shampoo (3A)

la **chaqueta** jacket (I)

charlar to chat (4B)

el **cheque:**

 cobrar un — to cash a check (3A)

 el — de viajero traveler's check (2B)

 el — (personal) (personal) check (2B)

la **chica** girl (I)

el **chico** boy (I)

chocar (c→qu) con to crash into, to collide with (5B)

la **chuleta de cerdo** pork chop (7B)

el **cielo** sky (7B)

cien one hundred (I)

las **ciencias:**

 la clase de — naturales science class (I)

 la clase de — sociales social studies class (I)

el **científico, la científica** scientist (9A)

(es) cierto (it is) certain (9B)

cinco five (I)

cincuenta fifty (I)

el **cine** movie theater (I)

la **cinta adhesiva** transparent tape (1A)

el **cinturón,** *pl.* **los cinturones** belt (2A)

la **cita** date (2A)

la **ciudad** city (I)

claro, -a light (color) (2B)

la **clase** class (I)

 la sala de clases classroom (I)

¿**Qué — de ...?** What kind of ...? (I)

el **club,** *pl.* **los clubes** club (1B)

 el — atlético athletic club (1B)

cobrar un cheque to cash a check (3A)

el **coche** car (I)

la **cocina** kitchen (I)

cocinar to cook (I)

el **codo** elbow (5B)

la **colección,** *pl.* **las colecciones** collection (4A)

coleccionar to collect (4A)

el **colegio** secondary school, high school (9A)

la **colina** hill (9B)

el **collar** necklace (I)

el **color,** *pl.* **los colores** color (I)

 ¿**De qué — ...?** What color ...? (I)

 de sólo un — solid-colored (2B)

la **comedia** comedy (I)

el **comedor** dining room (I)

el **comentario** commentary (6A)

comenzar (e →ie) (z →c) to start (5A)

comer to eat (I)

cómico, -a funny, comical (I)

la **comida** food, meal (I)

como like, as (I)

¿**Cómo?:**

 ¿**— eres?** What are you like? (I)¿**— es?** What is he / she like? (I)

 ¿**— está Ud.?** How are you? *formal* (I)

 ¿**— estás?** How are you? *fam.* (I)

 ¿**— lo pasaste?** How was it (for you)? (I)

 ¿**— se dice...?** How do you say ...? (I)

 ¿**— se escribe...?** How is...spelled? (I)

 ¿**— se hace...?** How do you make...? (7A)

 ¿**— se llama?** What's his / her name? (I)

 ¿**— se va...?** How do you go to...? (3B)

 ¿**— te llamas?** What is your name? (I)

 ¿**— te queda(n)?** How does it (do they) fit (you)? (I)

¡**Cómo no!** Of course! (3A)

la **cómoda** dresser (I)

cómodo, -a comfortable (2A)

compartir to share (I)

la **competencia** competition (6A)

competir (e→i) to compete (6A)

complicado, -a complicated (I, 3B)

la **composición,** *pl.* **las composiciones** composition (I)

comprar to buy (I)

comprar recuerdos to buy souvenirs (I)

comprender to understand (I)

la **computadora** computer (I)

 la — portátil laptop computer (I)

 usar la — to use the computer (I)

comunicarse (c→qu) to communicate (I)

 (tú) te comunicas you communicate (I)

 (yo) me comunico I communicate (I)

la **comunidad** community (I)

con with (I)

 — destino a going to (8A)

 — mis / tus amigos with my / your friends (I)

 ¿**— qué se sirve?** What do you serve it with? (7A)

 ¿**— quién?** With whom? (I)

el **concierto** concert (I)

el **concurso** contest (2A)

 el — de belleza beauty contest (6A)

 el programa de —s game show (I)

el **conductor, la conductora** driver (3B)

congelado, -a frozen (7A)

conmigo with me (I)

conocer (c→zc) to know, to be acquainted with (I, 1A)

conseguir (e → i) to obtain (8B)

consentido, -a spoiled (4A)

conservar to conserve (9B)

el **consultorio** doctor's /dentist's office (3A)

el **contador, la contadora** accountant (9A)

la **contaminación** pollution (9B)

contaminado, -a polluted (9B)

contar (o→ue) (chistes) to tell (jokes) (4B)

contento, -a happy (I)

contestar to answer (1A)

contigo with you (I)

contra against (9B)

la **corbata** tie (I)

el **coro** chorus, choir (1B)

el **correo** post office (3A)

el **correo electrónico** e-mail (I)

escribir por — to write e-mail (I)

correr to run (I)

cortar to cut (I, 7A)

— el césped to mow the lawn (I)

—se to cut oneself (5B)

—se el pelo to cut one's hair (2A)

cortés, *pl.* **corteses** polite (8B)

las **cortinas** curtains (I)

corto, -a short *(length)* (I)

los pantalones —s shorts (I)

la **cosa** thing (I)

costar (o→ue) to cost (I)

¿Cuánto cuesta(n)...? How much does (do) ... cost? (I)

la **costumbre** custom (4B)

crear to create (I)

— una página Web to create a Web page (1B)

creer (i→y):

Creo que... I think... (I)

Creo que no. I don't think so. (I)

Creo que sí. I think so. (I)

el **crimen** crime (6B)

el / la **criminal** criminal (6B)

el **crítico, la crítica** critic (6B)

el **cruce de calles** intersection (3B)

cruzar to cross (3B)

el **cuaderno** notebook (I)

la **cuadra** block (3B)

el **cuadro** painting (I)

¿Cuál? Which? What? (I)

¿— es la fecha? What is the date? (I)

¿Cuándo? When? (I)

¿Cuánto?:

¿— cuesta(n)...? How much does (do)...cost? (I)

¿— tiempo hace que...? How long...? (1B)

¿Cuántos, -as? How many? (I)

¿—s años tiene(n)...? How old is / are...? (I)

cuarenta forty (I)

cuarto, -a fourth (I)

y — quarter past *(in telling time)* (I)

el **cuarto** room (I)

cuatro four (I)

cuatrocientos, -as four hundred (I)

la **cuchara** spoon (I)

la **cucharada** tablespoon(ful) (7A)

el **cuchillo** knife (I)

el **cuello** neck (5B)

la **cuenta** bill (I)

la **cuerda** rope (4A)

el **cuero** leather (2B)

cuidar a to take care of (3A)

el **cumpleaños** birthday (I)

¡Feliz —! Happy birthday! (I)

cumplir años to have a birthday (4B)

el **cupón de regalo,** *pl.* **los cupones de regalo** gift certificate (2B)

el **curso: tomar un curso** to take a course (I)

D _____

dar to give (I)

— + *movie* or *TV program* to show (I)

— de comer al perro to feed the dog (I)

— puntadas to stitch *(surgically)* (5B)

— un discurso to give a speech (1A)

— una caminata to take a walk (7B)

dar(se) la mano to shake hands (4B)

de of, from (I)

— acuerdo. OK. Agreed. (3B)

— algodón cotton (2B)

— cuero leather (2B)

¿— dónde eres? Where are you from? (I)

— ida y vuelta round trip (8A)

— la mañana / la tarde / la noche in the morning / afternoon / evening (I)

— lana wool (2B)

— moda in fashion (2B)

— negocios business (9A)

— niño as a child (4A)

— oro gold (2A)

— pequeño as a child (4A)

— plata silver (2A)

— plato principal as a main dish (I)

— postre for dessert (I)

— prisa in a hurry (5A)

¿— qué color ...? What color ...? (I)

¿— qué está hecho, -a? What is it made of? (2B)

— repente suddenly (5A)

— seda silk (2B)

— sólo un color solid-colored (2B)

— tela sintética synthetic fabric (2B)

¿— veras? Really? (I)

— vez en cuando once in a while (4A)

debajo de underneath (I)

deber should, must (I)

decidir to decide (I)

décimo, -a tenth (I)

decir to say, to tell (I)

¿Cómo se dice ...? How do you say ...? (I)

dime tell me (I)

¡No me digas! You don't say! (I)

¿Qué quiere — ...? What does...mean? (I)

Quiere — ... It means ... (I)

Se dice... You say... (I)

las decoraciones decorations (I)

decorar to decorate (I)

el dedo finger (I)

Déjame en paz. Leave me alone. (3B)

dejar to leave *(something)*, to let (3B)

no dejes don't leave, don't let (7A)

delante de in front of (I)

delicioso, -a delicious (I)

los demás, las demás others (I)

demasiado too (I)

el / la dentista dentist (3A)

dentro de inside (7B)

depende it depends (2A)

el dependiente, la dependienta salesperson (I)

deportista athletic, sports-minded (I)

derecha: a la — (de) to the right (of) (I)

derecho straight (3B)

el derecho *(study of)* law (9A)

el desayuno breakfast (I)

en el — for breakfast (I)

descansar to rest, to relax (I)

los descuentos: la tienda de — discount store (I)

desde from, since (3B)

desear to wish (I)

¿Qué desean (Uds.)? What would you like? *formal* (I)

el desfile parade (4B)

el desierto desert (9B)

desobediente disobedient (4A)

el desodorante deodorant (2A)

desordenado, -a messy (I)

despacio slowly (3B)

el despacho office (home) (I)

despedirse (e→i) (de) to say good-bye *(to)* (4B)

el despertador alarm clock (I)

despertarse (e→ie) to wake up (2A)

después (de) afterwards, after (I)

destino: con — a going to (8A)

la destrucción destruction (9B)

destruir (i→y) to destroy (5A)

el / la detective detective (6B)

detrás de behind (I)

devolver (o→ue) (un libro) to return (a book) (3A)

el día day (I)

Buenos —s. Good morning. (I)

cada — every day (I)

el — festivo holiday (4B)

¿Qué — es hoy? What day is today? (I)

todos los —s every day (I)

la diapositiva slide (I)

dibujar to draw (I)

el diccionario dictionary (I)

diciembre December (I)

diecinueve nineteen (I)

dieciocho eighteen (I)

dieciséis sixteen (I)

diecisiete seventeen (I)

los dientes teeth (2A)

cepillarse — to brush one's teeth (2A)

el cepillo de — toothbrush (2A)

diez ten (I)

difícil difficult (I)

digital: la cámara — digital camera (I)

dime tell me (I)

el dinero money (I)

el dinosaurio dinosaur (4A)

la dirección, *pl.* **las direcciones** direction (6B)

la — electrónica e-mail address (I)

directo, -a direct (8A)

el director, la directora *(school)* principal (6B)

el disco compacto compact disc (I)

grabar un — to burn a CD (I)

el discurso speech (1A)

discutir to discuss (1A)

el diseñador, la diseñadora designer (9A)

disfrutar de to enjoy (8B)

el disquete diskette (I)

divertido, -a amusing, fun (I)

divertirse (e→ie) (e→i) to have fun (4B)

doblar to turn (3B)

doce twelve (I)

el documento document (I)

doler (o→ue) to hurt (I, 5B)

el dolor pain (5B)

domingo Sunday (I)

dónde:

¿—? Where? (I)

¿De — eres? Where are you from? (I)

dormido, -a asleep (5A)

dormir (o→ue) (o→u) to sleep (I)

—se to fall asleep (6A)

el dormitorio bedroom (I)

dos two (I)

los / las dos both (I)

doscientos, -as two hundred (I)

el **drama** drama (I)

la **ducha** shower (2A)

ducharse to take a shower (2A)

dudar to doubt (9B)

el **dueño, la dueña** owner (9A)

dulce sweet (7B)

los **dulces** candy (I)

durante during (I)

durar to last (I, 8A)

el **durazno** peach (7B)

E _____

echar una carta to mail a letter (3A)

ecológico, -a ecological (9B)

económico, -a economical (9B)

el **edificio de apartamentos** apartment building (5A)

la **educación física: la clase de —** physical education class (I)

efectivo: en — cash (2B)

los **efectos especiales** special effects (6B)

eficiente efficient (9B)

ejemplo: por — for example (2A)

el **ejercicio: hacer —** to exercise (I)

el *m. sing.* the (I)

él he (I)

la **electricidad** electricity (9B)

los **electrodomésticos: la tienda de —** household-appliance store (I)

electrónico, -a: la dirección — e-mail address (I)

elegante elegant (2A)

eliminar to eliminate (9B)

ella she (I)

ellas *f.* they (I)

ellos *m.* they (I)

emocionado, -a excited, emotional (6A)

emocionante touching (I)

el **empate** tie (6A)

empezar (e →ie) (z →c) to begin, to start (I, 1A)

el **empleado, la empleada** employee (8A)

en in, on (I)

— **+** *vehicle* by, in, on (I)

— **casa** at home (I)

— **efectivo** cash (2B)

— **la ... hora** in the ... hour (class period) (I)

— **la Red** online (I)

— **línea** online (1B)

— **medio de** in the middle of (3B)

— **peligro de extinción** endangered, in danger of extinction (9B)

— **punto** exactly *(time)* (8B)

¿— qué puedo servirle? How can I help you? (I)

— **realidad** really (2B)

— **seguida** right away (3A)

enamorado, -a de in love with (6B)

enamorarse (de) to fall in love (with) (6B)

encantado, -a delighted (I)

encantar to please very much, to love (I)

a él / ella le encanta(n) he / she loves (I)

me / te encanta(n)... I / you love ... (I)

encender (e →ie) to turn on, to light (7A)

encima de on top of (I)

encontrar (o →ue) to find (2B)

la **energía** energy (9B)

enero January (I)

el **enfermero, la enfermera** nurse (5B)

enfermo, -a sick (I)

enlatado, -a canned (7A)

enojado, -a angry (6A)

enojarse to get angry (6A)

enorme enormous (4B)

la **ensalada** salad (I)

la — de frutas fruit salad (I)

ensayar to rehearse (1B)

el **ensayo** rehearsal (1B)

enseñar to teach (I)

entender (e →ie) to understand (1A)

entonces then (I)

la **entrada** entrance (2B)

entrar to enter (I)

entre among, between (1B)

entregar to turn in (1A)

el **entrenador, la entrenadora** coach, trainer (6A)

la **entrevista** interview (6A)

entrevistar to interview (6A)

entusiasmado, -a excited (2A)

enviar (i →í) to send (I, 3A)

el **equipaje** luggage (8A)

facturar el — to check luggage (3A)

el **equipo** team (1B)

el — de sonido sound (stereo) system (I)

el — deportivo sports equipment (3A)

¿Eres...? Are you ...? (I)

es is; (he / she / it) is (I)

— **cierto** it's true (9B)

— **el** *(number)* **de** *(month)* **it is the... of...** *(in telling the date)* (I)

— **el primero de** *(month).* **It is the first of ...** (I)

— **la una.** It is one o'clock. (I)

— **necesario.** It's necessary. (I)

— **un(a) ...** It's a ... (I)

la **escala** stopover (8A)

la **escalera** stairs, stairway (I), ladder (5A)

escaparse to escape (5A)

la **escena** scene (6B)

escoger (g →j) to choose (2B)

esconder(se) to hide (oneself) (5A)

escribir:

¿Cómo se escribe ...? How

is ... spelled? (I)

 — cuentos to write stories (I)

 — por correo electrónico to write e-mail (I)

 — un informe sobre... to write a report about...

 Se escribe ... It's spelled ... (I)

el **escritor, la escritora** writer (9A)

el **escritorio** desk (I)

escuchar música to listen to music (I)

la **escuela primaria** primary school (I)

la **escuela técnica** technical school (9A)

ese, esa that (I, 2B)

eso: por — that's why, therefore (I)

esos, esas those (I, 2B)

el **espacio** (outer) space (9B)

los **espaguetis** spaghetti (I)

la **espalda** back (5B)

el **español: la clase de —** Spanish class (I)

especial special (2A)

especialmente especially (I)

el **espejo** mirror (I)

esperar to wait (3B)

la **esposa** wife (I)

el **esposo** husband (I)

el **esquí acuático** waterskiing (8B)

esquiar to ski (I)

la **esquina** corner (3B)

Está hecho, -a de ... It is made of ... (2B)

esta noche this evening (I)

esta tarde this afternoon (I)

la **estación,** *pl.* **las estaciones** season (I)

 la — de servicio service station (3A)

el **estadio** stadium (I)

el **estante** shelf, bookshelf (I)

estar to be (I)

 ¿Cómo está Ud.? How are

you? *formal* (I)

¿Cómo estás? How are you? fam. (I)

— + *present participle* to be + *present participle* (I)

— basado, -a en to be based on (6B)

— de moda to be in fashion (2B)

— en línea to be online (I, 1B)

— enamorado, -a de to be in love with (6B)

— seguro, -a to be sure (3B)

No estoy de acuerdo. I don't agree. (I)

la **estatua** statue (3B)

este, esta this (I, 2B)

este fin de semana this week end (I)

el **estilo** style (2B)

el **estómago** stomach (I)

estos, estas these (I, 2B)

 ¿Qué es esto? What is this? (I)

estrecho, -a narrow (3B)

la **estrella (del cine)** (movie) star (6B)

el / la **estudiante** student (I)

estudiar to study (I)

estudioso, -a studious (I)

la **estufa** stove (7A)

estupendo, -a stupendous, wonderful (8B)

el **evento especial** special event (2A)

exagerado, -a outrageous (2B)

el **éxito** success (6B)

 tener — to be successful (6B)

examinar to examine, to check (5B)

la **excursión,** *pl.* **las excursiones** excursion, short trip (8B)

la **experiencia** experience (I)

explicar to explain (1A)

la **explosión,** *pl.* **las explosiones** explosion (5A)

extracurricular extracurricular

(1B)

extranjero, -a foreign (8A)

el / la **extraterrestre** alien (6B)

F _____

fácil easy (I)

facturar to check (luggage) (8A)

la **falda** skirt (I)

faltar to be missing (I)

famoso, -a famous (8B)

fantástico, -a fantastic (I)

la **farmacia** pharmacy (3A)

fascinante fascinating (I)

fascinar to fascinate (6B)

favorito, -a favorite (I)

febrero February (I)

la **fecha: ¿Cuál es la —?** What is the date? (I)

¡Felicidades! Congratulations! (4B)

felicitar to congratulate (4B)

¡Feliz cumpleaños! Happy birthday! (I)

fenomenal phenomenal (6A)

feo, -a ugly (I)

la **fiesta** party (I)

 la — de sorpresa surprise party (4B)

el **fin de semana:**

 este — this weekend (I)

 los fines de semana on weekends (I)

final: al final at the end (6A)

flojo, -a loose (2B)

la **flor,** *pl.* **las flores** flower (I)

la **fogata** bonfire (7B)

el **fósforo** match (7B)

la **foto** photo (I)

la **fotografía** photography (1B)

el **fotógrafo, la fotógrafa** photographer (1B)

el **fracaso** failure (6B)

frecuentemente frequently (4B)

el **fregadero** sink (7A)

freír (e→í) to fry (7A)

las **fresas** strawberries (I)

fresco, -a fresh (7A)

los **frijoles** beans (7B)

el **frío:**

    Hace —. It's cold. (I)

    tener — to be cold (I)

frito, -a fried (7A)

fue it was (I)

    — un desastre. It was a disaster. (I)

el **fuego** fire (7A)

los **fuegos artificiales** fireworks (4B)

la **fuente** fountain (3B); source (9B)

fuera (de) outside (7B)

funcionar to function, to work (9B)

furioso, -a furious (6A)

el **fútbol: jugar al —** to play soccer (I)

el **fútbol americano: jugar al —** to play football (I)

el **futuro** future (9A)

G

el **galán,** *pl.* **los galanes** leading man (6B)

la **galleta** cookie (I)

ganar to win (I); to earn *(money)* (1B)

    —se la vida to make a living (9A)

la **ganga** bargain (2B)

el **garaje** garage (I)

la **gasolina** gasoline (3A)

gastar to spend (2B)

el **gato** cat (I)

el **gel** gel (2A)

generalmente generally (I)

generoso, -a generous (4A)

¡Genial! Great! (I)

la **gente** people (I)

el / la **gerente** manager (9A)

la **gimnasia** gymnastics (1B)

    hacer — to do gymnastics (1B)

el **gimnasio** gym (I)

gira: — hacer una — to take a tour (8B)

el **globo** balloon (I)

el **gol** goal (in sports) (6A)

    meter un — to score a goal (6A)

el **golf: jugar al —** to play golf (I)

la **gorra** cap (I)

grabar to record (1B)

    — un disco compacto to burn a CD (I)

gracias thank you (I)

gracioso, -a funny (I)

la **graduación,** *pl.* **las graduaciones** graduation (9A)

graduarse (u→ú) to graduate (9A)

los **gráficos** computer graphics (I)

grande large (I)

la **grapadora** stapler (1A)

grasoso, -a fatty (7B)

grave serious (9B)

gris gray (I)

gritar to scream (5A)

los **guantes** gloves (I)

guapo, -a good-looking (I)

la **guardería infantil** day-care center (4A)

la **guerra** war (9B)

el / la **guía** guide (8B)

la **guía** guidebook (8B)

los **guisantes** peas (I)

gustar:

    a él / ella le gusta(n) he / she likes (I)

    (A mí) me gusta ... I like to ... (I)

    (A mí) me gusta más... I like to ... better (I prefer to ...) (I)

    (A mí) me gusta mucho ... I like to ... a lot (I)

    (A mí) no me gusta ... I don't like to ... (I)

    (A mí) no me gusta nada ... I don't like to...at all. (I)

    Le gusta ... He / She likes... (I)

Me gusta ... I like... (I)

Me gustaría... I would like ... (I)

Me gustó. I liked it. (I)

No le gusta ... He / She doesn't like ... (I)

¿Qué te gusta hacer? What do you like to do? (I)

¿Qué te gusta hacer más? What do you like better (prefer) to do? (I)

Te gusta ... You like ... (I)

¿Te gusta ...? Do you like to ...? (I)

¿Te gustaría? Would you like? (I)

¿Te gustó? Did you like it? (I)

H

haber to have *(as an auxiliary verb)* (6B)

    había there was / there were (4B)

la **habitación,** *pl.* **las habitaciones** room (8B)

    la — doble double room (8B)

    la — individual single room (8B)

    hablar to talk (I)

    — por teléfono to talk on the phone (I)

habrá there will be (9A)

hacer to do (I)

    ¿Cómo se hace...? How do you make...? (7A)

    ¿Cuánto tiempo hace que...? How long...? (1B)

    hace + *time expression* ago (I)

    Hace + *time* **+ que ...** It has been ... (1B)

    Hace calor. It's hot. (I)

    Hace frío. It's cold. (I)

    Hace sol. It's sunny. (I)

    — ejercicio to exercise (I)

    — el papel de to play the role of (6B)

    — escala to stop over (8A)

    — gimnasia to do gymnastics

(1B)

— la cama to make the bed (I)

— la maleta to pack the suitcase (8A)

— ruido to make noise (8B)

— un picnic to have a picnic (4B)

— un viaje to take a trip (8A)

— un video to videotape (I)

— una búsqueda to do a search (1B)

— una gira to take a tour (8B)

— una parrillada to have a barbecue (7B)

— una pregunta to ask a question (1A)

¿Qué hiciste? What did you do? (I)

¿Qué tiempo hace? What is the weather like? (I)

(tú) haces you do (I)

(yo) hago I do (I)

hambre: Tengo —. I'm hungry. (I)

la **hamburguesa** hamburger (I)

la **harina** flour (7B)

has visto you have seen (6B)

hasta until (3A); as far as, up to (3B)

— luego. See you later. (I)

— mañana. See you tomorrow. (I)

— pronto. See you soon. (3A)

hay there is, there are (I)

— que one must (I)

haya *(subjunctive)* there is, there are (9B)

haz *(command)* do, make (I)

he visto I have seen (6B)

hecho: ¿De qué está — ? What is it made of? (2B)

el **helado** ice cream (I)

herido, -a injured (5A)

el **herido, la herida** injured person (5A)

el **hermano, la hermana** brother, sister (I)

el **hermanastro, la hermanastra** stepbrother, stepsister (I)

los **hermanos** brothers, brother(s) and sister(s) (I)

el **héroe** hero (5A)

la **heroína** heroine (5A)

hervir (e→ie) (e→i) to boil (7A)

el **hijo, la hija** son, daughter (I)

los **hijos** children, sons (I)

histórico, -a historical (8B)

el **hockey** hockey (1B)

la **hoja de papel** sheet of paper (I)

¡Hola! Hello! (I)

el **hombre** man (I)

el — de negocios businessman (9A)

el **hombro** shoulder (5B)

la **hora: en la... —** in the...hour (class period) (I)

¿A qué —? (At) what time? (I)

el **horario** schedule (I)

la **hormiga** ant (7B)

el **horno** oven (7A)

al — baked (7A)

horrible horrible (I)

el **horror: la película de —** horror movie (I)

el **hospital** hospital (I)

el **hotel** hotel (I)

hoy today (I)

hubo there was, there were (5A)

el **hueso** bone (5B)

los **huevos** eggs (I)

el **humo** smoke (5A)

el **huracán,** *pl.* **los huracanes** hurricane (5A)

I _____

ida y vuelta round-trip (8A)

identidad: carnet de — ID card

el **idioma** language (9A)

la **iglesia** church (I)

igualmente likewise (I)

impaciente impatient (I)

importante important (I)

importa(n): me/te — it matters (it's important)/they matter to me/to you (2B)

impresionante impressive (I)

el **incendio** fire (5A)

increíble incredible (I)

infantil childish (I)

la **información** information (I)

el **informe** report (I, 1A)

el **ingeniero, la ingeniera** engineer (9A)

el **inglés: la clase de —** English class (I)

el **ingrediente** ingredient (7A)

inmediatamente immediately (2B)

inolvidable unforgettable (I)

insistir en to insist (8A)

la **inspección,** *pl.* **las inspecciones de seguridad** security checkpoint (8A)

inteligente intelligent (I)

el **interés** interest (1B)

interesante interesting (I)

interesar to interest (I)

me interesa(n) it interests me (they interest me) (I)

la **inundación,** *pl.* **las inundaciones** flood (5A)

investigar (g → gu) to investigate (5A)

el **invierno** winter (I)

la **inyección,** *pl.* **las inyecciones** injection, shot (5B)

poner una — to give an injection (5B)

ir to go (I)

— a + *inf.* to be going to + *verb* (I)

— a la escuela to go to school (I)

— a pie to go on foot (3A)

— de cámping to go camping (I)

— de compras to go shopping (I)

— de pesca to go fishing (I)

— **de vacaciones** to go on vacation (I)

¡Vamos! Let's go! (I)

el **itinerario** itinerary (8B)

la **izquierda: a la — (de)** to the left (of) (I)

J

el **jabón** soap (3A)

el **jardín,** *pl.* **los jardines** garden, yard (I)

los **jeans** jeans (I)

joven *adj.* young (I)

el / la **joven** young man, young woman (I)

los **jóvenes** young people (1B)

las **joyas (de oro, de plata)** (gold, silver) jewelry (2A)

la **joyería** jewelry store (I)

las **judías verdes** green beans (I)

jueves Thursday (I)

el **juez, la jueza,** *pl.* **los jueces** judge (9A)

el **jugador, la jugadora** player (6A)

jugar (a) (u → ue) (g → gu) to play *(games, sports)* (I)

— **a los bolos** to bowl (1B)

— **al básquetbol** to play basketball (I)

— **al béisbol** to play baseball (I)

— **al fútbol** to play soccer (I)

— **al fútbol americano** to play football (I)

— **al golf** to play golf (I)

— **al tenis** to play tennis (I)

— **al vóleibol** to play volleyball (I)

— **videojuegos** to play video games (I)

el **jugo:**

el — **de manzana** apple juice (I)

el — **de naranja** orange juice (I)

el **juguete** toy (I)

julio July (I)

junio June (I)

juntarse to join (9B)

L

la the *f. sing.* (I); it, her *f. dir. obj. pron.* (I)

los **labios** lips (2A)

el **laboratorio** laboratory (I, 1A)

el **lado: al — de** next to (I)

el **ladrón, la ladrona,** *pl.* **los ladrones** thief (6B)

el **lago** lake (I)

la **lámpara** lamp (I)

la **lana** wool (2B)

el **lápiz,** *pl.* **los lápices** pencil (I)

largo, -a long (I)

las the *f. pl.;* them, you *formal pl. f. dir. obj. pron.* (I)

— **dos, los dos** both (I)

lástima: ¡Qué —! What a shame! (5B)

lastimarse to hurt oneself (5B)

la **lata** can (I)

lavar to wash (I)

— **el coche** to wash the car (I)

— **la ropa** to wash the clothes (I)

— **los platos** to wash the dishes (I)

—**se la cara** to wash one's face (2A)

le (to / for) him, her, you *formal sing. ind. obj. pron.* (I)

— **gusta ...** He / She likes... (I)

— **traigo ...** I will bring you ... (I)

No — gusta ... He / She doesn't like ... (I)

la **lección,** *pl.* **las lecciones de piano** piano lesson (class) (I)

tomar lecciones to take lessons (1B)

la **leche** milk (I)

la **lechuga** lettuce (I)

el **lector DVD** DVD player (I)

leer (i→y) revistas to read magazines (I)

lejos (de) far (from) (I)

lentamente slowly (2A)

la **leña** firewood (7B)

les (to / for) them; you *(formal) pl. ind. obj. pron.* (I)

el **letrero** sign (2B)

levantar pesas to lift weights (I)

levantarse to get up (2A)

la **ley** law (9A)

la **librería** bookstore (I)

el **libro** book (I)

la **liga** league (6A)

la **limonada** lemonade (I)

limpiar el baño to clean the bathroom (I)

limpio, -a clean (I)

la **línea:**

estar en — to be online (I, 1B)

la — aérea airline (8A)

la **liquidación,** *pl.* **las liquidaciones** sale (2B)

listo, -a ready (8A)

llamar:

— **por teléfono** to call on the phone (5A)

¿Cómo se llama? What's his / her name? (I)

¿Cómo te llamas? What is your name? (I)

Me llamo ... My name is ... (I)

la **llave** key (8B)

el **llavero** key chain (I)

la **llegada** arrival (8A)

llegar: llegar tarde to arrive late (1A)

llenar (el tanque) to fill (the tank) (3A)

llevar to wear (I); to take, to carry, to bring (I)

llevarse bien / mal to get along well / badly (4B)

llorar to cry (4B)

llover (o→ue) to rain (5A)

Llueve. It's raining. (I)

la **lluvia** rain (5A)

lo it, him, you *formal m. dir. obj. pron.* (I)

— **siento.** I'm sorry. (I)

lo que what (1A)

loco, -a: volverse (o→ue) — to go crazy (6A)

el **locutor, la locutora** announcer (5A)

los the *m. pl.* (I); them, you *formal pl. m. dir. obj. pron.* (I)

— **dos, las dos** both (I)

— **fines de semana** on weekends (I)

— **lunes, los martes...** on Mondays, on Tuesdays... (I)

luchar to fight (9B)

luego then (2A)

el **lugar** place (I)

la **Luna** the moon (9B)

lunes Monday (I)

los lunes on Mondays (I)

la **luz,** *pl.* **las luces** light (I)

M

la **madrastra** stepmother (I)

la **madre (mamá)** mother (I)

el **maíz** corn (7B)

mal bad, badly (I)

la **maleta** suitcase (8A)

hacer la — to pack the suitcase (8A)

malo, -a bad (I)

manejar to drive (3B)

la **manera** way, manner (9B)

la **mano** hand (I)

darse la — to shake hands (4B)

mantener: para — **la salud** to maintain one's health (I)

la **mantequilla** butter (I)

la **manzana** apple (I)

el jugo de — apple juice (I)

mañana tomorrow (I)

la **mañana:**

a las ocho de la — at eight

(o'clock) in the morning (I)

de la — in the morning (I)

el **maquillaje** make-up (2A)

el **mar** sea (I)

la **marca** brand (2B)

los **mariscos** shellfish (7A)

marrón *pl.* **marrones** brown (I)

martes Tuesday (I)

los martes on Tuesdays (I)

marzo March (I)

más:

¿**Qué** —? What else? (I)

— **...que** more...than (I)

— **de** more than (I)

— **o menos** more or less (I)

matar to kill (6B)

las **matemáticas: la clase de** — mathematics class (I)

los **materiales** supplies, materials (1A)

mayo May (I)

la **mayonesa** mayonnaise (7B)

mayor, *pl.* **mayores** *adj.* older (I)

los **mayores** grown-ups (4B)

me (to / for) me *dir., ind. obj. pron.* (I)

— **aburre(n)** it / they bore(s) me (I)

— **estás poniendo nervioso, -a.** You are making me nervous. (3B)

— **falta(n) ...** I need ... (I)

— **gustaría** I would like (I)

— **gustó.** I liked it. (I)

— **importa(n)** it matters (it's important) they matter to me (2B)

— **interesa(n)** it / they interest(s) me (I)

— **llamo ...** My name is ... (I)

— **parece que** it seems to me (2B)

— **queda(n) bien / mal.** It / They fit(s) me well / poorly. (I)

— **quedo en casa.** I stay at home. (I)

¿— **trae...?** Will you bring me ...? *formal* (I)

el **mecánico, la mecánica** mechanic (9A)

media, -o half (I)

y — thirty, half past (I)

mediano, -a medium (2B)

la **medicina** medicine (5B)

el **médico, la médica** doctor (3A)

medio ambiente environment (9B)

mejor:

el/ la —, **los / las** —**es** the best (I)

—**(es) que** better than (I)

mejorar to improve (9B)

el **melón,** *pl.* **los melones** melon (7B)

memoria: aprender de — to memorize (1A)

menor younger (I)

menos:

más o — more or less (I)

— **... que** less / fewer ... than (I)

— **de** less / fewer than (I)

mentir (e→ie) (e→i) to lie (4A)

el **menú** menu (I)

menudo: a — often (I)

el **mercado** market (2B)

el **mes** month (I)

la **mesa** table (I)

poner la — to set the table (I)

la **mesita** night table (I)

meter: — **un gol** to score a goal (6A)

el **metro** subway (3B)

mezclar to mix (7A)

la **mezquita** mosque (I)

mi, mis my (I)

mí:

a — **también** I do (like to) too (I)

a — **tampoco** I don't (like to) either (I)

para — in my opinion, for me (I)

el **microondas** microwave (7A)

el **miedo: tener** — **(de)** to be

scared (of), to be afraid (of) (I)

el **miembro** member (1B)

    ser — to be a member (1B)

mientras (que) while (4B)

miércoles Wednesday (I)

mil thousand (I)

militar *(adj.)* military (9A)

un **millón de / millones de** a million / millions of (6A)

mío, -a, -os, -as mine (2A)

mirar to look (at) (I)

mismo, -a same (I)

la **mochila** bookbag, backpack (I)

moda: de — in fashion (2B)

los **modales** manners (4B)

mojado, -a wet (7B)

molestar to bother (4A)

el **momento: un —** a moment (I)

la **moneda** coin (4A)

el **mono** monkey (I)

las **montañas** mountains (I)

montar:

    — a caballo to ride horse back (I)

    — en bicicleta to ride a bicycle (I)

    — en monopatín to skateboard (I)

el **monumento** monument (I)

morado, -a purple (I)

morirse (o →ue)(o →u) to die (6A)

    se murieron they died (5A)

la **mosca** fly (7B)

la **mostaza** mustard (7B)

la **moto acuática** jet skiing (8B)

moverse (o→ue) to move (5B)

mucho, -a a lot (I)

    — gusto pleased to meet you (I)

muchos, -as many (I)

los **muebles** furniture (5A)

muerto, -a dead (5A)

la **mujer** woman (I)

    la — de negocios

businesswoman (9A)

las **muletas** crutches (5B)

la **multa** ticket (3B)

el **mundo** world (4A)

la **muñeca** doll (4A); wrist (5B)

el **muñeco** action figure (4A)

el **músculo** muscle (5B)

el **museo** museum (I)

el **músico, la música** musician (1B)

muy very (I)

    — bien very well (I)

N

nacer to be born (4B)

nada nothing (I)

    (A mí) no me gusta — ... I don't like to...at all. (I)

nadar to swim (I)

nadie no one, nobody (1A)

la **naranja: el jugo de —** orange juice (I)

la **nariz,** *pl.* **las narices** nose (I)

la **natación** swimming (1B)

la **naturaleza** nature (9B)

navegar to sail, to navigate (8B) **— en la Red** to surf the Web (I, 1B)

    necesario: Es —. It's necessary. (I)

necesitar:

    necesitas you need (I)

    necesito I need (I)

los **negocios** business (9A)

    el hombre de — business man (9A)

    la mujer de — business woman (9A)

negro: el pelo negro black hair (I)

nervioso, -a nervous (2A)

nevar (e→ie) to snow (5A)

    Nieva. It's snowing. (I)

ni ... ni neither ... nor, not ... or (I)

ningún, ninguno, -a no, none, not any (1A)

el **niño, la niña** young boy, young girl (I)

los **niños** children (I)

No comas. Don't eat. (7A)

No dejes Don't leave, don't let (7A)

No escribas. Don't write. (7A)

No estoy de acuerdo. I don't agree. (I)

No hables. Don't speak. (7A)

¡No me digas! You don't say! (I)

no ... todavía not yet (6B)

la **noche:**

    a las ocho de la — at eight (o'clock) in the evening, at night (I)

    Buenas —s. Good evening. (I)

    de la — in the evening, at night (I)

    esta — this evening, tonight (I)

nos (to / for) us *dir., ind. obj. pron.* (I)

    ¡— vemos! See you later! (I)

nosotros, -as we (I)

la **nota** grade, mark (in school) (1A)

    sacar una buena — to get a good grade (1A)

el **noticiero** newscast (5A)

novecientos, -as nine hundred (I)

noveno, -a ninth (I)

noventa ninety (I)

noviembre November (I)

el **novio, la novia** boyfriend, girlfriend (I)

la **nube** cloud (7B)

nuestro, -a, -os, -as our, ours (I)

nueve nine (I)

nuevo, -a new (I)

el **número** shoe size (2B)

nunca never (I)

O

o or (I)

obedecer (c→zc) to obey (4A)

obediente obedient (4A)

la **obra de teatro** play (I)

observar to observe (8B)

ochenta eighty (I)

ocho eight (I)

ochocientos, -as eight hundred (I)

octavo, -a eighth (I)

octubre October (I)

ocupado, -a busy (I)

ocurrir to occur (5A)

ofender to offend (8B)

la **oficina** office (9A)

ofrecer (c→zc) to offer (4A)

oír to hear (5A)

el **ojo** eye (I)

la **olla** pot (7A)

el **olor** smell, odor (7B)

olvidarse de to forget about (7A)

    no te olvides de don't forget about / to (7A)

    se me olvidó I forgot (3A)

once eleven (I)

la **oportunidad** opportunity (1B)

ordenado, -a neat (I)

el **oro** gold (2A)

la **orquesta** orchestra (1B)

os (to / for) you *pl. fam. dir., ind. obj. pron.* (I)

oscuro, -a dark (2B)

el **oso** bear (I)

    el — de peluche teddy bear (4A)

el **otoño** fall, autumn (I)

otro, -a other, another (I)

otra vez again (I)

¡Oye! Hey! (I)

P

la **paciencia** patience (8A)

    tener — to be patient (8A)

paciente *adj.* patient (I)

el **padrastro** stepfather (I)

el **padre (papá)** father (I)

los **padres** parents (I)

pagar (por) to pay (for) (I)

la **página Web** Web page (I)

el **país** country (I)

el **pájaro** bird (I)

la **palabra** word (1A)

el **palacio** palace (8B)

el **palo de golf** golf club (3A)

el **pan** bread (I)

    el — tostado toast (I)

la **pantalla** (computer) screen (I)

los **pantalones** pants (I)

    los — cortos shorts (I)

las **papas** potatoes (I)

    las — fritas French fries (I)

el **papel** role (6B)

    el — picado cut-paper decorations (I)

    hacer el — de to play the role of (6B)

la **papelera** wastepaper basket (I)

para for (I)

    — + *inf.* in order to (I)

    — la salud for one's health (I)

    — mantener la salud to maintain one's health (I)

    — mí in my opinion, for me (I)

    ¿ — qué sirve? What's it (used) for? (I)

    — ti in your opinion, for you (I)

el **paramédico, la paramédica** paramedic (5A)

parar to stop (3B)

parecer:

    me parece que it seems to me (2B)

    ¿Qué te parece? What do you think? / How does it seem to you? (2B)

la **pared** wall (I)

los **parientes** relatives (4B)

el **parque** park (I)

    el — de diversiones amusement park (I)

    el — nacional national park (I)

parrilla: a la — on the grill (7B)

participar (en) to participate (in) (1B)

el **partido** game, match (I)

el **pasajero, la pasajera** passenger (8A)

el **pasaporte** passport (8A)

pasar to pass, to go (3B)

    ¿Cómo lo pasaste? How was it (for you)? (I)

    — la aspiradora to vacuum (I)

    — tiempo con amigos to spend time with friends (I)

    ¿Qué pasa? What's happening? (I)

    ¿Qué te pasó? What happened to you? (I, 5B)

el **pasatiempo** pastime (1B)

pasear en bote to go boating (I)

el **pasillo** aisle (8A)

la **pasta dental** toothpaste (3A)

pastel *adj.* pastel *(color)* (2B)

el **pastel** cake (I)

los **pasteles** pastries (I)

las **pastillas** pills (5B)

patinar to skate (I)

los **patines** skates (3A)

el **patio de recreo** playground (4A)

el **pavo** turkey (7B)

la **paz** peace (9B)

el **peatón,** *pl.* **los peatones** pedestrian (3B)

el **pedazo** piece, slice (7A)

pedir (e→i) to order, to ask for (I)

    — ayuda to ask for help (1A)

    — prestado, -a (a) to borrow (from) (2A)

el **peine** comb (2A)

pelar to peel (7A)

pelearse to fight (4A)

la **película** film, movie (I)

    la — de acción action film (6B)

    la — de ciencia ficción science fiction movie (I)

    la — de horror horror movie

(I)

la — policíaca crime movie, mystery (I)

la — romántica romantic movie (I)

ver una — to see a movie (I)

(en) peligro de extinción in danger of extinction, endangered (9B)

peligroso, -a dangerous (3B)

pelirrojo, -a red-haired (I)

el **pelo** hair (I, 2A)

  el — canoso gray hair (I)

  el — castaño brown (chestnut) hair (I)

  el — negro black hair (I)

  el — rubio blond hair (I)

la **pelota** ball (3A)

peluche: el oso de — teddy bear (4A)

pensar (e→ie) to plan, to think (I)

peor:

  el / la —, los / las —es the worst (I)

  —(es) que worse than (I)

pequeño, -a small (I)

perder (e→ie) to lose (6A)

Perdón. Excuse me. (I)

perezoso, -a lazy (I)

el **perfume** perfume (I)

el **periódico** newspaper (I)

el **permiso de manejar** driver's license (3B)

permitir to permit, to allow (4A)

pero but (I)

el **perrito caliente** hot dog (I)

el **perro** dog (I)

la **persona** person (I)

el **personaje principal** main character (6B)

pesas: levantar — to lift weights (I)

el **pescado** fish *(as a food)* (I)

el **pez,** *pl.* **los peces** fish (4A)

picante spicy (7B)

picar to chop (7A)

el **picnic** picnic (4B)

el **pie** foot (I)

la **piedra** rock (7B)

la **pierna** leg (I)

el / la **piloto** pilot (8A)

la **pimienta** pepper (I)

pintarse (las uñas) to paint, to polish (one's nails) (2A)

el **pintor, la pintora** painter (9A)

la **piña** pineapple (7B)

la **piñata** piñata (I)

la **piscina** swimming pool (I)

el **piso** story, floor (I)

  primer — second floor (I)

  segundo — third floor (I)

la **pizza** pizza (I)

planear to plan (8A)

la **planta** plant (9B)

la **planta baja** ground floor (I)

el **plástico** plastic (I)

la **plata** silver (2A)

el **plátano** banana (I)

el **plato** plate, dish (I)

  de — principal as a main dish (I)

  el — principal main dish (I)

la **playa** beach (I)

la **plaza** plaza (3B)

pobre poor (I)

pobrecito, -a poor thing (5B)

poco: un — (de) a little (I)

poder (o→ue) to be able to (I)

  (tú) puedes you can (I)

  (yo) puedo I can (I)

  se puede you can (7A)

el / la **policía** police officer (3B)

policíaca: la película — crime movie, mystery (I)

la **política** politics (9A)

el **político, la política** politician (9A)

el **pollo** chicken (I)

poner to put, to place (I)

  pon *(command)* put, place (I)

  — la mesa to set the table (I)

  — una inyección to give an injection (5B)

  — una multa to give a ticket (3B)

  —se to apply, to put on *(clothing, make up, etc.)* (2A); *+ adj.* to become (6A)

(tú) pones you put (I)

(yo) pongo I put (I)

por for (how long) (3A); by, around, along, through (3B)

  — ejemplo for example (2A)

  — eso that's why, therefore (I)

  — favor please (I)

  — lo general in general (4A)

  ¿— qué? Why? (I)

  — supuesto of course (I)

  — ... vez for the ... time (6A)

porque because (I)

portarse bien / mal to behave well / badly (4A)

la **posesión,** *pl.* **las posesiones** possession (I)

el **postre** dessert (I)

  de — for dessert (I)

la **práctica** practice (1B)

practicar (c→qu) deportes to play sports (I)

práctico, -a practical (I)

el **precio** price (I, 2B)

preferir (e→ie) (e→i) to prefer (I)

  (tú) prefieres you prefer (I)

  (yo) prefiero I prefer (I)

la **pregunta** question (1A)

  hacer una — to ask a question (1A)

el **premio** prize (6A)

preparar to prepare (I)

  —se to get ready (2A)

la **presentación,** *pl.* **las presentaciones** presentation (I)

el **presentador, la presentadora** presenter (6A)

prestar atención to pay attention (1A)

la **primavera** spring (I)

primer (primero), -a first (I)

    — piso second floor (I)

el **primo, la prima** cousin (I)

los **primos** cousins (I)

    prisa hurry (3B)

      de — in a hurry (5A)

      tener — to be in a hurry (3B)

    probar (o→ue) to taste, to try (7A)

    probarse (o→ue) to try on (2B)

el **problema** problem (I)

la **profesión,** *pl.* **las profesiones** profession (9A)

el **profesor, la profesora** teacher (I)

el **programa** program, show (I)

    el — de concursos game show (I)

    el — de dibujos animados cartoon (I)

    el — de entrevistas interview program (I)

    el — de estudios course of studies (9A)

    el — de la vida real reality program (I)

    el — de noticias news program (I)

    el — deportivo sports program (I)

    el — educativo educational program (I)

    el — musical musical program (I)

    prohibir: se prohíbe it is forbidden (1A)

    pronto soon (3A)

      Hasta —. See you soon. (3A)

la **propina** tip (8B)

    propio, -a own (I)

    proteger (g→j) to protect (9B)

el **proyecto** project (1A)

    el — de construcción construction project (I)

el **público** audience (6A)

el **pueblo** town (9B)

    puede: se — you can (7A)

    puedes: (tú) — you can (I)

    puedo: (yo) — I can (I)

el **puente** bridge (3B)

la **puerta** door (I)

    la — de embarque departure gate (8A)

    pues well *(to indicate pause)* (I)

el **puesto** (food) stand (7B)

la **pulsera** bracelet (I)

    el reloj — watch (I)

las **puntadas** stitches (5B)

    dar — to stitch *(surgically)* (5B)

    puntual punctual (8B)

el **pupitre** desk (I)

    puro, -a pure (9B)

Q

    que who, that (I)

    qué:

      ¿Para — sirve? What's it (used) for? (I)

      ¡— + *adj.!* How ...! (I)

      ¡— asco! How awful! (I)

      ¡— buena idea! What a good / nice idea! (I)

      ¿— clase de...? What kind of ... ? (I)

      ¿— desean (Uds.)? What would you like? *formal* (I)

      ¿— día es hoy? What day is today? (I)

      ¿— es esto? What is this? (I)

      ¿— hiciste? What did you do? (I)

      ¿— hora es? What time is it? (I)

      ¡— lástima! What a shame! (5B)

      ¿— más? What else? (I)

      ¿— pasa? What's happening? (I)

      ¡— pena! What a shame / pity! (I)

      ¿— quiere decir... ? What does ... mean? (I)

      ¿— tal? How are you? (I)

      ¿— tal es ...? How is (it)...? (6B)

      ¿— te gusta hacer? What do you like to do? (I)

      ¿— te gusta hacer más? What do you like better (prefer) to do? (I)

      ¿— te parece? What do you ˆ think? / How does it seem to you? (I, 2B)

      ¿— te pasó? What happened to you? (I, 5B)

      ¿— tiempo hace? What's the weather like? (I)

    quedar to fit, to be located (I, 3B)

    quedarse to stay (3A)

el **quehacer (de la casa)** (household) chore (I)

    quemar(se) to burn (oneself), to burn up (5A)

    querer (e→ie) to want (I)

      ¿Qué quiere decir...? What does...mean? (I)

      Quiere decir... It means... (I)

      quisiera I would like (I)

      (tú) quieres you want (I)

      (yo) quiero I want (I)

    ¿Quién? Who? (I)

    quince fifteen (I)

    quinientos, -as five hundred (I)

    quinto, -a fifth (I)

el **quiosco** newsstand (8B)

    quisiera I would like (I)

    quitar to take away, to remove (3B)

      — el polvo to dust (I)

    quizás maybe (I)

R

la **radiografía** X-ray (5B)

    sacar una — to take an X-ray (5B)

    rápidamente quickly (I, 2A)

la **raqueta de tenis** tennis racket (3A)

el **ratón,** *pl.* **los ratones** (computer) mouse (I)

    razón: tener — to be correct (I)

    realista realistic (I)

la **recepción** reception desk (8B)

la **receta** prescription (5B); recipe (7A)

recetar to prescribe (5B)

recibir to receive (I)

reciclar to recycle (I)

recientemente recently (2B)

recoger (g→j) to collect, to gather (I)

recomendar (e→ie) to recommend (6B)

recordar (o→ue) to remember (4B)

los **recuerdos** souvenirs (I)

comprar — to buy souvenirs (I)

la **Red:**

en la — online (I)

navegar (g→gu) en la — to surf the Web (I, 1B)

reducir to reduce (9B)

el **refresco** soft drink (I)

el **refrigerador** refrigerator (7A)

regalar to give (a gift) (4B)

el **regalo** gift, present (I)

regatear to bargain (8B)

registrar to inspect, to search (*luggage*) (8A)

la **regla** rule (1A)

regresar to return (I)

regular okay, so-so (I)

la **reina** queen (6A)

reírse (e→í) to laugh (4B)

el **reloj** clock (I)

el — pulsera watch (I)

repente: de — suddenly (5A)

repetir (e → i) to repeat (1A)

el **reportero, la reportera** reporter (5A)

rescatar to rescue (5A)

la **reservación,** *pl.* **las reservaciones** reservation (8A)

reservado, -a reserved, shy (I)

resolver (o→ue) to solve (9B)

respetar to respect (1A)

el **restaurante** restaurant (I)

resultar to result, to turn out (6A)

el **retraso** delay (8A)

la **reunión,** *pl.* **las reuniones** meeting (1B); gathering (4B)

reunirse (u→ú) to meet (4B)

el **rey,** king *pl.* **los reyes** king and queen (8B)

rico, -a rich, tasty (I)

el **río** river (I)

robar to rob, to steal (6B)

la **rodilla** knee (5B)

rojo, -a red (I)

romántico, -a: la película — romantic movie (I)

romper to break (I)

—se to break, to tear (5B)

la **ropa: la tienda de —** clothing store (I)

rosado, -a pink (I)

roto, -a broken (5B)

rubio, -a blond (I)

ruedas: silla de — wheelchair (5B)

el **ruido** noise (8B)

S

sábado Saturday (I)

saber to know (how) (I, 1B)

(tú) sabes you know (how to) (I)

(yo) sé I know (how to) (I)

el **sabor** taste (7B)

sabroso, -a tasty, flavorful (I)

el **sacapuntas,** *pl.* **los sacapuntas** pencil sharpener (I)

sacar (c→qu):

— fotos to take photos (I)

— la basura to take out the trash (I)

— un libro to take out, to check out a book (3A)

— una buena nota to get a good grade (1A)

— una radiografía to take an X-ray (5B)

la **sal** salt (I)

la **sala** living room (I)

la — de clases classroom (I)

la — de emergencia emergency room (5B)

el **salario** salary (9A)

la **salchicha** sausage (I)

la **salida** exit (2B); departure (8A)

salir to leave, to go out (I)

el **salón de belleza,** *pl.* **los salones de belleza** beauty salon (2A)

los **salones de chat** chat rooms (1B)

la **salsa** salsa, sauce (7A)

la — de tomate ketchup (7B)

saltar (a la cuerda) to jump (rope) (4A)

la **salud:**

para la — for one's health (I)

para mantener la — to maintain one's health (I)

saludar(se) to greet (4B)

salvar to save (5A)

la **sandía** watermelon (7B)

el **sándwich de jamón y queso** ham and cheese sandwich (I)

la **sangre** blood (5B)

la **sartén** frying pan (7A)

se abre opens (3A)

se cierra closes (3A)

se me olvidó I forgot (3A)

se murieron they died (5A)

se prohíbe ... it's forbidden ... (1A)

se puede you can (7A)

sé: (yo) — I know (how to) (I)

el **secador** blow dryer (2A)

secarse to dry (2A)

seco, -a dry (7B)

el **secretario, la secretaria** secretary (9A)

sed:

Tengo —. I'm thirsty. (I)

la **seda** silk (2B)

seguida: en — right away (3A)

seguir (e→i) to follow, to continue (3B)

— **una carrera** to pursue a career (9A)

según according to (I)

— **mi familia** according to my family (I)

segundo, -a second (I)

— **piso** third floor (I)

seguro, -a sure (3B)

seis six (I)

seiscientos, -as six hundred (I)

el **sello** stamp (3A)

la **selva tropical** rain forest (9B)

el **semáforo** stoplight (3B)

la **semana** week (I)

este fin de — this weekend (I)

la — pasada last week (I)

los fines de — on weekends (I)

el **sendero** trail (7B)

sentirse (e→ie) (e→i) to feel (5B)

la **señal** sign (3A)

la — de parada stop sign (3B)

señor (Sr.) sir, Mr. (I)

señora (Sra.) madam, Mrs. (I)

señorita (Srta.) miss, Miss (I)

separar to separate (I)

septiembre September (I)

séptimo, -a seventh (I)

ser to be (I)

¿Eres...? Are you...? (I)

es he / she is (I)

fue it was (I)

no soy I am not (I)

soy I am (I)

ser: será it, he, she will be (6B)

serio, -a serious (I)

la **servilleta** napkin (I)

servir (e→i) to serve, to be useful (I)

¿En qué puedo —le? How can I help you? (I)

¿Para qué sirve? What's it (used) for? (I)

sirve para it is used for (I)

sesenta sixty (I)

setecientos, -as seven hundred (I)

setenta seventy (I)

sexto, -a sixth (I)

si if, whether (I)

sí yes (I)

siempre always (I)

siento: Lo —. I'm sorry. (I)

siete seven (I)

siguiente next, following (8B)

la **silla** chair (I)

la — de ruedas wheelchair (5B)

simpático, -a nice, friendly (I)

sin without (I)

— **duda** without a doubt (5A)

la **sinagoga** synagogue (I)

el **sitio Web** Web site (I)

sobre on, about (I, 1A)

sociable sociable (I, 1A)

¡Socorro! Help! (5A)

el **software** software (I)

el **sol:**

Hace —. It's sunny. (I)

los anteojos de — sunglasses (I)

tomar el — to sunbathe (I)

solar solar (9B)

sólo only (I)

de — un color solid-colored (2B)

solo, -a alone (I)

Son las... It is ... *(in telling time)* (I)

sonreír (e→í) to smile (4B)

la **sopa de verduras** vegetable soup (I)

la **sorpresa** surprise (4B)

el **sótano** basement (I)

soy I am (I)

su, sus his, her, your *formal,* their (I)

subir to go up (5A)

sucio, -a dirty (I)

la **sudadera** sweatshirt (I)

el **suelo** ground, floor (7B)

sueño: tener — to be sleepy (I)

el **suéter** sweater (I)

sugerir (e→ie) (e→i) to suggest (8A)

el **supermercado** supermarket (3A)

supuesto: por — of course (I)

el **surf de vela** windsurfing (8B)

suyo,-a,-os,-as his, hers, yours, theirs (2A)

T

tal: ¿Qué — ? How are you? (I)

¿Qué — es? How is it? (6B)

tal vez maybe, perhaps (8B)

talentoso, -a talented (I)

la **talla** size (2B)

también also, too (I)

a mí — I do (like to) too (I)

tampoco: a mí — I don't (like to) either (I)

tan so (2B)

— + *adj.* so + adj. (2B)

— + *adj.* **+ como** as + *adj.* + as (1B)

el **tanque** tank (3A)

el **tanteo** score (6A)

tanto so much (I)

tantos, -as + *noun* **+ como** as much / many + *noun* + as (1B)

tarde late (I)

la — afternoon (I)

a la una de la — at one (o'clock) in the afternoon (I)

Buenas —s. Good afternoon.(I)

de la — in the afternoon (I)

esta — this afternoon (I)

llegar (g→gu) — to arrive late (1A)

la **tarea** homework (I)

la **tarjeta** card (I, 3A)

la — de crédito credit card (2B)

la — de embarque boarding pass (8A)

la — postal postcard (8B)

la **taza** cup (I)

te (to / for) you *sing. dir., ind. obj. pron.* (I)

¿**— gusta ... ?** Do you like to...? (I)

¿**— gustaría?** Would you like? (I)

¿**— gustó?** Did you like it? (I)

— importa(n) it matters (it's important), they matter to you (2B)

— ves (bien) you look (good) (2A)

el **té** tea (I)

el **— helado** iced tea (I)

el **teatro** theater (I)

el **teclado** (computer) keyboard (I)

el **técnico, la técnica** technician (9A)

la **tecnología** technology / computers (I)

la clase de — technology / computer class (I)

la **tela sintética** synthetic fabric (2B)

la **telenovela** soap opera (I)

el **televisor** television set (I)

el **templo** temple, Protestant church (I)

temprano early (I)

tendremos we will have

el **tenedor** fork (I)

tener to have (I)

¿**Cuántos años tiene(n) ...?** How old is / are...? (I)

— calor to be warm (I)

— cuidado to be careful (3B)

— éxito to succeed, to be successful (6B)

— frío to be cold (I)

— miedo (de) to be scared (of), to be afraid (of) (I)

— paciencia to be patient (8A)

— prisa to be in a hurry (3B)

— razón to be correct (I)

— sueño to be sleepy (I)

Tengo hambre. I'm hungry. (I)

Tengo que ... I have to... (I)

Tengo sed. I'm thirsty. (I)

Tiene(n)...años. He / She is / They are ... (years old). (I)

el **tenis: jugar al —** to play tennis (I)

tercer (tercero), -a third (I)

terminar to finish, to end (I)

el **terremoto** earthquake (5A)

ti you *fam. after prep.*

¿**Y a —?** And you? (I)

para — in your opinion, for you (I)

el **tiempo:**

a — on time (1A)

¿**Cuánto — hace que...?** How long have you been...? (1B)

el **— libre** free time (I)

pasar — con amigos to spend time with friends (I)

¿**Qué — hace?** What's the weather like? (I)

la **tienda** store (I)

la — de descuentos discount store (I)

la — de electrodomésticos household-appliance store (I)

la — de ropa clothing store (I)

Tiene(n)...años. He / She is / They are ... (years old). (I)

la **Tierra** Earth (9B)

las **tijeras** scissors (1A)

tímido, -a timid (4A)

típico, -a typical (8B)

el **tío, la tía** uncle, aunt (I)

los **tíos** uncles, aunt(s) and uncle(s) (I)

tirar to spill, to throw away (7A)

no tires don't spill, don't throw away (7A)

la **toalla** towel (2A)

el **tobillo** ankle (5B)

tocar (c→qu) la guitarra to play the guitar (I)

el **tocino** bacon (I)

todavía still (3A)

no... — not yet (6B)

todo el mundo everyone (4A)

todos, -as all (I)

— los días every day (I)

tomar:

— el sol to sunbathe (I)

— lecciones to take lessons (1B)

— un curso to take a course (I)

los **tomates** tomatoes (I)

tonto, -a silly, stupid (I)

torcerse (o→ue) (c→z) to twist, to sprain (5B)

la **tormenta** storm (5A)

la **tortuga** turtle (4A)

trabajador, -ora hardworking (I)

trabajar to work (I)

el **trabajo** work, job (I)

el **— voluntario** volunteer work (I)

traer:

Le traigo... I will bring you... (I)

¿**Me trae ...?** Will you bring me ...? *formal* (I)

el **tráfico** traffic (3B)

el **traje** suit (I)

el **— de baño** swimsuit (I)

tranquilo, -a calm (2A)

tratar de to try to (5A)

tratarse de to be about (6B)

travieso, -a naughty, mischievous (4A)

trece thirteen (I)

treinta thirty (I)

treinta y uno thirty-one (I)

tremendo, -a tremendous (I)

el **tren** train (I)

el **— eléctrico** electric train (4A)

tres three (I)

trescientos, -as three hundred (I)

el **triciclo** tricycle (4A)

triste sad (I)

tropezar (e→ie) (z→c) (con) to trip (over) (5B)

tu, tus your (I)

tú you *fam.* (I)

el / la **turista** tourist (8A)

tuyo, -a, -os, -as yours (2A)

U

Ud. (usted) you *formal sing.* (I)

Uds. (ustedes) you *formal pl.* (I)

¡Uf! ugh!, yuck! (I)

último, -a the last / final (6A)

un, una a, an (I)

— **poco (de)** a little (I)

la **una: a la —** at one o'clock (I)

la **universidad** university (9A)

uno one (I)

unos, -as some (I)

las **uñas** nails (2A)

usado, -a used (I)

usar la computadora to use the computer (I)

usted (Ud.) you *formal sing.* (I)

ustedes (Uds.) you *formal pl.* (I)

las **uvas** grapes (I)

V

las **vacaciones: ir de —** to go on vacation (I)

valiente brave (5A)

el **valle** valley (9B)

¡Vamos! Let's go! (I)

varios, -as various, several (3A)

el **vaso** glass (I)

el **vecino, la vecina** neighbor (4A)

veinte twenty (I)

veintiuno, -a (veintiún) twenty-one (I)

la **vela** sail (8B)

la **venda** bandage (5B)

el **vendedor, la vendedora** vendor (8B)

vender to sell (I)

venir to come (I)

la **ventana** window (I)

la **ventanilla** (airplane) window (8A)

ver to see (I)

a — ... Let's see... (I)

¡Nos vemos! See you later! (I)

te ves (bien) you look good (2A)

— **la tele** to watch television (I)

— **una película** to see a movie (I)

el **verano** summer (I)

veras: ¿De —? Really? (I)

la **verdad** truth (4A)

¿Verdad? Really? (I)

verde green (I)

el **vestido** dress (I)

vestirse (e→i) to get dressed (2A)

el **veterinario, la veterinaria** veterinarian (9A)

la **vez,** *pl.* **las veces:**

a veces sometimes (I)

de — en cuando once in a while 4A)

otra — again (I)

por ... — for the ... time (6A)

viajar to travel (I)

el **viaje** trip (I)

la **víctima** victim (6B)

la **vida** life (5A)

el **video** videocassette (I)

la **videocasetera** VCR (I)

los **videojuegos: jugar —** to play video games (I)

el **vidrio** glass (I)

viejo, -a old (I)

viernes Friday (I)

el **vinagre** vinegar (7A)

la **violencia** violence (6B)

violento, -a violent (I)

visitar to visit (I)

— **salones de chat** to visit chat rooms (I, 1B)

vivir to live (I)

vivo, -a bright (color) (2B); living, alive (5A)

el **vóleibol: jugar al —** to play volleyball (I)

volver (o→ue) to return (1B)

—**se loco, -a** to go crazy (6A)

la **voz,** *pl.* **las voces** voice (1B)

el **voluntario, la voluntaria** volunteer (I)

vosotros, -as you *fam. pl.* (I)

el **vuelo** flight (8A)

vuestro, -a, -os, -as your, yours (I)

W

Web: crear una página Web to create a Web page (1B)

Y

y and (I)

¿— a ti? And you? (I)

— **cuarto** quarter past (I)

— **media** thirty *(in telling time)* (I)

¿— tú? And you? *fam.* (I)

¿— usted (Ud.)? And you? *formal* (I)

ya already (I, 3B)

el **yeso** cast (5B)

yo I (I)

el **yogur** yogurt (I)

Z

las **zanahorias** carrots (I)

la **zapatería** shoe store (I)

los **zapatos** shoes (I)

el **zoológico** zoo (I)

English-Spanish Vocabulary

The *English-Spanish Vocabulary* contains all active vocabulary from the text, including vocabulary presented in the grammar sections.

A dash (—) represents the main entry word. For example, **to play** — after **baseball** means **to play baseball**

The number following each entry indicates the chapter in which the word or expression is presented. A Roman numeral (I) indicates that the word was presented in REALIDADES 1.

The following abbreviations are used in this list: *adj.* (adjective), *dir. obj.* (direct object), *f.* (feminine), *fam.*(familiar), *ind. obj.* (indirect object), *inf.* (infinitive), *m.* (masculine), *pl.* (plural), *prep.* (preposition), *pron.* (pronoun), *sing.* (singular).

A

a, an un, una (I)

a little un poco (de) (I)

a lot mucho, -a (I)

able: to be — to poder (o → ue) (I)

about sobre (I, 1A)

   to be — tratarse de (6B)

accident el accidente (5B)

to **accompany** acompañar (7B)

according to según (I)

   — my family según mi familia (I)

accountant el contador, la contadora (9A)

acquainted: to be — with conocer (c → zc) (I, 1B)

acting la actuación (6B)

action figure el muñeco (4A)

action film la película de acción (6B)

actor el actor (I)

actress la actriz, *pl.* las actrices (I)

to **add** añadir (7A)

addition: in — (to) además (de) (9B)

address: e-mail — la dirección electrónica (I)

afraid: to be — (of) tener miedo (de) (I)

after después de (I)

afternoon:

   at one (o'clock) in the afternoon a la una de la tarde (I)

   Good —. Buenas tardes. (I)

   in the — de la tarde (I)

   this — esta tarde (I)

afterwards después (I)

again otra vez (I)

against contra (9B)

agitated agitado, -a (6A)

ago hace + *time expression* (I)

agree:

   I —. Estoy de acuerdo. (I)

   I don't —. No estoy de acuerdo. (I)

Agreed. De acuerdo. (3B)

air conditioning el aire acondicionado (9B)

airline la línea aérea (8A)

airplane el avión (I)

airport el aeropuerto (8A)

aisle el pasillo (8A)

alarm clock el despertador (I)

alien el / la extraterrestre (6B)

alive vivo, -a (5A)

all todos, -as (I)

almost casi (I, 3A)

alone solo, -a (I)

along por (3B)

already ya (I, 3B)

also también (I)

always siempre (I)

am:

   I — (yo) soy (I)

   I — not (yo) no soy (I)

ambulance la ambulancia (5B)

among entre (1B)

amusement park el parque de diversiones (I)

amusing divertido, -a (I)

and y (I)

— you? ¿Y a ti? *fam.* (I); ¿Y tu? *fam.* (I); ¿Y usted (Ud.)? *formal* (I)

angry enojado, -a (6A)

   to get — enojarse (6A)

animal el animal (I)

ankle el tobillo (5B)

anniversary el aniversario (4B)

to **announce** anunciar (2B)

announcement el anuncio (8A)

announcer el locutor, la locutora (5A)

another otro, -a (I)

to **answer** contestar (1A)

ant la hormiga (7B)

antique antiguo, -a (4B)

any algunos, -as (1A)

anyone alguien (1A)

Anything else? ¿Algo más? (I)

apartment el apartamento (I)

   — building el edificio de apartamentos (5A)

to **applaud** aplaudir (6A)

apple la manzana (I)

   — juice el jugo de manzana (I)

approximately aproximadamente (3B)

April abril (I)

architect el arquitecto, la arquitecta (9A)

Are you ... ? ¿Eres ... ? (I)

arm el brazo (I)

around por (3A, 3B); alrededor de (4B)

to **arrest** arrestar (6B)

arrival la llegada (8A)

to **arrive late** llegar (g → gu) tarde (1A)

art class la clase de arte (I)

article el artículo (5A)

artist el artista, la artista (9A)

artistic artístico, -a (I)

arts las artes (9A)

   martial — las artes marciales (1B)

as como (I)

    — a child de niño (4A); de pequeño (4A)

    — a main dish de plato principal (I)

    — far as hasta (3B)

as much / many + *noun* **+ as** tantos, -as + *noun* + como

as + *adj.* **+ as** tan + *adj.* + como (1B)

to ask for pedir (e → i) (I)

    — help pedir ayuda (1A)

to ask a question hacer una pregunta (1A)

asleep dormido, -a (5A)

    to fall—dormirse (6A)

at:

    — eight (o'clock) a las ocho (I)

    — eight (o'clock) at night a las ocho de la noche (I)

    — eight (o'clock) in the evening a las ocho de la noche (I)

    — eight (o'clock) in the morning a las ocho de la mañana (I)

    — home en casa (I)

    — one (o'clock) a la una (I)

    — one (o'clock) in the afternoon a la una de la tarde (I)

    — the end al final (6A)

    — what time? ¿A qué hora? (I)

athlete el / la atleta (6A)

ATM el cajero automático (8B)

to attend asistir a (1B)

attentive atento, -a (8B)

attention: to pay — prestar atención (1A)

attraction(s) la atracción, *pl.* las atracciones (I)

audience el público (6A)

audition la audición, *pl.* las audiciones (2A)

auditorium el auditorio (6A)

August agosto (I)

aunt la tía (I)

aunt(s) and uncle(s) los tíos (I)

autumn el otoño (I)

avenue la avenida (3B)

avocado el aguacate (7B)

B ———————————

baby el / la bebé (4B)

back la espalda (5B)

backpack la mochila (I)

bacon el tocino (I)

bad malo, -a (I); mal (I)

badly mal (I)

bag la bolsa (I)

baked al horno (7A)

ball la pelota (3A)

balloon el globo (I)

banana el plátano (I)

band *(musical)* la banda (1B)

bandage la venda (5B)

bank el banco (3A)

barbecue: to have a — hacer una parrillada (7B)

bargain la ganga (2B)

to bargain regatear (8B)

baseball: to play — jugar al béisbol (I)

based: to be — on estar basado, -a en (6B)

basement el sótano (I)

basket la cesta (7B)

basketball: to play — jugar al básquetbol (I)

bathroom el baño (I)

to be ser (I); estar (I)

    He / She is / They are … (years old). Tiene(n) … años. (I)

    How old is / are … ? ¿Cuántos años tiene(n)…? (I)

    to — + *present participle* estar + *present participle* (I)

    to — a member ser miembro (1B)

    to — able to poder (o → ue) (I)

to — about tratarse de (6B)

to — acquainted with conocer (c → zc) (I)

to — afraid (of) tener miedo (de) (I)

to — based on estar basado, -a en (6B)

to — born nacer (4B)

to — careful tener cuidado (3B)

to — cold tener frío (I)

to — correct tener razón (I)

to — going to + *verb* ir a + *inf.* (I)

to — in a hurry tener prisa (3B)

to — in fashion estar de moda (2B)

to — in love with estar enamorado, -a de (6B)

to — located quedar (I, 3B)

to — online estar en línea (I, 1B)

to — scared (of) tener miedo (de) (I)

to — sleepy tener sueño (I)

to — sure estar seguro, -a (3B)

to — useful servir (I)

to — warm tener calor (I)

beach la playa (I)

beans los frijoles (7B)

bear el oso (I)

to beat batir (7A)

beautiful bello, -a (8B)

beauty contest el concurso de belleza (6A)

beauty salon el salón de belleza, *pl.* los salones de belleza (2A)

because porque (I)

    — of a causa de (5A)

to become ponerse (6A)

bed la cama (I)

    to go to — acostarse (o → ue) (2A)

    to make the — hacer la cama (I)

bedroom el dormitorio (I)

beefsteak el bistec (I)

before antes de (I, 2A)

to **begin** empezar (e → ie) (I)

to **behave well / badly** portarse bien / mal (4A)

behind detrás de (I)

belt el cinturón, *pl.* los cinturones (2A)

benefits los beneficios (9A)

besides además (de) (9B)

best: the — el / la mejor, los / las mejores (I)

better than mejor(es) que (I)

between entre (1B)

bicycle: to ride a — montar en bicicleta (I)

bilingual bilingüe (9A)

bill la cuenta (I)

binder: three-ring — la carpeta de argollas (I)

bird el pájaro (I)

birthday el cumpleaños (I)

    Happy —! ¡Feliz cumpleaños! (I)

    to have a — cumplir años (4B)

black hair el pelo negro (I)

block la cuadra (3B)

blocks los bloques (4A)

blond hair el pelo rubio (I)

blood la sangre (5B)

blouse la blusa (I)

blow dryer el secador (2A)

blue azul (I)

to **board** abordar (8A)

boarding pass la tarjeta de embarque (8A)

boat el barco (I)

    sail — el bote de vela (8B)

boating: to go — pasear en bote (I)

to **boil** hervir (e → ie) (e → i) (7A)

bone el hueso (5B)

bonfire la fogata (7B)

book el libro (I)

bookbag la mochila (I)

bookshelf el estante (I)

bookstore la librería (I)

boots las botas (I)

to **bore** aburrir (I)

    it / they bore(s) me aburre(n) (I)

    to get bored aburrirse (6A)

boring aburrido, -a (I)

born: to be — nacer (4B)

to **borrow (from)** pedir (e → i) prestado, -a (a) (2A)

both los dos, las dos (I)

to **bother** molestar (4A)

bottle la botella (I)

to **bowl** jugar a los bolos (1B)

box la caja (I)

boy el chico (I)

    young — el niño (I)

boyfriend el novio (I)

bracelet la pulsera (I)

brand la marca (2B)

brave valiente (5A)

bread el pan (I)

to **break** romper (I); romperse (5B)

breakfast el desayuno (I)

    for — en el desayuno (I)

bridge el puente (3B)

bright *(color)* vivo, -a (2B)

to **bring** traer (I); llevar (I)

    I will — you ... Le traigo ... (I)

    Will you — me ... ? ¿Me trae ... ? (I)

broken roto, -a (5B)

broth el caldo (7A)

brother el hermano (I)

brothers; brother(s) and sister(s) los hermanos (I)

brown marrón (I)

    — (chestnut) hair el pelo castaño (I)

brush el cepillo (2A)

    tooth — el cepillo de dientes (3A)

to **brush (one's teeth)** cepillarse (los dientes) (2A)

to **burn a CD** grabar un disco compacto (I)

to **burn (oneself), to burn up** quemar(se) (5A)

bus el autobús, *pl.* los autobuses (I)

business los negocios (9A)

    — man el hombre de negocios (9A)

    — woman la mujer de negocios (9A)

busy ocupado, -a (I)

but pero (I)

butter la mantequilla (I)

to **buy** comprar (I)

    — souvenirs comprar recuerdos (I)

by por (3B)

    — + *vehicle* en + *vehicle* (I)

C

café el café (I)

cake el pastel (I)

to **call: to — on the phone** llamar por teléfono (5A)

calculator la calculadora (I)

calm tranquilo, -a (2A)

camera la cámara (I)

    digital — la cámara digital (I)

camp el campamento (I)

can la lata (I)

can:

    I — (yo) puedo (I)

    you — (tú) puedes (I); se puede (7A)

candy los dulces (I)

canned enlatado, -a (7A)

cap la gorra (I)

to **capture** capturar (6B)

car el coche (I)

card la tarjeta (I, 3A)

    credit — la tarjeta de crédito (2B)

    ID — el carnet de identidad (I)

    post — la tarjeta postal (8B)

cardboard el cartón (I)

care: to take — of cuidar a (3A)

career la carrera (9A)

careful: to be — tener cuidado (3B)

carrots las zanahorias (I)

to **carry** llevar (I)

cartoon el programa de dibujos animados (I)

cash en efectivo (2B)

to **cash a check** cobrar un cheque (3A)

cash register la caja (2B)

cashier el cajero, la cajera (2B)

cast el yeso (5B)

castle el castillo (8B)

cat el gato (I)

cathedral la catedral (8B)

cause la causa (5A)

CD: to burn a — grabar un disco compacto (I)

to **celebrate** celebrar (I)

center el centro (I, 3A)

cereal el cereal (I)

certain: it is — es cierto (9B)

chain la cadena (I)

chair la silla (I)

   wheel — la silla de ruedas (5B)

champion el campeón, la campeona, *pl.* los campeones (6A)

championship el campeonato (6A)

to **change** cambiar (8B)

channel *(TV)* el canal (I)

character: main — el personaje principal (6B)

to **chat** charlar (4B)

chat rooms los salones de chat (1B)

cheap barato, -a (I)

check:
   to cash a — cobrar un cheque (3A)
   traveler's — el cheque de viajero (2B)
   personal — el cheque personal (2B)

to **check** *(luggage)* facturar (el equipaje) (8A); examinar (5B)

to **check out** sacar (c → qu) (3A)

cheerleader el animador, la animadora (1B)

cherry la cereza (7B)

chess el ajedrez (1B)

chicken el pollo (I)

child: as a — de niño (4A); de pequeño (4A)

childish infantil (I)

children los hijos (I); los niños (I)

choir el coro (1B)

to **chop** picar (c → qu) (7A)

chore: household — el quehacer (de la casa) (I)

chorus el coro (1B)

to **choose** escoger (g → j) (2B)

church la iglesia (I)
   Protestant — el templo (I)

city la ciudad (I)

class la clase (I)

classroom la sala de clases (I)

clean limpio, -a (I)

to **clean the bathroom** limpiar el baño (I)

clock el reloj (I)

to **close** cerrar (3A)

close (to) cerca (de) (I)

closed cerrado, -a (8A)

closes se cierra (3A)

closet el armario (I)

clothing store la tienda de ropa (I)

cloud la nube (7B)

club el club, *pl.* los clubes (1B)
   athletic — el club atlético (1B)

coach el entrenador, la entrenadora (6A)

coat el abrigo (I)

coffee el café (I)

coin la moneda (4A)

cold:
   It's —. Hace frío. (I)
   to be — tener frío (I)

to **collect** recoger (g → j) (I)

to **collect** coleccionar (4A)

collection la colección, *pl.* las colecciones (4A)

to **collide with** chocar (c → qu) con (5B)

cologne el agua de colonia (2A)

color:
   What — ...? ¿De qué color ...?   (I)
   —s los colores (I)

comb el peine (2A)

to **come** venir (I)

comedy la comedia (I)

comfortable cómodo, -a (2A)

comical cómico, -a (I)

commentary el comentario (6A)

to **communicate** comunicarse (c → qu) (I)
   I — (yo) me comunico (I)
   you — (tú) te comunicas (I)

community la comunidad (I)

compact disc el disco compacto (I)
   to burn a — grabar un disco compacto (I)

to **compete** competir (e → i) (6A)

competition la competencia (6A)

complicated complicado, -a (I, 3B)

composition la composición, *pl.* las composiciones (I)

computer la computadora (I)
   — graphics los gráficos (I)
   — keyboard el teclado (I)
   — mouse el ratón (I)
   — screen la pantalla (I)
   —s / technology la tecnología (I)
   laptop — la computadora portátil (I)
   to use the — usar la computadora (I)

concert el concierto (I)

to congratulate felicitar (4B)

Congratulations! ¡Felicidades! (4B)

to conserve conservar (9B)

construction project el proyecto de construcción (I)

contest el concurso (2A)

beauty — el concurso de belleza (6A)

to continue seguir (e → i) (3B)

to cook cocinar (I)

cookie la galleta (I)

cooking oil el aceite (7A)

corn el maíz (7B)

corner la esquina (3B)

correct: to be — tener razón (I)

to cost costar (o → ue) (I)

How much does (do) ... —? ¿Cuánto cuesta(n)? (I)

cotton el algodón (2B)

country el país, *pl.* los países (I)

countryside el campo (I)

course:

to take a — tomar un curso (I)

— of studies el programa de estudios (9A)

cousin la prima, el primo (I)

—s los primos (I)

to crash into chocar (c → qu) con (5B)

crazy: to go – volverse loco, -a (6A)

to create crear (I)

to — a Web page crear una página Web (1B)

credit card la tarjeta de crédito (2B)

crime el crimen (6B)

— movie la película policíaca (I)

criminal el / la criminal (6B)

critic el crítico, la crítica (6B)

to cross cruzar (3B)

crutches las muletas (5B)

to cry llorar (4B)

cup la taza (I)

currency exchange la casa de cambio (8B)

curtains las cortinas (I)

custom la costumbre (4B)

customs la aduana (8A)

customs officer el aduanero, la aduanera (8A)

to cut cortar (I, 7A)

to — oneself cortarse (5B)

to — one's hair cortarse el pelo (2A)

to — the lawn cortar el césped (I)

cut-paper decorations el papel picado (I)

D

dance el baile (I)

to dance bailar (I)

dancer el bailarín, la bailarina *pl.* los bailarines (1B)

dangerous peligroso, -a (3B)

daring atrevido, -a (I)

dark oscuro, -a (2B)

date: What is the —? ¿Cuál es la fecha? (I)

date la cita (2A)

daughter la hija (I)

day el día (I)

every — todos los días (I); cada día (I)

What — is today? ¿Qué día es hoy? (I)

day care center la guardería infantil (4A)

dead muerto, -a (5A)

December diciembre (I)

to decide decidir (I)

to decorate decorar (I)

decorations las decoraciones (I)

delay el retraso (8A)

delicious delicioso, -a (I)

delighted encantado, -a (I)

dentist el / la dentista (3A)

deodorant el desodorante (2A)

department store el almacén,

pl. los almacenes (I)

departure la salida (8A)

departure gate la puerta de embarque (8A)

depend: it depends depende (2A)

desert el desierto (9B)

designer el diseñador, la diseñadora (9A)

desk el pupitre (I); el escritorio (I)

dessert el postre (I)

for — de postre (I)

to destroy destruir (i → y) (5A)

destruction la destrucción (9B)

detective el / la detective (6B)

dictionary el diccionario (I)

Did you like it? ¿Te gustó? (I)

to die morirse (o → ue) (o → u) (6A)

difficult difícil (I)

digital camera la cámara digital (I)

dining room el comedor (I)

dinner la cena (I)

dinosaur el dinosaurio (4A)

direct directo, -a (8A)

direction la dirección, *pl.* las direcciones (6B)

director el director, la directora (6B)

dirty sucio, -a (I)

disaster: It was a —. Fue un desastre. (I)

discount store la tienda de descuentos (I)

to discuss discutir (1A)

dish el plato (I)

as a main — de plato principal (I)

main — el plato principal (I)

diskette el disquete (I)

disobedient desobediente (4A)

to do hacer (I)

— *(command)* haz (I)

— you like to ... ? ¿Te gusta ... ? (I)

I — (yo) hago (I)

to — a project hacer un proyecto (1A)

to — a search hacer una búsqueda (1B)

to — gymnastics hacer gimnasia (1B)

you — (tú) haces (I)

What did you —? ¿Qué hiciste? (I)

doctor el médico, la médica (3A)

doctor's / dentist's office el consultorio (3A)

document el documento (I)

dog el perro (I)

to feed the — dar de comer al perro (I)

doll la muñeca (4A)

Don't eat. No comas. (7A)

Don't leave, Don't let No dejes (7A)

Don't speak. No hables. (7A)

Don't write. No escribas. (7A)

door la puerta (I)

double room la habitación doble (8B)

doubt: without a — sin duda (5A)

to doubt dudar (9B)

to download bajar (información) (I)

downtown el centro (3A)

drama el drama (I)

to draw dibujar (I)

dress el vestido (I)

dressed: to get — vestirse (2A)

dresser la cómoda (I)

to drink beber (I)

drinks las bebidas (I)

to drive manejar (3B)

driver el conductor, la conductora (3B)

driver's license el permiso de manejar (3B)

dry seco, -a (7B)

to dry secarse (c → qu) (2A)

dryer: blow — secador (2A)

during durante (I)

to dust quitar el polvo (I)

DVD player el lector DVD (I)

E ────────────

e-mail:

— address la dirección electrónica (I)

to write — escribir por correo electrónico (I)

to earn ganar (1B)

to enjoy disfrutar de (8B)

early temprano (I)

to earn *(money)* ganar (1B)

earrings los aretes (I)

Earth la Tierra (9B)

earthquake el terremoto (5A)

easy fácil (I)

to eat comer (I)

ecological ecológico, -a (9B)

economical económico, -a (9B)

educational program el programa educativo (I)

efficient eficiente (9B)

eggs los huevos (I)

eight ocho (I)

eight hundred ochocientos, -as (I)

eighteen dieciocho (I)

eighth octavo, -a (I)

eighty ochenta (I)

either tampoco (I)

I don't (like to) — a mí tampoco (I)

elbow el codo (5B)

electric train el tren eléctrico (4A)

electricity la electricidad (9B)

elegant elegante (2A)

to eliminate eliminar (9B)

elevator el ascensor (8B)

eleven once (I)

else:

Anything —? ¿Algo más? (I)

What —? ¿Qué más? (I)

emergency room la sala de

emergencia (5B)

emotional emocionado, -a (6A)

employee el empleado, la empleada (8A)

end: at the — al final (6A)

to end terminar (I)

endangered en peligro de extinción (9B)

energy la energía (9B)

engineer el ingeniero, la ingeniera (9A)

English class la clase de inglés (I)

to enjoy disfrutar de (8B)

enormous enorme (4B)

enough bastante (I)

Enough! ¡Basta! (3B)

to enter entrar (I)

entrance la entrada (2B)

environment medio ambiente (9B)

to escape escaparse (5A)

especially especialmente (I)

evening:

Good —. Buenas noches. (I)

in the — de la noche (I)

this — esta noche (I)

every day cada día (I), todos los días (I)

everyone todo el mundo (4A)

exactly en punto (8B)

to examine examinar (5B)

example: for — por ejemplo (2A)

excited entusiasmado, -a (2A); emocionado, -a (6A)

exchange: currency — la casa de cambio (8B)

to exchange cambiar (8B)

excursion la excursión, *pl.* las excursiones (8B)

Excuse me. Perdón. (I)

to exercise hacer ejercicio (I)

exit la salida (2B)

expensive caro, -a (I)

experience la experiencia (I)

to **explain** explicar (c → qu) (1A)

explosion la explosión, *pl.* las explosiones (5A)

extinction: in danger of — en peligro de extinción (9B)

extracurricular extracurricular (1B)

    — activities las actividades extracurriculares (1B)

eye el ojo (I)

F _____

fabric: synthetic — la tela sintética (2B)

face la cara (2A)

face-to-face cara a cara (I)

failure el fracaso (6B)

to **fall** caerse (5B)

    I — (yo) me caigo (5B)

    to — asleep dormirse (o→ue) (o→u) (6A)

    to — in love (with) enamorarse (de) (6B)

    you — (tú) te caes (5B)

fall el otoño (I)

famous famoso, -a (8B)

fan el aficionado, la aficionada (6A)

fantastic fantástico, -a (I)

far (from) lejos (de) (I)

farmer el agricultor, la agricultora (9A)

to **fascinate** fascinar (6B)

fascinating fascinante (I)

fashion: to be in — estar de moda (2B)

fast rápidamente (I)

father el padre (papá) (I)

fatty grasoso, -a (7B)

favorite favorito, -a (I)

February febrero (I)

to **feed the dog** dar de comer al perro (I)

to **feel** sentirse (e → ie) (e → i) (5B)

fewer:

    — ... than menos ... que (I)

    — than ... menos de ... (I)

fifteen quince (I)

fifth quinto, -a (I)

fifty cincuenta (I)

to **fight** luchar (9B)

to **fight** pelearse (4A)

to **fill (the tank)** llenar (el tanque) (3A)

film la película (I)

final último, -a (6A)

to **find** encontrar (o → ue) (2B)

finger el dedo (I)

to **finish** terminar (I)

fire el incendio (5A); el fuego (7A)

firefighter el bombero, la bombera (5A)

firewood la leña (7B)

fireworks los fuegos artificiales (4B)

first primer (primero), -a (I)

fish el pescado (I); el pez, *pl.* los peces (4A)

    to go —ing ir de pesca (I)

to **fit: It / They —(s) me well / poorly.** Me queda(n) bien / mal. (I)

five cinco (I)

five hundred quinientos, -as (I)

to **fix (one's hair)** arreglarse (el pelo) (2A)

flag la bandera (I)

flavorful sabroso, -a (I)

flight el vuelo (8A)

flight attendant el / la auxiliar de vuelo (8A)

flood la inundación, *pl.* las inundaciones (5A)

floor el piso (I); el suelo (7B)

    ground — la planta baja (I)

    second — el primer piso (I)

    third — el segundo piso (I)

flour la harina (7B)

flower la flor, *pl.* las flores (I)

fly la mosca (7B)

folder la carpeta (I)

to **follow** seguir (e → i) (3B)

following siguiente (8B)

food la comida (I)

food stand el puesto (7B)

foot el pie (I)

football: to play — jugar (u → ue) (g → gu) al fútbol americano (I)

for para (I); por (3A)

    — breakfast en el desayuno (I)

    — example por ejemplo (2A)

    — lunch en el almuerzo (I)

    — me para mí (I)

    — the ... time por ... vez (6A)

    — you para ti (I)

for (how long) por (3A)

forbidden: It is —. Se prohíbe. (1A)

foreign extranjero, -a (8A)

forest el bosque (9B)

    rain — la selva tropical (9B)

to **forget about/to** olvidarse de (7A)

    don't — no te olvides de (7A)

forgot: I — se me olvidó (3A)

fork el tenedor (I)

fortunately afortunadamente (5A)

forty cuarenta (I)

fountain la fuente (3B)

four cuatro (I)

four hundred cuatrocientos, -as (I)

fourteen catorce (I)

fourth cuarto, -a (I)

free time el tiempo libre (I)

French fries las papas fritas (I)

frequently frecuentemente (4B)

fresh fresco, -a (7A)

Friday viernes (I)

fried frito, -a (7A)

friendly simpático, -a (I)

frightened asustado, -a (5A)

from de (I); desde (3B)

    Where are you —? ¿De dónde eres? (I)

frozen congelado, -a (7A)

fruit salad la ensalada de frutas (I)

to **fry** freír (e → i) (7A)

frying pan la sartén, *pl.* las sartenes (7A)

fun divertido, -a (I)

    to have — divertirse (e → ie) (e → i) (4B)

to **function** funcionar (9B)

funny gracioso, -a (I); cómico, -a (I)

furious furioso, -a (6A)

furniture los muebles (5A)

future el futuro (9A)

G

game el partido (I)

game show el programa de concursos (I)

garage el garaje (I)

garden el jardín, *pl.* los jardines (I)

garlic el ajo (7A)

gasoline la gasolina (3A)

to **gather** recoger (g → j) (I)

gathering la reunión, *pl.* las reuniones (4B)

gel el gel (2A)

general: in — por lo general (4A)

generally generalmente (I)

generous generoso, -a (4A)

get:

    to — a good grade sacar (c → qu) una buena nota (1A)

    to — along well / badly llevarse bien / mal (4B)

    to — angry enojarse (6A)

    to — bored aburrirse (6A)

    to — dressed vestirse (e → i) (2A)

    to — married casarse (con) (4B)

    to — ready prepararse (2A)

    to — up levantarse (2A)

gift el regalo (I)

gift certificate el cupón de

regalo, *pl.* los cupones de regalo (2B)

girl la chica (I)

    young — la niña (I)

girlfriend la novia (I)

to **give** dar (I); regalar (4B)

    to — a speech dar un discurso (1A)

    to — a ticket poner una multa (3B)

    to — an injection poner una inyección (5B)

glass el vaso (I); el vidrio (I)

gloves los guantes (I)

to **go** ir (I); pasar (3B)

    Let's —! ¡Vamos! (I)

    to be —ing to + *verb* ir a + *inf.* (I)

    to — to bed acostarse (o → ue) (2A)

    to — boating pasear en bote (I)

    to — camping ir de cámping (I)

    to — crazy volverse (o → ue) loco, -a (6A)

    to — down bajar (5A)

    to — fishing ir de pesca (I)

    to — on foot ir a pie (3A)

    to — on vacation ir de vacaciones (I)

    to — out salir (I)

    to — shopping ir de compras (I)

    to — to bed acostarse (o → ue) (2A)

    to — to school ir a la escuela (I)

    to — up subir (5A)

goal *(in sports)* el gol (6A)

    to score a — meter un gol (6A)

going to con destino a (8A)

gold el oro (2A)

golf:

    — club el palo de golf (3A)

    to play — jugar (u → ue) (g → gu) al golf (I)

good bueno (buen), -a (I)

    — afternoon. Buenas tardes. (I)

    — evening. Buenas noches. (I)

    — gracious caramba (3A)

    — morning. Buenos días. (I)

Good-bye! ¡Adiós! (I)

good-looking guapo, -a (I)

grade *(in school)* la nota (1A)

    to get a good — sacar una buena nota (1A)

to **graduate** graduarse (u → ú) (9A)

graduation la graduación, *pl.* las graduaciones (9A)

grandfather el abuelo (I)

grandmother la abuela (I)

grandparents los abuelos (I)

grapes las uvas (I)

gray gris (I)

    — hair el pelo canoso (I)

greasy grasoso, -a (7B)

Great! ¡Genial! (I)

green verde (I)

    — beans las judías verdes (I)

to **greet** saludar(se) (4B)

to **grill** asar (7B)

grill: on the — a la parrilla (7B)

grilled asado, -a (7B)

ground el suelo (7B)

ground floor la planta baja (I)

grown-ups los mayores (4B)

guide el / la guía (8B)

guidebook la guía (8B)

guitar: to play the — tocar la guitarra (I)

gym el gimnasio (I)

gymnastics la gimnasia (1B)

H

hair el pelo (I, 2A)

    black — el pelo negro (I)

    blond — el pelo rubio (I)

    brown (chestnut) — el pelo castaño (I)

gray — el pelo canoso (I)

  to cut one's — cortarse el pelo (2A)

  to fix one's — arreglarse el pelo (2A)

half media, -o (I)

  — **past** y media *(in telling time)* (I)

ham and cheese sandwich el sándwich de jamón y queso (I)

hamburger la hamburguesa (I)

hand la mano (I)

  to shake —**s** darse la mano (4B)

handicrafts la artesanía (8B)

happy contento, -a (I); alegre (6A)

  — **birthday!** ¡Feliz cumpleaños! (I)

hardworking trabajador, -ora (I)

to have tener (I)

  I — **to ...** tengo que + *inf.* (I)

  to — **a barbecue** hacer una parrillada (7B)

  to — **a birthday** cumplir años (4B)

  to — **a picnic** hacer un picnic (4B)

  to — **fun** divertirse (e → ie) (e → i) (4B)

  to — **just...** acabar de + *inf.* (I)

  to — **lunch** almorzar (o → ue) (z → c) (1A)

to have haber *(as an auxiliary verb)* (6B)

he él (I)

he / she is es (I)

  He / She is / They are ... (years old). Tiene(n) ... años. (I)

head la cabeza (I)

health:

  for one's — para la salud (I)

  to maintain one's — para mantener la salud (I)

to hear oír (5A)

heat el fuego (7A); la calefacción (9B)

to heat calentar (e → ie) (7A)

Hello! ¡Hola! (I)

to help ayudar (I)

  How can I — **you?** ¿En qué puedo servirle? (I)

help la ayuda (1A)

Help! ¡Socorro! (5A)

her su, sus *possessive adj.* (I); la *dir. obj. pron.* (I); le *ind. obj. pron.* (I)

hers suyo, -a (2A)

here aquí (I)

hero el héroe (5A)

heroine la heroína (5A)

Hey! ¡Oye! (I)

to hide (oneself) esconder(se) (5A)

high alto, -a (2B)

high school el colegio (9A)

highway la carretera (3B)

hill la colina (9B)

him lo *dir. obj. pron.* (I); le *ind. obj. pron.* (I)

his su, sus (I); suyo, -a (2A)

historical histórico, -a (8B)

hockey el hockey (1B)

holiday el día festivo (4B)

home la casa (I)

  at — en casa (I)

  — **office** el despacho (I)

  (to) — a casa (I)

homework la tarea (I)

horrible horrible (I)

horror movie la película de horror (I)

horseback: to ride — montar a caballo (I)

hospital el hospital (I)

hot caliente (7A)

  — **dog** el perrito caliente (I)

  It's —. Hace calor. (I)

hotel el hotel (I)

hour: in the ... — en la ... hora *(class period)* (I)

house la casa (I)

household:

—**appliance store** la tienda de electrodomésticos (I)

  — **chore** el quehacer (de la casa) (I)

how!

  — + *adj.!* ¡Qué + *adj.!* (I)

  — **awful!** ¡Qué asco! (I)

How? ¿Cómo? (I)

  — **are you?** ¿Cómo está Ud.? *formal* (I); ¿Cómo estás? *fam.* (I); ¿Qué tal? *fam.* (I)

  — **can I help you?** ¿En qué puedo servirle? (I)

  — **do you go to ... ?** ¿Cómo se va...? (3B)

  — **do you make ... ?** ¿Cómo se hace ...? (7A)

  — **do you say ... ?** ¿Cómo se dice... ? (I)

  — **does it (do they) fit (you)?** ¿Cómo te queda(n)? (I)

  — **does it seem to you?** ¿Qué te parece? (2B)

  — **is ... spelled?** ¿Cómo se escribe … ? (I)

  — **is (it) ... ?** ¿Qué tal es...? (6B)

  — **long ... ?** ¿Cuánto tiempo hace que...? (1B)

  — **many?** ¿Cuántos, -as? (I)

  — **much?** ¿Cuánto?

  — **much does (do) ... cost?** ¿Cuánto cuesta(n) ... ? (I)

  — **old is / are ... ?** ¿Cuántos años tiene(n) ... ? (I)

  — **was it (for you)?** ¿Cómo lo pasaste? (I)

to hug abrazar(se) (z → c) (4B)

hundred: one — cien(to) (I)

hungry: I'm —. Tengo hambre. (I)

hurricane el huracán, *pl.* los huracanes (5A)

hurt doler (o → ue) (I, 5B)

to hurt oneself lastimarse (5B)

hurry prisa (3B)

  in a — de prisa (5A)

  to be in a — tener prisa (3B)

husband el esposo (I)

I

I yo (I)

— **am** soy (I)

— **am not** no soy (I)

— **do too** a mí también (I)

— **don't either** a mí tampoco (I)

— **don't think so.** Creo que no. (I)

— **forgot** se me olvidó (3A)

— **have seen** he visto (6B)

— **stay at home.** Me quedo en casa. (I)

— **think ...** Creo que ... (I)

— **think so.** Creo que sí. (I)

— **will bring you ...** Le traigo ... (I)

— **would like** Me gustaría (I); quisiera (I)

—**'m hungry.** Tengo hambre. (I)

—**'m sorry.** Lo siento. (I)

—**'m thirsty.** Tengo sed. (I)

ice cream el helado (I)

iced tea el té helado (I)

ID card el carnet de identidad (1A)

if si (I)

immediately inmediatamente (2B)

impatient impaciente (I)

important importante (I)

impressive impresionante (I)

to **improve** mejorar (9B)

in en (I)

— **danger of extinction** en peligro de extinción (9B)

— **front of** delante de (I)

— **general** por lo general (4A)

— **love with** enamorado, -a de (6B)

— **my opinion** para mí (I)

— **order to** para + *inf.* (I)

— **the ... hour** en la ... hora *(class period)* (I)

— **the middle of** en medio de (3B)

— **your opinion** para ti (I)

incredible increíble (I)

inexpensive barato, -a (I)

information la información (I)

ingredient el ingrediente (7A)

injection la inyección, *pl.* las inyecciones (5B)

to give an — poner una inyección (5B)

injured herido, -a (5A)

injured person el herido, la herida (5A)

inside dentro de (7B)

to **insist** insistir en (8A)

to **inspect** registrar (8A)

intelligent inteligente (I)

interest el interés (1B)

to **interest** interesar (I)

it / they interest(s) me me interesa(n) (I)

interesting interesante (I)

intersection el cruce de calles (3B)

interview la entrevista (6A)

— **program** el programa de entrevistas (I)

to **interview** entrevistar (6A)

to **investigate** investigar (g → gu) (5A)

is es (I)

he / she — es (I)

it — **true** es cierto (9B)

it la, lo *dir. obj. pron.* (I)

— **depends** depende (2A)

— **fits (they fit) me well / poorly.** Me queda(n) bien / mal. (I)

— **has been ...** Hace + *time* + que ... (1B)

— **is ...** Son las *(in telling time)* (I)

— **is forbidden ...** Se prohíbe ... (1A)

— **is made of ...** Está hecho, -a de ... (2B)

— **is one o'clock.** Es la una. (I)

— **is the ... of ...** Es el *(number)* de *(month) (in telling the date)* (I)

— **is the first of ...** Es el primero de *(month).* (I)

— **seems to me** me parece que (2B)

— **was** fue (I)

— **was a disaster.** Fue un desastre. (I)

—**'s a ...** es un / una ... (I)

—**'s cold.** Hace frío. (I)

—**'s hot.** Hace calor. (I)

—**'s necessary.** Es necesario. (I)

—**'s raining.** Llueve. (I)

—**'s snowing.** Nieva. (I)

—**'s sunny.** Hace sol. (I)

it / he / she will be será (6B)

itinerary el itinerario (8B)

J

jacket la chaqueta (I)

January enero (I)

jeans los jeans (I)

jet skiing la moto acuática (8B)

jewelry (gold, silver) las joyas (de oro, de plata) (2A)

jewelry store la joyería (I)

job el trabajo (I)

to **join** juntarse (9B)

judge el juez, la jueza, *pl.* los jueces (9A)

juice:

apple — el jugo de manzana (I)

orange — el jugo de naranja (I)

July julio (I)

to **jump (rope)** saltar (a la cuerda) (4A)

June junio (I)

just: to have — ... acabar de + *inf.* (I)

K

ketchup la salsa de tomate (7B)

key la llave (8B)

key chain el llavero (I)

keyboard (computer) el teclado (I)

to **kill** matar (6B)

kind: What — of ... ? ¿Qué clase de ... ? (I)

king el rey (8B)

to **kiss** besar(se) (4B)

kitchen la cocina (I)

knee la rodilla (5B)

knife el cuchillo (I)

to **know** saber (I); conocer (c → zc) (I, 1A)

    I — (yo) conozco (I)

    I — (how to) (yo) sé (I)

    you — (tú) conoces (I)

    you — (how to) (tú) sabes (I)

L

laboratory el laboratorio (I, 1A)

ladder la escalera (5A)

lake el lago (I)

lamp la lámpara (I)

language el idioma (9A)

laptop computer la computadora portátil (I)

large grande (I)

last último, -a (6A)

last:

    — night anoche (I)

    — week la semana pasada (I)

    — year el año pasado (I)

to **last** durar (I, 8A)

late tarde (I)

to arrive — llegar tarde (1A)

later: See you — ¡Hasta luego!; ¡Nos vemos! (I)

to **laugh** reírse (e → í) (4B)

law la ley (9A); *(study of)* el derecho (9A)

lawyer el abogado, la abogada (9A)

lazy perezoso, -a (I)

leading man el galán, *pl.* los galanes (6B)

league la liga (6A)

to **learn** aprender (a) (I)

leather el cuero (2B)

to **leave** salir (I); *(something)* dejar (3B)

    don't — no dejes (7A)

Leave me alone. Déjame en paz. (3B)

left: to the — (of) a la izquierda (de) (I)

leg la pierna (I)

lemonade la limonada (I)

less:

    — ... than menos ... que (I)

    — than menos de (I)

lessons: to take — tomar lecciones (1B)

to **let** dejar (3B)

    don't — no dejes (7A)

Let's go! ¡Vamos! (I)

Let's see ... A ver ... (I)

letter la carta (I, 3A)

    to mail a — echar una carta (3A)

lettuce la lechuga (I)

library la biblioteca (I)

to **lie** mentir (e → ie) (e → i) (4A)

life la vida (5A)

to **lift weights** levantar pesas (I)

to **light** encender (e → ie) (7A)

light *(color)* claro, -a (2B); la luz, *pl.* las luces (I)

like como (I)

to **like:**

    Did you — it? ¿Te gustó? (I)

    Do you — to ... ? ¿Te gusta ... ? (I)

    He / She doesn't — ... No le gusta ... (I)

    He / She —s ... Le gusta ... (I); A él / ella le gusta(n) ... (I)

    I don't — to ... (A mí) no me gusta ... (I)

I don't — to ... at all. (A mí) no me gusta nada ... (I)

I — ... Me gusta ... (I)

I — to ... (A mí) me gusta ... (I)

I — to ... a lot (A mí) me gusta mucho ... (I)

I — to ... better (A mí) me gusta más ... (I)

I —d it. Me gustó. (I)

I would — Me gustaría (I); quisiera (I)

What do you — better (prefer) to do? ¿Qué te gusta hacer más? (I)

What do you — to do? ¿Qué te gusta hacer? (I)

What would you — ? ¿Qué desean (Uds.)? (I)

Would you —? ¿Te gustaría? (I)

You — ... Te gusta ... (I)

likewise igualmente (I)

lips los labios (2A)

to **listen to music** escuchar música (I)

little: a — un poco (de) (I)

to **live** vivir (I)

living vivo, -a (5A)

    to make a — ganarse la vida (9A)

living room la sala (I)

located: to be — quedar (3B)

locker el armario (1A)

long largo, -a (I)

    How — ? ¿Cuánto tiempo hace que ..? (1B)

to **look:**

    to — (at) mirar (I)

    to — for buscar (c → qu) (I)

    you — (good) te ves (bien) (2A)

loose flojo, -a (2B)

to **lose** perder (e → ie) (6A)

    lot: a — mucho, -a (I)

to **love** encantar (I)

    He / She —s ... A él / ella le encanta(n) ... (I)

I / You — ... Me / Te encanta(n) ... (I)

love el amor (6B)

to be in — with estar

You are making me nervous. Me estás poniendo nervioso, -a. (3B)

make-up el maquillaje (2A)

meal la comida (I)

to mean:
   It —s ... Quiere decir ... (I)
   What does ... —? ¿Qué quiere

How — is / are ... ? ¿Cuántos años tiene(n) ... ? (I)

—er mayor, *pl.* mayores (I)

—er man el anciano (I)

—er people los ancianos (I)

—er woman la anciana (I)

on en (I), sobre (1A)

— Mondays, on Tuesdays ... los lunes, los martes ... (I)

— the grill a la parrilla (7B)

— time a tiempo (1A)

— top of encima de (I)

— weekends los fines de semana (I)

once in a while de vez en cuando (4A)

one uno (un), -a (I)

at — (o'clock) a la una (I)

— hundred cien (I)

— must hay que (I)

— thousand mil (I)

onion la cebolla (I)

online en la Red (I)

to be — estar en línea (I, 1B)

only sólo (I)

to open abrir (I)

open abierto, -a (8A)

opens se abre (3A)

opinion: in my — para mí (I)

opportunity la oportunidad (1B)

or o (I)

orange anaranjado, -a (I)

— juice el jugo de naranja (I)

orchestra la orquesta (1B)

to order pedir (e→ i) (I)

other otro, -a (I)

others los / las demás (I)

our nuestro(s), -a(s) (I)

ours nuestro(s), nuestra(s) (2A)

outdoors al aire libre (7B)

outer space el espacio (9B)

outrageous exagerado, -a (2B)

outside fuera (de) (7B)

oven el horno (7A)

own propio, -a (I)

owner el dueño, la dueña (9A)

P

to pack the suitcase hacer la maleta (8A)

page: Web — la página Web (1B)

pain el dolor (5B)

to paint (one's nails) pintarse (las uñas) (2A)

painter el pintor, la pintora (9A)

painting el cuadro (I)

palace el palacio (8B)

pants los pantalones (I)

paper: sheet of — la hoja de papel (I)

parade el desfile (4B)

paramedic el paramédico, la paramédica (5A)

parents los padres (I)

park el parque (I)

amusement — el parque de diversiones (I)

national — el parque nacional (I)

to participate (in) participar (en) (1B)

party la fiesta (I)

surprise — la fiesta de sorpresa (4B)

to pass pasar (3B)

passenger el pasajero, la pasajera (8A)

passport el pasaporte (8A)

pastel *(colors)* pastel *adj.* (2B)

pastime el pasatiempo (1B)

pastries los pasteles (I)

patience la paciencia (8A)

patient paciente (I)

to be — tener paciencia (8A)

to pay (for) pagar (g → gu) (por) (I)

to pay attention prestar atención (1A)

peace la paz (9B)

peach el durazno (7B)

peas los guisantes (I)

pedestrian el peatón, *pl.* los peatones (3B)

to peel pelar (7A)

pen el bolígrafo (I)

pencil el lápiz, *pl.* los lápices (I)

— sharpener el sacapuntas, *pl.* los sacapuntas (I)

people la gente (I)

older — los ancianos (I)

young — los jóvenes (1B)

pepper la pimienta (I)

perfume el perfume (I)

perhaps tal vez (8B)

to permit, to allow permitir (4A)

person la persona (I)

pharmacy la farmacia (3A)

phenomenal fenomenal (6A)

phone: to talk on the — hablar por teléfono (I)

photo la foto (I)

to take —s sacar (c → qu) fotos (I)

photographer el fotógrafo, la fotógrafa (1B)

photography la fotografía (1B)

physical education class la clase de educación física (I)

piano lesson (class) la lección de piano (I)

picnic el picnic (4B)

piece el pedazo (7A)

pills las pastillas (5B)

pilot el / la piloto (8A)

piñata la piñata (I)

pineapple la piña (7B)

pink rosado, -a (I)

pizza la pizza (I)

place el lugar (I)

to place poner (I)

to plan pensar (e → ie) + *inf.* (I); planear (8A)

plant la planta (9B)

plastic el plástico (I)

plate el plato (I)

play la obra de teatro (I)

to play jugar (u → ue) (g → gu) (a) *(games, sports)* (I); tocar *(an instrument)* (I)

to — **baseball** jugar al béisbol (I)

to — **basketball** jugar al básquetbol (I)

to — **football** jugar al fútbol americano (I)

to — **golf** jugar al golf (I)

to — **soccer** jugar al fútbol (I)

to — **sports** practicar deportes (I)

to — **tennis** jugar al tenis (I)

to — **the guitar** tocar la guitarra (I)

to — **the role of** hacer el papel de (6B)

to — **video games** jugar videojuegos (I)

to — **volleyball** jugar al vóleibol (I)

player el jugador, la jugadora (6A)

playground el patio de recreo (4A)

plaza la plaza (3B)

please por favor (I)

to — **very much** encantar (I)

pleased to meet you mucho gusto (I)

plot el argumento (6B)

police officer el / la policía (3B)

to **polish (one's nails)** pintarse (las uñas) (2A)

polite cortés, pl. corteses (8B)

politician el político, la política (9A)

politics la política (9A)

polluted contaminado, -a (9B)

pollution la contaminación (9B)

pool la piscina (I)

poor pobre (I)

— **thing** pobrecito, -a (5B)

pork el cerdo (7B)

— **chop** la chuleta de cerdo (7B)

possession la posesión, pl. las posesiones (I)

postcard la tarjeta postal (8B)

post office el correo (3A)

poster el cartel (I)

pot la olla (7A)

potatoes las papas (I)

practical práctico, -a (I)

practice la práctica (1B)

to **prefer** preferir (e → ie) (e → i) (I)

I — (yo) prefiero (I)

I — **to ...** (a mí) me gusta más ... (I)

you — (tú) prefieres (I)

to **prepare** preparar (I)

to **prescribe** recetar (5B)

prescription la receta (5B)

present el regalo (I)

presentation la presentación, pl. las presentaciones (I)

presenter el presentador, la presentadora (6A)

pretty bonito, -a (I)

price el precio (I, 2B)

principal (of a school) el director, la directora (6B)

primary school la escuela primaria (I)

prize el premio (6A)

problem el problema (I)

profession la profesión, pl. las profesiones (9A)

program el programa (I)

project el proyecto (1A)

Protestant church el templo (I)

to **protect** proteger (g → j) (9B)

punctual puntual (8B)

pure puro, -a (9B)

purple morado, -a (I)

purse el bolso (I)

to **pursue a career** seguir (e → i) una carrera (9A)

to **put** poner (I)

— (command) pon (I)

I — (yo) pongo (I)

to — on (clothing, make-up, etc.) ponerse (2A)

to — out (fire) apagar (g → gu) (5A)

you — (tú) pones (I)

Q

quarter past y cuarto (I)

queen la reina (6A)

question la pregunta (1A)

to ask a — hacer una pregunta (1A)

quickly rápidamente (I, 2A)

R

rain la lluvia (5A)

rain forest la selva tropical (9B)

to **rain** llover (o → ue) (5A)

It's —ing. Llueve. (I)

rather bastante (I)

to **read magazines** leer revistas (I)

ready listo, -a (8A)

to get — prepararse (2A)

realistic realista (I)

reality program el programa de la vida real (I)

really en realidad (2B)

Really? ¿Verdad? (I); ¿De veras? (I)

to **receive** recibir (I)

recently recientemente (2B)

reception desk la recepción (8B)

recipe la receta (7A)

to **recommend** recomendar (e → ie) (6B)

to **record** grabar (1B)

to **recycle** reciclar (I)

recycling center el centro de reciclaje (I)

red rojo, -a (I)

—**haired** pelirrojo, -a (I)

to **reduce** reducir (9B)

refrigerator el refrigerador (7A)

rehearsal el ensayo (1B)

to **rehearse** ensayar (1B)

relatives los parientes (4B)

to **relax** descansar (I)

to **remember** recordar (o → ue) (4B)

to **remove** quitar (3B)

to rent alquilar (6B)

to repeat repetir (e → i) (1A)

report el informe (I, 1A)

reporter el reportero, la reportera (5A)

to rescue rescatar (5A)

reservation la reservación, *pl.* las reservaciones (8A)

reserved reservado, -a (I)

to respect respetar (1A)

to rest descansar (I)

restaurant el restaurante (I)

to result resultar (6A)

to return regresar (I); volver (o→ue) (1B)

    to — a book devolver (o → ue) (un libro) (3A)

rice el arroz (I)

rich rico, -a (I)

to ride:

    to — a bicycle montar en bicicleta (I)

    to — horseback montar a caballo (I)

right:

    to the — (of) a la derecha (de) (I)

    — away en seguida (3A)

ring el anillo (I)

river el río (I)

road la calle (I)

to roast asar (7B)

to rob robar (6B)

rock la piedra (7B)

role el papel (6B)

    to play the — of hacer el papel de (6B)

romantic movie la película romántica (I)

room el cuarto (I); la habitación, *pl.* las habitaciones (8B)

    chat — el salón de chat, *pl.* los salones de chat (1B)

    double — la habitación doble (8B)

    single — la habitación individual (8B)

to straighten up the — arreglar el cuarto (I)

rope la cuerda (4A)

round-trip ida y vuelta (8A)

ruins las ruinas (8B)

rug la alfombra (I)

rule la regla (1A)

to run correr (I)

S

sack la bolsa (I)

sad triste (I)

to sail navegar (g → gu) (8B)

sailboat el bote de vela (8B)

salad la ensalada (I)

    fruit — la ensalada de frutas (I)

salary el salario (9A)

sale la liquidación, *pl.* las liquidaciones (2B)

salesperson el dependiente, la dependienta (I)

salon: beauty — el salón de belleza, *pl.* los salones de belleza

salsa la salsa (7A)

salt la sal (I)

same mismo, -a (I)

sandwich: ham and cheese — el sándwich de jamón y queso (I)

Saturday sábado (I)

sausage la salchicha (I)

to save ahorrar (9B); salvar (5A)

to say decir (I)

    How do you —? ¿Cómo se dice? (I)

    to — good-bye despedirse (e → i) de (4B)

    You — … Se dice … (I)

    You don't —! ¡No me digas! (I)

scared: to be — (of) tener miedo (de) (I)

scene la escena (6B)

schedule el horario (I)

school la escuela (I)

    high — el colegio (9A)

primary — la escuela primaria (I)

technical — la escuela técnica (9A)

science:

    — class la clase de ciencias naturales (I)

    — fiction movie la película de ciencia ficción (I)

scientist el científico, la científica (9A)

scissors las tijeras (1A)

score el tanteo (6A)

to score (a goal) meter un gol (6A)

to scream gritar (5A)

screen: computer — la pantalla (I)

to scuba dive bucear (I)

sea el mar (I)

search la búsqueda (1B)

    to do a — hacer una búsqueda (1B)

to search (for) buscar (I)

season la estación, *pl.* las estaciones (I)

seat el asiento (1A)

second segundo, -a (I)

    — floor el primer piso (I)

secretary el secretario, la secretaria (9A)

security checkpoint la inspección, *pl.* las inspecciones de seguridad (8A)

to see ver (I)

    Let's — A ver … (I)

    — you later! ¡Nos vemos!; Hasta luego. (I)

    — you soon. Hasta pronto. (3A)

    — you tomorrow. Hasta mañana. (I)

    to — a movie ver una película (I)

seem:

    How does it — to you? ¿Qué te parece? (2B)

    it —s to me me parece que (2B)

it —s to me me parece que
(2B)

seen:

I have — he visto (6B)

you have — has visto (6B)

to sell vender (I)

to send enviar (i → í) (I, 3A)

to separate separar (I)

September septiembre (I)

serious serio, -a (I); grave (9B)

to serve servir (e → i) (I)

What do you — it with?
¿Con qué se sirve? (7A)

service station la estación de
servicio (3A)

to set the table poner la mesa (I)

seven siete (I)

seven hundred setecientos, -as
(I)

seventeen diecisiete (I)

seventh séptimo, -a (I)

seventy setenta (I)

several varios, -as (3A)

shake hands dar(se) la mano
(4B)

shame: What a —! ¡Qué lástima!
(5B)

shampoo el champú (3A)

to share compartir (I)

to shave afeitarse (2A)

she ella (I)

sheet of paper la hoja de papel
(I)

shelf el estante (I)

shellfish los mariscos (7A)

ship el barco (I)

shirt la camisa (I)

T— la camiseta (I)

shoe store la zapatería (I)

shoes los zapatos (I)

shoe size el número (2B)

short bajo, -a (stature); corto, -a
(length) (I)

shorts los pantalones cortos (I)

shot la inyección, pl. las
inyecciones (5B)

should deber (I)

shoulder el hombro (5B)

show el programa (I)

to show + movie or TV program
dar (I)

shower la ducha (2A)

to take a — ducharse (2A)

shrimp el camarón, pl. los
camarones (7A)

shy reservado, -a (I)

sick enfermo, -a (I)

sign el letrero (2B); la señal (3A)

stop — la señal de parada
(3B)

silk seda (2B)

silly tonto, -a (I)

silver la plata (2A)

since desde (3B)

to sing cantar (I)

singer el / la cantante (1B)

sink el fregadero (7A)

sir (el) señor (Sr.) (I)

sister la hermana (I)

site: Web — el sitio Web (I)

six seis (I)

six hundred seiscientos, -as (I)

sixteen dieciséis (I)

sixth sexto, -a (I)

sixty sesenta (I)

size (shoe) el número, la talla
(2B)

to skate patinar (I)

to skateboard montar en
monopatín (I)

skates los patines (3A)

to ski esquiar (i → í) (I)

skirt la falda (I)

sky el cielo (7B)

to sleep dormir (o→ue) (o → u) (I)

to fall asleep dormirse (o → ue)
(o → u) (6A)

sleepy: to be — tener sueño (I)

slice el pedazo (7A)

slide la diapositiva (I)

slowly lentamente (2A); despacio
(3B)

small pequeño, -a (I)

smell el olor (7B)

to smile sonreír (e → í) (4B)

smoke el humo (5A)

to snorkel bucear (I)

to snow: nevar (e → ie) (5A)

It's —ing. Nieva. (I)

so tan (2B)

so + adj. tan + adj. (1B)

so much tanto (I)

so-so regular (I)

soap el jabón (3A)

soap opera la telenovela (I)

soccer: to play — jugar
(u → ue) (g → gu) al fútbol (I)

sociable sociable (I)

social studies class la clase de
ciencias sociales (I)

socks los calcetines (I)

soft drink el refresco (I)

software el software (I)

solar solar (9B)

solid-colored de sólo un color
(2B)

to solve resolver (o → ue) (9B)

some unos, -as (I); algún, alguno,
-a (1A)

— day algún día (9A)

someone alguien (1A)

something algo (I)

sometimes a veces (I)

son el hijo (I)

—s; —(s) and daughter(s)
los hijos (I)

song la canción, pl. las canciones
(I, 1B)

soon pronto (3A)

See you —. Hasta pronto.
(3A)

sorry: I'm —. Lo siento. (I)

sound (stereo) system el
equipo de sonido (I)

soup: vegetable — la sopa de
verduras (I)

source la fuente (9B)

souvenirs los recuerdos (I)

to buy — comprar recuerdos (I)

space el espacio (9B)

spaghetti los espaguetis (I)

Spanish class la clase de español (I)

special especial (2A)

special effects los efectos especiales (6B)

special event el evento especial (2A)

speech el discurso (1A)

to spell:

   How is ... spelled? ¿Cómo se escribe ... ? (I)

   It's spelled ... Se escribe ... (I)

to spend gastar (2B)

   to — time with friends pasar tiempo con amigos (I)

spicy picante (7B)

to spill tirar (7A)

   don't — no tires (7A)

spoiled consentido, -a (4A)

spoon la cuchara (I)

sports:

   — equipment el equipo deportivo (3A)

   —-minded deportista (I)

   — program el programa deportivo (I)

   to play — practicar (c → qu) deportes (I)

spring la primavera (I)

stadium el estadio (I)

stairs, stairway la escalera (I)

stamp el sello (3A)

stand (food) el puesto (7B)

stapler la grapadora (1A)

star: movie — la estrella (del cine) (6B)

to start empezar (e → ie) (I); comenzar (e → ie) (z → c) (5A)

statue la estatua (3B)

to stay: quedarse (3A)

   I — at home. Me quedo en casa. (I)

steak la carne de res (7B)

to steal robar (6B)

stepbrother el hermanastro (I)

stepfather el padrastro (I)

stepmother la madrastra (I)

stepsister la hermanastra (I)

stereo system el equipo de sonido (I)

still todavía (3A)

to stitch (surgically) dar puntadas (5B)

stitches las puntadas (5B)

stomach el estómago (I)

to stop parar (3B)

to stop over hacer escala (8A)

stop sign la señal de parada (3B)

stoplight el semáforo (3B)

stopover la escala (8A)

store la tienda (I)

   book— la librería (I)

   clothing — la tienda de ropa (I)

   department — el almacén, pl. los almacenes (I)

   discount — la tienda de descuentos (I)

   household-appliance — la tienda de electrodomésticos (I)

   jewelry — la joyería (I)

   shoe — la zapatería (I)

stories: to write — escribir cuentos (I)

storm la tormenta (5A)

story el piso (I)

stove la estufa (7A)

to straighten up the room arreglar el cuarto (I)

straight derecho (3B)

strawberries las fresas (I)

street la calle (I)

student el / la estudiante (I)

studies: course of — el programa de estudios (9A)

studious estudioso, -a (I)

to study estudiar (I)

stupendous estupendo, -a (8B)

stupid tonto, -a (I)

style el estilo (2B)

subway el metro (3B)

to succeed tener éxito (6B)

success el éxito (6B)

   to be —ful tener éxito (6B)

suddenly de repente (5A)

sugar el azúcar (I)

to suggest sugerir (e → ie) (e → i) (8A)

suit el traje (I)

suitcase la maleta (8A)

summer el verano (I)

to sunbathe tomar el sol (I)

Sunday domingo (I)

sunglasses los anteojos de sol (I)

sunny: It's —. Hace sol. (I)

supermarket el supermercado (3A)

supplies los materiales (1A)

sure seguro, -a (3B)

to surf the Web navegar (g → gu) en la Red (I, 1B)

surprise la sorpresa (4B)

sweater el suéter (I)

sweatshirt la sudadera (I)

sweet dulce (7B)

to swim nadar (I)

swimming la natación (1B)

swimsuit el traje de baño (I)

synagogue la sinagoga (I)

synthetic fabric la tela sintética (2B)

T

T-shirt la camiseta (I)

table la mesa (I)

   to set the — poner la mesa (I)

tablespoon(ful) la cucharada (7A)

to take llevar (I)

   to — a bath bañarse (2A)

to — a course tomar un curso (I)

to — a shower ducharse (2A)

to — a tour hacer una gira (8B)

to — a trip hacer un viaje (8A)

to — a walk dar una caminata (7B)

to — away quitar (3B)

to — care of cuidar a (3A)

to — lessons tomar lecciones (1B)

to — out sacar (c → qu) (3A)

to — out the trash sacar la basura (I)

to — photos sacar fotos (I)

to — an X-ray sacar una radiografía (5B)

talented talentoso, -a (I)

to talk hablar (I)

    to — on the phone hablar por teléfono (I)

tall alto, -a (I)

tank el tanque (3A)

tape: transparent — la cinta adhesiva (1A)

taste el sabor (7B)

to taste probar (o → ue) (7A)

tasty sabroso, -a (I); rico, -a (I)

tea el té (I)

    iced — el té helado (I)

to teach enseñar (I)

teacher el profesor, la profesora (I)

team el equipo (1B)

to tear romperse (5B)

technical school la escuela técnica (9A)

technician el técnico, la técnica (9A)

technology / computers la tecnología (I)

technology / computer class la clase de tecnología (I)

teddy bear el oso de peluche (4A)

teeth los dientes (2A)

    to brush one's — cepillarse los dientes (2A)

television: to watch — ver la tele (I)

television set el televisor (I)

to tell decir (I)

    — me dime (I)

    to — jokes contar (o → ue) (chistes) (4B)

temple el templo (I)

ten diez (I)

tennis: to play — jugar (u → ue) (g → gu) al tenis (I)

tennis racket la raqueta de tenis (3A)

tenth décimo, -a (I)

thank you gracias (I)

that que (I); ese, esa (I); *(over there)* aquel, aquella (2B)

    —'s why por eso (I)

the el, la (I) los, las (I)

    — best el / la mejor, los / las mejores (I)

    — worst el / la peor, los / las peores (I)

theater el teatro (I)

    movie — el cine (I)

their su, sus (I)

theirs suyo, -a, suyos, -as (2A)

them las, los *dir. obj. pron.* (I), les *ind. obj. pron.* (I)

then entonces (I); luego (2A)

there allí (I)

    — is / are hay (I); haya *(subjunctive)* (9B)

    — was hubo (5A)

    — was / — were había (4B)

    — will be habrá (9A)

therefore por eso (I)

these estos, estas (I)

they ellos, ellas (I)

they died se murieron (5A)

thief el ladrón, la ladrona, *pl.* los ladrones (6B)

thing la cosa (I)

to think pensar (e → ie) (I)

    I don't — so. Creo que no. (I)

    I — ... Creo que ... (I)

    I — so. Creo que sí. (I)

    What do you — (about it)? ¿Qué te parece? (I)

third tercer (tercero), -a (I)

third floor el segundo piso (I)

thirsty: I'm —. Tengo sed. (I)

thirteen trece (I)

thirty treinta (I); y media *(in telling time)* (I)

thirty-one treinta y uno (I)

this este, esta (I)

    — afternoon esta tarde (I)

    — evening esta noche (I)

    — weekend este fin de semana (I)

    What is — ? ¿Qué es esto? (I)

those esos, esas (I); (over there) aquellos, aquellas (2B)

thousand: a — mil (I)

three tres (I)

three hundred trescientos, -as (I)

three-ring binder la carpeta de argollas (I)

through por (3B)

to throw away tirar (7A)

Thursday jueves (I)

ticket el boleto (I); la multa (3B)

    to give a — poner una multa (3B)

tie la corbata (I); el empate (6A)

tight apretado, -a (2B)

time:

    At what —? ¿A qué hora? (I)

    for the ... — por ... vez (6A)

    free — el tiempo libre (I)

    on — a tiempo (1A)

    to spend — with friends pasar tiempo con amigos (I)

    What — is it? ¿Qué hora es? (I)

timid tímido, -a (4A)

tip la propina (8B)

tired cansado, -a (I)

to a *prep.* (I)

    in order — para + *inf.* (I)

    — the a la, al (I)

    — the left (of) a la izquierda (de) (I)

    — the right (of) a la derecha (de) (I)

toast el pan tostado (I)

today hoy (I)

tomatoes los tomates (I)

tomorrow mañana (I)

    See you —. Hasta mañana. (I)

tonight esta noche (I)

too también (I); demasiado (I)

    I do (like to) — a mí también (I)

    me — a mí también (I)

toothbrush el cepillo de dientes (3A)

toothpaste la pasta dental (3A)

top: on — of encima de (I)

touching emocionante (I)

tour: to take a — hacer una gira (8B)

tourist el / la turista (8A)

towel la toalla (2A)

town el pueblo (9B)

toy el juguete (I)

traffic el tráfico (3B)

trail el sendero (7B)

train el tren (I)

    electric — el tren eléctrico (4A)

trainer el entrenador, la entrenadora (6A)

transparent tape la cinta adhesiva (1A)

to **travel** viajar (I)

travel agency la agencia de viajes (8A)

travel agent el / la agente de viajes (8A)

tree el árbol (I)

tremendous tremendo, -a (I)

tricycle el triciclo (4A)

trip el viaje (I)

    to take a — hacer un viaje (8A)

to **trip** (over) tropezar (e → ie) (z → c) (con) (5B)

tropical rain forest la selva tropical (9B)

truck el camión, *pl.* los camiones (3B)

truth la verdad (4A)

to **try** probar (o → ue) (7A)

to **try on** probarse (o → ue) (2B)

to **try to** tratar de (5A)

Tuesday martes (I)

    on —s los martes (I)

turkey el pavo (7B)

to **turn** doblar (3B)

    to — in entregar (g → gu) (1A)

    to — off apagar (g → gu) (7A)

    to — on encender (e → ie) (7A)

    to — out resultar (6A)

turtle la tortuga (4A)

TV channel el canal (I)

twelve doce (I)

twenty veinte (I)

twenty-one veintiuno (veintiún) (I)

to **twist** torcerse (o → ue) (c → z) (5B)

two dos (I)

two hundred doscientos, -as (I)

typical típico, -a (8B)

U

Ugh! ¡Uf! (I)

ugly feo, -a (I)

uncle el tío (I)

uncles; uncle(s) and aunt(s) los tíos (I)

underneath debajo de (I)

to **understand** comprender (I); entender (e → ie) (1A)

university la universidad (9A)

unforgettable inolvidable (I)

until hasta (3A)

up to hasta (3B)

us: (to / for) — nos *dir., ind. obj. pron.* (I)

to **use:**

    to — the computer usar la computadora (I)

    What's it —d for? ¿Para qué sirve? (I)

used usado, -a (I)

useful:

    to be — servir (e → i) (I)

    is — for sirve para (I)

V

vacation: to go on — ir de vacaciones (I)

to **vacuum** pasar la aspiradora (I)

valley el valle (9B)

various varios, -as (3A)

VCR la videocasetera (I)

vegetable soup la sopa de verduras (I)

vendor el vendedor, la vendedora (8B)

very muy (I)

    — well muy bien (I)

veterinarian el veterinario, la veterinaria (9A)

victim la víctima (6B)

video games: to play — jugar videojuegos (I)

videocassette el video (I)

to **videotape** hacer un video (I)

vinegar el vinagre (7A)

violence la violencia (6B)

violent violento, -a (I)

to **visit** visitar (I)

    to — chat rooms visitar salones de chat (I, 1B)

voice la voz, *pl.* las voces (1B)

volleyball: to play — jugar (u → ue) (g → gu) al vóleibol (I)

volunteer el voluntario, la voluntaria (I)

    — work el trabajo voluntario (I)

W

to **wait** esperar (3B)

waiter, waitress el camarero, la camarera (I)

to **wake up** despertarse (e → ie) (2A)

to **walk** caminar (I)

to take a — dar una caminata (7B)

wall la pared (I)

wallet la cartera (I)

to **want** querer (e → ie) (I)

I — (yo) quiero (I)

you — (tú) quieres (I)

war la guerra (9B)

warm: to be — tener calor (I)

was fue (I)

to **wash** lavar (I)

to — the car lavar el coche (I)

to — the clothes lavar la ropa (I)

to — the dishes lavar los platos (I)

to — one's face lavarse la cara (2A)

wastepaper basket la papelera (I)

watch el reloj pulsera (I)

to **watch television** ver la tele (I)

water el agua (I)

watermelon la sandía (7B)

waterskiing el esquí acuático (8B)

way la manera (9B)

we nosotros, -as (I)

to **wear** llevar (I)

weather: What's the — like? ¿Qué tiempo hace? (I)

Web:

to create a — page crear una página Web (1B)

to surf the — navegar (g → gu) en la Red (I, 1B)

— page la página Web (I, 1B)

— site el sitio Web (I)

Wednesday miércoles (I)

wedding la boda (2A)

week la semana (I)

last — la semana pasada (I)

weekend:

on —s los fines de semana (I)

this — este fin de semana (I)

welcome bienvenido, -a (8A)

well bien (I); pues ... *(to indicate pause)* (I)

very — muy bien (I)

— -behaved bien educado, -a (4A)

wet mojado, -a (7B)

What? ¿Cuál? ¿Qué? (I)

— are you like? ¿Cómo eres? (I)

(At) — time? ¿A qué hora? (I)

— color ... ? ¿De qué color ... ? (I)

— day is today? ¿Qué día es hoy? (I)

— did you do? ¿Qué hiciste? (I)

— do you like better (prefer) to do? ¿Qué te gusta hacer más? (I)

— do you like to do? ¿Qué te gusta hacer? (I)

— do you serve it with? ¿Con qué se sirve? (7A)

— do you think (about it)? ¿Qué te parece? (I, 2B)

— does ... mean? ¿Qué quiere decir ... ? (I)

— else? ¿Qué más? (I)

— happened to you? ¿Qué te pasó? (I, 5B)

— is it made of? ¿De qué está hecho, -a? (2B)

— is she / he like? ¿Cómo es? (I)

— is the date? ¿Cuál es la fecha? (I)

— is this? ¿Qué es esto? (I)

— is your name? ¿Cómo te llamas? (I)

— kind of ... ? ¿Qué clase

de ...? (I)

— time is it? ¿Qué hora es? (I)

— would you like? ¿Qué desean (Uds.)? (I)

—'s happening? ¿Qué pasa? (I)

—'s his / her name? ¿Cómo se llama? (I)

—'s it (used) for? ¿Para qué sirve? (I)

—'s the weather like? ¿Qué tiempo hace? (I)

what!:

— a good / nice idea! ¡Qué buena idea! (I)

— a shame / pity! ¡Qué pena! (I); ¡Qué lástima! (5B)

what lo que (4A)

wheelchair la silla de ruedas (5B)

When? ¿Cuándo? (I)

Where? ¿Dónde? (I)

— are you from? ¿De dónde eres? (I)

(To) —? ¿Adónde? (I)

whether si (I)

Which? ¿Cuál? ¿Cuáles? (I)

while mientras (que) (4B)

once in a — de vez en cuando (4A)

white blanco, -a (I)

who que (I)

Who? ¿Quién? (I)

Why? ¿Por qué? (I)

wide ancho, -a (3B)

wife la esposa (I)

will be será (6B)

Will you bring me ... ? ¿Me trae ... ? (I)

to **win** ganar (1B)

window la ventana (I)

window *(airplane)* la ventanilla (8A)

windsurfing el surf de vela (8B)

winter el invierno (I)

with con (I)

— me conmigo (I)

— my / your friends con mis / tus amigos (I)

— whom? ¿Con quién? (I)

— you *familiar* contigo (I)

What do you serve it —? ¿Con qué se sirve? (7A)

without sin (I)

— a doubt sin duda (5A)

woman la mujer (I)

older woman la anciana (I)

business— la mujer de negocios (9A)

wonderful estupendo, -a (8B)

wool la lana (2B)

word la palabra (1A)

work el trabajo (I)

volunteer — el trabajo voluntario (I)

to work trabajar (I); funcionar (9B)

world el mundo (4A)

worse than peor(es) que (I)

worst: the — el / la peor, los / las peores (I)

Would you like? ¿Te gustaría? (I)

wrist la muñeca (5B)

to write:

to — e-mail escribir por correo electrónico (I)

to — stories escribir cuentos (I)

writer el escritor, la escritora (9A)

X _____

X-ray la radiografía (5B)

Y _____

yard el jardín, *pl.* los jardines (I)

year el año (I)

last — el año pasado (I)

yellow amarillo, -a (I)

yes sí (I)

yesterday ayer (I)

yet: not — no ... todavía (6B)

yogurt el yogur (I)

you *fam. sing.* tú (I); *formal sing.* usted (Ud.) (I); *fam. pl.* vosotros, -as (I); *formal pl.* ustedes (Uds.) (I); *fam. after prep.* ti (I); *sing. ind., dir. obj. pron* te (I), *pl. fam. ind. obj. pron.* os (I), *formal ind. obj. pron.* le, les (I), *formal dir. obj. pron.* lo, la, los, las

And —? ¿Y a ti? (I)

for — para ti (I)

it matters (it's important), they matter to — te importa(n) (2B)

to / for — *fam. pl.* os (I)

to / for — *fam. sing.* te (I)

with — contigo (I)

— can se puede (7A)

— don't say! ¡No me digas! (I)

— have seen has visto (6B)

— look (good) te ves (bien) (2A)

— say ... Se dice ... (I)

young joven (I)

— boy / girl el niño, la niña (I)

— man el joven (I)

— people los jóvenes (1B)

— woman la joven (I)

—er menor, *pl.* menores (I)

—est el / la menor, los / las menores (I)

your *fam.* tu (I); *fam.* tus, vuestro(s), -a(s) (I); *formal* su, sus (I)

yours *fam.* tuyo, -a, -os, -as, *formal* suyo, -a, -os, -as (2A)

yuck! ¡Uf! (I)

Z _____

zero cero (I)

zoo el zoológico (I)

Grammar Index

Structures are most often presented first in *A primera vista,* where they are practiced lexically in conversational contexts. They are then explained in a *Gramática* section or are placed as reminders in a *¿Recuerdas?* or *Nota.* Lightface numbers refer to the pages where these structures are initially presented lexically or, after explanation, where student reminders occur. Lightface numbers also refer to pages that review structures first presented in Level 1. **Boldface numbers** refer to pages where new structures are explained.

a personal with **conocer** 56
absolute superlatives 183
accents:
    to separate diphthongs 254
    written 144
adjectives:
    agreement of 3
    demonstrative 102, 104, **114,** 124
    making comparisons with 47, **53**
    possessive 76, **88,** 96
    used as nouns **116**
adverbs, formation of 79
affirmative and negative words 19, 20, **31**

cardinal numbers 99
commands:
    affirmative *tú* 158–159, **168,** 353
    irregular affirmative *tú* 159, **168,** 180
    irregular negative *tú* **356,** 370
    negative *tú* 350, **356,** 370, 382
    usted, ustedes 375, **382,** 396
como: *see* comparisons
comparisons 46, 47, **53**
conocer:
    with **alguien, nadie** 32
    with personal **a** 32, 56
    vs. **saber** 56, 68
contractions 43
creer que + subjunctive 488
dar, preterite of 142

decir:
    affirmative *tú* command 168
    present 155
diéresis 459
diminutives **(-ito, -ita)** 183
direct object pronouns; *see* pronouns

estar vs. **ser** 86, 96
exclamations with **¡Qué!** 237
Exploración del lenguaje:
    antonyms 482
    compound words 383
    false cognates 272
    gestos 170
    origins of words from Arabic 113
    prefixes: **des-, im-, in-, ir-** 221
    suffix **-ero(a)** 436
    suffixes: **-oso(a), -dor(a)** 327
    verbs and corresponding **-ción** nouns 60

future tense:
    of regular verbs 452, **460,** 462, 463, 472
    of irregular verbs **decir, poner, querer, salir, venir** 463, **484,** 496
    of irregular verbs **haber, hacer, poder, saber, tener** 452, **462,** 463, 472, 484

haber:
    imperfect 222, **248**
    preterite 240, **248**
hacer:
    affirmative *tú* command 168
    irregular *yo* form of present tense 15, 155
    with time expressions 46, **58**
hay que 19

imperfect and preterite 248, 272, 307
imperfect progressive 288
    and preterite 266, **277**
imperfect tense:
    of **haber** 222, **248**

of irregular verbs **ir, ser, ver** 186, 189, **196,** 208
of **jugar, ser, tener** 208
of regular verbs 186, 188–189, **194**
other uses of **248**
to describe a situation 213, **219,** 234, 307
to describe weather; physical, mental, emotional states; states of being 241 **248**
impersonal **se** 350–351, **360**
indicative mood 410
    of stem-changing verbs 437
indirect object pronouns; *see* pronouns
infinitive:
    in verbal expressions 399
    used after prepositions 81
    with certain verbs and expressions 71
ir:
    affirmative *tú* command 168
    imperfect **196,** 208
    ir + a + infintive 43, 460
    present 43
    to indicate future 460

nationalities 6
nouns, making comparisons with 46, **53**
numbers:
    cardinal numbers 99
    in telling time 127

oír:
    ¡Oye! 250
    present **250,** 262
    preterite **250,** 262

para 24
parecer 116
past participles **331,** 342
personal **a,** with **conocer** 56
poner:
    affirmative *tú* command 168
    irregular *yo* form of present 15, 155

Acknowledgments

Cover Design Tamada Brown & Associates

Program Graphic Development Herman Adler Design

Technical Illustration Herman Adler Design; p. xxxi

Illustrations Wilkinson Studios Artists: Bob Brugger 029, 309, 327, 330, 436; Dennis Dzielak 092; Seitu Hayden 012, 081, 087, Reggie Holladay 023, 089, 130, 144, 186, 187, 212, 213, 266, 267, 330, 427 (l), 431; Tim Jones 004, 008, 019, 022, 058, 060, 074, 075, 087, 106, 145, 154, 158, 159, 190, 191, 217, 225, 241, 249, 270, 271 (tr), 272, 277, 281 (t), 306 (b), 374, 375, 402, 403; Albert Lorenz 164, 256; Judy Love 018, 079, 102, 103, 284, 348, 371, 452, 456, 457, 458 (r), 490; Miguel Luna 023, 228; Jonathan Massie 019 (tl), 036, 046, 047 (m), 051, 064, 083, 107, 135, 139, 163, 169, 271 (m), 277, 281 (br), 310, 320 (l), 352, 354, 390, 476; Tom McKee 034, 083, 114, 131, 134, 136, 229, 240, 244, 246, 248, 249, 251, 270, 295, 306 (tl), 308, 320 (tl), 321, 324, 332, 339; Donna Perrone 035; Tammy Smith 197, 459, 482; Shari Warren 221, 254, 255, 273, 278, 379, 384, 407, 416, 453 (l), 458; Nicole Wong 075, 111, 116, 199, 202 (m), 203 (t), 204, 272, 458, 480, 485.

Photography Corbis = CO. Front and back covers: Market day in Solola, near Lake Atitlán, Guatemala (background) Robert Frerck/Odyssey/Chicago; Indigenous woman at market carrying carrots, Guatemala (inset) Brian King/Leo de Wys Stock Photo Agency.

vi (m) David Woods/CO; vii Kevin Schafer; vii, (t) (tr) Joseph Sohm/Visions of America/Corbis; viii, © Nan Coulter/Dallas Morning News; ix John Morrison Photography; xi Jay Penni Photography; xii Carol Maglitta; xix Jay Penni Photography; xvi–xvii Danny Lehman/CO; xvi (l) xvi Heriberto Rodríguez Reuters NewMedia, Inc./CO; xvii Photograph by Araceli Gordobil, Madrid, Spain; xviii–xix Kevin Schafer/CO; xx (bl) Tom Bean/CO; xx–xxi Don Hebert/Taxi/GettyImages; xxii–xxiii Chris Huxley/eStock Photography/PictureQuest; xxiv–xxv Bob Krist/CO; xxvi (bl) V.C.L./Taxi/GettyImages; xxvi–xxvii Michael Busselle/CO; xxvii Sean Sprague/The Image Works; xxviii (bl) Bob Daemmrich/The Image Works; xxviii–xxix David Muench/CO; xxix Bill Ross/CO; xxix Jay Penni Photography; xxxi Pat LaCroix/The Image Bank/Getty Images, Inc.; xxxi Jay Penni Photography; xxxii (l) HIRB/Index Stock Imagery; xxxii (bl) John Phelan/DDB Stock Photo; 1 (t) Dan Gair Photographic/Index Stock Imagery; (b) Owen Franken/CO; 2 (bm) Bill Burlingham Photography; (tr) Jay Penni Photography; 3 (br) Reuters NewMedia, Inc./CO; 4 (tr) Richard T. Nowitz/CO; 7 (m) Digital Vision/GettyImages; (tm) Alamy Images; (bm) Digital Vision; (tl) Mad Cow Studio/firstlight/PictureQuest; (r) Thinkstock/PictureQuest; (m) Royalty-Free/CO; (ml) Barbara Penoyar/PhotoDisc/GettyImages; (tr) Royalty-Free/CO; (br) Stanley Fellerman/Royalty-Free/CO; 8(m) Jay Penni Photography; 11 Getty Images; 16 (bl) Silva, Simón, (b. 1961), El día del maestro; 16–17 (bg) Robert Frerck/Odyssey/Chicago; 18 (tl) Jay Penni Photography; 19 (mr) Jay Penni Photography; 24 (bl) Joe Viesti/Viesti Associates; 25 (tr) Bill Burlingham Photography; (br) Rudi von Briel/PhotoEdit; 26 (mr) David Young-Wolff/PhotoEdit; 28 (br) David Simson/Stock Boston; 29 (tr) Ralf-Finn Hestoft/Index Stock Imagery; 32 (br) Ulrike Welsch/Stock Boston; 33 Photo courtesy of Craig Reubelt; 35 (tr) Okapi Magazine, October, 2002.; 37 (tr) Jay Penni Photography; (br) Jay Penni Photography; 38 (br) Buddy Mays/CO; (mr) © 2003 Danny Lehman/CO; (tr) Jack Kurtz/The Image Works; 39 (m) Jan Murray/Alamy Limited; 39 (tr) © 2003 Danny Lehman/CO; 42 (b) Bob Daemmrich Photography; 44 (bl) Berni, Antonio (1905–1981), Club Atlético Nueva Chicago (New Chicago Athletic Club), 1942, oil on canvas, 6'3/4" x 9' 10-1/4", The Museum of Modern Art/licensed by SCALA, photo courtesy of Art Resource, NY.; (bg) Alfredo Caliz/Cover; 46 (ml) Jay Penni Photography; 47 (tr) Jay Penni Photography; (tl) Jay Penni Photography; 50 (mr) Emilio Guzmán/Reuters NewMedia, Inc/CO; 51 (mr) Todd Powell/Index Stock Imagery; 52 (tr) HIRB/Index Stock Imagery; (br) Robert Fried/Stock Boston; 52 (t) © Paul Buck/AP/Wide World Photos; 54 (b) David Young-Wolff/PhotoEdit; 55 (tm, tr) Fernando Botero, Courtesy, Marlborough Gallery, NY; 55 (br) Botero, Fernando (b. 1933), El pájaro (Little Bird), 1988–medium series, bronze sculpture, photo courtesy of Jeremy Horner/CO; 59 (bl) Tom & Dee Ann McCarthy/CO; 59 (bl) Michael Ochs Archives; (bl) Lucy Nicholson-AFP/CO; 60 (tm) Bill Burlingham Photography; 61 (tl) Getty Images, Inc.; (tr) A. Ramey/Stock Boston; (br) Ghislain & Marie David de Lossy/The Image Bank/GettyImages; 62 (br) Robert Fried Photography; (mr) Robert Frerck/Odyssey/Chicago; (bm Carlos Goldin/CO; 63 (br) Robert Frerck/Odyssey Productions, Inc.; Bonnie Kamin/Photo Edit 64 (both) Bill Burlingham Photography; 65 (all) Bill Burlingham Photography; 66(m) Stephen Simpson/Taxi/GettyImages; (br) Andre Jenny/Focus Group/PictureQuest; (tr) Michael S. Yamashita/CO; (mr) Danny Lehman/CO; 67 (tr) Macduff Everton/CO; 70 (tm) Bill Burlingham Photography; 72 (m) Paul Perez/Latin Focus.com; (bl) Rivera, Diego (1886–1957), Baile en Tehuantepec (Dance in Tehuantepec) 1935, charcoal and water, 13-15/16 x 23-7/8 in., Los Angeles County Museum of Art, Gift of Mr. and Mrs. Milton W. Lipper, From the Milton W. Lipper Estate photo courtesy of Museum Associates/LACMA; 74 (all) Bill Burlingham Photography; 75 (all) Bill Burlingham Photography; 79 (b) Ryan McVay/Getty Images, Inc.; 81 (tr) John Morrison Photography; 82 (tr) Bill Burlingham Photography; (t) © Digital Vision; (br) Bob Daemmrich Photography; 83 (tr Rob Lewine/CO; 84 (br) Bob Daemmrich/Stock Boston; 85 (ml) Jimmy Dorantes/Latin Focus.com; (tr) Bill Burlingham Photography; (br) © Nik Wheeler/CO; (bl) © Bob Daemmrich/The Image Works, Inc.; 86 (br) Bob Daemmrich Photography; 88 (br) Daniel Ciccone; 90 (m) Carlos Goldin/DDB Stock Photo; 90 (bl) Carlos Goldin/DDB Stock Photo; 91 (tr) Charlie Westerman/ImageState; 91 (mr) Robert Fried Photography; 92 (tr) Jeremy Horner/CO; (tr) Tiziana and Gianni Baldizzone/CO; 93 (tr) David Young-Wolff/PhotoEdit; (mr) Francesco Venturi/CO; (br) Nik Wheeler/CORBIS; 94 Danny Lehman/CO; 95 (all) Danny Lehman/CO; 98 (tm) Robert Frerck/Odyssey/Chicago; 100 (bg) Mark Antman/The Image Works; (bl) Infanta Margarita (1651–73) in Blue Dress, 1659 (oil on canvas) by Diego Rodríguez de Silva y Velázquez (1599–1660) Kunstistorisches Museum, Vienna, Austria/Bridgeman Art Library; 102 (bl) Bill Burlingham Photography; 108 (tr) Bill Burlingham Photography; 109 (tr) Isaac Hernández/MercuryPress.com; 112 (bl) Bob Daemmrich/Stock Boston; (br) The Granger Collection, New York; 113 Diaphor Agency/Index Stock Imagery, Inc.(bm) Bettmann/CO; (tr) Dallas & John Heaton/CO; 115 (tr) Robert Fried Photography; Daniel Ciccone 117 (both) AP/Wide World; 118 (bm) Royalty-Free/CO; (bl) Bettmann/CO; 119 (mr) Paul A. Souders/CO; (tr) Robert Fried/Stock Boston; (ml) Crabill/Bettmann/CO; 120 (tr) Tony Freeman/PhotoEdit; (br) Paul Rodriguez/© Jimmy Dorantes/LatinFocus.com; 121 (t) Getty Images, Inc.; (b) Robert Fried/Stock Boston; 123 © Jimmy Dorantes/Latin Focus.com; Courtesy, U.S. Latino and Latina WWII Oral History Project/UT Austin; KJ Historical/CO; 126 (tl) Robert Frerck/Odyssey/Chicago; (tr) Ray Juno/CO; 128 (bl) Julio Alpuy (b. 1919), Buenos Aires, 1957, photo courtesy of Cecilia de Torres, Ltd., New York.; 128–129 Jan Butchofsky-Houser/CO; 130 (all) Jay Penni Photography; 135 (br) Dave G. Houser/CO; 136 (br) Bill Burlingham Photography; 137 (tr) © Wolfgang Kaehler 2004 www.wkaehlerphoto.com; (br) Jay Penni Photography; (mr) Robert Fried Photography; 139 Bob Thomas/Stone/GettyImages; 140 (br) © Mug Shots/CO; 141 (tm) Hulton Archive/GettyImages; 142 (br) David Young-Wolff/PhotoEdit; 143 (both) PhotoDisc/GettyImages; 144 (br) Despotovic Dusko/CO Sygma; 145 (br) Jimmy Dorantes/Latin Focus.com; 147 Magano, Francisco Let's All Play Together, 2002, Sister Cities International Young Artists Program.; 148 (tr) Paul Almasy/CO; (mr) Jeremy Horner/CO; 149 (br) Robert Fried Photography; (tr) Gisela Damm/eStock Photo; 156 (bl) Rivera, Diego (1886–1957), La elaboración de un fresco (The Making of a Fresco), 1931, fresco, 271 x 357 in., San Francisco Art Institute, gift of William Gerstle, photo courtesy of David Wakely.; (bg) Stephen Wilkes/The Image Bank/GettyImages; 156 (background) © PhotoDisc; 158 (bl) Bill Burlingham Photography; 162 (m) Robert Frerck/Odyssey/Chicago; 164 (tr) © Wolfgang Kaehler 2004 www.wkaehlerphoto.com; (tl) Steve Vidler/eStock Photography; (bl) Robert Fried Photography; 165 (br) Robert Fried/Stock Boston; (br) © Sime s.a.s./eStock Photography/PictureQuest; 167 © 2003 age footstock. All rights reserved.; 169 (br) Bettmann/CO; 171 (br) Ferrer y Miró, Juan (b. 1850), An Exposition of Painting, 19th century, photo courtesy of Superstock.; 172 (br) Daniel Ciccone; 173 (m) (t) Kahlo, Frida (1907–1954), El camión (The Bus), 1929, oil on canvas, 26 x 55 cm., Fundación Dolores Olmeda/Schalkwijk/Art Resource, NY.; 173 (b)Washington DC Convention and Tourism Corporation; 174 (br) Bob Crandall/Stock Boston; 175 (mr) Rudi von Briel/PhotoEdit; (br) Robert Frerck/Odyssey/Chicago; 176 (mr) Richard Gaver/CO; 177 (tr) David Young-Wolff/PhotoEdit; (br) Robert Frerck/Odyssey/Chicago; 182 (tm) Robert Frerck/Odyssey/Chicago; 183 (tr) PhotoDisc/GettyImages; 184–185 Robert Frerck/Odyssey/Chicago; (bl) Picasso, Pablo (1881–1973), Primeros pasos (First Steps), 1943, Yale University Art Gallery/Gift of Stephen Carlton Clark,

B.A.; 186 (1) Paul Barton/Corbis; (2) Dorling Kindersley Media Library/Pearson; 3) Siede Preis/PhotoDisc/GettyImages; (4) PhotoDisc/GettyImages; (6) Royalty-Free/CO; (7) Definitive Stock; (8) Jay Penni Photography; (bl) Bill Burlingham Photography; (5) PhotoDisc/GettyImages; 190 (br) PhotoDisc/GettyImages; 191 (tr) Robert Van Der Hilst/Stone/GettyImages; 192 (br) Ellen Senisi/The Image Works; 193 (br) Carol Shanahan; 194 (br) Robert Frerck/Odyssey/Chicago; 195 Photo courtesy of Carol Shanahan; 196 (br) Rob Tringall, Jr./SportsChrome; 197 (tr) The Granger Collection, New York; 198 (mr) Hulton Archive/GettyImages; 200 (br) Lorenzo Armendariz/Latin Focus; (m) Robert Frerck/Odyssey/Chicago/National Museum of Anthropology; 201 (mr) Goya y Lucientes, Francisco José (1746–1828), Don Manuel Osorio Manrique de Zúñiga, 1788–9, 127 x 101 in., Metropolitan Museum of Art, NY/Bridgeman Art Library.; (bl) Spencer Grant/Painet; Mug Shots/CO; 205 Photo courtesy of Carol Shanahan; (t) © Bob Daemmrich/Bob Daemmrich Photography; 210–211 (bg) Robert Frerck/Odyssey/Chicago; 210 (ml) Ruiz, Antonio "El Corcito" (1897–1964), Desfile cívico escolar (Schoolchildren on Parade), 1936, oil on canvas, 24.5 x 33.5 cm., Col. Averco Patrimonial, Secretaria de Hacienda y Crédito Público.; 212 (tm, ml) Bill Burlingham Photography; (mr) Jay Penni Photography; 212 (m) Jay Penni Photography; 216 (br) Quim Llenas/COVER/The Image Works; 218 (br) Joe Viesti/Viesti Associates; 220 (tr) Bill Burlingham Photography; (br) Stewart Aitchison/DDB Stock Photo; 220 (bm) Courtesy Peggy Palo Boyles; (bl) Bill Burlingham Photography; 221 (tr) Tony Freeman/PhotoEdit; 222 (tr) Garza, Carmen Lomas (b. 1948), Tamalada (Making Tamales), 1988, oil on linen mounted on wood, 24" x 32", Collection of Paula Maciel-Benecke and Norbert Benecke, Aptos, California.; 223 (tr, br) Bettmann/CO; (mr) Goya, Francisco de (1746–1828), Los fusilamientos del 3 de mayo, 1808 (The Shooting of May 3, 1808), 1814, oil on canvas, 8'6" x 11'4", Museo del Prado, Madrid.; 224 (mr) Robert Frerck/Odyssey/Chicago; 225 (br) Steve Dunwell/Index Stock Imagery; 226 (tr) Jacques Janquox/Stone/GettyImages; 227 (tl) Addison Geary/Stock Boston; (bm) © www.andycaulfield.com; 228 (bm) Bill Burlingham Photography; 229 (bl) Suzanne Murphy-Larrone/DDB Stock Photo; (mr) Peggy Boyles; 230 (tr) David Simson/Stock Boston; (br) J.P. Courau/DDB Stock Photo; (b) Ryan McVay/PhotoDisc/GettyImages; 231 (tr) Robert Frerck/Odyssey/Chicago; 236 (tl) Royalty-Free/CO; (tm, tr) Massimo Listri/CO; 238–239 AFP/CO; (bl) Gotay de Anderson, Zulia, The Storm, 2002, oil on masonite, 24 x 30 in.; 240 (m) Bill Burlingham Photography; (bm) Bill Gentile/CO; (br) Jorge Silva/Reuters NewMedia, Inc./CO; (br) Tomas del Amo/Index Stock Imagery; (bl) Daniel Anguilar/Reuters NewMedia, Inc./CO; (tm) Robert Brenner/PhotoEdit; (mr) Nigel Shuttleworth/Life File/GettyImages; 241 (tl) Bill Burlingham Photography; 245 (br) Pablo Corral Vega/CO; 246 AFP/EPA/EFE/Robin Townsend/CO; 247 (b) Reuters NewMedia, Inc./CO; 251 (r) Oswaldo Rivas/Reuters NewMedia, Inc./CO; 252 (tr) Joe Viesti/Viesti Associates; (br) Botero, Fernando (b. 1933), Terremoto en Popayán (Earthquake in Popayán), 1999, oil on canvas, 173 x 112 cm., Museo Botero of the Banco de la República de Colombia.; 255 (b) AFP/CO; 256 (r) Bettmann/CO; 257 (tl) Bettmann/CO; 258 (br) Craig Lovell/CO; (tr) Dave G. Houser/CO; 259 (tr) Bill Burlingham Photography; (b) Bob Krist/CO; 264 (bl) Rivera, Diego (1886–1957), La medicina antigua y la moderna (The History of Medicine in Mexico), 1953, mural, 24-1/4 x 35-1/2 ft., Schalkwijk/Art Resource, NY.; 264–265 (m) Associated Press, Lake-Sumter Emergency Services; 271 (br) David Young-Wolff/PhotoEdit; 273 (br) Ted Spiegel/CO; 274 D.Donne Bryant Stock Photography; 276 (br) Ronnie Kaufman/CO; 278 (both) Patrulla Aérea Colombiana - Antioquia; 279 (t) Jim Cummins/CO; (b) Franck Sequin/TempSport/CO; 280 (t) AFP/Getty Images; (br) Pablo San Juan/CO; 282 (mr) Pan American Health Organization/Regional Office for the Americas of the World Health Organization; (b) Paul Fenton/Moonglow Photo Agency; 283 (tr) AFP/Omar Torres/CO; (tl) Vince Bucci/GettyImages; (mr) Medical Air for Children of Latin America; 284 (tr) Spencer Grant/PhotoEdit; (mr) PhotoDisc/GettyImages; 285 (tr) David Young-Wolff/PhotoEdit; (br) Tom Stewart/CO; 292–293 Despotovic Dusko/CO Sygma; 292 (bl) Dalí, Salvador (1904–1989), El futbolista (The Football Player), 1973, lithograph on zinc, 19 x 24 in., Gala-Salvador Dalí Foundation, Artists Right Society (ARS) New York, photo courtesy of Natalie Rubin.; 294 (tl) AFP/Jorge Uzon/CO; (tr) Henry Romero/Reuters NewMedia, Inc./CO; (ml) Jay Penni Photography; 298 (tr) Patricio Crooker/Fotosbolivia/The Image Works; 299 (ml) Francisco J. Rangel; 299 Victor Englebert; 300 Chris Trotman/Duomo/CO; (bm) Albert Gea/Reuters/Corbis; 301 (br) Mike Segar/Reuters/Landov; (tl) AP/Wide World; 303 (t) Clive Brunskill/Getty Images, (b) Mark Dadswell/Getty Images; 304 (mr) NASA; (tl) CO; (mr) Jan Butchofsky-Houser/CO; (tr) ABC News/GettyImages; 305 Luis Diez Solano/COVER/The Image Works; 307 (mr) Sapia, Mariano (b. 1964), Pantallas (Screens), 2002, oil on canvas, 120 x 170 cm., photo courtesy of Praxis International Art, NY.; Shelley Gazin/CO; 308 (tr) Despotovic Dusko/CO Sygma; 310 (br) Pan American Sports Organization; (l) AFP/John Gibson/CO; 311 (1) Comité Olímpico Cubano; (tl) Reprinted with permission of the United States Olympic Committee; (1) Comité Olímpico Argentino: (mr) Craig Lovell/Eagle Visions Photography/Alamy; (tr) Mike Finn-Kelcey/Getty Images; 312 (tr) Despierta América/Univisión Communications Inc. 2002, All Rights Reserved; 313 (tr) Spencer Rowell/Taxi/GettyImages; (br) CBS Photo Archive; 318–319 Maury Christian/CO Sygma; (tr) Servicio Postal Mexicano, 1996.; 325 (tr) Columbia Tristar Motion Pictures Group; (br) Billie L. Porter/Photofest; 326 (br) Sorel/Photofest; 328 (br) Photofest; 330 (bl) AP/Wide World; 332 (b) © 2004 Focus Features. All Rights Reserved; 334 (br) Keith Dannemiller/CO SABA; 335 (tr) Potier/Alamo/CO Sygma; 336 (both) Photofest; 337 (tl) Photofest; 338 (br) John Morrison Photography; (tr) Daniel Ciccone; (mr) HIRB/Index Stock Imagery; 344 (tm) Pat LaCroix/The Image Bank/GettyImages; 346–347 Owen Franken/CO; (bl) Silva, Simón, (b. 1961), Tomates (Tomatoes), 1997, gouache on canvas, 18 x 24 in.; 349 (all) Jay Penni Photography; 352 (br) Takehiko Sunada/HAGA/The Image Works; 353 (ml) Renee Comet Photography/StockFood; (bl) Michelle Garrett/CO; (mr) Becky Luigart-Stayner/CO; (br) Amy Reichman/Envision; 355 (br) Andre Baranowski/Envision; 357 (r) Comet/StockFood; 358 (br) Pablo Corral Vega/CO; (tr) Morton Beebe/CO; 359 (mr) Chris Everard/Stone/GettyImages; 360 (m) Nik Wheeler/CO; (1) Steven Needham/Envision; (2) Bruce Coleman Photography; (3) Photononstop/Envision; (4) Japack Company/CO; (5) Lynda Richardson/CO; (6) Michelle Garrett/CO; (7) Paul Webster/Stone/GettyImages; (8) Mark Ferri/Envision; 361 (mr) Photolibrary.com/Index Stock Imagery; 362 (tr) Danny Lehman/CO; 363 (b) Michael Newman/PhotoEdit; (br) © Jimmy Dorantes/Latin Focus.com; (tr) Danny Lehman/CO; 364 (all) Jay Penni Photography; 365 (Neruda) Hulton Archive/GettyImages; (all) Jay Penni Photography; 366 (tr) James Carrier/StockFood; (br) Jay Penni Photography; 367 (br) Jay Penni Photography; 372–373 Chuck Savage/CO; (bl) Garza, Carmen Lomas (b. 1948), Sandía (Watermelon), 1986, gouache painting on paper, 20 x 28 in., Collection of Dudley D. Brooks & Tomas Ybarra-Frausto, NY., photo courtesy of Wolfgang Dietze.; 377 Jay Penni Photography; 378 (br) Robert Frerck/Odyssey/Chicago; 380 (l) John Dominis/Index Stock Imagery/PictureQuest; (br) Robert Frerck/Odyssey/Chicago; (bl) PhotoDisc/GettyImages; 381 (br) Lois Ellen Frank/CO; 383 (tl) Climent, Elena (b. 1955), Tienda de legumbres (Vegetable Store), 1992, oil on canvas, 36 x 44-1/8 in., courtesy of Mary-Anne Martin/Fine Art, New York.; 384 (br) Thomas Hoeffgen/Taxi/GettyImages; 385 (br) Galen Rowell/CO; 386 (br) Alison Wright/CO; 387 (br) Latin Focus.com; 388 (br) James P. Blair/CO; 389 (tr) Robert Fried Photography; 390–391 John Mitchell/Photo Researchers; 390 (l) Angelina Lax/Photo Researchers; 390 (inset) Tom Bean/CO; 391 (tr) Chip and Rosa María de la Cueva Peterson; (m) Kevin Schafer/CO; (br) Bob Krist/CO; (br) Kevin Schafer/CO; 392 Latin Focus.com; 393 (t) Paul Barton/CO; (b) Lawrence Sawyer/Index Stock Imagery; 398 (1) Michael S. Yamashita/CO; (2) Doug Stamm/Seapics.com; (3) Paul Steel/CO; (4) Buddy Mays/CO; 400 (bl) García, Valencia (b. 1963), Playas de Oaxaca (Beach at Oaxaca), 2000, oil on canvas, 36 x 48 in.; 400–401 Mark Wagner/aviation-images.com; 402 (bl) Jay Penni Photography; (mr) John Morrison Photography; (br) Jay Penni Photography; 403 (mr) Najlah Feanny/CO SABA; (tr) James Marshall/CO; (tl) World Images News Service; (tm) Mark Peterson/CO SABA; 406 (br) Larry Luxner/Luxner News; 407 (br) Larry Luxner/Luxner News; 409 (tr) John Morrison Photography; (mr) Pablo Corral Vega/CO; 411 (tr) Alain Le Garsmeur/CO; 412 (mr) John Lei/Omni-Photo; 413 (br) Robert Frerck/Odyssey/Chicago; 415 (1) Abbie Enock; Travel Ink/CO; (2) Franz-Marc Frei/CO; (3) Giraud Philippe/CO Sygma; (4) Suzanne Murphy-Larronde; 417 (tr) Robert Fried/DDB; (br) Larry Luxner/Luxner News; 418 (b) Pablo Corral Vega/CO; (m) Paul Rodriguez/Latin Focus; (br) David Simson/DAS Photo; John Morrison Photography; 419 (tr) Owen Franken/CO; (m) Todd Wolf/CO; (tl) Albrecht G. Schaefer/CO; 420 (both) Benson Latin American Collection, University of Texas Library; 421 (tr) Erv Schowengerdt; 424 (bl) Jimmy Dorantes/Latin Focus; 424–425 Danny Lehman/CO; 426 (m) Jay Penni Photography; (bm) Nik Wheeler/CO; (t) Jay Penni Photography; (bl) David Young-Wolff/Alamy Limited; (br) José Fuste Raga/CO; 427 (others) John Morrison Photography; 430 Jan Butchofsky-Houser/CO; 431 (br) David Simchock/Vagabond Vistas Photography; 432 (tm) Jimmy Dorantes/Latin Focus; (tr) D. Stonek/Latin Focus; 433 (l) David Stoecklein/CO; (tr) Tony Arruza/CO; 434 (br) Suzanne Murphy-Larronde; 435 (mr) Jeremy Horner/CO; 436 (mr) Daniel Ciccone; 438 (tr) Sven Martson/The Image Works; 439 Joe Vesti/The Vesti Collection, Inc.; 440 (br) Alan Kearney/Viesti Associates; 442–443 Massimo Listri/CO; 442 (bl) Peter M. Wilson/CO; 443 (br) Larry Luxner/Luxner News; (tr) ML Sinibaldi/CO; 444 (tr) Sappa/Photo Researchers; (br) John Morrison Photography; 445 (tr) Bettmann/CO; (br) Hubert Stadler/CO;s 448 (tm) Paul A. Souders/CO; 450 (bl) Siqueiros, David Alfaro (1896–1974), El pueblo a la Universidad y la Universidad al Pueblo (The People for the University and the University for the People) detail, 1950–1954, photo courtesy of Paul Almasy/CO.; 450–451 Farrel Grehan/CO; 452 (bl) Jay Penni Photography; 453 (all) Jay Penni Photography (bl) Richard Haynes; 457 (tr) Jan

560 quinientos sesenta
Acknowledgments

Halaska/Index Stock Imagery; 458 (br) Daniel Ciccone; 460 (br) Bob Daemmrich Photography; 461 (t) Alamy Images; 463 (br) Hinojosa, Celina (b. 1961), The Lenten Harvest, 1999, acrylic on canvas, 30 x 40 in.; 465 (tr) Owen Franken/CO; (mr) Pablo Corral Vega/CO; 467 (t) Jeff Greenberg / Photo Edit, Inc.; Bob Daemmrich Photography; 468 (bl) Monika Graff/The Image Works; Daniel Ciccone; (mr) David Young-Wolff/PhotoEdit; 469 (tl) Bob Daemmrich/Stock Boston; (br) Bill Bachmann/Stock Boston; 470 (tr) Toaquiza, Julio. Targelia, Christmas Eve, 1990, photo courtesy of Pablo Corral Vega/CO.; (br) Louis, E., Xochimilco, San Miguel de Allende, Guanajuato, México, 20th century, photo courtesy of the Art Archive/Mireille Vautier.; 471 (tr) José Luis Pelaez/CO; 474 (bl) Arreguín, Alfredo (b. 1935), Las garzas (The Herons), 2002, oil on canvas, 42 x 60 in.; 474–475 Michael & Patricia Fogden/CO; 476 Jay Penni Photography; 477 Photo researchers, Inc.; (m inset) Fred Bruemmer/DRK Photo; (bl inset) Tom Bean/DRK Photo; (br) C. & J. Isenhart/Tom Stack & Associates; (tr inset) Brian Parker/Tom Stack & Associates; (tr) Darrell Gulin/DRK Photo; (l) Mark Garlick/Photo Researchers; 480 (br) Tom Till/DRK Photo; 481 (br) Charles Philip/Painet; 483 (eagle coin) David Macias/Photo Researchers; (other coins) Jay Penni Photography/Coins Courtesy of Don Bailey Numismatic Services; (bl) W. Perry Conway/CO; 484 (br) Frank Siteman/PhotoEdit; 485 (tr) Michael Fogden/DRK Photo; 490 (mr) Torres-García, Joaquín (1874–1949), Nueva York a vista de pájaro (New York City: Bird's Eye View), 1920, gouache and watercolor on cardboard, 33.8 x 48.5 cm., Yale University Art Gallery.; 490 (tr) Velásquez, José Antonio (1906-1983), Paisaje hondureño de San Antonio de Oriente, 1972, oil on canvas, 47-1/4 x 60-1/2 in., Art Museum of the Americas/Courtesy Organization of American States.; 491 (tr) David Stoecklein/CO; 491 (b) AFP/Getty Images; 492–493 (all) Carol Maglitta; 494 (tr) Michael Lawton/Panoramic Images; (mr) Mark Edwards/Peter Arnold; (br) World Resources Institute/Global Forest Watch; 495 (tr) SuperStock/SuperStock/PictureQuest.

Text Chapter 1A, p. 34: "Reglas de oro para estudiar mejor" from *Okapi*, Mayo 2002 © Okapi Bayard Presse. Used by permission. Chapter 3B, p. 174: "Manejo Defensivo" from Manual de Educación y Seguridad Vial www.costaricaweb.com. Chapter 5B, p. 282: "Campeones de la Salud" from Organización Panamericana de la Salud. Chapter 6A, p. 310: "Logos y Mascotas" from *Panamericanos Rio 2007*. Chapter 7A, p. 359: Excerpt from "Oda a las papas fritas" by Pablo Neruda. Chapter 7A, p. 364: Excerpt from "Oda al tomate" by Pablo Neruda. Chapter 7A, p. 365: Excerpt from "Oda a la cebolla" by Pablo Neruda. Chapter 7B, p. 389: Festival from Noel Productos. Chapter 7B, p. 390: General Trail Information from USDA Forest Service, Southern Region, Caribbean National Forest. Chapter 9A, p. 468: Helping You Plan, Apply, and Pay for College from www.ncmentor.org. Copyright © 2001 College Foundation Inc. All Rights Reserved. Chapter 9B, p. 483: "En Riesgo de extinción 20% de los animales en México" by Julián Sánchez from EL UNIVERSAL domingo, el 25 de agosto de 2002. Chapter 9B, p. 483: "¡Tú puedes ayudar a evitar su extinción!" from *Muy Interesante*, Año xviii, No. 07. Chapter 9B, p. 489: "Ssshhh . . . escucha" from Ayuntamiento de Madrid.

Note: Every effort has been made to locate the copyright owner of material used in this textbook. Omissions brought to our attention will be corrected in subsequent editions.